principles of educational psychology

SECOND CANADIAN EDITION

JEANNE ELLIS ORMROD
UNIVERSITY OF NORTHERN COLORADO (EMERITA)
UNIVERSITY OF NEW HAMPSHIRE

DONALD H. SAKLOFSKE
UNIVERSITY OF CALGARY

VICKI L. SCHWEAN
UNIVERSITY OF CALGARY

JAC J. W. ANDREWS
UNIVERSITY OF CALGARY

BRUCE M. SHORE
MCGILL UNIVERSITY

Pearson Canada
Toronto

Library and Archives Canada Cataloguing in Publication

Principles of educational psychology/Jeanne Ellis Ormrod . . . [et al.].—2nd Canadian ed.

Includes bibliographical references and index.
ISBN 978-0-13-500734-1

1. Educational psychology—Textbooks. 2. Teaching—Textbooks. 3. Learning—Textbooks. 4. Classroom management—Textbooks. I. Ormrod, Jeanne Ellis

LB1051.P725 2010   370.15   C2008-904274-3

Copyright © 2010, 2006 Pearson Education Canada, a division of Pearson Canada Inc., Toronto, Ontario.

Pearson Prentice Hall. All rights reserved. This publication is protected by copyright and permission should be obtained from the publisher prior to any prohibited reproduction, storage in a retrieval system, or transmission in any form or by any means, electronic, mechanical, photocopying, recording, or likewise. For information regarding permission, write to the Permissions Department.

Original edition published by Pearson Education, Inc., Upper Saddle River, New Jersey, USA. Copyright © 2008 Pearson Education, Inc.

This edition is authorized for sale only in Canada.

ISBN-13: 978-0-13-500734-1
ISBN-10: 0-13-500734-8

Vice President, Editorial Director: Gary Bennett
Editor-in-Chief: Ky Pruesse
Executive Acquisitions Editor: Christine Cozens
Marketing Manager: Loula March
Senior Developmental Editor: Jennifer Murray
Production Editors: Laura Neves, Söğüt Y. Güleç
Copy Editor: Laura Neves
Proofreaders: Melissa Hajek, Deborah Cooper-Bullock
Production Coordinator: Avinash Chandra
Compositor: Macmillan Publishing Solutions
Photo and Permissions Researcher: Julie Pratt
Art Director: Julia Hall
Cover and Interior Designer: Jennifer Stimson
Cover Image: Chris Strong/Getty Images

For permission to reproduce copyrighted material, the publisher gratefully acknowledges the copyright holders listed on page C-1 and in the sources throughout the text, which are considered extensions of this copyright page.

1 2 3 4 5   13 12 11 10 09

Printed and bound in the United States of America.

To our beautiful children who have taught us so much:
Jon and Alison—DHS
Micah—VLS
Jenna and Chad—JWA
John, Brenda, Darren, and Monica—BMS

Brief Contents

Chapter 1   Educational Psychology and Teacher Decision Making   2

PART 1   UNDERSTANDING STUDENT DEVELOPMENT AND DIVERSITY

Chapter 2   Cognitive and Linguistic Development   14

Chapter 3   Personal, Social, and Moral Development   46

Chapter 4   Individual and Group Differences   74

PART 2   UNDERSTANDING HOW STUDENTS LEARN

Chapter 5   Learning and Behaviour Processes   106

Chapter 6   Learning and Cognitive Processes   130

Chapter 7   Knowledge Construction and Higher-Level Thinking   158

Chapter 8   Social Cognitive Views of Learning   194

Chapter 9   Motivation, Affect, and Cognition   218

PART 3   UNDERSTANDING INSTRUCTIONAL PROCESSES

Chapter 10   Instructional Strategies   258

Chapter 11   Creating and Maintaining a Productive Classroom Environment   292

Chapter 12   Instructional Assessment   310

Contents

Preface xii

CHAPTER 1 Educational Psychology and Teacher Decision Making 2

Case Study *More Than Meets the Eye* 3
Teaching Connections 3
OOPS—A Pretest 3
Drawing Conclusions from Psychological and Educational Research 6
   Descriptive Studies 6
   Correlational Studies 6
   Experimental Studies 6
   A Cautionary Note 6
Using Principles and Theories in Classroom Decision Making 7
Importance of Ongoing Assessment in Classroom Decision Making 8
Developing as a Teacher 8
Looking Ahead to the Following Chapters 10
Studying Educational Psychology More Effectively 10
   Connecting Research to Teaching 12
   Principles, Theories, and Assessment in Decision Making 12
   Developing as a Teacher 12
   Reading about and Studying Educational Psychology 12
Teaching Constructions 13
   Key Concepts 13

PART 1
UNDERSTANDING STUDENT DEVELOPMENT AND DIVERSITY

CHAPTER 2 Cognitive and Linguistic Development 14

Case Study *How Do You Learn?* 15
Teaching Connections 15
Basic Principles of Human Development 15
Piaget's Theory of Cognitive Development 16
   Piaget's Basic Assumptions 16
   Piaget's Stages of Cognitive Development 18
   Current Perspectives on Piaget's Theory 22
Vygotsky's Theory of Cognitive Development 23
   Vygotsky's Basic Assumptions 23
   Current Perspectives on Vygotsky's Theory 26
An Information-Processing View of Cognitive Development 29
   Attention 29
   Learning Strategies 29
   Knowledge 31
   Metacognition 31
Linguistic Development 33
   Theoretical Perspectives on Language Development 33
   Trends in Language Development 34
   Learning a Second Language 38
Considering Diversity in Cognitive and Linguistic Development 40
   Accommodating Students with Exceptionalities 41
Summary of Cognitive and Linguistic Development 43
Teaching Constructions 44
   Key Concepts 44

CHAPTER 3 Personal, Social, and Moral Development 46

Case Study *The Bad Apple* 47
Teaching Connections 47
Factors That Influence Personal, Social, and Moral Development 47
   Temperamental Differences 48
   Effects of Parenting 48
   Effects of Culture 49
   Peer Influences 50
Development of a Sense of Self 50
   Factors Influencing the Development of Self-Views 51
   Developmental Changes in Students' Self-Views 53

Social Development 56
   Peer Relationships 56
   Fostering Social Skills 60
Moral and Prosocial Development 62
   Development of Moral Reasoning: Kohlberg's Theory 64
   Possible Sex Differences in Moral Reasoning: Gilligan's Theory 67
   Emotional Components of Moral Development 68
   Determinants of Moral Behaviour 69
   Promoting Moral Development in the Classroom 69
Accommodating Students in the Inclusive Classroom 71
General Themes in Personal, Social, and Moral Development 71
Teaching Constructions 73
   Key Concepts 73

CHAPTER 4 Individual and Group Differences 74

Case Study *Hidden Treasure* 75
Teaching Connections 75
Keeping Individual and Group Differences in Perspective 75
Intelligence 77
   Measuring Intelligence 77
   How Theorists Conceptualize Intelligence 78
   Heredity, Environment, and Group Differences in Intelligence 81
   Socioeconomic Difference, Ability, and Achievement 82
   Factors Interfering with School Success 82
   Being Optimistic about Students' Potential 85
Creativity 85
   Fostering Creativity in the Classroom 86
Cultural and Ethnic Differences 87
   Navigating Different Cultures at Home and at School 87
   Examples of Ethnic Diversity 88
   Creating a More Multicultural Classroom Environment 91
Sex Differences 93
   Origins of Sex Differences 93
Students at Risk 96
   Characteristics of Students at Risk 96
   Why Students Drop Out 97
   Helping Students at Risk Stay in School 97
   Fostering Resilience: A Lesson from Low Socioeconomic Status Children under Stress 99
   Building on Students' Strengths 100
Exceptional Students 100
Students in Inclusive Settings 101
   The Current Concept of Inclusion 103
   Classroom Strategies to Promote Inclusion 103
Teaching Constructions 105
   Key Concepts 105

PART 2

UNDERSTANDING HOW STUDENTS LEARN

CHAPTER 5 Learning and Behaviour Processes 106

Case Study *The Attention Getter* 107
Teaching Connections 107
Basic Assumptions of Behaviourism 107
Classical Conditioning 109
   Classical Conditioning of Emotional Responses 110
   Generalization 110
   Extinction 110
Operant Conditioning 111
   Contrasting Classical and Operant Conditioning 112
   Reinforcement in the Classroom 112
   Using Reinforcement Effectively 115
Shaping New Behaviours 117
Effects of Antecedent Stimuli and Responses 118
   Cueing 118
   Generalization 118
   Discrimination 118
Reducing and Eliminating Undesirable Behaviours 119
   Extinction 119
   Cueing Inappropriate Behaviours 120
   Reinforcing Incompatible Behaviours 120
   Punishment 120
Maintaining Desirable Behaviours over the Long Run 124
   Promoting Intrinsic Reinforcement 125
   Using Intermittent Reinforcement 125
Addressing Especially Difficult Classroom Behaviours 125
   Applied Behaviour Analysis 125
   Functional Analysis and Positive Behavioural Support 126
Considering Diversity in Student Behaviours 127
   Accommodating All Students 127
Strengths and Potential Limitations of Behavioural Approaches 127
Teaching Constructions 129
   Key Concepts 129

CHAPTER 6 Learning and Cognitive Processes 130

Case Study *Darren's Day at School* 131
Teaching Connections 131
Basic Assumptions of Cognitive Psychology 131
Basic Terminology in Cognitive Psychology 134
A Model of Human Memory 134
   The Nature of the Sensory Register 135
   Moving Information to Working Memory: The Role of Attention 135
   The Nature of Working (Short-Term) Memory 136
   Moving Information to Long-Term Memory: Connecting New Information with Prior Knowledge 137

   The Nature of Long-Term Memory   *138*
   Critiquing the Three-Component Model   *139*
Long-Term Memory Storage   140
   The Various Forms of Knowledge   *140*
   How Declarative Knowledge Is Learned   *141*
   How Procedural Knowledge Is Learned   *146*
   Prior Knowledge and Working Memory in Long-Term Memory Storage   *147*
   Using Mnemonics in the Absence of Relevant Prior Knowledge   *148*
Long-Term Memory Retrieval   149
   The Nature of Long-Term Memory Retrieval   *149*
   Factors Affecting Retrieval   *149*
   Why People Sometimes Forget   *152*
Giving Students Time to Process: Effects of Increasing Wait Time   154
Accommodating Diversity in Cognitive Processes   155
   Facilitating Cognitive Processing in All Students   *155*
Learning and the Brain: A Word of Caution about "Brain-Based" Teaching   157
Teaching Constructions   157
   Key Concepts   *157*

CHAPTER 7 Knowledge Construction and Higher-Level Thinking   158

Case Study *Earth-Shaking Summaries*   159
Teaching Connections   159
Constructive Processes in Learning and Memory   160
Knowledge Construction as a Social Process   160
   Benefits of Group Meaning-Making in the Classroom   *161*
Organizing Knowledge   161
   Concepts   *161*
   Schemas and Scripts   *162*
When Knowledge Construction Goes Awry: Origins and Effects of Misconceptions   163
Promoting Effective Knowledge Construction   165
   Providing Opportunities for Experimentation   *165*
   Presenting the Ideas of Others   *165*
   Emphasizing Conceptual Understanding   *165*
   Using Authentic Activities   *166*
   Promoting Dialogue   *166*
   Creating a Community of Learners   *167*
Promoting Conceptual Change   169
Considering Diversity in Constructive Processes   171
   Accommodating Students in Inclusive Classrooms   *171*
Metacognition and Learning Strategies   171
   Effective Learning Strategies   *173*
   Factors Affecting Strategy Use   *176*
Transfer   178
   Basic Concepts in Transfer   *178*
   Factors Affecting Transfer   *179*
   Importance of Retrieval in Transfer   *181*

Problem Solving   181
   Basic Concepts in Problem Solving   *181*
   Cognitive Factors Affecting Problem Solving   *183*
   Using Computer Technology to Promote Effective Problem Solving   *186*
Critical Thinking   186
   Identifying Memes   *188*
Considering Diversity in Higher-Level Thinking Processes   189
   Accommodating Students in Inclusive Classrooms   *189*
General Strategies for Promoting Higher-Level Thinking Skills   189
Teaching Constructions   192
   Key Concepts   *192*

CHAPTER 8 Social Cognitive Views of Learning   194

Case Study *It's all Ancient Greek to Me*   195
Teaching Connections   195
Basic Assumptions of Social Cognitive Theory   195
The Social Cognitive View of Reinforcement and Punishment   197
   Expectations   *197*
   Vicarious Experiences   *198*
   Cognitive Processing   *199*
   Choice of Behaviour   *199*
   Nonoccurrence of Expected Consequences   *199*
Modelling   199
   How Modelling Affects Behaviour   *200*
   Characteristics of Effective Models   *200*
   Helping Students Learn from Models   *202*
   Modelling and Aggression   *203*
Self-Efficacy   204
   How Self-Efficacy Affects Behaviour   *204*
   Factors in the Development of Self-Efficacy   *205*
Self-Regulation   207
   Self-Regulated Behaviour   *208*
   Self-Regulated Learning   *211*
   Self-Regulated Problem Solving   *212*
Reciprocal Causation   214
Promoting Self-Regulation in Students with Special Needs   215
Teaching Constructions   216
   Key Concepts   *216*

CHAPTER 9 Motivation, Affect, and Cognition   218

Case Study *Passing Algebra*   219
Teaching Connections   219
The Nature of Motivation   220
   How Motivation Affects Learning and Behaviour   *220*
   Intrinsic versus Extrinsic Motivation   *221*
Theoretical Perspectives of Motivation   222
   The Trait Perspective   *222*
   The Behaviourist Perspective   *223*
   The Social Cognitive Perspective   *223*
   The Cognitive Perspective   *224*

What Basic Needs Do People Have?   225
   Self-Worth   225
   Relatedness   226
Affect and Its Effects   228
   Hot Cognition   228
   Anxiety   229
Cognitions That Motivate   231
The Interplay of Cognition and Motivation   232
Self-Perceptions and Intrinsic Motivation   232
   Self-Efficacy   232
   Self-Determination   234
Expectancies and Values   236
   Internalizing the Values of Others   237
   Fostering Expectancies and Values in the Classroom   238
Interest   238
   Situational versus Personal Interest   238
   Promoting Interest in Classroom Subject Matter   239
Goals   240
   Mastery and Performance Goals   240
   Work-Avoidance Goals   242
   Social Goals   243
   Capitalizing on Students' Goals   243
Attributions: Perceived Causes of Success and Failure   245
   Dimensions Underlying Students' Attributions   245
   How Attributions Influence Affect, Cognition, and Behaviour   246
   Developmental Trends in Attributions   247
   Factors Influencing the Development of Attributions   247
   Mastery Orientation versus Learned Helplessness   248
Teacher Expectations and Attributions   249
   How Expectations and Attributions Affect Classroom Performance   250
   Forming Productive Expectations and Attributions for Student Performance   250
Considering Diversity in Motivation, Affect, and Cognition   252
   Ethnic Differences   252
   Sex Differences   253
   Socioeconomic Differences   254
   Accommodating Students in Inclusive Settings   255
Teaching Constructions   257
   Key Concepts   257

PART 3

UNDERSTANDING INSTRUCTIONAL PROCESSES

CHAPTER 10 Instructional Strategies   258

Case Study *Building Communities*   259
Teaching Connections   259
Overview of Instructional Strategies   260
Planning for Instruction   260
   Identifying the Goals of Instruction   260
   Conducting a Task Analysis   263
   Developing a Lesson Plan   264
Expository Approaches   265
   Lectures and Textbooks   265
   Mastery Learning   266
   Direct Instruction   268
   Information and Communication Technology Instruction   269
   E-learning and Online Research   273
Hands-On Approaches: Discovery Learning and In-Class Activities   274
   Discovery Learning   274
   In-Class Activities   275
Interactive and Collaborative Approaches   276
   Teacher Questions   276
   Class Discussions   276
   Cognitive Strategy Teaching   277
   Computer-Supported Collaborative Learning   280
   Co-operative Learning   281
   Peer Tutoring   284
Taking Student Diversity into Account   285
   Considering Group Differences   286
   Accommodating Students in Inclusive Settings   286
Teaching Constructions   288
   Key Concepts   288

CHAPTER 11 Creating and Maintaining a Productive Classroom Environment   292

Case Study *A Contagious Situation*   293
Teaching Connections   293
Creating an Environment Conducive to Learning   293
   Arranging the Classroom   295
   Creating an Effective Classroom Climate   295
   Setting Limits   298
   Planning Activities That Keep Students on Task   299
   Monitoring What Students Are Doing   301
   Modifying Instructional Strategies   301
Dealing with Misbehaviours   302
Taking Student Diversity into Account   303
   Creating a Supportive Climate   304
   Accommodating Students in the Inclusive Classroom   304
Coordinating Efforts with Others   304
   Working with Other Teachers   304
   Working with the Community at Large   306
   Working with Parents   306
Teaching Constructions   309
   Key Concepts   309

CHAPTER 12 Instructional Assessment   310

Case Study *Learning about Our Country*   311
Teaching Connections   311
Assessments as Tools   311
The Various Forms of Educational Assessment   312

Using Assessment for Different Purposes 314
   Promoting Learning 314
   Guiding Instructional Decision Making 315
   Diagnosing Learning and Performance Problems 315
   Promoting Self-Regulation 316
   Determining What Students Have Learned 316
Important Qualities of Good Assessments 316
   Reliability 316
   Standardization 319
   Validity 319
   Practicality 321
Standardized Tests 321
   Types of Standardized Tests 323
   Guidelines for Choosing and Using Standardized Tests 324
Types of Test Scores 325
   Raw Scores 325
   Criterion-Referenced Scores 325
   Norm-Referenced Scores 326
   Norm- versus Criterion-Referenced Scores in the Classroom 328
   Interpreting Test Scores Appropriately 329
High-Stakes Testing and Accountability 329
   Problems with High-Stakes Testing 329
   Potential Solutions to the Problems 330
Communication about Assessment Results 330
   Communicating Classroom Assessment Results 330
   Explaining Standardized Test Results 330
Taking Student Diversity into Account 330
   Developmental Differences 330
   Test Anxiety 331
   Cultural Bias 331
   Language Differences 332
   Testwiseness 332
   Accommodating Students with Special Needs 332
Assessment, Cognition, and Metacognition 334
Informal Assessment 334
   RSVP Characteristics of Informal Assessment 335

Planning a Formal Assessment 336
   Selecting Appropriate Tasks 336
   Obtaining a Representative Sample 337
Paper-Pencil Assessment 337
   Constructing the Assessment Instrument 337
   General Guidelines for Constructing Paper-Pencil Assessments 341
   Administering the Assessment 341
   Scoring Students' Responses 342
   RSVP Characteristics of Paper-Pencil Assessment 342
Performance Assessment 343
   Choosing Appropriate Performance Tasks 343
   Planning and Administering the Assessment 344
   Scoring Students' Responses 345
   RSVP Characteristics of Performance Assessment 347
Including Students in the Assessment Process 347
Encouraging Risk Taking 349
Evaluating a Test/Assessment through Item Analysis 349
Summarizing Students' Achievement 350
   Determining Final Class Grades 350
   Using Portfolios 353
Taking Student Diversity into Account 354
   Accommodating Students in the Inclusive Classroom 355
Teaching Constructions 356
   Key Concepts 357

GLOSSARY G-1

REFERENCES R-1

NAME INDEX N-1

SUBJECT INDEX S-1

PHOTO CREDITS C-1

Preface

Each time we enter a school building in our professional capacities as psychologists and educators, we are reminded of how exciting and energizing it can be to interact and work with children and adolescents. Our personal experiences as parents have only added to this excitement and wonderment. From both perspectives, we have come to recognize that the principles of educational psychology have clear relevance to understanding, encouraging, and assessing learning and to the decisions a classroom teacher must make on an ongoing basis. How children and adolescents learn and think, how they change as they grow and develop, why they do the things they do, how they are often very different from one another and at other times so much alike—our understanding of all these things has innumerable implications for classroom practice and, ultimately, for the lives of the next generation.

What drew the four Canadian authors of *Principles in Educational Psychology* to this project was the similarity of our thinking and views with those of Dr. Jeanne Ormrod, author of the U.S. editions of this text (titled *Educational Psychology: Developing Learners*), along with the desire to have the field of educational psychology captivate you the way it has captivated each of us. A rich and comprehensive foundation was already there in a book that was engaging, meaningful, and thought-provoking as well as informative. We share a definite philosophy about how future teachers can best learn and apply educational psychology—a philosophy that has guided us in writing both the first and now second Canadian edition of this book. More specifically, we believe that you can construct a more accurate and useful understanding of the principles of educational psychology when you:

- Truly understand the nature of learning
- Focus on core or central principles of the discipline
- Relate the principles to your own learning and behaviour
- Use the principles to understand the learning and behaviour of children and adolescents
- Consistently apply the principles to classroom practice

We have incorporated numerous features into the book that will encourage you to do all of these things. We hope that you will learn a great deal from what educational psychology has to offer, not only about the students you will be teaching but also about yourself as a lifelong learner. The following pages describe the features of this second Canadian edition, which has retained the best features of Dr. Ormod's previous U.S. editions and our first Canadian edition.

Our Second Canadian Edition

The advantages of modifying U.S. authored books is that these texts are comprehensive and exceptionally well written by leading experts, have already been field-tested and reviewed, and are recognized as outstanding, based on the number of adoptions in university courses. They are excellent examples of textbook production with supporting materials (CDs, student workbooks, test-item banks, etc.). Furthermore, Dr. Ormrod's book lends itself to being adapted to the Canadian context: we have retained the best of the content and features and enriched it with a Canadian focus. Chapters that are heavily grounded in core principles and theory, and research findings are sufficiently robust and fit into the textbooks of either country. Yet the Canadian cultural mosaic—with its unique children, teachers, and schools—must also be represented and discussed wherever it is relevant. Our efforts to achieve this blend range from adding Canadian-specific examples to rewriting whole sections of the book to reflect the Canadian context. Even in the few short years since the publication of our first edition, new research and applications to teaching and learning have inspired a number of changes to this second Canadian edition. We have again made every effort to list key Canadian websites that showcase contemporary information relevant to education and psychology, learners and learning, and teachers and best teaching practices.

As in the first Canadian edition, it has remained evident to us and our students that traditional educational psychology books (EDPSY) are often too lengthy. Most Canadian EDPSY courses are single-term, usually spanning about 12 to 13 weeks including exam time, thereby effectively reducing instructional time to 11 to 12 weeks. As well, these books are somewhat encyclopedic in volume, and sometimes include content that is now commonly taught in curriculum and special education courses. Thus it makes good sense in the process of Canadianizing first-rate texts such as Dr. Ormrod's *Educational Psychology: Developing Learners* and in revising our first Canadian edition to also ensure that this new edition reflects the realities of Canadian university courses in educational psychology.

In the first Canadian edition we compiled a 12-chapter book to capture the common essential learning objectives of most EDPSY university courses. Thus the original 16 chapters from the U.S. sixth edition have been reduced to 12 to better fit with the length and topic descriptions of most EDPSY courses that focus on learners and learning. Again, we have retained the briefer format so that this edition continues to be consistent with the content covered in a typical single-term course and should also fit more readily with intersession courses without losing any of the features that make the Ormrod texts among the best in the field. For students, a welcome bonus will be the "face validity" of a Canadian text that is more in line with the instructor's course outline.

Much of the content and all of the central themes from Dr. Ormrod's previous and current U.S. editions, also remain in this second Canadian edition. Again, this choice was based on our experiences in teaching EDPSY courses, the relevance of the chapters and content to teaching practice, and the very fact that Dr. Ormrod has produced six editions of a text that is regarded as exemplary of EDPSY textbooks. However, as stated above, we have attempted to keep the same length as our first Canadian edition, and thus this book is significantly shorter than Dr. Ormrod's text. We have not so much omitted content from the original U.S. edition, but rather have summarized and focused more directly on the key points and issues related to cognitive and social development and diversity, learning theories and understanding how students learn, instruction, and assessing student learning.

We were fortunate to have the opportunity to review and draw from other recent books by Dr. Ormrod (*Essentials of Educational Psychology*, 2006; *Human Learning*, Fifth Edition, 2008) but also to include new and relevant work published in Canada, the United States, and other countries. In keeping with our first Canadian edition, we have continued to introduce current Canadian research and applications about learners, learning, and instruction, and have provided the information needed for students to follow up on key topics (e.g., websites related to Canadian culture, exceptional students, assessment practices, etc.). For example, Chapter 4 was substantially rewritten in the first Canadian edition to reflect Canada's cultural diversity and this new edition has added further contemporary information of relevance to future teachers.

This second Canadian Edition also includes a change in authorship. Dr. Gina Harrison, who contributed greatly to the first Canadian edition, is now at the University of Victoria, B.C. and is engaged in new research pursuits requiring her full commitment. We were very fortunate to have Dr. Bruce M. Shore from the Department of Educational and Counselling Psychology at McGill University join our author team. Bruce is well known and highly respected in Canada and abroad as an education and psychology researcher and practitioner, and especially for his work in gifted education and school psychology. The four Canadian authors have engaged in a collaborative effort to ensure that the quality and integrity of Dr. Ormrod's books, as well as our first Canadian edition, were preserved. We are fully committed to creating a textbook to serve the needs of the students we teach in our introductory EDPSY courses.

A DEEPER, MORE APPLIED APPROACH TO THE UNDERSTANDING OF EDUCATIONAL PSYCHOLOGY

Understanding the Nature of Learning

One of the fundamental features of this educational psychology text is its direct focus on learners and learning, and understanding and assessing the conditions that influence the learning process and its outcomes.

We haven't just written about the nature of learning but have applied what we know about it to make your own role as a learner much easier as you read the book. For instance, we have continually applied two principles that are central to effective learning. First is the principle of meaningful learning: Students learn and remember information more effectively when they relate it to what they already know. Second is the principle of elaboration: Students learn and remember information more effectively, and are also more likely to use it in new situations, when they spontaneously go *beyond* what they read by drawing inferences, thinking of new examples, or speculating about possible applications. So as you read the book, you will be asked to relate new concepts to your own knowledge and experiences. In addition, many of the comments and questions in the margins will encourage you to recall ideas discussed in previous chapters, think of new examples, or speculate about applications.

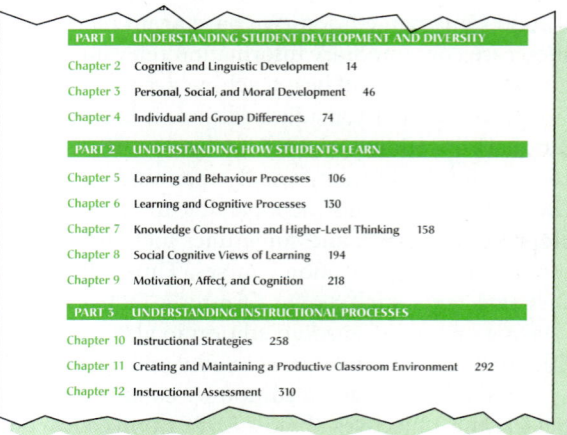

Focusing on Core Principles and Relating Principles to Your Own Learning and Behaviour

Rather than superficially explore every aspect of educational psychology, we remain committed in this second Canadian edition to providing an in-depth treatment of fundamental concepts and principles that have broad applicability to classroom practice. If we couldn't imagine how a concept or principle could possibly be of use to you, as a teacher, or was not one common to EDPSY courses in Canada, we left it out. Moreover, a central goal of this text is to help you discover more about yourself as a thinker and learner. If you can understand how *you* learn, you will be in a better position to understand how your students learn and, as a result, to help them do so more effectively. Throughout the book you will find exercises, reflective margin notes, webpage links, and other learning aids that will help you discover important points firsthand and thereby construct a more complete, meaningful understanding of the psychological principles of learning, development, motivation, and behaviour.

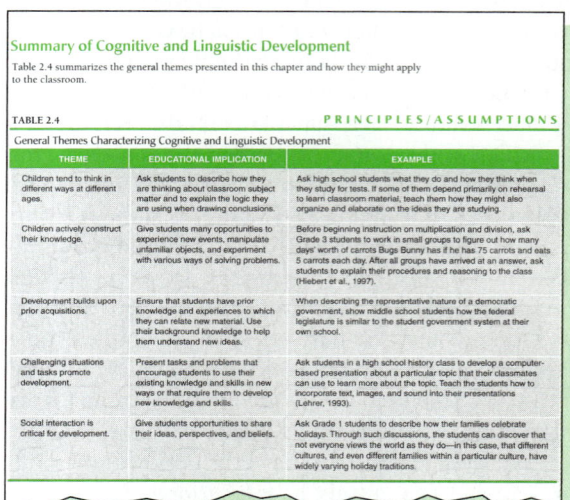

Applying Principles to Classroom Practice

Just as we have applied principles to an understanding of how *you* learn, so, too, will you use these to better understand how elementary and secondary school students learn and to make sense of what they do and say in the classroom. The Case Studies that begin each chapter, along with the Teaching Connections and Teaching Constructions sections, will help you think about the principles of learning, development, and motivation within classroom practice. In addition, the application of

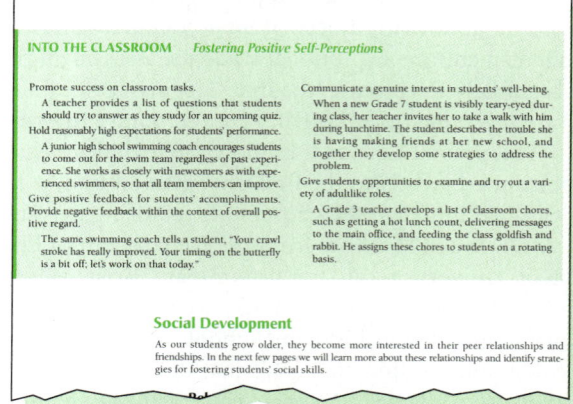

psychological concepts and principles to classroom practice is consistently highlighted as bulleted italicized statements within the text, or summarized through Into the Classroom features and Students in Inclusive Settings tables. Furthermore, you will find that the Teaching Constructions questions at the end of each chapter will help you apply ideas you have encountered in the chapter and make instructional decisions based on what you have learned. The many listed websites throughout this book will keep you connected with the rapidly growing body of information related to education, learning, and teaching. The websites cited in this text are intended to open a door into the extensive network of relevant information available online. We hope that you will continue to explore these resources, using the links in this text as starting points for even greater learning.

Supplements

To help both instructors and students get the most out of *Principles of Educational Psychology*, Second Canadian Edition, we have provided a number of useful supplements:

Instructor's Resource CD-ROM

For instructors, a handy Instructor's Resource CD-ROM (ISBN 0-13-506777-4) accompanies the text and contains all of the instructor-related supplements, including the Instructor's Manual, PowerPoint Slides, and the Test Item File.

Instructor's Manual. The Instructor's Manual includes suggestions for learning activities, supplementary lectures, case study analyses, discussion topics, group activities, and additional resources. These have been carefully selected to provide opportunities to support, enrich, and expand on what you read in the textbook.

PowerPoint Slides. The PowerPoint Slides include key concept summarizations, diagrams, and other graphic aids to enhance learning. They are designed to help students understand, organize, and remember core concepts and theories.

Test Item File. The Test Item File comprises over 1000 questions including multiple-choice and essay formats. The lower-level questions ask you to identify or explain concepts and principles, while the higher-level questions will ask you to apply those same concepts and principles to specific classroom situations—that is, to actual student behaviours and teaching strategies.

MyTest

A powerful assessment generation program, MyTest helps instructors easily create and print quizzes, tests, and exams. Questions and tests can all be authored online, allowing flexibility and the ability to efficiently manage assessments at any time, from anywhere. The MyTest can be accessed by visiting www.pearsonedmytest.com.

CourseSmart

CourseSmart is a new way for instructors and students to access textbooks online anytime from anywhere. With thousands of titles across hundreds of courses, CourseSmart helps instructors choose the best textbook for their class and give their students a new option for buying the assigned textbook as a lowercost eTextbook. For more information, visit www.coursesmart.com.

Technology Specialists

Pearson's Technology Specialists work with faculty and campus course designers to ensure that Pearson technology products, assessment tools, and online course materials are tailored to meet your specific needs. This highly qualified team is dedicated to helping schools take full advantage of a wide range of educational resources, by assisting in the integration of a variety of instructional materials and media formats. Your local Pearson Education sales representative can provide you with more details on this service program.

Acknowledgments

Many young people deserve thanks for letting me use their work. In particular, I want to acknowledge the contributions of Andrew and Katie Belcher; Noah and Shea Davis; Zachary Derr; Ben and Darcy Geraud; Dana Gogolin; Colin Hedges; Erin Islo; Laura Linton; Frederik Meissner; Meghan Milligan; Patrick Paddock; Alex, Jeff, and Tina Ormrod; Isabelle Peters; Ian Rhoades; Corey Ross; Ashton and Haley Russo; Connor Sheehan; Matt and Melinda Shump; and Grace Tober.

Last but certainly not least, I must thank my husband and children, who have been ever so patient as I have spent countless hours either buried in my books and journals or else glued to my computer. Without their continuing support and patience, this book would never have seen the light of day.
—Jeanne Ellis Ormrod

For this second Canadian edition, as in the first Canadian edition, we are indebted to Dr. Jeanne Ellis Ormrod for writing the textbook that we were invited to adapt for the Canadian context. Her brilliant writing reflects a comprehensive knowledge and practical understanding of learning, development, and teaching that we can all aspire to.

Dr. Laureen McIntyre from the University of Saskatchewan made an invaluable contribution to the chapter on Cognitive and Linguistic Development in the first edition that has carried over to this second edition. Her expertise in speech and language helped make this chapter especially meaningful for teachers. Thanks to Suzie Bisson, University of Calgary, for facilitating an understanding of how to support children from different ethnic backgrounds in Canadian schools. Danielle Droucker, also from the University of Calgary, provided invaluable assistance in locating Canadian research and websites. We are also grateful to Brenda Linn at McGill University for her additional contributions in bringing the sections on linguistic development fully up to date with the latest in psychological research on learning language and learning to read.

We are most grateful to the expert staff at Pearson Education Canada for their input at all stages of this book's development. Christine Cozens, as acquisitions editor, set the stage for this project and was encouraging from the very start. Jennifer Murray has worked with us on both editions of this book. She has been so very supportive throughout and, as developmental editor, has offered the kind of expert guidance that makes these books a reality. Laura Neves served as both production editor and copy editor and ensured that our words and ideas were successfully transferred to the printed pages of this book. We would be remiss if we did not repeat our very special thank you to Duncan MacKinnon for both his persistence in encouraging us to write the first Canadian edition of this book and his belief that we were the ones to do it.

The following individuals graciously gave up their time to provide constructive criticism of the various drafts of the revisions. We are grateful to these people, and to a few who wish to remain anonymous, for their many useful comments and suggestions.

Cheryl Bereziuk, Grande Prairie
Kerry Bernes, University of Lethbridge
Linda Chmiliar, Athabasca University
Diane Galambos, Sheridan College
Joseph Goulet, University of Winnipeg
Michael Harrison, University of Ottawa
Lori Levitt, Langara College
Tim Loreman, Concordia University College
Anne MacGregor, Douglas College
Karen Magro, University of Winnipeg
Michael Rodda, Grant MacEwan College
M. Stefan Sikora, Mount Royal College
Shelley Lynn Watson, Grant MacEwan College
Byrad Yyellan, Lakeland College

—Don Saklofske, Vicki Schwean,
Jac Andrews, Bruce Shore

principles of *educational* psychology

SECOND CANADIAN EDITION

1 Educational Psychology and Teacher Decision Making

CASE STUDY MORE THAN MEETS THE EYE

TEACHING CONNECTIONS

OOPS—A PRETEST

DRAWING CONCLUSIONS FROM PSYCHOLOGICAL AND EDUCATIONAL RESEARCH
Descriptive Studies • Correlational Studies • Experimental Studies • A Cautionary Note

USING PRINCIPLES AND THEORIES IN CLASSROOM DECISION MAKING

IMPORTANCE OF ONGOING ASSESSMENT IN CLASSROOM DECISION MAKING

DEVELOPING AS A TEACHER

LOOKING AHEAD TO THE FOLLOWING CHAPTERS

STUDYING EDUCATIONAL PSYCHOLOGY MORE EFFECTIVELY
Connecting Research to Teaching • Principles, Theories, and Assessment in Decision Making • Developing as a Teacher • Reading about and Studying Educational Psychology

TEACHING CONSTRUCTIONS

KEY CONCEPTS

CASE STUDY *More Than Meets the Eye*

Rosa is a personable, outgoing 12-year-old. Born in South America, she has lived in Canada for only three years, but she seems to have adjusted well to her new home. She now converses in English with just the slightest hint of an accent. She has made many friends and has an active after-school social life. She has blossomed into a talented athlete, seemingly a natural in almost any sport she tries, and is becoming especially proficient in volleyball and basketball. She also does well in art class and in the school choir, although she sometimes has trouble learning the lyrics.

But after three years in her new homeland, Rosa is still having difficulty in language arts, social studies, science, and mathematics. She often seems distracted in class and sometimes has trouble answering even the simplest questions her teachers ask her. Her test scores are inconsistent—sometimes quite high, but more frequently near the bottom of the class.

Rosa's teachers see occasional indicators that she is a bright and talented girl. For example, she is a skillful peacemaker who frequently steps in to help resolve interpersonal conflicts among her classmates. Her short stories, although often filled with grammatical and spelling errors, are imaginative and well developed. And of course there are the occasional high test scores. Rosa's teachers are convinced that Rosa is capable of achieving at a much higher level, but they are puzzled about just how to help her be more successful in her classroom activities.

TEACHING CONNECTIONS

In this first chapter you will get a taste of **educational psychology** by sampling research findings in development, learning, motivation, instruction, and classroom assessment practices. Most importantly, we will explore the ways in which psychology and your knowledge of psychology can be applied to teaching. As you read this chapter, then, consider the following questions in connecting theory with teaching practice:

- How much can common sense guide you in your efforts to help students learn and develop?
- What kinds of conclusions can you draw from psychological and educational research studies?
- How can psychological principles, theories, and research assist you in making decisions about how best to help students learn and achieve? How can your ongoing assessment of students' work and behaviours help you as well?
- How can you continue to improve throughout your professional teaching career?
- What are some possible explanations for Rosa's poor academic performance? Could the source of difficulty lie in her limited experience with English? In her cultural background? In her motivation? In her study skills? In the ways that her knowledge is assessed? Or perhaps in some combination of these things?
- Later in the chapter, we will have an overview of the book and discuss strategies for studying and learning educational psychology effectively.

Educational psychology A discipline encompassing psychological principles and theories related to learning, motivation, child and adolescent development, individual and group differences, and psychological assessment, especially as these topics relate to classroom practice.

OOPS—A Pretest

You probably have several hypotheses about why Rosa might be having difficulty. You've been a student for many years now, and in the process you've certainly learned a great deal about how students learn and develop and about how teachers can best help them achieve. But exactly how much *do* you know? To help you find out, we've developed a short pretest, Ormrod's Own Psychological Survey (OOPS).

EXPERIENCING FIRSTHAND *Ormrod's Own Psychological Survey (OOPS)*

Decide whether each of the following statements is *true* or *false*.
True/False

_____ 1. Most children 5 years of age and older are natural learners; they know the best way to learn something without having to be taught how to learn it.
_____ 2. When we compare boys and girls, we find that both groups are, on average, very similar in their mathematical and verbal aptitudes.
_____ 3. The best way to learn and remember a new fact is to repeat it over and over again.
_____ 4. Although students initially have many misconceptions about the world, they quickly revise their thinking once their teacher presents information that contradicts what they believe.
_____ 5. Students often misjudge how much they know about a topic.
_____ 6. Taking notes during a lecture usually interferes with learning more than it helps.
_____ 7. When a teacher rewards one student for appropriate behaviour, the behaviour of other students may also improve.
_____ 8. Anxiety sometimes helps students learn and perform more successfully in the classroom.
_____ 9. When we have children tutor their classmates in academic subject matter, we help only the students being tutored; the students doing the tutoring gain very little from the interaction.
_____ 10. The ways in which teachers assess students' learning influence what and how the students actually learn.

Now let's see how well you did on the OOPS. The answers, along with an explanation for each one, are as follows:

1. *Most children 5 years of age and older are natural learners; they know the best way to learn something without having to be taught how to learn it.* FALSE—Many students of all ages are relatively naive about how they can best learn something, and they often use inefficient strategies when they study. For example, most elementary students and a substantial number of high school students don't engage in **elaboration** as they study classroom material; that is, they don't analyze, interpret, or otherwise add their own ideas to the things they need to learn. Yet elaboration is one of the most effective ways of learning new information: Students learn the information more quickly and remember it better. We will look at developmental trends in elaboration as we discuss cognitive development in Chapter 2. We'll also explore the very important role that elaboration plays in long-term memory as we discuss cognitive processes in Chapter 6.

2. *When we compare boys and girls, we find that both groups are, on average, very similar in their mathematical and verbal aptitudes.* TRUE—Despite commonly held beliefs to the contrary, boys and girls tend to be similar in their ability to perform both mathematical and verbal academic tasks. Any differences in the average performance of boys and girls in these areas are usually too small for teachers to worry about. We will explore sex differences—and similarities as well—in Chapter 4.

3. *The best way to learn and remember a new fact is to repeat it over and over again.* FALSE—Although repeating information over and over again is better than doing nothing at all, repetition is a relatively *ineffective* way to learn. Students learn information more easily and remember it longer when they connect it with the things they already know and when they elaborate on it. Chapter 6 describes several cognitive processes that promote students' long-term retention of school subject matter.

4. *Although students initially have many misconceptions about the world, they quickly revise their thinking once their teacher presents information that contradicts what they believe.* FALSE—As you will discover in Chapter 7, students typically have many misconceptions about the world (e.g., they may believe that rivers always run south rather than north). They often hold strongly to these misconceptions even in the face of contradictory evidence or instruction. As teachers, one of our biggest challenges is to help students discard their erroneous beliefs in favour of more accurate and useful perspectives; some strategies for promoting such conceptual change appear in Chapter 7.

Elaboration A cognitive process in which learners expand on new information based on what they already know.

How often do you elaborate when you read your textbooks?

5. *Students often misjudge how much they know about a topic.* TRUE—Contrary to popular opinion, students are usually *not* the best judges of what they do and do not know. For example, many students think that if they've spent a long time studying a textbook chapter, they must know its content very well. Yet if they have spent most of their study time inefficiently (perhaps by "reading" without paying attention to meaning or by mindlessly copying definitions), they may know far less than they think they do. We will consider this *illusion of knowing* further in Chapter 7.

6. *Taking notes during a lecture usually interferes with learning more than it helps.* FALSE—In general, students who take notes learn more material from a lecture than students who don't take notes. Note taking appears to facilitate learning in at least two ways: It helps students put, or *store,* information into memory more effectively, and it allows them to review that information at a later time. Chapter 7 presents research concerning the effectiveness of note taking and other study strategies.

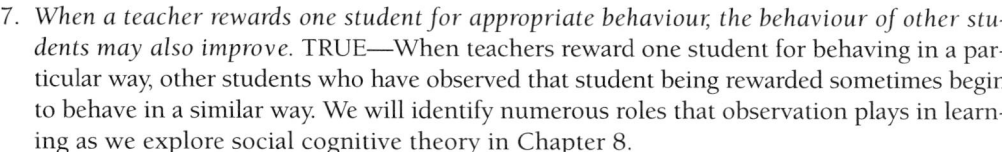
As a teacher, you will continually be making decisions about how best to help students learn, develop, and achieve.

7. *When a teacher rewards one student for appropriate behaviour, the behaviour of other students may also improve.* TRUE—When teachers reward one student for behaving in a particular way, other students who have observed that student being rewarded sometimes begin to behave in a similar way. We will identify numerous roles that observation plays in learning as we explore social cognitive theory in Chapter 8.

8. *Anxiety sometimes helps students learn and perform more successfully in the classroom.* TRUE—Many people think that anxiety is always a bad thing. Yet for some classroom tasks, and especially for relatively easy tasks, a moderate level of anxiety actually *improves* students' learning and performance. We will consider the effects of anxiety on learning and performance in more detail in Chapter 9.

9. *When we have children tutor their classmates in academic subject matter, we help only the students being tutored; the students doing the tutoring gain very little from the interaction.* FALSE—When students teach one another, the tutors often benefit as much as the students being tutored. For instance, in one research study, Grade 4 students who were doing relatively poorly in mathematics served as arithmetic tutors for Grade 1 and 2 students; the tutors themselves showed a substantial improvement in arithmetic skills (Inglis & Biemiller, 1997). We will look more closely at the effects of peer tutoring in Chapter 10.

10. *The ways in which teachers assess students' learning influence what and how the students actually learn.* TRUE—What and how students learn depend, in part, on how they expect their learning to be assessed. For example, students typically spend more time studying the things they think will be on a test than the things they think the test won't cover. And they are more likely to organize and integrate class material as they study if they expect assessment activities to require such organization and integration. Chapter 12 describes the effects of classroom assessment practices on students' learning.

How many of the OOPS items did you answer correctly? Did some of the false items seem convincing enough that you marked them true? Did some of the true items contradict certain beliefs you had? If either of these was the case, you are hardly alone. University students often agree with statements that seem obvious but are, in fact, completely wrong (Gage, 1991; Lennon, Ormrod, Burger, & Warren, 1990). Furthermore, many students in teacher education classes reject research findings when those findings appear to contradict their own personal beliefs and experiences (Borko & Putnam, 1996; Holt-Reynolds, 1992; Wideen, Mayer-Smith, & Moon, 1998).

Keep an open mind as you read this book. If you encounter ideas that at first seem incorrect, try to think of personal experiences and observations that support those ideas.

Chapter 1 Educational Psychology and Teacher Decision Making

Drawing Conclusions from Psychological and Educational Research

It's easy to be persuaded by "common sense" and become convinced that what seems logical must be reality. Yet common sense and logic do not always tell us the true story about how people actually learn and develop, nor do they always give us accurate information about how best to help students succeed in the classroom. Educational psychologists believe that knowledge about teaching and learning should come from a more objective source of information—that is, from psychological and educational research.

Most of the ideas presented in this book are based either directly or indirectly on the results of research studies. Let's take a look at three major types of research—descriptive, correlational, and experimental—and at the kinds of conclusions we can draw from each one.

Can you think of other questions that each type of research might address?

Descriptive study A research study that describes situations. Such a study enables researchers to draw conclusions about the current state of affairs but not about correlational or cause–effect relationships.

Correlational study A research study that explores relationships among variables. Such a study enables researchers to predict one variable on the basis of their knowledge of another but not to draw a conclusion about a cause–effect relationship.

Correlation The extent to which two variables are related to each other, such that when one variable increases, the other either increases or decreases in a somewhat predictable way.

Experimental study (experiment) A research study that involves the manipulation of one variable to determine its possible effect on another variable. It enables researchers to draw conclusions about cause–effect relationships.

Descriptive Studies

A **descriptive study** *describes* a situation. Descriptive studies might give us information about the characteristics of students, teachers, or schools; they might also provide information about the frequency with which certain events or behaviours occur. Descriptive studies allow us to draw conclusions about the way things are—the current state of affairs.

Correlational Studies

A **correlational study** explores relationships among different things. For instance, it might tell us how closely two human characteristics are associated with each other. Correlational studies enable us to draw conclusions about **correlation**—that is, about the extent to which two variables are interrelated. Correlations are often described numerically with a statistic known as a *correlation coefficient*.

Correlations between two variables allow us to make *predictions* about one variable if we know the status of the other. For example, if we find that older students are more capable of abstract thought than younger students, we can predict that Grade 10 students will benefit more from an abstract discussion of democratic government than Grade 4 students.

Experimental Studies

An **experimental study, or experiment**, is a study in which the researcher somehow changes, or *manipulates,* one or more aspects of the environment (*independent variables*) and then measures the effects of such changes on something else. The "something else" being affected (*dependent variable*) may be some aspect of student behaviour—perhaps an increase in achievement test scores or ability to interact appropriately with classmates. Experimental studies enable us to draw conclusions about *causation*—about *why* behaviours occur.

A Cautionary Note

To draw conclusions about causal relationships, we must eliminate other possible explanations for the outcomes we observe. Imagine that the Hometown School District wants to find out which of two reading programs, *Reading Is Great* (RIG) or *Reading and You* (RAY), leads to better reading in Grade 3. Grade 3 teachers choose one of these two reading programs and use it throughout a particular school year. End-of-year achievement test scores of students in the RIG and RAY classrooms show that RIG students achieve substantially higher reading comprehension scores than RAY students. We might quickly jump to the cause–effect conclusion that RIG promotes better reading comprehension than RAY. But is this really so?

Be careful that you don't jump too quickly to conclusions about what factors are affecting students' learning, development, and behaviour in particular situations. Scrutinize research carefully, always with this question in mind: *Have the researchers ruled out other possible explanations for their results?* Only when the answer to this question is an undeniable *yes* should you draw a conclusion about a cause–effect relationship.

Using Principles and Theories in Classroom Decision Making

When similar research studies yield similar results time after time, even under widely varying circumstances and with very different kinds of learners, educational psychologists derive general psychological **principles** describing specific factors that influence students' learning, development, and behaviour. Oftentimes, educational psychologists also speculate about why these principles are true; they develop **theories** that describe possible underlying, unobservable mechanisms regulating human learning, development, and behaviour. Psychological theories typically incorporate many principles and encompass a multitude of interrelationships. In essence, principles describe the *whats* of human behaviour—they describe what things happen under what conditions—whereas theories describe *why* those things happen.

Throughout the book we will be examining principles and theories related to student learning and classroom practice. Keep in mind that they are not necessarily set in stone; they simply represent our best guesses at the present time. With new research, our conceptions of human learning, development, and behaviour will continue to evolve into more complete and accurate explanations.

Yet, incomplete and tentative as current principles and theories in educational psychology may be, they provide numerous ideas and insights about how best to help our students achieve academic and social success. At some point, you may find yourself asking "Why aren't my students learning?" Following are just three of the many possible explanations:

- *They don't believe they can learn what you are trying to teach them:* One well-established principle of motivation is that people are more likely to try to learn something if they believe they are capable of learning and mastering it. Called *self-efficacy* by some theorists and *sense of competence* by others—it plays a significant role in social cognitive theory (Chapter 8) and may be particularly important for intrinsic (i.e., self-generated) motivation (Chapter 9).

- *They are having trouble comprehending something in the abstract manner you have explained it.* Jean Piaget proposed that children progress through four stages of increasingly complex and sophisticated thought and do not think abstractly until they reach the final stage, typically around age 11 or 12. Researchers have found partial support for Piaget's theory: Children show some evidence of abstract thought well before age 11, but they engage in it more frequently once they reach adolescence. (Piaget's theory is described in Chapter 2.)

- *They don't have enough background knowledge to understand the material you are presenting.* A basic principle of learning and cognitive development is that a learner's prior knowledge affects the learner's ability to acquire new information and skills. In general, the more students already know about a topic, the more quickly and easily they learn additional things about that topic. (See Chapters 2, 6, and 7.)

Each of these explanations leads to different instructional strategies for your class of 30 students. For instance, if your students don't believe they are capable of learning the knowledge or skills in question (i.e., if they have low self-efficacy), you might begin with fairly easy subject matter—something they can readily master—and gradually increase the difficulty level over time. Psychological principles and theories alone do not provide the answer. Ongoing assessment of students' achievement and progress is equally critical for teacher decision making.

Principle A description of how one variable influences another variable. It evolves when similar research studies yield similar results time after time.

Theory An organized body of concepts and principles developed to explain certain phenomena; a description of possible underlying mechanisms to explain why certain principles are true.

Importance of Ongoing Assessment in Classroom Decision Making

> The more accurate information you have about your students, the more effective you will be in promoting their learning.

Most teachers schedule regular assessments of what their students have learned, perhaps in the form of quizzes, compositions, projects, or presentations. But effective teachers don't limit themselves to such formal, planned evaluations. They continually observe their students in a variety of contexts—in the classroom, on the playground, on field trips, during extracurricular activities, with family members at parent–teacher conferences—for clues about what the students might be thinking, feeling, and learning. Students' comments, questions, facial expressions, body language, work habits, and interactions with friends and classmates can provide valuable insights into their learning, development, and behaviour. We will explore the topic of assessment in Chapter 12, but you will find implications for assessment in every chapter.

Developing as a Teacher

As a beginning teacher, you may initially find your role a bit overwhelming. So in the first few weeks or months, you may need to rely heavily on the standard lessons that curriculum development specialists provide. As you gain experience, you will be able to make decisions about routine situations and problems quickly and efficiently, giving you the time and energy to think creatively and flexibly about how best to teach your students (Borko & Putnam, 1996; Sternberg, 1996a).

The chapters that follow describe many ways you can help your students learn and develop. But it is equally important that *you* learn and develop as well, especially in your role as a teacher. Here are several strategies for doing so:

- *Continue to take courses in teacher education.* Additional coursework in teaching is one surefire way of keeping up to date on the latest theoretical perspectives and research results related to classroom practice. In general, teacher education definitely *does* enhance teaching effectiveness (Darling-Hammond, 1995).

- *Learn as much as you can about the subject matter you teach.* Effective teachers (those who are flexible in their approaches to instruction, help their students develop a thorough understanding of classroom subject matter, and convey obvious enthusiasm for whatever they are teaching) know their subject matter extremely well (Borko & Putnam, 1996; Cochran & Jones, 1998; Phillip, Flores, Sowder, & Schappelle, 1994).

- *Learn as much as you can about specific strategies for teaching your particular subject matter.* In addition to general teaching strategies, develop strategies specific to the topic you are teaching; a repertoire of such strategies is known as pedagogical content knowledge. Effective teachers typically have a large number of strategies for teaching various topics and skills (Borko & Putnam, 1996; Brophy, 1991; Cochran & Jones, 1998; L. S. Shulman, 1986). Furthermore, they can usually anticipate—and so can also address—the difficulties students will have, as well as the kinds of errors students will make, in the process of mastering a skill or body of knowledge (Borko & Putnam, 1996; D. C. Smith & Neale, 1991). Consider keeping a journal of effective teaching strategies you develop and use.

- *Learn as much as you can about the culture(s) of the community in which you are working.* We will be identifying numerous ways in which students from diverse cultural backgrounds may think and behave differently than the ways *you* thought and behaved as a child. Yet a textbook can give only a sample of the many possible differences. You can more effectively become aware of the beliefs and practices of your students' cultural groups by participating in local community activities and conversing with community members (McCarty & Watahomigie, 1998; H. L. Smith, 1998).

- *Conduct your own research.* The research literature on learning, motivation, development, and instructional practice grows by leaps and bounds every year. Nevertheless, teachers sometimes encounter problems in the classroom that existing research findings don't address. In such circumstances, we can conduct our own research. Conducting systematic studies of issues and problems in our schools, with the goal of seeking more effective interventions in the lives of our students, is **action research**.

Action research Research conducted by teachers and other school personnel to address issues and problems in their own schools or classrooms.

INTO THE CLASSROOM *Becoming a More Effective Teacher*

Use some of the standard lessons that curriculum development specialists provide, especially in your first few weeks or months in the classroom.

> A science teacher consults the teaching manual that accompanies her class textbook for ideas about how to make science come alive for her students.

As you gain experience and confidence as a teacher, begin to adapt standard lessons and develop your own lessons.

> When a high school social studies teacher begins using a new geography textbook, he peruses the teacher's manual that accompanies the book. He notices that the manual's lesson plans focus almost exclusively on meaningless memorization of geographic concepts and principles. Rather than use these lessons, he develops classroom activities of his own that will encourage his students to apply geography to real-life situations.

Keep a journal of the instructional strategies you use and their relative effectiveness.

> As a way of winding down at bedtime, a new teacher reflects on his day in the classroom. He picks up the notebook and pen on his bedside table and jots down notes about the strategies that did and did not work well in class that day.

Seek the advice and suggestions of your more experienced colleagues.

> A Grade 4 teacher is teaching her students long division, but after a week they still don't understand what they are supposed to do. In the teacher's lounge she consults with two of her fellow teachers for ideas about how she might approach the topic differently.

Continue your education, both formally and informally.

> A middle school science teacher takes advantage of a tour package to Costa Rica designed specifically for teachers. There she will study the plants, animals, and ecology of the rain forest.

Conduct your own research to answer questions about your students and about the effectiveness of your teaching practices.

> Over the course of the school year, a Grade 2 school teacher alternates among three different approaches to teaching the weekly spelling words. At the end of the school year, he compares his students' spelling quiz scores for each of the three methods and sees that one approach led to noticeably higher scores than the other two.

Remember that teaching, like any other complex skill, takes time and practice to master.

> A teacher continues to try new instructional techniques that he sees described in professional journals. As he does so, he adds to his repertoire of effective teaching strategies and becomes increasingly able to adjust his methods to the diverse population of students in his classroom.

Action research is a popular endeavour among teachers and other educational professionals. It takes a variety of forms; for example, it might involve assessing the effectiveness of a new teaching technique or conducting an in-depth case study of a particular student (Cochran-Smith & Lytle, 1993; Mills, 2000). Many colleges and universities now offer courses in action research; two other good sources of information are Geoffrey Mills' *Action Research* (2000) and the online journal *Action Research International* (www.scu.edu.au/schools/gcm/ar/ari/arihome.html).

■ *Believe that you can become an effective teacher.* Earlier we mentioned that students are more likely to try to learn something if they believe that they *can* learn it—in other words, if they have high self-efficacy. You, too, must have high self-efficacy. Believing that you can be a good teacher will help you persist in the face of occasional setbacks and ultimately be effective in the classroom. Students who achieve at the highest levels are most likely to be those whose teachers have confidence in what they *themselves* can do for their students (J. A. Langer, 2000; Tschannen-Moran, Woolfolk Hoy, & Hoy, 1998).

Teaching, like any other complex skill, takes time and practice to master. And you, like any other learner, will inevitably make a few mistakes, especially at the beginning. But you *will* improve over time. If you base classroom decisions on documented principles and sound educational practice, you can undoubtedly make a difference in the lives of your students (e.g., see Figure 1.1).

FIGURE 1.1 Twelve-year-old Grace describes her favourite teacher

> I know a great teacher and his name is Mr. Shipley. Mr. Shipley was my grade 6 teacher for Science, Social Studies, and Flex (or Study hall). This man is my favourite teacher for many reasons.
>
> I had Science during first period and since, I don't think that it is the most interesting subject, I would often get bored and lose interest in what he was saying. But every so often Mr. Shipley would do something crazy and funny to kind-of snap me out of my daze and put me back into class. I thank him for that!
>
> Mr. Shipley was always understanding and he seemed to have a special bond with kids. I was in his study hall and during that period, 6th period, the grade 7 students had lunch. That is a free time to do whatever you want, so the grade 7s would wander down to talk to him. (Of course they'd ask for a Jolly Rancher from his famous stash in his desk!) I admire and was amazed to see how he continued to bring students from years past, down to him.
>
> Not only was Mr. Shipley funny, understanding, and just a great, all around great teacher, he believed in me. Mr. Shipley had faith in me and that is something I knew my other teachers had, but rarely expressed. I always got an A or A+ in his classes and Language Arts, but Math was a struggle for me. I always ended up with a B+ in that class. But I tried harder and harder to get that B+ up to an A, but I just couldn't. So each time grade card time rolled around, I'd wind up with all A's and A+'s except for Math, a B+. I worked so hard all year for a 4.0 (straight A's) but wound up with an average of 3.899. Mr. Shipley always told me that I'd "get 'em next time." And I did! I am now in grade 7 with a 4.0, straight A's! Even in Math. I also made the tennis team, 1st doubles. Mr. Shipley believed in me all the way! So, I owe a lot to him.
>
> Mr. Shipley - the funny man, the understander, the believer: My favourite teacher!

Looking Ahead to the Following Chapters

As a teacher, you are a decision maker. And you are most likely to make wise decisions when, in the process, general questions such as these are considered:

- What characteristics do your students bring to the classroom?
- What do you know about how students learn?
- How can you convert our knowledge about development, diversity, and learning into effective teaching practice?

Figure 1.2 provides a graphic overview of this book, with examples of questions that each chapter addresses. Take a moment to think about specific topics you hope the book will cover and identify the chapters in which you are most likely to find them.

These students are engaged in discovery learning within the context of a co-operative learning activity. Discovery learning and co-operative learning are just two of the many instructional strategies we'll consider in Chapter 10.

Studying Educational Psychology More Effectively

As you read the book, you will gain insights about how you can help your students more effectively learn the things you want to teach them. At the same time, we hope you will also gain insights about how *you yourself* can learn course material. But rather than wait until we get to our discussion of learning in Part 2, let's look briefly at three general principles of effective learning that you can apply as you read and study this book:

- *Students learn more effectively when they relate new information to the things they already know.* Try to connect the ideas you read in the book with things you are already familiar with—for example, with your own past experiences, with your previous course work, with things you have observed in schools, or with your general knowledge about the world.

UNDERSTANDING STUDENT DEVELOPMENT AND DIVERSITY
- What characteristics do our students bring to the classroom?

Chapter 2. Cognitive and Linguistic Development
- How does logical thinking change with age?
- To what extent do students at different grade levels learn differently?
- How do students' language skills develop during the elementary and secondary school years?

Chapter 3. Personal, Social, and Moral Development
- What can we do to promote students' self-esteem?
- What roles do students' friends and classmates play in development?
- How do we help students develop a "conscience" about right and wrong?

Chapter 4. Individual and Group Differences
- What are intelligence and creativity?
- How do students' cultural backgrounds influence their classroom performance?
- How are boys and girls similar and different?
- In what ways are students with special needs different from their peers?
- What instructional strategies support students in inclusive settings?

UNDERSTANDING HOW STUDENTS LEARN
- What do we know about how students learn?

Chapter 5. Learning and Behaviour Processes
- What role does reinforcement play in learning?
- How can we encourage productive classroom behaviours?
- Should we ever use punishment and, if so, under what circumstances?

Chapter 6. Learning and Cognitive Processes
- What is learning?
- What thinking processes help students learn classroom subject matter effectively?
- Why do students sometimes forget what they've learned?

Chapter 7. Knowledge Construction and Higher-Level Thinking
- How can we help students learn new concepts?
- What effects do students' misconceptions about classroom topics have on learning?
- How can we help students learn to study effectively?
- How can we help students apply the things they learn to real-world situations?
- How can we facilitate problem solving and critical thinking skills?

Chapter 8. Social Cognitive Views of Learning
- What can students learn from watching others?
- How can we enhance students' self-confidence about performing classroom tasks?
- How can we help students regulate their own behaviour and learning?

Chapter 9. Motivation, Affect, and Cognition
- How does motivation affect learning and behaviour?
- What social needs are students likely to have?
- How do anxiety and other emotions affect learning?
- How can we foster intrinsic motivation to learn?
- Why do some students have trouble accepting responsibility for their own actions?
- How might our expectations for students lead to a self-fulfilling prophecy?

UNDERSTANDING INSTRUCTIONAL PROCESSES
- How can we convert our knowledge about development, diversity, and learning into effective teaching practice?

Chapter 10. Instructional Strategies
- Under what circumstances are verbal explanations (e.g., lectures) apt to be effective?
- In what situations might it be better to let students discover ideas for themselves?
- How do class discussions enhance students' learning?

Chapter 11. Creating and Maintaining a Productive Classroom Environment
- How can we get the school year off to a good start?
- How can we keep discipline problems to a minimum?
- How can we collaborate with parents to maximize students' classroom performance?

Chapter 12. Instructional Assessment
- How do classroom assessment practices affect students' learning?
- How do we know when the results of our assessments are accurate?
- What purposes can standardized tests serve?
- What classroom assessment tools can best determine whether students are achieving instructional objectives?
- What guidelines can help us develop good paper-pencil tests and performance tasks?
- On what criteria should we base final grades?

FIGURE 1.2 Overview of the book: Examples of questions addressed in each chapter

■ *Students learn more effectively when they elaborate on new information.* As you learned earlier, elaboration is a process of adding one's own ideas to new information. In most situations, elaboration enables us to learn information with greater understanding, remember it better, and apply it more readily when we need it. So try to think *beyond* the information you read. Generate new examples of concepts. Draw inferences from the research findings presented. Identify educational applications of various principles and theories.

■ *Students learn more effectively when they periodically check to make sure they have learned.* There are times when even the best of us don't concentrate on what we're reading—

How frequently do you apply these principles when you study?

> The key to successful learning is to make whatever you are learning *meaningful*. Reflect on your own educational history and recall those classes or topics that you did not fully grasp or understand; did you do well in that class, do you recall what you learned, or do you use this information today?

> Make a list of factors that you think have made you a successful learner. These factors might relate to specific learning situations and content; they might relate to you, your teacher, or other supports such as family and friends, technology, and so on.

when we are actually thinking about something else as our eyes go down the page. So stop once in a while (perhaps once every two or three pages) to make sure you have really learned and understood the things you've been reading. Try to summarize the material. Ask yourself questions about it. Make sure everything makes logical sense to you. Don't become a victim of that *illusion of knowing* we mentioned earlier.

Perhaps you are a student who has been following these principles for years. But in case you are someone for whom such learning strategies are relatively new, we've provided margin notes (designated by a green bar) to help you learn and study throughout the book. These notes will give you some suggestions for how you might think about the material in nearby paragraphs. With practice, the strategies recommended will eventually become second nature to you as you read and study in all your classes. Margin notes designated by a grey bar provide suggestions for further reading.

Furthermore, the case study in each chapter can help you relate chapter content to concrete classroom situations. These opening case studies introduce you to a variety of concepts and principles and are frequently referred to throughout the chapters. Each case study is followed by questions intended to connect theory with your own teaching practice.

Connecting Research to Teaching

As the OOPS test may have shown you, you (like everyone) almost certainly have a few misconceptions about how students typically learn and develop and about how teachers can most effectively promote students' classroom success. Psychological and educational research provides a reality check for such misconceptions and may yield insights that fly in the face of many common-sense, seemingly logical ideas about instructional practice.

Some research studies are *descriptive* in nature, in that they describe existing characteristics of students, teachers, or instructional practices. Other studies are *correlational*, in that they provide information about relationships among variables—perhaps relationships among two or more student characteristics, or perhaps relationships between students' behaviours and the kinds of environments in which students live. Still other studies are *experimental*: The researcher manipulates one or more aspects of the environment and measures the effects of that manipulation on some aspect of student behaviour. Correlational studies allow us to predict one characteristic when we have information about another, related characteristic, but only experimental studies allow us to draw conclusions about cause–effect relationships.

Principles, Theories, and Assessment in Decision Making

When research studies yield similar results time after time, educational psychologists derive principles and theories that describe and explain people's learning, development, and behaviour. Although such principles and theories provide a starting point for classroom decision making, we can ultimately identify the most effective classroom strategies for our own classrooms only when we assess students' knowledge, interpretations, and progress using both planned assignments and informal observations on an ongoing basis.

Developing as a Teacher

Researchers continually add to our knowledge about how children and adolescents think and learn. As a teacher, you must keep yourself abreast of research results, theoretical developments, and educational innovations. In your first few months as a classroom teacher, you may initially find your classroom a bit overwhelming, but with experience, continuing education, and the professional support of your teaching colleagues, you can almost certainly become an expert in the teaching profession.

Reading about and Studying Educational Psychology

As we explore the many ways that children and adolescents think and learn in the chapters that follow, you will undoubtedly discover many new strategies that can help you in your *own* learning. For the time being, however, keep these three strategies in mind as you read and study the book: (a) Relate new information to what you already know, (b) elaborate on that information, and (c) occasionally stop to test yourself on the content you've studied.

TEACHING CONSTRUCTIONS

In this first chapter we sampled critical themes in development, learning, motivation, instruction, and classroom assessment practices. Importantly, you were introduced to the relevance of psychology to teaching, learning, and the classroom. Given what you read in this chapter, consider the following questions:

- How do your personal beliefs fit with the applications of educational psychology in the classroom?
- How do you think psychological research informs your own teaching practice?
- Do you think you will be the same teacher 10 years from now?
- How would you adapt your classroom to enhance Rosa's personal, social, and academic success?

KEY CONCEPTS

Educational psychology (p. 3)
elaboration (p. 4)
descriptive study (p. 6)
correlational study (p. 6)
correlation (p. 6)
experimental study (experiment) (p. 6)
principle (p. 7)
theory (p. 7)
action research (p. 8)

2 Cognitive and Linguistic Development

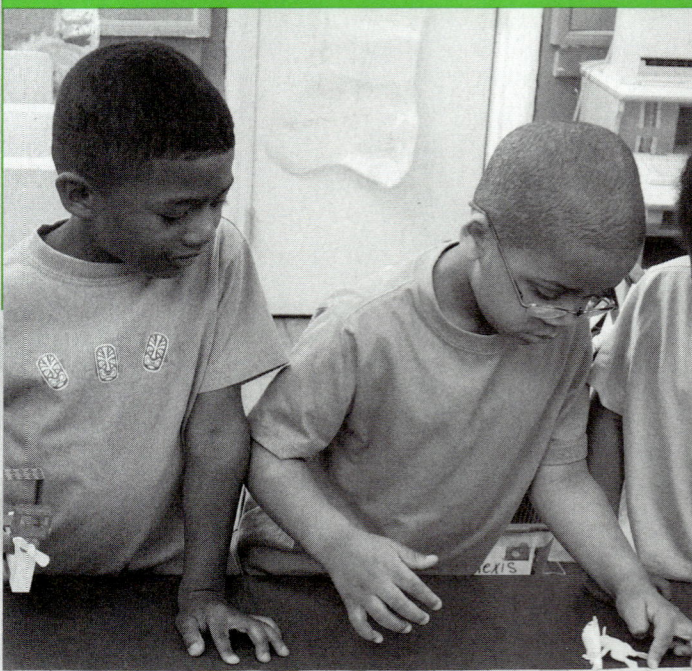

CASE STUDY HOW DO YOU LEARN?

TEACHING CONNECTIONS

BASIC PRINCIPLES OF HUMAN DEVELOPMENT

PIAGET'S THEORY OF COGNITIVE DEVELOPMENT
Piaget's Basic Assumptions • Piaget's Stages of Cognitive Development • Current Perspectives on Piaget's Theory

VYGOTSKY'S THEORY OF COGNITIVE DEVELOPMENT
Vygotsky's Basic Assumptions • Current Perspectives on Vygotsky's Theory

AN INFORMATION-PROCESSING VIEW OF COGNITIVE DEVELOPMENT
Attention • Learning Strategies • Knowledge • Metacognition

LINGUISTIC DEVELOPMENT
Theoretical Perspectives on Language Development • Trends in Language Development • Learning a Second Language

CONSIDERING DIVERSITY IN COGNITIVE AND LINGUISTIC DEVELOPMENT
Accommodating Students with Exceptionalities

SUMMARY OF COGNITIVE AND LINGUISTIC DEVELOPMENT

TEACHING CONSTRUCTIONS

KEY CONCEPTS

CASE STUDY *How Do You Learn?*

Are *you* prepared to be our case study? Think of a time when you were enrolled in an extremely challenging course that caused you to experience considerable frustration. Both the textbook and lectures in the course were hard to understand and there seemed to be an overwhelming amount of material to memorize. Reflect on factors that contributed to your difficulties in comprehending the textbook and lectures. What characteristics of the text seemed to be interfering with your understanding? For example, was the material too abstract? Did you have the necessary background information to help you make sense of the material? Were you motivated by the course content? Were you able to organize and elaborate on the material such that it facilitated your understanding? Were you clear about the objectives of the course?

Now take a moment and reflect on strategies you and the instructor might have used to better facilitate your learning. Could the instructor have presented the material in several smaller lessons or provided structure or guidelines about how the material could be better understood? Could you have been more effective in attempting to link new information presented in the class to information you had acquired in other related courses? As you journey through this chapter, try to identify other instructional strategies that you, as a teacher, can use to assist students in learning and remembering new information.

TEACHING CONNECTIONS

As we look at cognitive and linguistic development in this chapter, consider the following questions as you make connections between the theory and the practice of teaching:

- What principles and theories can guide you in your efforts to adapt instruction to students' cognitive abilities and to promote their further cognitive development?
- How do students' language abilities change with age, and what implications do such changes have for classroom practice?
- How might your students differ from one another in their cognitive and linguistic development, and how can you accommodate such differences?

Basic Principles of Human Development

By working through the case study, you hopefully came to some understandings about various impediments to your learning. As we study various theories of cognitive and linguistic development in the pages ahead, you will gain additional insights about how children and adolescents learn and the factors that enhance or impede their learning. But first, let's consider several principles that seem to hold true regardless of the aspect of development. Following are four important principles to keep in mind as you read Chapters 2 and 3:

- *Development proceeds in a somewhat orderly and predictable pattern.* Human development is often characterized by **developmental milestones** that occur in a predictable sequence. For example, children think logically about abstract ideas only after they have learned to think logically about concrete objects and observable events. To some extent, then, we see **universals** in development: We see similar patterns in how children change over time regardless of the specific environment in which they are being raised.

- *Different children develop at different rates.* Although research tells us the average ages at which children achieve developmental milestones (e.g., walking, talking), there is variability among children; some reach these milestones earlier and others later. Knowing the approximate ages at which children can perform certain behaviours and think in certain ways helps us to form general expectations about children's capabilities at a particular age level and to design curriculum and instructional strategies around these expectations.

Developmental milestone The appearance of a new behaviour that is developmentally more advanced.

Universals (in development) The similar patterns we see in how children change over time regardless of the specific environment in which they are raised.

Descriptive research on child development tells us the *average* age at which various developmental milestones are reached. But we must remember that individual children develop at different rates.

Maturation The unfolding of genetically controlled changes as a child develops.

Temperament A genetic predisposition to respond in particular ways to one's physical and social environments.

Sensitive period An age range during which a certain aspect of a child's development is especially susceptible to environmental conditions.

- *Periods of relatively rapid growth (spurts) may appear between periods of slower growth (plateaus).* Development does not always proceed at a constant rate. Toddlers may speak with a limited vocabulary and one-word "sentences" for months, yet sometime around their second birthday a virtual explosion in language development occurs: Vocabulary expands rapidly and sentences become longer and longer within weeks. Some theorists use such patterns of uneven growth and change as evidence for distinct, qualitatively different periods in development.

- *Development is continually affected by both nature (heredity) and nurture (environment).* Virtually all aspects of development are directly or indirectly affected by a child's genetic makeup. Not all inherited characteristics appear at birth; heredity influences a child's growth through the process of **maturation**, an unfolding of genetically controlled changes as the child develops. For example, motor skills such as walking, running, and jumping develop primarily as a result of neurological development, increased strength, and increased muscular control, all largely determined by heredity. Furthermore, children are genetically endowed with particular ways of responding to their physical and social environments, and such **temperaments** influence their tendency to be calm or irritable, outgoing or shy, adventuresome or cautious, cheerful or fearful (Kagan, 1998; Rothbart & Bates, 1998).

The environment is also critical in most aspects of development. For example, poverty compromises immediate and long-term health, social development, and cognitive ability. This finding is frightening: Over a million children in Canada live in poverty (Ross & Roberts, 1999).

Heredity and environment typically interact. We may never be able to disentangle the unique influences of nature and nurture on development (Collins, Maccoby, Steinberg, Hetherington, & Bornstein, 2000; Gottlieb, 2000; Turkheimer, 2000). Heredity may predetermine **sensitive periods**—age ranges during which a growing child can be especially influenced by environmental conditions. For instance, neurological developments during the preschool and elementary years may indicate these as sensitive periods in brain development and urge us to maximize children's educational experiences, especially for languages. However, others argue that we have no evidence of sensitive periods for academic subjects such as reading, writing, or mathematics (Bruer, 1999; Geary, 1998; Greenough, Black, & Wallace, 1987).

This question of *nature versus nurture* continues to be a source of controversy among developmental theorists. In your own opinion, how much are human characteristics influenced by heredity? By environment?

Piaget's Theory of Cognitive Development

Have you encountered Piaget's theory in other courses? What do you already know about his theory?

In the 1920s, Swiss biologist Jean Piaget began studying children's responses to problems. Piaget and his colleagues were curious about the origins of knowledge, a branch of philosophy known as *epistemology*, and the forms knowledge takes as it develops. Their studies provide many unique insights about how children think and learn about the world around them (e.g., Inhelder & Piaget, 1958; Piaget, 1928, 1952, 1959, 1970, 1980). Let's explore his basic assumptions and the four stages of logical thinking that he proposed.

Piaget's Basic Assumptions

Piaget introduced a number of ideas and concepts to describe and explain the changes in logical thinking that he observed in children and adolescents:

- *Children are active and motivated learners.* Children are not passive receivers of environmental stimulation; instead, they are naturally curious about their world and actively seek out information to help them understand and make sense of it. They continually experiment with the objects they encounter, manipulating things and observing the effects of their actions.

- *Children construct knowledge from their experiences.* Children's knowledge is not a collection of isolated pieces of information. Rather, children use their accumulated information to construct an overall view of how the world operates. Because Piaget proposed that children construct their knowledge from their experiences, his theory is often called a **constructivist** theory.

  In Piaget's terminology, what children learn and can do are organized as **schemes**—groups of related ideas or actions. For example, a teen may have a scheme for what is fashionable, allowing her to classify peers as either "totally awesome" or "complete dorks."

  With experience and over time, children's schemes become modified and better integrated with one another. For instance, children begin to recognize the hierarchical interrelationships of some schemes: They learn that poodles and cocker spaniels are both dogs, that dogs and cats are both animals, and so on. A progressively more organized body of knowledge and thought processes allows children to think in increasingly sophisticated and logical ways.

- *Children learn through the two complementary processes of assimilation and accommodation.* Children's schemes change over time, but the processes by which children develop them remain the same. Piaget proposed that learning and cognitive development occur as the result of two complementary processes: assimilation and accommodation. **Assimilation** is a process of dealing with a new object or event in a way that is consistent with an existing scheme. For example, the teen labels a new classmate as being either awesome or dorkish.

  Sometimes children cannot easily relate to a new object or event with their existing schemes. One of two forms of **accommodation** will then occur: They will either modify an existing scheme to deal with the new object or event, or form an entirely new scheme. For example, the teen may have to revise her existing scheme of fashion according to changes in what's cool or uncool and develop a new scheme for classmates who no longer fit pre-existing schemes.

  Assimilation and accommodation typically work together as children develop their knowledge and understanding of the world. Children interpret each new event within the context of their existing knowledge (assimilation) but at the same time may modify their knowledge as a result of the new event (accommodation). Our students can benefit from (accommodate to) new experiences only when they can relate those experiences to their current knowledge and beliefs.

- *Interaction with one's physical and social environments is essential for cognitive development.* New experiences are essential for learning and cognitive development. Hence, Piaget stressed encouraging children to interact with their physical environment. Manipulating the environment—for example, experimenting in a science lab—can promote understanding of cause–effect relationships, physical characteristics such as weight and volume, and so on.

  Social interaction is equally critical for cognitive development. Through interaction with others, children learn that different individuals see things differently and that their own view of the world is not necessarily a completely accurate or logical one. To illustrate, a preschool child may have difficulty seeing the world from anyone's perspective but his own. Through social interactions, both pleasant (e.g., a conversation) and unpleasant (e.g., an argument), he begins to realize that his own perspective is unique and not entirely shared by others.

Constructivism A theoretical perspective that proposes that learners construct a body of knowledge from their experiences—knowledge that may or may not be an accurate representation of external reality. Adherents to this perspective are called *constructivists*.

Scheme In Piaget's theory, an organized group of similar actions or thoughts. (The word *schema*—pronounced "skeema"—is also often used in the psychological literature; the plurals of schema are *schemata* or *schemas*.)

Assimilation In Piaget's theory, dealing with a new event in a way that is consistent with an existing scheme. (As a rough mental image, think of reshaping a new peg to fit an existing hole.)

Accommodation In Piaget's theory, dealing with a new event by either modifying an existing scheme or forming a new one. (As a rough mental image, think of remaking an existing hole to accommodate a new peg.)

From Piaget's perspective, both interaction with concrete objects (e.g., counting and handling money) and interaction with others (e.g., sharing perspectives about a topic or problem) are essential for cognitive development.

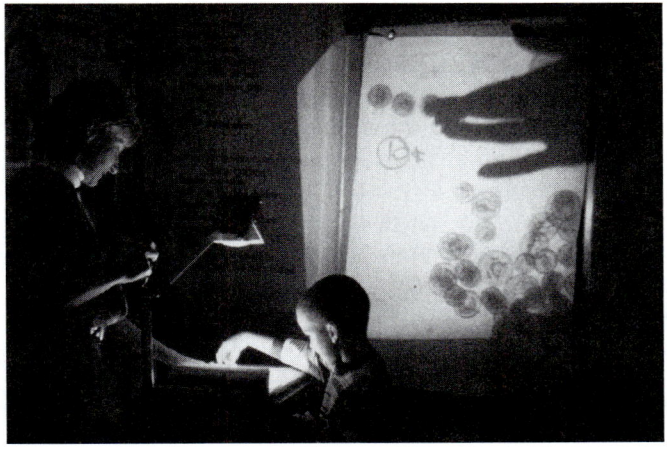

> *The process of equilibration promotes progression toward more complex thought levels.* For Piaget, when children can comfortably explain new events with existing schemes, they are in a state of **equilibrium**. When they encounter events they cannot adequately explain given their current understanding of the world, these events create **disequilibrium**, a sort of mental discomfort. Through replacing, reorganizing, or better integrating their schemes (i.e., accommodation) children become able to understand and explain those previously puzzling events. Moving to disequilibrium and back to equilibrium is a process known as **equilibration**. Equilibration and children's need to achieve equilibrium promote the development of more complex levels of thought and knowledge.

> *Cognitive development can proceed only after certain genetically controlled neurological changes occur.* Piaget speculated that cognitive development depends partly on brain maturation and, because of neurological immaturity, young children cannot think as adults do, no matter what parents or teachers might do to encourage adultlike thinking. Piaget hypothesized that major physiological changes take place at about age 2, again at 6 or 7, and again around puberty, and that these changes allow the development of increasingly complex thought. We should note that psychologists disagree about whether neurological advancements are truly responsible for the developmental changes that Piaget described (e.g., Rosser, 1994).

Equilibrium In Piaget's theory, a state of being able to explain new events by using existing schemes.

Disequilibrium In Piaget's theory, an inability to explain new events by using existing schemes.

Equilibration In Piaget's theory, the movement from equilibrium to disequilibrium and back to equilibrium—a process that promotes the development of more complex forms of thought and knowledge.

Sensorimotor stage Piaget's first stage of cognitive development, in which schemes are based on behaviours and perceptions.

Object permanence The realization that objects continue to exist even after they are removed from view.

Piaget's Stages of Cognitive Development

A major feature of Piaget's theory is his description of four stages of logical reasoning capabilities:

1. Sensorimotor stage (birth until 2 years)
2. Preoperational stage (2 years until 6 or 7 years)
3. Concrete operations stage (6 or 7 years until 11 or 12 years)
4. Formal operations stage (11 or 12 years through adulthood)

These stages are summarized in Figure 2.1. Each stage has unique characteristics and capabilities, and each builds upon the accomplishments of former stages, so in Piaget's view, children must progress through the four stages in the same, invariant sequence.

For reasons described later, many psychologists question whether cognitive development is as stagelike as Piaget proposed (Flavell, 1994; Siegler, 1998). Nevertheless, Piaget's stages do provide insights about children's thinking at different age levels, so it is helpful to examine the characteristics of each stage. Note that the ages given for each stage are *averages*; some children may reach a stage at a slightly younger age, and others may reach it at an older age. Also, some children may be *transitional* from one stage to the next and so may display characteristics of two adjacent stages during the same time period.

Sensorimotor Stage (birth until 2 years)

Piaget proposed that children in the **sensorimotor stage** develop schemes based primarily on behaviours and perceptions. They are not yet capable of *mental* schemes that enable them to think about objects beyond immediate view, partly because they lack words they can use to mentally represent things they cannot see.

Nevertheless, important cognitive capabilities emerge during the sensorimotor stage, especially as children begin to experiment with their environments through trial and error. For example, near the end of the stage, children develop **object permanence**, the realization that objects continue to exist when removed from view. After repeatedly observing that certain actions lead to certain consequences, they also begin to develop an understanding of *cause–effect relationships*. Object permanence, cause and effect, and other ideas that develop during the sensorimotor stage are basic building blocks of later cognitive development.

FIGURE 2.1 Piaget's stages of cognitive development

SENSORIMOTOR STAGE
(birth until about 2 years old)

Schemes are based on behaviours and perceptions; schemes don't yet represent objects beyond a child's immediate view.

PREOPERATIONAL STAGE
(2 until about 6 or 7 years old)

Schemes now represent objects beyond a child's immediate view, but the child does not yet reason in logical, adultlike ways.

CONCRETE OPERATIONS STAGE
(6 or 7 until about 11 or 12 years old)

Adultlike logic appears but is limited to reasoning about concrete reality.

FORMAL OPERATIONS STAGE
(11 or 12 through adulthood)

Logical reasoning processes are applied to abstract ideas as well as to concrete objects.

Preoperational Stage (2 years until 6 or 7 years)

Children in the **preoperational stage** can form schemes that are relatively independent of immediate perceptions and behaviours. This ability to represent external objects and events in one's mind (**symbolic thinking**) marks the beginning of true thought as Piaget defined it.

Language skills explode early in the preoperational stage. Children's rapidly increasing vocabularies provide labels for newly developed schemes and enable children to think about objects and events even when they are not in direct view. Language also provides the basis for a new form of social interaction—verbal communication. Children can now express their thoughts and receive information from other people in a way previously not possible.

At the same time, preoperational thinking has some definite limitations, especially when compared with concrete operational thinking (see Table 2.1). For example, children in this stage exhibit **preoperational egocentrism**, an inability to view situations from another person's perspective. They may have trouble understanding why they must share school supplies with a classmate or why they must be careful not to hurt someone else's feelings.

Preoperational stage Piaget's second stage of cognitive development, in which children can think about objects beyond their immediate view but do not yet reason in logical, adultlike ways.

Symbolic thinking The ability to represent and think about external objects and events in one's head.

Preoperational egocentrism In Piaget's theory, the inability of children in the preoperational stage to view situations from another person's perspective.

TABLE 2.1   COMPARE/CONTRAST

Preoperational versus Concrete Operational Thought

PREOPERATIONAL THOUGHT	CONCRETE OPERATIONAL THOUGHT
Preoperational Egocentrism Students do not see things from someone else's perspective; they think their own perspectives are the only ones possible. *Example:* A student tells a story without considering what prior knowledge the listener is likely to have.	**Differentiation of One's Own Perspective from the Perspectives of Others** Students recognize that others see things differently than they do; they realize that their own perspectives may be incorrect. *Example:* A student asks for validation of his own thoughts (e.g., "Did I get that right?").
Lack of Conservation Students believe that amount (e.g., number, mass) changes when a substance is reshaped or rearranged, even though nothing has been added or taken away. *Example:* A student asserts that two rows of five pennies similarly spaced have equal amounts; but when one row is spread out so that it is longer than the other, she says that it has more pennies.	**Conservation** Students recognize that amount stays the same if nothing has been added or taken away, even if the substance is reshaped or rearranged. *Example:* A student asserts that two rows of five pennies have the same number of pennies regardless of their spacing.
Irreversibility Students don't recognize that certain processes can be undone, or reversed. *Example:* A student doesn't realize that a row of five pennies made longer can be shortened back to its original length; the student also treats addition and subtraction as two unrelated processes (e.g., Baroody, 1999).	**Reversibility** Students understand that certain processes can be reversed. *Example:* A student moves the five pennies in the longer row close together again to demonstrate that both rows have the same amount; she also recognizes that subtraction is the reverse of addition.
Inability to Reason about Transformations Students focus on static situations; they have difficulty thinking about change processes. *Example:* A student refuses to believe that a caterpillar can turn into a butterfly, instead insisting that the caterpillar crawls away and the butterfly comes to replace it (K. R. Harris, 1986).	**Ability to Reason about Transformations** Students can reason about change and its effects. *Example:* A student understands that a caterpillar becomes a butterfly through the process of metamorphosis.
Single Classification Students are able to classify objects in only one way at any given time. *Example:* A student denies that a mother can also be a doctor.	**Multiple Classification** Students recognize that objects may belong to several categories simultaneously. *Example:* A student acknowledges that a mother can also be a doctor, a spouse, and an artist.
Transductive Reasoning Students reason by combining unrelated facts; for instance, they infer a cause–effect relationship simply because two events occur close together in time and space. *Example:* A student believes that clouds make the moon grow (Piaget, 1928).	**Deductive Reasoning** Students can draw a logical inference from two or more pieces of information. *Example:* A student deduces that if all children are human beings and if all human beings are living things, then all children must be living things.

FIGURE 2.2 Conservation of liquid: Do Glasses A and C contain the same amount of water?

Transductive reasoning Making a mental leap from one specific thing to another, such as identifying one event as the cause of another simply because the two events occur close together in time.

Conservation The realization that if nothing is added or taken away, amount (e.g., number, mass) stays the same regardless of any alterations in shape or arrangement.

Operations In Piaget's theory, organized and integrated systems of thought processes.

Concrete operations stage Piaget's third stage of cognitive development, in which adultlike logic appears but is limited to concrete reality.

Multiple classification The recognition that objects may belong to several categories simultaneously.

Deductive reasoning Drawing a logical inference about something that must be true, given other information that has already been presented as true.

Preoperational thinking is also illogical (at least from an adult's point of view), especially during the preschool years. Children in the stage may exhibit **transductive reasoning**, drawing erroneous causal inferences about two events that occur close together in time and space. For example, consider the following situation:

> You show 5-year-old Nathan the three glasses in Figure 2.2. Glasses A and B are identical in size and shape and contain an equal amount of water. You ask Nathan whether the two glasses of water contain the same amount, and he replies confidently that they do. You then pour the water from Glass B into Glass C. You ask him whether the two glasses of water (A and C) have the same amount. Nathan replies, "No, that glass [pointing to Glass A] has more because it's taller."

Nathan's response illustrates lack of **conservation**: He does not realize that because no water has been added or taken away, the amount of water in the two glasses must be equivalent. Young children often confuse changes in appearance with changes in amount.

As children approach the later part of the preoperational stage, perhaps at around 4 or 5 years of age, they show early signs of being logical. For example, they may correctly answer conservation problems (e.g., the water/glasses problem) but cannot yet explain *why* their conclusions are correct. Indeed, they base their conclusions on hunches and intuition rather than on any conscious awareness of underlying logical principles. When children move into the concrete operations stage, they become increasingly able both to make logical inferences and to explain the reasoning behind their conclusions.

Concrete Operations Stage (6 or 7 years until 11 or 12 years)

Piaget proposed that children's thought processes gradually become organized and integrated into larger systems of mental processes. These systems, or **operations**, allow children to assemble their thoughts so they make sense and, therefore, to think more logically. Such integrated and coordinated thought emerges at the beginning of the **concrete operations stage**.

Concrete operational thought differs from preoperational thought in several ways (see Table 2.1). Children now realize that their own thoughts and feelings are not necessarily shared by others and may reflect personal opinions rather than reality. As a result, they know that they can sometimes be wrong and begin to seek out external validation for their ideas. They also show conservation: They readily understand that amount stays the same, despite changes in shape or arrangement, if nothing is added or taken away. In addition, they are capable of **multiple classification**: They can readily classify objects into two categories simultaneously. And they demonstrate **deductive reasoning**: They can draw logical inferences from the facts they are given.

Children continue to develop their newly acquired logical thinking capabilities during the elementary school years. They become capable of dealing with increasingly complex conservation tasks. Some forms of conservation, such as conservation of liquid and number appear at 6 or 7 years of age, but other forms may not appear until several years later. Consider the task involving conservation of weight in Figure 2.3. Using a balance scale, an adult shows a child that two balls of clay have the same weight. One ball is removed from the scale and smashed into a pancake shape. Does the pancake weigh the same as the unsmashed ball, or do the two pieces of clay weigh different amounts? Children typically do not achieve conservation of weight—that is, they do not realize that the flattened pancake weighs the same as the round ball it was earlier—until sometime between age 9 and 12 (Sund, 1976).

FIGURE 2.3 Conservation of weight: Ball A and Ball B initially weigh the same amount. When Ball B is flattened into a pancake shape, how does its weight now compare with that of Ball A?

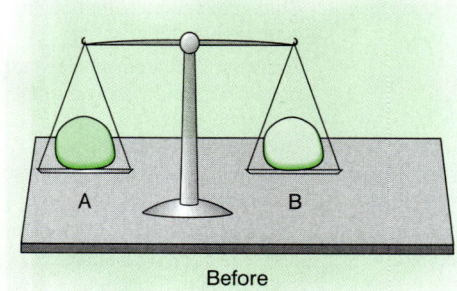
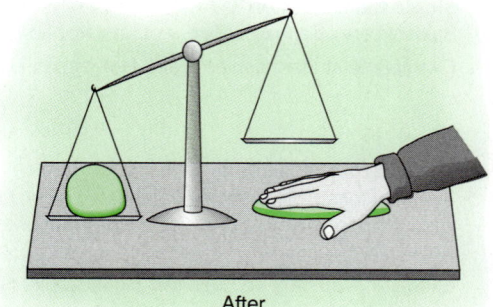

TABLE 2.2   COMPARE/CONTRAST

Concrete Operational versus Formal Operational Thought

CONCRETE OPERATIONAL THOUGHT	FORMAL OPERATIONAL THOUGHT
Dependence on Concrete Reality Students can reason logically about concrete objects they can observe; they are unable to reason about abstract, hypothetical, or contrary-to-fact ideas. *Example:* A student has difficulty with the concept of negative numbers, wondering how something can possibly be less than zero.	**Ability to Reason about Abstract, Hypothetical, and Contrary-to-Fact Ideas** Students can reason about things that are not tied directly to concrete, observable reality. *Example:* A student understands negative numbers and is able to use them effectively in mathematical procedures.
Inability to Formulate and Test Multiple Hypotheses When seeking an explanation for a scientific phenomenon, students identify and test only one hypothesis. *Example:* When asked what makes a pendulum swing faster or more slowly, a student says that the weight of the pendulum is the determining factor.	**Formulation and Testing of Multiple Hypotheses** Students seeking an explanation for a scientific phenomenon formulate and test several hypotheses about possible cause–effect relationships. *Example:* When asked what makes a pendulum swing faster or more slowly, a student says that weight, length, and strength of the initial push are all possible explanations.
Inability to Separate and Control Variables When attempting to confirm or disconfirm a particular hypothesis about cause–effect relationships, students test (and thereby confound) more than one variable simultaneously. *Example:* In testing possible factors influencing the oscillation rate of a pendulum, a student adds more weight to the pendulum while at the same time also shortening the length of the pendulum.	**Separation and Control of Variables** When attempting to confirm or disconfirm a particular hypothesis, students test one variable at a time while holding all other variables constant. *Example:* In testing factors that influence a pendulum's oscillation rate, a student tests the effect of weight while keeping length and strength of push constant; the student then tests the effect of length while keeping weight and push constant.
Lack of Proportional Reasoning Students do not understand the nature of proportions. *Example:* A student does not understand the relationship between fractions and decimals.	**Proportional Reasoning** Students understand proportions and can use them effectively in mathematical problem solving. *Example:* A student works easily with proportions, fractions, decimals, and ratios.

Although students displaying concrete operational thought show many signs of logical thinking, their cognitive development is not yet complete (see Table 2.2). For example, they have trouble understanding and reasoning about abstract and contrary-to-fact ideas, and they have difficulty handling problems that require them to consider many hypotheses or variables simultaneously. Such capabilities emerge in the final stage, formal operations.

Formal Operations Stage (11 or 12 years through adulthood)

Adolescents can increasingly envision and reason logically about alternatives to reality. Thinking about concepts with little or no basis in concrete reality—abstract, hypothetical, or contrary-to-fact concepts—is evidence of the **formal operations stage**. Students recognize that what is logically valid is different from what is true in the real world; for example, if all children are basketballs, and if all basketballs are jellybeans, then all children must be jellybeans, even though real children *aren't* jellybeans. Several abilities essential for sophisticated scientific and mathematical reasoning—formulating and testing multiple hypotheses, separating and controlling variables, and proportional reasoning—also emerge in the formal operations stage (see Table 2.2).

Let's consider how, from Piaget's perspective, students' capabilities in mathematics are likely to improve once formal operational thinking develops. Abstract problems, such as mathematical word problems, should become easier to solve. Students should become capable of understanding such concepts as *negative number, pi* (π), and *infinity*; for instance, they should now comprehend how temperature can be below zero and how two parallel lines will never touch even if they go on forever. And because they can now use proportions in their reasoning, they can study and understand fractions, ratios, and decimals, and they can use such proportions to solve problems.

Formal operations stage Piaget's fourth and final stage of cognitive development, in which logical reasoning processes are applied to abstract ideas as well as to concrete objects.

Scientific reasoning is also likely to improve once students are capable of formal operational thought. Three formal operational abilities—reasoning logically about hypothetical ideas, formulating and testing hypotheses, and separating and controlling variables—together allow formal operations individuals to use a *scientific method*, in which several possible explanations for an observed phenomenon are proposed and tested in a systematic manner.

Because students capable of formal operational reasoning can deal with hypothetical and contrary-to-fact ideas, they can envision how the world might be different—and possibly better. Thus, they may exhibit some idealism about social, political, ethical, or religious issues. Many secondary school students begin to show concern about world problems and to devote energy to worthy causes such as the environment or hunger. Their devotion may be evident more in their talk than in their actions, however (Elkind, 1984), and they may recommend changes that seem logical but aren't practical. For example, a teenager might argue that racism would disappear overnight if people would just begin to love one another. Piaget proposed that adolescent idealism reflects **formal operational egocentrism**, an inability to separate one's own logical abstractions from the perspectives of others or practical considerations. Only through experience do adolescents eventually begin to temper their optimism with some realism about what is possible in a given time frame and with limited resources.

Formal operational egocentrism The inability of individuals in Piaget's formal operations stage to separate their own abstract logic from the perspectives of others and from practical considerations.

In your own words, can you summarize the characteristics of each of Piaget's four stages?

Current Perspectives on Piaget's Theory

Piaget's theory sparked much research about children's cognitive development. Overall, this research supports the *sequence* in which different abilities emerge (Flavell, 1996; Siegler & Richards, 1982) and the order in which various conservation tasks are mastered. However, researchers do question the *ages* at which various abilities actually appear. They are also finding that students' logical reasoning capabilities may vary considerably depending on their previous knowledge and experiences related to the topic at hand.

Capabilities of Infants and Preschool Children

Infants and preschoolers appear more competent than Piaget's descriptions of the sensorimotor and preoperational stages suggest. For example, infants show preliminary signs of object permanence as young as 2.5 months and continue to firm up this understanding over many months (Baillargeon, 2004; Cohen & Cashon, 2006). And preschoolers don't always show egocentrism: They can often identify the emotions that others are feeling, and they sometimes realize that other people don't know what they themselves know (Lennon, Eisenberg, & Carroll, 1983; Wellman, Cross, & Watson, 2001). Under some circumstances, preschoolers are capable of class inclusion and conservation (Gelman & Baillargeon, 1983; Rosser, 1994).

Capabilities of Elementary School Children

Piaget may have underestimated the capabilities of elementary school students as well. Many occasionally show some ability to think abstractly and hypothetically (S. Carey, 1985; Metz, 1995). Also, some elementary school children can separate and control variables when a task is simplified in some way (Barchfeld, Sodian, Thoermer, & Buliock, 2005; Metz, 1995; Ruffman, Perner, Olson, & Doherty, 1993). Even Grade 1 and 2 students have some ability to understand and use simple proportions (e.g., fractions such as $\frac{1}{2}$, $\frac{1}{3}$, and $\frac{1}{4}$) if they can relate these to everyday objects (Empson, 1999; Van Dooren, De Bock, Hessels, Janssens, & Verschaffel, 2005).

Capabilities of Adolescents

Piaget probably *overestimated* what adolescents can do. Formal operational thinking processes emerge more gradually than Piaget suggested, and even high school students don't use them as regularly as he concluded (Flieller, 1999; Kuhn & Franklin, 2006; Schauble, 1996; Tourniaire & Pulos, 1985). Furthermore, students may demonstrate formal operational thought in one content domain while thinking concretely in another. Evidence of formal operational reasoning typically appears in the physical sciences earlier than in such subjects as history or geography. Students often have difficulty thinking about abstract and hypothetical ideas in social studies until well into the high school years (Lovell, 1979; Tamburrini, 1982) because they may contain a great deal of unfamiliar vocabulary.

Effects of Prior Knowledge and Experience

It is becoming increasingly apparent that the ability to think logically about a situation or topic depends greatly on a student's knowledge and background experiences. For instance, 9- to 11-year-olds become increasingly able to separate and control variables when they have numerous experiences that require them to do so (Schauble, 1990). Junior high and high school students, and adults as well, often apply formal operational thought to topics about which they have a great deal of knowledge and yet think concretely about topics with which they are unfamiliar (Girotto & Light, 1993; M. C. Linn, Clement, Pulos, & Sullivan, 1989; Schliemann & Carraher, 1993).

Piaget's Theory Reconsidered

Can cognitive development truly be characterized as a series of stages? Some contemporary theorists have proposed alternative stage theories to account for children's logical thinking (e.g., Case & Okamoto, 1996; Fischer & Bidell, 1991). Others believe that cognitive development is better described in terms of gradual *trends* that may be somewhat specific to different contexts and content areas (Flavell, 1994; Rosser, 1994; Siegler, 1998). Later, when we consider information-processing theory, we will identify several general developmental trends in children's ability to think and learn in the classroom.

When different children are at different stages, Piaget referred to this as a *vertical décalage*, or vertical gap. Individual students also move across vertical décalages as they move from one stage to another. Sometimes individual students may exhibit evidence of different stages in different contexts or subject areas (or in the same content when they are in transition). Piaget referred to this as a *horizontal décalage*. Juan Pascual-Leone (1976) of York University, also trained as a physician, suggested that this was a critical weak point in Piaget's theory because Piaget tried to use the idea of horizontal décalage to explain cognitive growth rather than to explore it in greater depth. This exploration has since been undertaken by others. The décalages exist, but they might be evidence of other processes than those envisaged by Piaget, some of which are addressed in the rest of this chapter.

Yet many of Piaget's basic assumptions (that children construct their own understandings of the world, that they must relate new experiences to what they already know, and that they can most effectively learn when they interact with their physical and social environments) have stood the test of time. The many tasks that Piaget developed to study children's reasoning abilities (tasks dealing with conservation, classification, etc.) give valuable insights about the "logic" students use when they think about their world and what engages them.

In the 1920s and 1930s, while Piaget was working in Switzerland, Russian psychologist Lev Vygotsky was also conducting research in an attempt to describe and explain children's cognitive development. Vygotsky's theory is quite different from Piaget's, and yet it, too, provides many valuable insights about how children's thinking skills develop over time.

Vygotsky's Theory of Cognitive Development

Vygotsky conducted many studies of students' thinking from the 1920s until his premature death from tuberculosis in 1934. Western psychologists were not aware of the importance of his work until decades later when his major writings were translated into English (e.g., Vygotsky, 1962, 1978, 1987, 1997). Vygotsky never had the chance to fully develop his theory, but his ideas are central to today's views of learning and instruction.

Vygotsky's Basic Assumptions

Piaget proposed that cognitive development is largely an individual enterprise; growing children do most of the mental work themselves. In contrast, Vygotsky believed that the adults in a society foster children's cognitive development in an intentional and somewhat systematic manner. They continually engage children in meaningful and challenging activities and help them perform those activities successfully. Because Vygotsky emphasized the importance of society and culture in promoting cognitive growth, his theory is sometimes referred to as the **sociocultural perspective**. Despite his emphasis on the social mediation of learning by adults or more

Sociocultural perspective A theoretical perspective that emphasizes the importance of society and culture for promoting cognitive development.

INTO THE CLASSROOM *Applying Piaget's Theory*

Provide hands-on experiences with physical objects, especially for elementary school students. Encourage students to explore and manipulate things.

A kindergarten teacher and his students work with small objects (e.g., blocks, buttons, pennies) to explore such basic elements of arithmetic as conservation of number and the reversibility of addition and subtraction.

Ask students to explain their reasoning, and challenge illogical explanations.

Students in a Grade 9 science class experiment with three variables (mass, length, and height from which a pendulum is released) to see which variables determine the rate at which a pendulum swings. When a student asserts that mass affects oscillation rate, his teacher points out that he has simultaneously varied mass and length in his experiment.

When students show signs of egocentric thought, express confusion or explain that others think differently.

A Grade 1 student asks, "What's this?" about an object that is out of the teacher's view. The teacher responds, "What's *what*? I can't see the thing you're looking at."

Be sure students have certain capabilities for mathematical and scientific reasoning (e.g., conservation of number, reversibility, proportional reasoning, separation and control of variables) before requiring them to perform complex tasks that depend on these capabilities.

In a unit on fractions in a Grade 7 math class, students express confusion about why $\frac{2}{3}$, $\frac{4}{6}$, and $\frac{8}{12}$ are all equivalent. Before beginning a lesson about how to add and subtract fractions with different denominators—processes that require an understanding of such equivalencies—their teacher uses concrete objects (e.g., sliced pizza pies, plastic rods that can be broken into small segments) to help students understand how two different fractions can be equal.

Relate abstract and hypothetical ideas to concrete objects and observable events.

To illustrate the idea that heavy and light objects fall at the same speed, a Grade 8 science teacher has students drop objects of various weights from a second-storey window.

In general, encourage students to invent their own procedures and to try to solve problems in different ways (Kamii, 1989).

Social constructivism A theoretical perspective that emphasizes that an individual's meaning-making (or learning in general) is mediated by adults or more knowledgeable peers, even though it is ultimately constructed by the individual learner.

knowledgeable peers, Vygotsky, like Piaget, believed that what a child or adolescent learns is ultimately his or her own construction. Learning theory informed by Vygotsky's work is therefore also sometimes referred to as **social constructivism**. The term is used, for example, in research on inquiry-based instruction (see Aulls & Shore, 2008). For more detail, refer to Chapter 7. The following major assumptions provide a summary of Vygotsky's sociocultural perspective:

■ *Complex mental processes begin as social activities; as children develop, they gradually internalize these processes and begin to use them independently.* Vygotsky believed that many thinking processes have their roots in social interactions. Children first talk about objects and events with adults and other knowledgeable individuals; in the process, they discover how the people around them think about those objects and events.

To Vygotsky, dialogue with others is essential to promote cognitive development. Gradually, children incorporate the ways that adults and others talk about and interpret the world into their own thinking. The process through which social activities become internal mental activities is **internalization**.

Internalization In Vygotsky's theory, the process through which social activities evolve into the individual's mental activities.

Mental processes also emerge as children interact with peers. For example, children often argue with one another about how best to carry out an activity, what games to play, and who did what to whom. Childhood arguments help children discover that there are often several ways to view the same situation. Eventually, children can, in essence, internalize the "arguing" process, developing the ability to look at a situation from several different angles *on their own*.

■ *Thought and language become increasingly interdependent in the first few years of life.* For adults, thought and language are closely interconnected. We often think using the specific words that our language provides; for example, when we think about household pets, our thoughts contain words such as *dog* and *cat*. In addition, we usually express our thoughts when we converse with others; as we sometimes put it, we "speak our minds."

Vygotsky proposed that thought and language are separate functions for infants and toddlers. When language appears, it is first used primarily as a means of communication rather than as a mechanism of thought. Sometime around age 2, thought and language become intertwined: Children begin to express their thoughts when they speak, and to think in words.

When thought and language merge, we begin to see **self-talk** (also known as *private speech*), children talking to themselves out loud. Recall Piaget's notion of *egocentric speech*, in which young children say things without taking into account the listener's perspective. Vygotsky proposed that such speech is better understood as talking to *oneself* than to someone else. Self-talk eventually evolves into **inner speech**: Children "talk" to themselves mentally rather than aloud. They continue to direct themselves verbally through tasks and activities, but others can no longer see or hear them do it. To Vygotsky, both self-talk and inner speech have a similar purpose: By talking to themselves, children learn to guide and direct their own behaviours through difficult tasks and complex manoeuvres much the same way that adults have previously guided them (also see Berk, 1994; Schimmoeller, 1998). Self-talk and inner speech, then, are examples of the internalization process: Children gradually internalize the directions that they have initially received from those around them, so that they eventually give *themselves* directions.

■ *Through both informal conversations and formal schooling, adults convey to children the ways in which their culture interprets the world.* Adults share with children the language of their culture, including the specific concepts and terminology used in various academic disciplines (Vygotsky, 1962). Although Vygotsky, like Piaget, saw value in allowing children to make some discoveries themselves, he also saw value in having adults describe the discoveries of previous generations, both in informal conversations and through formal education.

To the extent that specific cultures pass along unique concepts, ideas, and beliefs, children of different cultural backgrounds will develop somewhat different knowledge, skills, and ways of thinking. Vygotsky's theory leads us to expect greater diversity among children, at least in cognitive development, than Piaget's theory does.

■ *Children can perform more challenging tasks when assisted by more advanced and competent individuals.* At any particular point in a child's development, Vygotsky distinguished between the upper limit of tasks that the child can perform independently (without help from anyone else—the **actual developmental level**), and the child's **level of potential development** (the upper limit of tasks that he or she can perform with the assistance of a more competent individual). To get a true sense of children's cognitive development, Vygotsky suggested we should assess their capabilities both performing alone and with assistance.

Children can typically do more difficult things in collaboration with adults than they can do on their own. For example, children just learning how to hit a baseball are often more successful when adults guide their swing.

■ *Challenging tasks promote maximum cognitive growth.* The range of tasks that children cannot yet perform independently but *can* perform with the help and guidance of others, Vygotsky termed the **zone of proximal development (ZPD)**. A child's zone of proximal development includes learning and problem-solving abilities that are just beginning to develop—abilities in an immature, "embryonic" form. Any child's ZPD will change over time; as some tasks are mastered, other, more complex ones appear on the horizon to take their place. For example, think of the yardsticks in a North American football game as a team makes progress and "first downs" toward the opponent's goalposts. A connection between the ZPD and Piaget's theory is that learners need to be in the ZPD in order for accommodation to occur.

Vygotsky proposed that children learn little from performing tasks they can already do independently. Instead, they develop primarily by attempting tasks they can accomplish only in collaboration with a more competent individual—that is, when they attempt tasks within their zone of proximal development. Thus, it is the challenges in life—not the easy successes—that promote cognitive development.

As a teacher, you should assign some tasks that your students can perform successfully only with help from others. Such assistance may come from more skilled individuals, such as adults or older students. However, students of equal ability can also work together on difficult assignments, thereby jointly accomplishing tasks that none of them might be able to accomplish on their own. Students with different ZPD's may sometimes need different tasks and assignments—a strong case for providing as much individualized instruction as possible.

Self-talk Talking to oneself as a way of guiding oneself through a task; also known as *private speech*.

Inner speech "Talking" to oneself mentally rather than aloud.

Think about the situations in which you talk to yourself. Is it sometimes easier to perform a difficult task by talking your way through it?

Actual developmental level In Vygotsky's theory, the extent to which one can successfully perform a task independently.

Level of potential development In Vygotsky's theory, the extent to which one can successfully execute a task with the assistance of a more competent individual.

Zone of proximal development (ZPD) In Vygotsky's theory, the range of tasks between one's actual developmental level and one's level of potential development—that is, the range of tasks that one cannot yet perform independently but can perform with the help and guidance of others. The ZPD changes as the learner progresses.

Try to think of an example to illustrate the connection between ZPD and Piaget's theory.

According to Vygotsky, challenge is critical for cognitive development.
CALVIN AND HOBBES © Watterson. Reprinted with permission of Universal Press Syndicate. All rights reserved.

Current Perspectives on Vygotsky's Theory

Vygotsky's descriptions of developmental processes were, like Piaget's, often imprecise and lacking in detail. In addition, Vygotsky said little about the specific characteristics that children of particular ages are likely to exhibit. For such reasons, Vygotsky's theory has been especially difficult for researchers to either verify or challenge (Gauvain, 2001; Haenan, 1996; Wertsch, 1984).

Nevertheless, many contemporary theorists and practitioners have made considerable use of Vygotsky's ideas. They describe the value of teaching students how to give themselves instructions (i.e., how to self-talk) as they complete challenging tasks (see Chapter 8). They also encourage us to use mediate learning experience through *socially constructed meaning*, *guided participation*, *scaffolding*, *apprenticeships*, and *peer interaction* in promoting learning and cognitive development. Let's look briefly at each of these strategies.

Socially Constructed Meaning

When parents and teachers refrain from giving answers or imposing their own interpretations, but make comments that help children focus on important observations or directions in their conversations (Crowley & Jacobs, 2002; John-Steiner & Mahn, 1996), the interaction is called a **mediated learning experience**. The adult's emphasis is on the thinking process, the mediation, not the answer. At school such mediation is usually focused on a group of children working together. Many contemporary theorists are convinced of the value of such joint meaning-making dialogue in helping children acquire more complex understandings of their physical, social, and academic worlds. This idea, called social constructivism, is addressed again in Chapter 7.

Mediated learning experience A learning experience in which a learner or group of learners interact with a parent, teacher, or more knowledgeable peer, who focuses or prompts the learner's thinking processes but does not impose an adult interpretation.

Guided Participation

When you assist your students as they perform *adultlike* activities, you engage them in **guided participation** in the world of adults (Radziszewska & Rogoff, 1991; Rogoff, 1990, 1991). As you guide them, use some of the language that adults typically use in such contexts; for example, when students conduct scientific experiments, you should use words such as *hypothesis*, *evidence*, and *theory* as you help them evaluate their procedures and results (Perkins, 1992).

Guided participation Giving a child the necessary guidance and support to perform an activity in the adult world.

Scaffolding

Theorists have given considerable thought to the kinds of assistance that can help children complete challenging tasks. The term **scaffolding** is often used here: More competent individuals provide some form of guidance or structure that enables children to perform tasks in their zone of proximal development. As a teacher, you can provide a variety of support mechanisms to help students master tasks within their ZPD; here are some examples:

- Work with students to develop a plan for dealing with a new task.
- Demonstrate proper performance of the task in a way students can easily imitate.
- Divide a complex task into several smaller, simpler tasks.
- Provide structure or guidelines about how the task should be accomplished.
- Provide a calculator, computer software (word processing programs, spreadsheets, etc.), or other technology that makes some aspects of the task easier.
- Ask questions that get students thinking in appropriate ways about the task.
- Keep students' attention focused on the relevant aspects of the task.
- Keep students motivated to complete the task.
- Prompt students to keep their goal in mind (e.g., what a solution should look like).
- Give frequent feedback about how students are progressing. (Gallimore & Tharp, 1990; Good, McCaslin, & Reys, 1992; Lajoie & Derry, 1993; P. F. Merrill et al., 1996; Rogoff, 1990; Rosenshine & Meister, 1992; D. Wood, Bruner, & Ross, 1976)

As students become more adept at performing a task, scaffolding is ideally modified to nurture newly emerging skills (Puntambekar & Hübscher, 2005). You can gradually withdraw some of these support mechanisms—a process called *fading*—until students can do the task on their own.

Scaffolding A support mechanism, provided by a more competent individual, that helps a learner successfully perform a task within his or her zone of proximal development.

What task have you recently performed that was in your zone of proximal development? Who scaffolded your efforts so that you could successfully complete it?

Apprenticeships

In an **apprenticeship** a learner works intensively with an expert to accomplish complex tasks that he or she cannot do independently. The expert provides considerable structure and guidance throughout the process, gradually removing scaffolding and giving the learner more responsibility as competence increases (Rogoff, 1990, 1991).

Through an apprenticeship a student often learns both how to perform a task and how to *think about* a task; such a situation is sometimes called a **cognitive apprenticeship** (John-Steiner, 1997; Rogoff, 1990; W. Roth & Bowen, 1995). Although apprenticeships can differ widely from one context to another, they typically have some or all of these features (A. Collins, Brown, & Newman, 1989):

- *Modelling.* The teacher carries out the task, simultaneously thinking aloud about the process, while the student observes and listens.
- *Coaching.* As the student performs the task, the teacher gives frequent suggestions, hints, and feedback.
- *Scaffolding.* The teacher provides various forms of support for the student, perhaps by simplifying the task, breaking it into smaller and more manageable components, or providing less-complicated equipment.
- *Articulation.* The student explains what he or she is doing and why, allowing the teacher to examine the student's knowledge, reasoning, and problem-solving strategies.
- *Reflection.* The teacher asks the student to compare his or her performance with that of experts, or perhaps with an ideal model of how the task should be done.
- *Increasing complexity and diversity of tasks.* As the student gains greater proficiency, the teacher presents more complex, challenging, and varied tasks to complete.
- *Exploration.* The teacher encourages the student to frame questions and problems on his or her own and thereby to expand and refine acquired skills. (Inquiry begins here!)

Apprenticeship A situation in which a learner works intensively with an expert to learn how to accomplish complex tasks.

Cognitive apprenticeship A mentorship in which a teacher and a student work together to accomplish a challenging task or solve a difficult problem; in the process, the teacher provides guidance about how to think about the task or problem.

Chapter 2 Cognitive and Linguistic Development

INTO THE CLASSROOM *Applying Vygotsky's Theory*

Encourage students to talk themselves through difficult tasks.

As his students work on complex mathematical equations such as this one,

$$x = \frac{2(4 \times 9)^2}{6} + 3$$

a junior high school mathematics teacher gives students a mnemonic (**P**lease **e**xcuse **m**y **d**ear **A**unt **S**ally) they might repeat to themselves to help them remember the order in which they should perform various operations (**p**arentheses, **e**xponents, **m**ultiplication and **d**ivision, **a**ddition and **s**ubtraction).

Provide cognitive tools that students can use to make difficult tasks easier.

A high school chemistry teacher places two equal-size inflated balloons into two beakers of water, one heated to 25°C and the other heated to 50°C. The students all agree that the balloon placed in the warmer water expands more. "Now how much more did the 50-degree balloon expand?" the teacher asks. "Let's use Charles's law to figure it out."

Present some tasks that students can perform successfully only with assistance.

A Grade 5 teacher assigns students their first research paper, knowing that he will have to give them a great deal of guidance as they work on it.

Provide sufficient support, or scaffolding, to enable students to perform challenging tasks successfully; gradually withdraw the support as they become more proficient.

An elementary physical education teacher begins a lesson on tumbling by demonstrating forward and backward rolls in slow motion and physically guiding her students through the correct movements. As the students become more skillful, she stands back from the mat and gives verbal feedback about how to improve.

Have students work in small groups to accomplish complex, multifaceted tasks.

A middle school art teacher asks his students to work in groups of four or five to design large murals that depict various ecosystems—rain forest, desert, grassland, tundra, and so on—and the kinds of plant and animal species that live in each one. The groups then paint their murals on the walls of the school corridors.

Engage students in adult activities that are common in their culture.

A high school publishes a monthly school newspaper with news articles, editorials, cartoons, announcements of upcoming events, advertisements for local businesses, and classified ads. Students assume various roles, including reporters, cartoonists, marketers, editors, proofreaders, photocopiers, and distributors.

Give young children time to practise adult roles and behaviours through play.

A kindergarten teacher equips his classroom with many household items (dress-up clothes, cooking utensils, a toy telephone, etc.) so that students can play house during free-play time.

Peer Interaction

Students can often accomplish more difficult tasks when they work together rather than alone; in these situations, students essentially provide scaffolding for one another's efforts. Researchers and practitioners alike have become increasingly convinced that interactive approaches to instruction, in which students work collaboratively rather than in isolation, can be highly effective in promoting both cognitive development and classroom achievement. In Chapter 7 we'll consider the advantages and effects of peer interaction for classroom learning and achievement; in Chapter 10 we'll examine instructional strategies that promote such interaction.

Vygotsky described several mechanisms (e.g., internalization, self-talk) through which children gradually acquire adultlike ways of thinking about the world. Researchers have likewise studied mechanisms that promote cognitive development, even imagination (Gajdamaschko, 2005), and they have done so with greater precision than Vygotsky did. Recent research has also tried to characterize the nature of thinking processes at various ages, but rather than focus on reasoning and logic (as Piaget did), the focus is the development of cognition more generally. The perspective that many of these researchers have taken—information processing theory—is our next topic of discussion.

An Information-Processing View of Cognitive Development

Stop for a moment to consider what you have observed about children of different ages. Do you think children become better at paying attention as they grow older? Do you think older children remember more than younger children, or vice versa? In what ways do high school students learn and study differently from elementary students?

Such questions reflect information processing theory, an approach to cognitive development that has evolved largely within the last three or four decades. Drawing on the work of Canadian neuropsychologist Donald Hebb (1949) of McGill University, psychologists in the 1960s began to devise methods to isolate basic processes of cognition. Their new methods made it possible to study **cognitive processes** developmentally, for example, in terms of working memory, attention, and phonological and visual processing.

Because processes such as attention and working memory develop gradually and at different rates, even within individual children, some cognitive psychologists reject "stage theories" of development such as those of Piaget and Case (Case & Okamoto, 1996). Other critics have pointed out that a person's developmental "stage" depends upon his or her specific situation. Regardless of age or overall reading skill, a person faced with the word "snalgaplaft" will function at the "early stage" of letter-by-letter, phonics-based decoding (Chall, 1983; Share, 1995). However, other researchers defend the reality of age-related developmental stages, arguing that radical changes in a child's world-view, or Construction of Reality, as Piaget put it, emerge at critical points in the development of the various cognitive processes (e.g., Lewis, 2000).

Cognitive processes Specific operations involved in storing, remembering, classifying, retrieving and manipulating visual, spatial, verbal, and any other conceptual information.

Attention

Two trends in cognitive development relate to children's attention and its impact on learning:

- *Children become less distractible over time.* Young children's attention often moves quickly from one thing to another, and it is easily drawn to objects and events unrelated to the task at hand. But as children grow older, they become better able to focus their attention on a particular task and keep it there, and they are less likely to be distracted by irrelevant occurrences (Dempster & Corkill, 1999; Lane & Pearson, 1982; Ruff & Lawson, 1990). However, children whose distractability results from an Attention Deficit Disorder do not outgrow learning disabilities over time. Researchers from Dalhousie University and Toronto's Hospital for Sick Children have documented the lifelong challenges faced by children with serious attention deficits, noting that the nature of those challenges changes across the lifespan, but their seriousness does not diminish (A.-C. Bédard et al., 2002). Such children require ongoing support (psychological, educational, and medical) if they are to fulfill their full potential at school and in adult life.

- *How and what children learn depends increasingly on what they actually intend to learn.* Perhaps because of their distractibility, younger children often remember many things unrelated to what they are supposed to be doing or learning (DeMarie-Dreblow & Miller, 1988; Hagen & Stanovich, 1977). Older children, though, are better at learning and remembering the things they *intend* to learn; they are not necessarily better at learning irrelevant information.

Learning Strategies

Preschoolers often recognize the need to remember something but seem to have little idea of how to go about learning it, apart from looking or pointing at it (Kail, 1990; Wellman, 1988). As children grow older, they develop a number of **learning strategies**—specific methods of learning information—that help them learn and remember things. Following are four commonly observed trends in the development of learning strategies:

- *Rehearsal increases during the elementary school years.* What do you do if you need to remember a telephone number for a few minutes? Do you repeat it to yourself over and over again as a way of keeping it in your memory until you dial it? This process of **rehearsal** is rare in kindergarten children but increases in frequency and effectiveness throughout the elementary school years (Bjorklund & Coyle, 1995; Gathercole & Hitch, 1993; Kail, 1990). There are more effective rehearsal techniques, such as *elaborative rehearsal* (Craik, Routh, & Broadbent,

Learning strategy One or more cognitive processes used intentionally for a particular learning task.

Rehearsal A cognitive process in which information is repeated over and over as a possible way of learning and remembering it. When it is used to maintain information in working memory, it is called *maintenance rehearsal*.

1983) or *practising for variability* (P. Cohen, 2008; also see Chapter 6 of this book) in which the material to be memorized or learned is rehearsed in different ways, such as chanting, varying the rhythm, stating it in different words, and writing notes.

■ *Organization improves throughout the elementary and secondary grades.* Again, this developmental trend refers to what children do spontaneously, without formal or explicit guidance. Try the following exercise before reading ahead.

EXPERIENCING FIRSTHAND   *Mental Manoeuvre*

Read the twelve words below *one time only*. Then cover up the page and write the words down in the order they come to mind.

daisy	apple	dandelion
hammer	pear	wrench
tulip	pliers	peach
banana	rose	screwdriver

In what order did you remember the words? Did you recall them in their original order, or did you rearrange them somehow? If you are like most people, you grouped the words into three categories—flowers, tools, and fruit—and remembered one category at a time. In other words, you imposed **organization** on the information. What is more, you imposed order *unconsciously* and *automatically*.

Organized information is learned more easily and remembered more completely than unorganized information (see Chapter 6). As children grow older, they more frequently and more automatically organize the information they receive. This tendency to organize begins in early childhood and continues to develop well into the high school years (Bjorklund, Schneider, Cassel, & Ashley, 1994; M. Carr, Kurtz, Schneider, Turner, & Borkowski, 1989; DeLoache & Todd, 1988; Hacker, 1998a; Plumert, 1994). Younger children do not sort material spontaneously, at least not according to higher order categories. Teachers can facilitate learning by doing some organizing for or with pupils, for example, sort some words on a spelling list according to particular spelling patterns. (Sorting words by *meaning* does not help children remember how to spell them.)

■ *Elaboration emerges around puberty and increases throughout adolescence.* **Elaboration** means connecting information to knowledge you already have, drawing parallels, noting differences, and thinking about the implications and probable consequences of what you are trying to learn and remember. It is a deeper level of processing than simple rehearsal. The greater the depth of processing, the more easily material can be recalled (Lockhart & Craik, 1990). Elaboration creates a network of neural connections in the brain. The more connections we create with a particular concept, the more ideas and images will cue us when we try to remember that concept. The connections between cues become stronger and last longer if they are used frequently.

Children begin to elaborate on their experiences even before they begin school (Fivush, Haden, & Adam, 1995). Yet, as a strategy children *intentionally* use to help learn and make sense of new information, elaboration appears relatively late in development (usually around puberty) and gradually increases throughout the teens (Flavell, Miller, & Miller, 1993; Schneider & Pressley, 1989). Young children, as well as adults and adolescents, remember things better when they have engaged in deeper processing of the material. However, in the early grades, the teacher must assume more responsibility for pointing out connections, embedding them in stories, reinforcing them with pictures, and generally guiding the children through the elaboration process.

Both organization and elaboration are constructive in nature: You take new information, rearrange it or add to it based on what you already know, and so construct an understanding that is uniquely your own.

■ *Learning strategies become increasingly efficient and effective.* When children first acquire new learning strategies, they use them infrequently, with a great deal of effort, and often

---

Organization A cognitive process in which learners find connections (e.g., by forming categories, identifying hierarchies, determining cause–effect relationships) among the various pieces of information they need to learn.

Elaboration A cognitive process in which learners expand on new information based on what they already know.

We will examine rehearsal, organization, and elaboration in greater depth in Chapter 6.

ineffectively. With time and practice, they become increasingly adept at applying their strategies quickly, efficiently, and flexibly as they tackle challenging learning tasks. As they gain competence and confidence with more sophisticated strategies, they gradually leave less efficient ones behind (P. A. Alexander, Graham, & Harris, 1998; Flavell, Miller, & Miller, 1993; Siegler, 1998). It's often possible to get a sense of the strategies that students are (and are not) using by attending closely to what they say and write.

Knowledge

Students' ability to elaborate upon the information they are learning depends in part upon the extent of their **knowledge base**—their knowledge of specific topics and of the world in general. Their knowledge base changes in at least two ways as they develop:

■ *The amount of knowledge that children have increases over time.* There is no question that children acquire more and more information as they grow older. This increasing knowledge base is one reason why adults and older children learn new things more easily: They have more existing knowledge to help them understand and elaborate on new ideas and events (Flavell, Miller, & Miller, 1993; Halford, 1989; Kail, 1990). Older, more experienced children can use their elaborated understandings to better understand and remember new information. Younger children are less likely to make connections between a new situation and what they already know (A. L. Brown et al., 1977). In cases where children have more knowledge than adults, they are often the more effective learners (Chi, 1978; Rabinowitz & Glaser, 1985). Research by psychologist Keith Stanovich of the University of Toronto revealed that general knowledge and the ability to use that knowledge to reason logically are directly related to how much students read (Cunningham & Stanovich, 2003).

■ *Children's knowledge base becomes increasingly integrated.* Older children are more likely to organize information as they learn it and to make connections between new information and the things they already know. Not surprisingly, then, children's knowledge becomes increasingly integrated as they grow older. The knowledge base of older children includes many associations and interrelationships among concepts and ideas; that of younger children is more likely to consist of separate, isolated facts (Bjorklund, 1987; Flavell et al., 1993). The more integrated knowledge base of older children is probably one reason why, as Piaget discovered, they can think more logically and draw inferences more readily.

Knowledge base One's knowledge about specific topics and the world in general.

Metacognition

As an adult with many years of formal education behind you, you have probably learned a great deal about how you think and learn. You may have learned that you cannot absorb everything in a textbook the first time you read it, or that you remember information better when you elaborate on it, rather than when you simply repeat it over and over meaninglessly.

The term **metacognition** refers both to the knowledge people have about their own cognitive processes and to their intentional use of certain cognitive processes to facilitate learning and memory. The prefix "meta-" in psychology is used to mean "at one step removed." Thus, metacognition is cognition about cognition, or thinking about thinking. As children develop, their metacognitive knowledge and skills improve in the following ways:

Metacognition One's knowledge and beliefs about one's own cognitive processes, and one's resulting attempts to regulate those cognitive processes to maximize learning and memory.

■ *Children become more aware of the limitations of their memories.* Young children tend to be overly optimistic about how much they can remember. As they grow older and encounter a greater variety of learning tasks, they discover that some things are more difficult to learn than others (Bjorklund & Green, 1992; Flavell et al., 1993) and also realize that their memories are not perfect—that they cannot possibly remember everything they see or hear.

Let's consider an experiment with elementary school children (Flavell, Friedrichs, & Hoyt, 1970) as an example. Children in four age-groups (ranging from preschool to Grade 4) were shown strips of paper with pictures of 1 to 10 objects. The children were asked to predict how many of the objects they could remember over a short period of time. The average predictions of each age-group and the average number of objects the different groups actually *did* remember were as follows:

Age-Group	Predicted Number	Actual Number
Preschool	7.2	3.5
Kindergarten	8.0	3.6
Grade 2	6.0	4.4
Grade 4	6.1	5.5

Notice how all four age-groups predicted that they would remember more objects than they actually could. But the older children were more realistic about the limitations of their memories than the younger ones. The kindergartners predicted they would remember eight objects, but they actually remembered fewer than four!

■ *Children become better able to identify the things they do and do not know.* Young children in the early elementary grades often think they know or understand something before they actually do. As a result, they don't study classroom material as much as they should, and they often don't ask questions when they receive incomplete or confusing information (Markman, 1977; McDevitt, Spivey, Sheehan, Lennon, & Story, 1990).

Even high school and university students sometimes have difficulty assessing their own knowledge accurately. For example, they often think they can spell words they actually cannot spell (P. A. Adams & Adams, 1960; Ormrod & Wagner, 1987) or overestimate how well they will perform on an exam (Hacker, Bol, Horgan, & Rakow, 2000).

■ *Children become more knowledgeable about effective learning strategies.* As mentioned earlier, children show greater use of such learning strategies as rehearsal, organization, and elaboration as they grow older. With experience they also become increasingly aware of which strategies are effective in different situations (Lovett & Flavell, 1990; Short, Schatschneider, & Friebert, 1993; Wellman, 1985). Consider the simple idea that when you don't learn something the first time you try, you need to study it again. This is a strategy that 8-year-olds use but 6-year-olds do not (Masur, McIntyre, & Flavell, 1973). Similarly, Grade 10 students are more aware than Grade 8 students of the advantages of using elaboration to learn new information (Waters, 1982).

As children grow older, they become increasingly able to draw inferences from what they see, in part because they have a larger and better integrated knowledge base to help them interpret their experiences.

Even so, many students of all ages (university students included) seem relatively uninformed about which learning strategies work most effectively in different situations (Ormrod & Jenkins, 1989; J. W. Thomas, 1993b; Waters, 1982).

As a teacher, you must remember that your students are likely to be less efficient learners than you are. A variety of factors that affect their ability to learn—attention, intention to learn, prior knowledge, awareness and use of effective learning strategies, and so on—develop gradually throughout the school years. You should not expect that your students will always learn as quickly, or even in the same way, as you do.

Learning strategies make such a difference in students' classroom achievement that you shouldn't leave the development of these strategies to chance. As you ask your students to study and learn classroom subject matter, you should also give them suggestions about *how* they might study and learn it. This approach is consistent not only with information processing theory but also with Vygotsky's proposal that adults can better promote children's cognitive development by talking about how they themselves think about challenging tasks. Chapter 7 explores the nature of metacognitive knowledge and skills in more detail and provides suggestions for promoting students' metacognitive development.

No matter which theoretical perspective we take—Piaget's theory, Vygotsky's theory, or information processing theory—we find that children's language capabilities play a key role in their cognitive development. Piaget suggested that words help children mentally represent and think about external objects and events and that language in general is critical for the social interactions that enable children to think less egocentrically and more logically. In Vygotsky's view, verbal interaction and self-talk provide the

INTO THE CLASSROOM *Applying Information Processing Theory*

Minimize distractions, especially when working with young children.

> As his class begins a writing assignment, a Grade 1 teacher asks his students to put all objects except pencil and paper inside their desks.

Base instruction on what students already know.

> A music teacher introduces a new topic by saying, "We've already learned the scale in C major. Today we're going to study the scale in C minor and see how it is both similar to and different from C major."

Encourage learning strategies to suit different age groups.

> A Grade 3 teacher encourages her pupils to trace each of their spelling words several times, letter by letter, saying the sound of each letter or letter-group (e.g., *th* or *tion*) as they do so. Meanwhile, a high school history teacher asks her students to think about why certain historical events may have happened as they did; for example, she encourages them to speculate about the personal motives, economic circumstances, and political and social issues that may have influenced people's decision making at the time.

Identify situations in which various learning strategies are likely to be useful.

> A Grade 6 teacher says to his class, "We've studied several features of the nine planets in our solar system—size, colour, composition, distance from the sun, and duration of revolution around the sun. This sounds like a situation where a two-dimensional chart might help us organize the information."

Give students many opportunities to assess their own learning efforts and thereby to find out what they do and don't know.

> A junior high school health teacher has students read a textbook chapter at home and then gives them a non-graded quiz to help them identify parts of the chapter that they may need to read again.

---

means through which children gradually internalize and adopt the social processes and ways of thinking of the people around them. From an information processing point of view, much of the knowledge that children acquire about their world comes to them through conversations, explanations, books, and other verbal formats; furthermore, many of their learning strategies (e.g., rehearsal, organization, elaboration) are predominantly verbal in nature. We can better understand cognitive development, then, when we also know something about linguistic development.

Linguistic Development

Using human language is a very complex endeavour. To be truly effective, we must have a working knowledge of thousands of words, and we must be able to put these words together in particular ways. We must be able to identify and articulate the individual vowel sounds (e.g., *e* or *o*), diphthongs (*oi*), consonant sounds, and consonant blends (e.g., *s*, *th*, or *bl*) of which our words are composed. We also must follow certain social conventions as we speak; for instance, we should respond to someone else's greeting (e.g., "How are you?") with a greeting of our own (e.g., "Fine, thanks, and how about you?"), and we should let a person with whom we are conversing finish a sentence before we speak.

Theoretical Perspectives on Language Development

Psychologists once thought that language, like other skills, might be learned by a simple process of imitation and reinforcement (Skinner, 1953). It soon became clear that this was not so. The fact that most languages share certain characteristics, such as rules for forming negatives, and asking questions, led many linguists to believe that the ability to acquire language is somehow "hard wired" (N. Chomsky, 1965, 1972; Gopnik, 1997; Karmiloff-Smith, 1993). *Connectionist theorists* later challenged that view, suggesting that what is hard-wired is not a specific "language acquisition device," but an almost uncanny ability to detect patterns and to calculate probabilities (Kuhl, 2000; Kuhl et al., 2006; Seidenberg, 1992). In either case, there is no doubt that children are predisposed to pay attention to patterns related to language (Vouloumanos & Werker, 2007). This attention begins before birth and continues through early

Sensitive period An age range during which a certain aspect of a child's development is especially susceptible to environmental conditions.

childhood. There appear to be **sensitive periods** for different aspects of language acquisition: Children more easily master such things as verb tenses and flawless pronunciation if they are exposed to a language within the first 5 to 10 years of life (Bialystok, 1994a; Bruer, 1999; Newport, 1993, Ruben, 1999). However, other linguistic development, such as vocabulary acquisition, does not begin to slow down until mid-teens, and continues in an attenuated form throughout the lifespan.

Trends in Language Development

Children begin using recognizable words sometime around their first birthday and are putting these words together by their second birthday. During the preschool years, they become capable of forming longer and more complex sentences. By the time they begin school at age 5 or 6, they use language that seems adultlike in many respects. Yet students' language capabilities continue to develop and mature throughout the school years. Numerous changes occur in both **receptive language**—the ability to understand what is heard and read—and **expressive language**—the ability to communicate effectively through speaking and writing. Let's examine several aspects of linguistic development—phonological awareness, vocabulary, syntax, oral communication, and metalinguistic awareness—and their implications for teachers.

Receptive language The ability to understand the language that one hears or reads.

Expressive language The ability to communicate effectively through speaking and writing.

Aspects of Linguistic Development: Phonology, Semantics, Syntax, Pragmatics

Researchers have traditionally focused on three principal areas of linguistic growth, namely semantics (vocabulary), syntax (rules that govern sentence construction and grammar), and pragmatics (practical conventions such as turn taking). We shall consider these areas one by one, and see how each contributes to the overall mastery of language. But first, we shall look at some other aspects of language that have recently been attracting attention. These belong to the general category of phonology (sounds of a language), and include sensitivity to the rhythmic and melodic qualities of language (*prosody*), and *perception of phonemes* or individual speech sounds. There are two intriguing things about these latter aspects of language: First, infants become aware of them as soon as, or even before, they are born, and second, rather surprisingly, they appear to play a critical role in learning to read.

Development of Phonological Awareness

Every language has its own particular "music" created by distinctive patterns of inflection, stress, and rhythm. These prosodic patterns are so distinctive that you can often tell what language is heard from the next room, even without being able to make out the actual words. Infants can recognize their mother's language at birth on the basis of intonation and rhythm alone (Christophe & Morton, 1998). The musical qualities of language—pitch, tempo, rhythm, and volume—express both emotion and meaning. In Cantonese, the word *Sii* means "silk," "to try," "to matter," "time," "history," or "city," depending upon whether it is pronounced in a high or low voice, or one that rises or falls within the word. In English, the mood of a sentence also depends upon inflection: Try saying the sentence, "You're going with him" as a statement and then as a question. Notice how you indicate the differences by changes in pitch.

In addition to its rhythms and melodies, every language has a particular set of sounds (**phonemes**) that determine the meaning of words. Before they can learn to talk, infants must learn the phonemes of their language. This process begins at birth as a result of the chatter that takes place between infants and their caregivers, especially their mothers. By six months, they can coo all the vowels and babble all the consonants of every language in the world. They also can distinguish and classify all these sounds with the accuracy of a sound spectroscope. However, after a year, intensive mother–infant language lessons have actually "warped" the child's perception, so that variations of a single phoneme, however different acoustically, sound similar to the trained 1-year-old ear (these phonemic variations that do not affect meaning are called **allophones**). In Japanese, for example, infants learn to equate the sounds "l" and "r," because, in Japanese, the distinction between them makes no difference to the meaning of words. Kuhl and her team (2006) interpreted these findings as a remarkable instance of socially constructed knowledge: A learned, culture-specific "filter" actually changes the child's perception of physical stimuli.

Children's phonological sensitivity continues to develop during the preschool years, enabling most children to master the phonology of new languages until they are well into the

Phoneme The smallest unit of sound that makes a difference to the meaning of a word.

Allophone Variations of a single phoneme that do not make any difference to a word's meaning.

primary grades. At about 3 years of age, perhaps as a result of their growing vocabulary (Metsala & Walley, 1998), children begin to consciously notice parts of words. In kindergarten, they like to clap out syllables and play with rhymes. By Grade 1, they appreciate book titles and games based on alliteration (e.g., *If you give a moose a muffin,* [Numeroff, 1991]). As children approach high school, their phonological agility declines somewhat, making it more difficult for older children and adults to acquire a second language without "an accent."

Development of Vocabulary

As infants produce some version of *ma-ma, da-da, pa-pa, na-na,* almost invariably in that order, proud parents eagerly attach meaning to these syllables, and children soon learn to use words referentially. This marks the child's foray into **semantics**, or vocabulary acquisition. Vocabulary increases dramatically during childhood. It has been estimated that the average Grade 1 student knows the meanings of 8000 to 14 000 words, whereas the average high school graduate knows the meanings of at least 80 000 words (S. Carey, 1978; Nippold, 1988). Children learn some words through vocabulary instruction at school, especially instruction that is "early, direct, and sequential" (Biemiller, 2001). But they probably learn many more by inferring meaning from the contexts in which they hear or read the words (Nippold, 1988; Owens, 1996; Pinker, 1987, Stanovich, 2000).

Semantics The meanings of words and word combinations.

Students' knowledge of word meanings is not always an all-or-nothing thing. In many cases, their early understanding of a word's meaning is somewhat vague and "fuzzy"; they have a general idea of what the word means but define it imprecisely and sometimes use it incorrectly. Through repeated encounters with words in different contexts and through direct feedback when they use words incorrectly, students continue to refine their understandings of what various words mean.

Can you think of words whose meanings are still unclear to you?

One common error that students make in their understanding of words is **undergeneralization**: The meaning they attach to a word is too restricted, leaving out some situations to which the word applies. For example, one of the authors once asked her son, then 6 years old, to say what an *animal* is. He gave this definition:

Undergeneralization An overly restricted meaning for a word that excludes some situations to which the word does, in fact, apply; an overly narrow view of what objects or events a concept includes.

It has a head, tail, feet, paws, eyes, noses, ears, lots of hair.

As shown in this example, young elementary school children often restrict their meaning of *animal* primarily to mammals, such as dogs and horses, and insist that fish, birds, and insects are *not* animals (S. Carey, 1985; Saltz, 1971).

Another frequent error is **overgeneralization**: The meaning students attach to a word is too broad, and so they use it in situations where it's not appropriate. For example, when asking a 6-year-old to give you some examples of *insects,* he includes black widow spiders in his list. He overgeneralizes: All insects have six legs, so eight-legged spiders do not qualify.

Overgeneralization An overly broad meaning for a word that includes some situations where the word is not appropriate; an overly broad view of what objects or events a concept includes.

Sometimes even common words have subtleties that children don't master until the upper elementary grades or later. For example, 9-year-old children sometimes confuse situations in which they should use the articles *a* and *the* (Reich, 1986). Children in the upper elementary and junior high grades have trouble with many connectives, such as the words *but, although, yet, however,* and *unless* (Nippold, 1988; Owens, 1996). As an illustration, do the following exercise.

EXPERIENCING FIRSTHAND   *Using Connectives*

In each of the following pairs of sentences, identify the one that makes more sense:

Jimmie went to school, but he felt sick.

Jimmie went to school, but he felt fine.

The meal was good, although the pie was bad.

The meal was good, although the pie was good.

Even 12-year-olds have trouble identifying the correct sentence in pairs like these, reflecting only a vague understanding of the connectives *but* and *although* (Katz & Brent, 1968). (The first sentence is the correct one in both cases.)

Words such as *but* and *although* may be particularly difficult for elementary school children because their meanings are fairly abstract. Recall that abstract thinking emerges slowly (in Piaget's view, not until early adolescence). Young children in particular are apt to define words in terms of the obvious, concrete aspects of their world (Anglin, 1977; Ausubel, Novak, & Hanesian, 1978). For example, when Jeff was 4, he defined *summer* as the time of year when school is out and it's hot outside. But when he was in middle school, after he had developed a capacity for abstract reasoning and had studied the seasons in his science class, he was able to define summer in terms of the earth's tilt relative to the sun—a far more abstract notion.

Understanding figurative language expressions may also be difficult for children. As children get older, they become less dependent on context to understand what others say to them. They also become increasingly able to look beyond the literal meanings of messages (Owens, 1996; Winner, 1988). Children in the early elementary grades take the words they hear at face value; for instance, when we describe someone as being "tied up" or "hitting the roof," they are likely to take us literally. And they have little success drawing generalizations from such proverbs as "Look before you leap" or "Don't put the cart before the horse." Students' ability to interpret proverbs in a generalized, abstract fashion continues to develop even in the high school years (Owens, 1996). Therefore, children may need support to understand expressions with multiple meanings such as proverbs and idioms (Nippold, 1991). Teachers can foster students' understanding of multiple meaning expressions by using these expressions and explaining their meanings to students in the classroom environment.

To some extent, you must obviously tailor your lessons and reading materials to your students' vocabulary, yet you must not restrict instruction only to words that students already know. One way to promote students' semantic development is to teach vocabulary words and definitions directly—for instance, by having students define new vocabulary in their own words and use this vocabulary in a variety of contexts. You should also correct any misconceptions (e.g., under- or overgeneralizations) that reveal themselves in students' speech. And you must encourage your students to *read, read, read*: Children and adolescents learn many new words through their reading activities (Stanovich, 2000; Swanborn & de Glopper, 1999). The discussion of concept learning in Chapter 7 presents additional ways of teaching word meanings.

Development of Syntax

In early childhood, semantics and syntax are much the same thing. Infants' first sentences are "holophrastic." One word, such as "Doggy!" is used to express a complete thought: "May I pat the doggy?" "I am afraid of the doggy," or even "The cat is a doggy" (a fairly common example of overgeneralization). However, by the time a child is two, he or she will begin to put words together, and will do so according to predictable patterns. The rules that we use to put words together into grammatically correct sentences—rules of **syntax**—are incredibly complex, and to a great extent we aren't consciously aware of the nature of these rules (N. Chomsky, 1972; R. Ellis, 1994).

Syntax The set of rules that one uses (often unconsciously) to put words together into sentences.

By the time children begin school, they have already acquired many syntactic rules; nevertheless, their knowledge of correct syntax continues to develop throughout the elementary years (Owens, 1996; Reich, 1986). For instance, children in the early elementary grades often make an error known as **overregularization**: They apply syntactical rules in situations in which such rules don't apply (Bryant, Nunes, & Aidinis, 1999; Cazden, 1968; Marcus, 1996). To illustrate, young children might add *-ed* to indicate past tense or *-s* to indicate plural when such suffixes are inappropriate (e.g., "I *goed* to the store," "I have two *feets*"). This overregularization may suddenly appear in children who previously used the correct forms "went" and "feet." It marks a new awareness of the rules of syntax which will gradually be refined to accommodate exceptions.

Overregularization Applying syntactical rules in situations where those rules don't apply.

Children in the early elementary grades may also have difficulty interpreting passive sentences and sentences with two or more clauses (Karmiloff-Smith, 1979; O'Grady, 1997; Owens, 1996; Sheldon, 1974). Often they seem to rely on word order when interpreting such sentences. For instance, if Grade 1 students were to hear the sentence "Grandma was visited by her friends," they might conclude that Grandma did the visiting (O'Grady, 1997). If they heard the sentence "The horse kicked the pig after he jumped over the fence," many would say that the horse kicked the pig *before* it jumped over the fence, even though the word *after* clearly communicates the opposite sequence (E. V. Clark, 1971).

Students' knowledge of syntax and grammar continues to develop even at the secondary level (e.g., Perera, 1986). At this point, most syntactical development probably occurs as the result of formal language instruction—perhaps courses in language arts, English composition, and foreign language (Maratsos, 1998). Therefore, you should continue instruction and practice in grammar and composition throughout the high school years. Your students are more likely to improve their speech and writing when they have ample opportunities to express their ideas orally and on paper and when they receive direct feedback about ambiguities and grammatical errors in their speech and writing.

Development of Oral Communication Skills

In order to speak effectively, children must know how to pronounce words correctly. During the preschool and early elementary years, many children have difficulty pronouncing some English sounds, for example, *r, th, dr, sl,* and *str* (Owens, 1996). Most students master the sounds of English by age 8 or 9. However, early identification and intervention of speech and language difficulties is important. Parents and teachers should refer children experiencing speech or language difficulties to a speech-language pathologist. Do not wait to see if the children "grow out" of the difficulties they are experiencing.

To communicate their ideas effectively, children also need to consider the characteristics (e.g., age, prior knowledge, perspective) of the person receiving their message. Young children sometimes say things without considering the listener's perspective (Piaget called this *egocentric speech*). Even 4-year-olds can adapt their speech somewhat to the age of their listeners; for example, they use simpler language with 2-year-olds than with their peers (McDevitt & Ford, 1987; Shatz & Gelman, 1973). Yet elementary school children have difficulty taking other characteristics of their listeners into account, for example, what prior information their listeners are likely to have (Glucksberg & Krauss, 1967; McDevitt & Ford, 1987). As a teacher, you must let your students know exactly when you don't understand them. You can ask them to explain who or what they are talking about when they refer to people or things with which you are unfamiliar, and you can express your confusion when they describe events or ideas ambiguously.

The ability to adjust what you say to suit the listeners and the situation belongs to the aspect of language known as **pragmatics**. Pragmatics include not only rules of etiquette—taking turns speaking when conversing with others, saying goodbye when leaving, and so on—but also strategies for beginning and ending conversations, changing the subject, telling stories, and arguing effectively. Elementary school children differ in their beliefs about what to do when they don't understand something the teacher says. Many children, younger ones especially, apparently believe that it is inappropriate to ask for clarification, perhaps because they have previously been discouraged from asking questions at school or at home (McDevitt, 1990; McDevitt et al., 1990). For example, children growing up in certain cultures, including those in many Asian communities, may have learned that initiating a conversation with an adult is disrespectful (Delgado-Gaitan, 1994; Trawick-Smith, 2000). Children continue to refine their knowledge of pragmatics throughout the elementary grades (Owens, 1996); our own observations have been that this process continues into the middle and high school years (often even longer). When students haven't mastered certain social conventions—for instance, when they interrupt frequently or change the subject without warning—others may find their behaviour irritating or strange; a lack of pragmatic skills, then, can seriously interfere with students' relationships with their peers. It is important to observe students' pragmatic skills as they interact both with you and with their classmates and to give students guided practice in any skills they may be lacking.

Development of Metalinguistic Awareness

Throughout the school years, most students delight in "playing" with language by creating and reciting rhymes, skipping songs, chants, jokes, puns, secret codes, and so forth (Christie & Johnsen, 1983; Owens, 1996). Such wordplay is beneficial; for instance, rhymes help students discover the relationships between sounds and letters (L. Bradley & Bryant, 1991), and jokes and puns may help students come to realize that words and phrases often have more than one meaning (Cazden, 1976). In the latter case, students are developing **metalinguistic awareness**— the ability to think about the nature of language itself. Another example of metalinguistic awareness is children's understanding of the "Alphabetic Principle" that letters "have" (stand for) sounds. This is not obvious to many children, especially children who have weak phonological

---

You can find more information on how to identify students with speech or language difficulties in your classroom. Refer to the Canadian Association of Speech Language Pathologists and Audiologists (CASLPA) website at www.caslpa.ca.

Pragmatics Practical and social aspects of language, including social conventions guiding verbal interactions.

You can find more information on the social uses of language by referring to the information sheets entitled "Pragmatic Language Tips" and "Pragmatics: Socially Speaking," by the American Speech-Language-Hearing Association (ASHA) at www.asha.org/public/speech/development/pragmatics.htm and www.asha.org/public/speech/development/PragmaticLanguageTips.htm.

Metalinguistic awareness The extent to which one is able to think about the nature of language.

skills. Teaching the alphabetic principle in kindergarten greatly enhances children's ability to benefit from phonics instruction in Grade 1 (Cunningham, 1990).

Metalinguistic awareness seems to emerge relatively late. During the elementary years, students gradually become capable of determining when sentences are grammatically acceptable and when not (Bowey, 1986). In the upper elementary and middle school grades, they begin to consider the various functions of words in a sentence (nouns, verbs, adjectives, etc.); such growth is almost certainly due, at least in part, to the formal instruction they receive about parts of speech. High school students enhance their metalinguistic awareness still further as they consider the rhetorical and literary use of words in sentences, proverbs, poetry, and so on.

The Relationship between Oral and Written Language Development

In the early 1970s, the "psycholinguistic" theory of reading as a natural extension of speech prompted an explosion of psychological research. In fact, the study of reading has been called one of the triumphs of cognitive psychology. Drawing upon converging evidence from laboratory, classroom, and clinical settings, psychologists have been able to document in detail how we read, how we learn to read, why some of us have trouble, and what can be done about it.

One of things we know beyond a doubt is that **phonological awareness** is important to learning to read. Lesly Wade-Woolley at Queen's University is one of several researchers who have discovered that practice with the rhythm and stress patterns of language may help children with reading fluency, and in particular, may help them deal with polysyllabic words, giving them a sense of where to make syllable divisions and where to place accents (Wade-Woolley & Wood, 2006). **Phonemic awareness**, and the ability to segment words into their component sounds, is also extremely important in beginning reading (Adams, 1990; Bradley & Bryant, 1991; Juel, 1988; Torgesen et al., 2001; Siegel, 1988; Stanovich, 2000). Such awareness makes it possible for Grade 1 children to begin matching phonemes to **graphemes**, and so begin to decode. Children learning **phoneme–grapheme correspondences (PGCs)** in English benefit greatly from explicit, systematic, phonics-based instruction (an example of **explicit teaching and learning**), because in our rather complex spelling system, certain sounds are represented by more than one letter, and certain letters by more than one sound (Gillooly, 1973). Once mastered, however, the knowledge of phoneme-grapheme correspondences is generative knowledge. It permits us to read new and unpredictable words and add them to our vocabulary (Adams, 1990; Share, 1995). Good readers read many thousands more words than poor readers over the course of elementary school (Stanovich, 2000) and good readers are also more able to infer the meanings of new words from their contexts (Adams, 1990). Students' exposure to print also affects their mastery of syntax, because written language exposes them to much more complex and varied sentence structures than they would encounter in speech. The ability to deal with complex sentence structure may be one of the reasons that avid readers overtake less-avid readers in verbal reasoning ability during the course of their formal schooling (Cunningham & Stanovich, 2003).

Learning a Second Language

The need is greater than ever for children to learn one or more additional languages. As noted earlier, there may be a sensitive period for learning language, thus making exposure to a language in the first few years of life ideal. Yet research evidence regarding the best time to learn a *second* language is mixed and often tainted by serious methodological problems (Bialystok, 1994a; Hakuta & McLaughlin, 1996; Long, 1995; Newport, 1993). In general, early instruction in a second language is important for mastering correct pronunciations, especially if the language is very different from a student's native tongue, and perhaps also for mastering complex grammatical constructions (Bialystok, 1994a, 1994b; Bruer, 1999; Johnson & Newport, 1989). Aside from such possible limitations, children and adolescents can acquire fluency in a second language regardless of when they begin instruction.

Although there may be no hard-and-fast sensitive period for learning a second language, beginning instruction in the early years has definite advantages. Learning a second language facilitates achievement in such other academic areas as reading, vocabulary, and grammar (Diaz, 1983; Reich, 1986). It also sensitizes young children to the international and multicultural nature of the world. Students who learn a second language during the elementary school years express more positive attitudes toward people who speak that language and are more likely to enrol in second language classes in high school (Reich, 1986).

Phonological awareness The ability to discern separable units in the soundstream of oral language, for example, syllables within words, or phonemes within syllables. The ability to recognize and produce rhyme and alliteration are markers of phonological awareness in young children.

Phonemic awareness The ability to discern the individual phonemes that make up a word. Phonemic awareness is a subset of phonological awareness.

Grapheme A letter or group of letters that represents a single phoneme.

Phoneme–grapheme correspondences (PGCs) The regular relationships between sounds and the letters we use to represent them.

Explicit teaching and learning Teaching and learning in which the content is clearly articulated and consciously processed, not simply implied or inferred.

Bilingualism

A *bilingual* person speaks two languages fluently. Some bilingual children have been raised in families in which two languages are spoken regularly. Others have lived for a time in a community where one language is spoken and then moved to a community where a different language is spoken. Still others live in a bilingual society—for example, in Canada (where both English and French, as well as Aboriginal and ethnic languages, are spoken), Wales (where both English and Welsh are spoken), and certain ethnic communities in the United States (where a language such as Spanish or Chinese is spoken along with English).

There are advantages to being bilingual. For example, bilingual children, when they are truly fluent in both languages, tend to perform better on tasks requiring complex cognitive functioning (e.g., on intelligence tests or on tasks requiring creativity). They also appear to have greater metalinguistic awareness—a better understanding of the nature of language itself (Bialystok, 2001; Diaz & Klingler, 1991; García, 1994; C. E. Moran & Hakuta, 1995). Growing up bilingual also seems to offer children a head start in phonological awareness (Weikum et al., 2007). On the other hand, Canadian researcher Alex Gottardo and colleagues at Wilfrid Laurier University have shown that, for all alphabetic languages, children with weak phonological skills tend to have considerable difficulty with reading and writing, also in a second language (Gottardo, Colins, Baciu, & Gebotys, 2008). Fortunately, if children with phonological awareness difficulties are identified in kindergarten, and they are given an intensive program in phonological awareness, sound games, and explicit practice in separating the individual sounds in words before they begin Grade 1, *and* if their Grade 1 program is based on explicit, systematic phonics, most are able to keep up with their peers in Grade 1 (L. Bradley & Bryant, 1991; Juel, Griffiths, & Gough, 1986).

Promoting bilingualism. In some situations, learning a second language is critical, as for non-English-speaking students whose families become long-term or permanent residents of an English-speaking society. In other situations, learning a second language, though not essential, is highly desirable; this is the case for English-speaking students who may wish eventually to study or work in other societies. But bilingualism also has immediate social benefits in the classroom: If different students speak only one of two different languages (such as English or Spanish), teaching students one another's languages increases student interaction (A. Doyle, 1982).

You can find more information on bilingualism by referring to the information sheet entitled "Learning Two Languages" found on the ASHA website at www.asha.org/public/speech/development/BilingualChildren.htm.

INTO THE CLASSROOM *Facilitating Language Development*

Teach vocabulary related to topics being studied. Look for and correct students' misconceptions of word meanings.

- A science teacher explains and illustrates the concepts *speed* and *acceleration* and corrects students who erroneously use one term in place of the other.

Teach conventions of word usage and syntax.

- A high school English teacher describes the situations in which it is appropriate to use *who* and *whom* and then gives her students practice using both words correctly.

Help students understand that being good listeners involves understanding and remembering as well as paying attention.

- A Grade 4 teacher invites a police officer to speak to her class about bicycle safety. Following the officer's departure, she asks her students to summarize the important things to remember when riding a bicycle.

Give students lots of practice presenting their ideas orally to others. Provide specific and constructive feedback about how well they are communicating.

- A high school history teacher has each student give an oral report on a topic related to early Canadian history. After each report he speaks with the student individually, identifying parts of the report that were especially effective and providing suggestions for giving a better report the next time.

Spend time looking at the nature of language itself.

- A Grade 6 teacher asks, "Has anyone ever heard the expression 'A stitch in time saves nine'? What does that expression mean? Is it only about sewing?"

Encourage all students to learn a second language.

- A Grade 2 teacher spends a few minutes each day teaching her students some simple French vocabulary and phrases. She also encourages them to use their French during lunch and on the playground.

Immersion An approach to second-language instruction in which students hear and speak that language almost exclusively within the classroom.

Bilingual education An approach to second-language instruction in which students are instructed in academic subject areas in their native language while simultaneously being taught to speak and write in the second language. The amount of instruction delivered in the native language decreases as students become more proficient in the second language.

To learn more about the research that is being done related to immigration and immigrant integration into Canadian society, visit the website of the Prairie Centre of Excellence for Research on Immigration and Integration at http://pcerii.metropolis.net/.

FIGURE 2.4 Students exhibit considerable diversity in the age at which they acquire formal operational capabilities. Here 10-year-old Laura shows some ability to envision alternatives to reality. In Piaget's theory such an ability appears, on average, at age 11 or 12.

How can we help children become fluent in a second language? It appears that the best approach depends on the circumstances. For English-speaking students learning a second language while still living in their native country, total **immersion** in the second language—hearing and speaking it almost exclusively within the classroom—is the method of choice. Total immersion helps students become proficient in a second language relatively quickly, and any adverse effects of such immersion on students' achievement in other areas of the curriculum appear to be short-lived (Collier, 1992; Cunningham & Graham, 2000; Krashen, 1996; W. P. Thomas, Collier, & Abbott, 1993).

In contrast, for non-English-speaking students who have recently immigrated to this country, total immersion in English may actually be detrimental to their academic progress. For these students, **bilingual education**—wherein instruction in academic subject areas is given in students' native language while they are simultaneously taught to speak and write in English—leads to higher academic achievement (e.g., in reading, mathematics, and social studies), greater self-esteem, and a better attitude toward school (Moll & Diaz, 1985; C. E. Snow, 1990; Willig, 1985; S. C. Wright & Taylor, 1995).

Why does immersion work better for some students while bilingual education is more effective for others? As discussed earlier, language is critical for children's cognitive development, promoting social interaction and providing a symbolic means through which they can mentally represent and think about their world. We therefore need a method of teaching a second language without losing the first language in the process. English-speaking students immersed in a second language at school still have many opportunities—at home, with their friends, and in the local community and culture—to continue using and developing their English. But recent immigrants to this country often have little opportunity outside their immediate families to use their native language. If these students are taught exclusively in English, they may very well lose proficiency in one language (their native tongue) before developing proficiency in another (Pérez, 1998; Willig, 1985; S. C. Wright, Taylor, & Macarthur, 2000). Enrichment and gifted programs may also benefit from substantial use of the students' first languages (Karovitch, Shore, & Delcourt, 1996).

Given the many advantages of second-language learning and bilingualism, we should think seriously about promoting bilingualism in *all* students (Navarro, 1985; NCSS Task Force on Ethnic Studies Curriculum Guidelines, 1992). Doing so would not only promote our students' cognitive and linguistic development but also enhance communication, interaction, and interpersonal understanding among students with diverse linguistic and cultural backgrounds (Minami & Ovando, 1995).

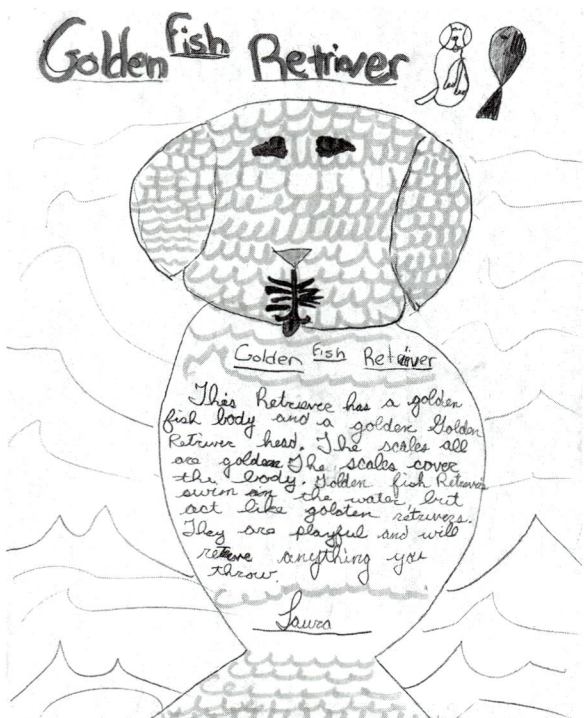

Considering Diversity in Cognitive and Linguistic Development

As previously noted, the *order* in which children acquire specific cognitive and linguistic capabilities is often similar from one child to the next, but the *rate* at which they acquire these abilities may differ considerably (e.g., see Figure 2.4). So for any particular age-group, you are likely to find considerable diversity in the developmental levels of your students. According to Piaget, you may see signs of both preoperational and concrete operational thinking in the primary grades; for example, some students may demonstrate conservation while others do not. Similarly, you may find evidence of both concrete and formal operational thinking at the middle school and high school levels; for example, some students will think more abstractly than others, and students will differ in such abilities as hypothetical reasoning, separation and control of variables, and proportional thought. Vygotsky suggested you will inevitably have students with different zones of proximal development: The cognitive challenges necessary for optimal cognitive development will vary from one student to the next. And from an information processing perspective, you will find diversity in the learning strategies that our students use, as well as in the background knowledge and experiences from which they can draw as they try to understand and elaborate on new information.

Children's cognitive development may also differ depending on the cultures in which they've been raised. Some of the logical reasoning abilities that Piaget described (e.g., conservation, separation, and control of variables) and some of the learning strategies (e.g., rehearsal) that information processing theorists have identified appear earlier in children raised in Western countries than in children raised in developing countries, presumably because such cognitive processes are more highly valued and more systematically promoted in Western culture (Berk, 2000; N. S. Cole, 1990; Trawick-Smith, 2000). When we consider cognitive abilities that other cultures value more than we do (e.g., the ability to judge the right amount of clay to use in making a pot, or the ability to locate food in a barren desert), children in our society fall short (Kearins, 1981; Price-Williams, Gordon, & Ramirez, 1969; Rogoff & Waddell, 1982).

You will find diversity in students' language capabilities as well. For example, students in kindergarten and Grade 1 will vary considerably in phonological awareness and this variation will have consequences for early reading and for second language learning. Students at all levels will vary in the size of their vocabulary and in their knowledge of complex syntactical structures. Some students may express themselves using a **dialect**—a form of English characteristic of a particular ethnic group or region of the country—different from the dialect we consider Standard English. Other students may have **limited English proficiency (LEP)**—they will be fluent in their native language but not in English—and so have difficulties both in communicating their ideas and in understanding others. Finally, your students are likely to have varying pragmatic skills—depending on individual aptitude, the families, and cultures in which they've been raised. We will identify strategies for accommodating some of these differences in our discussion of ethnicity in Chapter 4.

As a teacher, you must continually be aware of the specific cognitive and linguistic abilities and weaknesses that individual students possess and then tailor instruction accordingly. For example, your students will display more advanced reasoning skills when you ask them to deal with topics with which they are familiar. And as we have seen, students with limited English proficiency will achieve at higher levels in a bilingual education program.

Accommodating Students with Exceptionalities

You are especially likely to see differences in cognitive and linguistic development in your students with exceptionalities. For example, you may have a few students who show especially advanced cognitive development (e.g., students who are gifted); you may also have one or two who have not yet acquired the cognitive abilities typical of their age group (e.g., students with intellectual disabilities). You may have students with exceptional difficulties in specific aspects of cognition despite otherwise normal cognitive development (e.g., students with learning disabilities or attention-deficit hyperactivity disorder). Finally, you may have students who display speech and language difficulties that significantly interfere with their classroom performance. Chapter 4 looks more closely at all of these students with special needs.

Table 2.3 presents specific characteristics related to cognitive and linguistic development that we may see in students with a variety of special educational needs. It also presents numerous strategies for helping such students achieve academic success.

Dialect A form of English (or other language) characteristic of a particular region or ethnic group.

Limited English proficiency (LEP) A limited ability to understand and communicate in oral or written English, usually because English is not one's native language.

The Canadian Language and Literacy Research Network's vision is to improve the language and literacy skills of Canadian children. To learn more about the initiatives sponsored by the network, visit its website at www.cllrnet.ca. To learn more about psychological research on prevention and remediation of reading difficulties, visit the website of the International Dyslexia Association at www.interdys.org.

You can learn more about research and education issues relating to students with exceptionalities by visiting the Canadian Centre on Disability Studies' website at www.disabilitystudies.ca.

TABLE 2.3 STUDENTS IN INCLUSIVE SETTINGS

Promoting Cognitive and Linguistic Development in Students with Special Education Needs

CATEGORY	CHARACTERISTICS YOU MIGHT OBSERVE	SUGGESTED CLASSROOM STRATEGIES
Students with specific cognitive or academic difficulties	• Distractibility, difficulty paying and maintaining attention • Few effective learning strategies • Possible difficulties with abstract reasoning • Difficulties in listening comprehension • Difficulties in expressive language (e.g., in syntax) • Weak phonological skills, dysfluent reading	• Make sure you have students' attention before giving instructions or presenting information. • Keep distracting stimuli to a minimum. • Teach learning strategies within the context of classroom lessons. • Encourage students to use self-talk to help themselves deal with challenging situations. • Seek assistance from a speech pathologist when students have unusual difficulties with listening comprehension or spoken language. • Seek assistance of a reading specialist with expertise in phonological awareness and systematic phonics when students are having unusual difficulty with reading or spelling.
Students with social or behavioural problems	• Lack of attention, as reflected in restlessness, daydreaming, etc. • Delayed language development (some students with autism) • Uneven performance on cognitive tasks (some students with autism)	• Capture students' attention by gearing instruction toward their personal interests. • Provide intensive instruction and practice for any delayed cognitive or linguistic skills. (Also use strategies presented above for students with specific cognitive or academic difficulties.)
Students with general delays in cognitive and social functioning	• Reasoning abilities characteristic of younger children (e.g., preoperational thought in the upper elementary grades, inability to think abstractly in the secondary grades) • Lack of learning strategies such as rehearsal and organization • Less developed knowledge base to which new information can be related • Delayed language development (e.g., in vocabulary, listening comprehension)	• Present new information in a concrete, hands-on fashion. • Teach simple learning strategies (e.g., rehearsal) within the context of classroom lessons. • Give instructions in concrete and specific terms.
Students with physical or sensory challenges	• Less developed knowledge base to which new information can be related, due to limited experiences in the outside world • Possible cognitive or language deficiencies (if brain damage is present) • Delayed language development (if students have long-term hearing loss) • Difficulties with articulation (if students have limited muscular control or are congenitally deaf)	• Provide the basic life experiences that students may have missed because of their disabilities. • Identify any specific cognitive and/or language deficiencies, and adjust instruction and assessment practices accordingly. • Provide intensive instruction in the cognitive and/or language skills that students are lacking.
Students showing evidence of giftedness, talent, or high performance	• Appearance of formal operational thinking (e.g., abstract thought) at an earlier age • Tendency for many regular classroom tasks to be below students' zone of proximal development • Greater and better linked knowledge base to which new information can be related • Advanced vocabulary and enjoyment of language quirks • More sophisticated expressive language • More language-based sense of humor	• Provide opportunities through which students can explore classroom topics in greater depth or complexity. • Provide opportunities for students to proceed through the curriculum at a more rapid pace. • Provide systematic, explicit reading instruction, to close the gap as quickly as possible between what students can understand orally and what they can read independently. • Extend learning beyond the classroom to knowledge fairs, performances, local politics, writing for local media (explicitly address the meaning and importance of intellectual property, integrity, and plagiarism).

Summary of Cognitive and Linguistic Development

Table 2.4 summarizes the general themes presented in this chapter and how they might apply to the classroom.

TABLE 2.4   **PRINCIPLES/ASSUMPTIONS**

General Themes Characterizing Cognitive and Linguistic Development

THEME	EDUCATIONAL IMPLICATION	EXAMPLE
Children tend to think in different ways at different ages.	Ask students to describe how they are thinking about classroom subject matter and to explain the logic they are using when drawing conclusions.	Ask high school students what they do and how they think when they study for tests. If some of them depend primarily on rehearsal to learn classroom material, teach them how they might also organize and elaborate on the ideas they are studying.
Children actively construct their knowledge.	Give students many opportunities to experience new events, manipulate unfamiliar objects, and experiment with various ways of solving problems.	Before beginning instruction on multiplication and division, ask Grade 3 students to work in small groups to figure out how many days' worth of carrots Bugs Bunny has if he has 75 carrots and eats 5 carrots each day. After all groups have arrived at an answer, ask students to explain their procedures and reasoning to the class (Hiebert et al., 1997).
Development builds upon prior acquisitions.	Ensure that students have prior knowledge and experiences to which they can relate new material. Use their background knowledge to help them understand new ideas.	When describing the representative nature of a democratic government, show middle school students how the federal legislature is similar to the student government system at their own school.
Challenging situations and tasks promote development.	Present tasks and problems that encourage students to use their existing knowledge and skills in new ways or that require them to develop new knowledge and skills.	Ask students in a high school history class to develop a computer-based presentation about a particular topic that their classmates can use to learn more about the topic. Teach the students how to incorporate text, images, and sound into their presentations (Lehrer, 1993).
Social interaction is critical for development.	Give students opportunities to share their ideas, perspectives, and beliefs.	Ask Grade 1 students to describe how their families celebrate holidays. Through such discussions, the students can discover that not everyone views the world as they do—in this case, that different cultures, and even different families within a particular culture, have widely varying holiday traditions.

TEACHING CONSTRUCTIONS

In this chapter we have considered several theoretical perspectives of, as well as developmental trends in, cognitive and linguistic development. Considering what you have learned in this chapter, let's revisit our "self-analysis" case study:

- Describe how you learn differently today than when you were in elementary school.
- Is it possible to teach any content, such as physics or religion, to children of any age? What might be the constraints on children's versus adults' understanding?
- How does language influence your own learning?

KEY CONCEPTS

developmental milestone (p. 15)
universals (in development) (p. 15)
maturation (p. 16)
temperament (p. 16)
sensitive period (p. 16)
constructivism (p. 17)
scheme (p. 17)
assimilation (p. 17)
accommodation (p. 17)
equilibrium (p. 18)
disequilibrium (p. 18)
equilibration (p. 18)
sensorimotor stage (p. 18)
object permanence (p. 18)
preoperational stage (p. 19)
symbolic thinking (p. 19)
preoperational egocentrism (p. 19)
transductive reasoning (p. 20)
conservation (p. 20)
operations (p. 20)
concrete operations stage (p. 20)
multiple classification (p. 20)
deductive reasoning (p. 20)

formal operations stage (p. 21)
formal operational egocentrism (p. 22)
sociocultural perspective (p. 23)
social constructivism (p. 24)
internalization (p. 24)
self-talk (p. 25)
inner speech (p. 25)
actual developmental level (p. 25)
level of potential development (p. 25)
zone of proximal development (ZPD) (p. 25)
mediated learning experience (p. 26)
guided participation (p. 26)
scaffolding (p. 27)
apprenticeship (p. 27)
cognitive apprenticeship (p. 27)
cognitive processes (p. 29)
learning strategy (p. 29)
rehearsal (p. 29)
organization (p. 30)
elaboration (p. 30)
knowledge base (p. 31)
metacognition (p. 31)

sensitive periods (p. 34)
receptive language (p. 34)
expressive language (p. 34)
phoneme (p. 34)
allophone (p. 34)
semantics (p. 35)
undergeneralization (p. 35)
overgeneralization (p. 35)
syntax (p. 36)
overregularization (p. 36)
pragmatics (p. 37)
metalinguistic awareness (p. 37)
phonological awareness (p. 38)
phonemic awareness (p. 38)
grapheme (p. 38)
phoneme-grapheme correspondences (PGCs) (p. 38)
explicit teaching and learning (p. 38)
immersion (p. 40)
bilingual education (p. 40)
dialect (p. 41)
limited English proficiency (LEP) (p. 41)

3 Personal, Social, and Moral Development

CASE STUDY: THE BAD APPLE

TEACHING CONNECTIONS

FACTORS THAT INFLUENCE PERSONAL, SOCIAL, AND MORAL DEVELOPMENT
Temperamental Differences • Effects of Parenting • Effects of Culture • Peer Influences

DEVELOPMENT OF A SENSE OF SELF
Factors Influencing the Development of Self-Views • Developmental Changes in Students' Self-Views

SOCIAL DEVELOPMENT
Peer Relationships • Fostering Social Skills

MORAL AND PROSOCIAL DEVELOPMENT
Development of Moral Reasoning: Kohlberg's Theory • Possible Sex Differences in Moral Reasoning: Gilligan's Theory • Emotional Components of Moral Development • Determinants of Moral Behaviour • Promoting Moral Development in the Classroom

ACCOMMODATING STUDENTS IN THE INCLUSIVE CLASSROOM

GENERAL THEMES IN PERSONAL, SOCIAL, AND MORAL DEVELOPMENT

TEACHING CONSTRUCTIONS

KEY CONCEPTS

CASE STUDY *The Bad Apple*

Adam seems to cause problems wherever he goes. In the classroom he is rude and defiant. On a typical school day he comes to class late, slouches in his seat, rests his feet on his desk, yells obscenities at classmates and his teacher, and stubbornly refuses to participate in classroom activities.

Away from his teacher's watchful eye, Adam's behaviour is even worse. He shoves and pushes students in the hall, steals lunches from smaller boys in the cafeteria, and frequently initiates physical fights on the school grounds.

For obvious reasons, no one at school likes Adam very much. His classmates say that he's a bully, and their parents describe him as a "bad apple," rotten to the core. Even his teacher, who tries to find the best in all of her students, has seen few redeeming qualities in Adam and is beginning to write him off as a lost cause.

Adam doesn't seem to be bothered by the hostile feelings he generates. He's counting the days until he can legally drop out of school.

TEACHING CONNECTIONS

In this chapter we will consider children's personal development (their personalities and self-perceptions), social development (their ability to interact effectively with other people), and moral development (their understanding of right and wrong behaviour). While you read, consider the following questions in making connections between theory and teaching practice:

- How do heredity and environment influence students' personal, social, and moral development?
- How do students' self-concepts and self-esteem affect their classroom performance and academic achievement? How can you help students think positively about themselves and their abilities?
- How do peer relationships change with age? What cognitive abilities enhance such relationships?
- How can you help students learn effective ways of interacting with their peers?
- In what ways do students' moral reasoning and behaviour change over time, and how can you promote your students' moral and prosocial development?
- Why does Adam behave the way he does? What possible factors in his environment—perhaps at home, at school, or among his peers—might have contributed to his aggressiveness, impulsiveness, and apparent self-centredness?
- How might you as a teacher help Adam develop more appropriate and productive behaviour?

Factors That Influence Personal, Social, and Moral Development

What people in your life have had a significant impact on the kind of person you are today? How have parents or other family members influenced the ways that you think about yourself, the manner in which you interact with others, or the moral values that guide your decisions? Can you think of teachers who've had a major effect on your self-confidence, your interpersonal skills, or your moral values? In what ways have your friends and classmates also played a role in the development of these characteristics?

School is not just a place where students learn reading, writing, and arithmetic. It is also a place where they develop beliefs about their own abilities, acquire strategies for getting along with other people, and explore various perspectives on right and wrong. In other words, school is a place where students grow personally, socially, and morally as well as academically.

Temperamental Differences

Temperament A genetic predisposition to respond in particular ways to one's physical and social environments.

Children seem to have certain personalities almost from birth. For instance, some are cheerful and easy to care for; others are fussy and demanding. Such differences reflect **temperament**, a genetic predisposition to respond in particular ways to one's physical and social environments. Researchers have identified many characteristics that emerge early in life and appear to have genetic origins, including general activity level, adventurousness, shyness, irritability, and distractibility (Bouchard, Lykken, McGue, Segal, & Tellegen, 1990; Kagan, Snidman, & Arcus, 1992; Lanthier & Bates, 1997; Plomin, 1989).

Effects of Parenting

The behaviours of parents and other caregivers influence children's personalities from the very beginning of life. For example, when parents and their infants form a strong, affectionate bond (a process called **attachment**), the infants are likely to develop into amiable, independent, self-confident, and co-operative children who adjust easily to the classroom environment and establish productive relationships with teachers and peers. In contrast, those who do not become closely attached to a parent or some other individual early in life can be immature, dependent, unpopular, and prone to disruptive and aggressive behaviours later on (Hartup, 1989; Jacobson & Wille, 1986; S. Shulman, Elicker, & Sroufe, 1994; Sroufe, 1983; Sroufe, Carlson, & Schulman, 1993).

Attachment A strong, affectionate bond formed between a child and another individual (e.g., a parent); usually formed early in the child's life.

General patterns of childrearing—*parenting styles*—also appear to play a role in children's personal, social, and moral development. For most children, the ideal situation appears to be **authoritative parenting**, in which parents provide a loving and supportive home, hold high expectations and standards for performance, explain why some behaviours are acceptable and others are not, and enforce household rules consistently. Children from authoritative homes are happy, energetic, self-confident, and likable; they make friends easily and show self-control and concern for the rights and needs of others (Baumrind, 1989; W. A. Collins et al., 2000; Lamborn, Mounts, Steinberg, & Dornbusch, 1991; Maccoby & Martin, 1983; Rohner, 1998; L. Steinberg, Elmen, & Mounts, 1989). In contrast, children from very controlling homes tend to be unhappy, anxious, and lacking in social skills; those from very permissive homes tend to be selfish, unmotivated, impulsive, and disobedient (Baumrind, 1989; Maccoby & Martin, 1983). Children whose parents use harsh disciplinary methods can be defiant, explosive, and unpredictable; those from exceptionally abusive homes tend to have emotional difficulties and low **self-esteem**, which suggests they have a low view of their own general value and worth and can be oppositional and aggressive (Nix et al., 1999; R. A. Thompson & Wyatt, 1999). For example, two Canadian researchers, utilizing data from a representative sample of over 11 000 Canadian children across the 10 provinces from the National Longitudinal Survey of Children and Youth (NLSCY) were able to demonstrate that physical aggression in the family does negatively influence children's adjustment (Onyskiw & Hayduk, 2001; Statistics Canada, 1997).

Authoritative parenting A parenting style characterized by emotional warmth, high expectations and standards for behaviour, consistent enforcement of rules, explanations of the reasons behind these rules, and the inclusion of children in decision making.

Self-esteem Judgments and beliefs about one's own general value and worth.

Keep in mind, however, that research on parenting is typically *correlational* in nature: It shows relationships between parenting styles and children's characteristics but does not necessarily indicate that certain parenting behaviours *cause* certain characteristics in children. Many children do well despite unhappy conditions at home (Masten & Coatsworth, 1998; R. A. Thompson & Wyatt, 1999). In some cases, parents' behaviours are probably the result of how *their children* treat *them* (Clarke-Stewart, 1988; J. R. Harris, 1998; Maccoby & Martin, 1983; Stice & Barrera, 1995). Recall our earlier discussion of temperament: Some children are naturally quieter and more easygoing, whereas others are more lively or irritable. When children are quick to comply with their parents' wishes, parents may have no reason to be overly controlling. When children are hot-tempered, parents may have to impose more restrictions on behaviour and administer consequences for misbehaviours more frequently. Be careful that total credit or blame is not placed on parents for their parenting styles.

You, as a teacher, can serve as valuable resources to parents about possible strategies for promoting their children's development. With newsletters, parent–teacher conferences, and parent discussion groups, you can share ways of helping children develop age-appropriate behaviours. The important thing is to communicate information *without* pointing fingers or being judgmental about parenting behaviours. Visit the National Centre for Family and

Community Connections with Schools website at www.sedl.org/connections for research-based information and resources that can be used to connect schools, families, and communities. Also see the research paper by Debbie Pushor entitled *Parent engagement: Creating a shared world* (Ontario Education Research Symposium, 2007).

Effects of Culture

To some degree, different cultural groups encourage different behaviours. For example, in China, many children are raised to be shy, whereas in Zambia, smiling and sociability are apt to be the norm (X. Chen, Rubin, & Sun, 1992; Hale-Benson, 1986; D. Y. F. Ho, 1986, 1994). European-American families often encourage assertiveness and self-reliance, but families from many other countries (e.g., Mexico, China, Japan, India) encourage restraint, obedience, and deference to elders (Chao, 1994; Goodnow, 1992; Joshi & MacLean, 1994; Rothbaum, Weisz, Pott, Miyake, & Morelli, 2000; Trawick-Smith, 2000).

The process of moulding behaviour so that children fit in with a particular cultural group is called **socialization**. Through socialization children learn the culture's **norms**, the rules determining acceptable and unacceptable behaviour. They also learn the specific **roles** that different people occupy within their society—the patterns of behaviour acceptable for people having various functions within the group. For example, children usually learn that different behaviours are considered appropriate for the teachers and students in a classroom. Many children also develop the notion that boys and girls should behave differently and that men and women should do likewise. Each culture has its own norms regarding acceptable behaviour and defines the roles of various individuals (e.g., teachers vs. students, males vs. females) in a somewhat unique fashion.

Children typically learn their earliest lessons about society's expectations from parents and other family members, who teach them personal hygiene, table manners, rudimentary interpersonal skills (e.g., saying "please" and "thank you"), and so on. Yet teachers become equally important socialization agents once children reach school age. For example, in our society, teachers typically expect and encourage behaviours such as the following (Helton & Oakland, 1977; R. D. Hess & Holloway, 1984):

- Obeying school rules
- Behaving in an orderly fashion
- Showing respect for authority figures
- Controlling impulses
- Following instructions
- Working independently
- Completing assigned tasks
- Helping and co-operating with classmates
- Striving for academic excellence
- Delaying satisfaction of immediate needs and desires in order to attain long-term goals

Socialization The process of moulding a child's behaviour to fit the norms and roles of the child's society.

Norms As related to socialization, society's rules for acceptable and unacceptable behaviour. As related to testing practice, data regarding the typical performance of various groups of students on a standardized test or other norm-referenced assessment.

Roles Patterns of behaviour acceptable for individuals having different functions within a society.

Culture shock A sense of confusion that occurs when a student encounters a culture with very different expectations for behaviour than the expectations with which the student has been raised.

When behaviours expected of students at school differ from those expected at home, children may become confused, nonproductive, sometimes even resistant (R. D. Hess & Holloway, 1984). In other words, they may experience some **culture shock** when they first enter school.

You must especially encourage your students to exhibit those behaviours essential for long-term school success—behaviours such as obeying school rules, following instructions, and working independently. For example, when students are expected to work independently, even those students who have not had this expectation placed on them at home show improved work habits (J. L. Epstein, 1983). At the same time, students will need your guidance, support, and patience when your expectations differ from those of their family or cultural group.

Children may experience some culture shock when they first enter school, especially if behaviours expected at school are very different from those expected at home.

Peer Influences

Parents, teachers, and other adults in one's culture are hardly the only people to have a say in students' personal, social, and moral development. Peers, too, influence such development, and they do so in myriad ways—for instance by serving as examples of how one "should" behave, providing direct feedback and more subtle cues about students' social competence and likeability, offering comfort and support in times of stress or uncertainty, creating interpersonal conflicts that encourage students to learn skills in negotiation and compromise, and presenting multiple perspectives on moral issues. The effects of friends, classmates, and other peers will be a key focus throughout this chapter.

Development of a Sense of Self

Students tend to have an overall, general feeling of self-worth: They believe either that they are good, capable individuals or that they are somehow inept or unworthy (Harter, 1990; H. W. Marsh & Craven, 1997). At the same time, they are usually aware that they have both strengths and weaknesses, that they do some things well and other things poorly (Harter, 1982; H. W. Marsh & Craven, 1997; H. W. Marsh & Yeung, 1997, 1998). For example, students may have somewhat different views about themselves in these areas (Harter, 1982):

- *Cognitive competence.* Students have general beliefs about their academic ability and performance. For example, they may describe themselves as being smart and performing academic tasks successfully, or perhaps instead as being stupid and doing poorly in school.
- *Social competence.* Students have general beliefs about their ability to relate to other people, especially their peers. For example, they may describe themselves as having many friends and being liked, or instead as having trouble making friends and being unpopular.
- *Physical competence.* Students have general beliefs about their ability to engage in physical activities such as sports and outdoor games. For example, they may describe themselves as being athletic and often selected for team sports, or instead as being uncoordinated and frequently excluded from team sports.

Students typically make still finer distinctions when judging themselves, especially as they get older (D. Hart, 1988; Harter, Whitesell, & Junkin, 1998; Marsh, 1990b; Schell, Klein, & Babey, 1996). For example, students may define themselves as poor readers but good in mathematics. They also are likely to see a difference between at least two aspects of their physical selves—their athletic capabilities and their physical attractiveness to others. Thus, **self-concept** (one's perceptions of, and beliefs about, oneself) appears to have several levels of specificity, as Figure 3.1 illustrates.

> In which of these three areas do you perceive yourself to be strongest?

Self-concept One's perceptions of, and beliefs about, oneself.

FIGURE 3.1 Self-concept is multifaceted and hierarchical in nature.

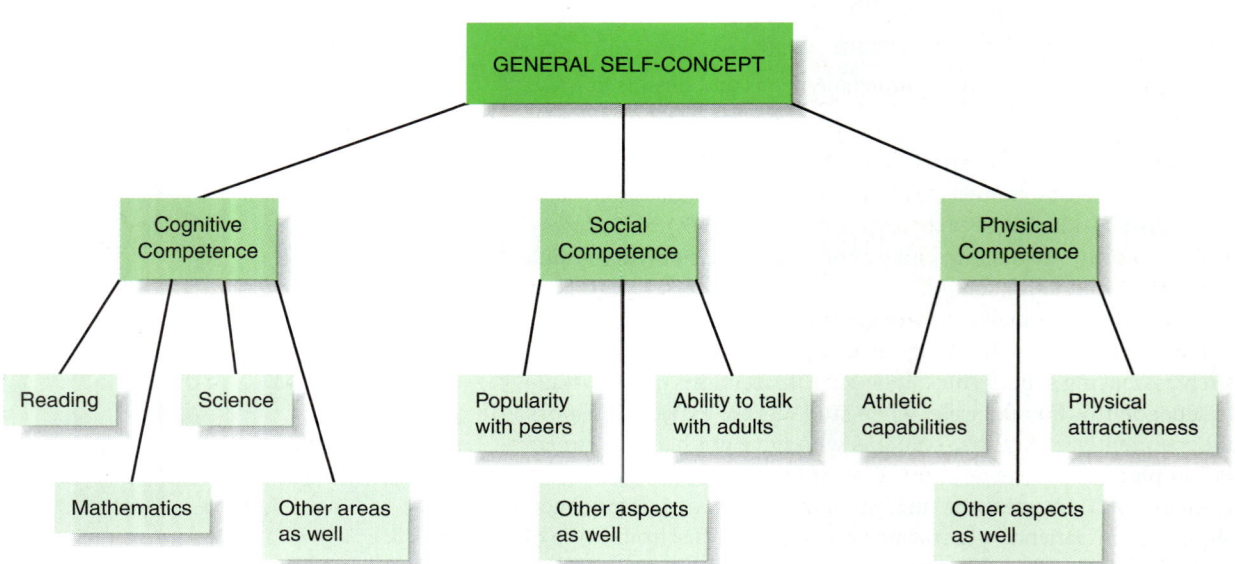

Students may even have differing beliefs about themselves regarding specific tasks and situations within a particular domain. For instance, although a person might not think of herself as very popular, she might have many people who like her. And although she might not think of herself as a great athlete—as a result of being older and less flexible—she could consider herself fairly decent at golf and skiing. When we talk about people's self-beliefs in such specific areas, we are talking about their **self-efficacy**—their beliefs about whether they are capable of achieving certain goals or outcomes (e.g., Bandura, 1982, 1997). Students tend to behave in ways that mirror their beliefs about themselves, and those who have positive self-views are more likely to succeed academically, socially, and physically (Assor & Connell, 1992; Ma & Kishor, 1997; Pintrich & Garcia, 1994; Yu, Elder, & Urdan, 1995). Those who see themselves as "good students" are more likely to pay attention, follow directions in class, use effective learning strategies, work independently and persistently to solve difficult problems, and enrol in challenging courses. In contrast, those who believe they are "poor students" are likely to misbehave in class, study infrequently or not at all, neglect to turn in homework assignments, and avoid taking difficult subjects. Along a similar vein, students who see themselves as friendly and likable are apt to seek the company of their classmates and perhaps run for student council, whereas those who believe they are disliked by classmates may keep to themselves or act with hostility and aggression toward their peers. Students with a high sense of physical competence will go out for extracurricular athletics, whereas those who see themselves as total klutzes probably will not.

Self-efficacy The belief that one is capable of executing certain behaviours or reaching certain goals.

Before you read ahead, can you predict what some of the factors affecting self-concept might be?

Factors Influencing the Development of Self-Views

Simply telling students that they are "good" or "smart" or "popular" is unlikely to make much of a dent in low self-esteem (Damon, 1991; L. Katz, 1993; H. W. Marsh & Craven, 1997). Furthermore, vague, abstract statements such as "You're special" have little meaning in the concrete realities of young children (McMillan, Singh, & Simonetta, 1994). However, two factors definitely *do* influence whether students form positive or negative self-concepts: students' own prior behaviours and performance, and the behaviours of other individuals. Each one offers insights as to how, as a teacher, you can enhance your students' sense of self.

Students' Prior Behaviours and Performance

As we have seen, students' self-concepts influence the ways in which they behave. Yet the reverse is true as well: Students' self-assessments depend on how successfully they have behaved in the past (Damon, 1991; Marsh, 1990a). Students are more likely to believe that they have an aptitude for mathematics if they have been successful in previous math classes, to believe that they are likeable individuals if they have been able to make and keep friends, or to believe that they are capable athletes if they have been victorious in athletic competitions.

The interplay between self-perceptions and behaviour can create a vicious cycle: A poor self-concept leads to less productive behaviour, which leads to fewer successes, which perpetuates the poor self-concept. To break the cycle, make sure that students have numerous opportunities to succeed at academic, social, and physical tasks (Damon, 1991; L. Katz, 1993; Leary, 1999; H. W. Marsh & Craven, 1997). For example, you can gear assignments to their developmental levels and cognitive capabilities, and you can make sure they have mastered the necessary prerequisite knowledge and skills *before* you assign new tasks. But remember that success in very *easy* activities is unlikely to have much of an impact. Instead, assign challenging tasks, giving students the structure and support (the scaffolding) they need to accomplish those tasks successfully.

Behaviours of Others

Other people's behaviours influence students' self-perceptions in at least two ways. First, how students evaluate their own performances depends to some extent on how they compare to the performances of those around them, and especially to that of their peers (Guay, Boivin, & Hodges, 1999; Marsh, Chessor, Craven, & Roche, 1995; Nicholls, 1984). Older students in particular are likely to judge themselves in comparison with classmates: Those who see themselves performing better than others are likely to develop more positive self-perceptions than those who consistently find themselves falling short. To help students develop positive self-concepts, then, you probably want to minimize competition and other situations in which students might compare themselves unfavourably with others.

Second, students' self-perceptions are affected by how others behave *toward* them (Harter, 1988, 1996; Hartup, 1989; Ryan & Lynch, 1989). Through their behaviours, adults and peers communicate their evaluations of a student and their beliefs about his or her worth as a person. For example, parents who accept their children as they are and who treat their children's interests and problems as important are likely to have children with positive self-concepts and high self-esteem. Parents who punish their children for the things they cannot do, without also praising for things done well, are likely to have children with low self-esteem (Griffore, 1981; Harter, 1983b). When parents and teachers have high expectations and offer support and encouragement for the attainment of challenging goals, students tend to have more positive self-concepts and greater confidence in their own academic capabilities (Eccles, Jacobs, Harold-Goldsmith, Jayaratne, & Yee, 1989; Eccles [Parsons], 1983; M. J. Harris & Rosenthal, 1985). Meanwhile, peers communicate information about students' social competence—perhaps by seeking out a student's companionship, ridiculing a student in front of others, and so on.

Obviously you can't always control how other people treat your students. But you can make sure that *you* respond to students in ways that will boost rather than lower self-esteem. Students who misbehave usually capture our attention more readily than those who behave appropriately, so it is often easier to criticize undesirable behaviour than to praise desirable behaviour. As a teacher, make a concerted effort to catch students in the act of doing something well and praise them accordingly. Be specific about what you are praising, because you will

> Have you ever heard a student say something that threatens a classmate's self-esteem? How might a teacher intervene in such a situation?

FIGURE 3.2 Erikson's eight stages of psychosocial development

Erik Erikson (1963, 1972) described a series of eight "psychosocial" stages through which people proceed over the course of development. Each stage presents a unique developmental task, and the way in which an individual deals with each task has a particular impact on that individual's personal development.

Trust versus mistrust (infancy). According to Erikson, the major developmental task of infants is to learn whether or not other people can be trusted to satisfy basic needs. A child's parents and other primary caretakers play a key role here. When caretakers can be depended on to feed a hungry stomach, change an uncomfortable diaper, and provide physical affection at regular intervals, an infant learns *trust*—that others are consistently dependable and reliable. When caretakers ignore the infant's needs, are inconsistent in attending to them, or are even abusive, the infant may instead learn *mistrust*—that the world is an undependable, unpredictable, and possibly dangerous place.

Autonomy versus shame and doubt (toddler years). With the increased muscular coordination that results from physiological maturation and the increased mobility that accompanies learning to crawl and walk, toddlers become capable of satisfying some of their own needs. They are learning to feed themselves, wash and dress themselves, and use the bathroom. When parents and other caretakers encourage self-sufficient behaviour, toddlers develop a sense of *autonomy*—a sense of being able to handle many problems on their own. But when caretakers demand too much too soon, refuse to let children perform tasks of which they are capable, or ridicule early attempts at self-sufficiency, children may instead develop *shame and doubt* about their ability to handle the problems that the environment presents.

Initiative versus guilt (preschool years). During the preschool years, children become increasingly capable of accomplishing tasks on their own, rather than depending on adults to do those tasks for them. With this growing independence, they begin to make their own decisions about the activities they want to pursue. Sometimes they initiate projects that they can readily accomplish, but at other times they undertake projects that are beyond their limited capabilities or that interfere with the plans and activities of others. When parents and preschool teachers encourage and support their efforts, while also helping them make realistic choices that do not conflict with the needs of others, children develop *initiative*—independence in planning and undertaking activities.[a] When adults instead discourage the pursuit of independent activities or dismiss them as silly and bothersome, then children may develop *guilt* about their needs and desires.

Industry versus inferiority (elementary school years). Erikson proposed that the elementary school years are critical for the development of self-confidence. Ideally, elementary school provides

[a]Erikson did not address the very important role that culture plays in personal and emotional development. For example, many cultures intentionally discourage autonomy, initiative, and self-assertiveness in young children, sometimes as a way of protecting them from the very real dangers of their environments (X. Chen et al., 1992; Harwood, Miller, & Irizarry, 1995; G. J. Powell, 1983).

usually be more successful in improving particular aspects of your students' self-concepts than in improving their overall sense of self-worth (Marsh, 1990b). More generally, you must treat your students with respect—for example, by asking them about their personal views and opinions about academic subject matter, seeking their input in important classroom decisions, and communicating a genuine interest in their well-being (e.g., L. Katz, 1993).

Developmental Changes in Students' Self-Views

One early theorist, Erik Erikson, proposed that people's views of both themselves and others change in significant ways throughout the lifespan. His theory of eight psychosocial stages, presented in Figure 3.2, was a prominent and influential perspective of personal development in the 1960s and 1970s. Since then, developmental theorists have taken issue with several of Erikson's stages (see the footnotes in Figure 3.2). Although Erikson's theory provides a general idea of the ages at which various issues in personal development are likely to emerge, considerable flexibility and diversity exist in these timelines.

Let's look now at what more recent researchers have found about developmental changes during childhood and adolescence.

Childhood

During the preschool and elementary school years, children tend to define themselves in terms of concrete, easily observable characteristics and behaviours (D. Hart, 1988; Harter, 1983a). Most preschoolers have positive self-concepts and high self-esteem; in fact, they often believe

---

FIGURE 3.2 continued

---

many opportunities for children to achieve the recognition of teachers, parents, and peers by producing things (*industry*)—for example, by drawing pictures, solving addition problems, and writing sentences. When children are encouraged to make and do things and are then praised for their accomplishments, they begin to demonstrate industry by being diligent, persevering at tasks until they complete them, and putting work before pleasure. If children are instead ridiculed or punished for their efforts or if they find that they are incapable of meeting their teachers' and parents' expectations, they may develop feelings of *inferiority* and inadequacy about their own capabilities.

Identity versus role confusion (adolescence). As they make the transition from childhood to adulthood, adolescents ponder the roles they will play in the adult world. Initially, they are likely to experience some *role confusion*—mixed ideas and feelings about the specific ways in which they will fit into society—and may experiment with a variety of behaviours and activities (e.g., tinkering with cars, baby-sitting for neighbours, engaging in extracurricular activities at school, affiliating with particular political or religious groups). Eventually, Erikson proposed, most adolescents achieve a sense of *identity* regarding who they are and where their lives are headed.[b]

Intimacy versus isolation (young adulthood). Once people have established their identities, they are ready to make commitments to one or more other individuals. They become capable of forming *intimate*, reciprocal relationships with others (e.g., through marriage or close friendships) and willingly make the sacrifices and compromises that such relationships require.[c] When people cannot form these intimate relationships (perhaps because of their reluctance or inability to forego the satisfaction of their own needs), then a sense of *isolation* may result.

Generativity versus stagnation (middle age). During middle age, the primary developmental task is one of contributing to society and helping to guide future generations. When an individual makes a contribution during this period, perhaps by raising a family or by working toward the betterment of society, a sense of *generativity*—a sense of productivity and accomplishment—results. In contrast, an individual who is self-centred and unable or unwilling to help society move forward develops a feeling of *stagnation*—a dissatisfaction with the relative lack of productivity.

Integrity versus despair (retirement years). According to Erikson, the final developmental task is retrospection. Individuals look back on their lives and accomplishments. They develop feelings of contentment and *integrity* if they believe that they have led a happy, productive life. They may instead develop a sense of *despair* if they look back on a life of disappointments and unachieved goals.

---

[b]Most people probably do not achieve a sense of identity as early or as easily as Erikson suggested (see the section "Late Adolescence" on p. 55).

[c]Erikson based his stages on his work with men; for many women, a focus on intimacy occurs simultaneously with, and in some cases may even precede, a focus on identity (Josselson, 1988).

they are more capable than they actually are (Flavell, Miller, & Miller, 1993). One reason for this overconfidence may be that they have few opportunities to compare their own performance to that of their age-mates. Instead, their self-assessments are probably based primarily on the progress they continue to make in accomplishing "big boy" and "big girl" tasks.

Children's self-esteem often drops soon after they begin elementary school (Harter, 1990; Stipek, 1981), perhaps because of the many new challenges—both academic and social—that school presents. As children have more and more opportunities to compare themselves with their classmates during the elementary grades, their self-assessments become increasingly realistic (Chapman, Tunmer, & Prochnow, 2000; Paris & Cunningham, 1996; Pintrich & Schunk, 2002). For example, researchers at the Université du Québec à Montréal found in their study of 115 elementary schoolchildren that as children mature and gain more schooling experience, they tend to bring their self-perceptions into line with their actual performance. Moreover, the results of their study suggest that boys are earlier than girls in consolidating their self-system, whereas girls are more precocious in differentiating their competence and intrinsic motivation according to academic domain. Hence, this would allow girls to structure a self-system that is less global and more domain specific earlier than boys (Bouffard, Marcoux, Vezeau, & Bordeleau, 2003).

Tina drew this self-portrait in Grade 2. Young children think largely of observable characteristics and behaviours when they define themselves.

Early Adolescence

As children reach adolescence and gain an increasing capability for abstract thought, they begin to think of themselves in terms of general traits, such as "smart," "athletic," or "friendly" (Harter, 1988; Rosenberg, 1986). Social acceptance and physical appearance are far more important to most young adolescents than academic competence (D. Hart, 1988; Harter, 1990; Harter et al., 1998).

Students' self-concepts and self-esteem often drop as they make the transition from elementary school to junior high school, with the drop being more pronounced for girls (Eccles & Midgley, 1989; Marsh, 1990b; Sadker & Sadker, 1994; Wigfield & Eccles, 1994). In her study of 2014 twelve- and thirteen-year-old boys and girls, Angela MacPhee (2004) at the University of Calgary found that being dissatisfied with self and holding a view of self as ineffective and lacking in positive qualities places early adolescents at substantial risk for depressive symptoms. Moreover, at this age level, girls tend to have a significantly higher level of depressive symptoms than boys. The physiological changes that occur with puberty may be a factor: Although students' self-concepts depend increasingly on their beliefs about their appearances and popularity, boys and girls alike tend to think of themselves as being somewhat less attractive once they reach adolescence (Bender, 1997; Cornell et al., 1990; Harter, 1990). The changing school environment probably also has a negative impact. Traditional junior high schools often differ from elementary schools in several ways (Eccles & Midgley, 1989). For one thing, students don't have the opportunity to form the close-knit, supportive relationships with teachers that many of them had in elementary school. Students may also discover that their school grades are based more on competitive criteria—that is, on how well they perform in comparison with their classmates. Two additional phenomena characterize the self-perceptions of young adolescents. First, these students often believe that, in any social situation, everyone else's attention is focused squarely on them—a phenomenon known as the **imaginary audience** (Elkind, 1981; Lapsley, 1993; R. M. Ryan & Kuczkowski, 1994). Because they believe themselves to be the centre of attention, young teenagers (girls especially) are often preoccupied with their physical appearance and are quite critical of themselves, assuming that everyone else is equally observant and critical. Extreme sensitivity to embarrassment, when coupled with inadequate social skills, can lead some adolescents to respond with undue violence when their peers insult or verbally attack them (Lowry, Sleet, Duncan, Powell, & Kolbe, 1995).

A second noteworthy phenomenon in early adolescence is the **personal fable**: Young teenagers often believe themselves to be completely unlike anyone else (Elkind, 1981; Lapsley, 1993). For instance, they often think that their own feelings are completely unique—that those around them have never experienced such emotions. Hence, they may insist that no one else, least of all parents and teachers, could possibly know how they feel. Furthermore, they may have a sense of invulnerability and immortality, believing that they are immune to the normal dangers of life. Thus, many adolescents take seemingly foolish risks, such as experimenting with drugs and alcohol, having unprotected sexual intercourse, or driving at high speeds (Arnett, 1995; DeRidder, 1993; Packard, 1983; S. P. Thomas, Groër, & Droppleman, 1993).

Imaginary audience The belief that one is the centre of attention in any social situation.

Personal fable The belief that one is completely unlike anyone else and so cannot be understood by other individuals.

The development of both the imaginary audience and personal fable may, to some extent, reflect students' changing cognitive abilities during the adolescent years. Some theorists have proposed that both the imaginary audience and the personal fable are symptoms of the *adolescent egocentrism* that Piaget described (Elkind, 1981). Others suggest that the two phenomena result from adolescents' increasing ability to look at the world from other people's perspectives and their growing concern about what others think of them (Lapsley, 1993; R. M. Ryan & Kuczkowski, 1994). Still others believe that adolescents' risk-taking behaviours may be partly the result of developmental changes in the brain (Spear, 2000). Whatever the origins of these phenomena, they appear to peak in early adolescence and then slowly decline (Lapsley, 1993).

Late Adolescence

By late adolescence, most students have sufficiently recovered from the "double whammy" of puberty and a changing school environment that they enjoy positive self-concepts and general mental health (Nottelmann, 1987; S. I. Powers, Hauser, & Kilner, 1989; Wigfield & Eccles, 1994). As they reach the high school years, their self-concepts begin to include a sense of **identity**: a self-constructed definition of who they are, what things they find important, and what goals they want to accomplish in life. Memberships in various groups—perhaps informal cliques at school, organized clubs or teams, or ethnic neighbourhoods or communities—often play a key role in adolescents' identities (Phinney, 1989; Trawick-Smith, 2000; Wigfield, Eccles, & Pintrich, 1996). Not only do such groups help students define who they are, but they also endorse values and goals that students may adopt for themselves. Furthermore, a strong sense of ethnic or racial identity and pride can often help students from minority groups deal with the racist behaviours that they sometimes face (McAdoo, 1985; Spencer & Markstrom-Adams, 1990).

Erik Erikson proposed that most people achieve a sense of identity by the end of adolescence (see Figure 3.2). But more recent evidence indicates that, even by the high school years, only a small minority of students have begun to think seriously about the eventual role they will play in society and to identify lifelong goals (Archer, 1982; Durkin, 1995; Marcia, 1980, 1988). Most adolescents need considerable time to explore various options for themselves—options related to careers, political beliefs, religious affiliations, and so on—before they achieve a true sense of their adult identity. Marcia (1980) has observed four distinct patterns of behaviour that may characterize the status of an adolescent's search for identity:

- *Identity diffusion.* The adolescent has made no commitment to a particular career path or ideological belief system. Some haphazard experimentation with particular roles or beliefs may have taken place, but the individual has not yet embarked on a serious exploration of issues related to self-definition.
- *Foreclosure.* The adolescent has made a firm commitment to an occupation, a particular set of beliefs, or both. The choices have been based largely on what others (especially parents) have prescribed, without an earnest exploration of other possibilities.
- *Moratorium.* The adolescent has no strong commitment to a particular career or set of beliefs but is actively exploring and considering a variety of professions and ideologies. In essence, the individual is undergoing an identity crisis.
- *Identity achievement.* The adolescent has previously gone through a period of moratorium and emerged with a commitment to particular political or religious beliefs, a clear choice of occupation, or both.

The ideal situation is to proceed through a period of moratorium—a period of searching and experimentation that may continue into early adulthood—before finally settling on a clear identity (Berzonsky, 1988; Marcia, 1988). Foreclosure—identity choice *without* prior exploration—rules out potentially more productive alternatives, and identity diffusion leaves young people without a clear sense of direction in life.

As students get older, they increasingly include abstract qualities in their self-descriptions. In this self-description, 12-year-old Melinda identifies several abstract characteristics: musical, lovable, imaginative, noble, and animal-lover.

Identity A self-constructed definition of who a person thinks he or she is and what things are important in life.

> **INTO THE CLASSROOM** *Fostering Positive Self-Perceptions*
>
> Promote success on classroom tasks.
>
> > A teacher provides a list of questions that students should try to answer as they study for an upcoming quiz.
>
> Hold reasonably high expectations for students' performance.
>
> > A junior high school swimming coach encourages students to come out for the swim team regardless of past experience. She works as closely with newcomers as with experienced swimmers, so that all team members can improve.
>
> Give positive feedback for students' accomplishments. Provide negative feedback within the context of overall positive regard.
>
> > The same swimming coach tells a student, "Your crawl stroke has really improved. Your timing on the butterfly is a bit off; let's work on that today."
>
> Communicate a genuine interest in students' well-being.
>
> > When a new Grade 7 student is visibly teary-eyed during class, her teacher invites her to take a walk with him during lunchtime. The student describes the trouble she is having making friends at her new school, and together they develop some strategies to address the problem.
>
> Give students opportunities to examine and try out a variety of adultlike roles.
>
> > A Grade 3 teacher develops a list of classroom chores, such as getting a hot lunch count, delivering messages to the main office, and feeding the class goldfish and rabbit. He assigns these chores to students on a rotating basis.

Social Development

As our students grow older, they become more interested in their peer relationships and friendships. In the next few pages we will learn more about these relationships and identify strategies for fostering students' social skills.

Peer Relationships

The classroom is very much a "social" place: Students interact regularly with one another, and most of them actively seek out friendly relationships with classmates. In fact, for many students, socializing with and gaining the acceptance of peers are more important than classroom learning and achievement (B. B. Brown, 1993; Dowson & McInerney, 2001; W. Doyle, 1986a). Peer relationships, especially friendships, serve several functions in children's and adolescents' personal and social development:

- *Peer interactions provide an arena for learning and practising social skills.* A child's relationships with parents and teachers are usually lopsided, unequal ones, such that the adults have the upper hand and control the nature of interactions. But in most relationships with peers, each individual is an equal partner. This equality provides a situation in which a child can begin to develop skills in negotiation, persuasion, co-operation, compromise, emotional control, and conflict resolution (Asher & Parker, 1989; Erwin, 1993; Maxmell, Jarrett, & Dickerson, 1998; Sutton-Smith, 1979).

- *Peers offer social and emotional support.* Young children see their age-mates primarily as sources of recreation (Youniss & Volpe, 1978). As they grow older, they find that friendships provide comfort and safety—a group with whom to eat lunch, a "safe haven" from playground bullies, and so on—as well (Eckert, 1989; Pellegrini & Bartini, 2000). Once children reach puberty, they rely increasingly on their peers for emotional support, especially in times of trouble or confusion (Levitt, Guacci-Franco, & Levitt, 1993; R. M. Ryan, Stiller, & Lynch, 1994). Although some students adjust quite successfully on their own, as a general rule those students who have the acceptance and support of their peers have higher self-esteem, fewer emotional problems (e.g., depression), and higher school achievement (Buhrmester, 1992; Guay et al., 1999; Levitt et al., 1999; R. M. Ryan et al., 1994; Wentzel, 1999).

Many adolescents (particularly girls) may reveal their innermost thoughts to their friends (Basinger, Gibbs, & Fuller, 1995; Levitt et al., 1993). Friends often understand a teenager's perspective—the preoccupation with physical appearance, the concerns about the opposite sex, and so on—when no one else seems to. By sharing their thoughts and feelings with one another, students may discover that they aren't as unique as they once thought and gradually abandon the personal fable we spoke of earlier (Elkind, 1981).

■ *Peers are influential socialization agents.* Children and adolescents socialize one another in several ways (Erwin, 1993; Ginsberg, Gottman, & Parker, 1986; J. R. Harris, 1998; A. M. Ryan, 2000). They define options for leisure time, perhaps getting together in a study group or smoking cigarettes on the corner. They offer new ideas and perspectives, perhaps demonstrating how to do an "Ollie" on a skateboard or presenting arguments for becoming a vegetarian. They serve as role models and provide standards for acceptable behaviour, showing what is possible, what is admirable, what is cool. They reinforce one another for acting in ways deemed appropriate for their age, sex, or ethnic group. And they sanction one another for stepping beyond acceptable bounds, perhaps through ridicule, gossip, or ostracism. Such **peer pressure** has its greatest effects during the junior high school years, and teenagers who have weak emotional bonds to their families seem to be especially vulnerable (Berndt, Laychak, & Park, 1990; Erwin, 1993; R. M. Ryan & Lynch, 1989; Urdan & Maehr, 1995).

Young adolescents often strive to look cool in the eyes of their peers, as this drawing by 11-year-old Marci illustrates.

Peer pressure A phenomenon whereby a student's peers strongly encourage some behaviours and discourage others.

Most students want to be accepted by their classmates. As they reach puberty, their heightened concern for how others might evaluate them (recall our discussion of the *imaginary audience*) can lead them to be quite conforming—that is, to rigidly imitate their peers' choices in dress, music, slang, and behaviour. By looking and sounding like others, they may feel that they better fit in with their classmates (Hartup, 1983; Owens, 1996).

Many peers encourage such desirable qualities as truthfulness, fairness, co-operation, and abstinence from drugs and alcohol (Berndt & Keefe, 1996; Damon, 1988; McCallum & Bracken, 1993). Others, however, encourage violence, criminal activity, and other antisocial behaviours (Berndt, Hawkins, & Jiao, 1999; Dishion, Spracklen, Andrews, & Patterson, 1996; Gottfredson, 2001; Lowry et al., 1995). Some peers encourage academic achievement, yet others convey the message that academic achievement is undesirable, perhaps by making fun of "brainy" students or by encouraging such behaviours as cheating on homework, cutting class, and skipping school (Berndt, 1992; B. B. Brown, 1993; Knapp & Woolverton, 1995).

Keep in mind that, while peer pressure certainly exists, its effects on children's behaviours have probably been overrated (Berndt & Keefe, 1996). Most children and adolescents acquire a strong set of values and behavioural standards from their families, and they do not necessarily discard these values and standards once they enter the school building (B. B. Brown, 1990; W. A. Collins et al., 2000; Hartup, 1983). Furthermore, students tend to choose friends who are similar to them in motives, styles of behaviour, academic achievement, and leisure-time activities (W. A. Collins et al., 2000; Kindermann, McCollam, & Gibson, 1996; A. M. Ryan, 2000). They also actively think about and evaluate what their peers ask them to do; they rarely accept anyone's suggestions without question (B. B. Brown, 1990). In some cases, students lead "double lives" that enable them to attain academic success while maintaining peer acceptance; for example, although they attend class and do their homework faithfully, they may feign disinterest in scholarly activities, disrupt class with jokes or goofy behaviours, and express surprise at receiving high grades (B. B. Brown, 1993; Covington, 1992). You can help these students maintain their "image" by sometimes allowing them to demonstrate their achievements privately—through written assignments or in one-on-one conversations—instead of in front of their classmates.

Friendships

Close friends tend to be similar in age and are usually of the same sex, although some older children and adolescents have close friends of the opposite sex as well (Gottman, 1986; Hartup, 1992; Kovacs, Parker, & Hoffman, 1996). Friends also tend to be of the same race; cross-race friendships are more common when the number of available peers is relatively small—for instance, in small classes or rural communities (Hallinan & Teixeria, 1987; Roopnarine, Lasker, Sacks, & Stores, 1998).

As children get older, and especially as they reach adolescence, they increasingly think of friends as people who can be trusted and relied upon. Yet to some degree, even Grade 1 students realize that friends provide more than recreation, as this description by 6-year-old Katie (who depicts herself and friend Meghan playing with dolls) illustrates.

Clique Moderately stable friendship group of perhaps 3 to 10 members.

Subculture A group that resists the ways of the dominant culture and adopts its own norms for behaviour

Were you part of a social group in adolescence? If so, how would you characterize it?

Gang A cohesive social group characterized by initiation rites, distinctive colours and symbols, territorial orientation, and feuds with rival groups.

Friends find activities that are mutually meaningful and enjoyable, and over time they acquire a common set of experiences that enable them to share certain perspectives on life (Gottman, 1986; Suttles, 1970). Friends care for and help one another, and ultimately how they *feel* about one another is more important than what they *do* with one another (J. L. Epstein, 1986; Rubin, Bukowski, & Parker, 1998). Because friends have an emotional investment in their relationship, they work hard to look at a situation from one another's point of view and to resolve any disputes that threaten to separate them; as a result, they develop increased perspective-taking and conflict-resolution skills (Basinger et al., 1995; DeVries, 1997; Newcomb & Bagwell, 1995). Close friendships foster self-esteem and, especially at the secondary school level, provide a sense of identity for students—a sense that they "belong" to a particular group (Berndt, 1992; Knapp & Woolverton, 1995).

In their study of Canadian adolescents, researchers from Concordia University found sex differences in friendship stability. Their findings indicated that girls are more sensitive to contextual influences (such as school size) on peer relationships than are boys. In addition, adolescent girls are more concerned about friends' loyalty and intimacy than are boys (Hardy, Bukowski, & Sippola, 2002).

Larger Social Groups

Most children and adolescents interact regularly with, and clearly enjoy the company of, many peers besides their close friends. Over time, many form larger social groups that regularly associate and socialize (Eisenberg, Martin, & Fabes, 1996; Gottman & Mettetal, 1986). Initially, such groups usually comprise a single sex, but in adolescence they often include both boys and girls (Gottman & Mettetal, 1986; J. R. Harris, 1995).

Once children or adolescents gel as a group, they prefer other group members over non-members, and they develop feelings of loyalty to individuals within the group. In some cases, they also develop feelings of hostility and rivalry toward members of other groups (J. R. Harris, 1995, 1998; Sherif, Harvey, White, Hood, & Sherif, 1961). If you look back on your own adolescent years, you may recall that you and your friends attached names to members of different groups—perhaps "brains," "jocks," "druggies," or "geeks" (Eckert, 1989; J. R. Harris, 1995; Pipher, 1994).

Larger groups become a particularly prominent feature of students' social worlds once they reach puberty. Researchers have described at least three distinct types of groups during the adolescent years: cliques, subcultures, and gangs. **Cliques** are moderately stable friendship groups of perhaps 3 to 10 individuals, and such groups provide the setting for most voluntary social interactions (Crockett, Losoff, & Peterson, 1984; J. L. Epstein, 1986; Kindermann et al., 1996). Clique boundaries tend to be fairly rigid and exclusive (some people are "in," others are "out"), and memberships in various cliques often affect students' social status (Wigfield et al., 1996).

Some teenagers also affiliate with a well-defined **subculture**, a group that resists a powerful dominant culture by adopting a significantly different way of life (J. S. Epstein, 1998). Such a group may be considerably larger than a clique and may not have the tight-knit cohesiveness and carefully drawn boundaries of a clique. Instead, it is defined by common values, beliefs, and behaviour patterns. Some subcultures are relatively benign. Others are more worrisome, such as those that endorse racist and anti-Semitic behaviours (e.g., "skinheads") and those that practise Satanic worship and rituals (C. C. Clark, 1992). Adolescents are more likely to affiliate with subcultures when they feel alienated from the dominant culture (perhaps that of their school or that of society more generally) and want to distinguish themselves from it in some way (C. C. Clark, 1992; J. R. Harris, 1998).

A **gang** is a cohesive social group characterized by initiation rites, distinctive colours and symbols, ownership of a specific "territory," and feuds with one or more rival groups (A. Campbell, 1984). Typically, gangs are governed by strict rules for behaviour, with stiff penalties for rule violations. Adolescents (and sometimes children as well) affiliate with gangs for a variety of reasons (A. Campbell, 1984; C. C. Clark, 1992; Parks, 1995; Simons, Whitbeck, Conger, & Conger, 1991). Some do so as a way of demonstrating their loyalty to their family, friends, or neighbourhood. Some seek the status and prestige that gang membership brings. Some have poor academic records and perceive the gang as an alternative arena in which they might gain recognition for their accomplishments. Many members of gangs have had troubled relationships with their families, or they have been consistently rejected by peers, and so they turn to gangs to get the emotional support they can find nowhere else. As a teacher, you can definitely make a difference in the lives of any gang members who might be in your classes (S. G. Freedman, 1990; Parks, 1995). You must, first and foremost, show these students that you truly care about them and their well-being—for instance, by being a willing listener in times of trouble and by providing the support they need to achieve both academic and social success. You must also have some awareness of students' backgrounds—their cultural values, economic circumstances, and so on—so that you can better understand the issues they may be dealing with.

Romantic Relationships

As students move through the middle school and high school grades, the biological changes of puberty are accompanied by new, often unsettling, feelings and sexual desires (Larson, Clore, & Wood, 1999). Not surprisingly, then, romance is often on adolescents' minds and is a frequent topic of conversation at school (B. B. Brown, Feiring, & Furman, 1999). From a developmental standpoint, romantic relationships have definite benefits: They can address students' needs for companionship, affection, and security, and they provide an opportunity to experiment with new social skills and interpersonal behaviours (Furman & Simon, 1999; B. C. Miller & Benson, 1999). At the same time, romance can wreak havoc with adolescents' emotions (Larson et al., 1999). Adolescents have more extreme mood swings than younger children or adults, and for many, this instability may be due, in part, to the excitement and frustrations of being romantically involved (or *not* involved) (Arnett, 1999; Larson et al., 1999).

Once students reach puberty, romance may often be on their minds and distract them from their schoolwork.

Initially, "romances" often exist more in students' minds than in reality (Gottman & Mettetal, 1986). For example, consider Sandy's recollection of her first foray into couplehood:

> In about fifth and sixth grade, all our little group that we had . . . was like, "OK," you know, "we're getting ready for junior high," you know, "it's time we all have to get a boyfriend." So I remember, it was funny, Carol, like, there were two guys who were just the heartthrobs of our class, you know . . . so, um, I guess it was Carol and Cindy really, they were, like, sort of the leaders of our group, you know, they were the, yeah, they were just the leaders, and they got Tim and Joe, each of those you know. Carol had Tim and Cindy had Joe. And then, you know, everyone else, then it kind of went down the line, everyone else found someone. I remember thinking, "Well, who am I gonna get? I don't even like anybody," you know. I remember, you know, all sitting around, we were saying, "OK, who can we find for Sandy?" you know, looking, so finally we decided, you know, we were trying to decide between Al and Dave and so finally I took Dave, you know. (Eckert, 1989, p. 84)

Middle school students' romantic thoughts may also involve crushes on people who are out of reach—perhaps favourite teachers, movie idols, or rock stars (B. B. Brown et al., 1999; Miller & Benson, 1999).

Eventually, however, many students begin to date, especially if their friends are also dating. Students' early choices in dating partners are often based on physical attractiveness or social status, and their dates involve only limited and superficial interaction (B. B. Brown et al., 1999; Collins & Sroufe, 1999; Downey, Bonica, & Rincón, 1999). As students move into the high school grades, some form more intense, affectionate, and long-term relationships with members of the opposite sex, and these relationships often (but by no means always) lead to some degree of sexual intimacy (B. B. Brown et al., 1999; Connolly & Goldberg, 1999). The age of first sexual intercourse has decreased steadily over the last few decades, perhaps in part because the media often communicate the message that sexual activity is appropriate (Brooks-Gunn & Paikoff, 1993; Larson et al., 1999).

As they reach high school (perhaps even earlier), some students find themselves attracted to their own sex, either instead of or in addition to the opposite sex. Adolescence is a particularly confusing time for homosexual and bisexual students. Some students actively try to ignore or stifle what they perceive to be deviant urges. Others accept their sexual yearnings yet struggle to form an identity while feeling different and isolated from peers (Morrow, 1997; C. J. Patterson, 1995). Many gay, lesbian, and bisexual students describe feelings of anger and depression, some entertain thoughts of suicide, and a higher than average proportion drop out of school (Elia, 1994; Patterson, 1995). According to Kevin Alderson (2002) at the University of Calgary, school counsellors should provide a safe place for youth to talk openly about their feelings and frustrations, help teenagers address family problems that might emerge as a result of disclosing their sexual identity and orientation, and promote school-wide respect for diversity and equality.

Teenagers often have mixed feelings about their early sexual experiences (Alapack, 1991), and those around them—parents, teachers, peers—are often uncertain about how to handle the topic (Katchadourian, 1990). When parents and teachers do broach the topic of sexuality, they often raise it in conjunction with *problems,* such as irresponsible behaviour, substance abuse, disease, and unwanted pregnancy. They rarely raise the topic of homosexuality except within the context of acquired immune deficiency syndrome (AIDS) and other risks (M. B. Harris, 1997).

The extent to which you talk about sexuality with your students must, in part, be dictated by the policies of the school and the values of the community in which you work. At the same time, especially if you are teaching at the middle school or high school level, you must be aware that romantic and sexual relationships, whether real or imagined, are a considerable source of excitement, frustration, confusion, and distraction for your students, and you must lend a sympathetic and open-minded ear to those students who seek your counsel and support.

Fostering Social Skills

Social skills Behaviours that enable a person to interact effectively with others.

Prosocial behaviour Behaviour directed toward promoting the well-being of someone else.

Social skills are the things that we do to interact effectively with other people—showing courtesy, initiating conversations, negotiating, co-operating, and so on. Some social skills are aimed at benefiting someone else more than ourselves; such **prosocial behaviours** include sharing, helping, comforting, and showing empathy for another person's feelings. According to Jac Andrews (University of Calgary), social skills are important because they affect the quality of our lives. For most people, social skills are acquired incidentally. Most of us can learn to successfully interact with others, make friends, and solve our social problems without specific interventions. However, some people need systematic instruction and/or organized activities to help them acquire and perform the social skills and behaviours that promote positive social relationships in various situations. Because of limitations in their social skills, some children do not experience personally satisfying and beneficial relationships with others (Andrews, 2006). As you might expect, students who have better social skills tend to have more friends, and their friendships tend to be of higher quality (Fabes et al., 1999; A. J. Rose & Asher, 1999).

Schools and classrooms, because they present complex social situations, provide an ideal context in which social skills and prosocial behaviours can develop (Deutsch, 1993; S. N. Elliott & Busse, 1991). You can do many things to help students acquire effective ways of interacting with others and forming productive interpersonal relationships. Following are several possibilities:

■ *Provide numerous opportunities for social interaction.* Students gain considerable information about which social behaviours are and are not effective simply by interacting with one another. For instance, students' play activities—whether they are the fantasy play of preschoolers and kindergartners or the rule-based games of older children and adolescents—can promote co-operation, sharing, perspective taking, and conflict resolution skills (Creasey, Jarvis, & Berk, 1998; Gottman, 1986; Rubin, 1982). Students are, of course, more likely to learn effective social skills when they have opportunities to interact with classmates who exhibit prosocial behaviours, rather than with those who are disruptive and aggressive (Dishion, McCord, & Poulin, 1999).

■ *Plan co-operative activities.* When students participate in co-operative games, rather than in competitive ones, their aggressive behaviours toward one another decrease (Bay-Hinitz, Peterson, & Quilitch, 1994). Further, when they engage in co-operative classroom assignments, they can learn and practise help-giving, help-seeking, and conflict-resolution skills, and they develop a better sense of justice and fairness regarding their peers (Damon, 1988; Lickona, 1991; Webb & Farivar, 1994).

■ *Prevent and manage peer harassment.* The prevalence of peer harassment (bullying) in Canadian schools has been studied a number of times and is considered a significant school problem. Ziegler and Rosenstein-Manner (1991) reported that 15 percent of the students they surveyed in Toronto admitted that they bullied other students more than once during a school term. Noelle Bidwell (1997) found that 10 percent of students surveyed within a school division in Saskatoon, Saskatchewan, reported being bullied on an ongoing weekly basis. Beran and Tutty (2002) found, in their study of 472 students in Grades 1 to 6 in Calgary, Alberta, that about 27 percent of students experienced both physical and verbal bullying, 21 percent experienced verbal bullying, and 5 percent reported physical bullying. In addressing this problem there should be student-based and school-based strategies. For example, at the student level, teachers should demonstrate care and empathy for victimized students, and help students develop solutions and safety plans (Beran & Tutty, 2002). At the same time, bullies need to be identified and counselled. At the school level, staff awareness of bullying should be increased, school discipline policies should be developed, collaborative input from parents should be promoted, and classroom lesson plans should be created and implemented that encourage students to openly discuss harassment and ways to deal with it. According to Beran (2006c), it is most important that school personnel actively work at creating a positive school environment in which students feel respected, supported, and nurtured.

Peer relationships are critical for social and emotional development.

- *Help students interpret social situations in an accurate and productive way.* Students will interact more appropriately with their peers if they can accurately interpret their peers' behaviours and intentions (Graham, 1997; Guerra & Slaby, 1990). For example, in one research study involving boys in Grades 3 through 5, students attended a series of training sessions in which, through role-playing, discussions of personal experiences, brainstorming, and similar activities, they practised making inferences about other people's intentions and identifying appropriate courses of action (Hudley & Graham, 1993). They also learned several guidelines to remind them of how to behave in various situations; for example, they might think to themselves, "When I don't have the information to tell what he meant, I should act as if it were an accident" (p. 128). Following the training, the students were less likely to presume hostile intent or endorse aggressive retaliation in interpersonal situations, and their teachers rated them as less aggressive than control-group students.

- *Teach specific social skills, provide opportunities for students to practise them, and give feedback.* Teach students appropriate ways of behaving both through explicit verbal instructions and through modelling desired behaviours. Such instruction is especially likely to be effective when you also ask students to practise their newly learned social skills (perhaps through role playing) and give them concrete feedback about how they are doing (S. N. Elliott & Busse, 1991; S. Vaughn, 1991; Zirpoli & Melloy, 2001).

- *Label and praise appropriate behaviours when they occur.* Identify and praise the specific social skills that you see your students exhibit (Vorrath, 1985; Wittmer & Honig, 1994). For example, you might say, "Thank you for being so helpful," or, "I'm glad that you two were able to co-operate so well as you worked on your project."

- *Describe students as having desirable social behaviours.* Openly describe your students as being helpful, courteous, or generous (Grusec & Redler, 1980; Wittmer & Honig, 1994). For example, an 8-year-old who is told, "You're the kind of person who likes to help others whenever you can," will be more likely to share belongings with others at a later date (Grusec & Redler, 1980).

- *Teach social problem-solving strategies.* Some students lack productive strategies for solving social problems; for example, they may barge into a game without asking or respond aggressively to any provocation (Hughes, 1988; Neel, Jenkins, & Meadows, 1990). One strategy you can teach is for students to think carefully about a situation before responding and then talk themselves through the appropriate behaviours for dealing with it (Hughes, 1988). A second strategy, for the classroom as a whole, is *mediation training*, which teaches students how to mediate conflicts among classmates by asking the opposing sides to express their differing points of view and then work together to devise a reasonable resolution (Deutsch, 1993; Sanchez & Anderson, 1990; Stevahn, Johnson, Johnson, & Real, 1996).

Aggressive behaviour Action intentionally taken to hurt another, either physically or psychologically.

- *Establish and enforce firm rules for acceptable classroom behaviour.* In addition to encouraging appropriate social behaviours, actively *discourage* such inappropriate behaviours as inconsiderateness, aggression, and prejudicial remarks (Bierman, Miller, & Stabb, 1987; Braukmann, Kirigin, & Wolf, 1981; Schofield, 1995). You must have clear guidelines for classroom behaviour and impose consequences when such guidelines are not followed. By establishing and enforcing firm rules about **aggressive behaviour** and other antisocial behaviours while simultaneously teaching appropriate social skills, you will often see noticeable improvements in behaviour.

Moral and Prosocial Development

The domain of morality includes such traits as honesty, fairness, dependability, concern for the rights and welfare of others, and prosocial behaviour—helping, sharing, comforting, and so on. The term *immoral behaviour* typically refers to actions that are unfair, cause physical or emotional harm, or violate the rights of others (Smetana, 1983; Turiel, 1983).

Students' beliefs about moral and immoral behaviour—their beliefs about what's right and wrong—affect their actions at school and in the classroom. For example, there will be fewer instances of theft or violence when students respect the property and safety of their classmates, and fewer cases of cheating when students believe that cheating is morally unacceptable. By acting morally and prosocially, students will gain greater support from their teachers and classmates and thereby achieve greater academic and social success over the long run (Caprara et al., 2000).

Students' beliefs about morality also affect how they think about and understand the topics they study in school. For instance, students' moral values are likely to influence their reactions when they read descriptions of the Holocaust during World War II or discuss recent acts of terrorism around the world. Their sense of human dignity may enter in when they read the anti-Semitic statements that some characters in Shakespeare's *The Merchant of Venice* make about a Jewish money-lender. And the importance of fairness and respect for the rights of others certainly come into play in any discussions about good sportsmanship on the athletic field. Students simply cannot avoid moral issues in their school activities.

Shelley Hymel, Kimberly Schonert-Reichl, and Lynn Miller from the University of British Columbia strongly advocate that schools support the social-emotional development of children and youth in schools, not only because it provides a foundation for academic growth, but also because it creates a safe and caring community of learners that fosters moral qualities (such as fairness, compassion, and respect) that underlie socially responsible citizenship (2006).

As teachers, you play a significant role in the moral and prosocial development of your students (Pollard, Kurtines, Carlo, Dancs, & Mayock, 1991; Rushton, 1980). Consider the teacher who prepares a class for the arrival of a new student, first by discussing the feelings of uncertainty, apprehension, and loneliness that the student is likely to have, and then by helping the class identify steps it can take to make the student feel at home. This teacher is facilitating perspective taking and setting the stage for students to behave prosocially toward the newcomer. Now consider the teacher who ignores incidents of selfishness and aggression in class and on the playground, perhaps using the rationale that students should always work things out among themselves. This teacher is doing little to promote students' social and moral growth and in fact may inadvertently be sending them the message that antisocial behaviour is quite acceptable. It is important to note that along with promoting academic development, a primary function of schooling is to develop citizenship skills and moral character (Wentzel, 1991). In fact, this mandate is evident in the mission and vision statements of the majority of ministries and departments of education across Canada (as shown in Figure 3.3).

In the pages that follow, we explore the multidimensional nature of moral development. We will first consider moral reasoning, with a particular emphasis on the work of Lawrence Kohlberg and Carol Gilligan. Later, we will consider the role that emotions—guilt, shame, empathy, and sympathy—and other factors play in moral decision making and behaviour. Finally, we will identify strategies for promoting moral and prosocial development in the classroom.

FIGURE 3.3 Educational mission and vision statements of Canadian provinces and territories

PROVINCE/ TERRITORY	EDUCATIONAL MISSION OR VISION STATEMENT
Alberta	Ministers' Message: *We need to ensure that our students' education includes learning the values and behaviours necessary to be good citizens.* (www.education.alberta.ca/department/annualreport/2006-2007.aspx)
British Columbia	*The mission of the Ministry of Education is to set the legal, financial, curricular, and accountability frameworks so as to enable all learners to develop their individual potential and to acquire the knowledge, skills, and attitudes needed to contribute to a healthy, democratic, and pluralistic society and a prosperous, sustainable economy.* (www.gov.bc.ca/bced)
Manitoba	*Manitoba Education, Citizenship and Youth's goal is to work with partners to provide access to relevant, engaging, high-quality and responsive education that meets the needs of every learner. The primary responsibilities of Manitoba Education, Citizenship and Youth are to facilitate the improvement of learning at the kindergarten to Senior 4 (K to S4) levels, to enhance citizenship development, and to address transition (career development) issues for youth.* (www.edu.gov.mb.ca/ar_ecy_0506/report.pdf)
New Brunswick	Mission Statement: *To have each student develop the attributes needed to be a lifelong learner, to achieve personal fulfillment, and to contribute to a productive, just, and democratic society.* (www.gnb.ca/0000/about-e.asp)
Newfoundland and Labrador	Mission Statement: *To enable and encourage every individual to acquire through lifelong learning, the knowledge, skills, and values necessary for personal growth and the development of society.* (www.edu.gov.nl.ca/rights/intro.htm)
Northwest Territories	Purpose: *To invest in and provide for the development of the people of the Northwest Territories, enabling them to reach their potential, to lead fulfilled lives, and to contribute to a strong and prosperous society.* (www.ece.gov.nt.ca/index.htm)
Nova Scotia	*Our mission is [. . .] to provide excellence in education and training for personal fulfillment and for a productive, prosperous society.* (www.ednet.ns.ca)
Nunavut	Mission Statement: *Education provides the path and guides the life-long learning journey of Nunavummiut by providing excellence in education and training so that Nunavummiut benefit from their past and create their own future for a productive, prosperous society.* (www.gov.nu.ca/education/eng/)
Ontario	*Our plan to promote a strong, vibrant, publicly funded education system is focused on three goals:* • *High levels of student achievement* • *Reduced gaps in student achievement* • *High levels of public confidence in public education* *To achieve these goals we will focus our activities on:* • *Identifying and supporting effective teaching, learning, and assessment practices* • *Identifying and supporting effective gap-reducing practices* • *Engaging students, families, and communities in building a supportive learning environment* • *Increasing system effectiveness, efficiency, transparency and responsiveness* (www.edu.gov.on.ca/eng/about/whatwedo.html)
Prince Edward Island	Our Vision: *Prince Edward Island is a place where education is highly valued. All individuals have the opportunity to develop their full social, intellectual, economic, cultural, and physical potential. The Department of Education is the leader in assuring equitable opportunities for lifelong learning.* Our Mission: *Our mission is to provide leadership in the pursuit of excellence, and to create effective learning opportunities for all.* (www.gov.pe.ca/educ/index.php3?number=78487&lang=E)
Quebec	*The Ministere l'Education is the government authority responsible for seeing that Quebec's citizens receive the educational services they need in order to develop as individuals and become active, contributing members of society.* (www.mels.gouv.qc.ca/ADMINIST/plan_strategique/PlanStrat0003/Anglais.pdf)
Saskatchewan	Our Vision: *Through lifelong learning, all Saskatchewan people become knowledgeable and skilled citizens contributing to and benefiting from society and the economy. The province in enriched socially, culturally, and economically through the leadership of its learning sector.* (www.sasked.gov.sk.ca)
Yukon	*. . . the goal of the Yukon education system is to work in co-operation with parents to develop the whole child including the intellectual, physical, social, emotional, cultural, and aesthetic potential of all students to the extent of their abilities so that they may become productive, responsible, and self-reliant members of society while leading personally rewarding lives in a changing world . . .* (www.education.gov.yk.ca/publications.html)

Source: Adapted from Hymel, Schonert-Reichl, & Miller, 2006.

Development of Moral Reasoning: Kohlberg's Theory

EXPERIENCING FIRSTHAND   *Heinz's Dilemma*

In Europe, a woman was near death from a rare form of cancer. There was one drug that the doctors thought might save her, a form of radium that a druggist in the same town had recently discovered. The druggist was charging $2000, ten times what the drug cost him to make. The sick woman's husband, Heinz, went to everyone he knew to borrow the money, but he could only get together about half of what the drug cost. He told the druggist that his wife was dying and asked him to sell it cheaper or let him pay later. But the druggist said no. So Heinz got desperate and broke into the man's store to steal the drug for his wife. (Kohlberg, 1984, p. 186)

- Should Heinz have stolen the drug? What would *you* have done if you were Heinz? Which is worse, stealing something that belongs to someone else or letting another person die a preventable death? Why?
- Do you think that people younger than yourself might answer the same questions differently? How do you think a typical Grade 5 student might respond? A typical high school student?

Moral dilemma A situation in which there is no clear-cut answer regarding the morally correct thing to do.

The story of Heinz and his dying wife illustrates a **moral dilemma**, a situation to which there is no clear-cut right or wrong response. Lawrence Kohlberg presented a number of moral dilemmas to people of various ages and asked them to propose solutions for each one. Here are three solutions to Heinz's dilemma proposed by elementary and secondary school students. The students have been given fictitious names so we can refer to them again later.

> **James (a Grade 5 student):** Maybe his wife is an important person and runs a store, and the man buys stuff from her and can't get it any other place. The police would blame the owner that he didn't save the wife. He didn't save an important person, and that's just like killing with a gun or a knife. You can get the electric chair for that. (Kohlberg, 1981, pp. 265–266)
>
> **Jesse (a high school student):** If he cares enough for her to steal for her, he should steal it. If not he should let her die. It's up to him. (Kohlberg, 1981, p. 132)
>
> **Jules (a high school student):** In that particular situation Heinz was right to do it. In the eyes of the law he would not be doing the right thing, but in the eyes of the moral law he would. If he had exhausted every other alternative I think it would be worth it to save a life. (Kohlberg, 1984, pp. 446–447)

Each student offers a different reason to justify why Heinz should steal the lifesaving drug. James bases his decision on the possible advantages and disadvantages of stealing or not stealing the drug for Heinz alone; he does not consider the perspective of the dying woman at all. Likewise, Jesse takes a very self-serving view, proposing that the decision to either steal or not steal the drug depends on how much Heinz loves his wife. Only Jules considers the value of human life in justifying why Heinz should break the law.

After obtaining hundreds of responses to moral dilemmas, Kohlberg proposed that the development of moral reasoning is characterized by a series of qualitatively distinct stages (e.g., Colby, Kohlberg, Gibbs, & Lieberman, 1983; Kohlberg, 1984). These stages, as in any stage theory, form an invariant sequence: An individual progresses through them in order, without skipping any. Each stage builds upon the foundation laid by earlier stages but reflects a more integrated and logically consistent set of moral beliefs than those before it. Kohlberg grouped his stages into three *levels* of morality: the preconventional, conventional, and postconventional levels. These three levels and the two stages within each one are described in Table 3.1.

Preconventional morality A lack of internalized standards about right and wrong; making decisions based on what is best for oneself, without regard for others' needs and feelings.

As you can see, **preconventional morality** is the earliest and least mature form of morality, in that the individual has not yet adopted or internalized society's conventions regarding what is right or wrong. The preconventional individual's judgments about the morality of behaviour are determined primarily by physical consequences: Behaviours that lead to rewards and pleasure are "right," and behaviours that lead to punishment are "wrong."

Why is this level called *preconventional*?

James's response to the Heinz dilemma is a good example of preconventional (Stage 1) thinking: He considers the consequences of Heinz's actions only for Heinz himself. Kohlberg also classified Jesse's response as a preconventional (in particular, a Stage 2) response. Jesse is beginning to recognize the importance of saving someone else's life, but the decision to do so ultimately depends on whether or not Heinz loves his wife; in other words, it depends on *his* feelings alone.

TABLE 3.1 COMPARE/CONTRAST

Kohlberg's Three Levels and Six Stages of Moral Reasoning

LEVEL	AGE RANGE	STAGE	NATURE OF MORAL REASONING
Level I: Preconventional morality	Seen in preschool children, most elementary school students, some junior high school students, and a few high school students	Stage 1: Punishment-avoidance and obedience	Individuals make decisions based on what is best for themselves, without regard for others' needs or feelings. They obey rules only if established by more powerful individuals; they disobey when they can do so without getting caught. The only "wrong" behaviours are ones that will be punished.
		Stage 2: Exchange of favours	Individuals begin to recognize that others also have needs. They may attempt to satisfy others' needs if their own needs are also met in the process ("you scratch my back, I'll scratch yours"). They continue to define right and wrong primarily in terms of consequences to themselves.
Level II: Conventional morality	Seen in a few older elementary school students, some junior high school students, and many high school students (Stage 4 typically does not appear until the high school years)	Stage 3: Good boy/good girl	Individuals make decisions based on what actions will please others, especially authority figures (e.g., parents, teachers, popular classmates). They are concerned about maintaining interpersonal relationships through sharing, trust, and loyalty, and they take other people's perspectives and intentions into account in their decision making.
		Stage 4: Law and order	Individuals look to society as a whole for guidelines concerning what is right or wrong. They know that rules are necessary for keeping society running smoothly and believe it is their "duty" to obey them. However, they perceive rules to be inflexible; they don't necessarily recognize that as society's needs change, rules should change as well.
Level III: Postconventional morality	Rarely seen before post-secondary school (Stage 6 is extremely rare even in adults)	Stage 5: Social contract	Individuals recognize that rules represent an agreement among many people about appropriate behaviour. They think of such rules as being useful mechanisms that maintain the general social order and protect individual human rights, rather than as absolute dictates that must be obeyed simply because they are "the law." They also recognize the flexibility of rules; rules that no longer serve society's best interests can and should be changed.
		Stage 6: Universal ethical principle	Individuals adhere to a few abstract, universal principles (e.g., equality of all people, respect for human dignity and rights, commitment to justice) that transcend specific norms and rules for behaviour. They answer to a strong inner conscience and willingly disobey laws that violate their own ethical principles. Stage 6 is an "ideal" stage that few people ever reach.

Sources: Colby & Kohlberg, 1984; Colby et al., 1983; Kohlberg, 1976, 1984, 1986; Reimer, Paolitto, & Hersh, 1983; Snarey, 1995.

Conventional morality is characterized by an acceptance of society's conventions concerning right and wrong: The individual obeys rules and follows society's norms even when there is no reward for obedience and no punishment for disobedience. Adherence to rules and conventions is somewhat rigid; a rule's appropriateness or fairness is seldom questioned. Conventional individuals believe in the Golden Rule ("Treat others as you would like them to treat you") and in the importance of keeping promises and commitments.

People who exhibit **postconventional morality** have developed their own set of abstract principles to define what actions are morally right and wrong—principles that typically include such basic human rights as life, liberty, and justice. They tend to obey rules consistent with their own abstract principles, and they may *dis*obey rules inconsistent with those principles. Jules's response to the Heinz dilemma illustrates postconventional (Stage 5) reasoning: Jules proposed that the woman's well-being would be better served by breaking the law than by obeying it. Most

Conventional morality
Acceptance of society's conventions regarding right and wrong; behaving to please others or to live up to society's expectations for appropriate behaviour.

Postconventional morality
Behaving in accordance with one's own, self-developed, abstract principles regarding right and wrong.

people never reach postconventional reasoning (even in adulthood), and Kohlberg found Stage 6 reasoning to be extremely rare (Colby & Kohlberg, 1984, 1987; Reimer et al., 1983). We find an example of Stage 6 reasoning in Martin Luther King Jr.'s "Letter from a Birmingham Jail":

> One may well ask, "How can you advocate breaking some laws and obeying others?" The answer lies in the fact that one has not only a legal but a moral responsibility to obey just laws. One has a moral responsibility to disobey unjust laws, though one must do so openly, lovingly and with a willingness to accept the penalty. An individual who breaks a law that conscience tells him is unjust, and accepts the penalty to arouse the conscience of the community, is expressing in reality the highest respect for law. An unjust law is a human law not rooted in eternal law and natural law. A law that uplifts human personality is just; one which degrades human personality is unjust. (King, 1965, cited in Kohlberg, 1981, pp. 318–319)

Factors Affecting Progression through Kohlberg's Stages

As you may have inferred from the age ranges given in Table 3.1, students at any particular grade level are not always reasoning at the same level and stage. We see the greatest variability in high school students, some of whom may show Stage 4 reasoning while others are still reasoning at Stage 1. Kohlberg drew on two aspects of Piaget's theory of cognitive development—the stages of logical reasoning and the concept of disequilibrium—to explain the progression to higher stages of moral reasoning.

First, Kohlberg proposed that advanced moral reasoning requires formal operational thought (Kohlberg, 1976). Postconventional reasoning is based on abstract principles, and even Stage 4 reasoning requires an abstract understanding of the purpose of laws and rules: to help society run smoothly. Hence, the latter stages of moral reasoning typically do not appear until adolescence. At the same time, progression to an advanced stage of cognitive development does not guarantee equivalent moral development; for example, it is quite possible to be formal operational in logical reasoning but preconventional in moral reasoning. In other words, Kohlberg maintained that cognitive development is a *necessary but insufficient* condition for moral development to occur.

Do you know anyone who is very intelligent yet reasons at a preconventional level?

Kohlberg suggested that individuals progress to a higher stage of moral development only when they experience *disequilibrium*—that is, when they realize that their beliefs about morality cannot adequately address the events and dilemmas they experience. By struggling with the various dilemmas and challenges they face, individuals gradually restructure their thoughts about morality and, as a result, move from one stage to the next. As a teacher, you can best create disequilibrium by presenting a moral argument just one stage above the stage at which a student is currently reasoning—for instance, by presenting "law and order" logic (Stage 4) to a student who is concerned primarily with gaining the approval of others (Stage 3). If our moral argument is too much higher than the student's current stage, then the student is unlikely to understand and remember what you are saying (e.g., Narváez, 1998) and so unlikely to experience disequilibrium.

What Research Tells Us about Kohlberg's Theory

A great deal of research on moral development has followed on the heels of Kohlberg's theory. Some research supports Kohlberg's sequence of stages: Generally speaking, people seem to progress through the stages in the order Kohlberg proposed (Colby & Kohlberg, 1984; Reimer et al., 1983; Snarey, 1995; Stewart & Pascual-Leone, 1992). At the same time, it appears that people are not always completely in one stage: Their moral thought usually reflects a particular stage, but they also show occasional instances of reasoning in the two surrounding stages. Furthermore, although the first four stages are found in a wide variety of cultural groups, postconventional moral reasoning is not seen in all cultures (Snarey, 1995).

Researchers have found, too, that young children are probably more advanced than Kohlberg suggested. Even preschoolers have some internal standards of right and wrong, regardless of what authority figures might tell them and regardless of what consequences certain behaviours may or may not bring (Laupa & Turiel, 1995; Smetana, 1981; Tisak, 1993). By the time they are 6 or 7, most children clearly recognize that certain behaviours that are harmful or unfair to others are inherently wrong, whereas behaviours that violate commonly accepted *social conventions* (e.g., burping in public, calling teachers by their first names) are less serious (P. Davidson, Turiel, & Black, 1983; Nucci & Nucci, 1982a, 1982b; Turiel, 1983).

An additional problem is that, although Kohlberg's stages suggest that people's moral reasoning should be relatively consistent from one occasion to the next, in fact people's reasoning depends considerably on situational variables (Rest, Narvaez, Bebeau, & Thoma, 1999; Turiel, 1998). For example, students are more likely to think of lying as immoral if it causes someone else harm than if it has no adverse effect—that is, if it is just a "white lie" (Turiel, Smetana, & Killen, 1991). And moral reasoning influences students' decisions about using drugs only when they view drug use as potentially harmful to others (Berkowitz, Guerra, & Nucci, 1991).[1]

Finally, Kohlberg's theory has been criticized for focusing on moral *thinking* rather than on moral *behaviour*. Some researchers have found that people at higher stages of moral reasoning do tend to behave more morally as well (Bear & Richards, 1981; Blasi, 1980; Reimer et al., 1983). For example, students at the higher stages are less likely to cheat in the classroom, more likely to help people in need, more likely to disobey orders that would cause harm to another individual, and less likely to engage in criminal and other delinquent activities (Blasi, 1980; Chandler & Moran, 1990; Kohlberg, 1975; Kohlberg & Candee, 1984). Generally speaking, however, the relationship between moral reasoning and moral behaviour is a weak one at best (Blasi, 1980; Eisenberg, 1987). Clearly, then, Kohlberg's theory does not give us the total picture of how morality develops.

Despite such weaknesses, Kohlberg's theory offers valuable insights into the nature and development of children's and adolescents' moral thinking. For example, it shows us that children's moral reasoning does not simply result from adults handing down particular moral values and preachings but instead emerges out of children's own, personally constructed beliefs (hence, Kohlberg's theory is very much a *constructivist* approach). Kohlberg's theory also highlights the importance of social interaction in creating disequilibrium and thereby nudging students toward more advanced and complex views of morality.

Possible Sex Differences in Moral Reasoning: Gilligan's Theory

Kohlberg developed his stages after studying how people solved moral dilemmas, but consider this quirk in his research: Subjects in his early studies were predominantly males. Carol Gilligan (1982, 1987) believes that Kohlberg's theory does not adequately describe female moral development. Kohlberg's stages emphasize issues of fairness and justice but omit other aspects of morality, especially compassion and caring for those in need, that Gilligan suggests are more characteristic of the moral reasoning and behaviour of females. She argues that females are socialized to stress interpersonal relationships and to take responsibility for the well-being of others to a greater extent than males; therefore, females develop a morality that emphasizes a greater concern for others' welfare.

EXPERIENCING FIRSTHAND   *The Porcupine Dilemma*

A group of industrious, prudent moles have spent the summer digging a burrow where they will spend the winter. A lazy, improvident porcupine who has not prepared a winter shelter approaches the moles and pleads to share their burrow. The moles take pity on the porcupine and agree to let him in. Unfortunately, the moles did not anticipate the problem the porcupine's sharp quills would pose in close quarters. Once the porcupine has moved in, the moles are constantly being stabbed. The question is, what should the moles do? (Meyers, 1987, p. 141; adapted from Gilligan, 1985)

According to Gilligan, males are more likely to view the problem as that of someone's rights being violated. For example, they might point out that the burrow belongs to the moles, and so the moles can legitimately throw the porcupine out. If the porcupine refuses to leave, some may argue that the moles are well within their rights to kill him. In contrast, females are

---

[1] To account for such inconsistent, situation-specific reasoning, some theorists have proposed a *neo-Kohlbergian* theory: Over time, individuals acquire three distinct moral belief systems, or *schemas*: (a) a "personal interests" schema (reflecting preconventional thinking), (b) a "maintaining norms" schema (reflecting conventional thinking), and (c) a "postconventional" schema. The first emerges in childhood, the second and third in adolescence or adulthood. As people grow older, many begin to prefer the "maintaining norms" schema over the "personal interests" schema and, later, the "postconventional" schema over the other two. However, even morally advanced adults may show an occasional preference for their own personal interests (Rest et al., 1999).

```
hopes
goals
dreams
happiness
    broken
    destroyed
    eliminated
    exterminated
no steps forward
no evolution
no prosperity
no hope
But
maybe
perhaps
except
if we
help
together
we stand
a chance.
```

In this poem Matt, a middle school student, shows empathy for victims of the Holocaust.

Shame A feeling of embarrassment or humiliation that children feel after failing to meet the standards for moral behaviour that adults have set.

Guilt The feeling of discomfort that individuals experience when they know that they have caused someone else pain or distress.

Empathy Experiencing the same feelings as someone in unfortunate circumstances.

Sympathy A feeling of sorrow or concern for another person's problems or distress.

more likely to show compassion and caring when addressing the dilemma. For example, they may suggest that the moles simply cover the porcupine with a blanket; this way, his quills won't annoy anyone and everyone's needs will be met (Meyers, 1987).

Gilligan raises a good point: Males and females are often socialized quite differently. Furthermore, by including compassion for other human beings as well as consideration for their rights, she broadens our conception of what morality *is* (L. J. Walker, 1995). But in fact, most research studies do *not* find major sex differences in moral reasoning (Eisenberg et al., 1996; Nunner-Winkler, 1984; L. J. Walker, 1991). And as Gilligan herself has acknowledged, males and females alike reveal concern for both justice and compassion in their moral reasoning (L. M. Brown, Tappan, & Gilligan, 1995; Gilligan & Attanucci, 1988; Turiel, 1998; L. J. Walker, 1995).

Both Kohlberg and Gilligan portray moral development largely in terms of logic and reasoning. Yet other developmentalists suggest that morality has an affective (emotional) component as well. Let's look at some of their findings.

Emotional Components of Moral Development

How do you feel when you inadvertently cause inconvenience for someone else? When you hurt someone else's feelings? When a friend suddenly and unexpectedly loses a close family member? Perhaps such feelings as shame, guilt, empathy, and sympathy come to mind. All of these emotions are associated with moral development.

By the time children reach the middle elementary grades, most of them occasionally feel **shame**: They feel embarrassed or humiliated when they fail to meet the standards for moral behaviour that parents and teachers have set for them (Damon, 1988). Shortly thereafter, as they begin to develop their *own* standards for behaviour, they sometimes experience **guilt**—a feeling of discomfort when they know that they have caused someone else pain or distress (Damon, 1988; Hoffman, 1991). Both shame and guilt, though unpleasant in nature, are good signs that students are developing a sense of right and wrong and that their future behaviours will improve.

Shame and guilt emerge when children believe they have done something wrong. In contrast, **empathy**—experiencing the same feelings as someone in unfortunate circumstances—motivates moral and prosocial behaviour even in the absence of wrongdoing (Damon, 1988; Eisenberg, 1982; Hoffman, 1991). Empathy is especially likely to promote such behaviour when it leads to **sympathy**, whereby children not only assume another person's feelings but also have concerns for the individual's well-being (Eisenberg & Fabes, 1991; Turiel, 1998).

Empathy continues to develop throughout the elementary school years and often during the high school years as well (Eisenberg, 1982). At the primary grade levels, students show empathy only to people they know, such as friends and classmates. But by the late elementary school years, students may also begin to feel empathy for people they *don't* know—perhaps for the poor, the homeless, or those in catastrophic circumstances (Damon, 1988; Hoffman, 1991).

Nancy Eisenberg and her colleagues (Eisenberg, 1982; Eisenberg, Carlo, Murphy, & Van Court, 1995; Eisenberg, Lennon, & Pasternack, 1986) have identified five levels of prosocial reasoning, reflecting different degrees of empathy and sympathy, which can help us predict how students of different ages are likely to behave in situations that call for altruism and other prosocial behaviours. These five levels or orientations (selfish and self-centred; superficial "needs of others"; approval and stereotypic good boy/girl; empathic; and internalized values) are not true stages, in that children and adolescents do not necessarily progress through them in a sequential or universal fashion. Instead, children may reason at two or more different levels in any particular time period (Eisenberg, Miller, Shell, McNalley, & Shea, 1991). Generally speaking, however, children and adolescents show increasing use of the upper levels, and less frequent use of lower ones, as they grow older (Eisenberg et al., 1995).

You are often in a position to foster empathy and prosocial behaviour in your students. For instance, you can ask students to imagine how people must have felt during particularly traumatic and stressful events in history, or possibly even have them role-play such events (Brophy & Alleman, 1996; Brophy & VanSledright, 1997). You can encourage them to engage in such prosocial behaviours as co-operating and sharing with one another and comforting classmates whose feelings have been hurt, and you can acknowledge and reward such behaviours when you see them. Furthermore, as the curriculum provides an increasingly broader view of the country and world in which we all live, you can expose your students to situations in which other people's needs may be far greater than their own.

Determinants of Moral Behaviour

Most children act more morally and prosocially as they grow older; for example, they become increasingly generous (Eisenberg, 1982; Rushton, 1980). Gains in moral reasoning, perspective taking, and empathy are, of course, partly responsible for this trend. Yet motivational factors come into play as well. Children and adolescents typically have many goals: Although they may want to do the right thing, they may also be concerned about whether others will approve of their actions and about what positive or negative consequences might result. Students are more likely to act in accordance with their moral standards if the benefits are high (e.g., they gain others' approval or respect) and the personal costs are low (e.g., an act of altruism involves little sacrifice) (Batson & Thompson, 2001; Eisenberg, 1987; Narváez & Rest, 1995).

In adolescence some students begin to integrate a commitment to moral values into their overall sense of identity (Arnold, 2000; Blasi, 1995; Kurtines, Berman, Ittel, & Williamson, 1995; Youniss & Yates, 1999). They think of themselves as moral, caring individuals and place a high priority on demonstrating these values. Their acts of altruism and compassion are not limited to their friends and acquaintances, but extend to the community at large.

Promoting Moral Development in the Classroom

Some well-meaning individuals have suggested that society is in a sharp moral decline and urge parents and educators to impart desirable moral traits (honesty, integrity, loyalty, responsibility, etc.) through lectures at home and in school, as well as through firm control of children's behaviour. In fact, there is no evidence to indicate that the present generation of young people is in any way less "moral" than previous generations (Turiel, 1998). Furthermore, lecturing students about morally appropriate behaviour and imposing firm control on their actions do little to instil a particular set of moral values (Damon, 1988; Higgins, 1995; Turiel, 1998). Research suggests, however, that several other strategies *can* make a difference:

■ *Give reasons why some behaviours are unacceptable.* Although it is important to impose consequences for immoral or antisocial behaviours, punishment by itself often focuses children's attention primarily on their own hurt and distress (Hoffman, 1975). To promote moral development, focus students' attention on the hurt and distress their behaviours have caused *others*. Thus, give students reasons that certain behaviours are unacceptable—an approach known as **induction** (Hoffman, 1970, 1975). For example, you might describe how a behaviour harms someone else either physically ("Having your hair pulled the way you just pulled Mai's can really be painful") or emotionally ("You probably hurt John's feelings when you call him names like that"). You might also show students how they have caused someone else inconvenience ("Because you ruined Marie's jacket, her parents are making her work around the house to earn the money for a new one"). Still another approach is to explain someone else's perspective, intention, or motive ("This science project you've just ridiculed may not be as fancy as yours, but I know that Michael spent many hours working on it and is quite proud of what he's done").

Induction A method for encouraging moral development in which one explains why a certain behaviour is unacceptable, often with a focus on the pain or distress that someone has caused another.

Induction is victim-centred: It helps students focus on the distress of others and recognize that they themselves have been the cause of it (Hoffman, 1970). The consistent use of induction in disciplining children, particularly when accompanied by *mild* punishment for misbehaviour, appears to promote co-operation with rules and facilitate the development of such prosocial characteristics as empathy, compassion, and altruism (Baumrind, 1971; G. H. Brody & Shaffer, 1982; Hoffman, 1975; Maccoby & Martin, 1983; Rushton, 1980).

■ *Provide practice in recognizing others' emotional states.* There is less need to explain someone else's feelings if your students are able to recognize those feelings on their own. Yet many students, young ones especially, are poor judges of the emotional states of others. With preschoolers, you can orally label a classmate's feelings as "sadness," "disappointment," or "anger" (Chalmers & Townsend, 1990; Wittmer & Honig, 1994). In later years, you might ask students to describe to one another exactly how they feel about particular misbehaviours directed toward them (Doescher & Sugawara, 1989). Or, you might ask them how they themselves would feel in the same situation (Hoffman, 1991). As a teacher, you also should describe your own emotional reactions to any inappropriate behaviours (Damon, 1988).

■ *Expose students to numerous models of moral behaviour.* Children and adolescents are more likely to exhibit moral and prosocial behaviour when they see others behaving in morally appropriate ways. For example, when adults or peers are generous and show concern for others, children tend to do likewise (Rushton, 1980; C. C. Wilson, Piazza, & Nagle, 1990). Yet by the same token, when children see their peers cheating, they themselves are more likely to cheat (Sherrill, Horowitz, Friedman, & Salisbury, 1970). Television, too, provides both prosocial and antisocial models for children. When children watch television shows that emphasize perspective taking and prosocial actions (e.g., *Sesame Street, Mister Rogers' Neighbourhood, Barney & Friends*), they are more likely to exhibit such behaviours themselves; when they see violence on television, they, too, are more likely to be violent (Hearold, 1986; Rushton, 1980; Singer & Singer, 1994).

■ *Encourage discussions about moral issues and dilemmas.* Kohlberg proposed that children develop morally when they are challenged by moral dilemmas they cannot adequately deal with at their current stage of moral reasoning. Research confirms his belief: Classroom discussions of controversial topics and moral issues appear to promote increased perspective taking and the transition to more advanced moral reasoning (De Lisi & Golbeck, 1999; DeVries & Zan, 1996; D. W. Johnson & Johnson, 1988; Power, Higgins, & Kohlberg, 1989; Schlaefli, Rest, & Thoma, 1985).

Social and moral issues often arise at school. Sometimes these issues relate to inappropriate student behaviours that occur in most classrooms at one time or another (e.g., cheating, plagiarism, theft, interpersonal conflicts). At other times they are intrinsic in course content. Consider the following questions that might emerge in discussions related to history, social studies, science, or literature:

- Is it appropriate to engage in armed conflict, and hence to kill others, when two groups of people disagree about political or religious issues?
- Is military retaliation for acts of terrorism justified even when it may involve killing innocent people?
- How can a capitalistic society encourage free enterprise while at the same time protecting the rights of citizens and the ecology of the environment?
- Should laboratory rats be used to study the effects of cancer-producing agents?
- Was Hamlet justified in killing Claudius to avenge the murder of his father?

INTO THE CLASSROOM   *Promoting Moral and Prosocial Development*

Encourage prosocial behaviour, and acknowledge and reward it when it occurs.

A kindergarten teacher commends a student for consoling a classmate whose feelings have been hurt.

Talk about reasons why some behaviours are inappropriate, noting especially the harm or inconvenience that those behaviours have caused.

A Grade 2 teacher explains to Sarah that because she has thoughtlessly left her chewing gum on Margaret's chair, Margaret's mother must now pay to have Margaret's new pants professionally cleaned.

Model appropriate moral and prosocial behaviour.

A junior high school teacher mentions that he will be working at a Habitat for Humanity project on Saturday and asks if any of his students would like to join him.

Incorporate moral issues and dilemmas into classroom discussions.

When discussing the war in Iraq, a high school teacher mentions that Canada refused to participate with the United States in the war. He asks his students to decide whether or not they think this was the right decision and to explain their reasoning.

Remember that standards for what is "moral" and "immoral" differ somewhat from one culture to another.

A teacher sees a student inadvertently knock a classmate's jacket off its hook. The teacher mentions the incident to the student, but he denies that he had anything to do with the fallen jacket. Remembering that in this student's culture, lying is an acceptable way of saving face, the teacher doesn't chastise the student; instead, she asks him to do her the "favour" of returning the jacket to its hook. A short time later, she engages her class in a conversation about the importance of being careful around other people's belongings.

Social and moral issues will not always have right or wrong answers. As teachers, you can encourage student discussions of such issues in a variety of ways (Reimer et al., 1983). First, you can provide a trusting and nonthreatening classroom atmosphere in which students feel free to express their ideas without censure or embarrassment. Second, you can help students identify all aspects of a dilemma, including the needs and perspectives of the various individuals involved. Third, you can help students explore their reasons for thinking as they do—that is, to clarify and examine the principles on which their moral judgments are based.

- *Engage students in community service.* As we have seen, adolescents are more likely to act in moral and prosocial ways when they have integrated a commitment to moral ideals into their overall sense of identity. Such integration is more probable when students become actively involved in service to others even before they reach puberty (Youniss & Yates, 1999). Through ongoing community service activities—food and clothing drives, visits to homes for the elderly, community cleanup efforts, and so on—elementary and secondary students alike learn that they have the skills and the responsibility for helping those less fortunate than themselves and can make the world a better place in which to live. In the process, they also begin to think of themselves as concerned, compassionate, and moral citizens (Youniss & Yates, 1999). For more information about the social–emotional side of education, see the article "Reading, 'riting,' rithmetic and relationships: Considering the social side of education" by Hymel, Schonert-Reichl, and Miller (2006). In addition, see the list below for online materials, readings, and lesson plans that educators can use to promote students' social–emotional development, character, and moral education (adapted from Hymel, Schonert-Reichl, and Miller, 2006).

- Development Studies Center (Child Development Project) www.devstu.org
- Center for Social and Emotional Education www.csee.net
- Center for the Fourth & Fifth Rs: Respect and Responsibility www.cortland.edu/character
- Studies in Moral Development and Education http://tigger.uic.edu/~lnucci/MoralEd/
- Roots of Empathy Primary Prevention Program www.rootsofempathy.org
- Collaborative for Academic, Social, and Emotional Learning (CASEL) www.casel.org
- The Search Institute www.search-institute.org

Accommodating Students in the Inclusive Classroom

Some of our students will have special education needs related to their personal, social, and moral development. Table 3.2 describes some of the characteristics you might observe along with some suggested classroom strategies.

General Themes in Personal, Social, and Moral Development

Themes evident throughout this chapter along with educational implications and examples are summarized in Table 3.3.

TABLE 3.2 STUDENTS IN INCLUSIVE SETTINGS

Promoting Personal, Social, and Moral Development in Students with Special Educational Needs

CATEGORY	CHARACTERISTICS YOU MIGHT OBSERVE	SUGGESTED CLASSROOM STRATEGIES
Students with specific cognitive or academic difficulties	• Low self-esteem related to areas of academic difficulty • Greater susceptibility to peer pressure (if students have learning disabilities or ADHD) • Difficulty in perspective taking or accurately interpreting social situations (for some students with learning disabilities or ADHD) • In some cases, poor social skills and few friendships; tendency to act without thinking through the consequences of one's actions (especially if students have ADHD)	• Promote academic success (e.g., by providing extra scaffolding for classroom tasks). • Give students the opportunity to "show off" the things they do well. • Use induction to promote perspective taking (e.g., focus students' attention on how their behaviours have caused harm or distress to others). • Teach any missing social skills.
Students with social or behavioural problems	• Rejection by peers; few friendships • Difficulty in perspective taking and recognizing others' emotional states • Deficits in ability to interpret social cues (e.g., perceiving hostile intent in innocent interactions) • Poor social skills and social problem-solving ability; limited awareness of how poor their social skills actually are • Poor impulse control; difficulty controlling emotions • Less empathy for others	• Explicitly teach social skills, provide opportunities to practise them, and give feedback. • Establish and enforce firm rules regarding acceptable classroom behaviour. • Label and praise appropriate behaviours. • Teach social problem-solving strategies (e.g., through mediation training). • Provide opportunities for students to make new friends (e.g., through co-operative learning activities). • Help students recognize the outward signs of various emotions. • Use induction to promote empathy and perspective taking.
Students with general delays in cognitive and social functioning	• Generally low self-esteem • Social skills typical of younger children • Difficulty identifying and interpreting social cues • Concrete, often preconventional, ideas of right and wrong	• Scaffold academic success. • Teach social skills, provide opportunities to practise them, and give feedback. • Specify rules for classroom behaviour in specific, concrete terms. • Label and praise appropriate behaviours.
Students with physical or sensory challenges	• Fewer friends and possible social isolation • Fewer opportunities to develop appropriate social skills	• Maximize opportunities for students to interact with their classmates. • Assign "buddies"—classmates who can assist students with tasks that they cannot perform themselves due to a disability. • Teach any missing social skills.
Students showing evidence of giftedness, talent, or high performance	• Above-average social development and emotional adjustment (although some extremely gifted students may have difficulty because they are so *very* different from their peers) • High self-esteem with regard to academic tasks (more typical of males than females) • Conflicts (especially for females) between the need to develop and display abilities on the one hand and to gain peer acceptance on the other • For some students, more advanced moral reasoning • Concerns about moral and ethical issues at a younger age than peers • Greater perspective taking	• Be sensitive to students' concerns about how their exceptional abilities may affect their relationships with classmates. • Engage students in conversations about ethical issues and moral dilemmas. • Involve students in projects that address social problems at a community, national, or international level. • Include curricular activities that encourage all students to come to know their identities, including heritage, their interests, their learning strengths, what motivates them, and the ways they dream about contributing to the world. • Where possible, facilitate mentor relationships with role models for individuals and groups of two or three students. (Mentors need to be screened in the same ways as all other school personnel.)

Sources: Barkley, 1998; Beirne-Smith et al., 2002; Bierman et al., 1987; Cartledge & Milburn, 1995; Coie & Cillessen, 1993; Dempster & Corkill, 1999; Flavell et al., 1993; Gresham & MacMillan, 1997; Grinberg & McLean-Heywood, 1999; Harter et al., 1998; Heward, 2000; Hughes, 1988; Juvonen & Weiner, 1993; B. K. Keogh & MacMillan, 1996; Lind, 1994; Maker & Schiever, 1989; H. W. Marsh & Craven, 1997; Mercer, 1997; Milch-Reich et al., 1999; Neel et al., 1990; Piirto, 1999; Schonert-Reichl, 1993; Schumaker & Hazel, 1984; Tomlinson et al., 2002; Turnbull et al., 1999; Winner, 1997; Zeaman & House, 1979; Zirpoli & Melloy, 2001.

TABLE 3.3   PRINCIPLES/ASSUMPTIONS

General Themes Characterizing Personal, Social, and Moral Development

THEME	EDUCATIONAL IMPLICATION	EXAMPLE
Standards for acceptable behaviour, along with the reasons behind them, are essential for development.	Establish rules and expectations for classroom behaviour that preserve all students' rights and welfare. When students do not adhere to such standards, administer appropriate consequences and help students understand how their actions have caused harm or inconvenience to someone else.	If a student maliciously ruins a classmate's work (e.g., a homework assignment or art project), point out that the classmate spent quite a bit of time completing the work and insist that the student make amends.
Interaction with peers provides the impetus for many advancements.	Include many opportunities to interact with peers in the daily schedule, both in and outside the classroom.	When teaching art in the lower elementary grades, provide one set of art supplies (e.g., crayons, scissors, glue) for each table, so that children sitting at the same table must share. Give the children some guidelines about how to share the materials fairly.
Development is best fostered in a warm, supportive environment.	Continually communicate the message that you like students and want them to succeed. Design lessons and activities in which students co-operate with and help one another, and assign projects to which every student has something valuable to contribute.	In a co-operative learning activity, have students work in groups of three to read and study a section of their textbook. Group members take one of three roles: (a) *reader* (who reads a paragraph), (b) *questioner* (who develops two or three thought-provoking questions about the material presented), and (c) *responder* (who answers the questions). The students rotate these three roles for succeeding paragraphs.
Personal, social, and moral understandings are self-constructed.	Encourage students to exchange views about social and moral issues. When students have difficulty getting along with their peers, help them reflect on their peers' perspectives and intentions.	Hold a classroom debate on the pros and cons of capital punishment, perhaps after first having students conduct library research to support their perspectives.

TEACHING CONSTRUCTIONS

Now that you have learned about personal, social, and moral development in students of different ages, let's revisit Adam at the beginning of this chapter. Based on what you now know:

- How would you as Adam's teacher help Adam to think more positively about himself and to interact more positively with his peers and in the school setting?
- How would you describe Adam's sense of self and his level of personal, social, and moral development?

KEY CONCEPTS

temperament (p. 48)
attachment (p. 48)
authoritative parenting (p. 48)
self-esteem (p. 48)
socialization (p. 49)
norms (p. 49)
roles (p. 49)
culture shock (p. 49)
self-concept (p. 50)
self-efficacy (p. 51)

imaginary audience (p. 54)
personal fable (p. 54)
identity (p. 55)
peer pressure (p. 57)
clique (p. 58)
subculture (p. 58)
gang (p. 58)
social skills (p. 60)
prosocial behaviour (p. 60)
aggressive behaviour (p. 62)

moral dilemma (p. 64)
preconventional morality (p. 64)
conventional morality (p. 65)
postconventional morality (p. 65)
shame (p. 68)
guilt (p. 68)
empathy (p. 68)
sympathy (p. 68)
induction (p. 69)

4 Individual and Group Differences

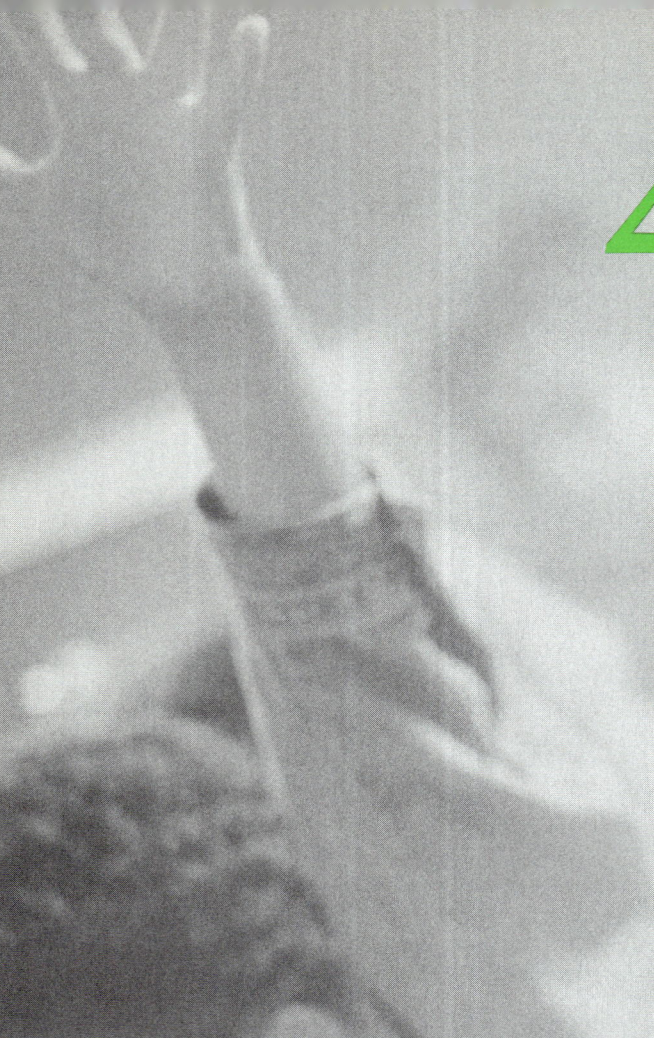

CASE STUDY HIDDEN TREASURE

TEACHING CONNECTIONS

KEEPING INDIVIDUAL AND GROUP DIFFERENCES IN PERSPECTIVE

INTELLIGENCE
Measuring Intelligence • How Theorists Conceptualize Intelligence • Heredity, Environment, and Group Differences in Intelligence • Socioeconomic Difference, Ability, and Achievement • Factors Interfering with School Success • Being Optimistic about Students' Potential

CREATIVITY
Fostering Creativity in the Classroom

CULTURAL AND ETHNIC DIFFERENCES
Navigating Different Cultures at Home and at School • Examples of Ethnic Diversity • Creating a More Multicultural Classroom Environment

SEX DIFFERENCES
Origins of Sex Differences

STUDENTS AT RISK
Characteristics of Students at Risk • Why Students Drop Out • Helping Students at Risk Stay in School • Fostering Resilience: A Lesson from Low Socioeconomic Status Children under Stress • Building on Students' Strengths

EXCEPTIONAL STUDENTS

STUDENTS IN INCLUSIVE SETTINGS
The Current Concept of Inclusion • Classroom Strategies to Promote Inclusion

TEACHING CONSTRUCTIONS

KEY CONCEPTS

CASE STUDY *Hidden Treasure*

Eight-year-old Dijana has just enrolled in Ms. Padilla's Grade 3 classroom in Toronto. The daughter of new Canadians, Dijana has been raised in Croatia by her parents, who had limited financial resources and were able to provide very few playthings such as toys, puzzles, crayons, and scissors. Ms. Padilla rarely calls on Dijana in class because of her apparent lack of academic skills; she is afraid of embarrassing her in front of her classmates. By mid-year, Ms. Padilla is very concerned about Dijana's apparent lack of progress.

Dijana is always quiet and well behaved in class; in fact, she's so quiet that Ms. Padilla sometimes forgets she's even there. Yet a researcher's video camera captures a different side to Dijana. On one occasion, she is quick to finish her Language Arts assignment and so begins to work on a puzzle during her free time. A classmate, also recently arrived from Croatia, approaches, and he and Dijana begin playing with a box of toys. A teacher assistant asks the boy whether he has finished his Language Arts assignment, implying that he should return to complete it, but the boy does not understand the aide's subtle message. Dijana gently persuades the boy to go back and finish his work. She then returns to her puzzle and successfully fits most of it together. Two classmates having difficulty with their own puzzles request her assistance, and she competently and patiently shows them how to assemble puzzles and how to help each other.

Ms. Padilla is amazed when she views the videotape, which shows Dijana to be a competent girl with strong teaching and leadership skills. This is in contrast to Ms. Padilla's overall classroom observations that Dijana had not met the academic expectations. Ms. Padilla and her aides begin working closely with Dijana on academic skills, and they often allow her to take a leadership role in group activities. At the end of the school year, Dijana obtains teacher-based and standardized achievement test scores indicating grade-level competence across all subject areas. She is clearly ready for Grade 4.

TEACHING CONNECTIONS

In this chapter, we will describe how you may adapt your own classroom practices to accommodate **individual** and **group differences**. As you read, keep the following questions in mind in making connections between the issue described and your own teaching practice:

- To what extent will knowledge about individual and group differences enable us to draw conclusions about particular students?
- What do we mean by the term *intelligence*, and how can we promote intelligent behaviour and creativity in all of our students?
- In what ways are students from various cultural, ethnic, and socioeconomic groups apt to be alike and different from one another? What implications do their differences have for classroom practice?
- What general principles can guide us in our efforts to provide maximally beneficial classroom experiences for all students with special needs?
- What characteristics can help us identify students at risk for school failure, and how can we help these students achieve academic success?
- Why might a teacher believe that Dijana has poor academic skills? Might Dijana's background be a reason? Might her classroom behaviour be a reason?
- What might have happened to Dijana if her behaviour with classmates had gone unnoticed? How might her academic life have been different?

Individual differences The ways in which people of the same age are different from one another.

Group differences Consistently observed differences, on average, among certain groups of individuals.

Keeping Individual and Group Differences in Perspective

We will inevitably find that some students learn more easily than others. For example, Dijana finishes assignments and completes puzzles more quickly than some of her classmates. We will also find differences in how accurately our students remember information, how readily they connect ideas with one another, and how easily and creatively they apply their knowledge to new situations and problems.

Some of Dijana's behaviours may be partly due to either her Croatian heritage or her sex. For example, she is proficient in her native language and displays the co-operative attitude

Chapter 4 Individual and Group Differences 75

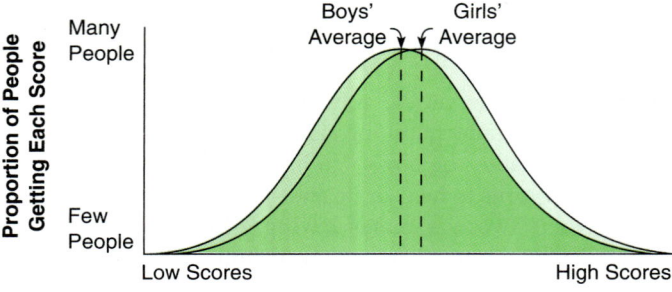

FIGURE 4.1 Typical "difference" between boys and girls on tests of verbal ability

For more information on this point, see the section "Teacher Expectations and Attributions" in Chapter 9.

encouraged in many cultures. She is so quiet in class that her teacher often forgets she's there; as we will discover later, girls are, on average, less assertive in whole-class situations than boys.

In observing our students day after day, we are likely to draw inferences about their academic capabilities, just as Ms. Padilla did for Dijana. Yet we must be careful that such inferences are never set in stone—that we keep an open mind about how each student is likely to perform in future situations. For example, we will soon discover that creativity is domain-specific: Some students may be creative in science, whereas others are more creative in fine arts. We will find, too, that intelligence can change over time, especially during the early years, and that students often behave more intelligently in some contexts than in others.

When considering group differences, such as those among diverse ethnic groups and those between males and females, we need to keep in mind two very important points. First, *there is a great deal of individual variability within any group*. We will be describing how students of different groups behave *on average*, yet some students may be very different from that "average" description. Second, *there is almost always a great deal of overlap between two groups*. Figure 4.1 shows the typical overlap between boys and girls on measures of verbal ability: Notice how many of the boys are *better* than some of the girls despite the average advantage for girls (Halpern & LaMay, 2000).

As we shall discover in Chapter 9, teachers' preconceived notions about how students will behave may actually *increase* the differences among those students. At the same time, if we are to maximize the learning and development of all students, then we should be aware of individual and group differences that may influence students' classroom performance. Several general principles regarding student diversity are presented in Table 4.1.

This chapter identifies many differences that are likely to affect our students' academic achievement, as well as strategies for accommodating those differences. We should never ask ourselves whether particular students can learn and achieve in the classroom. We should instead ask how we, as teachers, can most effectively help *every* student master the knowledge and skills essential for school and lifelong success.

TABLE 4.1   PRINCIPLES/ASSUMPTIONS

General Principles Regarding Students' Diversity

GENERAL PRINCIPLE	EDUCATIONAL IMPLICATION	EXAMPLE
Differences among students are subject to change over time; they are not necessarily permanent differences.	Never make long-range predictions about students' future success or failure based on their present behaviours.	Although a student currently shows little creativity, believe that creative behaviour is possible, and plan instructional activities that promote such creativity.
There is a great deal of variability among members of any single ethnic group, sex, or socioeconomic group.	Be careful not to draw conclusions about students' characteristics and abilities simply on the basis of their sex, ethnic background, or other group membership.	Have considerable optimism that, with reasonable support from you and your colleagues, many students from lower socioeconomic backgrounds can pursue post-secondary degrees. Share your optimism about students' potential with them. They need to know that there is hope.
When two groups differ *on average* in terms of a particular characteristic, considerable overlap usually exists between the two groups with respect to that characteristic.	Remember that average differences between groups don't necessarily apply to individual members of those groups.	Although boys have historically developed their athletic abilities more than girls (on average), nevertheless provide equal opportunities for both sexes to achieve athletic success.
Students achieve at higher levels when instruction takes individual and group differences into account.	Consider students' unique backgrounds and abilities when planning instructional activities.	Use co-operative learning activities more frequently when students' cultural backgrounds emphasize the value of co-operation and group achievement.

Intelligence

What exactly *is* intelligence? Clearly it is more than a simple, single entity, but psychologists have not yet reached consensus on the answer to this question. Here are several components of what many theorists construe **intelligence** to be:

- It is adaptive.
- It is related to *learning ability*.
- It involves the *use of prior knowledge* to analyze and understand new situations effectively.
- It involves the complex interaction and coordination of *many different mental processes*.
- It may be seen in *different arenas*—for example, on academic tasks or in social situations.
- It is both general and culture-specific.

While somewhat distinct from what a person has actually learned (e.g., as reflected in school achievement), intelligent thinking and intelligent behaviour do depend on prior learning. Intelligence is not necessarily a permanent, unchanging characteristic. As you will soon discover, it can be modified through experience and learning.

Measuring Intelligence

In the early 1900s, school officials in France asked Alfred Binet to develop a method of identifying those students unlikely to benefit from regular school instruction and therefore in need of special educational services. Binet devised a test that measured general knowledge, vocabulary, perception, memory, and abstract thought. In doing so, he designed the earliest version of what we now call an **intelligence test**. Although these tests have evolved considerably since Binet's time, they continue to measure many of the same abilities that Binet's original test did.

IQ Scores

"Intelligence quotient," or **IQ scores**, are determined by comparing a student's performance on an intelligence test with the performance of others in the same age-group. A score of 100 indicates average performance: Students with this score have performed better than half of their age-mates on the test and not as well as the other half. Usually, scores less than 85 indicate below-average performance on the test and scores above 115 indicate above-average performance. For children, the IQ score is valid only for two years following the date when the intelligence test was administered.

Figure 4.2 shows the percentage of students getting scores at different points along the scale (e.g., 12.9 percent get scores between 100 and 105). Notice how the curve is high in the middle and low at both ends; we have many more students obtaining scores close to 100 than we have students scoring very much higher or lower than 100. For example, adding up the percentages

> What kinds of behaviours lead you to believe that someone is "intelligent"? Do you think that intelligence is a general ability that contributes to success in many different areas? Or is it possible for an individual to be intelligent in one area yet not in another?

> **Intelligence** The ability to modify and adjust one's behaviours in order to accomplish new tasks successfully. It involves many different mental processes, and its nature may vary, depending on the culture in which one lives.

> Think of someone you think is intelligent. Does that individual's behaviour fit these criteria?

> One component of intelligence is the ability to use prior knowledge to analyze new situations. These students are trying to calculate the volume of the large pyramid by applying geometric principles they've learned in their math class.

> **Intelligence test** A general measure of current cognitive abilities, used in schools primarily to predict academic achievement over the short run. Intelligence tests may also assist in the assessment and diagnosis of various learning difficulties.

> **IQ score** A composite score on an intelligence test. It is determined by comparing one's performance on the test with the performance of others in the same age-group; for most tests, it is a standard score with a mean of 100 and a standard deviation of 15.

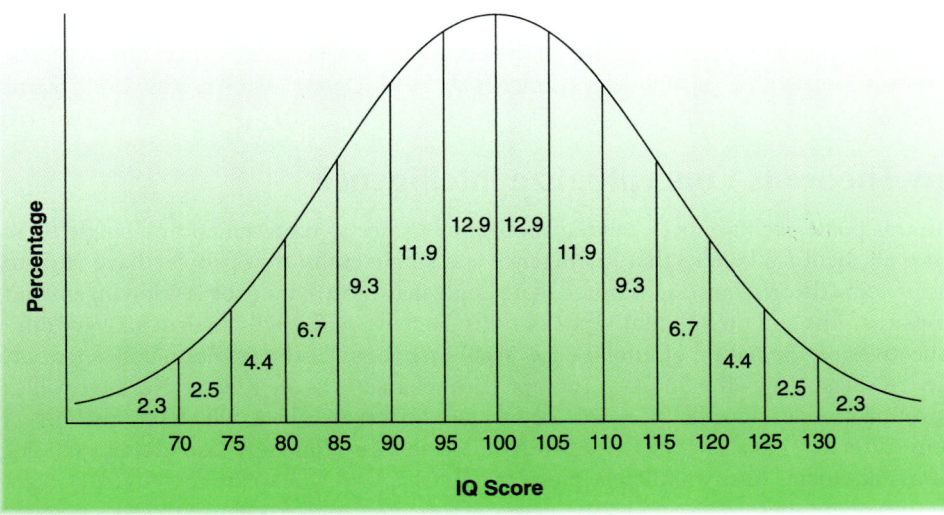

FIGURE 4.2 Percentage of IQ scores in different ranges

Canadian psychologists Dr. Lynne Beal and Dr. Don Saklofske, respectively, were the project directors that established Canadian test norms for the Wechsler intelligence tests for children (WISC-III) and adults (WAIS-III). The new WISC-IV has also been standardized in Canada by Harcourt Assessment (see Chapter 12).

When might it be appropriate for a teacher to use intelligence test results? What potential dangers are there in relying solely on IQ scores as a measure of students' abilities?

in different parts of Figure 4.2, approximately two-thirds (68 percent) of students score within 15 points of 100 (i.e., between 85 and 115). In contrast, only 2 percent of students score as low as 70, and only 2 percent score as high as 130. This symmetric and predictable distribution of intelligence test scores was created by psychologists to intentionally yield such a distribution. (You can find a more detailed explanation of IQ scores in the discussion of *standard scores* in Chapter 12.)

IQ and School Achievement

Modern intelligence tests have been designed with Binet's original purpose in mind: to predict how well individual students are likely to perform in the classroom and similar situations. Studies repeatedly show that performance on intelligence tests is correlated with school achievement (N. Brody, 1997; Gustafsson & Undheim, 1996; Sattler, 2008). On average, children with higher IQ scores do better on standardized achievement tests, have higher school grades, and complete more years of education. In other words, IQ scores often *do* predict school achievement, albeit imprecisely. As a result, intelligence tests are frequently used by school psychologists and other specialists to identify and assess the cognitive abilities of those students who may have special educational needs.

While recognizing the relationship between intelligence test scores and school achievement, we must also keep three points in mind about this relationship:

- Intelligence does not necessarily *cause* achievement; it is simply correlated with it.
- The relationship between IQ scores and achievement is not a perfect one; there are exceptions to the rule.
- IQ scores simply reflect a student's performance on a particular test at a particular time, and some change is to be expected over the years.

Limitations of Intelligence Tests

"True" intelligence cannot be measured, and intelligence tests do not and cannot tell you all that you need to know about your students. It is critical, then, to be aware of the following limitations of traditional intelligence tests:

See Chapter 12 for a description of test validity and reliability.

- Different kinds of intelligence tests often yield somewhat different scores.
- A student's performance on any test is inevitably affected by many temporary factors present at the time the test is taken, such as general health, mood, fatigue, time of day, and the number of distracting stimuli. Such temporary factors affect a test's *reliability*—a concept we will consider in Chapter 12.
- Test items focus on a limited set of skills that are important in mainstream Western culture, and particularly in school settings; they do not necessarily tap into skills that may be more highly valued in other contexts or other societies.
- Some students may be unfamiliar with the content or types of tasks involved in particular test items and perform poorly on those items as a result.

Are any of your prior beliefs about intelligence tests inconsistent with what you've just read? If so, can you resolve the inconsistencies?

- Students with limited English proficiency (LEP) are at an obvious disadvantage when an intelligence test is administered in English.
- Some students may not be motivated to perform at their best and so may obtain scores that underestimate their capabilities. (Neisser et al., 1996; Ogbu, 1994; Perkins, 1995; Sternberg, 1996b)

How Theorists Conceptualize Intelligence

Up to this point, we have been talking about intelligence as represented by a single IQ score. Yet not all theorists believe that intelligence is a single entity that people "have" in varying degrees; some theorists instead propose that people may behave more or less intelligently in different situations and on different kinds of tasks. Here we will briefly look at six very different perspectives on the nature of intelligence. We'll first consider the traditional idea that intelligence is a single, generalized trait—a concept often referred to as the g factor. Next, we will examine two theories developed by Howard Gardner and Robert Sternberg, which portray intelligence as multidimensional and context-dependent. Models developed by Canadian psychologists J. P. Das and Robbie Case will then be presented. In Chapter 6 we explore cognitive-psychological meanings of abilities.

Spearman's Concept of g

Whenever we use an IQ score as an estimate of a person's cognitive ability, we are, to some extent, buying into the notion that intelligence is a single entity. Historically, considerable evidence has supported this idea (Neisser et al., 1996). Charles Spearman (1904, 1927) called this single entity a *general factor,* or **g**.[1] Some contemporary information processing theorists believe that g is a reflection of the speed and efficiency with which people can process information, learning tasks, and problem situations (N. Brody, 1992; Dempster & Corkill, 1999).

g (general factor in intelligence) The theoretical notion that intelligence includes a general factor that influences people's ability to learn in a wide variety of content domains.

Gardner's Theory of Multiple Intelligences

In contrast to viewing intelligence as a general or composite ability, Howard Gardner (1983, 1998, 1999) suggests that there are at least eight different and relatively independent abilities, or *intelligences* (see Table 4.2).[2] Thus, some students may show exceptional promise in

In which of Gardner's intelligences are you most "intelligent"?

TABLE 4.2   COMPARE/CONTRAST

Gardner's Multiple Intelligences

TYPE OF INTELLIGENCE	EXAMPLES OF RELEVANT BEHAVIOURS
Linguistic Intelligence The ability to use language effectively	• Making persuasive arguments • Writing poetry • Being sensitive to subtle nuances in word meanings
Logical-Mathematical Intelligence The ability to reason logically, especially in mathematics and science	• Solving mathematical problems quickly • Generating mathematical proofs • Formulating and testing hypotheses about observed phenomena[a]
Spatial Intelligence The ability to notice details of what one sees and to imagine and manipulate visual objects in one's mind	• Conjuring up images in one's mind • Drawing a visual likeness of an object • Making fine discriminations among very similar objects
Musical Intelligence The ability to create, comprehend, and appreciate music	• Playing a musical instrument • Composing a musical work • Having a keen awareness of the underlying structure of music
Bodily-Kinesthetic Intelligence The ability to use one's body skillfully	• Dancing • Playing basketball • Performing pantomime
Interpersonal Intelligence The ability to notice subtle aspects of other people's behaviours	• Reading another's mood • Detecting another's underlying intentions and desires • Using knowledge of others to influence their thoughts and behaviours
Intrapersonal Intelligence Awareness of one's own feelings, motives, and desires	• Discriminating among such similar emotions as sadness and regret • Identifying the motives guiding one's own behaviour • Using self-knowledge to relate more effectively with others
Naturalist Intelligence The ability to recognize patterns in nature and differences among various life-forms and natural objects	• Identifying members of particular plant or animal species • Classifying natural forms (e.g., rocks, types of mountains) • Applying one's knowledge of nature in such activities as farming, landscaping, or animal training

[a]This example may remind you of Piaget's theory of cognitive development. Many of the stage-specific characteristics that Piaget described fall within the realm of logical-mathematical intelligence.

---

[1]Spearman suggested that several more specific (s) factors come into play as well, with different factors having greater or lesser influence depending on the task.

[2]Gardner (1999) suggests that there may also be a ninth intelligence, *existential intelligence,* that involves the "capacity to locate oneself with respect to the furthest reaches of the cosmos . . . and the related capacity to locate oneself with respect to such existential features of the human conditions as the significance of life . . ." (Gardner, 1999, p. 60). Gardner acknowledges that the evidence for existential intelligence is somewhat weaker than that for the other eight intelligences—hence its exclusion from Table 4.2.

language, others may be talented in music, and still others may be able to learn mathematics more easily than their classmates.

Gardner also proposes that the various intelligences manifest themselves somewhat differently in different cultures. For example, in our culture, spatial intelligence might be reflected in painting, sculpture, or geometry. But among the Gikwe bushmen of the Kalahari Desert, it might be reflected in one's ability to recognize and remember many specific locations over a large area (perhaps over several hundred square kilometres), identifying each location by its rocks, bushes, and other landmarks (Gardner, 1983).

Some psychologists do not accept that Gardner's evidence is sufficiently compelling to support the notion of eight distinctly different abilities (Berk, 2000; N. Brody, 1992; Kail, 1998), or that abilities in specific domains, such as in music or bodily movement, are really "intelligence" per se (Bracken, McCallum, & Shaughnessy, 1999; Sattler, 2008). However, many educators have embraced Gardner's theory of multiple intelligences because of its optimistic view of human potential. This perspective encourages us to use many different teaching methods so that we may capitalize on students' diverse abilities (L. Campbell, Campbell, & Dickinson, 1998; Gardner, 1995, 2000). In this sense there is heuristic value to Gardner's model, but teachers should also be cautious not to let *belief trump evidence*.

Sternberg's Triarchic Theory

Whereas Gardner describes different kinds of intelligence, Robert Sternberg focuses more on the nature of intelligence itself. Sternberg (1998, 2005) suggests that intelligent behaviour involves an interplay of three factors, all of which may vary from one occasion to the next: (a) the environmental *context* in which the behaviour occurs, (b) the way in which one's prior *experiences* are brought to bear on a particular task, and (c) the *cognitive processes* required by that task. These three dimensions are summarized in Figure 4.3.

To date, research neither supports nor refutes Sternberg's belief that intelligence has this "triarchic" nature, and in fact Sternberg's theory is sufficiently vague that it is difficult to test empirically (Sattler, 2008; Siegler, 1998). At the same time, the theory reminds us that an individual's ability to behave "intelligently" may vary considerably depending on the particular context and on the specific knowledge, skills, and cognitive processes that a task requires. Some theorists believe that context makes all the difference in the world—a belief that is clearly evident in the concept of *distributed intelligence*.

While this concept is not a direct tenet of Sternberg's theory, he does support the idea that intelligent behaviour depends on people's physical and social support systems (e.g., scaffolding), sometimes referred to as **distributed intelligence**. People can "distribute" their thinking (and therefore think more intelligently) in at least three ways (Perkins, 1992, 1995). First, they can use physical objects, and especially technology (e.g., calculators, computers), to handle and manipulate large amounts of information. Second, they can work with other people to explore ideas and solve problems; after all, two heads are usually better than one. And third, they can represent and think about the situations they encounter using the various symbolic systems their culture provides—for instance, the words, diagrams, charts, mathematical equations, and so on that help them simplify or summarize complex topics and problems. As teachers, rather than asking the question, "How intelligent are our students?" we should instead be asking, "How can we help our students think as intelligently as possible? What tools, social networks, and symbolic systems can we provide?"

Distributed intelligence The idea that people are more likely to act "intelligently" when they have physical and/or social support systems to assist them.

What implications does such environmental support have for the *development* of intelligence? Use Vygotsky's concept of *zone of proximal development* (see Chapter 2) in your answer.

FIGURE 4.3 Sternberg's three dimensions of intelligence

Environmental Context
- Adapts behaviour to fit the environment
- Adapts the environment to fit one's needs
- Selects an environment conducive to success

Prior Experience
- Deals with a new situation by drawing on past experience
- Deals with a familiar situation quickly and efficiently

Cognitive Processes
- Interprets new situations in useful ways
- Separates important information from irrelevant details
- Identifies effective problem-solving strategies
- Finds relationships among seemingly different ideas
- Makes effective use of feedback
- Applies other cognitive processes

J. P. Das and the PASS Model

J. P. Das at the University of Alberta and his colleagues, including John Kirby (Queen's University), the late Ron Jarman (University of British Columbia), and more recently Jack Naglieri (George Mason University) have extended the theoretical and empirical foundations of the original neurocognitive model developed by A. R. Luria. This work has recently led to the publication of a test called the Cognitive Assessment System (Naglieri & Das, 1997). Essentially this model examines the cognitive processes of attention, simultaneous and successive processing, and planning (commonly called the PASS model). Rather than viewing each component as discrete, this is an interactive model. For example, planning offers the "means to employ simultaneous and successive processes for tasks that are the focus of attention" (Das, Naglieri, & Kirby, 1994, p. 27).

The concept of distributed intelligence suggests that students can often think more intelligently by using technology to manipulate large bodies of data, brainstorming possible problem solutions with classmates, and using symbolic systems (words, mathematical symbols, charts, diagrams, etc.) to simplify complex ideas and processes.

Arguing that single measure ("g") tests have little diagnostic and prescriptive utility, a number of studies are reported in the 1997 technical manual and numerous publications. For example, research conducted at the University of Saskatchewan (Saklofske & Schwean, 1993) has examined the effects of methylphenidate (Ritalin) on the PASS abilities of children with attention-deficit hyperactivity disorder (ADHD), with results suggesting some positive effects on specific planning and simultaneous tasks.

More recently, Das has developed PREP, a remediation program based on the PASS model. PREP is intended to induce successive and simultaneous processing while involving the training of planning and promoting selective attention (Das, Naglieri, & Kirby, 1994). Studies carried out at the University of Alberta by Krywaniuk, Kaufman, and Janzen have provided promising results with low-achieving First Nations children and children diagnosed as educable mentally handicapped; similar studies have been conducted in the United States by Naglieri and colleagues. Das, together with Henry and Troy Janzen at the University of Alberta and Don Saklofske, now at the University of Calgary, have initiated a study to examine the effects of PREP on the reading skills of First Nations children. Results are forthcoming, but interested readers may contact Dr. Janzen at troy.janzen@taylor-edu.ca.

Robbie Case and the Neo-Piagetian Theory of Cognitive Development

Another Canadian psychologist, Robbie Case, passed away at a very early age in May, 2000. He was, strictly speaking, a cognitive and social constructivist who developed not so much a theory of intelligence as an explanation of the cognitive development of children, grounded in neo-Piagetian perspectives (Case, 1997; Case, Griffin, & Kelly, 1999a, 1999b). His analysis and synthesis of some of the key ideas proposed by Piaget (see Chapter 2), meshed with current cognitive and information processing research, have resulted in a theory that has practical applications to the classroom. Case suggests that children progress through four cognitive stages: sensorimotor (0–$1\frac{1}{2}$ years), interrelational ($1\frac{1}{2}$–5 years), dimensional (5–11 years), and vectorial (11–19 years). These stages are tied to such specific domains as a child's understanding of numerical concepts and spatial concepts, and to social and interpersonal themes.

Progression through these stages is largely dependent on working memory capacity and efficiency. This capacity to hold and manipulate information in memory is facilitated by increased myelination, practice to the point of automatization, social and cultural experiences, and the acquisition of central conceptual structures. Clearly, learning opportunities within the classroom—but also the educational opportunities of the larger world context—are critical for cognitive development and the creation and transmission of knowledge. In this sense, teachers play a significant role in guiding student learning, by ensuring that both instruction and the content of instruction are aligned with the child's working memory capacities.

Heredity, Environment, and Group Differences in Intelligence

Research tells us that heredity does play a role in intelligence. Identical twins tend to have more similar IQ scores than fraternal twins do, even when each is raised in a different home (Bouchard, 1997; Plomin, 1994). The cognitive abilities of adopted children more closely resemble those of their biological parents than those of their adoptive parents, particularly as the children grow older (Plomin, Fulker, Corley, & DeFries, 1997; McGue, Bouchard, Iacono, &

Lykken, 1993). It may be reasonable to assume that heredity and genetics account for about half of the variance in intelligence test scores. While teachers cannot change heredity, they can significantly affect that side of intelligence that is based on life's many experiences.

Environment clearly has an effect on IQ scores. For instance, poor nutrition in the early years of development (including the nine months before birth) leads to lower IQ scores, as does a mother's excessive use of alcohol during pregnancy (Neisser et al., 1996; Ricciuti, 1993). Attending school has a consistently positive effect on IQ scores (Ceci & Williams, 1997). Changing a child's environment from an impoverished one to a more stimulating one (e.g., through adoption) can result in IQ gains of 15 points or more (Capron & Duyme, 1989; Scarr & Weinberg, 1976; Zigler & Seitz, 1982). Furthermore, researchers are finding that, worldwide, there is a slow but steady increase in people's IQ scores—a trend that is probably due to better nutrition, better schooling, an increased amount of daily stimulation (through increased access to television, reading materials, etc.), and other improvements in people's environments (Flynn, 2007; Neisser, 1998).

Many psychologists believe that it may ultimately be impossible to separate the effects of heredity and environment—that the two interact to influence children's cognitive development and measured IQ in ways that cannot be disentangled (Bidell & Fischer, 1997; Petrill & Wilkerson, 2000; Simonton, 2001; Wahlsten & Gottlieb, 1997).

Socioeconomic Difference, Ability, and Achievement

Environments may be defined and construed in many ways. In studying intelligence, but also in understanding the role of other factors in success in school and beyond, socioeconomic factors appear to be one of the most salient reasons for differences between groups. As a case in point, First Nations peoples are one of the most economically disadvantaged groups in Canada. This is reflected in lower educational achievement and early school leaving, lower incomes, and increased representation in unemployment and incarceration statistics. The cycle of poverty, marginalization, discrimination, and a host of historical factors are certainly germane in understanding, but also changing, this deplorable human situation.

Socioeconomic status (SES)
One's general social and economic standing in society, encompassing such variables as family income, occupation, and level of education.

The concept of **socioeconomic status** (often abbreviated as **SES**) encompasses a number of variables, including family income, parents' occupations, and parents' levels of education. Students' school performance is correlated with socioeconomic status: Higher-SES students tend to have higher academic achievement, and lower-SES students tend to be at greater risk for dropping out of school (McLoyd, 1998; L. S. Miller, 1995; Portes, 1996; Stevenson, Chen, & Uttal, 1990). As students from lower-SES families move through the grade levels, they fall further and further behind their higher-SES peers (Jimerson, Egeland, & Teo, 1999).

Factors Interfering with School Success

Several factors, described in the following paragraphs, probably contribute to the generally lower school achievement of low-SES students. Students who face only one or two of the challenges listed here often do quite well in school, but those who face most or all of them are at high risk for academic failure (Grissmer, Williamson, Kirby, & Berends, 1998).

Poor nutrition. Poor nutrition in the early developmental years is associated with lower IQ scores; it is also associated with poorer attention and memory, impaired learning ability, and lower school achievement (D'Amato et al., 1992; L. S. Miller, 1995). Poor nutrition can influence school achievement both directly (for instance, by hampering early brain development) and indirectly (for instance, by leaving children listless and inattentive in class) (Sigman & Whaley, 1998; R. A. Thompson & Nelson, 2001). As teachers, you must take any necessary culturally-responsive steps to ensure that your students are adequately fed.

Emotional stress. Students function less effectively when they are under emotional stress. Family violence is a stressor that occurs in approximately 37 percent of all households, is not limited to a particular socioeconomic group, and negatively impacts children's learning abilities (Deuvergne & Johnson, 2001). Further, many low-SES families live in chronically anxious and stressful conditions (McLoyd, 1998). Perhaps as a result, students from lower-income families show higher-than-average rates of depression and other emotional problems (Caspi, Taylor,

Moffitt, & Plomin, 2000; Seaton et al., 1999). As teachers, we must continually be on the lookout for signs that our students are undergoing unusual stress at home and provide whatever support we can for these students.

Traumatic experiences. Many immigrant and refugee students have experienced traumatic events (e.g., war, persecution, uprooting, or losses), which can impact their learning abilities (B. D. Perry, 2006). When children experience a traumatic event, they will attempt to make sense of it, just as adults do. While few children will develop a post-traumatic or an anxiety disorder, they may need to tell and retell or draw and redraw their trauma a number of times until they experience some form of resolution (Frater-Mathieson, 2004). They may also display signs of increased anxiety and fear during occasionally-occurring school safety procedures such as lockdowns (safety procedures that consist of locking all of the school's inside and outside doors, placing paper in door windows, and remaining seated quietly until the school principal signals that the school is safe). Further, since many immigrant and refugee students remain informed about various events impacting their country of origin, they may relive their trauma or experience guilt, worry, or sadness when friends and family members living back home struggle to overcome the negative consequences of specific events. Consequently, students' ability to be present and engaged with their academic activities during times of unrest will be impeded by past and ongoing traumatic events (Frater-Mathieson, 2004).

As teachers, we must be attentive to signs of trauma such as extensive tiredness (a sign of recurrent nightmares or sleep problems), anxious behaviours (e.g., always looking behind for the purpose of scanning the environment), and what appear to be memory issues (during a flashback, individuals will function as per usual but they will have red and watery eyes; when the flashback is over, the person will not remember what happened or what was said—they will know, however, that they were re-living a feared situation [B. D. Perry, 2006]). When experience of trauma is suspected, it is crucial for teachers to connect with students' parents or legal guardians to encourage them to seek out mental health support. Further, teachers can help students by taking the time to develop a positive relationship where students feel safe to ask questions and bring up concerns. For such a relationship to develop, teachers' body language must be congruent with their words as students who have experienced traumatic events have come to learn that body language overrides spoken language. Moreover, as teachers, we must remember that students' stories are not *our* stories. Thus, we are not asked to share the burden of these stories but rather to support the students who have experienced them.

Parents' acculturative stress. Immigrant and refugee students' well-being depends largely on their parents' ability to adapt to their new home country (Frater-Mathieson, 2004). When parents struggle to adjust successfully, children are expected to compensate. Children, for instance, will often act as an English interpreter for their parents and, in the process, a role reversal occurs where parents become dependent on their children in order to be able to function within society. Over time, students may report feeling confused about their dual roles as both children and care-takers, depending on how much their parents rely on them to handle social situations. Parents' acculturative stress contributes to students' school absenteeism, especially when parents have important appointments to attend or when they are in need of childcare. As teachers, we must demonstrate flexibility and understanding while expecting the best out of our students.

Students' acculturative stress. Schools are one of the primary environments in which students are expected to acculturate. For immigrant and refugee students, not only they must acculturate to a new country and a new culture, but also they must adapt to the curriculum and learning style of the school (A. Anderson, 2004). Further, given their varied experiences, immigrant and refugee students often feel older than their peers and consequently have difficulty relating with students who were born in their new home country (Terr, 1991). When combined, students experience a series of acknowledged and unacknowledged acculturative stressors that impact their ability to learn and keep up with the schools' expectations. As teachers, we must remember to be patient with immigrant and refugee students who have recently relocated as they are learning a lot more than the required subjects.

Fewer early experiences that foster school readiness. Many students from low-SES families lack some of the basic knowledge and skills (e.g., familiarity with letters and numbers) on which successful school learning so often depends (Case & Okamoto, 1996; McLoyd, 1998; Portes,

As shown by a multinational research team from Canada, Greece, the Netherlands, and the United States, intelligence appears to be related to both the affluence and education levels in a country (Georgas, Weiss, van de Vijver, & Saklofske, 2003).

See Chapter 3 and Chapter 8 for further discussions of bullying. The PREVNET (Promoting Relationships and Eliminating Violence) website (www.prevnet.ca) presents the research findings and applications from leading Canadian researchers including scientific co-directors Drs. Wendy Craig and Debra Pepler and their colleagues (Drs. Michel Boivin, Tina Daniels, Shelley Hymel, John LeBlanc, and Darcy Santor).

Research published by University of Calgary professor Don Saklofske and colleagues has shown that children's intelligence tests scores are related to the expectations that parents hold for their children (Weiss, Saklofske, Prifitera, & Holdnack, 2006).

Some lower-income parents often have difficulty getting time off work, finding suitable child care, and arranging transportation to visit the school and meet with teachers (Finders & Lewis, 1994; Heymann & Earle, 2000; Salend & Taylor, 1993). What accommodations can you make to ensure the active participation of these parents?

1996). Access to early educational opportunities that might develop such skills is always somewhat dependent on a family's financial resources and the quality of their environment. Low-income parents may have little time or energy to consider how they might promote their children's cognitive development. Furthermore, many low-SES parents have poor reading skills and so can provide few reading experiences to lay a foundation for reading instruction in the early elementary years (R. D. Hess & Holloway, 1984; Laosa, 1982). As teachers, it is essential that you identify and teach any missing basic skills; when you do so, there will likely be significant improvements in your students' classroom performance (S. A. Griffin, Case, & Capodilupo, 1995; McLoyd, 1998).

Lower quality schools. In the United States, students who are in most need of a good education are those least likely to have access to it. In Canada, this is less of an issue in urban areas, but our huge geographic expanse and a rural population that is spread both thinly and widely, especially in northern Canada, may place limitations on educational opportunities. Further, not all students who have recently moved to Canada will have had the opportunity to attend school regularly in their country of origin. As teachers, we must remember to meet students at their academic level and not to assume that their academic level will be congruent with their developmental level.

Peer rejection. Bullying is a form of peer rejection that occurs in most schools but not in all classes (Atria, Strohmeier, & Spiel, 2007) and can negatively impact children's mental and physical health (C. Hunt, 2007). For instance, students from lower-income families are often rejected by their more economically fortunate classmates; as a result, they may have fewer opportunities to become actively involved in school activities (Knapp & Woolverton, 1995). The strategies described in Chapter 3 should prove useful in helping these students forge new friendships.

Lower aspirations. Students from low-SES backgrounds, especially girls, typically have lower aspirations for educational and career achievement (Knapp & Woolverton, 1995; S. M. Taylor, 1994). Teachers, too—even those who teach kindergarten and Grade 1—often have lower expectations for students from lower-income families (McLoyd, 1998; Portes, 1996). Certainly you must encourage *all* of your students to aim high in their educational and professional goals. Teachers must also provide the extra support students need to achieve such goals.

Less parental involvement in children's education. The great majority of parents at all income levels want their children to get a good education (H. W. Stevenson et al., 1990). Some parents in lower-SES households are actively involved in their children's learning and education, and their children achieve at higher levels as a result (Jimerson et al., 1999). But many others may not be capable of helping their children with assigned schoolwork (Finders & Lewis, 1994), and cultural or economic factors may prevent some parents from becoming actively involved in their children's schooling (Hamilton, 2004). Some parents may feel uncomfortable in a school setting (Finders & Lewis, 1994) or they may not be aware that it is culturally appropriate to discuss their child's academic achievements (or lack of) directly with the teacher (Hamilton, 2004). As teachers, we should be especially flexible about when and where we meet with the parents of lower-income students or parents whose cultural understanding of the school system differs from what the family may have previously experienced; we should also be especially conscientious about establishing comfortable, trusting, and culturally-appropriate relationships with them (Finders & Lewis, 1994; Hamilton, 2004; Salend & Taylor, 1993).

English as a second language (ESL). The number of ESL students entering the school system is increasing rapidly (Hinkel, 2005) and only recently has the Ministry of Education recognized that students entering the school system may not have been exposed to the English language to the point of fluency even though they were born in Canada (Alberta Education, 2003). While changes in ESL policies have increased ESL funding, the drop-out rate for ESL students remains at 74 percent (Watt & Roessingh, 2001). Yet, we all know that being able to communicate using the English language facilitates the adaptation process of immigrant and refugee students and their families (Hamilton & Moore, 2004) and improves a person's capacity to live a fulfilling life in Canada. As teachers, we must remember that learning English as a second language is a lengthy process that requires continuous support in various settings and over a number of years.

Being Optimistic about Students' Potential

Contemporary views of intelligence give us reason to be optimistic about our students' abilities. If intelligence is as multifaceted as theorists such as Gardner and Sternberg believe, then scores from any single IQ test cannot possibly give a complete picture of students' "intelligence" (Neisser et al., 1996). In fact, we are likely to see intelligent behaviour in many of our students—perhaps in *all* of them—in one way or another (Gardner, 1995). Furthermore, as both research and Sternberg's triarchic theory point out, intelligent behaviour draws on a variety of cognitive processes that can clearly improve over time with experience and practice (Sternberg et al., 2000). And the notion of distributed intelligence suggests that intelligent behaviour should be relatively commonplace when students have the right tools, social groups, and symbolic systems with which to work.

For optimal intellectual development, students need a variety of stimulating experiences throughout the childhood years, including age-appropriate toys and books, frequent verbal interactions with adults and other children, and numerous opportunities to practise important behavioural and cognitive skills (R. H. Bradley & Caldwell, 1984; Brooks-Gunn, Klebanov, & Duncan, 1996; Ericsson & Chalmers, 1994). As we discussed above, SES disadvantage may also exacerbate problems in school and learning. When parents and other caretakers cannot provide such experiences, most welcome the availability of enriching pre-school and after-school programs. Regularly attending such programs can greatly enhance a student's cognitive development and potential to lead a productive life (F. A. Campbell & Ramey, 1994, 1995; Slaughter-Defoe, 2001).

We must remember, too, that to the extent that intelligence is culture-dependent, intelligent behaviour is likely to take different forms in children from different ethnic backgrounds (Gardner, 1995; Neisser et al., 1996; Perkins, 1995; Sternberg, 1985). For example, in our case study of Dijana, we saw a young girl with an exceptional ability to work co-operatively with others. Co-operation is a valued skill among many cultural groups. In Canada, our mix of cultures also reflects such values as collectivism versus individualism; of interest is that this cultural and ethnic diversity will continue to grow such that in the next dozen years, about 25 percent of Canada's children will be members of *visible* minority groups. The intelligence of some First Nations students may be reflected in their ability to help their family and tribal nation, to perform cultural rituals, or to demonstrate expert craftsmanship (Kirschenbaum, 1989). We must be careful not to limit our conception of intelligence only to students' ability to succeed at traditional academic tasks.

Finally, intelligence—no matter how we define it—can never be the only characteristic that affects our students' academic achievement. Learning strategies, motivation, and creativity also play important roles. It is to creativity that we now turn.

> Visit the website of Statistics Canada (www.statcan.ca) for a full description of Canada's population.
>
> See Chapters 6 and 9 for a discussion of learning strategies and motivation.

Creativity

Like intelligence, **creativity** is often defined differently by different people. But most definitions of creativity (Ripple, 1989; Runco & Chand, 1995) include two components:

- New and original behaviour: Behaviour not specifically learned from someone else
- An appropriate and productive result: A useful product or effective problem solution

Both criteria must be met before we identify behaviour as creative.

Although a certain degree of intelligence is necessary for creative thinking, intelligence and creativity are somewhat independent abilities (Sternberg, 1985; I. A. Taylor, 1976; Torrance, 1976). In other words, highly intelligent students are not always the most creative ones. Many theorists believe that the cognitive processes involved in intelligence and creativity may be somewhat different (e.g., see Kogan, 1983). Tasks on intelligence tests often involve **convergent thinking**—pulling several pieces of information together to draw a conclusion or to solve a problem. In contrast, creativity often involves **divergent thinking**—starting with one idea and taking it in many different directions.

Creativity is probably *not* a single entity that people either have or don't have (e.g., Hocevar & Bachelor, 1989). Rather, it is probably a combination of many specific characteristics, thinking processes, and behaviours. Among other things, creative individuals tend to

- Interpret problems and situations in a flexible manner
- Possess a great deal of information relevant to a task
- Combine existing information and ideas in new ways

> **Creativity** New and original behaviour that yields an appropriate and productive result.
>
> **Convergent thinking** Pulling several pieces of information together to draw a conclusion or solve a problem.
>
> **Divergent thinking** Taking a single idea in many different directions.

Are these views of creativity similar to Gardner's and Sternberg's theories of intelligence?

- Evaluate their accomplishments in accordance with high standards
- Have a passion for—and therefore invest much time and effort in—what they are doing (Csikszentmihalyi, 1996; Glover, Ronning, & Reynolds, 1989; Runco & Chand, 1995; Russ, 1993; Simonton, 2000; Weisberg, 1993)

Furthermore, creativity is probably somewhat specific to different situations and different content areas (R. T. Brown, 1989; Ripple, 1989). Students may show creativity in art, writing, or science, but they aren't necessarily creative in all those areas. As teachers, we must be careful not to label particular students as "creative" or "not creative." Instead we should keep our eyes and minds open for instances of creative thinking or behaviour in many (perhaps *all*) of our students.

Creativity is specific to different content domains. Some students may be creative artists, others creative writers, and still others creative scientists.

Fostering Creativity in the Classroom

Certain aspects of creative thinking may have a hereditary component, but environmental factors clearly play an equally important role in creativity's development (Esquivel, 1995; Ripple, 1989; Simonton, 2000; Torrance, 1976). And culture very much determines what is viewed and valued as creative. Research studies suggest several strategies for promoting creativity in the classroom:

- *Show students that creativity is valued.* We are more likely to foster creativity when we show students that we value creative thoughts and behaviours. Engaging in creative activities ourselves also shows that we value creativity (Feldhusen & Treffinger, 1980; Hennessey & Amabile, 1987; Parnes, 1967; Torrance & Myers, 1970).

- *Focus students' attention on internal rather than external rewards.* Students are more creative when they engage in activities because they enjoy them and take pride in what they have done; they are less creative when they work for external rewards such as grades (Hennessey, 1995; Lubart, 1994).

Here we are distinguishing between intrinsic *and* extrinsic *motivation,* concepts we will explore in Chapter 9.

- *Promote mastery of a subject area.* Creativity in a particular subject area is more likely to occur when students have considerable mastery of the subject; it is unlikely to occur when students have little or no understanding of the topic (Simonton, 2000).

- *Ask thought-provoking questions.* Students are more likely to think creatively when we ask them questions that require them to use previously learned information in a new way (these are frequently called **higher-level questions**). Questions that ask students to engage in divergent thinking may be particularly helpful (Feldhusen & Treffinger, 1980; Feldhusen, Treffinger, & Bahlke, 1970; Perkins, 1990; Torrance & Myers, 1970).

Higher-level question A question that requires students to do something new with information they have learned—for example, to apply, analyze, synthesize, or evaluate it.

- *Give students the freedom and security to take risks.* Creativity is more likely to appear when students feel comfortable taking risks; it is unlikely to appear when they are afraid of failing (Houtz, 1990).

- *Provide the time that creativity requires.* Students need time to experiment with new materials and ideas, to think in divergent directions, and occasionally to make mistakes (Feldhusen & Treffinger, 1980; Pruitt, 1989).

We will look at the nature of higher-level thinking in greater depth in Chapter 7 and at the value of higher-level questions in Chapter 10.

Like intelligence, creativity often takes different forms in different cultures: What constitutes a work of art or "good music" might vary from one culture to another. As we shall see now, the diverse cultural and ethnic backgrounds among our students will manifest themselves in many other ways as well.

Cultural and Ethnic Differences

When we use the term **culture**, we are referring to the behaviours and belief systems that characterize a social group. Or, an alternate definition by Pedersen is: "the context in which all behaviours are learned and displayed" (2001). One's cultural background influences the perspectives and values that one acquires, the skills that one masters and finds important, and the adult roles to which one aspires. It also guides the development of language and communication skills, expression and regulation of emotions, and formation of a sense of self.

Cultural identity is a term that refers to an individual's unique cultural sense of self. Cultural identity formation results from a combination of factors, including personal identity factors (e.g., experiences, personality), cultural factors (e.g., cultural heritage, ethnicity), contextual factors (e.g., social norms, historical context), and universal factors (e.g., spirituality, language use) (S. Collins & Arthur, 2005). Each person's cultural identity is unique and guides their understanding of the world.

An **ethnic group** derives a sense of identity from a common national origin, religion, and sometimes, physical characteristics. The group shares common values, beliefs, language, customs, and traditions. It is important to underscore that we cannot always determine a student's ethnic heritage strictly on the basis of physical characteristics (e.g., race) or birthplace (Wlodkowski & Ginsberg, 1995).

Within Canada, it is becoming increasingly apparent that our schools are struggling to meet the needs of the diverse cultural and ethnic groups they serve. Health Canada reports that cultural background, including ethnicity, has an effect on academic success (see www.hc-sc.gc.ca/dca-dea/publications/healthy_dev_partb_10_e.html):

> Despite some emphasis on multicultural education, Canadian schools generally reproduce the cultures and values of the dominant group.... Language and communication problems cause a disproportionate number of children from certain cultural groups to be placed in special and vocational education classes.... The result has been that the future education and careers of these children are seriously limited.... (Health Canada, 2000, p. 168)

In an earlier book (McCown et al., 1999), two of the authors of this text (Saklofske and Schwean) provided an in-depth discussion of cultural diversity and values from a Canadian perspective. Issues that we addressed included sources of cultural diversity, how ethnic and linguistic differences contribute to diversity, the importance of socioeconomic factors in contributing to diversity, the reasons for cultural conflicts in the classroom, the dimensions of multicultural education, and the position on cultural diversity taken by Canadian schools. You are encouraged to consult this material to gain greater insight into the sources of diversity that affect teaching and learning in the classroom.

Navigating Different Cultures at Home and at School

Many immigrants and refugees, as well as Aboriginal people and other ethnic group members, are likely to experience "acculturative stress" from a variety of sources including their economic circumstances, social and personal isolation, negative attitudes, and threatened or actual violence (Health Canada, 2000). Entering school for the first time may also cause significant acculturative stress for children from non-dominant groups. This culture shock is more intense for some groups of students than for others (Casanova, 1987; Ramsey, 1987). Most schools in North America and Western Europe are based largely on European-American, middle-class, "mainstream" culture, so students with this cultural background often adjust quickly to the classroom environment. But students who come from other cultural backgrounds, sometimes with very different norms regarding acceptable behaviour, may initially find school a confusing and incomprehensible place. For example, recent immigrants may not know what to expect from others or what behaviours others expect of them (C. R. Harris, 1991; Igoa, 1995). Children raised in a society where sex roles are clearly differentiated—where males and females are expected to behave very differently—may have difficulty adjusting to a school in which similar expectations are held for boys and girls (Kirschenbaum, 1989; Vasquez, 1988). Any such **cultural mismatch** between home and school cultures can interfere with students' adjustment to the school setting, and ultimately with their academic achievement as well (García, 1995; C. D. Lee & Slaughter-Defoe, 1995; Phelan, Yu, & Davidson, 1994).

Culture Behaviours and belief systems of a particular social group; or, the context in which all behaviours are learned and displayed.

Cultural identity A person's unique cultural sense of self.

Ethnic group A group of people with a common set of values, beliefs, and behaviours. The group's roots either precede the creation of, or are external to, the country in which the group resides.

Cultural mismatch A situation in which a child's home culture and the school culture hold conflicting expectations for the child's behaviour.

> Can you think of ways in which your own school environment was mismatched with the culture in which you were raised?

Cultural mismatch is compounded when teachers misinterpret the behaviours of students from ethnic minority groups. When students' behaviours differ enough from our own and we misinterpret them as being inappropriate, unacceptable, or just plain "odd," we may jump to the conclusion that these students are unable or unwilling to be successful in the classroom (B. T. Bowman, 1989; Hilliard & Vaughn-Scott, 1982).

As students gain experience with the culture of their school, they become increasingly aware of their teacher's and peers' expectations for behaviour and ways of thinking, and many eventually become adept at switching their cultural vantage point as they move from home to school and then back home again (Hong, Morris, Chiu, & Benet-Martínez, 2000; LaFromboise, Coleman, & Gerton, 1993; Phelan et al., 1994).

> See the article (2001) by Edith Samuel from the Ontario Institute for Studies in Education and co-authors Eva Krugly-Smolska and Wendy Warren from Queen's University analyzing the school achievement of students from minority/ethno-cultural groups in Canada.

Not all students make an easy adjustment, however. Some students actively resist adapting to the school culture, perhaps because they view it as being inconsistent with—even contradictory to—their own cultural background and identity (Ogbu, 1994, 1999; Phelan et al., 1994). Still others try desperately to fit in at school yet find inconsistencies between home and school difficult to resolve, as a teacher who worked with Muslim children from Pakistan and Afghanistan reports:

> During the days of preparation for Ramadan Feast, the children fasted with the adults. They were awakened by their parents before dawn. They had breakfast and then went back to sleep until it was time to get themselves ready for school. In school they refrained from food or drink—even a drop of water—until sunset. By noon, especially on warm days, they were a bit listless. I had observed that they refrained from praying in a public school even though prayer was a part of their cultural attitude. They spoke about their obligation to pray five times daily. In their writing they expressed the conflict within:
>
> > I always think about my country. I think about going there one day, seeing it and practicing my religion with no problems. Here we don't have enough priests. We call them mullah. Here we have only the mosque. The mullah is important because we learn the Koran from him. I can't practice my religion. Before sunrise, I can pray with my family. But at school we can't say to my teacher, "Please, teacher, I need to pray." (Igoa, 1995, p. 135)

As teachers, we will rarely, if ever, have a classroom in which all students share our own cultural heritage. Clearly, then, we must educate ourselves about the ways in which students from various ethnic backgrounds are likely to be different from one another and from ourselves.

Examples of Ethnic Diversity

Tremendous cultural variation exists within ethnic groups residing in Canada. We must therefore be careful not to form and to support stereotypes about any group. At the same time, we must be aware of group differences that may exist so that we can better understand why our students sometimes learn and behave as they do.

> If you are interested in knowing more about ethnic diversity in Canada, including the ethno-cultural makeup of the Canadian population, be sure to consult the Ethnic Diversity Survey at the Statistics Canada website: www.statcan.ca/Daily/English/030929/d030929a.htm.

Researchers have identified a variety of ways in which the cultures of some ethnic minority students may be different from the culture of a typical Canadian classroom. In the next few pages, we will discuss potential differences in several areas:

- Language and dialect
- Sociolinguistic conventions
- Co-operation versus competition
- Private versus public performance

> Before you read further, can you predict what some of these cultural differences might be? Can you think of other ways in which the cultures of minority students may be different from the culture of a typical Canadian classroom? Consider factors such as worldviews, family relationships and expectations, and so on.

Language and Dialect

Many students come to school with limited English proficiency or a dialect that is considered nonstandard English. Their language or **dialect** links them to particular ethnic minorities; language, as an important form of communication, is the primary medium through which ethnicity is shared. When ethnic groups do not share many of the values prized by the dominant cultural group in the local public schools, the stage is set for potential conflicts. Further, when teachers and students are linguistically different, there is the additional potential for communication difficulties to occur. These may cause a student to experience academic problems or to withdraw from the school's society (McCown et al., 1999).

> **Dialect** A form of English (or other language) characteristic of a particular region or ethnic group.

In 2006, over six million foreign-born people resided in Canada. They accounted for virtually one in five (or 20 percent) of the total population, the highest proportion in 75 years. Recent immigrants born in Asia (including the Middle East) made up the largest proportion of newcomers to Canada (58.3 percent) while newcomers born in Europe comprise the second largest group (16.1 percent). In addition, an estimated 10.8 percent of recent immigrants were born in Central and South America and the Caribbean, and another 10.6 percent of newcomers to Canada in 2006 were born in Africa. A majority (70.2 percent) of the foreign-born population in 2006 reported a mother tongue other than English or French. Among the foreign-born who had a non-English, non-French mother tongue, the largest proportion reported Chinese languages (18.6 percent), followed by Italian (6.6 percent), Punjabi (5.9 percent), Spanish (5.8 percent), German (5.4 percent), Tagalog (4.8 percent), and Arabic (4.7 percent) (Chui, Tran, & Maheux, 2007). For more information, see "Immigration in Canada: A Portrait of the Foreign-born Population, 2006 Census: Findings" and "The Evolving Linguistic Portrait, 2006 Census: Findings," both available from Statistics Canada.

Although it is recognized that not all children with limited English proficiency are participating in specialized language educational programs, statistics do indicate that approximately 300 000 Canadian children (outside of Quebec) are enrolled in second language immersion programs. Many more are likely being educated within regular classrooms.

Canada recognizes two official languages—French and English—and has translated this recognition into a policy of bilingualism (i.e., the official charter of both languages). It has also adopted the policy of multiculturalism, which encourages the preservation of other cultures and languages but stops short of advocating additional official languages. The Canadian policy of multiculturalism supports educational programs designed to teach heritage languages other than English or French but ultimately, depending on province of residency, all school children in Canada must acquire primary proficiency in either English or French.

Most educators recommend that all students develop proficiency in the official language(s) because success in mainstream adult society will be difficult to achieve without it, and members of ethnic communities typically echo this view (Casanova, 1987; Craft, 1984; Ogbu, 1999). At the same time, we should recognize that other languages and dialects are very appropriate means of communication in many situations (Fairchild & Edwards-Evans, 1990; C. D. Lee & Slaughter-Defoe, 1995; Ulichny, 1994). For example, although we may wish to encourage the official language(s) in most written work or in formal oral presentations, we might find other dialects quite appropriate in creative writing or informal classroom discussions (Smitherman, 1994). Ideally, we should encourage students to be proficient in *both* the official language(s) and their local language or dialect, so that they can communicate effectively in a wide variety of contexts (Ogbu, 1999; A. R. Warren & McCloskey, 1993).

Sociolinguistic Conventions

In our discussion of linguistic development in Chapter 2, the concept of *pragmatics*—general behavioural skills important for conversing effectively with others—was introduced. Pragmatics include **sociolinguistic conventions**: specific language-related behaviours that appear in some cultures or ethnic groups but not in others. For example, in an article focusing on Qitiqliq Secondary School in the hamlet of Arviat in the Keewatin region of the Northwest Territories, Macguire and McAlpine (1996) outlined the difficulties that mainstream teachers have in communicating with Aboriginal children and their families:

> . . . problems of communication between Aboriginal and mainstream English-speakers stem from basic differences in the social organization of discourse and communication patterns between the two groups, as well as from different expectations of teaching and learning. These differences lead to miscommunication and misunderstanding and frustrate the efforts of teachers and students to work effectively. Through the organization of home visits, members of the Inuit and Qallunaat cultures in Arviat and this community school are attempting to transform the negative images that are frequently attributed to each of them in the literature on home-school discontinuities. (p. 230)

We also see ethnic differences in the amount of time that individuals wait before they respond to other people's comments or questions. For instance, students from some Aboriginal communities pause before answering a question as a way of showing respect, as this statement illustrates:

> Even if I had a quick answer to your question, I would never answer immediately. That would be saying that your question was not worth thinking about. (Gilliland, 1988, p. 27)

According to Statistics Canada, by 2017 about 20 percent of Canada's population, or anywhere from 6.3 million to 8.5 million people, could be visible minorities. Close to half are projected to be South Asian or Chinese. The highest growth rates are projected for West Asian, Korean and Arab groups, whose populations could more than double by 2017 but would remain small relative to the South Asian, Chinese, and African populations. In 2017, 95 percent of the visible minority population will live in a census metropolitan area (Statistics Canada, 2007).

We consider students to have limited English proficiency when English is not their first language and they depend primarily on their first language for communication and understanding. A dialect is a distinctive version of a language or a variation within a language. Differences among dialects may be evident in, for example, variations in pronunciation or vocabulary.

Sociolinguistic conventions Specific language-related behaviours that appear in some cultures or ethnic groups but not in others.

Wait time The length of time a teacher pauses, either after asking a question or hearing a student's comment, before saying something else.

Negative wait time The tendency to interrupt someone who has not yet finished speaking.

Why do you think some teachers encourage competition among their students?

In some cultures, such as in many Aboriginal communities, group achievement is valued over individual or competitive achievement. Children from such cultures are therefore more accustomed to working co-operatively. This emphasis on collectivism is also found in many Asian cultures.

Teachers frequently ask questions of their students and then wait for an answer. But exactly how long *do* they wait? Research indicates that most teachers wait a second or even less for students to reply. Research also indicates that when teachers wait for longer periods of time—for three seconds or even longer—students, especially those from ethnic minority groups, are more likely to answer teachers' questions and participate in class discussions (Mohatt & Erickson, 1981; M. B. Rowe, 1987; Tharp, 1989). Not only does such an extended **wait time** allow students to show respect, but it also gives students with limited English proficiency some mental "translation" time (Gilliland, 1988).

Yet we should also be aware that some other minority students, rather than wanting time to think or show respect, may have a preference for **negative wait time**: They often interrupt teachers or classmates who haven't finished speaking. Such interruptions, which many might interpret as rude, are instead a sign of personal involvement in the community culture of those students (Tharp, 1994).

Co-operation versus Competition

School achievement in a traditional classroom is often a solitary, individual endeavour. Students receive praise, stickers, and good grades when they perform at a high level, regardless of how their classmates are performing. Sometimes, though, school achievement is quite competitive: A student's performance is evaluated in comparison with the performance of classmates. For example, some teachers may identify the "best" papers or drawings in the class; others may grade "on a curve," with some students doing very well and others inevitably failing.

Yet in some cultures, it is neither individual achievement nor competitive achievement that is recognized, but rather *group* achievement: The success of the village or community is valued over individual success. Students from such cultures are more accustomed to working co-operatively than competitively, and for the benefit of the community rather than for themselves (García, 1992; Lomawaima, 1995; Tharp, 1994). They may therefore resist when asked to compete against their classmates; 16-year-old Maria put it this way:

> I love sports, but not competitive sports. [My brother is] the same way. I think we learned that from our folks. They both try to set things up so that everyone wins in our family and no one is competing for anything. (Pipher, 1994, p. 280)

Students from co-operative cultures may also be confused when teachers scold them for helping one another on assignments or for "sharing" answers, and they may feel uncomfortable when their individual achievements are publicly acknowledged. Group work, with an emphasis on co-operation rather than competition, often facilitates the school achievement of these students (García, 1995; Losey, 1995; McAlpine & Taylor, 1993; L. S. Miller, 1995).

Private versus Public Performance

In many classrooms, learning is a very public enterprise. Individual students are often asked to answer questions or demonstrate skills in full view of their classmates, and they are encouraged to ask questions themselves when they don't understand. Such practices, which many teachers take for granted, may confuse or even alienate the students of some ethnic groups (Eriks-Brophy & Crago, 1994; García, 1994; Lomawaima, 1995). For example, children from some ethnic backgrounds, including many Aboriginal groups, have been taught that speaking directly and assertively to adults is rude (Hidalgo, Siu, Bright, Swap, & Epstein, 1995; Lomawaima, 1995). Many Aboriginal children are also accustomed to practising a skill privately at first, performing in front of a group only after they have attained a reasonable level of mastery (García, 1994; S. Sanders, 1987; Suina & Smolkin, 1994). As you might guess, then, many students from diverse ethnic backgrounds perform better when they can work one-on-one with the teacher or in a co-operative setting with a small group of classmates (Cazden & Leggett, 1981; Vasquez, 1990). They may also feel more comfortable practising new skills in privacy until they have sufficiently mastered them (Fuller, 2001).

Creating a More Multicultural Classroom Environment

Clearly, we must be sensitive to the ways in which students of various ethnic groups are likely to act and think differently from one another. But it is just as important that we help our students develop the same sensitivity: As adults, they will inevitably have to work co-operatively with people from a wide variety of backgrounds. It is in our students' best interests, then, that we promote awareness and understanding of numerous cultures in our classrooms. We can do so through strategies such as the following:

- Incorporating the values, beliefs, and traditions of many cultures into the curriculum
- Working to break down ethnic stereotypes
- Promoting positive social interactions among students from various ethnic groups
- Fostering democratic ideals

Incorporating the Values, Beliefs, and Traditions of Many Cultures into the Curriculum

Multicultural education should not be limited to cooking ethnic foods or celebrating Robbie Burns day. Rather, effective **multicultural education** integrates the perspectives and experiences of numerous cultural groups throughout the curriculum and gives all students reason for pride in their own cultural heritage (Banks, 1995; García, 1995; Hollins, 1996; NCSS Task Force on Ethnic Studies Curriculum Guidelines, 1992).

As teachers, we can incorporate content from different ethnic groups into many aspects of the school curriculum. Here are some examples:

- In literature, read the work of minority authors and poets.
- In art, consider the creations and techniques of artists from around the world.
- In physical education, learn games or folk dances from other countries and cultures.
- In mathematics, use mathematical principles to address multicultural tasks and problems (e.g., using graph paper to design an Iranian rug).
- In social studies, look at different religious beliefs and their effects on people's behaviours.
- In current events, consider such issues as discrimination and oppression. (Boutte & McCormick, 1992; Casanova, 1987; Cottrol, 1990; K. Freedman, 1996; NCSS Task Force on Ethnic Studies Curriculum Guidelines, 1992; Nelson-Barber & Estrin, 1995; Pang, 1995; Sleeter & Grant, 1999; Ulichny, 1994)

As we explore various cultures, we should look for commonalities as well as differences. For example, we might study how various cultural groups celebrate the beginning of a new year, discovering that "out with the old and in with the new" is a common theme among many such celebrations (Ramsey, 1987). At the middle school or high school level, it can be beneficial to explore issues that adolescents of all cultures face: gaining the respect of elders, forming trusting relationships with peers, and finding a meaningful place in society (Ulichny, 1994). One important goal of multicultural education should be to communicate that, underneath it all, people are more alike than different.

Breaking Down Ethnic Stereotypes

Although we and our students should certainly be aware of true differences among various ethnic groups, it is counterproductive to hold a **stereotype**—a rigid, simplistic, and inevitably erroneous caricature—of any particular group. As teachers, we must make a concerted effort to develop and select curriculum materials that represent all cultural groups in a positive and competent light; for example, we should choose textbooks, works of fiction, and videotapes that portray people of diverse ethnic backgrounds as legitimate participants in mainstream society, rather

Multicultural education Education that integrates the perspectives and experiences of numerous cultural groups throughout the curriculum.

See www.safehealthyschools.org/whatsnew/racism.htm for links to many of the multicultural education programs found across Canada. See the Working to Improve Schools and Education site (www.ithaca.edu/wise/topics/multicultural.htm) for resources on multicultural education and responsive teaching. The 2008 Multicultural Education Internet Resource Guide (http://jan.ucc.nau.edu/~jar/Multi.html) is another excellent resource.

For further reading, see *Multicultural education policies in Canada and the United States*, edited by Reva Joshee and Lauri Johnson (2007).

Stereotype A rigid, simplistic, and erroneous caricature of a particular group of people.

than as exotic "curiosities" who live in a separate world. And we must definitely avoid or modify curriculum materials that portray members of minority groups in an overly simplistic, romanticized, exaggerated, or otherwise stereotypical fashion (Banks, 1994; Boutte & McCormick, 1992; Ladson-Billings, 1994b; Pang, 1995).

Stereotypes don't exist only in curriculum materials; they exist in society at large as well. We can help break down ethnic stereotypes in several simple yet effective ways. For one thing, we can arrange opportunities for students to meet and talk with successful minority models. We can also explore the historical roots of cultural differences with our students—for example, by explaining that such differences sometimes reflect the various economic and social circumstances in which particular ethnic groups have historically found themselves. And finally, we must emphasize that individual members of any single ethnic group will often be very different from one another (García, 1994; Lee & Slaughter-Defoe, 1995; McAlpine & Taylor, 1993; Spencer & Markstrom-Adams, 1990; Trueba, 1988).

Promoting Positive Social Interactions among Students from Various Cultural Groups

When students from various cultural groups interact regularly, and particularly when they come together as equals, work toward a common goal, and see themselves as members of the same "team," they are more likely to accept one another's differences—and perhaps even *value* them (Dovidio & Gaertner, 1999; Oskamp, 2000; Ramsey, 1995). Such interactions can sometimes occur within the context of planned classroom activities; for example, we can hold classroom discussions in which our students describe the traditions, conventions, and perceptions of their own ethnic or racial groups (K. Schultz, Buck, & Niesz, 2000). We can also promote friendships among students of diverse ethnic backgrounds by co-operative learning activities, teaching the rudiments of other students' native languages, and encouraging schoolwide participation in extracurricular activities. By learning to appreciate the multicultural differences within a single classroom, our students take an important first step toward appreciating the multicultural nature of the world at large (Casanova, 1987).

Unfortunately, not all schools have a culturally diverse population. In such homogeneous schools, we may have to take our students, either physically or vicariously, beyond school boundaries. For example, we can engage our students in community action projects that provide services to particular ethnic groups—perhaps in preschools, nursing homes, or city cultural centres. Or we can initiate a "Sister Schools Program" in which students from two ethnically

---

INTO THE CLASSROOM   *Accommodating Cultural and Ethnic Differences*

Build on students' background experiences.

A teacher asks students from different cultural and ethnic groups to demonstrate how they would greet a new student.

Use curriculum materials that represent all ethnic groups in a positive and competent light.

A history teacher peruses a history textbook to make sure that it portrays members of all ethnic groups in a nonstereotypical manner. He supplements the text with readings that highlight the important roles that members of various ethnic groups have played in Canadian history.

Expose students to successful models from various ethnic backgrounds.

A teacher invites several successful professionals from minority groups to speak with her class about their careers. When some students seem especially interested in one or more of these careers, she arranges for the students to spend time with the professionals in their workplaces.

Provide opportunities for students of different backgrounds to get to know one another better.

For a co-operative learning activity, a teacher forms groups that integrate students from various neighbourhoods and ethnic groups.

Educate yourself about the cultures in which students have been raised.

A teacher accepts invitations to attend the meetings of several cultural heritage associations such as the French, Ukranian, and Chinese. Here she is able to observe various traditions as well as observe her students in this context.

different communities regularly communicate through the mail or the internet, possibly exchanging news, stories, photographs, art projects, and various artifacts from the local environment (Koeppel & Mulrooney, 1992).

Fostering Democratic Ideals

Ultimately, any multicultural education program must include such democratic ideals as human dignity, equality, justice, and appreciation of diverse viewpoints (Cottrol, 1990; NCSS Task Force on Ethnic Studies Curriculum Guidelines, 1992; Sleeter & Grant, 1999). We better prepare our students to function effectively in a democratic society when we help them understand that virtually any nation includes a diversity of cultures and that such diversity provides a richness of ideas and perspectives that will inevitably yield a more creative, productive society overall. The following passage that 16-year-old Randy wrote for his Canadian history class illustrates:

> To me, diversity is not only a fact of life, but it is life. To be different and unique is what allows people to live a fulfilling life. To learn and admire other people's differences is perhaps one of the keys to life and without that key, there will be too many doors that will be locked, keeping you out and not allowing you to succeed. To learn that a majority of one kind in one place may be a minority of another kind in another place can help to initiate an outlook on life that promotes perspective and reason of any situation.

A democracy involves **equity**—freedom from bias or favouritism—as well as equality. To help students achieve maximal classroom success, we must be equitable in our treatment of them; in other words, we must tailor instruction to meet the unique characteristics of each and every one. The notion of equitable treatment applies not only to students of diverse ethnic backgrounds but also to both boys and girls. Let's consider how boys and girls are likely to be different and how we can help students of both sexes achieve academic success.

Equity (in instruction)
Instruction without favouritism or bias toward particular individuals or groups of students.

Sex Differences

In their academic abilities, boys and girls are probably more similar than you think. But in other respects, they may be more different than you realize. Researchers have investigated possible differences between males and females in numerous areas; general trends in their findings, along with educational implications, are presented in Table 4.3. It appears that girls and boys are similar in general intellectual ability; any differences in aptitudes for specific academic areas are small, with a great deal of overlap between the two groups. As teachers, we should expect our male and female students to have similar academic aptitudes for different subject areas; furthermore, we should encourage both groups to achieve in all areas of the curriculum.

What differences between boys and girls did you notice when you were in elementary school? When you were in high school? What differences do you see now that you are taking university classes?

Are the findings in Table 4.3 consistent with your own observations of males' and females' behaviours? If not, can you resolve the discrepancies?

Origins of Sex Differences

Obviously, heredity determines the differences in physical characteristics we see in males and females both at birth and when they reach puberty. Because of heredity, girls reach puberty earlier than boys, and after puberty, boys are taller and have more muscle tissue than girls. Courtesy of male hormones, adolescent males are better than their female age-mates at tasks involving strength and have a greater inclination toward aggression (Collaer & Hines, 1995; J. R. Thomas & French, 1985). Both hormonal differences and subtle differences in brain structure may be partly responsible for the small sex differences in verbal and visual-spatial abilities (Halpern & LaMay, 2000; O'Boyle & Gill, 1998). A more likely explanation for many sex-based differences is socialization: Boys and girls are taught that some behaviours are more appropriate for males and that others are more appropriate for females.

While males have traditionally been viewed as being more aggressive and more likely to engage in fighting than girls, there is growing concern about bullying and physical abuse (as well as psychological abuse) among both male and female students. These range from verbal abuse and intimidation to the killings that occurred in September 2006 at Dawson College in downtown Montreal and in May 2007 at a Toronto high school.

In what ways is the environment different for boys and girls? Can you generate some hypotheses before you read further?

Janet Hyde has recently argued that males and females may be more alike than different (J. Hyde, 2005).

TABLE 4.3   COMPARE/CONTRAST

Sex Differences and Their Educational Implications

CHARACTERISTIC	SIMILARITIES AND DIFFERENCES	EDUCATIONAL IMPLICATION
Scholastic abilities	Boys and girls have similar general intellectual ability (e.g., IQ scores). Girls are often slightly better at verbal (language-based) tasks. Especially after puberty, boys may be somewhat better at visual-spatial tasks and mathematical problem solving (although girls often do better in computation). In recent years, boys and girls have become increasingly *similar* in their academic performance.	Expect boys and girls to have similar aptitudes for all academic subject areas.
Physical and motor skills	Boys are temperamentally disposed to be more active than girls. Before puberty, boys and girls have similar physiological capability, but boys tend to develop their physical and motor skills more than girls. After puberty, boys have the advantage in height and muscular strength. Girls have better fine motor skills.	Assume that both sexes have similar potential for developing physical and motor skills, especially during the elementary school years.
Motivation for school tasks	Girls are generally more concerned about doing well in school. They tend to work harder on school assignments, earn higher grades, and are more likely to graduate from high school. Boys exert more effort in stereotypically masculine areas (e.g., mathematics, science, mechanical skills); girls work harder in stereotypically feminine areas (e.g., reading, literature, art). Boys are more active in both positive ways (e.g., they talk and ask questions more in class) and negative ways (e.g., they exhibit more behaviour problems).	Encourage both boys and girls to achieve in all areas of the curriculum.
Self-esteem	Boys are more likely to have self-confidence in their ability to control the world and solve problems; girls are more likely to see themselves as competent in interpersonal relationships. Boys and girls also tend to have greater self-confidence in areas consistent with their own stereotypes about what males and females should do. In general, boys tend to rate their performance on tasks more positively than girls do, even when actual performance is the same for both sexes.	Show students that they can be successful in counterstereotypical subject areas. For example, show girls that they can have just as much success in learning mathematics and science as boys do and show boys that they can have just as much success in learning creative writing as girls do.
Explanations for success and failure	Especially in stereotypically masculine domains (e.g., math), boys and girls interpret success and failure differently. Boys tend to attribute successes to enduring ability (e.g., intelligence, natural talent) and failures to a lack of effort. In contrast, girls attribute successes to effort (working hard) and failures to a lack of ability. Boys' beliefs in greater natural ability make them more optimistic about their chances for future success.	Convince girls that their past and present successes indicate an ability to succeed and that they can avoid or overcome failure with sufficient effort.
Expectations and career aspirations	Although girls are more likely to see themselves as college-bound, boys have higher long-term expectations for themselves, especially in stereotypically masculine areas. Career aspirations tend to be consistent with sex stereotypes; furthermore, girls (but not boys) tend to choose careers that won't interfere with their future roles as spouses and parents.	Expose students to successful male and female models in a variety of roles and professions. Also, provide examples of people successfully juggling careers with marriage and parenthood.
Interpersonal relationships	Boys exhibit more physical aggression, although girls can be just as aggressive as boys in more subtle and less physical ways (e.g., by tattling, gossiping, or snubbing peers). Girls are more affiliative: They form closer and more intimate interpersonal relationships, seem to be more aware of others' feelings and intentions, and are more concerned about maintaining group harmony. Boys feel more comfortable than girls in competitive situations; girls prefer co-operative environments that offer social support.	Teach both sexes less aggressive and more prosocial ways of interacting with one another. To accommodate girls' more affiliative nature, provide opportunities for co-operative group work and frequent interaction with classmates.

Sources: Becker, 1986; Binns, Steinberg, Amorosi, & Cuevas, 1997; Block, 1983; Bornholt, Goodnow, & Cooney, 1994; Bosacki, 2000; D. A. Cole, Martin, Peeke, Seroczynski, & Fier, 1999; Collaer & Hines, 1995; Crick & Grotpeter, 1995; Deaux, 1984; Durkin, 1987; W. O. Eaton & Enns, 1986; Eccles, 1989; Eccles, Wigfield, & Schiefele, 1998; Eccles (Parsons), 1984; Eisenberg et al., 1996; Fennema, 1987; Gustafsson & Undheim, 1996; Halpern, 1997b; Halpern & LaMay, 2000; Hedges & Nowell, 1995; Hegarty & Kozhevnikov, 1999; Hyde, Fennema, & Lamon, 1990; Hyde & Linn, 1988; Inglehart, Brown, & Vida, 1994; Jacklin, 1989; G. P. Jones & Dembo, 1989; Jovanovic & King, 1998; A. Kelly & Smail, 1986; M. C. Linn & Hyde, 1989; M. C. Linn & Petersen, 1985; Loeber & Stouthamer-Loeber, 1998; H. M. Marks, 2000; McCall, 1994; McCallum & Bracken, 1993; J. D. Nichols, Ludwin, & Iadicola, 1999; Pajares & Valiante, 1999; K. Paulson & Johnson, 1983; E. Rowe, 1999; J. Smith & Russell, 1984; Stipek, 1984; J. R. Thomas & French, 1985; Vermeer, Boekaerts, & Seegers, 2000.

Dealing with aggression in children is a priority for Canadians. This is reflected in results from an opinion poll conducted by the Centre of Excellence for Early Childhood Development in 2002 (Centre of Excellence for Early Childhood Development, 2002). Canadians viewed youth violence as second only to poverty as a major concern. A call for greater investment in violence prevention programs for children and youth was among the highest-rated priorities. A 1993 Environics poll (Saskatchewan School Trustees Association, 1994) revealed that Canadians believed school-based youth violence to be the single most important issue facing public education. More recent data indicates that the level of public concern for youth violence has not declined (Solicitor General Canada, 2000).

Many aspects of society conspire to teach growing children to conform to sex stereotypes. For example, parents are more likely to encourage their sons to be independent, athletic, and aggressive, and they tend to have higher career expectations for their sons than for their daughters, especially in stereotypically male professions (Block, 1983; Fagot, Hagan, Leinbach, & Kronsberg, 1985; Parsons, Adler, & Kaczala, 1982; Ruble, 1988; J. R. Thomas & French, 1985). In addition, girls and boys are given different toys and play different games (Block, 1983; P. A. Campbell, 1986; Etaugh, 1983) that foster the development of verbal and social skills in girls and the greater development of visual-spatial skills in boys (Frost, Shin, & Jacobs, 1998; Liss, 1983; Sprafkin, Serbin, Denier, & Connor, 1983). Although sex-stereotypical expectations for males and females are evident in virtually any society, they are more pronounced in some cultures than in others (Fuller, 2001).

The media promote sex-stereotypical behaviour as well: Males are aggressive leaders and successful problem solvers, whereas females are domestic, demure, and obedient followers (Durkin, 1987; Huston et al., 1992; Ruble & Ruble, 1982; Sadker & Sadker, 1994). Furthermore, males appear much more prominently in history and science textbooks than females do (Eisenberg, Martin, & Fabes, 1996; Sadker, Sadker, & Klein, 1991). As teachers, we must make a concerted effort to develop and select curriculum materials that represent both sexes in a positive and competent light; nonsexist materials reduce sex stereotypes when students are exposed to them on a continual and consistent basis (Fennema, 1987; D. D. Horgan, 1995; Sadker & Miller, 1982). As noted in Chapter 3, schools are important socialization agents for children, and such socialization often includes further encouragement of sex-stereotypical behaviours. Two particularly influential groups of people—peers and teachers—also promote the development of sex differences.

We must empower girls to recognize that they have just as much potential for learning such subjects as mathematics and science as boys do.

Peer Behaviours

Playmates and classmates often encourage adherence to traditional sex stereotypes. They tend to respond more positively to children who play in "sex appropriate" ways and more negatively to those who do not (Eisenberg et al., 1996; Fagot & Leinbach, 1983; Huston, 1983). They may also ridicule or avoid students who enroll and excel in "sex inappropriate" subjects, such as high

---

INTO THE CLASSROOM   *Promoting Sex Equity*

Use your knowledge of typical sex differences to create greater equity for males and females, *not* to form expectations about how successful males and females are likely to be in various activities.

Be on the lookout for sex stereotypes in classroom materials, and use some materials that portray both sexes in a counterstereotypical fashion.

Occasionally ask students to work together in single-sex pairs or groups.

Monitor yourself to see if you are unintentionally treating boys and girls differently.

school girls who excel in science and mathematics (Casserly, 1980; Sadker & Sadker, 1994; Schubert, 1986).

Remember how quiet and passive Dijana was in our opening case study? Boys often take a more active role in class than girls, especially when the two are asked to work together; for example, when paired in a science lab, boys handle the equipment and perform experiments while girls watch or take notes (Eccles, 1989; Jovanovic & King, 1998; Kahle & Lakes, 1983). For this reason, it may sometimes be beneficial to group girls with girls, and boys with boys, to ensure that girls participate more actively in classroom activities (Kahle & Lakes, 1983; MacLean, Sasse, Keating, Stewart, & Miller, 1995). Girls are also more likely to assume the role of leader in same-sex groups and, in the process, to develop valuable leadership skills (Fennema, 1987).

Teacher Behaviours

During the past 20 years, schools have shown increasing efforts to treat boys and girls similarly (Eccles, 1989). Girls' sports are enjoying more publicity and financial support than ever before (for example, recall the success of Canada's women's hockey team in international competition). Nevertheless, differences in the treatment of boys and girls continue. For instance, teachers tend to give more attention to boys—partly because, on average, boys ask more questions and present more discipline problems (Altermatt, Jovanovic, & Perry, 1998; Sadker & Sadker, 1994; L. C. Wilkinson & Marrett, 1985). When girls cannot answer a question, their teachers tend to tell them the correct answer; but when boys have equal difficulty, their teachers usually help them think through the correct answer on their own (Sadker & Sadker, 1985). Boys are told to try harder when they fail; girls are simply praised for trying (P. A. Campbell, 1986; Eccles & Jacobs, 1986; L. H. Fox, 1981).

In most cases, teachers are probably unaware that they discriminate between boys and girls the way they do. The first step toward ensuring more equitable treatment of males and females is to become aware of existing inequities. Then we can try to correct those inequities—for example, by interacting frequently with *all* of our students, helping them think through correct answers, encouraging them to persist when they experience difficulty, and holding high expectations for everyone.

Students at Risk

Do you remember classmates in elementary school who never seemed to complete assignments or get their homework done? Do you remember classmates in high school who did poorly in most of their classes and rarely participated in extracurricular activities? How many of those students eventually graduated from high school? What are they doing now?

Students at risk are students with a high probability of failing to acquire the minimum academic skills necessary for success in the adult world. Many of them drop out before high school graduation; many others graduate without basic skills in reading or mathematics (National Assessment of Educational Progress, 1985; Slavin, 1989). Such individuals are often ill equipped to make productive contributions to their families, communities, or society at large.

Characteristics of Students at Risk

Some students at risk are those with identified special educational needs; for example, they may have learning disabilities or emotional and behavioural problems that interfere with learning and achievement. Others may be students whose cultural backgrounds don't mesh easily with the dominant culture at school. Still others may be students from home environments in which academic success is neither supported nor encouraged.

Students at risk come from all socioeconomic levels, but children of poor, single-parent families are especially likely to leave school before high school graduation. Boys are more likely to drop out than girls. Children from low socioeconomic status are at higher risk of leaving school than are children from socioeconomically advantaged backgrounds. Students in large cities and rural areas are more likely to drop out than students in the suburbs. Students at greatest risk

---

Students at risk Students who have a high probability of failing to acquire the minimal academic skills necessary for success in the adult world.

Carol Leroy and Brent Symes (2001) at the University of Alberta wrote an insightful paper on the beliefs held by teachers on the family backgrounds of children considered to be at risk for school and later life failure. Risk factors included child abuse, alcoholism, and single or absent parents.

for dropping out are those whose families speak little or no English and whose own knowledge of English is also quite limited (García, 1995; Hardre & Reeve, 2001; L. S. Miller, 1995; Nieto, 1995; Portes, 1996; Raber, 1990; Roderick & Camburn, 1999; Rumberger, 1995; L. Steinberg, Blinde, & Chan, 1984; U.S. Department of Education, 1997).

In addition, students at risk, especially those who eventually drop out of school, typically have some or all of the following characteristics:

- *A history of academic failure.* High school dropouts often have a history of poor academic achievement going back as far as Grade 3 (Garnier, Stein, & Jacobs, 1997; Lloyd, 1978). On average, they have less effective study skills, earn lower grades, obtain lower achievement test scores, and are more likely to have repeated a grade level than their classmates who graduate (Battin-Pearson et al., 2000; Jozefowicz, Arbreton, Eccles, Barber, & Colarossi, 1994; Raber, 1990; Steinberg et al., 1984; L. D. Wilkinson & Frazer, 1990).

- *Older age in comparison with classmates.* Because low achievers are more likely to have repeated a grade, they are often older than their classmates (Raber, 1990; L. D. Wilkinson & Frazer, 1990). Some (though not all) research studies find that students who are overage in comparison with classmates are those most likely to drop out of school (D. C. Gottfredson, Fink, & Graham, 1994; Roderick, 1994; Rumberger, 1995).

- *Emotional and behavioural problems.* Potential dropouts tend to have lower self-esteem than their more successful classmates. They also are more likely to exhibit disruptive behaviour, create discipline problems, use drugs, and engage in criminal activities (Finn, 1991; Garnier et al., 1997; Jozefowicz et al., 1994; Rumberger, 1995; U.S. Department of Education, 1992).

- *Lack of psychological attachment to school.* Students who are at risk for academic failure are less likely to identify with their school or to perceive themselves as a vital part of the school community; for example, they engage in fewer extracurricular activities and are more likely to express dissatisfaction with school in general (Finn, 1989; Hymel, Comfort, Schonert-Reichl, & McDougall, 1996; Rumberger, 1995).

- *Increasing disinvolvement with school.* Dropping out is not necessarily an all-or-none thing. In fact, many high school dropouts show lesser forms of "dropping out" many years before they officially leave school. For example, future dropouts are absent from school more frequently than their peers, even in the early elementary grades (Finn, 1989; G. A. Hess, Lyons, & Corsino, 1990; Jozefowicz et al., 1994). They are more likely to have been suspended from school, and they are more likely to show a long-term pattern of dropping out, returning to school, and dropping out again (Raber, 1990). Over time, then, we see decreasing involvement—physical, academic, and social—in school activities.

The characteristics just listed are by no means sure-fire indicators of which students will drop out, however. For instance, many dropouts are from two-parent, middle-income homes, and many are involved in school activities (Hymel et al., 1996; Janosz, Le Blanc, Boulerice, & Tremblay, 2000).

Why Students Drop Out

Students drop out for a variety of reasons. A few have little family support or encouragement for school success. Others have extenuating life circumstances; for example, they may have medical problems, take an outside job to help support the family, or become pregnant. Many simply become dissatisfied with school: They don't do well in their classes, have trouble getting along with their classmates, find the school environment too dangerous or restrictive, or perceive the curriculum to be boring and irrelevant to their needs (Hardre & Reeve, 2001; Portes, 1996; Raber, 1990; Rumberger, 1995; Steinberg et al., 1984).

Helping Students at Risk Stay in School

Students who are at risk for academic failure are a diverse group of individuals with a diverse set of needs, and there is probably no single strategy that can keep every student in school until

---

What are possible reasons why some students don't participate in their school's extracurricular activities?

A conference held in February, 2008, at Carleton University brought together researchers and practitioners from across Canada to address student dropout and retention in post-secondary settings. A list of the presenters and their PowerPoint presentations can be found at www.carleton.ca/artsone/FirstYearInFocusConferenceSchedule.html.

high school graduation (Finn, 1991; Janosz et al., 2000). Nevertheless, we can do several things to help many students at risk succeed and stay in school:

- *Identify students at risk as early as possible.* We begin to see indicators of "dropping out," such as low school achievement and high absenteeism, as early as elementary school. And such other signs as low self-esteem, disruptive behaviour, and lack of involvement in school activities often appear years before students officially withdraw from school. So it is quite possible to identify at-risk students early in their school careers and to take steps to prevent or remediate academic difficulties before they become insurmountable. Research clearly indicates that for students at risk, prevention and early intervention are more effective than later intervention efforts (Ramey & Ramey, 1998; Slavin, Karweit, & Madden, 1989).

- *Create a warm, supportive school and classroom atmosphere.* Schools that have high success rates with students at risk for academic failure tend to be schools that communicate a sense of caring, concern, and high regard for students (L. W. Anderson & Pellicer, 1998). Chapter 11 presents several strategies for creating a warm and supportive atmosphere in its section "Creating an Effective Classroom Climate."

- *Make the curriculum relevant to students' lives and needs.* Students are more likely to stay in school, and also more likely to learn and achieve at high levels, if they find the curriculum relevant to their own cultural values, life experiences, and personal needs (Knapp, Turnbull, & Shields, 1990; Lee-Pearce, Plowman, & Touchstone, 1998; Ramey & Ramey, 1998). To increase the relevance of school for students at risk, we should place academic skills within the context of real-world tasks, and particularly within the context of students' local environments. As an example, a mathematics teacher at an inner-city middle school consistently encouraged her students to identify problems in their community and work to solve them (Tate, 1995). One of her classes expressed concern about the 13 liquor stores located within 300 meters of their school, in part because of the inebriated customers and drug dealers that the stores attracted. The students used yardsticks and maps to calculate the distance of each store from the school, gathered information about zoning restrictions and other city government regulations, identified potential violations, met with a local newspaper editor (who published an editorial describing the situation), and eventually met with state legislators and the city council. As a result of their efforts, city police monitored the liquor stores more closely, major violations were identified (leading to the closing of two stores), and the city council made it illegal to consume alcohol within 200 meters of the school (Tate, 1995).

- *Communicate high expectations for academic success.* Although many students at risk have a history of academic failure, under *no* circumstances should we write these students off. On the contrary, we should communicate to them that school success is both possible and expected and, furthermore, that they are capable of achieving at high levels (L. W. Anderson & Pellicer, 1998; García, 1994; Garibaldi, 1993; Ladson-Billings, 1994a). We can acknowledge past learning problems but let students know that there are ways to overcome those problems and that we will help them acquire the knowledge and skills they need for classroom success (Alderman, 1990).

- *Provide extra academic support.* Because students at risk often have a history of academic failure and may have little support for academic achievement at home, these students may need more than the usual amount of assistance from teachers and other school personnel to succeed. Here are some specific ways to facilitate their academic success:

  - Help them develop more effective reading and learning strategies.
  - Adapt instruction to their current skills and knowledge.
  - Give them relatively structured tasks and tell them exactly what is expected.
  - Allow them to develop mastery of one skill before moving to a more difficult one.
  - Assess their progress frequently and give them specific criteria for measuring their own success.
  - Increase one-on-one teacher–student interactions.
  - Deliver as much instruction as possible within the context of general education; make any necessary instruction in self-contained settings as brief as possible.

Such a project might enhance students' *collective self-efficacy*—the belief that, working together, they can make a difference (see Chapter 10).

- Solicit parent and community co-operation with the school program. (Alderman, 1990; Covington & Beery, 1976; Garibaldi, 1993; Slavin et al., 1989)
- Connect them to after-school homework clubs (e.g., the Bridge program).

As you may have noticed, these recommendations would be helpful for *any* student. Research indicates that the most effective programs for students at risk are those that incorporate common, educationally sound teaching practices (Slavin et al., 1989).

- *Show students that they are the ones who have made success possible.* When we help students at risk improve academically, we must help them recognize that *they themselves* are responsible for their success (Alderman, 1990). For example, we might give messages such as these:

- "Wow, look how much you've improved! That extra practice really helped."
- "You really deserved this A. You are writing in complete sentences now, and you are checking your work for spelling and punctuation errors."

With such messages we increase students' *self-efficacy* through the *attributions* we give for their success. We will discuss these concepts in Chapters 8 and 9.

- *Encourage and facilitate identification with school.* Students at risk may need extra encouragement to become involved in academic and social activities at school. To help them become more involved in, and feel more psychologically attached to, the school community, we can do the following:

- Establish close working relationships with students.
- Include instructional techniques that promote active class involvement (e.g., class discussions, co-operative learning).
- Encourage participation in athletic programs, extracurricular activities, and student government. (This is especially important when students are having academic difficulties, because it provides an alternative way of experiencing school success.)
- Involve students in school policy and management decisions.
- Give students positions of responsibility in managing school activities.
- Provide rewards (e.g., trips to a local amusement park) for good attendance records. (Finn, 1989; Garibaldi, 1992; Newmann, 1981; M. G. Sanders, 1996)

Students are far more likely to stay in school and try to succeed in school activities when they feel as if they truly belong there.

Fostering Resilience: A Lesson from Low Socioeconomic Status Children under Stress

Fortunately, many students of low-income families succeed in school despite exceptional hardships (Humphreys, 1992; Nieto, 1995; B. Williams & Newcombe, 1994). Some seem to be **resilient students**: They develop characteristics and coping skills that help them rise above their adverse circumstances. Thus, low SES and low ability are not necessarily correlated and certainly are not always causally connected. As a group, resilient students have likable personalities, positive self-concepts, strong motivation to succeed, and high yet realistic goals. They believe that success comes with hard work, and their bad experiences serve as constant reminders of the importance of getting a good education (Masten & Coatsworth, 1998; McMillan & Reed, 1994; Werner, 1995). Resilient students usually have one or more individuals in their lives whom they trust and can turn to in difficult times (Masten, 2001; McLoyd, 1998; Werner, 1995). Such individuals may be family members, neighbours, or school personnel; for example, resilient students often mention teachers who have taken a personal interest in them and been instrumental in their school success (McMillan & Reed, 1994; Paris & Cunningham, 1996).

As a teacher, you are most likely to promote resilience in low-SES students when you show them that you like and respect them, are available and willing to listen to their views and concerns, hold high expectations for their performance, and provide the encouragement and support they need to succeed both inside and outside of the classroom (see Masten & Coatsworth, 1998; McMillan & Reed, 1994; Werner, 1995).

Resilient students Students who succeed in school despite exceptional hardships in their lives.

Resiliency is the capacity to manage and cope with everyday and extraordinary stressors and to "bounce back" in the face of adversity. A special 2008 issue of the *Canadian Journal of School Psychology* (volume 23, no. 1), titled "Resiliency: Translating Theory into Applications for Children and Adolescents," includes many relevant and useful articles for teachers. See http://cjs.sagepub.com.

> **INTO THE CLASSROOM** *Helping Students at Risk for Academic Failure and Dropping Out*
>
> Identify at-risk students as early as possible.
>
> > A Grade 2 teacher speaks with the principal and school counsellor about possible ways to help a student who is frequently absent from school and seems to have little interest in her schoolwork.
>
> Use students' strengths to promote high self-esteem.
>
> > A school forms a singing group (the "Jazz Cats") for which students in a low-income, inner-city elementary school must try out. The group performs at a variety of community events, and the students enjoy considerable visibility for their talent. Group members exhibit increased self-esteem, improvement in other school subjects, and greater teamwork and leadership skills (Jenlink, 1994).
>
> Communicate high expectations for students' performance.
>
> > A mathematics teacher tells a group of junior high school students, "Yes, I know that you're finding fractions difficult right now. But I also know that you can learn fractions if you try hard and practise using them. Why don't we try a different approach to learning them today—one that might work a little better for us?"
>
> Provide extra support for academic success.
>
> > A high school English teacher meets with a small group of low-reading-level students to read and discuss print materials in their areas of interest.
>
> Show students that they are personally responsible for their successes.
>
> > A teacher says to a student, "Your essay about recent hate crimes in the city is very powerful. You've given the topic considerable thought, and you've clearly mastered some of the techniques of persuasive writing that we've talked about this semester. I'd like you to think seriously about submitting your essay to the local paper for its editorial page. Can we spend some time during lunch tomorrow fine-tuning the grammar and spelling?"
>
> Help students to identify with their school.
>
> > A teacher encourages a student with a strong throwing arm to try out for the school baseball team and introduces the student to the baseball coach. The coach, in turn, expresses his enthusiasm for having the student join the team and asks several current team members to help him feel at home during team practices.

Building on Students' Strengths

Although many students from lower-SES backgrounds may lag behind their classmates in such basic academic skills as reading, writing, and computation, they bring other strengths to the classroom. For example, they may be more adept at improvising with everyday objects (Torrance, 1995), which is related to creativity (discussed earlier). If they work part-time, they may have a good understanding of the working world. If they are children of single, working parents, they may know far more than their classmates about cooking, cleaning house, and taking care of younger siblings. If financial resources have been particularly scarce, they may know firsthand what it is like to be hungry for days at a time or to live in an unheated apartment in the winter; they may therefore have a special appreciation for basic human needs and true empathy for victims of war or famine around the world. As a teacher, then, you must remember that students who have grown up in poverty may, in some respects, have more knowledge and skills than their more economically advantaged peers. Such knowledge and skills can often provide a basis for teaching classroom subject matter. Furthermore, students who are willing to talk about the challenges they've faced can sensitize their classmates to the serious inequities that currently exist in our society.

Exceptional Students

Students with special needs
Students who are different enough from their peers that they require specially adapted instructional materials and practices.

We will sometimes see the individual and group differences discussed in this chapter reflected in the characteristics of our **students with special needs**. For instance, students from lower socioeconomic backgrounds are more likely to be identified as having either cognitive or behavioural difficulties that require special educational services (U.S. Department of Education, 1996). Some cultures discourage females, even those with high IQ scores and considerable academic promise, from pursuing advanced educational opportunities; as a result, some female students are reluctant to make the most of their advanced cognitive abilities (M. L. Nichols & Ganschow, 1992). Other sex differences exist as well; for example, we will more often see specific cognitive or academic difficulties (e.g., learning disabilities) among boys than girls, and we are likely to observe different kinds of problems in boys and girls with emotional and behavioural disorders (Caseau, Luckasson, & Kroth, 1994; Halpern, 1997b; U.S. Department of Education, 1992).

All students have strengths and talents that we can foster, and *all* students have the potential to develop new skills and abilities. Furthermore, the unique background and qualities that each student brings to class—for example, the realization by many girls that career aspirations must ultimately be balanced against dedication to family, the preference of students from some ethnic backgrounds for co-operative rather than competitive endeavours, and the first-hand awareness of some students from low-income homes regarding such social issues as poverty and homelessness—together create a situation in which we and our students have much to learn from one another.

The special needs of exceptional students have received formal recognition in Canada. Although there is no federal legislation, aside from the Declaration of Human Rights, outlining or guaranteeing the rights of children with exceptionalities, each of the provinces is responsible for passing legislation and developing policies pertaining to the education of children within its respective jurisdiction (Winzer, 1995). In Ontario, for example, provincial legislation adopted in 1980 requires that school divisions provide services to students with disabilities. Within this legislation, principles such as universal access; financial responsibility of the province for the education of exceptional students; the appeal process; and ongoing assessment, diagnosis, and programming are outlined (Winzer, 1995).

Most types of exceptionality stem from a disability. The terms *disability* and *handicap* are often used interchangeably in everyday language. Even so, the terms are distinctive, and the distinction is important for teachers to understand. "A disability is an inability to do something, a diminished capacity to perform in a specific way. A handicap, on the other hand, is a disadvantage imposed on an individual. A disability may or may not be a handicap, depending on the circumstances" (Hallahan & Kauffman, 1994, p. 6). Recent Canadian statistics suggest that there are approximately 550 000 children and youth between 0 and 19 years of age that have at least one disability. This number represents about 7 to 8 percent of all children in Canada. The rate of disability varies by age group, with children 0 to 4 years showing the lowest percentage (4.5 percent) and children aged 10 to 14 years the highest (9.0 percent). Forty-six percent of children aged 0 to 14 years with disabilities had a disability or long-term health condition that limited or prevented them from participating fully in school, play, or other normal activities. Thirty-five percent had sensory difficulties and almost eleven percent had a long-term emotional, psychological, nervous, or mental health condition that limited their activity (Canadian Institute of Child Health, 1996; www.cich.ca).

Before we discuss the service delivery model of **inclusion** and specific kinds of curricular materials and instructional practices that are likely to be most effective for students with special educational needs, see Table 4.4 for the various categories of exceptionality within special education.

Inclusion The practice of educating all students, including those with severe and multiple disabilities, in neighbourhood schools and general education classrooms.

As we have seen, students in any single classroom will be diverse in terms of both individual differences (e.g., those based on intelligence or creativity) and group differences (e.g., those based on ethnicity, sex, or SES). Yet we must repeatedly remind ourselves that there is *considerable individual variability within any group* and a *great deal of overlap between any two groups*. Thus, we must never jump to conclusions about individual students based solely on IQ scores, data about creative potential, or group membership.

Students in Inclusive Settings

In Canada, inclusion continues to be the service delivery of choice for children with disabilities. According to Stainback and Stainback (1990), an inclusive school is a place where everyone belongs, is accepted, supports, and is supported by his or her peers and other members of the school community in the course of having his or her educational needs met. How one achieves an inclusive school, however, varies among provinces and school divisions across Canada. For example, Alberta Learning states that inclusion, by definition, refers not merely to

TABLE 4.4 STUDENTS IN INCLUSIVE SETTINGS

General and Specific Categories of Student with Special Needs

GENERAL CATEGORY	SPECIFIC CATEGORIES	DESCRIPTION
Students with specific cognitive or academic difficulties	Learning disabilities	Difficulties in specific cognitive processes (e.g., in perception, language, memory, or metacognition) that cannot be attributed to such other disabilities as mental retardation, emotional or behavioural disorders, or sensory impairments
	Attention-deficit hyperactivity disorder (ADHD)	Disorder marked by either or both of these characteristics: (a) difficulty focusing and maintaining attention and (b) frequent hyperactive and impulsive behaviour
	Speech and communication disorders	Impairments in spoken language (e.g., mispronunciations of certain sounds, stuttering, or abnormal syntactical patterns) or language comprehension that significantly interfere with classroom performance
Students with social or behavioural problems	Emotional or behavioural disorders	Emotional states or behaviours that are present over a substantial period of time and significantly disrupt academic learning and performance
	Autism	Condition marked by varying degrees of impaired social interaction and communication, repetitive behaviours, and restricted interests; a strong need for a predictable environment also commonly observed
Students with general delays in cognitive and social functioning	Mental retardation	Condition marked by significantly below-average general intelligence and deficits in adaptive behaviour (i.e., in practical and social intelligence)
Students with physical or sensory challenges	Physical and health impairments	Physical or medical conditions (usually long-term) marked by one or more of these three characteristics: limited energy and strength, reduced mental alertness, or little muscle control
	Visual impairments	Malfunctions of the eyes or optic nerves that prevent normal vision even with corrective lenses
	Hearing loss	Malfunctions of the ear or associated nerves that interfere with the perception of sounds within the frequency range of normal speech
	Severe and multiple disabilities	Presence of two or more disabilities, the combination of which requires significant adaptations and highly specialized educational services
Students showing evidence of giftedness, talent, or high performance	Giftedness	Unusually high ability or aptitude in one or more of these areas: general intellectual ability, aptitude in a specific academic field, creativity, visual or performing arts, or leadership; such ability or aptitude is not always realized in performance, depending on opportunity; giftedness may also be regarded as evolving expertise either in thinking processes or one or more subject domains

setting but to specifically designed instruction and support for students with special needs in regular classrooms and neighbourhood schools (see www.learning.gov.ab.ca). Saskatchewan Learning, on the other hand, has more broadly defined inclusion by focusing on the integration of the philosophy of inclusion with community education principles and practices to create a learning community that promotes the well-being of all students within the broader context of the community (see www.sasked.gov.sk.ca).

Despite the endorsement of inclusion throughout Canada, this practice continues to be controversial and hotly debated among both theorists and practitioners (Brantlinger, 1997; B. K. Keogh & MacMillan, 1996; W. Stainback & Stainback, 1992). Some experts worry that when students with special needs are in a regular classroom for the entire school day, they cannot possibly get the intense specialized instruction that many need to achieve essential basic skills in reading, mathematics, and so on (Manset & Semmel, 1997; Zigmond et al., 1995). Others voice the concern that the trend to educate all students in general education classrooms is based more on philosophical grounds than on research results (Lieberman, 1992). Others argue that placement in general education classrooms can have benefits such as academic achievement equivalent to (and sometimes higher than) what it would be in a **self-contained class**; more positive self-concept and greater self-esteem; more frequent interaction with nondisabled peers; better social skills; and more appropriate classroom behaviour.

We are especially likely to see such benefits when regular classroom materials and instruction are tailored to students' specific educational needs and academic levels (Halvorsen & Sailor, 1990; P. Hunt & Goetz, 1997; Scruggs & Mastropieri, 1994; Slavin, 1987; S. Stainback & Stainback, 1992). It is important to note, however, that many studies comparing the effectiveness of regular class versus special class placement are correlational rather than experimental studies, making it difficult to draw firm conclusions about causal relationships (Madden & Slavin, 1983; D. M. Murphy, 1996). Furthermore, research has focused more on students with mild disabilities than severe disabilities and more on the elementary grades than on secondary grades (B. K. Keogh & MacMillan, 1996).

> **Self-contained class** A class in which students with special needs are educated as a group apart from other students.

The Current Concept of Inclusion

Despite varying definitions of inclusion, there would appear to be consensus on two points. First, truly inclusive practices require individualization of instruction for all students, not just those with identified needs. Such individualization must necessarily entail a major overhaul of traditional curriculum materials and instructional practices, rather than just occasional "add-ons" and modifications. Second, effective teaching is seen as involving an equal, collaborative partnership between regular classroom teachers and special educators; thus, we are likely to see a great deal of **co-operative teaching**, in which at least two teachers teach all students—both those with disabilities and those without—throughout the school day (e.g., Thousand, Villa, & Nevin, 1994).

> **Co-operative teaching** A general education teacher and special education teacher collaborating to teach all students in a class, including students both with and without special educational needs, throughout the school day.

Classroom Strategies to Promote Inclusion

Table 4.5 outlines suggested classroom strategies that will facilitate the achievement of students with special needs within the inclusive classroom.

TABLE 4.5 — STUDENTS IN INCLUSIVE SETTINGS

Considering Individual and Group Differences in Students with Special Educational Needs

CATEGORY	CHARACTERISTICS YOU MIGHT OBSERVE	SUGGESTED CLASSROOM STRATEGIES
Students with specific cognitive or academic difficulties	• In most cases, average or above-average scores on traditional intelligence tests • Greater frequency in males than females (for learning disabilities and attention-deficit hyperactivity disorder) • Higher than average dropout rate (students with learning disabilities)	• Remember that students with difficulties in one area (e.g., those with specific learning disabilities) may nevertheless be capable of average or above-average performance in other areas. • Minimize potentially distracting stimuli. • Use multiple modalities to present information. • Analyze students' errors for clues about their processing difficulties. • Teach learning and memory strategies. • Provide study aids.
Students with social or behavioural problems	• Sex differences in the specific problems exhibited, with males more likely to exhibit overt misbehaviours (e.g., aggression, antisocial behaviour) and females more likely to exhibit internalized problems (e.g., depression, social withdrawal, excessive anxiety) • Greater frequency in lower-SES students • Higher dropout rate than for any other category of special needs	• Be on the lookout for possible emotional problems when students (especially girls) are exceptionally quiet or withdrawn. • Take steps to decrease the likelihood of students dropping out (e.g., make the curriculum relevant, provide extra support for academic success). • Modify students' schedules and work environments. • Teach attention-maintaining strategies. • Provide outlets for excess energy. • Help students organize and use their time effectively. • Teach and encourage appropriate classroom behaviours. • Show an interest in students' well-being. • Make classroom activities relevant to students' interests. • Give students a sense that they have some control. • Communicate clear expectations for behaviour. • Try to anticipate problems and then nip them in the bud. • Specify and follow through on consequences.

(continued)

TABLE 4.5 (continued)

Considering Individual and Group Differences in Students with Special Educational Needs

CATEGORY	CHARACTERISTICS YOU MIGHT OBSERVE	SUGGESTED CLASSROOM STRATEGIES
Students with general delays in cognitive and social functioning	• Low scores on traditional intelligence tests • Sex and socioeconomic differences, with delays (e.g., mental retardation) being more common in males and in students from lower-SES backgrounds • Higher than average dropout rate	• Look for and nurture individual students' strengths in the various intelligences identified by Gardner. • Remember that the great majority of students from low-SES backgrounds have average or above-average intelligence. • Promote success on academic tasks. • Clearly describe expectations for academic performance. • Consider students' reading skills when assigning reading materials. • Take steps to enhance self-confidence and motivation. • Pace instruction slowly enough to ensure a high rate of success. • Explain tasks concretely, specifically, and completely. • Provide considerable scaffolding to facilitate effective cognitive processing. • Include vocational and general life skills in the curriculum.
Students with physical or sensory challenges	• Average intelligence in most cases • Chronic illness more common in students from lower-income families	• Assume an average ability to learn classroom subject matter unless there is compelling evidence to the contrary. • Be sensitive to specific needs and disabilities, and accommodate them flexibly. • Know what to do in emergency situations. • If the student and parents give their permission, educate classmates about the nature of the disability. • Orient students ahead of time to the physical layout of the classroom. • Use visual materials with sharp contrast for students with partial sight. • Minimize irrelevant noise. • Supplement auditory presentations with visual information and hands-on experiences. • Take steps to maximize students' hearing capabilities and ability to speechread. • Occasionally check for understanding by asking students to repeat what you've said. • Address deficiencies in reading and other language skills. • Teach elements of American Sign Language and finger spelling to other class members. • Identify and teach those behaviours and skills most essential for a student's general welfare and successful inclusion in the classroom. • Pair students with and without disabilities in the same activity. • Keep the mind-set that all students can and should participate in regular classroom activities to the fullest extent possible. • Provide access to the same educational opportunities that other students have. • Provide assistance only when students truly need it. • Use technological innovations to facilitate instruction and performance.
Students showing evidence of giftedness, talent, or high performance	• High scores on traditional intelligence tests (less true for students from culturally diverse backgrounds) • Often, exceptional talents only in specific domains (e.g., language, math, music) • Divergent thinking (e.g., asking unusual questions, giving novel responses) • Giftedness possibly manifested in different ways in different cultures (e.g., richness of oral language among African American students, exceptional sensitivity to others' perspectives among First Nations students) • More self-doubt about own abilities among females than males • In some cultures, discouragement of females from acting too "intelligently" or pursuing advanced education • Little exposure to female and minority high-ability role models	• Recognize that giftedness may reveal itself differently in students from diverse backgrounds. • Accept and encourage divergent thinking, including responses that you haven't anticipated. • Help students accurately appraise their own abilities. • Encourage females as well as males to achieve at high levels, while also identifying avenues whereby students can demonstrate their talents in ways that their families and local cultures value. • Expose students to talented female and minority role models. • Individualize instruction in accordance with students' specific talents. • Form study groups of students with similar abilities and interests. • Encourage students to set high goals for themselves. • Seek outside resources to help students develop their exceptional talents. • Teach complex cognitive skills within the context of specific subject areas. • Provide opportunities for independent study. • Create permanent or semi-permanent cluster groups within the classroom to help gifted students learn in their zone of proximal development. • Make available learning materials appropriate to gifted students' interests and intellectual and creative abilities. • Consider acceleration (e.g., two years in one), compression of the time devoted to the core curriculum, and grade skipping as viable options.

Sources: Alderman, 1990; American Psychiatric Association, 1994; Barga, 1996; Barkley, 1998; Beirne-Smith et al., 2002; Davis & Rimm, 2004; Eisenberg et al., 1996; Finn, 1989; Garibaldi, 1993; Halpern, 1997b; Heward, 2000; Knapp et al., 1990; Maker & Schiever, 1989; McLoyd, 1998; M. L. Nichols & Ganschow, 1992; Nolen-Hoeksema, 2001; Piirto, 1999; Pressley, 1995; Sadker & Sadker, 1994; Torrance, 1989; Turnbull et al., 1999; U.S. Department. of Education, 1992, 1997.

TEACHING CONSTRUCTIONS

Now that you have learned about the many sources of diversity in a typical classroom, consider how this has enhanced your personal sensitivity about your students' individual differences. Let's revisit Dijana, whom you met at the beginning of this chapter.

- How is Dijana the same as the other children in her class? How is she different?
- If you were Dijana's teacher, how would you use the issues discussed in this chapter to encourage her personal, social, and educational development?

As we have seen, students in any single classroom will be diverse in terms of individual differences and group differences. Yet we must continue to remind ourselves that there is considerable individual variability within any group and a great deal of overlap between any two groups. Thus we must never jump to conclusions about individual students based solely on IQ scores, data about creative potential, or group membership (e.g., sex, culture, socioeconomic status, exceptionality).

KEY CONCEPTS

individual differences (p. 75)
group differences (p. 75)
intelligence (p. 77)
intelligence test (p. 77)
IQ score (p. 77)
g (general factor in intelligence) (p. 79)
distributed intelligence (p. 80)
socioeconomic status (SES) (p. 82)
creativity (p. 85)
convergent thinking (p. 85)

divergent thinking (p. 85)
higher-level question (p. 86)
culture (p. 87)
cultural identity (p. 87)
ethnic group (p. 87)
cultural mismatch (p. 87)
dialect (p. 88)
sociolinguistic conventions (p. 89)
wait time (p. 90)
negative wait time (p. 90)

multicultural education (p. 91)
stereotype (p. 91)
equity (in instruction) (p. 93)
students at risk (p. 96)
resilient students (p. 99)
students with special needs (p. 100)
inclusion (p. 101)
self-contained class (p. 103)
co-operative teaching (p. 103)

5 Learning and Behaviour Processes

CASE STUDY: THE ATTENTION GETTER

TEACHING CONNECTIONS

BASIC ASSUMPTIONS OF BEHAVIOURISM

CLASSICAL CONDITIONING
Classical Conditioning of Emotional Responses • Generalization • Extinction

OPERANT CONDITIONING
Contrasting Classical and Operant Conditioning • Reinforcement in the Classroom • Using Reinforcement Effectively

SHAPING NEW BEHAVIOURS

EFFECTS OF ANTECEDENT STIMULI AND RESPONSES
Cueing • Generalization • Discrimination

REDUCING AND ELIMINATING UNDESIRABLE BEHAVIOURS
Extinction • Cueing Inappropriate Behaviours • Reinforcing Incompatible Behaviours • Punishment

MAINTAINING DESIRABLE BEHAVIOURS OVER THE LONG RUN
Promoting Intrinsic Reinforcement • Using Intermittent Reinforcement

ADDRESSING ESPECIALLY DIFFICULT CLASSROOM BEHAVIOURS
Applied Behaviour Analysis • Functional Analysis and Positive Behavioural Support

CONSIDERING DIVERSITY IN STUDENT BEHAVIOURS
Accommodating All Students

STRENGTHS AND POTENTIAL LIMITATIONS OF BEHAVIOURAL APPROACHES

TEACHING CONSTRUCTIONS

KEY CONCEPTS

CASE STUDY The Attention Getter

James is the sixth child in a family of nine children. He likes many things such as rock music, comic books, basketball, and strawberry ice cream. But more than anything else, James craves the attention of others.

James is a skillful attention getter. He gets his teacher's attention by blurting out answers in class, throwing paper clips and erasers in the teacher's direction, and refusing to turn in classroom assignments. He gets his classmates' attention by teasing them, poking them, or writing obscenities on the rest room walls. By the middle of the school year, James is getting an extra bonus as well: His antics send him to the main office often enough that he has the school principal's attention at least once a week.

TEACHING CONNECTIONS

In this chapter we will look more closely at behaviour processes and use behaviourist theories to understand how, as teachers, we can help students acquire more complex, productive, or positive behaviours. As you read, ask yourself the following questions in making connections between this theory and teaching practice:

- Why do you think James chooses such inappropriate behaviours (rather than more appropriate ones) as a way of getting the attention of others? Can you speculate on possible reasons?
- Exactly what has James learned? Can you derive a principle of learning from James's attention-getting behaviour?
- What basic assumptions are central to behaviourists' beliefs about learning?
- How can you explain students' emotional responses (e.g., test anxiety) to classroom events using the behaviourist notion of classical conditioning?
- What strategies can you use to encourage desirable behaviours in the classroom?
- What behaviourist principles can assist you in your efforts to reduce inappropriate classroom behaviours?
- How can you apply behaviourist principles systematically to address especially difficult classroom behaviours?

Basic Assumptions of Behaviourism

Think back to your own experiences as a student in elementary and secondary school. Which students received the most attention—those who behaved appropriately or those who behaved inappropriately? Chances are that it was the *mis*behaving students to whom your teachers and classmates paid the most attention (J. C. Taylor & Romanczyk, 1994). Our case study illustrates a basic assumption of **behaviourism**: our behaviours are largely the result of experiences. Key assumptions that underlie behaviourist views of learning (summarized in Table 5.1) are as follows:

- *Students' behaviours are largely the result of their experiences with environmental stimuli.* With the exception of a few simple reflexes, a person is born as a "blank slate" (the Latin term is *tabula rasa*), with no inherited tendency to behave one way or another. Over time, the environment "writes" on this slate, slowly moulding, or **conditioning**, the individual into an adult who has unique characteristics and ways of behaving. Thus, by changing the environmental events, we may also be able to change behaviour.

- *Learning can be described in terms of relationships among observable events—that is, relationships among stimuli and responses.* Behaviourists contend that thoughts, beliefs, feelings, etc. occurring inside a person cannot be observed and so cannot be studied scientifically. Some behaviourists describe a person as a "black box"—something that cannot

Behaviourism A theoretical perspective in which learning and behaviour are described and explained in terms of stimulus–response (S–R) relationships. Adherents to this perspective are called behaviourists.

Conditioning Another word for learning; commonly used by behaviourists.

Is this "blank slate" assumption inconsistent with anything you've read in earlier chapters?

TABLE 5.1 — **PRINCIPLES/ASSUMPTIONS**

Basic Assumptions of Behaviourism and Their Educational Implications

ASSUMPTION	EDUCATIONAL IMPLICATION	EXAMPLE
Influence of the environment	Develop a classroom environment that fosters desirable student behaviours.	When a student often has trouble working independently, inconspicuously praise her every time she completes an assignment without having to be prompted.
Focus on observable events (stimuli and responses)	Identify specific stimuli (including your own behaviours) that may be influencing the behaviours that students exhibit.	If a student frequently engages in disruptive classroom behaviour, consider whether you might be encouraging such behaviour by giving the student attention every time it occurs.
Learning as a behaviour change	Don't assume that learning has occurred unless students exhibit a change in classroom performance.	Look for concrete evidence that learning has taken place rather than assume that students have learned simply because they say they understand what they are studying.
Contiguity of events	If you want students to associate two events (stimuli and/or responses) with each other, make sure those events occur close together in time.	Include enjoyable yet educational activities in each day's schedule as a way of helping students associate school subject matter with pleasurable feelings.
Similarity of learning principles across species	Remember that research with nonhuman species often has relevance for classroom practice.	Reinforce a hyperactive student for sitting quietly for successively longer periods of time—a *shaping* process based on early research studies with rats and pigeons.

Stimulus (S) (pl. stimuli) A specific object or event that influences an individual's learning or behaviour.

Response (R) A specific behaviour that an individual exhibits.

be opened for inspection. Instead they focus on observable **stimuli** (Ss) and **responses** (Rs) that can be studied objectively (e.g., Kimble, 2000).

Not all behaviourists hold firmly to the black box assumption. In recent years, cognitive processes and other internal phenomena have been integrated into their theoretical explanations (DeGrandpre, 2000; Forsyth & Eifert, 1998; Rachlin, 1991). Many behaviourists recognize how thinking affects our explanations of learning and behaviour.

■ *Learning involves a behaviour change.* Learning is something that can be observed and documented and should be defined as a change in behaviour. This definition can be especially useful for teachers. To illustrate, consider this scenario:

> Your students look at you attentively as you explain a difficult concept. When you finish, you ask, "Any questions?" You look around the room, and not a single hand is raised. "Good," you think, "they all understand."

But you really have no idea whether they do or not. Only observable behaviour changes—perhaps an improvement in test scores, a greater frequency of independent reading, or a reduction in hitting and kicking—can ultimately tell you that learning has occurred. Accordingly, this idea will resurface as we begin our discussion of assessment in Chapter 12.

■ *Learning is most likely to take place when stimuli and responses occur close together in time.* For stimulus–response relationships to develop, they must occur at more or less the same time so that there is **contiguity** between them. The following two examples illustrate contiguity:

Contiguity The occurrence of two or more events at the same time. *Contiguous* is the adjective used to refer to events having contiguity.

> One of your instructors scowls at you as she hands back the exam she has just corrected. You discover that you have gotten a D on the exam, and you get an uncomfortable feeling in the pit of your stomach. The next time your instructor scowls at you, that same uncomfortable feeling returns.

> Another instructor smiles and calls on you most times you raise your hand and always acknowledges your contributions to the class. Although you are fairly quiet in other classes, you raise your hand and speak up more and more frequently in this one.

In the first situation, the instructor's scowl and the D on your exam are presented more or less simultaneously (contiguity between two stimuli). In the second situation, your response of raising your hand is followed immediately by the instructor's smile and his calling on you; in this case, we see contiguity between a response and two stimuli (although smiling and calling on you are responses that the instructor makes, they are *stimuli* for *you*). Both situations have changed your behaviour: You've learned to respond with an unpleasant feeling in your stomach every time a particular instructor scowls, and you've learned to raise your hand and speak more frequently in another instructor's class.

■ *Many species of animals, including humans, learn in similar ways.* Behaviourist theories, particularly classical and operant conditioning developed from the study of nonhuman animals, often explain human behaviour. What animals have you observed learning something new? Can you think of any similarities in the ways that animals and people learn?

"Stimulus, response! Stimulus, response! Don't you ever *think*?"

Classical Conditioning

Alan has always loved baseball. But in a game last year, he was badly hurt by a wild pitch while he was up at bat. Now, although he still plays baseball, he gets anxious whenever it is his turn at bat, to the point where his heart rate increases and he often backs away from the ball instead of swinging at it.

One possible explanation of Alan's learning is **classical conditioning**, a theory that explains how we sometimes learn new responses as a result of two stimuli (in this case, the sight of an oncoming baseball and the pain of the ball's impact) being present at approximately the same time. Alan's current responses to a pitched ball—his feelings of anxiety and his backing away—are ones that he didn't exhibit before his painful experience with a baseball; thus, learning has occurred.

Classical conditioning was first described by Ivan Pavlov, a Russian physiologist who was conducting research about salivation. Pavlov often used dogs as his research subjects and presented meat to get them to salivate. He noticed that the dogs frequently began to salivate as soon as they heard the lab assistant coming down the hall, even though they could not yet smell or see the meat the assistant was carrying. Pavlov then conducted experiments to examine more systematically how a dog learns to salivate to a new stimulus.

Classical conditioning often helps us understand students' feelings about various school activities.

1. It begins with a stimulus–response association that already exists—an *unconditioned* stimulus–response association. Pavlov's dog salivates automatically whenever it smells meat, and Alan becomes anxious and backs away whenever he encounters a painful stimulus; no learning is involved in either case. When a stimulus leads to a particular response without prior learning, we say that an **unconditioned stimulus (UCS)** *elicits* an **unconditioned response (UCR)**. The unconditioned response is typically an automatic, involuntary one—one over which the learner has little or no control.

2. Conditioning begins when a **neutral stimulus**—one that doesn't elicit any particular response—is presented immediately before the unconditioned stimulus. In Pavlov's early studies, a light was presented immediately before the meat; for Alan, a baseball is pitched immediately before the painful hit. Conditioning is especially likely to occur when both stimuli are presented together on several occasions and when the neutral stimulus occurs *only* when the unconditioned stimulus is about to follow (R. R. Miller & Barnet, 1993; Rachlin, 1991).

3. Before long, the new and previously neutral stimulus also elicits a response, usually one very similar to the unconditioned response. The neutral stimulus has become a

Classical conditioning A form of learning whereby a new, involuntary response is acquired as a result of two stimuli being presented at the same time.

A very comprehensive overview of behavioural psychology and the principles of behaviourism can be found at http://psych.athabascau.ca/html/aupr/ba.shtml.

Unconditioned stimulus (UCS) A stimulus that, without prior learning, elicits a particular response.

Unconditioned response (UCR) A response that, without prior learning, is elicited by a particular stimulus.

Neutral stimulus A stimulus that does not elicit any particular response.

The word *elicit*, meaning "draw forth or bring out," is frequently used in descriptions of classical conditioning.

Chapter 5 Learning and Behaviour Processes

Classical conditioning often helps us understand students' feelings about various school activities. This boy's feelings about soccer will be influenced both by his success at the sport and by the quality of his interactions with teammates.

Conditioned stimulus (CS) A stimulus that, through classical conditioning, begins to elicit a particular response.

Conditioned response (CR) A response that, through classical conditioning, begins to be elicited by a particular stimulus.

The best part of Grade 3 was
division
algebra
multiplication
math
reading

In a personal "yearbook," Ashton identifies math and reading as being the best part of his Grade 3 year. He clearly associates these subjects with pleasure rather than anxiety.

Do you remember the earlier example of learning to respond negatively to an instructor's scowl? Can you explain your learning from the perspective of classical conditioning?

Generalization A phenomenon whereby an individual learns a response to a particular stimulus and then makes the same response in the presence of similar stimuli.

Extinction, in classical conditioning The eventual disappearance of a conditioned response as a result of the conditioned stimulus being repeatedly presented alone (i.e., in the absence of the unconditioned stimulus).

conditioned stimulus (CS) and the response to it a **conditioned response (CR)**. Pavlov's dog acquires a conditioned response of salivation to a new, conditioned stimulus—the light. Likewise, Alan acquires conditioned responses of anxiety and backing away to a pitched baseball. Like the unconditioned response, the conditioned response is an involuntary one; it occurs automatically every time the conditioned stimulus is presented.

Classical Conditioning of Emotional Responses

Classical conditioning is frequently used to explain why people sometimes respond emotionally to what might otherwise be fairly "neutral" stimuli. Teachers must maintain a classroom (including our own behaviours toward students) that will elicit such responses as enjoyment or relaxation, *not* fear or anxiety. When students associate school with pleasant stimuli—positive feedback, enjoyable activities, and so on—they soon learn that school is a place where they want to be. But when they instead encounter unpleasant stimuli in school—negative comments, public humiliation, bullying, or constant frustration and failure—they may eventually learn to fear or dislike a particular activity, subject area, teacher, or school in general. This can range from minor discomfort in the classroom to school phobia. Classrooms where students do not feel successful or valued will most likely result in behaviour problems, underachievement, and even early school leaving (drop-out).

Generalization

When people learn a conditioned response to a new stimulus, they may also respond in the same way to other similar stimuli—a phenomenon known as **generalization**. For example, a boy who learns to feel anxious about long division tasks may generalize that anxiety to other aspects of mathematics. Generalization is the primary means through which learners *transfer* what they have learned in one setting to new situations. Students' knowledge but also their reactions to school and class activities may generalize (transfer) to situations far beyond the classroom itself. When students associate school with pleasant stimuli, they learn that school is an enjoyable place to be.

Extinction

Conditioned responses don't necessarily last forever. By pairing a light with meat, Pavlov conditioned a dog to salivate to the light alone. But later, when he flashed the light repeatedly without ever again following it with meat, the dog salivated less and less. Eventually, the dog no longer salivated when it saw the light flash. When a conditioned stimulus occurs repeatedly *in the absence of* the unconditioned stimulus, the conditioned response may decrease and eventually disappear. In other words, **extinction** occurs.

Many conditioned responses fade over time. Unfortunately, many others do not; a person's fear of water or anxiety about mathematics may persist for years. People tend to avoid situations that cause such emotional reactions. If they stay away from a stimulus that makes them fearful, they never have a chance to experience that stimulus in the absence of the unconditioned stimulus with which it was originally paired. As a result, they have no opportunity to learn *not* to be afraid—they have no opportunity for the response to undergo extinction.

Psychologists have learned that one way to extinguish a negative emotional reaction to a particular conditioned stimulus is to introduce that stimulus *slowly and gradually* while the student is happy or relaxed (M. C. Jones, 1924; Wolpe, 1969). If Bobby gets overly anxious every time he attempts a mathematics problem, you might revert back to easier problems—those he can readily solve—and gradually increase the difficulty of his assignments only as he demonstrates greater competence and self-confidence.

There is nothing like success to help students feel good about being in the classroom. One thing you can do to promote student success is structure the classroom environment so that

> **INTO THE CLASSROOM** *Applying Principles of Classical Conditioning*
>
> Create a positive classroom environment.
>
> A Grade 3 teacher plans many activities that make classroom learning enjoyable. He never ridicules students for mistakes they may make.
>
> Be sure that students associate success with all areas of the curriculum.
>
> A high school mathematics teacher takes a mastery approach to teaching algebra, making sure that her students master each concept and procedure before moving to more advanced material.
>
> When a particular subject or task arouses anxiety in students, present it slowly and gradually while they are happy and relaxed and ensure they are successful.
>
> When teaching a fearful child to swim, a swimming instructor begins the first lesson by playing games in the baby pool, moving to deeper water very gradually as the child seems comfortable about doing so.

appropriate behaviours are reinforced and inappropriate behaviours are not. It is to the role that reinforcement plays in learning—to operant conditioning—that we turn now.

We will consider the nature and effects of anxiety in more detail in Chapter 9.

Operant Conditioning

Mark is a student in Ms. Ferguson's geography class. This is what happens to Mark during the first week in October:

Monday. Ms. Ferguson asks the class to locate Colombia on the globe. Mark knows where Colombia is, and he sits smiling, with his hands in his lap, hoping that Ms. Ferguson will call on him. Instead, Ms. Ferguson calls on another student.

Tuesday. Ms. Ferguson asks the class where Colombia got its name. Mark knows that Colombia is named after Christopher Columbus, so he raises his hand a few inches. Ms. Ferguson calls on another student.

Wednesday. Ms. Ferguson asks the class why people in Colombia speak Spanish rather than English or French. Mark knows that Colombians speak Spanish because the country's early European settlers came from Spain. He raises his hand high in the air. Ms. Ferguson calls on another student.

Thursday. Ms. Ferguson asks the class why Colombia grows coffee but Canada does not. Mark knows that coffee can be grown only in certain climates. He raises his hand high and waves it wildly back and forth. Ms. Ferguson calls on him.

Friday. Whenever Ms. Ferguson asks a question that Mark can answer, Mark raises his hand high and waves it wildly about.

Notice how several of Mark's behaviours in geography class, such as sitting quietly, smiling, and raising his hand politely, bring no results. But waving his hand wildly does bring Mark the result that he wants: his teacher's attention. The response that has attracted Ms. Ferguson's attention continues. Other responses disappear.

The change in Mark's behaviour illustrates **operant conditioning**, a form of learning described by many behaviourists and most notably by B. F. Skinner (e.g., 1953, 1954, 1968). The basic principle of operant conditioning is a simple one:

A response that is followed by a reinforcing stimulus (a reinforcer) is more likely to occur again.

Operant conditioning A form of learning whereby a response increases in frequency as a result of its being followed by reinforcement.

When behaviours are followed by desirable consequences, they tend to increase in frequency. When behaviours don't produce results, they typically decrease and may even disappear altogether.

Students often learn and demonstrate new behaviours for the consequences those behaviours bring. Following are some examples:

Sergio brings a fancy new bicycle to school and finds himself surrounded by classmates who want to ride it. Suddenly Sergio has several new "friends."

Shawn studies hard for his French vocabulary quiz. He gets an A on the quiz.

Sharon copies her answers to the French quiz from Shawn's paper. She, too, gets an A on the quiz.

Contingency A situation in which one event happens only after another event has already occurred. One event is *contingent* on another's prior occurrence.

As a teacher, be aware of and know what you are reinforcing; reinforce those behaviours that you want to increase (e.g., completing homework assignments) and be careful not to reinforce behaviours that you wish to see decreased or eliminated (e.g., pushing other students).

How is the concept of *contingency* different from *contiguity*?

Operant conditioning can occur only under two conditions. First, the learner must make a response; that is, the learner must *do* something. Behaviourists believe that little is accomplished by having students sit quietly and listen passively to their teacher; instead, students are more likely to learn when they are making active, overt responses in the classroom (e.g., Drevno et al., 1994). Second, the reinforcer should be **contingent** on the learner's response; that is, it should occur when, and *only* when, the desired response has occurred. Teacher praise only when students behave appropriately is making reinforcement contingent on desired behaviour. In contrast, the teacher who laughs at the antics of a chronically misbehaving student is providing reinforcement even when an acceptable response hasn't occurred.

You should be sure to reinforce the behaviours you want your students to learn and acquire. If you want students to read frequently, volunteer in class, demonstrate good form and accuracy in passing a soccer ball, or work co-operatively with their classmates, you should reinforce such behaviours as they occur. However, you should be careful *not* to reinforce any inappropriate and counterproductive behaviours that students exhibit. If you repeatedly allow Jane to turn in assignments late because she tells you that she forgot her homework and if you often let Jake get his way by bullying his classmates on the playground, then you are reinforcing (and hence increasing) Jane's excuse making and Jake's aggressiveness.

Contrasting Classical and Operant Conditioning

Operant conditioning is different from classical conditioning in two important ways:

- *The way in which conditioning comes about.* Classical conditioning results from the pairing of two stimuli, the UCS that initially elicits a response and the CS that begins to elicit the same or a similar response. In contrast, operant conditioning occurs when *a response is followed by a reinforcer.*

- *The nature of the response.* In classical conditioning, the response is involuntary. In operant conditioning, the response is usually a voluntary one: the learner can control whether or not it occurs. In our case study, James is willingly behaving in these ways; no particular stimulus is forcing him to do so.

Reinforcement in the Classroom

We often talk about giving students rewards for their academic achievements and for appropriate classroom behaviours. The word *reward* brings to mind things we would all agree are pleasant and desirable—things such as candy, praise, money, trophies, or special privileges. But some individuals increase their behaviour for consequences that others would not find so appealing. Thus, a **reinforcer** is *any consequence that increases the frequency of a particular behaviour,* whether other people find that consequence pleasant or not. Following a particular response with a reinforcer is called **reinforcement**.

James learned that he could get his teacher's attention by blurting out answers in class, throwing objects around the room, and refusing to turn in classroom assignments. We can assume that James's teacher is not smiling or praising him for such behaviour. Probably the teacher is frowning, scolding, or even yelling. We don't usually think of these types of responses as rewards, yet they are leading to an increase in James's misbehaviours, so they are apparently reinforcers for James.

In the next few pages we will look at primary versus secondary reinforcers, and positive versus negative reinforcement—and in the process will identify a number of potentially effective reinforcers in classroom settings. It is important to understand that a reinforcer is only a reinforcer if it increases the target behaviour. Thus, you will need to consider using a variety of reinforcers in your classroom. For example, McGill University researchers Derevensky and Leckerman (1997) found that teachers in special education classrooms use many more types of reinforcement than regular class teachers. We will then consider how both timing and motivation influence a reinforcer's effectiveness.

Primary versus Secondary Reinforcers

A **primary reinforcer** satisfies a basic physiological need; food, water, warmth, and oxygen are all examples; physical affection and cuddling may address biological needs as well (Harlow &

Reinforcer A consequence (stimulus) of a response that leads to an increased frequency of that response.

Reinforcement The act of following a particular response with a reinforcer and thereby increasing the frequency of that response.

Recall that behaviourists focus on stimuli and responses. Which of these is reinforcement: a *stimulus* or a *response*?

Primary reinforcer A stimulus that satisfies a basic physiological need.

Attention can be a very effective social reinforcer.

Garfield © Paws, Inc. Reprinted with permission of UNIVERSAL PRESS SYNDICATE. All rights reserved.

Zimmerman, 1959; Vollmer & Hackenberg, 2001). For an adolescent addicted to an illegal substance, the next "fix" is also a primary reinforcer (Lejuez, Schaal, & O'Donnell, 1998).

A **secondary reinforcer** does not satisfy any physiological need yet becomes reinforcing over time through its association with another reinforcer. Perhaps praise was once associated with a special candy treat from Mom, or a good grade was associated with a hug from Dad. Through such associations, consequences such as praise, good grades, money, feelings of success, and perhaps even scolding become reinforcing in their own right: They become secondary reinforcers and are *learned* reinforcers. Although most of our students will probably respond positively to such consequences as praise or a good grade, a few students may not.

Secondary reinforcer A stimulus that becomes reinforcing over time through its association with another reinforcer; it is sometimes called a conditioned reinforcer.

Positive versus Negative Reinforcement

Up to this point, we have been speaking of reinforcement as the *presentation* of a particular reinforcing stimulus. But, we can also reinforce a behaviour through the *removal* of a stimulus. Operant conditioning theorists distinguish between these two situations by using the terms *positive reinforcement* and *negative reinforcement*.

Positive reinforcement. Whenever a particular stimulus is *presented* after a behaviour, and the behaviour increases as a result, **positive reinforcement** has occurred. This is the case whether or not the presented stimulus is one that others would agree is pleasant and desirable. For instance, some students will make a response to get a teacher's praise, but others (like James in our case study) may behave to get themselves a scolding. Following are examples of the forms that positive reinforcement may take:

- A **concrete reinforcer** is an actual object (e.g., a snack, sticker, or toy) and is especially likely to be effective with young children (e.g., Rimm & Masters, 1974).

- A **social reinforcer** is a gesture or sign (e.g., a smile, a hug, attention, praise, or "thank you") that one person gives another for a certain behaviour. Teachers often use simple social gestures—smiles, compliments, and nods of approval—as classroom reinforcers (L. Katz, 1993; Piersel, 1987).

- An **activity reinforcer** is an opportunity to engage in a favourite activity. According to the **Premack principle** (Premack, 1959, 1963), students will often do even something they don't like to do if it enables them to do something they do enjoy. Students are more likely to sit quietly if being quiet enables them to go to lunch. Students at risk for dropping out of school are more likely to come to school regularly if a good attendance record will earn them a trip to a local amusement park (M. G. Sanders, 1996).

- Sometimes the simple message that an answer is correct or that a task has been done well— **positive feedback**—is reinforcement enough. Positive feedback is most effective when it tells students in explicit terms what they are doing well and what they can do to improve their performance even further (D. L. Butler & Winne, 1995; Feltz, Chaase, Moritz, & Sullivan, 1999). As an example, see Figure 5.1.

The reinforcers just listed are **extrinsic reinforcers**, those provided by the external environment (often by other people). Positive reinforcers may also be **intrinsic reinforcers**, those supplied by learners themselves or inherent in the tasks being performed. Students engage in some activities simply because they enjoy those activities or because they like to feel competent and

Positive reinforcement A consequence that brings about the increase of a behaviour through the presentation (rather than removal) of a stimulus.

Concrete reinforcer A reinforcer that can be touched.

Social reinforcer A gesture or sign that one person gives another to communicate positive regard.

Activity reinforcer An opportunity to engage in a favourite activity.

Premack principle A phenomenon whereby individuals do less-preferred activities in order to engage in more-preferred activities.

Positive feedback A message that an answer is correct or a task has been well done.

Extrinsic reinforcer A reinforcer that comes from the outside environment, rather than from within the individual.

Intrinsic reinforcer A reinforcer provided by oneself or inherent in the task being performed.

Chapter 5 Learning and Behaviour Processes

successful. When students perform certain behaviours in the absence of any observable reinforcers—when they do extra classwork without being asked, when they practise on their electric guitars into the wee hours of the morning—they are probably working for the intrinsic reinforcement that such behaviours yield. We will talk more about such *intrinsic motivation* in Chapter 9.

Negative reinforcement. In contrast to positive reinforcement, **negative reinforcement** brings about a behaviour increase through the *removal* of a stimulus (typically an unpleasant one).[1] When people make a response to get rid of something, they are being negatively reinforced. When James misbehaved, he was often sent to the principal's office; this negatively reinforced his behaviour because it enabled him to *get out of class*, thereby removing a stimulus—the class environment—that may have been aversive for him. (If James liked spending time with the principal, then he was receiving positive reinforcement as well.)

Following are additional examples of negative reinforcement:

Rhonda must read *Ivanhoe* for her English literature class before the end of the month. She doesn't like having this assignment hanging over her head, so she finishes it early. When she's done, she no longer has to worry about it.

Reuben is in the same literature class. Whenever he sits down at home to read *Ivanhoe,* he finds the novel confusing and difficult to understand. He quickly ends his study sessions by finding other things that he "needs" to do instead—things like playing basketball with his friends, for example.

In these examples, notice how negative reinforcement sometimes promotes desirable behaviours (such as completing an assignment early) and at other times promotes undesirable behaviours (such as procrastination). Notice, as well, how students are not the only ones who respond to reinforcement in the classroom. After all, teachers are human beings too!

Teachers want to create a classroom environment in which there are few stimuli that students want to be rid of. Nevertheless, negative reinforcement *does* have an effect on behaviour. When certain responses enable students to remove unpleasant stimuli—perhaps classroom assignments or perhaps even the classroom itself—those responses will increase in frequency.

Importance of Timing

B. F. Skinner argued that reinforcement is likely to be effective only if it occurs *immediately* after a desired response has occurred. Research indicates the more closely a reinforcer follows a response, the more effective it is likely to be (Rachlin, 1991).

Yet as children get older, they become better able to **delay gratification**. They can forego small, immediate reinforcers for the larger reinforcers that their long-term efforts are likely to bring down the road (Green, Fry, & Myerson, 1994; Rotenberg & Mayer, 1990). Whereas a preschooler is likely to choose a small reinforcer she can have *now* over a larger and more attractive reinforcer she cannot get until tomorrow, an 8-year-old is more willing to wait a day or two for the more appealing item. Many adolescents can delay gratification for weeks at a time. For instance, 16-year-old Jeff worked long hours stocking shelves at the local grocery store to earn enough money to pay half the cost of a $400-a-night limousine for the high school prom.

However, even 4- and 5-year-olds can learn to delay gratification for a few hours if their teachers tell them that rewards for desired behaviours (such as sharing toys with other children) will be coming later in the day (Fowler & Baer, 1981). Teaching children effective "waiting" strategies—for example, encouraging them to focus their attention on something else during the duration, or teaching them such self-talk as "If I wait a little longer, I will get the bigger one"—enhances their ability to delay gratification as well (Binder, Dixon, & Ghezzi, 2000).

---

[1] You might draw an analogy between positive and negative reinforcement and positive and negative numbers. Positive numbers and positive reinforcement both *add* something to a situation. Negative numbers and negative reinforcement both *subtract* something from a situation.

FIGURE 5.1 In commenting on Matt's book project, the teacher is explicit about what he can do to improve but vague about what he has done well. Knowing what *specific* things made his summary and project description "very good" would help Matt repeat these things in the future.

Negative reinforcement A consequence that brings about the increase of a behaviour through the removal (rather than the presentation) of a stimulus.

Delay of gratification The ability to forego small, immediate reinforcers in order to obtain larger ones later on.

How might you determine which reinforcers are most effective for your students?

What stimulus is removed? What response is being reinforced as a result?

Role of Motivation

In the opening case study, James engages in a variety of inappropriate behaviours to gain the attention of his teacher, his classmates, and sometimes his principal. Students are far more likely to misbehave if they have very little social contact with others *unless* they misbehave (McGill, 1999). James might prefer more appropriate interactions with adults and peers, yet for whatever reasons (perhaps because his academic performance rarely gains his teacher's praise, perhaps because his social skills are insufficient to make and maintain friendships) he seldom has such interactions.

We will look at motivation in more detail in Chapter 9, but for now we should note that motivation plays a significant role in determining the consequences that students find reinforcing (Michael, 2000). Some students may respond well to praise, but others (for example, those who don't want to be labelled "teacher's pet" by their peers) may view a teacher's praise as a fate worse than death (e.g., Pfiffner, Rosen, & O'Leary, 1985). Remember that *different stimuli are reinforcing for different individuals;* never make assumptions about what specific events are reinforcing for particular students.

Ideally, students should perceive class activities as interesting and enjoyable challenges rather than as boring, tedious tasks to complete as quickly as possible. In other words, positive reinforcement should be far more common than negative reinforcement.

Using Reinforcement Effectively

As a teacher, you will want to use reinforcement to help students behave more productively. Several strategies will increase the likelihood that your use of reinforcement is effective:

- *Specify the desired behaviour at the beginning.* Behaviourists recommend that teachers describe, up front, what they want students to learn and to describe this end result—the **terminal behaviour**—in specific, concrete, observable terms. Rather than say that students should "learn responsibility," you might state that students will follow instructions, bring the necessary books and supplies to class every day, and turn in assignments by the due date. By specifying the terminal behaviour from the start, you give both yourself and your students a target to shoot for and you can better determine whether you are, in fact, making progress toward that target.

S. R. Flora's 2004 book, The Power of Reinforcement, addresses many of the myths and criticisms directed at the use of reinforcement.

- *Identify consequences that are truly reinforcing for each student.* The use of reinforcement is far more effective when tailored to individual students than when the same consequences are used for everyone (e.g., Pfiffner et al., 1985). Teachers can ask students (or perhaps their parents) about the consequences they find especially appealing. They can observe students, keeping a lookout for consequences that students seem to appreciate. The one thing that you don't want to do is *guess* about the reinforcers you should use.

Terminal behaviour The form and frequency of a desired response that a teacher or other practitioner is shaping through operant conditioning.

Students may choose their own reinforcers, and perhaps even choose different reinforcers on different occasions (L. G. Bowman, Piazza, Fisher, Hagopian, & Kogan, 1997; Fisher & Mazur, 1997). One mechanism through which you can do this is a **token economy**, whereby students who exhibit desired behaviours receive *tokens* (poker chips, specially marked pieces of coloured paper, etc.) that they can later use to "purchase" a variety of **backup reinforcers**—perhaps small treats, free time in the reading centre, or a prime position in the lunch line—from a reinforcement menu. Philips, Schwean, and Saklofske (1997) conducted a study at the University of Saskatchewan demonstrating the effectiveness of token economies in a school-based program for aggressive children.

Token economy A technique whereby desired behaviours are reinforced by tokens, reinforcers that students can use to "purchase" a variety of other reinforcers.

Backup reinforcer A reinforcer that a student can "purchase" with one or more tokens earned in a token economy.

Concrete reinforcers can be expensive, and they also distract students' attention away from the task at hand—their schoolwork. Fortunately, many nontangible reinforcers are effective with students, including positive feedback, special privileges, favourite activities, and parental reinforcement at home for school behaviours (e.g., Feltz et al., 1999; Kelley & Carper, 1988).

- *When trying to encourage the same behaviour in a group of students, consider using a group contingency.* When a teacher uses a **group contingency**, students are reinforced only when *everyone* in a particular group (perhaps a co-operative learning group, perhaps an entire class) achieves or behaves at a certain level. Group contingencies are clearly effective in improving academic achievement and classroom behaviour, provided that everyone in the group

Group contingency A situation in which everyone in a group must make a particular response before reinforcement occurs.

Playing a team sport is an example of a behaviour reinforced by a group contingency: The team wins together or loses together.

is capable of making the desired response (Barbetta, 1990; Lentz, 1988). Consider the following example as evidence:

> Of 32 Grade 4 students, on average, only 12 students (38 percent) had perfect spelling tests in any given week. Their teacher announced that any student with a perfect test score would get free time later in the week. The new reinforcement program had a noticeable effect: The average number of perfect spelling tests rose to 25 a week (80 percent). But then the teacher added a group contingency: Whenever the entire class achieved perfect spelling tests by Friday, the class could listen to the radio for 15 minutes. The group contingency produced an average of 30 perfect spelling tests (94 percent) a week (Lovitt, Guppy, & Blattner, 1969).

Group contingencies are probably effective for at least two reasons. One reason may be peer pressure: Students encourage their classmates to achieve and behave appropriately, and they then reinforce those classmates for doing so (O'Leary & O'Leary, 1972). Furthermore, students begin to tutor one another in academic subjects, a practice that enhances achievement (e.g., Pigott, Fantuzzo, & Clement, 1986). Group contingencies play an important role in *co-operative learning,* an instructional strategy we will discuss in Chapter 10. However, group contingencies may have some negative effects for those students who, for various reasons, may not be able to contribute as effectively as others, leading to a sense of having let down the group to overt actions of exclusion and rejection from the group. Teachers must be very aware of how they form groups to ensure that they achieve their purposes and are positive experiences for the individuals.

■ *Make response-consequence contingencies explicit.* Reinforcement is more likely to be effective when students know exactly what consequences will follow various behaviours. Kindergarten students are more likely to respond appropriately when they are told, "The quietest group will be first to get in line for lunch." Calgary junior high school students are more likely to complete their Western Canada history assignments if they know that by doing so they will be able to take a field trip to Heritage Park.

Contingency contract A formal agreement between a teacher and a student that identifies behaviours the student will exhibit and the reinforcers that will follow those behaviours.

One explicit way of communicating our expectations is through a **contingency contract**. Beginning with a discussion of the problem behaviour (e.g., perhaps the student has a tendency to talk to friends during independent seatwork), the teacher and student together identify and agree on desired behaviours that the student will demonstrate (e.g., completing seatwork assignments within a certain time frame). They also agree on one or more reinforcers for those behaviours (e.g., a certain amount of free time or points earned toward a particular privilege or prize) and then write and sign a contract that describes both the behaviours that the student will perform and the reinforcers that will result. Contingency contracts are an effective strategy for improving a wide variety of academic and social behaviours (Brooke & Ruthren, 1984; D. L. Miller & Kelley, 1994; Rueger & Liberman, 1984; Welch, 1985).

■ *When giving reinforcement publicly, make sure that all students have an opportunity to earn it.* In your attempts to improve the behaviour of some students, you may unintentionally ignore other, equally deserving students. For example, Jeff Derevensky and Randie Leckerman (1997) reported that reinforcement is not used similarly or systematically by all Canadian teachers. In integrated classrooms, "regular students" received more praise and reinforcement than children with special needs.

Furthermore, some students may be unable to exhibit particular behaviours through no fault of their own. Consider the case of a Vietnamese immigrant boy whose family circumstances were such that he was always late to school:

> [E]very week on Friday after school, the teacher would give little presents to students that were good during the week. And if you were tardy, you wouldn't get a present . . . I would never get one because I would always come to school late, and that hurt at first. I had a terrible time. I didn't look forward to going to school. (Igoa, 1995, p. 95)

School should be a place where *all* of your students can earn reinforcement and in other ways be successful. Classrooms are busy places and it may be all too easy to overlook a few students who desperately want and need your attention. In such cases, you can explicitly *teach* them appropriate ways of seeking out and getting reinforcement—for instance, by raising their hands or walking quietly to their desks at an appropriate time, asking questions (e.g., "How am I doing?" "What do I do next?"), and keeping you informed of their progress ("Look, I'm all finished!") (K. A. Meyer, 1999).

- *Administer reinforcement consistently.* Responses increase more quickly when they are reinforced each and every time they occur. **Continuous reinforcement** is most important when students are first *learning* a behaviour. Once mastered and exhibited frequently, you may want to reinforce it less often (more about the advantages of such *intermittent reinforcement* later in the chapter).

- *Monitor students' progress.* To determine behaviour change and reinforcement effectiveness, assess the frequency of the terminal behaviour both before and during your attempts to increase it through operant conditioning. The frequency, whether high or low, of a behaviour *before* you intentionally begin reinforcement is called the **baseline** level of that behaviour.

By comparing the baseline response frequency of a behaviour with its frequency after you begin reinforcing it, you can determine whether the reinforcer you are using is actually bringing about a behaviour change. In the opening case study, James rarely turns in classroom assignments; a behaviour with a low baseline. An obvious reinforcer to use with James is attention, a consequence that, until now, has effectively reinforced such non-desired behaviours as blurting out answers in class and throwing objects. When our attention is contingent on James's turning in assignments, rather than on his refusals to do so, we should see an almost immediate increase in the number of assignments we receive from James. If we see no significant change in James's behaviour, we need to consider alternative reinforcers.

But if a desired behaviour has a baseline level of *zero,* the process of shaping is required.

Continuous reinforcement Reinforcing a response every time it occurs.

Baseline The frequency of a response before operant conditioning takes place.

Shaping New Behaviours

Cam is very shy and withdrawn, rarely interacting with other students, either in class or on the playground. In a situation where he must interact with a classmate, he doesn't seem to know how to behave. To help students like Cam develop appropriate social behaviours, you can use a procedure called **shaping**, which is a process of reinforcing a series of responses that increasingly resemble the desired terminal behaviour; that is, it involves reinforcing successively closer and closer approximations to that behaviour as follows:

1. First reinforce any response that in some way resembles the terminal behaviour
2. Then reinforce a response that more closely approximates the terminal behaviour (no longer reinforcing the previously reinforced response)
3. Then reinforce a response that resembles the terminal behaviour even more closely
4. Continue reinforcing closer and closer approximations to the terminal behaviour
5. Finally reinforce only the terminal behaviour

Each response in the sequence is reinforced every time it occurs until you see it regularly. Only at that point do we begin reinforcing a behaviour that more closely approaches the terminal behaviour.

To illustrate this process, let's consider how you might shape Cam's social behaviour. You can first reinforce him for something that he occasionally does, such as smiling at a classmate. After you begin to see him smiling frequently (perhaps after a few days or weeks), you then reinforce him only when he makes a verbal response to the comments or questions of a classmate. When that behaviour occurs frequently, you reinforce him only when he initiates a conversation. Later steps to take would be reinforcing Cam for approaching a group of peers, for suggesting a group activity, and so on.

It may often be unreasonable to expect students to make drastic changes in their behaviour overnight. Teachers may need to shape a student's behaviour by first reinforcing one small step in the right direction, then by reinforcing another small step, and then yet another, until eventually the desired terminal behaviour is achieved. We can (and often do) use shaping to teach students to work independently on classroom assignments. We begin by giving Grade 1 students structured tasks that may take only 5 to 10 minutes to complete. As students move through the elementary school years, we expect them to work independently for longer periods of time, and we also give

Shaping A process of reinforcing successively closer and closer approximations of a desired terminal behaviour.

How might you use shaping to teach an 8-year-old cursive writing; a 12-year-old to swing a baseball bat; an aggressive high school student to behave prosocially?

Chapter 5 Learning and Behaviour Processes 117

them short assignments to do at home. By high school, students have extended study halls (where, with luck, they study independently) and complete lengthy assignments at home. In the post-secondary years, student assignments require a great deal of independence and self-direction.

Effects of Antecedent Stimuli and Responses

In our discussion of operant conditioning so far, we have focused on the *consequences* of desired behaviours. Yet some behaviours are more likely to be reinforced in some situations than in others. For example, the behaviour of looking up a word to find its correct spelling is more likely to be reinforced when you are writing a research paper than when you are writing a note to a friend; we could diagram the situation this way:

$$S_{Paper} \rightarrow R \rightarrow S_{Reinforcement}$$
$$S_{Note} \rightarrow R \rightarrow \text{(no consequence)}$$

Similarly, talking about effective teaching practices is more likely to be reinforced when you are sitting in your educational psychology class than when you are at a party or the movies. You are more likely to make a particular response when already making similar kinds of responses.

Researchers have found that the stimuli and responses that precede a particular desired response (i.e., the **antecedent stimuli** and **antecedent responses**) often influence the frequency of the response. Here we will look at four phenomena—cueing, setting events, generalization, and discrimination—that involve antecedent stimuli and one—behavioural momentum—that involves antecedent responses.

Antecedent stimulus A stimulus that increases the likelihood that a particular response will follow.

Antecedent response A response that increases the likelihood that another, particular response will follow.

Cueing A teacher's use of signals to indicate that a particular behaviour is desired or that a particular behaviour should stop.

Cueing

Students are more likely to behave appropriately when they are given reminders (often called *cues* or *prompts*) that certain behaviours are expected of them (Northup et al., 1995). **Cueing** sometimes involves a nonverbal signal (turning the lights on and off a few times to give the signal that students must be quiet and attend to the teacher). At other times, it involves a verbal reminder, either direct or indirect, about what students should be doing:

- "*After you have all read pages 14 through 19 in your textbooks,* I will hand out information about the school ski trip."
- "I see some *art supplies that still need to be put back on the shelves* before you can go home."

Generalization

Once people have learned that a response is likely to be reinforced in one set of circumstances (i.e., in the presence of one antecedent stimulus), they are likely to make the same response in a similar situation; in other words, they show generalization. After Cam has learned how to make friends at school, he may begin to apply the same skills in his out-of-school activities. In classical conditioning, generalization involves an automatic, involuntary response, but in operant conditioning it is a voluntary response.

Discrimination

Sometimes people learn that responses are reinforced only when certain stimuli (certain environmental conditions) are present. Cam might discover that a classmate who smiles at him is more likely to reinforce his attempts at being friendly than a classmate who scowls. When people learn that responses are reinforced in the presence of one stimulus but not in the presence of another (perhaps very similar) stimulus, they have learned **discrimination** between the two stimuli.

Occasionally students may overgeneralize, exhibiting responses they have learned in situations where such responses are unproductive or inappropriate. In such cases, you must teach them to discriminate between suitable and unsuitable stimulus conditions. For instance, you should describe in very concrete terms the circumstances in which certain behaviours are and are not productive and acceptable. You then must be sure that you reinforce students for exhibiting behaviours *only* in situations where those behaviours are appropriate.

Discrimination A phenomenon in operant conditioning whereby an individual learns that a response is reinforced in the presence of one stimulus but not in the presence of another, similar stimulus.

> **INTO THE CLASSROOM** *Encouraging Productive Classroom Behaviours through Operant Conditioning*
>
> Reinforce desirable behaviours.
>
> > To a student who has just completed an excellent oral book report, a teacher says, "Nice job, Monica. You made the book sound so interesting. *I* certainly want to read it now, and I suspect that many of your classmates do as well."
>
> Give feedback about specific behaviours rather than general areas of performance.
>
> > As his kindergartners are cleaning up after a class art project, a teacher says, "I like how everyone is remembering to pick up the scraps of paper around their desks. And look at how LaMarr and Julia are collecting every group's boxes of markers and bottles of glue without my even having to ask them!"
>
> Provide opportunities for students to practise correct behaviours.
>
> > In a unit on basketball, a physical education teacher makes sure that every student has several successful shots at the basket.
>
> Remember that different things are reinforcing to different students. A teacher allows students to engage in favourite activities during the free time they earn each day. Some students work on the classroom computer, others work on art projects, and still others converse with friends.
>
> When the baseline level of a desired behaviour is low, gradually shape the behaviour over time by reinforcing closer and closer approximations.
>
> > A teacher praises a shy and withdrawn boy for smiling or making eye contact with his classmates. After such behaviours become more frequent, the teacher begins praising him when he responds to classmates' questions or comments. As the latter behaviour also increases, the teacher praises the boy only when he initiates a conversation with someone else.
>
> Cue appropriate behaviours.
>
> > As students are busily working on co-operative group projects, their teacher sees that one group's discussion is being dominated by a single student. She announces to the class, "Please remember a point that I made earlier: You are more likely to create a good product when *all* group members contribute their ideas."
>
> Once students are exhibiting desired behaviours frequently, continue to reinforce them intermittently so that they don't undergo extinction.
>
> > After a formerly aggressive student has developed appropriate social skills and is using them consistently in the classroom, her teacher occasionally commends her for her prosocial behaviour.

Reducing and Eliminating Undesirable Behaviours

Our focus up to this point has been on promoting desirable behaviours. Yet you will also need to address *un*desirable behaviours—those that interfere with students' own learning and achievement, and possibly with the learning and achievement of their classmates as well. To decrease, perhaps even eliminate, such behaviours, several possible strategies include extinction, cueing inappropriate behaviours, reinforcing incompatible behaviours, and punishment.

Extinction

We earlier considered extinction in relation to classical conditioning and now extend this to operant conditioning. When a response is no longer reinforced, it decreases in frequency and usually returns to its baseline level. The decrease of a nonreinforced response in operant conditioning also is known as **extinction**. For example, the class clown whose jokes are ignored may stop telling jokes. One way of reducing the frequency of an inappropriate behaviour, then, is simply to make sure it is never reinforced.

Unfortunately, teachers and other adults often inadvertently reinforce the very behaviours they want to eliminate. A girl who copies her homework assignment word for word from a classmate and then receives a high grade for that assignment is reinforced for representing someone else's work as her own. As a teacher, you must look reflectively at your own behaviours in the classroom, being careful *not* to reinforce those responses that are unlikely to help your students over the long run.

There are several points to keep in mind about extinction. First, once reinforcement stops, a previously reinforced response doesn't always decrease immediately. Sometimes the

Extinction, in operant conditioning The eventual disappearance of a response that is no longer being reinforced.

How is extinction similar in classical and operant conditioning? How is it different?

Simple body language is often an effective cue. While this teacher is temporarily preoccupied, her hand on a student's shoulder provides a subtle reminder about what he should and should not be doing.

behaviour initially *increases* for a short time (Lerman & Iwata, 1995; McGill, 1999). The class clown who is now being ignored may tell more jokes at first before learning that such behaviours no longer produce the desired results.

Second, you may sometimes find situations in which a response doesn't decrease even when you remove a reinforcer. When extinction doesn't occur, chances are that you haven't been able to remove *all* reinforcers of the response. Perhaps the behaviour is leading to a naturally reinforcing consequence; for example, a class clown's peers may continue to snicker even when the teacher ignores his jokes. Or perhaps the response is intrinsically reinforcing; for example, a student's physically aggressive behaviour may release pent-up energy (and so may "feel good") even if it doesn't otherwise get her what she wants. Only when all reinforcers are removed will extinction occur.

Finally, extinction of desirable behaviours occurs as easily as with undesirable ones. The student who is never called on in class may stop raising his hand. The student who never passes a paper–pencil test no matter how hard she studies may eventually stop studying. Counterproductive classroom behaviours are not to be reinforced, but productive responses *are* to be reinforced, either through such extrinsic reinforcers as attention, praise, or favourite activities or through the intrinsic satisfaction that classroom accomplishments bring.

Cueing Inappropriate Behaviours

You can use cueing to remind students about what they should be doing and what they should *not* be doing. For example, you might use *body language*—perhaps making eye contact, or frowning—to let students know that you disapprove of their behaviour and would like it to cease. When body language doesn't get the attention of a misbehaving student, a more obvious cue is *physical proximity:* moving closer to the student and standing there until the problem behaviour stops (Emmer, 1987; Woolfolk & Brooks, 1985). Particularly if you are walking around the room anyway during a classroom activity, this strategy can attract the attention of the guilty party without at the same time drawing undue attention from classmates.

Sometimes you will have to be more explicit. A brief *verbal cue*—stating a student's name, reminding a student about correct behaviour, or (if necessary) pointing out an inappropriate behaviour—may be in order (Northup et al., 1995). For example, you might say something as simple as, "Please keep your eyes on your own work."

Reinforcing Incompatible Behaviours

Incompatible behaviours Two or more behaviours that cannot be performed simultaneously.

Two behaviours are **incompatible** when they cannot be performed simultaneously. For example, sitting is incompatible with standing. Eating crackers is incompatible with singing, or at least with singing *well*. In each case, it is physically impossible to perform both activities at exactly the same time.

In addition to cueing and extinction, another way to reduce an inappropriate behaviour is to reinforce an incompatible (and presumably more desirable) one; the inappropriate response must inevitably decrease as the incompatible one increases (Zirpoli & Melloy, 2001). When reinforcing an overactive student for sitting down, you are showing them that sitting is incompatible with getting-out-of-seat and roaming-around-the-room behaviours. You might use this to deal with forgetfulness (we reinforce students when they remember to do what they were supposed to do), being off-task (we reinforce on-task behaviour), and verbal abusiveness (we reinforce prosocial statements).

Punishment

Some misbehaviours require an immediate remedy—they interfere significantly with students' learning, and they may threaten students' physical safety or psychological well-being as well. You cannot simply wait for gradual improvements over time.

TABLE 5.2   COMPARE/CONTRAST

Distinguishing among Positive Reinforcement, Negative Reinforcement, and Punishment

CONSEQUENCE	EFFECT	EXAMPLES
Positive reinforcement	Response *increases* when a new stimulus (presumably one that the person finds desirable) is *presented*.	• A student *is praised* for writing an assignment in cursive. She begins to write other assignments in cursive as well. • A student *gets his lunch money* by bullying a girl into surrendering hers. He begins bullying his classmates more frequently.
Negative reinforcement	Response *increases* when a previously existing stimulus (presumably one that the person finds undesirable) is *removed*.	• A student *no longer has to worry* about a research paper he has completed several days before the due date. He begins to do his assignments ahead of time whenever possible. • A student *escapes the principal's wrath* by lying about her role in a recent incident of school vandalism. She begins lying to school faculty whenever she finds herself in an uncomfortable situation.
Presentation punishment	Response *decreases* when a new stimulus (presumably one that the person finds undesirable) is *presented*.	• A student *is scolded* for taunting other students. She taunts others less frequently after that. • A student *is ridiculed by classmates* for asking a "stupid" question during a lecture. He stops asking questions in class.
Removal punishment	Response *decreases* when a previously existing stimulus (presumably one that the person finds desirable) is *removed*.	• A student *is removed from the softball team for a week* for showing poor sportsmanship. She rarely shows poor sportsmanship in future games. • A student *loses points on a test* for answering a question in a creative but unusual way. He takes fewer risks on future tests.

Bonnie doesn't handle frustration very well. Whenever she encounters a difficulty or obstacle that she cannot immediately overcome, she responds by hitting, kicking, or breaking something. Over the course of the school year, she has knocked over furniture, broken two windows and innumerable pencils, and made several dents in the wall.

Bonnie's inappropriate behaviours are difficult to extinguish because they aren't really being reinforced to begin with (not extrinsically, at least). They are also behaviours with no obvious incompatible responses that we can reinforce. We can reasonably assume that Bonnie's teacher has already cued her about her inappropriate behaviour on many occasions. When other strategies are inapplicable or ineffective, punishment may be a useful alternative.

Earlier, we defined a reinforcer as a consequence that increases the frequency of a particular behaviour. **Punishment** is defined as a consequence that *decreases* the frequency of the response it follows.

Punishing consequences fall into one of two groups. **Presentation punishment** involves presenting a new stimulus, presumably something that a student finds unpleasant and doesn't want. Scoldings and teacher scowls, if they lead to a reduction in the behaviour they follow, are all instances of presentation punishment. **Removal punishment** involves removing a previously existing stimulus, presumably one that a student finds desirable and doesn't want to lose. The loss of a privilege, a fine (involving the loss of tokens or points), and "grounding" (when certain pleasurable outside activities are missed) are all possible examples of removal punishment. Table 5.2 should help you understand how negative reinforcement, presentation punishment, and removal punishment are all very different concepts.

Strictly speaking, punishment is not a part of operant conditioning. Many early behaviourists believed that punishment is a relatively *in*effective means of changing behaviour—that it may temporarily suppress a response but can never eliminate it—and suggested that teachers focus their efforts on reinforcing desirable behaviours, rather than on punishing undesirable ones. However, behaviourists have found that some forms of punishment can be quite effective in reducing problem behaviours.

Effective Forms of Punishment

As a general rule, you will want to use relatively mild forms of punishment in the classroom; severe consequences may lead to such unwanted side effects as resentment, hostility, or truancy.

Punishment A consequence that decreases the frequency of the response it follows.

Presentation punishment A form of punishment involving the presentation of a new stimulus, presumably one that an individual finds unpleasant.

Removal punishment A form of punishment involving the removal of an existing stimulus, presumably one that an individual views as desirable and doesn't want to lose.

Can you describe positive reinforcement, negative reinforcement, presentation punishment, and removal punishment in your own words? Can you think of examples of each concept?

Chapter 5   Learning and Behaviour Processes

Researchers and educators have identified several forms of mild punishment that can be effective in reducing classroom misbehaviours: reprimands, response cost, logical consequences, and time-out.

Verbal reprimand A scolding for inappropriate behaviour.

Verbal reprimands (scolding). Most students, particularly if they are scolded relatively infrequently, find **verbal reprimands** to be unpleasant and punishing (Pfiffner & O'Leary, 1993; Van Houten, Nau, MacKenzie-Keating, Sameoto, & Colavecchia, 1982). Reprimands are more effective when they are immediate, brief, and unemotional; they also work better when they are given in a calm voice and in close proximity to the student, perhaps because they are less likely to be noticed and so less likely to draw the attention of classmates (O'Leary, Kaufman, Kass, & Drabman, 1970; Pfiffner & O'Leary, 1993). Reprimands should be given in private whenever possible: When scolded in front of their classmates, some students may relish the peer attention, but others may feel totally humiliated (Fuller, 2001).

Response cost The loss of either a previously earned reinforcer or an opportunity to obtain reinforcement.

Response cost. **Response cost** involves the loss of either a previously earned reinforcer or an opportunity to obtain reinforcement; it is an instance of removal punishment. Teachers of students with chronic behaviour problems sometimes incorporate response cost into a point system or token economy: They award points, check marks, plastic chips, or the like for good behaviour (reinforcement) and take away these things for inappropriate behaviour (response cost). Students who accumulate a sufficient number of points or tokens can use them to "buy" objects, privileges, or enjoyable activities that are otherwise not available. Response cost is especially effective when coupled with reinforcement of appropriate behaviour (Iwata & Bailey, 1974; Lentz, 1988; Rapport, Murphy, & Bailey, 1982).

Logical consequence A consequence that follows logically from a student's misbehaviour; in other words, the punishment fits the crime.

Logical consequences. A **logical consequence** follows naturally or logically from a student's misbehaviour; in other words, the punishment fits the crime. If two close friends talk so much that they aren't getting their assignments done, a reasonable consequence is for them to be separated. The use of logical consequences makes "logical" sense, and numerous research studies and case studies vouch for its effectiveness (Dreikurs, 1998; Lyon, 1984; Schloss & Smith, 1994; L. S. Wright, 1982).

Time-out A procedure whereby a misbehaving student is placed in a dull, boring situation with no opportunity to interact with others and no opportunity to obtain reinforcement.

Time-out. In **time-out**, a misbehaving student is placed in a dull, uninteresting (but not scary) situation—perhaps a separate room designed especially for time-outs, or a remote corner of the classroom. A student undergoing time-out has no opportunity to interact with classmates and no opportunity to obtain reinforcement. Time-outs are often quite short (perhaps 2 to 10 minutes, depending on the age of the student), but the student is not released from the time-out situation until inappropriate behaviour (e.g., screaming, kicking) has stopped. Time-outs have been used successfully to reduce a variety of noncompliant, disruptive, and aggressive behaviours (e.g., Pfiffner & Barkley, 1998; Rortvedt & Miltenberger, 1994).

Can you explain how *release* from a time-out situation is *negative reinforcement*?

Just as you must use different reinforcers for different students, punishment is also individualized. Some students enjoy the attention that verbal reprimands bring (remember James in the opening case study). A few may even appreciate the peace and quiet of an occasional time-out (Pfiffner & Barkley, 1998). If we find that a particular form of punishment produces no substantial decrease in a student's behaviour, you should conclude that it isn't really a punishing consequence for that student and that a different form of punishment is called for in the future.

Guidelines for using time-outs can be found on the website of the Special Programs Branch of Alberta Learning: http://education.alberta.ca/media/547960/timeout_oct_2002.pdf.

Ineffective Forms of Punishment

Several forms of punishment are typically *not* recommended: physical punishment, psychological punishment, extra classwork, and out-of-school suspension.

We encourage you to consult your local and provincial teacher associations on the issue of using punishment in schools. An informative project may be to interview several teachers about their views on punishment and how they manage to promote positive personal, social, and learning behaviours in their classrooms.

Physical punishment. Physical punishment is not advised for school-age children (W. Doyle, 1990; Zirpoli & Melloy, 2001); furthermore, its use in the classroom is illegal in many places and we would further endorse the position stated by an anonymous reviewer of this book: "Physical and psychological punishment is inappropriate, unethical, inhumane, and should not be practised by any teacher or school administrator regardless of legality."

The Board of the Canadian Psychological Association in March 2004 approved in principle the following public statement: "Physical punishment has been consistently demonstrated to be an ineffective and potentially harmful method of managing children's behaviour. It places children at risk of physical injury and may interfere with psychological adjustment" (C. Lee, 2004; see also www.cheo.on.ca/english/pdf/joint_statement_e.pdf).

Psychological punishment Any consequence that seriously threatens a student's self-concept and self-esteem.

Psychological punishment. **Psychological punishment**—any consequence that seriously threatens a student's self-esteem—is also not recommended (J. E. Walker & Shea, 1995). Embarrassing remarks and public humiliation can lead to some of the same side effects as physical punishment and have the potential to inflict long-term psychological harm. Deflating students' self-perceptions may also lower students' expectations for future performance and their motivation to learn and achieve (more on this point in the discussion of *self-efficacy* in Chapters 8 and 9).

Extra classwork. Asking a student to complete make-up work for time missed in school is a reasonable and justifiable request. But assigning extra classwork or homework beyond that required for other students is inappropriate if it is assigned simply to punish a student's wrongdoing (Cooper, 1989; Corno, 1996). In this case, you have a very different side effect: You inadvertently communicate the message that "schoolwork is unpleasant."

Out-of-school suspension. Teachers and administrators are negatively reinforced when they suspend a problem student. After all, they get rid of something they don't want—a problem! But out-of-school suspension is usually not an effective means of changing a student's behaviour (J. D. Nichols, Ludwin, & Iadicola, 1999; Pfiffner & Barkley, 1998). In the first place, this may be exactly what the student wants, in which case inappropriate behaviours are being reinforced rather than punished. Second, because many students with chronic behaviour problems also tend to do poorly in their schoolwork, suspension involves a loss of valuable instructional time and interferes with any psychological "attachment" to school, thereby decreasing even further the students' chances for academic and social success (J. D. Nichols et al., 1999).

Suspension from school may actually reinforce inappropriate school behaviour rather than punish it.

An additional form of punishment—missing recess—gets mixed reviews regarding its effectiveness. In some situations, missing recess may be a logical consequence for students who fail to complete their schoolwork during regular class time due to off-task behaviour. Yet research tells us that, at least at the elementary level, students can more effectively concentrate on school tasks when they have occasional breaks from academic activities (Pellegrini, Huberty, & Jones, 1995). Perhaps the best advice here is to withdraw recess privileges infrequently, if at all, and to monitor the effectiveness of such a consequence on students' classroom behaviour over the long run.

Using Punishment Humanely

A frequent criticism of using punishment is that it is "inhumane," or somehow cruel and barbaric. Indeed, certain forms of punishment, such as physical abuse or public humiliation, do constitute inhumane treatment. You must be *extremely careful* in your use of punishment in the classroom. When administered judiciously, however, some forms of mild punishment (e.g., losing a privilege) can lead to a rapid reduction in misbehaviour without causing physical or psychological harm. And when you can decrease counterproductive classroom behaviours quickly and effectively—especially when those behaviours are harmful to self or others—then punishment may, in fact, be one of the most humane approaches you can take. Following are several guidelines for using punishment effectively and humanely:

- *Inform students ahead of time that certain behaviours will be punished, and explain how those behaviours will be punished.* When students are informed of response–punishment contingencies ahead of time, they are less likely to engage in the forbidden behaviours; they are also less likely to be surprised or resentful if punishment must be administered (G. D. Gottfredson & Gottfredson, 1985; Moles, 1990). Ultimately, students should learn that their behaviours influence the consequences that they experience—that they have some control over what happens to them (see *attribution theory* in Chapter 9).

- *Follow through with specified consequences.* One mistake that some teachers make is to continually threaten punishment without ever following through. One warning is desirable, but repeated warnings are not. The teacher who says, "If you bring that rubber snake to class one more time, Tommy, I'm going to take it away," but never does, is giving the message that no response–punishment contingency really exists.

- *Administer punishment privately.* By administering punishment such as a verbal reprimand, in private, you protect your students from public embarrassment or humiliation. You also eliminate the possibility that the punishment will draw the attention of classmates—a potential reinforcer for the very behaviour you are trying to eliminate.

INTO THE CLASSROOM   *Decreasing and Eliminating Undesirable Behaviours*

Don't inadvertently reinforce undesirable behaviours.

A teacher realizes that a particular "problem" student, a girl who makes frequent inappropriate remarks in class, seems to thrive on any kind of attention. He also realizes that the girl's behaviour has gotten worse instead of better. Rather than continue to reinforce the girl by scolding her publicly, he meets with her after school and together they develop a contingency contract designed to improve her behaviour.

Cue students when you see them behaving inappropriately.

As she describes the morning's assignment, a teacher notices that two boys on the other side of the classroom are whispering, giggling, and obviously not paying attention. While continuing her description of the assignment, she walks slowly across the room and stands next to the boys.

Reinforce behaviours that are incompatible with undesirable behaviours.

A student is out of her seat so frequently that she gets little of her own work done and often distracts her classmates from doing theirs. Her teacher discusses the problem behaviour with her, and together they decide that she will earn points for staying in her seat and keeping on task; she may use the points to "buy" time with her friends at the end of the day.

When a misbehaviour must be suppressed quickly, choose a mild punishment, yet one that is likely to deter the behaviour in the future.

When members of the school soccer team have an unexcused absence from team practice, they are not allowed to play in that week's soccer game.

Describe both appropriate and inappropriate behaviours, as well as their consequences, in concrete and explicit terms.

The soccer coach reminds students that those who miss practice will sit out at the next game and all students who *do* make practice will play at least part of the game.

When misbehaviours continue despite all reasonable efforts to correct them, seek the advice of experts.

A teacher consults with the school psychologist about three students who are often physically aggressive in their interactions with classmates. Together they develop a strategy to help these students.

■ *Explain why the punished behaviour is unacceptable.* You must explain exactly why a certain behaviour cannot be tolerated in the classroom (perhaps because it interferes with learning, threatens the safety or self-esteem of other students, or damages school property). Punishment is far more effective when accompanied by one or more reasons why the punished behaviour is unacceptable (Cheyne & Walters, 1970; Parke, 1974; D. G. Perry & Perry, 1983). (Recall our discussion of *induction* in Chapter 3.)

■ *Emphasize that it is the behaviour that is undesirable, not the student.* As a teacher, you must emphasize to students that certain behaviours interfere with their success in learning—that their behaviour is preventing them from becoming the very best that they can be.

■ *Simultaneously teach and reinforce desirable alternative behaviours.* Punishment of misbehaviour is almost always more effective when appropriate behaviours are being reinforced at the same time (Pfiffner & Barkley, 1998; Ruef, Higgins, Glaeser, & Patnode, 1998). By reinforcing desirable responses as well as punishing undesirable ones, you give students the positive, optimistic message that behaviour can and will improve. Ultimately, the overall classroom atmosphere you create must be a positive one that highlights the good things that students do and deemphasizes the "bad" (R. E. Smith & Smoll, 1997).

Saskatchewan Learning has published a practical and comprehensive guide called "Promoting Positive Behaviour," available at www.sasked.gov.sk.ca/branches/curr/special_ed/docs/createopp/creatopp.shtml.

Maintaining Desirable Behaviours over the Long Run

How can you ensure that your students will continue to behave in productive ways over the long run? Two viable strategies are promoting intrinsic reinforcement and using intermittent reinforcement.

Promoting Intrinsic Reinforcement

Intrinsic reinforcers come from students themselves, rather than from some outside source. Students will often engage in activities that are enjoyable or that satisfy their curiosity. They will also exhibit behaviours that lead to success and to feelings of mastery, accomplishment, and pride. Such internal consequences are most effective in sustaining productive behaviours both in the classroom and in the outside world.

Yet success is not always achieved easily and effortlessly. Many of the tasks that students will tackle in school—reading, writing, solving mathematical problems, reasoning scientifically, understanding historical and social events, participating skilfully in team sports, learning to play a musical instrument—are complex, challenging, and at times, frustrating. When students struggle with a challenging task and encounter frequent failure, teachers should provide extrinsic reinforcement for the little improvements they make. When you must break down a complex task into smaller pieces that, though easier to accomplish, are less fulfilling in their own right (e.g., when you assign drill-and-practice exercises to foster basic reading or math skills), you will probably need to reinforce students' many seemingly small successes. Once mastered tasks and skills bring students frequent successes and feelings of mastery, extrinsic reinforcers should no longer be necessary (M. V. Covington, 1992; Lepper, 1981). In fact, for reasons that you will discover in Chapter 9, it may actually be counterproductive to provide extrinsic reinforcers when students are already finding intrinsic reinforcement in the things they are doing.

Using Intermittent Reinforcement

Earlier, we stated that desired responses increase more quickly when they are reinforced every time they occur. Yet once those responses are occurring regularly, such *continuous reinforcement* may not be optimal. You may instead want to switch to **intermittent reinforcement**, reinforcing desired behaviour on some occasions and not doing so on others.

Intermittent reinforcement Reinforcing a response only occasionally, with some occurrences of the response going unreinforced.

Behaviours that have previously been reinforced intermittently decrease slowly (if at all) once reinforcement stops; in other words, they are more *resistant to extinction* (e.g., Freeland & Noell, 1999). Once students have acquired a desired terminal behaviour, you should continue to reinforce that behaviour intermittently, especially if it does not otherwise lead to intrinsic reinforcement. A teacher doesn't need to call on a student every time his or her hand is raised but he should certainly call on this student once in a while. In a similar manner, you might occasionally reinforce diligent study habits, completed homework assignments, prosocial behaviours, and so on, even for the best of students, as a way of encouraging such responses to continue.

Which form of reinforcement, continuous or intermittent, would you use to teach your students to persist at difficult tasks?

Addressing Especially Difficult Classroom Behaviours

Educators and other practitioners sometimes apply behaviourism in a very systematic way, especially when they want to address difficult and chronic behaviour problems. Here we consider three systematic approaches for modifying especially challenging behaviours: applied behaviour analysis, functional analysis, and positive behavioural support.

For other examples of addressing behaviours that can interfere with classroom learning and management, see www.bced.gov.bc.ca/specialed/landbdif/55.htm.

Applied Behaviour Analysis

A group of procedures that systematically apply traditional behaviourist principles are collectively known as **applied behaviour analysis** (**ABA**; also called *behaviour modification, behaviour therapy,* or *contingency management*). ABA assumes that behaviour problems result from past and present environmental circumstances and that modifying a student's present environment will promote more productive responses. When teachers and therapists use ABA to help a student acquire more appropriate classroom behaviour, they typically use strategies such as these:

- Describe both the present behaviours and the desired terminal behaviours in observable, measurable terms.
- Identify one or more effective reinforcers.
- Develop a specific intervention or treatment plan—one that may involve reinforcement of desired behaviours, shaping, extinction, reinforcement of incompatible behaviours, punishment, or some combination of these.

Applied behaviour analysis (ABA) The systematic application of behaviourist principles in educational and therapeutic settings; sometimes known as *behaviour modification*.

> ABA has been applied to children with a wide range of exceptionalities, for example, Autism Spectrum Disorders. Comprehensive descriptions can be found on various Canadian education and mental health websites including: www.edu.gov.mb.ca/k12/specedu/aut/pdf/chapter4.pdf, www.autism.ca/educsugg.htm, and www.edu.gov.on.ca/extra/eng/ppm/140.html.

- Measure the frequency of desired and/or undesirable behaviours both before treatment (i.e., at baseline level) and during treatment.
- Monitor the treatment program for effectiveness by observing how various behaviours change over time, and modify the program if necessary.
- Take steps to promote generalization of newly acquired behaviours (e.g., by having the student practise the behaviours in a variety of realistic situations).
- Gradually phase out the treatment (e.g., through intermittent reinforcement) after the desired behaviours are acquired.

Hundreds of research studies tell us that the systematic use of behaviourist principles can lead to significant improvements in academic performance and classroom behaviour. When you reinforce appropriate classroom behaviours, such as paying attention and interacting cooperatively and prosocially with classmates, misbehaviours decrease (Ormrod, 1999). In many situations, ABA is effective when other approaches have not been (Emmer & Evertson, 1981; Piersel, 1987).

ABA often works so well because students know exactly what is expected of them. Consistent use of reinforcement for appropriate responses gives a clear message about which behaviours are acceptable and which are not. Further, through the gradual process of *shaping*, students begin to learn new behaviours only when they are truly ready to acquire them, increasing the probability of achieving both success and reinforcement.

> Can you think of other possible reasons for the success of behaviourist techniques?

Functional Analysis and Positive Behavioural Support

Traditional ABA focuses on changing response–reinforcement contingencies to bring about more appropriate behaviour. You may also consider the purposes, or *functions*, that students' inappropriate behaviours may serve. You can identify the specific conditions (i.e., antecedent stimuli) present when students tend to misbehave and also the consequences (i.e., reinforcers and/or punishments) that typically follow such misbehaviours, like so:

$$\text{Antecedent} \rightarrow \text{Behaviour} \rightarrow \text{Consequence}$$

> Contemporary evidence-based research findings on the efficacy of ABA and other behavioural techniques can be found on websites such as PsycINFO and PsycARTICLES; see also "Psychology Works" at the Canadian Psychological Association's website (www.cpa.ca).
>
> **Functional analysis** Examining a student's inappropriate behaviour, as well as its antecedents and consequences, to determine the function(s) that the behaviour might serve for the student.

Such an approach is known as **functional analysis**. We have speculated that James, in our opening case study, misbehaves to get the attention he apparently cannot get in any other way. Students with chronic classroom behaviour problems often misbehave when they are asked to do difficult or unpleasant tasks (this is the *antecedent*) and their misbehaviour either (a) allows them to avoid having to do such tasks or (b) gains the attention of their teacher or peers (these are possible *consequences*) (K. M. Jones, Drew, & Weber, 2000; K. A. Meyer, 1999; Van Camp et al., 2000).

Another approach takes the process a step further: After identifying the purposes that a student's inappropriate behaviours may serve, the teacher also identifies more productive behaviours to serve the same purposes and designs an environment to encourage those productive behaviours. This approach, sometimes known as **positive behavioural support**, involves strategies such as these (Koegel, Koegel, & Dunlap, 1996; Ruef et al., 1998):

> **Positive behavioural support** A modification of traditional applied behaviour analysis that includes identifying the purpose that an undesirable behaviour serves for a student and providing an alternative way for the student to achieve the same purpose.

- Teach desirable behaviours that can serve the same purpose as—and can therefore replace—the inappropriate behaviours.
- Consistently reinforce desired behaviours in ways that the student truly appreciates.
- Modify the classroom environment to minimize conditions that might trigger inappropriate behaviours.
- Establish a predictable daily routine as a way of minimizing anxiety and making the student feel more comfortable and secure.
- Give the student frequent opportunities to make choices; in this way, the student can often gain desired outcomes without having to resort to inappropriate behaviours.
- Make adaptations in the curriculum, instruction, or both to maximize the likelihood of academic success (e.g., by building on the student's interests and preferred activities, presenting material at a slower pace, or interspersing challenging tasks among easier and more enjoyable ones).

Considering Diversity in Student Behaviours

When you take a behaviourist perspective, you realize that each of your students bring their own unique set of prior experiences to the classroom; such diversity in previous environments (e.g., home, community, culture) is undoubtedly one of the reasons for the different behaviours you see in the classroom. For one thing, your students will have been reinforced and punished—by their parents, siblings, previous teachers, peers, and so on—for different kinds of behaviours. Some students may have been reinforced for completing tasks in a careful and thorough manner, whereas others may have been reinforced for completing tasks quickly but sloppily. Some diversity in students' classroom responses will also be due to the different behaviours that varying cultures encourage (reinforce) and discourage (punish) in their children.

Furthermore, you will see differences in the secondary reinforcers to which students respond. The relative effectiveness of praise and positive feedback will depend on the extent to which such associations have been made. For example, some First Nations students may feel uncomfortable when praised for their work as individuals yet feel quite proud when they receive praise for group success (Fuller, 2001). Such preference for group praise is consistent with the co-operative spirit by which these students have been raised (see the discussion of ethnic differences in Chapter 4).

Finally, your students will have had varying experiences with the specific stimuli and general activities they will encounter at school. For example, when they throw a softball for the first time at school, some may be able to generalize from previous experiences throwing a baseball, whereas others may have to start from scratch in developing the skill.

With such diversity in mind, effective reinforcers, baseline rates of desired behaviours, and responses to particular stimuli will all be different for each student.

Accommodating All Students

A behaviourist approach allows us to consider characteristics of students with special needs from a somewhat different angle than we have in previous chapters. Table 5.3 illustrates how responses, reinforcement, generalization, and discrimination may be somewhat different in some students with special needs.

Again, we suggest you see www.sasklearning.gov.sk.ca/branches/curr/special_ed/docs/createopp/chap/chap12 for a helpful overview on applying a range of behaviourist psychology principles to promote positive behaviours.

Strengths and Potential Limitations of Behavioural Approaches

Behaviourist techniques are especially helpful in addressing chronic classroom behaviour problems. Although such approaches as applied behaviour analysis, functional analysis, and positive behavioural support can be quite time-consuming (J. N. Hughes, 1988), they are often effective when other approaches have not been.

Psychologists have had mixed feelings about the value of behaviourist techniques in addressing *academic* problems, however. Although reinforcement and other behaviourist strategies often lead to improved academic performance, you should note that extrinsic reinforcement may undermine learning that is already intrinsically motivated and that we may inadvertently reinforce children for quickly rather than thoroughly finishing a task. Furthermore, attempts at changing only behaviours ignore cognitive factors that may be interfering with learning. When students are capable of learning a new skill but are not motivated to do so, the use of reinforcement may be all that is needed to bring about the desired behaviour change. But when cognitive deficiencies interfere with the acquisition of a new skill (e.g., perhaps a student has little background knowledge or ineffective study strategies), reinforcement alone may be insufficient. In the latter situation, you may need to employ teaching techniques based more on the cognitive theories we will examine in Chapter 6.

TABLE 5.3

Encouraging Appropriate Behaviours in Students with Special Educational Needs

CATEGORY	CHARACTERISTICS YOU MIGHT OBSERVE	POSSIBLE CLASSROOM STRATEGIES
Students with specific cognitive or academic difficulties	• Inappropriate classroom behaviours (in some students) • Difficulty discriminating among similar stimuli, especially when perceptual deficits exist • Difficulty generalizing responses from one situation to another	• Be explicit about, and consistently reinforce, desired classroom behaviours. • Emphasize differences among similar stimuli (e.g., the letters *b*, *d*, *p*, and *q*) and provide opportunities to practise making subtle discriminations. • Promote generalization of new responses (e.g., by pointing out similarities among different situations and by teaching skills in real-world contexts).
Students with social or behavioural problems	• Inappropriate responses, especially in social situations; difficulty determining when and where particular responses are appropriate • A history of inappropriate behaviours being reinforced (e.g., intrinsically or by teacher attention) • Responsiveness to teacher praise if given in private (for students with emotional and behavioural disorders) • Difficulty generalizing appropriate responses to new situations	• Describe desired behaviours clearly. • Give precise feedback regarding students' behaviour. • Reinforce desired behaviours using teacher attention, private praise, activity reinforcers, group contingencies (for students with emotional and behavioural disorders). • Reinforce accomplishments immediately using concrete reinforcers, activity reinforcers, or praise (especially for students with autism). • Shape desired behaviours over time; expect gradual improvement rather than immediate perfection. • Punish inappropriate behaviours (e.g., using time-out or response cost); consider ABA, functional analysis, or positive behavioural support for persistently challenging behaviours. • Promote generalization of new responses to appropriate situations (e.g., by teaching skills in real-world contexts and providing opportunities to role-play new responses).
Students with general delays in cognitive and social functioning	• High reinforcing value of extrinsic reinforcers • Behaviours more likely to increase when reinforcement is immediate rather than delayed • Inappropriate responses in social situations • Difficulty discriminating between important and unimportant stimuli • Difficulty generalizing responses from one situation to another	• Cue students regarding appropriate behaviours. • Reinforce accomplishments immediately (e.g., using concrete reinforcers, activity reinforcers, praise). • Use continuous reinforcement during the acquisition of new responses. • Shape desired behaviours over time; expect gradual improvement rather than immediate perfection. • Reprimand minor misbehaviours; use time-out or response cost for more serious and chronic misbehaviours. • Emphasize the stimuli to which you want students to attend. • Promote generalization of new responses (e.g., by teaching skills in real-world contexts and by reinforcing generalization).
Students with physical or sensory challenges	• Loss of some previously learned behaviours if students have had a traumatic brain injury	• Shape desired behaviours over time; expect gradual improvement rather than immediate perfection.
Students showing evidence of giftedness, talent, or high performance	• Unusual and sometimes creative responses to classroom tasks	• Keep an open mind regarding acceptable responses to classroom assignments. • Require fewer examples in general, perhaps avoiding the excessively simple ones, invite them to create interesting questions for themselves, and generally avoid "busywork" or other assignments that may encourage either boredom or justified objections that may be acted out rather than openly discussed.

Sources: Barbetta, 1990; Barbetta, Heward, Bradley, & Miller, 1994; Beirne-Smith et al., 2002; Buchoff, 1990; E. S. Ellis & Friend, 1991; Gearheart, Weishahn, & Gearheart, 1992; Heward, 2000; Landau & McAninch, 1993; Mercer, 1997; Morgan & Jenson, 1988; Patton, Blackbourn, & Fad, 1996; Pfiffner & Barkley, 1998; Piirto, 1999; Pressley, 1995; Turnbull et al., 1999.

TEACHING CONSTRUCTIONS

We can understand a great deal about the way students learn and behave by looking at stimulus–response principles. Conditions already present in a learner's environment—antecedent stimuli—tend to evoke certain kinds of responses either involuntarily (in classical conditioning) or voluntarily (in operant conditioning). Those responses, in turn, may lead to changes in the learner's environment; for instance, they may lead to reinforcement or punishment. If you think of reinforcing and punishing consequences as *stimuli* (because indeed they are), then you see a continuing interaction between the learner and his or her environment. By changing any part of this chain of events—whether by altering the classroom environment or by teaching students a more effective way of responding to that environment—you can help students acquire more productive classroom behaviours. But remember, helpful as they may be, stimulus–response principles alone do not give you a complete picture of human learning; motivation and cognition are critically important, as are developmental level and the influence of culture.

Now that you have studied behaviourist views of learning, let's revisit James, whom you met at the start of this chapter. Based on what you have learned:

- Describe James's behaviour using either operant or classical conditioning.
- Create a program using one or more of the principles in this chapter that you hypothesize would be effective in changing James's in-class behaviour.

KEY CONCEPTS

- behaviourism (p. 107)
- conditioning (p. 107)
- stimulus (S) (p. 108)
- response (R) (p. 108)
- contiguity (p. 108)
- classical conditioning (p. 109)
- unconditioned stimulus (UCS) (p. 109)
- unconditioned response (UCR) (p. 109)
- neutral stimulus (p. 109)
- conditioned stimulus (CS) (p. 110)
- conditioned response (CR) (p. 110)
- generalization (p. 110)
- extinction, in classical conditioning (p. 110)
- operant conditioning (p. 111)
- contingency (p. 112)
- reinforcer (p. 112)
- reinforcement (p. 112)
- primary reinforcer (p. 112)
- secondary reinforcer (p. 113)
- positive reinforcement (p. 113)
- concrete reinforcer (p. 113)
- social reinforcer (p. 113)
- activity reinforcer (p. 113)
- Premack principle (p. 113)
- positive feedback (p. 113)
- extrinsic reinforcer (p. 113)
- intrinsic reinforcer (p. 113)
- negative reinforcement (p. 114)
- delay of gratification (p. 114)
- terminal behaviour (p. 115)
- token economy (p. 115)
- backup reinforcer (p. 115)
- group contingency (p. 115)
- contingency contract (p. 116)
- continuous reinforcement (p. 117)
- baseline (p. 117)
- shaping (p. 117)
- antecedent stimulus (p. 118)
- antecedent response (p. 118)
- cueing (p. 118)
- discrimination (p. 118)
- extinction, in operant conditioning (p. 119)
- incompatible behaviours (p. 120)
- punishment (p. 121)
- presentation punishment (p. 121)
- removal punishment (p. 121)
- verbal reprimand (p. 122)
- response cost (p. 122)
- logical consequence (p. 122)
- time-out (p. 122)
- psychological punishment (p. 122)
- intermittent reinforcement (p. 125)
- applied behaviour analysis (ABA) (p. 125)
- functional analysis (p. 126)
- positive behavioural support (p. 126)

Chapter 5 Learning and Behaviour Processes

6 Learning and Cognitive Processes

CASE STUDY DARREN'S DAY AT SCHOOL

TEACHING CONNECTIONS

BASIC ASSUMPTIONS OF COGNITIVE PSYCHOLOGY

BASIC TERMINOLOGY IN COGNITIVE PSYCHOLOGY

A MODEL OF HUMAN MEMORY
The Nature of the Sensory Register • Moving Information to Working Memory: The Role of Attention • The Nature of Working (Short-Term) Memory • Moving Information to Long-Term Memory: Connecting New Information with Prior Knowledge • The Nature of Long-Term Memory • Critiquing the Three-Component Model

LONG-TERM MEMORY STORAGE
The Various Forms of Knowledge • How Declarative Knowledge Is Learned • How Procedural Knowledge Is Learned • Prior Knowledge and Working Memory in Long-Term Memory Storage • Using Mnemonics in the Absence of Relevant Prior Knowledge

LONG-TERM MEMORY RETRIEVAL
The Nature of Long-Term Memory Retrieval • Factors Affecting Retrieval • Why People Sometimes Forget

GIVING STUDENTS TIME TO PROCESS: EFFECTS OF INCREASING WAIT TIME

ACCOMMODATING DIVERSITY IN COGNITIVE PROCESSES

FACILITATING COGNITIVE PROCESSING IN ALL STUDENTS

LEARNING AND THE BRAIN: A WORD OF CAUTION ABOUT "BRAIN-BASED" TEACHING

TEACHING CONSTRUCTIONS

KEY CONCEPTS

CASE STUDY Darren's Day at School

At the dinner table one night, Darren's mother asks him, "How was your day at school?" Darren shrugs, thinks for a moment, and says, "OK, I guess." "What did you learn?" his father asks. "Nothing much," Darren replies. Nothing much, indeed! Let's look at several slices of Darren's school day and see how much he actually *did* learn.

In his daily lesson, Darren is studying the multiplication tables for the number 9. He finds that some multiplication facts are easy to learn because he can relate them to things he already knows; for example, $9 \times 2 = 18$ is like adding 9 plus 9, and $9 \times 5 = 45$ can be derived from counting by fives. Others, such as $9 \times 4 = 36$ and $9 \times 8 = 72$, are more difficult because he can't connect them to any number facts he has learned before. When Ms. Caffarella finds Darren and a few others struggling, she teaches the class two tricks for learning the nines multiplication table:

1. The first digit in the product is 1 less than the number by which 9 is being multiplied. For 9×6, the first digit in the product must be $6 - 1$, or 5.

2. The two digits of the product, when added together, equal nine. Because 5 plus 4 equal 9, the product of 9×6 must be 54.

With these two tricks, Darren discovers a pattern in the nines table that helps him recite the table correctly.

During a geography lesson, Ms. Caffarella describes the trip she took to Greece. She holds up a picture postcard of the Parthenon and explains that the building is constructed entirely of marble. Darren is sitting near the back of the room and can't see the picture very clearly; he envisions a building made entirely of marbles and silently wonders how the ancient Greeks managed to glue them all together.

Darren's art class is making papier-mâché masks. His friend Carla gives her mask a very large nose by adding a crumpled wad of paper below the eye holes and then covering and shaping the wad with several pieces of glued paper. Darren watches her closely and then makes a nose for his mask in a similar way.

TEACHING CONNECTIONS

We will consider cognitive processes involved in learning in this chapter, focusing on basic principles of cognition and information processing. As you read the chapter, consider the following questions in making connections between this theory and your own teaching practice:

- What basic assumptions and concepts are central to cognitive psychologists' beliefs about learning?
- What is the nature of human memory?
- What cognitive processes are involved in learning *(storing)* something new, and how can teachers best help students use these processes?
- What factors influence students' ability to remember *(retrieve)* information over the long run, and why do students sometimes forget what they've previously learned?
- What are the advantages of giving students time to process classroom material?

Basic Assumptions of Cognitive Psychology

Underlying **cognitive psychology** are several basic assumptions about how people learn. These assumptions, summarized in Table 6.1, are as follows:

- *Cognitive processes influence the nature of what is learned.* Cognitive psychologists view learning as an internal mental phenomenon, not an external behaviour change as we learned in Chapter 5. Furthermore, how people think about and interpret their experiences affects what they learn from those experiences. Cognitive psychologists have offered numerous explanations for how people mentally process information; many of these theories are collectively known as **information processing theory**.

As an illustration of the role that cognitive processes play, consider how Darren relates $9 \times 2 = 18$ to $9 + 9 = 18$ and relates $9 \times 5 = 45$ to counting by fives. Consider, too, how the

Cognitive psychology A theoretical perspective that focuses on the mental processes underlying human learning and behaviour. Adherents to this perspective are sometimes called *cognitivists*.

Information processing theory A theoretical perspective that focuses on the specific ways in which individuals mentally think about and "process" the information they receive.

TABLE 6.1 — PRINCIPLES/ASSUMPTIONS

Basic Assumptions of Cognitive Psychology and Their Educational Implications

ASSUMPTION	EDUCATIONAL IMPLICATION	EXAMPLE
Influence of cognitive processes	Encourage students to think about class material in ways that will help them remember it.	When introducing the concept *mammal*, ask students to identify numerous examples.
Selectivity about what is learned	Help students identify the most important things for them to learn. Also help them understand why these things are important.	Give students questions that they should try to answer as they read their textbooks. Include questions that ask them to apply what they read to their own lives.
Construction of meaning	Provide experiences that will help students make sense of the topics they are studying.	When studying Nathaniel Hawthorne's *The Scarlet Letter*, ask students to get together in small groups to discuss possible reasons why Reverend Arthur Dimmesdale refuses to acknowledge that he is the father of Hester Prynne's baby.
Role of prior knowledge and beliefs	Relate new ideas to what students already know and believe about the world.	When introducing a unit on "ocean animals" to elementary students, have them relate what they already know about the ocean, either from visiting the ocean or an aquarium or from reading books or watching popular movies involving ocean animals, to learn how organisms may survive in such an environment.
Active involvement in learning	Plan classroom activities that get students actively thinking about and using classroom subject matter.	To help students understand latitude and longitude, ask them to track the path of a hurricane using a series of latitude–longitude coordinates obtained on the internet.

teacher's description of a pattern in the nines table helps Darren remember more difficult facts such as $9 \times 8 = 72$. These two examples illustrate two principles from cognitive psychology: (a) *People learn new information more easily when they can relate it to something they already know,* and (b) *People learn several pieces of new information more easily when they can relate them to an overall organizational structure.*

This focus on the nature of cognitive processes can be extremely helpful to you as a teacher. You must consider not only *what* students are to learn but also *how* they can most effectively learn it.

■ *Students are selective about what they process and learn.* We are constantly bombarded with information and can handle only so much information at a given time. We must therefore be selective. Students are no different, and focus on what they think is important and ignore everything else. As a teacher, you must help your students make wise decisions about the pieces of information they choose to attend to, process, and save.

It is useful to distinguish between *sensation*—one's ability to sense stimuli in the environment—and *perception*—one's interpretation of stimuli. What the body senses is not always perceived (interpreted).

■ *Meaning is constructed by the learner, rather than being derived directly from the environment.* The process of **construction** lies at the core of many cognitive theories of learning: People take many separate pieces of information and use them to create an understanding or interpretation of the world around them (e.g., Bransford & Franks, 1971; Hegland & Andre, 1992; Marshall, 1992; Neisser, 1967). To experience the process of construction firsthand, try the following exercise.

Construction A mental process in which a learner takes many separate pieces of information and uses them to build an overall understanding or interpretation of an event.

EXPERIENCING FIRSTHAND   *Three Faces*

What do you see in each picture? Most people perceive the picture on the left as that of a woman, even though many of her features are missing. Enough features are visible—an eye, parts of the nose, mouth, chin, and hair—to construct a meaningful perception from them. Is enough information available in the other two figures? Construction of a face from the figure on the right may take you a while, but it can be done.

FIGURE 6.1 Can you construct a person from each of these pictures?

Source: From "Age in the Development of Closure Ability in Children" by C. M. Mooney, 1957, *Canadian Journal of Psychology*, 11, p. 220. Copyright 1957. Canadian Psychological Association. Reprinted with permission.

Knowing how human faces typically appear was probably enough to enable you to add the missing features (mentally) and perceive a complete picture. Curiously, once you have constructed faces from the pictures, they then seem obvious. If you were to close this book now and not pick it up again for a week or more, you would probably see the faces almost immediately, even if you had had considerable difficulty perceiving them originally.

We see the process of construction in our case study as well. When Ms. Caffarella describes the Parthenon's marble construction, Darren envisions a building made of marbles similar to the ones he has at home (such a misconception has been described by Sosniak & Stodolsky, 1994). He combines new information with what he already knows to construct meaning.

Some cognitive theories focus primarily on the ways that learners construct knowledge; many of these theories are collectively known as **constructivism**. We first encountered the constructivist perspective in Chapter 2: As early as the 1920s, Jean Piaget proposed that children construct their own understandings of the world based on their experiences with their physical and social environments.

Your students won't necessarily learn information exactly as you presented it to them; in fact, they will each interpret classroom subject matter in their own, idiosyncratic ways. In some cases, students like Darren may even learn *mis*information. You will therefore need to frequently monitor students' understanding by asking questions, encouraging dialogue, and listening carefully to students' ideas and explanations.

■ *Prior knowledge and beliefs play a major role in the meanings that people construct.* Perhaps the major reason that different students in the same classroom learn different things is that they have their own personal histories and experiences. Existing understandings of the world have a major influence on what and how effectively people can learn from their experiences. We will repeatedly see the effects of prior knowledge and beliefs in this and the next chapter.

■ *Students are actively involved in their own learning.* Students do not simply "absorb" knowledge from their surroundings. Instead, they are, and in fact *must be*, active participants in their own learning. Cognitive processing and knowledge construction require a certain amount of mental "work." In our discussion of memory in the pages ahead, we will begin to find out what our students must do (mentally) to learn effectively.

Constructivism A theoretical perspective that proposes that learners construct a body of knowledge from their experiences—knowledge that may or may not be an accurate representation of external reality. Adherents to this perspective are called constructivists.

This student might have more prior knowledge about shellfish and other sea creatures because of her recent trip to Vancouver Island.

Basic Terminology in Cognitive Psychology

Four concepts—memory, storage, encoding, and retrieval—will be important in our upcoming discussions of the cognitive processes involved in learning.

Memory A learner's ability to save something (mentally) that he or she has previously learned, *or* the mental "location" where such information is saved.

Memory. The term *memory* refers to learners' ability to "save" things (mentally) that they have previously learned. In some instances, we will use the term to refer to the actual process of saving learned knowledge or skills over a period of time. In other instances, it will refer to a "location"—perhaps working memory or long-term memory—where learners "put" what they learn.

Storage The process of "putting" new information into memory.

Storage. The term *storage* refers to the acquisition of new knowledge—the process of putting what is learned into memory in the first place. For example, your students, you hope, have been storing the ideas that you have been teaching on the wildlife indigenous to the Canadian Arctic.

Encoding Changing the format of new information as it is being stored in memory.

Encoding. We don't always store information exactly as we receive it. We usually modify it in some way; that is, we *encode* it. For example, when you listen to a story, you may picture some of the story's events in your mind.

People frequently store information in a different way from how it was presented. For example, they may change information from auditory to visual form, as when they form a mental picture of a story to which they are listening. They may change information from visual to auditory form, as when they read aloud a passage from a book. Encoding often involves assigning specific *meanings* and *interpretations* to stimuli and events. For example, when students reflect on something they have just read, they often don't remember *each and every detail* about what they have read. Instead, students, like the rest of us, store the gist (its general meaning) without necessarily storing the specific words. This tendency to encode gist rather than verbatim information increases as children get older (Brainerd, Reyna, Howe, & Kingma, 1990).

Think of an exam you have taken recently. Which student would have done better on that exam: one who had encoded course information verbatim or one who had encoded its meanings in relation to prior knowledge?

Retrieval The process of "finding" information previously stored in memory.

Retrieval. After you have stored information in your memory, you may discover that you need to use the information. The process of remembering previously stored information—"finding" the information in memory—is called *retrieval*. The following exercise illustrates this process.

EXPERIENCING FIRSTHAND   *Retrieval Practice*

See how quickly you can answer each of the following questions:

1. What is your name?
2. In what year did World War II end?
3. What is the capital of Spain?
4. What did you have for dinner three years ago today?
5. When talking about serving appetizers at a party, we sometimes use a French term instead of the word *appetizer*. What is that French term, and how is it spelled?

As you probably just noticed when you tried to answer these questions, retrieving information from memory is sometimes an easy, effortless process; for example, you undoubtedly had little difficulty remembering your name. But other things stored in memory can be retrieved only after some thought and effort; for example, it may have taken you some time to remember that World War II ended in 1945 or that the capital of Spain is Madrid. Other things, even though stored in memory at one time, may never be retrieved at all; perhaps a dinner menu three years ago and the correct spelling of *hors d'oeuvre* fall into this category.

How is information stored and encoded in memory? What factors influence the ease with which we can retrieve it? Let's take a look at a model of how human memory might work.

A Model of Human Memory

Cognitive psychologists do not agree about the exact nature of human memory. But many of them believe that memory may have three components: a sensory register, a working (short-term)

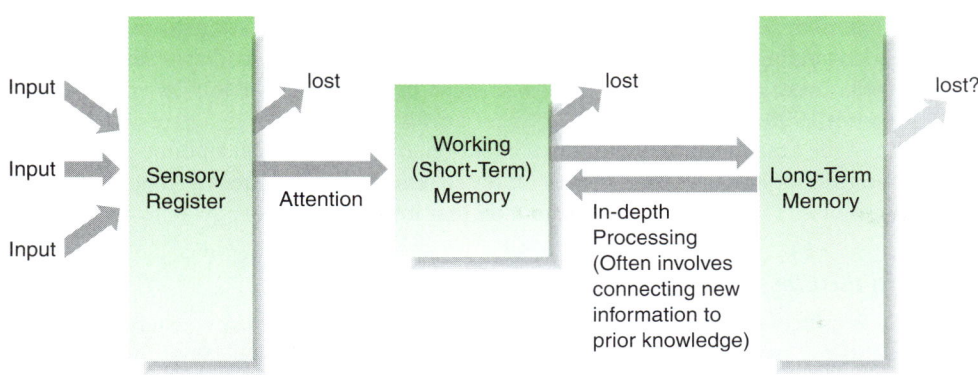

FIGURE 6.2 A model of the human memory system.

memory, and a long-term memory.[1] A three-component model of human memory, based loosely on one proposed by Atkinson and Shiffrin in 1968 but modified to reflect more recent research findings, is presented in Figure 6.2. Please note that in referring to three components of memory, we are *not* necessarily referring to three separate parts of the brain. The model of memory that is described has been derived from studies of human behaviour, not from studies of the brain. In the pages that follow, we will look at the characteristics of each component of memory and at how information is moved from one component to the next.

The Nature of the Sensory Register

The **sensory register** is the component of memory that holds the information that students receive—*input*—in more or less its original, *un*encoded form. Probably everything that they are capable of seeing, hearing, and otherwise sensing is stored in the sensory register. In other words, the sensory register has a *large capacity*; it can hold a great deal of information at one time.

That's the good news. The bad news is that information stored in the sensory register doesn't last very long (Cowan, 1995; Wingfield & Byrnes, 1981). Visual information—what students *see*—probably lasts for less than a second. Auditory information—what students *hear*—probably lasts slightly longer, perhaps for two or three seconds. To keep information for any time at all, then, it needs to move to *working memory*. Whatever information isn't moved is probably lost, or forgotten.

Sensory register A component of memory that holds incoming information in an unanalyzed form for a very brief period of time (probably less than a second for visual input and two or three seconds for auditory input).

Moving Information to Working Memory: The Role of Attention

The first step in making sensory information memorable is **attention**: *Whatever students pay attention to (mentally) moves into working memory.* Anything in the sensory register that does not get a student's attention disappears from the memory system. For example, imagine yourself reading a textbook for one of your classes. Your eyes are moving down each page, but meanwhile you are thinking about something altogether different—a recent fight with a friend, a high-paying job advertised in the newspaper, or your growling stomach. What have you learned and remembered from the textbook? Absolutely nothing. Even though your eyes were focused on the words in your book, you weren't really paying attention to those words.

Unfortunately, students can attend to only a very small amount of information at any one time—i.e., attention has a *limited capacity*. For example, if one of your students is seated in front of two other students who are talking, as you are delivering a lesson, this student will be able to attend to—and therefore learn from—only one of those conversations; this phenomenon is sometimes called the *cocktail party phenomenon* (Cherry, 1953; Norman, 1969).

Exactly *how* limited is the limited capacity of human attention? People can often perform two or three well-learned, automatic tasks at once; for example, we can walk and chew gum simultaneously. But when a stimulus or event is detailed and complex (as is true for listening

Attention The focusing of mental processes on particular environmental stimuli.

---

[1]Some models of memory also include a *central executive*, which oversees the flow of information throughout the memory system. However, theorists have yet to pin down its exact nature, and its functions seem to overlap with those of working memory (Kimberg, D'Esposito, & Farah, 1997). For simplicity, we have left a central executive out of the model presented here.

to the teacher and the conversation of the students in front) or when a task requires considerable thought (understanding a lecture and driving a car on an icy mountain road are examples of tasks requiring one's utmost concentration), then people can usually attend to only *one* thing at a time (J. R. Anderson, 1990; Reisberg, 1997).

Because of the limited capacity of human attention, only a very small amount of information stored in one's sensory register ever moves on to working memory. The vast majority of information that the body initially receives is quickly lost from the memory system.

Attention in the Classroom

Obviously, it is critical that students pay attention in order to learn. To some extent, you can tell which students are paying attention by their overt behaviours (Grabe, 1986; Piontkowski & Calfee, 1979). But appearances can be deceiving. For example, you can probably think of times when, as a student, you looked at a teacher without really hearing anything the teacher said. You can probably also think of times when you looked at a textbook without a single word on the page sinking in. Attention is not just a behaviour, it is also a mental process. It is not enough that students' eyes and ears are directed toward their classroom material. Their minds must be directed toward it as well.

How can you be sure that your students are really paying attention? First, you can ask questions that test students' understanding of the ideas you are presenting; students are more likely to keep their minds on instruction or on an assignment if they know that they will be immediately tested on it (Carney & Levin, 1998; Grabe, 1986; Piontkowski & Calfee, 1979). Second, you can ask students to put new information to use—for example, by having them draw an inference or solve a problem using it. Third, encourage older students to take notes; note taking usually helps students learn information, partly because it makes them pay attention to what they are hearing or reading (Di Vesta & Gray, 1972; Kiewra, 1989). Furthermore, having students **reconstruct** and elaborate notes after class, and especially doing this with partners, further enhances learning quality beyond what is written down in class (Kiewra, 2002). Fourth, in a technique developed at McGill University, have students make up questions about the class content or readings to test one another in pairs and evaluate one anothers' answers compared to what they thought should be the best answer—this is an application of the "learning cell," one of many useful forms of dyadic learning in which the teacher and students share roles of constructing new knowledge (see Schermerhorn, Goldschmid, & Shore, 1975, and Tabach, Hershkowitz, & Schwartz, 2006).

Reconstruction (as a complement to note taking) Creating notes from classes or other events in one's own words without consulting original notes and then revising them or comparing them with others' notes for an enhanced learning experience.

Every classroom has students who have difficulty keeping their minds on school subject matter. Such students more likely focus when they are seated near their teacher (Pfiffner & Barkley, 1998; Schwebel & Cherlin, 1972). You can also help by providing a stimulating classroom environment in which everyone *wants* to pay attention. Students are more likely to be attentive when they find exciting new things to learn every day, when you use a variety of methods to present classroom material, and when you are lively and enthusiastic about a topic.

Of course, students cannot keep their minds on any particular topic forever. They need occasional breaks from intensive mental activity (Pellegrini & Bjorklund, 1997). Some breaks are built into the daily school schedule—recess is an example. You may also want to give students additional mental breathers as well—perhaps by asking them to perform a physical task related to the topic at hand or perhaps, after an intensive work session, by giving them a chance to take a one-minute stretch.

The discussion of motivation in Chapter 9 offers additional ideas for capturing and keeping students' attention.

The Nature of Working (Short-Term) Memory

Working memory, sometimes known as short-term memory, is the component of memory where new information stays while it is mentally processed; you might think of it as a temporary holding bin for new information. Working memory is also where much of thinking, or cognitive processing, occurs. It is where students try to make sense of instruction, understand a passage they have read, or solve a problem. Working memory probably has several components for different kinds of information—for example, for visual versus auditory information (e.g., Baddeley, 1986; E. E. Smith, 2000)—but descriptions of them are beyond the scope of this discussion.

Working memory A component of memory that holds and processes a limited amount of information; also known as *short-term memory*. The duration of information stored in working memory is probably about 5 to 20 seconds.

Generally speaking, working memory is the component that probably does most of the work of the memory system. It has two characteristics that are particularly worth noting: a short duration and a limited capacity.

Short Duration

Imagine that you need to call a friend, so you look up the friend's telephone number in the phone book. Once you have the number in your head, you discover that someone else is using the phone. You have no paper and pencil handy. What do you do to remember the number until the phone is available?

Because you've paid attention to the number, it is presumably in your working memory. But working memory, as its alternative name "short-term memory" implies, is *short*. Unless you do something further with the telephone number, it will probably last only 5 to 20 seconds at the most (e.g., L. R. Peterson & Peterson, 1959). To keep it in your head until the phone is available, you might simply repeat it to yourself over and over again. This process, known as **maintenance rehearsal**, keeps information in working memory for as long as you're willing to continue talking to yourself. But once you stop, the number quickly disappears (e.g., Landauer, 1962; Sperling, 1967).

We sometimes hear students talking about putting class material in "short-term memory" so that they can do well on an upcoming exam. Such a statement reflects the misconception that this component of memory lasts for several days, weeks, or even months. No: Information stored in working memory lasts less than half a minute unless it is processed further. Working memory is *not* the "place" to leave information that you need for an exam later in the week, or even for information that you'll need for a class later in the day.

Mainteance rehearsal Repeating information to oneself to retain it in working memory.

Do you see why this process is called *maintenance* rehearsal?

Did you have this misconception about short-term memory before you read this section?

Limited Capacity

Let's put your working memory to work for a moment.

EXPERIENCING FIRSTHAND *A Divisive Situation*

Try computing the answer to this division problem in your head:

$$59\overline{)49\,383}$$

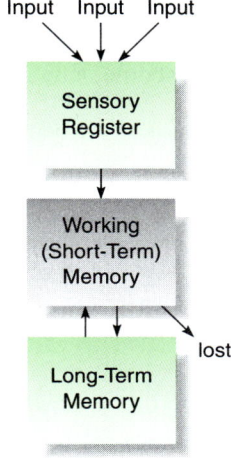

Did you find yourself having trouble remembering some parts of the problem while you were dealing with other parts? Did you ever arrive at the correct answer of 837? Most people cannot solve a division problem with this many digits unless they can write the problem on paper. The fact is, working memory just doesn't have room to hold all that information at once—it has a *limited capacity* (G. A. Miller, 1956; Simon, 1974).

Students have limited space in their working memories, so they learn only so much so fast. Keep this in mind as you plan lessons and activities. Many new teachers present too much information too quickly, and their students' working memories simply can't keep up. New information should be presented in ways that students have time to process it all. Slow the pace, repeat the same idea several times (perhaps rewording it each time), write important points on the chalkboard, and provide numerous examples and illustrations to your students.

Even when the pace of instruction is appropriate, students can probably never learn *everything* presented to them in class or a textbook. Most teachers and textbooks present much more information than students can store (Calfee, 1981). For example, one psychologist (E. D. Gagné, 1985) estimated that students likely learn only about one to six new ideas from each minute of a lecture—a small fraction of the ideas typically presented during that time! Although they must continually make choices about what to learn and what *not* to learn, students aren't always the best judges of what is important (Garner, Alexander, Gillingham, Kulikowich, & Brown, 1991; Mayer, 1984; R. E. Reynolds & Shirey, 1988). You can help your students make the right choices if you tell them what information is most important, give them guidelines on how and what to study, and omit unnecessary details from your lessons.

Ultimately, we hope that the information that students are learning stays with them and in turn is useful and meaningful in their future learning endeavours. How new information is connected with students' prior knowledge and is also retained for future use will now be considered.

Moving Information to Long-Term Memory: Connecting New Information with Prior Knowledge

In the memory model depicted in Figure 6.2 (see page 135), you will notice that the arrows between working memory and long-term memory go in both directions. The process of storing

"Mr. Osborne, may I be excused? My brain is full."

Working memory is a bottleneck in the human memory system, in that it has a very limited capacity. In contrast, long-term memory probably has as much room as we would ever need.

The Far Side® by Gary Larson © 1986 FarWorks, Inc. All Rights Reserved. Used with permission.

Long-term memory The component of memory that holds knowledge and skills for a relatively long period of time.

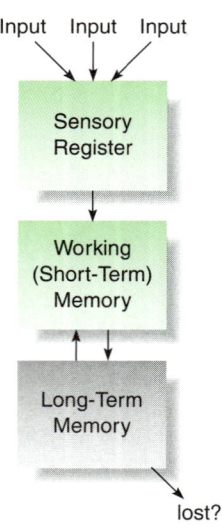

new information in long-term memory usually involves drawing on "old" information already stored there; in other words, it necessitates using prior knowledge. Here are two examples:

Paul discovers that the initial letters of each of the five Great Lakes—Huron, Ontario, Michigan, Erie, and Superior—spell the word *HOMES*.

Like many young children, Jessie believes that the world is flat. When her teacher tells her that the world is round, Jessie pictures a flat, circular disk (which is, of course, round *and* flat).

Each student is connecting new information with something he or she already knows or believes. Paul connects the five Great Lakes with a familiar word. Jessie relates the idea that the world is round to her previous conception of a flat world and to the many flat, circular objects (e.g., coins, pizzas) with which she has had experience.

Before we look more closely at the processes through which information is stored in long-term memory, let's examine the characteristics of long-term memory and the nature of the "old" information stored within it.

The Nature of Long-Term Memory

Long-term memory is the final component of the human memory system. This component holds information for a relatively long time—perhaps a day, a week, a month, a year, or one's entire lifetime. Long-term memory has three characteristics especially worth noting: a long duration, an essentially unlimited capacity, and a rich network of interconnections.

(Indefinitely) Long Duration

Information stored in long-term memory lasts much longer than information in working memory. But exactly *how* long is long-term memory? Some psychologists believe that information may slowly "weaken" and possibly disappear from long-term memory, especially if it is not used regularly (J. R. Anderson, 1990; Reisberg, 1997; D. L. Schacter, 1999). Others believe instead that once information is stored in long-term memory, it remains there permanently but some information may be extremely difficult to retrieve (Loftus & Loftus, 1980). The exact duration of long-term memory has not been determined and perhaps never can be (Eysenck & Keane, 1990).

Unlimited Capacity

Long-term memory seems to be capable of holding as much information as a learner needs to store there—there is probably no such thing as "running out of room." In fact, for reasons you will discover shortly, the more information already stored in long-term memory, the easier it is to learn new things.

Interconnectedness

Theorists have discovered that the information stored in long-term memory is organized and interconnected to some extent. For example, try the following exercise.

EXPERIENCING FIRSTHAND *Horse #1*

What is the first word that comes to your mind when you hear the word *horse*? And what word does that second word remind you of? And what does that third word remind you of? Beginning with the word *horse,* follow your train of thought, letting each word remind you of another one, for a sequence of at least eight words. Write down your sequence of words as each word comes to mind.

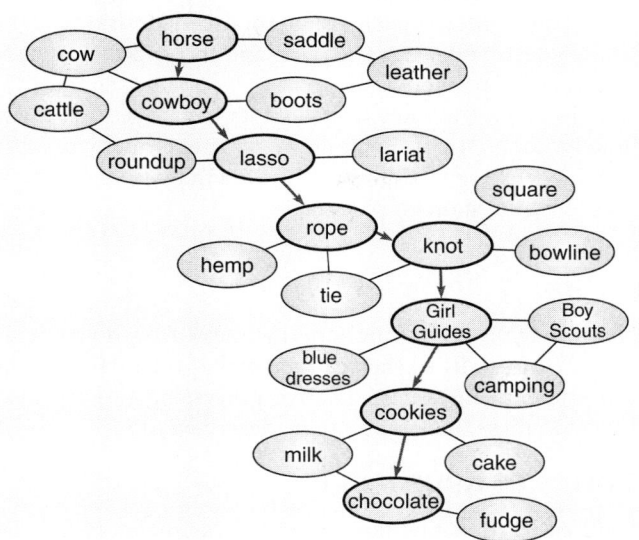

FIGURE 6.3
Interconnectedness in long-term memory

Long-term memory is organized, such that related pieces of information are often associated with one another. Here we can follow the author's train of thought from "horse" to "chocolate."

You probably found yourself easily following a train of thought from the word *horse*, perhaps something like this:

horse → Calgary Stampede → summer → road trip → friends → camping → tent → rain

The last word in your sequence might be one with little or no obvious relationship to horses. Yet *you* can probably see a logical connection between each pair of words in the sequence. Cognitive psychologists believe that related pieces of information in long-term memory are often connected with one another, perhaps in a network similar to the one depicted in Figure 6.3.

This is a type of concept map (see Chapter 7). In addition to generating and linking the ideas or concepts, it is also important that students explain what the links mean. Creating stronger and more descriptive associations will produce a higher **quality of concept links**. Research by graduate students working with Canadian educational psychologist Bruce Shore has shown that concept mapping enhances meaningful learning and the ability to transfer this learning to original situations with complex problems (Austin & Shore, 1995).

Critiquing the Three-Component Model

In the last few pages we have considered the sensory register, working memory, and long-term memory. But are there really three separate components of human memory, and are they as distinctly different from one another as described? Not all cognitive psychologists agree that the three-component model is an accurate representation of how human memory works, and research yields mixed results as to whether the different components of memory can be neatly distinguished (Cowan, 1995; Crowder, 1993; Eysenck & Keane, 1990).

Some psychologists such as J. R. Anderson (1995), Cowan (1995), and Canadian researcher Alan Paivio and his colleagues (e.g., Sadoski & Paivio, 2001) proposed that working and long-term memory are not separate components but instead simply reflect different **activation** states of a single memory. Based on this view, all information stored in memory is in either an active or inactive state. Active information is what students are paying attention to and processing—the information that is in working memory, as previously described. Other information in memory becomes activated as attention shifts, and previously activated information gradually becomes inactive. Most information stored in memory is in an inactive state, so that we are not consciously aware of it—this is the information that is in long-term memory.

The three-component model, though not perfect, is similar to how many cognitive psychologists conceptualize human memory. This model also emphasizes aspects of memory

Can you summarize the model of memory described in the last few pages?

Quality of concept links In a concept map, pairs of concepts can be more or less strongly linked, and the description of the link can be more or less complete and detailed. When creating a concept map, the quality of the links is at least as important as having well-chosen or well-understood concepts.

Activation The degree to which a particular piece of information in memory is currently being attended to and mentally processed.

that are important for us to keep in mind as we teach. For example, it highlights the importance of *attention* in learning, the *limited capacity* of attention and working memory, the *interconnectedness* of the knowledge that learners acquire, and the importance of *relating* new information with things learned on previous occasions.

Regardless of whether there are three truly distinct components of memory, some aspects of memory are definitely "long-term." Certainly we remember many things for a considerable length of time, and in this sense, at least, these things are in long-term memory. Let's look more closely at the nature of long-term memory storage.

Long-Term Memory Storage

What forms does "knowledge" take in long-term memory? How do students think about and process new information and skills so they can remember them later? What can you do as a teacher to help your students engage in effective processing to keep information in long-term memory? Answers to these questions will be described next.

The Various Forms of Knowledge

Information is probably encoded in long-term memory in a number of different forms (e.g., J. R. Anderson, 1995; E. D. Gagné, 1985; Sadoski & Paivio, 2001). For example, some information is stored in a *verbal* form, perhaps as actual words. Things that students remember word for word—for example, their name, their address—are all verbally encoded. Other information is encoded in the form of *imagery,* or how that information appears perceptually. For example, if, in your mind, you can "see" the face of a relative or "hear" that person's voice, then you are retrieving images. Finally, a great deal of information in long-term memory is encoded *semantically,* as underlying meanings. For example, when you listen to a lecture or read a textbook, you probably store the gist of the message more frequently than you store the words themselves. All of these examples are instances of **declarative knowledge**—knowledge that declares *how things are.*

Students also acquire **procedural knowledge**; in other words, they learn *how to do things* (e.g., J. R. Anderson, 1983; Phye, 1997; Tulving, 1983). To perform such actions successfully, students must adapt their behaviour to changing conditions; for example, in learning to ride a bicycle, they must be able to turn left or right when an object blocks their path, and they must be able to come to a complete stop at their destination. Accordingly, procedural knowledge must include information about how to respond under different circumstances.

Information encoded in multiple ways is more easily retrieved from long-term memory than information encoded just one way. For example, students more readily learn and remember information that they receive in both a verbal form (e.g., a lecture or textbook passage) and a graphic form (e.g., a picture, map, or diagram) (Kulhavy, Lee, & Caterino, 1985; Sadoski & Paivio, 2001; Winn, 1991). Thus, presenting information to students in multiple modalities, or asking them to represent it in at least two different ways (e.g., see Figure 6.4), increases the likelihood that they will be able to remember it over the long run.

Declarative knowledge
Knowledge related to "what is," to the nature of how things are, were, or will be (as opposed to *procedural knowledge,* which relates to how to do something).

Procedural knowledge
Knowledge concerning how to do something (as opposed to *declarative knowledge,* which relates to how things are).

FIGURE 6.4 Students learn and remember information more effectively if they encode it in a variety of ways. Here, 9-year-old Nicholas records his findings from a Grade 3 science experiment in both words and a picture. Nick has difficulties with written language skills that qualify him for special educational services. Notice how he misspells many words and writes up from the bottom of the page. (Translation: "We poured so many cubes [that] the cup overflowed. The blocks took up all the room.")

How Declarative Knowledge Is Learned

The specific cognitive processes that students use when trying to learn new information affect their ability to remember and use that information later. In the next few pages, we will consider five processes (summarized in Table 6.2) that people use in storing declarative information in long-term memory: rehearsal, meaningful learning, organization, elaboration, and visual imagery.

Rehearsal

Earlier we described how maintenance rehearsal—repeating something over and over again verbally—helps keep information in working memory indefinitely. Early theorists (e.g., R. C. Atkinson & Shiffrin, 1968) believed that **rehearsal** is also a means through which information is stored in long-term memory. In other words, if we repeat something often enough, it might eventually sink in.

The main disadvantage of rehearsal is that we make few, if any, connections between new information and the knowledge already in our long-term memory. Thus, we are engaging in **rote learning**: learning information verbatim, without attaching any meaning to it. Contrary to what many students think, rote (meaningless) learning is a slow and relatively ineffective way of storing information in long-term memory (J. R. Anderson, 1995; Ausubel, 1968; Craik & Watkins, 1973). Information stored by rote learning is more difficult to retrieve later.

If you have already read the discussion of cognitive development in Chapter 2, then you may remember that rehearsal is one of the first strategies that students develop (usually in the early elementary school years). Verbally rehearsing information is probably better than not processing it at all, and in cases where students have little, if any, prior knowledge to draw on to help them understand new material, rehearsal may be one of the few strategies that they can use

> **Rehearsal** A cognitive process in which information is repeated over and over as a possible way of learning and remembering it. When it is used to maintain information in working memory, it is called *maintenance rehearsal*.
>
> **Rote learning** Learning information primarily through verbatim repetition, without attaching any meaning to it.

TABLE 6.2   COMPARE/CONTRAST

Five Possible Ways of Learning Declarative Knowledge

PROCESS	DEFINITION	EXAMPLE	EFFECTIVENESS	EDUCATIONAL IMPLICATION
Rehearsal	Repeating information verbatim, either mentally or aloud	Repeating a word-for-word definition of *inertia*	Relatively ineffective: Storage is slow, and later retrieval is difficult	Suggest that students use rehearsal as a last resort only.
Meaningful learning	Making connections between new information and prior knowledge	Putting a definition of *inertia* into one's own words or identifying examples of inertia in one's own life experiences	Effective if associations made with prior knowledge are appropriate ones	Help students connect new information to things they already know.
Organization	Making connections among various pieces of new information	Studying how one's lines in a play relate to the play's overall story line	Effective if organizational structure is legitimate and if it consists of more than just a "list" of separate facts	Present material in an organized way, and point out the organizational structure and interrelationships in the material.
Elaboration	Adding additional ideas to new information based on what one already knows	Thinking about possible reasons why historical figures behaved as they did	Effective if the ideas added are appropriate inferences	Encourage students to go beyond the information itself—for example, to draw inferences and speculate about possible implications.
Visual imagery	Forming a mental picture of information	Imagining how various characters and events in *Ivanhoe* might have looked	Individual differences in effectiveness; especially beneficial when used to supplement meaningful learning, organization, or elaboration	Illustrate verbal instruction with visual materials (e.g., pictures, maps, diagrams).

(E. Wood, Willoughby, Reilley, Elliott, & DuCharme, 1994). But regardless of your students' age or experience, you should encourage them to use other, more effective methods—meaningful learning, organization, elaboration, and visual imagery—whenever possible.

Meaningful Learning

Meaningful learning A cognitive process in which learners relate new information to the things they already know.

The process of **meaningful learning** involves recognizing a relationship between new information and something else already stored in long-term memory. When we use words like *comprehension* or *understanding,* we are talking about meaningful learning.

Research clearly indicates that meaningful learning is more effective than rote learning (Ausubel, Novak, & Hanesian, 1978; Bransford & Johnson, 1972; Mayer, 1996). As illustrations of the effectiveness of meaningful learning, try the following two exercises.

EXPERIENCING FIRSTHAND *Two Letter Strings, Two Pictures*

1. Study each of the following strings of letters until you can remember them perfectly:

    AIIRODFMLAWRS   FAMILIARWORDS

2. Study each of the two pictures below until you can reproduce them accurately from memory.

Figures are from "Comprehension and Memory for Pictures" by G. H. Bower, M. B. Karlin, and A. Dueck, 1975, *Memory and Cognition, 3*, p. 217. Reprinted by permission of Psychonomic Society, Inc.

No doubt the second letter string was easier for you to learn because you could relate it to something you already knew: "familiar words." How easily were you able to learn the two pictures? Do you think that you could draw them from memory a week from now? Do you think that you would be able to remember them more easily if they had meaningful titles such as "a child playing a trombone in a telephone booth" and "an early bird who caught a very strong worm"? The answer to the latter question is a definite yes (Bower et al., 1975).

Some students approach school assignments with meaningful learning in mind: They turn to what they already know to try to make sense of new information. These students are likely to be the high achievers in the classroom. Other students instead use rote learning strategies, such as repeating something over and over to themselves without really thinking about what they are saying. As you might guess, these students learn less successfully (Britton, Stimson, Stennett, & Gülgöz, 1998; Novak, 1998; Van Rossum & Schenk, 1984).

Why do some students learn meaningfully, whereas others persist in rote memorization? At least three conditions probably facilitate meaningful learning (Ausubel et al., 1978):

■ *The student has a meaningful learning set.* When students approach a learning task believing that they can make sense of the information—that is, when they have a **meaningful learning set**—they are more likely to learn that information meaningfully.

Meaningful learning set An attitude that one can make sense of the information one is studying.

If meaningful learning relies on relevant prior knowledge, what are the implications for teaching students from diverse cultural backgrounds?

How we present a task affects the likelihood students will adopt a meaningful learning set (Ausubel et al., 1978). We must communicate confidence that students *can* and *should* make sense of the things they study. We can ask students to define new vocabulary or give examples of certain concepts by putting definitions in their own words, or by generating new concept examples rather than repeating textbook or teacher-generated definitions and descriptions.

Meaningful learning is especially effective when people relate new ideas not only to the things they already know but also to *themselves* (e.g., T. B. Rogers, Kuiper, & Kirker, 1977). Here, 6-year-old Nadia thinks about the four seasons in terms of what she does during each one.

■ *The student has previous knowledge to which the new information can be related.* Meaningful learning can occur only when long-term memory contains a relevant **knowledge base**, information to which a new idea can be connected. The more information a student has already stored in long-term memory, the easier it is for that student to learn new information, because there are more things with which that new information can be associated. For example, a student who saw the dinosaur skeletons at Drumheller, Alberta, last summer, or in a natural history museum, will better understand how large the dinosaurs really were.

Knowledge base One's knowledge about specific topics and the world in general.

Calvin and Hobbes   by Bill Watterson

Calvin is trying to learn new information meaningfully, but his efforts are in vain because the word *feudal* is not in his knowledge base.

Calvin and Hobbes © Watterson. Reprinted with permission of Universal Press Syndicate. All rights reserved.

■ *The student is aware that previously learned information is related to new information.* Students often don't make the connection between new and prior information; as a result, they resort to rote learning strategies unnecessarily. Oftentimes we can promote meaningful learning by reminding students of things they know that bear directly on a topic of classroom study (Machiels-Bongaerts, Schmidt, & Boshuizen, 1991; L. B. Resnick, 1989; Spires & Donley, 1998). For example, we can tie science to students' day-to-day observations and experiences.

The two storage processes discussed next—organization and elaboration—also involve relating new information to prior knowledge; hence, both of these processes incorporate meaningful learning but each one includes an additional twist.

Organization

We learn and remember a body of new information more easily when we organize it in some way (e.g., Bjorklund et al., 1994; Mandler & Pearlstone, 1966; Tulving, 1962). Such **organization** invariably involves making connections among various pieces of new information; it often involves making connections with existing knowledge as well.

Learners are more likely to organize information if the material fits an organizational structure with which they are already familiar—for example, if the material can be placed into discrete categories or into a hierarchical arrangement (Bousfield, 1953; Bransford & Franks, 1971; DuBois, Kiewra, & Fraley, 1988; Gauntt, 1991). They are also more likely to organize new material if it has been presented to them with its organizational structure laid out. As an illustration, let's consider the results of a classic experiment (Bower, Clark, Lesgold, & Winzenz, 1969).

Organization A cognitive process in which learners find connections (e.g., by forming categories, identifying hierarchies, determining cause–effect relationships) among the various pieces of information they need to learn.

FIGURE 6.5 We remember information more easily when it is organized in some way.

Figure from "Hierarchical Retrieval Schemes in Recall of Categorized Word Lists" by G. H. Bower, M. C. Clark, A. M. Lesgold, and D. Winzenz in *Journal of Verbal Learning and Verbal Behaviour, 8,* 323–343, copyright 1969, Elsevier Science (USA), reproduced by permission of the publisher.

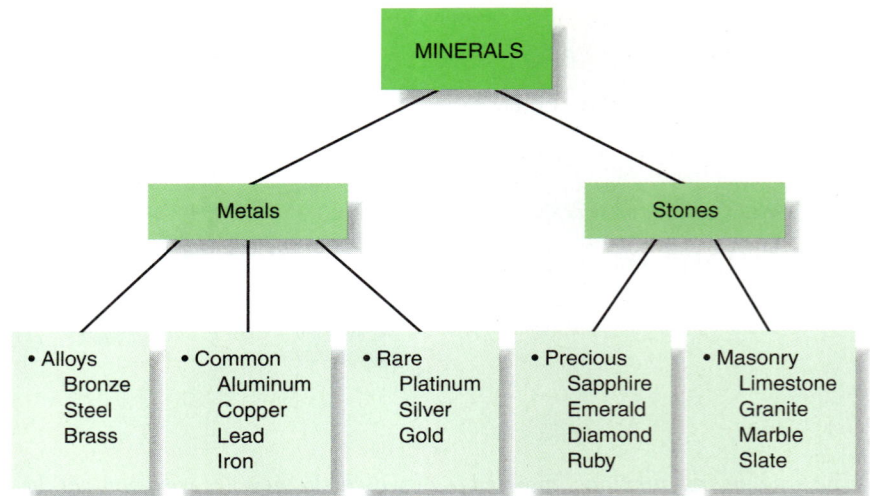

University students were given four study trials in which to learn 112 words falling into four categories (e.g., minerals, plants). For some students, the words were arranged in an organized fashion (Figure 6.5 is an example). For other students, the words were arranged randomly. Look at the average number of words that each group remembered after one study period (about four minutes) and again after three additional study periods:

Number of Study Periods	Organized Words	Unorganized Words
1	73 (65%)	21 (19%)
4	112 (100%)	70 (63%)

Notice that, after studying the words one time, students with organized words remembered more than three times as many words as students who received them in mixed-up order. After four study periods, students with the organized words remembered the entire list of 112!

Unfortunately, many students tend to "organize" the things they study merely as a list of separate facts, rather than as a set of interrelated ideas (Kletzien, 1988; B. J. F. Meyer, Brandt, & Bluth, 1980). Research at McGill University has demonstrated that able learners will more likely organize a group of problems in terms of "deep" important similarities such as similar underlying meaning, rather than "surface" qualities such as wording, length, or format. When reminded to group ideas, students at all levels were able to sort the problems into meaningful groups and subgroups to some degree, even before they tried to solve the problems (Pelletier & Shore, 2003). As students learn more about a topic, they not only discover new categories, but also better recognize the unique features of each category, which reduces confusion and interference (discussed later in this chapter) when storing information (Clapper, 2007). Thus, you should initially organize new material in a logical way for your students before you present it. You can then draw students' attention to this organizational structure. For example, you might point out the categories in which facts can be grouped, the hierarchical nature of concepts, or the important interrelationships (e.g., cause-and-effect) among various ideas. You can also present related pieces of information close together in time; students are more likely to associate related ideas when they encounter those ideas together (Glanzer & Nolan, 1986; Hayes-Roth & Thorndyke, 1979). Also let them try alternative ways to organize the material and to explain to each other the ways in which the categories group ideas and how they differ.

Additional strategies are *concept mapping* (Chapter 7) and *advance organizers* (Chapter 10).

Elaboration

Elaboration A cognitive process in which learners expand on new information based on what they already know.

The process of adding to newly acquired information in some way is called **elaboration**. In most cases, the more students elaborate on new material—the more they use what they already know to help them understand and interpret the material—the more effectively they will store it in long-term memory (J. R. Anderson, 1995). Students who elaborate on the things they learn in school are usually better students than those who simply take information at face value (McDaniel & Einstein, 1989; Pressley, 1982; Waters, 1982). For example:

> Maria learns that an allosaur had powerful jaws and sharp, pointed teeth. "Allosaurs must have been meat eaters," she deduces.
>
> Marcus gets a note from a friend who writes, "Meat me by the bak door after skool." Marcus translates his friend's message as, "Meet me by the back door after school."

As a teacher, you will often want your students to go beyond the information actually presented to them. You can help them to elaborate in numerous ways. For example, you can ask frequent questions along these lines:

- Why do you think this happens?
- Can you think of some examples of this concept?
- How could we use this idea in our everyday lives?
- What things can you conclude from this information?

You can also encourage students to talk about a topic among themselves, ask them to explain an idea on paper, or simply give them time to think about new information.

Visual Imagery

Numerous research studies indicate that **visual imagery**—forming mental pictures of objects or ideas—can be a particularly effective method of storing information (Dewhurst & Conway, 1994; Johnson-Glenberg, 2000; Sadoski, Goetz, & Fritz, 1993; Sadoski & Paivio, 2001). To show you how effective visual imagery can be, let us teach you a few of the Mandarin Chinese words the first author studied in high school.

Visual imagery The process of forming mental pictures of objects or ideas.

EXPERIENCING FIRSTHAND   *Five Chinese Words*

Try learning these five Chinese words by forming the visual images described (don't worry about learning the marks over the words):

Chinese Word	English Meaning	Image
fáng	house	Picture a *house* with *fangs* growing on its roof and walls.
mén	door	Picture a rest room *door* with the word *MEN* painted on it.
ké	guest	Picture someone giving someone else (the *guest*) a *key* to the house.
fàn	food	Picture a plate of *food* being cooled by a *fan*.
shū	book	Picture a *shoe* with a *book* sticking out of it.

At this point, find something else to do for a couple of minutes. Stand up and stretch, get a glass of water, or use the bathroom. But be sure to come back to your reading in just a minute or two. . . .

Now that you're back, cover the list of Chinese words, English meanings, and visual images. Try to remember what each word means:

ké   fàn   mén   fáng   shū

Did the Chinese words remind you of the visual images that you stored? Did the images help you remember the English meanings of the Chinese words?

You may have remembered all five words easily, or you may have remembered only one or two. People differ in their ability to use visual imagery: Some form visual images quickly and easily, whereas others form them only slowly and with difficulty (Behrmann, 2000; J. M. Clark & Paivio, 1991; Kosslyn, 1985). For those in the former category, imagery can be a powerful means of storing information in long-term memory.

As a teacher, you can promote the use of visual imagery in several ways. You can ask students to imagine how certain events in literature or history might have looked (Sadoski & Paivio,

INTO THE CLASSROOM   *Helping Students Learn New Information*

Let students know what information is most important to learn.

> When a history teacher prepares his students for an upcoming exam on World War I, he reminds them, "When you study for the test, you should try to understand how the specific events that we discussed contributed to the progress and eventual outcome of the war. Know when each event occurred in relation to other events, but don't try to learn each and every date."

Present the same ideas in more than one form.

> A biology teacher shows her class a diagram of the human heart. She traces the flow of blood with her finger as she describes how the heart pumps blood through the body.

Communicate the belief that students can and should make sense of the things they study.

> Students in a high school first-aid class have learned that when people suffer from traumatic shock, many normal bodily functions are depressed because insufficient blood is circulating through the body. The teacher asks, "Given what you have learned about traumatic shock, why do experts recommend that if we find a person in shock, we have them lie down and keep them warm but not hot?"

Show students how new material relates to things they already know.

> When describing the law of gravity, a teacher asks, "What happens when you let go of something? Which way does it fall? Have you ever seen anything fall *up*?"

Present information in an organized fashion.

> A teacher groups new spelling words by letter pattern. For example, she gives students a list of *uff* words (e.g., *buff, muff, stuff*) and *ough* words (e.g., *rough, tough, enough*).

Encourage students to elaborate on class material.

> A social studies teacher describes a general principle of geography: New settlements often spring up at the junctions of two or more major transportation routes. She then asks her class, "Why do you think that might be so?"

Encourage students to form visual images that capture the things they are studying.

> An elementary teacher is reading a short story to his class. After reading a description of the story's main character, he stops and asks his class to imagine the person just as the author has described her—a woman with tousled grey hair, twinkling brown eyes, and a warm, welcoming smile.

Begin at a level consistent with students' existing knowledge base.

> At the beginning of the school year, a mathematics teacher gives her students a pretest covering the mathematical concepts and operations they studied the year before. She finds that many students still have difficulty computing the perimeter and area of a rectangle. She reviews these procedures and gives students additional practice with them before beginning a unit on computing the volume of objects with rectangular sides.

Have students work in pairs organizing ideas, generating questions, and reconstructing notes.

> A high school teacher introduces students to a new unit about angles and triangles. Before assigning problems for practice in class or at home, the teacher asks the students to work in pairs grouping the problems according to similarities they identify, to ask questions of each other about why they are grouped as they are, and to make shared notes about the important points to remember when trying to solve these kinds of geometry problems.

2001). You can provide visual materials (pictures, charts, graphs, etc.) that illustrate important, but possibly abstract, ideas (R. K. Atkinson et al., 1999; Verdi, Kulhavy, Stock, Rittschof, & Johnson, 1996). And you can ask students to draw their *own* illustrations or diagrams of the things they are learning (Edens & Potter, 2001; Van Meter, 2001).

How Procedural Knowledge Is Learned

Some of the procedures that people learn—for example, driving a stick shift, baking a cake, and serving a volleyball—consist primarily of overt behaviours. Many others—for instance, solving for *x* in an algebraic equation, making sense of difficult reading material, and surfing the internet—are largely mental in nature. Most procedures obviously involve a combination of physical behaviours and mental activities. Procedural knowledge ranges from relatively simple actions (e.g., holding a pencil correctly or using scissors) to far more complex ones. Complex procedures are usually learned slowly over time, often only with a great deal of practice (J. R. Anderson, 1983; Ericsson & Chalmers, 1994; Proctor & Dutta, 1995).

To some extent, of course, learners store procedures as actual behaviours. Yet many procedures, particularly complex ones, may begin largely as declarative knowledge—in other

> **INTO THE CLASSROOM** *Helping Students Acquire New Procedures*
>
> Help students understand the logic behind the procedures they are learning.
>
> > As a teacher demonstrates the correct way to swing a tennis racket, she asks her students, "Why is it important to have your feet apart rather than together? Why is it important to hold your arm straight as you swing?"
>
> When skills are especially complex, break them into simpler tasks that students can practise one at a time.
>
> > Knowing how overwhelming the task of driving a car can initially be, a driver-education teacher begins behind-the-wheel instruction by having students practise steering and braking in an empty school parking lot. Only later, after students have mastered these skills, does he have them drive in traffic on city streets.
>
> Provide mnemonics that can help students remember a sequence of steps.
>
> > In a unit on basketball, a teacher coaches her students on an effective approach to making a free throw. "Just remember BEEF," she says. "*B*alance the ball, put your *e*lbows in, *e*levate your arms, and *f*ollow through."
>
> Give students many opportunities to practise new skills, and provide the feedback they need to help them improve.
>
> > A science teacher asks his students to write lab reports after each week's lab activity. Many of his students have had little or no previous experience in scientific writing, so when he grades the reports, he writes numerous comments as well. Some comments describe the strengths that he sees, and others provide suggestions for making the reports more objective, precise, or clear.

words, as *information* about how to execute a procedure rather than as the actual *ability* to execute it (J. R. Anderson, 1983, 1987). When learners use declarative knowledge to guide them as they carry out a new procedure, their performance is slow and laborious, the activity consumes a great deal of mental effort, and they often talk themselves through their actions. As they continue to perform the activity, however, their declarative knowledge gradually evolves into procedural knowledge. This knowledge becomes fine-tuned over time and eventually allows learners to perform an activity quickly, efficiently, and effortlessly (J. R. Anderson, 1983, 1987).

Theorists have suggested several teaching strategies that seem to help students learn and remember procedures more effectively. For instance, we can demonstrate a procedure or show pictures of its specific steps (R. M. Gagné, 1985). We can verbalize our thoughts, thereby demonstrating *mental* procedures, as we engage in a complex task (Schunk, 1981). We can encourage students to use verbal rehearsal as they learn a new skill—in other words, to repeat the required steps over and over to themselves (Weiss & Klint, 1987). And, as you might guess, our students will be more likely to remember a procedure when we give them a chance to carry it out themselves and when we provide regular feedback about how they are doing (R. L. Cohen, 1989; Heindel & Kose, 1990; Proctor & Dutta, 1995). When procedures are fairly complicated, we may want to break them down into smaller tasks and have students practise each one separately at first (J. R. Anderson, Reder, & Simon, 1996). Chapter 7 describes additional strategies for facilitating the acquisition of procedural knowledge within the context of such complex cognitive processes as metacognition and problem solving.

Which of these strategies remind you of Vygotsky's theory of cognitive development (described in Chapter 2)?

Prior Knowledge and Working Memory in Long-Term Memory Storage

In general, a relevant knowledge base helps students store classroom subject matter much more effectively (P. A. Alexander, Kulikowich, & Schulze, 1994; Hamman et al., 1995; Schneider, 1993). Students' prior knowledge contributes to their learning in several ways:

- It helps them determine what is most important to learn; thus, it helps them direct their *attention* appropriately.
- It enables them to understand something—that is, to engage in *meaningful learning*—instead of learning it by rote.

- It provides a framework for *organizing* new information.
- It helps them *elaborate* on information—for example, by filling in missing details, clarifying ambiguities, or drawing inferences. (Ausubel et al., 1978; Bjorklund, Muir-Broaddus, & Schneider, 1990; Carpenter & Just, 1986; Lindberg, 1991; Rumelhart & Ortony, 1977; West, Farmer, & Wolff, 1991; P. T. Wilson & Anderson, 1986)

Yet, as noted in our discussion of meaningful learning, it is not enough that students have the knowledge they need to interpret new material; they must also be *aware* that the knowledge is relevant. They must then retrieve it from long-term memory while thinking about the new material, so that they have both the "old" and "new" simultaneously in working memory and can make good connections (Bellezza, 1986; Glanzer & Nolan, 1986).

You will need to keep students' existing knowledge in mind and use it as a starting point whenever you introduce a new topic. For example, you might begin a Grade 1 unit on plants by asking students to describe what their parents do to keep flowers or vegetable gardens growing. Or, in a secondary English literature class, you might introduce Sir Walter Scott's *Ivanhoe* (in which Robin Hood is a major character) by asking students to tell the tale of Robin Hood as they know it. Remember that students from diverse cultural backgrounds are likely to have different knowledge bases and modify your starting points accordingly.

Using Mnemonics in the Absence of Relevant Prior Knowledge

Mnemonic A special memory aid or trick designed to help students learn and remember a specific piece of information.

When students are likely to have trouble finding relationships between new material and their prior knowledge, or when a body of information has an organizational structure with no apparent logic behind it (e.g., as for many lists), special memory aids known as **mnemonics** can help them learn new material more effectively. Three commonly used mnemonics are verbal mediation, the keyword method, and superimposed meaningful structures.

Verbal Mediation

Verbal mediator A word or phrase that forms a logical connection or "bridge" between two pieces of information; used as a *mnemonic.*

A **verbal mediator** is a word or phrase that creates a logical connection, or "bridge," between two pieces of information. Verbal mediators can be used for such paired pieces of information as foreign language words and their English meanings, countries and their capitals, chemical elements and their symbols, and words and their spellings. Following are some examples:

Information to Be Learned	Verbal Mediator
Handschuh is German for "glove."	A glove is a *shoe* for the *hand*.
Quito is the capital of Ecuador.	Mos*quitos* at the *equator*.
Au is the symbol for gold.	'*Ay, you* stole my gold watch!
The word *principal* ends in *pal* (not *ple*).	The principal is my *pal*.

Keyword Method

Keyword method A mnemonic technique in which an association is made between two ideas by forming a visual image of one or more concrete objects (keywords) that either sound similar to, or symbolically represent, those ideas.

Like verbal mediation, the **keyword method** aids memory by making a connection between two things. This technique is especially helpful when there is no logical verbal mediator to fill the gap—for example, when there is no obvious sentence or phrase to relate a foreign language word to its English meaning. The keyword method involves two steps, which we will illustrate using the French word *amour* and its English meaning *love*:

1. Identify a concrete object to represent each piece of information. The object may be either a commonly used symbol (e.g., a heart to symbolize *love*) or a sound-alike word (e.g., a suit of armour to represent *amour*). Such objects are keywords.

2. Form a picture in your mind of the two objects together. To remember that *amour* means *love*, you might picture a knight in a suit of armour with a huge red heart painted on his chest.

You used the keyword method when you did the "Five Chinese Words" exercise earlier.

Superimposed Meaningful Structure

A larger body of information (e.g., a list of items) can often be learned by superimposing a meaningful organization—a familiar shape, word, sentence, rhythm, poem, or story—on that information. Here are some examples of such **superimposed meaningful structures**:

Information to Be Learned	Superimposed Meaningful Structure
The shape of Italy	A "boot"
The shape of France	A "bearskin rug"
The Great Lakes (Huron, Ontario, Michigan, Erie, Superior)	HOMES
Lines on the treble clef (EGBDF)	Elvis's guitar broke down Friday, *or* every good boy does fine.
The distinction between stalagmites and stalactites	When the "mites" go up, the "tites" come down.
The number of days in each month	Thirty days has September . . .

Superimposed meaningful structure A familiar shape, word, sentence, poem, or story imposed on information to make it easier to recall; used as a *mnemonic*.

Research consistently supports the effectiveness of mnemonics in student learning (Bower & Clark, 1969; Bulgren, Schumaker, & Deshler, 1994; M. S. Jones, Levin, Levin, & Beitzel, 2000; Pressley, Levin, & Delaney, 1982; Scruggs & Mastropieri, 1989). In addition to helping students store information and procedures in long-term memory, mnemonics also appear to help students retrieve what they stored at an earlier time. We now turn to the topic of retrieval.

Long-Term Memory Retrieval

As noted earlier in the chapter, some information is easily retrieved from long-term memory. But it may take considerable time to "find" some other information you have stored there. For example, can you still remember what the Mandarin Chinese words *ké, fàn, mén, fáng,* and *shu* mean? Can you retrieve the visual images you stored to help remember these words?

The Nature of Long-Term Memory Retrieval

Retrieving information from long-term memory appears to be a process of following a "pathway" of associations. One idea reminds us of another idea, which reminds us of still another, and so on, just as we saw in the "Horse #1" exercise earlier in the chapter. Retrieval is successful only when we eventually stumble on the information we are looking for. We are most likely to do so if we have connected the desired information to something else—presumably something logically related to it—in long-term memory.

Factors Affecting Retrieval

Even when we connect new information to our existing knowledge, we can't always find it when needed. At least four factors promote ability to retrieve information from long-term memory:

- Making multiple connections with existing knowledge
- Learning information to mastery and beyond
- Using knowledge frequently
- Having a relevant retrieval cue

Making Multiple Connections with Existing Knowledge

We are more likely to retrieve information when we have many possible pathways to it—in other words, when we have associated the information with many other things in our existing knowledge base.

As a teacher, you can help students more effectively remember classroom content over the long run if you help them connect it to numerous pieces of information in their existing knowledge base. For example, show them and ask them to suggest how new material relates to

- Concepts and ideas within the same subject area (e.g., showing them how multiplication is related to addition)
- Concepts and ideas in other subject areas (e.g., talking about how scientific discoveries have affected historical events)
- Students' general knowledge of the world (e.g., drawing parallels between the "Black Death" of the fourteenth century and the modern-day AIDS epidemic)
- Students' personal experiences (e.g., finding similarities between the family feud in *Romeo and Juliet* and students' own interpersonal conflicts)
- Students' current activities and needs outside of the classroom (e.g., showing how persuasive writing skills might be used to craft a personal essay for a university application)

The more interrelationships your students actively form among pieces of information in long-term memory, the more easily they can retrieve those pieces later on.

Learning Things to Mastery and Beyond

Research tells us that students are far more likely to retrieve the material they have learned if they continue to study and practise it, ideally in a variety of contexts (Graham, Harris, & Fink, 2000; Semb & Ellis, 1994; Shepard, 2000; Underwood, 1954).

When students continue to practise information and skills they have already mastered, they eventually achieve **automaticity**: They can retrieve what they've learned quickly and effortlessly and can use it almost without thinking (J. R. Anderson, 1983; Cheng, 1985; Proctor & Dutta, 1995; Schneider & Shiffrin, 1977). As an example, think of a complicated skill—perhaps driving a car—that you can perform easily. Your first attempts at driving many years ago probably required a great deal of mental effort. But now you can drive without having to pay conscious attention to the position of your foot on the pedals or the orientation of the steering wheel—you execute these skills automatically.

Remember, working memory has a limited capacity. When much of its capacity must be used for retrieving single facts or executing simple procedures, little room is left for understanding more complex situations or dealing with more difficult tasks. One key reason for learning some facts and procedures to automaticity, then, is to free up enough working memory capacity for students to tackle the complex tasks that require those facts and procedures, as Keith Stanovich (2000) at the University of Toronto and others (e.g., Jones & Christensen, 1999; Proctor & Dutta, 1995; L. B. Resnick, 1989) have noted. For example, Grade 2 students reading a story can better focus their efforts on understanding it if they don't have to sound out words like *before* and *after*. Grade 4 students faced with the multiplication problem

$$\begin{array}{r} 87 \\ \times\ 59 \\ \hline \end{array}$$

can solve it more easily if they can quickly retrieve such basic facts as $9 \times 8 = 72$ and $5 \times 7 = 35$. High school chemistry students can more easily interpret Na_2CO_3 (sodium carbonate) if they don't have to stop to think about what the symbols *Na, C,* and *O* represent.

Unfortunately, automaticity is achieved in only one way: practice, practice, and more practice. This is not to say, however, that we must continually assign drill-and-practice exercises involving isolated facts and procedures. Quite the contrary, such activities are often boring and unlikely to convince students of the value of what they are learning. A more effective approach is to routinely incorporate basic knowledge and skills into a variety of meaningful and enjoyable activities, such as problem-solving tasks, group projects, games, brainteasers, and so on. Internationally known Canadian music-performance coach Philip Cohen (2008) cautioned against rehearsing for replicability; rather, he recommends practising for **creative variability**, playing and *playing with* the task at hand so that it is constantly experienced in intentionally new ways. He compared it to sketching. This is both more fun and more effective for applying the learning in new contexts.

A popular joke, often attributed in various forms to violinist Jascha Heifetz, goes something like this:

Tourist in New York: How do you get to Carnegie Hall?
Reply: Practice, practice, practice!

Automaticity The ability to respond quickly and efficiently while mentally processing or physically performing a task.

What kinds of assessment procedures are most likely to encourage automaticity? What kinds are least likely to encourage it?

Creative variability Conceptualizing (or "playing with") the learning process in different ways or in different contexts so that practice or rehearsal lead to more effective learning.

Sometimes the punch line is just "Practice!" and T-shirts on sale at Carnegie Hall state "Practice, Practice" on the back. But what kinds of practice favour meaningful learning?

Using Knowledge Frequently

Frequently used knowledge is retrieved more easily than knowledge that is used rarely or not at all (R. Brown & McNeill, 1966; Yarmey, 1973). It is easier to remember your own birthday than the birthday of a friend or relative, or the current year than the year of Confederation.

Classroom activities that require your students to review what they have learned earlier in the year or in previous years will enhance retrieval. For example, have occasional refresher discussions of "old" material, or ask students to use the material to understand new topics or solve new problems. Occasional review enhances students' memory for information, especially when reviews are spread out over several months or years (Bahrick, Bahrick, Bahrick, & Bahrick, 1993; Dempster, 1991; Di Vesta & Smith, 1979; McDaniel & Masson, 1985).

Having a Relevant Retrieval Cue

If you were educated in North America, then you probably learned the names of the five Great Lakes at one time or another. Yet you may have trouble retrieving all five names, even though they are all still stored in your long-term memory. Perhaps Lake Michigan doesn't come to mind when you retrieve the other four. The *HOMES* mnemonic provides a **retrieval cue**, or hint about where to "look" in long-term memory. The mnemonic tells you that one lake begins with the letter *M*, and so you search among the *M* words in your long-term memory until (we hope) you find "Michigan." Learners are more likely to retrieve information when relevant retrieval cues are present to start their search of long-term memory in the right direction (e.g., Tulving, 1983; Tulving & Thomson, 1973).

For another example of how retrieval cues can aid retrieval, try the following exercise.

EXPERIENCING FIRSTHAND   *Recall versus Recognition*

Earlier in the chapter, we described a process that keeps information in working memory for longer than the usual 5 to 20 seconds. Can you retrieve the name of that process from your long-term memory? See if you can before you read any further.

If you can't remember the term to which we're referring, then try answering the same question posed in a multiple-choice format:

What do we call the process that keeps information in working memory for longer than the usual 5 to 20 seconds?

    a. facilitative construction
    b. internal organization
    c. short-term memorization
    d. maintenance rehearsal

Did you experience an "Aha, now I remember" feeling? The correct answer is *d*. Perhaps the multiple-choice format offered a retrieval cue, directing you to the correct answer you had stored in long-term memory. Generally, it is easier to remember something in a **recognition task** (in which you simply need to recognize correct information among irrelevant or incorrect information) than in a **recall task** (in which the correct information must be retrieved in its entirety from long-term memory) (Semb, Ellis, & Araujo, 1993). A recognition task is easier because it provides more retrieval cues to aid you in your search of long-term memory.

As a teacher, you won't always want to help students retrieve information by putting that information right in front of them. Nevertheless, there will be occasions when providing hints is certainly appropriate. For example, when Sheri asks how the word *liquidation* is spelled, we might say, "*Liquidation* means to make something liquid. How do you spell *liquid*?" When Shawn wants to know what the symbol *Au* stands for, we might help him retrieve the answer with a hint like this one: "In class we talked about how *Au* comes from the Latin word *aurum*. And there can be an "aura" of success. Can you now remember what aurum means?"

In the early grades, teachers typically provide many retrieval cues for their students: They remind students about the tasks they need to do and when they need to do them ("I hear

Developing automaticity does not necessarily require the drill and practice in which Connor engages in his Grade 6 music class. Automaticity can also develop when basic concepts and skills are repeatedly embedded in more meaningful activities.

Retrieval cue A hint about where to "look" for a piece of information in long-term memory.

Recognition task A memory task in which one must identify correct information among irrelevant information or incorrect statements.

Recall task A memory task in which one must retrieve information in its entirety from long-term memory.

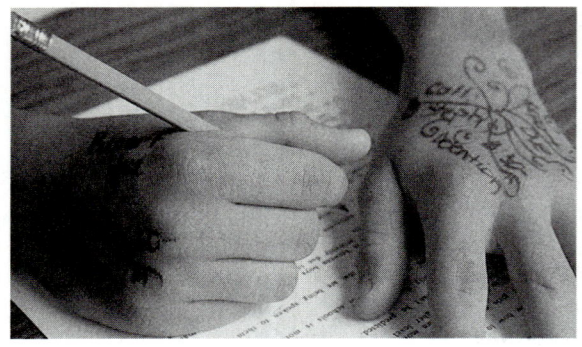

Ultimately, students must learn to develop their own retrieval cues. This student has written notes to himself on his hands.

the fire alarm. Remember, we all walk quietly during a fire drill"; or "It's time to go home. Do you all have the field-trip permission slip to take to your parents?"). But as they grow older, students must develop greater independence, relying more on themselves and less on their teachers for the things they need to remember. At all grade levels, we can teach students ways of providing retrieval cues for *themselves*. For example, if we expect Grade 1 students to bring back those permission slips tomorrow, we might ask them to write a reminder on a piece of masking tape that they put on their jackets or lunch boxes. If we give junior high school students a major assignment due several weeks later, we might suggest that they help themselves remember the due date by taping a note to their bedside tables or by making an entry on their kitchen calendars.

Why People Sometimes Forget

Fortunately, we don't need to remember everything. Much of the information we encounter is—like junk mail—not worth keeping, and forgetting enables us to get rid of that needless clutter (D. L. Schacter, 1999).

But as we have just seen, we sometimes have trouble recalling what we *do* need. Psychologists have numerous explanations for why people seem to forget. Here we consider five of them: failure to retrieve, reconstruction error, interference, decay, and failure to store.

Failure to Retrieve

Inability to retrieve Failing to locate information that currently exists in long-term memory.

One reason we forget is an **inability to retrieve**: We can't locate information stored in long-term memory (e.g., Schacter, 1999). Sometimes we stumble on the information later, while "looking" for something else. But sometimes we never do retrieve the information, perhaps because we learned it by rote or because we don't have sufficient retrieval cues.

Reconstruction Error

Reconstruction error Constructing a logical but incorrect "memory" by using information retrieved from long-term memory plus one's general knowledge and beliefs about the world.

Retrieval isn't necessarily an all-or-nothing phenomenon. Sometimes we retrieve part of the information we are seeking from long-term memory but cannot recall the rest. In such situations we may fill in the gaps using our general knowledge and assumptions about the world (Kolodner, 1985; Roediger & McDermott, 2000; P. T. Wilson & Anderson, 1986). Even though the gaps are filled in "logically," they aren't always filled in correctly—a form of forgetting called **reconstruction error**. Chapter 7 looks at the reconstructive nature of retrieval in greater detail.

Interference

EXPERIENCING FIRSTHAND   *Six Chinese Words*

Here are six more Mandarin Chinese words and their English meanings (for simplicity, "tone" marks on the words are omitted). Read them two or three times and try to store them in your long-term memory. But don't do anything special to learn the words; for example, don't intentionally develop mnemonics to help you remember them.

Chinese	**English**
jung	middle
ting	listen
sung	deliver
peng	friend
ching	please
deng	wait

Now cover up the list of words and test yourself. What was the word for *friend*? *please*? *listen*? *wait*?

INTO THE CLASSROOM   *Maximizing Retrieval and Minimizing Forgetting*

Where important information is concerned, never assume that once is enough.

> A language arts teacher introduces the parts of speech (e.g., nouns, verbs, adjectives) early in the school year. Because these concepts will be important for students to know when they study a foreign language in later grades, he continues to review them throughout the year—for example, by frequently incorporating them into classroom activities.

When information must be retrieved rapidly, occasionally assign drill-and-practice exercises that enable students to learn it to automaticity.

> An elementary school teacher gives frequent practice in addition and subtraction until each student can add and subtract single digits quickly and accurately. To make such practice both motivating and informative, she has students vary how they practice (e.g., on paper, orally, in games, or in different orders), time their performance each day, and chart their continuing improvement on graph paper.

Teach students to develop their own retrieval cues for things they need to remember.

> A teacher suggests that students tape a note to their jackets, reminding them to return their permission slips the next day.

When important details are difficult to fill in logically, make sure students learn them well.

> A teacher gives students extra practice in troublesome spelling words, such as those that are spelled differently than they are pronounced (e.g., *people, February*).

Provide retrieval cues when appropriate.

> When a student puzzles over how to compute the area of a circle, her teacher says, "We studied this last week. Do you remember the formula?" When the student shakes her head, the teacher continues, "Because the problem involves a circle, the formula probably includes *pi,* doesn't it?"

Did you find yourself getting confused, perhaps forgetting which English meaning went with each Chinese word? If you did, then you were the victim of **interference**. The various pieces of information that you stored in your long-term memory were interfering with one another; in a sense, the pieces were getting "mixed up." Notice that we told you *not* to use mnemonics to learn the Chinese words. Interference is especially likely to occur when pieces of information are similar to one another and when they are learned by rote (e.g., Dempster, 1985; Postman & Underwood, 1973; Underwood, 1948, 1957).

Interference A phenomenon whereby something stored in long-term memory inhibits one's ability to remember something else correctly.

Decay

As noted earlier, some psychologists believe that information remains in long-term memory forever. But others propose that information may weaken over time and perhaps disappear altogether, especially if it is not used frequently (J. R. Anderson, 1990; Reisberg, 1997; D. L. Schacter, 1999). Theorists sometimes use the word **decay** when describing this gradual fading process.

Decay A hypothesized weakening over time of information stored in long-term memory, especially if the information is used infrequently or not at all.

Failure to Store

Another reason for forgetting is **failure to store**: Information never reached long-term memory to begin with. Perhaps attention wasn't paid to the information, so it never went beyond the sensory register. Or perhaps the learner, after attending to it, didn't process it any further, so it went no further in the memory system than working memory. Obviously, failure to store is not an explanation of information loss; however, it is one possible reason why students who *think* they have learned something cannot recall it later on (D. L. Schacter, 1999).

Failure to store One's failure to mentally process information in ways that promote its storage in long-term memory.

All five explanations for forgetting underscore the importance of the instructional strategies that were identified earlier: For instance, make sure your students are paying attention, help them relate new material to things they already know, and give them opportunities to review, practise, and apply that material frequently.

Yet even when effective storage processes are encouraged, and even when students are given helpful retrieval cues, long-term memory storage and retrieval processes don't always happen instantaneously. For example, it may take time for students to relate new material to their existing knowledge and, at some later date, to retrieve all the "pieces" of what they have learned. What happens when teachers give students more time to process and retrieve information? The results can be quite dramatic, as we shall see now.

When students informally test themselves as they learn and study, failure to store is less likely to be a problem. We will consider this process of *monitoring comprehension* in Chapter 7.

Giving Students Time to Process: Effects of Increasing Wait Time

Consider the following situation.

Mr. Smith likes to ask questions in his classroom. He also likes to keep class sessions going at a rapid pace. A typical day goes something like this:

Mr. Smith:	Why is it warmer in summer than in winter?
Amelia:	Because the sun is hotter.
Mr. Smith:	Well, yes, the sun *feels* hotter. What changes in the earth make it feel hotter?
Arnold:	The earth is closer to the sun in the summer.
Mr. Smith:	That's a possibility, Arnold. But there's something we need to consider here. When it's summer in the Northern Hemisphere, it's winter in the Southern Hemisphere. When North America is having its warmest days, Australia is having its coldest days. Can we use the earth's distance from the sun to explain that?
Arnold:	Uh . . . I guess not.
Mr. Smith:	So . . . why is it warmer in summer than in winter? (No one responds.) Do you know, Angela? (She shakes her head.) How about you, Andrew?
Andrew:	Nope.
Mr. Smith:	Can you think of anything we discussed yesterday that might help us with an explanation? (No one responds.) Remember, yesterday we talked about how the earth's axis of rotation is not perpendicular to its orbit around the sun. This annual change in the north and south hemisphere's tilt toward the sun explains why the length of days and temperatures change over the year, except close to the equator.

Mr. Smith is hoping that his students will draw a connection between information they learned yesterday (changes in the earth's axis of rotation relative to the sun) and today's topic (the seasons). Unfortunately, Mr. Smith is moving too quickly from one question to the next and from one student to another. His students don't make the connections he expects because he doesn't give them enough time to do so. He also overpowers short-term memory by not helping them to rehearse and reconnect their conceptual learning in reasonable quantities.

The first problem with Mr. Smith's lesson is one seen in many classrooms: too short a **wait time**. When teachers ask students a question, they typically wait one second or less for a response. If students don't respond in that short time interval, teachers tend to speak again—sometimes by asking different students the same question, sometimes by rephrasing the question, sometimes even by answering the question themselves (M. B. Rowe, 1974, 1987). Teachers are equally reluctant to let much time lapse after students answer questions or make comments in class; once again, they typically allow *one second or less* of silence before responding to a statement or asking another question (M. B. Rowe, 1987).

If we consider basic principles of cognitive psychology—for example, the importance of relating new information to prior knowledge and the difficulty often associated with retrieving information from long-term memory—then we realize that one second is a very short time indeed for students to develop their responses. When teachers instead allow at least *three seconds* to elapse after their own questions and after students' comments, dramatic changes can occur in both students' and teachers' behaviours:

Changes in students' behaviours:

- *More class participation.* More students participate, especially females and students from ethnic minority groups. Students are more likely to answer questions correctly and to contribute spontaneously to a discussion, perhaps by asking their own questions, presenting their own perspectives, or responding to one another's comments.

- *Better quality of responses.* Students give a greater variety of responses to the same question, and their responses are longer and more sophisticated. They are more likely to support their reasoning with evidence or logic and more likely to speculate when they don't know an answer.

Wait time The length of time a teacher pauses, either after asking a question or hearing a student's comment, before saying something else.

- *Better overall classroom performance.* Students are more likely to feel confident that they can master the material and more motivated to learn it. Academic achievement increases, and discipline problems decrease.

Changes in teachers' behaviours:

- *Different kinds of questions.* Teachers ask fewer "simple" questions (e.g., those requiring recall of facts) and a greater number of complex questions (e.g., those requiring students to elaborate or develop alternative explanations).
- *Increased flexibility in teaching.* Teachers modify the direction of discussion to accommodate students' comments and questions, and allow their classes to pursue a topic in greater depth than originally anticipated.
- *Higher expectations.* Teachers' expectations for many students, especially previously low-achieving students, begin to improve. (Mohatt & Erickson, 1981; M. B. Rowe, 1974, 1987; Tharp, 1989; Tobin, 1987)

When teachers increase wait time to three seconds or longer, students participate more actively and give more complex responses to questions.

From the perspective of cognitive psychology, increasing wait time has two benefits for student learning (Tobin, 1987). First, it allows students more time to process and be actively engaged with the classroom subject matter. Second, it appears to change the very nature of teacher–student discussions; for example, teachers are more likely to ask challenging, thought-provoking questions. In fact, the nature of the questions teachers ask is probably as important as—and perhaps even more important than—the amount of wait time per se (Giaconia, 1988).

When our objective is simple recall—when students need to retrieve classroom material very quickly, to "know it cold"—then wait time should be short. As we have seen, students may sometimes need rapid-fire drill-and-practice to learn information and skills to automaticity. But when our objectives include more complex processing of ideas and issues, longer wait time may provide both teachers and students the time that they need to think things through.

Accommodating Diversity in Cognitive Processes

As we've explored basic principles of cognitive psychology in this chapter, we've considered many factors—attention, working memory capacity, long-term memory storage processes, prior knowledge, retrieval, and so on—that influence what and how well our students are likely to learn and remember classroom material. Naturally, our students will differ considerably with regard to these factors; for example, they will have unique knowledge bases on which to draw, and they will elaborate differently on the ideas we present (e.g., Cothern, Konopak, & Willis, 1990; Grant & Gomez, 2001; R. E. Reynolds, Taylor, Steffensen, Shirley, & Anderson, 1982). They may also have had varying experiences with different kinds of memory tasks. For instance, students from traditional North American classrooms are likely to have had more experience learning lists of things, whereas students from some African countries may have an easier time remembering stories (Flavell et al., 1993). Furthermore, as noted in Chapter 4, students from diverse backgrounds will especially benefit from extended wait time; for instance, those with limited proficiency in English may require some "mental translation" time.

Facilitating Cognitive Processing in All Students

Some of our students with special educational needs may have particular trouble attending to and processing classroom subject matter in an effective manner. This will certainly be true for students with learning disabilities (by definition, they have difficulty with certain cognitive processes), and it will often be true for students with ADHD as well (Barkley, 1998; Lorch et al., 1999; Mercer, 1997). Furthermore, students with mental retardation will typically process information more slowly than their classmates, and students with emotional and behavioural disorders may have trouble keeping their attention on the task at hand (Courchesne et al., 1994; Turnbull et al., 1999).

In contrast, gifted students are likely to process new ideas more rapidly and in a more complex manner than many of their classmates (B. Clark, 1997; Heward, 2000). In fact, many of the instructional strategies in Table 6.3—getting students' attention, analyzing their errors, teaching them mnemonics, and so on—need not be limited to use with students with special needs. *All* of our students can benefit from help in processing information more effectively.

TABLE 6.3 — STUDENTS IN INCLUSIVE SETTINGS

Facilitating Cognitive Processing in Students with Special Educational Needs

CATEGORY	CHARACTERISTICS YOU MIGHT OBSERVE	SUGGESTED CLASSROOM STRATEGIES
Students with specific cognitive or academic difficulties	• Deficiencies in one or more specific cognitive processes (e.g., perception, encoding) • Distractibility, inability to sustain attention (in some students) • Difficulty screening out irrelevant stimuli • Less working memory capacity, or less efficient use of working memory • Impulsivity in responding	• Analyze students' errors as a way of identifying possible processing difficulties. • Identify weaknesses in specific cognitive processes and provide instruction that enables students to compensate for these weaknesses. • Present information in an organized fashion and make frequent connections to students' prior knowledge as ways of promoting more effective long-term memory storage. • Teach mnemonics to aid long-term memory storage and retrieval. • Encourage greater reflection before responding—for instance, by reinforcing accuracy rather than speed, or by teaching self-instructions (see Chapter 8). • Intersperse activities that require sustained attention with opportunities for physical exercise.
Students with social or behavioural problems	• Lack of attention because of off-task thoughts and behaviours • Difficulty shifting attention quickly (for students with autism) • Possible difficulties in other cognitive processes (e.g., undiagnosed learning disabilities)	• Make sure you have students' attention before giving instructions or presenting information. • Refer students to a school psychologist for evaluation and diagnosis of possible learning disabilities.
Students with general delays in cognitive and social functioning	• Slower cognitive processing • Difficulty with attention to task-relevant information • Reduced working memory capacity, or less efficient use of working memory • Smaller knowledge base on which to build new learning	• Keep instructional materials simple, emphasizing relevant stimuli and minimizing irrelevant stimuli. • Provide clear instructions that focus students' attention on desired behaviours (e.g., "Listen," "Write," "Stop"). • Pace instruction to allow students enough time to think about and process information adequately (e.g., provide ample wait time after questions). • Assume little prior knowledge about new topics (i.e., "begin at the beginning").
Students with physical or sensory challenges	• Normal cognitive processing ability in most students • Less general knowledge due to limited experiences in the outside world	• Assume equal ability for learning and understanding new information and skills, but consider how students' physical and sensory challenges may interfere with some learning processes. • Expose students to life experiences they may have missed due to their disabilities.
Students showing evidence of giftedness, talent, or high performance	• More rapid cognitive processing • Larger knowledge base (the nature of which will vary, depending on students' cultural backgrounds) • More and better interconnections among ideas in long-term memory • More rapid retrieval of information from long-term memory	• Proceed through topics more quickly or in greater depth. • Create interdisciplinary lessons to foster integration of material in long-term memory. • Have students propose and implement their own ideas for learning new material and evaluating their successes.

Sources: Austin & Shore, 1995; Barkley, 1998; Beirne-Smith et al., 2002; Bulgren et al., 1994; Butterfield & Ferretti, 1987; B. Clark, 1997; Courchesne et al., 1994; Heward, 2000; Landau & McAninch, 1993; Lorch et al., 1999; Mercer, 1997; Morgan & Jenson, 1988; Piirto, 1999; Pressley, 1995; Rabinowitz & Glaser, 1985; H. L. Swanson et al., 1998; A. Turnbull et al., 1999.

Learning and the Brain: A Word of Caution about "Brain-Based" Teaching

The neuropsychology of learning is a very young science and, to date, gives us only the most general picture of how and where learning occurs. For example, we know from animal studies that learning results in an increase in the size and number of the interconnections (**synapses**) between brain cells (**neurons**) (R. D. Hawkins & Bower, 1989; A. M. Turner & Greenough, 1985). We know, too, that most of the mental "action" during learning and memory tasks takes place in the upper, caplike part of the brain known as the **cortex** (e.g., Kimberg, D'Esposito, & Farah, 1997; Nadel & Jacobs, 1998; E. E. Smith, 2000).

More and more often we are hearing the teachers with whom we are working speak about the workshops and in-services they have attended across Canada on applying "brain research" in the classroom. When we listen closely to what is actually being presented, these workshops are typically concerned with what we have learned from studies of *behaviour* rather than from studies of brain anatomy and physiology. Although studies of the brain may someday give us ideas about how best to help children and adolescents learn, it is premature to turn to biology, rather than psychology, for guidance about effective teaching strategies (e.g., Bruer, 1997).

Synapse A junction between two neurons that allows messages to be transmitted from one to the other.

Neuron A cell in the brain or another part of the nervous system that transmits information to other cells.

Cortex The upper part of the brain; site of conscious and higher-level thinking processes.

TEACHING CONSTRUCTIONS

Let's revisit Darren, whom you met at the start of this chapter. Based on what you have now learned about cognitive processing and cognitive theories of learning, consider the following:

- Describe the ways in which Darren was actively engaged in learning during his day at school.
- What information from today will he likely remember for his next day of school? Why? How can you, as his teacher, help Darren retrieve information that he learned today for the next time he needs to use it?

Theories of cognitive processing are central to how students receive, process, and retrieve the information they are learning in the classroom. To learn and remember something effectively, learners must, first and foremost, give it their undivided attention; that is, they must mentally focus on it and, for at least a brief time, make it the psychological centre of their cognitive universe. Learners must then actively try to make it more meaningful, organized, logical, and vivid—for instance, by identifying ways in which it is similar to things they already know, finding interconnections among its various pieces, drawing inferences from it, or forming a visual image that helps understanding. Emphasizing the importance of *understanding* rather than rote memorization in your instructional techniques and strategies is critical. Such an approach will not only make students' learning more meaningful and memorable but also enhance their belief that classroom topics are interesting, enjoyable, and in some way relevant to their own lives.

KEY CONCEPTS

cognitive psychology (p. 131)
information processing theory (p. 131)
construction (p. 132)
constructivism (p. 133)
memory (p. 134)
storage (p. 134)
encoding (p. 134)
retrieval (p. 134)
sensory register (p. 135)
attention (p. 135)
reconstruction (as a complement to note taking) (p. 136)
working memory (p. 136)
maintenance rehearsal (p. 137)
long-term memory (p. 138)

quality of concept links (p. 139)
activation (p. 139)
declarative knowledge (p. 140)
procedural knowledge (p. 140)
rehearsal (p. 141)
rote learning (p. 141)
meaningful learning (p. 142)
meaningful learning set (p. 142)
knowledge base (p. 143)
organization (p. 143)
elaboration (p. 144)
visual imagery (p. 145)
mnemonic (p. 148)
verbal mediator (p. 148)
keyword method (p. 148)

superimposed meaningful structure (p. 149)
automaticity (p. 150)
creative variability (p. 150)
retrieval cue (p. 151)
recognition task (p. 151)
recall task (p. 151)
inability to retrieve (p. 152)
reconstruction error (p. 152)
interference (p. 153)
decay (p. 153)
failure to store (p. 153)
wait time (p. 154)
synapse (p. 157)
neuron (p. 157)
cortex (p. 157)

7 Knowledge Construction and Higher-Level Thinking

CASE STUDY EARTH-SHAKING SUMMARIES

TEACHING CONNECTIONS

CONSTRUCTIVE PROCESSES IN LEARNING AND MEMORY

KNOWLEDGE CONSTRUCTION AS A SOCIAL PROCESS
Benefits of Group Meaning-Making in the Classroom

ORGANIZING KNOWLEDGE
Concepts • Schemas and Scripts

WHEN KNOWLEDGE CONSTRUCTION GOES AWRY: ORIGINS AND EFFECTS OF MISCONCEPTIONS

PROMOTING EFFECTIVE KNOWLEDGE CONSTRUCTION
Providing Opportunities for Experimentation • Presenting the Ideas of Others • Emphasizing Conceptual Understanding • Using Authentic Activities • Promoting Dialogue • Creating a Community of Learners

PROMOTING CONCEPTUAL CHANGE

CONSIDERING DIVERSITY IN CONSTRUCTIVE PROCESSES
Accommodating Students in Inclusive Classrooms

METACOGNITION AND LEARNING STRATEGIES
Effective Learning Strategies • Factors Affecting Strategy Use

TRANSFER
Basic Concepts in Transfer • Factors Affecting Transfer • Importance of Retrieval in Transfer

PROBLEM SOLVING
Basic Concepts in Problem Solving • Cognitive Factors Affecting Problem Solving • Using Computer Technology to Promote Effective Problem Solving

CRITICAL THINKING
Identifying Memes

CONSIDERING DIVERSITY IN HIGHER-LEVEL THINKING PROCESSES
Accommodating Students in Inclusive Classrooms

GENERAL STRATEGIES FOR PROMOTING HIGHER-LEVEL THINKING SKILLS

TEACHING CONSTRUCTIONS

KEY CONCEPTS

CASE STUDY *Earth-Shaking Summaries*

Ms. LaRiviere is beginning a new science unit on earthquakes with her Grade 3 students at a French Immersion school in Calgary. She spends the first 30 minutes discussing how earthquakes occur and sharing examples of recent earthquakes throughout the world. One of her students, Ethan, has recently moved to Calgary from Vancouver and shares his stories about earthquake drills that he practised at his old school. Ms. LaRiviere introduces the theory of *plate tectonics*—the notion that the earth's crust is made up of many separate pieces (*plates*) that rest upon a layer of hot, molten rock (the *mantle*). She explains that plates occasionally shift and rub against each other, making the immediate area shake and leaving *faults* in the earth's surface. She has brought in a picture to demonstrate this theory.

Her students listen attentively throughout her explanation. When she finishes, she asks whether there are any questions. Finding that there are none, she says, "Great! I'm glad you all understand. What I'd like you to do now is to take out a piece of paper and write a paragraph answering this question: *Why do we have earthquakes*?" She knows from her courses in educational psychology that asking students to summarize what they've learned often helps them to remember it better later on, and she figures that the task she's just assigned is an excellent way to encourage summarization.

Ms. LaRiviere collects students' papers as they prepare for the next class. As she glances quickly through the stack, she is distressed by what she sees. Some of her students, including Ethan, have provided a relatively complete and accurate description of plate tectonics. But the responses of others are vague enough to make her uneasy about how thoroughly they understood her explanation; here are three examples:

Frank: The earth's crust shifts around and shakes us up.

Ethan: The earth's crust is like plates that lie on hot rock and the plates shake and make big cracks in the earth.

Mitchell: Earthquakes happen when really big plates on the earth move around.

And three of her students clearly have made little sense of the lesson:

Adrienne: Scientists use technology to understand how earthquakes happen. They use computers and stuff.

Tori: When there are earthquakes, people's plates move around the house.

Jonathan: Earthquakes aren't anybody's fault. They just happen.

Ms. LaRiviere sighs, clearly discouraged by the feedback she's just received from most of her students about her first earthquake lesson. "I guess I still have a lot to learn about teaching this material," she concludes.

TEACHING CONNECTIONS

Chapter 6 described how students learn and remember declarative and procedural knowledge. Formal explicit learning requires effort and focused attention, and is relatively slow in the beginning but worth it in the long run. This chapter focuses on building students' ability to construct knowledge from their own learning experiences, how students understand and direct their own learning processes, and how students use and evaluate what they learn. As you read, try to make connections between theory and teaching practice by considering the following questions:

- Why is Ms. LaRiviere not convinced that Frank and Mitchell have mastered the material? What critical aspects of the lesson did each boy omit in his response?
- Ethan provides a good summary; what do you think has influenced his performance? How has his knowledge about earthquakes been constructed differently than the other students'?
- What pieces of information from the lesson did Adrienne, Tori, and Jonathan apparently use when answering their teacher's question? Try to explain their responses using the concept of knowledge construction.
- What instructional strategies might Ms. LaRiviere have used to help her students gain a better understanding of plate tectonics, and how might the students work together to construct meaning?
- How does *metacognition*—students' knowledge and beliefs about their own cognitive processes—influence their ability to learn successfully? How could Ms. LaRiviere have encouraged her students to be more *metacognitive*?

- What *study strategies* seem to facilitate academic achievement, and how can you help your students acquire these strategies?
- Under what circumstances are learners most likely to apply (*transfer*) what they've learned to new situations and what cognitive processes are involved in effective *problem solving*? How can you help students solve problems more successfully?
- What is *critical thinking*, and how can you promote it in your classroom?

Constructive Processes in Learning and Memory

As noted in Chapter 6, retrieval isn't always an all-or-nothing phenomenon. Sometimes we retrieve only parts of the information we seek in long-term memory. In such situations, we may construct our "memory" of an event by combining the tidbits we can retrieve with our general knowledge and assumptions about the world (Kolodner, 1985; Loftus, 1991; Rumelhart & Ortony, 1977). As an example of how retrieval of a specific event or idea often involves drawing on our knowledge about other things as well, try the following exercise.

EXPERIENCING FIRSTHAND   *Missing Letters*

Can you fill in the missing letters of these five words?

_____   1. sep - rate
_____   2. exist - nce
_____   3. adole - - - nce.
_____   4. retr - - val
_____   5. hors d'o - - - - -

Were you able to retrieve the missing letters from your long-term memory? If not, then you may have made reasonable guesses, using either your knowledge of how the words are pronounced or your knowledge of how words in the English language are typically spelled.

When people fill in the gaps in what they've retrieved based on what seems "logical," they often make mistakes—a phenomenon known as **reconstruction error**. Your students will sometimes fall victim to reconstruction error, pulling together what they can recall in ways we may hardly recognize (Leichtman & Ceci, 1995; Roediger & McDermott, 2000). If important details are difficult to fill in logically, you must make sure your students learn them well enough to retrieve them directly from long-term memory.

Up to this point, we have been talking about construction as a process that occurs within a single learner. Theories that focus on how people, as individuals, construct meaning from events are collectively known as **individual constructivism**. Views about memory storage processes such as organization, elaboration, and visual imagery (see Chapter 6) have an element of individual constructivism, as do Piaget's theory of cognitive development and many explanations of language development (see Chapter 2). Yet sometimes people work together to construct meaning and knowledge, as we shall see now.

Knowledge Construction as a Social Process

Think about times when you've been confused about material in one of your own classes. In such situations, did you ever work co-operatively with classmates (who were just as confused as you were) to make sense of the material *together*? Quite possibly, by sharing your various interpretations, you jointly constructed a better understanding of the subject matter than any of you could have constructed on your own. Unlike individually constructed knowledge, which may differ considerably from one individual to another, socially constructed knowledge is shared by two or more people simultaneously. A perspective known as **social constructivism** focuses, in one interpretation, on such collective efforts to impose meaning on the world (this may be a good or bad thing, depending on one's perspective or circumstances) and how different social groups see the world in very diverse ways (Hong et al., 2000; O. Lee, 1999; Tomasello, 2000). Another interpretation is an important pedagogical meaning based on Vygotsky (see

---

Reconstruction error Constructing a logical but incorrect "memory" by using information retrieved from long-term memory plus one's general knowledge and beliefs about the world.

What implications does the notion of reconstruction error have for the credibility of eyewitness testimony?

Individual constructivism A theoretical perspective that focuses on how people, as individuals, construct meaning from the events around them.

Social constructivism A theoretical perspective that emphasizes that an individual's meaning-making (or learning in general) is mediated by adults or more knowledgeable peers, even though it is ultimately constructed by the individual learner.

Chapter 2), who proposed that a major part of meaningful learning requires interactions with others and necessarily, by extension, with larger society. McGill University educational psychologists Mark Aulls and Bruce Shore have placed constructivist and social constructivist philosophical principles at the heart of **inquiry-based instruction** and have argued that the practice of inquiry and the exercise of the skills and processes of inquiry are not curricular options or enrichment, but central to teaching and learning in the twenty-first century (Aulls & Shore, 2008; Shore, Aulls, & Delcourt, 2008). The discussion of communities of learners, later in this chapter, further explores this topic.

Inquiry-based instruction Teaching based on social-constructivist principles, in which students learn tasks as well as answer questions, and especially characterized by learning based on student interests and role exchanges between teachers and learners.

Benefits of Group Meaning-Making in the Classroom

Increasingly, theorists and practitioners are recognizing the value of having students work together to construct meaning about classroom subject matter—for instance, to explore, explain, discuss, and debate certain topics either in small groups or as an entire class. Sharing ideas and perspectives enhances students' understanding in several ways:

- Students can clarify and organize their ideas well enough to verbalize them to others.
- Students have opportunities to elaborate on what they have learned—for example, by drawing inferences, generating hypotheses, and asking questions.
- Students are exposed to the views of others—views that may reflect a more accurate understanding of the topics under discussion.
- Students discover flaws and inconsistencies in their own thinking, thereby helping them identify gaps in their understanding.
- Students discover how people from different cultural and ethnic backgrounds may interpret the world in different, yet perhaps equally valid, ways. (L. M. Anderson, 1993; Banks, 1991; Barnes, 1976; M. Carr & Biddlecomb, 1998; Fosnot, 1996; Hatano & Inagaki, 1993; E. H. Hiebert & Raphael, 1996; K. Hogan, Nastasi, & Pressley 2000; A. King, 1999; Schwarz, Neuman, & Biezuner, 2000; Webb & Palincsar, 1996)

Students who share their interpretations with one another often construct more complex understandings of the subject matter than they could have constructed on their own.

As a result, students who work as a group are likely to construct a more complex understanding of a topic than any single student could do alone. Some theorists, such as Canadian researcher Marlene Scardamalia and her colleagues (e.g., Hewitt & Scardamalia, 1998), and others (e.g., A. L. Brown et al. 1993; Salomon, 1993a, 1993b), refer to such "group thinking" as **distributed cognition**, a concept that overlaps with *distributed intelligence* (Chapter 4).

Distributed cognition A process whereby people think about an issue or problem together, sharing ideas and working collaboratively to draw conclusions or develop solutions.

Organizing Knowledge

In the process of constructing knowledge, people organize it in a variety of ways, creating the interconnected long-term memory described in Chapter 6. This section introduces several ways in which people organize the things they learn: *concepts, schemas, scripts,* and *personal theories*. Of these, we will spend the most time looking at concepts because researchers have been studying them for a longer time and so have a better understanding of them.

Concepts

A **concept** is a way of mentally grouping or categorizing objects or events. For instance, the concept *furniture* encompasses such objects as chairs, tables, beds, and desks. Students learn thousands of concepts during their school years. They learn some concepts quickly and easily. They acquire others more gradually and continue to modify them over time; in the meantime, they may have an "almost-but-not-quite" understanding of what the concepts are. Following are two examples of such partial understanding:

Concept A mental grouping of objects or events that have something in common.

> Taylor thinks of an *animal* as something with four legs and fur. He is quite surprised when his teacher says that fish, birds, and insects are also animals.

> Lisa correctly defines a *rectangle* as a geometric figure composed of two sets of parallel lines that are joined by right angles; this definition appropriately includes squares as examples of rectangles. Yet when she is shown a variety of shapes and asked to pick out all the rectangles, she doesn't identify the squares as being rectangles (P. S. Wilson, 1988).

> **INTO THE CLASSROOM**   *Teaching Strategies to Facilitate Concept Learning*
>
> Provide a definition of the concept.
>
> > A geometry teacher defines a *sphere* as "the set of points in three-dimensional space that are equidistant from a single point."
>
> Make defining features concrete and salient.
>
> > A teacher illustrates the concept *insect* with a line drawing that emphasizes its defining features, such as three body parts and three pairs of legs, in bold black lines. At the same time, the drawing downplays other, irrelevant characteristics that students might see, such as the insect's colour or the presence of wings.
>
> Present a variety of positive instances.
>
> > A music teacher plays a *primary chord* in several keys.
>
> Present a "best example," or prototype.
>
> > To illustrate the concept *democracy*, a social studies teacher describes a hypothetical, "ideal" government.
>
> Present negative instances—especially "near misses"—to show what the concept is not.
>
> > When a teacher describes what a *mammal* is, he shows students frogs and lizards and explains why these animals are not mammals.
>
> Ask students to identify positive and negative instances from among numerous possibilities.
>
> > A language arts teacher gives students a list of sentences and asks them to identify the sentences containing a *dangling participle*.
>
> Ask students to generate their own positive instances of the concept.
>
> > A teacher asks students to think of examples of *adjectives* that they use frequently in their own conversations.
>
> Show students how various concepts are related to one another.
>
> > A science teacher explains that the concepts *velocity* and *acceleration* have somewhat different meanings, even though they both involve speed.

Undergeneralization An overly restricted meaning for a word that excludes some situations to which the word does, in fact, apply; an overly narrow view of what objects or events a concept includes.

Overgeneralization An overly broad meaning for a word that includes some situations where the word is not appropriate; an overly broad view of what objects or events a concept includes.

Positive instance A specific example of a concept.

Negative instance A nonexample of a concept.

In some cases, students **undergeneralize** a concept: They have too narrow a view as to which objects or events are included. Taylor undergeneralizes when he excludes fish, birds, and insects from his concept of *animal*. Lisa's current conception of a *rectangle* is an undergeneralization because she doesn't realize that squares are also rectangles. On other occasions, students may **overgeneralize** a concept: They may identify objects and events as examples of a concept when in fact they are nonexamples. Students don't fully understand what a concept is until they can identify both examples (**positive instances**) and nonexamples (**negative instances**) of the concept with complete accuracy.

Interconnectedness of Concepts

In addition to learning concepts, students also learn how concepts are interrelated. In many situations, concepts are nested within one another in a hierarchical fashion. For instance, as a student, you learned that *dogs* and *cats* are both *mammals*, that *mammals* and *birds* are *vertebrates*, and that *vertebrates* and *invertebrates* are *animals*. The more general, all-encompassing concepts (near the top of the hierarchy) tend to be relatively abstract, whereas the more specific ones (near the bottom of the hierarchy) tend to be fairly concrete (Flavell et al., 1993; Rosch, Mervis, Gray Johnson, & Boyes-Braem, 1976). As you learned in Chapter 2, children generally learn the specific (concrete) concepts earlier than they learn the more general (abstract) ones. However, children are able to categorize objects in two or more ways simultaneously when they learn how various concepts are interrelated—knowledge that is likely to evolve, at least in part, as a result of formal education (Flavell et al., 1993).

Schemas and Scripts

Schema In contemporary cognitive psychology, an organized body of knowledge about a specific topic.

Some theorists propose that much of the information stored in long-term memory is organized as **schemas**—organized bodies of knowledge about particular objects or phenomena (e.g., Rumelhart & Ortony, 1977). Schemas give us an idea of how things "typically" are. Not only do schemas provide a means for organizing information, but they also influence how we interpret new situations. As an example, try the following exercise.

EXPERIENCING FIRSTHAND *John*

Read the following passage *once only*:

> John was feeling bad today so he decided to go see the family doctor. He checked in with the doctor's receptionist, and then looked through several medical magazines that were on the table by his chair. Finally, the nurse came and asked him to take off his clothes. The doctor was very nice to him. He eventually prescribed some pills for John. Then John left the doctor's office and headed home. (Bower, Black, & Turner, 1979, p. 190)

You probably had no trouble understanding the passage because you have been to a doctor's office yourself and have a schema for how those visits usually go. You can therefore fill in a number of details that the passage doesn't ever tell you. For example, you probably inferred that John must have *gone* to the doctor's office, although the story omits this essential step. Likewise, you probably concluded that John took his clothes off in the examination room, *not* in the waiting room, even though the story never makes it clear where John did his striptease. When a schema involves a predictable sequence of events related to a particular activity, as is the case in a visit to the doctor's office, it is sometimes called a **script**.

Students from diverse cultural backgrounds may sometimes come to school with different schemas and scripts and so may interpret the same classroom materials or activities differently (Lipson, 1983; R. E. Reynolds et al., 1982; Steffensen, Joag-Dev, & Anderson, 1979). Thus, as a teacher, you need to find out whether your students have the appropriate schemas and scripts— the organized bodies of knowledge about specific topics and events—to understand the subject matter you are teaching. When your students *don't* have such knowledge, you may sometimes need to back up and help them develop it before you forge full-steam ahead with new material.

Long before they start school, children begin to construct general belief systems—**personal theories**—about how the world operates (Keil, 1989, 1994; Wellman & Gelman, 1998). These theories include many concepts and the relationships (e.g., correlational and cause-effect relations) among them.

Students' personal theories about the world seem to guide them as they identify potential defining features of the concepts they are learning (Keil, 1987). For example, if you were trying to learn what a *horse* is, knowing that it is an animal would lead you to conclude that its location (in a stable, a pasture, a shopping mall, etc.) is irrelevant. In contrast, if you were trying to learn what the *equator* is, knowing that it is something on a map of the world should lead you to suspect that location is of the utmost importance.

By the time children reach school age, they have developed some preliminary theories and beliefs about the physical world, the biological world, and even the mental world—that is, the nature of thinking (Wellman & Gelman, 1998). These theories and beliefs have often evolved with little or no guidance from other, more knowledgeable individuals; as a result, they may include some erroneous beliefs, or **misconceptions**, about how the world operates. Let's look at the origins and effects of such misconceptions.

Script A schema that involves a predictable sequence of events related to a common activity.

What is a typical script for a trip to the grocery store? To the movies? To a fast-food restaurant?

Personal theory A self-constructed explanation for one's observations about a particular aspect of the world; it may or may not be consistent with generally accepted explanations of scientific phenomena.

Misconception Previously learned but incorrect information.

When Knowledge Construction Goes Awry: Origins and Effects of Misconceptions

When learners construct their own understandings, there is, of course, no guarantee that they will construct accurate ones. Consider how 7-year-old Rob thinks about how mountains are formed:

Interviewer:	How were the mountains made?
Rob:	Some dirt was taken from outside and it was put on the mountain and then mountains were made with it.
Interviewer:	Who did that?
Rob:	It takes a lot of men to make mountains, there must have been at least four. They gave them the dirt and then they made themselves all alone.
Interviewer:	But if they wanted to make another mountain?
Rob:	They pull one mountain down and then they could make a prettier one. (dialogue from Piaget, 1929, p. 348)

Construction workers and professional landscapers apparently play a major role in Rob's personal theory about the physical world.

Children and adolescents typically have many misconceptions about the world around them. One common one in the elementary grades is the assumption that living creatures and nonliving natural objects (rocks, mountains, etc.) exist for a particular purpose; for example, children might think that some rocks are pointy so that animals living nearby can scratch themselves when they get an itch (Kelemen, 1999). Figure 7.1 lists other common misconceptions.

Students' misconceptions probably have a variety of sources. Sometimes they result from how things *appear* to be (diSessa, 1996; Duit, 1991; Reiner, Slotta, Chi, & Resnick, 2000); for example, from our perspective on the earth's surface, the sun looks as if it moves around the earth, rather than vice versa. Sometimes misconceptions are encouraged by common expressions in language; for instance, we often talk about the sun "rising" and "setting" (Duit, 1991; Mintzes, Trowbridge, Arnaudin, & Wandersee, 1991). Sometimes learners infer incorrect cause–effect relationships between two events simply because those events often occur at the same time (Byrnes, 1996; Keil, 1991). Perhaps even fairy tales and television cartoon shows play a role in promoting misconceptions (Glynn, Yeany, & Britton, 1991). Often students' misconceptions simply arise out of their own well-intended efforts to make sense of what they see. Consider this teacher's anecdote about a young boy's interpretation of evaporating water:

> Wesley and I had become friends over a forlorn empty fish tank. It *did* contain big rocks and enough water to cover them. He had recounted to me that they had to put water in the tank almost every week, and I had asked him where he thought that water went. Wesley had answered, "Into the rocks." (F. P. L. Hawkins, 1997, p. 337)

FIGURE 7.1 Common student misconceptions

ASTRONOMY

Fact: The earth revolves around the sun.
Misconception: The sun revolves around the earth. It "rises" in the morning and "sets" in the evening, at which point it "goes" to the other side of the earth.

Fact: The earth is shaped more or less like a sphere.
Misconception: The earth is shaped like a round, flat disk.

BIOLOGY

Fact: A living thing is something that carries on such life processes as metabolism, growth, and reproduction.
Misconception: A living thing is something that moves and/or grows. The sun, wind, clouds, and fire are living things.

Fact: A plant is a food producer.
Misconception: A plant grows in a garden and is relatively small. Carrots and cabbage are vegetables, not plants. Trees are plants only if they are small.

PHYSICS

Fact: An object remains in uniform motion until a force acts upon it; a force is needed only to *change* speed or direction.
Misconception: Any moving object has a force acting upon it. For example, a ball thrown in the air continues to be pushed upward by the force of the throw until it begins its descent.

Fact: Gravity is the force whereby any two masses are attracted together.
Misconception: Gravity is "glue" or "sticky stuff" that holds people to the earth.

GEOGRAPHY

Fact: The Great Lakes contain fresh water.
Misconception: The Great Lakes contain salt water.

Fact: Rivers run from higher elevation to lower elevation.
Misconception: Rivers run from north to south (going "down" on a map). For example, rivers can run from Canada into the United States, but not vice versa.

Sources: S. Carey, 1986; Kyle & Shymensky 1989; Lennon et al., 1990; Maria, 1998; J. Nussbaum, 1985; Sneider & Pulos, 1983; Vosniadou, 1994; Vosniadou & Brewer, 1987; geography misconceptions courtesy of R. K. Ormrod.

Unfortunately, students' misconceptions can wreak havoc on new learning (Lipson, 1982; Reiner et al., 2000; K. J. Roth & Anderson, 1988). Thanks to the processes of meaningful learning and elaboration—these usually facilitate learning—students may change or distort new information to fit their existing misbeliefs. Students can then spend a great deal of time learning the wrong thing!

Effective teachers help students construct accurate understandings of the world around them, and encourage students to discard erroneous beliefs they have previously constructed. We will now consider strategies to promote both knowledge construction and conceptual change.

Even university students have been known to ignore information presented in class when it is inconsistent with their prior beliefs (Holt-Reynolds, 1992).

Promoting Effective Knowledge Construction

Knowing that learning is a constructive process does not necessarily tell us how we can most effectively promote such learning (K. R. Harris & Alexander, 1998; Hirsch, 1996; Nuthall, 1996). In fact, cognitive psychologists believe there are many ways to help students construct a rich and sophisticated knowledge base. A few possibilities are as follows.

Providing Opportunities for Experimentation

By interacting and experimenting with the objects around them, students can discover many characteristics and principles of the world firsthand (e.g., Fosnot, 1996). Teachers can create numerous hands-on opportunities for students to touch, manipulate, modify, combine, and recombine concrete objects.

Teachers often teach students clearly delineated, step-by-step procedures for accomplishing certain tasks. Yet on some occasions, it might be more helpful to let students develop such procedures *on their own* through experimentation. For example, when teaching cooking, it may sometimes be more productive to cast aside recipes and instead let students try different combinations and proportions of ingredients (Hatano & Inagaki, 1993).

Presenting the Ideas of Others

Although it may sometimes be beneficial to have students discover basic principles for themselves (reinventing the wheel, so to speak), students should also be given opportunities to hear and read about the ideas of others—the concepts, principles, theories, and so on, that society has developed to explain both the physical and psychological aspects of human experience (Driver, 1995; Vygotsky, 1962). Knowledge, after all, is socially constructed. Your students are most likely to construct a productive view of the world when they have the benefit of experiencing the world firsthand *and* the benefit of learning how those before them have interpreted human experience.

Students can more effectively construct meaningful interpretations of events when they examine how others have interpreted similar events. For example, by reading classic works of literature, they view daily life from the perspectives of numerous authors.

Emphasizing Conceptual Understanding

Without a doubt, students benefit more from acquiring facts, concepts, and ideas in an integrated, interrelated, and meaningful fashion; in other words, they benefit from developing a **conceptual understanding** of academic subject matter (L. M. Anderson, 1993; Bédard & Chi, 1992; J. J. White & Rumsey, 1994). For example, rather than simply memorize basic mathematical computation procedures, students also learn how those procedures reflect underlying principles of mathematics.

Conceptual understanding Knowledge acquired in an integrated and meaningful fashion.

Following are several ways in which you might help students develop a conceptual understanding of classroom subject matter:

- Organize units around a few core ideas and themes, always relating specific content back to this core.
- Explore each topic in depth—for example, by considering many examples, examining cause–effect relationships, and discovering how specific details relate to more general principles.
- Explain how new ideas relate to students' own experiences and to things they have previously learned.

In a 1998 talk to the students and staff at the University of Toronto Schools, Canadian chemist and Nobel Laureate John Polanyi proposed that all of education is about learning to recognize patterns. He said that finding patterns is how we bring order, another word for meaning or understanding, into teaching and learning. Help students learn to look for, give meaning to, remember, compare, evaluate, and use patterns in what they hear, see, read, touch, smell, and so on.

- Show students—through the things you say, the assignments you give, and the criteria you use to evaluate learning—that conceptual understanding of classroom subject matter is far more important than knowledge of isolated facts.
- Ask students to teach what they have learned to others—a task that encourages them to focus on main ideas and pull them together in a way that makes sense. (L. M. Anderson, 1993; Brophy & Alleman, 1992; Hatano & Inagaki, 1993; Prawat, 1993; VanSledright & Brophy, 1992; J. J. White & Rumsey, 1994)

Construction of an integrated understanding of any complex topic will inevitably take time. Accordingly, many educators advocate a *less is more* principle: *Less* material studied more thoroughly is learned *more* completely and with greater understanding (Brophy & Alleman, 1992; Kyle & Shymansky, 1989; Marshall, 1992; Sizer, 1992).

Using Authentic Activities

Many educational researchers suggest that students can construct a more useful, productive, and integrated knowledge base if they learn classroom subject matter within the context of **authentic activities**—activities similar to those encountered in the outside world. For example, students practise their writing skills by sending letters to real people. Students' writing improves in both quality and quantity when they engage in such authentic writing tasks (E. H. Hiebert & Fisher, 1992).

Authentic activity A classroom activity similar to one students are likely to encounter in the outside world.

Authentic activities can relate to virtually any area of the curriculum. For example, we might ask students to:

Give an oral report	Play in an athletic event
Write an editorial	Complete an art project
Participate in a debate	Perform in a concert
Find information in the library	Tutor a classmate
Conduct an experiment	Make a videotape
Graph data	Perform a workplace routine
Construct a chart or model	Develop classroom webpages to showcase special projects
Create and distribute a class newsletter	
Converse in a foreign language	

In many cases, these activities may require considerable support (scaffolding) to ensure that students carry them out successfully. As such, they may remind you of the *guided participation* described within the context of Vygotsky's theory in Chapter 2.

By placing classroom activities in real-world contexts, students discover the reasons why they are learning academic subject matter. The likelihood that, later on, they will actually use the information and skills that have been taught to them is also increased (A. Collins, Brown, & Newman, 1989; De Corte, Greer, & Verschaffel, 1996).

Promoting Dialogue

We have already identified numerous advantages to having students talk with one another about classroom topics and many theorists recommend that classroom dialogues be a regular feature of instruction (J. Hiebert et al., 1997; Marshall, 1992; Paris & Cunningham, 1996; Sosniak & Stodolsky, 1994).

As an example of how students might work together to construct meaning, let's look in on Ms. Lombard's Grade 4 class in Winnipeg, which has been studying fractions. Ms. Lombard has never taught her students how to divide a number by a fraction. Nevertheless, she gives them the following problem, which can be solved by dividing 20 by $\frac{3}{4}$:[1]

---

[1] In case your memory of how to divide by a fraction is rusty, you can approach the problem $20 \div \frac{3}{4}$ by inverting the fraction and multiplying, like so: $20 \times \frac{4}{3} = \frac{80}{3} = 26\frac{2}{3}$. Thus, Mom can make 26 tarts and have enough apples to make two-thirds of another tart. If she has two-thirds of the three-fourths of an apple she needs to make another whole tart, then she has half an apple left over ($\frac{2}{3} \times \frac{3}{4} = \frac{1}{2}$).

Mom makes small apple tarts, using $\frac{3}{4}$ of an apple for each small tart. She has 20 apples. How many small apple tarts can she make? (J. Hiebert et al., 1997, p. 118)

Ms. Lombard asks the students to work in teams to plan how they might solve the problem. One group of four girls—Jeanette, Liz, Kerri, and Nina—has been working on the problem for some time and so far has arrived at such answers as 15, 38, and 23. We join them midway through their discussion, when they've already agreed that they can use three-fourths of each apple to make a total of 20 tarts:

Jeanette:	In each apple there is a quarter left. In each apple there is a quarter left, so you've used, you've made twenty tarts already and you've got a quarter of twenty see—
Liz:	So you've got twenty quarters *left*.
Jeanette:	Yes, . . . and twenty quarters is equal to five apples, . . . so five apples divided by—
Liz:	Six, seven, eight.
Jeanette:	But three-quarters equals three.
Kerri:	But she can't make only three apple tarts!
Jeanette:	No, you've still got twenty.
Liz:	But you've got twenty quarters, if you've got twenty quarters you might be right.
Jeanette:	I'll show you.
Liz:	No, I've drawn them all here.
Kerri:	How many quarters have you got? Twenty?
Liz:	Yes, one quarter makes five apples and out of five apples she can make five tarts which will make that twenty-five tarts and then she will have, wait, one, two, three, four, five quarters, she'll have one, two, three, four, five quarters. . . .
Nina:	I've got a better . . .
Kerri:	Yes?
Liz:	Twenty-six quarters and a remainder of one quarter left. (J. Hiebert et al., 1997, p. 121)

The discussion and occasional disagreements continue, and the girls eventually arrive at the correct answer: Mom can make 26 tarts and then will have half an apple left over.

As the preceding conversation illustrates, classroom dialogues can help students achieve a conceptual understanding of classroom subject matter—for instance, a conceptual understanding of what it means to divide by a fraction (J. Hiebert et al., 1997; Lampert, Rittenhouse, & Crumbaugh, 1996). Classroom dialogues also have an important benefit for teachers as well: By carefully monitoring students' comments and questions, you can identify and address any misconceptions that might interfere with students' ability to acquire further knowledge and skills (Presseisen & Beyer, 1994; Sosniak & Stodolsky, 1994).

Creating a Community of Learners

With the benefits of dialogue and other forms of student interaction in mind, and with the goal of promoting the social construction of meaning, some psychologists and educators suggest that we create a **community of learners**—a classroom in which you and your students consistently work to help one another learn (A. L. Brown & Campione, 1994; Prawat, 1992; Rogoff,

Many cognitive psychologists advocate authentic activities that resemble tasks students may eventually encounter in the outside world. As an example, 12-year-old Mary Lynn created this map of the area between her home and school.

Chapter 10 describes strategies for promoting student dialogue through class discussion, reciprocal teaching, computer technology, and co-operative learning.

Community of learners A classroom in which teacher and students actively and collaboratively work to help one another learn.

Matusov, & White, 1996). A classroom that operates as a community of learners is likely to have characteristics such as the following:

- All students are active participants in classroom activities.
- Discussion and collaboration among two or more students are common occurrences and play a key role in learning.
- Diversity in students' interests and rates of progress is expected and respected.
- Students and teacher coordinate their efforts at helping one another learn; no one has exclusive responsibility for teaching others.
- Everyone is a potential resource for the others; different individuals are likely to serve as resources on different occasions, depending on the topics and tasks at hand.
- The teacher provides some guidance and direction for classroom activities, but students may also contribute to such guidance and direction.
- Students regularly critique one another's work.
- The process of learning is emphasized as much as, and sometimes more than, the finished product. (A. L. Brown & Campione, 1994, 1996; Campione, Shapiro, & Brown, 1995; Rogoff, 1994; Rogoff et al., 1996)

As one example of how a community of learners might be structured (A. L. Brown & Campione, 1994), students are divided into small groups to study different subtopics falling within a general theme. The class then reassembles into new groups that include at least one representative from each of the previous groups; within these groups, the students teach one another the things they have learned.

We can also use a computer network to promote a community of learners, according to Canadian researcher Marlene Scardamalia and colleagues at the Ontario Institute for Studies in Education at the University of Toronto (e.g., Scardamalia & Bereiter, 1996; Hewitt & Scardamalia, 1998). For instance, we can create ongoing "chat rooms" in which students present questions or issues to which others respond. Such online discussions may be especially valuable for students who are shy or for other reasons feel uncomfortable communicating with their classmates in a more public fashion (Hewitt & Scardamalia, 1998).

INTO THE CLASSROOM *Promoting Knowledge Construction*

Provide opportunities for experimentation.

A teacher has students experiment with clay and water to discover the principle that a certain quantity of a solid displaces the same amount of water regardless of the shape that the solid takes.

Expose students to others' interpretations of the world.

A teacher has students read poetry from a variety of countries and cultures.

Focus on an in-depth understanding of a few key ideas instead of covering many topics superficially.

A teacher tells his class, "As we study the geography of South America, we aren't going to worry about memorizing a lot of place names. Instead, we will look at how topography and climate have influenced the economic and cultural development of different regions of the continent."

Include authentic activities in the curriculum.

A teacher has students develop and cook a menu that includes all the basic food groups.

Create opportunities for small-group or whole-class discussions in which students can freely exchange their views.

A teacher asks students to speculate on how the Japanese people must have felt after the atomic bomb was dropped over Hiroshima.

Have students work in groups to research certain topics and then teach one another what they have learned.

In a unit on zoology, different groups of students "major" in different classes of invertebrates (e.g., mollusks, segmented worms, sponges) and then prepare illustrated "textbooks" that they share with their classmates in other groups.

Promote an inquiry climate by exchanging roles with students and sharing the construction of the curriculum.

In any class activity at any level, encourage students to propose topics to be explored, individual and group activities to support the learning, and ways in which they will be able to recognize that meaningful learning has taken place; then make these a part of the curriculum.

Ultimately, a community of learners can help create a *sense of community* in the classroom—a sense that we and our students have shared goals, are mutually respectful and supportive of one another's efforts, and believe that everyone makes an important contribution to classroom learning. We will look at this idea more closely in Chapter 11.

At the same time, we should note a couple of potential weaknesses that communities of learners, and group discussions more generally, may have (A. L. Brown & Campione, 1994; Hynd, 1998). For one thing, what students learn will inevitably be limited to the knowledge that they themselves acquire and share with one another. Second, students may occasionally pass on their own misconceptions to their classmates. Obviously, then, when we conduct classroom discussions or structure our classrooms as communities of learners, we must carefully monitor student interactions to make sure that students ultimately acquire thorough and accurate understandings of the subject matter they are studying. If they do not, we may need to take active steps to encourage conceptual change. We look at strategies for doing so now.

Promoting Conceptual Change

Teachers often present new information in class with the expectation that such information will replace any erroneous beliefs that students currently have. Yet research indicates that students of all ages often hold quite stubbornly to their misconceptions, even after considerable instruction that explicitly contradicts those misconceptions (S. Carey, 1986; Chambliss, 1994; Chinn & Brewer, 1993; Shuell, 1996). Consider the following situation described by J. F. Eaton, Anderson, and Smith (1984):

> A Grade 5 class was about to study a unit on light and vision. A pretest revealed that most students believed incorrectly that vision occurs simply as the result of light shining on an object and making it bright. During the unit, the teacher presented the correct explanation of human vision: Light must be reflected off an object *and then travel to the eye* before the object can be seen. Even though students both read and heard the correct explanation of how people see objects, most of them "learned" what they already believed: that an object can be seen as soon as light hits it. Posttest results indicated that only 24 percent of the class had learned the correct explanation.

Why are students' misconceptions often so resistant to change? Possible explanations include:

- As noted earlier, students' existing misconceptions may often colour their understanding of new information. Learners are likely to interpret new information in ways that are consistent with what they already "know" about the world.
- Students also tend to look for information that confirms their existing beliefs and to ignore or discredit any *dis*confirming evidence (Duit, 1991; Gunstone & White, 1981; Hynd, 1998; Kuhn, Amsel, & O'Loughlin, 1988).
- Students' existing beliefs are often consistent with their everyday experiences; in contrast, more accurate explanations (perhaps commonly accepted scientific principles or theories) may be fairly abstract and difficult to relate to everyday reality (P. A. Alexander, 1997; R. Driver, Asoko, Leach, Mortimer, & Scott, 1994; M. C. Linn, Songer, & Eylon, 1996).
- Some erroneous beliefs are integrated into cohesive personal theories, with many interrelationships existing among various ideas; in such a situation, changing misconceptions involves changing an entire organized body of knowledge rather than a single belief (Chambliss, 1994; Derry, 1996; C. L. Smith, Maclin, Grosslight, & Davis, 1997). For example, the belief that the sun revolves around the earth may be part of a more general "earth-centred" view of things, perhaps one that includes the moon, stars, and various other heavenly bodies revolving around the earth. The earth-centred view is a much easier one to understand and accept (on the surface, at least), and everything seemingly fits together quite nicely.
- In many situations, students learn new information without letting go of their prior beliefs, so that two inconsistent ideas are kept in memory simultaneously (Chambliss, 1994; Keil & Silberstein, 1996; Mintzes et al., 1991; Winer & Cottrell, 1996). Sometimes this happens because students learn the new information by rote, without relating it to what they already know and believe (Chambliss, 1994; Strike & Posner, 1992).

Students often have erroneous beliefs about how the earth, sun, and moon move in relation to one another. These students are trying to get a better understanding of the solar system through computer simulations and a multimedia presentation.

Conceptual change Revising one's knowledge and understanding of a topic in response to new information about that topic.

When your students hold misconceptions about the world, you must help them revise their thinking, to undergo **conceptual change**. Table 7.1 identifies four principles regarding how conceptual change may come about. The following strategies are derived from these four principles:

- *Identify existing misconceptions before instruction begins.* Informal pretesting will be particularly important in your first few years of teaching. As you gain experience teaching a particular topic year after year, you may eventually find that you can anticipate what your students' prior beliefs and misbeliefs about the topic are likely to be.

- *Convince students that their existing beliefs are inadequate.* Several strategies include:
  - Asking questions that challenge students' current beliefs
  - Presenting phenomena that students cannot adequately explain within their existing perspectives, then asking them to explain why these phenomena might have occurred
  - Engaging students in discussions of the pros and cons of various explanations
  - Explicitly pointing out the differences between students' beliefs and "reality"
  - Showing how the correct explanation of an event or phenomenon is more plausible (i.e., makes more sense) than students' existing explanations. (Chan, Burtis, & Bereiter, 1997; Hynd, 1998; Pine & Messer, 2000; Posner, Strike, Hewson, & Gertzog, 1982; Prawat, 1989; K. J. Roth, 1990; Slusher & Anderson, 1996; Vosniadou & Brewer, 1987)

Students will notice inconsistencies between new information and their previously acquired beliefs only if they try to make connections between the "new" and the "old"—in other words, if they engage in meaningful learning (Chinn & Brewer, 1993; O. Lee & Anderson, 1993; Pintrich, Marx, & Boyle, 1993; Slusher & Anderson, 1996). In Chapter 6 we found that students who engage in meaningful rather than rote learning acquire new information more quickly and retrieve it more easily. Here we see an additional reason to encourage meaningful learning: It helps "undo" existing misconceptions.

TABLE 7.1   **PRINCIPLES/ASSUMPTIONS**

Principles for Promoting Conceptual Change

PRINCIPLE	EDUCATIONAL IMPLICATION	EXAMPLE
Conceptual change is more likely to occur when existing misconceptions are identified before instruction begins.	Probe students' understanding of a topic through a short pretest or a series of discussion questions.	When beginning a unit on gravity, ask, "If we were to drop a penny and a golf ball from a second-storey window at exactly the same time, would one of them land sooner than the other, or would they both land at the same time?" If students predict that a golf ball would land sooner than a penny, have them conduct an experiment to test their prediction.
Students are most likely to revise their current beliefs about the world when they become convinced that these beliefs are incorrect.	Show students how new information contradicts the things they currently believe.	If students believe that sweaters keep people warm by generating heat, leave a sweater outside during a cold night, then ask students whether it feels warm the following morning (Gardner, 2000).
Students must be motivated to learn correct explanations for the phenomena they observe.	Show students how correct explanations relate to their own personal interests.	Demonstrate how the laws of physics relate to auto mechanics and, indirectly, to auto repair.
Some misconceptions may persist despite instruction designed to contradict them.	Carefully scrutinize what students say and write, not only during a lesson but after the lesson as well, for signs of partial or total misunderstanding.	When a student says that a spider is an *insect*, respond: "A spider is actually an *arachnid*, not an insect. Think back to what we learned about insects. Why don't spiders fit in that category?"

- *Motivate students to learn correct explanations.* Students are most likely to engage in meaningful learning and undergo conceptual change when they are motivated to do so (O. Lee & Anderson, 1993; Pintrich et al., 1993).

- *Monitor what students say and write for persistent misconceptions.* Because of students' natural tendency to reinterpret new information within the context of what they already know and believe, some misconceptions may be especially resistant to change despite your best efforts. These misconceptions are sometimes blatantly incorrect; at other times, they may be sort-of-but-not-quite correct.

Throughout each lesson, continue to check students' beliefs about the topic at hand, looking for subtle signs that their understanding is not quite accurate and giving corrective feedback when necessary.

Considering Diversity in Constructive Processes

As you help your students construct a meaningful understanding of the world around them, you can increase their multicultural awareness by promoting *multiple constructions* of the same situation. For example, we might present the western migration across Canada during the 1700s and 1800s from two different perspectives: that of the European settlers and that of the First Nations already residing on the land. One simple way to do this is to point out that migrating peoples are referred to as *pioneers* or *settlers* in most history books but might instead have been called *foreigners* or *invaders* by the First Nations (Banks, 1991). Or we could discuss how in 1519, Aztec emperor Montezuma II welcomed the conquistador Cortés as the god Quetzalcoatl returning from his journey east—clearly a different perspective than the Spanish might have had (PBS, n.d.). Ultimately, help your students to understand the very complex nature of human "knowledge" and to appreciate the fact that there may be several equally valid interpretations of any single event, and some of these may have tragic consequences.

A community of learners may be especially valuable when we have a diverse classroom of students (García, 1994; Ladson-Billings, 1995). Such a community values the contributions of all students, using everyone's individual backgrounds, cultural perspectives, and unique abilities to enhance the overall performance of the class.

How might you introduce multiple perspectives into the subject matter you will be teaching?

Accommodating Students in Inclusive Classrooms

Table 7.2 identifies some patterns that researchers have found in the constructive processes of students with special needs; it also presents suggestions for helping all students acquire appropriate meanings from academic and social situations.

The cornerstone of cognitive theories of learning is that students are actively engaged in the learning process. We have learned about how knowledge may be constructed by students. Now we turn our attention to how students themselves can be actively engaged in learning and the kinds of strategies students themselves can use to promote the construction of knowledge and higher-level thinking.

Metacognition and Learning Strategies

Higher-level thinking involves application, analysis, synthesis, evaluation, and other elaborative processes. The concept of **metacognition** includes learners' knowledge and beliefs regarding their own cognitive processes, as well as their attempts to regulate those cognitive processes to maximize learning and memory. Metacognition involves the activation of students' **higher-level thinking** skills. For example, metacognition includes:

- Knowing the extent and limits of one's own repertoire of learning and memory capabilities
- Knowing what learning tasks one can realistically accomplish within a certain amount of time
- Evaluating which learning strategies are effective and which are not, in general and in context
- Planning an approach to a learning task that is likely to be successful

Metacognition One's knowledge and beliefs about one's own cognitive processes, and one's resulting attempts to regulate those cognitive processes to maximize learning and memory.

Higher-level thinking Thought that involves going beyond information specifically learned (e.g., application, analysis, synthesis, evaluation).

TABLE 7.2 STUDENTS IN INCLUSIVE SETTINGS

Promoting Knowledge Construction in Students with Special Education Needs

CATEGORY	CHARACTERISTICS YOU MIGHT OBSERVE	SUGGESTED CLASSROOM STRATEGIES
Students with specific cognitive or academic difficulties	• Possible holes in students' knowledge base that may limit meaningful understanding of some classroom topics • Occasional unusual or inappropriate interpretations of prose • Occasional misinterpretations of social situations	• Determine students' prior knowledge about a new topic; remind them of what they *do* know about the topic. • Monitor students' comprehension of prose; correct misinterpretations. • Present alternative interpretations of others' behaviours.
Students with social or behavioural problems	• Frequent misinterpretations of social situations	• Present alternative interpretations of others' behaviours and identify suitable courses of action based on the most reasonable interpretation of a given situation.
Students with general delays in cognitive and social functioning	• Smaller knowledge base from which to draw • Difficulty constructing an accurate interpretation when information is ambiguous or incomplete	• Assume little if any prior knowledge about topics unless you have evidence to the contrary; remind students of what they *do* know about a topic. • Present information clearly and unambiguously.
Students with physical or sensory challenges	• Limited knowledge base to which students can relate new information, due to fewer opportunities to interact with the outside world	• Provide the background experiences (e.g., field trips) that students need to make sense of classroom subject matter.
Students showing evidence of giftedness, talent, or high performance	• Larger knowledge base from which to draw • Rapid concept learning • Greater conceptual understanding of classroom material (e.g., greater understanding of cause–effect relationships) • Greater ability to draw inferences	• Assign challenging tasks that enable students to develop and use their advanced understanding of topics. • Ask thought-provoking questions that encourage inference drawing.

Sources: Butterfield & Ferretti, 1987; Graham & Hudley, 1994; Hughes, 1988; Lochman & Dodge, 1994; Patton, Blackbourn, & Fad, 1996; Piirto, 1999; Pressley, 1995; Schumaker & Hazel, 1984; A. Turnbull et al., 1999; J. P. Williams, 1991.

■ Using effective learning strategies to process and learn new material

■ Monitoring one's own knowledge and comprehension—in other words, knowing when information has been successfully learned and when it has not

■ Using effective strategies for retrieval of previously stored information

The more students know about effective learning strategies—the greater their metacognitive awareness—the higher their classroom achievement is likely to be (Baker, 1989; Perkins, 1995; P. L. Peterson, 1988). Furthermore, students who use more sophisticated metacognitive strategies are more likely to undergo conceptual change when such change is warranted (Gunstone, 1994; Wittrock, 1994).

Did you have misconceptions about how best to study before you read this book?

Unfortunately, many students are unaware of how they can best learn and remember information. Younger children (those in the elementary grades) are especially naive about effective learning strategies (see the sections "Learning Strategies" and "Metacognition" in Chapter 2). But older students are also prone to misconceptions about how they can best learn and remember. For example, many students at all grade levels (even those in university) erroneously believe that rote learning is an effective way to study (Barnett, 2001; Pintrich & De Groot, 1990; Prawat, 1989; Schommer, 1994a).

With each transition to a higher educational level, teachers expect students to learn more material and think about it in a more sophisticated fashion. Yet all too often, teachers teach academic content areas without also teaching students *how to learn* in those content areas (Hamman, Berthelot, Saia, & Crowley, 2000; Pressley et al., 1990; E. Wood, Motz, & Willoughby, 1997). When left to their own devices, most students develop effective strategies very slowly (if at all) and so over the years encounter increasing difficulty in their attempts to master classroom subject matter. And when they *don't* master it, they may not know why they have failed, nor may they know how to improve their chances of succeeding the next time around (Hacker et al., 2000; Loranger, 1994; O'Sullivan & Joy, 1990).

In the upcoming sections we review research findings on a variety of learning strategies. We then consider factors that influence students' use of such strategies, as well as ways in which you can help your students learn more effectively.

Effective Learning Strategies

Research studies point to a number of effective study strategies, including the following.

Identifying Important Information

Students often have difficulty separating central and important information from the trivial and unimportant. Here are some features of books and classroom lectures on which students often inappropriately focus:

Students often need help distinguishing important ideas from more trivial information, especially when they first begin to learn a topic.

- *The first sentence of a lesson or paragraph.* Many students erroneously believe that the main idea (and perhaps *only* idea) of a paragraph is always found in the first sentence (Mayer, 1984).

- *Items that look different.* Definitions and formulas often stand out in a textbook, perhaps because they appear in *italics* or **boldface type** or perhaps because they are

    set apart

from the rest of the text. As a result, students often focus on them to the exclusion of other, potentially more important information (Mayer, 1984).

- *Items presented in more than one way.* Students are more likely to view material as important when it is presented in several different ways. For example, they are more likely to pay attention to things that teachers describe verbally *and* write on the chalkboard (Kiewra, 1989).

- *Items that are intrinsically interesting.* Students at all levels attend more to interesting statements than to uninteresting ones even if the most interesting statements are relatively unimportant (P. A. Alexander & Jetton, 1996; Garner, Brown, Sanders, & Menke, 1992; Harp & Mayer, 1998).

You can help your students learn more effectively by telling them what ideas are most important in your teaching and reading materials. Some strategies include the following:

- Provide a list of objectives for a lesson.
- Write key concepts and major ideas on the chalkboard.
- Ask questions that focus students' attention on important ideas.

Students (especially low-achieving ones) are more likely to learn the important points of a lesson when such "prompts" are provided for them (Kiewra, 1989; R. E. Reynolds & Shirey, 1988; Schraw & Wade, 1991). As your students become better able to distinguish important from unimportant information on their own, you can gradually phase out your guidance.

Do such prompts remind you of the concept of scaffolding?

Taking Notes

The process of note taking seems to serve two very important functions (Barnett, Di Vesta, & Rogozinski, 1981; Di Vesta & Gray, 1972; Kiewra, 1989). First, it helps learners pay attention to and *encode* information, thus allowing for more effective storage in memory. Second, it provides a means of *external storage* for the information. Long-term memory is often unreliable (recall our discussion of forgetting in Chapter 6), whereas notebooks are fairly dependable and allow students to review the material on one or more later occasions.

Why is review important? (For the answer, see the section "Using Knowledge Frequently" in Chapter 6.)

Particularly in the years when students are first starting to take notes in class (typically in the middle school or junior high grades), you will want to scaffold their efforts by giving them an idea about what things are most important to include (Pressley, Yokoi, van Meter, Van Etten, & Freebern, 1997; Yokoi, 1997). One approach is to provide a specific structure to use. Another strategy to consider, especially if your students are novice note-takers, is to occasionally check their notebooks for accuracy and appropriate emphasis and then give constructive feedback.

Retrieving Relevant Prior Knowledge

Students can engage in meaningful learning only to the extent that they have previous knowledge to which they can relate new information and are also *aware* of the potential relationship (Ausubel et al., 1978). A strategy that encourages students to think about the things they already know as they encounter new information is to read aloud a portion of a textbook, stopping occasionally to tie an idea in the text to something previously present in class or tied to your own personal experience. You can then encourage students to do likewise, giving suggestions and guiding their efforts as they proceed (Spires, Donley, & Penrose, 1990). Especially when working in the elementary grades, provide specific questions that remind students to think about what they already know as they read and study.

With time and practice, your students should eventually get in the habit of retrieving relevant prior knowledge with little or no assistance (Spires et al., 1990).

Organizing

As we discovered in Chapter 6, organized information is stored and retrieved more easily than unorganized information. When students engage in activities that help them organize what they are studying, they learn more effectively (DuBois et al., 1988; M. A. McDaniel & Einstein, 1989; Mintzes, Wandersee, & Novak, 1997). For example, one useful way of organizing information is *outlining* the material—a strategy that may be especially helpful to low-achieving students (Baker, 1989; McDaniel & Einstein, 1989; Wade, 1992).

Concept map A diagram of concepts within an instructional unit and the interrelationships among them.

Another strategy that promotes organization is making a **concept map**, a diagram that depicts the concepts of a unit and their interrelationships (Novak, 1998; Novak & Gowin, 1984). Figure 7.2 shows concept maps constructed by two Grade 5 students after they watched a slide lecture on Australia. The concepts themselves are in circles; their interrelationships are designated by lines and phrases that link pairs of concepts. The map on the right shows many more and better described interconnections among concepts than does the map on the left, and we can reasonably assume that the student who drew the right-hand map learned the subject matter more effectively. (Also look back at Figure 6.3 and the related discussion on page 139.)

By focusing on how key concepts relate to one another, students organize material better. They are also more likely to notice how new concepts are related to concepts they already know; thus, they are more likely to learn the material meaningfully and therefore more memorably. Furthermore, when students construct a concept map from verbal material (e.g., from a class presentation or a textbook), they can encode that material in long-term memory visually as well as verbally. The very process of concept mapping promotes a more sophisticated perspective of what learning *is*: Students may begin to realize that learning is not a process of just "absorbing" information but instead involves actively making connections among ideas (Holley & Dansereau, 1984; Mintzes et al., 1997; Novak, 1998; Novak & Gowin, 1984).

Not only do concept maps help students, they can also help you as a teacher. When you develop a concept map for a lesson, the organizational scheme of that lesson becomes clearer, and you have a better idea about how to sequence the presentation of ideas. When you examine the concept maps that your students have constructed, students' understandings of a lesson

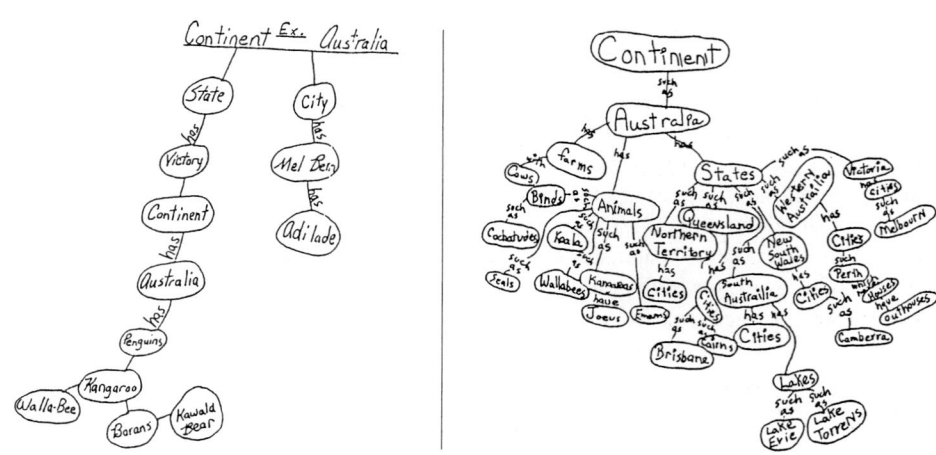

FIGURE 7.2 Concept maps constructed by two Grade 5 students after watching a slide lecture on Australia

From *Learning How to Learn* (pp. 100–101) by J. D. Novak and D. B. Gowin, 1984, Cambridge, England: Cambridge University Press. Copyright 1984 by Cambridge University Press. Reprinted with the permission of Cambridge University Press.

becomes readily apparent, as do any misconceptions (Novak, 1998; Novak & Gowin, 1984; Novak & Musonda, 1991).

Elaborating

Whether they are reading, taking notes in class, or studying for an exam, students typically do better when they elaborate on course material—for example, when they draw inferences from it or consider its implications.

When you model retrieval of relevant prior knowledge, you can model elaboration as well—for example, by stopping to identify your own examples of a concept you are reading about, to consider the implications of a new principle, and so on. You can also give students specific questions to consider as they listen to a class presentation or read their textbook; for example:

- Explain why . . .
- How would you use . . . to . . . ?
- What is a new example of . . . ?
- What do you think would happen if . . . ?
- What is the difference between . . . and . . . ?
(questions from A. King, 1992, p. 309)

In this book report, 7-year-old Ashton shows some elaboration when he says that Toad's habit of singing and reading to his seeds is "very silly." However, most children don't *intentionally* elaborate as a way to learn and remember information until sometime around puberty (see Chapter 2).

Elaborative interrogation A study strategy in which students develop and answer knowledge-expanding (elaborative) questions about the material they are trying to learn.

Another approach is to teach your students to develop and answer their *own* elaborative questions using a strategy known as **elaborative interrogation**[2] (Kahl & Woloshyn, 1994; A. King, 1992, 1994, 1999; Rosenshine, Meister, & Chapman, 1996; E. Wood et al., 1999). For example, let's say your students are studying this fact in a unit on plants indigenous to the Canadian prairies: Many current-day medicines have been derived from these plants. Encourage students to ask themselves, "*How* were the medicines discovered in plants in the first place?" Students will generate answers to their questions as they actively engage with the material.

Elaborative interrogation is often not an easy strategy for students to acquire. They may sometimes use it more effectively, at least at first, when they work in pairs or small groups to develop and answer questions (A. King, 1994; Rosenshine et al., 1996; E. Wood et al., 1999).

In Chapter 10 we will look at *reciprocal teaching*, another effective means of showing students how to elaborate as they read.

Summarizing

Another important learning strategy is summarizing the material being studied (Dole, Duffy, Roehler, & Pearson, 1991; Hidi & Anderson, 1986; A. King, 1992). Effective summarizing usually entails at least three processes (Hidi & Anderson, 1986; Spivey, 1997):

- Separating important from unimportant information
- Condensing details into more general ideas
- Identifying important relationships among those general ideas

Many students have trouble summarizing material even at the high-school level (V. Anderson & Hidi, 1988/1989). Probably the best way of helping students develop this strategy is to ask them to summarize what they hear and read on a regular basis (e.g., see Figure 7.3). For example, you might ask students to work in co-operative groups to develop a brief oral presentation that condenses information they've learned about a particular topic. At first you should restrict summarizing assignments to short, simple, and well-organized passages involving material with which students are familiar; you can assign more challenging material as students become more proficient summarizers (V. Anderson & Hidi, 1988/1989).

FIGURE 7.3 Eight-year-old Nathan summarizes a lesson about glaciers.

---
[2]You may also see the term *guided peer questioning*.

Monitoring Comprehension

Successful learners engage in **comprehension monitoring**: They periodically check themselves to ensure they understand what they are reading or hearing. Then they take steps to correct the situation when they *don't* comprehend, perhaps by rereading a section of a textbook or asking a question in class (Hacker, 1998b; Haller, Child, & Walberg, 1988; Stone, 2000). In contrast, low achievers seldom check for understanding or take appropriate action when they don't comprehend. Poor readers, for instance, rarely reread paragraphs that they haven't sufficiently understood the first time around (Baker & Brown, 1984).

Many students at all grade levels engage in little if any comprehension monitoring (Dole et al., 1991; Markman, 1979; J. W. Thomas, 1993a). When students don't monitor their own comprehension, they don't know what they know and what they don't know: They may think they have mastered something when they really haven't, according to Canadian researchers Deborah Butler and Philip Winne (1995) and others (e.g., Hacker, 1998b; Stone, 2000). This **illusion of knowing** is seen in students at all levels, even college students (Baker, 1989).

To be successful learners—and more specifically, to *know what they know*—students should monitor their comprehension both *while* they are learning and *after* they have learned (Hacker et al., 2000; T. O. Nelson & Dunlosky, 1991; Spires, 1990). You can promote better comprehension-monitoring skills in your students by helping them use **self-questioning**—formulating and asking *themselves*. Ultimately, the goal is to get students actively engaged in the content of instruction, to make it relevant and meaningful to them, and to ensure that important content remains with students to draw on at a later time.

In elaborative interrogation, students learn how to ask one another questions that encourage application, analysis, and other higher-level thinking skills.

Comprehension monitoring The process of checking oneself to make sure one understands the things being read or heard.

Illusion of knowing Thinking one knows something that one actually does not know.

Self-questioning The process of asking oneself questions as a way of checking one's understanding of a topic.

Epistemological beliefs One's beliefs about the nature of knowledge and knowledge acquisition.

Factors Affecting Strategy Use

At least four factors appear to influence students' choice and use of strategies: knowledge base, previous comprehension monitoring, beliefs about the nature of knowledge and knowledge acquisition, and training in learning strategies. Students are more likely to use effective strategies when they have a fair amount of prior knowledge about a topic (Greene, 1994; Schneider, 1993; E. Wood et al., 1994). Students are also likely to acquire and use new, more effective strategies only if they realize that their prior strategies have been *in*effective. They will come to such a conclusion only if they monitor their comprehension regularly and so are aware that they are not learning and understanding classroom subject matter as well as they would like (Kuhn, Garcia-Mila, Zohar, & Andersen, 1995; Lodico, Ghatala, Levin, Pressley, & Bell, 1983; Loranger, 1994). It also plays a pivotal role in the development of *other* metacognitive strategies.

Students have differing views about the nature of knowledge and knowledge acquisition; in other words, they have differing **epistemological beliefs**. Students' epistemological beliefs often influence how they study and learn (Hofer & Pintrich, 1997; Purdie, Hattie, & Douglas, 1996; Schommer, 1997). For example, many students believe that knowledge or ideas are indisputably either right or wrong, and that you either have that knowledge or you don't. But other students recognize that there may be different, equally valid viewpoints on the same topic that could all legitimately be called "knowledge." The former students are more likely to believe that learning should be a relatively rapid process, and so they will give up quickly if they find themselves struggling to understand classroom material (Schommer, 1994b).

As a teacher, it is important to communicate to your students—in what you *say* as well as what you *do* (e.g., what activities you assign, how you assess students' learning)—what you yourself have already learned about knowledge and knowledge acquisition (Hofer & Pintrich, 1997; Schommer, 1994b):

- Knowledge does not always mean having clear-cut answers to difficult, complex issues.
- Knowledge involves knowing the interrelationships among ideas, as well as the ideas themselves.
- Learning involves active construction of knowledge, rather than just a passive "reception" of it.
- Understanding a body of information and ideas sometimes requires persistence and hard work.

In doing so, you will increase the likelihood that your students will apply effective learning strategies, critically evaluate classroom subject matter, and undergo conceptual change when they encounter explanations that contradict their current beliefs (Hofer & Pintrich, 1997; Purdie et al., 1996; Schommer, 1994b; C. L. Smith, Maclin, Houghton, & Hennessey, 2000; Strike & Posner, 1992).

"Learning" Learning Strategies

Students can be taught to study and learn more effectively (see the reference list at the bottom of Table 7.3). Study skills training programs often include the following components:

TABLE 7.3 — PRINCIPLES/ASSUMPTIONS
Promoting More Effective Learning Strategies

PRINCIPLE	EDUCATIONAL IMPLICATION	EXAMPLE
Learning strategies are most effectively learned within the context of particular content domains.	When presenting academic content through lectures, reading assignments, and so on, simultaneously teach students how to study that content.	Give students specific questions to ask themselves (thereby facilitating comprehension monitoring) as they read their textbooks.
Group learning situations often promote the development of effective strategies, perhaps because students verbalize and model various ways to think about classroom subject matter.	Occasionally ask students to study instructional materials in pairs or small co-operative learning groups.	Have students work in pairs to develop and answer questions that require them to elaborate on textbook content.
Students are more likely to acquire sophisticated learning strategies when their initial efforts are scaffolded to promote success.	Scaffold students' attempts to use new strategies—for instance, by modelling the strategies, giving clues about when to use them, and giving feedback on appropriate and inappropriate strategy use.	To encourage students to organize material in a particular way, provide an organizational chart that co-operative learning groups fill out.
Students learn more effectively when their learning strategies are numerous and varied.	As opportunities arise, continue to introduce new strategies—note taking, elaboration, self-questioning, mnemonics, and so on—throughout the school year.	Suggest that students use such mnemonics as verbal mediation and the keyword method to learn the capitals of South American countries or the meanings of Japanese vocabulary words.
Students are more likely to use effective learning strategies when they understand why those strategies are useful.	Explain the usefulness of various strategies in ways that students understand.	Show students how note taking helps them keep their minds from wandering during class and how comprehension monitoring enables them to identify gaps in their knowledge.
Students use strategies more effectively if they know when each one is most appropriate.	Point out occasions in which particular strategies are likely to be helpful.	Give students opportunities to elaborate on material—by drawing implications, generating new examples, and so on—when they must apply it to new situations.
Students are most likely to master effective strategies when they can practise them regularly across a wide variety of tasks.	Give students numerous and varied opportunities to apply metacognitive strategies.	Ask students' previous teachers what strategies they have taught and then explain how such strategies are applicable for current learning tasks as well.
Students are likely to use effective strategies only when they believe such strategies can ultimately help them learn more effectively.	When teaching study strategies, make sure each student is eventually able to apply them successfully. Also, expose students to peers who model effective use of the strategies.	After a lecture, place students in small groups in which they look at the notes each group member has taken and then combine all notes into a single, comprehensive set.

Sources: P. A. Alexander et al., 1998; R. C. Anderson et al., 2001; Barnett et al., 1981; Borkowski, Carr, Rellinger, & Pressley, 1990; D. L. Butler & Winne, 1995; A. Collins et al., 1989; Hacker, 1998b; Hattie, Biggs, & Purdie, 1996; Kahl & Woloshyn, 1994; A. King, 1992, 1994; Kucan & Beck, 1997; Kuhn et al., 1995; Mayer & Wittrock, 1996; Meloth & Deering, 1994; Nist, Simpson, Olejnik, & Mealey, 1991; Palincsar & Brown, 1984; Paris, 1988; Paris & Winograd, 1990; Pintrich, García, & De Groot, 1994; Pressley, Borkowski, & Schneider, 1987; Pressley, El-Dinary, Marks, et al., 1992; Pressley, Harris, & Marks, 1992; Rosenshine & Meister, 1992; Rosenshine et al., 1996; Starr & Lovett, 2000; J. W. Thomas, 1993a; Vygotsky, 1978; C. E. Weinstein, Goetz, & Alexander, 1988; West et al., 1991; Winne, 1995; E. Wood et al., 1994.

- Time management (e.g., planning when and how long to study)
- Effective learning and reading strategies
- Note-taking strategies
- Specific memory techniques (e.g., mnemonics)
- Comprehension-monitoring strategies
- Test-taking strategies

Graduates of successful study skills training programs are more confident about their ability to succeed in the classroom and, in fact, do achieve at higher levels (e.g., Paris, 1988; Pressley, El-Dinary, Marks, Brown, & Stein, 1992; J. E. Wilson, 1988).

How can we help students *learn how to learn?* Researchers have identified several principles that describe the conditions under which students are most likely to acquire and use effective learning skills. Table 7.3 presents these principles, along with their implications for classroom practice.

How students learn school subject matter has implications not only for how effectively they can remember it but also for how likely they are to *use* this knowledge on later occasions, as we shall see in our upcoming exploration of transfer.

Transfer

Transfer A phenomenon or process wherein something that an individual has learned at one time affects how the individual learns or performs in a later situation.

When something students have previously learned affects how they learn or perform in another situation, **transfer** is occurring. Ideally, transfer of knowledge should be a major objective for classrooms at all grade levels. For example, when people cannot use their basic arithmetic skills to compute correct change, balance a chequebook, or solve a chemistry equation, then we have to wonder whether the time spent learning the arithmetic might have been better spent doing something else. As we explore the nature of transfer in this section, we will identify numerous ways to help students apply classroom subject matter to new situations, both in their future academic studies and in the outside world.

Basic Concepts in Transfer

We begin our discussion by distinguishing between various kinds of transfer—in particular, between positive and negative transfer, and between specific and general transfer.

Positive versus Negative Transfer

Positive transfer A phenomenon whereby something learned at one time facilitates learning or performance at a later time.

Negative transfer A phenomenon whereby something learned at one time interferes with learning or performance at a later time.

Positive transfer occurs when something that a person has learned in one situation *helps* that person learn or perform in another situation. For example, Céline speaks French and English fluently. She is currently taking Spanish and realizes that her knowledge of French will help her to learn Spanish vocabulary.

In contrast, **negative transfer** occurs when prior knowledge *hinders* a person's learning or performance at a later time. For example, if Céline were to transfer the rules of pronunciation and grammar from French to Spanish (e.g., Littlewood, 1984).

Earlier in this chapter we discovered that previously acquired misconceptions can have a negative impact on learning. Here we see that *correct* ideas and information sometimes have a negative impact as well, in that students may apply them inappropriately in new situations.

Can you think of a recent situation in which you exhibited positive transfer? Negative transfer?

Specific versus General Transfer

Specific transfer An instance of transfer in which the original learning task and the transfer task overlap in content.

General transfer An instance of transfer in which the original learning task and the transfer task do not overlap in content.

When transfer occurs because the original learning task and the transfer task overlap in content, we have **specific transfer**. When learning in one situation affects learning and performance in a somewhat dissimilar situation, we have **general transfer**.

Within the past few years, however, theorists such as Canadian psychologist Carl Bereiter (1997) and others (e.g., J. R. Anderson, Greeno, Reder, & Simon, 2000; J. R. Anderson, Reder, & Simon, 1996, 1997) have increasingly come to realize that the knowledge and skills learned in school are *not* always limited to the specific contexts in which they have been acquired. For instance, we frequently see general transfer in metacognition: When students acquire effective learning strategies within the context of one academic discipline, those strategies often transfer positively to learning in a very different discipline (Brooks & Dansereau, 1987; Perkins, 1995; Pressley, Snyder, & Cariglia-Bull, 1987). In addition, many students apply some of the skills they learn in school, such as skills in reading and arithmetic, to a broad range of out-of-school tasks (J. R. Anderson et al., 1996).

Factors Affecting Transfer

Although both specific and general transfer do occur, students often *don't* transfer the knowledge and skills they learn in school on occasions when such knowledge and skills are clearly applicable (Mayer & Wittrock, 1996; Perkins, 1992; Renkl, Mandl, & Gruber, 1996). Research has revealed that a number of factors influence the extent to which transfer occurs. These factors are summarized as general principles in Table 7.4. Let's look briefly at each one.

TABLE 7.4   PRINCIPLES/ASSUMPTIONS

Basic Principles of Transfer

PRINCIPLE	EDUCATIONAL IMPLICATION	EXAMPLE
As **instructional time** increases, the probability of transfer also increases.	To promote transfer, teach a few topics in depth, rather than many topics superficially.	When teaching a unit on the geography of South America, focus on environmental and cultural similarities and differences across the continent, instead of presenting a lengthy, encyclopedia-like list of facts about each country.
Meaningful learning leads to greater transfer than rote learning.	Encourage students to relate new material to the things they already know.	When introducing the concept *gravity* to Grade 3 students, ask them to think about what happens whenever they throw an object into the air (i.e., it comes back down).
Principles transfer more readily than facts.	Teach general principles (e.g., cause–effect relationships) related to each topic, along with general strategies based on those principles.	When teaching a unit on softball, basketball, soccer, or tennis, tell students, "Keep your eye on the ball," and explain why such vigilance is important.
Numerous and varied **examples** and **opportunities for practice** promote transfer.	Illustrate new concepts and principles with a variety of examples, and engage students in activities that let them practise new skills in different contexts.	After teaching students what a complete sentence is, have them practise writing complete sentences in essays, short stories, and class newsletter articles.
As the **similarity** between two situations increases, so does the probability of transfer from one situation to the other.	Make school tasks as similar as possible to the tasks that students are likely to encounter in the outside world.	When teaching students about the foods that make a balanced diet, have them prepare a healthful lunch with groceries from a local food store.
Transfer is more likely when only a **short amount of time** has elapsed after students have studied a topic.	Present topics as close in time as possible to the occasions when students may need to use those topics.	After having students learn and play the F Major scale in an instrumental music class, have them practise several musical pieces in the key of F Major.
Transfer is more likely when students perceive classroom material to be **context-free** rather than context-bound.	Relate topics in one discipline to topics in other disciplines and to tasks in the outside world. Ensure that students perceive the topic as a whole and its component parts, each in relation to other knowledge.	When teaching students how to solve for *x* in algebra, give them word problems in which they must solve for an unknown in such contexts as physics, building construction, and sewing. Give students examples and practise breaking down tasks into their subtasks and component ideas, which makes it easier to draw meaningful and multiple connections at different levels.

Amount (and quality) of instructional time. Instructional time is clearly an important variable affecting transfer: The more time students spend studying a particular topic, the more likely they are to transfer what they learn to a new situation (Gick & Holyoak, 1987; Schmidt & Bjork, 1992; Voss, 1987). Students are also more likely to transfer their school learning to new situations, including those beyond the classroom, when students study a few things in depth and learn them well, rather than study many topics superficially (J. E. Brophy, 1992; Porter, 1989).

Extent to which learning is meaningful. In Chapter 6 we identified two advantages of meaningful learning over rote learning: Information is stored more quickly and is retrieved more easily. An additional advantage is that information learned in a meaningful fashion is more likely to be transferred or applied to a new situation (Bereiter, 1995; Brooks & Dansereau, 1987; Mayer & Wittrock, 1996).

Remember, meaningful learning involves connecting information with what one already knows. The more associations students make between new information and the various other things in their long-term memories, the more likely it is that they will "find" (retrieve) that information at a time when it will be useful.

> Think about the subject matter you will be teaching. How can you ensure that the general principles you are teaching have wide transfer for students?

Extent to which principles rather than facts are learned. People can transfer general (and perhaps somewhat abstract) principles more easily than specific, concrete facts (J. R. Anderson et al., 1996; Judd, 1932; Perkins & Salomon, 1987).

Variety of examples and opportunities for practice. Students are more likely to apply something they learn if, within the course of instruction, they are given many examples and opportunities to practise in different situations (Cox, 1997; Reimann & Schult, 1996; J. A. Ross, 1988; Schmidt & Bjork, 1992). By using knowledge in many contexts, students store that knowledge in association with all those contexts and so are more likely to retrieve the information on a future occasion (Perkins & Salomon, 1987; Voss, 1987).

Similarity of the two situations. Transfer is more likely to occur when a new situation appears to be similar to a previous situation (Bassok, 1990; Blake & Clark, 1990; Di Vesta & Peverly, 1984). Here we see the value of authentic activities in the curriculum. The examples and opportunities for practice that you give your students should be very similar to the situations that they are likely to encounter in future studies or in the outside world (Perkins, 1992).

Yet we should note that the similarity of two situations, while promoting positive transfer, might promote negative transfer as well. It is important that you explicitly point out the differences between two superficially similar topics to students in order to prevent such negative transfer.

Length of time between the two situations. Students are most likely to apply new information soon after they have learned it (Gick & Holyoak, 1987). Thus, whenever possible try to present topics to students at a time close to when students will need to use those topics.

> What implications does this idea have for classroom assessment practices?

Perception of information as context-free rather than context-bound. In many cases, we would like students to transfer their knowledge in one content domain to a different domain—for example, to transfer mathematics to physics and grammar to creative writing. Yet students tend to think of academic subject areas as being distinct, unrelated disciplines; they also tend to think of their school learning as being separate from real-world concerns (Perkins & Simmons, 1988; Rakow, 1984) or context-bound. Transfer will therefore be difficult outside of that context (P. A. Alexander & Judy, 1988; J. R. Anderson et al., 1996; Bassok, 1996; diSessa, 1982; Renkl et al., 1996). Transfer is also difficult if students think of knowledge as immutable "wholes" rather than made up of parts with which they can experiment mentally or physically by creatively rearranging, adding, deleting, or elaborating. Using the building blocks of learning in these ways (i.e., not being overly constrained by an original context) is called **generativity** (R. Epstein, 1993; the term is also used in personality and computer theory). Generativity facilitates transfer both by treating knowledge as constructed and by implicitly and explicitly empowering learners to "play with" what they are learning and to create their own new meanings that can be tested in dialogue with classmates and teachers (Chapter 6).

> **Generativity** Creating new learning from previous learning, including new combinations and new contexts or application. Also, the feeling of empowerment to take such initiatives and "play with" knowledge.

When teaching within a particular content area, then, it is important to relate that material to other disciplines and to the outside world as often as possible (Blake & Clark, 1990; Perkins, 1992). Students should also be encouraged to brainstorm specific situations in which they could apply what they are learning in class (J. R. Anderson et al., 1996). Ideally, students should use what they learn in many different contexts, including a variety of authentic activities, so that eventually their knowledge and skills become *context-free* (A. Collins et al., 1989).

Importance of Retrieval in Transfer

The factors we've just examined point to a key principle in transfer: From a cognitive perspective, information learned in one situation helps in another situation only if the information is *retrieved* within the context of that second situation (Cormier, 1987; Gick & Holyoak, 1987; Halpern, 1998). Several factors—in-depth study, meaningful learning, focus on general principles, variety of examples and practice opportunities, and perception of a domain as context-free—encourage students to make numerous connections between class material and other aspects of their world, and such multiple connections will invariably enhance the likelihood of retrieving that material on occasions where it is potentially relevant.

Another factor—similarity between the learning situation and transfer situation—is related to retrieval as well. Students are more likely to transfer what they learn in one situation to a similar (rather than dissimilar) situation because a similar situation provides *retrieval cues* that remind students of specific, relevant things they have already learned (Gick & Holyoak, 1987; Perkins & Salomon, 1989; Sternberg & Frensch, 1993).

The factors that affect transfer also affect one very important form of transfer: solving problems. Cognitive psychologists have offered additional insights about problem solving as well, as you shall see now.

Children are more likely to transfer their knowledge of fractions and ratios to future situations if they practise using fractions and ratios in a variety of contexts.

Problem Solving

This section of the chapter explores the multifaceted nature of human problem solving. After defining several basic concepts, we will examine cognitive factors that help or hinder successful problem solving; in the process, we will also identify strategies for helping your own students become more successful problem solvers.

Basic Concepts in Problem Solving

The problems that students need to solve differ widely in their content and scope and require different strategies to reach a solution. Virtually all problems can be considered as either *well-defined* or *ill-defined*, and most problem-solving strategies can be categorized as either *algorithms* or *heuristics*.

Well-Defined and Ill-Defined Problems

Problems differ in the extent to which they are clearly specified and structured. A **well-defined problem** is one in which the goal is clearly stated, all information needed to solve the problem is present, and only one correct answer exists. Calculating the amount of change one gets from a loonie to purchase a cookie from the school's bake sale is an example of a well-defined problem: we know exactly what is required to solve the problem.

In contrast, an **ill-defined problem** is one in which the desired goal is unclear, information needed to solve the problem is missing, or several possible solutions to the problem exist. The deforestation of the rain forest is an example of an ill-defined problem. First, the goal—curtailing deforestation—is ambiguous. Do we want to stop deforestation altogether or just slow it down a bit? If we just want to decrease the rate, what rate is acceptable? Second, we undoubtedly need more information to solve the problem. For example, it would be helpful to determine whether previously cleared and farmed lands can be reclaimed and rejuvenated, and to identify economically reasonable alternatives to slash-and-burn farming practices. Some of this needed information may require extensive research. Finally, there is no single "correct" solution: Curtailing deforestation will undoubtedly require a number of steps taken more or less simultaneously. Ill-defined problems, then, are usually more difficult to solve than well-defined ones and require further definition by students.

One way to help your students learn to solve problems is to teach them techniques for better defining ill-defined problems. For example, teaching students how to break large problems into smaller, well-defined ones. You can also teach them to distinguish information they need from information they may *not* need. You can also teach techniques for finding missing information.

Well-defined problem A problem in which the goal is clearly stated, all information needed to solve the problem is present, and only one correct answer exists.

Ill-defined problem A problem in which the desired goal is unclear, information needed to solve the problem is missing, and/or several possible solutions to the problem exist.

Problem-Solving Strategies: Algorithms and Heuristics

Algorithm A prescribed sequence of steps that guarantees a correct problem solution.

Some problems can be successfully solved by following specific, step-by-step instructions—that is, by using an **algorithm**. For example, we can put a new bicycle together by following the "Directions for Assembly" that come with it. When we follow an algorithm faithfully, we invariably arrive at a correct solution.

Yet not all problems come equipped with directions for assembly. There are no rules we can follow to help us solve the deforestation problem described earlier. When there is no algorithm for solving a problem, people may instead use a **heuristic**, a general problem-solving strategy that may or may not yield a workable solution.

Heuristic A general problem-solving strategy that may or may not yield a problem solution.

Students in our classrooms get far more practice solving well-defined problems than ill-defined ones, and they are taught many more algorithms than heuristics. For example, they are likely to spend more school time learning problem-solving strategies useful in determining the amount of change from a loonie than strategies applicable to the problem of deforestation. Yet many real-world problems—problems that your students will encounter after graduation—probably cannot be solved with cut-and-dried algorithms. Furthermore, few true algorithms exist for solving problems outside the domains of mathematics and science.

Problem-solving strategies, algorithms and heuristics alike, are often specific to a particular content domain. But here are three general problem-solving heuristics that your students may find helpful in a variety of contexts:

- *Identify subgoals.* Break a problem into two or more subproblems that can be better defined and more easily solved.
- *Work backward.* Begin at the goal of the problem (i.e., the solution needed) and work backward, one step at a time, toward the initial problem statement.
- *Draw an analogy.* Identify a situation analogous to the problem situation and derive potential problem solutions from that analogy.

Teaching problem-solving strategies. How can you help your students acquire effective problem-solving strategies? Here are a number of possibilities:

For teaching algorithms:

- Describe and demonstrate specific algorithms and situations in which they can be used.
- Provide worked-out examples of algorithms being applied.
- Help students understand why particular algorithms are relevant and effective in certain situations.
- When a student's application of an algorithm yields an incorrect answer, look closely at the specific steps the student has taken until the trouble spot is located.

For teaching heuristics:

- Give students practice in defining ill-defined problems.
- Teach heuristics that students can use in situations where no specific algorithms apply; for example, encourage such strategies as rounding, identifying subgoals, working backward, and drawing analogies.

For teaching both algorithms and heuristics:

- Teach problem-solving strategies within the context of specific subject areas (*not* as a topic separate from academic content).
- Provide scaffolding for difficult problems—for example, by breaking them into smaller and simpler problems, giving hints about possible strategies, or providing partial solutions.
- Ask students to explain what they are doing as they work through a problem.
- Have students solve problems in small groups, sharing ideas about problem-solving strategies, modelling various approaches for one another, and discussing the merits of each approach. (R. K. Atkinson, Derry, Renkl, & Wortham, 2000; Barron, 2000; Crowley & Siegler, 1999; Heller & Hungate, 1985; Mayer, 1985, 1992; Noddings, 1985; Reimann & Schult, 1996; L. B. Resnick, 1983)

As we have seen, well-defined problems are usually more easily solved than ill-defined ones, and problems that can be solved with algorithms are generally easier than those that require heuristics. But there are several other factors, all cognitive in nature, that affect problem-solving success as well.

Cognitive Factors Affecting Problem Solving

Cognitive psychologists have identified several factors that affect problem-solving success:

Working Memory Capacity

Working memory has a limited capacity: It can hold only a few pieces of information and can accommodate only so much cognitive processing at any one time. If a problem requires an individual to deal with too much information at once or to manipulate that information in a very complex way, working memory capacity may be insufficient for effective problem processing. Once working memory capacity is exceeded, the problem cannot be solved (Johnstone & El-Banna, 1986; Perkins, 1995).

Students who learn basic skills to automaticity have more working memory capacity to handle complex tasks that require such skills.

Students can overcome the limits of their working memories in at least two ways. One obvious way is to create an external record of information relevant to the problem—for example, by writing that information on a piece of paper. Another way to overcome working memory capacity is to learn some skills to a level of automaticity (look again at this section in Chapter 6)—in other words, to learn them to a point where they can be retrieved quickly, easily, and almost without conscious thought (N. Frederiksen, 1984a; Mayer & Wittrock, 1996; Rabinowitz & Glaser, 1985; Schneider & Shiffrin, 1977).

Encoding of the Problem

When we discussed cognitive processes in Chapter 6, we talked about *encoding,* changing the form of new information while storing it in memory. Encoding is clearly a factor that affects problem-solving ability. Sometimes students have trouble encoding a problem in any way that allows them to begin working to solve it. Students often have trouble solving mathematical word problems because they don't know how to translate those problems into procedures or operations with which they are familiar (Mayer, 1992; L. B. Resnick, 1989; Reusser, 1990). At other times, students may encode a problem in a seemingly logical way that nevertheless fails to yield a correct problem solution. As an example, take a stab at the problem in the following exercise.

EXPERIENCING FIRSTHAND   *The Candle Problem*

You are in a room with a bulletin board firmly affixed to the wall about 1 metre above the floor. Your task is to *stand a candle upright* in front of the bulletin board. You do not want the candle touching the bulletin board, because the candle's flame must not singe the bulletin board. Instead, you need to place the candle about 1 centimetre away. How can you accomplish the task with the following materials?

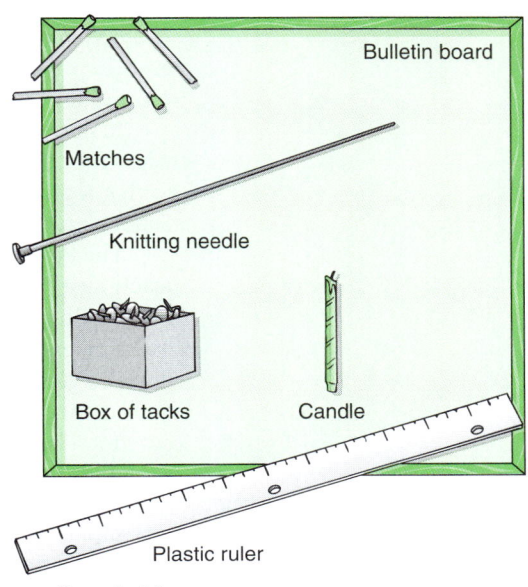

- Small candle
- Metal knitting needle
- Matches
- Box of thumbtacks
- 30-centimetre plastic ruler
- See whether you can solve the problem before you read further.

Based on Duncker, 1945

As it turns out, the ruler and knitting needle are useless in solving the candle problem (if you try to puncture the candle with the knitting needle, you will probably break the candle; if you try to balance the ruler on a few tacks, it will probably fall down). The easiest solution is to fasten the thumbtack box to the bulletin board with tacks

Mental set Encoding (or, more generally, creating a mental representation of a problem in a way that excludes potential problem solutions.

and then attach the candle to the top of the box with either a tack or some melted wax. Many people don't consider this solution, however, because they encode the box only as a *container of tacks,* thereby overlooking its potential use as a candle stand. When we encode a problem in a way that excludes potential solutions, we are the victims of a **mental set**.

Mental sets in problem solving sometimes emerge when students practise solving a particular kind of problem (e.g., doing subtraction problems in math) without also practising other kinds of problems at the same time (E. J. Langer, 2000; Luchins, 1942). Such repetitive practice can lead students to encode problems in a particular way without really thinking about the problems; that is, it can lead to automaticity in encoding. Although automaticity in the basic information and skills needed for problem solving is often an advantage (it frees up working memory capacity), automaticity in *encoding* problems may lead students to solve them incorrectly and so in many cases is a *dis*advantage (E. J. Langer, 2000).

Following are several strategies we can use to help students encode problems more effectively yet not fall victim to counterproductive mental sets:

- Present problems in a concrete way; for example, provide real objects that students can manipulate or an illustration of a problem's components (A. S. Luchins & Luchins, 1950; Mayer, 1992).
- Encourage students to make problems concrete *for themselves;* for example, encourage them to draw a picture or diagram of a problem (Anzai, 1991; Mayer, 1986; Prawat, 1989; K. Schultz & Lochhead, 1991).
- Point out any features of problems that students *can* solve, and when those features appear again in a different problem, indicate that the same information can be applied or the same approach to problem solution can be used (Prawat, 1989).
- Give problems that look very different on the surface yet require the same or similar problem-solving procedures (Z. Chen, 1999).
- Mix up the kinds of problems that students tackle in any given practice session (E. J. Langer, 2000).
- Have students work in co-operative groups to identify different ways of representing a single problem—perhaps as a formula, a table, and a graph (Brenner et al., 1997; J. C. Turner, Meyer, et al., 1998).

Depth and Integration of One's Knowledge Relevant to the Problem

Research consistently indicates that when students have a thorough, conceptual understanding of a topic—when they have stored a great deal of information about it, with various pieces of information appropriately organized and interrelated in long-term memory—they can more easily use their knowledge to solve problems (P. A. Alexander & Judy, 1988; Heller & Hungate, 1985; Voss, Greene, Post, & Penner, 1983). For example, students are more likely to apply a principle of physics to a specific situation if they understand the concepts underlying that principle and the situations to which it relates.

In contrast, when students have limited knowledge about a certain topic, and particularly when they don't have a conceptual understanding of it, they are likely to encode problems related to that topic on the basis of superficial problem characteristics (Chi, Feltovich, & Glaser, 1981; Schoenfeld & Hermann, 1982).

The fact that conceptual understanding facilitates problem solving is yet another reason for teaching a few topics thoroughly, rather than many topics superficially (the *less is more* notion once again). It also suggests that, for any given procedure or principle, we should provide many and different examples and opportunities for practice. For example, students can study arithmetic operations by using such diverse examples as balancing a chequebook, calculating change, or predicting the possible profits and necessary supplies (number of cups, amount of lemonade mix, etc.) for a lemonade stand. Only by spending time with a certain topic and studying a variety of examples can students learn that topic in a meaningful fashion and make multiple connections with situations to which that subject matter applies. All too often, students don't have these critical opportunities (e.g., Porter, 1989).

Your students are also more likely to make connections between classroom material and its potential applications when they anticipate situations in which they might need to use the material to solve problems (J. R. Anderson et al., 1996). Not only should classroom instruction

In what areas do you have the depth of knowledge necessary for solving problems successfully? In what areas has your relative lack of knowledge been a handicap?

be focused on the application of information, but assessment procedures should focus on application as well (Bransford, Franks, Vye, & Sherwood, 1989; Sternberg & Frensch, 1993), as you will learn in Chapter 12.

Retrieval of Relevant Information from Long-Term Memory

Obviously, students cannot solve a problem unless they retrieve from long-term memory the information necessary to solve it. But as we discovered in Chapter 6, long-term memory contains a great deal of information, and students cannot possibly retrieve it all in any given situation. Successful problem solving therefore requires that students search the right "places" in long-term memory at the right time. The parts of long-term memory that a student searches depends on how the student encoded the problem in the first place.

Metacognitive Processes

Earlier in the chapter we discovered the importance of metacognition for effective learning and studying. Metacognitive processes play an important role in problem solving as well. For instance, effective problem solvers tend to

- Identify one or more goals that reflect problem solutions
- Break a complex problem into two or more subproblems
- Plan a systematic, sequential approach to solving the problem and any subproblems
- Continually monitor and evaluate their progress toward their goal(s)
- Identify any obstacles that may be impeding their progress
- Change to a new strategy if the current one does not seem to be working (J. E. Davidson & Sternberg, 1998; Dominowski, 1998)

Such metacognitive processes enable students to use problem-solving strategies flexibly, to apply them to more complex problem situations, and to know when particular strategies are and are not appropriate (J. E. Davidson & Sternberg, 1998; Dominowski, 1998). In contrast, *ineffective* problem solvers tend to apply problem-solving procedures mindlessly, without any real understanding of what they are doing or why they are doing it (M. Carr & Biddlecomb, 1998; J. E. Davidson & Sternberg, 1998).

> How many of your exams have tested your ability to remember information, but not *apply* information? Did such exams give you the message that knowing something was important but using it was not?

INTO THE CLASSROOM   *Promoting Successful Transfer and Problem Solving*

Tie class material to what students already know.

> After teaching that water expands when it freezes, a science teacher explains that many of the bumps seen in country roads are frost heaves caused by freezing water.

Give students practice in dealing with ill-defined problems and show them how to make such problems more well-defined.

> A teacher asks students in an interdisciplinary class to wrestle with the problem of diminishing rain forests. He starts them off by asking, "What should be the final goal of preservation efforts?" and "What are some of the biological, social, and political factors that you need to consider as you try to solve this problem?"

Teach the basic information and skills needed in problem solving to a level of automaticity.

> An elementary school teacher makes sure that his students have thoroughly mastered the basic multiplication and division facts before teaching them long division.

Provide opportunities for students to apply what they have learned to new situations and problems.

> A social studies teacher asks students to apply their knowledge of human settlement patterns in explaining why the populations of various countries are distributed as they are.

Ask students to apply what they know in tests and other assessment activities.

> A science teacher asks students to use principles of physics to describe how they might singlehandedly move a 200-kilogram object to a location 6 meters away.

Make school tasks similar to the tasks that students are likely to encounter in the outside world.

> An art teacher and a language arts teacher develop a joint project in which students develop posters and email messages to advertise the school's knowledge fairs and annual theatre productions.

Students' metacognitive awareness can be enhanced when you ask students to explain what they are doing, and why they are doing it, as they work on a problem (Dominowski, 1998; Johanning, D'Agostino, Steele, & Shumow, 1999). You can also give them questions they can ask *themselves* as they work on a problem—questions such as "What are we trying to do here?" "Are we getting closer to our goal?" "What didn't work?" (A. King, 1999, p. 101). Such approaches are especially effective when students work in pairs or small groups on challenging problems and must explain and defend their reasoning to one another (Johanning et al., 1999; A. King, 1999).

> Such instructional strategies are more likely to be helpful for average-ability rather than high-ability students (J. E. Davidson & Sternberg, 1998). Why might this be so?

Using Computer Technology to Promote Effective Problem Solving

Throughout our discussion of problem solving, we have identified numerous strategies for enhancing students' problem-solving effectiveness. Most of these have relied on fairly traditional classroom resources and techniques, yet you can also capitalize on computer technology to foster students' problem-solving capabilities as well. For instance,

- Use computer-based tutoring programs to promote mathematical and scientific reasoning and problem solving
- Show students how to use spreadsheets to analyze complex sets of data
- Use computer simulations that allow students to formulate hypotheses, design experiments to test those hypotheses, interpret the virtual results, and state new hypotheses
- Present complex real-world problems (i.e., authentic activities) that students must solve (Cognition and Technology Group at Vanderbilt, 1990, 1996; Vye et al., 1998)

Critical Thinking

Critical thinking Evaluating the accuracy and worth of information or arguments.

Critical thinking involves evaluating the accuracy and worth of information or arguments (Beyer, 1985), especially "in terms of their logical and empirical foundations" (B. Linn & Shore, 2008, p. 155). Critical thinking may take a variety of forms, depending on the context. For instance, it may involve any one or more of the following (Halpern, 1997a, 1998):

- *Verbal reasoning:* Understanding and evaluating the persuasive techniques found in oral and written language (e.g., deductive and inductive logic).
- *Argument analysis:* Discriminating between reasons that do and do not support a particular conclusion. For example, imagine this situation:

  > You have a beat-up old car and it would cost several thousand dollars to get it in working order. You can sell the car in its present condition for $1500, or you can invest a couple of thousand dollars on more repairs and then sell it for $3000. What should you do? (modelled after Halpern, 1998)

  Obviously, it makes more sense to sell the car now: If you sell the car for $3000 after making $2000 worth of repairs, you make $500 less than you would otherwise. Yet many people mistakenly believe that their *past* investments justify making additional ones, when in fact past investments are irrelevant to the present state of affairs (Halpern, 1998).

- *Probabilistic reasoning:* Determining the likelihood and uncertainties associated with various events. As an example, consider the following situation:

  > You have been rolling a typical six-sided die (i.e., one member of a pair of dice). You know for a fact that the die is not "loaded" (it's not heavier on one side than another), and yet in the past 30 rolls you have not rolled a number 4 even once. What are the odds that you will get a 4 in the next roll?

  Many people mistakenly believe that a roll of 4 is long overdue and so is more likely in the next roll than it would be otherwise.[3] In fact, on any roll of an unloaded (fair) die, the probability is 1 in 6 that its outcome will be a 4, *regardless* of the outcomes of any previous rolls.

---

[3] Such reasoning is sometimes called the *gambler's fallacy*.

- *Hypothesis testing:* Evaluating the value of data and research results in terms of the methods used to obtain them and their potential relevance to particular conclusions. When hypothesis testing includes critical thinking, it involves considering questions such as these:

    Was an appropriate method used to measure a particular outcome?

    Have other possible explanations or conclusions been eliminated?

    Can the results obtained in one situation be reasonably generalized to other situations?

- *Decision making:* Identifying several alternatives and selecting the best alternative.

All too often, students at all grade levels (even university students) take the information they see in textbooks, advertisements, media reports, and elsewhere at face value; in other words, they engage in little or no critical thinking as they consider its accuracy and worth. Students are more likely to look analytically and critically at new information if they believe that even experts' understanding of any single topic continues to evolve as new evidence accumulates; they are less likely to engage in critical thinking if they believe that "knowledge" is an absolute, unchanging entity (Kardash & Scholes, 1996; Kuhn, 2001; Schommer-Aikins, 2001). In other words, students' *epistemological beliefs* enter into the critical thinking process. So do their linguistic skills and command of language (Chapter 2), without which students would have little ability to use reason in the ways demanded by critical thinking.

Canadian psychologist Keith Stanovich at the University of Toronto has extensively studied critical thinking and identified four thinking dispositions essential to critical thinking: active and intentional cognition, cognitive flexibility, awareness of and sensibility to different sources of bias, and decontextualizing (B. Linn & Shore, 2008; Stanovich, 1999, 2004).

Some suggestions for promoting critical thinking in your classroom include:

- Teach fewer topics, but in greater depth—the *less is more* principle yet again (Onosko, 1989; Onosko & Newmann, 1994).
- Encourage some intellectual skepticism—for instance, by urging students to question and challenge the ideas that they read and hear—and communicate the message that our knowledge and understanding of any single topic will continue to change over time (Kardash & Scholes, 1996; Kuhn, 2001; Onosko, 1989).
- Model and have students practise seeking and comparing **convergent evidence** from multiple sources (sometimes called triangulation) as a way to build and verify good arguments (Stanovich, 2007).
- Model critical thinking—for instance, by thinking aloud while analyzing a persuasive argument or scientific report (Onosko & Newmann, 1994).
- Show students that critical thinking involves considerable mental effort, but that the benefits often make the effort worthwhile (Halpern, 1998).
- Give students many and varied opportunities to practise critical thinking—for instance, by identifying flaws in the logical arguments presented in persuasive essays and by evaluating the quality and usefulness of scientific findings (Halpern, 1998).
- Ask questions such as these to encourage critical thinking:

    What additional information do I need?

    What information is relevant to this situation? What information is irrelevant?

    What persuasive technique is the author using? Is it valid, or is it designed to mislead the reader?

    What reasons support the conclusion? What reasons do *not* support the conclusion?

    What actions might I take to improve the design of this study? (based on Halpern, 1998, p. 454)

- Have students debate controversial issues from several perspectives, occasionally asking them to take a perspective quite different from their own (Reiter, 1994).
- Embed critical thinking skills within the context of authentic activities as a way of helping students retrieve those skills later on, both in the workplace and in other aspects of adult life (Derry et al., 1998; Halpern, 1998).

McGill University researchers Brenda Linn and Bruce Shore (2008) have suggested two elaborations on traditional approaches to teaching critical thinking:

Convergent evidence Multiple sources or types of support for an observation, argument, theory, or practice, all pointing to a common conclusion.

> **INTO THE CLASSROOM** *Fostering Critical Thinking*
>
> Teach elements of critical thinking.
>
> > In a unit on persuasion and argumentation, a middle school language arts teacher explains that a sound argument meets three criteria (Halpern, 1997a): (a) The evidence presented to justify the argument is accurate and consistent; (b) the evidence is relevant to, and provides sufficient support for, the conclusion; and (c) there is little or no missing information that, if present, would lead to a contradictory conclusion. The teacher then has students practise applying these criteria to a variety of persuasive and argumentative essays.
>
> Foster epistemological beliefs that encourage critical thinking.
>
> > Rather than teach history as a collection of facts to be memorized, a high school history teacher portrays the discipline as an attempt by informed but inevitably biased scholars to interpret and make sense of historical events. On several occasions, he asks his students to read two or three different historians' accounts of the same incident and to look for evidence of personal bias in each one (Paxton, 1999).
>
> Embed critical thinking skills within the context of authentic activities.
>
> > In a unit on statistical and scientific reasoning, a Grade 8 class studies concepts related to probability, correlation, and experimental control. Then, as part of a simulated "legislative hearing," the students work in small groups to develop arguments for or against a legislative bill concerning the marketing and use of vitamins and other dietary supplements. To find evidence to support their arguments, the students apply what they've learned about statistics and experimentation as they read and analyze journal articles and government reports about the possible benefits and drawbacks of nutritional supplements (Derry, Levin, Osana, & Jones, 1998).

- Students can learn to recognize the tasks and "traps" in both theoretical and practical situations that might lead to misconceptions or dangerous interpretations, and they can learn to select and practise ways to avoid these traps (p. 162).
- Students can learn to recognize the thinking dispositions that affect their ability to be objective and analytical and they can learn to apply appropriate dispositions in new circumstances (p. 162).

Both of these involve learners and teachers in analyzing their own thinking and the cognitive demands of tasks they engage in. These are complex examples of using metacognition, introduced earlier in this chapter.

Identifying Memes

We and our students can learn from positive examples of a concept, and also negative examples. A negative example of critical thinking is the idea of a "*meme*" (rhymes with cream). This word was coined by geneticist Richard Dawkins to describe shared ideas that, like genes, have somehow managed to become self-replicating in a culture and that are commonly believed or referred to by people as though they had some accuracy or worth, but have not (by the meme-user, at least) been subject to critical examination. Memes can interfere with critical analysis since they might lead students to make unwarranted assumptions in their thinking.

Some examples of memes include the idea of race except for the human race as a whole; expressions such as "sunset" (the sun does not set, the earth rotates), "an apple a day keeps the doctor away," or "way to go!"; nursery rhymes (who can explain what Miss Muffet sat on?); automatically passing on a chain letter; computer virus warnings that are later withdrawn; iconic advertising messages (e.g., Apple computers are intuitive, Juan Valdéz picks coffee beans in Columbia, Chiquita Banana is a woman); or that we all know what democracy is.

EXPERIENCING FIRSTHAND *Identifying Memes*

Ask your students to critically analyze some of these examples and to come up with other examples of widely held and shared ideas that are worthy of critical examination. Explore with them, in a sensitive way, whether or not challenging some of the memes they come up with would cause their friends to think they are unpatriotic, racist, or (for teenagers especially) "uncool."

Considering Diversity in Higher-Level Thinking Processes

We have noted the importance of a solid knowledge base for effective study strategies and successful problem solving. Students with different backgrounds will, of course, have different knowledge bases, and such diversity will naturally affect their ability to deal with higher-level thinking tasks. For instance, our students will use more effective study strategies when they read textbook materials consistent with their own cultural experiences (Pritchard, 1990).

Furthermore, students' previous experiences may have influenced the particular thinking skills they've developed. For example, in some cultures respect for one's elders may be highly valued, and so critical thinking and analysis of elders' beliefs may be strongly discouraged (Delgado-Gaitan, 1994). Students whose previous educational experiences have focused on drills and rote memorization (e.g., as is true in some schools in Asia) may have little awareness of the value of such learning strategies as meaningful learning and elaboration (D. Y. F. Ho, 1994; Purdie & Hattie, 1996).

Accommodating Students in Inclusive Classrooms

We are especially apt to find diversity in the higher-level thinking skills of our students with special needs. Table 7.5 presents characteristics common in these students.

Particularly noteworthy is the diversity in students' metacognitive awareness and use of learning strategies. Canadian researcher Bernice Wong (1991a) and others (e.g., McGlynn, 1998; H. L. Swanson, 1993) have noted that many students with learning disabilities, and some with emotional or behavioural disorders, demonstrate difficulty using learning strategies effectively. Students with mental retardation likely show even greater deficits in metacognitive skills and they often have difficulty transferring any strategies they learn to new situations (Campione, Brown, & Bryant, 1985). In contrast, gifted students typically have more sophisticated learning strategies than their classmates (Candler-Lotven, Tallent-Runnels, Olivárez, & Hildreth, 1994; Pelletier & Shore, 2003).

For many students with special needs, you may have to teach complex cognitive skills explicitly and with considerable **metacognitive scaffolding**—that is, with close guidance and assistance in the use of specific learning strategies. For example, you might provide partially filled-in outlines to guide students' note taking; Figure 7.4 presents an example of such an outline. Students need numerous opportunities to practise newly acquired strategies, along with feedback about how effectively they are using each one (E. S. Ellis & Friend, 1991).

If the focus of class time and activities is on *doing things with* information—for instance, understanding, organizing, elaborating, applying, analyzing, and critically evaluating it—rather than merely rote memorizing and recalling facts, then your students should acquire the cognitive processes, skills, and dispositions that will serve them well in the world beyond the classroom. This view fits Robert Sternberg's theory of intelligence presented in Chapter 4.

Metacognitive scaffolding A support structure that guides students in their use of metacognitive strategies.

General Strategies for Promoting Higher-Level Thinking Skills

Throughout the chapter we've identified numerous strategies for fostering effective study strategies, transfer, problem solving, and critical thinking. These strategies include the following:

- *Emphasize meaningful learning and conceptual understanding over rote memorization.* Students can better apply and critique classroom subject matter when they acquire an integrated, cohesive, and thorough understanding of that subject matter. Thus, we have repeatedly encountered the *less is more* principle: Teaching a few topics in depth is ultimately more effective than skimming over the surface of a great many.

- *Teach higher-level thinking skills within the context of specific topics.* For example, teaching critical thinking and problem-solving skills as we study science or teaching creative thinking as we study writing (M. C. Linn et al., 1989; Porath, 1988; Pulos & Linn, 1981; Stanley, 1980).

- *Communicate that much of what we "know" about the world is subject to change as new evidence comes in.* Learners' epistemological beliefs about a particular academic discipline, as well as about knowledge and learning more generally, have a significant impact on

TABLE 7.5   STUDENTS IN INCLUSIVE SETTINGS

Promoting Higher-Level Thinking Skills in Students with Special Educational Needs

CATEGORY	CHARACTERISTICS YOU MIGHT OBSERVE	SUGGESTED CLASSROOM STRATEGIES
Students with specific cognitive or academic difficulties	• Less metacognitive awareness or control of learning • Use of few and relatively inefficient learning strategies • Increased strategy use after training • Difficulty in transferring learned information to new situations • Difficulties in problem solving, perhaps because of limited working memory capacity, inability to identify important aspects of a problem, inability to retrieve appropriate problem-solving strategies, or limited metacognitive problem-solving skills	• Teach more effective learning strategies (e.g., taking notes, using mnemonics, finding general themes in reading material) and identify occasions when each strategy is likely to be useful. • Scaffold students' use of new learning strategies (e.g., provide outlines to guide note taking, ask questions that encourage retrieval of prior knowledge). • Present simple problems at first, then gradually move to more difficult ones as students gain proficiency and self-confidence. • Teach techniques for minimizing the load on working memory during problem solving (e.g., writing the parts of a problem on paper, making a diagram of the problem situation).
Students with social or behavioural problems	• Limited metacognitive awareness of own processing difficulties (for some students) • Few effective learning strategies (for some students) • Deficiencies in social problem-solving skills	• Provide guidance in using effective learning and study strategies (e.g., give outlines that guide note taking and ask questions that encourage retrieval of prior knowledge). • Teach social problem-solving skills (see Chapter 8 for ideas).
Students with general delays in cognitive and social functioning	• Lack of metacognitive awareness or control of learning • Lack of learning strategies, especially in the absence of strategies training • Difficulty in transferring information and skills to new situations • Few effective problem-solving strategies	• Teach relatively simple learning strategies (e.g., rehearsal, specific mnemonics) and give students ample practice using them. • Teach new information and skills in the specific contexts and situations in which you want students to use them. • Present simple problems and guide students through each step of the solutions.
Students with physical or sensory challenges	• No consistent deficits in higher-level thinking processes; any deficits observed may be due to students' limited experiences with tasks that require higher-level thinking	• Address any deficits in higher-level thinking skills using strategies that you would use with nondisabled students, making appropriate accommodations for physical and sensory limitations.
Students showing evidence of giftedness, talent, or high performance	• Use of relatively sophisticated learning strategies • Greater transfer of learning to new situations • Greater effectiveness in problem solving, more sophisticated problem-solving strategies, greater flexibility in strategy use, less susceptibility to mental sets, use of metacognition, and willingness and ability to critically examine ideas	• Place greater emphasis on higher-level thinking skills (e.g., transfer, problem solving) within the curriculum. • Teach higher-level thinking skills within the context of specific classroom topics rather than in isolation from academic content. • Use inquiry-based instruction so students can apply knowledge and skills in areas of student interest.

Sources: Beirne-Smith et al., 2002; Brownell, Mellard, & Deshler, 1993; Campione et al., 1985; Candler-Lotven et al., 1994; B. Clark, 1997; DuPaul & Eckert, 1994; N. R. Ellis, 1979; Frasier, 1989; Grodzinsky & Diamond, 1992; K. R. Harris, 1982; Heward, 2000; M. C. Linn et al., 1989; Maker, 1993; Mastropieri & Scruggs, 2000; McGlynn, 1998; Meichenbaum, 1977; Mercer, 1997; Piirto, 1999; Porath, 1988; Pressley, 1995; Pulos & Linn, 1981; Robinson, Shore, & Enerson, 2006; Scruggs & Mastropieri, 1992; Shore & Kanevsky, 1993; Slife, Weiss, & Bell, 1985; Stanley, 1980; H. L. Swanson, 1993; Torrance, 1989; A. Turnbull et al., 1999; Wilder & Williams, 2001; Wong, 1991a.

how learners study, what they learn, how readily they apply classroom subject matter, and how often they critically evaluate it. Some classroom topics are fairly certain, to be sure; 2 + 2 will always equal 4 (as long as we're working with a base-10 number system). Yet many other things—how the brain works, why some historical figures behaved as they did, and so on—are still a source of considerable debate, and students should be aware of this.

■ *Scrutinize new ideas in open discussion with students.* Look for patterns that group ideas together, explore their component parts, and discuss what happens when these elements are recombined in new ways—whether they are building blocks in a kindergarten, characters in a novel, or elements in high-school chemistry.

MUSCLES

A. Number of Muscles

    1. There are approximately _____ muscles in the human body.

B. How Muscles Work

    1. Muscles work in two ways:

        a. They _____, or shorten.

        b. They _____, or lengthen.

C. Kinds of Muscles

    1. _____ muscles are attached to the bones by _____.

        a. These muscles are _____ (voluntary/involuntary).

        b. The purpose of these muscles is to _____.

    2. _____ muscles line some of the body's _____.

        a. These muscles are _____ (voluntary/involuntary).

        b. The purpose of these muscles is to _____.

    3. The _____ muscle is the only one of its kind; it is also called the _____.

        a. This muscle is _____ (voluntary/ involuntary).

            The purpose of this muscle is to _____.

FIGURE 7.4 An example of metacognitive scaffolding: A partially filled-in outline that can guide students' note taking

- *Encourage higher-level thinking through group discussions and projects.* When students talk with one another, they must verbalize (and therefore become more metacognitively aware of) what and how they themselves are thinking. They also hear other (possibly better) interpretations, problem-solving strategies, and critical analyses. Invariably, too, they scaffold one another's attempts at higher-level tasks that might be too difficult for any of them to accomplish individually.

- *Use authentic activities to promote transfer of thinking skills to real-life settings.* Use authentic activities as a regular part of the school curriculum so students may find relevance in the skills they are learning for their own lives.

- *Foster dispositions as well as skills.* Students are more likely to apply higher-level thinking skills to classroom tasks—and to situations and problems in their outside lives as well—if they are in the *habit* of doing so. Undoubtedly the best place for this habit to develop is where students most frequently encounter new ideas, perspectives, and ways of doing things: at school.

- *Explicitly incorporate critical thinking in classroom discussions.* Pause to identify important assertions, assess the quality and convergence of evidence for and against an argument, and propose and evaluate alternative interpretations.

- *Incorporate higher-level thinking into assessment activities.* As you will discover in Chapter 12, it is fairly easy to construct assignments and tests that assess knowledge of basic facts and procedures. But it is ultimately more important that we assess what students can *do* with that knowledge. In Chapter 12 we will identify a variety of strategies for assessing higher-level thinking skills.

TEACHING CONSTRUCTIONS

Now that you have studied the ways in which knowledge might be organized, as well as strategies for promoting knowledge construction and strategic learning, let's revisit the lesson on earthquakes at the beginning of this chapter:

- How are these children constructing knowledge differently?
- If you were teaching this lesson, what would you do to capitalize on what you now know about how knowledge is constructed?
- How could you help students to activate their higher-level thinking skills in this and other subject areas?

Many cognitive psychologists believe that students *construct* knowledge from their experience, rather than simply absorb it in the form presented to them; their resulting "reality" is not necessarily identical to the reality of the external world, however. Constructive processes may occur both when information is being received (during storage) and when it is later recalled (during retrieval). Students also organize what they learn in a variety of ways. As a teacher, you can help your students construct accurate interpretations of the world around them and pull such interpretations into a well-integrated *conceptual understanding* of classroom topics. There are also numerous learning strategies for fostering effective transfer, problem solving, and critical thinking—strategies that ultimately help integrate information for conceptual understanding.

KEY CONCEPTS

reconstruction error (p. 160)
individual constructivism (p. 160)
social constructivism (p. 160)
inquiry-based instruction (p. 161)
distributed cognition (p. 161)
concept (p. 161)
undergeneralization (p. 162)
overgeneralization (p. 162)
positive instance (p. 162)
negative instance (p. 162)
schema (p. 162)
script (p. 163)
personal theory (p. 163)
misconception (p. 163)

conceptual understanding (p. 165)
authentic activity (p. 166)
community of learners (p. 167)
conceptual change (p. 170)
metacognition (p. 171)
higher-level thinking (p. 171)
concept map (p. 174)
elaborative interrogation (p. 175)
comprehension monitoring (p. 176)
illusion of knowing (p. 176)
self-questioning (p. 176)
epistemological beliefs (p. 176)
transfer (p. 178)
positive transfer (p. 178)

negative transfer (p. 178)
specific transfer (p. 178)
general transfer (p. 178)
generativity (p. 180)
well-defined problem (p. 181)
ill-defined problem (p. 181)
algorithm (p. 182)
heuristic (p. 182)
mental set (p. 184)
critical thinking (p. 186)
convergent evidence (p. 187)
metacognitive scaffolding (p. 189)

8 Social Cognitive Views of Learning

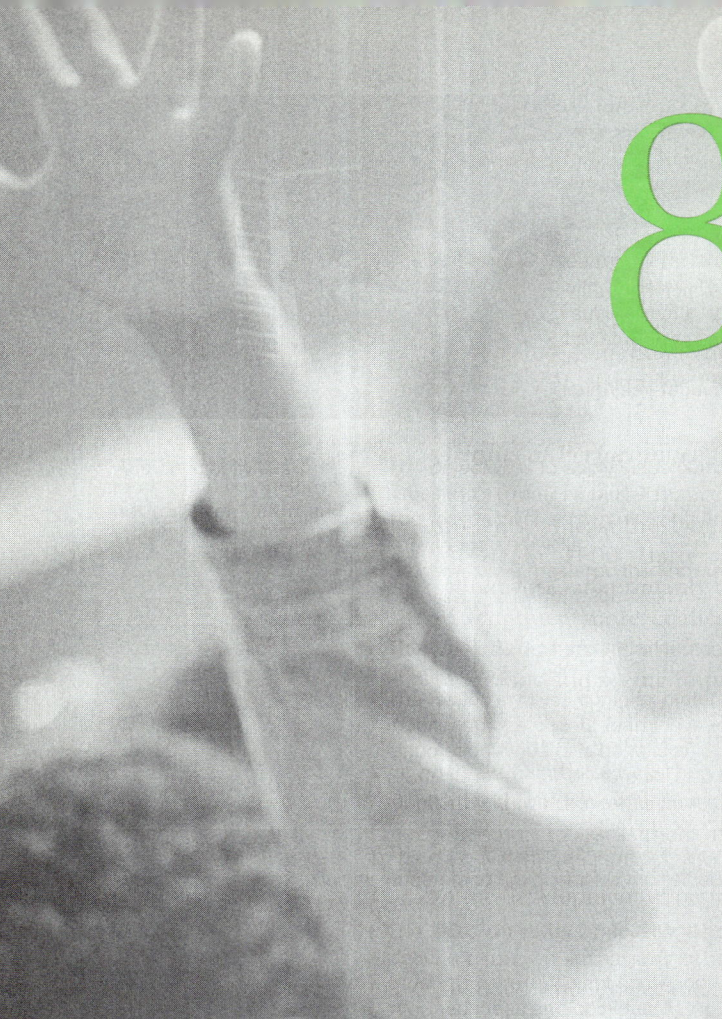

CASE STUDY IT'S ALL ANCIENT GREEK TO ME

TEACHING CONNECTIONS

BASIC ASSUMPTIONS OF SOCIAL COGNITIVE THEORY

THE SOCIAL COGNITIVE VIEW OF REINFORCEMENT AND PUNISHMENT
Expectations • Vicarious Experiences • Cognitive Processing • Choice of Behaviour • Nonoccurrence of Expected Consequences

MODELLING
How Modelling Affects Behaviour • Characteristics of Effective Models • Helping Students Learn from Models • Modelling and Aggression

SELF-EFFICACY
How Self-Efficacy Affects Behaviour • Factors in the Development of Self-Efficacy

SELF-REGULATION
Self-Regulated Behaviour • Self-Regulated Learning • Self-Regulated Problem Solving

RECIPROCAL CAUSATION

PROMOTING SELF-REGULATION IN STUDENTS WITH SPECIAL NEEDS

TEACHING CONSTRUCTIONS

KEY CONCEPTS

CASE STUDY *It's all Ancient Greek to Me*

Nathan isn't taking Latin because he wants to; he has enrolled in Latin I only because his mother insisted. Although he does well in his other high school courses, he's convinced that he will be a failure in Latin. After all, three friends who took Latin last year got mostly Ds and Fs on quizzes and homework, and two of them dropped the class after the first semester.

On the first day of Latin class, Nathan notices that most of his classmates are girls; the few boys in the class are students he doesn't know very well. He sits sullenly in the back row, convinced that he will do no better in Latin than his friends did. "I do OK in math and science, but I'm just no good at learning languages," he tells himself. "Besides, learning Latin is a 'girl' thing."

Although Nathan comes to class every day, his mind usually wanders to other topics as his teacher explains simple syntactical structures and demonstrates the correct pronunciation of new vocabulary words. He makes feeble attempts at homework assignments but quickly puts them aside whenever he encounters anything he doesn't immediately understand.

Sure enough, Nathan is right: He can't do Latin. He gets a D– on his first exam.

TEACHING CONNECTIONS

In this chapter we will explore **social cognitive theory** (also called *social learning theory*), a perspective that can help us understand what, when, and how people learn by observing others, and how people ultimately begin to assume some control over their own behaviour. As you read, consider the following questions in applying these principles to teaching:

- What basic assumptions are central to the social cognitive perspective of learning?
- How do cognitive processes influence the effects that reinforcement and punishment have on behaviour?
- How can we effectively use modelling to facilitate students' learning?
- What role does *self-efficacy* play in learning, and how can we enhance it in our students?
- How can we help students take control of their own behaviour and learning? In other words, how can we promote *self-regulation*?
- What has Nathan learned about Latin by observing other people?
- Why do Nathan's beliefs lead to a self-fulfilling prophecy?

Social cognitive theory A theoretical perspective in which learning by observing others is the focus of study.

Basic Assumptions of Social Cognitive Theory

You might initially think that Nathan has learned nothing from observing others because he has apparently not benefited from his teacher's explanations and demonstrations. Yet at second glance, you might realize that Nathan *has* learned something through observation after all: He has seen what happened to his three friends and concluded that *he* probably won't succeed in Latin class either. As we proceed through the chapter, you will discover some reasons why Nathan has apparently learned more from his friends than he has from his teacher.

Social cognitive theory has its roots in behaviourism, but over the past few decades it has increasingly incorporated cognitive processes into its explanations of learning; it now provides a nice blend of ideas from behaviourism and cognitive psychology. Yet it addresses *motivation* to a greater degree than either the cognitive or behaviourist perspective; accordingly, it provides a good transition to our discussion of motivation in Chapter 9. Social cognitive theory has developed in large part through the research efforts of Albert Bandura at Stanford University. You will find references to Bandura and others who build on his ideas (e.g., Dale Schunk, Barry Zimmerman) throughout the chapter.

Albert Bandura was born on December 4, 1925, in Mundara, a small town in Alberta, and obtained his undergraduate degree from the University of British Columbia. His M.A. and Ph.D. degrees were granted by the University of Iowa.

As you read the chapter, look for references to motivation in the sections on modelling, self-efficacy, and self-regulation.

In our case study of Nathan, we can see one basic assumption underlying social cognitive theory: People can learn from observing others. This and several other assumptions are summarized in Table 8.1. Let's look at them more closely:

- *People can learn by observing others.* In our discussion of operant conditioning in Chapter 5, we found that learning is sometimes a process of trial and error: People try many different responses, increasing the ones that bring about desirable consequences and eliminating the unproductive ones. Social cognitive theorists contend that people don't always have to "experiment" in this way; instead, they can acquire many new responses simply by observing the behaviours of people around them.

- *Learning is an internal process that may or may not result in a behaviour change.* Some of the things people learn appear in their behaviour immediately, other things affect their behaviour at a later time, and still others may never influence their behaviour at all. For example, you might attempt to swing a tennis racket as soon as you learn the correct form. But you probably won't demonstrate that you've learned how to apologize tactfully until a time when an apology is necessary. And you might *never* walk barefoot over hot coals, no matter how many times you see someone else do it. Social cognitive theory, like cognitive psychology, defines learning as an internal mental process that may or may not be reflected in the learner's behaviour.

- *Behaviour is directed toward particular goals.* Because you are reading this book, you probably want to become a teacher or enter some related profession, and you are taking an educational psychology class to help you attain that goal. Social cognitive theorists propose that people often set goals for themselves and direct their behaviour accordingly; in essence, they are *motivated* to accomplish their goals. Throughout the chapter we will see the relevance of such goals for learning and behaviour.

- *Behaviour eventually becomes self-regulated.* From a behaviourist perspective, people's behaviours are governed largely by the things that happen *to* them—the stimuli they encounter,

TABLE 8.1   PRINCIPLES/ASSUMPTIONS

Basic Assumptions of Social Cognitive Theory and Their Educational Implications

ASSUMPTION	EDUCATIONAL IMPLICATION	EXAMPLE
Learning by observation	Help students acquire new behaviours more quickly by demonstrating those behaviours yourself.	Demonstrate appropriate ways to deal with and resolve interpersonal conflicts. Then ask students to role-play conflict resolution in small groups, and commend those who use prosocial strategies.
Learning as an internal process that may or may not be reflected in behaviour	Remember that learning does not always appear immediately, but may instead be reflected in students' later behaviours.	When one student engages in disruptive classroom behaviour, take appropriate steps to discourage it. Otherwise, classmates who have witnessed the misbehaviour may be similarly disruptive in the future.
Goal-directed behaviour	Encourage students to set goals for themselves, especially goals that are challenging yet achievable.	When teaching American Sign Language to students to help them communicate with a classmate who is deaf, ask them to predict how many new words and phrases they can learn each week.
Self-regulation of behaviour	Teach students strategies for helping themselves learn effectively and behave appropriately.	Give students some concrete suggestions about how they can remind themselves to bring needed supplies to school each day.
Indirect effects of reinforcement and punishment	Ensure that the consequences of students' behaviours communicate the right messages about which actions are and are not acceptable in the classroom.	To encourage students to speak in Cree, respond to questions only if students make a reasonable attempt to ask the question in Cree.

the reinforcers that follow their behaviours, and so on. In contrast, social cognitive theorists believe that people eventually begin to regulate their *own* learning and behaviour. As an example, let's consider Shih-tai, a Grade 3 student who is learning to write in cursive. A traditional behaviourist might tell us that Shih-tai can best learn cursive if her teacher reinforces her for increasingly more appropriate responses, thereby shaping skilful penmanship over a period of several weeks or months. But a social cognitive theorist might suggest that Shih-tai can learn to write cursive letters more effectively by looking carefully at the examples her teacher has written on the chalkboard, copying those letters as closely as possible, and then comparing the letters she has written with those on the board. If she is happy with her work, she will give herself a mental pat on the back; if she is not, she may continue to practise until her letters are comparable with those of the teacher. From the social cognitive perspective, people often set their own standards for acceptable and unacceptable behaviour and then strive to behave in accordance with those standards.

Do you think your own behaviours are regulated more by the environment or by your own standards for what is acceptable and what is not?

- *Reinforcement and punishment have several indirect effects (rather than a direct effect) on learning and behaviour.* Operant conditioning theorists believe that reinforcement is necessary for learning, in that responses increase only when they are reinforced. Some behaviourists have also argued that punishment is an effective counterpart to reinforcement, decreasing the frequency of a behaviour it follows. Implied in the behaviourist perspective is the idea that reinforcement and punishment are directly responsible for the behaviour changes we see.

Reinforcement and punishment are less critical in social cognitive theory, but they have several indirect effects on learning and behaviour. In the section that follows, we will find out exactly how reinforcement and punishment fit into the social cognitive perspective.

The Social Cognitive View of Reinforcement and Punishment

According to social cognitive theorists (e.g., Bandura, 1977, 1986; T. L. Rosenthal & Zimmerman, 1978), both reinforcement and punishment influence learning and behaviour in several ways:

- People form *expectations* about the likely consequences of future responses based on how current responses are reinforced or punished.
- People's expectations are also influenced by their observations of the consequences that follow other people's behaviours—in other words, by *vicarious experiences*.
- Expectations about probable future consequences affect how people *cognitively process* new information.
- Expectations also affect how people *choose to behave*.
- The *nonoccurrence of an expected consequence* may have a reinforcing or punishing effect in and of itself.

Let's see how each of these factors plays out in social cognitive theory.

Expectations

Perhaps you have taken a course in which all the exam questions were based on the textbook, without a single question coming from class lectures. After the first exam, did you find yourself studying the textbook very carefully but skipping class frequently? On the other hand, perhaps you have taken a course in which exams were based almost *entirely* on class lectures and activities. In that situation, did you go to class regularly but seldom bother to open your textbook?

According to social cognitive theory, people form expectations about the consequences likely to result from various behaviours. When we find that a particular response is reinforced every time we make it, we typically expect to be reinforced for behaving that way in future situations. When we discover that a response frequently leads to punishment, we expect that response to be punished on later occasions as well.

Can you think of an occasion when you chose not to do something because of the ridicule you thought it might bring you?

From the social cognitive perspective, reinforcement increases the frequency of a behaviour only when students think or know that the behaviour is being reinforced—that is, when they are *aware* of a response–reinforcement contingency (Bandura, 1986). As teachers, then, we should be very clear about what we are reinforcing, so that our students know the real response–reinforcement contingencies operating in the classroom. For example, if Sam gets an A on an essay but we don't let him know *why* he earned that grade, he won't necessarily know how to get an A the next time. To improve Sam's performance, we might tell him that the essay earned an A because he supported his opinion with a logical train of thought.

Vicarious Experiences

Our expectations about the consequences of certain responses come not only from making those responses ourselves but also from observing what happens when others make them. In other words, we sometimes experience reinforcement and punishment *vicariously*.

People who observe someone else getting reinforced for a particular behaviour tend to exhibit that behaviour more frequently themselves—a phenomenon known as **vicarious reinforcement**. For example, by watching the consequences that their classmates experience, students might learn that studying hard leads to good grades, that being elected to class office brings status and popularity, or that neatness counts.

Conversely, when we see someone else get punished for a certain behaviour, we are *less* likely to behave that way ourselves—a phenomenon known as **vicarious punishment**. For example, when a coach benches a hockey player for unsportsmanlike conduct, other players will be less likely to mimic such behaviour. But unfortunately, vicarious punishment may suppress desirable behaviours as well. For example, when a teacher belittles a student for asking a "silly" question, other students may be reluctant to ask questions of their own.

As teachers, we must be extremely careful that we don't vicariously reinforce undesirable behaviours or vicariously punish desirable ones. If we give too much attention to a misbehaving student, others who want our attention may misbehave as well. If we ridicule a student who unwittingly volunteers an incorrect answer or erroneous belief, classmates will hardly be eager to respond to our questions or express their ideas and opinions.

Vicarious reinforcement
A phenomenon whereby a response increases in frequency when another (observed) person is reinforced for that response.

Vicarious punishment
A phenomenon whereby a response decreases in frequency when another (observed) person is punished for that response.

INTO THE CLASSROOM   *Administering Consequences from a Social Cognitive Perspective*

Describe the specific behaviours you are reinforcing, so that students are aware of the response–reinforcement contingencies operating in the classroom.

> A teacher tells his class, "Because everyone got at least 80 percent of the math problems correct this morning, we will have 10 minutes of free time at the end of the day."

Make sure students believe that they can achieve the incentives offered in the classroom.

> A teacher realizes that if she were to grade her students' science projects on a curve, only a few students could possibly get As. Instead, she gives her students a checklist of the specific criteria she will use to grade the projects; she tells her class that any project meeting all the criteria will get an A.

Tell students what behaviours are unacceptable in the classroom and describe the consequences that will result when those behaviours occur.

> A teacher reminds students that anyone seen pushing in the lunch line will go to the end of the line.

Follow through with the reinforcements you have promised for desirable student behaviours; also follow through with the adverse consequences students expect for undesirable behaviours.

> When announcing tryouts for an upcoming holiday play, a teacher tells students that only those who sign up ahead of time may try out. Although she later regrets making this statement—some of the most talented students don't sign up in time—she sticks to her word during tryout sessions and turns away anyone whose name does not appear on her sign-up sheet.

Remember that the consequences you administer for a particular student's behaviour have a potential effect on any students who observe those consequences.

> The student council president, even though she is well liked and highly respected by both students and teachers, is nevertheless punished in accordance with school rules when she is caught cheating on an exam.

Cognitive Processing

When we believe that we will be reinforced for learning something, we are more likely to pay attention to it and mentally process it in an effective fashion. When we *don't* expect to be reinforced for learning it, we are far less likely to think about or process it in any significant way. As an example of the latter situation, let's return to Nathan in our opening case study. Already convinced that he can't learn Latin, Nathan pays little attention to what his teacher says in class, and he makes only half-hearted efforts to complete his homework assignments.

Choice of Behaviour

Students learn many things that they never demonstrate because there is no reinforcement for doing so. They learn facts and figures, they learn ways of getting their teacher's attention, and they may even learn such tiny details as which classmate stores chocolate bars in his desk. Of all the things they learn, students will be most likely to demonstrate the ones they think will bring them reinforcement. The things they think will *not* be reinforced may remain hidden forever.

When students work diligently for a reinforcer that they hope to obtain in the future, they are working for an **incentive**. Incentives are never guaranteed: Students never know that they are going to get an A on a test when they study for it. An incentive is an expected or hoped-for consequence, one that may or may not actually occur.

Incentive A hoped-for, but not certain, consequence of behaviour.

Students don't work for incentives they don't believe they can achieve. For example, in a classroom of 30 Grade 7 students, a competition in which one prize will be awarded for the highest test score provides an incentive to just a handful of top achievers. An incentive is effective only if it is obtainable and a student perceives it as such. Therefore, when we provide incentives for student achievement, we should make sure our students believe they have some chance of achieving those incentives.

Nonoccurrence of Expected Consequences

Social cognitive theorists propose that the nonoccurrence of expected reinforcement is a form of punishment (e.g., Bandura, 1986). When people think that a certain response is going to be reinforced, yet the response is *not* reinforced, they are less likely to exhibit that behaviour in the future.

Perhaps you can think of a time when you broke a rule, expecting to be punished, but got away with your crime. Or perhaps you can remember seeing someone else break a rule without being caught. When nothing bad happens after a forbidden behaviour, people may actually feel as if they have been reinforced for that behaviour. Just as the nonoccurrence of reinforcement is a form of punishment, the nonoccurrence of punishment is a form of reinforcement (Bandura, 1986).

Can you recall an occasion when, as a student, you did not receive the reinforcement you expected? How did you feel and behave when that happened?

When students work hard to achieve a desired end result—perhaps a compliment, high grade, or special privilege—and the anticipated result doesn't materialize, they will be unlikely to work as hard the next time. And when students break school rules yet are not punished for doing so, they are more likely to break those rules again. As teachers, it is important that we follow through with promised reinforcements for desirable student behaviours. It is equally important that we impose the consequences students have come to expect for undesirable behaviours.

As we have seen, students learn many behaviours from observing those around them. But they don't necessarily model everything they see someone else do. When do students imitate the behaviours they see? And what kinds of people are they most likely to imitate? It is to such questions about *modelling* that we turn now.

Modelling

Consider these research findings:

- In one experiment, young children were taught not to speak to strangers through one of two techniques. One group of children heard a lecture about the dangers of following strangers and about the things they should do if a stranger tried to entice them; nevertheless, very few of these children tried to resist a friendly stranger who later appeared on the playground. A second group of children actually observed another child demonstrate techniques for resisting strangers; most of these children resisted the stranger's advances (Poche, Yoder, & Miltenberger, 1988).

> Think of specific people who might serve as positive role models (either real or symbolic) for your own students.

- When children see aggressive models—whether those models are people the children know, people on television, or cartoon characters—they are more likely to be aggressive themselves. Boys in particular are likely to model the aggressive behaviours they observe (Bandura, Ross, & Ross, 1961, 1963; Bushman & Anderson, 2001; Lowry et al., 1995).

- After watching adults demonstrate such behaviours as co-operation, sympathy, sharing, and generosity, children are more likely to demonstrate similar prosocial behaviours (R. Elliott & Vasta, 1970; Radke-Yarrow, Zahn-Waxler, & Chapman, 1983; Rushton, 1980).

- When a model preaches one set of moral values and practises another, observers are more likely to do what the model *does* than what the model *says* (J. H. Bryan, 1975).

We learn many different things through modelling. We learn such motor skills as holding a pencil, whittling a piece of wood, and dribbling a basketball by seeing how other people do these things. We also acquire skills in such academic areas as arithmetic, reading, and art more readily by observing others. And we develop interpersonal skills and moral values, at least in part, by watching and imitating the people around us.

Most of the models from which we learn are **live models**—real people that we actually see doing something. In a classroom setting, students may learn something by watching their teacher solve an algebraic equation, observing a visiting police officer demonstrate important rules of bicycle safety, or seeing a classmate perform a flawless hook shot on the basketball court. But we are also influenced by **symbolic models**—real or fictional characters portrayed in books, in films, on television, and through various other media. For example, students can learn valuable lessons from studying the behaviours of important figures in history or reading stories about people who accomplish great things in the face of adversity.

Live model An individual whose behaviour is observed "in the flesh."

Symbolic model A real or fictional character portrayed in the media (television, books, etc.) that influences an observer's behaviour.

How Modelling Affects Behaviour

Social cognitive theorists (e.g., Bandura, 1977, 1986; T. L. Rosenthal & Zimmerman, 1978) propose that modelling has several possible effects on human behaviour: observational learning, response facilitation, response inhibition, and response disinhibition.

The **observational learning effect** occurs when *the observer acquires a new behaviour demonstrated by the model*. By seeing and hearing models, students learn how to dissect an earthworm, swim the elementary backstroke, and pronounce correctly "*Est-ce-que tu étudies le français?*"

The **response facilitation effect** occurs when *the observer displays a previously learned behaviour more frequently after seeing a model being reinforced for that behaviour* (i.e., after receiving vicarious reinforcement). Our students are more likely to wear ragged old jeans if their classmates appear to be winning popularity with this attire.

The **response inhibition effect** occurs when *the observer displays a previously learned behaviour less frequently after seeing a model being punished for that behaviour* (i.e., after receiving vicarious punishment). Students tend to inhibit (*not* engage in) behaviours that result in adverse consequences for those around them.

Response disinhibition effect occurs when the observer displays a previously forbidden or punished behaviour more frequently after seeing a model exhibit the behaviour without adverse consequences. Although students will inhibit behaviours leading to punishment, they may begin to engage in behaviours they have previously inhibited if they observe those behaviours going unpunished for other people. For example, students are more likely to chew gum, copy homework from classmates, or fight in the corridors if they see other students getting away with such behaviours.

However, students don't always model the people around them. What factors determine when students are most likely to imitate the behaviours they see? A look at characteristics of effective models will help us with the answer.

Observational learning effect Occurs when an observer acquires a new behaviour after watching someone else demonstrate it.

Response facilitation effect Occurs when an observer displays a previously learned behaviour more frequently after seeing someone else being reinforced for that behaviour.

Response inhibition effect Occurs when an observer displays a previously learned behaviour less frequently after seeing someone else being punished for that behaviour.

Response disinhibition effect Occurs when an observer displays a previously forbidden or punished behaviour more frequently after seeing someone else exhibit that behaviour without adverse consequences.

Characteristics of Effective Models

Social cognitive theorists have found some consistency in the types of models that others are most likely to imitate (Bandura, 1986; T. L. Rosenthal & Bandura, 1978). Effective models typically exhibit one or more of the following characteristics.

Competence. Students will typically try to imitate people who do something well, not those who do it poorly. For example, they will try to imitate the basketball skills of a professional basketball player rather than those of the class klutz, or copy the fashions of a popular classmate rather than those of a student who is socially isolated.

Prestige and power. Children and adolescents often imitate people who are famous or powerful. Some effective models—a world leader, a renowned athlete, a popular rock star—are famous at a national or international level. The prestige and power of other models—a head cheerleader, the captain of the high school hockey or soccer team, a gang leader—may be limited to a more local environment.

In addition to modelling desired behaviours ourselves, we can expose our students to a variety of models that they are likely to view as prestigious and powerful. For example, we might invite respected professionals (e.g., a police officer, nurse, or newspaper reporter) to visit our classrooms and talk with students about topics within their areas of expertise.

"Sex appropriate" behaviour. Remember Nathan's belief that Latin is a "girl" thing? Students are most likely to model behaviours they believe are appropriate for their sex (with different students inevitably defining sex appropriate somewhat differently). For example, many girls and boys limit their academic choices and career aspirations to the subjects and professions they believe are "for women" and "for men," respectively. Some girls may shy away from careers in mathematics as being too "masculine." Some boys may not take typing because they perceive it to be a secretarial skill, and most secretaries are women. Yet mathematics and keyboarding are useful skills for both sexes. Exposure to numerous examples of people in so-called nontraditional careers—female mathematicians and engineers, male secretaries and nurses—can help broaden students' perceptions as to what behaviours are sex appropriate. In the process, such models can also broaden students' academic choices and possibly enhance their career aspirations.

Behaviour relevant to the learner's own situation. Students are most likely to model the behaviours they believe will help them in their own circumstances. A boy may wear the torn jeans that his popular classmates wear if he thinks he can become popular with such attire; however, he will have less reason to dress this way if he thinks that his thick glasses and adolescent acne will prevent him from ever being popular regardless of his clothing.

In the classroom we are likely to model a variety of behaviours throughout the day. But our students will adopt these behaviours only if they believe that such responses will truly be useful and productive for them. Therefore, we must show them how the problem-solving methods we teach, the writing skills we demonstrate, and the physical fitness regimen we advocate are all applicable to their own situations.

Our students are less likely to perceive the relevance of modelled behaviours when the model is different from them in some obvious way. For example, students from cultures other than our own may think that some of the things we try to teach them don't apply to their own cultural circumstances. Similarly, students with disabilities may believe that they are incapable of accomplishing the things a nondisabled teacher demonstrates. So it is important that we include individuals from minority cultures and individuals with disabilities in the models we present to our students. Minority students benefit from observing successful minority adults, and students with disabilities become more optimistic about their own futures when they meet adults successfully coping with and overcoming their own disabilities (Pang, 1995; L. E. Powers, Sowers, & Stevens, 1995).

You can probably think of teachers you admired and wanted to be like. Most teachers have one or more characteristics of an effective model; for example, students typically view their teachers as being competent and having power, at least within the school environment. So as teachers, we "teach" not only by what we say but also by what we do. It is critical that we model appropriate behaviours and *not* model inappropriate ones. Do we model fairness to all students, or favouritism to a small few? Do we model enthusiasm and excitement about the subject matter being taught, or merely tolerance for a dreary topic that the class must muddle through as best it can? Do we expound on the virtues of innovation and creativity yet use the same curriculum materials year after year? Our actions often speak louder than our words.

In the Bleachers by Steve Moore

Not all the people in children's lives model desirable behaviours. A child is most apt to imitate undesirable behaviours that appear to have no adverse consequences and that seem to lead to reinforcement.
IN THE BLEACHERS © Steve Moore. Reprinted with permission of Universal Press Syndicate. All rights reserved.

How are the response facilitation and response disinhibition effects similar? How are they different?

IN THE BLEACHERS
by Steve Moore

"Don't cry, Megan. Remember, it's not whether Daddy wins the brawl in the stands that's important. It's how you played the game."

When we work with children, our actions will often speak louder than our words.
IN THE BLEACHERS © Steve Moore. Reprinted with permission of Universal Press Syndicate. All rights reserved.

Yet even when models are competent and prestigious and even when they exhibit behaviours that students think are appropriate for themselves as well, successful modelling does not necessarily occur. What must students do to learn modelled behaviour effectively? Let's find out.

Helping Students Learn from Models

According to social cognitive theorists (e.g., Bandura, 1986), four conditions are necessary before a student can successfully model someone else's behaviour: attention, retention, motor reproduction, and motivation.

Attention. In the opening case study, Nathan paid little attention to his Latin teacher. Yet to learn effectively, the learner must pay attention to the model. Before imitation is possible, our students must observe carefully as we show proper procedures in the science lab, watch closely as we demonstrate the elementary backstroke, or listen attentively as we pronounce *Comment allez-vous?*

Retention. After paying attention, the learner must remember what the model does. If you have already read the discussion of cognitive processes in Chapter 6, then you know that students are more likely to remember information they have encoded in memory in more than one way—perhaps both as a visual image and as a verbal representation. As teachers, then, we may often want to describe what we are doing as we demonstrate behaviours. For example, we should explain what we are doing as we model the process of long division, perhaps like so:

> First I have to decide what number to divide 4 into. I take 276, start on the left and move toward the right until I have a number the same as or larger than 4. Is 2 larger than 4? No. Is 27 larger than 4? Yes. So my first division will be 4 into 27. Now I need to multiply 4 by a number that will give an answer the same as or slightly smaller than 27. How about 5? 5 × 4 = 20. No, too small. Let's try 6. 6 × 4 = 24. Maybe. Let's try 7. 7 × 4 = 28. No, too large. So 6 is correct. (Schunk, 1998, p. 146)

We may also want to give descriptive labels to complex behaviours that might otherwise be difficult to remember (Gerst, 1971; T. L. Rosenthal, Alford, & Rasp, 1972). To illustrate, when teaching swimming, an easy way to help students remember the sequence of arm positions in the elementary backstroke is to teach them "chicken" (arms bent with hands tucked under armpits), "airplane" (arms straight out to the side), and "soldier" (arms straight and held close to the torso). It may be especially helpful for students to repeat such labels aloud as they copy a model's actions (R. L. Cohen, 1989; Mace, Belfiore, & Shea, 1989; Schunk, 1989c). As an example, consider the following set of self-instructions taught to students who are first learning a basic tennis stroke:

1. Say *ball* to remind yourself to look at the ball.
2. Say *bounce* to remind yourself to follow the ball with your eyes as it approaches you.
3. Say *hit* to remind yourself to focus on contacting the ball with the racket.
4. Say *ready* to get yourself into position for the next ball to come your way. (Ziegler, 1987)

Tennis students taught to give themselves these simple instructions—*ball, bounce, hit,* and *ready*—improve the accuracy of their returns more quickly than students not taught to do so (Ziegler, 1987).

Motor reproduction. In addition to attending and remembering, the learner must be physically capable of reproducing the modelled behaviour. When a student lacks the ability to reproduce an observed behaviour, motor reproduction obviously cannot occur. For example, Grade 1 students who watch a high school student throw a softball do not possess the muscular coordination to mimic that throw.

It will often be useful to have students imitate a desired behaviour immediately after they watch us demonstrate it. When they do so, we can give them the feedback they need to improve their performance. Modelling accompanied by verbal guidance and frequent feedback—a technique sometimes known as *coaching*—is often more effective than modelling alone (S. N. Elliott & Busse,

1991; Kitsantis, Zimmerman, & Cleary, 2000; Zirpoli & Melloy, 2001). At the same time, we must keep in mind a point made in Chapter 4: Students from some ethnic groups may prefer to practise new behaviours in private at first, showing us what they have learned only after they have achieved sufficient mastery.

Motivation. Finally, the learner must be motivated to demonstrate the modelled behaviour. Some students may be eager to show what they have observed and remembered; for example, they may have seen the model reinforced for a certain behaviour and so have already been vicariously reinforced. But other students may not have any motivation to demonstrate something they have seen a model do, perhaps because the model was punished or perhaps because they don't see the model's actions as being appropriate for themselves. In Chapter 9 we will identify numerous strategies for increasing students' motivation to exhibit desired behaviours.

When all four factors—attention, retention, motor reproduction, and motivation—are present, modelling can be an extremely powerful teaching technique (e.g., Kitsantis et al., 2000; Schloss & Smith, 1994; Schunk & Hanson, 1985).

Modelling and Aggression

Students can also learn negative behaviours from models. In particular, aggression in schools has of late become a priority for Canadians. A 1993 Environics poll (Saskatchewan School Trustees Association, 1994) revealed that Canadians believed school-based youth violence to be the single most important issue facing public education. More current data indicates that the level of public concern for youth violence has not declined (Solicitor General Canada, 2000). Teachers have reported dramatic increases in the type, frequency, and severity of anti-social, aggressive, and violent behaviour in classrooms (P. Carney, 1999; Solicitor General Canada, 1994; Saskatchewan School Trustees Association, 1994). Baillargeon, Tremblay, & Willms (1999), analyzing data from the National Longitudinal Survey of Children and Youth, reported that physical aggression affects a significant segment of the Canadian population of children. They estimated that 3.5 percent of 2- to 4-year-old children in the Canadian population are physically aggressive. This percentage was nearly the same for boys between 5 and 11 years of age (3.3 percent), whereas it was substantially lower for girls (0.6 percent). Of concern, however, are reports of increasing rates of assault and other violent crimes perpetrated by girls in Canada (Artz & Nicholson, 2001).

Aggressive behaviour in children is not only a concern due to the immediate negative consequences to peers, caregivers, and the community, but also due to the long-term consequences for the child. Concerns include increased risk for academic underachievement, alcohol and drug abuse, violent crimes, depression, suicide attempts, spouse abuse, and neglectful and abusive parenting (Cote, Vaillancourt, LeBlanc, Nagin, & Tremblay, 2006; Tremblay et al., 2004). There are also long-term consequences for the environment in which the child lives, including the home, school, and community.

What causes aggression in children? Aggression in children cannot be attributed to one single causal factor. Indeed, the most comprehensive explanatory models view aggression as "resulting from the interplay among predisposing child, family, community, and cultural characteristics, and ongoing experiences" (Mash & Wolfe, 1999, p. 211). Bandura's social learning theory is an integral component of such comprehensive models in that some kinds of aggression are learned through past experiences and social conditions for which children are directly or vicariously rewarded. Patterson and colleagues (1992), for example, have convincingly demonstrated that coercive parent–child interactions serve as a training ground for the development of aggression. Further, aggressive behaviour in children is more prevalent in neighbourhoods that encourage, model, or condone antisocial behaviour (Caspi & Moffitt, 1995). Social-cognitive models, such as that proposed by Dodge and others (Crick & Dodge, 1994), also show how the reciprocal effect of a child's cognition, parent and peer appraisal and interactions, and emotional- and social-interaction processes can be instrumental in the development of aggression.

Bullying

Bullying is a form of aggression that may be aimed directly at a targeted peer (e.g., hitting, slapping, name calling) or indirectly through peers (e.g., gossiping, excluding). Bullying is differentiated from other forms of aggression in that the targeted person cannot defend him/herself

(Beran, 2006a). Cyber-bullying (cyber-harassment) has emerged as another form of bullying whereby children use technology such as cell phones, emails, and instant messaging to send harassing messages to their peers, and, in some cases, adults (Beran & Li, 2007).

Across Canadian studies, the proportion of students in Grades 1 to 6 who report being victimized ranges from 5 to 27 percent (Beran & Tutty, 2002). The percentage of students in these same grades who self-report bullying others ranges from 6 to 17 percent. In a study of 6500 Canadian students from Grades 6 to 10, Craig (2004) found that more boys than girls report being victimized, and boys report higher frequency of bullying than do girls. Bullying and victimization was at the highest level in Grade 10 for boys and Grade 8 for girls. The majority of victims reported being bullied by teasing and by being excluded or having rumours spread about them. Boys were twice as likely to report physical victimization than were girls, who tend to use non-physical aggression (Craig & Pepler, 1997).

Children who are bullied report numerous physical, emotional, cognitive, and behavioural problems (Beran, 2006b; Beran, Hughes, & Lupart, 2008). Children who witness bullying may also experience levels of helplessness and fear similar to those felt by children being bullied (Beran, 2006b). Interestingly, children who bully also report experiencing negative outcomes. Past research has shown that they are more likely to use other forms of aggression, sexual harassment, and dating violence in adolescence and are also more likely to engage in illegal activities, such as delinquency and substance use (Craig, 2004).

What do social cognitive theories tell us about bullying? Craig and Pepler (1997) conducted observations of bullying and victimization in the schoolyard. They found that peers were involved in some capacity in 85 percent of the bullying episodes. Peers actively took part in 48 percent of the episodes by being either actively involved (i.e., being physically or verbally abusive to the victim), observing the aggressive interaction, being involved in the same activity as the bully prior to the episode, or intervening to terminate the interaction. In 81 percent of the episodes, the peers reinforced the bullying episode. Interestingly, peers were significantly more likely to be respectful to bullies (74 percent of the episodes) than victims (23 percent of the episodes). The researchers concluded that these findings provide preliminary evidence to support the following peer processes in bullying: reinforcement, modelling, emotional contagion, and a weakening of control against aggressive tendencies. Further, emotional arousal and contagion can arise because bullies likely derive some sense of satisfaction and pleasure from their attacks on victims.

The Promoting Relationships and Eliminating Violence Network (PREVNet) is a coalition of Canadians concerned about bullying. The primary goal of PREVNet is to translate and exchange knowledge about bullying to enhance awareness, provide assessment and intervention tools, and promote policy related to the problems of bullying. Their website (www.prevnet.ca) is designed to be a rich and instructive resource that provides immediate and easy access to age-specific information for every user.

Self-Efficacy

People are more likely to engage in certain behaviours when they believe they are capable of executing those behaviours successfully—that is, when they have high **self-efficacy** (e.g., Bandura, 1997). For example, I hope you believe that, with careful thought about what you read, you will be able to understand the ideas in this textbook; in other words, I hope you have high self-efficacy for learning educational psychology.

Self-efficacy The belief that one is capable of executing certain behaviours or reaching certain goals.

The concept of self-efficacy is similar to the concept of *self-concept*, but with an important difference. Self-concept is conceptualized as pervading a wide variety of activities; for instance, we tend to describe people as having a generally positive or negative self-concept. Self-efficacy is more situation-specific; for example, people may have high self-efficacy about understanding an educational psychology textbook but not about understanding a book about neurosurgery. They may have high self-efficacy about learning to perform a swan dive but not about swimming the entire length of a swimming pool underwater.

How do students' feelings of self-efficacy affect their behaviour? And how do feelings of high or low self-efficacy develop? In the next few pages, we will identify several answers to these two questions.

How Self-Efficacy Affects Behaviour

According to social cognitive theorists, people's sense of self-efficacy affects their choice of activities, their effort and persistence, and their learning and achievement (Bandura, 1982, 2000; Schunk, 1989c; Zimmerman, Bandura, & Martinez-Pons, 1992):

Choice of activities. People tend to choose tasks and activities at which they believe they can succeed and to avoid those at which they think they will fail. Students who believe that they can succeed at mathematics are more likely to take math courses than students who believe that they are mathematically incompetent. Students who believe that they can win a role in the school musical are more likely to try out than students with little faith in their acting or singing ability.

Effort and persistence. Students with a high sense of self-efficacy are more likely to exert effort in attempting to accomplish a task. They are also more likely to persist (to "try, try again") when faced with obstacles to their success. In contrast, students with low self-efficacy about a particular task will put in little effort and will give up quickly when they encounter obstacles. Such effort and persistence reflect the intrinsic motivation of students with high self-efficacy (more about this concept in Chapter 9).

Learning and achievement. Students with high self-efficacy tend to learn and achieve more than students with low self-efficacy even when actual ability levels are the same (Bandura, 1986; Eccles, Wigfield, et al., 1989). In other words, among students of equal ability, those students who believe they can do a task are more likely to accomplish it successfully than those who believe they are incapable of success. Students with high self-efficacy may achieve at superior levels partly because they engage in cognitive processes that promote learning—paying attention, organizing, elaborating, and so on (Pintrich & Schunk, 2002). As teachers, then, we should do whatever we can to enhance our students' beliefs that they can be successful at school tasks.

A student must believe that she has the ability to make friends before she will actually try to make them.

Factors in the Development of Self-Efficacy

Perceptions of self-efficacy are usually fairly accurate: Students typically have a good sense of what they can and cannot do (Bandura, 1986). Ideally, it is probably best that they slightly *over*rate their competence; by doing so, they are more likely to try challenging tasks that help them develop new skills and abilities (Assor & Connell, 1992; Bandura, 1997). But sometimes students (girls especially) *under*estimate their chances of success, perhaps because of a few bad experiences (D. A. Cole et al., 1999; D. Phillips & Zimmerman, 1990). For example, a girl who gets a C in science from a teacher with exceptionally strict grading criteria may erroneously believe that she is "no good" in science. Students who underestimate their capabilities try less hard and are less persistent at challenging school tasks (D. Phillips & Zimmerman, 1990).

What factors in Nathan's situation may have contributed to his low self-efficacy for learning Latin?

According to social cognitive theorists (e.g., Bandura, 1986, 1989, 1997; Schunk, 1989a; Schunk, Hanson, & Cox, 1987), several factors affect the development of self-efficacy:

- One's own previous successes and failures
- Messages from others
- Successes and failures of others
- Successes and failures of the group as a whole

One's Own Successes and Failures

Students feel more confident that they can succeed at a task when they have succeeded at that task or at similar ones in the past (Bandura, 1986). For example, Edward is more likely to believe that he can learn to divide fractions if he has already mastered the process of multiplying fractions. One important strategy for promoting our students' self-efficacy, then, is to help them be successful in various academic disciplines—for instance, by teaching important basic skills to mastery and by providing the necessary instructional support that enables students to make noticeable progress on difficult and complex tasks.

We find developmental differences in *how far back* students look when they consider their prior successes and failures. Perhaps because of more limited cognitive abilities, children in the early elementary grades typically recall only their most recent experiences when judging their competence to perform a particular activity; in contrast, older children and adolescents are likely to consider a long-term pattern of successes and failures (Eccles et al., 1998). We can help students of all ages develop high self-efficacy by showing them in a concrete way—for instance, by comparing earlier work samples with their current efforts—just how much they've improved over time (R. Butler, 1998a). We can also show them how their successes are the result of their own hard work and so are hardly a fluke (Pintrich & Schunk, 2002).

Resilient self-efficacy The belief that one can perform a task successfully even after experiencing setbacks; includes the belief that effort and perseverance are essential for success.

Once students have developed a high sense of self-efficacy, an occasional failure is unlikely to dampen their optimism. In fact, when these students encounter small setbacks on the way to achieving success, they learn that sustained effort and perseverance are key ingredients of that success; in other words, they develop **resilient self-efficacy** (Bandura, 1989). When students *consistently* fail at an activity, however, they tend to have little confidence about their ability to succeed at that activity in the future. For instance, students with learning disabilities—students who typically have encountered failure after failure in classroom activities—often have low self-efficacy for mastering school subject matter (Schunk, 1989c).

Messages from Others

We can sometimes enhance students' self-efficacy by assuring them that they can, in fact, be successful (e.g., Zeldin & Pajares, 2000). Statements such as "You can do this problem if you work at it" or "I bet Judy will play with you if you just ask her" do give students a slight boost in self-confidence. But this boost will be short-lived unless students' efforts at a task ultimately meet with success (Schunk, 1989a).

Sometimes the messages we give students are implied rather than directly stated, yet such messages can have just as much of an effect on self-efficacy. For example, by giving constructive criticism about how to improve a poorly written research paper—criticism that indirectly communicates the message that "I know that you can do better, and here are some suggestions how"—we can enhance students' self-confidence about writing such research papers (Parsons, Kaczala, & Meece, 1982; Pintrich & Schunk, 2002). In some cases, we communicate our beliefs about students' competence through our actions rather than our words. For example, if we give struggling students more assistance than they really need, we may inadvertently communicate the message that "I don't think you can do this on your own" (Schunk, 1989b).

Successes and Failures of Others

We often form opinions about our own self-efficacy by observing the successes and failures of other people, especially those similar to ourselves (Eccles et al., 1998; Zeldin & Pajares, 2000). Students often consider the successes and failures of their classmates, especially those of similar ability, when appraising their own chances of success. So we can enhance students' self-efficacy, and ultimately their willingness to try to master classroom subject matter, by pointing out that others like themselves have mastered that material (Schunk, 1983b, 1989c). When students actually *see* others of similar age and ability successfully reaching a goal, they are especially likely to believe that they, too, can achieve that goal. Hence, students sometimes develop greater self-efficacy when they see a fellow student model a behaviour than when they see their teacher model that same behaviour. For example, in one study (Schunk & Hanson, 1985), elementary school children having trouble with subtraction were given 25 subtraction problems to complete. Children who had seen another student successfully complete the problems got an average of 19 correct, whereas those who saw a teacher complete the problems got only 13 correct, and those who saw no model at all solved only 8!

So another way to enhance our students' self-efficacy for academic tasks is to have them observe their peers successfully accomplishing those tasks. It may be especially beneficial for students to see one or more peers struggling with a task or problem at first—something they themselves are likely to do—and then eventually mastering it (Kitsantis et al., 2000; Schunk et al., 1987; Schunk & Zimmerman, 1997).

Successes and Failures of the Group as a Whole

Collective self-efficacy People's beliefs about their ability to be successful when they work together on a task.

Students may have greater self-efficacy when they work in a group than when they work alone. Such **collective self-efficacy** depends not only on students' perceptions of their own and others' capabilities but also on their perceptions of how effectively they can work together and coordinate their roles and responsibilities (Bandura, 1997, 2000).

The concept of collective self-efficacy is fairly new, and research to date has focused primarily on adults (Bandura, 1997; Goddard, 2001; Tschannen-Moran et al., 1998). Yet we can reasonably assume that students are likely to have higher self-efficacy when they work in groups, provided that those groups are functioning smoothly and effectively. We will consider strategies for fostering effective group work in our discussion of co-operative learning in Chapter 10.

INTO THE CLASSROOM *Enhancing Self-Efficacy*

Teach basic skills to mastery.

> A biology teacher makes sure all students clearly understand the basic structure of DNA before moving to mitosis and meiosis, two topics that require a knowledge of DNA's structure.

Help students make noticeable progress on difficult tasks.

> In November a creative writing teacher shows students samples of their work from September and points out ways in which each student has improved over the two-month period.

Present some tasks that are challenging but achievable so that students succeed at them only with effort and perseverance.

> A physical education teacher tells her students, "Today we've seen how far each of you can go in the long jump. We will continue to practise a little bit every week. Let's see if one of you can jump at least five centimetres further when I test you again at the end of the month."

Assure students that they can be successful and remind them that others like themselves have succeeded before them.

> Students in the beginning band express frustration about learning to play their instruments. Their teacher reminds them that students in last year's band—like themselves—started out with little knowledge but eventually mastered their instruments.

Have students see successful peer models.

> The students in beginning band class hear the school's advanced band (last year's beginning band class) play a medley from the Broadway musical *Cats*.

Provide opportunities to work in small groups on especially challenging tasks.

> A Grade 5 teacher has students work in groups of three or four to write research papers about early colonial life in Canada. The teacher makes sure that the students in each group collectively have the skills in library research, writing, word processing, and art necessary to complete the task. She also makes sure that every student has some unique skills to contribute to the group effort.

We should note here that teachers, too, can have collective self-efficacy. If the teachers at a school believe that, as a group, they can make a significant difference in the lives of their students, their students achieve at higher levels and have higher self-efficacy (Goddard, 2001; Goddard, Hoy, & Woolfolk Hoy, 2000; Tschannen-Moran et al., 1998).

When students have high self-efficacy about accomplishing classroom tasks and mastering academic subject matter, they have a critical prerequisite for directing and regulating their own learning. We turn to this process of *self-regulation* now.

Self-Regulation

The standards we set for ourselves, the ways in which we monitor and evaluate our own cognitive processes and behaviours, and the consequences we impose on ourselves for our successes and failures are all aspects of **self-regulation**. If our thoughts and actions are under our *own* control, rather than being controlled by the people and circumstances around us, we are self-regulating individuals (Zimmerman, 1998).

You will likely be more successful in promoting behavioural self-regulation if you also promote academic self-regulation. Over the past decade, Deborah Butler at the University of British Columbia and her colleagues (D. L. Butler, 1994, 1995, 2002; D. L. Butler & Winne, 1995; D. L. Butler, Elaschuk, & Poole, 2000) have looked at ways to promote self-regulated learning with secondary and post-secondary students as well as with younger students. This research highlights the importance for teachers to help students identify task demands, reflect on the learning process, recognize successes, evaluate strategies, revise ineffective approaches, and personalize their strategies. Nancy Perry, also at the University of British Columbia, has shown that very young children can also engage in self-regulated learning and behaviour in classrooms (N. E. Perry, Vandekamp, Mercer, & Nordby, 2002). N. E. Perry, Nordby, and Vandekamp (2003) also contend that parents and teachers should share ways to promote self-regulation and build on children's home experiences.

Self-regulation The process of setting standards and goals for oneself and engaging in cognitive processes and behaviours that lead to the accomplishment of those standards and goals.

Ideally, our students should become increasingly self-regulated as they grow older, and in fact many of them do (Bronson, 2000; Eccles et al., 1998; van Kraayenoord & Paris, 1997). Once they reach adulthood and leave the relatively structured and protective environments of home and school, they will make most of their own decisions about what they should accomplish and how they should behave. Ultimately, we want them to make wise choices that enable them to achieve their goals and make productive contributions to society.

In the pages that follow, we will identify some of the things that learners do when they engage in *self-regulated behaviour*. We will then use what we have learned to consider how we might promote *self-regulated learning* and *self-regulated problem solving*.

Self-Regulated Behaviour

By observing how our environment reacts when we behave in particular ways—by discovering that some behaviours are reinforced and others are punished or in some other way discouraged—we begin to distinguish between appropriate and inappropriate responses. As we develop an understanding about which responses are appropriate (for ourselves, at least) and which are not, we begin to control and monitor our own behaviour (Bandura, 1986). Five aspects of such **self-regulated behaviour** are summarized in Figure 8.1. Let's look at the nature and potential implications of each one.

Self-Determined Goals and Standards

As human beings, we tend to identify certain goals for ourselves and then engage in the kinds of behaviours that can help us achieve those goals. We also set standards for our own behaviour; in other words, we determine criteria for evaluating our own performance.

Different students will inevitably adopt different goals and standards for themselves. For example, Robert may be striving for a report card with straight As, whereas Richard is content with Cs. To some extent, the goals and standards that students set for themselves are modelled after those that they see other people adopt (Bandura, 1986; Locke & Latham, 1990).

Students are more likely to be motivated to work toward goals—and thus more likely to accomplish them—when they have set those goals for themselves, rather than when others have imposed goals on them (M. E. Ford, 1992; Spaulding, 1992). So one way we can help students develop self-regulation is to provide situations in which they set their own goals. Ideally, we should encourage our students to establish goals and standards that are challenging yet realistic. When students have goals and standards that are too low—for instance, when intelligent students are content getting Cs on classroom assignments—then they will not achieve at maximal levels. In contrast, when students' standards are too high—for example, when they are satisfied only if every grade is 100 percent—then they are doomed to frequent failure and equally frequent self-recrimination. Such students may become excessively anxious or depressed when they can't achieve the impossible goals they have set for themselves (Bandura, 1986; Covington, 1992).

To facilitate appropriate goal setting, we can show our students that challenging goals are attainable, perhaps by describing individuals of similar ability who have attained them with reasonable effort. In some situations, we might even want to provide incentives that encourage students to set and achieve challenging goals (Stipek, 1996). At the same time, we must help

---

Self-regulated behaviour
Engaging in self-chosen behaviours that lead to the accomplishment of personally chosen standards and goals.

Students from low-income families typically set low goals for themselves in terms of career aspirations (Durkin, 1995). Can you explain this fact in light of the discussion here?

FIGURE 8.1 Components of self-regulated behaviour

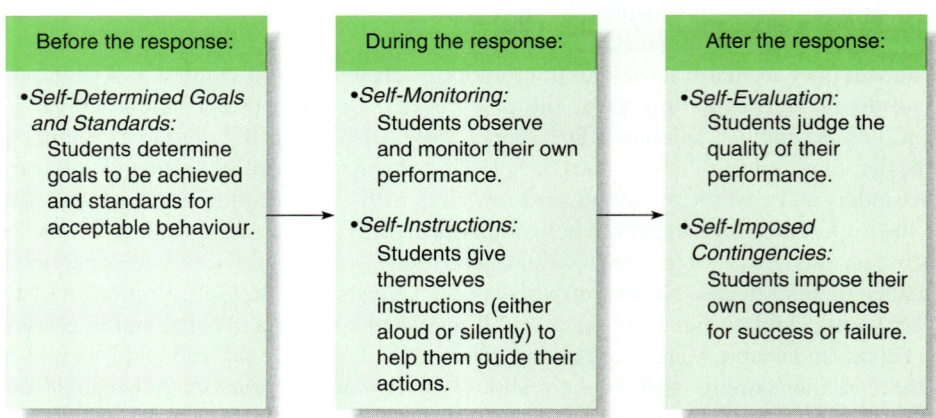

any overly ambitious students understand and accept the fact that no one is perfect and that an occasional failure is nothing to be ashamed of.

Self-Monitoring

An important part of self-regulation is to observe oneself in action—a process known as **self-monitoring** (also known as *self-observation*). To make progress toward important goals, we must be aware of how well we are doing currently; we must know which aspects of our performance are working well and which need improvement. Furthermore, when we see ourselves making progress toward our goals, we are more likely to continue with our efforts (Schunk & Zimmerman, 1997).

Yet students aren't necessarily accurate observers of their own behaviour; they aren't always aware of how frequently they do something wrong or how *in*frequently they do something right. To help students attend to the things that they do and don't do, we can have them observe and record their own behaviour. If Olivia has trouble staying on task during assigned activities, we can ask her to stop and reflect on her behaviour every few minutes (perhaps with the aid of an egg timer), determining whether she was staying on task during each interval.

Research indicates clearly that such self-focused observation and recording can bring about changes (sometimes dramatic ones) in student behaviour. For example, self-observation can be used to increase students' attention to their work (their *time on task*) and the number of assignments they are likely to complete. It is also effective in reducing aggressive responses and such disruptive classroom behaviours as talking out of turn and getting out of one's seat (Allen, 1998; Belfiore & Hornyak, 1998; Webber, Scheuermann, McCall, & Coleman, 1993).

Self-Instructions

Consider the formerly "forgetful" student who, before leaving the house each morning, now asks herself, "Do I have everything I need for my classes? I have my math homework for period 1, my history book for period 2, my change of clothes for gym during period 3. . . ." And consider the once impulsive student who now pauses before beginning a new assignment and says to himself, "OK, what am I supposed to do? Let's see . . . I need to read the directions first. What do the directions tell me to do?" And consider as well the formerly aggressive student who has learned to count to 10 every time she gets angry—an action that gives her a chance to cool off.

Sometimes students simply need a reminder about how to respond in particular situations. By teaching students how to talk themselves through these situations using **self-instructions**, we provide them with a means through which *they remind themselves* about appropriate actions, thereby helping them to control their own behaviour. Such a strategy is often effective in working with students who otherwise seem to behave without thinking (Casey & Burton, 1982; Meichenbaum, 1985).

Donald Meichenbaum is one of the founders of the "cognitive revolution." Meichenbaum, a professor of psychology at the University of Waterloo in Ontario, and author of many publications that focus on cognitive approaches to learning (1977, 1985; Meichenbaum & Biemiller, 1998; Meichenbaum & Goodman, 1971), has described an effective way of teaching students to give themselves instructions involving five steps (Meichenbaum, 1977):

1. The teacher models self-instruction by repeating instructions aloud while simultaneously performing the activity.
2. The teacher repeats the instructions aloud while the student performs the activity.
3. The student repeats the instructions aloud while performing the activity.
4. The student whispers the instructions while performing the activity.
5. The student simply "thinks" the instructions while performing the activity.

Through these five steps, impulsive elementary school children can effectively learn to slow themselves down and think through what they are doing (Meichenbaum & Goodman, 1971). For example, notice how one formerly impulsive student was able to talk his way through a matching task in which he needed to find two identical pictures among several very similar ones:

> I have to remember to go slowly to get it right. Look carefully at this one, now look at these carefully. Is this one different? Yes, it has an extra leaf. Good, I can eliminate this one. Now, let's look at this one. I think it's this one, but let me first check the others. Good, I'm going slow and carefully. Okay, I think it's this one. (Meichenbaum & Goodman, 1971, p. 121)

Self-monitoring The process of observing and recording one's own behaviour.

Self-selected goals promote a greater sense of *self-determination*, a topic we will consider in Chapter 9.

Self-instructions Instructions that students give themselves as they perform a complex behaviour.

Can you relate steps 3, 4, and 5 to Vygotsky's notions of *self-talk* and *inner speech* (Chapter 2)?

Self-Evaluation

Self-evaluation The process of evaluating one's own performance or behaviour.

Both at home and in school, students' behaviours are frequently judged by others—their parents, teachers, classmates, and so on. But eventually our students should also begin to judge their *own* behaviour; in other words, they should engage in **self-evaluation**. Their ability to evaluate themselves with some degree of objectivity and accuracy will be critical for their long-term success in the adult world (Vye et al., 1998).

Once our students have developed appropriate goals and standards, and some objective techniques for observing their own behaviour, there are many ways in which we can encourage them to evaluate their own performance. For example, we can have them

- Assemble portfolios of what they think is their best work, with self-evaluations of each entry
- Write in daily or weekly journals, in which they address the strengths and weaknesses of their performance
- Participate in peer conferences, in which several students discuss their reactions to one another's work (Paris & Ayres, 1994; Paris & Paris, 2001)

Chapter 12 describes *portfolios* in greater depth.

We might also have students complete self-assessment instruments that show them what to look for as they judge their work (Paris & Ayres, 1994). For example, to evaluate a project they have just completed, students might respond to questions such as these:

- What did you like about this project?
- What would have made this project better?
- What grade do you feel you earned on this project? Justify your response. (Based on Paris & Ayres, 1994, p. 78)

Students who hold different standards for themselves will naturally judge the same behaviour in different ways. For example, if Robert and Richard both get all Bs on their report cards, Robert (with the straight-A standard) will judge his performance to be unacceptable, whereas Richard (with acceptability defined as C) will go home and celebrate. It is essential, then, that we help our students use appropriate criteria for evaluating their performance (Yell, Robinson, & Drasgow, 2001; Zuckerman, 1994).

Self-Imposed Contingencies

When you accomplish something you've set out to do, especially if the task is complex and challenging, you probably feel quite proud of yourself and give yourself a mental pat on the back. In contrast, when you fail to accomplish that task, you are probably unhappy with your performance; you may also feel guilty, regretful, or ashamed. Likewise, as our students become increasingly self-regulated, they will begin to reinforce themselves (perhaps by feeling proud or telling themselves they did a good job) when they accomplish their goals. And they will also begin to punish themselves (perhaps by feeling sorry, guilty, or ashamed) when they do something that does not meet their own performance standards.

Self-imposed contingencies Contingencies that students provide for themselves; the self-reinforcements and self-punishments that follow various behaviours.

Yet such **self-imposed contingencies** are not necessarily confined to people's emotional reactions to their own behaviours. Many self-regulating individuals reinforce themselves in far more concrete ways when they accomplish something successfully. For example, after obtaining a terrific mark on a tough examination, you might decide to treat yourself to a dinner out or a shopping spree!

Thus, an additional way to help students become more self-regulating is to teach them self-reinforcement. When students begin to reinforce themselves for appropriate responses—perhaps by giving themselves some free time, allowing themselves to engage in a favourite activity, or simply praising themselves—their classroom behaviour often improves significantly (K. R. Harris, 1986; S. C. Hayes et al., 1985). For example, in one research study, students who were performing poorly in arithmetic were taught to give themselves points when they did well on their assignments; they could later use these points to "buy" a variety of items and privileges. Within a few weeks, these students were doing as well as their classmates on both in-class assignments and homework (H. C. Stevenson & Fantuzzo, 1986). In some instances, self-reinforcement is just as effective as reinforcement administered by a teacher (Bandura, 1977).

Self-Regulated Learning

Social learning theorists and cognitive psychologists alike are beginning to realize that to be truly effective learners, students must engage in self-regulating activities. In fact, not only must students regulate their own behaviours, but they must also regulate their own cognitive processes. In particular, **self-regulated learning** includes the following processes, many of which are *metacognitive*:

- *Goal-setting.* Self-regulated learners know what they want to accomplish when they read or study. For instance, they may want to learn specific facts, get an overall understanding of the ideas being presented, or simply acquire enough knowledge to do well on a classroom exam (Nolen, 1996; Winne & Hadwin, 1998; Wolters, 1998; Zimmerman, 1998).

- *Planning.* Self-regulated learners determine ahead of time how best to use the time and resources they have available for a learning task (Zimmerman, 1998; Zimmerman & Risemberg, 1997).

- *Attention control.* Self-regulated learners try to focus their attention on the subject matter at hand and to clear their minds of potentially distracting thoughts and emotions (Corno, 1993; Harnishfeger, 1995; Kuhl, 1985; Schutz & Davis, 2000; Winne, 1995).

- *Application of learning strategies.* Self-regulated learners choose different learning strategies depending on the specific goal they hope to accomplish. For example, the way they read a magazine article depends on whether they are reading it for entertainment or studying for an exam (Linderholm, Gustafson, van den Broek, & Lorch, 1997; Winne, 1995).

Self-regulated learners seek assistance when they need it and are especially likely to ask for help with skills that will make them more independent.

- *Self-motivational strategies.* Self-regulated learners keep themselves on task with a variety of strategies, such as competing against their own prior performance, finding ways to make a boring activity more interesting or challenging, imagining themselves completing an activity successfully, or varying the procedures they use for successive tasks or problems (Corno, 1993; Kuhl, 1987; Sansone, Weir, Harpster, & Morgan, 1992).

- *Solicitation of outside help when needed.* Truly self-regulated learners don't necessarily try to do everything on their own. On the contrary, they recognize when they need other people's help and seek out such assistance; they are especially likely to ask for the kind of help that will enable them to work more independently in the future (R. Butler, 1998b; A. M. Ryan, Pintrich, & Midgley, 2001).

- *Self-monitoring.* Self-regulated learners continually monitor their progress toward their goals, and they change their learning strategies or modify their goals if necessary (D. L. Butler & Winne, 1995; Carver & Scheier, 1990; Zimmerman & Risemberg, 1997). *Comprehension monitoring* (described in Chapter 7) is an example of such self-monitoring.

- *Self-evaluation.* Self-regulated learners determine whether what they have learned fulfills the goals they have set for themselves, according to Canadian researchers Butler and Winne (1995) and others (e.g., Schraw & Moshman, 1995; Zimmerman & Risemberg, 1997). Ideally, they also use their self-evaluations to modify their selection and use of various learning strategies on future occasions (Winne & Hadwin, 1998).

In addition to such activities, self-regulated learning requires **intrinsic motivation**—motivation that comes from within the individual, rather than from such outside influences as extrinsic reinforcers (Bronson, 2000; Zimmerman & Risemberg, 1997). One important factor in intrinsic motivation is high self-efficacy: Students must believe that they have the ability to accomplish the learning task successfully (more about this point in Chapter 9).

When students are self-regulated learners, they set more ambitious academic goals for themselves, learn more effectively, and achieve at higher levels in the classroom (D. L. Butler & Winne, 1995; Zimmerman & Risemberg, 1997). Furthermore, a great deal of adolescent and adult learning—doing homework, reading, surfing the internet, and so on—occurs in isolation from other people and so requires considerable self-regulation (Winne, 1995).

Self-regulated learning Regulating one's own cognitive processes to learn successfully; includes goal setting, planning, attention control, use of effective learning strategies, self-monitoring, and self-evaluation.

Do you reinforce yourself in some tangible way for your accomplishments? If so, how?

Intrinsic motivation The internal desire to perform a particular task.

Unfortunately, however, few students develop a high level of self-regulated learning, perhaps in part because traditional instructional practices do little to encourage it (Paris & Ayres, 1994; Zimmerman & Risemberg, 1997).

To promote self-regulated learning, we must, of course, teach students the kinds of cognitive processes that facilitate learning and memory (see the discussion of metacognition in Chapter 7). In addition, theorists have suggested the following strategies:

- Encourage students to set some of their own goals for learning and then to monitor their progress toward those goals.

- Give students opportunities to learn and achieve without teacher direction or assistance, including both independent learning activities in which students study by themselves (e.g., seatwork assignments, homework) and group activities in which students help one another learn (e.g., peer tutoring, co-operative learning).

- Occasionally assign activities (e.g., research papers, creative projects) in which students have considerable leeway regarding goals, use of time, and so on.

- Provide scaffolding as needed to help students acquire self-regulating strategies (e.g., show them how to use checklists to identify what they need to do each day and to determine when they have completed all assigned work).

- Model self-regulating cognitive processes by "thinking aloud" about such processes, and then give students constructive feedback as they engage in similar processes.

- Consistently ask students to evaluate their own performance, and have them compare their self-assessments to teacher assessments. (Belfiore & Hornyak, 1998; Bronson, 2000; A. King, 1997; McCaslin & Good, 1996; Paris & Paris, 2001; N. E. Perry, 1998; Schunk & Zimmerman, 1997; J. W. Thomas, 1993b; Winne & Hadwin, 1998; Zimmerman & Risemberg, 1997)

Self-Regulated Problem Solving

We can sometimes use self-regulation techniques (especially self-instructions) to help students develop more effective problem-solving skills. For example, to promote greater creativity in their solutions to academic problems, we might encourage them to give themselves instructions such as these:

> I want to think of something no one else will think of, something unique. Be freewheeling, no hangups. I don't care what anyone thinks; just suspend judgment. I'm not sure what I'll come up with; it will be a surprise. The ideas can just flow through me.... (Meichenbaum, 1977, p. 62)

To help students deal more effectively with social conflicts and other interpersonal problems, we might ask them to take steps such as these:

1. Define the problem.
2. Identify several possible solutions.
3. Predict the likely consequences of each solution.
4. Choose the best solution.
5. Identify the steps required to carry out the solution.
6. Carry the steps out.
7. Evaluate the results. (S. N. Elliott & Busse, 1991; Meichenbaum, 1977; Weissburg, 1985; Yell et al., 2001)

Self-regulated problem-solving strategy A strategy that helps students solve their own interpersonal problems.

Mediation training Training that involves teaching students how to mediate conflicts among classmates by asking opposing sides to express their differing viewpoints and then work together to devise a reasonable resolution.

Such **self-regulated problem-solving strategies** often help students who have difficulty interacting appropriately with their peers (e.g., students who are either socially withdrawn or overly aggressive) to develop more effective interpersonal skills (K. R. Harris, 1982; Meichenbaum, 1977; Yell et al., 2001).

Another approach is **mediation training**, a strategy for helping students *help one another* solve interpersonal problems. More specifically, we teach students how to mediate conflicts among classmates by asking the opposing sides to express their differing points of view and then working together to devise a reasonable resolution (Deutsch, 1993; D. W. Johnson & Johnson, 1996, 2001; Stevahn, Oberle, Johnson, & Johnson, 2001). For example, in a study involving several classrooms at Grade 2 through 5 levels (D. W. Johnson, Johnson, Dudley, Ward, &

INTO THE CLASSROOM   *Fostering Self-Regulation*

Help students set challenging yet realistic goals and standards.

> A teacher encourages a pregnant student to stay in school until she graduates. Together they discuss strategies for juggling motherhood and schoolwork.

Have students observe and record their own behaviour.

> A student with attention-deficit hyperactivity disorder frequently tips his chair back to the point where he is likely to topple over. Concerned for the student's safety, his teacher asks him to record each instance of such behaviour on a sheet of graph paper. Both student and teacher notice how quickly the behaviour disappears once the student has become aware of his bad habit.

Teach students instructions they can give themselves to remind them of what they need to do.

> To help a student control her impulsive behaviour on multiple-choice tests, her teacher has her mentally say this to herself as she reads each question: "Read the entire question. Then look at each answer carefully and decide whether it is correct or incorrect. Then choose the answer that seems most correct."

Encourage students to evaluate their own performance.

> A science teacher gives students a list of criteria to evaluate the lab reports they have written. In assigning grades, she considers how accurately students have evaluated their own reports.

Teach students to reinforce themselves for appropriate behaviour.

> A teacher helps students develop more regular study habits by encouraging them to make a favourite activity—for example, shooting baskets, watching television, or calling a friend on the telephone—contingent on completing their homework first.

Give students opportunities to practise learning with little or no help from their teacher.

> A middle school social studies teacher distributes various magazine articles related to current events in the Middle East, making sure that each student receives an article appropriate for his or her reading level. He asks students to read their articles over the weekend and prepare a one-paragraph summary to share with other class members. He also provides guidelines about what information students should include in their summaries.

Provide strategies that students can use to solve interpersonal problems.

> A teacher teaches her students a sequence to follow when they find themselves in a conflict with a classmate: *identify* the source of the conflict, *listen* to each other's perspectives, *verbalize* each other's perspectives, and *develop* a solution that provides a reasonable compromise.

Magnuson, 1995), students were trained to help their peers resolve interpersonal conflicts by asking the opposing sides to do the following:

1. Define the conflict (the problem)
2. Explain their own perspectives and needs
3. Explain the *other* person's perspectives and needs
4. Identify at least three possible solutions to the conflict
5. Reach an agreement that addresses the needs of both parties

The students took turns serving as mediator for their classmates, such that everyone had experience resolving the conflicts of others. In comparison to students in an untrained control group, students who completed the training more frequently resolved their *own* interpersonal conflicts in ways that addressed the needs of both parties, and they were less likely to ask for adult intervention. Similarly, in a case study involving adolescent gang members (Sanchez & Anderson, 1990), students were given mediation training and asked to be responsible for mediating gang-related disputes. After only one month of training, rival gang members were exchanging friendly greetings in the corridors, giving one another the "high five" sign, and interacting at lunch; meanwhile, gang-related fights virtually disappeared from the scene.

As we consider how best to help our students become self-regulated learners and problem solvers, we should keep in mind a point that Lev Vygotsky made many years ago: Many complex cognitive processes have their roots in social interactions, including interactions with teachers and classmates. Over time, the things that students may initially do on a social level—setting group goals, identifying effective ways to approach a particular learning task or solve a particular problem, discussing appropriate evaluation criteria, guiding others' learning and behaviour, and

> Conflict resolution and peer mediation programs are active in school divisions throughout Canada, from Vancouver to Prince Edward Island. The aim of these programs is to help create safe, caring, and just schools. If you are interested in obtaining further information about Canadian examples of these programs, see the Peer Resources website: Peer Helping Programs, www.peer.ca/helping.html.

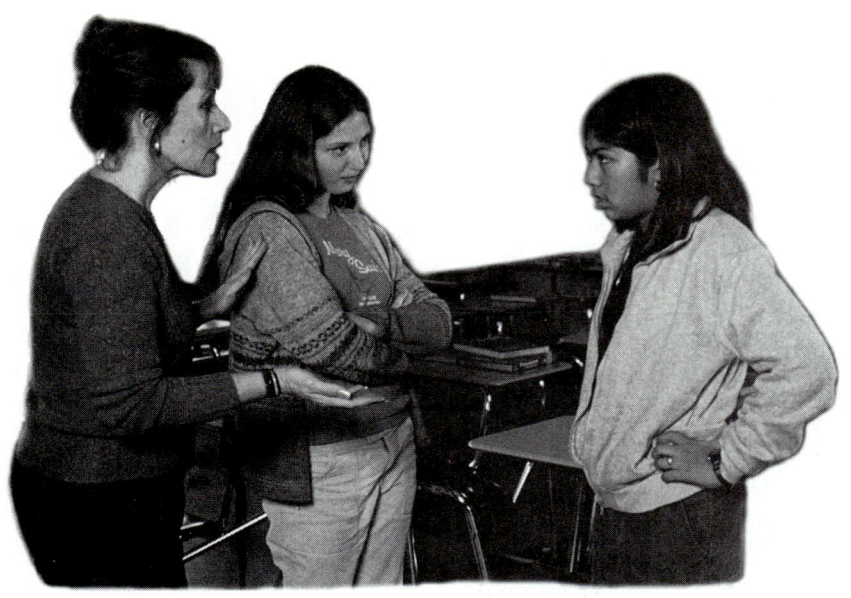

so on—eventually become internalized in the form of mental processes that students can use to guide their *own* learning and behaviour (Biemiller, Shany, Inglis, & Meichenbaum, 1998; Zimmerman, 1998).

When students set challenging goals for themselves and achieve those self-chosen goals through their own efforts, their self-efficacy is enhanced and their motivation to undertake new challenges increases (Bandura, 1989; Bandura & Schunk, 1981). And when students have a high sense of self-efficacy and engage in self-regulating activities, they are more likely to believe that they control their environment, rather than that their environment controls them. In fact, social cognitive theorists assert that people, their behaviours, and the environment all have a somewhat "controlling" influence on one another, as we shall see now.

Teachers sometimes intervene when students have an interpersonal conflict. But *mediation training*, whereby students learn how to help one another resolve their differences, is more likely to promote self-regulation.

Reciprocal causation The interdependence of environment, behaviour, and personal variables as these three factors influence learning.

Reciprocal Causation

Throughout the chapter we've discussed aspects of learners' environments and the behaviours that result from various environmental conditions. We have also talked about such personal variables as expectations and self-efficacy that learners bring with them to a task. Now which one of these three factors—environment, behaviour, or person—lays the foundation for learning? According to social cognitive theorists, all three are essential ingredients, and each one influences the other two. This interdependence among environment, behaviour, and person is known as **reciprocal causation** (Bandura, 1989). Some examples of how each factor affects the other two are listed in Table 8.2.

As you can see from Table 8.2, the things we do in the classroom—the *environment* we create—affect both the behaviours that students exhibit and the personal factors that influence

TABLE 8.2 COMPARE/CONTRAST

Mutual Influences (Reciprocal Causation) among Environment, Behaviour, and Person

		A GENERAL EXAMPLE	AN EXAMPLE OF NEGATIVE EXPECTATIONS	AN EXAMPLE OF POSITIVE EXPECTATIONS
Effect of Environment	On Behaviour	Reinforcement and punishment affect future behaviour.	Teacher's ignoring student leads to future classroom failure.	New instructional methods lead to improved academic performance.
	On Person	Feedback from others affects sense of self-efficacy.	Teacher's ignoring student perpetuates low self-efficacy.	New instructional methods capture student's interest and attention.
Effect of Behaviour	On Environment	Specific behaviours affect the amount of reinforcement and punishment received.	Poor classroom performance leads to the teacher meeting privately with student, then eventually ignoring her.	Better academic performance leads to more reinforcement from the teacher.
	On Person	Success and failure affect expectations for future performance.	Poor classroom performance leads to low self-efficacy.	Better academic performance leads to higher self-efficacy.
Effect of Person	On Environment	Self-efficacy affects choices of activities and therefore the specific environment encountered.	Attention to classmates rather than classroom activities affects environment experienced.	Attention to classroom activities leads to greater influence of teacher's instruction.
	On Behaviour	Attention, retention, motor reproduction, and motivation affect degree to which one imitates modelled behaviour.	Attention to classmates rather than classroom activities leads to academic failure.	Greater self-efficacy and increased motivation lead to more persistent study habits.

their learning. Students' behaviours and personal factors, in turn, influence the future classroom environment that they experience. As teachers, we must create and maintain a classroom environment that helps students develop the behaviours (e.g., academic and social skills) and personal characteristics (e.g., high self-efficacy and the expectation that their efforts will be rewarded) that are likely to bring them academic and personal success.

Can you explain reciprocal causation in your own words? Can you provide an example from your own experience?

Promoting Self-Regulation in Students with Special Needs

Most of our students will undoubtedly stand to gain from teaching strategies that promote greater self-regulation. But students with special educational needs will often be among those in greatest need of becoming more self-regulated (Sands & Wehmeyer, 1996). Such students are especially likely to benefit when we encourage them to set and strive for their own goals, particularly when those goals are concrete, specific, and accomplishable within a short period of time. Students with special needs will also be well served when we teach them self-observation, self-reinforcement techniques, and self-regulated problem-solving skills (Abery & Zajac, 1996; C. E. Cunningham & Cunningham, 1998; L. E. Powers et al., 1996; Yell et al., 2001).

To better understand the relationship of constructs such as self-esteem, self-determination, motivation, and perseverance in children with learning disabilities, see the literature review, *Putting a Canadian Face on Learning Disabilities*, published by the Learning Disabilities Association of Canada (www.pacfold.ca).

Table 8.3 presents a social cognitive perspective of characteristics commonly seen in students with special needs; it also presents a number of strategies for promoting the academic and social success of these students. As you will undoubtedly notice, the concepts *modelling, self-efficacy,* and *self-regulation* appear repeatedly throughout the table.

Dr. Charles E. Cunningham, Professor of Psychiatry and Behavioural Neurosciences in the Faculty of Health Sciences at McMaster University, has been actively involved in the development and evaluation of services for children with a wide variety of behaviour problems.

TABLE 8.3 STUDENTS IN INCLUSIVE SETTINGS

Promoting Social Learning in Students with Special Educational Needs

CATEGORY	CHARACTERISTICS YOU MIGHT OBSERVE	SUGGESTED CLASSROOM STRATEGIES
Students with specific cognitive or academic difficulties	• Difficulty predicting the consequences of specific behaviours • Low self-efficacy for academic tasks in areas where there has been a history of failure • Less self-regulation of learning and behaviour	• Help students form more realistic expectations about the consequences of their behaviours. • Scaffold students' efforts on academic tasks to increase the probability of success. • Identify students' areas of strength and provide opportunities to tutor other students in those areas. • Promote self-regulation (e.g., by teaching self-observation, self-instructions, self-reinforcement).
Students with social or behavioural problems	• Unusual difficulty in learning from the social environment (for students with autism) • Difficulties predicting the consequences of specific behaviours • Friendships with peers who are poor models of effective social skills or prosocial behaviour (for students with emotional and behavioural disorders) • Little self-regulation of behaviour • Deficits in social problem solving	• Help students recognize and interpret social cues and nonverbal language. • Discuss possible consequences of various courses of action in social conflict situations (for students with emotional and behavioural disorders). • Model appropriate classroom behaviours; for students with autism, combine modelling with explicit verbal instruction, and use visual aids to communicate desired behaviours. • Provide opportunities for students to interact with peers who model effective social and prosocial behaviours. • Videotape students exhibiting appropriate behaviours and then have them view themselves as models for such behaviour. • Teach self-regulation (e.g., self-observation, self-instructions, self-regulated problem-solving strategies).
Students with general delays in cognitive and social functioning	• Low self-efficacy for academic tasks • Tendency to watch others for guidance about how to behave • Low goals for achievement (possibly as a way of avoiding failure) • Little if any self-regulation of learning and behaviour	• Scaffold students' efforts on academic tasks to increase the probability of success. • Model desired behaviours; identify peers who can also serve as appropriate models. • Encourage students to set high yet realistic goals for their own achievement. • Promote self-regulation (e.g., by teaching self-observation, self-instructions, self-reinforcement).

(continued)

TABLE 8.3 (continued)

Promoting Social Learning in Students with Special Educational Needs

CATEGORY	CHARACTERISTICS YOU MIGHT OBSERVE	SUGGESTED CLASSROOM STRATEGIES
Students with physical or sensory challenges	• Few opportunities to develop self-regulation skills due to health limitations, a tightly controlled environment, or both	• Teach skills that promote self-sufficiency and independence. • Teach students to make positive self-statements (e.g., "I can do it!") to enhance their self-efficacy for acting independently.
Students showing evidence of giftedness, talent, or high performance	• High self-efficacy for academic tasks • High goals for performance • More effective self-regulated learning • For some students, a history of easy successes and, hence, little experience dealing with failure effectively	• Provide the academic support that students need to reach their goals. • Provide opportunities for independent study. • Provide challenging tasks at which students may sometimes fail; teach constructive strategies for dealing with failure (e.g., persistence, using errors to guide future practice efforts).

Sources: Balla & Zigler, 1979; Bandura, 1989; Beirne-Smith et al., 2002; Biemiller et al., 1998; C. E. Cunningham & Cunningham, 1998; E. S. Ellis & Friend, 1991; Hughes, 1988; Kehle, Clark, Jenson, & Wampold, 1986; Lupart, 1995; Mercer, 1997; Morgan & Jenson, 1988; J. R. Nelson, Smith, Young, & Dodd, 1991; Piirto, 1999; Sands & Wehmeyer, 1996; Schumaker & Hazel, 1984; Schunk et al., 1987; Turnbull et al., 1999; Yell et al., 2001.

TEACHING CONSTRUCTIONS

Now that you have read about the fundamental principles of social cognitive views of learning, let's revisit Nathan who was struggling with his Latin classes. Given what you now know, consider the following questions:

- What basic assumptions from the social cognitive perspective can help to explain Nathan's difficulties learning Latin?
- If you were Nathan's Latin teacher, how could you help him to enhance his sense of self-efficacy?
- As his teacher, how would you help Nathan regulate his learning?

KEY CONCEPTS

social cognitive theory (p. 195)
vicarious reinforcement (p. 198)
vicarious punishment (p. 198)
incentive (p. 199)
live model (p. 200)
symbolic model (p. 200)
observational learning effect (p. 200)
response facilitation effect (p. 200)
response inhibition effect (p. 200)

response disinhibition effect (p. 200)
self-efficacy (p. 204)
resilient self-efficacy (p. 206)
collective self-efficacy (p. 206)
self-regulation (p. 207)
self-regulated behaviour (p. 208)
self-monitoring (p. 209)
self-instructions (p. 209)
self-evaluation (p. 210)

self-imposed contingencies (p. 210)
self-regulated learning (p. 211)
intrinsic motivation (p. 211)
self-regulated problem-solving strategy (p. 212)
mediation training (p. 212)
reciprocal causation (p. 214)

9 Motivation, Affect, and Cognition

CASE STUDY PASSING ALGEBRA

TEACHING CONNECTIONS

THE NATURE OF MOTIVATION
How Motivation Affects Learning and Behaviour • Intrinsic versus Extrinsic Motivation

THEORETICAL PERSPECTIVES OF MOTIVATION
The Trait Perspective • The Behaviourist Perspective • The Social Cognitive Perspective • The Cognitive Perspective

WHAT BASIC NEEDS DO PEOPLE HAVE?
Self-Worth • Relatedness

AFFECT AND ITS EFFECTS
Hot Cognition • Anxiety

COGNITIONS THAT MOTIVATE

THE INTERPLAY OF COGNITION AND MOTIVATION

SELF-PERCEPTIONS AND INTRINSIC MOTIVATION
Self-Efficacy • Self-Determination

EXPECTANCIES AND VALUES
Internalizing the Values of Others • Fostering Expectancies and Values in the Classroom

INTEREST
Situational versus Personal Interest • Promoting Interest in Classroom Subject Matter

GOALS
Mastery and Performance Goals • Work-Avoidance Goals • Social Goals • Capitalizing on Students' Goals

ATTRIBUTIONS: PERCEIVED CAUSES OF SUCCESS AND FAILURE
Dimensions Underlying Students' Attributions • How Attributions Influence Affect, Cognition, and Behaviour • Developmental Trends in Attributions • Factors Influencing the Development of Attributions • Mastery Orientation versus Learned Helplessness

TEACHER EXPECTATIONS AND ATTRIBUTIONS
How Expectations and Attributions Affect Classroom Performance • Forming Productive Expectations and Attributions for Student Performance

CONSIDERING DIVERSITY IN MOTIVATION, AFFECT, AND COGNITION
Ethnic Differences • Sex Differences • Socioeconomic Differences • Accommodating Students in Inclusive Settings

TEACHING CONSTRUCTIONS

KEY CONCEPTS

CASE STUDY *Passing Algebra*

Fourteen-year-old Michael has been getting failing grades in his Grade 8 algebra class, and so his family asks graduate student Valerie Tucker to tutor him. In their initial tutoring session, Michael tells Ms. Tucker that he has no hope of passing algebra because he has little aptitude for math and his teacher doesn't teach the subject matter very well. In his mind, he is powerless to change either his own ability or his teacher's instructional strategies, and so continuing failure is inevitable. Michael reports that he is feeling increasingly anxious but also unmotivated to do math.

As Ms. Tucker works with Michael over the next several weeks, she encourages him to think more about what *he* can do to master algebra and less about what his teacher may or may not be doing to help him. She points out that he has done well in math in earlier grades and so he clearly does have the ability to learn algebra if he puts his mind to it. She also teaches him a variety of strategies for understanding and applying algebraic principles. Michael takes a first giant step forward when he finally realizes that his own efforts play a role in his classroom success:

> [M]aybe I can try a little harder. . . . The teacher is still bad, but maybe some of this other stuff can work. (Tucker & Anderman, 1999, p. 5)

As Michael sees gradual improvement on his algebra assignments and quizzes, he becomes increasingly aware that the specific *strategies* he uses are just as important as his effort:

> I learned that I need to understand information before I can hold it in my mind. . . . Now I do things in math step by step and listen to each step. I realize now that even if I don't like the teacher or don't think he is a good teacher, it is my responsibility to listen. I listen better now and ask questions more. . . . (Tucker & Anderman, 1999, p. 5)

As Michael's performance in algebra continues to improve in the weeks ahead, he gains greater confidence that he *can* master algebra after all, and he comes to realize that his classroom success is ultimately up to him:

> [T]he teacher does most of his part, but it's no use to me unless I do my part. . . . [N]ow I try and comprehend, ask questions and figure out how he got the answer. . . . I used to just listen and not even take notes. I always told myself I would remember but I always seemed to forget. Now I take notes and I study at home every day except Friday, even if I don't have homework. Now I study so that I know that I have it. I don't just hope I'll remember. (Tucker & Anderman, 1999, p. 6)

TEACHING CONNECTIONS

In this chapter we will examine various theoretical perspectives of motivation, consider some of the basic needs that students may have, and how emotion (or *affect*) as well as external influences (e.g., teacher's attributions and expectations) influence motivation. We will also examine how a student's perceptions, beliefs, expectations, values, interests, goals, and attributions (i.e., *cognitions*) influence their motivation. As you read about how these perspectives inform your teaching practice, consider the following questions:

- What factors influence a student's preferences for particular classes and subjects in school?
- On what factors does Michael initially blame his failure? What effects do his early beliefs appear to have on his classroom behaviour and study habits?
- To what factors does Michael later attribute his success? How have his changing beliefs affected his learning strategies?

Students from more than 41 countries, including Canada, recently participated in a study conducted by the Programme for International Student Achievement (PISA) that explored student achievement in mathematics. Of interest to the researchers was the relationship of achievement in mathematics to variables such as student engagement and confidence, anxiety, motivation, and family factors. Findings revealed that 15-year-old Canadian students are well motivated to learn mathematics, believing that it is useful to their future employment and education. These youth reported above-average levels of confidence and perceived ability in mathematics. In addition, the Canadian students reported slightly lower levels of anxiety in dealing with mathematics. Overall, girls reported less confidence in their ability to solve mathematical problems, lower perceived ability to learn mathematics, higher levels of anxiety, and lower levels of interest and enjoyment in mathematics. Relationships were also observed between various family factors and mathematics achievement. For example, mathematics scores of students whose parents had a high-school education or less were significantly lower than the average scores of students who had parents with post-secondary education. Moreover, students from families with higher socioeconomic status also tended to perform better in mathematics (Bussière, Cartwright, & Knighton, 2004; McMullen, 2004).

A more recent PISA study focused on achievement in science literacy relative to factors such as sex, minority language school systems, immigrant status, engagement, and family factors (Bussière, Knighton, & Pennock, 2007). Canadian 15-year-old students in all 10 provinces performed well in science, scoring above the international average. No sex differences were observed amongst Canadian students on the combined science scale with the exception of Newfoundland and Labrador, where girls performed slightly better than boys. Students enrolled in French-language school systems in Nova Scotia, New Brunswick, Ontario, and Manitoba performed significantly lower on the combined science scale than students in the English-language school systems. In contrast, within Quebec, there was a small but statistically significant difference, with results favouring students enrolled in the French-language school system. Immigrant youth in Canada also performed above the overall international average in science. Moreover, when compared to the average for 15-year-olds in all participating countries, Canadian 15-year-olds reported higher levels of confidence in performing science-related tasks and a more positive perception of their ability to learn science. Science achievement was significantly higher among youth with at least one parent who had completed a postsecondary education compared to youth whose parents had high-school education or less. Family socioeconomic status also showed a positive relationship to student science performance.

In this chapter we will explore what motivates students to learn and how motivation affects student learning, confidence, and achievement. We will also examine how we as teachers might improve student motivation.

The Nature of Motivation

Motivation A state that energizes, directs, and sustains behaviour.

Motivation is something that energizes, directs, and sustains behaviour; it gets students moving, points them in a particular direction, and keeps them going. We often see students' motivation reflected in *personal investment* and *cognitive engagement* in an activity (Maehr & Meyer, 1997; Paris & Paris, 2001; Steinberg, 1996).

Virtually all students are motivated in one way or another. One student may be keenly interested in classroom subject matter and so may seek out challenging coursework, participate actively in class discussions, and earn high marks on assigned projects. Another student may be more concerned with the social side of school, interacting with classmates frequently, attending extracurricular activities almost every day, and perhaps even running for a student government office.

Some students may bring a strong interest in art to the classroom. Yet motivation is not always something that people "carry around" inside of them; it can also be influenced by environmental conditions. When we talk about how the environment can enhance a person's motivation to learn particular things or behave in particular ways, we are talking about **situated motivation** (Paris & Turner, 1994; Rueda & Moll, 1994). As we proceed through this chapter, we will find that, as teachers, we can do many things to create a classroom environment that motivates students to learn and behave in ways that will promote their long-term success.

Situated motivation A phenomenon whereby aspects of one's immediate environment enhance one's motivation to learn particular things or behave in particular ways.

How Motivation Affects Learning and Behaviour

Motivation has several effects on students' learning and behaviour, which are summarized in Figure 9.1:

- *It directs behaviour toward particular goals.* Social cognitive theorists propose that individuals set goals for themselves and direct their behaviour toward those goals. Motivation determines the specific goals toward which people strive (Maehr & Meyer, 1997; Pintrich et al., 1993). Thus, it affects the choices that students make—whether to enrol in trigonometry or studio art,

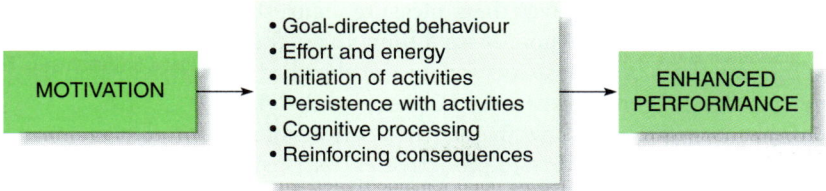

FIGURE 9.1 How motivation affects learning and behaviour

whether to watch the Vancouver Canucks versus the Montreal Canadiens game or write an assigned research paper.

- *It leads to increased effort and energy.* Motivation increases the amount of effort and energy that students expend in activities directly related to their needs and goals (Csikszentmihalyi & Nakamura, 1989; Maehr, 1984; Pintrich et al., 1993). It determines whether students pursue a task enthusiastically and wholeheartedly on the one hand, or apathetically and lackadaisically on the other.

- *It increases initiation of, and persistence in, activities.* Students are more likely to begin a task that they actually *want* to do. They are also more likely to continue that task until they've completed it, even when they are occasionally interrupted or frustrated in their efforts to do so (Larson, 2000; Maehr, 1984; Wigfield, 1994).

- *It enhances cognitive processing.* Motivation affects what and how information is processed (Eccles & Wigfield, 1985; Pintrich & Schunk, 2002; Voss & Schauble, 1992). For one thing, motivated students are more likely to pay attention, and as we know, attention is critical for getting information into both working memory and long-term memory. They also try to understand material—to learn it meaningfully—rather than simply "go through the motions" of learning in a superficial, rote fashion.

- *It determines what consequences are reinforcing.* The more students are motivated to achieve academic success, the more proud they will be of an A and the more upset they will be by an F or perhaps even by a B. The more students want to be accepted and respected by their peers, the more meaningful membership in the "in group" will be, and the more painful the ridicule of classmates will seem.

- *It leads to improved performance.* Because of these other effects—goal-directed behaviour, energy and effort, initiation and persistence, cognitive processing, and reinforcement—motivation often leads to improved performance. As you might guess, then, our students who are most motivated to learn and excel in classroom activities will also tend to be our highest achievers (A. E. Gottfried, 1990; Schiefele, Krapp, & Winteler, 1992; Walberg & Uguroglu, 1980). Conversely, students who are least motivated are at high risk for dropping out before they graduate from high school (Hardre & Reeve, 2001; Hymel et al., 1996; Vallerand, Fortier, & Guay, 1997).

Intrinsic versus Extrinsic Motivation

Consider these two students in a trigonometry class:

> Sheryl detests mathematics and is taking the class for only one reason: Earning a C or better in trigonometry is a requirement for a scholarship at the University of Alberta. She desperately wants to attend that university.

> Shannon has always liked math. Trigonometry will help her get a scholarship at the University of Manitoba, but in addition, Shannon truly wants to understand how to use trigonometry. She sees its usefulness for her future profession as an architect. Besides, she's discovering that trigonometry is actually a lot of fun.

Sheryl exhibits **extrinsic motivation**: She is motivated by factors external to herself and unrelated to the task she is performing. Students who are extrinsically motivated may want the good grades, money, or recognition that particular activities and accomplishments bring. Essentially, they are motivated to perform a task as a means to an end, not as an end in and of itself. In contrast, Shannon exhibits **intrinsic motivation**: She is motivated by factors within herself and inherent in the task she is performing. Students who are intrinsically motivated may

Dr. Philip H. Winne at Simon Fraser University holds a Canada Research Chair in Self-Regulated Learning and Learning Technologies (see www.educ.sfu.ca/fri/winne/). His research team has developed software tools that help learners cognitively engage with multimedia information in strategic ways, collaborate, and develop and practice skills that support lifelong learning (see www.learningkit.sfu.ca and www.learningkit.sfu.ca/publications.htm).

Dr. F. Guay at Université Laval holds a Canada Research Chair on Motivation and Academic Success. Guay is an expert in academic motivation, social factors, and academic success. His studies aim to better understand academic persistence and success among children and adolescents based on contextual (parents, teachers, and peers) and motivational factors (see www.motivation.chaire.ulaval.ca).

Extrinsic motivation Motivation promoted by factors external to the individual and unrelated to the task being performed.

Intrinsic motivation The internal desire to perform a particular task.

Some researchers believe that our schools foster extrinsic motivation far more often than intrinsic motivation (R. M. Ryan, Connell, & Grolnick, 1992; Spaulding, 1992). Has this been true in your own experience?

engage in an activity because it gives them pleasure, helps them develop a skill they think is important, or is the ethically and morally right thing to do. Students with a high level of intrinsic motivation sometimes become so focused on and absorbed in an activity that they lose track of time and completely ignore other tasks (Csikszentmihalyi, 1990, 1996).

Students are most likely to show the beneficial effects of motivation when they are *intrinsically* motivated to engage in classroom activities. Intrinsically motivated students tackle assigned tasks willingly and are eager to learn classroom material, are more likely to process information in effective ways (e.g., by engaging in meaningful learning, elaboration, and visual imagery), and more likely to achieve at high levels. In contrast, extrinsically motivated students may have to be enticed or prodded, may process information only superficially, and are often interested in performing only easy tasks and meeting minimal classroom requirements (A. E. Gottfried, Fleming, & Gottfried, 2001; Larson, 2000; Schiefele, 1991; Spaulding, 1992; Tobias, 1994; Voss & Schauble, 1992).

Many researchers have found that students' intrinsic motivation for learning school subject matter declines during the school years. In the early elementary grades, children are often eager and excited to learn new things at school. But sometime between Grades 3 and 9, children become less intrinsically motivated, and more *extrinsically* motivated, to learn and master school subject matter (Covington & Müeller, 2001; Harter, 1992; J. M. T. Walker, 2001). Their intrinsic motivation may be especially low when they make the often anxiety-arousing transition from elementary to secondary school.

This decline in intrinsic motivation for academic subject matter is probably the result of several factors. As students move through the grade levels, they are increasingly reminded of the importance of good grades (extrinsic motivators) for promotion, graduation, and university admission, and many begin to realize that they are not necessarily "at the top of the heap" in comparison with their peers (Covington & Müeller, 2001; Harter, 1992). Furthermore, they become more cognitively able to set and strive for long-term goals, and they begin to evaluate school subjects in terms of their relevance to such goals, rather than in terms of any intrinsic appeal. And they may grow increasingly impatient with the overly structured, repetitive, and boring activities that they too often find at school (Battistich, Solomon, Kim, Watson, & Schaps, 1995; Larson, 2000).

Students learn more and are more likely to engage in meaningful learning and elaboration when they are genuinely interested in what they are learning.

This is not to say, however, that extrinsic motivation is necessarily a bad thing. Oftentimes students are motivated by both intrinsic and extrinsic factors simultaneously (Bronson, 2000; Covington, 2000; Hidi & Harackiewicz, 2000). For example, although Shannon enjoys studying trigonometry, she also knows that a good grade in her trigonometry course will help her get a scholarship at the University of Manitoba. Furthermore, good grades and other external rewards for her achievements may confirm that she is, in fact, mastering the subject matter she is studying. Indeed, extrinsic motivation, perhaps in the form of extrinsic reinforcers for academic achievement or productive behaviour, may be essential for getting some students on the road to successful classroom learning and productivity. Yet intrinsic motivation is ultimately what will sustain our students over the long run: It will encourage them to make sense of and apply the things they are studying, and it will increase the odds that they continue to read and learn about science, history, and other academic subject matter long after they have graduated and ventured out into the adult world.

Researchers at universities all across Canada are studying factors critical to motivation and affect. For example, the Motivation and Academic Achievement (MAACH) Research Group out of the University of Manitoba is dedicated to the study of cognitive, motivational, and social factors affecting academic performance, and to developing intervention strategies to assist at-risk students.

The origins of both extrinsic and intrinsic motivation have been the source of considerable debate for many years. Let's look at how various researchers have studied and tried to explain the nature of motivation and how it emerges.

Theoretical Perspectives of Motivation

Researchers and theorists have approached the study of motivation from four major angles: the trait, behaviourist, social cognitive, and cognitive perspectives.

The Trait Perspective

Trait theory of motivation A theoretical perspective portraying motivation as involving enduring personality characteristics that people have to a greater or lesser extent.

Trait theorists propose that motivation takes the form of relatively enduring personality characteristics that people have to a greater or lesser extent. For example, children and adolescents differ in their tendency to forge friendly relationships with others and in their desire to gain other people's regard and respect (more about such needs for *affiliation* and *approval* shortly). They may also differ in the extent to which they seek out new, exciting, and possibly dangerous experiences—that is, in the extent to which they are *sensation seekers* (Snow, Corno, & Jackson, 1996).

Of the various needs that people might have, the majority of research has focused on the need for achievement, more often called **achievement motivation**. Achievement motivation is the need for excellence for its own sake, without regard for any external rewards that one's accomplishments might bring (e.g., J. W. Atkinson & Feather, 1966; McClelland, Atkinson, Clark, & Lowell, 1953; Veroff, McClelland, & Ruhland, 1975). Children with high achievement motivation seek out challenging tasks that they know they can accomplish with effort and persistence. They rarely rest on their laurels; instead, they set increasingly higher standards for excellence as their current standards are met (Eccles et al., 1998; Veroff et al., 1975).

In its earliest conceptualization, achievement motivation was thought to be a general characteristic that students exhibit consistently in a variety of tasks across many domains. More recently, however, many theorists have proposed that this need may instead be somewhat specific to particular tasks and occasions (e.g., Dweck & Elliott, 1983; Stipek, 1996; Wigfield, 1997). Theorists are also beginning to explain achievement motivation in terms of specific cognitive factors that influence the choices students make and the tasks they pursue. Thus, explanations of achievement motivation have shifted away from a "trait" approach to a more cognitive approach.

Although the trait approach to motivation is losing prominence in contemporary theory and research, personality characteristics clearly *do* influence the motives that students exhibit in the classroom.

Achievement motivation The need for excellence for its own sake, without regard for any external rewards that one's accomplishments might bring.

The Behaviourist Perspective

From a behaviourist perspective, people behave primarily to obtain reinforcing outcomes (or perhaps to avoid punishing ones), and many of the behaviours they exhibit are those responses that have been reinforced in the past. For instance, students might study hard if their teacher praises them for their efforts, and they might misbehave in class if doing so gains them the attention of their teacher and classmates.

Early behaviourists proposed that specific consequences are reinforcing only if they address a particular **drive**, an internal state in which something necessary for optimal functioning (food, water, warmth, etc.) is missing. For example, a hungry person finds food reinforcing, a thirsty person enjoys water, a cold person enjoys a fire and warm blanket, and so on. In recent years, however, motivation theorists have largely left drive reduction theory by the wayside (Bolles, 1975; Graham & Weiner, 1996). For one thing, learning sometimes occurs without satisfying, or reducing, any apparent drive (e.g., Sheffield, Wulff, & Backer, 1951). And a great deal of human behaviour seems to be aimed at accomplishing long-term goals rather than fulfilling short-term needs (Pintrich & Schunk, 2002). Furthermore, people sometimes behave in ways that actually *increase* drive (Rachlin, 1991), perhaps by going to scary movies or riding roller coasters.

Drive A motivational state in which something necessary for optimal functioning (food, water, etc.) is missing.

Rather than focusing on physiological needs and drives, many behaviourists now look more generally at the purposes that particular behaviours may serve for people. Other theorists, whether or not they take a behaviourist approach to learning and motivation, nevertheless recognize that the consequences of behaviours can certainly affect students' motivation to exhibit those behaviours. For instance, psychologists of a variety of theoretical persuasions have studied the circumstances under which *feedback* is likely to be effective. In general, feedback is most effective when it provides information that students cannot get on their own, identifies specific strengths that students have and specific weaknesses that can be addressed, and maintains students' self-efficacy and self-esteem (Kluger & DeNisi, 1998; Little, Oettingen, Stetsenko, & Baltes, 1995; Pintrich & Schunk, 2002).

The Social Cognitive Perspective

Social cognitive theory has contributed in several important ways to our understanding of motivation. For instance, this perspective places heavy emphasis on the *goals* for which people are striving, as reflected in the choices they make and the behaviours they exhibit. It also acknowledges that the reinforcement and punishment that follow various behaviours affect people's *expectations* for the consequences of their future behaviours. And it points out that people's beliefs about their own capability to perform a particular activity (their *self-efficacy*) is a key factor in their decision to engage in and persist at that activity.

The Cognitive Perspective

As you might guess, cognitive psychologists focus on how mental processes affect motivation. They propose that human beings are naturally inclined to make sense of their world, that their curiosity is often piqued by new and puzzling events, and that they are especially motivated by perceived discrepancies between new information and their existing beliefs. People try to make sense of the things that happen to them as well—for instance, by identifying possible causes of (*attributions* for) their successes and failures ("I got an A on my report because I'm smart," "I didn't get to start in Saturday's game because the coach doesn't like me," etc.). This need to make sense of one's environment and experiences is undoubtedly a primary source of intrinsic motivation, but it is probably not the only source. For instance, some cognitive theorists propose that two other conditions are essential for intrinsic motivation: (a) People must have some sense of mastery over their world (i.e., they must have a *sense of competence* or *self-efficacy*), and (b) they must believe that they have some control over the direction their lives are taking (i.e., they must have a *sense of self-determination*).

Within the last two or three decades, the cognitive and social cognitive perspectives have dominated theory and research in motivation (A. M. Ryan, 2000; Winne & Marx, 1989). Yet we must keep in mind that no single theory gives us a complete picture of human motivation. Each of the perspectives just summarized provides pieces of the motivation "puzzle," and so each offers useful ideas about how we can motivate students in classroom settings. Table 9.1 contrasts the four perspectives and describes the general educational implications of each one.

To motivate students in the classroom, a cognitive psychologist might propose capitalizing on their natural curiosity by presenting new and puzzling situations.

TABLE 9.1 — COMPARE/CONTRAST

Comparing Theoretical Perspectives of Motivation

ISSUE	TRAIT THEORIES	BEHAVIOURISM	SOCIAL COGNITIVE THEORY	COGNITIVE PSYCHOLOGY
Sources of motivation are . . .	relatively stable characteristics and personality traits.	the consequences of various behaviours.	personal goals, beliefs about one's own ability to perform tasks successfully, and expectations regarding the likely outcomes of future efforts.	inconsistencies between current beliefs and new experiences, interpretations of past successes and failures, and perceptions of personal competence and control.
Examples of motivational concepts are . . .	achievement motivation, need for affiliation, need for approval.	drive, reinforcement, punishment, functional analysis, feedback.	goals, self-efficacy, expectations.	curiosity, interest, disequilibrium, attributions, sense of competence, sense of self-determination.
Educational implications focus on . . .	identifying motivational traits and using instructional strategies that address students' individual needs.	administering consequences that increase desirable behaviours and decrease nonproductive ones.	encouraging efforts toward self-chosen goals and facilitating success through instruction, modelling, and ongoing guidance and support.	pointing out how new information contradicts students' existing beliefs, showing students how their successes and failures are due to factors within their control (e.g., effort, learning strategies), and providing opportunities for choice and self-direction.

What Basic Needs Do People Have?

As we described the four perspectives of motivation in the preceding section, we occasionally talked about *needs*; for instance, we mentioned the needs for affiliation and approval, the need for achievement, and the need to make sense of the world. Over the years, psychologists have speculated that people have a wide variety of needs, some of which are essential for physical survival and others of which are important for psychological well-being.

As an example, one early theorist, Abraham Maslow (e.g., 1973, 1987), proposed that people have five basic needs that they try to satisfy:

1. *Physiological*: Needs related to physical survival (needs for food, water, oxygen, warmth, etc.)
2. *Safety*: The need to feel safe and secure in one's environment
3. *Love and belonging*: The need to have affectionate relationships with others and to be accepted as part of a group
4. *Esteem*: The need to feel good about oneself and to believe that others also perceive oneself favourably
5. *Self-actualization*: The need to reach one's full potential—to become all that one is capable of becoming

Maslow further proposed that these needs form a hierarchy, such that people satisfy the most basic ones before addressing the others. More specifically, they will try to satisfy their physiological needs first, then their need for safety, and still later their needs for love, belonging, and esteem. Only when such needs have been met do they strive for self-actualization, whereby they explore areas of interest, learn for the sake of learning, and so on. Unfortunately, Maslow's hierarchy of needs was based on very little hard evidence, and so many theorists continue to regard his theory as being more conjecture than fact. Nevertheless, it provides a helpful reminder for us as teachers: Our students are unlikely to pursue classroom tasks with much interest or energy until their more basic needs (e.g., an adequate diet, a safe classroom environment, the positive regard of their teacher and classmates) have been addressed.

Self-Worth

One early theorist proposed that people have an intrinsic need to feel *competent*—to believe that they can deal effectively with their environment (R. White, 1959). To achieve this sense of competence, children spend a great deal of time engaged in exploring and attempting to master the world. The need for competence may have evolutionary significance: It pushes people to develop ways of dealing more effectively with environmental conditions and thus increases their chances of survival.

More recently, Martin Covington (1992) has proposed that *protecting* one's sense of competence—something he calls **self-worth**—is one of people's highest priorities. Obviously, achieving success on a regular basis is one way of maintaining, perhaps even enhancing, this self-worth. But consistent success isn't always possible, especially when people face challenging tasks. In such instances, students may protect their sense of self-worth by making excuses that seemingly justify their poor performance, or they may refuse to engage in certain tasks at all (Covington, 1992). Furthermore, some may do things that actually *undermine* their chances of success—a phenomenon known as **self-handicapping**. Self-handicapping takes a variety of forms, including these:

- *Setting unattainably high goals*: Working toward goals that even the most able individuals couldn't achieve
- *Procrastinating*: Putting a task off until success is virtually impossible
- *Reducing effort*: Putting forth an obviously insufficient amount of effort to succeed
- *Using alcohol or drugs*: Taking substances that will inevitably reduce performance (Covington, 1992; M. E. Ford, 1996; E. E. Jones & Berglas, 1978; Riggs, 1992; Urdan & Midgley, 2001)

It might seem paradoxical that students who want to be successful would engage in such behaviours. But if they believe they are unlikely to succeed at a particular task, they increase their chances of *justifying* their failure (and therefore maintaining self-worth) by acknowledging that,

Self-worth Beliefs about one's own general ability to deal effectively with the environment.

Self-handicapping Undermining one's own success, often as a way of protecting one's sense of self-worth when being asked to perform difficult tasks.

> TRACE—Teaching Resources and Continuing Education, at the University of Waterloo, publishes the tip sheet "Motivating Students: Creating an Inspiring Environment." The strategies listed focus on paying attention to students' sense of inclusion, their attitudes toward learning, the meaning they make of course material, and their feelings of competence (see www.adm.uwaterloo.ca/infotrac/tips_challenges.html).

under the circumstances, success wasn't very likely to begin with (Covington, 1992; E. E. Jones & Berglas, 1978; Riggs, 1992).

Students who have a strong sense of self-worth rarely engage in self-handicapping and so, as you might guess, achieve at higher levels than those who consistently self-handicap (Urdan & Midgley, 2001). Curiously, students are *less* likely to engage in self-handicapping when their chances of success are slim; in such situations, failure does not indicate low ability and so does not threaten their sense of self-worth (Covington, 1992).

Ideally, students' sense of self-worth should be based on a reasonably accurate appraisal of what they can and cannot accomplish. Students who underestimate their abilities will set unnecessarily low goals for themselves and give up easily after only minor setbacks. Those who overestimate their abilities (perhaps because they have been lavished with praise by parents or teachers, or perhaps because school assignments have been consistently easy and nonchallenging) may set themselves up for failure by forming unrealistically high expectations for themselves or by not exerting a sufficient amount of effort to succeed (Paris & Cunningham, 1996; D. Phillips & Zimmerman, 1990; Pintrich & Schunk, 2002; H. W. Stevenson et al., 1990). The strategies we've previously identified for enhancing students' self-concept, self-esteem, and self-efficacy—for instance, scaffolding their efforts at challenging tasks—can also help them maintain a healthy sense of self-worth.

Relatedness

To some extent, we are all social creatures: We live, work, and play with our fellow human beings. Some theorists have proposed that people of all ages have a fundamental need to feel socially connected and to secure the love and respect of others; in other words, they have a **need for relatedness** (Connell, 1990; Connell & Wellborn, 1991). As is true for the need for competence, the need for relatedness may be important from an evolutionary standpoint, in that people who live in cohesive, co-operative social groups are more likely to survive than people who go it alone (R. Wright, 1994).

> **Need for relatedness** The need to feel socially connected to others, as well as to secure their love and respect.

Students' need for relatedness may manifest itself in a wide variety of behaviours. Many children and adolescents place high priority on interacting with friends, often at the expense of getting their schoolwork done (Dowson & McInerney, 2001; W. Doyle, 1986a; Wigfield, Eccles, Mac Iver, Reuman, & Midgley, 1991). They may also be concerned about projecting a favourable public image—that is, by looking smart, popular, athletic, or cool to others (Juvonen, 2000). And some may exhibit their need for relatedness by showing concern for other people's welfare or helping peers who are struggling with classroom assignments (Dowson & McInerney, 2001; M. E. Ford, 1996). The need for relatedness seems to be especially high in the middle school years (B. B. Brown, Eicher, & Petrie, 1986; Juvonen, 2000; A. M. Ryan & Patrick, 2001). Young adolescents tend to be overly concerned about what others think, prefer to hang out in tight-knit groups, and are especially susceptible to peer influence.

As teachers, we must remember that social relationships will be among our students' highest priorities (Dowson & McInerney, 2001; Geary, 1998). Our students are more likely to be academically successful—and more likely to stay in school rather than drop out—when they believe that their teachers and peers like and respect them and when they feel that they belong to the classroom community (Goodenow, 1993; Hymel et al., 1996; Ladd, 1990; A. M. Ryan & Patrick, 2001).

Individual Differences in the Need for Relatedness

Although the need for relatedness may be universal, some children and adolescents seem to have a greater need for interpersonal relationships than others (Kupersmidt, Buchele, Voegler, & Sedikides, 1996). Let's briefly take a "trait" approach to motivation as we consider research related to needs for affiliation and approval.

> **Need for affiliation** The tendency to seek out friendly relationships with others.

Need for affiliation. Students differ in the extent to which they desire and actively seek out friendly relationships with others; in other words, they differ in their **need for affiliation**. Students' needs for affiliation will be reflected in the choices they make at school (Boyatzis, 1973; French, 1956; Wigfield et al., 1996). For example, students with a low need for affiliation may prefer to work alone, whereas students with a high need for affiliation more often prefer to work in small groups. When choosing work partners, students with a low affiliation need are apt to choose classmates whom they believe to be competent at the task to be performed; students with a high affiliation need are apt to choose their friends even if these friends are relatively incompetent. In high school, students with a low need for affiliation are likely to choose a class schedule that meets their own interests and ambitions, whereas students with a high need for affiliation are more likely to choose one that enables them to be with their friends. As you can see, then, a high need for affiliation often interferes with maximal classroom learning and achievement (Urdan & Maehr, 1995; Wentzel & Wigfield, 1998).

As teachers, we cannot ignore the high need for affiliation that many students bring to the classroom. On the contrary, as we plan our daily lessons and classroom activities, we must provide opportunities for students to interact with one another. Ideally, we should find ways to help students learn academic subject matter *and* meet their affiliation needs simultaneously (Wentzel & Wigfield, 1998). Although some classroom objectives may be best accomplished when students work independently, others can be accomplished just as easily (perhaps even more so) when students work together. Group-based activities, such as discussions, debates, role-playing, co-operative learning tasks, and competitions among two or more teams of equal ability, all provide the means through which students can satisfy their need for affiliation while simultaneously acquiring new knowledge and skills (J. E. Brophy, 1987; Urdan & Maehr, 1995).

We must remember, too, that many of our students will want to affiliate not only with their classmates but with teachers as well. Therefore, we should show our students that we like them, enjoy being with them, and are concerned about their well-being (McKeachie, Lin, Milholland, & Isaacson, 1966; Stipek, 1996). We can communicate our fondness for students in numerous ways—for example, by expressing an interest in their outside activities and accomplishments, providing extra help or support when it is needed, or lending a sympathetic ear. These "caring" messages may be especially important for students from culturally different backgrounds: Such students are more likely to succeed in our classroom if we show interest in their lives and concern for their individual needs (Phelan, Davidson, & Cao, 1991).

Need for approval. Another need in which we see individual differences is the **need for approval**, a desire to gain the acceptance and positive judgments of other people (Igoe & Sullivan, 1991; Juvonen & Weiner, 1993; Urdan & Maehr, 1995). Students with a high need for approval are overly concerned with pleasing others and tend to give in easily to peer pressure, for fear that they might otherwise be rejected (Crowne & Marlowe, 1964; Wentzel & Wigfield, 1998). Whereas other students might engage in a school task for the pleasure that success at the task brings, students with a high need for approval are likely to engage in the task primarily to please their teacher and will persist at it only as long as their teacher praises them for doing so (Harter, 1975; S. C. Rose & Thornburg, 1984).

In the early years, children are most apt to seek the approval of adults, such as parents and teachers. As they get older, and especially as they move into adolescence, they are usually more interested in gaining the approval of their peers (Juvonen & Weiner, 1993; Urdan & Maehr, 1995). Cultural background may also influence whether children and adolescents prefer adult or peer approval; for instance, many teenagers from Asian cultures highly value the approval of adult authority figures (e.g., Dien, 1998).

When students have a high need for approval, we can promote their classroom achievement by praising them frequently for the things they do well. At the same time, we must keep in mind that some students (especially at the secondary level) may be more concerned about gaining the approval of *peers* and that those peers may disapprove of high academic achievement (Juvonen & Weiner, 1993; L. Steinberg, 1996; Wigfield et al., 1996). If being a high achiever is not the socially acceptable thing to do, many students will prefer that their accomplishments be praised privately rather than publicly. Ultimately, how well our students are accomplishing instructional objectives is no one's business but theirs, their parents', and ours.

Relationships with peers and teachers are, for many students, a source of considerable pleasure and enjoyment. Conversely, difficulties in interpersonal interactions, which may impede students' ability to satisfy their need for relatedness, are often a source of sadness and anxiety. Pleasure, enjoyment, anxiety—all of these are examples of feelings, emotions, or what psychologists call *affect*. We turn to this topic now.

> **Need for approval** A desire to gain the approval and acceptance of others.

INTO THE CLASSROOM *Addressing Students' Social Needs*

Have students work together on some learning tasks.

A high school history teacher incorporates classroom debates, small-group discussions, and co-operative learning tasks into every month's activities.

Continually communicate the message that you like and respect your students.

A middle school teacher tells one of his students that he saw her dancing troupe's performance at the local mall over the weekend. "I had no idea you were so talented," he says. "How many years have you been studying dance?"

Create a classroom culture in which respect for *everyone's* needs and well-being is paramount.

When a Grade 5 teacher overhears two boys making fun of a fellow student who stutters, she discretely pulls them aside, explains that the classmate is extremely self-conscious about his disability and is working hard to overcome it, and reminds the boys that they, too, have imperfections as well as strengths.

Provide a means through which every student can feel part of a small, close-knit group.

During the first week of school, a Grade 9 math teacher establishes *base groups*—groups of three or four students who provide support and assistance for one another throughout the school year—in each of his classes. At the beginning or end of every class period, the teacher gives the groups five minutes to help one another with questions and concerns about daily lessons and homework assignments.

Give frequent praise to students who have a high need for approval.

Several students in a Grade 2 class have difficulty staying on task during independent assignments. Their teacher has found that they are more likely to stay on task when she commends them for doing so.

Praise students privately when being a high achiever is not sanctioned by their peer group.

While reading a stack of short stories that his students have written, a high school English teacher discovers that one of his students—a young woman who, he knows, is quite concerned about looking cool in front of her classmates—has written a particularly creative story. On the second page of her story (where the student's classmates won't be likely to see what he has written), he writes, "This is great work, Brigitta! I think it's good enough to enter into the provincial writing contest. I'd like to meet with you before or after school some day this week to talk more about the contest."

Affect and Its Effects

Affect The feelings and emotions that an individual brings to bear on a task.

When we speak of motivation, we must also consider **affect**—the feelings and emotions that an individual brings to bear on a task. Motivation and affect are closely intertwined. In this section we examine two aspects of affect that are particularly relevant to our work as teachers: hot cognition and anxiety.

Hot Cognition

Hot cognition Learning or cognitive processing that is emotionally charged.

Sometimes learning and cognitive processing are emotionally charged—a phenomenon known as **hot cognition** (e.g., Hoffman, 1991; P. H. Miller, 1993). For example, students might get excited when they read about advances in science that could lead to effective treatments of spinal cord injuries, cancer, AIDS, or mental illness. They may feel sad when they read about the living conditions in certain parts of the world. They will, we hope, get angry when they learn about the atrocities committed against millions of Jewish people and members of other minority groups during World War II.

Affect is clearly intertwined with learning and cognition. Students are more likely to pay attention to things that evoke strong emotions, such as excitement, sadness, or anger (LaBar & Phelps, 1998; Reisberg & Heuer, 1992). When they are interested in a topic about which they are reading (perhaps finding it exciting or upsetting), they process information more effectively—for example by engaging in more meaningful learning and visual imagery (Hidi & Anderson, 1992; Tobias, 1994). In addition, students can usually retrieve information with high emotional content more easily than they can recall relatively nonemotional information (Barkley, 1996; LaBar & Phelps, 1998; Reisberg & Heuer, 1992). In general, then, students will learn and remember more when they become involved in classroom subject matter not only cognitively but emotionally as well.

Problem solving also is easier when students enjoy what they're doing, and successful problem solutions are often accompanied by feelings of excitement, pleasure, and pride (McLeod & Adams, 1989; M. U. Smith, 1991). In contrast, students are likely to feel frustrated and anxious when they fail at a learning or problem-solving activity, especially if it appears to be an easy one, and they are apt to develop a dislike for what they've been doing (Carver & Scheier, 1990; Stodolsky, Salk, & Glaessner, 1991).

Anxiety

Imagine that you have been asked to present a talk to your university class on a topic that is unfamiliar to you. Although you try to prepare for the talk, you do not have enough time to adequately familiarize yourself with the material. By the day of your talk, you are a nervous wreck: Your heart is pounding wildly, your palms are sweaty, and your stomach is in a knot.

You are a victim of **anxiety**: You have a feeling of uneasiness and apprehension about an event because you're not sure what its outcome will be. This feeling is accompanied by a variety of physiological symptoms, including a rapid heartbeat, increased perspiration, and muscular tension (e.g., a "knot" or "butterflies" in the stomach). Anxiety is similar to fear, but different in one important respect: Although we are usually *afraid* of something in particular (a roaring lion, a lightning storm, or the bogeymen under the bed), we usually don't know exactly why we're *anxious*. And it's difficult to deal with anxiety when we can't pinpoint its cause.

The concept of *hot cognition* tells us that students are more likely to attend to and remember things that not only stimulate their thinking but also elicit emotional reactions.

Anxiety A feeling of uneasiness and apprehension concerning a situation with an uncertain outcome.

State Anxiety versus Trait Anxiety

Almost everyone is anxious at one time or another. Many students become anxious just before a test they know is going to be difficult, and most get nervous when they have to give a prepared speech in front of their classmates. Such temporary feelings of anxiety are instances of **state anxiety**. Yet some students are anxious a good part of the time, even when the situation is not particularly dangerous or threatening. For example, some students may get excessively nervous even before very easy exams, and others may be so anxious about mathematics that they can't concentrate on the simplest math assignment. When an individual shows a pattern of responding with anxiety even in nonthreatening situations, we have a case of **trait anxiety**. It is our trait-anxious students whose performance is most hampered by anxiety and for whom we may have to go the extra mile to convince them that they can succeed at classroom tasks.

State anxiety A temporary feeling of anxiety elicited by a threatening situation.

Trait anxiety A pattern of responding with anxiety even in nonthreatening situations.

How Anxiety Affects Classroom Performance

Imagine, for a moment, that you are not at all anxious—not even the teeniest bit—about your oral presentation to the class. Without any anxiety at all, would you have tried to prepare for the talk? If you have no anxiety whatsoever, you might not even attend the class that day!

A small amount of anxiety often improves performance: It is **facilitating anxiety**. A little anxiety spurs people into action; for instance, it makes them go to class, read the textbook, do assignments, and study for exams. It also makes them approach their classwork carefully and reflect before making their responses (Shipman & Shipman, 1985). Yet too much anxiety often interferes with effective performance: It is **debilitating anxiety**. Excessive anxiety distracts people and interferes with their attention to the task at hand.

Facilitating anxiety Anxiety that enhances performance. Relatively low levels of anxiety are usually facilitating.

Debilitating anxiety Anxiety that interferes with performance. A high level of anxiety is likely to be debilitating.

At what point does anxiety stop facilitating and begin debilitating performance? In general, very easy tasks—things that students can do almost without thinking (e.g., running)—are facilitated by high levels of anxiety. But more difficult tasks—those that require considerable thought and effort—are best performed with only a small or moderate level of anxiety (Kirkland, 1971; Yerkes & Dodson, 1908). An excessive level of anxiety in difficult situations can interfere with several processes critical for successful learning and performance:

- Paying attention to what needs to be learned
- Processing information effectively (e.g., engaging in meaningful learning, organization, or elaboration)

- Remembering information and demonstrating skills that have already been learned (Covington, 1992; Eysenck, 1992; Hagtvet & Johnsen, 1992; I. G. Sarason, 1980)

Anxiety is especially likely to interfere with such processes when a task places heavy demands on working memory or long-term memory—for instance, when a task involves creativity or problem solving (Eysenck, 1992; McLeod & Adams, 1989; Mueller, 1980; Tobias, 1985).

As you might expect, highly anxious students tend to achieve at levels below their potential; in other words, they are underachievers (K. T. Hill, 1984; Tobias, 1980; Zeidner, 1998). Highly anxious students are often so preoccupied about doing poorly that they simply can't get their minds on what they need to accomplish (Eccles & Wigfield, 1985; Wine, 1980).

Sources of Anxiety

Under what circumstances are our students likely to experience debilitating anxiety? Students sometimes develop feelings of anxiety about particular stimuli through the process of classical conditioning. Students are also more likely to experience debilitating anxiety when they face a **threat**—a situation in which they believe that they have little or no chance of succeeding—than when they face a **challenge**—a situation in which they believe they can probably achieve success with a significant yet reasonable amount of effort (Combs, Richards, & Richards, 1976; Csikszentmihalyi & Nakamura, 1989; Deci & Ryan, 1992). Furthermore, many school-age children and adolescents experience a certain amount of anxiety about the following:

- *Physical appearance.* For example, students may be concerned about being too fat or thin or about reaching puberty either earlier or later than their classmates.
- *A new situation.* For example, students may experience uncertainty when moving to a new community.
- *Judgment or evaluation by others.* For example, students may be worried about being liked and accepted by classmates or about receiving a low grade from a teacher.
- *Classroom tests.* For example, students may panic at the mere thought of having to take an exam.
- *Excessive classroom demands.* For example, students are likely to feel anxious when teachers expect them to learn a great deal of material in a very short amount of time.
- *The future.* For example, adolescents may worry about how they will make a living after they graduate from high school.
- *Any situation in which self-esteem is threatened.* For example, students may feel anxious when they perform a task awkwardly or incorrectly in front of others. (Covington, 1992; Harter, 1992; Hembree, 1988; N. J. King & Ollendick, 1989; Phelan, Yu, & Davidson, 1994; I. G. Sarason, 1980; S. B. Sarason, 1972; Stipek, 1993; Stodolsky et al., 1991; Wigfield & Meece, 1988)

Keeping Students' Anxiety at a Facilitative Level

As a teacher, you probably can't eliminate all sources of anxiety for your students; things such as physical appearance, acceptance by peers, and students' future circumstances are often beyond your control. Nevertheless, you can take several steps to keep students' anxiety about classroom tasks and activities at a productive and facilitative level. For one thing, you can reduce the uncertainty of the classroom environment by communicating your expectations for students' performance clearly and concretely. Highly anxious students, in particular, are likely to perform better in a well-structured classroom in which expectations for academic achievement and social behaviour are explicitly laid out (Hembree, 1988; Stipek, 1993; Tobias, 1977).

In addition, it is important to make sure students have a good chance of achieving classroom success and give them reasons to believe they can succeed with effort; in other words, make sure they have high self-efficacy about classroom tasks. Therefore, you are more likely to keep students' anxiety at a facilitative level when you

- Set realistic expectations for performance, taking such factors as students' ability and prior performance level into account
- Match the level of instruction to students' cognitive levels and capabilities—for example, by using concrete materials to teach mathematics to students not yet capable of abstract thought

---

Threat A situation in which people believe that they have little or no chance of success.

Challenge A situation in which a person believes that he or she can probably succeed with sufficient effort.

Waddell (2007), using figures derived from epidemiological surveys of Canadian children, ages 4 to 17 years, reports that approximately 340 000 children experience clinical levels of anxiety (see www.firstcallbc.org/pdfs/Communities/4-alliance.pdf).

INTO THE CLASSROOM *Keeping Students' Anxiety at a Facilitative Level*

Be aware of situations in which students are especially likely to be anxious, and take steps to reduce their anxiety on those occasions.

> The day before students are scheduled to take a standardized test, their teacher tells them, "The best way to prepare for the test is to get a good night's sleep and eat a good breakfast in the morning. As you take the test tomorrow, you certainly want to do the very best that you can do. But keep in mind that you aren't expected to know the answers to *all* of the questions. If you find a question you cannot answer, just skip it and go on to the next one. Return to it later if you have time."

Develop classroom routines that help create a comfortable and somewhat predictable work environment.

> An elementary teacher has a list of classroom chores—getting a lunch count, feeding the fish, handing out paper, and so on—that are assigned to individual students on a rotating basis.

Communicate expectations for student performance clearly and concretely.

> A high school history teacher begins a unit on World War II this way: "We will focus on the major battles that contributed to the Allied forces' victory. As you read your textbook, look for reasons why certain battles played a role in the war's final outcome. I will *not* expect you to memorize all the details—dates, generals, numbers of troops, and so on—of every single battle."

Make sure students have a reasonable chance of success and give them reasons to believe that they can succeed with effort.

> A science teacher describes an upcoming quiz: "On the quizzes you've taken so far this year, you've had to describe only the basic principles of chemistry we've studied. But on the next quiz I'm going to ask you to apply what you know about chemistry to new situations and problems. I'll give you several practice questions this week so you'll know what to expect. I'll also give you two chances to take the quiz. If you don't do well the first time, we'll work together on your trouble spots, and then you can take the quiz again."

- Provide supplementary sources of support for learning subject matter (e.g., additional practice, individual tutoring, a structure for taking notes) until mastery is attained
- Teach strategies (e.g., effective study skills) that enhance learning and performance
- Assess students' performance independently of how well their peers are doing, and encourage students to assess their own performance in a similar manner
- Provide feedback about specific behaviours, rather than global evaluations of students' performance
- Allow students to correct errors, so that no single mistake is ever a "fatal" one (J. E. Brophy, 1986; K. T. Hill & Wigfield, 1984; McCoy, 1990; I. G. Sarason, 1980; Stipek, 1993; Tryon, 1980; Zeidner, 1998)

As a teacher, you must continually be on the lookout for how students' feelings of anxiety and other emotions are likely to affect their classroom learning and achievement. Sometimes students will actually tell us how they are feeling; for example, they may express their apprehensiveness about an upcoming exam. In other instances, you may see indications in their behaviour; for example, you may observe that some students are clearly excited about an upcoming activity whereas others seem less enthusiastic. In still other cases, students' writing will uncover their feelings about classroom activities.

Cognitions That Motivate

Think about the university courses you've taken in recent years. In which courses were you more interested in the grade you received than in anything you might learn in class? In which courses did you truly want to learn the subject matter, and why? Did you perceive some topics to be relevant to your own needs and goals? Were other topics so fascinating that you simply had to find out more about them? Did your instructors do anything in particular that made certain topics intriguing, thought-provoking, or just plain fun?

In the rest of this chapter, we will look at how students' perceptions, beliefs, expectations, values, interests, goals, and attributions influence their motivation; in other words, we will focus on "cognitions that motivate." We will also examine the effects that *teacher* cognition—especially teachers' attributions and expectations regarding students' behaviours and accomplishments—has on students' performance and achievement.

The Interplay of Cognition and Motivation

In the opening case study, Michael believes he is failing algebra because of two things he cannot control—his own low ability and his teacher's poor instruction—and so he doesn't listen very attentively or take notes in class. With Ms. Tucker's guidance, however, Michael acquires a better understanding of algebra and learns how to use it to solve mathematical problems. He also discovers that increased effort and better strategies (taking notes, asking questions when he doesn't understand, studying regularly, etc.) *do* affect his classroom performance. Suddenly Michael himself—not his teacher, and not some predetermined inability that lurks within him—is in control of the situation, and his confidence skyrockets.

Michael's dramatic turnaround illustrates that *motivation affects cognitive processing*. Like Michael, motivated students are more likely to pay attention, engage in meaningful learning, and seek help when they don't understand. Yet the case illustrates the reverse as well: *Cognitive processes affect motivation*. Michael's initial beliefs about his own ability (his self-efficacy) and his explanations for poor performance (low ability and poor instruction) contribute to a lackadaisical attitude: He simply *hopes* that he'll remember (but usually forgets) his teacher's explanations. Later, when Michael's appraisal of the situation changes (when his self-efficacy increases and he attributes success to effort and better strategies), he is a much more engaged and proactive learner.

As we explore the cognitive aspects of motivation (perceptions, expectancies, values, interests, goals, and attributions) in the pages that follow, we will frequently see how cognition and motivation interact in their effects on learning and behaviour. We begin by looking at two self-perceptions that play key roles in intrinsic motivation: self-efficacy and self-determination.

Self-Perceptions and Intrinsic Motivation

A number of theorists have proposed that people are most likely to be intrinsically motivated to do something (to perform a particular task or engage in a particular activity) when two conditions exist:

1. They have high **self-efficacy**: They believe that they are capable of successfully accomplishing the task or activity.
2. They have a sense of **self-determination**: They believe that they are in control of their own destinies and can make choices regarding the directions that their lives will take. (Boggiano & Pittman, 1992; Corno & Rohrkemper, 1985; Deci & Ryan, 1985, 1992; R. M. Ryan & Deci, 2000; Spaulding, 1992)

Self-Efficacy

Our students are more likely to be intrinsically motivated to engage in classroom activities when they have high self-efficacy—what some motivation theorists call a *sense of competence*—about their ability to perform those activities successfully. Most 4- to 6-year-olds are quite confident about their ability to perform various tasks; in fact, they often overestimate what they are capable of doing (R. Butler, 1990; Eccles et al., 1998; Nicholls, 1979). As they move through the elementary grades, however, they can better recall their past successes and failures, and they become increasingly aware of how their performance compares with that of their classmates (Eccles et al., 1998; Feld, Ruhland, & Gold, 1979). Presumably as a result of these changes, they become less confident, though usually more realistic, about what they can and cannot do. In some situations, however, students significantly *under*estimate their capabilities. For instance, in the opening case, Michael's self-efficacy for passing his algebra class is initially rock-bottom:

Self-efficacy The belief that one is capable of executing certain behaviours or reaching certain goals.

Self-determination A sense that one has some choice and control regarding the future course of one's life.

The Social Sciences and Humanities Research Council of Canada (SSHRC) financially supports scholarly research focusing on emotional reactions, cognitive style, self-concept, and self-perception. Visit their website at www.sshrc.ca.

In his mind, he doesn't have the ability to succeed, and his teacher does little to help the situation.

In our discussion of social cognitive theory in Chapter 8, we identified several factors that affect the development of self-efficacy and, in the process, derived several strategies for enhancing it in the classroom:

- Make sure students master basic skills.
- Help them make noticeable progress on difficult tasks.
- Communicate confidence in students' abilities through both words and actions.
- Expose students to successful peers.

Motivation theorists have offered additional recommendations for enhancing students' self-efficacy and, indirectly, increasing intrinsic motivation:

- *Provide competence-promoting feedback.* Positive feedback is often an effective reinforcer for students. Positive feedback may also promote intrinsic motivation, especially if it conveys the message that students have the ability to perform the task successfully and thereby enhances their self-efficacy. In fact, even negative feedback can promote high self-efficacy if it tells students how they can improve their performance and communicates confidence that improvement is likely (Deci & Ryan, 1985; Pintrich & Schunk, 2002). Here are some examples of negative feedback that might positively influence student motivation:
    - "I can see from the past few homework assignments that you're having trouble with long division. I think I know what the problem is. Here, let me show you what you need to do differently."
    - "In the first draft of your research paper, many of your paragraphs don't lead logically to the ones that follow. A few headings and transitional sentences would make a world of difference. Let's find a time to discuss how you might use these techniques to improve the flow of your paper."

- *Promote mastery on challenging tasks.* A challenge is a situation in which success is not guaranteed but can probably be achieved with reasonable effort. A challenge encourages people to stretch themselves to their limits—perhaps to think in new ways or experiment with new strategies. In Chapter 2 we found that challenging activities promote cognitive development. In addition, mastery of challenges enhances self-efficacy and, as a result, promotes intrinsic motivation. Students who master challenging tasks experience considerable pleasure, satisfaction, and pride in their accomplishments (Csikszentmihalyi & Nakamura, 1989; Deci & Ryan, 1992; Shernoff, Knauth, & Makris, 2000; A. G. Thompson & Thompson, 1989; J. C. Turner, 1995).

Once students are intrinsically motivated, they frequently pursue further challenges of their own accord. They also exhibit considerable persistence in the face of difficulty, and they continue to remain interested in an activity even when they make frequent errors (Covington, 1992; Deci, 1992; Harter, 1992). As you can see, then, challenges and intrinsic motivation mutually enhance one another, leading to a "vicious" cycle of the most desirable sort.

As teachers, we are more likely to encourage students to tackle challenging tasks when, through the feedback we give and the criteria we use for evaluation, we create an environment in which our students feel free to take risks and make mistakes (Clifford, 1990). We can also provide greater rewards for succeeding at challenging tasks than for achieving easy successes; for example, we might give students a choice between doing an easy task or a more difficult one but give them more points for accomplishing the difficult one (Clifford, 1990; Lan, Repman, Bradley, & Weller, 1994).

At the same time, however, we must tailor the level of challenge to students' current self-efficacy levels: Students who (like Michael) have little or no confidence in their ability to perform a particular activity may initially respond more favourably when we give them tasks at which they will likely do well (Stipek, 1996). Furthermore, the school day shouldn't necessarily be one challenge after another. Such a state of affairs would be absolutely exhausting, and probably quite discouraging as well. Instead, we should probably strike a balance between easy tasks—those that will boost students' self-confidence over the short run—and the challenging tasks so critical for a long-term sense of competence and self-efficacy (Spaulding, 1992; Stipek, 1993, 1996).

- *Promote self-comparison rather than comparison with others.* If we define success in terms of task accomplishment, skill improvement, or academic progress, then virtually all of our students can be successful. If we instead define success in terms of how well students perform

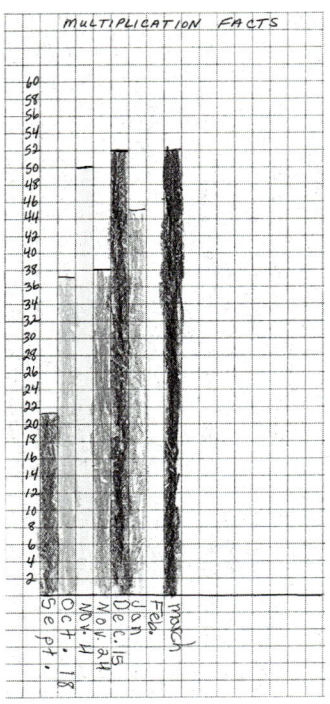

FIGURE 9.2 Nine-year-old Sophie charts her monthly progress in remembering multiplication facts. Although she has minor setbacks, her general progress is upward. (She was absent for February's assessment.)

in comparison with their peers, many will fare poorly. Such competition may motivate a few students who believe they can rise to meet the challenge; however, it will undermine the intrinsic motivation of the majority of their classmates, who will see failure as the most likely outcome (Deci & Ryan, 1992; Shih & Alexander, 2000; Stipek, 1996). Furthermore, some students may resist competing if they believe that their own successes will contribute to their classmates' failures (Grant & Gomez, 2001).

As noted earlier, over time students become increasingly aware of how their performance compares with that of classmates. Inevitably, then, some students begin to believe that they simply don't measure up to their peers. As teachers, we shouldn't compound the problem. Most of our students will achieve at higher levels if we encourage them to define success in terms of their own improvement, rather than in terms of how they stack up against others (Covington, 1992; Graham & Golen, 1991).

You can do at least two things to encourage students to make self-comparisons rather than comparisons with others. First, you can minimize their awareness of their classmates' performance levels. For example, you can use absolute rather than comparative criteria to assess their work (awarding high grades to all students who meet those criteria rather than grading on a curve), keep performance on assignments confidential, and give feedback in private. Second, you can provide opportunities for students to assess their own performance and monitor their improvement over time. Remember that children and adolescents are often impatient, expecting success overnight when in fact the development of knowledge and skills may take several days, months, or even years. You can help them focus on their successes rather than their imperfections by providing them with concrete mechanisms that highlight improvement—for example, by giving them progress charts that they can fill in themselves (e.g., see Figure 9.2) and providing frequent verbal or written feedback about the "little things" they are doing well.

■ *Be sure errors occur within an overall context of success.* At one time, many educators proposed that students should never be allowed to fail. But whether we like it or not, occasional failures are a normal, inevitable, and often beneficial part of the learning process, and students need to learn to take them in stride. When students never make mistakes, we can reasonably assume they are not being challenged by the tasks we are assigning. Furthermore, students unaccustomed to failure in their school curriculum have difficulty coping with failure when they eventually do encounter it (Dweck, 1986).

Yet when students encounter failure *too* frequently, they (like Michael) develop low self-efficacy, believing that nothing they do will produce positive results. Ideally, then, students should experience occasional failure within the context of overall success. This way, they learn that they *can* succeed if they try, while also developing a realistic attitude about failure—that it at worst is a temporary setback and at best can give them useful information about how to improve their performance.

Self-Determination

Students are more likely to be intrinsically motivated when they have a sense of self-determination—in other words, when they have some feeling of *autonomy* regarding the things they do and the directions their lives take (Boggiano & Pittman, 1992; deCharms, 1972; Deci, 1992; Deci & Ryan, 1992; Spaulding, 1992; J. C. Turner, 1995). A sense of self-determination increases the likelihood that students will become actively engaged in in-class and extracurricular activities and that they will stay in school rather than drop out before graduation (Hardre & Reeve, 2001; E. J. Langer, 1997; J. Reeve, Bolt, & Cai, 1999; Shernoff et al., 2000). Even kindergartners seem to value classroom activities of their own choosing, and students' perceptions of autonomy versus control are often seen in their notions of "play" and "work" (E. J. Langer, 1997; Paley, 1984).

Naturally, we can't always give students total freedom about what they will and will not do in the classroom. Nor can we always convince them that classroom activities are really play rather than work. Nevertheless, we can do several things to enhance students' sense of self-determination about school-related tasks and assignments:

■ *Present rules and instructions in an informational rather than controlling manner.* Virtually any classroom needs a few rules and procedures to ensure that students act appropriately and that class activities run smoothly. Furthermore, for a variety of reasons, teachers must often impose guidelines and restrictions related to how students carry out their assignments. The challenge is to present these rules, procedures, guidelines, and restrictions without communicating a message of *control*. As Richard Koestner, psychology professor at McGill University, has found, you can instead present them as *information*—for instance, as conditions that can help students accomplish classroom objectives (Deci, 1992; Koestner, Ryan, Bernieri, & Holt, 1984). Here are a couple of examples of rules or instructions presented in an informational rather than controlling manner:

- "We can make sure everyone has an equal chance to speak and be heard if we listen without interrupting and if we raise our hands when we want to contribute to the discussion."

- "I'm giving you a particular format to follow when you do your math homework. If you use this format, it will be easier for me to find your answers and to figure out how I can help you improve."

■ *Provide opportunities for students to make choices.* Sometimes there is only one way to accomplish a particular instructional objective. But, more often, a variety of routes will lead to the same destination. In such cases, why not let students choose how they want to get there? For example, you might allow them to make decisions, either individually or as a group, about some or all of the following:

- Rules and procedures to make the class run more smoothly
- Ways of achieving mastery of a classroom objective (e.g., which of several possible procedures to use, whether to work individually or in small groups)
- Specific topics for research or writing projects
- Specific works of literature to be read
- Due dates for some assignments
- The order in which specific tasks are accomplished during the school day
- Ways of demonstrating that an objective has been mastered
- Criteria by which some assignments will be evaluated (Kohn, 1993; Meece, 1994; Stipek, 1993)

When students can make choices such as these, they are more likely to be interested in what they are doing, to work diligently, to complete assignments quickly and efficiently, and to take pride in their work (Deci & Ryan, 1992; Lepper & Hodell, 1989; J. A. Ross, 1988; J. C. Turner, 1995). Furthermore, students who are given choices—even students with serious behaviour problems—are less likely to misbehave in class (Dunlap et al., 1994; S. Powell & Nelson, 1997; B. J. Vaughn & Horner, 1997).

■ *Give students considerable autonomy within their organized extracurricular activities.* Ideally, students' extracurricular activities (clubs, theatre groups, community service projects, etc.) can provide both the challenges that enhance students' self-efficacy and the autonomy that enhances their sense of self-determination (Larson, 2000). When we supervise such activities, then, we can foster intrinsic motivation—not to mention the development of initiative and skills in planning and negotiation—by giving students considerable freedom and responsibility in determining the direction the activities take (Larson, 2000). At the same time, we will often need to provide the guidance students may need to tackle challenges, for instance by helping them think through the likely outcomes of various courses of action (Larson, 2000).

■ *Evaluate students' performance in a noncontrolling fashion.* As teachers, we will inevitably need to evaluate students' accomplishments. But we must keep in mind that external evaluations may undermine students' intrinsic motivation, especially if communicated in a controlling manner (Deci & Ryan, 1992; Harter, Whitesell, & Kowalski, 1992). Ideally, we should present our evaluations of students' work, not as "judgments" to remind students of how they *should* perform, but as information that can help them improve their knowledge and skills (Stipek, 1996). Furthermore, we can give students criteria by which they can evaluate *themselves* in the self-comparative manner described earlier.

■ *Minimize reliance on extrinsic reinforcers, but use them when necessary.* Previous discussions emphasized the importance of relying on intrinsic reinforcers—for example, on students' own feelings of pride and satisfaction about their accomplishments—as often as possible. A problem with using extrinsic reinforcers—praise, stickers, favourite activities, and so on—is that they may undermine intrinsic motivation, especially when students perceive them as controlling behaviour and limiting choices (Deci, 1992; A. E. Gottfried, Fleming & Gottfried, 1994; Lepper & Hodell, 1989). Extrinsic reinforcers may also communicate the message that classroom tasks are unpleasant "chores" (why else would a reinforcer be necessary?), rather than activities to be carried out and enjoyed for their own sakes (Hennessey, 1995; Stipek, 1993).

Intrinsic motivation and extrinsic motivation are not necessarily incompatible; oftentimes students are simultaneously motivated by both the extrinsic reinforcers and the intrinsic feelings of pleasure that their actions bring (Cameron & Pierce, 1994; Deci, 1998). Furthermore, students may sometimes need occasional extrinsic reinforcers to carry them through the more tedious and boring topics and skills they must learn in order to master a complex task or content domain (Covington, 2000; Deci, Koestner, & Ryan, 1999; Hidi & Harackiewicz, 2000). So how can we use extrinsic reinforcers without diminishing students' sense of self-determination? For one thing, we can use reinforcers such as praise to communicate information rather than to control behaviour (Deci, 1992; R. M. Ryan, Mims, & Koestner, 1983); consider these statements as examples:

- "Your description of the main character in your short story makes her come alive."
- "This poster clearly states the hypothesis, method, results, and conclusions of your science project. Your use of a bar graph makes the differences between your treatment and control groups easy to see and interpret."

Furthermore, we may want to encourage *self*-reinforcement—a practice that clearly keeps control in the hands of students.

- *Help students keep externally imposed constraints in proper perspective.* Our students will often encounter circumstances that cast a "controlling" light on school activities: Competitions, extrinsic rewards, and external evaluation are frequent events in most schools.

For example, students often compete in athletic contests, spelling bees, and science fairs. They may make the Honour Roll, win a first-place ribbon at an art exhibit, or receive a free pizza coupon for reading a certain number of books each month.

To help our students keep such external constraints in perspective as they engage in a learning task, we should remind them that although competition, extrinsic rewards, or evaluation may be present, the most important thing is for them to focus on the inherent value of the task itself (Amabile & Hennessey, 1992; Hennessey, 1995).

Self-efficacy and self-determination are not necessarily the only factors involved in intrinsic motivation. Students' expectations and values are also important, as we shall see now.

Expectancies and Values

Some theorists (e.g., Eccles [Parsons], 1983; Feather, 1982; Weiner, 2000; Wigfield, 1994; Wigfield & Eccles, 2000) have proposed that motivation for performing a particular task depends on two variables, both of which are fairly subjective. First of all, students must have a high expectation, or **expectancy**, that they will be successful. Certainly students' self-efficacy about their ability to perform a task has a strong influence on their expectation for success. But other factors affect expectancy level as well, including the perceived difficulty of the task, the availability of environment resources and support, the quality of instruction (remember Michael's concerns about his algebra teacher), and the amount of effort that may be necessary (Dweck & Elliott, 1983; Wigfield & Eccles, 1992; Zimmerman et al., 1992). From factors such as these, students come to a conclusion—perhaps correct, perhaps not—about their chances of success.

Equally important is **value**: Students must believe that there are direct or indirect benefits in performing a task. Theorists have suggested several possible reasons why value might be high or low (Eccles [Parsons], 1983; Eccles & Wigfield, 1985). Some activities are valued because they are associated with certain personal qualities; for example, a boy who wants to be smart and thinks that smart people do well in school will place a premium on academic success. Other activities have high value because they are seen as means to a desired goal; for example, much as she found mathematics confusing and frustrating, Sheryl struggled through four years of high school math classes because many universities require that much math. Still other activities are valued simply because they bring pleasure and enjoyment.

Expectancy In motivation theory, the belief that one will be successful in accomplishing a task or achieving a goal.

Value The belief that an activity has direct or indirect benefits.

We can also anticipate the circumstances in which students will probably *not* value an activity very much (Eccles [Parsons], 1983; Eccles & Wigfield, 1985). Some activities may require a lot more effort than they are worth; for example, you could probably become an expert on some little-known topic (e.g., the nature of rats' dreams, animal-eating plants of Borneo), but I'm guessing that you have more important things to which to devote your time and energy right now. Other activities may be associated with too many bad feelings; for example, if students become frustrated often enough in their efforts to understand mathematics, they may eventually begin to steer clear of the subject whenever possible. And, of course, anything likely to threaten a student's sense of self-worth is a "must" to avoid.

In the early elementary years, students often pursue activities they find interesting and enjoyable, regardless of their expectations for success (Wigfield, 1994). As they get older, however, they attach greater value to activities for which they have high expectations for success and to activities that they think will help them meet their long-term goals (Wigfield, 1994). Sadly, the value students find in many school subjects (e.g., math, English, music, and sports) declines markedly over the school years (Eccles et al., 1998; Wigfield et al., 1991). As one 16-year-old put it, "School's fun because you can hang out with your friends, but I know I won't use much of this stuff when I leave here" (Valente, 2001).

These girls may be motivated in their math class because they *expect* to be successful in it and because they find *value* in the problem-solving skills they are learning.

Internalizing the Values of Others

As they get older, most students begin to adopt some of the values of the people around them. Such **internalized motivation** typically develops gradually over time, perhaps in the following sequence (Deci & Ryan, 1995):

1. *External regulation.* Students are motivated to behave (or not behave) in certain ways based primarily on the external consequences that will follow behaviours; in other words, they are extrinsically motivated. For instance, students may do schoolwork mostly to avoid being punished for poor grades, and they are likely to need a lot of prodding to get their work done.

2. *Introjection.* Students behave in particular ways to gain the approval of others; for example, they may willingly complete an easy, boring assignment as a means of gaining their teacher's praise. At this point, students feel some internal pressure to adopt certain behaviours; for instance, they may feel guilty when they violate certain standards or rules. However, they do not fully understand the rationale behind such standards and rules; instead, their primary motives appear to be avoiding a negative self-evaluation and protecting their sense of self-worth.

3. *Identification.* Students now see behaviours as being personally important or valuable. For instance, they may value learning and academic success in and of themselves, perceive assigned classroom tasks as being essential for helping them learn, and so need little prodding to get their work done.

4. *Integration.* Students have fully accepted the desirability of certain behaviours and integrated them into an overall system of motives and values. For example, a student might have acquired a keen interest in science as a career goal; if so, we are likely to see that interest reflected in many things the student does regularly.

Internalized motivation The adoption of behaviours that others value, without regard for the external consequences of such behaviours.

As you can see, then, extrinsic and intrinsic motivation are not necessarily either/or phenomena; in some situations, extrinsic motivation gradually evolves into internalized values.

Theorists have suggested that three conditions promote the development of internalized motivation (R. M. Ryan et al., 1992). First, growing children need a *warm, responsive, and supportive environment* in which they gain a feeling of relatedness to important individuals (e.g., their parents and teachers) in their lives. Second, they need *some degree of autonomy,* so that they have a sense of self-determination as they make choices and decisions. Finally, they need *appropriate guidance and structure*, including information about expected behaviours and why they're important, as well as clear consequences for inappropriate behaviours. Fostering the development of internalized motivation, then, involves a delicate balancing act between giving students enough opportunities to experience self-determination and providing some guidance about appropriate behaviour. In a sense, we need to "scaffold" desired behaviours at first, gradually reducing such scaffolding as our students exhibit those behaviours more easily and frequently.

Fostering Expectancies and Values in the Classroom

Three Canadian researchers set out to explore why high school students lack motivation in the classroom. Their study found that lack of motivation was tied to four factors: lack of belief in their ability, lack of belief in their effort capacity, unappealing characteristics of the academic task, and a lack of value placed on the task (Legualt, Green-Demers, & Pelletier, 2006).

Teachers should give students reasons why they should expect to succeed at classroom tasks—for instance, by providing the necessary resources, support, and strategies that will enable them to do so (recall how Ms. Tucker taught Michael strategies for mastering algebra). We must also help them find value in school activities.

Theorists and practitioners have offered several suggestions for fostering value for academic subject matter. For instance, we can show how we ourselves value academic activities—for example, by sharing our fascination with certain topics and describing how we apply the things we've learned in school (J. E. Brophy, 1987; Brophy & Alleman, 1991). We can embed the use of many basic skills within the context of meaningful, real-world (authentic) tasks (e.g., Newmann & Wehlage, 1993). And we should refrain from asking students to engage in activities with little long-term benefit—memorizing trivial facts for no good reason, reading material that is clearly beyond students' comprehension level, and so on (J. E. Brophy, 1987).

One common reason that we value something is that we find it interesting. Let's find out what theorists have to say about the role of interest in human motivation.

Interest

Interest A feeling that a topic is intriguing or enticing.

When we say that people have **interest** in a particular topic or activity, we mean that they find the topic or activity intriguing and enticing. Interest, then, is a form of intrinsic motivation. Positive affect accompanies interest; for example, people pursuing a task in which they are interested experience such feelings as pleasure, excitement, and liking (Hidi & Anderson, 1992).

Students who are interested in a particular topic show greater cognitive engagement in that topic (Pintrich et al., 1994; Wigfield, 1994). They are also more likely to learn in a meaningful and elaborative fashion—for example, by relating new material to things they already know, drawing inferences, forming visual images, generating their own examples, and identifying potential applications (Hidi & Anderson, 1992; Pintrich & Schrauben, 1992; Schiefele, 1991, 1992; Tobias, 1994). Thus, as you might guess, students who are interested in what they are studying are more likely to remember it over the long run and use it as a foundation for future learning (Garner et al., 1991; Renninger, Hidi, & Krapp, 1992; Scholes & Kardash, 1996; Wigfield, 1994).

Situational versus Personal Interest

Situational interest Interest evoked temporarily by something in the environment.

Theorists distinguish between two general types of interest (Hidi & Harackiewicz, 2000; Renninger et al., 1992; Schraw & Lehman, 2001). **Situational interest** is evoked by something in the immediate environment. Things that are new, different, unexpected, or especially vivid often generate situational interest, as do things with a high activity level or intense emotions (Hidi, 1990; Mitchell, 1993; Renninger et al., 1992; Schank, 1979). Furthermore, certain topics—for example, death, destruction, danger, money, romance, and sex—appear to be inherently interesting for human beings (Schank, 1979). Works of fiction (novels, short stories, movies, and so on) are more interesting and engaging when they include themes and characters with which people can personally identify (Hidi & Harackiewicz, 2000; Schank, 1979; Wade, 1992). Nonfiction is more interesting when it is easy to understand and relationships among ideas are clear (Schraw & Lehman, 2001; Wade, 1992). And challenging tasks are often more interesting than easy ones (Danner & Lonky, 1981; Harter, 1978).

Personal interest A long-term, relatively stable interest in a particular topic or activity.

Other interests lie within: Students tend to have personal preferences regarding the topics they pursue and the activities in which they engage. Because such **personal interests** are relatively stable over time, we see a consistent pattern in the choices students make.

The origins of personal interest have not been investigated as fully as sources of situational interest have. Many personal interests probably come from students' prior experiences with various activities and topics; for example, events and subject matter that initially invoke situational interest may provide the seeds from which personal interests will eventually grow (Hidi & Harackiewicz, 2000). Students may also find that acquiring more knowledge and skill in a particular area enhances their sense of self-efficacy, thereby enhancing their intrinsic motivation. Often, interest and knowledge seem to perpetuate each other: Personal interest in a topic fuels a quest to learn more about the topic, and the increased knowledge gained, in turn, promotes greater interest (Hidi & McLaren, 1990; Kintsch, 1980; Tobias, 1994).

In the early grades, interests are largely situational: Young children are readily attracted to novel, attention-getting events and stimuli. By the middle to upper elementary grades, however, students acquire specific interests—perhaps in reptiles, ballet, or outer space—that persist over time (Eccles et al., 1998). By and large, students form interests in activities that they can do well and that are stereotypically appropriate for their sex and social class (L. S. Gottfredson, 1981; Wigfield, 1994).

Promoting Interest in Classroom Subject Matter

Students' personal interests provide the force that will ultimately sustain their involvement in an activity over the long run (P. A. Alexander et al., 1994). As a teacher, you can certainly capitalize on students' personal interests by allowing some flexibility in the topics about which students read, learn, write, and study (e.g., see Figure 9.3). Furthermore, you can tie traditional classroom subjects to things students are naturally curious about; for example, you might explain how we could use latitude and longitude to help locate the *Titanic* (J. E. Brophy, 1986). Students are often interested in topics related to people and culture (e.g., disease, violence, holidays), nature (e.g., dinosaurs, weather, the sea), and current events (e.g., television shows, popular music, substance abuse, gangs) (Zahorik, 1994).

On other occasions, you can temporarily pique students' interest, and in the process perhaps stimulate the beginnings of more enduring personal interests, by the activities you develop and the ways you present information. In particular, you can

- Include variety and novelty in classroom materials or procedures
- Present inconsistent or discrepant information
- Encourage occasional fantasy and make-believe
- Convey your own enthusiasm for a topic
- Provide opportunities for students to get actively involved with the subject matter
- Ask students to apply new knowledge and skills to events and concerns in their personal lives
- Ask students to teach what they learn to others (Anand & Ross, 1987; J. Brophy, 1999; J. E. Brophy, 1987; Covington, 1992; Deci, 1992; Deci & Ryan, 1992; Hidi & Anderson, 1992; Hidi, Weiss, Berndorff, & Nolan, 1998; Lepper & Hodell, 1989; R. P. Perry, 1985; J. A. Ross, 1988; Wade, 1992; Zahorik, 1994)

To illustrate, here are some specific things you might do:

- In a unit on musical instruments, let students experiment with a variety of simple instruments.
- In a lesson about sedimentary, metamorphic, and igneous rocks, give co-operative groups a bag of rocks and have them categorize each one.
- In a lesson about alcoholic beverages, have students role-play being at a party and being tempted to have a beer or wine cooler.

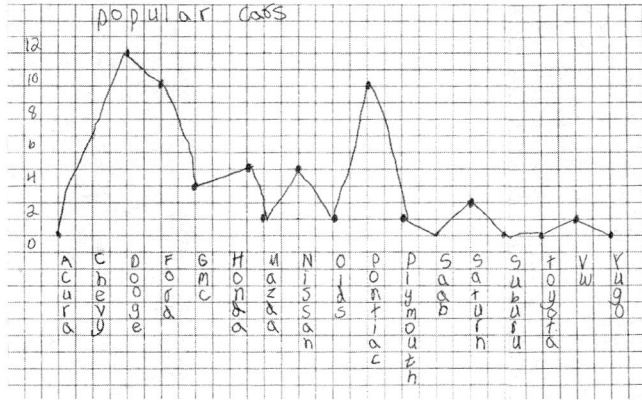

FIGURE 9.3 Teachers can capitalize on students' personal interests by allowing flexibility in the topics that students explore as they work on basic skills. Here 12-year-old Connor practises basic research and graphing skills by surveying his fellow students about one of his favourite topics: cars.

Yet another strategy for generating interest is to relate classroom subject matter to students' short-term and long-term goals (J. E. Brophy, 1987; Parsons, Adler, et al., 1982; Parsons, Kaczala et al., 1982). Let's look at the kinds of goals your students are likely to have.

Goals

As you discovered earlier, social cognitive theorists propose that much of human behaviour is goal-directed. Many motivation theorists echo this idea: People set goals for themselves and choose courses of action that they think will help them achieve those goals (e.g., Dweck & Elliott, 1983; M. E. Ford, 1996; Kaplan, 1998; Locke & Latham, 1994). Some goals (e.g., "I want to finish reading my dinosaur book") are short-term and transitory; others (e.g., "I want to be a paleontologist") are long-term and relatively enduring. Students' goals influence the extent to which they actively engage themselves in academic tasks and the kinds of learning strategies they use as they read and study (E. M. Anderman & Maehr, 1994; Nolen, 1996; Winne & Marx, 1989).

Goal setting is also an important component of self-regulated learning: Self-regulated learners know what they want to accomplish when they read or study, direct their thoughts and learning strategies accordingly, and continually monitor their progress toward their goals (Carver & Scheier, 1990; Schunk & Zimmerman, 1994). Furthermore, by achieving their goals in a particular domain, students enhance their self-efficacy for tasks and activities within that domain (Bandura & Schunk, 1981). To produce these benefits, however, goals must be accomplishable; if they are unrealistically high, consistent failure to achieve them may result in anxiety or depression (Bandura, 1986).

Children and adolescents typically have a wide variety of goals: Being happy and healthy, doing well in school, being popular with classmates, gaining recognition for accomplishments, defeating others in competitive events, earning money, and finding a long-term mate are just a few of the many possibilities (M. E. Ford, 1996; Schutz, 1994). Yet among their many goals are certain **core goals** that drive much of what they do (Schutz, 1994). For instance, students who attain high levels of academic achievement typically make classroom learning a high priority; students who achieve at lower levels are often more concerned with social relationships (Wentzel & Wigfield, 1998; Wigfield et al., 1996).

Core goal A long-term goal that drives much of what a person does.

Here we look at research findings related to several kinds of goals: mastery and performance goals, work-avoidance goals, social goals, and career goals. We then identify ways to capitalize on students' goals in order to enhance their motivation to learn and achieve in the classroom.

Mastery and Performance Goals

Mr. Wesolowski, the physical education teacher, is teaching a unit on basketball. He asks Tim, Travis, and Tony to get on the court and try dribbling, passing, and shooting baskets. In Tim's case, he hopes that his performance will impress Mr. Wesolowski and his friends and so he wants to maximize opportunities to demonstrate his skill on the court. Travis, on the other hand is concerned about making mistakes. While he, too, is focusing on the impression he makes, it is because he does not want to look *bad*. Unlike Tim and Travis, Tony isn't thinking about how his performance will appear to others. Instead, he is interested mainly in developing his skill in the game and doesn't expect immediate success. For Tony, making mistakes is an inevitable part of learning a new skill, not a source of embarrassment or humiliation.

Mastery goal A desire to acquire additional knowledge or master new skills.

Performance goal A desire either to look good and receive favourable judgments from others, or else *not* to look bad and receive unfavourable judgments.

Performance-approach goal A desire to look good and receive favourable judgments from others.

Performance-avoidance goal A desire not to look bad and receive unfavourable judgments from others.

Tony's approach to basketball illustrates a **mastery goal** (also known as a *learning goal*), a desire to acquire additional knowledge or master new skills. Tim and Travis are each setting a **performance goal**, a desire to present oneself as competent in the eyes of others. More specifically, Tim has a **performance-approach goal**: He wants to look good and receive favourable judgments from others. In contrast, Travis has a **performance-avoidance goal**: He wants to *avoid* looking bad and receiving unfavourable judgments. In some instances, performance goals also have an element of social comparison, in that students are concerned about how their accomplishments compare to those of their peers (Elliot & McGregor, 2000; Elliot & Thrash, 2001; Midgley et al., 1998).

Mastery goals, performance-approach goals, and performance-avoidance goals are not necessarily mutually exclusive; students may simultaneously have two kinds, or even all three (Covington & Müeller, 2001; Hidi & Harackiewicz, 2000; Meece & Holt, 1993). For example, returning to our basketball example, we could imagine another boy, Trey, who wants to improve his basketball skills *and* look good in front of his classmates *and* not come across as a klutz.

Effects of Mastery and Performance Goals

A considerable body of research indicates that mastery goals are the optimal situation. As Table 9.2 illustrates, students with mastery goals tend to engage in the very activities that will help them learn: They pay attention in class, process information in ways that promote effective long-term memory storage, and learn from their mistakes. Furthermore, students with mastery goals have a healthy perspective about learning, effort, and failure: They realize that learning is a process of trying hard and continuing to persevere even in the face of temporary setbacks. Consequently, it is usually these students who benefit the most from their classroom experiences.

In contrast, students with performance goals—especially those with performance-*avoidance* goals—may stay away from some of the very tasks that, because of their challenging nature, would do the most to help them master new skills. Furthermore, these students often experience debilitating anxiety about tests and other classroom tasks (Middleton & Midgley, 1997; Skaalvik, 1997; J. C. Turner, Thorpe, & Meyer, 1998). Performance-*approach* goals are a mixed bag: They sometimes have very positive effects, spurring students on to achieve at high levels, especially

> In which of these goal(s) do you see intrinsic motivation? In which do you see extrinsic motivation?

> In what areas do you have mastery goals? In what areas are you interested only in how you appear to others? How is your learning affected by the particular goals you have?

TABLE 9.2 — COMPARE/CONTRAST

Students with Mastery versus Performance Goals

STUDENTS WITH MASTERY GOALS	STUDENTS WITH PERFORMANCE GOALS (ESPECIALLY THOSE WITH PERFORMANCE-AVOIDANCE GOALS)
Believe that competence develops over time through practice and effort	Believe that competence is a stable characteristic—that people either have talent or they don't
Choose tasks that maximize opportunities for learning	Choose tasks that maximize opportunities for demonstrating competence; avoid tasks and actions (e.g., asking for help) that make them look incompetent
React to easy tasks with feelings of boredom or disappointment	React to easy tasks with feelings of pride or relief
View effort as something necessary to improve competence	View effort as a sign of low competence; think that competent people shouldn't have to try very hard
Are more likely to be intrinsically motivated to learn course material	Are more likely to be extrinsically motivated—that is, by expectations of external reinforcement and punishment—and are more likely to cheat to obtain good grades
Exhibit more self-regulated learning and behaviour	Exhibit less self-regulation
Use learning strategies that promote true comprehension of course material (e.g., meaningful learning, elaboration, comprehension monitoring)	Use learning strategies that promote only rote learning (e.g., repetition, copying, word-for-word memorization)
Willingly collaborate with peers when doing so is likely to enhance learning	Are willing to collaborate with peers primarily when such collaboration offers opportunities to look competent or enhance social status
Evaluate their own performance in terms of the progress they make	Evaluate their own performance in terms of how they compare with others
Interpret failure as a sign that they need to exert more effort	Interpret failure as a sign of low ability and therefore predictive of future failures
View errors as a normal and useful part of the learning process; use errors to help improve performance	View errors as a sign of failure and incompetence; engage in self-handicapping to provide apparent justification for errors and failures
Are satisfied with their performance if they try hard, even if their efforts result in failure	Are satisfied with their performance only if they succeed
View their teacher as a resource and guide to help them learn	View their teacher as a judge and as a rewarder or punisher

Sources: Ablard & Lipschultz, 1998; C. Ames & Archer, 1988; E. M. Anderman, Griesinger, & Westerfield, 1998; E. M. Anderman & Maehr, 1994; Dweck, 1986; Dweck & Elliott, 1983; Jagacinski & Nicholls, 1984, 1987; Kaplan & Midgley, 1999; Meece, 1994; P. K. Murphy, 2000; Newman & Schwager, 1995; Nolen, 1996; Rawsthorne & Elliot, 1999; A. M. Ryan et al., 2001; Urdan & Midgley, 2001; Urdan, Midgley, & Anderman, 1998.

Students with mastery goals recognize that competence comes only from effort and practice.

in the secondary grades and especially in combination with mastery goals (Hidi & Harackiewicz, 2000; McNeil & Alibali, 2000; Pintrich, 2000; Rawsthorne & Elliott, 1999; Urdan, 1997). Yet by themselves, performance-approach goals may be less beneficial than mastery goals: To achieve them, students may use relatively superficial learning strategies (e.g., rote memorization), exert only the minimal effort necessary to achieve desired outcomes, engage in self-handicapping, and perhaps even cheat (E. M. Anderman et al., 1998; J. E. Brophy, 1987; Midgley, Kaplan, & Middleton, 2001). Performance-approach goals appear to be most detrimental when students have low self-efficacy for classroom tasks (Hidi & Harackiewicz, 2000).

Origins of Performance Goals

Unfortunately, performance goals seem to be far more prevalent than mastery goals among today's students, at least those in the secondary grades (Blumenfeld, 1992; W. Doyle, 1986b; Elliot & McGregor, 2000; Harter, 1992). Most students, if they are motivated to succeed in their schoolwork, are primarily concerned about getting good grades, and they prefer short, easy tasks to lengthier, more challenging ones. Performance goals are also common in team sports, where the focus is often more on winning and gaining public recognition than on developing new skills and seeing improvement over time (Roberts, Treasure, & Kavussanu, 1997).

In some instances, students adopt performance goals as a means of protecting their sense of self-worth or gaining status with peers (L. H. Anderman & Anderman, 1999; Covington, 1992). In other cases, they may adopt performance goals because they believe that ability is something that they either have or don't have (rather than something they can increase with hard work) and so try to assess their "natural" ability by continually comparing their own performance with that of others (Dweck, 1999). Yet many common teaching and coaching practices also contribute to the development of performance goals. Scoring tests on a curve, reminding students that they need to get good grades if they want to go to university, displaying grades for everyone to see, focusing on surpassing other schools and teams—all of these strategies, though undoubtedly well intended, encourage students to focus their attention more on looking good than on learning.

Fostering Mastery Goals

Performance goals are probably inevitable in today's schools and in society at large (R. Butler, 1989; Elliot & McGregor, 2000). Children and adolescents will invariably look to their peers' performance as one means of evaluating their own performance, and many aspects of the adult world (gaining admission to university, seeking employment, working in private industry, playing professional sports, etc.) are inherently competitive in nature. Yet we do our students a disservice when we focus their attention primarily on how they appear to others and how often they do or do not surpass their classmates. When we instead point out how school subject matter will be useful in the future, encourage students to engage in meaningful learning rather than rote memorization, show students that they are making progress, and acknowledge that effective learning requires exerting effort and making mistakes, we are emphasizing goals that will help students better understand and more thoroughly master subject matter (C. Ames, 1992; E. M. Anderman & Maehr, 1994; Bong, 2001; Graham & Weiner, 1996; Meece, 1994). Focusing learners' attention on mastery goals, especially when those goals relate to learners' own lives, may especially benefit students from diverse ethnic backgrounds and students at risk for academic failure (Alderman, 1990; García, 1992; Wlodkowski & Ginsberg, 1995).

Work-Avoidance Goals

As we have just seen, students sometimes want to avoid looking bad as they perform classroom tasks. On other occasions, they may want to avoid having to do classroom tasks *at all*, or at least they will try to put as little effort as possible into those tasks. In other words, they may have a **work-avoidance goal** (Dowson & McInerney, 2001; Gallini, 2000; Nicholls, Cobb, Yackel, Wood, & Wheatley, 1990).

To date, research on work-avoidance goals has focused on the middle school grades, where such goals seem to be far too common (Dowson & McInerney, 2001; Gallini, 2000). Students with work-avoidance goals use a variety of strategies to minimize their workload; for instance, they may engage in off-task behaviour, solicit help on easy tasks and problems, pretend they don't

Work-avoidance goal A desire to avoid having to perform classroom tasks or to complete them with only minimal effort.

understand something even when they do, complain loudly about challenging assignments, and select the least taxing alternatives whenever choices are given (Dowson & McInerney, 2001). They rarely use effective learning strategies or pull their weight in small-group activities (Dowson & McInerney, 2001; Gallini, 2000).

Given the current paucity of research findings on work-avoidance goals, we can only speculate about how these goals originate. But we can reasonably guess that students are most likely to adopt them when they find little value or interest in classroom academic subject matter, have low self-efficacy for learning it, and see no long-term payoffs for mastering it. In other words, students are most likely to have work-avoidance goals when they have neither intrinsic nor extrinsic motivation to achieve instructional objectives. Students with work-avoidance goals may thus be our biggest challenges, and we will have to use a wide variety of motivational strategies—probably including extrinsic reinforcement—to get them truly engaged in, and eventually committed to mastering, academic subject matter.

Social Goals

We noted earlier in this chapter that most students make social relationships a high priority, and in fact all students probably have some need for relatedness. Students are apt to have a variety of social goals, perhaps including the following:

- Forming and maintaining friendly or intimate relationships with others
- Becoming part of a cohesive, mutually supportive group
- Gaining other people's approval
- Achieving status and prestige among peers
- Meeting social obligations and keeping interpersonal commitments
- Assisting and supporting others, and ensuring their welfare (Dowson & McInerney, 2001; M. E. Ford, 1996; Hicks, 1997; Schutz, 1994)

The nature of students' social goals will undoubtedly affect their classroom behaviour and academic performance. If students want to gain their teacher's attention and approval, they are apt to strive for good grades and in other ways shoot for performance goals (Hinkley, McInerney, & Marsh, 2001). If they want to gain the approval of low-achieving peers, they may exert little effort in their studies and possibly even adopt work-avoidance goals. If they are seeking friendly relationships with classmates or are concerned about others' welfare, they may eagerly and actively engage in such activities as co-operative learning and peer tutoring (Dowson & McInerney, 2001). Teachers must continually consider how they can help students achieve their social goals at the same time that students work toward more academically oriented ones—for example, by making ample use of group work, enlisting students' assistance in schoolwide and community service projects, and providing opportunities for all students to "shine" in some way and thereby gain the admiration of their peers.

Capitalizing on Students' Goals

As we've explored some of the goals that students are likely to have, we've also considered the implications of these goals for instructional practice. We now look at a few more general ways in which we can use students' goals to foster their academic achievement:

- *Plan activities that enable students to meet several goals at once.* Most students have numerous goals at any one time and use a variety of strategies to juggle them. Sometimes students find activities that allow them to achieve two or more goals simultaneously; for instance, they may satisfy both academic and social goals by forming a study group to prepare for a test. But in other situations they may believe they have to abandon one goal to satisfy another (McCaslin & Good, 1996; Phelan, Yu, & Davidson, 1994).

Our students will, of course, be most successful when their multiple goals all lead them in the same direction (M. E. Ford, 1992; Wentzel, 1999). For example, students might work toward mastery goals by learning and practising new skills within the context of group projects (thus meeting their social goals) and with evaluation criteria that allow for risk taking and mistakes (thus also meeting their performance goals). Students are *un*likely to strive for mastery goals when our assignments ask little of them, when we insist that they compete with one another for resources or high test scores (thereby interfering with their social goals), and when any single failure has a significant impact on their final grades (thereby thwarting their progress toward performance goals).

- *Relate classroom subject matter to students' present lives and future goals.* Some classroom activities will be naturally fun, interesting, or otherwise intrinsically motivating for students. But others—perhaps the drill and practice so essential for developing automaticity of basic skills, or perhaps the complex topics and procedures with which students must initially struggle—may sometimes be less than exciting. Students will be more apt to engage themselves in unenticing classroom subject matter, and more likely to use effective cognitive processes as they learn it, when they see how it relates to their personal lives and professional aspirations (C. Ames, 1992; J. E. Brophy & Alleman, 1991; Pintrich et al., 1993). In other words, students learn classroom material more effectively when they have a self-perceived *need to know* that material. Thus, we might illustrate how mathematics plays a role in shopping and budgeting an allowance, how science helps us solve everyday problems, and how physical fitness helps us look and feel better.

- *Encourage students to set specific, short-term goals for their learning and achievement.* Oftentimes students respond more favourably to goals they set for themselves rather than those that others set for them (Wentzel, 1999), possibly because self-chosen goals help them maintain a sense of self-determination. Although we should certainly encourage students to develop long-term goals (e.g., going to university, becoming an environmental scientist), such goals are often too general and abstract to guide students' immediate behaviour (Bandura, 1997; Husman & Freeman, 1999). Many students (younger ones especially) initially respond more favourably

INTO THE CLASSROOM *Promoting Intrinsic Motivation*

Define success as eventual, rather than immediate, mastery of class material, and acknowledge that occasional mistakes are to be expected.

> When a middle school student is disappointed in her mediocre performance on a difficult assignment, her teacher consoles her by saying, "You're a very talented student, and you're probably used to having your schoolwork come easily. But remember, as you move into the upper grades, your assignments will become more challenging. They *have* to challenge you, or else you wouldn't grow. With a little more study and practice, I know you'll improve quite a bit."

Encourage self-comparison, rather than comparison with other students.

> In January an elementary school teacher asks his students to write a short story. After reading students' stories and writing feedback in the margins, he returns the stories to the authors; he also returns stories that the students wrote in early September. "Do you see how much your writing has improved over the past four months?" he asks. "The stories that you wrote this week are longer and better developed, and you made fewer spelling and grammatical errors."

Enhance students' sense of self-determination regarding classroom assignments and activities.

> A high school science teacher tells her students, "I know you can't always complete your lab reports the same day that you did a lab in class. Let's see whether we can set some reasonable due dates for your reports so that *you* have time to write them and *I* have time to read them and give you feedback before the next lab activity."

Communicate the belief that students *want* to learn.

> Early in the school year, a social studies teacher explains that her class will help students become "social scientists." She frequently refers back to this idea—for example, by saying, "Since you are social scientists, you will recognize that the description of this area as a tropical rain forest has implications about what kinds of crops will grow there," or "Thinking as social scientists, what conclusions might we draw from this information?" (J. E. Brophy, 1986, p. 46)

Relate classroom material to students' personal interests.

> An elementary school teacher asks students to bring in objects they use to celebrate holidays at home. He incorporates these objects into a lesson on how holiday traditions differ not only from religion to religion but also from family to family.

Grab students' attention and pique their interest by occasionally introducing variety and novelty into classroom activities.

> After clearing her strategy with the school principal, a high school psychology teacher brings Taffy, her mild-mannered cocker spaniel, to class for the day. She uses Taffy to demonstrate the various ways in which reinforcement (in this case, dog biscuits) can influence behaviour.

to short-term, concrete goals—perhaps learning a list of spelling words or solving a certain number of mathematics problems (Bandura & Schunk, 1981; Good & Brophy, 1994; Schunk & Rice, 1989). By setting and working for a series of short-term goals, students get regular feedback about the progress they are making, develop a greater sense of self-efficacy that they can master school subject matter, and achieve at higher levels (Bandura, 1981; Kluger & DeNisi, 1998; Page-Voth & Graham, 1999; Schunk, 1996).

The topics we've explored so far have suggested numerous ideas about how we can enhance students' intrinsic motivation to learn academic subject matter. The feature "Promoting Intrinsic Motivation" identifies and illustrates just a few of them. We turn now to yet another cognitive factor affecting motivation: students' attributions for their successes and failures.

Attributions: Perceived Causes of Success and Failure

Attributions are the causal explanations for success and failure that students assign to the things that happen to them—their beliefs about *what causes what*. These causal attributions in turn guide their future behaviour. The theoretical examination of these attributions and their influence on behaviour is known as **attribution theory** (e.g., Dweck, 1986; Weiner, 1984, 1986, 1994, 2000).

Attribution An internally constructed causal explanation for one's success or failure.

Attribution theory A theoretical perspective that focuses on people's attributions concerning the causes of events that befall them, as well as on the behaviours that result from such attributions.

Dimensions Underlying Students' Attributions

Your students may form a variety of attributions about the causes of classroom events; they will have beliefs about why they do well or poorly on tests and assignments, why they are popular with their classmates or have trouble making friends, why they are skilled athletes or total klutzes, and so on. They may attribute their school successes and failures to such factors as aptitude or ability (how smart or proficient they are), effort (how hard they tried), other people (how well you taught or how much their classmates like them), task difficulty (how easy or hard something is), luck, mood, illness, fatigue, or physical appearance. These various attributions differ from one another in three primary ways: locus, stability, and controllability (Weiner, 1986, 2000).

1. *Locus ("place"): Internal versus external.* Students sometimes attribute the causes of events to *internal* things—to factors within themselves. Thinking that a good grade is due to your own hard work and believing that a poor grade is due to your lack of ability are examples of internal attributions. At other times, students attribute events to *external* things—to factors outside themselves. Concluding that you received a scholarship because you "lucked out" and interpreting a classmate's scowl as a sign of her bad mood (rather than the result of anything you might have done) are examples of external attributions.

2. *Stability: Stable versus unstable.* Sometimes students believe that events are due to *stable* factors—to things that probably won't change much in the near future. For example, if you believe that you do well in science because of your innate intelligence or that you have trouble making friends because you're overweight, then you are attributing events to stable, relatively long-term causes. But sometimes students instead believe that events result from *unstable* factors—things that can change from one time to the next. Thinking that winning a tennis game was just a matter of luck and believing that you got a bad test grade because you were tired when you took the test are examples of attributions involving unstable factors.[1]

3. *Controllability: Controllable versus uncontrollable.* On some occasions, students attribute events to *controllable* factors—to things they can influence and change. For example, if you believe that a classmate invited you to his birthday party because you always smile and say nice things to him, and if you think that you probably failed a test simply because you didn't study the right things, then you are attributing these events to controllable factors. On other occasions, students attribute events to *uncontrollable* factors—to things over which they themselves have no influence. For example, if you think that you were chosen for the lead in the school play only because the drama teacher thinks you look "right" for the part or that you played a lousy game of basketball because you were sick, then you are attributing these events to uncontrollable factors.

---

[1] People occasionally think of *effort* and *luck* as being relatively stable, long-term characteristics (Weiner, 1986). To be consistent with much of the literature in attribution theory, however, we will use both terms to refer to a temporary state of affairs.

Students are usually happy when they succeed at classroom tasks. But whether they also feel proud and satisfied, on the one hand, or relieved and grateful, on the other, depends on whether they attribute their success to internal or external causes. (Self-portrait by Corey, age 9)

In general, students tend to attribute their successes to internal causes (e.g., high ability, hard work) and their failures to external causes (e.g., luck, behaviours of others) (Marsh, 1990a; Whitley & Frieze, 1985). By patting themselves on the back for the things they do well and putting the blame elsewhere for poor performance, they are able to maintain their sense of self-worth (Clifford, 1990; Paris & Byrnes, 1989). Attributions don't always reflect the true state of affairs, however; for example, a student may blame a low test grade on a "tricky" test or an "unfair" teacher when the cause is really the student's own lack of effort or poor study skills (e.g., Horgan, 1990).

How Attributions Influence Affect, Cognition, and Behaviour

We have already alluded to some of the effects that attributions may have. In the following paragraphs, we look more closely at such effects.

Emotional reactions to success and failure. Naturally, students will be happy when they succeed. But they will also have feelings of pride and satisfaction when they attribute their successes to internal causes—that is, to something they themselves have done. When they instead credit their successes to the actions of another person or to some other external force, they are apt to feel grateful rather than proud (Weiner, Russell, & Lerman, 1978, 1979). In a similar vein, students will usually feel a certain amount of sadness after a failure. They will also feel guilty or ashamed when they blame their failures on internal causes, such as their own lack of ability or effort. But when they blame their failures on external causes—to events and people outside of themselves—they are likely to be angry (Weiner et al., 1978, 1979).

Expectations for future success or failure. When students attribute their successes and failures to stable factors, they expect their future performance to be similar to their current performance. In other words, successful students anticipate that they will continue to succeed, and failing students believe that they will always be failures. In contrast, when students attribute their successes and failures to unstable factors such as effort or luck, then their current success rate will have less influence on their expectation for future success, and a few failures won't put much of a dent in their self-efficacy (Dweck, 1978; Schunk, 1990; Weiner, 1986). The most optimistic students—those with the highest expectations for future success—are the ones who attribute their successes to stable factors such as innate ability and their failures to unstable factors such as lack of effort or inappropriate strategies (Fennema, 1987; Schunk, 1990; Weiner, 1984).

Expenditure of effort. When students believe that their failures result from their own lack of effort, they are likely to try harder in future situations and to persist in the face of difficulty (Dweck, 1975; Feather, 1982; Weiner, 1984). But when students instead attribute failure to a lack of innate ability (they couldn't do it even if they tried), they give up easily and sometimes can't even perform tasks they have previously accomplished successfully (Dweck, 1978; Eccles [Parsons], 1983).

Help-seeking behaviour. Students who believe that success is a result of their own doing—those who attribute success to internal and controllable causes—are more inclined to seek the support that will facilitate their future learning. For instance, they may ask for their teacher's assistance if they don't understand course material, or they may voluntarily attend the extra help sessions that are offered (R. Ames, 1983). In contrast, students who believe that their learning successes and failures are beyond their control are unlikely to seek outside support even when it's readily available.

Classroom performance. We find consistent correlations between students' attributions and their academic achievement. For example, students who expect to succeed get better grades than students of equal ability who expect to fail (Eccles [Parsons], 1983). Students who expect to succeed are apt to approach problem-solving tasks in a logical, systematic manner; students who expect to fail are apt to solve problems through random trial and error or to memorize problem-solving procedures in a rote, meaningless fashion (Tyler, 1958).

Future choices. As you might expect, students whose attributions lead them to expect success in a particular subject area are more likely to pursue that area—for example, by enrolling in more courses in the same discipline (Eccles [Parsons], 1984; Stipek & Gralinski, 1990; Weiner, 1986). Students who believe that their chances for future success in an activity are slim will avoid that activity whenever they can. And naturally, when students don't continue to pursue an activity, they can't possibly get better at it.

Developmental Trends in Attributions

Students become increasingly able to distinguish among various attributions as they get older. In the preschool years, children don't have a clear understanding of the differences among the possible causes—effort, ability, luck, task difficulty, and so on—of their successes and failures (Eccles et al., 1998; Nicholls, 1990). Especially troublesome is the distinction between effort and ability, which they gradually get a better handle on over time (Nicholls, 1990). At about age 6, they begin to recognize that effort and ability are separate qualities but see them as positively correlated: People who try hardest have the greatest ability, and effort is the primary determinant of success. Sometime around age 9, they begin to understand that effort and ability often compensate for one another and that people with less ability may have to exert greater effort to achieve the same outcome as their more able peers. By age 13 or so, they make a clear distinction between effort and ability: They realize that people differ both in their inherent ability to perform a task and in the amount of effort they exert on a task. They also know that ability and effort can compensate for each other but that a lack of ability sometimes precludes success no matter *how* much effort a person puts forth.

A related trend is an increasing tendency to attribute success and failure to ability rather than to effort (M. V. Covington, 1992; Dweck & Elliott, 1983; Nicholls, 1990). In the early elementary grades, students tend to attribute their successes to hard work and practice; therefore, they are usually relatively optimistic about their chances for success and so may try harder when they fail. As students get older, many of them begin to attribute their successes and failures to an inherited ability—for instance, to "intelligence"—that they perceive to be fairly stable and beyond their control. If these students are usually successful at school tasks, then they will have high self-efficacy about such tasks; if failures are frequent, their self-efficacy may plummet (Dweck, 1986; Eccles [Parsons], 1983; Schunk, 1990).

Whether intelligence is actually a stable or unstable characteristic is a matter of considerable controversy, and even school-age children and adolescents have differing opinions on this matter. Students with an **entity view** believe that intelligence is a "thing" that is fairly permanent and unchangeable. Students with an incremental view believe that intelligence can and does improve with effort and practice (Dweck & Leggett, 1988; Weiner, 1994). As you might guess, students who have an **incremental view** of intelligence and other abilities are more likely to attribute their failures to a temporary and unstable, rather than permanent, state of affairs.

Entity view of intelligence A belief that intelligence is a "thing" that is relatively permanent and unchangeable.

Incremental view of intelligence The belief that intelligence can and does improve with effort and practice.

Factors Influencing the Development of Attributions

Why does one student see a certain failure as a temporary setback due to her own insufficient effort, whereas another thinks it reveals a lack of ability and so signals more failures to come, and still another blames the failure on a teacher's capricious and unpredictable actions? Researchers have identified several factors that influence students' attributions: past successes and failures, reinforcement and punishment, messages from adults, and image management.

Past successes and failures. Students' attributions are partly the result of their previous success and failure experiences (M. V. Covington, 1987; Hong, Chiu, & Dweck, 1995; Klein, 1990). Students who usually succeed when they give a task their best shot are likely to credit success to internal factors such as effort or high ability. Those who frequently fail despite their best efforts are likely to attribute success to something beyond their control—perhaps to an ability they don't possess or to such external factors as luck or a teacher's arbitrary judgment. Here we find yet another reason to promote student success on a regular basis: In doing so, teachers also promote more internal, and thus more productive, attributions.

When you know that your students have high self-efficacy about the subject matter in question, you may occasionally want to give them a series of tasks that they can perform successfully only if they exert considerable time and mental effort. In doing so, you can promote **learned industriousness**: Students will begin to realize that they can succeed at some tasks only with effort, persistence, and well-chosen strategies (Eisenberger, 1992; Winne, 1995).

Learned industriousness The recognition that one can succeed at some tasks only with effort, persistence, and well-chosen strategies.

Reinforcement and punishment. In general, children are more likely to attribute events to internal, controllable causes when adults reinforce their successes but don't punish their failures. Conversely, they are more likely to make external attributions when adults punish failures and ignore successes (Katkovsky, Crandall, & Good, 1967). It appears that our students will be more apt to accept responsibility for their failures if, as teachers, we don't make a big deal out of them.

As noted in Chapter 5, however, mild punishment is sometimes necessary to discourage behaviours that seriously interfere with classroom learning. On such occasions, it is important to make response–consequence contingencies clear—for example, by describing unacceptable behaviours in advance and by using punishment in a consistent, predictable fashion. In the process, you help students learn that their *own behaviours* lead to desirable and undesirable consequences and that they can therefore influence the events that occur by changing how they behave. Hence, you help them develop internal attributions regarding the consequences they experience and a greater sense of control over classroom events.

Messages from adults. Adults communicate their beliefs about students' strengths and weaknesses in a variety of subtle, and sometimes not so subtle, ways (more about these ways in the upcoming section on "Teacher Expectations and Attributions"). When adults communicate their belief that students are incapable of mastering a task, students are likely to attribute their failures to low ability and may therefore conclude that they will gain little by trying harder (Butler, 1994; Weiner, 2000; D. K. Yee & Eccles, 1988). In some instances, adults may directly offer attributions for students' successes and failures (Parsons, Kaczala, & Meece, 1982; Schunk, 1982).

Image management. As students get older, they discover that different kinds of attributions elicit different kinds of reactions from other people, and so they begin to modify their attributions for the particular audience at hand. One attribution theorist calls this phenomenon *face-saving* (Juvonen, 2000); we think the term *image management* is more descriptive. For example, teachers are often sympathetic and forgiving when students fail because of something beyond their control (illness, lack of ability, etc.) but frequently get angry when students fail because they didn't try very hard. By the time students reach Grade 4, most of them are aware of this fact and so may verbalize attributions that are likely to elicit a favourable reaction (Juvonen, 2000).

Students become equally adept at tailoring their attributions for the ears of their classmates. Generally speaking, Grade 4 students believe that their peers value diligence and hard work, and so they are likely to tell their classmates that they did well on an assignment because they worked hard. By Grade 8, however, many students believe that their peers will disapprove of those who exert much effort on academic tasks, and so they often prefer to convey the impression that they *aren't* working very hard. For instance, they might tell peers that they "didn't study very much" for an important exam (Juvonen, 2000).

For reasons we've just identified, different students may interpret the same events in very different ways. As they grow older, students gradually develop predictable patterns of attributions and expectations for their future performance, as we shall see now.

Mastery Orientation versus Learned Helplessness

Consider these two students, keeping in mind that *their actual academic ability is the same*:

> Jared is an enthusiastic, energetic learner. He seems to enjoy working hard at school activities and takes obvious pleasure in doing well. He likes challenges and especially likes to solve the "brain teaser" problems that his teacher assigns as extra credit work each day. He can't always solve the problems, but he takes failure in stride and is eager for more problems the following day.

> Jerry is an anxious, fidgety student. He doesn't seem to have much confidence in his ability to accomplish school tasks successfully. In fact, he is always underestimating what he can do: Even when he has succeeded, he doubts that he can do it again. He seems to prefer filling out drill-and-practice worksheets that help him practise skills he's already mastered, rather than attempting new tasks and problems. As for those daily brain teasers, he sometimes takes a stab at them, but he gives up quickly if the answer isn't obvious.

Over time, some students, like Jared, develop a general sense of optimism that they can master new tasks and succeed in a variety of endeavours. They attribute their accomplishments to their own ability and effort and have an *I can do it* attitude known as a **mastery orientation**. Other students, like Jerry, who are either unsure of their chances for success or else convinced that they can*not* succeed, display a growing sense of futility about their chances for future success. They have an *I can't do it* attitude known as **learned helplessness**.

Even though students with a mastery orientation and those with learned helplessness may have equal ability initially, those with a mastery orientation behave in ways that lead to higher achievement over the long run: They set ambitious goals, seek challenging situations, and persist in the face of failure. Students with learned helplessness behave very differently: Because

---

Mastery orientation A general belief that one is capable of accomplishing challenging tasks.

Learned helplessness A general belief that one is incapable of accomplishing tasks and has little or no control of the environment.

they underestimate their own ability, they set goals they can easily accomplish, avoid the challenges likely to maximize their learning and growth, and respond to failure in counter-productive ways (e.g., giving up quickly) that almost guarantee future failure (Dweck, 1986; Graham, 1989; C. Peterson, 1990; Seligman, 1991).

Even preschoolers can develop learned helplessness about a particular task if they consistently encounter failure when attempting it (Burhans & Dweck, 1995). As a general rule, however, children younger than 8 rarely exhibit learned helplessness, perhaps because they still believe that success is due largely to their own efforts (Eccles et al., 1998; Paris & Cunningham, 1996). By early adolescence, feelings of helplessness are more common: Some middle schoolers believe they cannot control what happens to them and are at a loss for strategies about how to avert future failures (Paris & Cunningham, 1996; C. Peterson, Maier, & Seligman, 1993).

As mentioned earlier, the messages that teachers and other adults give students can have a significant influence on the attributions that students form. We now look more closely at the effects that teachers' expectations and attributions are likely to have. As we do so, we'll identify additional strategies for promoting productive attributions.

> Think of the distinction between a mastery orientation and learned helplessness as a continuum of individual differences rather than a complete dichotomy. You might also look at it as a difference between *optimists* and *pessimists* (C. Peterson, 1990; Seligman, 1991).

Teacher Expectations and Attributions

Teachers typically draw conclusions about their students relatively early in the school year, forming opinions about each one's strengths, weaknesses, and potential for academic success. In many instances, teachers size up their students fairly accurately: They know which ones need help with reading skills, which ones have short attention spans, which ones have trouble working together in the same co-operative group, and so on, and they can adapt their instruction and assistance accordingly (Goldenberg, 1992; Good & Brophy, 1994; Good & Nichols, 2001).

Yet even the best teachers inevitably make errors in their judgments. For example, B. Corenblum (1996) has employed a model of identity development that integrates both motivational and cognitive developmental perspectives to explain identity development in First Nations children. Corenblum's research shows that because of their own expectations and beliefs, teachers may not be sensitive to the assessment of minority children.

Teachers often underestimate the abilities of students who:

- Are physically unattractive
- Misbehave frequently in class
- Speak in dialects other than Standard English
- Are members of ethnic minority groups
- Are recent immigrants
- Come from low-income backgrounds (Banks & Banks, 1995; Bennett, Gottesman, Rock, & Cerullo, 1993; Knapp & Woolverton, 1995; McLoyd, 1998; Oakes & Guiton, 1995; Ritts, Patterson, & Tubbs, 1992)

All too often, teachers perceive students' ability levels to be relatively fixed and stable; in other words, they have an *entity* view of intelligence (Oakes & Guiton, 1995; Reyna, 2000). Their beliefs about these "stable" abilities affect their expectations for students' performance, which in turn lead them to behave differently toward different students. For example, when teachers have high expectations for students, they create a warmer classroom climate, interact with students more frequently, provide more opportunities for students to respond, and give more positive feedback; they also present more course material and more challenging topics. In contrast, when teachers have low expectations for certain students, they offer fewer opportunities for speaking in class, ask easier questions, give less feedback about students' responses, and present few if any challenging assignments (Babad, 1993; Good & Brophy, 1994; Graham, 1990; R. Rosenthal, 1994).

Teachers' beliefs about students' abilities also affect their attributions for students' successes and failures (Weiner, 2000). Consider the following interpretations of a student's success:

- "You did it! You're so smart!"
- "That's wonderful. Your hard work has really paid off, hasn't it?"
- "You've done very well. It's clear that you really know how to study."
- "This is certainly your lucky day."

> Minority students with a history of academic failure are especially likely to be the recipients of teacher behaviours that signal low ability (Graham, 1990).

And now consider these interpretations of a student's failure:

- "Hmmm, maybe this just isn't something you're good at. Perhaps we should try a different activity."
- "Why don't you practise a little more and then try again?"
- "Let's see whether we can come up with some study strategies that might work better for you."
- "Maybe you're just having a bad day."

Teachers who hold high expectations for their students are more likely to give specific feedback about the strengths and weaknesses of students' responses.

All of these comments are presumably intended to make a student feel good. But notice the different attributions they imply. The student's success or failure is attributed in some cases to uncontrollable abilities (being smart or not "good at" something); in other cases to controllable—and therefore changeable—student behaviours (hard work, lack of practice, effective or ineffective study strategies); and in still other cases to external, uncontrollable causes (a lucky break, a bad day).

Sometimes teachers communicate their attributions for students' successes and failure in more subtle ways—for instance, through the emotions they convey, such as pity and sympathy (Reyna, 2000; Reyna & Weiner, 2001; Weiner, 2000). Some teachers might even punish students for their poor performance (Reyna & Weiner, 2001).

How Expectations and Attributions Affect Classroom Performance

Most children and adolescents are well aware of their teachers' differential treatment of individual students and use such treatment to draw logical inferences about their own and others' abilities (Butler, 1994; Good & Nichols, 2001; R. S. Weinstein, 1993). When their teachers repeatedly give them low-ability messages, they may begin to see themselves as their teachers see them. Furthermore, their behaviour may mirror their self-perceptions; for example, they may exert little effort on academic tasks, or they may frequently misbehave in class (Marachi, Friedel, & Midgley, 2001; Murdock, 1999). In some cases, then, teachers' expectations and attributions may lead to a **self-fulfilling prophecy**: What teachers expect students to achieve becomes what students actually *do* achieve.

Self-fulfilling prophecy A situation in which one's expectations for an outcome either directly or indirectly lead to the expected result.

Certainly teacher expectations don't always lead to self-fulfilling prophecies. In some cases, teachers follow up on low expectations by offering the kinds of instruction and assistance that students need to improve, and so students *do* improve (Goldenberg, 1992). In other cases, students may develop an "I'll show *you*" attitude that spurs them on to greater effort and achievement than a teacher anticipated (Good & Nichols, 2001). In still other cases, assertive parents may step in and offer evidence that their children are more capable than a teacher initially thought (Good & Nichols, 2001).

So how prevalent are self-fulfilling prophecies? In other words, to what extent do teacher expectations affect students' classroom performance and overall academic growth? Research on this topic yields mixed results (Eccles et al., 1998; Goldenberg, 1992; R. Rosenthal, 1994). Some research indicates that girls, students from low-income families, and students from ethnic minority groups are more susceptible to teacher expectations than boys from Caucasian backgrounds (Graham, 1990; Jussim, Eccles, & Madon, 1996). Teacher expectations also appear to have a greater influence in the early elementary school years (Grades 1 and 2), in the first year of secondary school, and, more generally, within the first few weeks of school—in other words, at times when students are entering new and unfamiliar school environments (Jussim et al., 1996; Raudenbush, 1984; R. S. Weinstein, Madison, & Kuklinski, 1995).

University researchers in Alberta, J. Lupart, C. Barva, and E. Cannon, explored the relationship between personal values, achievement-related choices, and life satisfaction in two groups of high-achieving women to enhance understanding of female career choice and decision making. One major finding was the importance of sex-specific subjective task value in making achievement-related choices (i.e., the importance of values, intrinsic interests, self-image, and long-term goals). Compared to males, females in the study were more likely to emphasize personal values and interests as important influences in their occupational choice.

Forming Productive Expectations and Attributions for Student Performance

Sometimes teacher expectations are based on completely erroneous information. More often, however, teachers' initial impressions of students are reasonably accurate. In the latter case, a problem emerges when teachers don't *change* their expectations in light of new data (Cooper & Good, 1983; Good & Brophy, 1994). The constructive nature of learning and memory often gets in the way here: People's prior beliefs and expectations influence how they interpret new information.

Unfortunately, teachers' beliefs about students' ability, as well as their attributions for students' performance, are sometimes affected by sex and ethnic stereotypes (Deaux, 1984; C. B. Murray & Jackson, 1982/1983; Reyna, 2000). For instance, a high school math teacher who believes that "girls aren't good in math" is likely to express pity and offer considerable help with classroom tasks. A Grade 4 teacher who believes that a particular ethnic group is "lazy" and "doesn't care about education" is apt to blame members of that group for their own failures and so give them little emotional support or assistance.

As a teacher, you are most likely to facilitate your students' learning and to motivate them to achieve at high levels if you have optimistic expectations for their performance (within realistic limits, of course) and if you attribute their successes and failures to things over which either they or you have control (*their* effort, *your* instructional methods, etc.). Several strategies are helpful here:

■ *Remember that teachers can definitely make a difference.* You are more likely to have high expectations for your students when you are confident in your ability to help them achieve academic and social success (Ashton, 1985; R. S. Weinstein et al., 1995). It is important to keep in mind that ability can and does change over time, especially when environmental conditions are conducive to such change. For this reason, you should take an *incremental view* of your students' intelligence and other abilities (Pintrich & Schunk, 2002). Accordingly, you must continually reassess your expectations and attributions for individual students, modifying them as new evidence presents itself.

■ *Look for strengths in every student.* Sometimes students' weaknesses are all too evident. It is essential that you also look for the many unique qualities and strengths that your students will inevitably have. All students have their strengths; for instance, some are good readers, others are inquisitive scientists, and still others are creative storytellers. As a teacher, you are more likely to have high expectations for students when you look for things they do *well* rather than focus entirely on their weaknesses.

■ *Communicate optimistic and controllable attributions.* As a teacher, you must be careful about the attributions you make about student performance. Probably the optimal course of action is to attribute success partly to a relatively stable ability (thus promoting optimism about future success) and partly to such controllable factors as effort and learning strategies (thereby emphasizing that continued success will come only with hard work). When considering possible causes for failure, however, you should focus primarily on factors that are internal, unstable, and controllable; thus, attributions for failures should focus on effort and learning strategies, rather than on low ability (which students are likely to believe is stable and uncontrollable) or external factors (Pressley, Borkowski, & Schneider, 1987; Schunk, 1983a; C. E. Weinstein, Hagen, & Meyer, 1991).

You can communicate optimistic attributions and expectations for student performance through statements such as these:

■ "You've done very well. Obviously you're good at this, and you've been trying very hard to get better."
■ "Your project shows a lot of talent and a lot of hard work."
■ "The more you practise, the better you will get."

Studies have shown that when students' failures are consistently attributed to ineffective learning strategies or a lack of effort, rather than to low ability or uncontrollable external factors, and when new strategies or increased effort *do* produce success, then students work harder, persist longer in the face of failure, and seek help when they need it (Dweck & Elliott, 1983; Eccles & Wigfield, 1985; Graham, 1991; Paris & Paris, 2001).

■ *Learn more about students' backgrounds and home environments.* Teachers are most likely to have low expectations for students' performance when they have formed rigid stereotypes about students from certain ethnic or socioeconomic groups (McLoyd, 1998; R. E. Snow et al., 1996). Such stereotypes often stem from ignorance about students' cultures and home environments (K. L. Alexander, Entwisle, & Thompson, 1987). So education is the key here: Learn as much as you can about your students' backgrounds and local communities. When you have a clear picture of their activities, habits, values, and families, you are far more likely to think of them as individuals than as stereotypical members of any particular group.

- *Assess students' progress regularly and objectively.* Because your expectations for students' performance are likely to colour your informal evaluations of what they actually accomplish, you need to identify more objective ways of assessing learning and achievement. Furthermore, you should assess students' progress frequently, so that you have ongoing and reasonably accurate information with which to make instructional decisions (Goldenberg, 1992).

Considering Diversity in Motivation, Affect, and Cognition

We've seen numerous instances of student diversity in our discussion of cognitive factors in motivation. For instance, we've learned that students have widely varying personal interests and will find greater or lesser value in particular subject areas. Furthermore, the degree to which students have high self-efficacy, mastery goals, productive attributions, and a mastery orientation will influence whether they prefer challenges, persist at difficult tasks, and take failure in stride. Let's look at some of the specific ways in which the cognitive aspects of motivation are likely to vary because of ethnicity, sex, socioeconomic background, and special educational needs.

Ethnic Differences

Immigrant children and children of immigrants represent a growing component of the Canadian population, and will make up an increasing proportion of Canada's population in the future. It is estimated that today, 20 percent of Canada's young people under age 18 are immigrants or children of immigrants (Canadian Council on Social Development, 2006). They tend to be concentrated in a few major cities across Canada (Toronto, Vancouver, and Montreal), and many are living in neighbourhoods of high immigrant density within those cities. Many live in poverty. Measures of school success, especially dropout rates, indicate that immigrant children and youth are falling

---

INTO THE CLASSROOM   *Promoting Productive Attributions*

Communicate high expectations for student performance.

In September a high school teacher tells his class, "Next spring, I will ask you to write a 15-page research paper. Fifteen pages may seem like a lot now, but in the next few months we will work on the various skills you will need to research and write your paper. By April, 15 pages won't seem like a big deal at all!"

Attribute students' successes to a combination of high ability and such controllable factors as effort and learning strategies.

In a unit on basketball, a physical education teacher tells his class, "From what I've seen so far, you all have the capability to play a good game of basketball. And it appears that many of you have been practising after school."

Attribute students' successes to effort only when they have actually exerted that effort.

A teacher observes that his students complete a particular assignment more quickly and easily than he expected. He briefly acknowledges their success and then moves on to a more challenging task.

Attribute students' failures to factors that are controllable and easily changed.

A high school student seeks his teacher's advice as to how he might do better in her class. "I know you can do better than you have been, Frank," she replies. "I'm wondering if part of the problem might be that, with your part-time job and all your extracurricular activities, you just don't have enough time to study. Let's sit down before school tomorrow and look at what and how much you're doing to prepare for class."

When students fail despite obvious effort, attribute their failures to a lack of effective strategies and then help them acquire such strategies.

A student in an advanced science class is having difficulty on the teacher's challenging weekly quizzes. The student works diligently on her science every night and attends the after-school help sessions her teacher offers on Thursdays, yet to no avail. Her teacher observes that the student is trying to learn the material by rote—an ineffective strategy for answering the higher-level questions the quizzes typically ask—and helps the student develop strategies that promote more meaningful learning.

behind their peers in education. A study using data from the National Longitudinal Study compared the academic performance of children of immigrants in Canada to that of children of non-immigrants (Worswick, 2001). Results indicated that despite the economic disadvantage that some immigrants face, children of immigrants generally achieve at levels commensurate with their peers, although they may initially have weaker reading skills. Interestingly, children of immigrants who speak English or French as their first language tend to outperform children of non-immigrants. Moreover, children of immigrants attain more university education than their Canadian-born peers.

Researchers have found that students' motivation often varies as a function of their ethnic background. For instance, although all students almost certainly have a need for relatedness, they may satisfy this need in somewhat different ways. In comparison to other groups, Asian students tend to spend less time socializing with their peers and place greater importance on gaining their teachers' attention and approval (Dien, 1998; L. Steinberg, 1996). Furthermore, whereas Asian students are likely to have friends who encourage academic achievement, students from many other ethnic groups (boys especially) may be subject to considerable peer pressure *not* to achieve at high levels. An additional factor in students' need for relatedness is their family ties: Students from many ethnic groups have especially strong loyalties to their family and may have been raised to achieve for their community, rather than just for themselves as individuals.

Ethnicity and sex can be important factors influencing students' motivation, yet all students have certain basic motives, such as the need for self-worth and relatedness.

Students from various ethnic backgrounds may also differ in their levels and sources of anxiety. For instance, students from some Asian families may feel considerable family pressure to perform well in school, to the point where they experience debilitating test anxiety (Pang, 1995). And students who are recent immigrants are frequently anxious about a variety of things in their new country—how to behave, how to interpret others' behaviours, how to make friends, and, more generally, how to make sense of the strange new culture in which they now find themselves (Dien, 1998; Igoa, 1995).

Children and adolescents from most ethnic groups place high value on getting a good education, but those from some minority groups have lower expectancies for academic and professional success, perhaps as a result of the discriminatory practices they often encounter in society (Eccles et al., 1998; Fordham & Ogbu, 1986). Furthermore, students from different groups may define academic success differently and so set different goals for themselves. For instance, Asian students, on average, shoot for higher grades than students in other ethnic groups, in part because, they report, their parents would be angry if they got grades lower than As (Steinberg, 1996). Students raised in cultures that value group achievement over individual achievement (e.g., many First Nations groups) may focus their goals not on how much they alone can improve, but instead on how much they and their classmates can improve (Kaplan, 1998).

Students' ethnic backgrounds influence their attributions as well. For instance, students from Asian backgrounds are more likely to attribute classroom success and failure to unstable factors—effort in the case of academic achievement, and temporary situational factors in the case of appropriate or inappropriate behaviours—than students brought up in mainstream Western culture (R. D. Hess, Chih-Mei, & McDevitt, 1987; Lillard, 1997; L. Steinberg, 1996). To some extent, racial prejudice may contribute to learned helplessness: Some students may begin to believe that, because of the colour of their skin, they have little chance of success no matter what they do (Sue & Chin, 1983; van Laar, 2000).

For more information on immigrant children and youth, see the Canadian Coalition for Immigrant Children and Youth website at www.lerc.educ.ubc.ca/CCICY/.

Sex Differences

We are apt to see sex differences in motivation as well. For example, girls are more likely than boys to have a high need for affiliation; perhaps for this reason, they achieve at higher levels when their teachers encourage co-operation rather than competition (Block, 1983; Eccles, 1989; Inglehart et al.,

1994). Girls are also more concerned about doing well in school: They work harder on assignments, earn higher grades, engage in less self-handicapping, and are more likely to graduate from high school (Halpern, 1992; McCall, 1994; Urdan & Midgley, 2001). We will typically find more boys than girls achieving at levels far below their potential (Eccles et al., 1998; McCall, 1994). Despite such differences, boys tend to have greater confidence in their academic ability and greater expectations for their future success (D. A. Cole et al., 1999; Deaux, 1984; Eccles et al., 1998).

Boys and girls may find greater or lesser value in various academic domains depending on whether they view these domains as being stereotypically appropriate for boys or girls. Many (but by no means all) students perceive some domains (e.g., writing, instrumental music) to be for girls and others (e.g., math, science) to be for boys (Eccles et al., 1998; Kahle, 1983; Pajares & Valiante, 1999), and such perceptions invariably influence their effort and course selection.

A sex difference appears in students' long-term goals as well. As we have seen, girls tend to have lower long-term aspirations for themselves; this is true despite the fact that they have higher average school achievement than boys. Two research findings may help explain this seeming paradox. First, girls sometimes report lower self-efficacy for academic tasks than boys do, especially in stereotypically male domains. When sex differences in self-efficacy are seen, they may reflect a tendency for girls to *under*estimate their competence and for boys to *over*estimate it (D. A. Cole et al., 1999; Eccles et al., 1998; Middleton, 1999).

> Have you observed this difference in the males and females you know? Can you think of individuals who are exceptions to the pattern?

Second, girls are more likely to be discouraged by their failures than boys are (Dweck, 1986), a difference we can explain, at least in part, by looking at sex differences in attributions. Some research studies indicate that boys have a tendency to attribute their successes to a fairly stable ability and their failures to lack of effort, thus having the attitude that *I know I can do this*. Girls show the reverse pattern: They attribute their successes to effort and their failures to lack of ability, believing that *I don't know whether I can keep on doing it, because I'm not very good at this type of thing*. Such differences, which can appear even when boys' and girls' previous levels of achievement are equivalent, are more frequently observed in stereotypically male domains such as mathematics and sports (Eccles & Jacobs, 1986; Fennema, 1987; Stipek, 1984; Vermeer et al., 2000).

As we work to encourage high levels of motivation in all of our students, we may want to focus our efforts in somewhat different directions for males and females. For boys, we may need to stress the relationship of high classroom achievement to their own long-term goals. For girls, we may need to encourage openmindedness about a wide variety of career options (including traditionally "masculine" ones) and demonstrate quite clearly that these options are, with effort and appropriate strategies, well within their grasp.

Socioeconomic Differences

As we teachers consider how students from different groups are likely to be different, we must remember that those who are *least* likely to be motivated to do well in school—and those who are at greatest risk for failing and dropping out of school—are students from low socioeconomic backgrounds. It is for these students especially that we must make a concerted effort to make school a source of pleasure, companionship, emotional support, and success.

When working with students from lower socioeconomic backgrounds, you should remember that two conditions—self-efficacy and self-determination—are probably essential for intrinsic motivation. You are most likely to enhance students' self-efficacy if you have high (yet realistic) expectations for their performance and if you provide the academic support through which they can meet those expectations (Brophy & Evertson, 1976). And when you give them a sense of self-determination and control over their lives—for instance, when you involve them in classroom decision making and teach them effective ways of bringing about change in their local communities—they will attend school more regularly and achieve at higher levels (deCharms, 1972; NCSS Task Force on Ethnic Studies Curriculum Guidelines, 1992).

In addition, you can increase the perceived value of school activities by making those activities relevant to students' own lives and experiences (P. A. Alexander et al., 1994; Knapp et al., 1990; Tobias, 1994; Wlodkowski & Ginsberg, 1995). As you present new topics, draw on the knowledge that the students are apt to have, thereby increasing the likelihood of meaningful learning; for instance, you might keep in mind that these students are more likely to have encountered dogs and cats than elephants and zebras, more likely to have seen a grocery store or city park than a dairy farm or airport. You should also relate classroom tasks and activities to students' specific, day-to-day needs and interests; for example, it is important to teach academic subject matter within the context of authentic activities as often as we can. And you can occasionally solicit students' ideas about issues and questions that they'd like to study in class.

Accommodating Students in Inclusive Settings

Students with special educational needs will typically be among those who show the greatest diversity in motivation. For example, students with learning disabilities may be easily discouraged by challenging tasks, yet students who are gifted may become bored if classroom activities *don't* challenge their abilities (Mercer, 1997; Winner, 2000b). Canadian researchers, McInerney and Kerns, at the University of Victoria, have linked motivation to the performance of children with ADHD. Furthermore, although some students with special needs are quite adept at social relationships, others will have greater-than-average difficulty satisfying their need for relatedness, perhaps as a result of few opportunities to interact with age-mates (true for many students with physical disabilities), poor social skills (true for many students with emotional and behavioural disorders), or interests and ability levels that are significantly different from those of classmates (true for some students who are highly gifted). Table 9.3 identifies additional ways in which

Research shows that adolescents with learning disabilities frequently exhibit anxiety in mastery situations, fear failure, and have a low expectancy for success based on past performances. Strategies to facilitate independence and motivation in students with learning disabilities are listed on the website of the Learning Disabilities Association of Canada: www.ldac-taac.ca.

TABLE 9.3 STUDENTS IN INCLUSIVE SETTINGS

Enhancing Motivation in Students in the Inclusive Classroom

CATEGORY	CHARACTERISTICS YOU MIGHT OBSERVE	SUGGESTED CLASSROOM STRATEGIES
Students with specific cognitive or academic difficulties	• Less intrinsic motivation to succeed at academic tasks • High test anxiety • Reluctance to ask questions or seek assistance, especially at the secondary level	• Use extrinsic reinforcers to encourage students' classroom effort and achievement; gradually phase them out as students show signs of intrinsic motivation. • Minimize anxiety-arousing statements and procedures during testing situations (see Chapter 12). • Offer assistance when you think that students may really need it, but refrain from offering help when you know that students are capable of succeeding on their own.
Students with social or behavioural problems	• Desire to succeed in the classroom, despite behaviours that may indicate a lack of motivation • Stronger desire for power over classmates than for affiliation with them (for some students with emotional and behavioural disorders) • Need for predictability; debilitating anxiety in new or unpredictable situations (for students with autism) • Excessive anxiety and uneasiness (for students with anxiety disorders)	• Provide the guidance and support that students need to succeed at classroom tasks. • Help students discover the benefits of equitable and prosocial (rather than domineering) interactions with classmates. • Create a structured and predictable classroom environment, especially for students with autism.
Students with general delays in cognitive and social functioning	• Less intrinsic motivation than age-mates; responsiveness to extrinsic motivators • Tendency to give up easily in the face of difficulty	• Use extrinsic reinforcers to encourage productive behaviours; gradually phase them out as students show signs of intrinsic motivation. • Reinforce persistence as well as success.
Students with physical or sensory challenges	• Fewer opportunities to satisfy affiliation needs	• Assign "buddies" who can help students with assigned tasks or provide companionship at lunch and on the playground. • Collaborate with parents to promote interaction with classmates outside of school.
Students showing evidence of giftedness, talent, or high performance	• High intrinsic motivation (e.g., curiosity about how things work) • Strong commitment to specific (especially self-chosen) tasks • Persistence in the face of failure (although some may give up easily if they aren't accustomed to failure) • Social isolation (for some students who are exceptionally gifted) • Possible self-handicapping if there is a strong desire to affiliate with low-achieving peers	• Provide opportunities for students to pursue complex tasks and activities over an extended time. • Give assignments that students find stimulating and challenging. • Form special-interest groups for students who might otherwise be socially isolated. • Keep students' exceptional achievements confidential if their friends don't value high achievement.

Sources: Beirne-Smith et al., 2002; B. Clark, 1997; Covington, 1992; Friedel, 1993; Good & Brophy, 1994; A. W. Gottfried, Gottfried, Bathurst, & Guerin 1994; Heward, 2000; Mercer, 1997; Morgan & Jenson, 1988; Patrick, 1997; Patton, Blackbourn, & Fad, 1996; B. N. Phillips, Pitcher, Worsham, & Miller, 1980; Piirto, 1999; S. Powell & Nelson, 1997; Renzulli, 1978; Sanborn, 1979; G. F. Schultz & Switzky, 1990; Turnbull et al., 1999; Winner, 1997, 2000b.

students with exceptionalities are likely to show different motivational characteristics and behaviours than their peers; it also offers suggestions for addressing these students' unique needs.

Students with specific or general academic difficulties (e.g., those with learning disabilities, those with mental retardation) may also show signs of learned helplessness with regard to classroom tasks, especially if their past efforts have repeatedly met with failure (Deshler & Schumaker, 1988; Jacobsen, Lowery, & DuCette, 1986; Seligman, 1975). Students who have difficulty getting along with their classmates (e.g., those with emotional and behavioural disorders) may inappropriately attribute their social failures to factors beyond their control. Table 9.4 presents a summary of these and other motivational patterns in students with special needs.

In recent years, special educators have become especially concerned about the need for students with disabilities to develop a sense of self-determination—to believe that they have some control over the direction that their lives take (Sands & Wehmeyer, 1996). Many of these students, especially those with physical or sensory challenges, may live in sheltered environments in which other people are calling most of the shots (Wehmeyer, 1996). As a teacher, you can do many simple things to enhance the self-determination that these students feel; for instance, you can let them make choices and set some of their own goals, help them develop skills that enable them to gain increasing independence, and teach the many self-regulation strategies that we identified in Chapter 8 (Abery & Zajac, 1996; L. E. Powers et al., 1996).

TABLE 9.4   **STUDENTS IN INCLUSIVE SETTINGS**

Promoting "Cognitions That Motivate" Students in the Inclusive Classroom

CATEGORY	CHARACTERISTICS YOU MIGHT OBSERVE	SUGGESTED CLASSROOM STRATEGIES
Students with specific cognitive or academic difficulties	• Low self-efficacy for many classroom tasks • Tendency to attribute poor achievement to low ability rather than to more controllable factors; tendency to attribute successes to external causes (e.g., luck) • Tendency to give up easily; learned helplessness regarding performance on some classroom tasks	• Establish challenging yet realistic goals for achievement. • Teach effective learning strategies and encourage students to attribute their successes to such strategies. • Encourage students to develop more productive attributions regarding their achievement difficulties (e.g., attributing failures to insufficient effort or ineffective strategies).
Students with social or behavioural problems	• Tendency to interpret praise as an attempt to control them (when students exhibit defiance or oppositional behaviour) • Perception of classroom tasks as having little relevance to personal needs and goals • Tendency to attribute negative consequences to uncontrollable factors (things just "happen")	• When students are concerned about control issues, use subtle reinforcers (e.g., leave notes describing productive behaviours) rather than more obvious and seemingly controlling ones. • Provide choices about academic activities as a way of increasing a sense of self-determination. • Relate the curriculum to specific needs and interests that students may have. • Teach behaviours that lead to desired consequences; stress cause–effect relationships between actions and outcomes.
Students with general delays in cognitive and social functioning	• Limited (if any) ability to conceptualize long-term goals • Tendency to attribute poor achievement to low ability or to external sources rather than to more controllable factors; in some situations, a sense of learned helplessness	• Set specific, short-term goals for performance. • Help students see the relationship between their own actions and the consequences that result.
Students with physical or sensory challenges	• Low sense of self-determination regarding the course that their lives are taking	• Give students some choices within the curriculum. • Teach self-regulating behaviours and independence skills.
Students showing evidence of giftedness, talent, or high performance	• High self-efficacy • Boredom when classroom tasks don't challenge their abilities • May seek out challenges on their own • Variety of interests, sometimes pursued with a passion • Higher than average goal-directedness	• Encourage students to set high goals, but without expecting perfection. • Promote learned industriousness by assigning a series of tasks that require considerable effort and persistence. • Do not publicly use them or their work any more than others as models for other students to emulate.

Sources: Beirne-Smith et al., 2002; M. Carr & Borkowski, 1989; B. Clark, 1997; Duchardt, Deshler, & Schumaker, 1995; Dunlap et al., 1994; Foster-Johnson, Ferro, & Dunlap, 1994; A. E. Gottfried et al., 1994; Heward, 2000; Hoge & Renzulli, 1993; Jacobsen et al., 1986; Knowlton, 1995; D. P. Morgan & Jenson, 1988; Piirto, 1999; S. Powell & Nelson, 1997; Sands & Wehmeyer, 1996; Turnbull et al., 1999; U.S. Department of Education, 1992; Winner, 1997, 2000a, 2000b; Wong, 1991b.

TEACHING CONSTRUCTIONS

Now that you've considered various motivational factors that affect student learning, let's revisit the case study presented at the beginning of this chapter:

- As a teacher what will you do to enhance Michael's and other students' interest and motivation especially in classes that may be less intrinsically motivating for some students?
- What can you do as a teacher to alter Michael's beliefs in his successes and failures and also his attitudes toward particular academic activities?
- Describe how beliefs about oneself as a learner interact with achievement in the classroom. How would this apply to Michael?

KEY CONCEPTS

motivation (p. 220)
situated motivation (p. 220)
extrinsic motivation (p. 221)
intrinsic motivation (p. 221)
trait theory of motivation (p. 222)
achievement motivation (p. 223)
drive (p. 223)
self-worth (p. 225)
self-handicapping (p. 225)
need for relatedness (p. 226)
need for affiliation (p. 226)
need for approval (p. 227)
affect (p. 228)
hot cognition (p. 228)
anxiety (p. 229)

state anxiety (p. 229)
trait anxiety (p. 229)
facilitating anxiety (p. 229)
debilitating anxiety (p. 229)
threat (p. 230)
challenge (p. 230)
self-efficacy (p. 232)
self-determination (p. 232)
expectancy (p. 236)
value (p. 236)
internalized motivation (p. 237)
interest (p. 238)
situational interest (p. 238)
personal interest (p. 238)
core goal (p. 240)

mastery goal (p. 240)
performance goal (p. 240)
performance-approach goal (p. 240)
performance-avoidance goal (p. 240)
work-avoidance goal (p. 242)
attribution (p. 245)
attribution theory (p. 245)
entity view of intelligence (p. 247)
incremental view of intelligence (p. 247)
learned industriousness (p. 247)
mastery orientation (p. 248)
learned helplessness (p. 248)
self-fulfilling prophecy (p. 250)

10 Instructional Strategies

CASE STUDY: BUILDING COMMUNITIES

TEACHING CONNECTIONS

OVERVIEW OF INSTRUCTIONAL STRATEGIES

PLANNING FOR INSTRUCTION
Identifying the Goals of Instruction • Conducting a Task Analysis • Developing a Lesson Plan

EXPOSITORY APPROACHES
Lectures and Textbooks • Mastery Learning • Direct Instruction • Information and Communication Technology Instruction • E-Learning and Online Research

HANDS-ON APPROACHES: DISCOVERY LEARNING AND IN-CLASS ACTIVITIES
Discovery Learning • In-Class Activities

INTERACTIVE AND COLLABORATIVE APPROACHES
Teacher Questions • Class Discussions • Cognitive Strategy Teaching • Computer Supported Collaborative Learning • Co-operative Learning • Peer Tutoring

TAKING STUDENT DIVERSITY INTO ACCOUNT
Considering Group Differences • Accommodating Students in Inclusive Settings

TEACHING CONSTRUCTIONS

KEY CONCEPTS

CASE STUDY Building Communities

Grade 4 teacher Deborah Hamilton has recently begun a social studies unit on building communities. Today's lesson focuses on how it feels to be a new person in a town or city and what can be done to address this issue.

"Being alone in a new place can be scary, boring, and lonely," Ms. Hamilton tells her class. She has her students think to themselves for a minute about being alone in a new place and what they might do to about it. After a minute of self-reflection, Ms. Hamilton tells her students to turn to a student beside them and share with each other the things they thought about that might help them with their feelings of boredom and loneliness. After a few minutes of sharing their views with one another, the students are asked by Ms. Hamilton to share their ideas with the entire class. The following discussion ensues with the students and Ms. Hamilton.

Ms. H.: What is one thing a person could do if he or she is lonely?

Samantha: One thing I would want to do right away is make some friends!

Jason: I would want to do something about my fear of being alone.

Ms. H: These are two very good suggestions. Does anyone else have any other ideas?

Chad: I guess I would want to get involved in something.

Ms. H: Well class, I think these are some very good beginning ideas about what you can do when you are by yourself in a new place. I would like the class to split up into three groups, and you can discuss with one another things you would need to consider with respect to making friends, dealing with fear, and getting involved. Everyone with last names beginning with the letters "A" to "H" go to this corner and get ready to discuss considerations for making friends. Everyone with last names beginning with the letters "I" to "P" go to this corner and get ready to discuss considerations for dealing with fear. Everyone with last names beginning with the letters "Q" to "Z" go to this corner and get ready to discuss considerations for getting involved.

Once all of the students have gone to their respective corners of the room, Ms. Hamilton distributes journals to each group, in which students can write their responses. She gives them a couple of minutes to get organized and reminds them that they have to pick people for different task roles—for example, facilitator of discussion, recorder, checker for understanding, time keeper, noise monitor, and consensus taker. Also, she reminds everyone that they have 20 minutes to discuss their subject matter and that they must be prepared to share their ideas with the rest of the class after this 20-minute period.

TEACHING CONNECTIONS

In this chapter, we will consider how planning and carrying out instruction are essential aspects of effective teaching and have an impact on what students ultimately learn and achieve. It is important to keep in mind that planning, instruction, the classroom environment, and assessment practices affect one another and that they both influence and are influenced by student behaviours and characteristics (see Figure 10.1). Consider the following questions as you read and make connections between research and teaching practice:

- How can you plan effectively for instruction, both on a daily basis and over the course of the school year?
- How can you effectively teach new material through *expository instruction*—that is, by directly presenting the information you want your students to know, understand, and apply?
- How can you also help students acquire new knowledge and skills through more *hands-on* approaches?
- What strategies can maximize students' ability to learn *from one another* as well as from the teacher?
- How can you best accommodate students' diverse backgrounds, characteristics, and needs when you plan and implement classroom instruction?
- Are the students in Ms. Hamilton's class engaged in the lesson? What evidence is there to indicate active learning?
- What specific instructional strategies is Ms. Hamilton using to engage and motivate her students?

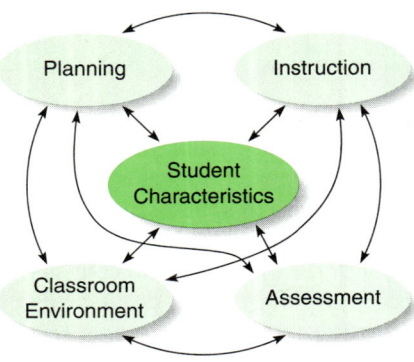

FIGURE 10.1 Planning, instruction, the classroom environment, assessment, and student characteristics are not independent; each one influences the others.

Overview of Instructional Strategies

The students in Ms. Hamilton's class are clearly engaged in the lesson (e.g., they are actively responding to her questions). Ms. Hamilton uses several collaborative learning strategies (e.g., "Think–Pair–Share," "Corners") and structures learning activities to ensure that the students practise social and cognitive skills as they are introduced in group work (see Andrews & Lupart, 2000). By establishing and using roles such as facilitator, recorder, and consensus taker, Ms. Hamilton provides meaningful context for practice. When skills such as these become natural, students will become more independent, requiring less direction from the teacher. Moreover, time on task will increase, and the quality of discussion and learning will improve.

Planning for Instruction

Effective teaching begins long before students enter the classroom. Good teachers engage in considerable advance planning: They identify the knowledge and skills they want their students to acquire, determine an appropriate sequence in which to foster such knowledge and skills, and develop classroom activities that will promote maximal learning and keep students continually motivated and on task. Here we consider three aspects of instructional planning: identifying the goals of instruction, conducting a task analysis, and developing lesson plans.

Identifying the Goals of Instruction

An essential part of planning is identifying the specific things you want your students to learn during a lesson or unit, as well as the things you want them to accomplish over the course of the semester or school year. Educators use a variety of terms for such goals (e.g., *outcomes, proficiencies, targets, benchmarks*), but the term **instructional objectives** is probably the most common.

When you identify your objectives before you begin teaching, you are in a better position to choose an effective method of instruction; you can also develop an appropriate means of evaluating your students' achievement. For example, if your objective for a unit on addition is *knowledge* of number facts, then you may want to use drill and practice (perhaps flash cards, perhaps gamelike computer software) to enhance students' automaticity for these facts, and you may want to use a timed test to measure students' ability to recall them quickly and easily. But if your objective is *application* of number facts, then you may want to focus instruction and assessment methods on word problems, or perhaps on activities involving real objects, hands-on measurements, and so on.

Students, too, benefit from knowing the objectives for a lesson or unit. When they know what their teacher hopes they will accomplish, they can make more informed decisions about how to focus their efforts and allocate their study time, and they can more effectively monitor their comprehension as they read and study (Gronlund, 2000; McAshan, 1979). For example, if you tell students that you expect them to "apply mathematics procedures to everyday situations," they will probably think about and study mathematics very differently than if you were to tell them to "know all the definitions by heart."

Choosing Appropriate Objectives

School districts typically identify numerous objectives for students at different grade levels. Yet as teachers, you will undoubtedly add your own objectives to any list that the school district provides. For example, you may want to use classifications (*taxonomies*) of knowledge and skills that have been developed by educators.

When students are actively involved in designing and carrying out classroom projects, they can develop important self-regulatory skills.

Instructional objective A statement describing a final goal or outcome of instruction.

Have you ever been in a situation where you couldn't figure out what a teacher expected you to learn? Do you remember feeling confused, frustrated, or otherwise "lost" in that situation?

Why is the third domain called *affective*?

You don't necessarily want to limit your objectives just to the acquisition and use of information—in other words, to the **cognitive domain**. Other important objectives might involve body movements and actions (the **psychomotor domain**), and still others might involve students' feelings, attitudes, and values about what they learn (the **affective domain**). Educators have developed taxonomies in each of these domains that describe a variety of possible educational objectives; Table 10.1 presents three classic ones. Although certainly not exhaustive lists, such taxonomies can nevertheless give an idea of the kinds of objectives to consider (Krathwohl, 1994).

Instructional objectives should be developed that can guide you as you plan instructional activities and assessment procedures. Following are several strategies for developing useful objectives:

- *Include objectives at varying degrees of complexity and sophistication.* The taxonomies presented in Table 10.1 include activities that range from very simple to fairly complex. For instance, the taxonomy for the cognitive domain (often called **Bloom's taxonomy**) includes both lower-level skills (remembering, understanding) and higher-level skills (applying, analyzing, evaluating, creating). You will undoubtedly want to include *both* kinds of skills in your objectives. As an illustration, consider these objectives for a lesson on the physics of light:
  - Students will describe laws related to the reflection and refraction of light.
  - Students will identify examples of reflection and refraction in their own lives (e.g., mirrors, eyeglasses).
  - Students will use the law of reflection and laws of geometry to determine the actual location of objects viewed in a mirror.
  - Students will use the law of refraction to explain how microscopes and telescopes make objects appear larger.

Although all four objectives lie within the cognitive domain, they reflect different levels of that domain. The first objective focuses exclusively on knowledge/remembering of separate facts that students might conceivably learn by rote, in isolation from anything else they know. But the other three objectives, which involve application and analysis, should encourage students to engage in meaningful learning and can therefore promote effective concept learning, transfer, and problem solving.

- *Describe the expected outcomes of instruction.* Consider these objectives for a French class:
  - Students will study the meanings of French words.
  - Students will practise pronouncing French words.
  - Students will learn how to conjugate French verbs.

These objectives describe what students will do during French class; in other words, they describe learning *processes*. Yet objectives are usually more helpful when they tell us what students should be able to do at the end of instruction—in other words, when they describe *outcomes* (Gronlund, 2000). With this point in mind, the French class objectives may be revised as follows:

- Students will give the English meanings of French words.
- Students will pronounce French words correctly.
- Students will correctly conjugate common French verbs in the present and past tenses.

- *Identify both short-term and long-term goals.* Ideally, your instructional goals should include both **short-term objectives**—those that can be accomplished within a limited period of time (perhaps within a single lesson or unit, and certainly within a single school year)—and **long-term objectives**—those that require months or years of instruction and practice before they are achieved (Brophy & Alleman, 1991; N. S. Cole, 1990; Gronlund, 2000). When you want students to use effective learning strategies as they study, read critically rather than take everything at face value, and apply scientific methods as they try to understand and explain the world around them, you are setting long-term objectives.

Some short-term objectives are "minimum essentials": Students *must* accomplish them before proceeding to the next unit, course, or grade level (Gronlund, 2000). For example, elementary school students must know how to add before they move to multiplication, and high school students must know the symbols for the chemical elements before they learn how to symbolize

Cognitive domain The domain of learning tasks that includes knowledge of information, as well as ways of thinking about and using that information.

Psychomotor domain The domain of learning tasks that includes simple and complex physical movements and actions.

Affective domain The domain of learning tasks that includes attitudes and values about the things one learns.

Bloom's taxonomy A taxonomy in which six learning tasks, varying in degrees of complexity, are identified for the cognitive domain: remembering, understanding, applying, analyzing, evaluating, and creating.

Short-term objective An objective that can typically be accomplished within the course of a single lesson or unit.

Long-term objective An objective that requires months or years of instruction and practice to be accomplished.

TABLE 10.1   COMPARE/CONTRAST

Writing Objectives at Different Levels and in Different Domains

LEVEL AND DEFINITION	EXAMPLES
The Cognitive Domain (Bloom's Taxonomy) (adapted from Bloom, Engelhart, Furst, Hill, & Krathwohl, 1956; revised by Anderson & Krathwohl, 2001)	
1. *Remembering* (previous labelled Knowledge): Rote memorizing of information in a basically word-for-word fashion	• Reciting definitions of terms • Recognizing faces of classmates • Remembering lists of items
2. *Understanding* (Comprehension): Translating information into one's own words	• Rewording a definition • Paraphrasing a rule
3. *Applying:* Using information in a new situation	• Applying mathematical principles to the solution of word problems • Applying psychological theories of learning to educational practice
4. *Analyzing:* Breaking information down into its constituent parts	• Discovering the assumptions underlying a philosophical essay • Identifying fallacies in a logical argument
5. *Evaluating:* Placing a value judgment on data	• Critiquing a theory • Examining the internal and external validity of an experiment
6. *Creating* (Synthesis): Constructing something new by integrating several pieces of information	• Developing a theory • Presenting a logical defence of a particular viewpoint within a debate
The Psychomotor Domain (adapted from Harrow, 1972)	
1. *Reflex movements:* Responding to a stimulus involuntarily, without conscious thought	• Ducking to avoid being hit by an oncoming object • Shifting weight to help maintain one's balance
2. *Basic-fundamental movements:* Making basic voluntary movements directed toward a particular purpose	• Walking • Holding a pencil
3. *Perceptual abilities:* Responding appropriately to information received through the senses	• Following a moving object with one's eyes • Maintaining eye-hand coordination
4. *Physical abilities:* Developing general abilities in the areas of endurance, strength, flexibility, and agility	• Running a long distance • Exercising with weights • Changing direction quickly
5. *Skilled movements:* Performing a complex action with some proficiency or mastery	• Swimming • Throwing a football • Sawing a piece of wood
6. *Nondiscursive communication:* Communicating feelings and emotions through bodily actions	• Doing pantomime • Dancing to communicate the mood of a musical piece
The Affective Domain (adapted from Krathwohl, Bloom, & Masia, 1964)	
1. *Receiving:* Being aware of, or paying attention to, something	• Recognizing that there may be two sides to a story • Knowing that there are differences among people of different cultural backgrounds
2. *Responding:* Making an active and willing response to something	• Obeying playground rules • Reading books for pleasure
3. *Valuing:* Consistently demonstrating interest in a particular activity so that ongoing involvement in or commitment to the activity is reflected	• Writing a letter to a newspaper regarding an issue one feels strongly about • Consistently eating a balanced diet
4. *Organization:* Integrating a new value into one's existing set of values and building a value system	• Forming judgments about the directions in which society should move • Setting priorities for one's life
5. *Characterization by a value or value complex:* Consistently behaving in accordance with an organized value system and integrating that system into a total philosophy of life	• Perceiving situations objectively, realistically, and with tolerance • Relying increasingly on scientific methods to answer questions about the world and society

chemical reactions. In contrast, many long-term objectives can be thought of as "developmental" in nature: They include skills and abilities that continue to evolve and improve throughout the school years, and perhaps into adulthood as well (Gronlund, 2000). Yet even when long-term objectives cannot be completely accomplished within the course of students' formal education, they are often among the most important ones to set for students and must therefore have a prominent place in your list of objectives.

■ *Incorporate opportunities for self-regulation and self-determination.* On some occasions, it is both appropriate and desirable for students to identify their *own* objectives. For example, different students might choose different authors to read, different athletic skills to master, or different art media to use. By allowing students to establish some of their own objectives, you are encouraging the *goal setting* that, from the perspective of social cognitive theory, is an important aspect of self-regulation. You are also fostering the sense of *self-determination* that many theorists believe is so critical for intrinsic motivation.

How do you break down a large instructional task—for example, a course in government, a unit on basketball, or a driver education class—into specific objectives? Several procedures known collectively as *task analysis* can help us analyze the components of a complex topic or skill.

Conducting a Task Analysis

Consider these two teachers:

> Ms. Begay plans to teach her Grade 3 students how to solve arithmetic word problems. She also wants to help her students learn more effectively from the things they read.

> Mr. McKenzie must teach the students in his high school driver education class how to drive a car safely through the city streets.

Both teachers have something in common: They want to teach complex topics or skills. Both of them should probably conduct a **task analysis**: They should identify the specific knowledge and behaviours necessary to master the subject matter in question. Such a task analysis can then guide them as they select the most appropriate methods and sequence in which to teach that subject matter.

Figure 10.2 illustrates three general approaches to task analysis (Jonassen, Hannum, & Tessmer, 1989):

Task analysis A process of identifying the specific knowledge and/or behaviours necessary to master a particular subject area or skill.

■ *Behavioural analysis.* One way of analyzing a complex task is to identify the specific behaviours required to perform it (much as a behaviourist might do). For example, Mr. McKenzie can identify the actions required in driving an automobile with a standard transmission—turning on the ignition, steering, accelerating, stepping on the clutch, shifting gears, releasing the clutch, and braking.

■ *Subject matter analysis.* Another approach is to break down the subject matter into the specific topics, concepts, and principles that it includes. To illustrate, a teacher can identify various aspects of the judicial system (concepts such as "innocent until proven guilty" and "reasonable doubt," the roles that judges and juries play, etc.) and their interrelationships.

FIGURE 10.2 Three ways of analyzing a task

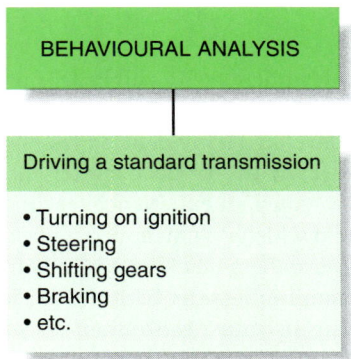
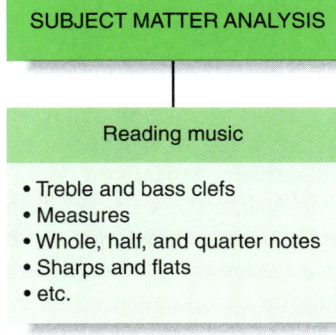
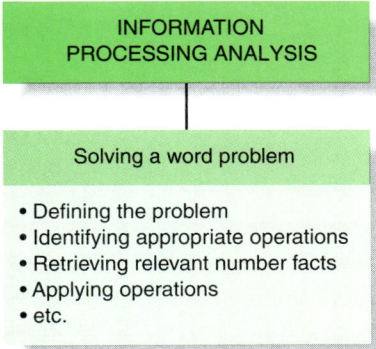

Subject matter analysis is especially important when the subject matter being taught includes many interrelated ideas and concepts. From the perspective of cognitive psychology, you can help students learn class material more meaningfully, organize it better in their long-term memories, and remember it more effectively if you teach them the interconnections among various ideas and concepts along with the ideas and concepts themselves.

- *Information processing analysis.* A third approach, using a cognitive perspective once again, is to specify the cognitive processes involved in a task. To illustrate, Ms. Begay can identify the mental processes involved in successfully solving an arithmetic word problem, such as correct classification (encoding) of the problem (determining what operations—addition, subtraction, and so on—to perform) and rapid retrieval of basic number facts. Similarly, she can identify some global cognitive strategies useful in reading comprehension, such as finding main ideas, elaborating, and summarizing.

Conducting task analyses for complex skills and topics has at least two advantages (Desberg & Taylor, 1986; Jonassen et al., 1989). First, when you identify a task's specific components—whether those components are behaviours, concepts and ideas, or cognitive processes—you have a better sense of what things your students need to learn and the order in which they can most effectively learn them. For example, Mr. McKenzie must teach his driver education students how to control the clutch before he can teach them how to shift gears.

A second advantage in conducting a task analysis is that it helps you choose appropriate instructional strategies. Different tasks—and perhaps even different components of a single task—may require different approaches to instruction. For example, if one necessary component of solving arithmetic word problems is the rapid retrieval of math facts from memory, then repeated practice of these facts may be critical for developing automaticity. If another component of solving these problems is identifying the appropriate operation to apply in various situations, then promoting a true understanding of mathematical concepts and principles (perhaps by using concrete manipulatives or authentic activities) is essential.

Sometimes a task analysis will lead you to conclude that you can most effectively teach a complex task by teaching some or all of its components separately from one another. Ms. Begay should almost certainly teach her students the processes involved in learning effectively from reading materials—elaborating, summarizing, and so on—primarily within the context of authentic reading tasks.

A task analysis of a topic or skill can help you identify the specific things to teach and appropriate strategies for teaching them.

Developing a Lesson Plan

Once they have identified their goals for instruction, and perhaps conducted a task analysis as well, effective teachers develop a lesson plan to guide them during instruction. A lesson plan typically includes the following:

- The objective(s) of instruction
- The instructional strategies used, and in what sequence
- Instructional materials (e.g., textbooks, handouts) and equipment required
- The assessment method(s) planned

Any lesson plan should, of course, take into account the students who will be learning—their developmental levels, prior knowledge, cultural backgrounds, and so on.

As a beginning teacher, you will probably want to develop a fairly detailed lesson plan that describes how you are going to help your students learn the subject matter in question (Calderhead, 1996; Sternberg & Horvath, 1995). But as you gain experience teaching certain topics, you will learn which strategies work effectively and which do not, and you may use some of the effective ones frequently enough that you can retrieve them quickly and easily from long-term memory. As time goes on, you will find that planning lessons becomes far less time-consuming and that you can do a lot of your planning in your head rather than on paper (Calderhead, 1996).

Lesson plans are more guides than recipes—in other words, a general plan of attack that you can and should adjust as the situation warrants (Calderhead, 1996). For instance, during the course of a lesson, you may find that your students have less prior knowledge than you realized, and so you may have to "back up" and teach material you thought they had already mastered. Or, if your students express curiosity or have intriguing insights about a particular topic, you may want to spend more time exploring that topic than you had originally intended.

As you proceed through the school year, your long-range plans will also change somewhat. For instance, you may find that your task analyses of desired knowledge and skills were overly simplistic. Or you may discover that the expectations you have for students' achievement, as reflected in the instructional objectives you've developed, are either unrealistically high or unnecessarily low. You must continually revise your plans as instruction proceeds and as classroom assessments reveal how well your students are learning and achieving.

In planning lessons, choose instructional strategies that are suitable for your objectives. As we examine various strategies in the pages that follow, we will identify the circumstances in which each one might be most appropriate and effective.

See the *Free Stuff for Canadian Teachers* website (www.thecanadianteacher.com) for links to news, articles, resources, lesson plans, and other materials.

Expository Approaches

Without a doubt, the most widely used approach to teaching is **expository instruction**: Information is presented (*exposed*) in essentially the same form that students are expected to learn it. Some forms of expository instruction are largely "one-way" in nature, in that information goes primarily from teacher to student; textbooks are the best example of such one-way communication. Other forms are more interactive, in that they incorporate an exchange of information between teacher (or perhaps a "virtual" teacher, such as a computer) and student. In this section we consider several instructional formats and methods that are primarily expository: lectures and textbooks, mastery learning, direct instruction, information and communication technology (ICT) instruction, and e-learning and online research.[1]

Expository instruction An approach to instruction whereby information is presented in more or less the same form in which students are expected to learn it.

Educational videos and field trips are two additional forms of expository instruction. What particular benefits might these forms of instruction have?

Lectures and Textbooks

Some theorists have criticized lectures and textbooks for putting students in a passive role. For instance, from a behaviourist perspective, students learn only when they are actively making responses (and perhaps getting reinforced for those responses), and students make very few observable responses when they sit quietly listening to a lecture or reading a textbook (Skinner, 1968). However, many cognitivists argue that students are often *mentally* active during such seemingly passive activities (Ausubel et al., 1978; Pressley, 1995; Weinert & Helmke, 1995). From the perspective of cognitive psychology, the degree to which students learn from expository instruction depends on how they process information—that is, on the particular cognitive responses they make. The more students pay attention, and the more they engage in meaningful learning, organization, elaboration, and so on, the more they are likely to benefit from the lectures they hear and the textbooks they read.

Unfortunately, lectures and textbooks don't always present information in ways that facilitate learning. For instance, you can undoubtedly think of high school or college instructors you've had whose lectures were dry, disorganized, confusing, or in some other way *non*motivating and *non*informative. And analyses of school textbooks in such diverse disciplines as history, geography, and science have found that the focus of most texts is on teaching specific facts, with little attention to helping students learn these facts in a meaningful way (Bochenhauer, 1990; Calfee & Chambliss, 1988; Chambliss, Calfee, & Wong, 1990; McKeown & Beck, 1990).

Researchers have identified several factors that facilitate students' learning from lectures, textbooks, and other forms of expository instruction. Table 10.2 describes and illustrates these factors as general principles that can help you whenever you need to present information in a largely "one-way" fashion.

---

[1] Many theorists use the term *expository instruction* primarily in reference to lectures and textbooks. We are using the term more broadly to refer to any approach that centres around the *transmission* of information from expert (e.g., classroom teacher, textbook writer, computer software designer) to student.

TABLE 10.2 Principles of Expository Instruction

PRINCIPLES/ASSUMPTIONS

PRINCIPLE	EDUCATIONAL IMPLICATION	EXAMPLE
An **advance organizer**—a verbal or graphic introduction that lays out the general organizational framework of the material—helps students organize and interrelate the things they learn.	Introduce a new unit by describing the major ideas and concepts to be discussed and showing how they are interrelated.	Introduce a unit on vertebrates by saying something like this: "Vertebrates all have backbones. We will be talking about five phyla of vertebrates—mammals, birds, reptiles, amphibians, and fish—which differ from one another in several ways, including whether their members are warm-blooded or cold-blooded; whether they have hair, scales, or feathers; and whether they lay eggs or bear live young."
Connections to prior knowledge help students learn classroom material more meaningfully, provided that their prior "knowledge" is accurate. (See the section "When Knowledge Construction Goes Awry" in Chapter 7.)	Remind students of something they already know and point out how a new idea is similar. This strategy is known as **prior knowledge activation**.	Draw an analogy between *peristalsis* (muscular contractions that push food through the digestive tract) and the process of squeezing ketchup from a packet: "You squeeze the packet near one corner and run your fingers along the length of the packet toward an opening at the other corner. When you do this, you push the ketchup through the packet, in one direction, ahead of your fingers, until it comes out of the opening" (Newby, Ertmer, & Stepich, 1994, p. 4).
An **organized presentation** of material helps students make appropriate interconnections among ideas.	Help students organize material in a particular way by presenting the information using that same organizational structure.	Use a *concept map* to depict the main concepts and ideas of a topic and their interrelationships (see the section "Organizing Knowledge" in Chapter 7).
Various **signals** built into a presentation (e.g., italicized print, interspersed questions) can draw students' attention to important points.	Stress important points—for instance, by writing them on the chalkboard, asking questions about them, or simply telling students what things are most important to learn.	When assigning a textbook chapter for homework, identify several questions that students should try to answer as they read the chapter.
Visual aids help students encode material visually as well as verbally.	Illustrate new material through pictures, photographs, diagrams, maps, physical models, and demonstrations.	When describing major battles of the American Civil War, present a map illustrating where each battle took place and point out that some battles were fought in especially strategic locations.
Appropriate **pacing** gives students adequate time to process information.	Pace a presentation slowly enough that students can engage in meaningful learning, elaboration, and other effective storage processes.	Intersperse lengthy explanations with demonstrations or hands-on activities that illustrate some of the principles you are describing.
Summaries help students review and organize material and identify main ideas.	After a lecture or reading assignment, summarize the key points of the lesson.	At the end of a unit on Emily Dickinson, summarize her work by describing the characteristics that made her poetry so unique and influential.

Sources: Ausubel et al., 1978; Bulgren, Deshler, Schumaker, & Lenz, 2000; Corkill, 1992; Dansereau, 1995; Donnelly & McDaniel, 1993; E. L. Ferguson & Hegarty, 1995; Hall & O'Donnell, 1994; Hansen & Pearson, 1983; Hartley & Trueman, 1982; Krajcik, 1991; J. R. Levin & Mayer, 1993; M. C. Linn et al., 1996; R. F. Lorch, Lorch, & Inman, 1993; Mayer, 1989; Mayer & Gallini, 1990; McDaniel & Einstein, 1989; Newby, Ertmer, & Stepich 1994; Pittman & Beth-Halachmy, 1997; R. E. Reynolds & Shirey, 1988; Sadoski & Paivio, 2001; Scevak, Moore, & Kirby, 1993; M. Y. Small, Lovett, & Scher, 1993; Tennyson & Cocchiarella, 1986; Wade, 1992; P. T. Wilson & Anderson, 1986; Winn, 1991; Zook, 1991; Zook & Di Vesta, 1991.

Lectures, textbooks, and other one-way forms of instruction have a distinct advantage: They allow teachers to present information quickly and efficiently. A major *dis*advantage is that, in and of themselves, they do not allow us to assess students' progress in learning the subject matter. When you need to make sure that students master information and skills that are prerequisites for later lessons, mastery learning may be a better approach.

Mastery Learning

Mastery learning An approach to instruction whereby students learn one topic thoroughly before moving to a more difficult one.

When you move through lessons without making sure that all students master the content of each one, you lose more and more students as you go along, particularly if early lessons provide the foundation for later ones. **Mastery learning**, in which students demonstrate mastery of one topic before proceeding to the next, minimizes the likelihood that you leave students in the dust as you move to increasingly challenging material (e.g., Bloom, 1981; Guskey, 1985; Hunter, 1982; J. F. Lee & Pruitt, 1984). This approach is based on three underlying assumptions:

- Almost every student can learn a particular topic to mastery.
- Some students need more time to master a topic than others.
- Some students need more assistance than others.

As you can see, mastery learning represents a very optimistic approach to instruction: It assumes that most children *can* learn school subject matter if they are given sufficient time and instruction to do so.

Mastery learning usually includes the following components:

1. *Small, discrete units.* The subject matter is broken up into a number of separate units or lessons, with each one covering a limited amount of material and aimed at accomplishing a small number (perhaps one to three) of instructional objectives.
2. *A logical sequence.* Units are sequenced such that basic, foundational concepts and procedures are learned first and more complex concepts and procedures are learned later. For example, a unit in which students learn what a fraction is would obviously come before a unit in which they learn how to add two fractions.
3. *Demonstration of mastery at the completion of each unit.* Before moving from one unit to the next, students must show that they have mastered the current unit, often by taking a test on the content of that unit. (Here is an example of how instruction and assessment often work hand in hand.)
4. *A concrete, observable criterion for mastery of each unit.* Mastery of a topic is defined in specific and concrete terms. For example, to "pass" a unit on adding fractions with the same denominator, students might have to answer at least 90 percent of test items correctly.
5. *Additional "remedial" activities for students needing extra help or practice to attain mastery.* Students do not always demonstrate mastery on the first try. Additional support and resources (perhaps alternative approaches to instruction, different materials, workbooks, study groups, and individual tutoring) are provided for students who need them.

Students engaged in mastery learning often proceed through the various units at their own speeds; hence, different students may be studying different units at any given time. But it is also possible for an entire class to proceed through a sequence at the same time: Students who master a unit earlier than their classmates can pursue various enrichment activities, or they can serve as tutors for those still working on the unit (Block, 1980; Guskey, 1985).

We find justification for mastery learning in several theoretical perspectives. Operant conditioning theorists tell us that complex behaviours are often more easily learned through *shaping*, whereby a simple response is reinforced until it occurs frequently (i.e., until it is mastered), then a slightly more difficult response is reinforced, and so on. Cognitive psychologists point out that information and skills that need to be retrieved rapidly or used in complex problem-solving situations must be practised and learned thoroughly so that *automaticity* is attained. Finally, as social cognitive theorists have noted, the ability to perform a particular task successfully and easily is likely to enhance students' sense of self-efficacy for performing similar tasks.

Research indicates that mastery learning has several advantages over nonmastery approaches. In particular, students tend to

- Learn more and perform better on classroom assessments
- Maintain better study habits, studying regularly rather than procrastinating and cramming
- Enjoy their classes and teachers more
- Have greater interest in the subject
- Have more self-confidence about their ability to learn the subject (Block & Burns, 1976; Born & Davis, 1974; C. C. Kulik, Kulik, & Bangert-Drowns, 1990; J. A. Kulik, Kulik, & Cohen, 1979; Shuell, 1996)

Mastery learning is most appropriate when the subject matter is hierarchical in nature—that is, certain concepts and skills provide the foundation for future learning. When instructional objectives deal with such basics as word recognition, rules of grammar, addition and subtraction, or key scientific concepts, instruction designed to promote mastery learning may be in order. Nevertheless, the very notion of mastery may be *in*appropriate for some of your long-term objectives. As noted earlier, skills such as critical reading, scientific reasoning, and creative writing may continue to improve over the years without ever really being mastered.

Direct Instruction

Direct instruction An approach to instruction that uses a variety of techniques (brief explanations, teacher questioning, rapid pacing, guided and independent practice) to promote learning of basic skills.

An approach incorporating elements of both expository instruction and mastery learning is **direct instruction**, which uses a variety of techniques designed to keep students continually and actively engaged in learning and applying classroom subject matter (Englemann & Carnine. 1982; R. M. Gagné, 1985; Rosenshine & Stevens, 1986; Tarver, 1992; Weinert & Helmke, 1995). To some extent, direct instruction is based on behaviourist principles of learning; for instance, it requires learners to make frequent overt responses and provides immediate reinforcement of correct responses through teacher feedback. But it also considers principles from cognitive psychology, including the importance of attention and long-term memory storage processes in learning, the limited capacity of working memory, and the value of learning basic skills to automaticity (Rosenshine & Stevens, 1986).

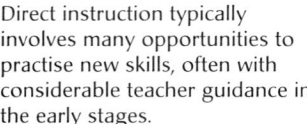

See the National Institute for Direct Instruction (www.nifdi.org) and www.directinstruction.org for more information about the nature and use of direct instruction within the school curriculum and related references, resources, and materials.

Different theorists describe and implement direct instruction somewhat differently. But in general, this approach involves small and carefully sequenced steps, fast pacing, and a great deal of teacher–student interaction. Each lesson typically involves most or all of the following components (Rosenshine & Stevens, 1986):

1. *Review of previously learned material.* The teacher reviews relevant content from previous lessons, checks homework assignments involving that content and, if necessary, reteaches any information or skills that students have apparently not yet mastered.

2. *Statement of the goals of the lesson.* The teacher describes one or more objectives that students should accomplish during the new lesson.

3. *Presentation of new material in small, carefully sequenced steps.* The teacher presents a small amount of information or a specific skill using an expository approach—perhaps through a verbal explanation, modelling, and one or more examples. The teacher may also provide an advance organizer, ask questions, or in other ways scaffold students' efforts to process and remember the material.

4. *Guided student practice and assessment after each step.* Students have frequent opportunities to practise what they are learning, perhaps by answering questions, solving problems, or performing modelled procedures. The teacher gives hints during students' early responses, provides immediate feedback about their performance, makes suggestions about how to improve, and provides remedial instruction as needed.

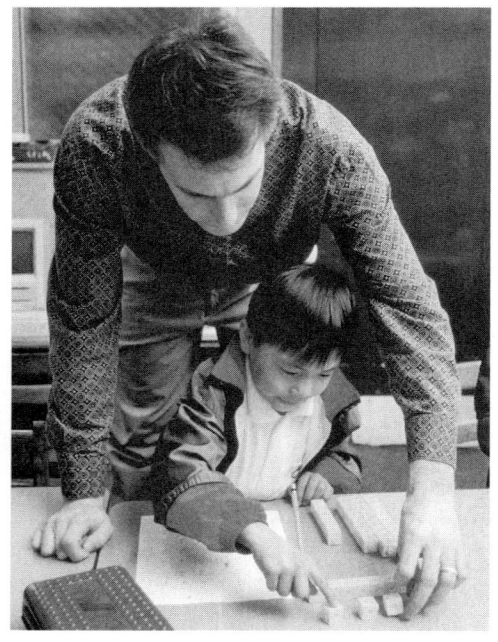

Direct instruction typically involves many opportunities to practise new skills, often with considerable teacher guidance in the early stages.

5. *Assessment of student progress.* After students have completed guided practice, the teacher checks to be sure they have mastered the information or skill in question, perhaps by having them answer a series of follow-up questions or summarize what they've learned.

6. *Independent practice.* Once students have acquired some mastery (e.g., by answering 80 percent of questions correctly), they engage in further practice either independently or in small, co-operative groups. By doing so, they work toward achieving automaticity for the material in question.

7. *Frequent follow-up reviews.* The teacher provides many opportunities for students to review previously learned material over the course of the school year—perhaps through homework assignments, writing assignments, or paper–pencil quizzes.

The teacher proceeds back and forth among these steps as necessary to ensure that all students are truly mastering the subject matter.

Like mastery learning, direct instruction is most suitable for teaching information and skills that are well defined and should be taught in a step-by-step sequence (Rosenshine & Stevens, 1986). Because of the high degree of teacher–student interaction, it is often more easily implemented with small groups of students rather than with an entire classroom. Under such circumstances, research indicates that it can be a highly effective instructional technique, leading to substantial gains in achievement of both basic skills and higher-level thinking processes, high student interest and self-efficacy for the subject matter in question, and low rates of student misbehaviour (Rosenshine & Stevens, 1986; Tarver, 1992; Weinert & Helmke, 1995).

One advantage of both mastery learning and direct instruction approaches is that because students must demonstrate mastery at the completion of each unit, they receive frequent feedback about the progress they are making. Yet another approach—information and communication technology instruction—may provide even *more* frequent feedback, as we shall see now.

Information and Communication Technology Instruction

Over the past four decades there has been enormous growth in the application of information and communication technology (ICT) and new educational technologies to instruction. This growth began with early work on programmed instruction and teaching machines that was adapted to early microcomputers in order to provide computer assisted instruction. With the rapid increase in memory and processing capabilities, new educational technologies became "intelligent tools" that could be used to enhance learning, communication, and personal productivity in myriad ways. We can briefly trace this evolution as follows.

Programmed Instruction

In behaviourism's heyday in the middle decades of the twentieth century, B. F. Skinner (1954, 1968) demonstrated how **programmed instruction** could be used to provide active and engaging learning activities for students. According to Skinner, programmed instruction offered a means of putting the three principles of operant conditioning into practice for teaching new material:

1. *Active Responding:* The learner is continually active in making responses—for instance by answering questions or filling in blanks to complete words and statements.

2. *Shaping:* Instruction begins with information the learner already knows, then it breaks new information into tiny pieces and presents them one at a time over the course of a lesson. As the learner acquires more information and answers questions of increasing difficulty, the desired terminal behaviour (mastery of the subject matter) is gradually shaped.

3. *Immediate Reinforcement:* Because instruction involves a gradual progression through the material, mastery of each piece is almost guaranteed. Hence, the learner has a high probability of responding correctly to the questions asked and is reinforced immediately by receiving feedback that the answers are correct.

Programmed instruction An approach to instruction whereby students independently study a topic that has been broken into small, carefully sequenced segments.

In the 1950s and 1960s, programmed instruction was commonly presented through books and other printed materials. There was, however, an increasing use of mainframe computers that were programmed to provide simple forms of **computer-assisted instruction (CAI)** in practical academic areas such as reading, spelling, and arithmetic operations. A well-known computer-assisted instruction research project for teaching mathematics to elementary school students began at Stanford University's Institute for Mathematical Studies in Social Sciences (IMSSS) in 1963. The study consisted of 41 Grade 4 students who were given daily arithmetic drill-practice lessons in their classroom. These lessons were given on a teletype machine that was connected to the Institute's computer by telephone lines (Suppes & Macken, 1978).

Computer-assisted instruction (CAI) Programmed instruction presented by means of a computer; it is one form of computer-based instruction.

ICT as an Educational Tool

With the increasing availability and affordability of microcomputers in the 1970s and 1980s, computer-assisted instruction gained momentum as an educational tool for home and school use. Early CAI provided repetitive drill and practice sessions designed to promote mastery of basic knowledge and skills (e.g., math facts, typing, fundamentals of music), helping students to develop automaticity in these areas (Merrill et al., 1996). This type of software presented information in carefully graded steps, clearly laid out the rules for success, and provided immediate feedback on progress. Many students, especially those with special education needs, enjoy using such software packages and there is evidence that some make good progress with them (Curzon, Ryba, & Selby, 2005; Ryba, Curzon, & Selby, 2004). However, there are many concerns about the transfer of skills to other contexts. For example, a student may learn to add coin values to $10 but checking the change they receive at the supermarket may remain a mystery. Successful use of CAI software appears to depend on whether the CAI activities can be supplemented by functional, real-life opportunities to integrate and transfer skills to other familiar settings where they are required. Educational games, drill and practice, and tutorial programs can be used in innovative ways to assist with the development of specific skills.

More recently, the increasing capacity of new educational technology has enabled sophisticated forms of **computer-based instruction (CBI)** to skilfully guide students through complex subject matter and address a wide range of learning difficulties (Lajoie & Derry, 1993). Multimedia applications are now routinely applied to create realistic problem-solving scenarios. For example, Kid Pix is a multimedia program that combines photos, text, graphics, and sound. This can be used to set up computer-based instruction that uses realistic instructional materials (e.g., digital camera photos, scanned images, hyperlinks) to guide students through a series of learning events. Contemporary educational software often incorporates cognitive as well as behavioural principles that focus on actively engaging students in constructing their own meaning (Grennon Brooks & Brooks, 1993).

Computer-based instruction (CBI) Instruction provided via computer technology.

Numerous research studies have documented the effectiveness of CBI. Research has shown that certain forms of CBI result in students having higher academic achievement and better attitudes toward their schoolwork compared with peers who have been taught through more traditional methods (J. A. Kulik, Kulik, & Cohen, 1980; Lepper & Gertner, 1989; Merrill et al., 1996; Roblyer, Castine & King, 1988; Tudor, 1995; Wise & Olsen, 1998). There is also evidence that students who study academic materials on a computer can potentially gain an increased sense of control over their own learning, thereby developing more intrinsic motivation to learn (Swan, Mitrani, Guerrero, Cheung & Schoener, 1990).

ICT as a Learning Partner

Working with ICT as an "intellectual partner" enables students to participate in many activities and do many things that were not previously accessible to them. For example, they can engage in simulated activities, such as moving through a forest in search of rare plants and insects, or carry out complex scientific experiments. These highly interactive and advanced educational applications not only provide realistic instruction but also offer a means of enhancing the learning potential of students in a number of important ways:

- *Zone of proximal development (ZPD)*—According to Vygotsky, learners' interactions with others in the zone of proximal development (ZPD) enable them to jointly carry out cognitive processes that are more advanced than would be possible if attempted independently, and these shared problem-solving processes serve as a basis for subsequent independent efforts (see Chapter 2 for more discussion on Vygotsky's theory of cognitive development). Interestingly, computer learning environments can function as the ZPD in which students' partner with intelligent new educational technologies to advance their learning.

- *Motivation and active engagement*—ICT provides students with opportunities to work and collaborate with others and to use the technology in ways that are meaningful to them. For example, students in New Zealand and Canada have collaborated on ecology projects that compare and contrast the natural evolution of both countries. They communicate via the multimedia platform Elluminate Live!, which enables them to talk to one another, show PowerPoint presentations, break into discussion groups, and work together on an interactive whiteboard.

- *Internal attributions and locus of control*—ICT offers a situation in which the students can take control. This might simply be at the level of taking a digital photo or adjusting the size of an image on a screen. At a more complex level, students can produce audio-enhanced PowerPoint slides using a platform such as Adobe Acrobat Connect Professional and then "publish" their presentations on the internet so that they are available for others to see.

- *Repeated opportunities for success*—It does not matter how many times a learner uses a particular computer tool or instructional program, they can experience repeated success. For example, 10-year-old Nikolai likes making slide presentations with PowerPoint. He knows how to insert digital photos and videoclips into slides and he can also pick and choose different images for each presentation. The computer learning environment provides Nikolai with a framework in which he can make decisions and experience success through preparing creative presentations.

- *Self-pacing and consistent operating procedures*—Most computer software follows a logical sequence of steps that enables students to learn the correct operating procedures even if they require a lot of practice and over-learning. Students with learning difficulties can especially benefit by the consistent and self-pacing procedures in that they can practice for as long as they need to learn a set of operations. For example, it took Tom a lot of trial and error to learn how to load photos into Kid Pix but he succeeded in the end and was proud of his efforts. Tom's teacher was impressed with his persistence and the amount of time he put into learning how to upload the photos.

- *Exploration of personal interests*—Computers and other forms of information communication technology have opened many doors for students to explore their personal interests. Erica, a 12-year-old student, has a collection of Living Books. Living Books are software-based story experiences that make extensive use of music, speech, and sound effects. They provide a lot of opportunities for Erica to make choices by creating her own stories or following one of the pre-programmed branching stories.

ICT for Building New Conceptions of Intelligent Behaviour

ICT is more than an instructional learning tool. It is a way of amplifying students' cognitive development through a number of important processes. Recent research by Ryba and Selby (2005) has shown how computers can be used in teaching as a means of promoting students' self awareness and self-regulation of thinking and problem solving (metacognition), and also to engage students in a way in which they can see themselves successfully performing tasks that they have not yet mastered. The following projects illustrate new educational technologies that can be used to build intelligent behaviour:

- *Mental imagery training*—The availability of low-cost digital cameras and their ease of operation offer some interesting new methods for using mental imagery as a tool for education and cognitive development. The advantage of digital cameras is that they are highly portable and can be easily used to augment learning and communication in a range of settings. For example, photos can be used to document learning sequences and actual field experiments. Tasks can be analyzed and recorded through the use of photos and videoclips. The digital images can be integrated with presentation software (e.g., PowerPoint) to support the development of class presentations. Mental imagery training has been successfully used to teach Canadian students with special needs how to operate complex equipment (for copying, enlarging, and collating documents) by following visual, auditory, tactile, and kinaesthetic cues in the correct sequence (Ryba, Selby, & Brown, 2004).

- *Feed forward*—This is an intervention approach that emphasizes the potential to learn from observing one's own successful actions, in particular to learn from "successes" that the learner has not yet had (Dowrick, 2000). This is accomplished by providing "feed forward" as opposed to "feedback," in which images of adaptive behaviour or skills that have not yet been achieved are edited together. By building up pictures of the students performing skills that are already available (images to think with), students can see themselves performing new tasks that they have not yet mastered. For example, a student can be taught to get to and from school safely by preparing and following a sequence of digital images in which she is shown correctly performing the required steps (e.g., stay on the footpath, check traffic left and right before crossing the street, etc.). This approach is based largely on the concept of self-modelling, in which learners receive "feed forward" about what they will be able to do in the future as opposed to traditional forms of feedback about what they have done in the past (Keys & Dowrick, 2001).

ICT as a Means of Differentiating Instruction

Effective teaching and learning in the twenty-first century will require teachers and students to utilize interactive and collaborative approaches (see the following section) that can engage the diversity of students in classrooms as well as facilitate the ability of teachers to provide differentiated instruction for their wide range of students. Advances in computer-based technology provide alternatives to traditional teaching and learning methods that can increase teacher and learner engagement in the teaching–learning transaction. However, all students, including students with culturally and linguistically diverse backgrounds, students living in poverty, and students with disabilities, must be provided access and training in order to the use technology in their homes and schools.

Differentiated instruction (by way of individual instruction, small groups, and large-group instruction) can be done by using interactive electronic whiteboards (IWBs), which enable users to present relevant information (including images, video, and sound) through multimedia programs such as SMART Board (by SMART Technologies) or Activboard (by Promethean UK). It can also be supplemented by using technology that allows teachers and students to do such things as interact with computer-displayed material and images from anywhere in the room (for example, using wireless pads and electronic pens). Other supports include the use of laptops for student note taking, the use of digital pens to help student organize and edit their notes, and the use of technology such as Elluminate Live! (www.elluminate.com) to foster the use of co-operative and collaborative arrangements among students.

Differentiating curricular instruction can be done by utilizing technological innovations such as digital textbooks, or e-textbooks, which are electronic versions of textbooks that can be read aloud to students by way of computers or handheld devices (Hasselbring & Bausch, 2006). E-textbooks have advantages over traditional textbooks because they can help students access textbook content through online multimedia resources such as graphics, audio, video, built-in dictionaries, and strategic learning prompts (Salend, 2008). Teachers and students can also access books and other print materials in a range of digital formats via a number of websites. Other ways to use technology to support the teaching of curricular areas include:

- Taking students on virtual field trips to various museums and scientific and historical sites via the internet (Chiappetta & Koballa, 2006)
- Providing students with a variety of digital learning materials and resources (for example, www.ipl.org)
- Teaching students how to obtain information on various topics and access online references and resources (for example, Digital Universe, www.digitaluniverse.net)
- Providing students with opportunities to do learning activities related to mathematics (for example, Mathematics on the Internet, wims.unice.fr/wims/en_home.html) or do scientific experiments (for example, Try Science, www.tryscience.org)
- Using educational computer games related to mathematics, social studies, and science to teach a variety of topics (for example, Ology, http://ology.amnh.org)
- Using specialized technology to support second-language students and students with sensory disabilities (Kapperman & Sticken, 2002)

See www.digital.library.upenn.edu/books for a list of online books and digital resources.

Reading skills can be enhanced through the use of computer technology (Elder-Hinshaw et al., 2006). For example, reading fluency difficulties can be aided by using text-to-speech and optical character recognition systems in order to access reading materials, scan individual words, adjust the size and format of texts, and help students decode unknown words (Salend, 2008; E. L. Higgins & Raskind, 2005). Some other ways technology can support students' literacy development include:

- Developing word recognition skills and word meanings with software programs such as TELE-Web or Visual Thesaurus (www.visualthesaurus.com)
- Providing students with online reading material (D. Johnson, 2004)
- Using PowerPoint slides with audio to teach phonetic-based words (Coleman-Martin, Heller, Cihak, & Irvine, 2005)
- Using digital storytelling to facilitate students' reading and writing (Ohler, 2006)
- Having students collaborate with online peers on writing projects

Examples of computer reading tools include Readingpen (www.readingpen.com) and myReader2 (www.humanware.com).

Integration of New Educational Technologies into Schools

A number of Canadian researchers have provided us with insight and understanding about how to integrate new educational technologies into schools and how teacher self-efficacy with using computers impacts student achievement and self-efficacy beliefs. For example, Scott Reid (2002) at the University of Ottawa found that although most teachers are enthusiastic about the possibilities of computer-based instruction, there are a number of potential issues that can hinder the success of CBI as a learning partner if they are not addressed. Reid's study further showed that teachers are concerned about students becoming overly absorbed in a form of virtual reality when working with technology, thus affecting socialization in the real world. Other concerns include the increased need for technical support in schools, the inequity of computer access because students come from varied home environments, the addition of new demands on teachers (particularly with respect to their time), and the need for teacher training to facilitate the effective integration of technology.

On the point of teacher training, a study by Ross, Hogaboam-Gray, and Hannay (2001) at the Ontario Institute for Studies in Education, University of Toronto, strengthens the claim that teacher efficacy in computer skills affects student learning. This study of 387 students aged 6 to 9 found that student achievement increased when students were taught by teachers with greater confidence in their ability to achieve learning goals requiring computer skills or in their ability to teach students how to use computers. Hence, school districts need to consider providing teacher professional development that focuses on increasing teacher self-efficacy. However, this might be easier said than done unless teachers are given the time and support needed to learn new technological skills and ways to effectively apply them in their classrooms.

E-learning and Online Research

E-learning has the power to transform the way students learn and the way teachers teach. The central challenge is to exploit technologies in all areas of learning by using ICT effectively across the curriculum as a means of connecting schools with communities and creating better conditions for learning and teaching practice. Student internet connections at home, together with local area networks of computers in schools, provide access to a growing number of electronic databases and information sources online. Web search engines (e.g., www.yahoo.com, www.google.com) provide students with ready access to a large number of websites on virtually any topic. Many provinces and school divisions now make use of distributed learning systems that enable flexible e-learning in English or French so that students can participate in collaborative learning between schools, often from remote locations. Recognizing the importance of e-learning, Alberta Education (2007) has announced a Distributed Learning Strategy to facilitate new opportunities for students and teachers to go beyond classroom walls and experience meaningful learning through broader social and information networks.

Educators are just beginning to explore the vast potential of the internet for students' learning, and we still await systematic research on the potential benefits and liabilities. Recent research on interactive electronic whiteboards by Ken Ryba (2005) in New Zealand has shown that whole-class and collaborative school projects can be successfully undertaken in many subject areas, including geography, social studies, and English at elementary, junior high, and secondary levels. In New York, teams of mostly middle school special education students held online debates via Elluminate Live!, a virtual classroom platform that includes interactive tools (such as an electronic whiteboard, a chat function, and video capabilities) that allow synchronous communication between users (Boettcher, 2008). But despite the growing body of evidence on the beneficial uses of online resources (e.g., finding information for research papers and oral presentations) there is growing concern that students may sometimes venture into unproductive domains (e.g., stumbling upon websites that promote racist attitudes or offer pornographic images). There are issues also about cyber bullying and the potential for students to use the technology for harmful and intimidating purposes both inside and outside of school (Beran & Li, 2007). Clearly, e-learning and the use of online facilities need to be carefully planned and monitored so that they are applied in beneficial ways to enhance student learning.

The further evolution of e-learning and online resources and the development of new technologies will play a key role in twenty-first-century education. However, in order to make effective use of the many online options now available, students need to develop their digital literacy along with the traditional literacies—reading, writing, and arithmetic—as essential skills. Digital (ICT) literacy is "the set of abilities that enables learners to access, manage, integrate, evaluate, communicate, and create diverse information in an ethical way, and to meaningfully engage with a range of ICT-mediated communities" (New Zealand Ministry of Education, 2006, p. 2). Concerns have been raised, however, about whether schools are providing sufficient opportunities for children to develop their ICT literacy. In this regard, the results of a study of 19 Grade 6 classrooms by Marlene Asselin (2001) at the University of British Columbia found that students lacked sufficient instruction on the cognitive processes of research. For example, Asselin observed no instruction on how to read or evaluate internet resources.

Importantly, internet technology allows for collaborative knowledge building within a knowledge-building environment (see Scardamalia, 2000; Scardamalia & Bereiter, 1999). According to Scardamalia and Bereiter (2003), it is important to engage learners in the full process of knowledge generation from an early age. They point out that in a knowledge-building environment, ideas are real things that are available for use by the community in a form that allows them to be discussed and revised. For example, the CSILE Knowledge Forum (www.knowledgeforum.com) is an example of an internet platform that provides opportunities for students to be collaboratively engaged in developing new knowledge (see "Computer-Supported Collaborative Learning" on pp. 280–281).

Hands-On Approaches: Discovery Learning and In-Class Activities

Discovery Learning

Think about something you've learned through your own research or experimentation. How thoroughly did you learn that information or skill? Do you think you learned it more thoroughly and understood it better than you would have if you had simply read about it in a book or heard about it from another person?

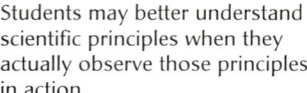

Discovery learning An approach to instruction whereby students develop an understanding of a topic through firsthand interaction with the physical or social environment.

Unlike expository instruction, where information is presented in its final form, **discovery learning** is a process through which students interact with their physical or social environment—for example, by exploring and manipulating objects, performing experiments, or wrestling with questions and controversies—and derive information for themselves. Common examples of discovery learning are laboratory experiments, library research projects, and opportunities for students to learn by trial and error (e.g., as they "fiddle" with computer software, a soccer ball, or watercolour paints). Research studies indicate that people often remember and transfer information more effectively when they construct it for themselves rather than when they simply read it in expository material (de Jong & van Joolingen, 1998; McDaniel & Schlager, 1990; McNamara & Healy, 1995). We can easily explain this finding using principles of cognitive psychology (Bruner, 1961, 1966; McDaniel, Waddill, & Einstein, 1988; B. Y. White & Frederiksen, 1998). When learners discover something on their own, they typically give more thought to (process) that information or skill than they might otherwise, and so they are more likely to engage in meaningful learning. In addition, learners often learn classroom subject matter in a more complete and integrated way (i.e., they achieve greater *conceptual understanding*) when they have opportunities to explore and manipulate their environment firsthand. Furthermore,

Students may better understand scientific principles when they actually observe those principles in action.

when learners *see* something as well as hear or read about it, they can encode it in long-term memory visually as well as verbally. And from a developmental perspective, many students, especially those in the elementary grades, understand concrete experiences more easily than abstract ideas.

Psychologists and educators have offered numerous suggestions for making discovery learning effective (e.g., see the Into the Classroom feature "Promoting Discovery Learning"). Two general guidelines are probably most critical:

■ *Make sure students have the knowledge they need to interpret their findings appropriately.* Students are most likely to benefit from a discovery learning activity when they can draw on prior knowledge to interpret their observations (Bruner, 1966; de Jong & van Joolingen, 1998; N. Frederiksen, 1984a). For example, having students conduct experiments to determine the influence of gravity on the velocity of a falling object will typically be more beneficial if students are already familiar with the concepts of gravity and velocity. As cognitive psychologists tell us, meaningful learning can occur only when students have appropriate knowledge to which they can relate new experiences. And from Vygotsky's perspective, students must ultimately tie their discoveries to the ways in which their cultures interpret the world. The central concepts and principles of various academic disciplines are, indeed, a very important part of those cultures.

INTO THE CLASSROOM *Promoting Discovery Learning*

Identify a concept or principle about which students can learn through interaction with their physical or social environment.

> A mathematics teacher realizes that rather than tell students how to calculate the area of a triangle, she can help them discover the procedure for themselves.

Make sure students have the necessary prior knowledge for discovering new ideas and principles.

> After students in a physics class have studied velocity, acceleration, and gravity, their teacher has them measure the speed of a metal ball rolling down ramps of varying degrees of incline.

Structure the experience so that students proceed logically toward any discoveries you want them to make.

> To demonstrate the effects of prejudice, a social studies teacher creates a situation in which each student, because of an arbitrarily chosen physical characteristic that he or she possesses, experiences the prejudice of classmates.

Show puzzling results to arouse curiosity.

> A science teacher shows her class two glasses of water. In one glass an egg is floating at the water's surface; in the other glass an egg has sunk to the bottom. The students give a simple and logical explanation for the difference: One egg has more air inside, so it is lighter. But then the teacher switches the eggs into opposite glasses. The egg that the students believe to be "heavier" now floats, and the "lighter" egg sinks to the bottom. The students are quite surprised to observe this result and demand to know what is going on. (Ordinarily, water is less dense than an egg, so an egg placed in it will quickly sink. But in this situation, one glass contains salt water—a mixture denser than an egg and therefore capable of keeping it afloat.) (based on Palmer, 1965)

Have students record their findings.

> A biology teacher has students make sketches of the specific organs they observe as they dissect an earthworm.

Help students relate their findings to concepts and principles in the academic discipline they are studying.

> After students in a social studies class have collected data on average incomes and voting patterns in different communities within their province, their teacher asks, "How can we interpret these data given what we've learned about the relative wealth of members of the major political parties?"

- *Provide some structure to guide students' discovery activities.* Young children often learn from random exploration of their environment—for example, by experimenting with, and thereby discovering the properties of, dry sand, wet sand, and water (Hutt, Tyler, Hutt, & Christopherson, 1989). At the elementary and secondary school levels, however, students are more likely to benefit from carefully planned and structured activities that help them construct appropriate interpretations (Hickey, 1997; Minstrell & Stimpson, 1996; B. Y. White & Frederiksen, 1998). In science, for example, such structure (scaffolding) might take the form of questions that guide students' thinking; here are three examples:

  - In what ways has the culture in this petri dish changed since yesterday?
  - How can we measure an object's rate of acceleration in an objective way?
  - When we add these two chemicals together and then heat them, how can we be sure the heat, rather than some other variable, is bringing about the change that we see?

In-Class Activities

In-class activities should be assigned first and foremost that will help students accomplish instructional objectives (Brophy & Alleman, 1992; W. Doyle, 1983). In some cases, these objectives may be at a "knowledge" level; for instance, you may want students to conjugate the French verb *être* ("to be"), know members of different biological classes and orders, and be familiar with current events around the globe. But in other cases, you may have higher-level objectives; for instance, you may want your students to write a persuasive essay, use scientific principles to interpret physical phenomena, or use arithmetic operations to solve real-world problems. Particularly when such higher-level objectives are involved, you will want to assign activities that help students learn classroom material in a meaningful, integrated way.

In addition to matching your in-class activities to your objectives, you are more likely to facilitate students' learning and achievement when you assign activities that

- Accommodate student diversity in abilities and interests
- Clearly define each task and its purpose
- Generate students' interest in accomplishing the task
- Begin at an appropriate difficulty level for students—ideally, presenting a task that challenges students to "stretch" their knowledge and skills (a task within students' zone of proximal development)
- Provide sufficient scaffolding to promote success
- Progress in difficulty and complexity as students become more proficient
- Provide opportunities for frequent teacher monitoring and feedback on students' progress
- Encourage students to reflect on and evaluate the work they've completed (Brophy & Alleman, 1991, 1992; Brophy & Good, 1986)

Interactive and Collaborative Approaches

In this section we examine six interactive and collaborative strategies: teacher questions, class discussions, cognitive strategy teaching, computer-supported collaborative learning, co-operative learning, and peer tutoring.

Teacher Questions

Lower-level question A question that requires students to express what they have learned in essentially the same way they learned it—for example, by reciting a textbook's definition of a concept or describing an application their teacher presented in class.

Teacher questioning is a widely used teaching strategy (e.g., Mehan, 1979). Many teacher questions are **lower-level questions** that ask students to retrieve information they've presumably already learned. Such questions have several benefits (Airasian, 1994; F. W. Connolly & Eisenberg, 1990; P. W. Fox & LeCount, 1991; Wixson, 1984). First, they enable us to determine what students' prior knowledge and misconceptions about a topic are likely to be. Second, they tend to keep students' attention on the lesson in progress. Third, they help us assess whether students are learning class material successfully or are confused about particular points; even very experienced teachers sometimes overestimate what students are actually learning during expository instruction. Fourth, they give students the opportunity to monitor their *own* comprehension—to determine whether they understand the information being presented or whether they should ask for help or clarification. Finally, when questions ask students about material they've studied earlier, they encourage review of that material, which should promote greater recall later on.

Higher-level question A question that requires students to do something new with information they have learned—for example, applying, analyzing, evaluating, creating, planning, and using metacognitive strategies.

You can encourage student elaboration of content, and therefore also encourage new knowledge construction, by asking **higher-level questions**—those that require students to go beyond the information they have learned (Meece, 1994; Minstrell & Stimpson, 1996). For instance, a higher-level question might ask students to think of their own examples of a concept, use a new principle to solve a problem, or speculate about possible explanations for a cause–effect relationship. As an illustration, consider these questions from a lesson on the telegraph:

> Was the need for a rapid communications system [in North America] greater during the first part of the nineteenth century than it had been during the latter part of the eighteenth century? Why do you think so? (Torrance & Myers, 1970, p. 214)

To answer these questions, students must recall what they know about the eighteenth and nineteenth centuries (including the increasing movement of settlers to distant western territories) and pull that knowledge together in a way they have perhaps never done before.

Class Discussions

Social constructivists propose that learners often work together to construct meaningful interpretations of their world. Class discussions in which students feel that they can speak freely, asking questions and presenting their ideas and opinions in either a whole-class or small-group context, obviously provide an important mechanism for promoting such socially constructed understandings (Haseman, 1999; G. J. Kelly & Chen, 1998; Marshall, 1992).

Class discussions lend themselves readily to a variety of academic disciplines. For example, students may discuss various interpretations of classic works of literature, addressing questions that have no easy or "right" answers; when they do so, they are more likely to relate what they are reading to their personal lives and understand it better as a result (Eeds & Wells, 1989; E. H. Hiebert & Raphael, 1996; L. M. McGee, 1992). In history classes, students may study and discuss various documents related to a single historical event and so begin to recognize that history is not necessarily as cut-and-dried as traditional history textbooks portray it (Leinhardt, 1994). In science classes, discussions of various and conflicting explanations of observed phenomena may enhance scientific reasoning skills, promote conceptual change, and help students begin to understand that science is not "fact" as much as it is a dynamic and continually evolving understanding of the world (Bereiter, 1994; K. Hogan et al., 2000; Schwarz et al., 2000). And in mathematics, class discussions that focus on alternative approaches to solving the same problem can promote a more meaningful understanding of mathematical principles and lead to better transfer of those principles to new situations and problems (Cobb et al., 1991; J. Hiebert & Wearne, 1996; Lampert, 1990).

Although students typically do most of the talking in classroom discussions, teachers nevertheless play a critical role. Theorists have offered several guidelines for how you can promote effective classroom discussions:

■ *Focus on topics that lend themselves to multiple perspectives, explanations, or approaches* (L. M. Anderson, 1993; E. H. Hiebert & Raphael, 1996; Lampert, 1990; Onosko, 1996). Controversial topics appear to have several benefits: Students are more likely to express their views to their classmates, seek out new information that resolves seemingly contradictory data, re-evaluate their own positions on the issues under discussion, and develop a meaningful and well-integrated understanding of the subject matter (E. G. Cohen, 1994; D. W. Johnson & Johnson, 1985; Kuhn, Shaw, & Felton, 1997; K. Smith, Johnson, & Johnson, 1981).

■ *Make sure students have enough prior knowledge about a topic to discuss it intelligently.* Such knowledge may come either from previous class sessions or from students' personal experiences (Bruning, Schraw, & Ronning, 1995). In many cases, it is likely to come from studying a particular topic in depth (Onosko, 1996).

■ *Use small-group discussions as a way of encouraging all students to participate.* Students are more likely to speak openly when their audience is a handful of classmates rather than the class as a whole; the difference is especially noticeable for girls (Théberge, 1994). On some occasions, then, you may want to have students discuss an issue in small groups first, thereby giving them the chance to test and possibly gain support for their ideas in a relatively private context; you can then bring them together for a whole-class discussion (Minstrell & Stimpson, 1996; Onosko, 1996).

■ *Provide a structure to guide the discussion.* Your class discussions are likely to be more effective when you structure them in some way. For example, as noted earlier, you might ask one or more thought-provoking (higher-level) questions to get the discussion underway. You might ask the class to examine a textbook or other source of information with a particular goal in mind (Calfee, Dunlap, & Wat, 1994). Before conducting an experiment, you might ask students to make predictions about what will happen and to explain and defend their predictions; later, after students have observed the outcome of the experiment, you might ask them to explain what happened and why (Hatano & Inagaki, 1991; B. Y. White & Frederiksen, 1998).

Many students feel more comfortable discussing issues in a small group than in front of the entire class.

Cognitive Strategy Teaching

Over the past few decades, developments occurring in the fields of education and psychology have culminated in the intensification of the cognitive education movement. This movement typically emphasizes the teaching of a broad range of cognitive and metacognitive strategies relevant to the acquisition, storage, retrieval, and application of knowledge. Some of the better known programs and/or approaches using cognitive strategy teaching are:

- Reciprocal Teaching (Palincsar, 1986; Palincsar & Brown, 1984; A. L. Brown & Palincsar, 1987; Palincsar & Herrenkohl, 1999)
- Informed Strategies for Learning (Paris, 1986; Paris, Cross, & Lipson, 1984; Paris & Oka, 1986)
- The Learning Strategies Curriculum (Deshler, Alley, & Carlson, 1980; Deshler, Warner, Schumaker, & Alley, 1983)
- Transactional Strategies (Pressley et al., 1992)

In addition, Mulcahy and his colleagues (Mulcahy, Marfo, Peat, & Andrews, 1986; Mulcahy, Marfo, Peat, Andrews, & Clifford, 1986) developed a program entitled "Strategies Program for Effective Learning and Thinking" (SPELT), which was tested as part of a longitudinal research project in the Province of Alberta (Mulcahy et al., 1989). Unlike many other programs, this project developed a curriculum with inclusive learning and thinking strategies that could be implemented across all subject areas within elementary, junior high, and high school curricula. Like current orientations to **cognitive strategy instruction**, the SPELT instructional sequence was premised on the view that the highest level of cognitive performance is characterized by efficient and spontaneous use of strategies. The SPELT instructional sequence reflects a general style of teaching that actively involves students in the learning process. Accordingly, teachers are to raise the cognitive and metacognitive awareness of their students; lead students to discover for themselves instead of revealing facts to them; and constantly challenge students to be critical, systematic, and strategic in their behaviour and attitude toward learning. For every single strategy that is taught (for example, memory strategy, organizational strategy, elaboration strategy, comprehension strategy, problem-solving strategy), the teacher should provide information, either directly or through class instruction, about the significance of the strategy, how and when to use it, and what modifications may be made to it in order to apply it to a broader range of learning problems. Teaching moves from a focus on recommended strategies for improving learning and performance in content areas such as language arts, mathematics, social studies, and science to a focus on student control and generation of their own effective strategies.

The SPELT program was evaluated over a four-year period involving over 900 average, learning disabled, and gifted students in Grades 4 to 9. The results were positive in that the use and awareness of cognitive strategies improved in all grade levels and for all groups. Moreover, parents, teachers, and administrators responded favourably to the program. In addition, a year after the termination of the research project, 85 percent of the teachers reported that they continued to use aspects of the program in their teaching.

Cognitive strategy teaching is typically used when the teacher identifies a problem students are having in their learning and/or performance. For example, a teacher might discover during student oral presentations in class that the students are not presenting information effectively. For example, the teacher observes that the students are not accommodating the needs of the audience, keeping focused on the task, and showing interest in their report. Hence, the teacher decides to inform the students that their performance was ineffective and needing improvement. The teacher leads the discussion with her students about what they think defines an effective oral report:

Cognitive strategy instruction
A teaching approach that enables students to regulate and control their learning.

Teacher: There are some things I noticed when you were giving your oral reports that could be improved. What are some things that you think should be considered when giving an oral report?

Susan: I think the speaker should show that she is interested in what she has to say.

Teacher: That is an interesting point, Susan. Why do you think it is important for the speaker to be interested in what she or he is saying?

Mark: If the speaker is interested in what he is saying, his enthusiasm will likely get the audience to pay more close attention to the presentation.

Teacher: OK! So the speaker should show that he or she wants to be heard by the audience. What else should the speaker consider when giving an oral report?

Sara: I think the speaker should make sure that the audience understands what she is saying.

Teacher: Good! Anything else?

(No more suggestions come from the class, so the teacher cues the students.)

Teacher: Class, when you are giving an oral report, what is something you don't like the audience to do?

Sam: I do not like when the audience seems not to care what you are saying and either looks away or does something else that indicates that they are not listening to me.

Teacher: Yes, I think that would be a little disturbing. So is there anything you can do about this?

Sam: Well, I guess I could make sure that the audience is ready to listen before I start speaking and try to keep them focused on my presentation.

Jenna: I think it helps if you look at your audience and show that you are paying attention to them as well.

Teacher: Very good, class! I think you have made some very good suggestions. In fact, you have noted all of the things that I noticed you were not doing during your presentations. Sometimes, even when we know what to do, we do not do it. Sometimes we need reminders to help us make sure we do things the way they should be done. I think the things you suggested for giving an oral report can form a strategy we can use to help us when we do our oral report presentations.

The teacher then presents to the class a mnemonic strategy (CHECK) that the students can use as a memory cue when giving oral reports, which uses their suggestions:

C: Check the audience. Is everyone ready to listen?

H: Have eye contact with the audience

E: Expressive

C: Clear. Make sure you speak so everyone understands

K: Keen to be heard. Show you are interested in what you are saying. Be enthusiastic

After showing a strategy to the class, typically teachers will reinforce the rationale for the strategy (for example, to be able to provide a better and more efficient oral presentation). Next, teachers should model the strategy to be learned by using a "think aloud" procedure. For example, for CHECK, the teacher might say something like: "Now let's see, 'C' stands for 'check the audience,' so now I will make sure my audience is ready for me to begin my presentation . . ."

Next, the steps of the strategy are memorized by the students—for example, by use of drills with the class:

Teacher: C (Teacher points or says a student's name)

Student: Check the audience.

Teacher: Good. H.

Student: Have eye contact with the audience.

Teacher: Yes. E.

Student: Expressive.

Teacher: Good. C.

Student: Clear—make sure everyone understands.

Teacher: OK. K.

Student: Keen to be heard.

This type of activity continues with the class until the steps can be verbalized both quickly and accurately without visual cues by the students. Discussions will also take place where the teacher makes sure that the students know where and when to use the strategy and why it should be used. After the strategy has been learned, the students are given many opportunities to practise the strategy and are given feedback from the teacher as well as one another until mastery is accomplished. After students have been shown that the strategy works (i.e., their oral reports are evaluated as being better and more effective after use of the strategy) the teacher will begin to encourage much more flexibility in the use of strategies taught to the students. This will be done so that students understand that strategies are not "carved in stone" but can be modified to better suit their needs and different contexts. This personalizes the strategies and acts as a stepping stone in the students' ability to self-generate effective learning strategies. To this end, the teacher will encourage strategy use across different tasks and content areas. As the activities change, the teacher and students discuss adaptations, modifications, and/or extensions, emphasizing how they improve the strategies.

The central concept in teaching strategies is for the teacher to act as the catalyst for the students to reason for themselves. Students are asked to identify other settings and task situations where strategies previously taught could be applied, and to evaluate the effectiveness of these strategies as they employ them in new situations. Later, the teacher will nurture in students the ability to generate strategies on their own as well as apply previously acquired strategies spontaneously. To this end, the teacher will typically employ a problem-solving approach to instruction, in which content-free and content-related problems and tasks are assigned to students, with the expectation that students come up with their own strategies for learning and performing the tasks. Individual as well as total class discussions of such assignments focus on the analysis of task requirements, alternative strategies, and avenues for ascertaining the relative effectiveness of useful strategies. The teacher can take advantage of group or paired problem-solving techniques, or incidentally occurring situations in the classroom for generating effective strategies for solving learning and performance problems. Continued exposure to this type of teaching is expected to lead students toward automatization of strategy generation and utilization and improved learning and performance.

> For more information regarding the application of strategies in the areas of reading, writing, mathematics, and study skills, see www.unl.edu/csi/teachingstrategy.shtml.

Computer-Supported Collaborative Learning

The vast range of currently available computer software provides many contexts and opportunities for fostering social interaction and collaborative learning. Numerous studies across different age groups lead to the same conclusions: Computer technology enables students to communicate with their peers (either in their own classroom or elsewhere), exchange perspectives, and build one another's ideas (Fabos & Young, 1999; Jessup, Egbert, & Connolly, 1995; Hewitt & Scardmalia, 1996; J. Schacter, 2000; Wizer, 1995). This communication can occur through such mechanisms as email, web-based chat rooms, and electronic bulletin boards.

One of the most significant areas of development has been computer-supported collaborative learning (CSCL), computer-based network systems that enable individual students and groups to work together for a common purpose (Randall & Macgregor, 2005). The purpose of CSCL is to scaffold or support students in learning together effectively. The rationale for CSCL is based on the premise that computer-supported systems can support and facilitate group process and group dynamics in ways that are more difficult to achieve in face-to-face situations. CSCL systems are typically designed for use by multiple learners working together on the same workstation or across a computer network. These systems can support access to information and documents, communication of ideas and information, and feedback on problem-solving activities.

There are many sites available to support school-based collaborative online projects. For example, the 2Learn.ca Portal (www.2Learn.ca) is an educational alliance supported by Alberta Education, the Alberta Teachers' Association, and other educational partners, that provides a platform for online classroom collaboration. Wendy Nero, a teacher in Alberta, carried out an innovative computer collaboration project called People in our World. Nero connected her elementary school students with classes in South Africa, India, Martinique, England, Australia, Venezuela, Thailand, Czech Republic, and the United States. The project was developed because of a need to access up-to-date information on the topic "People in the World" for Grade 2 Social Studies. As Nero described the project,

> "We shared information on how we meet our basic needs. The information was posted on our website, and we used that as a resource to contrast and compare the ways that others in the world meet their needs. The students were thrilled to be able to send emails around the world, with information about our community. They were equally excited when they received emails from other countries to add to our database. The insight they gained from communicating with students who are their age, all around the world, was priceless. They became excited about locating these countries on a map and their understanding of the world outside their own narrow existence was one of the biggest learning curves for them." (Wendy Nero, quoted in 2Learn.ca Education Society, 2008).

In the Netherlands, R. J. Simons and colleagues (1999), from Utrecht University, carried out a large-scale European study of CSCL. In it, they explored the effectiveness of computer-supported collaborative learning networks in creating a community of learners that used educational technology to build knowledge together through learning environments. Experimenting with different kinds of educational software, the project studied 25 teachers from 20 schools and almost 600 students from primary (aged 10–12), secondary (aged 13–16), and vocational (aged 18–24) education in five countries (Belgium, Finland, Greece, Italy, and the Netherlands). Results showed that to be successful, CSCL requires teachers and students to adopt an educational philosophy that focuses on "knowledge building" rather than "knowledge reproduction" as the main learning activity. This is characterized by an approach to learning that involves active, self-regulated, constructive, and contextualized learning by groups of students, more or less independently (Simons et al., 1999). The computer support added value by making collaborative learning in the classroom easier to organize, improving visibility of collaborative processes, making thinking processes and strategies clear, and helping students learn to build knowledge collectively and meaningfully.

In Canada, researchers at the University of Toronto developed software that allows students to communicate regularly using a class-wide database (Hewitt & Scardmalia, 1996; Lamon, Chan, Scardmalia, Burtis and Brett, 1993).[2] Students use the database to share questions, ideas, notes, writing products, and graphic constructions. Their classmates (and sometimes a subject matter expert as well) respond regularly, perhaps by giving feedback, building on ideas, offering alternative perspectives, or summarizing what has been learned. As an example, in an anthropology unit on "Prehistory in the New World", Grade 5 and 6 students worked in groups of three or four to study particular topics and then shared their findings through their computer database (Hewitt, Brett, Scardmailia, Frecker, & Webb, 1995). One group, which studied various theories about how human beings first migrated from Asia to the Americas, reported the following:

> **What we have learned**: We know that we have learned lots on this project, but the more that we learned the more we got confused about what is fact and what is fiction. The problem within this problem is that there isn't any real proof to say when they came or how. The theory that is most believed is the Bering Strait theory in which people from Asia walk over a land bridge. Another theory is that they kayaked the distance between the two continents. We have unfortunately found racist theories done by people who hate people unlike their own saying that the people of the New World are these people because of human sacrifices and only this race of people would do that." (Hewitt et al., 1995, p. 7)

In New York, teams of mostly middle school special education students held online debates via Elluminate *Live!* (Boettcher, 2008). The participating students took on some serious subjects such as cell phone usage in schools, immigration, the Iraq war, and other global issues. Students worked collaboratively in teams to prepare the elements of a debate (opening statements, positions, cross-examinations). The experience proved valuable for building the students' confidence, improving their social skills, and increasing their understanding of how to work collaboratively and engage in thoughtful debate with a live audience.

As you can see, computer software enables a classroom to become a *community of learners* in which students regularly co-operate with one another and contribute to one another's learning and achievement. We now look at other approaches for promoting co-operative learning.

Co-operative Learning

Co-operative learning is an approach to instruction in which students work in small groups to help one another learn. Unlike an individualistic classroom where one student's success is unrelated to classmates' achievement or a competitive classroom where one student's success actually depends on the failure of others, students in a co-operative learning environment work together to achieve common successes. In other words, they *sink or swim together* (D. W. Johnson & Johnson, 1991).

Co-operative learning An approach to instruction whereby students work with their classmates to achieve group goals and help one another learn.

---

[2] An early version of this software was known as Computer Supported Intentional Learning Environment, or CSILE (pronounced like the name Cecil). A second generation of CSILE, called Knowledge Forum® (available commercially from Learning in Motion), allows collaboration across schools and other institutions. You can visit the CSILE and Knowledge Forum websites at http://ikit.org and www.knowledgeforum.com.

See www.co-operation.org for more discussion and examples of co-operative learning in action.

We find justification for co-operative learning in several theoretical frameworks. From the perspective of cognitive psychology, co-operative learning yields the same benefits that emerge from class discussions: greater comprehension and integration of the subject matter, recognition of inadequacies or misconceptions in understanding, and increased perspective taking. Furthermore, when students help one another learn, they create scaffolding for one another's efforts, and they may jointly construct more sophisticated ideas and strategies than any single group member might be able to construct alone (Good et al., 1992; Hatano & Inagaki, 1991; O'Donnell & O'Kelly, 1994; N. M. Webb & Palincsar, 1996). From a behaviourist point of view, reinforcing group success is consistent with the operant conditioning notion of a *group contingency*. From a social cognitive perspective, students are likely to have higher self-efficacy for performing a task when they know that they will have the help of other group members; furthermore, students can model effective learning and problem-solving strategies for one another (A. L. Brown & Palincsar, 1989; Good et al., 1992). And theorists of various theoretical persuasions point out that co-operative ventures are important elements of scientific inquiry and adult work environments (Greeno, 1997; D. W. Johnson & Johnson, 1991).

How often do adults need to collaborate in the workplace? Do you think they might have benefited from co-operative experiences during their school years?

Numerous research studies indicate that co-operative learning activities, when designed and structured appropriately, are effective in many ways. For one thing, students of all ability levels show higher academic achievement; females, members of minority groups, and students at risk for academic failure are especially likely to show increased achievement (Lou et al., 1996; Nichols, 1996; Pérez, 1998; Qin, Johnson, & Johnson, 1995; Shachar & Sharan, 1994; R. J. Stevens & Slavin, 1995). Co-operative learning activities may also promote higher-level thinking skills: Students essentially "think aloud," modelling various learning and problem-solving strategies for one another and developing greater metacognitive awareness as a result (Good et al., 1992; A. King, 1999; Paris & Winograd, 1990).

The benefits of co-operative learning activities are not limited to gains in learning and achievement. Students have greater confidence about the likelihood of success (i.e., higher self-efficacy), express more intrinsic motivation to learn school subject matter, and participate more actively in classroom activities. They better understand the perspectives of others and more frequently engage in prosocial behaviour—making decisions about how to divide a task fairly and equitably, resolving interpersonal conflicts, and encouraging and supporting one another's learning. In classrooms that emphasize co-operative learning, students are more likely to believe they are liked and accepted by their classmates, and friendships across racial and ethnic groups and between students with and without disabilities are more apt to form (Lou et al., 1996; H. W. Marsh & Craven, 1997; J. D. Nichols, 1996; Slavin, 1990; R. J. Stevens & Slavin, 1995; N. M. Webb & Palincsar, 1996).

However, there are also some potential pitfalls in co-operative learning. Some students may be less interested in mastering the material than they are in meeting social and performance goals (e.g., making friends, creating a good impression, getting the right answer), and their willingness to assist one another or ask for help may be compromised as a result (Levy, Kaplan, & Patrick, 2000; M. C. Linn et al., 1996; Moje & Shepardson, 1998). The students who do most of the work and most of the talking are likely to learn more than other group members (Blumenfeld, 1992; Gayford, 1992; N. M. Webb, 1989). Students may occasionally agree to use an incorrect strategy or method that a particular group member has suggested, or they may share misconceptions about the topic they are studying (Good et al., 1992; Stacey, 1992). In some cases, students may simply not have the skills to help one another learn (D. M. Hogan & Tudge, 1999; O'Donnell & O'Kelly, 1994). Clearly, then, you must keep a close eye on the discussions that co-operative groups have and the products that they create, providing additional structure and guidance when necessary to promote maximal learning and achievement.

Co-operative learning has personal and social benefits as well as academic ones. For instance, it often promotes self-efficacy, intrinsic motivation, social skills, and cross-cultural friendships.

As you can see, co-operative learning is not simply a process of putting students in groups and setting them loose to work on an assignment together. Oftentimes, your students will be more accustomed to competitive and individualistic classroom situations than they are to working co-operatively with their classmates. For a co-operative learning activity to be successful, structure the activity in such a way that co-operation is not only helpful for academic success but in fact even necessary for it (D. W. Johnson & Johnson, 1991). Following are several strategies that enhance the effectiveness of co-operative groups:

- *Form groups based on which students are likely to work effectively with one another.* Co-operative groups are typically comprised of two to six members; groups of three to four students are especially effective (Hatano & Inagaki, 1991; Lou et al., 1996). In most cases, you should form the groups, identifying combinations of students that are likely to be productive (D. W. Johnson & Johnson, 1991).

- *Give group members one or more common goals to work toward.* At the beginning of a co-operative group activity, you should specify clearly and concretely what each group should accomplish (Crook, 1995; D. W. Johnson & Johnson, 1991).

- *Provide clear guidelines about how to behave.* Without instruction about appropriate group behaviours, students may act in a decidedly uncooperative manner; for example, they may try to dominate discussions, ridicule one another's ideas, or exert pressure to complete the task in a particular way (Blumenfeld, Marx, Soloway, & Krajcik, 1996; N. M. Webb & Palincsar, 1996). Instruction on such group skills as these seems to increase co-operative and productive group behaviours:

  - Listening to others politely and attentively
  - Giving encouragement to others
  - Making sure everyone has an equal chance to participate
  - Refraining from insulting or yelling at others
  - Offering assistance to those who need it
  - Asking clear, precise questions when one doesn't understand (E. G. Cohen, 1994; Deutsch, 1993; Gillies & Ashman, 1998; Lou et al., 1996; O'Donnell & O'Kelly, 1994; N. M. Webb & Farivar, 1999)

- *Structure tasks so that group members are dependent on one another for their success.* You should structure co-operative learning activities in such a way that each student's success depends on the help and participation of other group members; furthermore, each student must believe it is to his or her advantage that other group members do well (Deutsch, 1993; Karau & Williams, 1995; Lou et al., 1996). For instance, tasks that involve creative problem solving and have more than one right answer are likely to encourage students to work co-operatively with one another, presumably because students recognize that several heads will be better than one in solving them (Blumenfeld et al., 1996). In some situations, each student might have a unique and essential function within the group, perhaps serving as group leader, critic, bookkeeper, summarizer, and so on (A. L. Brown & Palincsar, 1989; D. W. Johnson & Johnson, 1991). In other situations, the **jigsaw technique** is useful: New information is divided equally among all group members, and each student must teach his or her portion to the other group members (Aronson & Patnoe, 1997). Still another approach is to assign projects that require such a wide range of talents and skills that every group member is likely to have something truly unique and useful to contribute to the group's overall success (E. G. Cohen, 1994; Schofield, 1995).

When students are novices at co-operative learning, it is often helpful to give them a set of steps (a "script" to follow) that guides their interaction (A. King, 1999; Meloth & Deering, 1994; N. M. Webb & Palincsar, 1996). In one approach, known as **scripted co-operation**, students work together in pairs to read and study expository text. One member of the pair might act as "recaller," summarizing the contents of a textbook passage. The other student acts as "listener," correcting any errors and recalling additional important information. For the next passage, the two students switch roles. Such an approach can help students improve such learning strategies as elaboration, summarizing, and comprehension monitoring (Dansereau, 1988; O'Donnell, 1999).

- *Make students individually accountable for their achievement, but also reinforce them for group success.* Students are more likely to learn assigned classroom subject matter during co-operative learning activities when they know that they will have to demonstrate individual mastery or accomplishment of the group's goal—for example, by taking a quiz or answering questions in class. Such an approach minimizes the likelihood that some students will do most or all of the work while others get a "free ride" (Karau & Williams, 1995; Slavin, 1990; N. M. Webb & Palincsar, 1996).

In addition to holding students accountable for their own learning and achievement, you should also reinforce group members for the success of the group as a whole—a group contingency

Jigsaw technique An instructional technique in which instructional materials are divided among members of a co-operative learning group, with individual students being responsible for learning different material and then teaching that material to other group members.

Scripted co-operation In co-operative learning, a technique in which co-operative groups follow a set of steps or a "script" that guides members' verbal interactions.

in action (Lou et al., 1996; Slavin, 1990; Stipek, 1996). Such group rewards often promote higher achievement overall, perhaps because students have a vested interest in helping one another learn and so make a concerted effort to help fellow group members understand the material that the group is studying (Slavin, 1983; R. J. Stevens & Slavin, 1995). One commonly used approach is to give students a quiz on material they have studied in their co-operative groups and then award bonus points when all group members perform at or above a certain level.

■ *At the end of an activity, have the groups evaluate their effectiveness.* After co-operative groups have accomplished their goals, you should have them look analytically and critically (perhaps with your assistance) at the ways in which they have functioned effectively and the ways in which they need to improve (E. G. Cohen, 1994; Deutsch, 1993; D. W. Johnson & Johnson, 1991). You might ask them to consider some of the same issues you kept in mind as you monitored the activity—for instance, whether everyone participated equally, whether group members asked one another questions when they didn't understand, and whether everyone criticized ideas rather than people.

■ *Consider forming long-term co-operative groups.* Many groups are formed on a short-term basis to accomplish specific tasks—perhaps to study new material, solve a problem, or complete an assigned project. Yet on other occasions, it may be beneficial to form groups that work toward long-term classroom goals. For instance, **base groups** are co-operative groups that work together the entire semester or school year; they provide a means through which students can clarify assignments for one another, help one another with class notes, and give one another a general sense of support and belonging in the classroom (D. W. Johnson & Johnson, 1991).

Base group A co-operative learning group that works together for an entire semester or school year and provides a means through which students can be mutually supportive of one another's academic efforts and activities.

One of the reasons that co-operative learning is so often effective is that students tutor one another in the subject matter they are studying. Such peer tutoring is our next topic of discussion.

Peer Tutoring

As noted in our earlier discussion of mastery learning, some students may need more time to master a topic than others; hence, they may need more instructional time, and perhaps more individualized instruction, than their classmates. As a teacher, you can't always devote much time to one-on-one instruction. **Peer tutoring**—students who have mastered a topic teaching those who have not—can provide an effective alternative for teaching fundamental knowledge and skills. In some cases, students within a single class tutor one another. In other situations, older students teach younger ones; for instance, Grade 4 or 5 students might tutor students in kindergarten or Grade 1 (A. L. Brown & Campione, 1994; Inglis & Biemiller, 1997; Kermani & Moallem, 1997).

Peer tutoring An approach to instruction whereby students who have mastered a topic teach those who have not.

Like mastery learning, direct instruction, and computer-based instruction, peer tutoring sessions give students many opportunities to make the active responses that, from a behaviourist perspective, are so essential to learning. From a more cognitive framework, tutoring encourages students to organize and elaborate on what they have already learned in order to make the material clear to someone else. And cross-age tutoring is consistent with Vygotsky's belief that older and more competent individuals are invaluable in promoting the cognitive development of younger children.

In some cases, peer tutoring leads to greater academic gains than either mastery learning or more traditional whole-class instruction (D. Fuchs, Fuchs, Mathes, & Simmons, 1997; Greenwood, Carta, & Hall, 1988). One possible reason for its effectiveness is that it provides a context in which struggling students may be more comfortable asking questions when they don't understand something. In one study (Graesser & Person, 1994), students asked 240 times as many questions during peer tutoring as they did during whole-class instruction!

Why might teaching younger students a particular skill enhance tutors' self-regulation related to that skill?

Peer tutoring typically benefits tutors as well as those being tutored (D. Fuchs et al., 1997; Inglis & Biemiller, 1997; Semb et al., 1993; N. M. Webb & Palincsar, 1996). When students study material with the expectation that they will be teaching it to someone else, they are more intrinsically motivated to learn it, find it more interesting, process it in a more meaningful way, and remember it longer (Benware & Deci, 1984; Semb et al., 1993). Furthermore, when students who are relatively weak in a particular domain (compared to their age-mates) guide younger students in that domain, they develop greater ability to guide *themselves* (i.e., they develop greater self-regulation) in that domain (Biemiller et al., 1998). Peer tutoring has nonacademic benefits as well. Co-operation and other social skills improve, classroom behaviour problems diminish, and friendships develop among students of different ethnic groups and between students with and without disabilities (DuPaul, Ervin, Hook, & McGoey, 1998; Greenwood et al., 1988).

Like other interactive approaches to instruction, peer tutoring is most effective when teachers follow certain guidelines in its use. Following are several suggestions for using peer tutoring effectively:

- *Make sure tutors have mastered the material they are teaching and use effective instructional techniques.* Good tutors have a meaningful understanding of the subject matter they are teaching and provide explanations that focus on such understanding; poor tutors are more likely to describe procedures without explaining why the procedures are useful (L. S. Fuchs et al., 1996). Good tutors also use teaching strategies that are likely to promote learning: They ask questions, give hints, scaffold responses when necessary, provide feedback, and so on (Lepper, Aspinwall, Mumme, & Chabay, 1990).

- *Provide a structure for students' interactions.* Providing a structure for tutoring sessions can often help students tutor their classmates more effectively (Fantuzzo, King, & Heller, 1992; D. Fuchs et al., 1997; L. S. Fuchs et al., 1996; A. King, 1999).

- *Use peer tutoring to help students with special educational needs.* Peer tutoring has been used effectively to help students with learning disabilities, physical disabilities, and other special educational needs (Cushing & Kennedy, 1997; DuPaul, Barkley, & Connor, 1998; D. Fuchs et al., 1997). For example, in one study (Cushing & Kennedy, 1997), low-achieving students were assigned as tutors for classmates who had moderate or severe intellectual or physical disabilities. The student tutors clearly benefited from their tutoring assignments: They became more attentive in class, completed classroom tasks more frequently, and participated in class more regularly. We suspect that the opportunity to tutor classmates less capable than themselves may have enhanced their own self-efficacy for learning classroom subject matter, which in turn would encourage them to engage in the kinds of behaviours that would ensure academic success.

- *Make sure that all students have experience tutoring their classmates.* Ideally, you should make sure that all of your students have an opportunity to tutor their classmates at one time or another (Greenwood, 1991). This is often easier said than done, as a few of your students may show consistently lower achievement than most of their peers. One potentially effective strategy in such situations is to teach those students specific tasks or procedures that they can share with their higher-achieving, but in this case uninformed, classmates (E. G. Cohen, Lockheed, & Lohman, 1976; N. M. Webb & Palincsar, 1996).

In fact, how to best accommodate student diversity must be a top consideration no matter which instructional strategy you use. We turn now to a more focused discussion of individual and group differences and their potential implications for various instructional strategies.

In many cases, when one student tutors another, the tutor learns as much from the experience as the student being tutored.

Have you ever tutored a student who had a disability? If so, what benefits did *you* gain from the experience?

Taking Student Diversity into Account

The instructional strategies you choose will inevitably depend on the particular students you will be teaching, as described in Chapter 4. You must base your decisions, in part, on your students' ages and developmental levels. Strategies that involve teaching well-defined topics, require a great deal of active student responding, and provide frequent feedback (e.g., mastery learning, direct instruction, computer-based instruction) will often be more appropriate for younger students than for older ones (Rosenshine & Stevens, 1986). Lectures (which are often somewhat abstract) and homework assignments appear to be more effective with older students (Ausubel et al., 1978; Cooper & Valentine, 2001).

The knowledge and skills that your students bring to a topic should also be a consideration (Gustafsson & Undheim, 1996; Rosenshine & Stevens, 1986). Structured, teacher-directed approaches are probably most appropriate for students who know little or nothing about the subject matter. Students who have already mastered basic knowledge and skills, and particularly those who are self-regulated learners, should begin directing some of their own learning, perhaps in group discussions, authentic activities, or use of hypermedia and the internet. In general, however, virtually *any* student should have experience with a wide variety of instructional methods. For instance, although some students may need to spend considerable time on basic skills, too much time spent in structured, teacher-directed activities may minimize opportunities to choose what and how to study and learn and, as a result, may prevent students from developing a sense of self-determination (Battistich et al., 1995). Some instructional strategies adapt themselves readily to a wide variety of student abilities and needs. For example, mastery learning provides a means through which students can learn at their own pace. Computer-based instructional programs often tailor instruction to students' prior knowledge and skills.

Considering Group Differences

Your students' ethnic and cultural backgrounds may sometimes guide your choice of instructional strategies. Recent immigrants from some Asian countries, for example, may be more accustomed to teacher-directed instruction than to student-directed classroom activities (Igoa, 1995). Yet students from cultures that place a high premium on interpersonal co-operation are likely to achieve at higher levels in classrooms with many interactive and collaborative activities (García, 1994, 1995; McAlpine & Taylor, 1993; N. M. Webb & Palincsar, 1996). In situations where students have limited English skills, technology can often come to your assistance, perhaps in the form of English-language tutorials, computer programs that "read" electronic books to a student, and word processing programs with spelling and grammar checkers (P. F. Merrill et al., 1996).

Collaborative and co-operative approaches to instruction may also be helpful for your female students. Small-group discussions and activities encourage girls to participate more actively than they typically do during whole-class instruction (Théberge, 1994). We should note, however, that boys sometimes take control during small-group activities. If you regularly see such male dominance, you may occasionally want to form all-female groups; by doing so, you are likely to increase girls' participation in group activities and encourage them to take leadership roles (Fennema, 1987; MacLean et al., 1995).

Interactive strategies are especially valuable when your objectives include promoting social development as well as academic achievement. Peer tutoring encourages friendly relationships across ethnic and racial lines (Greenwood et al., 1988). Co-operative learning groups, especially when students work on tasks involving a number of different skills and abilities, can foster an appreciation for the various strengths that students with diverse backgrounds are likely to contribute (E. G. Cohen, 1994; E. G. Cohen & Lotan, 1995). And virtually any "co-operative" approach to instruction—co-operative learning, peer tutoring—may help students begin to recognize that despite the obvious diversity among them, they are more similar to one another than they are different (Schofield, 1995).

Accommodating Students in Inclusive Settings

You may sometimes want to tailor your instructional objectives to students' specific cognitive abilities or disabilities; for example, you may need to modify your expectations in some academic areas for students with learning disabilities, and you may find it beneficial to set more challenging goals for students who are gifted. In addition, different instructional strategies may be more or less useful for students with special educational needs. For instance, strictly expository instruction (e.g., a lecture) may provide a quick and efficient means of presenting new ideas to students who think abstractly and process information quickly yet be incomprehensible and overwhelming to students with low cognitive ability. Similarly, discovery learning is often effective in enhancing the academic achievement of students with high ability; however, it may actually be detrimental to the achievement of lower-ability students who have not yet mastered basic concepts and skills (Corno & Snow, 1986). Mastery learning and direct instruction have also been shown to be effective with students who have learning difficulties, including many students with special educational needs, yet they may prevent rapid learners from progressing at a rate commensurate with their abilities (Arlin, 1984; DuPaul, Ervin, Hook, & McGoey, 1998; Leinhardt & Pallay, 1982; Rosenshine & Stevens, 1986).

There will often be a need to adapt instructional strategies to the unique strengths and weaknesses of particular students with special needs. For example, when students have difficulty with certain aspects of information processing (e.g., when they have certain learning disabilities), it may be especially important to provide a variety of supports (advance organizers, visual aids, study guides, etc.) during expository instruction (Mercer, 1997). When students have social or behavioural problems, you may find that you need to provide close supervision and frequent encouragement and feedback during independent in-class assignments. Table 10.3 provides a "memory refresher" for some of the characteristics of students with special needs that we have considered in previous chapters; it also presents some instructional strategies we can use to accommodate such characteristics.

TABLE 10.3 STUDENTS IN INCLUSIVE SETTINGS

Identifying Objectives and Instructional Strategies Especially Suitable for Students with Special Educational Needs

CATEGORY	CHARACTERISTICS YOU MIGHT OBSERVE	SUGGESTED CLASSROOM STRATEGIES
Students with specific cognitive or academic difficulties	• Uneven patterns of achievement • Difficulty with complex cognitive tasks in some content domains • Difficulty processing or remembering information presented in particular modalities • Poor listening and/or reading skills • Greater-than-average difficulty in completing homework	• Establish challenging yet realistic objectives; tailor objectives to individual students' strengths and weaknesses. • Use an information processing analysis to identify the specific cognitive skills involved in a complex task; consider teaching each skill separately. • Use mastery learning, direct instruction, computer-based instruction, co-operative learning, and peer tutoring to help students master basic knowledge and skills. • During expository instruction, provide information through multiple modalities (e.g., with videotapes, audiotapes, graphic materials), and provide advance organizers and study guides. • Have students use computer tools (e.g., grammar and spelling checkers) to compensate for areas of weakness. • Assign homework that provides additional practice in basic skills; individualize assignments for students' unique abilities and needs; provide extra scaffolding (e.g., solicit parents' help, explicitly teach effective study habits). • Use reciprocal teaching to promote listening and reading comprehension.
Students with social or behavioural problems	• Frequent off-task behaviour • Inability to work independently for extended periods • Poor social skills	• Provide small-group direct instruction and peer tutoring as ways of providing one-on-one attention. • Keep unsupervised seatwork assignments to a minimum. • Use co-operative learning to foster social skills and friendships. • Give explicit guidelines about how to behave during interactive learning sessions. (As appropriate, also use strategies above for students with specific cognitive or academic difficulties.)
Students with general delays in cognitive and social functioning	• Difficulty with complex tasks • Difficulty thinking abstractly • Need for a great deal of repetition and practice of basic information and skills • Difficulty transferring information and skills to new situations	• Establish realistic objectives in both the academic and social arenas. • Use task analysis to break complex behaviours into simpler responses that students can more easily learn. • Present information as concretely as possible (e.g., by engaging students in hands-on experiences). • Use direct instruction, computer-assisted instruction, and in-class activities to provide extended practice in basic skills. • Embed basic skills within authentic tasks to promote transfer to the outside world. • Use peer tutoring as a means of promoting friendships with nondisabled classmates; identify skills that students have mastered and can teach to their classmates or to younger students.
Students with physical or sensory challenges	• Average intelligence in most instances • Tendency to tire easily (for some) • Limited motor skills (for some) • Difficulty with speech (for some)	• Aim for instructional objectives similar to those for nondisabled students unless there is a compelling reason to do otherwise. • Allow frequent breaks from strenuous or intensive activities. • Use computer-based instruction (perhaps with specially adapted input mechanisms) to allow students to progress through material at their own pace and to make active responses during instruction. • When students have difficulty speaking, provide another means of enabling them to participate actively in class discussions and co-operative learning groups (perhaps through technology).
Students showing evidence of giftedness, talent, or high performance	• Greater frequency of responses at higher levels of Bloom's taxonomy (e.g., analysis, synthesis) • Rapid learning • Greater ability to think abstractly; appearance of abstract thinking at a younger age • Greater conceptual understanding of classroom material • Ability to learn independently	• Identify standards and objectives that challenge students and encourage them to develop to their full potential. • Provide opportunities to pursue topics in greater depth (e.g., through assigned readings, computer-based instruction, or homogeneous co-operative groups). • Teach strategies that enable students to learn on their own (e.g., library skills, scientific methods, use of hypermedia and the internet). • Encourage students to communicate via the internet with others who have similar interests and abilities. • Ask predominantly higher-level questions. • Use advanced students as peer tutors only if both tutors and learners will benefit. • Encourage these students (and eventually others, as your teaching skills and ability to adapt instruction grow) to select topics of individual interest in or related to the curriculum and to work with you in an inquiry-based manner, initially in a shorter time frame but gradually expanding.

Sources: Aulls & Shore, 2008; T. Bryan, Burstein, & Bryan, 2001; Carnine, 1989; DuNann & Weber, 1976; DuPaul, Ervin, Hook, & McGoey, 1998; Fiedler, Lange, & Winebrenner, 1993; Greenwood et al., 1988; Heward, 2000; C. C. Kulik et al., 1990; Mercer, 1997; P. F. Merrill et al., 1996; Morgan & Jenson, 1988; Piirto, 1999; A. Robinson, 1991; Ruef et al., 1998; Schiffman, Tobin, & Buchanan, 1984; Spicker, 1992; R. J. Stevens & Slavin, 1995; Tarver, 1992; Turnbull et al., 1999; J. W. Wood & Rosbe, 1985.

TEACHING CONSTRUCTIONS

When you consider which instructional strategies to use in the classroom, remember that there is no single best approach to classroom instruction. Table 10.4 presents general conditions and specific examples in which many commonly used strategies might be most appropriate.

Now that you have learned about effective instructional strategies, let's revisit Ms. Hamilton's class, presented at the beginning of this chapter:

- What kinds of instructional strategies was Ms. Hamilton using in her lesson?
- If this was your lesson, what are some instructional strategies that you would incorporate into a lesson on building communities?
- In what ways did Ms. Hamilton incorporate both expository and co-operative instructional strategies in her teaching?
- How might Ms. Hamilton have used CBI to facilitate student learning and instruction?

KEY CONCEPTS

instructional objective (p. 260)
cognitive domain (p. 261)
psychomotor domain (p. 261)
affective domain (p. 261)
Bloom's taxonomy (p. 261)
short-term objective (p. 261)
long-term objective (p. 261)
task analysis (p. 263)

expository instruction (p. 265)
mastery learning (p. 266)
direct instruction (p. 268)
programmed instruction (p. 269)
computer-assisted instruction (CAI) (p. 269)
computer-based instruction (CBI) (p. 270)
discovery learning (p. 274)

lower-level question (p. 276)
higher-level question (p. 276)
cognitive strategy instruction (p. 278)
co-operative learning (p. 281)
jigsaw technique (p. 283)
scripted co-operation (p. 283)
base group (p. 284)
peer tutoring (p. 284)

TABLE 10.4   COMPARE/CONTRAST

Choosing an Instructional Strategy

YOU MIGHT USE	WHEN	FOR EXAMPLE, YOU MIGHT
Lectures and/or textbook readings	• The *objective* is to acquire knowledge within the cognitive domain. • The *lesson* involves information best learned within a specific organizational structure. • *Students* are capable of abstract thought, have knowledge to which they can relate new material, and have adequate reading skills and learning strategies for assigned readings.	• Enumerate the critical battles of World War I to advanced history students. • Demonstrate several defensive strategies to the soccer team.
Mastery learning	• The *objective* is to learn knowledge or skills to mastery (perhaps to automaticity). • The *lesson* provides critical information or skills for later instructional units. • *Students* vary in the time they need to achieve mastery.	• Have each student in instrumental music practise the C major scale until he or she can perform it perfectly. • Have students practise 100 single-digit addition facts until they can answer all the facts correctly within a five-minute period.
Direct instruction	• The *objective* is to learn a well-defined body of knowledge and skills. • The *lesson* provides critical information or skills for later instructional units. • *Students* are likely to need considerable guidance and practice in order to learn successfully.	• Explain how to add fractions with different denominators and give students practice in adding such fractions both in class and through homework. • Demonstrate how to use a jigsaw and watch carefully as students use the tool to cut irregularly shaped pieces of wood.
Computer-based instruction	• The *objective* is to acquire knowledge and skills within the cognitive domain. • The *lesson* involves information that students can learn from reading text or from watching and listening to multimedia presentations. • *Students* have some familiarity with computers and can work with only minimal guidance from their teacher.	• Use a typing-skills tutorial that helps students develop automaticity in keyboarding. • Assign a research project that requires the use of a computer-based, multimedia encyclopedia.
Online research	• The *objective* is to gain expertise in finding information available on the World Wide Web. • The *lesson* requires information not readily available in the classroom. • *Students* have some familiarity with internet software (e.g., web browsers) and search engines.	• Ask students to identify demographic differences among various regions of Canada using data from the Canadian Census Bureau. • Have students read about current events on the websites of national news bureaus and newsmagazines.
Discovery learning	• The *objective* is to develop firsthand knowledge of physical or social phenomena. • The *lesson* involves information that can be correctly deduced from hands-on experimentation with concrete objects or from direct social interaction with others. • *Students* have enough knowledge to interpret their findings correctly but sometimes have difficulty learning from strictly abstract material.	• Ask students to find out what happens when two primary colours of paint (red and yellow, red and blue, or yellow and blue) are mixed together. • Create a classroom situation in which students discover firsthand how it feels to experience "taxation without representation."
In-class activities	• The *objective* is to practise using new information or skills. • The *lesson* requires considerable teacher monitoring and scaffolding. • *Students* cannot yet work independently on the task.	• Have beginning tennis students practise their serves. • Have students work in pairs to draw portraits of their classmates.
Computer simulations and applications	• The *objective* is to gain experience in a domain that can be explored more easily in a "virtual" world *or* to gain experience with computer tools. • The *lesson* involves any task for which simulation software is available *or* that lends itself to a computer application. • *Students* have some familiarity with computers and can work with only minimal guidance from their teacher.	• Have students explore human anatomy through a computer simulation that gives an inside "look" at various anatomical structures. • Have students write a resumé using a word processing program.

(continued)

TABLE 10.4 (continued) COMPARE/CONTRAST

Choosing an Instructional Strategy

YOU MIGHT USE	WHEN	FOR EXAMPLE, YOU MIGHT
Homework	• The *objective* is to learn new yet simple material, obtain additional practice with familiar information and procedures, or relate classroom subject matter to the outside world. • The *lesson* is one that students can complete with little, if any, help from others. • *Students* exhibit enough self-regulation to perform the task independently.	• Have students read the next chapter in their health book. • In a unit on migration, have students find out what province, state, or country their parents and grandparents were born in.
Authentic activities	• The *objective* is to apply classroom material to real-world situations. • The *lesson* involves synthesizing and applying a variety of knowledge and skills. • *Students* have mastered the knowledge and skills necessary to perform the task.	• Have students grow sunflowers using varying amounts of water, plant food, and sunlight. • Have students construct maps of their local community, using appropriate symbols to convey direction, scale, physical features, and so on.
Teacher questions	• The *objective* is to understand and elaborate on a topic in greater depth. • The *lesson* involves complex material, such that frequent monitoring of students' learning is essential, mental elaboration of ideas is beneficial, or both. • *Students* are not likely to elaborate spontaneously or to monitor their own comprehension effectively.	• Ask questions that promote recall and review of the previous day's lesson. • Ask students for examples of how nonrenewable resources are recycled in their own community.
Class discussion	• The *objective* is to achieve greater conceptual understanding, acquire a multisided perspective of a topic, or both. • The *lesson* involves complex and possibly controversial issues. • *Students* have sufficient knowledge about the topic to voice informed ideas and opinions.	• Ask students to discuss the ethical implications of the United States' decision to drop an atomic bomb on Hiroshima. • Ask groups of four or five students to prepare arguments for an upcoming debate regarding the pros and cons of increasing the minimum wage.
Reciprocal teaching	• The *objective* is to develop reading comprehension and learning strategies. • The *lesson* requires students to cognitively process material in relatively complex ways. • *Students* have poor reading comprehension and learning strategies.	• Model four types of questions—summarizing, questioning, clarifying, and predicting—as students read aloud a passage from a textbook. • Ask students to take turns being "teacher" and ask similar questions of their classmates.
Technology-based discussion	• The *objective* is to construct new knowledge as a group and continue to revise it over time. • The *lesson* involves a topic that is sufficiently multifaceted that all students have something to contribute. • *Students* have adequate reading comprehension skills to learn independently or in small groups, and adequate computer literacy to exchange information electronically.	• In a community where students have easy access to computers and the internet, set up an electronic bulletin board that allows students to share their questions and ideas about homework assignments. • On the classroom computer's desktop, create several "folders" in which students can save essays for one another to read and critique.
Co-operative learning	• The *objective* is to develop the ability to work co-operatively with others on academic tasks. • The *lesson* involves tasks that are too large or difficult for a single student to accomplish independently. • *Students*' cultural backgrounds emphasize co-operation rather than competition.	• Have groups of two or three students work together on mathematics "brain teasers." • Have students in a French class work in small groups to write and videotape a soap opera spoken entirely in French.
Peer tutoring	• The *objective* is to learn basic knowledge or skills. • The *lesson* contains material that can effectively be taught by students. • *Students* vary in their mastery of the material, yet even the most advanced can gain increased understanding by teaching it to someone else.	• Have students work in pairs to practise conjugating irregular French verbs. • Have some students help others work through simple mathematical word problems.

11 Creating and Maintaining a Productive Classroom Environment

CASE STUDY A CONTAGIOUS SITUATION

TEACHING CONNECTIONS

CREATING AN ENVIRONMENT CONDUCIVE TO LEARNING
Arranging the Classroom • Creating an Effective Classroom Climate • Setting Limits • Planning Activities That Keep Students on Task • Monitoring What Students Are Doing • Modifying Instructional Strategies

DEALING WITH MISBEHAVIOURS

TAKING STUDENT DIVERSITY INTO ACCOUNT
Creating a Supportive Climate • Accommodating Students in the Inclusive Classroom

COORDINATING EFFORTS WITH OTHERS
Working with Other Teachers • Working with the Community at Large • Working with Parents

TEACHING CONSTRUCTIONS

KEY CONCEPTS

CASE STUDY *A Contagious Situation*

Ms. Cornell received her teaching certificate in May; soon after, she accepted a position as a Grade 5 teacher at Twin Pines Elementary School. She spent the summer planning her classroom curriculum: She identified the objectives she wanted her students to accomplish during the year and developed numerous activities to help them meet those objectives. She now feels well prepared for her first year in the classroom.

After the long, hot summer, most of Ms. Cornell's students seem happy to be back at school. So on the very first day of school, Ms. Cornell jumps headlong into the curriculum she has planned. But three problems quickly present themselves—problems in the form of Eli, Jake, and Vanessa.

These three students seem determined to disrupt the class at every possible opportunity. They move about the room without permission, making a point of annoying others as they walk to the pencil sharpener or wastebasket. They talk out of turn, sometimes being rude and disrespectful to their teacher and classmates and at other times belittling the classroom activities that Ms. Cornell has so carefully planned. They rarely complete their in-class assignments, preferring instead to engage in horseplay or practical jokes. They seem particularly prone to misbehaviour at "down" times in the class schedule—for example, at the beginning and end of the school day, before and after recess and lunch, and on occasions when Ms. Cornell is preoccupied with other students.

Ms. Cornell continues to follow her daily lesson plans, ignoring her problem students and hoping they will begin to see the error of their ways. Yet, with the three of them egging one another on, the disruptive behaviour continues. Furthermore, it begins to spread to other students. By the middle of October, Ms. Cornell's class is a three-ring circus, with general chaos reigning in the classroom and instructional objectives rarely being accomplished. The few students who still seem intent on learning something are having a difficult time doing so.

TEACHING CONNECTIONS

Effective teachers not only choose instructional strategies that promote effective learning and cognitive processing, but they also create an environment that keeps students busily engaged in classroom activities. In this chapter we will consider how to plan and create a classroom environment conducive to students' learning and achievement. Consider the following questions as you read and make connections between theory and your own teaching practice:

- How can you create a classroom environment that promotes student learning and minimizes off-task behaviour?
- How can you effectively deal with the misbehaviours that *do* occur?
- How can you coordinate your efforts with other teachers, community agencies, and students' parents?
- In what ways has Ms. Cornell planned for her classroom in advance? In what ways has she *not* planned?
- Why are Eli, Jake, and Vanessa so disruptive right from the start? Can you think of possible reasons related to how Ms. Cornell has begun the school year? Can you think of possible reasons related to the classroom activities Ms. Cornell has planned?
- Why does the misbehaviour of the three problem students continue? Why does it spread to other students in the classroom? Why is it particularly common during "down" times in the school day?

Creating an Environment Conducive to Learning

As a first-year teacher, Ms. Cornell is well prepared in some respects but not at all prepared in others. She has carefully identified her objectives and the activities through which she intends to accomplish those objectives. But she has neglected to think about how she might keep students on task or how she might adjust her lesson plans based on how students are progressing. And she has not considered how she might nip behaviour problems in the bud, before such misbehaviours begin to interfere with students' learning. In the absence of such planning, no curriculum—not even one grounded firmly in principles of learning and development—is likely to promote student achievement.

Students learn more effectively in some classroom environments than in others. Consider these four classrooms as examples:

> Mr. Aragon's class is calm and orderly. The students are working independently at their seats, and all of them appear to be concentrating on their assigned tasks. Occasionally, students approach Mr. Aragon to seek clarification of an assignment or to get feedback about a task they've completed, and he confers quietly with them.
>
> Mr. Boitano's class is chaotic and noisy. A few students are doing their schoolwork, but most are engaged in very nonacademic activities. One girl is painting her nails behind a large dictionary propped up on her desk, a boy nearby is picking wads of gum off the underside of his desk, several students are exchanging the latest school gossip, and a group of boys is re-enacting the Battle of Waterloo with rubber bands and paper clips.
>
> Mr. Cavalini's classroom is as noisy as Boitano's. But rather than exchanging gossip or waging war, students are debating (often loudly and passionately) about the pros and cons of nuclear energy. After 20 minutes of heated discussion, Cavalini stops them, lists their various arguments on the board, and then explains in simple philosophical terms why there is no easy or "correct" resolution of the issue.
>
> Mr. Durocher believes that students learn most effectively when rules for their behaviour are clearly spelled out. So he has rules for almost every conceivable occasion—53 rules in all. Following is a small sample:

- Be in your seat before the bell rings.
- Use a ballpoint pen with blue or black ink for all assignments.
- Use white lined paper with straight edges; do not use paper with loose-leaf holes or spiral notebook "fringe."
- Raise your hand if you wish to speak, and then speak only when called upon.
- Do not ask questions unrelated to the topic being studied.
- Never leave your seat without permission.

> Durocher punishes each infraction severely enough that students follow the rules to the letter. So his students are a quiet and obedient (if somewhat anxious) bunch, but they never seem to learn as much as Durocher knows they are capable of learning.

Two of these classrooms are quiet and orderly; the other two are active and noisy. Yet as you can see, the activity and noise levels are not good indicators of how much students are learning. Students are learning both in Mr. Aragon's quiet classroom and in Mr. Cavalini's rambunctious one. At the same time, neither the students in Mr. Boitano's loud, chaotic battlefield nor those in Mr. Durocher's peaceful military dictatorship seem to be learning much at all.

Effective **classroom management**—creating and maintaining a classroom environment conducive to learning and achievement—has little to do with noise or activity level. A well-managed classroom is one in which students are consistently engaged in productive learning activities and in which students' behaviours rarely interfere with the achievement of instructional objectives (W. Doyle, 1990; Emmer & Evertson, 1981; Munn, Johnstone, & Chalmers, 1990).

To create and maintain a productive learning environment, effective teachers typically

- Physically arrange the classroom in a way that facilitates teacher–student interactions and keeps distracting influences to a minimum
- Create a classroom climate in which students have a sense of belonging and an intrinsic motivation to learn
- Set reasonable limits for student behaviour
- Plan classroom activities that encourage on-task behaviour
- Continually monitor what all students are doing
- Modify instructional strategies when necessary

In the pages that follow, we will consider specific ways to implement each of these strategies.

Classroom management
Establishing and maintaining a classroom environment conducive to learning and achievement.

Is it possible to *over*manage a classroom? If so, what might be the negative ramifications of doing so? See the SMARTeacher Education Resource Centre of the University of Prince Edward Island, which provides resources for classroom management (www.upei.ca/smarteacher/).

Arranging the Classroom

As you arrange the furniture in the classroom, decide where to put various instructional materials and pieces of equipment, and think about where each student might sit, you should consider the effects that various arrangements are likely to have on students' behaviours (see the National Clearinghouse for Educational Facilities created by the U.S. Department of Education at www.edfacilities.org for ideas about how to design a classroom). Ultimately, you want a situation in which you can

- Minimize distractions
- Interact easily with any student
- Survey the entire class at any given time

Minimizing Distractions

Stuart is more likely to poke a classmate with his pencil if he has to brush past the classmate to get to the pencil sharpener. Marlene is more likely to fiddle with instructional materials at an inappropriate time if they are within easy reach of her desk. David is more likely to gossip with a friend if that friend is sitting right beside him. Arrange your classroom in ways that minimize the probability that such off-task behaviours will occur (Emmer, Evertson, Clements, & Worsham, 1994; Sabers, Cushing, & Berliner, 1991). For example, you can establish traffic patterns that allow students to move around the classroom without disturbing one another, keep intriguing materials out of sight and reach until it is time to use them, and situate overly chatty friends on opposite sides of the room.

A well-managed classroom is one in which students are consistently engaged in learning. It is not necessarily one in which everyone is quiet.

Facilitating Teacher–Student Interaction

Ideally, you should arrange desks, tables, and chairs so that you can easily interact and converse with your students (Davis & Thomas, 1989). Students seated near us are more likely to pay attention, interact with us, and become actively involved in classroom activities; hence, you may want to place chronically misbehaving or uninvolved students close at hand (W. Doyle, 1986a; Schwebel & Cherlin, 1972; C. S. Weinstein, 1979; Woolfolk & Brooks, 1985).

Surveying the Entire Class

As you proceed through various lessons and activities—even when you're working with a single individual or small group—you should ideally be able to see *all* of your students (Emmer et al., 1994). By occasionally surveying the classroom for possible signs of confusion, frustration, or boredom, you can more easily detect minor student difficulties and misbehaviours before they develop into serious problems.

Creating an Effective Classroom Climate

Think back on your many years as a student. Can you remember a class in which you were afraid of being ridiculed if you asked a "stupid" question? Can you remember one in which you and your fellow students spent more time goofing off than getting your work done because no one seemed to take the class seriously? Can you remember one in which you never knew what to expect because your instructor was continually changing expectations and giving last-minute assignments without warning?

In addition to the classroom's physical environment, you must also consider the psychological environment, or **classroom climate**, that you create. Ideally, you want a classroom in which students make their own learning a high priority and feel free to take the risks and make the mistakes so critical for long-term academic success. To create such a classroom climate,

Classroom climate The psychological atmosphere of the classroom.

- Communicate acceptance of, respect for, and caring about your students as human beings
- Give students some control over classroom activities
- Create a sense of community among the students

Visit www.udel.edu/cte/Tabook/climate.html for information on how to promote a positive classroom climate.

Showing Acceptance, Respect, and Caring

Human beings may have a fundamental need to feel socially connected with others. This *need for relatedness* expresses itself somewhat differently in different students. Many students have a high need for affiliation: They actively seek out friendly relationships with others. Many also have a high need for approval: They want to gain the acceptance and high regard of those around them.

You can help your students meet such needs through your own actions, including the many little things you do daily. For example, you can give students a smile and warm greeting at the beginning of each class day. You can compliment them when they get a new haircut, excel in an extracurricular activity, or receive recognition in the local newspaper. You can ask them for information or advice about a topic of particular interest to them. You can offer your support when they struggle at challenging classroom tasks and let them know you're pleased when they eventually succeed at such tasks. You can be a good listener when they come to school angry or upset. And you can show them how you, too, are a fallible human being by sharing some of your own concerns, problems, and frustrations (Diamond, 1991; Spaulding, 1992).

> Such teacher behaviours may be particularly beneficial for those students who have few caring relationships to draw on at home (Diamond, 1991).

Research is clear on this point: Effective teachers are warm, caring individuals who, through a variety of statements and actions, communicate a respect for students, an acceptance of them as they are, and a genuine concern about their well-being. When students believe that their teachers are genuinely caring and supportive, they have higher self-efficacy, find classroom subject matter more interesting and enjoyable, are more likely to ask for help when they need it, are less likely to cheat on classroom assignments, and achieve at higher levels (C. B. Hayes, Ryan, & Zseller, 1994; Kim, Solomon, & Roberts, 1995; Murdock, Hale, Weber, Tucker, & Briggs, 1999; Osterman, 2000; A. M. Ryan & Patrick, 2001; A. M. Ryan et al., 2001; Wentzel & Wigfield, 1998). In a study aimed at examining students' perceptions of teacher characteristics that support or inhibit help seeking, Le Mare and Sohbat (2002) at Simon Fraser University in British Columbia found that when students from Grades 2 to 7 believe their teachers know them and relate to them beyond academic matters, they seem more comfortable in asking for help when they need it. When teachers show little interest in their students' initiatives because they are busy, speak discourteously to them, use judgmental vocabulary, and pay superficial attention to what they say, they convey attitudes of insensitivity, lack of acceptance, and disrespect. On the other hand, when teachers let students know they care for them and that they are approachable, students will more likely seek their help.

Giving Students a Sense of Control

To make sure your students accomplish instructional goals, you must control the direction of classroom events to some extent. Nevertheless, you can give your students a sense that they, too, control some aspects of classroom life. For example, you can use strategies such as these (Spaulding, 1992):

- Give students advance notice of upcoming activities and assignments (enabling them to plan ahead).
- Create regular routines for accomplishing assignments (enabling students to complete the assignments successfully with minimal guidance from you).
- Allow students to set some of their own deadlines for completing assignments (enabling them to establish a reasonable timeframe for themselves).
- Provide opportunities for students to make choices about how to complete assignments or spend some of their class time (enabling them to set some of their own priorities).

By giving students opportunities to work independently and choose some of their own means of achieving classroom objectives, you promote the sense of self-determination so important for intrinsic motivation. You also promote the self-regulated learning so essential for students' long-term academic success. In this regard, Seifert at Memorial University in St. John's, Newfoundland, and his associates (Seifert & O'Keefe, 2001; Jarvis & Seifert, 2002), have found in their work with students from elementary school to high school in eastern Canada that the relationship between teachers and students is critical for developing intrinsic motivation and self-regulated learning. They have found in their studies that instructional practices that challenge students as well as help them develop a sense of competence and self-determination foster students who are intrinsically motivated. In order to behave in an intrinsically motivated manner, students need to feel confident and have a sense that they have some control over their learning. They also need to believe that the work they do is meaningful. According to Seifert (1997), when students view their teachers as nurturing, respectful, and guiding their thinking, it leads to the development of a sense of self-assuredness and control within them and to the pursuit of learning goals.

Creating a Sense of Community

Occasionally, competition among *groups* of students can be productive *if* all groups have an equal chance of winning—for instance, if every group has diverse abilities and talents represented—and *if* the final outcome is determined more by student effort than by intelligence or other seemingly uncontrollable factors (Stipek, 1996).

In general, however, a competitive classroom environment is often counterproductive. For one thing, competitive situations focus students' attention on performance goals rather than mastery goals (Nicholls, 1984; Spaulding, 1992); hence, students are more likely to worry about how competent they appear to their teacher and classmates than about how well they understand classroom material. Second, competition creates a situation in which most students become losers rather than winners; their self-efficacy decreases as a result, and their intrinsic motivation to learn is undermined (Deci & Ryan, 1985, 1992). Finally, when students consistently see others performing more successfully than themselves, they are more likely to attribute their own failures to a lack of ability: They conclude that they simply don't have what it takes to succeed at classroom tasks (C. Ames, 1984).

Ideally your students will be more productive if they co-operate, rather than compete, with one another (C. Ames, 1984; Deci & Ryan, 1985). Not only can they support one another in their efforts to master classroom topics, but they can also nurture the peer relationships that, for many, are so important for their social development and psychological well-being. Students have higher academic self-efficacy, are more motivated to learn and achieve, and are more consistently on task when they can collaborate with their classmates on assignments, believe that their peers accept and respect them, and have little fear that others will ridicule them if they make errors or ask for help (Osterman, 2000; A. M. Ryan & Patrick, 2001; A. M. Ryan et al., 2001). For example, in a study of 951 students from four Canadian high schools, Ferguson and Dorman (2001) found that improved levels of student involvement in class (e.g., participating in discussions), investigation (e.g., use of inquiry and problem-solving skills), and task orientation (e.g., completing subject matter activities) are significantly associated with academic efficacy.

Ultimately, you want to create a **sense of community** in the classroom—a sense that you and your students have shared goals, are mutually respectful and supportive of one another's efforts, and believe that everyone makes an important contribution to classroom learning (Hom & Battistich, 1995; Kim et al., 1995; Lickona, 1991; Osterman, 2000). Theorists have identified several strategies that can help create a sense of classroom community:

- Make frequent use of interactive and collaborative teaching strategies (class discussions, co-operative learning activities, etc.).
- Solicit students' ideas and opinions, and incorporate them into classroom discussions and activities.
- Provide opportunities for students to help one another (e.g., by asking, "Who has a problem that someone else might be able to help you solve?").
- Work on social skills with those students whose interpersonal behaviours may alienate others.
- Provide public recognition of students' contributions to the overall success of the classroom.
- Convey the general message that *all* students deserve the respect of their classmates and are important members of the classroom community. (Emmer et al., 1994; Kim et al., 1995; Lickona, 1991; Osterman, 2000; A. M. Ryan & Patrick, 2001; Sapon-Shevin, Dobbelaere, Corrigan, Goodman, & Mastin, 1998; Turnbull, Pereira, & Blue-Banning, 2000)

Sense of community In the classroom, a widely shared feeling that teacher and students have common goals, are mutually respectful and supportive of one another's efforts, and believe that everyone makes an important contribution to classroom learning.

Students achieve at higher levels in the classroom when they have a *sense of community*—that is, when they have shared goals and are respectful and supportive of one another's efforts.

When students share a sense of community, they are more likely to exhibit prosocial behaviour, stay on task, express enthusiasm about classroom activities, and achieve at high levels. Furthermore, a sense of classroom community is associated with lower rates of emotional distress, disruptive classroom behaviour, truancy, violence, drug use, and dropping out (D. C. Gottfredson, 2001; Hom & Battistich, 1995; Kim et al., 1995; Osterman, 2000; M. D. Resnick et al., 1997).

Setting Limits

A class without guidelines for appropriate behaviour is apt to be chaotic and unproductive. And students must learn that certain behaviours—especially those that cause injury, damage school property, or interfere with classmates' learning and performance—will definitely not be tolerated. Setting reasonable limits on classroom behaviour not only promotes a more productive learning environment but also contributes to students' socialization by encouraging them to develop behaviours essential for successful participation in the adult world.

Experienced educators have offered several suggestions for setting reasonable limits on students' classroom behaviour. For example, they suggest that you establish a few rules and procedures at the beginning of the year and periodically review the usefulness of existing rules and procedures.

Establishing Initial Rules and Procedures

The first few days and weeks of the school year are critical ones for establishing classroom procedures and setting expectations for student behaviour. Effective classroom managers establish and communicate certain rules and procedures right from the start (Borko & Putnam, 1996; Davis & Thomas, 1989; W. Doyle, 1986a, 1990). They identify acceptable and unacceptable behaviours. They develop consistent procedures and routines for such things as completing seatwork, asking for help, and turning in assignments. And they have procedures in place for nonroutine events such as school assemblies, field trips, and fire drills.

Ideally, your students should understand that rules and procedures are not merely the result of your personal whims but are designed to help the classroom run smoothly and efficiently. One way of promoting such understanding is to include students in decision making about the rules and procedures by which the class will operate (Davis & Thomas, 1989; Fuller, 2001; Lickona, 1991). For example, you might solicit students' suggestions for making sure that unnecessary distractions are kept to a minimum and that everyone has a chance to speak during class discussions. By incorporating students' ideas and concerns regarding the limits you set, you help students understand the reasons for—and thereby help them adhere to—those limits (Emmer et al., 1994).

Once rules and procedures have been formulated, you should communicate them clearly and explicitly, describe the consequences of noncompliance, and enforce them consistently. Taking time to clarify and enforce rules and procedures seems to be especially important in the early elementary grades, when students may not be as familiar with "how things are done" at school (Evertson & Emmer, 1982; Gettinger, 1988).

Keep in mind that rules and procedures are easier to remember and therefore easier to follow if they are relatively simple and few in number (Davis & Thomas, 1989). Effective classroom managers tend to stress only the most important rules and procedures at the beginning of the school year; they introduce other rules and procedures later on as needed (W. Doyle, 1986a). Also keep in mind that, although some order and predictability are essential for student productivity, *too much* order may make your classroom a rather boring, routine place—one without an element of fun and spontaneity. You don't necessarily need rules and procedures for everything!

Reviewing Existing Rules and Procedures

As the school year progresses, you may occasionally want to revise the rules and procedures you established earlier. For instance, you may find that rules about when students can and cannot move around the room are overly restrictive or that procedures for turning in homework don't adequately accommodate students who must sometimes leave class early to attend athletic events.

Regularly scheduled class meetings provide one mechanism through which you and your students can periodically review classroom rules and procedures (D. E. Campbell, 1996; Glasser, 1969). Consider this scenario as an example:

> Every Friday at 2:00, Ms. Ayotte's students move their chairs into one large circle, and the weekly class meeting begins. First on the agenda is a review of the past week's successes, including both academic achievements and socially productive events. Next, the group identifies problems that have emerged during the week and brainstorms possible ways to avert such problems in the future. Finally, the students consider whether existing classroom rules and procedures are serving their purpose. They may decide to modify some existing rules and procedures or may establish new ones.
>
> During the first few class meetings, Ms. Ayotte leads the group discussions. But once students have gotten the hang of things, she begins to relinquish control of the meetings to one or another of her students on a rotating basis.

By providing such opportunities for students to revise classroom policies frequently, teachers find one more way of giving them a sense of ownership in such policies. Furthermore, perhaps because of the authoritative atmosphere and the conversations about moral dilemmas that student decision making may entail, more advanced levels of moral reasoning may result (Power et al., 1989; Power & Power, 1992).

With this point in mind, how might Ms. Cornell (in the opening case study) have gotten the year off to a better start?

Planning Activities That Keep Students on Task

Effective teachers plan their lessons ahead of time. Furthermore, they plan activities that not only facilitate students' learning and cognitive processing but also motivate students to *want* to learn. For instance, they think about how to make subject matter interesting and incorporate variety into lessons, perhaps by employing colourful audiovisual aids, using novel activities (e.g., small-group discussions, class debates), or moving to a different location (e.g., the media centre or school yard) (Davis & Thomas, 1989; Munn et al., 1990).

As you plan your upcoming classroom activities, then, you should simultaneously plan specific ways of keeping your students on task. For example:

- Be sure students will always be busy and engaged
- Choose tasks at an appropriate academic level
- Provide a reasonable amount of structure for activities and assignments
- Make special plans for transition times in the school day

Keeping Students Busy and Engaged

Effective classroom managers make sure that there is little "empty" time in which nothing is going on. As teachers, you can use numerous strategies to keep your students busy and engaged; for example, you can

- Have something specific for students to do each day, even on the first day of class
- Have materials organized and equipment set up before class
- Have activities that ensure *all* students' involvement and participation
- Maintain a brisk pace throughout each lesson (although not so fast that students can't keep up)
- Have a system in place that ensures that students who finish an assigned task quickly have something else to do (perhaps writing in a class journal or reading a book) (Davis & Thomas, 1989; W. Doyle, 1986a; Emmer et al., 1994; Evertson & Harris, 1992; Gettinger, 1988; Munn et al., 1990)

Students who are busily engaged in classroom activities rarely exhibit problem behaviours.

Choosing Tasks at an Appropriate Level

Your students are more likely to get involved in their classwork, rather than in off-task behaviour, when they have academic tasks and assignments appropriate for their current ability levels (W. Doyle, 1986a; Emmer et al., 1994). They are apt to misbehave when they are asked to do things that are probably too difficult for them—in other words, when they are incapable of completing assigned tasks successfully. Thus, classroom misbehaviours are more often observed in students who have a history of struggling in their coursework (W. Doyle, 1986a).

This is not to suggest that you should plan activities so easy that your students are not challenged and learn nothing new in doing them. One workable strategy is to *begin* the school year with relatively easy tasks that students can readily complete. Such early tasks enable students to practise normal classroom routines and procedures; they also give students a sense that they can enjoy and be successful in classroom activities. Once a supportive classroom climate has been established and students are comfortable with classroom procedures, you can gradually introduce more difficult and challenging assignments (W. Doyle, 1990; Emmer et al., 1994; Evertson & Emmer, 1982). You might take a similar approach when introducing new instructional strategies; for instance, when you first ask students to engage in co-operative activities, you might have them work with relatively familiar content so that they can focus on mastering effective group interaction skills (asking for help, giving explanations, etc.) without being distracted by difficult subject matter (N. M. Webb & Farivar, 1999).

Providing Structure

EXPERIENCING FIRSTHAND   *Take Five More*

Grab a blank sheet of paper and a pen or pencil, and complete these two tasks:

- Task A: Using short phrases, list six characteristics of an effective teacher.
- Task B: Describe *schooling*.

Don't continue reading until you've spent a total of at least *five minutes* on these tasks.

Once you have completed the two tasks, answer either "Task A" or "Task B" to each of the following questions:

1. For which task did you have a better understanding of what you were being asked to do?
2. During which task did your mind more frequently wander to irrelevant topics?
3. During which task did you engage in more off-task behaviours (e.g., looking around the room, doodling on the paper, getting out of your seat)?

You probably found the first task to be relatively straightforward, whereas the second wasn't at all clear-cut. Did Task B's ambiguity lead to more irrelevant thoughts and off-task behaviours for you?

Just as may have been the case for you in the preceding exercise, off-task behaviour in the classroom occurs more frequently when activities are so loosely structured that students don't have a clear sense of what they are supposed to do. Effective teachers tend to give assignments with some degree of structure. They also give clear directions about how to proceed with a task and a great deal of feedback about appropriate responses, especially during the first few weeks of class (W. Doyle, 1990; Evertson & Emmer, 1982; Munn et al., 1990; Weinert & Helmke, 1995).

Yet you need to strike a happy medium here. You don't want to structure classroom tasks to the point where students never make their own decisions about how to proceed or to the point where only lower-level thinking skills are required. Ultimately, you want students to develop and use higher-level processes—for example, to think analytically, critically, and creatively—and have classroom assignments and activities that promote such processes (W. Doyle, 1986a; Weinert & Helmke, 1995).

Planning for Transitions

Transition times—as students end one activity and begin a second, or as they move from one classroom to another—are times when misbehaviours are especially likely to occur. Effective classroom managers take steps to ensure that such transitions proceed quickly and without a loss of momentum (Arlin, 1979; W. Doyle, 1984; Emmer et al., 1994). For example, they establish procedures for moving from one activity to the next. They ensure that there is little slack time in which students have nothing to do. And especially at the secondary level, where students change classes every hour or so, effective classroom managers typically have a task for students to perform as soon as class begins.

How might you plan for the various transitions that occur throughout the school day? Here are some examples:

- An elementary school teacher has students follow the same procedure each day as lunchtime approaches. Students must (a) place completed assignments in a basket on the teacher's desk, (b) put away classroom supplies (e.g., pencils, paint, scissors) they have been using, (c) get their lunch boxes from the coatroom, and (d) line up quietly by the classroom door.
- A junior high school history teacher has formed long-term co-operative learning groups (*base groups*) of three or four students each. The groups are given a few minutes at the end of each class to compare notes on material presented that day and to get a head start on the evening's reading assignment.
- A high school English composition teacher writes a topic or question (e.g., "My biggest pet peeve," "Whatever happened to hula hoops?") on the chalkboard at the beginning of each class period. Students know that when they come to class, they should immediately take out a pencil and paper and begin to write on the topic or question of the day.

All of these strategies, though very different in nature, share the common goal of keeping students focused on their schoolwork.

Monitoring What Students Are Doing

Effective teachers communicate something called **withitness**: They know (and their students *know* that they know) what students are doing at all times in the classroom. In a sense, "with-it" teachers act as if they have eyes in the back of their heads. They make it clear that they are aware of what everyone is doing. They regularly scan the classroom and make frequent eye contact with individual students. They know what misbehaviours are occurring *when* those misbehaviours occur, and they know who the perpetrators are (Davis & Thomas, 1989; Emmer et al., 1994; Kounin, 1970). Consider the following scenario as an example:

> An hour and a half of each morning in Mr. Rennaker's elementary school classroom is devoted to reading. Students know that, for part of this time, they will meet with Mr. Rennaker in their small reading groups. They spend the remainder of the time working on independent assignments tailored to their individual reading skills. As Mr. Rennaker works with each reading group in one corner of the classroom, he situates himself with his back to the wall so that he can simultaneously keep one eye on students working independently at their seats. He sends a quick and subtle signal—perhaps a stern expression, a finger to the lips, or a call of a student's name—to any student who begins to be disruptive.

When you demonstrate such withitness, especially at the beginning of the school year, your students are more likely to stay on task and display appropriate classroom behaviour (W. Doyle, 1986a; Woolfolk & Brooks, 1985). Not surprisingly, they are also more likely to achieve at high levels (W. Doyle, 1986a).

Withitness The appearance that a teacher knows what all students are doing at all times.

From your own perspective, what are the key ingredients of a successfully managed classroom?

Modifying Instructional Strategies

As we have repeatedly seen, principles of effective classroom management go hand in hand with principles of learning and motivation. When your students are learning and achieving successfully and when they clearly want to pursue the curriculum that the classroom offers, they are likely to be busily engaged in productive classroom activities for most of the school day (W. Doyle, 1990). In contrast, when they have difficulty understanding classroom subject matter or when they have little interest in learning it, they are likely to exhibit the nonproductive or even counterproductive classroom behaviours that result from frustration or boredom.

Research tell us that when students misbehave, beginning teachers often think about what the students are doing wrong. In contrast, experienced, "expert" teachers are more apt to think about what *they themselves* can do differently to keep students on task, and they modify their plans accordingly (Emmer & Stough, 2001; Sabers et al., 1991; H. L. Swanson, O'Connor, &

INTO THE CLASSROOM *Creating and Maintaining an Environment Conducive to Learning*

Physically arrange the classroom in a way that facilitates constructive student–student interaction, enables teacher monitoring or intervention as needed, and keeps distracting influences to a minimum.

> An elementary school teacher has arranged the 28 student desks in his classroom into 7 clusters of 4 desks each. The students who sit together in clusters form base groups for many of the classroom's co-operative learning activities. The teacher occasionally asks students to move their chairs into a large circle for whole-class discussions.

Show students that you care about and respect them as human beings, and give them some say about what happens in the classroom.

> A high school teacher realizes that she is continually admonishing one particular student for his off-task behaviour. To establish a more positive relationship with the student, she makes a point to greet him warmly in the hallway before school every day. At the end of one day in which his behaviour has been especially disruptive, she catches him briefly to express her concern, and the two agree to meet the following morning to discuss ways of helping him stay on task more regularly.

Set reasonable limits for student behaviour.

> After describing the objectives of an instrumental music class on the first day of school, a junior high school teacher tells his students, "There is one rule for this class to which I will hold firm. You must not engage in any behaviour that will interfere with your own learning or with that of your classmates."

Plan classroom activities that encourage on-task behaviour.

> Before each class, a creative writing teacher writes the day's topic on the chalkboard. Her students know that when they arrive at class, they are to take out a pencil and paper and begin an essay addressing that topic.

Show students that you are continually aware of what they are doing.

> While meeting with each reading group in one corner of the classroom, an elementary school teacher sits with his back to the wall so that he can keep an eye on those students who are working together in centres or independently at their desks.

Modify your plans for instruction when necessary.

> A teacher discovers that students quickly complete the activity she thought would take them an entire class period. She wraps up the activity after 15 minutes and then begins the lesson she had originally planned for the following day.

Cooney, 1990). So when behaviour problems crop up, start thinking as the experts do, by considering questions such as the following:

- How can I alter instructional strategies to capture students' interest and excitement?
- Are instructional materials so difficult that students are becoming frustrated? Or are they so easy that students are bored?
- How can I address students' motives and goals (e.g., their desire to affiliate with classmates) while simultaneously helping them achieve classroom objectives?

Answering such questions helps you focus your efforts on your ultimate goal: to help students *learn*.

Despite your best efforts, students may sometimes behave in ways that disrupt classroom activities and interfere with student learning. Effective teachers not only plan and structure a classroom that minimizes potential behaviour problems but they also deal with the misbehaviours that do occur (W. Doyle, 1990). What strategies are most effective in dealing with student misbehaviours? We turn to this topic now.

Dealing with Misbehaviours

Misbehaviour An action that has the potential to disrupt students' learning and planned classroom activities.

For purposes of our discussion, we will define a **misbehaviour** as any action that can potentially disrupt classroom learning and planned classroom activities (W. Doyle, 1990). Some classroom misbehaviours are relatively minor ones that have little long-term impact on students' achievement. Such behaviours as talking out of turn, writing notes to classmates during a lecture, and submitting homework assignments after their due dates—particularly if such behaviours occur infrequently—generally fall in this category. Other misbehaviours are far more serious, in that they definitely interfere with the learning and achievement of one or more students. For example, when

TABLE 11.1 — **PRINCIPLES/ASSUMPTIONS**

Six Strategies for Dealing with Student Misbehaviour

STRATEGY	SITUATIONS IN WHICH IT'S APPROPRIATE	POSSIBLE EXAMPLES
Ignoring the behaviour	• The misbehaviour is unlikely to be repeated. • The misbehaviour is unlikely to spread to other students. • Unusual circumstances elicit the misbehaviour temporarily. • The misbehaviour does not seriously interfere with learning.	• One student surreptitiously passes a note to another student just before the end of class. • A student accidentally drops her books, startling other students and temporarily distracting them from their work. • An entire class is hyperactive on the last afternoon before spring break.
Cueing the student	• The misbehaviour is a minor infraction yet interferes with students' learning. • The behaviour is likely to change with a subtle reminder.	• A student forgets to close his notebook at the beginning of a test. • A co-operative learning group is talking unnecessarily loudly. • Several students are exchanging jokes during an independent seatwork assignment.
Discussing the problem privately with the student	• Cueing has been ineffective in changing the behaviour. • The reasons for the misbehaviour, if made clear, might suggest possible strategies for reducing it.	• A student is frequently late to class. • A student refuses to do certain kinds of assignments. • A student shows a sudden drop in motivation for no apparent reason.
Promoting self-regulation	• The student has a strong desire to improve his or her behaviour.	• A student doesn't realize how frequently she interrupts her classmates. • A student seeks help in learning to control his anger. • A student wants to develop more regular study habits.
Using behaviourist techniques	• The misbehaviour has continued over a period of time and significantly interferes with student learning. • The student seems unwilling or unable to use self-regulation techniques.	• A student has unusual difficulty sitting still for reasonable periods of time. • A student's obscene remarks continue even though her teacher has spoken with her about the behaviour on several occasions. • A member of the football team displays unsportsmanlike conduct that is potentially dangerous to other players.
Conferring with parents	• The source of the problem may lie outside school walls. • Parents are likely to work collaboratively with school personnel to bring about a behaviour change.	• A student does well in class but rarely turns in required homework assignments. • A student is caught stealing, vandalizing school property, or engaging in other unethical or illegal behaviour. • A student falls asleep in class almost every day.

students scream at their teachers, hit their classmates, or habitually refuse to participate in classroom activities, then classroom learning—certainly the learning of the "guilty party," and often the learning of other students as well—may be adversely affected. Furthermore, such behaviours may, in some cases, threaten the physical safety or psychological well-being of others in the classroom.

As a teacher, you plan ahead about how to respond to the variety of misbehaviours you may see in the classroom. As you do so, keep in mind that different strategies may be appropriate under different circumstances. In Table 11.1 we present six general strategies and the situations in which each is likely to be appropriate.

See http://drwilliampmartin.tripod.com/classm.html for an extensive list of online classroom management resources.

Taking Student Diversity into Account

As you plan for a productive classroom environment, you must always take the diverse characteristics and needs of your students into account. For instance, you should make an extra effort to establish a supportive classroom climate, especially for students of ethnic minority groups and for students from lower-income neighbourhoods. Also, you may often have to make special accommodations for students with special educational needs. Let's briefly consider each of these issues.

Creating a Supportive Climate

Earlier in the chapter we noted the value of creating a warm, supportive classroom atmosphere. Such an atmosphere may be especially important for students from ethnic minority groups (García, 1995; Ladson-Billings, 1994a). For example, First Nations students in one Grade 8 social studies class were asked why they liked their teacher so much. Their responses were very revealing:

"She listens to us!"

"She respects us!"

"She lets us express our opinions!"

"She looks us in the eye when she talks to us!"

"She smiles at us!"

"She speaks to us when she sees us in the hall or in the cafeteria!" (Ladson-Billings, 1994a, p. 68)

A warm, supportive classroom climate may be especially important for students from diverse ethnic backgrounds.

Simple gestures such as these go a long way toward establishing the kinds of teacher–student relationships that lead to a productive learning environment. It's essential, too, that you create a sense of community in the classroom—a sense that you and your students share common goals and are mutually supportive of everyone reaching those goals.

Accommodating Students in the Inclusive Classroom

As you create a classroom environment that promotes student learning, you must take into account any special educational needs of your students. In general, an orderly classroom—one in which procedures for performing certain tasks are specified, expectations for student behaviour are clear, and misbehaviours are treated consistently—makes it easier for students with special needs to adapt comfortably to a general education setting (Pfiffner & Barkley, 1998; M. C. Reynolds & Birch, 1988; Scruggs & Mastropieri, 1994).

When students have a history of behaviour problems (e.g., as those with emotional and behavioural disorders often do), you may need to provide a great deal of guidance and support to help them develop productive classroom behaviour. Furthermore, many students with special needs may need explicit feedback about their classroom performance. When praising desirable behaviour, rather than saying "well done" or "nice work," you should describe exactly what responses you are praising. For example, you might say, "You did a good job following my instructions on your math assignment today," or "Thank you for remembering to sign yourself out when you went down the hall to use the drinking fountain just now." Similarly, when students display inappropriate behaviour, you should tell them exactly what they have done wrong. For example, when speaking with a student with chronic behaviour problems, you might say, "You borrowed Austin's book without asking him first. You know that taking other students' possessions without their permission is against the class rules we all agreed on at the beginning of the year." Additional suggestions for accommodating students with special needs are presented in Table 11.2.

Coordinating Efforts with Others

As you work to promote students' learning and development, you will be far more effective when you coordinate your efforts with the other people in students' lives. In particular, you must work cooperatively with other teachers, with the community at large, and, most importantly, with parents.

Working with Other Teachers

Although teachers spend much of the school day working in individual classrooms, they are far more effective when they

- Have common objectives regarding what students should learn and achieve
- Work together to identify obstacles to students' learning and to develop strategies for overcoming those obstacles

TABLE 11.2

Planning for Students with Special Education Needs

CATEGORY	CHARACTERISTICS YOU MIGHT OBSERVE	SUGGESTED CLASSROOM STRATEGIES
Students with specific cognitive or academic difficulties	• Difficulty staying on task • Misbehaviours such as hyperactivity, impulsiveness, disruptiveness, or inattentiveness (in some students) • Poor time management skills and/or a disorganized approach to accomplishing tasks (in some students)	• Closely monitor students during independent assignments. • Make sure students understand their assignments; if appropriate, give them extra time to complete the assignments. • Make expectations for behaviour clear, and enforce classroom rules consistently. • Cue students regarding appropriate behaviour. • Reinforce (e.g., praise) desired behaviours immediately. • For hyperactive students, plan short activities that help them settle down after periods of physical activity (e.g., after recess, lunch, or physical education). • For impulsive students, teach self-instructions (see Chapter 8). • Teach students strategies for organizing their time and work (e.g., tape a schedule of daily activities to their desks, provide folders they can use to carry assignments between school and home).
Students with social or behavioural problems	• Frequent overt misbehaviours, such as acting out, aggression, noncompliance, destructiveness, or stealing (in some students) • Difficulty inhibiting impulses • Misbehaviours triggered by changes in the environment or daily routine or by sensory overstimulation (for students with autism) • Difficulty interacting effectively with classmates • Difficulty staying on task • Tendency to engage in power struggles with the teacher (for some students)	• Specify in precise terms what behaviours are acceptable and unacceptable in the classroom; establish and enforce rules for behaviour. • Maintain a predictable schedule; warn students ahead of time about changes in the routine. • Use self-regulation techniques and behaviourist approaches to promote productive classroom behaviours. • Teach social skills (see Chapter 3). • Closely monitor students during independent assignments. • Give students a sense of self-determination about some aspects of classroom life; minimize the use of coercive techniques. • Make an extra effort to show students that you care about them as human beings.
Students with general delays in cognitive and social functioning	• Occasionally disruptive classroom behaviour • Dependence on others for guidance about how to behave • More appropriate classroom behaviour when expectations are clear	• Establish clear, concrete rules for classroom behaviour. • Cue students regarding appropriate behaviour; keep directions simple. • Use self-regulation techniques and behaviourist approaches to promote desired behaviours. • Give explicit feedback about what students are and are not doing appropriately.
Students with physical or sensory challenges	• Social isolation from classmates (for some students) • Difficulty accomplishing tasks as quickly as other students • Difficulty interpreting spoken messages (if students have hearing loss)	• Establish a strong sense of community within the classroom. • When appropriate, give extra time to complete assignments. • Keep unnecessary classroom noise to a minimum if one or more students have hearing loss.
Students showing evidence of giftedness, talent, or high performance	• Off-task behaviour in some students, often due to boredom during easy assignments and activities	• Assign tasks appropriate to students' cognitive abilities. • Ensure that these students can look forward to and actually have opportunities to learn and interact with their intellectual peers and students with similar interests. This might occur in class groups, between-class groups, or permanent groups. Also ensure that students are not ignored as a result of the false presumption that they will always succeed on their own.

Sources: Achenbach & Edelbrock, 1981; Barkley, 1998; Beirne-Smith et al., 2002; Buchoff, 1990; B. Clark, 1997; Dempster & Corkill, 1999; Diamond, 1991; Friedel, 1993; Granger, Whalen, Henker, & Cantwell, 1996; Heward, 2000; Koegel et al., 1996; Landau & McAninch, 1993; Mercer, 1997; D. P. Morgan & Jenson, 1988; Ogden & Germinario, 1988; Patton, Blackbourn, & Fad, 1996; Pellegrini & Horvat, 1995; Piirto, 1999; M. C. Reynolds & Birch, 1988; Turnbull et al., 1999; Winner, 1997.

- Are committed, as a group, to promoting equality and multicultural sensitivity throughout the school community (Battistich, Solomon, Watson, & Schaps, 1997; D. C. Gottfredson, 2001; J. A. Langer, 2000; Levine & Lezotte, 1995)

Sense of school community The sense that all faculty and students within a school are working together to help every student learn and succeed.

Ideally, you should not only create a sense of community within your individual classrooms but also create an overall **sense of school community** (Battistich et al., 1995, 1997). Your students should get the same message from every teacher—that you are working together to help them become informed, successful, and productive citizens, and that they can and should *help one another* as well.

When teachers and other school personnel communicate an overall sense of school community, students have more positive attitudes toward school, are more motivated to achieve at high levels, and exhibit more prosocial behaviour, and students from diverse backgrounds are more likely to interact with one another. Furthermore, teachers have higher expectations for students' achievement and a greater sense of self-efficacy about their own teaching effectiveness (Battistich et al., 1995, 1997; J. A. Langer, 2000). In fact, when teachers work together, they may have higher **collective self-efficacy**—a belief that, working as a group, they can definitely have an impact on students' learning and achievement—and this collective self-confidence is indeed related to students' performance (Bandura, 2000; Goddard et al., 2000). Such a "team spirit" has an additional advantage for beginning teachers: It provides the support structure (the scaffolding) they may need, especially when working with students who are at risk for school failure.

Collective self-efficacy People's beliefs about their ability to be successful when they work together on a task.

Working with the Community at Large

Students almost always have regular contact with other institutions besides school—possibly with youth groups, community organizations, social services, religious groups, hospitals, mental health clinics, or local judicial systems. And some of them are probably growing up in cultural environments unfamiliar to many teachers.

Effective teachers understand the environments within which their students live and think of themselves as part of a larger team that promotes their students' long-term development. For example, educate yourself about students' cultural backgrounds, perhaps by taking coursework or getting involved in local community events after school hours (Hadaway, Florez, Larke, & Wiseman, 1993; Ladson-Billings, 1994a). You must also keep in contact with other people and institutions who play major roles in students' lives, coordinating your efforts whenever possible (J. L. Epstein, 1996).

Not all students come from traditional two-parent families, such as this one drawn by 5-year-old Haley. Many children have single parents, grandparents, aunts and uncles, foster parents, or other individuals as their primary caretakers.

Working with Parents

Above all, work co-operatively with students' parents or other primary caretakers. You can best think of your relationship with parents as a *partnership* in which you collaborate to promote students' long-term development and learning (Hidalgo et al., 1995). Such a relationship may be especially important when working with students from diverse cultural backgrounds (Hidalgo et al., 1995; Salend & Taylor, 1993). It is *essential* when working with students who have special educational needs.

It is important to recognize that families come in a variety of forms and that students' primary caretakers are not always their parents. For example, in some ethnic minority communities, grandmothers take the primary responsibility for raising children (Stack & Burton, 1993; M. Wilson, 1989). For simplicity, the term *parents* is used in upcoming discussions, but it in fact refers to all primary caretakers.

Communicating with Parents

At the very minimum, you must stay in regular contact with parents about the progress students are making. You must inform them of their children's accomplishments and alert them to any behaviours that are consistently interfering with learning and achievement. Regular communication also provides a means through which parents can give *us* information. Such information might suggest ideas about how you can best assist or motivate their children; at the least, it will help us understand why your students sometimes behave as they do. Finally, you can coordinate your classroom strategies with those that parents use at home; your efforts to help students succeed will almost certainly yield greater returns if expectations for academic performance and social behaviour are similar both in and out of school. The following paragraphs describe several ways in which you can communicate regularly with parents.

Parent–teacher conferences. In most school districts, formal parent–teacher conferences are scheduled one or more times a year. Oftentimes you will want to include students in these conferences, and in some instances you might even ask students to *lead* them (Popham, 1995; Stiggins, 2001). When students play an active role in a parent conference, you increase the likelihood that parents will come to the conference, you encourage students to reflect on their own academic progress, and you give them practice in communication and leadership skills. Furthermore, teachers, students, and parents alike are apt to leave such meetings with a shared understanding of the progress that has been made and the steps to be taken next. Several suggestions for conducting effective conferences are presented in Figure 11.1.

Written communication. Written communication can take a variety of forms. It can be a regularly scheduled, teacher-constructed checklist or grade sheet that documents a student's academic progress. It can be a quick, informal note acknowledging a significant accomplishment. Or it can be a general newsletter describing noteworthy classroom activities. All of these have something in common: They let parents know what is happening at school while also conveying your intention to stay in touch on an ongoing basis.

Telephone conversations. Telephone calls are useful when issues require immediate attention. You might call a parent to express your concern when a student's behaviour deteriorates unexpectedly and without apparent provocation. But you might also call to express your excitement about an important step forward that a student has made. Parents, too, should feel

FIGURE 11.1 Conducting effective parent–teacher conferences

Suggestions for any conference:
- Schedule each conference at a time that accommodates parents' work schedules and other obligations.
- Prepare for the conference ahead of time; for example, organize your notes, review information you have about the student, plan an agenda for your meeting, and have examples of the student's work at hand.
- Create a warm, nonjudgmental atmosphere. For example, express your appreciation that the parents have come, actively encourage them to express their thoughts and perspectives, and give them sufficient time to do so. Remember that your objective is to work co-operatively and constructively together to create the best educational program possible for the student.
- Express your thoughts clearly, concisely, and honestly.
- Avoid educational jargon with which parents may be unfamiliar; describe the student's performance in ways a noneducator can understand.
- End the conference on a positive note—for instance, with a review of a student's many strengths and the progress he or she has made.
- After the conference, follow through with anything you have said you will do.

Additional suggestions for a student-led conference:
- Meet with the student ahead of time to agree on appropriate work samples to share.
- Model and role-play effective conferences in class, and give students time to practise with their classmates.
- Schedule a backup "audience" (e.g., one of the student's former teachers, a trusted friend) who can sit in if the parents don't show up.
- Offer additional time in which you can meet without the student present if the parents so desire.
- Talk with the student afterward about what went well and how, together, you might improve the next conference.

Sources: R. L. Linn & Gronlund, 2000; Polloway & Patton, 1993; Salend & Taylor, 1993; Stiggins, 2001.

free to call you. Keep in mind that many parents are at work during the school day; hence, it is often helpful to accept and encourage calls at home during the early evening hours.

Parent discussion groups. In some instances, you may want to assemble a group of parents to discuss issues of mutual concern. For example, you might use such a group as a sounding board when you can pick and choose among topics to include in your classroom curriculum, or perhaps when you are thinking about assigning controversial yet potentially valuable works of literature (e.g., Rudman, 1993). Alternatively, you might want to use a discussion group as a mechanism through which you can all share ideas about how best to promote students' academic, personal, and social development (e.g., J. L. Epstein, 1996).

None of the communication strategies just described will, in and of themselves, guarantee a successful working relationship with parents. Parent–teacher conferences and parent discussion groups typically occur infrequently. Written communication is ineffective with parents who have limited literacy skills. And, of course, not everyone has a telephone. Ideally, you want not only to communicate with parents but to get them actively involved in school activities as well.

Getting Parents Involved in School Activities

Effective teachers get parents and other important family members (e.g., grandparents, older siblings) actively involved in school life and in their children's learning (Davis & Thomas, 1989; J. L. Epstein, 1996; Levine & Lezotte, 1995). Students whose parents are involved in school activities have better attendance records, higher achievement, and more positive attitudes toward school (J. L. Epstein, 1996).

Most parents become involved in school activities only when they have a specific invitation to do so and when they know that school personnel genuinely *want* them to be involved (A. A. Carr, 1997; Hoover-Dempsey & Sandler, 1997). For example, you might invite parents to an open house or choir performance in the evening, or you might request their help with a fundraiser on a Saturday afternoon. You might seek volunteers to help with field trips, special projects, or individual tutoring during the school day. And you should certainly use parents and other community members as resources to give you a multicultural perspective of the community in which you work (McCarty & Watahomigie, 1998; Minami & Ovando, 1995; H. L. Smith, 1998).

In Canada, parents have been seen by educators as important contributors to school activities. For example, over the years, school districts in Canada have elected parents as school board members or school trustees who are responsible for monitoring district policy and finances. In addition, an increasing number of schools have invited parents to participate in local advisory committees or school councils (Dukacz & McCarthy, 1995; Hrycauk, 1997). For example, Alberta Education amended the *School Act* in 1995 to increase parental involvement in local schools by actively engaging in decision making and developing school philosophy (Alberta Education, 1996).

Encouraging "Reluctant" Parents

Despite your best efforts, a few parents will remain uninvolved in their children's education; for example, some parents may rarely, if ever, attend scheduled parent–teacher conferences. Before you jump too quickly to the conclusion that these parents are also *uninterested* in their children's education, you must recognize several possible reasons why parents might be reluctant to make contact with you. Some may have an exhausting work schedule or lack adequate child care. Others may have difficulty communicating in English or finding their way through the school system to the people they most need to talk with (H.-Z. Ho, Hinckley, Fox, Brown, & Dixon, 2001; Salend & Taylor, 1993). Still others may believe that it's inappropriate to bother teachers with questions about their children's progress or to offer information and suggestions (Hidalgo et al., 1995; Olneck, 1995; Pérez, 1998). And a few may simply have had bad experiences with school when they themselves were children (Salend & Taylor, 1993).

Educators have offered numerous suggestions for getting reluctant parents more involved in their children's schooling:

- Make an extra effort to establish parents' trust and confidence—for instance, by demonstrating that you value their input and would never make them appear foolish.
- Invite other important family members (e.g., grandparents, aunts, uncles) to participate in school activities, especially if a student's cultural background is one that places high value on the extended family.

- Give parents suggestions about learning activities they can easily do with their children at home.
- Find out what various parents do exceptionally well (e.g., carpentry, cooking) and ask them to share their talents with the class.
- Conduct parent–teacher conferences or parent discussions at times and locations more convenient for families; make use of home visits *if* such visits are welcomed.
- Offer resources for parents at the school building (e.g., contacts with social and health services; classes in English, literacy, home repairs, arts and crafts, etc.). (J. L. Epstein, 1996; Finders & Lewis, 1994; Hidalgo et al., 1995; H.-Z. Ho et al., 2001; Howe, 1994; G. R. López, 2001; Salend & Taylor, 1993; M. G. Sanders, 1996)

Discussing Problem Behaviours with Parents

As noted earlier, you may sometimes need to speak with parents about a chronic behaviour problem at school. You will be more effective when working with parents if you set a positive, upbeat tone in any communication. For one thing, you will always want to couch any negative aspects of a student's classroom performance within the context of the many things that the student does *well*. (For example, rather than starting out by complaining about a student's behaviour, you might begin by saying that Tommy is a bright and capable young man with many friends and a good sense of humour.) And you must be clear about your commitment to working *together* with parents to help a student succeed in the classroom.

See Chapter 5 for a discussion of punishment.

Following are some additional suggestions for enhancing your chances for a successful outcome when you must speak with a parent about a problem behaviour:

- *Don't place blame; instead, acknowledge that raising children is rarely easy.* Parents are more apt to respond constructively to your concerns if you don't blame them for their child's misbehaviour.
- *Express your desire for whatever support they can give you.* Parents are more likely to be co-operative if you present the problem as one that can be effectively addressed if everyone works together to understand and solve it.
- *Ask for information and be a good listener.* If you show that you truly want to hear their perspective, parents are more likely to share their ideas regarding possible causes of the problem and possible ways of addressing it.
- *Agree on a strategy.* You are more likely to bring about an improvement in behaviour if both you and a student's parents have similar expectations for behaviour and similar consequences when those expectations are not met. Some parents, if making decisions on their own, may administer excessive or ineffective forms of punishment; agreement during your discussion as to what consequences are appropriate may avert such a situation (derived from suggestions by Emmer et al., 1994).

TEACHING CONSTRUCTIONS

You have just learned about many strategies you can use in your classroom to promote an environment that keeps students actively engaged in learning. Considering what you now know, let's revisit Ms. Cornell's class, presented at the beginning of this chapter:

- What are some effective strategies that Ms. Cornell could have used early on to respond to Eli, Jake, and Vanessa's inappropriate behaviour?
- How might Ms. Cornell have involved each child's parents/caregivers in addressing each child's behaviour?
- What specific plans do you have to promote a conducive learning environment in your own classroom?

KEY CONCEPTS

classroom management (p. 294)
classroom climate (p. 295)
sense of community (p. 297)
withitness (p. 301)
misbehaviour (p. 302)
sense of school community (p. 306)
collective self-efficacy (p. 306)

12 Instructional Assessment

CASE STUDY LEARNING ABOUT OUR COUNTRY

TEACHING CONNECTIONS

ASSESSMENTS AS TOOLS

THE VARIOUS FORMS OF EDUCATIONAL ASSESSMENT

USING ASSESSMENT FOR DIFFERENT PURPOSES
Promoting Learning • Guiding Instructional Decision Making • Diagnosing Learning and Performance Problems • Promoting Self-Regulation • Determining What Students Have Learned

IMPORTANT QUALITIES OF GOOD ASSESSMENTS
Reliability • Standardization • Validity • Practicality

STANDARDIZED TESTS
Types of Standardized Tests • Guidelines for Choosing and Using Standardized Tests

TYPES OF TEST SCORES
Raw Scores • Criterion-Referenced Scores • Norm-Referenced Scores • Norm- versus Criterion-Referenced Scores in the Classroom • Interpreting Test Scores Appropriately

HIGH-STAKES TESTING AND ACCOUNTABILITY
Problems with High-Stakes Testing • Potential Solutions to the Problems

COMMUNICATION ABOUT ASSESSMENT RESULTS
Communicating Classroom Assessment Results • Explaining Standardized Test Results

TAKING STUDENT DIVERSITY INTO ACCOUNT
Developmental Differences • Test Anxiety • Cultural Bias • Language Differences • Testwiseness • Accommodating Students with Special Needs

ASSESSMENT, COGNITION, AND METACOGNITION

INFORMAL ASSESSMENT
RSVP Characteristics of Informal Assessment

PLANNING A FORMAL ASSESSMENT
Selecting Appropriate Tasks • Obtaining a Representative Sample

PAPER-PENCIL ASSESSMENT
Constructing the Assessment Instrument • General Guidelines for Constructing Paper-Pencil Assessments • Administering the Assessment • Scoring Students' Responses • RSVP Characteristics of Paper-Pencil Assessment

PERFORMANCE ASSESSMENT
Choosing Appropriate Performance Tasks • Planning and Administering the Assessment • Scoring Students' Responses • RSVP Characteristics of Performance Assessment

INCLUDING STUDENTS IN THE ASSESSMENT PROCESS

ENCOURAGING RISK TAKING

EVALUATING A TEST/ASSESSMENT THROUGH ITEM ANALYSIS

SUMMARIZING STUDENTS' ACHIEVEMENT
Determining Final Class Grades • Using Portfolios

TAKING STUDENT DIVERSITY INTO ACCOUNT
Accommodating Students in the Inclusive Classroom

TEACHING CONSTRUCTIONS

KEY CONCEPTS

CASE STUDY *Learning about Our Country*

Ellen and Roslyn are taking geography this year. Although they have different teachers, they both have the same textbook and often study together. In fact, they are each taking a test on Chapter 6 in their respective classes tomorrow. Here is a snippet of their conversation as they study the night before:

Ellen: Let's see . . . What's the capital of Newfoundland?

Roz: St. John's, I think. Why?

Ellen: Because I need to memorize the capitals of the provinces in Canada. I know most of them. Now I better move on and memorize my notes and the textbook material on the geography and then the economy of Canada.

Roz: Geez, are you expected to know all those things?

Ellen: Oh, yeah. For our test, Ms. Peterson will give us a map of Canada and ask us to label all the provinces, their capitals, and the major geographical features.

Roz: Wow! That's not what we're doing in Ms. Montgomery's class at all. We're supposed to learn about the topography, climate, economy, and culture of all the Canadian provinces. Ms. Montgomery says she'll ask us to use what we know about these things to explain why each province, and Canada as a country, imports and exports the products that it does.

Ellen: That sounds like a really hard test—much harder than mine.

Roz: Oh, I don't know. It all depends on what you're used to. Ms. Montgomery has been giving tests like this all year.

TEACHING CONNECTIONS

In this chapter, you will learn about the use of assessment techniques that accurately reflect what your students know and can do and how these techniques promote students' learning and achievement over the long run. As you read, consider the following questions in making connections between theory and practice:

- What do we mean by *assessment*, and what different forms can it take in classroom settings?
- What qualities characterize useful educational assessment instruments?
- How do you interpret various types of test scores?
- Who should know the results of students' test performance, and how can you communicate those results in an understandable manner?
- What issues must you consider as you assess students with diverse backgrounds and needs?
- In what situations is informal assessment most appropriate and useful?
- What steps should you take as you plan a test, assignment, or other formal assessment of students' learning?
- How can you get students actively involved in the assessment process? How can you encourage them to take risks even when their performance is being evaluated?
- What approaches can you take to summarize students' achievement?
- How do the different assessment methods described by Ellen and Roz affect students' learning of instructional content?

Assessments as Tools

Your assessment practices influence and reflect virtually every other aspect of the classroom: student learning and retention (e.g., what you want your students to learn and what they think they should know), your future planning and instruction (e.g., what you teach and how you teach it), the classroom environment (e.g., whether it feels threatening or psychologically

Principles for Fair Student Assessment Practices for Education in Canada may be obtained from the Centre for Research in Applied Measurement and Evaluation, 3-104, Education Building North, University of Alberta, Edmonton, Alberta, T6G 2G5, or visit the CRAME website of the University of Alberta: www.education.ualberta.ca/educ/psych/crame/files/eng_prin.pdf.

Assessment The process of observing a sample of students' behaviour and drawing inferences about their knowledge and abilities.

Can you think of classroom tests you've taken that were probably *not* good samples of what they were supposed to measure?

"safe"), and students' motivation and affect (e.g., whether students develop mastery or performance goals, whether they feel confident or anxious). Frank Nezavdal (2003) at Brock University views "teaching and assessing as inseparable parts of a complete process" (p. 65). Furthermore, learning and assessment are inseparable. The Western and Northern Canadian Protocol for Collaboration in Education (2006) has produced a comprehensive document that examines assessment *for* learning, *as* learning, and *of* learning. Only when you consider the very integral role that assessment plays in the classroom can you truly harness its benefits to help your students achieve important instructional objectives. *Rethinking Classroom Assessment with Purpose in Mind* is a "must-read" on this topic for all teachers. The report places assessment in the context of learners, learning, and teaching. Find it at www.wncp.ca/assessment/rethink.pdf.

Paper-pencil tests provide only one means through which you can assess student achievement. The statements students make in class, the ways they respond to questions, the questions *they* ask—all of these tell us something about what they have learned, or not yet learned. You can observe how well students use a pair of scissors, how carefully they set up laboratory equipment, or how they perform on physical fitness tasks. Some forms of assessment take only a few seconds, whereas others may take several hours or even several days. Some are planned and developed in advance; others occur spontaneously during the course of a lesson or classroom activities. Clearly, assessment is both an ongoing and continuous feature of your classroom. The following definition sums up the major features of assessment:

> **Assessment** is a process of observing a sample of students' behaviour and drawing inferences about their knowledge and abilities.

Some tests involve paper and pencil, but others do not. In this industrial arts class, the students have designed and constructed rockets and their teacher is assessing how well each rocket performs.

First, you are looking at students' *behaviour*. As behaviourists have pointed out, it's impossible to look inside students' heads and see what knowledge lurks there; you can see only how students actually respond in the classroom. Second, you typically use just a *sample* of students' classroom behaviour; you certainly cannot observe and keep track of every single thing that every single student does during every minute of the school day. Finally, you must draw *inferences* from the specific behaviours you do observe to make judgments about students' overall classroom achievement—a tricky business at best. In this chapter, we will discuss how to select behaviours that can give you a reasonably accurate estimate of what your students know and can do. Notice that our definition of assessment doesn't include anything about decision making. Assessment instruments do not, in and of themselves, dictate the decisions that should be made. Instead, *people*—teachers, administrators, government officials, parents, and even students themselves—interpret assessment results and make judgments and decisions based on them.

Before beginning the study of student assessment, we encourage you to review the *Principles for Fair Student Assessment Practices for Education in Canada* (1993), available from the Centre for Research in Applied Measurement and Evaluation. The Canadian Psychological Association also recommends that test users and developers consult the *Standards for Educational and Psychological Testing* (1999) and become familiar with the *Standards for Educational and Psychological Testing* approved by the American Educational Research Association, the American Psychological Association, and the National Council on Measurement in Education, found on the APA website (www.apa.org/science/standards.html). Another relevant document is *Recommendations from the Canadian Psychological Association for Improving the North American Safeguards that Help Protect the Public Against Test Misuse* (Canadian Psychological Association, 1994) (see also www.cpa.ca/publications/).

The Various Forms of Educational Assessment

Figure 12.1 summarizes four distinctions that educators often make regarding classroom assessment instruments. Let's look more closely at each one.

Informal assessment
Assessment that results from teachers' spontaneous, day-to-day observations of how students behave and perform in class.

Informal versus formal assessment. Spontaneous, day-to-day observations of how students perform in class constitute **informal assessment**. Here, you rarely have a specific agenda in

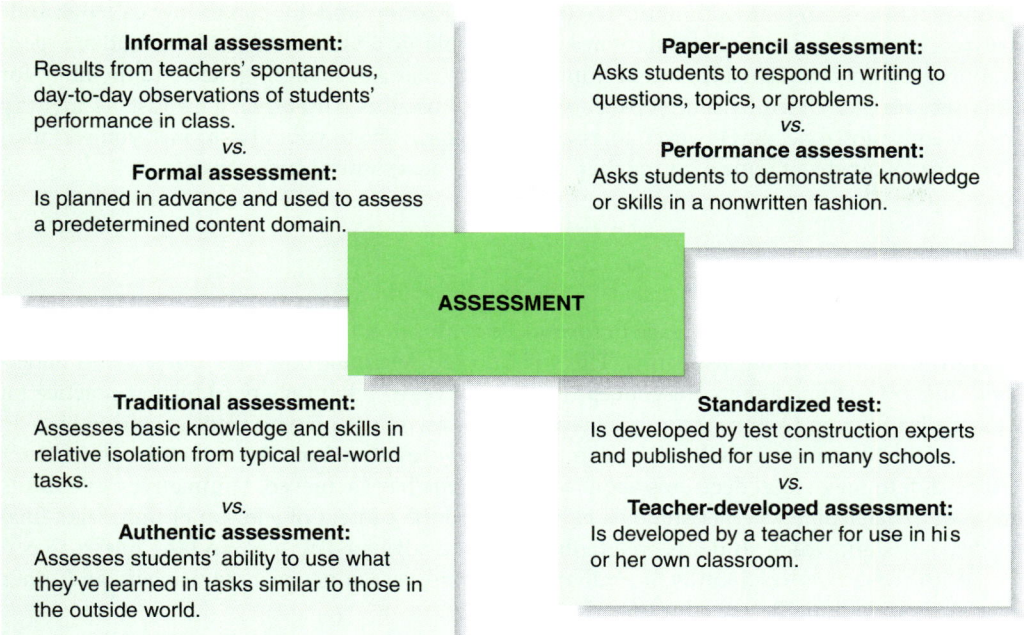

FIGURE 12.1 The various forms that classroom assessment can take

mind, and you are likely to learn different things about different students. You may discover that Tony has a misconception about gravity when he asks, "How come people in Australia don't fall into space?" In contrast, **formal assessment** is typically planned in advance and used for a specific purpose—perhaps to determine whether students can solve word problems requiring addition and subtraction, or to compare their strength and agility with those of students nationwide. It is "formal" in the sense that a particular time is set aside for it, students can prepare for it ahead of time, and it is intended to yield information about particular instructional objectives.

Paper-pencil versus performance assessment. As a teacher, you may sometimes choose **paper-pencil assessment**, in which you present questions to answer, topics to address, or problems to solve, and your students must write their responses on paper. Yet you may also find it helpful to use **performance assessment**, in which students demonstrate (perform) their abilities—for example, by giving an oral presentation, using a computer spreadsheet, jumping hurdles, or identifying acids and bases in a chemistry lab. More information on performance assessment can be found in *Performance Assessments: A Wealth of Possibilities, Connecting the Pieces*, published by the Saskatchewan Professional Development Unit (2003).

Traditional versus authentic assessment. Historically, educational assessment instruments have focused on measuring basic knowledge and skills in relative isolation from tasks typically found in the outside world. Spelling quizzes, mathematics word problems, and physical fitness tests are examples of such **traditional assessment**. Yet ultimately, your students must be able to understand and apply their knowledge and skills to complex tasks outside the classroom. **Authentic assessment**—measuring the actual knowledge and skills you want students to demonstrate in a real-life context—is gaining increasing popularity among educators (Lester, Lambdin, & Preston, 1997; Paris & Paris, 2001). This distinction represents a continuum rather than an either-or situation: Assessment tasks can resemble real-world situations to varying degrees. For further descriptions of classroom assessment practices and ideas across Canada, visit the websites of the provincial Departments of Education (e.g., http://education.alberta.ca/; www.gov.bc.ca/bced/), local school boards (e.g., http://schools.hpedsb.on.ca/), and education agencies (e.g., www.aac.ab.ca).

Standardized test versus teacher-developed assessment. Sometimes classroom assessments involve tests developed by test construction experts in Canadian Departments of Education or by test publishing companies in Canada (such as Pearson Assessment/ PsychCorp, http://pearsonassess.ca/haiweb/Cultures/en-CA/default.htm). These tests are

Formal assessment A systematic attempt to ascertain what students have learned. It is typically planned in advance and used for a specific purpose.

Paper-pencil assessment Assessment in which students provide written responses to written items.

Performance assessment Assessment in which students demonstrate their knowledge and skills in a nonwritten fashion.

Traditional assessment Assessment that focuses on measuring basic knowledge and skills in relative isolation from tasks more typical of the outside world.

Authentic assessment Assessment of students' knowledge and skills in an authentic, "real-life" context; in many cases, an integral part of instruction rather than a separate activity.

Standardized test A test developed by test construction experts and published for use in many different schools and classrooms.

Teacher-developed assessment instrument An assessment tool developed by an individual teacher for use in his or her own classroom.

published for use in many different schools and classrooms and are commonly called **standardized tests**. They can be helpful in measuring scholastic abilities and tracking students' general progress in various achievement domains. Tests that assess intelligence and memory, for example, are often used by school psychologists, counsellors, and other specialists to identify special educational needs. However, to assess learning specific to your classrooms, you will usually want to construct your own **teacher-developed assessment instruments**.

Using Assessment for Different Purposes

Formative evaluation An evaluation conducted during instruction to facilitate students' learning.

On some occasions, you will engage in **formative evaluation** that assesses what students know and can do *before or during instruction*. This will help you determine how well your students understand the topic at hand, what misconceptions they have, whether they need further practice on a particular skill, and so on. You can then develop or revise your lesson plans accordingly.

Summative evaluation An evaluation conducted after instruction is completed and used to assess students' final achievement.

At other times, you will engage in **summative evaluation**. Assessment occurs *after instruction* to make final decisions about what students have achieved. Summative evaluations are used to determine whether students have mastered the content of a lesson or unit, what final grades to assign, which students are eligible for more advanced classes, and the like.

With these two basic kinds of evaluation in mind, let's consider how teachers and other school personnel might use educational assessments.

Promoting Learning

Informative articles on assessment practices in Canada may be found in the *Alberta Journal of Educational Research, Canadian Journal of School Psychology, Canadian Journal of Education,* and the *McGill Journal of Education.* Visit also the website for the Canadian Psychological Association (www.cpa.ca).

Assessment can inform teachers about the effectiveness of their teaching practices and about student learning.

Assessments as motivators. Most students study class material more and learn it better when they are told they will be tested on it or in some other way held accountable for it, rather than when they are simply told to "learn it" (Blumenfeld, Hamilton, Bossert, Wessels, & Meece, 1983; N. Frederiksen, 1984b; Halpin & Halpin, 1982). Assessments are especially effective as motivators when students see them as good measures of course objectives and feel challenged to do their very best (Natriello & Dornbusch, 1984; Paris, Lawton, Turner, & Roth, 1991).

Assessments as mechanisms for review. As we discovered in Chapter 6, long-term memory is not necessarily "forever": for a variety of reasons, people tend to forget things as time goes on. Students have a better chance of remembering classroom subject matter over the long run when they review it at a later time. Studying for formal assessments provides one way of reviewing material related to important instructional objectives (Dempster, 1991; Kiewra, 1989).

What and how students study is, in part, a function of how they expect their learning will be assessed.

Assessments as influences on cognitive processing. What and how students learn depend partly on how students expect their learning to be assessed. Students will typically spend more time studying the things they think will be on a test than the things they think the test won't cover (Corbett & Wilson, 1988; J. R. Frederiksen & Collins, 1989; N. Frederiksen, 1984b). Their expectations about the kinds of tasks they will need to perform and the questions they will need to answer also will influence whether they memorize isolated facts or strive to learn a meaningful, integrated body of information (L. A. Shepard, 2000).

Assessments as learning experiences. You can probably recall classroom assessments that actually taught you something. In general, the very process of completing an assessment on class material helps students learn the material better, particularly if the assessment tasks ask students to elaborate on it in some way (Fall, Webb, & Chudowsky, 2000; Foos & Fisher, 1988; N. Frederiksen, 1984b). But two qualifications are important to note here. First, an assessment may help students learn only the material it specifically addresses (N. Frederiksen, 1984b). Second, when you present incorrect information on an assessment (as is the case for true-false and multiple-choice questions), students may eventually remember that misinformation as being true rather than false (A. S. Brown, Schilling, & Hockensmith, 1999; Voss, 1974).

Assessments as feedback. Regular classroom assessments can provide valuable feedback to students about which things have and have not been mastered. But simply knowing one's final test score (e.g., knowing the percentage of items answered correctly) is not very helpful. To facilitate student learning, assessment results must include concrete information about where students have succeeded and where they've had difficulty (Baron, 1987; Krampen, 1987).

> See the "Assessment as Learning" section in *Rethinking Classroom Assessment with Purpose in Mind* for more on this topic (www.wncp.ca/assessment/rethink.pdf).

Guiding Instructional Decision Making

In some cases, you might actually want to assess students' knowledge and understanding *before* you teach a topic; for instance, a quick pretest can help us determine a suitable point at which to begin instruction. You will also want to monitor students' learning throughout a lesson or unit (through either formal assessments or more informal means) to get ongoing information about the appropriateness of your instructional objectives and the effectiveness of your instructional strategies.

Diagnosing Learning and Performance Problems

Many standardized tests have been designed specifically to identify the special academic, social, and emotional needs of students. Many of these tests require explicit training in their use and so are often administered and interpreted by specialists (school psychologists, counsellors, speech and language pathologists, etc.). Yet teacher-developed assessment instruments can provide considerable diagnostic information as well, especially when they suggest where students are going wrong and why. In other words, they can, and ideally they *should*, provide information you can use to help students improve (Baek, 1994; Baxter, Elder, & Glaser, 1996; Covington, 1992).

INTO THE CLASSROOM   *Using Assessment to Promote Students' Learning and Achievement*

Give a formal or informal pretest to determine where to begin instruction.

> When beginning a new unit on cultural geography, a teacher gives a pretest designed to identify misconceptions that students may have about various cultural groups—misconceptions he can then address during instruction.

Choose or develop an assessment instrument that reflects the actual knowledge and skills you want students to achieve.

> When planning how to assess his students' achievement, a teacher initially decides to use questions from the test bank that accompanies his textbook. However, he discovers that the items measure only knowledge of isolated facts. Instead, he develops several authentic assessment tasks that better reflect his primary instructional objective: Students should be able to apply what they've learned to real-world problems.

Construct assessment instruments that reflect how you want students to process information when they study.

> A teacher tells her students, "As you study for next week's vocabulary test, remember that the test questions will ask you to put definitions in your own words and give your own examples to show what each word means."

Use an assessment task as a learning experience in and of itself.

> A high school science teacher has students collect samples of the local drinking water and test them for bacterial content. She is assessing her students' ability to use procedures she has taught them, but she also hopes they will learn something about their community's natural resources.

Use an assessment to give students specific feedback about what they have and have not mastered.

> As he grades students' persuasive essays, a teacher writes numerous notes in the margins of students' papers to indicate places where they have analyzed a situation correctly or incorrectly, identified a relevant or irrelevant example, proposed an appropriate or inappropriate solution, and so on.

Provide criteria that students can use to evaluate their *own* performance.

> The teacher of a "foods and nutrition" class gives her students a checklist of qualities to look for in the pies they have baked.

Promoting Self-Regulation

In our discussion of self-regulation in Chapter 8, we noted the importance of *self-monitoring* (students must be aware of how well they are doing as they study and learn) and *self-evaluation* (students must be able to assess their final performance accurately). An important function of your classroom assessment practices should be to help students engage in such self-regulating processes (Covington, 1992; Paris & Ayres, 1994; Vye et al., 1998). The significance of self-regulation to both student learning and achievement has been demonstrated by Phil Winne, Canada Research Chair at Simon Fraser University (Winne, 2006; Winne, Nesbitt, Kumar et al., 2006). In order to help students think about how they learn, study, and think, Winne and his colleagues have developed The Learning Kit Project, which is extensively described at www.learningkit.sfu.ca.

Determining What Students Have Learned

You will almost certainly use one or more formal assessments to determine whether students have achieved instructional objectives. Such information will be essential if you are using a mastery-learning approach to instruction; it will also be important as you assign final grades. School counsellors and administrators, too, may use assessment results for making placement decisions, such as deciding which students are most likely to do well in advanced classes, who might need additional coursework in basic skills, and so on.

In some cases, assessments of students' achievement are used to make major decisions about students, teachers, and schools. For instance, some school districts use one or more assessments to determine which students will graduate, which teachers get raises, and which schools get extra funds and other resources. As you might guess, such *high-stakes* assessments are a source of considerable controversy, and so we will look at them more closely later in the chapter.

Important Qualities of Good Assessments

A quick review: What do we call a memory aid such as *RSVP*? (You can find the answer in Chapters 6 and 7.)

As a student, have you ever been assessed in a way you thought was unfair? If so, *why* was it unfair? For example:

1. Did the teacher evaluate students' responses inconsistently?
2. Were some students assessed under more favourable conditions than others?
3. Was it a poor measure of what you had learned?
4. Was the assessment so time-consuming that, after a while, you no longer cared how well you performed?

In light of your experiences, what characteristics do *you* think are essential for a good classroom assessment instrument?

The four numbered questions just posed reflect, respectively, four "RSVP" characteristics of good classroom assessment:

- Reliability
- Standardization
- Validity
- Practicality

These RSVP characteristics are summarized in Table 12.1. Let's look more closely at each one.

Reliability

Reliability The extent to which an assessment instrument yields consistent information about the knowledge, skills, or abilities one is trying to measure.

The **reliability** of an assessment technique is the extent to which it yields consistent information about the knowledge, skills, or abilities you are trying to measure. You must be confident that your conclusions will be essentially the same regardless of whether you give the assessment Monday or Wednesday, or whether the weather is sunny or rainy. The same assessment instrument will rarely give us *exactly* the same results for the same student on two different occasions, even if the knowledge or ability you are assessing (e.g., the extent to which a student knows basic

TABLE 12.1

COMPARE/CONTRAST

The RSVP Characteristic of Good Assessment

CHARACTERISTIC	DEFINITION	RELEVANT QUESTIONS TO CONSIDER
Reliability	The extent to which the assessment instrument yields consistent results for each student	• How much are students' scores affected by temporary conditions unrelated to the characteristic being measured (*test-retest reliability*)? • Do different people score students' performance similarly (*scorer reliability*, also known as *interrater reliability*)? • Do different parts of a single assessment instrument lead to similar conclusions about a student's achievement (*internal consistency reliability*)?
Standardization	The extent to which assessment procedures are similar for all students	• Are all students assessed on identical or similar content? • Do all students have the same types of tasks to perform? • Are instructions the same for everyone? • Do all students have similar time constraints? • Is everyone's performance evaluated using the same criteria?
Validity	The extent to which an assessment instrument measures what it is supposed to measure	• Does the assessment tap into a representative sample of the content domain being assessed (*content validity*)? • Do students' scores predict their success at a later task (*predictive validity*)? • Does the instrument measure a particular psychological or educational characteristic (*construct validity*)?
Practicality	The extent to which an assessment is easy and inexpensive to use	• How much class time does the assessment take? • How quickly and easily can students' responses be scored? • Is special training required to administer or score the assessment? • Does the assessment require specialized materials that must be purchased?

addition facts) remains the same. Many temporary conditions unrelated to what you are trying to measure are likely to affect students' performance, including:

- *Day-to-day changes in students*—for example, changes in health, motivation, mood, and energy level
- *Variations in the physical environment*—for example, variations in room temperature, noise level, and outside distractions
- *Variations in administration of the assessment*—for example, variations in instructions, timing, and the teacher's responses to students' questions
- *Characteristics of the assessment instrument*—for example, the length of the task, and ambiguous or excessively difficult tasks (longer tasks tend to be more reliable because small errors have less of an impact on overall results; ambiguous and very difficult tasks increase students' tendency to guess randomly)
- *Subjectivity in scoring*—for example, tasks for which the teacher must make judgments about "rightness" or "wrongness" and situations in which students' responses are scored on the basis of vague, imprecise criteria

There are several ways of determining the reliability of tests and test scores. If you assess students using the same instrument on two different occasions, you get information about *test-retest reliability*, the degree to which the instrument yields similar information over a short time interval. If you ask two

Informal observations of student performance can give us valuable information, but ultimately you should draw firm conclusions about students' achievement only when you know that your assessment methods are *reliable*, yielding consistent results about individual students time after time.

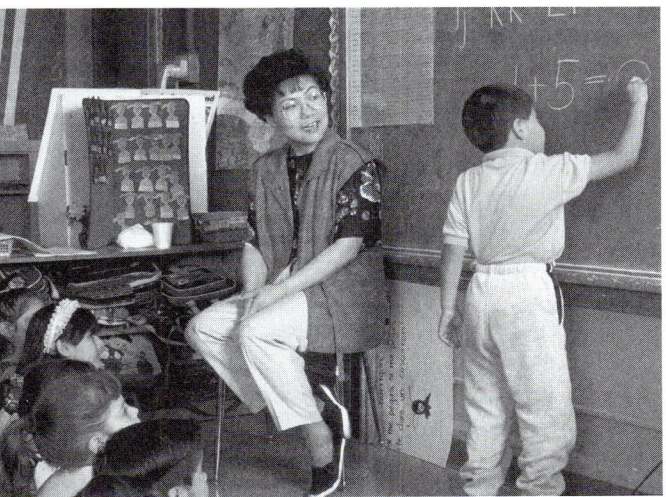

FIGURE 12.2 A graphic representation of Susan's scores on the Basic Skills Test (BST)

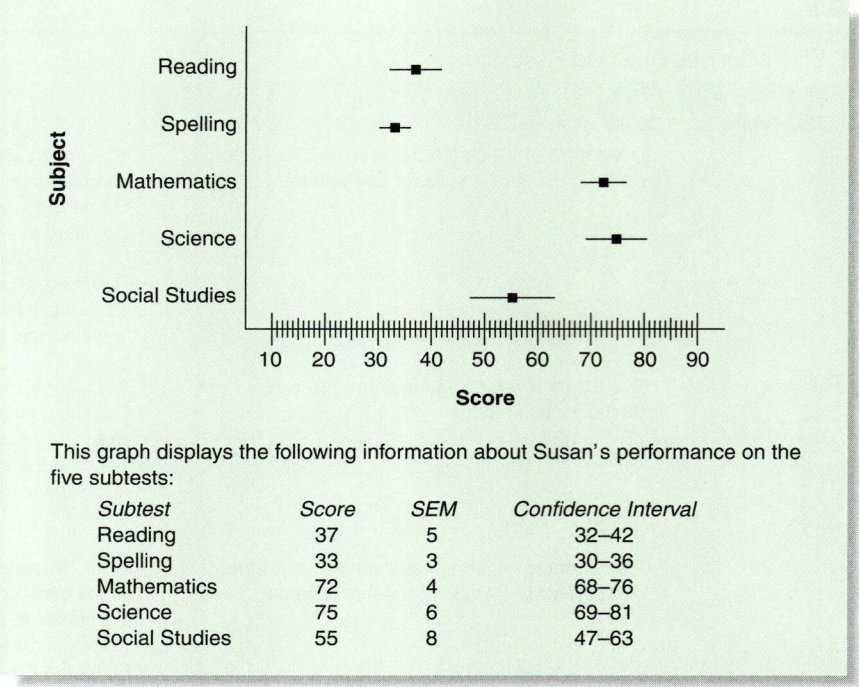

Reliability coefficient A numerical index of an assessment tool's reliability; ranges from 0 to 1, with higher numbers indicating higher reliability.

Standard error of measurement (SEM) A statistic estimating the amount of error likely to be present in a particular score on a test or other assessment instrument.

Confidence interval A range around an assessment score reflecting the amount of error likely to be affecting the score's accuracy.

or more people to judge students' performance (to grade the same set of essay papers, rate the same performance of gymnastic skills, etc.), you get information about *scorer reliability*, the degree to which different experts are likely to agree in their assessment of complex behaviours. If you compute two or more subscores for different items on the same instrument and look at how similar those subscores are, you get information about *internal consistency reliability*, the extent to which different parts of the instrument are all measuring the same characteristic.

Once you have two sets of scores for a group of students, you can determine how similar they are by computing a statistic known as a *correlation coefficient*; in this case, it is more frequently called a **reliability coefficient**.[1] As reliability coefficients decrease, they indicate more error in your assessment results—error due to temporary, and in most cases, irrelevant factors. Publishers of regional and national achievement and ability tests typically calculate and report reliability coefficients for the various scores and subscores that the tests yield.

Estimating Error in Assessment Results

How close is a particular student's reading, mathematics, or intelligence test score (called an "observed score") to what it actually should be (the "true score") if we could measure these skills or abilities with complete accuracy? The **standard error of measurement (SEM)** gives us an estimate of how close or far off you might be. Because almost any assessment score includes a certain amount of error, assessment results are sometimes reported not as a specific score, but as a range or **confidence interval** extending one SEM to either side of the actual test score. Figure 12.2 shows how you might report the scores of a student, Susan, on different subtests of a provincial standardized achievement test. Notice that the confidence intervals for the different subtests are different lengths, because each subtest has a different standard error of measurement.[2]

---

[1]Theoretically, reliability coefficients can range from +1 to −1. A negative coefficient would be obtained only when an inverse relationship between the two sets of scores exists—that is, when students who get the highest scores one time get the lowest scores the other time, and vice versa. Such an outcome is highly unlikely.

[2]When you use a single standard error of measurement (SEM) to determine the confidence interval, there is a 68 percent chance that the student's true score lies within that interval. If you instead use two SEMs to determine the interval (for Susan's reading score, identifying an interval of 27 to 47), you can be 95 percent confident that the true score lies within it. If you have some familiarity with descriptive statistics, it may help you to know that the SEM is the standard deviation for the hypothetical distribution of all possible scores that a student with a particular true score might get.

Enhancing the Reliability of Classroom Assessments

To maximize the extent to which any single instrument gives us reliable results, you should

- Include several tasks in each instrument and look for consistency in students' performance from one task to another
- Define each task clearly enough that students know exactly what they are being asked to do
- Identify specific, concrete criteria with which to evaluate students' performance
- Try not to let expectations for students' performance influence judgments
- Avoid assessing students' learning when they are obviously ill, tired, or out of sorts
- Administer the assessment in similar ways and under similar conditions (i.e., standardized) for all students

Standardization

A second important characteristic of good assessment is **standardization**: An assessment instrument is said to be standardized when it involves similar content and format and is administered and scored in the same way for everyone. In most situations, all students should be given the same instructions, perform identical or similar tasks, have the same time limits, and work under the same constraints (making appropriate adjustments for students with special needs). Furthermore, students' responses should be scored as consistently as possible; for example, you shouldn't use tougher standards for one student than for another.

Many tests constructed and published by testing experts are called *standardized* tests; this label indicates that such tests have explicit procedures for administration and scoring that are consistently applied whenever the tests are used. Yet standardization is important in your own classroom assessments as well: It reduces the error in your assessment results, especially error due to variation in test administration or subjectivity in scoring. The more an assessment is standardized for all students, then, the higher its reliability. Equity is an additional consideration: Except in unusual situations, it is only fair to ask all students to be evaluated under similar conditions. But in an era of mainstreaming, it is quite likely that any given classroom will comprise a wide range of students who may require special consideration related to test content, time to complete the exam, exam environment, and so on. The teacher is in the best position to determine how to most accurately assess student learning in heterogeneous classrooms that may require alternative assessment methods.

Standardization The extent to which assessment instruments and procedures involve similar content and format and are administered and scored in the same way for everyone.

Consult the websites and catalogues of major Canadian test developers and distribution companies such as Pearson Assessment, Nelson Canada, and Psycan for a description of the many standardized tests used by psychologists.

Validity

The **validity** of an assessment instrument is the extent to which it measures what it is supposed to measure. Does the Canadian Cognitive Abilities Test measure intelligence? Are scores on the Canadian Achievement Test (CAT-3) a good indication of a student's basic academic skills? Does your science test on cell biology measure the major objectives for this unit that you expect your students to know and understand? When your assessments don't do these things well—when they are poor measures of students' knowledge and abilities—then you have a validity problem.

As noted earlier, numerous irrelevant factors due to temporary conditions that lead to fluctuation in your assessment results can lower reliability. But other irrelevant factors—perhaps reading ability, self-efficacy, trait anxiety—are more stable, and so their effects on your assessment results will be relatively constant. If Joe has poor reading skills, he may get consistently low scores on paper-pencil, multiple-choice achievement tests in science and social studies regardless of how much he has actually learned in science, mathematics, or social studies. When your assessment results continue to be affected by the same irrelevant variables, then you must question the validity of your instruments.

There are three kinds of validity of particular interest to educators and other practitioners: content validity, predictive validity, and construct validity.

Validity The extent to which an assessment instrument actually measures what it is intended to measure.

Content Validity

As a teacher, you will usually be most concerned with **content validity**, the extent to which the tasks you ask students to perform are a representative sample of the knowledge and skills you are trying to assess. Test items and performance tasks must provide a representative sample and

Content validity The extent to which an assessment includes a representative sample of tasks within the content domain being assessed.

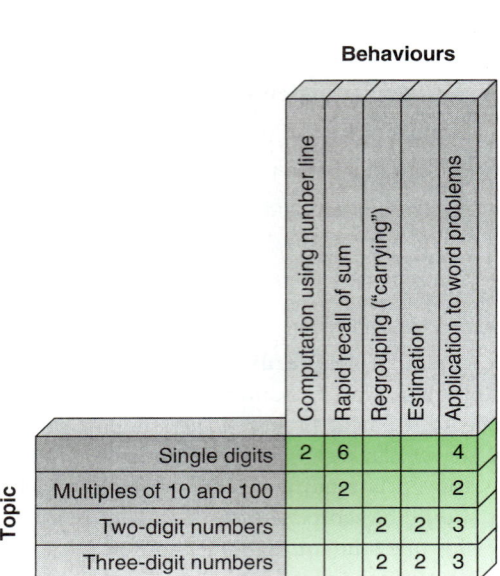

FIGURE 12.3 Two examples of a table of specifications

This table provides specifications for a 30-item paper-pencil test on addition. It assigns different weights (different numbers of items) to different topic–behaviour combinations, with some combinations not being measured at all.

This table provides specifications for a combination paper-pencil and performance assessment on simple machines. It assigns equal importance (the same percentage of points) to each topic–behaviour combination

Table of specifications A two-way grid that indicates both the topics to be covered in an assessment and the things that students should be able to do with each topic.

reflect all parts of the content domain in appropriate proportions and require the particular behaviours and skills identified in instructional objectives. High content validity is *essential* when determining what students have ultimately learned in your classes. A *blueprint* identifies the specific things you want to measure and the proportion of the instrument that addresses each one. This blueprint frequently takes the form of a **table of specifications**: a two-way grid that indicates both the topics to be covered and the behaviours associated with them. In each cell of the grid, you indicate the relative importance of each topic–behaviour combination, perhaps as a particular number or percentage of tasks or test items to be included in the overall assessment. Figure 12.3 shows two examples, one for a paper-pencil test on addition and a second for a combined paper-pencil and performance assessment on simple machines.

Sometimes the behaviours listed in a table of specifications are those in Bloom's taxonomy, such as "knowledge," "comprehension," and "application."

Content validity is important not only for teacher-developed assessments but also for any published achievement tests that you use in your school districts. Because these tests have already been constructed, you can follow the steps for ensuring content validity in reverse order. By looking at the items on the test, you can identify the topics covered and the behaviours (e.g., recalling information, applying procedures, solving problems) required.

Predictive Validity

To get an idea of her chances for future math success, Shantel takes the Mathematics Aptitude Test (we'll call it the MAT). She does quite well on the MAT, renewing her confidence that she will succeed in a mathematics career. But does the MAT actually measure a student's potential for future success in mathematics? This is a question of **predictive validity**, the extent to which an assessment instrument predicts future performance in some arena.

Predictive validity The extent to which the results of an assessment predict future performance.

Publishers of widely used ability tests often determine the accuracy with which test scores predict later success in certain domains. They first give a test to a group of people; at a later time, they measure the same group's success or competence in the behaviour being predicted (the criterion behaviour). They then calculate the **validity coefficient** between the test scores and the criterion behaviour, with higher numbers (e.g., in the .60s and .70s) indicating greater predictive validity. Lower predictive validity (e.g., coefficients in the .30s or .40s) are less accurate and will lead to more mistakes in your predictions.

Validity coefficient A numerical index of an assessment tool's predictive validity; ranges from 0 to 1, with higher numbers indicating more accurate predictions.

Construct Validity

Psychologists use the term *construct* to refer to a hypothesized internal trait that cannot be directly observed but must instead be inferred from the consistencies we see in people's behaviour. *Motivation*, *self-esteem*, *intelligence*, and personality factors such as *extroversion* are all constructs; we can't actually *see* any of them but must instead draw conclusions about them from the things that students do and don't do. By **construct validity**, then, we mean the extent to which an assessment instrument actually measures a general, abstract characteristic.

For instance, measurement experts might determine how well test scores correlate with other tests designed to measure the same trait (e.g., do scores on one intelligence test correlate with the scores on other IQ tests?). They might find out whether older students perform better than younger students on instruments measuring traits that presumably increase with age (e.g., do 12-year-olds correctly answer more items on an intelligence test than 6-year-olds?). When data from a variety of sources are consistent with what you would expect if the instrument were a measure of the characteristic in question, you conclude that it probably *does* have construct validity.

One principle that applies to all three forms of validity is this: *An assessment tool may be more valid for some purposes than for others*. A mathematics achievement test may be a valid measure of how well students can add and subtract but a terrible measure of how well they can use addition and subtraction in real-life situations. A paper-pencil test on the rules of tennis may accurately assess students' knowledge of how many games are in a set, what *deuce* means, and so on, but it probably won't tell us much about how well students can actually play the game. We should note, too, that *reliability is a necessary condition for validity*: Assessments can yield valid results only when they also yield reliable results—results that are only minimally affected by variations in administration, subjectivity in scoring, and so on. Reliability does not guarantee validity.

> **Construct validity** The extent to which an assessment accurately measures an unobservable educational or psychological characteristic.

Practicality

The last of the four RSVP characteristics is **practicality**, the extent to which assessment instruments and procedures are relatively easy to use, and includes such concerns as:

- How much time will it take to develop the instrument?
- How easily can the assessment be administered to a large group of students?
- Are expensive materials involved?
- How much time will the assessment take away from instructional activities?
- How quickly and easily can students' performance be evaluated?

There is often a trade-off between practicality and such other characteristics as validity and reliability. For example, a true–false test on tennis will be easier to construct and administer than a performance test, but a performance assessment in which students actually demonstrate their tennis skills is undoubtedly a more valid measure of how well students have mastered the game.

Of the four RSVP characteristics, validity is the most important: You *must* have an assessment technique that measures what you want it to measure. Reliability ensures the dependability of your assessment results (in doing so, it indirectly affects their validity), and standardization can enhance the reliability of those results. Practicality should be a consideration only when validity, reliability, and standardization are not seriously jeopardized.

Now that we have examined the characteristics of good assessments, let's apply what we have learned as we examine the nature of standardized tests.

> **Practicality** The extent to which an assessment instrument or procedure is inexpensive and easy to use and takes only a small amount of time to administer and score.

> Without looking back at Table 12.1, test yourself by describing the four characteristics of good assessment.

Standardized Tests

Standardized tests are *standardized* in several ways: All students are given the same instructions and time limits, respond to the same (or very similar) questions or tasks, and have their responses evaluated in accordance with the same criteria. Standardized tests come with test manuals that describe the instructions to give students, the time limits to impose, and explicit scoring criteria. These manuals also provide information about test reliability and validity.

Occasionally, standardized tests are designed to yield **criterion-referenced scores**, which indicate specifically what a student can and cannot do in relation to certain standards or criteria. More often, however, they are designed to yield **norm-referenced scores**, which are derived by

> **Criterion-referenced score** A test score that specifically indicates what students know and can do.
>
> **Norm-referenced score** A score that indicates how a student's performance on an assessment compares with the average performance of other students (i.e., with the performance of a norm group).

INTO THE CLASSROOM   *Considering the RSVP Characteristics of Assessment Instruments*

Remember that all assessment tools have some degree of error—that none is totally reliable.

> A teacher uses several test scores plus numerous other assessments of classroom performance to determine students' final grades.

Include confidence intervals when reporting standardized test results to students and their parents.

> At a parent–teacher conference, a teacher gives a student and her parents a computer-printed report. The teacher tells them, "Here are Mary's scores on the achievement test she took in November. Please remember that these scores are only approximate indicators of Mary's achievement. The bars on this graph indicate the likely margin of error for each score."

When holding some or all students to the same standards for achievement, be sure that assessments of their accomplishments are identical or equivalent in content, format, administration, and scoring criteria (making appropriate exceptions for students with disabilities).

> When three students are absent on the day of an important quiz, their teacher constructs an alternative quiz for them based on the same table of specifications he used in constructing the first one.

Follow the prescribed directions for administering and scoring a standardized test.

> As a teacher administers a nationwide achievement test, she reads the instructions in the test manual word for word. She also uses a stopwatch to make sure she gives students the prescribed amount of time to take the test.

Construct classroom assessment instruments that reflect both the topics you want to assess and the things you expect students to do with those topics.

> A teacher follows the table of specifications he has developed when writing a paper-pencil test, making sure that the items assess both lower-level and higher-level skills.

When using test scores to judge students' capabilities, consider recent assessment results only.

> When talking with a colleague, a high school teacher expresses her concern that one student, Mark, is having trouble grasping essential mathematics concepts. The colleague volunteers, "I had Mark four or five years ago when I was teaching middle school. As I recall, his standardized test scores showed a poor aptitude for quantitative ability. Maybe he's just not cut out for math." Mark's current teacher decides to ignore this information. Instead, she consults with the school psychologist about possible strategies for determining where Mark's problem may lie.

Make a classroom assessment instrument as practical as you can without sacrificing reliability, standardization, and validity.

> When trying to decide whether to use a paper-pencil test or several performance tasks to assess students' achievement in a particular unit, a teacher realizes that performance tasks are the only valid way to assess whether students have met the instrumental objectives. He identifies three performance tasks that can be administered to the class as a whole and will adequately represent the domain he wants to assess.

Norms As related to socialization, society's rules for acceptable and unacceptable behaviour. As related to testing practice, data regarding the typical performance of various groups of students on a standardized test or other norm-referenced assessment.

comparing a student's performance with that of other students on the same task(s). Hence, most standardized tests are accompanied by data regarding the typical performance (**norms**) of different groups of students, and these norms are used in calculating overall test scores.

Standardized testing is a common practice in Canadian schools and frequently is part of what has been termed high-stakes testing. Not only do such tests provide an open and public indication of how well students are performing in various skill and curriculum areas, but in some places they are also used for such critical decisions as student graduation. However, standardized test use is not without its critics in Canada. Headlines such as "Teachers must hold firm against standardized testing" (*Saskatchewan Bulletin*, 1997, 64, 3) and journal articles with titles such as "The Standardized Testing Movement: Equitable or Excessive?" (Nezavdal, 2003) are not uncommon. Marita Moll firmly stated in her book, *Passing the Test: The False Promises of Standardized Testing*, that standardized tests have no role or relevance in the teaching–learning process (2004). Marvin Simner (2000) has summarized the views (and concerns) of the Canadian Psychological Association and the Canadian Association of School Psychologists regarding this matter (see www.cpa.ca/documents/joint_position.html). In spite of the critics, there is also good evidence to show that standardized tests used in schools do provide important and relevant information to teachers. Canadian researchers Berthelot, Tremblay, and Ross (2001) have shown how the results from standardized tests can inform teachers about the learning needs of their students.

The School Indicators Achievement Program (SAIP), implemented about 12 years ago by the Council of Ministers of Education, Canada, is an attempt to gauge the achievement of Canadian students across the country in the areas of reading, writing, mathematics, and science. The results of these assessments may be viewed at www.cmec.ca, and from there, reports on the results of the first, second, and third cycles of assessment are available. More recently, the Program for International Student Assessment (PISA) was created to assess the achievement of 15-year-old students in 32 countries, including Canada. To view how Canadian students compared in the various subject areas, go to www.pisa.oecd.org and follow the links.

You will find an ongoing commentary on test use in most Canadian education publications and you may wish to regularly consult credible websites (e.g., provincial departments of education, the Canadian Society for Studies in Education) as well as books and journal articles.

> Remember, tests don't make decisions, teachers do. It is what we do with tests that make them good or bad, useful or useless!

Types of Standardized Tests

A wide variety of standardized tests is currently available.[3] The kinds that school districts use most frequently are group-administered tests of achievement, general ability, and specific aptitude. Critical aspects of these tests are summarized in Table 12.2. Diagnostic tests, including individually administered intelligence tests such as the Canadian adaptation of the WISC-IV and WIAT-II are used by school psychologists and other specialists in the schools and will not be discussed here. In general, teachers will not be direct users of restricted standardized tests such as intelligence and personality measures but should be aware of both their pros and cons, and their relevance to student learning.

Achievement Tests

Standardized achievement tests are designed to assess how much students have learned from the things they have specifically been taught. Test items are, at least in theory, written to reflect the curriculum and common essential learnings of most schools; for example, a history test will focus on national or world history rather than the history of a particular state, province, or community.

TABLE 12.2   COMPARE/CONTRAST

Comparing Standardized Tests of Achievement, General Ability, and Specific Aptitude

KIND OF TEST	PURPOSE	RELIABILITY AND VALIDITY	SPECIAL CONSIDERATIONS
Achievement tests	To assess how much students have learned from what they have specifically been taught	• *Reliability* coefficients are often .90 or higher; they are typically higher for secondary students than for elementary students. Coefficients may be somewhat lower for subtest scores. • *Content validity* must be determined for each situation.	• These tests are usually more appropriate for measuring broad areas of achievement than specific knowledge or skills.
Ability tests	To assess students' general capability to learn; to predict their general academic success over the short run	• *Reliability* coefficients are often .90 or higher; they are typically higher for secondary students than for elementary students. • *Predictive validity* for academic success ranges from .40 to .70, depending on the situation and student population.	• Test scores should not be construed as an indication of learning potential over the long run. • Individually administered tests (in which the tester works one-on-one with a particular student) are preferable when students' verbal skills are limited or when significant exceptionality is suspected.
Specific aptitude tests	To predict how well students are likely to perform in a specific content domain	• *Reliability* coefficients are often .90 or higher. • *Predictive validity* for academic success often falls below .50.	• Test scores should not be construed as an indication of learning potential over the long run.

---

[3] You can find descriptions of widely used standardized tests at www.ctb.com (for CTB and McGraw-Hill), www.riverpub.com (for Riverside Publishing), and http://pearsonassess.ca (for Pearson Assessment/PsychCorp).

> What non-teacher-made tests (if any) did you take when applying to university or during your school years? Would you characterize these tests as achievement tests or aptitude tests?

The overall test scores usually reflect achievement in a very broad sense: They tell us how much a student has learned about mathematics or language mechanics (relative to a norm group) but not necessarily whether the student knows how to multiply fractions or use commas appropriately.

Standardized achievement tests are useful in at least two ways (Ansley, 1997). First, they enable us to determine how well our students' performance compares with that of students elsewhere; this information may indirectly tell us something about the effectiveness of instructional programs. Second, they provide a means of tracking students' general progress over time and raising red flags about potential trouble spots. Content validity is your main concern when you assess achievement, and you need to determine each test's validity for your own situation. The most often-used group achievement tests include the Canadian Test of Basic Skills (CTBS, Nelson) and the Canadian Achievement Tests (CAT-III, Canadian Test Centre).

Ability Tests

Achievement tests are designed to assess what students have learned from the school curriculum. In contrast, **ability tests** are designed to assess a general or, in some instances, a specific *capacity* to learn. Traditionally, many of these tests have been called *intelligence tests* or IQ tests (recall your discussion of such tests in Chapter 4). Other commonly used terms are *general aptitude test*, *scholastic ability test*, and *cognitive ability test*.

> **Ability test** A test designed to assess one's general capacity to learn; typically used to predict students' success in future learning situations.

Regardless of what you call them, tests that fall in this category are often used for prediction—that is, to estimate how well students are likely to learn and perform in a future academic situation, and to aid in diagnosis and program planning for children who present with various learning problems. One way to predict how well students can learn in the future is to assess what they have learned already, and in fact achievement tests can be quite useful as predictors of later academic performance (Jencks & Crouse, 1982; Sax, 1989; J. J. Stevens & Clauser, 1996). But rather than focus on what students have specifically been taught in school, ability tests typically assess how much students have learned and deduced from their general, everyday experiences. A frequently used group test is the Canadian Cognitive Abilities Test (CCAT, Nelson).

When you are interested in how well students are apt to perform in a particular area—perhaps in art, music, or auto mechanics—then **specific aptitude tests** are more appropriate. These tests are sometimes used by school personnel to select students for specific instructional programs. They may also be used for counselling students about future educational plans and career choices. Both general ability and specific aptitude tests are based on the notion that one's ability to learn in a specific area is fairly stable. In recent years, many educators have begun to argue that teachers should focus more on developing abilities in *all* students.

> **Specific aptitude test** A test designed to predict students' ability to learn in a particular content domain.

Furthermore, some standardized tests are administered one-on-one. Such tests enable the examiner to observe a student's attention span, motivation, and other factors that may affect academic performance. For this reason, individualized tests are typically used when identifying special needs.

> How do these views on the use of ability and aptitude tests in schools relate to Gardner's description of the different kinds of intelligence, discussed in Chapter 4?

Guidelines for Choosing and Using Standardized Tests

As a teacher, you will sometimes have input into the selection of standardized tests for your districts, and you will often be involved in administering them. Some guidelines for choosing and using standardized tests appropriately include the following:

- Choose a test that has high validity for your particular purpose and high reliability for students similar to your own.
- Make sure that the test's norm group is relevant to your own population.
- When administering the test, follow the directions closely, and report any unusual conditions or circumstances that may impact (positively or negatively) the test scores of individual students or groups.

We again remind you of the *Principles for Fair Student Assessment Practices in Canada*, which provides excellent advice and guidelines for selecting, administering, and using the results of standardized tests in Canadian schools. Once you have administered a standardized test, you need to make good use of its results. We look now at various types of test scores and at strategies for interpreting them appropriately.

Types of Test Scores

Not all assessment instruments yield quantitative information. One method of summarizing students' achievement—portfolios—is more useful for the *qualitative* information it yields. However, many teacher-developed assessments do lend themselves to quantitative analysis, and virtually all standardized tests do. These *test scores* typically take one of three forms: raw scores, criterion-referenced scores (see page 321), and norm-referenced scores (see page 321). (Table 12.3 includes a summary of these three test score types).

Raw Scores

A score based solely on the number or point value of correct responses is a **raw score**. However, without knowing what kinds of tasks an assessment instrument includes or how other students have performed on the same assessment, you have no way to determine how good or bad a score of 29 out of 38, or 76 percent really is.

Raw score A test score based solely on the number or point value of correctly answered items.

Criterion-Referenced Scores

A *criterion-referenced score* tells us what students have achieved in relation to specific instructional objectives. They indicate that a student has passed or failed a unit, mastered or not mastered a skill, or met or not met an objective. Others indicate various levels of competence or achievement.

If a particular assessment instrument is designed to assess several objectives simultaneously, a student's performance may be reported as a list of the various objectives passed and not passed. As an example, a student's performance in a swimming class is often reported in a multiple-objective, criterion-referenced fashion (see Figure 12.4). You will often want to use a criterion-referenced approach to summarize what your students have learned, particularly when you are assessing basic skills that are essential prerequisites for later learning.

TABLE 12.3 COMPARE/CONTRAST

Interpreting Different Kinds of Scores

SCORE	HOW SCORE IS DETERMINED	USES	POTENTIAL DRAWBACKS
Raw score	By counting the number (or calculating a percentage) of correct responses or points earned	Often used in teacher-developed assessment instruments	Scores may be difficult to interpret without knowledge of how performance relates to either a specific criterion or a norm group.
Criterion-referenced score	By comparing performance to one or more criteria or standards for success	Useful when determining whether specific instructional objectives have been achieved	Criteria for assessing mastery of complex skills may be difficult to identify.
Age or grade equivalent (norm-referenced)	By equating a student's performance to the average performance of students at a particular age or grade level	Useful when explaining norm-referenced test performance to people unfamiliar with standard scores	Scores are frequently misinterpreted, especially by parents. Scores may be inappropriately used as a standard that all students must meet. Scores are often inapplicable when achievement at the secondary level or higher is being assessed.
Percentile rank (norm-referenced)	By determining the percentage of students at the same age or grade level who obtained lower scores	Useful when explaining norm-referenced test performance to people unfamiliar with standard scores	Scores overestimate differences near the mean and underestimate differences at the extremes.
Standard score (norm-referenced)	By determining how far the performance is from the mean (for the age or grade level) with respect to standard deviation units	Useful when describing a student's standing within the norm group	Scores are not easily understood by people without some knowledge of statistics.

FIGURE 12.4 In this swimming class, students' performance is reported in a criterion-referenced fashion.

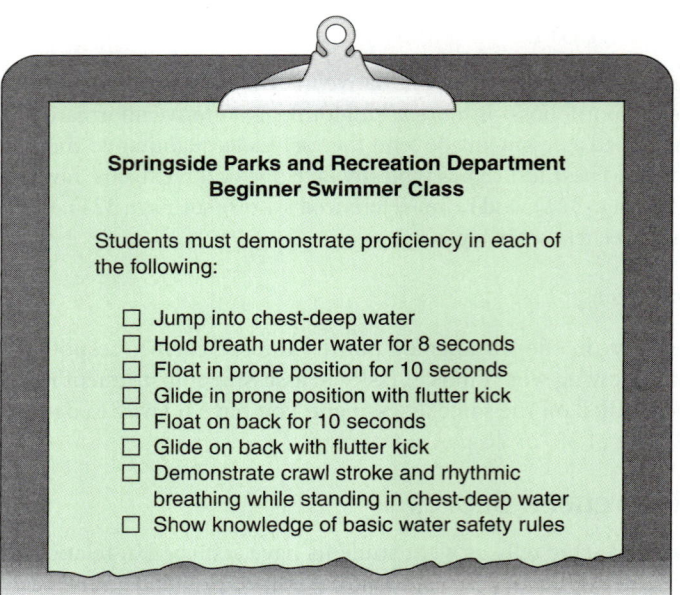

Norm-Referenced Scores

A *norm-referenced score* is derived by comparing a student's performance with the performance of other students, perhaps that of classmates or that of a nationwide norm group. Rather than tell us specifically what a student has or has not learned, such a score tells us how well the student stacks up against others at the same age or grade level.

Most scores on published standardized tests are norm-referenced scores, several of which are described here.

Grade-Equivalents and Age-Equivalents

Imagine that Shawn takes the Reading Achievement Test (RAT) and gets 46 of the 60 test items correct (46 is his raw score). You turn to the norms reported in the test manual and find the average raw scores for students at different grade and age levels:

Normative Data for the RAT

Norms for Grade Levels		Norms for Age Levels	
Grade	Average Raw Score	Age	Average Raw Score
5	19	10	18
6	25	11	24
7	30	12	28
8	34	13	33
9	39	14	37
10	43	15	41
11	46	16	44
12	50	17	48

Shawn's raw score of 46 is the same as the average score of Grade 11 students in the norm group, so he has a **grade-equivalent score** of 11. His score is halfway between the average score of 16-year-old and 17-year-old students, so he has an **age-equivalent score** of about 16 1/2. Shawn himself is 13 years old and in Grade 8, so he has obviously done well on the RAT.

More generally, grade- and age-equivalents are determined by matching a student's raw score to a particular grade or age level in the norm group. A student who performs as well as the average Grade 2 student on a reading test will get a grade-equivalent of 2, regardless of what grade level the student is actually in. A student who gets the same raw score as the average 10-year-old on a physical fitness test will get an age-equivalent of 10, regardless of whether that student is 5, 10, or 15 years old. Grade- and age-equivalents are frequently used because they seem so simple and straightforward, but they give us no idea of the typical *range* of performance for students at a particular age or grade level.

Grade-equivalent score A test score that indicates the grade level of students to whom a student's test performance is most similar.

Age-equivalent score A test score that indicates the age level of students to whom a student's test performance is most similar.

Percentile Ranks

A different approach is to compare students only with others at the same age or grade level using a **percentile rank**: the percentage of people getting a raw score less than or equal to the student's raw score. Because Shawn is in Grade 8, you turn to the Grade 8 norms and discover that his raw score of 46 is at the 98th percentile. Shawn has done as well as or better than 98 percent of Grade 8 students in the norm group on the Reading Achievement Test. A student getting a percentile rank of 25 has performed better than 25 percent of the norm group. It is important to note that percentile ranks refer to a percentage of *people,* not to the percentage of correct items.

In general, percentiles tend to *over*estimate differences in the middle range of the characteristic being measured: Scores a few points apart reflect similar achievement or ability. Meanwhile, they *under*estimate differences at the lower and upper extremes: Scores only a few points apart often reflect significant differences in achievement or ability. You avoid this problem when you use standard scores.

Percentile rank (percentile) A test score that indicates the percentage of people in the norm group getting a raw score less than or equal to a particular student's raw score.

Standard Scores

Many believe that educational and psychological characteristics (achievement and aptitude included) typically follow the same pattern we see for height: Most people are close to average, with fewer and fewer people as we move further from this average. This theoretical pattern of educational and psychological characteristics is called the **normal distribution** (or **normal curve**) and looks like this:

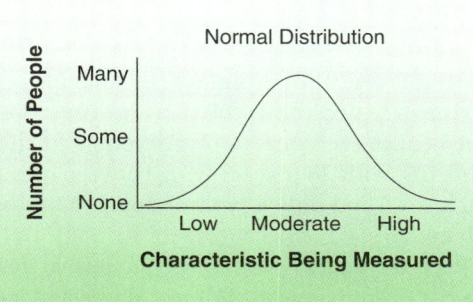

Normal distribution (normal curve) A theoretical pattern of educational and psychological characteristics in which most individuals lie somewhere in the middle range and only a few lie at either extreme.

Standard scores are test scores that reflect this normal distribution: Many students get scores in the middle range, and only a few get very high or very low scores.

Before we examine standard scores in more detail, we need to understand two numbers we use to derive these scores—the mean and standard deviation. The **mean (M)** is the average of a set of scores: We add all the scores together and divide by the total number of scores (or people). The **standard deviation (SD)** indicates the *variability* of a set of scores. A small number tells us that, generally speaking, the scores are close together, and a large number tells us that they are spread far apart.

The mean and standard deviation can be used to divide the normal distribution into several parts, as shown in Figure 12.5. The vertical line at the middle of the curve shows the mean; for a normal distribution, it is at the midpoint and highest point of the curve. The thinner lines to either side reflect the standard deviation: You count out a standard deviation's worth higher and lower than the mean and mark those spots with two lines, and then count another standard deviation to either side and draw two more lines. When you divide

Standard score A test score that indicates how far a student's performance is from the mean with respect to standard deviation units.

Mean (M) The arithmetic average of a set of scores. It is calculated by adding all the scores and then dividing by the total number of people who have obtained those scores.

Standard deviation (SD) A statistic that reflects how close together or far apart a set of scores are and thereby indicates the variability of the scores.

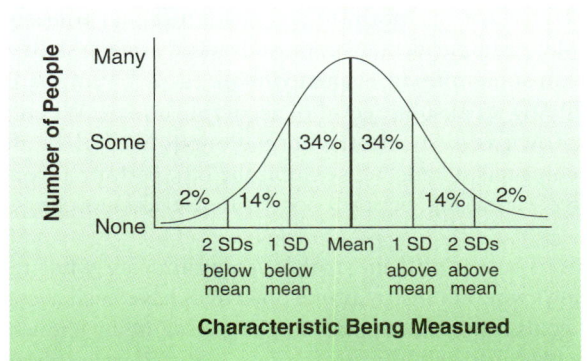

FIGURE 12.5 Normal distribution divided by the mean and standard deviation

Chapter 12 Instructional Assessment 327

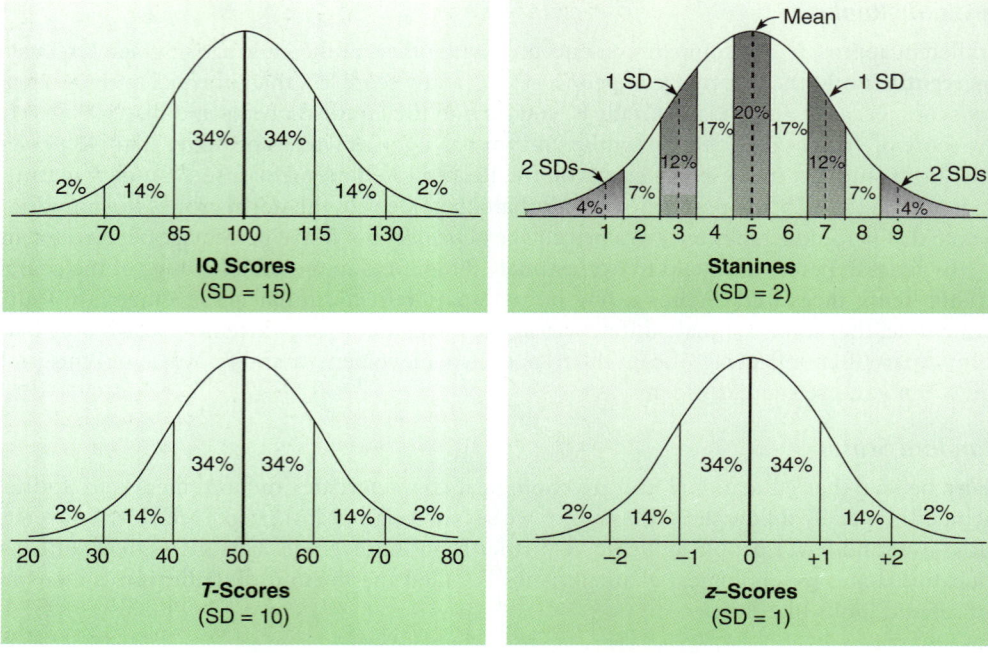

FIGURE 12.6 Distributions of four types of standard scores

the normal distribution in this way, the percentages of students getting scores in each part are always the same. Approximately two-thirds (68 percent) get scores within one standard deviation of the mean (34 percent in each direction). As you go further away from the mean, you find fewer and fewer students, with 28 percent lying between one and two standard deviations away (14 percent on each side) and only 4 percent being more than two standard deviations away (2 percent at each end).

A standard score reflects a student's position in the normal distribution: It tells us how far the student's performance is from the mean with respect to standard deviation units. Different scores have different means and standard deviations. Four commonly used standard scores, depicted graphically in Figure 12.6, are:

- **IQ scores**. IQ scores are frequently used to report students' performance on intelligence tests. They most often have a *mean of 100* and a *standard deviation of 15*.
- **Stanines**. Stanines (short for *standard nines*) are often used to report standardized achievement test results. They have a *mean of 5* and a *standard deviation of 2*. Because they are always reported as whole numbers, each score reflects a *range* of test performance (reflected by the shaded and nonshaded portions of the curve in Figure 12.6).
- **z-scores** and **T-scores** Standard scores known as z-scores are often used by statisticians. They have a *mean of 0* and a *standard deviation of 1*. A T-score simply converts these values to a mean of 50 and a standard deviation of 10.

IQ score A score on an intelligence test. It is determined by comparing one's performance on the test with the performance of others in the same age-group; for most tests, it is a standard score with a mean of 100 and a standard deviation of 15.

Stanine A standard score with a mean of 5 and a standard deviation of 2; it is always reported as a whole number.

z-score A standard score with a mean of 0 and a standard deviation of 1.

T-score A standard score with a mean of 50 and a standard deviation of 10.

Norm- versus Criterion-Referenced Scores in the Classroom

For teacher-developed assessments, norm-referenced scores may occasionally be appropriate. Some complex tasks—for example, demonstrating advanced athletic skills, or critically analyzing works of literature—can sometimes be evaluated more easily by comparing students with one another than by specifying an absolute level of accomplishment. When you assign norm-referenced scores on your own assessments, the norm group is likely to be all the students in your class: You give high scores to students who exhibit the best performance and low scores to students who, comparatively speaking, perform poorly. To use common lingo, you are "grading on the curve."

Some educators believe that classroom assessment scores should *always* be criterion-referenced. What do you think? Is it more meaningful to know that a student can add two-digit numbers with greater than 95 percent accuracy or that he scores in the top 10 percent of students in his class?

Criterion-referenced scores will most often communicate what teachers and students alike most need to know: whether instructional objectives have been accomplished. They focus attention on mastery goals rather than performance goals and, by showing improvement over time, should enhance students' self-efficacy for learning academic subject matter.

Interpreting Test Scores Appropriately

In and of themselves, test scores tell us only so much. Following are several guidelines to keep in mind when interpreting test scores (see also *Principles for Fair Student Assessment Practices for Education in Canada*):

- *Compare two norm-referenced test scores only when those scores are derived from the same or equivalent norm group(s)*. When two or more scores are from the same test, however, you can use the confidence intervals for the scores to make meaningful comparisons (see Figure 12.2). Overlapping confidence intervals for any two subtests indicate that the student has performed equally well in the two areas. If the intervals show no overlap, you can reasonably conclude that the student has done better in one area than the other.

- *Have a clear and justifiable rationale for establishing cutoff scores for "acceptable" performance*. If you want to use test results to make either-or decisions—for instance, whether a student should move to a more advanced math course or be exempt from a basic writing course—you must have a clear rationale for identifying the cutoff score. This process can be relatively easy for criterion-referenced scores, provided that they truly reflect mastery and nonmastery of the subject matter. It is far more difficult for norm-referenced scores: At what point does a student's performance become "acceptable"? At the 20th percentile? The 50th percentile? A stanine of 5? A z-score of 0.5? Without more information about what knowledge and skills such scores represent, there is no way of knowing.

Thus, it is not a matter of Sally scoring higher (93 percent) than Lukas (90 percent) on a Canadian history test, but that both students have achieved the goal of scoring above 85 percent that was established as the test score needed to demonstrate mastery of the content.

- *Never use a single test score to make important decisions*. No test, no matter how carefully constructed and widely used, has perfect reliability and validity. Every test is fallible, and students may do poorly on them for a variety of reasons. Thus, you should never use a single assessment instrument or single test score to make important decisions about individual students. Nor should you use single test scores to make important decisions about large groups of students or about the teachers who teach them.

High-Stakes Testing and Accountability

Within the past two or three decades, many politicians, business leaders, and other public figures have lamented what appear to be low achievement levels among our students and have called for major overhauls of the educational system. Many of these "reform-minded" individuals equate high achievement with high scores on standardized tests and, conversely, low achievement with low test scores and have been putting considerable pressure on teachers and educational administrators to get the test scores up! Here we are talking about both **high-stakes testing**—making major decisions on the basis of single assessments—and **accountability**—holding teachers, administrators, and other school personnel responsible for students' performance on those assessments.

Sometimes students too are held accountable for their performance on schoolwide assessments. Some school districts have used students' performance on tests or other assessments as a basis for promotion to the next grade level or for awarding high school diplomas (e.g., Boschee & Baron, 1993; Guskey, 1994).[4]

High-stakes testing Using students' performance on a single assessment instrument to make major decisions about students or school personnel.

Accountability Holding teachers and other school personnel responsible for students' performance on high-stakes assessments.

Problems with High-Stakes Testing

Experts have identified several problems with the heavy reliance on high-stakes tests to make decisions about students, educators, and school programs:

- The tests don't necessarily reflect important instructional objectives.
- Teachers spend a great deal of time teaching to the tests.
- School personnel have disincentives to include the test results of students with special educational needs and other low achievers.
- Different criteria lead to different conclusions about which students and schools are performing at high levels.
- Not enough emphasis may be placed on helping low-achieving students and schools.

---

[4]Such approaches go by a variety of names; *outcomes-based education* and *minimum competency testing* are two common ones.

Potential Solutions to the Problems

Public concerns about students' achievement levels are not going away any time soon, nor should they. Many students *are* achieving at low levels, particularly those in low-income school districts, those with diverse cultural backgrounds, and those with special educational needs (see Chapter 4).

Several potential solutions that, in combination, may alleviate some of the problems just identified are as follows:

- Identify and assess those things that are most important for students to know and do.
- Educate the public about what standardized tests can and cannot do for us.
- Look at alternatives to traditional objective tests.
- Advocate for the use of multiple measures in any high-stakes decisions. The more (multi-method) and better (reliable, valid) the information you have about your students, the better the decisions you can make.
- Most importantly, address the reasons for low achievement and lack of school success, whether at the classroom, school, or community level. This may require an interdisciplinary and multi-agency approach to change major conditions that have a negative effect on student learning, ranging from poverty to systemic discrimination.

> It would be interesting to look at local statistics in your community to know how many students do not complete high school or drop out of university before graduation.

Communication about Assessment Results

Communicating Classroom Assessment Results

Whenever you assess your students' achievement and abilities, remember that your primary purpose is to *help students learn and achieve more effectively* (Stiggins, 2001). Ultimately, you must think of yourself as working in co-operation with students and parents for something that all of us want—students' classroom success. Your primary goal in communicating classroom assessment results is to share information that will help us achieve that end. "Working with Parents" in Chapter 11 includes several strategies for creating partnerships with parents to facilitate students' success at school. Later in this chapter we will consider strategies for getting students actively involved in their own assessment.

Explaining Standardized Test Results

To describe tests and test results to students and parents who, in all likelihood, have never read a chapter on assessment in an educational psychology textbook, here are some general guidelines:

- Make sure you understand the results yourself.
- Remember that, in many cases, it is sufficient to describe the test and students' test performance in broad, general terms.
- When reporting specific test scores, use percentile ranks rather than grade equivalents or IQs.
- If you know the standard error of measurement, give parents the confidence interval for a test score; this is in fact a more accurate description than a single score.
- Focus on the student and not the test scores.

Taking Student Diversity into Account

As you identify and implement ways to assess learning and achievement, you must remember that students often differ from one another in ways that affect their performance in assessment situations.

In this section, we will consider how you might adapt your classroom assessment procedures to reflect student diversity and also accommodate students with special needs.

Developmental Differences

As we have seen, a variety of irrelevant factors affect an instrument's reliability and so indirectly affect its validity as well. Such sources of error in students' test scores and other assessment results are especially common in young children, who may have less-developed language skills and

TABLE 12.4 — COMPARE/CONTRAST

Keeping Students' Test Anxiety at a Facilitative Level

WHAT TO DO	WHAT *NOT* TO DO
Point out the value of the assessment as a feedback mechanism to improve learning.	Stress the fact that students' competence is being evaluated.
Administer a practice assessment or pretest that gives students an idea of what the final assessment instrument will be like.	Keep the nature of the assessment a secret until the day it is administered.
Encourage students to do their best.	Remind students that failing will have dire consequences.
Provide or allow the use of memory aids (e.g., a list of formulas or a single note card containing key facts) when instructional objectives do not require students to commit information to memory.	Insist that students commit even trivial facts to memory.
Eliminate time limits unless speed is an important part of the skill being measured.	Give more questions or tasks than students can possibly respond to in the time allotted.
Be available to answer students' questions during the assessment.	Hover over students, watching them closely as they respond.
Use unannounced ("pop") quizzes only for formative evaluation (e.g., to determine an appropriate starting point for instruction).	Give occasional pop quizzes to motivate students to study regularly and to punish those who do not.
Use the results of several assessments to make decisions (e.g., to assign grades).	Evaluate students on the basis of a single assessment.

Sources: Brophy, 1986; Gaudry & Bradshaw, 1971; K. T. Hill, 1984; K. T. Hill & Wigfield, 1984; Popham, 1990; Sax, 1989; Sieber, Kameya, & Paulson, 1970.

attention spans, little motivation to do their best, and low tolerance for frustration (Bracken & Walker, 1997; Messick, 1983). Furthermore, young children's less-consistent behaviour may make it difficult to maintain standardized testing conditions (Wodtke, Harper, & Schommer, 1989).

Test Anxiety

How anxious do you get when you know you will be taking a test in class? Students are typically not anxious about learning new knowledge and skills but many of them *are* anxious at the thought that they will be evaluated and judged and perhaps found to be "stupid" or in some other way inadequate. Their performance is apt to be impaired when they have very high **test anxiety**, particularly when assigned tasks require them to use what they have learned in a flexible and creative manner (Hagtvet & Johnsen, 1992; Kirkland, 1971).

When students are going to be taking a standardized test, you can encourage them to do their best without describing the test as a life-or-death matter (Sax, 1989). Fortunately, you have more control over how you administer the assessment instruments you develop yourself. Table 12.4 distinguishes between classroom practices that are likely to lead to facilitating anxiety and those that may produce debilitating anxiety.

Test anxiety Excessive anxiety about a particular test or about assessment in general.

A comprehensive book on this topic is M. Zeidner's (1998) *Test Anxiety: The State of the Art.*

Cultural Bias

An assessment instrument has **cultural bias** if any of its items either offend or unfairly penalize some students on the basis of their ethnicity, sex, or socioeconomic status (e.g., Popham, 1995). An assessment instrument isn't necessarily biased just because one group gets higher test scores than another group. It is biased only if the groups' scores are different when the characteristic you're trying to measure *isn't* different, or if the instrument has higher predictive validity for one group than for another.

This is a major area of controversy in Canada, particularly around the use of standardized tests of intelligence. A discussion of this topic is provided in the second Canadian edition of our previous textbook *Educational Psychology* (McCown et al., 1999) and other recently Canadianized texts (e.g., Chapter 13 in Woolfolk, Winne, and Perry's *Educational Psychology* [2004]). Most companies that publish large-scale standardized tests now employ individuals who represent numerous minority groups, and they actively screen their test items for possible sources of bias (R. L. Linn & Gronlund, 2000). Tests such as the third and fourth editions of the Wechsler Intelligence Scale for Children have been standardized and normed in Canada. However, classroom teachers

Cultural bias The extent to which the items or tasks of an assessment instrument either offend or unfairly penalize some students because of their ethnicity, sex, or socioeconomic status.

Is this discussion of cultural bias consistent with your previous beliefs about the topic? If not, can you reconcile the inconsistencies?

should be continually on the lookout for any unintentional cultural bias in the assessment instruments that they themselves construct.

Language Differences

Most ability tests show similar predictive validity for various groups *provided that the members of those groups are native English speakers*. Without question, students' facility with the English language will affect their performance on English-based classroom assessments. Poor reading and writing skills are likely to interfere with success on paper-pencil tasks; poor speaking skills will adversely influence students' ability to accomplish performance tasks such as classroom debates or oral reports. You may want to minimize the dependence on language to assess such areas as music or sport activities.

> When a child's language and culture both vary from the mainstream, this adds an even more complex dimension to student learning and evaluation, and certainly classroom instruction and teaching.

Testwiseness

Testwiseness is said to occur when students use test-taking strategies that enhance their test performance. Todd Rogers and Pinn Yang (1996) from the University of Alberta state that test-takers who are test-wise and possess relevant partial knowledge will take advantage of susceptible test items, resulting in improved or higher scores.

Testwiseness includes strategies such as these:

- *Using time efficiently*—for example, allocating enough time for each task and saving difficult items for last
- *Avoiding sloppy errors*—for example, checking answers a second time and erasing any stray pencil marks on a computer-scored answer sheet
- *Deductive reasoning*—for example, eliminating two alternatives that say the same thing and using information from one question to answer another (i.e., detecting flaws in a test item that will increase the chances of a correct response)
- *Guessing*—for example, eliminating obviously wrong alternatives and then guessing one of the others, and guessing randomly if time runs out and there is no penalty for guessing (Millman, Bishop, & Ebel, 1965; Petersen, Sudweeks, & Baird, 1990)

> **Testwiseness** Test-taking know-how that enhances test performance.

The sources of diversity just described point to the need for considerable flexibility in your approaches to classroom assessment; they also underscore the importance of assessing students' achievement in a variety of ways (multi-method assessment) rather than depending too much on a single instrument (Baek, 1994; Drake, 1993; C. Hill & Larsen, 1992). Ultimately, your assessment practices must be fair and equitable for students of all ages, backgrounds, and group memberships.

Accommodating Students with Special Needs

The *Standards for Educational and Psychological Testing* (American Educational Research Association, American Psychological Association, & National Council on Measurement in Education, 1999) ask us to consider six types of accommodations for students who have been identified as having special educational needs:

- Modifying the presentation format of the assessment (e.g., using Braille or American Sign Language to present test items and other assessment tasks)
- Modifying the response format (e.g., dictating answers, using a word processor)
- Modifying the timing (e.g., giving extra time or frequent breaks)
- Modifying the assessment setting (e.g., having a student take a standardized paper-pencil test alone in a quiet room)
- Administering part but not all of an instrument
- Using instruments different from those given nondisabled classmates, to be more compatible with students' ability levels and needs

Table 12.5 provides examples of specific accommodations to consider when administering standardized tests, and later we will identify accommodations that have more relevance to teacher-developed assessments.

Whenever educational assessment instruments are modified for students with special needs, you must recognize that there is a trade-off between two of your RSVP characteristics:

TABLE 12.5 — STUDENTS IN INCLUSIVE SETTINGS

Using Standardized Tests with Students with Special Educational Needs

CATEGORY	CHARACTERISTICS YOU MIGHT OBSERVE	SUGGESTED CLASSROOM STRATEGIES
Students with specific cognitive or academic difficulties	• Poor listening, reading, and/or writing skills (for some students) • Tendency for test scores to underestimate overall achievement levels (if students have poor reading skills) • Inconsistent performance due to off-task behaviours (e.g., hyperactivity, inattentiveness), affecting reliability and validity of scores (for some students with learning disabilities or ADHD) • Higher than average test anxiety	• Modify test administration procedures to accommodate disabilities identified in students' Individual Education Programs (IEPs) (e.g., when administering a standardized essay test, allow students with writing disabilities to use a word processor and spell checker). • Have students take tests in a room with minimal distractions. • Make sure students understand what they are being asked to do. • Be sure students are motivated to do their best but are not overly anxious. • Use classroom assessments (both formal and informal) to either confirm or disconfirm results of standardized test results. • Record and report all modifications made.
Students with social or behavioural problems	• Inconsistent performance due to off-task behaviours or lack of motivation, affecting reliability and validity of scores (for some students)	• Modify test administration procedures to accommodate disabilities identified in students' IEPs (e.g., when students are easily distracted, administer tests individually in a quiet room). • Use classroom assessments (both formal and informal) to either confirm or disconfirm results of standardized test results. • Record and report all modifications made.
Students with general delays in cognitive and social functioning	• Slow learning and cognitive processing • Limited if any reading skills • Poor listening skills	• Choose instruments appropriate for students' cognitive abilities and reading and writing skills. • Minimize use of instruments that are administered to an entire class at once; rely more on instruments that are administered to one student at a time. • Make sure students understand what they are being asked to do.
Students with physical or sensory challenges	• Mobility problems (for some students with physical challenges) • Tendency to tire easily (for some students with physical challenges) • Less developed language skills, affecting reading and writing ability (for some students with hearing loss)	• Obtain modified test materials for students with visual impairments (e.g., large-print or Braille test booklets). • Modify test administration procedures to accommodate students' unique needs (e.g., have a sign language interpreter give directions to students with hearing loss, have students with limited muscle control dictate their answers). • If reading and writing skills are impaired, read test items to students. • Break lengthy assessments into segments that can be administered on separate occasions. • Schedule tests at times when students feel rested and alert. • Record and report all modifications made. • Don't compare a student's performance to the norm group if significant modifications have been made.
Students showing evidence of giftedness, talent, or high performance	• Greater interest and engagement in challenging tests • Tendency in some students to hide giftedness to avoid possible ridicule by peers (e.g., some minority students may want to avoid "acting white") • In some instances, ability levels beyond the scope of typical tests for the grade level	• Keep assessment results confidential. • When students consistently earn perfect or near-perfect scores (e.g., percentile ranks of 99), request individualized testing that can more accurately assess actual ability levels. • Use above-level testing materials (e.g., an upper-elementary reading test for primary students, or a senior high school instrument for younger gifted teens). • Keep and report separately the grades and scores for what everyone in the class is expected to do, and for undertakings that are more challenging or advanced.

Sources: Barkley, 1998; Beirne-Smith et al. 2002; D. Y. Ford & Harris, 1992; A. W. Gottfried et al., 1994; Mastropieri & Scruggs, 2000; Mercer, 1997; M. S. Meyer, 2000; B. N. Phillips et al., 1980; Piirto, 1999; Pitoniak & Royer, 2001; Turnbull et al., 1999; Venn, 2000.

> An excellent resource for classroom applications for students with learning difficulties is the Learning Disabilities Association of Canada website: www.ldac-taac.ca/index-e.asp. See also the *Special Education Handbook: A Practical Guide for All Teachers* published by the Elementary Teachers' Federation of Ontario, 2007 (available at http://shopetfo.etfo.ca).

standardization versus validity. There is no magic formula for determining the right balance between standardization and validity for students with special needs; as a teacher, you must use your best professional judgment (and perhaps seek the advice of specialists as well) in each situation. Furthermore, while standardized testing procedures and norm-referenced scores are sometimes appropriate for students with special needs when your purpose is to identify existing learning and performance difficulties, criterion-referenced scores and a close inspection of students' responses to particular tasks and items may be more helpful when you are later concerned about how to modify instructional methods and materials to *address* those difficulties.

Regardless of your reasons for assessing students' knowledge and abilities, the following general principles can guide you in your efforts:

- All assessment instruments and practices should be evaluated with respect to the RSVP characteristics.
- Most assessment instruments focus on cognitive factors affecting learning and achievement; remember that other factors may be equally influential in students' classroom performance.
- Considerable information is lost when students' performance is summarized by a single test score.
- Classroom assessment practices have a significant influence on what and how students learn.
- Educational assessments are useful yet imperfect tools.

Assessment, Cognition, and Metacognition

In the case study at the beginning of this chapter, Ellen's teacher wants students to learn where Canadian provinces are located and what their capitals are, among other things. In other words, she wants them to learn facts—an objective that involves lower-level skills. Roz's teacher asks students to use what they've learned about topography, climate, economics, and culture to explain each province's and Canada's imports and exports—an objective that requires such higher-level skills as application, analysis, and synthesis. If both girls want to do well on their tests, they are wise to study differently, with Ellen focusing on isolated facts and Roz focusing on cause–effect relationships. Ellen may very well accomplish her goal simply by memorizing place names, but Roz will have to engage in meaningful learning and elaboration to understand why various provinces and Canada as a country have certain imports and exports. Most probably, then, Roz will remember what she has learned more effectively than Ellen.

> You can refresh your memory about epistemological beliefs by rereading the section "Factors Affecting Strategy Use" in Chapter 7.

Your students will draw inferences about your instructional objectives from the ways you assess their learning, and different assessment tasks may lead them to study and learn differently (J. R. Frederiksen & Collins, 1989; Lundeberg & Fox, 1991; Newmann, 1997; Poole, 1994). Your assessment practices will influence not only students' cognitive processes, but their metacognition as well. They will be served better in the long run by discovering that they can succeed on classroom assessments only if they construct an integrated understanding of a topic (a task that requires meaningful learning, organization, and elaboration) than if they find that learning discrete facts is sufficient.

How you assess students' learning is also likely to affect their views about the nature of various academic disciplines—that is, their *epistemological beliefs*. When Ms. Peterson asks students to label provinces, cities, and rivers on a blank map, they may very well conclude that, as a discipline, geography is little more than knowledge about the locations of various natural and human-made features. When Ms. Montgomery asks students to explain why Canada and the provinces import and export certain products, she is communicating a very different message: Geography involves understanding relationships between people and their environments.

In the upcoming pages we will explore both informal and formal approaches to classroom assessment. As we go along, we will consider the instructional objectives for which different assessment strategies might be most appropriate and the RSVP characteristics (reliability, standardization, validity, and practicality) of each type of assessment.

Informal Assessment

From your daily observations of and interactions with students, you can often draw conclusions about what students have and have not learned and make reasonable decisions about how future instruction should proceed. Such informal assessment takes many forms, including the following:

Assessment of verbal behaviours:

- Asking questions
- Listening to whole-class and small-group discussions
- Having students write daily or weekly entries in personal journals
- Holding brief conferences with individual students

Assessment of nonverbal behaviours:

- Observing how well students perform physical skills
- Looking at the relative frequency of on-task and off-task behaviours
- Identifying the activities in which students engage voluntarily
- Watching the "body language" that may reflect students' feelings about classroom tasks

Informal assessment provides continuing feedback about the effectiveness of the day's instructional tasks and activities. Second, it is easily adjusted at a moment's notice; for example, when students express misconceptions about a particular topic, you can ask follow-up questions that probe their beliefs and reasoning processes. Third, informal assessment provides information that may either support or call into question the data you obtain from more formal assessments such as paper-pencil tests. Finally, informal procedures provide clues about social, emotional, and motivational factors affecting students' classroom performance and may often be the only practical means through which you can assess such objectives as "shows courtesy" or "enjoys reading."

RSVP Characteristics of Informal Assessment

It is important that you be aware of the strengths and limitations of informal assessment with respect to reliability, standardization, validity, and practicality.

Reliability

Most informal assessments are quite short; for example, you may notice that Naomi is off task during an activity, or you may have a brief conversation with Jacquie after school about her interest in science. But such snippets of students' behaviour can be unreliable indicators of their overall accomplishments and dispositions. Perhaps you happen to look at Naomi during the *only* time she is off task. Perhaps you misinterpret what Jacquie is trying to say during your conversation with her. You should therefore base your conclusions on many observations over a longer period (Airasian, 1994) and keep ongoing, written records of the things you see and hear (R. L. Linn & Gronlund, 2000; Stiggins, 2001).

Standardization

Your informal assessments will rarely, if ever, be standardized; for example, you will ask different questions of different students, and you will probably observe each student's behaviour in different contexts. Hence, such assessments will definitely *not* give you the same information for each student. You will rarely be able to make legitimate comparisons among your students on the basis of casual observations alone.

Validity

Even if you see consistency in students' behaviour over time, you will not always get accurate data about what they have learned (Airasian, 1994; Stiggins, 2001). For instance, Margot may be reluctant to say anything at all because she is embarrassed by a speech impediment, not because she doesn't know the answer. In general, when you use in-class questions to assess students' learning, be aware that some students (e.g., students from certain ethnic minority groups) will be less eager to respond than others (B. Kerr, 1991; Sadker & Sadker, 1994; Villegas, 1991).

Your own biases and expectations can affect your interpretations of students' behaviours, inevitably affecting the accuracy of your conclusions (Farwell & Weiner, 1996; Ritts et al., 1992; Stiggins, 2001). You may expect academic or social competence from a student you like or admire and so are likely to perceive that student's actions in a positive light—a phenomenon known as the **halo effect**. In much the same way, you might expect inappropriate behaviour from a

Why do you think affective outcomes are usually assessed informally rather than formally?

Halo effect A phenomenon whereby people are more likely to perceive positive behaviours in a person they like or admire.

> ### INTO THE CLASSROOM — *Using Teacher Questions to Assess Learning and Achievement*
>
> Direct questions to the entire class, not just to a few who seem eager to respond.
>
> > The girls in a high school science class rarely volunteer when their teacher asks questions. Although the teacher often calls on students who raise their hands, he occasionally calls on those who do not, and he makes sure that he calls on *every* student at least once a week.
>
> Have students "vote" when a question has only a few possible answers.
>
> > When beginning a lesson on dividing one fraction by another, a middle school math teacher writes this problem on the chalkboard:
> >
> > $$\frac{3}{4} \div \frac{1}{2} = ?$$
> >
> > She asks, "Before we talk about how we solve this problem, how many of you think the answer will be less than 1? How many think it will be greater than 1? How many think it will be *exactly* 1?" She tallies the number of hands that go up after each question and then says, "Hmmm, most of you think the answer will be less than 1. Let's look at how we solve a problem like this. Then each of you will know whether you were right or wrong."
>
> Ask follow-up questions to probe students' reasoning.
>
> > In a geography lesson on Quebec, a Grade 4 teacher points out the St. Lawrence River on a map. "Which way does the water flow—toward the ocean or away from it?" One student shouts out, "Away from it." "Why do you think so?" the teacher asks. The student's explanation reveals a common misconception: that rivers can flow only from north to south, never vice versa.

We often hear expressions such as "he talks like a politician" or "she has the look of success." Can you think of some physical or social characteristics of your students that might influence your expectations of them?

student with a history of misbehaviour, and your observations may be biased accordingly (we could call this the "horns effect"). As we discovered in Chapter 9, teachers' expectations for their students are often influenced by students' ethnicity, sex, and socioeconomic status, and such expectations may unfairly bias teachers' judgments of student performance.

Practicality

The greatest strength of informal assessment is its practicality. It is time efficient and flexible: You can adapt your assessment procedures on the spur of the moment, altering them as events in the classroom change. Despite the practicality of informal assessment, we have noted serious problems regarding its reliability, standardization, and validity. Hence, you should treat any conclusions you draw only as *hypotheses* that you must either confirm or disconfirm through other means such as formal assessment techniques.

Planning a Formal Assessment

Formal assessments are most likely to be valid and reliable when they have been carefully planned ahead of time. Such planning involves addressing two key questions:

- What types of tasks will best measure students' achievement?
- How can you get a representative sample of the domain?

Selecting Appropriate Tasks

Content validity is maximized when assessment tasks reflect instructional objectives. In some situations, asking students to respond to multiple-choice or short-answer questions on a paper-pencil test may be both valid and practical. In other situations, essay questions that require students to follow a logical line of reasoning may be appropriate. Yet many skills—cooking a hard-boiled egg, executing a front dismount from the parallel bars, identifying specific microorganisms through a microscope—are difficult (perhaps impossible) to assess with paper and a pencil. In such situations, only performance assessment can give us reasonable content validity. Performance assessment can also be especially useful when you are concerned about students' ability to apply classroom subject matter to real-world situations. In the end, you may find that the most valid yet practical approach is a combination of both paper-pencil and performance tasks (Messick, 1994; Stiggins, 2001; D. B. Swanson et al., 1995). Using multiple assessment methods will also help you reduce assessment bias—psychologists call this "mixed-method" assessment.

Obtaining a Representative Sample

A test of any kind should have content validity. As described earlier, a *table of specifications* identifies both the topics to be covered and the things that students should be able to do with those topics. Once you have decided on the general nature of your assessment instrument, you should turn your attention to specific questions and tasks, administration procedures, and scoring criteria. We will address these issues separately for paper-pencil and performance assessment.

What kinds of performance tasks might be appropriate in the subject area you will be teaching? What methods might you use to determine if students understand and can apply what they have learned in an industrial arts class such as metal work?

Paper-Pencil Assessment

Questions that require brief responses, such as short-answer, matching, true-false, and multiple-choice, are often suitable for assessing students' knowledge of facts. Paper-pencil tasks that require extended responses—essays, for instance—lend themselves more easily to assessing such higher-level skills as problem solving, critical thinking, and synthesis of ideas (J. R. Frederiksen & Collins, 1989; Popham, 1995; Stiggins, 2001). Yet item type alone does not tell us whether you are assessing lower-level or higher-level skills. Although many classroom teachers use multiple-choice items primarily to assess knowledge of basic facts, you can also construct multiple-choice items that assess higher-level skills. With a little ingenuity, you can even develop relatively "authentic" paper-pencil tasks that assess students' ability to apply classroom subject matter to real-world tasks (Gronlund, 1993; D. B. Swanson et al., 1995).

An additional consideration is whether recognition or recall tasks better match your instructional objectives. **Recognition tasks** ask students to identify correct answers within the context of incorrect statements or irrelevant information; examples include multiple-choice, true-false, and matching questions. **Recall tasks** require students to generate the correct answers themselves; examples include short-answer questions, essays, and word problems. As noted in Chapter 6, recognition tasks are typically easier than recall tasks because they provide more retrieval cues to aid recall of relevant information from long-term memory.

You must weigh such advantages and disadvantages when deciding whether to use recognition items, recall items, or a combination of the two. Students can often answer many recognition questions in a short time; hence, such questions allow us to sample a wide range of knowledge and skills. You can score students' responses quickly and consistently, thus addressing your needs for practicality and reliability. However, recognition tasks may overestimate achievement: Students can sometimes guess correctly when they don't know the material.

When you want to assess students' ability to remember knowledge and skills without the benefit of having the correct answer in front of them, then recall tasks obviously have greater validity for assessing your instructional objectives. They are suited to assessing students' ability to organize information, follow a line of reasoning, design an experiment, or justify their position on a controversial topic. Yet because of the time needed to respond, you will be able to ask fewer items in a single assessment session (affecting reliability) and tap a more limited sample of the content domain (affecting content validity). Also, you will typically take longer to score such items (a practicality issue) and possibly make more errors in scoring them (an additional reliability issue).

Recognition task A memory task in which one must identify correct information among irrelevant information or incorrect statements.

Recall task A memory task in which one must retrieve information in its entirety from long-term memory.

Remember that your educational objectives—what it is the you want students to be able to do—will determine if you should use recall or recognition tasks to assess their learning outcomes.

Students tend to study more for essay tests than for multiple-choice tests (D'Ydewalle, Swerts, & De Corte, 1983; G. Warren, 1979). Why might this be so?

There are many excellent books that provide direct guidelines for constructing tests. We recommend the Canadian edition (2004) of Assessment of Student Achievement, *by Norman Gronlund and Ian Cameron at the University of Victoria.*

Constructing the Assessment Instrument

Writing good paper-pencil assessment items, especially those that assess higher-level thinking skills, takes considerable time and practice. In the following pages we will look at several formats that assess recognition and recall and then identify several general guidelines for constructing a paper-pencil assessment instrument.

Recognition Tasks

Alternative-response items. An alternative-response item is one for which there are only two or three possible answers, perhaps true versus false, or fact versus opinion. Such items are typically used to assess knowledge of discrete facts, although they can also be used for assessing such higher-level skills as discriminating between facts and opinions or identifying cause–effect relationships (R. L. Linn & Gronlund, 2000). If the subject matter lends itself easily to assessment in an either-or fashion, these items allow us to ask a large number of questions in a short time and so may enhance your ability to sample the domain in question. Remember that students have a 50 percent chance of correctly guessing each item. Following are a few guidelines for writing good alternative-response items:

- *Rephrase ideas presented in class or the textbook.* When students know that assessment items will be taken word for word from class material, they may try to learn that material verbatim. When they instead know that you will check for understanding by using different words and phrases to express the same idea, they will be more likely to engage in meaningful learning.

- *Write statements that clearly reflect one alternative or the other (e.g., statements that are clearly true or false).* A knowledgeable student should be able to respond to each item with certainty. When items are "sort of" true or "possibly" false, or they contain words with imprecise meanings (e.g., *sometimes, often*), then even your best students must resort to guessing what you had in mind when you wrote the items, resulting in lower test reliability.

- *Avoid excessive use of negatives, especially for false statements.* Negative words and prefixes in true-false items (e.g., *no, not, never, un-, mis-*) often lead to confusion, especially when the statements themselves are false.

Matching items. A matching item presents two columns of words, phrases, or data; students must match each item in the first column with an appropriate item in the second. Matching items lend themselves most readily to factual knowledge and ideas that can be easily paired—words and their meanings, countries and their capitals, parts of the body and their functions, and so on. Two basic guidelines to keep in mind when constructing these items are as follows:

- *Keep the items in each column homogeneous.* Consider this matching question from a Canadian social studies test:

Match each item on the left with its description on the right:

a. Current Prime Minister of Canada   1. 1867
b. The year of Canadian confederation   2. Regina
c. The capital city of Saskatchewan   3. oil
d. The major source of Alberta's wealth   4. Prime Minister Harper

Developing paper-pencil items that reflect important instructional objectives often takes considerable planning and creativity.

Even if you know nothing about Canada, you should be able to match the items easily because the different categories represented in the answers make only one possible answer for each question. To avoid this situation, the items in each column should all be members of the same category (perhaps dates, generals, capital cities, or word definitions) so as to give students few clues to the correct response.

- *Have more items in the answer or right-side column than in the question column.* Even if you don't know much about the question content, you can probably identify some of the correct answers, particularly the last one or two by a simple process of elimination. Therefore, consider placing more items in the answer column or using answers more than once.

Multiple-choice items. A multiple-choice item consists of a question or incomplete statement (the stem) followed by a series of alternatives. In most cases, only one alternative correctly answers the question or completes the statement; the other (incorrect) alternatives are distractors.

Most assessment experts recommend multiple-choice items for two reasons. First, the number of items that students get correct simply by guessing is relatively low (e.g., when an item has four possible answers, students have only a 25 percent chance of being right through guessing alone). The multiple-choice format also lends itself most readily to measuring higher-level thinking skills. These items cannot assess *everything*, of course; for instance, they can't assess students' ability to organize and express ideas coherently, nor can they assess what students would actually do in a real-life situation.

Following are several guidelines to keep in mind:

- *Present distractors that are clearly wrong to students who know the material but plausible to students who haven't mastered it.* Distractors should not be obviously incorrect. Instead, they should reflect common errors and misunderstandings.

- *Avoid putting negatives in both the stem and the alternatives.* Having negatives such as *not* and *don't* in two places at once amounts to a double negative that students have trouble understanding.

- *Use "all of the above" or "none of the above" seldom if at all.* Many of our students tell us that "all of the above" is the correct choice more often than not. And if at least one answer is correct, then "none of the above" can be ruled out.

- *Avoid giving logical clues about the correct answer.* Following are several ways to avoid giving logical clues about the correct alternative:
  - Make all alternatives grammatically consistent with the stem, so that each one, when combined with the stem, forms a complete sentence.
  - Make all alternatives different in meaning (don't present two or more alternatives that say essentially the same thing).
  - Make all alternatives equally long and precise. (Novice test writers tend to make the correct alternative longer and more specific/detailed than the distractors.)

Recall Tasks

Short-answer and completion items. A short-answer item poses a question to be answered with a single word or number, a phrase, or a couple of sentences. A completion item presents a sentence with a blank for students to fill in. Both formats require recall of information, but they lend themselves most readily to measuring lower-level skills, and scoring students' responses becomes more subjective, thereby decreasing reliability. Following are two guidelines to keep in mind when writing short-answer and completion items:

- *Indicate the type of response required.* Consider this item from a middle school science test:

Explain why it is colder in winter than in summer.

A student could conceivably write several paragraphs on this topic. Fortunately, the teacher who wrote the item gave students some guidance about how to respond to it and the other short-answer items on her test:

Provide a short answer (1–2 sentences) for each of the following questions. You must use complete and clearly stated sentences. Please use part of the question to introduce your response.

- *For completion items, include only one or two blanks per item.* Too many blanks make an item difficult, perhaps impossible, to interpret. To see what we mean, try filling in the blanks in this statement concerning material presented earlier in this chapter:

Constructing an assessment instrument with high _____ _____ for one's instructional _____ can be accomplished by developing a _____ that describes both the _____ and the _____.

There are so many blanks that it's hard to know what information is being called for. (The answers we had in mind are "content validity," "objectives," "table of specifications," "topic to be covered [or content]," and "student behaviours related to each topic [or learning outcomes]," or words to that effect.)

Problems and interpretive exercises. In a problem, students must manipulate or synthesize data and develop a solution to a new problem situation. We most often see this item type as word problems in mathematics and the sciences, as in the following example:

> You have a four-litre container of hot water (60°C) and a one-litre container of cold water (10°C). If you mix the water in the two containers together, what temperature will the water be?

Problems and interpretive exercises are especially suitable for assessing students' ability to transfer what they have learned to new situations; they may also involve such higher-level skills as analysis, synthesis, and critical thinking. They can be time-consuming to develop, but this time is well spent if greater validity is gained in assessing important instructional objectives.

> Remember that these are only suggestions; how you assess student learning is grounded in the realistic and relevant objectives you have established for the material to be learned.

Essay tasks. An essay task requires a student to write a lengthy verbal response—at least a paragraph, and perhaps as much as several pages. Essays are especially useful when you want students to show their writing ability or to demonstrate higher-level thinking skills (e.g., to analyze a piece of literature, compare and contrast two points of view, or apply scientific principles to explain various phenomena) in a written format. Essay items have two serious limitations, however. First, students can respond to only a small number of questions in a single assessment, thereby limiting sampling of the content domain (and hence limiting content validity). Second, scoring is time-consuming and more subjective, especially when the questions require lengthy, relatively unstructured responses. These guidelines maximize the information you can get from students' essays while simultaneously ensuring reasonable validity and reliability:

■ *Have several essays requiring shorter responses rather than one essay requiring a lengthy response.* Unless you are confident that one or two essay questions *do* provide a representative sample of the domain being tested and, furthermore, that each question yields responses that can be scored consistently, you probably want to either have several shorter essay questions or combine one or two lengthy essays with other item types that can be answered quickly and easily.

■ *Give students a structure for responding.* You may remember essay tests you've taken that provided little information or structure about how to respond. For example:

> List the events leading to the Riel Rebellion.

You may remember other tests that provided clear guidance about the nature of the responses required, such as this item does:

> Identify three key events that led to the formation of the Canadian Confederation in 1867. Explain in three to five sentences how each of these events contributed to the unification of Canada.

When you ask a totally unstructured question, students' responses may go in so many different directions that you will have difficulty scoring them consistently and reliably. Especially in situations where a great deal of material is potentially relevant, you should give students some guidance about the length and completeness of the desired response and about the things they should specifically address.

■ *Ask questions that can clearly be scored as correct or incorrect.* Consider these two essay questions:

> How can the dilemma of the world's diminishing rain forests best be solved?

> Develop and explain a possible solution to the problem of the world's diminishing rain forests. Show how your solution addresses at least two of the economic, social, or political factors contributing to rain forest devastation.

Students' responses can be judged on how well their proposed solutions address factors that contribute to deforestation—factors that were presumably discussed in class or presented in the textbook.

General Guidelines for Constructing Paper-Pencil Assessments

Regardless of the kinds of items you use, you should follow several guidelines as you construct and administer a paper-pencil assessment instrument:

- *Define tasks clearly and unambiguously.* Contrary to what some teachers believe, little is to be gained from assigning ambiguous tasks to assess students' learning and achievement (Sax, 1989).

- *Decide whether students should have access to reference materials.* In some cases, you may want your students to have only one resource—their long-term memory; in others, it may be appropriate to let them use reference materials when your objective is for students to locate and use information rather than memorize it.

- *Specify scoring criteria in advance.* You will typically want to identify correct responses at the same time that you develop your assessment items. In situations where there will be more than one correct answer, you should identify the components of a good response. You may want to share your scoring criteria with students; doing so gives them guidance about how they can best prepare and maximize their performance. Furthermore, you should develop policies to guide your scoring when students give partially correct answers, respond correctly but include additional *incorrect* information, or write responses with numerous grammatical and spelling errors.

With easy access to computers and unlimited sources of information, it is possible for a student to find information on any topic in the school curriculum. Teaching students how to use this resource and to critically assess the information gleaned from websites may be an important learning experience in its own right!

- *Place easier and shorter items at the beginning of the test; place more challenging ones near the end.* By beginning an assessment with short, relatively easy items, you put students at ease (thereby keeping test anxiety at a facilitative level) and ensure that they show us some of what they know.

Having students use reference materials during a formal assessment is quite appropriate when instructional objectives focus on the ability to find and apply, rather than recall, information.

- *Set parameters for students' responses.* Develop directions that specify the following:
  - *Time limits*—for example, how long students should spend on each item, and whether they have a limited time to complete the overall assessment
  - *Nature of desired responses*—for example, whether they should choose a single best answer on each multiple-choice question or instead mark all correct alternatives
  - *Method of recording responses*—for example, whether students should indicate their answers on the instrument itself or on a separate answer sheet
  - *Acceptability of guessing*—for example, whether students should guess if they're not sure, or whether points will be subtracted for wrong answers (many assessment experts recommend that you encourage guessing rather than penalize for it)

Administering the Assessment

Your concern about maximizing the validity of a paper-pencil assessment cannot end once you've constructed the assessment instrument. Also consider validity as you administer the instrument and score students' responses. Three additional strategies that are likely to increase the validity of your results are as follows:

- *Provide a quiet and comfortable environment.* This comfort factor may be especially important for students who are easily distracted, unaccustomed to formal assessments, or unmotivated to perform well on them.

- *Encourage students to ask questions when tasks are not clear.* You should encourage them to ask for clarification whenever they are uncertain about a task.

- *Take steps to discourage cheating.* The prevalence of cheating increases as students get older, and at the secondary level, more than 40 percent of students are likely to cheat at one time or another (Evans & Craig, 1990; Paris et al., 1991). The best approach is prevention—making sure students don't cheat in the first place. If, despite reasonable precautions, an incident of cheating

Recent instances in Canada of students sharing information about course assignments on websites and chat rooms have led to concerns by university faculty that this may be akin to cheating. What is your view on this?

One expert recommends that the consequence for cheating *not* be a low (or failing) grade for a course in which the student has, in other graded assignments, demonstrated mastery of the subject matter (Stiggins, 2001). Do you agree with Stiggins? Why or why not?

FIGURE 12.7 Example of a rubric for teacher and student evaluation of Grade 5 mathematics word problems

Elements	Possible Points	Points Earned Self	Points Earned Teacher
1. You highlighted the question(s) to solve.	2	___	___
2. You picked an appropriate strategy.	2	___	___
3. Work is neat and organized.	2	___	___
4. Calculations are accurate.	2	___	___
5. Question(s) answered.	2	___	___
6. You have explained in words how you solved the problem.	5	___	___
TOTAL	___	___	___

does occur, you should administer a consequence severe enough to discourage a student from cheating again, yet not so severe that the student's motivation and chances for academic success are affected over the long run. Your final grades should ultimately reflect what a student has and has not learned.

Scoring Students' Responses

Several strategies can help you score students' responses in an objective, reliable, and standardized manner:

- *Specify scoring criteria in concrete terms.* Whenever an assessment task involves subjective evaluation of a complex performance, you should list the components that a correct response must include or the characteristics you will consider as you judge it. Such a list is sometimes known as a **rubric** (Figure 12.7).

- *Unless specifically assessing writing skills, score grammar and spelling separately from the content of students' responses to the extent possible.* This recommendation is especially important when assessing students with limited English proficiency (Hamp-Lyons, 1992; Scarcella, 1990).

- *Skim a sample of students' responses ahead of time, looking for unanticipated responses and revising the criteria if necessary.* If you need to change your scoring criteria, you are more likely to score student responses consistently, fairly, and reliably if you change those criteria *before* you begin scoring rather than midway through a stack of papers.

- *Score item by item rather than test by test.* Score all students' responses to the first question, then all their responses to the second question, and so on.

- *Try not to let prior expectations for students' performance influence judgments of their actual performance.* Strategies such as shuffling papers after grading one question and using small self-stick notes to cover up students' names can help you keep your expectations from inappropriately influencing your judgments.

- *Accompany any overall scores with detailed feedback.* Your assessments should promote students' future learning as well as determine current achievement levels. Accordingly, give students detailed comments about their responses that tell them what they did well, where their weaknesses lie, and how they can improve (Bangert-Drowns, Kulik, Kulik, & Morgan 1991; Deci & Ryan, 1985; Krampen, 1987).

RSVP Characteristics of Paper-Pencil Assessment

Reliability

When your test questions elicit objectively scorable responses, you can evaluate students' responses with a high degree of consistency and reliability. When your questions require that you make subjective judgments about the relative rightness or wrongness of students' responses, reliability will inevitably decrease.

Rubric A list of components that performance on an assessment task should ideally include; used to guide the scoring of students' responses.

Examples of using rubrics to guide the scoring of student assessments can be found on the websites of several provincial departments of education, such as www.edu.gov.mb.ca/k12.

Standardization

Paper-pencil instruments present similar tasks and instructions to all students, provide similar time limits and environmental conditions, and score everyone's responses in more or less the same way. But you may also need to tailor assessment tasks to the particular abilities and disabilities of your students with special needs.

Validity

Tests that require only short, simple responses sample students' knowledge about many topics within a relatively short period of time and can give you greater content validity. Yet in some situations, you may need to be satisfied with a few tasks requiring lengthy responses.

Practicality

Because paper-pencil assessment is so practical, it should generally be your method of choice *if* it can also yield a valid measure of what students know and can do. However, you may need to sacrifice such practicality to gain the greater validity that a performance assessment provides.

Performance Assessment

A wide variety of performance tasks can be used to assess students' mastery of instructional objectives. Here are just a few of the many possibilities:

- Playing a musical instrument
- Conversing in a foreign language
- Identifying an unknown chemical substance
- Engaging in a debate about social issues
- Taking dictation in shorthand
- Diagnosing and repairing a malfunctioning machine
- Role-playing a job interview
- Performing a workplace routine
- Creating a computer simulation of a real-world task (Gronlund, 1993; C. Hill & Larsen, 1992; D. B. Swanson et al., 1995).

Performance assessment lends itself particularly well to the assessment of complex achievements, such as those that involve coordinating a number of skills simultaneously. It may also be quite helpful in assessing such higher-level cognitive skills as problem solving, critical thinking, and creativity. Furthermore, performance tasks are often more meaningful and thought-provoking, and so often more motivating, than paper-pencil tasks (Khattri & Sweet, 1996; Paris & Paris, 2001; D. P. Resnick & Resnick, 1996).

> In which category do most performance tasks fall—*recognition* or *recall* tasks?

Choosing Appropriate Performance Tasks

Let's look at four distinctions that can help us zero in on the tasks most appropriate for your purposes: products versus processes, individual versus group performance, restricted versus extended performance, and static versus dynamic assessment.

Products versus Processes

In performance assessment you can focus on products, processes, or both (E. H. Hiebert, Valencia, & Afflerbach, 1994; Messick, 1994; Paris & Paris, 2001). In some situations, you can look at tangible *products* that students have created—perhaps a pen-and-ink drawing, a scientific invention, or a poster display. In situations with no tangible product, you must instead look at the specific *processes and behaviours* that students exhibit—perhaps giving an oral presentation, demonstrating a forward roll, or playing an instrumental solo. In the latter case, you can sometimes ascertain students' *thinking processes* as well.

Individual versus Group Performance

Many performance tasks require *individual* students to complete them with little or no assistance from others. Other tasks are sufficiently complex that they are best accomplished by a *group* of students. For instance, you might assess high school students' mastery of a unit on urban geography using a field-based co-operative group project. Such a task might require students to collect data systematically, use the data to draw conclusions and make predictions and, more generally, think as an urban planner would think (Newmann, 1997). Teachers may consider individual students' behaviours and achievements (e.g., what and how much a student contributes to the group effort) in addition to, or perhaps instead of, the entire group's accomplishments (Lester et al., 1997; Stiggins, 2001).

Restricted versus Extended Performance

Some of your performance tasks are apt to be quite short; that is, they involve *restricted performance*. In a chemistry class you might ask students to demonstrate mastery of basic safety procedures before beginning their lab experiments. You assess *extended performance* when you want to determine what students are capable of doing over days or weeks (Alleman & Brophy, 1997; De Corte et al., 1996; Lester et al., 1997). Extended performance tasks might provide opportunities for students to collect data, engage in collaborative problem solving, and edit and revise their work. Many extended performance tasks embody authentic assessment: They closely resemble the situations and problems that students may eventually encounter in the outside world.

Static versus Dynamic Assessment

Most assessments focus on identifying students' existing abilities and achievements (i.e., *static* indicators) in contrast to assessing students' ability to learn in new situations, perhaps with the assistance of a teacher (Calfee & Masuda, 1997; Feuerstein, Feuerstein, & Gross, 1997; L. A. Shepard, 2000). This latter approach, sometimes called **dynamic assessment**, reflects Vygotsky's *zone of proximal development* and can give us an idea of what your students are likely to be able to accomplish with appropriate structure and guidance. Hence, it is most appropriate for formative (rather than summative) evaluation.

Dynamic assessment Examining how a student's knowledge or reasoning may change over the course of performing a specific task.

Dynamic assessment appears to be especially helpful in assessing students' cognitive processes and deficiencies, as well as in gathering information about students' dispositions and motivation (Feuerstein et al., 1997; Hamers & Ruijssenaars, 1997; Tzuriel, 2000). Furthermore, it often yields more optimistic evaluations of students' cognitive abilities than traditional assessment tasks do and may be particularly useful in assessing the abilities of students from diverse cultural backgrounds and lower-income families (Feuerstein, 1979; Tzuriel, 2000).

Planning and Administering the Assessment

Several of the guidelines presented in the section on paper-pencil assessment are equally relevant for performance assessment. In particular, you should

- Define tasks clearly and unambiguously
- Specify scoring criteria in advance (more about this point shortly)
- Standardize administration procedures as much as possible
- Encourage students to ask questions when tasks are not clear

Three additional guidelines pertain specifically to conducting performance assessments:

- *Consider incorporating the assessment into normal instructional activities.* You make more efficient use of your limited time with students if you can combine instruction and assessment into one activity. In addition, you may reduce the "evaluative" climate in your classroom. In other situations, then, you may want to conduct an assessment separately from instructional activities, announce it in advance, and give students some guidance as to how they can maximize their performance (Stiggins, 2001).

- *Provide an appropriate amount of structure.* You will probably want to structure performance tasks to some degree; this helps to standardize the assessment and so enables you to evaluate students' performance more reliably. Yet too much structure will reduce the authenticity of a task, so you must consider both reliability and validity as you determine the appropriate amount of structure to impose in any performance assessment.

- *Plan classroom management strategies for the assessment activity.* Effective teachers are continually aware of what their students are doing (the notion of *withitness*), and they make sure all students are busy and engaged. In situations when you must assess only a few students (or perhaps only one) at a time, you must make sure other students are actively involved in a learning activity (L. M. Carey, 1994).

Scoring Students' Responses

Occasionally, responses to performance assessment tasks are objectively scorable; for example, you can easily count the errors on a typing test or time students' performance in a 100-metre dash. But more often than not, you will find yourself making somewhat subjective decisions when you assess performance.

Especially for summative evaluations, carefully consider the criteria to use as you judge students' responses and develop a rubric that identifies these criteria. A rubric can guide you during the evaluation process, and later on, it can serve as a written record of what you have observed. The following strategies can help you design and use scoring rubrics effectively when you conduct performance assessments:

- *Consider using checklists, rating scales, or both in your rubric.* Some tasks lend themselves well to **checklists**, with which you evaluate student performance by indicating whether specific behaviours or qualities are present or absent. Other tasks are more appropriately evaluated with **rating scales**, with which you evaluate student performance by rating aspects of the performance on one or more continua (see Figure 12.8). Reliability of scoring and instructional benefits are enhanced: They identify any specific areas of difficulty for a student and so give feedback about how performance can be improved.

Checklist An assessment tool with which a teacher evaluates student performance by indicating whether specific behaviours or qualities are present or absent.

Rating scale An assessment tool with which a teacher evaluates student performance by rating aspects of the performance on one or more continua.

FIGURE 12.8 Examples of checklists and rating scales

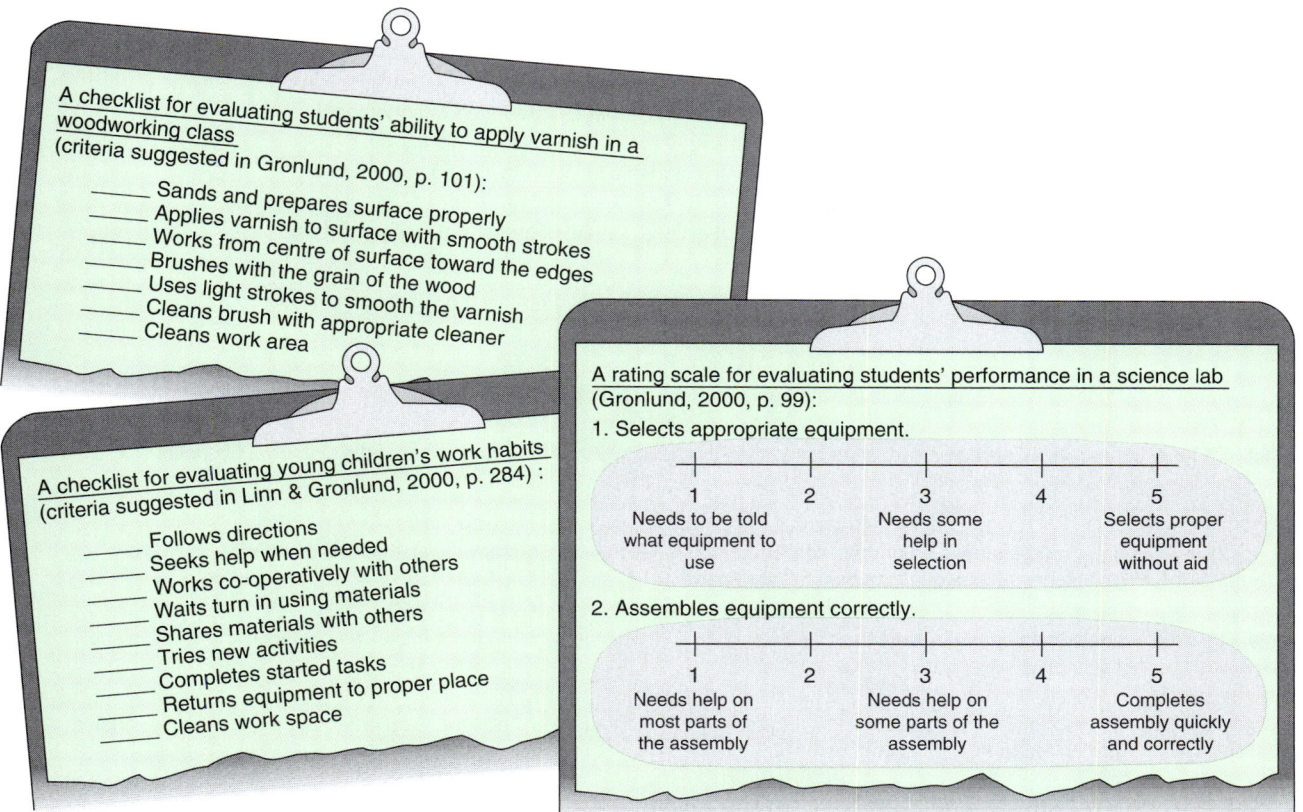

Chapter 12 Instructional Assessment 345

Analytic scoring Scoring students' performance on an assessment by evaluating various aspects of their performance separately.

Holistic scoring Summarizing students' performance on an assessment with a single score.

Which approach do raters use at Olympic events such as springboard diving and figure skating: analytic or holistic?

Use the concept of working memory (Chapter 6) to explain the value of having only a few criteria.

FIGURE 12.9 Grade 8 history teacher Mark Nichols uses this rubric (only partly shown here) to evaluate students' performance in co-operative group projects about pre–Confederation Canada

- *Decide whether analytic or holistic scoring better serves your purpose(s) in conducting the assessment.* When you need detailed information about students' performance, you may want to use **analytic scoring**, in which you evaluate various aspects of the performance separately, perhaps with a checklist or several rating scales. When you need to summarize students' performance in a single score, you should probably use **holistic scoring**, in which you consider all relevant criteria when making a single judgment. Analytic scoring is typically more useful in conducting formative evaluations and promoting students' learning, whereas holistic scoring is often used in summative evaluation.

- *Limit the criteria to the most important aspects of the desired response.* Your criteria should focus on aspects of the performance that are critical for a "good" response and most relevant to your instructional objectives (Stiggins, 2001; Wiggins, 1992). They should also be relatively few in number (perhaps five or six at the most) so that you can keep track of them as you observe each student's performance (Airasian, 1994; Gronlund, 1993; Popham, 1995).

- *Describe the criteria as explicitly and concretely as possible.* Criteria such as "very good" and "needs improvement" don't tell us very much, nor do they offer much feedback for students. You can score students' performance more objectively and reliably, and provide more constructive feedback, when your criteria focus on specific, observable qualities of students' products or behaviours (R. L. Linn & Gronlund, 2000; Stiggins, 2001; Wiggins, 1992). Figure 12.9 presents a partial rubric that a teacher uses to evaluate students' performance in a co-operative group activity.

- *Make note of any other significant aspects of a student's performance that the rubric doesn't address.* Rubrics are rarely perfect. You may occasionally want to jot down other noteworthy characteristics of students' performance. While neither standardized nor reliable, it can sometimes be useful in identifying students' unique strengths and needs and assist in your future instructional planning.

Colonial Economies Rubric

The following rubric will help the student to understand the expectations for each component of the group project. The number value represents the level of mastery. Higher numbers reflect greater mastery.

Outline: The outline is organized and concise while summarizing important information.

   Organization: The outline is formatted according to the style discussed in class and aligned with the book.
      5   4   3   2   1

   Clarity: The text of the outline is organized in a manner that helps students to fully understand the material.
      5   4   3   2   1

   Information: The outline information is to the point and does not exceed 1 sheet of paper (both sides).
      5   4   3   2   1

Artistic Interpretation: The creative project displays some of the important information within the subchapter.

   Creativity: The product reflects prior thought, effort, and artistry.
      5   4   3   2   1

   Interpretation: The product properly represents the material within the subchapter.
      5   4   3   2   1

   Attraction: The final product reflects organization and engages the audience through colour, size, and a high level of quality.
      5   4   3   2   1

Presentations:

   Preparedness: The group members are each prepared for the presentation with thorough knowledge of the material. They show preparedness through a sense of confidence in their presentation.
      5   4   3   2   1

   Clarity: The information presented is well organized and clearly stated. Members of the group make eye contact with the class and engage each student with understanding of the material.
      5   4   3   2   1

   Organization: The members of the group successfully organize the presentation so that there is an order and a pace that will enable students to gain a clear understanding of the material.
      5   4   3   2   1

RSVP Characteristics of Performance Assessment

Let's consider the four RSVP characteristics of performance assessments.

Reliability

The reliability of performance assessments, in many cases, is inconsistent over time, and different teachers may rate the same performance differently (S. Burger & Burger, 1994; R. L. Linn, 1994; Shavelson, Baxter, & Pine, 1992; D. B. Swanson et al., 1995). Students don't always behave consistently; even in a task as simple as shooting a basketball. When evaluating various aspects of complex behaviours relatively quickly, you may miss important parts of a student's performance. In addition, *internal consistency*, one form of reliability, is simply inappropriate for complex, multifaceted behaviours.

Accordingly, ask students to demonstrate behaviours related to important instructional objectives on more than one occasion (Airasian, 1994; L. M. Carey, 1994). And whenever possible, you should have more than one rater evaluate each student's performance (Stiggins, 2001; R. M. Thorndike, 1997).

Standardization

Some performance assessments are easily standardized (e.g., typing skills, driving tests), but others are not. In such nonstandardized situations, it is especially important to use multiple assessments and look for consistency in students' performance across several occasions.

Validity

Students' responses to a *single* performance assessment task are frequently *not* a good indication of their overall achievement (Koretz, Stecher, Klein, & McCaffrey, 1994; R. L. Linn, 1994; Shavelson et al., 1992; D. B. Swanson et al., 1995). Content validity is at stake here. In addition, any biases that affect your judgments may distort the conclusions you draw from their performance, further reducing the validity of your assessments (Airasian, 1994; L. M. Carey, 1994).

You will typically want to administer several *different* performance assessments, or perhaps administer the same task under different conditions (R. L. Linn, 1994; Messick, 1994; Stiggins, 2001; D. B. Swanson et al., 1995). For efficiency, you may want to incorporate some of these assessment activities into everyday instructional activities (Shavelson & Baxter, 1992).

Practicality

Unfortunately, performance assessments are often less practical (e.g., time consuming, expensive) than more traditional paper-pencil assessments (L. M. Carey, 1994; Hambleton, 1996; Popham, 1995). Clearly, then, you must carefully consider whether the benefits of a performance assessment outweigh its impracticality (Messick, 1994; Tzuriel, 2000; Worthen & Leopold, 1992).

Despite the limitations of performance assessments, they may more closely resemble the long-term objectives you have for your students, and in this sense they may be more valid indicators of students' achievement. The most reliable, valid, and practical assessment strategy overall may be to use *both* paper-pencil and performance assessments (multi-method assessment) when drawing conclusions about what your students have achieved (Gronlund, 1993; R. L. Linn, 1994).

At this point, you should be in a fairly good position to distinguish useful and dependable assessments from less valid and reliable ones. Table 12.6 presents a summary of our RSVP analyses of informal assessment, formal paper-pencil assessment, and formal performance assessment. We now turn your attention to strategies for including students in the assessment process.

Including Students in the Assessment Process

Earlier in this chapter, we noted that classroom assessments provide an externally imposed reason for learning school subject matter and achieving instructional objectives. Ideally, however, you want students to be *intrinsically* motivated to learn and achieve in the classroom, and they are more likely to be so if they have some sense of self-determination about classroom activities. Furthermore, if students are to become successful self-regulated learners, they must acquire skills in self-monitoring and self-evaluation. For such reasons, students should be regular and active participants in the assessment of their learning and performance. As teachers, you should think of

TABLE 12.6   COMPARE/CONTRAST

Evaluating the RSVP Characteristics of Different Types of Assessment

ASSESSMENT TYPE	RELIABILITY	STANDARDIZATION	VALIDITY	PRACTICALITY
Informal assessment	A single, brief assessment is not a reliable indicator of achievement. We must look for consistency in a student's performance across time and in different contexts.	Informal observations are rarely, if ever, standardized. Thus, we should not compare one student to another on the basis of informal assessment alone.	Students' "public" behaviour in the classroom is not always a valid indicator of their achievement (e.g., some may try to hide high achievement from peers).	Informal assessment is definitely practical: It is flexible and can occur spontaneously during instruction.
Formal paper-pencil assessment	Objectively scorable items are highly reliable. We can enhance the reliability of subjectively scorable items by specifying scoring criteria in concrete terms.	In most instances, paper-pencil instruments are easily standardized for all students. Giving students choices (e.g., about topics to write about or questions to answer), although advantageous from a motivational standpoint, reduces standardization.	Using numerous questions that require short, simple responses can make an assessment a more representative sample of the content domain. But tasks requiring lengthier responses may sometimes more closely match objectives.	Paper-pencil assessment is usually practical: All students can be assessed at once, and no special materials are required.
Formal performance assessment	It is often difficult to score performance assessment tasks reliably. We can enhance reliability by specifying scoring criteria in concrete terms.	Some performance assessment tasks are easily standardized, whereas others are not.	Performance tasks may sometimes be more consistent with instructional objectives than paper-pencil tasks. A single performance task may not provide a representative sample of the content domain; several tasks may be necessary to ensure content validity.	Performance assessment is typically less practical than other approaches: It may involve special materials, and it can take a fair amount of classroom time, especially if students must be assessed one at a time.

FIGURE 12.10 At the end of his Grade 3 year, 9-year-old Philip reviewed his work over the course of the year and identified his strengths and weaknesses.

assessment as something you do *with* students rather than *to* them. Furthermore assessment should be integrated as much as possible in the everyday learning environment of the classroom.

Students become increasingly skilful in self-assessment as they grow older (van Kraayenoord & Paris, 1997), but even students in the elementary grades have some ability to evaluate their own performance if they have the tools to do so (see Figure 12.10). Following are several strategies for including students in the assessment process and helping them develop important self-monitoring and self-evaluation skills:

- Make evaluation criteria explicit and easily observable (e.g., the criteria in Figure 12.9 were given to students at the beginning of the "pre-Confederation" unit).

- Provide examples of "good" and "poor" products and ask students to compare them on the basis of several criteria.

- Solicit students' ideas about evaluation criteria and rubric design.

- Have students compare self-ratings with teacher ratings

- Have students keep ongoing records of their performance and chart their progress over time.

- Have students reflect on their work in daily or weekly journal entries, where they can keep track of objectives they have and have not achieved, as well as learning strategies that have and have not been effective.

- Ask students to write practice questions similar to those they expect to see on upcoming quizzes and tests.

- Ask students to lead parent conferences. (A. L. Brown & Campione, 1996; R. L. Linn & Gronlund, 2000; Paris & Ayres, 1994; L. A. Shepard, 2000; Stiggins, 2001; Valencia, Hiebert, & Afflerbach, 1994)

An additional strategy is having students compile portfolios of their work; we will look at portfolios more closely later in the chapter.

Encouraging Risk Taking

Not only should students be actively involved in assessing their own learning and performance, but they should also feel comfortable enough about the assessment process that they feel free to take risks and make mistakes: Only under these circumstances will students tackle the challenging tasks that are likely to maximize their learning and cognitive development (Clifford, 1990) and feel a reasonable comfort level about classroom assessments.

Frequent assessments. Frequent assessment is important for several reasons. First, it provides ongoing information to both students and you about the progress that students are making and about areas of weakness that need attention. Second, students are less likely to experience debilitating anxiety when they have a number of assessments that each contributes only a small amount to their final grades (e.g., Sax, 1989). Third, frequent assessment motivates students, especially those with lower ability, to study regularly (Sax, 1989). Fourth, with the pressure off to perform well on every single test and assignment, students are less likely to cheat to obtain good grades (E. D. Evans & Craig, 1990). The bottom line is that students who are assessed frequently learn and achieve at higher levels than students who are assessed infrequently (Crooks, 1988; Gaynor & Millham, 1976; Glover, 1989).

> As a general rule in measurement and evaluation, the more assessment information you gather as a teacher, and the better that information is, the better your decisions and evaluations will be.

Retakes. As noted in the discussion of mastery learning in Chapter 10, some students will invariably need more time to master a topic than others and may therefore need to be assessed on the same material more than once. If you truly want students to master course material but also to take risks in their learning and classroom performance, then you may want to make retakes a regular practice.

Opportunities to correct errors. Students may learn as much—possibly even more—by correcting the errors they've made on an assessment task. One high school mathematics teacher, Dan Wagner, uses what he calls a mastery reform as a way of allowing students to make mistakes and then learn from them. When it is clear from classroom assessments that students haven't demonstrated mastery of a mathematical procedure, Dan has them complete an assignment that includes the following:

To encourage risk taking and reduce anxiety about classroom assessments, assess frequently and provide opportunities for students to correct errors. Here a teacher uses a student's errors on a paper-pencil assessment to guide her future studying efforts.

1. *Identification of the error.* Students describe in a short paragraph exactly what it is that they do not yet know how to do.
2. *Statement of the process.* Students explain the steps involved in the procedure they are trying to master; in doing so, they must demonstrate their understanding by using words rather than mathematical symbols.
3. *Practice.* Students show their mastery of the procedure by completing three new problems similar to the problem(s) they previously solved incorrectly.
4. *Statement of mastery.* Students state in a sentence or two that they have now mastered the procedure.

By completing the four prescribed steps, students can replace a grade on a previous assessment with the higher one that they earn by attaining mastery. Such assignments can have long-term benefits as well: many of Dan's students eventually incorporate the four steps into their regular, more internalized learning strategies.

Evaluating a Test/Assessment through Item Analysis

In the process of scoring students' performance on an assessment instrument, you may discover that some items or tasks simply don't provide the information you had hoped they would. For example, it may become obvious that one item is not measuring the knowledge or skill you had in mind (a validity problem) and that another is hard to score consistently (a reliability problem

Item analysis An analysis of students' responses to the individual items of an assessment instrument; used to identify possibly flawed items.

Item difficulty (*p*) The proportion of students getting a particular assessment item correct. A high *p* value indicates an easy item; a low *p* value indicates a difficult item.

that indirectly affects validity as well). An **item analysis** typically involves an examination of both the difficulty level and discriminative power of each item on the assessment instrument.

Item difficulty. The **item difficulty (*p*)** of an item is the proportion of students responding correctly relative to the total number of students who took the assessment:

$$p = \frac{\text{Number of students getting the item correct}}{\text{Number of students taking the assessment}}$$

This formula yields a number between 0.0 and 1.0. A high *p* value indicates that the item was a relatively easy one for students; for example, a *p* of .85 means that 85 percent of the students answered it correctly. A low *p* value indicates that the item was difficult; for example, a *p* of .10 means that only 10 percent gave a correct response.

Ideal *p* values are somewhere between .30 and .70, indicating that the items are difficult enough that some, but not all, students get them wrong. When almost all students answer an item in the same way—either correctly (a very high *p*) or incorrectly (a very low *p*)—you get little if any information about how the students differ from one another.

On criterion-referenced tests (such as many teacher-developed assessments), there is no "best" item difficulty value. In this case, *p* values help us determine how effectively you are accomplishing your instructional objectives. A low *p* value tells us either that your students haven't learned what you are assessing or that the item doesn't accurately reflect what students *did* learn.

Item discrimination (*D*) The relative proportion of high-scoring and low-scoring students getting a particular assessment item correct. A positive *D* indicates that an item appears to discriminate between knowledgeable and unknowledgeable students; a negative *D* indicates that the item may be providing misinformation about what students know and can do.

Item discrimination. You would expect the students who do well on any one item to be the same ones who perform well on the test overall. When an item "discriminates" among informed and uninformed students inaccurately, you have a problem with **item discrimination (*D*)**.

Item discrimination is determined by using two groups of students, the 20 to 30 percent who have the highest overall scores and the 20 to 30 percent who have the lowest scores. You then compare the proportions of students in the two groups getting each item correct, like this:

$$D = \frac{\text{Number of high-scoring students getting item correct}}{\text{Total number of high-scoring students}} - \frac{\text{Number of low-scoring students getting item correct}}{\text{Total number of low-scoring students}}$$

The *D* formula yields a number ranging from −1.0 to +1.0. Positive *D* values tell us that a greater proportion of high-scoring students have done well on an item than low-scoring students. In contrast, negative *D* values suggest that low-scoring students are answering the item correctly, but high-scoring students are not. A negative *D* is often a sign that something is wrong with the item; perhaps it misleads knowledgeable students to choose what was intended to be an incorrect response, or perhaps you have marked an incorrect answer on the answer key.

Many teachers save their good assessment items in an item file for use on future occasions. As they continue to add items to their files over the years, they eventually have a large enough collection that they don't have to use any one item very often.

Students who do well on any single item should be the same ones who perform well overall. Here we are talking about *internal consistency reliability*, the extent to which different parts of an assessment instrument are all measuring more or less the same thing. When the items or tasks on an assessment instrument are all designed to measure very *different* things, then this procedure is helpful in evaluating item effectiveness.

Summarizing Students' Achievement

Many of your assessments will provide a considerable amount of information regarding students' strengths and weaknesses, and you must eventually boil it down into more general indicators of what your students have accomplished. Two widely used approaches are *final class grades* and *portfolios*.

Determining Final Class Grades

Can you think of a time that you disagreed with a teacher's mark or grade assigned to you? What was the basis for the disagreement?

Over the years, teachers' grading practices have been a source of considerable controversy. First, because individual assessment instruments have less than perfect validity and reliability, grades based on these measures may also be somewhat inaccurate. Second, different teachers use different criteria to assign grades. Third, in heterogeneous classes, different students may be working to accomplish different instructional objectives. Fourth, typical grading practices promote performance goals rather than mastery goals and may encourage students to go for the "easy A" rather than take risks (Stipek, 1993; S. Thomas & Oldfather, 1997). Finally, students under pressure to achieve high grades may resort to undesirable behaviours (e.g., cheating, plagiarism) to attain those grades. Of course, very high and low grades are easier to arrive at and communicate overall excellent or "below par" achievement; grades in the middle range can mean very different things from student to student.

Despite such problems, final grades continue to be the most common method of summarizing students' overall classroom achievement. As a teacher, you can take several steps to ensure that the grades you assign are as accurate a reflection of what each student has accomplished as you can possibly make them:

- *Take the job of grading seriously.* Students' final class grades are often the *only* data that appear in their school records. You must take the time and make the effort to ensure that those grades are accurate. Many computer software packages are now available to assist with record keeping and grading.

- *Base grades on hard data.* Some teachers are better judges than others (Gaines & Davis, 1990; Hoge & Coladarci, 1989). Although teachers can generally judge the achievement of high-ability students with some accuracy, they are less accurate when they subjectively assess the achievement of low-ability students (Hoge & Coladarci, 1989), students from minority groups, and students from low socioeconomic backgrounds (Gaines & Davis, 1990). You should base grades on objective and observable information derived from formal assessment instruments, *not* from your subjective impressions.

- *Be selective about the assessments used to determine grades.* Using multiple assessments to determine final grades can help us compensate for the imperfect reliability and validity of any single assessment instrument. Many assessments may be more appropriately used for formative evaluation purposes—to help students learn—than for summative evaluation (Frisbie & Waltman, 1992).

- *Identify a reasonable grading system and stick to it.* If you want to give your students a sense that they have some control over their grades (recall the discussion of attribution theory in Chapter 9), you must tell them early in the semester or school year what your grading criteria will be. If you find that your criteria are overly stringent, you may need to "lighten up" in some way, perhaps by adjusting cutoffs or by allowing retakes of critical assessments. But you must never change your criteria midstream in a way that unfairly penalizes some students or imposes additional, unanticipated requirements.

Considering Improvement, Effort, and Extra Credit

Our discussion so far has been based on the assumption that class grades should reflect students' achievement of instructional objectives. Yet some educators suggest that students be graded on the basis of how much they improve, how hard they try, or how much extra work they do (e.g., Kane, 1983). Let's consider the implications of incorporating each of these factors into your final class grades.

Grading improvement. There are two good arguments against basing final grades solely on students' improvement over the course of a semester or school year. Some students may come to the first day of class already possessing some of the knowledge and skills in the curriculum you've planned, and so there is little room for improvement. Students trying to "beat the system" may quickly learn that they can achieve high grades simply by performing as poorly as possible at the beginning of the year (Airasian, 1994; Sax, 1989).

Yet in our discussion of promoting self-efficacy and intrinsic motivation in Chapter 9 we noted the importance of focusing students' attention on their own improvement, rather than on how their performance compares with that of their peers. One reasonable compromise here is to assign greater weight to assessments conducted at the end of the semester or school year, after *all* students have had a reasonable opportunity to achieve instructional objectives (Lester et al., 1997). Other strategies include administering retakes (perhaps using items or tasks different from those presented the first time) and giving students a chance to correct their errors and, in the process, demonstrate their mastery of the subject matter.

Grading effort. Most assessment experts recommend that you not base final grades on the amount of effort that students exert in the classroom. Students who begin the year already performing at a high level are penalized because they may not have to work as hard as their less knowledgeable classmates. Furthermore, "effort" is something that you can evaluate only subjectively and imprecisely at best (R. L. Linn & Gronlund, 2000; Sax, 1989; Stiggins, 2001). Some school systems have multidimensional grading systems that allow teachers to assign separate grades to the various aspects of students' classroom performance. Letters to parents, parent–teacher conferences, and letters of recommendation provide an additional means by which you can describe the multifaceted nature of students' classroom performance.

> Would a student who does little work all semester but pulls off a passing grade by doing an extra-credit project "learn a lesson" and develop more regular study habits? Why or why not?

Giving extra credit. Course grades are based on the extent to which students achieve instructional objectives, as determined by their performance on tests and assignments that are the same or equivalent (therefore standardized and fair) for all students. Extra-credit projects assigned to only one or two students (typically those achieving at the lowest levels) are insufficient to demonstrate mastery of the subject matter, and they are not standardized for the entire class.

Certainly, you can consider some extra-credit work as you assign grades, provided that the work relates to classroom objectives and all students are given the same opportunity to complete it. But incorporating extra credit into final evaluations is not the most appropriate way to help a failing student—one who has not met course objectives—achieve a passing grade.

Choosing Criterion- or Norm-Referenced Grades

As a general rule, final grades should reflect mastery of classroom subject matter and instructional objectives (e.g., Stiggins, 2001; Terwilliger, 1989). Criterion-referenced grades are especially appropriate during the elementary years: Much of the elementary curriculum consists of basic skills that are either mastered or not mastered, and there is little need to use grades as a basis for comparing students to one another.

At the secondary level, students' grades are sometimes used to choose college applicants, award scholarships, and so on. There are good reasons why high school grades should be criterion-referenced to the extent that such is possible. The most critical decisions for which grades are used—decisions about promotion and graduation—should be based on students' mastery or nonmastery of the school curriculum, not on their standing relative to others. Furthermore, different classes of students often differ in ability level; if grading were strictly norm-referenced, then a student's performance in one class (e.g., honours math) might be graded as C, whereas the same performance in another class (e.g., general math) might warrant an A.

When you set up a criterion-referenced grading system, you must determine as concretely as possible what you want each grade to communicate about students' achievement. For example, if you are using traditional letter grades, you might use criteria such as the following:

Grade	Criteria
A	The student has a firm command of both basic and advanced knowledge and skills in the content domain. He or she is well prepared for future learning tasks.
B	The student has mastered all basic knowledge and skills; mastery at a more advanced level is evident in some, but not all, areas. In most respects, he or she is ready for future learning tasks.
C	The student has mastered basic knowledge and skills but has difficulty with more advanced aspects of the subject matter. He or she lacks a few of the prerequisites critical for future learning tasks.
D	The student has acquired some but not all of the basics in the content domain. He or she lacks many prerequisites for future learning tasks.
F	The student shows little if any mastery of instructional objectives and cannot demonstrate the most elementary knowledge and skills. He or she lacks most of the prerequisites essential for success in future learning tasks. (based on criteria described by Frisbie & Waltman, 1992)

Summarizing students' many achievements with a single class grade can be quite challenging, and you inevitably lose a great deal of information in the process (Delandshere & Petrosky, 1998). Hence, some educators suggest that you communicate what students have achieved through other techniques that reflect the multifaceted nature of students' accomplishments. One strategy now gaining wide acceptance is portfolios.

INTO THE CLASSROOM   *Summarizing Students' Achievement*

Base final grades on objective and observable data.

> Carolyn always sits passively at the back of the classroom and never contributes to class discussions. Her teacher is surprised when she earns high scores on his first two classroom tests. He eventually realizes that, despite her lack of class participation, Carolyn is definitely achieving his instructional objectives and so grades her accordingly.

Use as many sources of data as is reasonably possible to determine grades.

> When determining semester grades, a high school teacher considers her students' performance on five paper-pencil tests, three formal performance assessments, a research paper, and numerous smaller assignments.

Don't count everything.

> A teacher frequently assigns homework as a way of encouraging students to practise new skills. He gives students feedback on their work but does not consider these assignments when determining course grades.

Evaluate actual achievement separately from such other factors as effort, improvement, and extra-credit projects.

> At a parent–teacher conference, a teacher describes Stan's performance this way: "Stan has gotten all Bs and Cs this term—grades that indicate adequate but not exceptional achievement. I have noticed a great deal of inconsistency in his classroom performance. When he puts forth the effort, he learns class material quite well; otherwise, he does poorly."

Assign criterion-referenced grades unless there is a compelling reason to do otherwise.

> A teacher assigns criterion-referenced grades for Algebra I, knowing that those grades will be used by school counsellors to determine an appropriate math class for each student next year.

Use portfolios to summarize students' accomplishment of complex, multifaceted tasks.

> A teacher has students develop portfolios of their fiction and nonfiction writing. These portfolios, which document students' mastery of some writing skills and progress on others, are shared with parents at the end of the school year.

Using Portfolios

A **portfolio** is a systematic collection of a student's work over a lengthy period. It need not be limited to paper-pencil products that students have developed; it might also include photographs, audiotapes, videotapes, or objects that a student has created (e.g., see Figure 12.11). Some portfolios are "developmental" in nature: Various products are included to show how a student has improved over a period of time. Others may include only the student's best work as a reflection of his or her final achievement (Spandel, 1997; Winograd & Jones, 1992).

Portfolios have several advantages (C. Hill & Larsen, 1992; Paris & Paris, 2001; F. L. Paulson, Paulson, & Meyer, 1991; Popham, 1995; Spandel, 1997). First, they capture the complex nature of students' achievement, often over a prolonged period, in ways that single letter grades can't possibly do. Dan Bachor (1990) at Victoria University states that the use of portfolios in the context of authentic assessment lessens the measurement errors that occur from single time or time-bound measurements. Second, they provide a mechanism through which you can easily intertwine assessment with instruction: Students typically include products that you may have assigned primarily for instructional purposes. Third, the process of constructing a portfolio encourages students to reflect on and evaluate their accomplishments. And fourth, portfolios sometimes influence the very nature of the instruction that takes place; because the focus is on complex skills, teachers may be more likely to *teach* those skills (Koretz et al., 1994). Leslie McLean (1988, 1990) at the Ontario Institute for Studies in Education asserts that portfolios are a most promising tool for the assessment of authentic achievement in the classroom (and perhaps accountability as well). He argues that they are "promising ways to truly integrate student evaluation with the rest of teaching and learning" (p. 78). And Bartley (1997) at Lakehead University further contends that portfolios encourage the valuing of teacher reflection.

However, RSVP characteristics are often a source of concern for portfolios, particularly if they are being used to evaluate, rather than simply communicate, students' learning and achievement. There may be little agreement among teachers about how any particular portfolio should be rated (Koretz et al., 1994; Popham, 1995). In addition, there is an obvious standardization problem: Because each portfolio will include a unique set of products, you will be evaluating each student on the basis of different information. Validity may or may not be a problem: A portfolio must

Portfolio A systematic collection of a student's work over a lengthy period of time.

include a sufficient number of work samples to provide a representative sample of what students have accomplished relative to instructional objectives (Arter & Spandel, 1992; Koretz et al., 1994). Last but not least, you must realize that portfolios, if used properly, are likely to take a great deal of your time, both during class and after hours (Airasian, 1994; Koretz et al., 1994; Popham, 1995); in this sense at least, they are less practical than other methods of summarizing achievement. Thus, you should be sure the potential benefits outweigh the disadvantages when you ask students to compile them, and you must use them cautiously when they serve as summative evaluations of what students have accomplished.

Advocates of portfolios have offered several suggestions for using portfolios effectively:

- *Consider the specific purpose for which a portfolio will be used.* Developmental portfolios, which include products from the entire school year or even longer, are most useful to determine whether your students are making reasonable progress toward long-term instructional objectives. Such portfolios are also invaluable for showing students *themselves* how much they've improved. "Best work" portfolios are more useful for summarizing students' final achievement, perhaps as a way of communicating students' accomplishments to parents, students' future teachers, or college admissions officers (Spandel, 1997).

- *Involve students in the selection of a portfolio's contents.* In most cases, students should decide for themselves which products to include in their portfolios (F. L. Paulson et al., 1991; Popham, 1995; Spandel, 1997), giving an enhanced sense of "ownership," self-determination, and intrinsic motivation to learn. Help students make appropriate choices by scheduling periodic one-on-one conferences in which you jointly discuss the products that best reflect their achievements (Popham, 1995). You can show them examples of portfolios that other students have created (make sure to get permission and respect confidentiality).

- *Identify the criteria by which products should be selected and evaluated.* Students are more likely to make wise selections when they have guidelines for making their selections and (if applicable) when they know the criteria by which their portfolio will eventually be evaluated (Popham, 1995; Spandel, 1997; Stiggins, 2001). If you are using portfolios for final evaluations, you will also want to develop a rubric for scoring it and, in some instances, you may want to include students themselves in the process of identifying the criteria to be used (Popham, 1995). Such a strategy further enhances students' self-determination and their ability to self-evaluate in future projects and assignments.

- *Ask students to reflect on the products they include.* In addition to examples of students' work, many portfolios include documentation that describes each product and the reason it was included. This encourages students to reflect on and judge their own work in ways that teachers typically do (Airasian, 1994; Arter & Spandel, 1992; Popham, 1995). Thus, it is likely to promote the self-monitoring and self-evaluation skills so essential for self-regulated learning.

Taking Student Diversity into Account

Standardization of assessment instruments and procedures is important for fairness, reliability, and (indirectly) validity in your assessment results. Yet it may limit your ability to accommodate students' diverse backgrounds and needs, capitalize on their individual strengths, and help them compensate for any areas of weakness.

Standardization in classroom assessment practices is essential if you want to make comparisons among your students, and especially if you also intend to use your assessment results to make decisions that may significantly affect students' future lives. In other situations, standardization is less critical; you may find that the best way of assessing one student's learning is a relatively *ineffective* way of assessing another's. Remind yourself of a few sources of diversity by reviewing Chapter 4.

Meghan makes arrangements of six in math.

Meghan displays her collection of 100.

FIGURE 12.11 In a kindergarten portfolio, Meghan and her teacher included these two digital photographs that illustrate Meghan's developing math skills.

While we have advocated for an RSVP view of assessment, is standardization of assessment really feasible in the heterogeneous classrooms of today?

Such factors as sex, language, and culture (described in Chapter 4) will, of course, affect students' ability to learn and achieve on your informal and formal assessments *independently* of their learning. This is yet another reason why you should consider multiple measures—as well as several different kinds of measures—whenever you are using your classroom assessment results to assign grades and make other important decisions.

Accommodating Students in the Inclusive Classroom

Earlier in this chapter, we noted the importance of making appropriate accommodations for students with special needs: You are unlikely to get valid results unless you *do* make such accommodations. The specific modifications to your assessment instruments and procedures must, of course, be tailored to students' particular disabilities. For example, you may need to break a lengthy assessment task into several shorter tasks for students with a limited attention span (e.g., for some students with ADHD or emotional and behavioural disorders). And you may have to construct individualized assessment instruments when instructional objectives differ for some of your students (e.g., as may often be the case for students with mental retardation). Additional accommodations for students with special needs are presented in Table 12.7.

> It is very likely that you will need to create Individual Educational Programs (IEPs) for students presenting with various exceptionalities. Arrange for a discussion with practising teachers about how IEP's are developed and consult your provincial education department to determine their guidelines for when an IEP is required and the implications this has for the student and teacher.

TABLE 12.7 — STUDENTS IN INCLUSIVE SETTINGS

Using Classroom Assessments with Students in the Inclusive Classroom

CATEGORY	CHARACTERISTICS YOU MIGHT OBSERVE	SUGGESTED CLASSROOM STRATEGIES
Students with specific cognitive or academic difficulties	• Poor listening, reading, and/or writing skills • Inconsistent performance due to off-task behaviours (for some students with learning disabilities or ADHD) • Difficulty processing specific kinds of information • Higher than average test anxiety	• Make paper-pencil instruments easy to respond to; for instance, type (rather than hand-write) tests, space items far apart, and have students respond directly on their test papers rather than on separate answer sheets. • Minimize reliance on reading and writing skills if appropriate. • Let students take tests in a quiet place (e.g., the school's resource room). • Give explicit directions. • Be sure students are motivated to do their best but not overly anxious. • Provide extra time to complete assessments. • Score responses separately for content and quality of writing. • Look at students' errors for clues about processing difficulties. • Use informal assessments to either confirm or disconfirm results of formal assessments.
Students with social or behavioural problems	• Inconsistent performance on classroom assessments due to off-task behaviours or lack of motivation (for some students)	• Make modifications in assessment procedures as necessary (see strategies presented above for students with specific cognitive or academic difficulties). • Use informal assessments to either confirm or disconfirm results of formal classroom assessments.
Students with general delays in cognitive and social functioning	• Slow learning and cognitive processing • Limited if any reading skills • Poor listening skills	• Be explicit about what you are asking students to do. • Make sure any reading materials are appropriate for students' reading level. • Use performance assessments that require little reading or writing. • Allow sufficient time for students to complete assigned tasks.
Students with physical or sensory challenges	• Mobility problems (for some students with physical challenges) • Tendency to tire easily (for some students with physical challenges) • Less developed language abilities (for some students with hearing loss)	• Use written rather than oral assessments (for students with hearing loss). • Minimize reliance on visual materials (for students with visual impairments). • Use appropriate technology to facilitate students' performance. • Provide extra time to complete assessments. • Limit assessments to short time periods and give frequent breaks. • Use simple language if students have language difficulties.
Students showing evidence of giftedness, talent, or high performance	• Greater ability to perform exceptionally complex tasks • Unusual, sometimes creative, responses to classroom assessment instruments • Tendency in some students to hide giftedness to avoid possible ridicule by peers	• Use performance assessments to assess complex activities. • Establish scoring criteria that allow unusual and creative responses. • Provide opportunities for students to demonstrate their achievements privately. • Keep assessment results confidential.

Sources: Barkley, 1998; Beirne-Smith et al., 2002; D. Y. Ford & Harris, 1992; Mercer, 1997; Morgan & Jenson, 1988; Piirto, 1999; Turnbull et al., 1999.

For an extensive listing of further classroom assessment methods, see *Rethinking Classroom Assessment with Purpose in Mind* published by the Western and Northern Canadian Protocol for Collaboration in Education (2006), available at www.wncp.ca/assessment/rethink.pdf.

You should also keep students' unique needs and disabilities in mind when you summarize and communicate their final achievements. Letter grades alone communicate very little definitive information about what students have learned and achieved; if you change the criteria for a particular student, the grades communicate even *less* information. Portfolios (perhaps including teacher checklists, photographs, audiotapes, and videotapes, as well as students' written work) can be particularly helpful for conveying the progress and achievements of students with a variety of disabilities and special needs (Mastropieri & Scruggs, 2000; Venn, 2000).

TEACHING CONSTRUCTIONS

This chapter has presented a wide variety of strategies for assessing students' learning and numerous guidelines for using them. Learning how to construct good classroom assessment instruments and evaluate student learning will likely be one of your most challenging tasks as a teacher. Give considerable thought to how you can best determine what your students are learning and devote considerable time and effort to designing your assessment instruments. Your assessments will indirectly affect students' learning and achievement through their influences on planning, instruction, and the classroom environment; they will also have several more direct effects on learning related to student motivation, self-efficacy and self-regulation, study habits, and present and future goals. Your ultimate goal as a teacher should be to *help students learn better*.

Several key suggestions drawn from this chapter should apply across the board:

- Match assessment instruments and practices to important instructional objectives.
- Consider the RSVP characteristics of every assessment.
- Specify scoring criteria as explicitly as possible.
- Look at students' errors for clues about where their difficulties lie.
- Don't summarize students' achievement any more than necessary.
- Evaluate assessment instruments after their use to be sure they have yielded the needed information, and look for ways to improve them in the future.

Now that you have considered the complex issues involved in assessing student learning, let's revisit Ellen and Roz, whom we met at the beginning of the chapter. Given what you have learned about instructional assessment, consider the following questions:

- What does assessment mean to you and to your students? Do you think it means the same to Ellen and Roz?
- Imagine you are Ellen and Roz's teacher. What alternative ways could you use to assess their knowledge and understanding about Canada's economy and geography?
- How will you ensure the quality and fairness of assessment practices in your classroom?
- How will students use assessments as learning opportunities? Do you think that Ellen and Roz will approach other learning tasks and how they study in the same or different ways, based on their classroom experience?

KEY CONCEPTS

assessment (p. 312)
informal assessment (p. 312)
formal assessment (p. 313)
paper-pencil assessment (p. 313)
performance assessment (p. 313)
traditional assessment (p. 313)
authentic assessment (p. 313)
standardized test (p. 314)
teacher-developed assessment instrument (p. 314)
formative evaluation (p. 314)
summative evaluation (p. 314)
reliability (p. 316)
reliability coefficient (p. 318)
standard error of measurement (SEM) (p. 318)
confidence interval (p. 318)
standardization (p. 319)
validity (p. 319)
content validity (p. 319)

table of specifications (p. 320)
predictive validity (p. 320)
validity coefficient (p. 320)
construct validity (p. 321)
practicality (p. 321)
criterion-referenced score (p. 321)
norm-referenced score (p. 321)
norms (p. 322)
ability test (p. 324)
specific aptitude test (p. 324)
raw score (p. 325)
grade-equivalent score (p. 326)
age-equivalent score (p. 326)
percentile rank (percentile) (p. 327)
normal distribution (normal curve) (p. 327)
standard score (p. 327)
mean (M) (p. 327)
standard deviation (SD) (p. 327)
IQ score (p. 328)
stanine (p. 328)

z-score (p. 328)
T-score (p. 328)
high-stakes testing (p. 329)
accountability (p. 329)
test anxiety (p. 331)
cultural bias (p. 331)
testwiseness (p. 332)
halo effect (p. 335)
recognition task (p. 337)
recall task (p. 337)
rubric (p. 342)
dynamic assessment (p. 344)
checklist (p. 345)
rating scale (p. 345)
analytic scoring (p. 346)
holistic scoring (p. 346)
item analysis (p. 350)
item difficulty (p) (p. 350)
item discrimination (D) (p. 350)
portfolio (p. 353)

Glossary

Ability test A test designed to assess one's general capacity to learn; typically used to predict students' success in future learning situations.

Accommodation In Piaget's theory, dealing with a new event by either modifying an existing scheme or forming a new one.

Accountability Holding teachers and other school personnel responsible for students' performance on high-stakes assessments.

Achievement motivation The need for excellence for its own sake, without regard for any external rewards that one's accomplishments might bring.

Action research Research conducted by teachers and other school personnel to address issues and problems in their own schools or classrooms.

Activation The degree to which a particular piece of information in memory is currently being attended to and mentally processed.

Activity reinforcer An opportunity to engage in a favourite activity.

Actual developmental level In Vygotsky's theory, the extent to which one can successfully perform a task independently.

Affect The feelings and emotions that an individual brings to bear on a task.

Affective domain The domain of learning tasks that includes attitudes and values about the things one learns.

Age-equivalent score A test score that indicates the age level of students to whom a student's test performance is most similar.

Aggressive behaviour Action intentionally taken to hurt another, either physically or psychologically.

Algorithm A prescribed sequence of steps guaranteeing a correct problem solution.

Allophone Variations of a single phoneme that do not make any difference to a word's meaning.

Analytic scoring Scoring students' performance on an assessment by evaluating various aspects of their performance separately.

Antecedent response A response that increases the likelihood that another, particular response will follow.

Antecedent stimulus A stimulus that increases the likelihood that a particular response will follow.

Anxiety A feeling of uneasiness and apprehension concerning a situation with an uncertain outcome.

Applied behaviour analysis (ABA) The systematic application of behaviourist principles in educational and therapeutic settings; sometimes known as *behaviour modification*.

Apprenticeship A situation in which a learner works intensively with an expert to learn how to accomplish complex tasks.

Assessment The process of observing a sample of students' behaviour and drawing inferences about their knowledge and abilities.

Assimilation In Piaget's theory, dealing with a new event in a way that is consistent with an existing scheme.

Attachment A strong, affectionate bond formed between a child and another individual (e.g., a parent); usually formed early in the child's life.

Attention The focusing of mental processes on particular environmental stimuli.

Attribution An internally constructed causal explanation for one's success or failure.

Attribution theory A theoretical perspective that focuses on people's attributions concerning the causes of events that befall them, as well as on the behaviours that result from such attributions.

Authentic activity A classroom activity similar to one students are likely to encounter in the outside world.

Authentic assessment Assessment of students' knowledge and skills in an authentic, "real-life" context; in many cases, an integral part of instruction rather than a separate activity.

Authoritative parenting A parenting style characterized by emotional warmth, high expectations and standards for behaviour, consistent enforcement of rules, explanations of the reasons behind these rules, and the inclusion of children in decision making.

Automaticity The ability to respond quickly and efficiently while mentally processing or physically performing a task.

Backup reinforcer A reinforcer that a student can "purchase" with one or more tokens earned in a token economy.

Base group A co-operative learning group that works together for an entire semester or school year and provides a means through which students can be mutually supportive of one another's academic efforts and activities.

Baseline The frequency of a response before operant conditioning takes place.

Behaviourism A theoretical perspective in which learning and behaviour are described and explained in terms of stimulus–response (S–R) relationships. Adherents to this perspective are called behaviourists.

Bilingual education An approach to second-language instruction in which students are instructed in academic subject areas in their native language while simultaneously being taught to speak and write in the second language. The amount of instruction delivered in the native language decreases as students become more proficient in the second language.

Bloom's taxonomy A taxonomy in which six learning tasks, varying in degrees of complexity, are identified for the cognitive domain: remembering, understanding, applying, analyzing, and creating.

Challenge A situation in which a person believes that he or she can probably succeed with sufficient effort.

Checklist An assessment tool with which a teacher evaluates student performance by indicating whether specific behaviours or qualities are present or absent.

Classical conditioning A form of learning whereby a new, involuntary response is acquired as a result of two stimuli being presented at the same time.

Classroom climate The psychological atmosphere of the classroom.

Classroom management Establishing and maintaining a classroom environment conducive to learning and achievement.

Clique A moderately stable friendship group of perhaps 3 to 10 members.

Co-operative learning An approach to instruction whereby students work with their classmates to achieve group goals and help one another learn.

Co-operative teaching A general education teacher and special education teacher collaborating to teach all students in a class, including students both with and without special educational needs, throughout the school day.

Cognitive apprenticeship A mentorship in which a teacher and a student work together to accomplish a challenging task or solve a difficult problem; in the process, the teacher provides guidance about how to think about the task or problem.

Cognitive domain The domain of learning tasks that includes knowledge of information, as well as ways of thinking about and using that information.

Cognitive processes Specific operations involved in storing, remembering, classifying, retrieving and manipulating visual, spatial, verbal, and any other conceptual information.

Cognitive psychology A theoretical perspective that focuses on the mental processes underlying human learning and behaviour. Adherents to this perspective are sometimes called *cognitivists*.

Cognitive strategy instruction A teaching approach that enables students to regulate and control their learning.

Collective self-efficacy People's beliefs about their ability to be successful when they work together on a task.

Community of learners A classroom in which teacher and students actively and collaboratively work to help one another learn.

Comprehension monitoring The process of checking oneself to make sure one understands the things being read or heard.

Computer-assisted instruction (CAI) Programmed instruction presented by means of a computer; it is one form of computer-based instruction.

Computer-based instruction (CBI) Instruction provided via computer technology.

Concept A mental grouping of objects or events that have something in common.

Concept map A diagram of concepts within an instructional unit and the interrelationships among them.

Conceptual change Revising one's knowledge and understanding of a topic in response to new information about that topic.

Conceptual understanding Knowledge acquired in an integrated and meaningful fashion.

Concrete operations stage Piaget's third stage of cognitive development, in which adultlike logic appears but is limited to concrete reality.

Concrete reinforcer A reinforcer that can be touched.

Conditioned response (CR) A response that, through classical conditioning, begins to be elicited by a particular stimulus.

Conditioned stimulus (CS) A stimulus that, through classical conditioning, begins to elicit a particular response.

Conditioning Another word for learning; commonly used by behaviourists.

Confidence interval A range around an assessment score reflecting the amount of error likely to be affecting the score's accuracy.

Conservation The concept that if nothing is added or taken away, an amount (e.g., number, mass) stays the same regardless of any alteration in shape or arrangement.

Construct validity The extent to which an assessment accurately measures an unobservable educational or psychological characteristic.

Construction A mental process in which a learner takes many separate pieces of information and uses them to build an overall understanding or interpretation of an event.

Constructivism A theoretical perspective that proposes that learners construct a body of knowledge from their experiences—knowledge that may or may not be an accurate representation of external reality. Adherents to this perspective are called *constructivists*.

Content validity The extent to which an assessment includes a representative sample of tasks within the content domain being assessed.

Contiguity The occurrence of two or more events at the same time. *Contiguous* is the adjective used to refer to events having *contiguity*.

Contingency A situation in which one event happens only after another event has already occurred. One event is contingent on another's prior occurrence.

Contingency contract A formal agreement between a teacher and a student that identifies behaviours the student will exhibit and the reinforcers that will follow those behaviours.

Continuous reinforcement Reinforcing a response every time it occurs.

Conventional morality Acceptance of society's conventions regarding right and wrong; behaving to please others or to live up to society's expectations for appropriate behaviour.

Convergent evidence Multiple sources or types of support for an observation, argument, theory, or practice, all pointing to a common conclusion.

Convergent thinking Pulling several pieces of information together to draw a conclusion or solve a problem.

Core goal A long-term goal that drives much of what a person does.

Correlation The extent to which two variables are related to each other, such that when one variable increases, the other either increases or decreases in a somewhat predictable way.

Correlational study A research study that explores relationships among variables. Such a study enables researchers to predict one variable on the basis of their knowledge of another but not to draw a conclusion about a cause–effect relationship.

Cortex The upper part of the brain; site of conscious and higher-level thinking processes.

Creative variability Conceptualizing (or "playing with") the learning process in different ways or in different contexts so that practice or rehearsal lead to more effective learning.

Creativity New and original behaviour that yields an appropriate and productive result.

Criterion-referenced score A test score that specifically indicates what students know and can do.

Critical thinking Evaluating the accuracy and worth of information or arguments.

Cueing A teacher's use of signals to indicate that a particular behaviour is desired or that a particular behaviour should stop.

Cultural bias The extent to which the items or tasks of an assessment instrument either offend or unfairly penalize some students because of their ethnicity, sex, or socioeconomic status.

Cultural identity A person's unique cultural sense of self.

Cultural mismatch A situation in which a child's home culture and the school culture hold conflicting expectations for the child's behaviour.

Culture Behaviours and belief systems of a particular social group; or, the context in which all behaviours are learned and displayed.

Culture shock A sense of confusion that occurs when a student encounters a culture with very different expectations for behaviour than the expectations with which the student has been raised.

Debilitating anxiety Anxiety that interferes with performance. A high level of anxiety is likely to be debilitating.

Decay A hypothesized weakening over time of information stored in long-term memory, especially if the information is used infrequently or not at all.

Declarative knowledge Knowledge related to "what is," to the nature of how things are, were, or will be (as opposed to *procedural knowledge*, which relates to how to do something).

Deductive reasoning Drawing a logical inference about something that must be true, given other information that has already been presented as true.

Delay of gratification The ability to forego small, immediate reinforcers in order to obtain larger ones later on.

Descriptive study A research study that describes situations. Such a study enables researchers to draw conclusions about the current state of affairs but not about correlational or cause–effect relationships.

Developmental milestone The appearance of a new behaviour that is developmentally more advanced.

Dialect A form of language characteristic of a particular region or ethnic group.

Direct instruction An approach to instruction that uses a variety of techniques (brief explanations, teacher questioning, rapid pacing, guided and independent practice) to promote learning of basic skills.

Discovery learning An approach to instruction whereby students develop an understanding of a topic through firsthand interaction with the physical or social environment.

Discrimination A phenomenon in operant conditioning whereby an individual learns that a response is reinforced in the presence of one stimulus but not in the presence of another, similar stimulus.

Disequilibrium In Piaget's theory, an inability to explain new events by using existing schemes.

Distributed cognition A process whereby people think about an issue or problem together, sharing ideas and working collaboratively to draw conclusions or develop solutions.

Distributed intelligence The idea that people are more likely to act "intelligently" when they have physical and/or social support systems to assist them.

Divergent thinking Taking a single idea in many different directions.

Drive A motivational state in which something necessary for optimal functioning (food, water, etc.) is missing.

Dynamic assessment Examining how a student's knowledge or reasoning may change over the course of performing a specific task.

Educational psychology A discipline encompassing psychological principles and theories related to learning, motivation, child and adolescent development, individual and group differences, and psychological assessment, especially as these topics relate to classroom practice.

Elaboration A cognitive process in which learners expand on new information based on what they already know.

Elaborative interrogation A study strategy in which students develop and answer knowledge-expanding (elaborative) questions about the material they are trying to learn.

Empathy Experiencing the same feelings as someone in unfortunate circumstances.

Encoding Changing the format of new information as it is being stored in memory.

Entity view of intelligence A belief that intelligence is a "thing" that is relatively permanent and unchangeable.

Epistemological beliefs One's beliefs about the nature of knowledge and knowledge acquisition.

Equilibration In Piaget's theory, the movement from equilibrium to disequilibrium and back to equilibrium—a process that promotes the development of more complex forms of thought and knowledge.

Equilibrium In Piaget's theory, a state of being able to explain new events by using existing schemes.

Equity (in instruction) Instruction without favouritism or bias toward particular individuals or groups of students.

Ethnic group A group of people with a common set of values, beliefs, and behaviours. The group's roots either precede the creation of, or are external to, the country in which the group resides.

Expectancy In motivation theory, the belief that one will be successful in accomplishing a task or achieving a goal.

Experimental study (experiment) A research study that involves the manipulation of one variable to determine its possible effect on another variable. It enables researchers to draw conclusions about cause–effect relationships.

Explicit teaching and learning Teaching and learning in which the content is clearly articulated and consciously processed, not simply implied or inferred.

Expository instruction An approach to instruction whereby information is presented in more or less the same form in which students are expected to learn it.

Expressive language The ability to communicate effectively through speaking and writing.

Extinction, in classical conditioning The eventual disappearance of a conditioned response as a result of the conditioned stimulus being repeatedly presented alone (i.e., in the absence of the unconditioned stimulus).

Extinction, in operant conditioning The eventual disappearance of a response that is no longer being reinforced.

Extrinsic motivation Motivation promoted by factors external to the individual and unrelated to the task being performed.

Extrinsic reinforcer A reinforcer that comes from the outside environment, rather than from within the individual.

Facilitating anxiety Anxiety that enhances performance. Relatively low levels of anxiety are usually facilitating.

Failure to store One's failure to mentally process information in ways that promote its storage in long-term memory.

Formal assessment A systematic attempt to ascertain what students have learned. It is typically planned in advance and used for a specific purpose.

Formal operational egocentrism The inability of individuals in Piaget's formal operations stage to separate their own abstract logic from the perspectives of others and from practical considerations.

Formal operations stage Piaget's fourth and final stage of cognitive development, in which logical reasoning processes are applied to abstract ideas as well as to concrete objects.

Formative evaluation An evaluation conducted during instruction to facilitate students' learning.

Functional analysis Examining a student's inappropriate behaviour, as well as its antecedents and consequences, to determine the function(s) that the behaviour might serve for the student.

g (general factor in intelligence) The theoretical notion that intelligence includes a *general factor* that influences people's ability to learn in a wide variety of content domains.

Gang A cohesive social group characterized by initiation rites, distinctive colours and symbols, territorial orientation, and feuds with rival groups.

General transfer An instance of transfer in which the original learning task and the transfer task do not overlap in content.

Generalization A phenomenon whereby an individual learns a response to a particular stimulus and then makes the same response in the presence of similar stimuli.

Generativity Creating new learning from previous learning, including new combinations and new contexts or application. Also, the feeling of empowerment to take such initiatives and "play with" knowledge.

Grade-equivalent score A test score that indicates the grade level of students to whom a student's test performance is most similar.

Grapheme A letter or group of letters that represents a single phoneme.

Group contingency A situation in which everyone in a group must make a particular response before reinforcement occurs.

Group differences Consistently observed differences, on average, among certain groups of individuals.

Guided participation Giving a child the necessary guidance and support to perform an activity in the adult world.

Guilt The feeling of discomfort that individuals experience when they know that they have caused someone else pain or distress.

Halo effect A phenomenon whereby people are more likely to perceive positive behaviours in a person they like or admire.

Heuristic A general problem-solving strategy that may or may not yield a problem solution.

High-stakes testing Using students' performance on a single assessment instrument to make major decisions about students or school personnel.

Higher-level question A question that requires students to do something new with information they have learned—for example, to apply, analyze, synthesize, or evaluate it.

Higher-level thinking Thought that involves going beyond information specifically learned (e.g., application, analysis, synthesis, evaluation).

Holistic scoring Summarizing students' performance on an assessment with a single score.

Hot cognition Learning or cognitive processing that is emotionally charged.

Identity A self-constructed definition of who a person thinks he or she is and what things are important in life.

Ill-defined problem A problem in which the desired goal is unclear, information needed to solve the problem is missing, and/or several possible solutions to the problem exist.

Illusion of knowing Thinking one knows something that one actually does not know.

Imaginary audience The belief that one is the centre of attention in any social situation.

Immersion An approach to second-language instruction in which students hear and speak that language almost exclusively within the classroom.

Inability to retrieve Failing to locate information that currently exists in long-term memory.

Incentive A hoped-for, but not certain, consequence of behaviour.

Inclusion The practice of educating all students, including those with severe and multiple disabilities, in neighbourhood schools and general education classrooms.

Incompatible behaviours Two or more behaviours that cannot be performed simultaneously.

Incremental view of intelligence The belief that intelligence can and does improve with effort and practice.

Individual constructivism A theoretical perspective that focuses on how people, as individuals, construct meaning from the events around them.

Individual differences The ways in which people of the same age are different from one another.

Induction A method for encouraging moral development in which one explains why a certain behaviour is unacceptable, often with a focus on the pain or distress that someone has caused another.

Informal assessment Assessment that results from teachers' spontaneous, day-to-day observations of how students behave and perform in class.

Information processing theory A theoretical perspective that focuses on the specific ways in which individuals mentally think about and "process" the information they receive.

Inner speech "Talking" to oneself mentally rather than aloud.

Inquiry-based instruction Teaching based on social-constructivist principles, in which students learn tasks as well as answer questions, and especially characterized by learning based on student interests and role exchanges between teachers and learners.

Instructional objective A statement describing a final goal or outcome of instruction.

Intelligence The ability to modify and adjust one's behaviours in order to accomplish new tasks successfully. It involves many different mental processes, and its nature may vary, depending on the culture in which one lives.

Intelligence test A general measure of current cognitive abilities, used in schools primarily to predict academic achievement over the short run. Intelligence tests may also assist in the assessment and diagnosis of various learning difficulties.

Interest A feeling that a topic is intriguing or enticing.

Interference A phenomenon whereby something stored in long-term memory inhibits one's ability to remember something else correctly.

Intermittent reinforcement Reinforcing a response only occasionally, with some occurrences of the response going unreinforced.

Internalization In Vygotsky's theory, the process through which social activities evolve into mental activities.

Internalized motivation The adoption of behaviours that others value, without regard for the external consequences of such behaviours.

Intrinsic motivation The internal desire to perform a particular task.

Intrinsic reinforcer A reinforcer provided by oneself or inherent in the task being performed.

IQ score A composite score on an intelligence test. It is determined by comparing one's performance on the test to the performance of others in the same age-group; for most tests, it is a standard score with a mean of 100 and a standard deviation of 15.

Item analysis An analysis of students' responses to the individual items of an assessment instrument; used to identify possibly flawed items.

Item difficulty (p) The proportion of students getting a particular assessment item correct. A high p value indicates an easy item; a low p value indicates a difficult item.

Item discrimination (D) The relative proportion of high-scoring and low-scoring students getting a particular assessment item correct. A positive D indicates that an item appears to discriminate between knowledgeable and unknowledgeable students; a negative D indicates that the item may be providing misinformation about what students know and can do.

Jigsaw technique An instructional technique in which materials are divided among members of a co-operative learning group, with individual students being responsible for learning different material and then teaching that material to other group members.

Keyword method A mnemonic technique in which an association is made between two ideas by forming a visual image of one or more concrete objects (keywords) that either sound similar to, or symbolically represent, those ideas.

Knowledge base One's knowledge about specific topics and the world in general.

Learned helplessness A general belief that one is incapable of accomplishing tasks and has little or no control of the environment.

Learned industriousness The recognition that one can succeed at some tasks only with effort, persistence, and well-chosen strategies.

Learning strategy One or more cognitive processes used intentionally for a particular learning task.

Level of potential development In Vygotsky's theory, the extent to which one can successfully execute a task with the assistance of a more competent individual.

Limited English proficiency (LEP) A limited ability to understand and communicate in oral or written English, usually because English is not one's native language.

Live model An individual whose behaviour is observed "in the flesh."

Logical consequence A consequence that follows logically from a student's misbehaviour; in other words, the punishment fits the crime.

Long-term memory The component of memory that holds knowledge and skills for a relatively long period of time.

Long-term objective An objective that requires months or years of instruction and practice to be accomplished.

Lower-level question A question that requires students to express what they have learned in essentially the same way they learned it—for example, by reciting a textbook's definition of a concept or by describing an application their teacher presented in class.

Maintenance rehearsal Repeating information to oneself to retain it in working memory.

Mastery goal A desire to acquire additional knowledge or master new skills.

Mastery learning An approach to instruction whereby students learn one topic thoroughly before moving to a more difficult one.

Mastery orientation A general belief that one is capable of accomplishing challenging tasks.

Maturation The unfolding of genetically controlled changes as a child develops.

Mean (M) The arithmetic average of a set of scores. It is calculated by adding all the scores and then dividing by the total number of people who have obtained those scores.

Meaningful learning A cognitive process in which learners relate new information to the things they already know.

Meaningful learning set An attitude that one can make sense of the information one is studying.

Mediated learning experience A learning experience in which a learner or group of learners interact with a parent, teacher, or more knowledgeable peer, who focuses or prompts the learner's thinking processes but does not impose an adult interpretation.

Mediation training Training that involves teaching students how to mediate conflicts among classmates by asking opposing sides to express their differing viewpoints and then work together to devise a reasonable resolution.

Memory A learner's ability to save something (mentally) that he or she has previously learned, *or* the mental "location" where such information is saved.

Mental set Encoding (or, more generally, creating a mental representation of) a problem in a way that excludes potential problem solutions.

Metacognition One's knowledge and beliefs about one's own cognitive processes, and one's resulting attempts to regulate those cognitive processes to maximize learning and memory.

Metacognitive scaffolding A support structure that guides students in their use of metacognitive strategies.

Metalinguistic awareness The extent to which one is able to think about the nature of language.

Misbehaviour An action that has the potential to disrupt students' learning and planned classroom activities.

Misconception Previously learned but incorrect information.

Mnemonic A special memory aid or trick designed to help students learn and remember a specific piece of information.

Moral dilemma A situation in which there is no clear-cut answer regarding the morally correct thing to do.

Motivation A state that energizes, directs, and sustains behaviour.

Multicultural education Education that integrates the perspectives and experiences of numerous cultural groups throughout the curriculum.

Multiple classification The recognition that objects may belong to several categories simultaneously.

Need for affiliation The tendency to seek out friendly relationships with others.

Need for approval A desire to gain the approval and acceptance of others.

Need for relatedness The need to feel socially connected to others, as well as to secure their love and respect.

Negative instance A nonexample of a concept.

Negative reinforcement A consequence that brings about the increase of a behaviour through the removal (rather than the presentation) of a stimulus.

Negative transfer A phenomenon whereby something learned at one time interferes with learning or performance at a later time.

Negative wait time The tendency to interrupt someone who has not yet finished speaking.

Neuron A cell in the brain or another part of the nervous system that transmits information to other cells.

Neutral stimulus A stimulus that does not elicit any particular response.

Norm-referenced score A score that indicates how a student's performance on an assessment compares with the average performance of other students (i.e., with the performance of a norm group).

Normal distribution (normal curve) A theoretical pattern of educational and psychological characteristics in which most individuals lie somewhere in the middle range and only a few lie at either extreme.

Norms As related to socialization, society's rules for acceptable and unacceptable behaviour. As related to testing practice, data regarding the typical performance of various groups of students on a standardized test or other norm-referenced assessment.

Object permanence The concept that objects continue to exist even after they are removed from view.

Observational learning effect Occurs when an observer acquires a new behaviour after watching someone else demonstrate it.

Operant conditioning A form of learning whereby a response increases in frequency as a result of being followed by reinforcement.

Operations In Piaget's theory, organized and integrated systems of thought processes.

Organization A cognitive process in which learners find connections (e.g., by forming categories, identifying hierarchies, determining cause–effect relationships) among the various pieces of information they need to learn.

Overgeneralization An overly broad meaning for a word that includes some situations where the word is not appropriate; an overly broad view of what objects or events a concept includes.

Overregularization Applying syntactical rules in situations where those rules don't apply.

Paper-pencil assessment An assessment in which students provide written responses to written items.

Peer pressure A phenomenon whereby a student's peers strongly encourage some behaviours and discourage others.

Peer tutoring An approach to instruction whereby students who have mastered a topic teach those who have not.

Percentile rank (percentile) A test score that indicates the percentage of people in the norm group getting a raw score less than or equal to a particular student's raw score.

Performance-approach goal A desire to look good and receive favourable judgments from others.

Performance-avoidance goal A desire not to look bad and receive unfavourable judgments from others.

Performance assessment Assessment in which students demonstrate their knowledge and skills in a nonwritten fashion.

Performance goal A desire either to look good and receive favourable judgments from others, or else *not* to look bad and receive unfavourable judgments.

Personal fable The belief that one is completely unlike anyone else and so cannot be understood by other individuals.

Personal interest A long-term, relatively stable interest in a particular topic or activity.

Personal theory A self-constructed explanation for one's observations about a particular aspect of the world; it may or may not be consistent with generally accepted explanations of scientific phenomena.

Phoneme The smallest unit of sound that makes a difference to the meaning of a word.

Phoneme–grapheme correspondences (PGCs) The regular relationships between sounds and the letters we use to represent them.

Phonemic awareness The ability to discern the individual phonemes that make up a word. Phonemic awareness is a subset of phonological awareness.

Phonological awareness The ability to discern separable units in the soundstream of oral language, for example, syllables within words, or phonemes within syllables. The ability to recognize and produce rhyme and alliteration are markers of phonological awareness in young children.

Portfolio A systematic collection of a student's work over a long period of time.

Positive behavioural support A modification of traditional applied behaviour analysis that includes identifying the purpose that an undesirable behaviour serves for a student and providing an alternative way for the student to achieve the same purpose.

Positive feedback A message that an answer is correct or a task has been well done.

Positive instance A specific example of a concept.

Positive reinforcement A consequence that brings about the increase of a behaviour through the presentation (rather than removal) of a stimulus.

Positive transfer A phenomenon whereby something learned at one time facilitates learning or performance at a later time.

Postconventional morality Behaving in accordance with one's own, self-developed, abstract principles regarding right and wrong.

Practicality The extent to which an assessment instrument or procedure is inexpensive and easy to use and takes only a small amount of time to administer and score.

Pragmatics Knowledge about the culture-specific social conventions guiding verbal interactions.

Preconventional morality A lack of internalized standards about right and wrong; making decisions based on what is best for oneself, without regard for others' needs and feelings.

Predictive validity The extent to which the results of an assessment predict future performance.

Premack principle A phenomenon whereby individuals do less-preferred activities in order to engage in more-preferred activities.

Preoperational egocentrism In Piaget's theory, the inability of children in the preoperational stage to view situations from another person's perspective.

Preoperational stage Piaget's second stage of cognitive development, in which children can think about objects beyond their immediate view but do not yet reason in logical, adultlike ways.

Presentation punishment A form of punishment involving the presentation of a new stimulus, presumably one that an individual finds unpleasant.

Primary reinforcer A stimulus that satisfies a basic physiological need.

Principle A description of how one variable influences another variable. It evolves when similar research studies yield similar results time after time.

Procedural knowledge Knowledge concerning how to do something (as opposed to *declarative knowledge*, which relates to how things are).

Programmed instruction An approach to instruction whereby students independently study a topic that has been broken into small, carefully sequenced segments.

Prosocial behaviour Behaviour directed toward promoting the well-being of someone else.

Psychological punishment Any consequence that seriously threatens a student's self-concept and self-esteem.

Psychomotor domain The domain of learning tasks that includes simple and complex physical movements and actions.

Punishment A consequence that decreases the frequency of the response it follows.

Quality of concept links In a concept map, pairs of concepts can be more or less strongly linked, and the description of the link can be more or less complete and detailed. When creating a concept map, the quality of the links is at least as important as having well-chosen or well-understood concepts.

Rating scale An assessment tool with which a teacher evaluates student performance by rating aspects of the performance on one or more continua.

Raw score A test score based solely on the number or point value of correctly answered items.

Recall task A memory task in which one must retrieve information in its entirety from long-term memory.

Receptive language The ability to understand the language that one hears or reads.

Reciprocal causation The interdependence of environment, behaviour, and personal variables as these three factors influence learning.

Recognition task A memory task in which one must identify correct information among irrelevant information or incorrect statements.

Reconstruction (as a complement to note taking) Creating notes from classes or other events in one's own words without consulting original notes and then revising them or comparing them with others' notes for an enhanced learning experience.

Reconstruction error Constructing a logical but incorrect "memory" by using information retrieved from long-term memory plus one's general knowledge and beliefs about the world.

Rehearsal A cognitive process in which information is repeated over and over as a possible way of learning and remembering it. When it is used to maintain information in working memory, it is called *maintenance rehearsal*.

Reinforcement The act of following a particular response with a reinforcer and thereby increasing the frequency of that response.

Reinforcer A consequence (stimulus) of a response that leads to an increased frequency of that response.

Reliability The extent to which an assessment instrument yields consistent information about the knowledge, skills, or abilities one is trying to measure.

Reliability coefficient A numerical index of an assessment tool's reliability; ranges from 0 to 1, with higher numbers indicating higher reliability.

Removal punishment A form of punishment involving the removal of an existing stimulus, presumably one that an individual views as desirable and doesn't want to lose.

Resilient self-efficacy The belief that one can perform a task successfully even after experiencing setbacks; includes the belief that effort and perseverance are essential for success.

Resilient students Students who succeed in school despite exceptional hardships in their lives.

Response (R) A specific behaviour that an individual exhibits.

Response cost The loss of either a previously earned reinforcer or an opportunity to obtain reinforcement.

Response disinhibition effect Occurs when an observer displays a previously forbidden or punished behaviour more frequently after seeing someone else exhibit that behaviour without adverse consequences.

Response facilitation effect Occurs when an observer displays a previously learned behaviour more frequently after seeing someone else being reinforced for that behaviour.

Response inhibition effect Occurs when an observer displays a previously learned behaviour less frequently after seeing someone else being punished for that behaviour.

Retrieval The process of "finding" information previously stored in memory.

Retrieval cue A hint about where to "look" for a piece of information in long-term memory.

Roles Patterns of behaviour acceptable for individuals having different functions within a society.

Rote learning Learning information primarily through verbatim repetition, without attaching any meaning to it.

Rubric A list of components that performance on an assessment task should ideally include; used to guide the scoring of students' responses.

Scaffolding A support mechanism, provided by a more competent individual, that helps a learner successfully perform a task within his or her zone of proximal development.

Schema In contemporary cognitive psychology, an organized body of knowledge about a specific topic.

Scheme In Piaget's theory, an organized group of similar actions or thoughts.

Script A schema that involves a predictable sequence of events related to a common activity.

Scripted co-operation In co-operative learning, a technique in which co-operative groups follow a set of steps or "script" that guides members' verbal interactions.

Secondary reinforcer A stimulus that becomes reinforcing over time through its association with another reinforcer; it is sometimes called a *conditioned reinforcer*.

Self-concept One's perceptions of, and beliefs about, oneself.

Self-contained class A class in which students with special needs are educated as a group apart from other students.

Self-determination A sense that one has some choice and control regarding the future course of one's life.

Self-efficacy The belief that one is capable of executing certain behaviours or reaching certain goals.

Self-esteem Judgments and beliefs about one's own general value and worth.

Self-evaluation The process of evaluating one's own performance or behaviour.

Self-fulfilling prophecy A situation in which one's expectations for an outcome either directly or indirectly lead to the expected result.

Self-handicapping Undermining one's own success, often as a way of protecting one's sense of self-worth when being asked to perform difficult tasks.

Self-imposed contingencies Contingencies that students provide for themselves; the self-reinforcements and self-punishments that follow various behaviours.

Self-instructions Instructions that students give themselves as they perform a complex behaviour.

Self-monitoring The process of observing and recording one's own behaviour.

Self-questioning The process of asking oneself questions as a way of checking one's understanding of a topic.

Self-regulated behaviour Engaging in chosen behaviours that lead to the accomplishment of personally chosen standards and goals.

Self-regulated learning Regulating one's own cognitive processes to learn successfully; includes goal setting, planning, attention control, use of effective learning strategies, self-monitoring, and self-evaluation.

Self-regulated problem-solving strategy A strategy that helps students solve their own interpersonal problems.

Self-regulation The process of setting standards and goals for oneself and engaging in cognitive processes and behaviours that lead to the accomplishment of those standards and goals.

Self-talk Talking to oneself as a way of guiding oneself through a task; also known as *private speech*.

Self-worth Beliefs about one's own general ability to deal effectively with the environment.

Semantics The meanings of words and word combinations.

Sense of community In the classroom, a widely shared feeling that teacher and students have common goals, are mutually respectful and supportive of one another's efforts, and believe that everyone makes an important contribution to classroom learning.

Sense of school community The sense that all faculty and students within a school are working together to help every student learn and succeed.

Sensitive period An age range during which a certain aspect of a child's development is especially susceptible to environmental conditions.

Sensorimotor stage Piaget's first stage of cognitive development, in which schemes are based on behaviours and perceptions.

Sensory register A component of memory that holds incoming information in an unanalyzed form for a very brief period of time (probably less than a second for visual input and two or three seconds for auditory input).

Shame A feeling of embarrassment or humiliation that children feel after failing to meet the standards for moral behaviour that adults have set.

Shaping A process of reinforcing successively closer and closer approximations of a desired terminal behaviour.

Short-term objective An objective that can typically be accomplished within the course of a single lesson or unit.

Situated motivation A phenomenon whereby aspects of one's immediate environment enhance one's motivation to learn particular things or behave in particular ways.

Situational interest Interest evoked temporarily by something in the environment.

Social cognitive theory A theoretical perspective in which learning by observing others is the focus of study.

Social constructivism A theoretical perspective that emphasizes that an individual's meaning-making (or learning in general) is mediated by adults or more knowledgeable peers, even though it is ultimately constructed by the individual learner.

Social reinforcer A gesture or sign that one person gives another to communicate positive regard.

Social skills Behaviours that enable a person to interact effectively with others.

Socialization The process of moulding a child's behaviour to fit the norms and roles of the child's society.

Sociocultural perspective A theoretical perspective that emphasizes the importance of society and culture for promoting cognitive development.

Socioeconomic status (SES) One's general social and economic standing in society, encompassing such variables as family income, occupation, and level of education.

Sociolinguistic conventions Specific language-related behaviours that appear in some cultures or ethnic groups but not in others.

Specific aptitude test A test designed to predict students' ability to learn in a particular content domain.

Specific transfer An instance of transfer in which the original learning task and the transfer task overlap in content.

Standard deviation (SD) A statistic that reflects how close together or far apart a set of scores are and thereby indicates the variability of the scores.

Standard error of measurement (SEM) A statistic estimating the amount of error likely to be present in a particular score on a test or other assessment instrument.

Standard score A test score that indicates how far a student's performance is from the mean with respect to standard deviation units.

Standardization The extent to which assessment instruments and procedures involve similar content and format and are administered and scored in the same way for everyone.

Standardized test A test developed by test construction experts and published for use in many different schools and classrooms.

Stanine A standard score with a mean of 5 and a standard deviation of 2; it is always reported as a whole number.

State anxiety A temporary feeling of anxiety elicited by a threatening situation.

Stereotype A rigid, simplistic, and erroneous caricature of a particular group of people.

Stimulus (S) (pl. stimuli) A specific object or event that influences an individual's learning or behaviour.

Storage The process of "putting" new information into memory.

Students at risk Students who have a high probability of failing to acquire the minimal academic skills necessary for success in the adult world.

Students with special needs Students who are different enough from their peers that they require specially adapted instructional materials and practices.

Subculture A group that resists the ways of the dominant culture and adopts its own norms for behaviour.

Summative evaluation An evaluation conducted after instruction is completed and used to assess students' final achievement.

Superimposed meaningful structure A familiar shape, word, sentence, poem, or story imposed on information to make it easier to recall; used as a *mnemonic*.

Symbolic model A real or fictional character portrayed in the media (television, books, etc.) that influences an observer's behaviour.

Symbolic thinking The ability to represent and think about external objects and events in one's head.

Sympathy A feeling of sorrow or concern for another person's problems or distress.

Synapse A junction between two neurons that allows messages to be transmitted from one to the other.

Syntax The set of rules that one uses (often unconsciously) to put words together into sentences.

T-score A standard score with a mean of 50 and a standard deviation of 10.

Table of specifications A two-way grid that indicates both the topics to be covered in an assessment and the things that students should be able to do with each topic.

Task analysis A process of identifying the specific knowledge and/or behaviours necessary to master a particular subject area or skill.

Teacher-developed assessment instrument An assessment tool developed by an individual teacher for use in his or her own classroom.

Temperament A genetic predisposition to respond in particular ways to one's physical and social environments.

Terminal behaviour The form and frequency of a desired response that a teacher or other practitioner is shaping through operant conditioning.

Test anxiety Excessive anxiety about a particular test or about assessment in general.

Testwiseness Test-taking know-how that enhances test performance.

Theory An organized body of concepts and principles developed to explain certain phenomena; a description of possible underlying mechanisms to explain why certain principles are true.

Threat A situation in which people believe that they have little or no chance of success.

Time-out A procedure whereby a misbehaving student is placed in a dull, boring situation with no opportunity to interact with others and no opportunity to obtain reinforcement.

Token economy A technique whereby desired behaviours are reinforced by tokens, reinforcers that students can use to "purchase" a variety of other reinforcers.

Traditional assessment Assessment that focuses on measuring basic knowledge and skills in relative isolation from tasks more typical of the outside world.

Trait anxiety A pattern of responding with anxiety even in nonthreatening situations.

Trait theory of motivation A theoretical perspective portraying motivation as involving enduring personality characteristics that people have to a greater or lesser extent.

Transductive reasoning Making a mental leap from one specific thing to another, such as identifying one event as the cause of another simply because the two events occur close together in time.

Transfer A phenomenon whereby something that an individual has learned at one time affects how the individual learns or performs in a later situation.

Unconditioned response (UCR) A response that, without prior learning, is elicited by a particular stimulus.

Unconditioned stimulus (UCS) A stimulus that, without prior learning, elicits a particular response.

Undergeneralization An overly restricted meaning for a word that excludes some situations to which the word does, in fact, apply; an overly narrow view of what objects or events a concept includes.

Universals (in development) The similar patterns we see in how children change over time regardless of the specific environment in which they are raised.

Validity The extent to which an assessment instrument actually measures what it is intended to measure.

Validity coefficient A numerical index of an assessment tool's predictive validity; ranges from 0 to 1, with higher numbers indicating more accurate predictions.

Value The belief that an activity has direct or indirect benefits.

Verbal mediator A word or phrase that forms a logical connection or "bridge" between two pieces of information; used as a *mnemonic*.

Verbal reprimand A scolding for inappropriate behaviour.

Vicarious punishment A phenomenon whereby a response decreases in frequency when another (observed) person is punished for that response.

Vicarious reinforcement A phenomenon whereby a response increases in frequency when another (observed) person is reinforced for that response.

Visual imagery The process of forming mental pictures of objects or ideas.

Wait time The length of time a teacher pauses, either after asking a question or hearing a student's comment, before saying something else.

Well-defined problem A problem in which the goal is clearly stated, all information needed to solve the problem is present, and only one correct answer exists.

Withitness The appearance that a teacher knows what all students are doing at all times.

Work-avoidance goal A desire to avoid having to perform classroom tasks or to complete them with only minimal effort.

Working memory A component of memory that holds and processes a limited amount of information; also known as *short-term memory*. The duration of information stored in working memory is probably about 5 to 20 seconds.

z-score A standard score with a mean of 0 and a standard deviation of 1.

Zone of proximal development (ZPD) In Vygotsky's theory, the range of tasks between one's actual developmental level and one's level of potential development—that is, the range of tasks that one cannot yet perform independently but can perform with the help and guidance of others.

References

2Learn.ca Education Society. (2008). "Project Centre: Tell Me Stories: A Conversation with Wendy Nero." *2Learn.ca*. Retrieved August 12, 2008, from http://www.2learn.ca/Projects/Together/STORIES/nero.html.

Abery, B., & Zajac, R. (1996). Self-determination as a goal of early childhood and elementary education. In D. J. Sands & M. L. Wehmeyer (Eds.), *Self-determination across the life span: Independence and choice for people with disabilities*. Baltimore: Brookes.

Ablard, K. E., & Lipschultz, R. E. (1998). Self-regulated learning in high-achieving students: Relations to advanced reasoning, achievement goals, and gender. *Journal of Educational Psychology, 90*, 94–101.

Achenbach, T. M., & Edelbrock, C. S. (1981). Behavioral problems and competencies reported by parents of normal and disturbed children aged four through sixteen. *Monographs of the Society for Research in Child Development, 46*(1, Serial No. 188).

Adams, M. J. (1990). *Beginning to read: Thinking and learning about print*. Cambridge, MA: MIT Press.

Adams, P. A., & Adams, J. K. (1960). Confidence in the recognition and reproduction of words difficult to spell. *American Journal of Psychology, 73*, 544–552.

Airasian, P. W. (1994). *Classroom assessment* (2nd ed.). New York: McGraw-Hill.

Alapack, R. (1991). The adolescent first kiss. *Humanistic Psychologist, 19*, 48–67.

Alberta Education. (1996). *Partners during changing times*. Edmonton: Special Education Branch.

Alberta Education. (2003). *Policy 1.5.1 English as a second language*. Retrieved May 15, 2008, from http://www.education.alberta.ca/department/policy/k-12manual/section1/esl.aspx.

Alberta Education. (2007). *Distributed Learning Strategy*. Unpublished manuscript.

Alderman, M. K. (1990). Motivation for at-risk students. *Educational Leadership, 48*(1), 27–30.

Alderson, K. (2002). Reflecting on shattered glass: Some thoughts about gay youth in schools. *The Alberta Counsellor, 27*(2), 3–11.

Alexander, K. L., Entwisle, D. R., & Thompson, M. (1987). School performance, status relations, and the structure of sentiment: Bringing the teacher back in. *American Sociological Review, 52*, 665–682.

Alexander, P. A. (1997). Mapping the multidimensional nature of domain learning: The interplay of cognitive, motivational, and strategic forces. In P. R. Pintrich & M. L. Maehr (Eds.), *Advances in motivation and achievement* (Vol. 10). Greenwich, CT: JAI Press.

Alexander, P. A., Graham, S., & Harris, K. R. (1998). A perspective on strategy research: Progress and prospects. *Educational Psychology Review, 10*, 129–154.

Alexander, P. A., & Jetton, T. L. (1996). The role of importance and interest in the processing of text. *Educational Psychology Review, 8*, 89–121.

Alexander, P. A., & Judy, J. E. (1988). The interaction of domain-specific and strategic knowledge in academic performance. *Review of Educational Research, 58*, 375–404.

Alexander, P. A., Kulikowich, J. M., & Schulze, S. K. (1994). How subject-matter knowledge affects recall and interest. *American Educational Research Journal, 31*, 313–337.

Alleman, J., & Brophy, J. (1997). Elementary social studies: Instruments, activities, and standards. In G. D. Phye (Ed.), *Handbook of classroom assessment: Learning, achievement, and adjustment*. San Diego, CA: Academic Press.

Allen, K. D. (1998). The use of an enhanced simplified habit-reversal procedure to reduce disruptive outbursts during athletic performance. *Journal of Applied Behavior Analysis, 31*, 489–492.

Altermatt, E. R., Jovanovic, J., & Perry, M. (1998). Bias or responsivity? Sex and achievement-level effects on teachers' classroom questioning practices. *Journal of Educational Psychology, 90*, 516–527.

Amabile, T. M., & Hennessey, B. A. (1992). The motivation for creativity in children. In A. K. Boggiano & T. S. Pittman (Eds.), *Achievement and motivation: A social-developmental perspective*. Cambridge, England: Cambridge University Press.

American Educational Research Association, American Psychological Association, & National Council on Measurement in Education. (1999). *Standards for educational and psychological testing* (2nd ed.). Washington, DC: American Educational Research Association.

American Psychiatric Association. (1994). *Diagnostic and statistical manual of mental disorders* (4th ed.). Washington, DC: Author.

Ames, C. (1984). Competitive, cooperative, and individualistic goal structures: A cognitive-motivational analysis. In R. Ames & C. Ames (Eds.), *Research on motivation in education: Vol. 1. Student motivation*. San Diego, CA: Academic Press.

Ames, C. (1992). Classrooms: Goals, structures, and student motivation. *Journal of Educational Psychology, 84*, 261–271.

Ames, C., & Archer, J. (1988). Achievement goals in the classroom: Students' learning strategies and motivation processes. *Journal of Educational Psychology, 80*, 260–267.

Ames, R. (1983). Help-seeking and achievement orientation: Perspectives from attribution theory. In A. Nadler, J. Fisher, & B. DePaulo (Eds.), *New directions in helping* (Vol. 2). New York: Academic Press.

Anand, P., & Ross, S. (1987). A computer-based strategy for personalizing verbal problems in teaching mathematics. *Educational Communication and Technology Journal, 35*, 151–162.

Anderman, E. M., Griesinger, T., & Westerfield, G. (1998). Motivation and cheating during early adolescence. *Journal of Educational Psychology, 90*, 84–93.

Anderman, E. M., & Maehr, M. L. (1994). Motivation and schooling in the middle grades. *Review of Educational Research, 64*, 287–309.

Anderman, L. H., & Anderman, E. M. (1999). Social predictors of changes in students' achievement goal orientation. *Contemporary Educational Psychology, 25*, 21–37.

Anderson, A. (2004). Issues of migration. In R. Hamilton & D. Moore (Eds.) *Educational interventions for refugee children: Theoretical perspectives and implementing best practice* (pp. 64–82). New York: Routledge.

Anderson, J. R. (1983). *The architecture of cognition*. Cambridge, MA: Harvard University Press.

Anderson, J. R. (1987). Skill acquisition: Compilation of weak-method problem solutions. *Psychological Review, 94*, 192–210.

Anderson, J. R. (1990). *Cognitive psychology and its implications* (3rd ed.). New York: Freeman.

Anderson, J. R. (1995). *Learning and memory: An integrated approach*. New York: Wiley.

Anderson, J. R., Greeno, J. G., Reder, L. M., & Simon, H. A. (2000). Perspectives on learning, thinking, and activity. *Educational Researcher, 29*(4), 11–13.

Anderson, J. R., Reder, L. M., & Simon, H. A. (1996). Situated learning and education. *Educational Researcher, 25*(4), 5–11.

Anderson, J. R., Reder, L. M., & Simon, H. A. (1997). Situative versus cognitive perspectives: Form versus substance. *Educational Researcher, 26*(1), 18–21.

Anderson, L. M. (1993). Auxiliary materials that accompany textbooks: Can they promote "higher-order" learning? In B. K. Britton, A. Woodward, & M. Binkley (Eds.), *Learning from textbooks: Theory and practice*. Hillsdale, NJ: Erlbaum.

Anderson, L. W., & Krathwohl, D. R. (Eds.). (2001). *A taxonomy for learning, teaching and assessing: A revision of Bloom's Taxonomy of educational objectives: Complete edition*. New York: Longman.

Anderson, L. W., & Pellicer, L. O. (1998). Toward an understanding of unusually successful programs for economically disadvantaged students. *Journal of Education for Students Placed at Risk, 3*, 237–263.

Anderson, R. C., Nguyen-Jahiel, K., McNurlen, B., Archodidou, A., Kim, S.-Y., Reznitskaya, A., Tillmanns, M., & Gilbert, L. (2001). The snowball phenomenon: Spread of ways of talking and ways of thinking across groups of children. *Cognition and Instruction, 19*, 1–46.

Anderson, V., & Hidi, S. (1988/1989). Teaching students to summarize. *Educational Leadership, 46*(4), 26–28.

Andrews, J. (2006). Conceptualizing and developing social competence: A guide for school counselors of adolescents. *Alberta Counsellor, 28*(2), 15–20.

Andrews, J., & Lupart, J. (2000). *The inclusive classroom: Educating exceptional children* (2nd ed.). Scarborough, ON: Nelson Thomson Learning.

Anglin, J. M. (1977). *Word, object, and conceptual development*. New York: Norton.

Ansley, T. (1997). The role of standardized achievement tests in grades K-12. In G. D. Phye (Ed.), *Handbook of classroom assessment: Learning, achievement, and adjustment*. San Diego, CA: Academic Press.

Anzai, Y. (1991). Learning and use of representations for physics expertise. In K. A. Ericsson & J. Smith (Eds.), *Toward a general theory of expertise: Prospects and limits*. Cambridge, England: Cambridge University Press.

Archer, S. L. (1982). The lower age boundaries of identity development. *Child Development, 53,* 1551–1556.

Arlin, M. (1979). Teacher transitions can disrupt time flow in classrooms. *American Educational Research Journal, 16,* 42–56.

Arlin, M. (1984). Time, equality, and mastery learning. *Review of Educational Research, 54,* 65–86.

Arnett, J. (1995). The young and the reckless: Adolescent reckless behavior. *Current Directions in Psychological Science, 4,* 67–71.

Arnett, J. J. (1999). Adolescent storm and stress, reconsidered. *American Psychologist, 54,* 317–326.

Arnold, M. L. (2000). Stage, sequence, and sequels: Changing conceptions of morality, post-Kohlberg. *Educational Psychology Review, 12,* 365–383.

Aronson, E., & Patnoe, S. (1997). *The jigsaw classroom: Building cooperation in the classroom* (2nd ed.). New York: Longman.

Arter, J. A., & Spandel, V. (1992). Using portfolios of student work in instruction and assessment. *Educational Measurement: Issues and Practice, 11*(1), 36–44.

Artz, S., & Nicholson, D. (2001). Understanding aggressive girls in Canada: A literature review. ERIC, ED476558.

Asher, S. R., & Parker, J. G. (1989). Significance of peer relationship problems in childhood. In B. H. Schneider, G. Attili, J. Nadel, & R. P. Weissberg (Eds.), *Social competence in the developmental perspective.* Dordrecht, Netherlands: Kluwer.

Ashton, P. (1985). Motivation and the teacher's sense of efficacy. In C. Ames & R. Ames (Eds.), *Research on motivation in education: Vol. 2. The classroom milieu.* San Diego, CA: Academic Press.

Asselin, M. (2001). Grade 6 research process instruction: An observation study. *The Alberta Journal of Educational Research, 47*(2), 123–140.

Assor, A., & Connell, J. P. (1992). The validity of students' self-reports as measures of performance affecting self-appraisals. In D. H. Schunk & J. L. Meece (Eds.), *Student perceptions in the classroom.* Hillsdale, NJ: Erlbaum.

Atkinson, J. W., & Feather, N. T. (Eds.). (1966). *A theory of achievement motivation.* New York: Wiley.

Atkinson, R. C., & Shiffrin, R. M. (1968). Human memory: A proposed system and its control processes. In K. W. Spence & J. T. Spence (Eds.), *The psychology of learning and motivation: Advances in research and theory* (Vol. 2). San Diego, CA: Academic Press.

Atkinson, R. K., Derry, S. J., Renkl, A., & Wortham, D. (2000). Learning from examples: Instructional principles from the worked examples research. *Review of Educational Research, 70,* 181–214.

Atkinson, R. K., Levin, J. R., Kiewra, K. A., Meyers, T., Kim, S., Atkinson, L. A., Renandya, W. A., & Hwang, Y. (1999). Matrix and mnemonic text-processing adjuncts: Comparing and combining their components. *Journal of Educational Psychology, 91,* 342–357.

Atria, M., Strohmeier, D., & Spiel, C. (2007). The relevance of the **school** class as social unit for the prevalence of **bullying** and victimization. *European Journal of Developmental Psychology, 4*(4), 372–387.

Aulls, M. W., & Shore, B. M. (2008). *Inquiry in education (Vol. I): The conceptual foundations for research as a curricular imperative.* New York: Erlbaum.

Austin, L. B., & Shore, B. M. (1995). Using concept mapping for assessment in physics. *Physics Education, 30*(1), 41–45.

Ausubel, D. P. (1968). *Educational psychology: A cognitive view.* New York: Holt, Rinehart & Winston.

Ausubel, D. P., Novak, J. D., & Hanesian, H. (1978). *Educational psychology: A cognitive view* (2nd ed.). New York: Holt, Rinehart & Winston.

Babad, E. (1993). Teachers' differential behavior. *Educational Psychology Review, 5,* 347–376.

Bachor, D. (1990). Toward improving assessment of students with special needs: Expanding the data base to include classroom performance. *The Alberta Journal of Educational Research, 36,* 65–77.

Baddeley, A. D. (1986). *Working memory.* New York: Oxford University Press.

Baek, S. (1994). Implications of cognitive psychology for educational testing. *Educational Psychology Review, 6,* 373–389.

Bahrick, H. P., Bahrick, L. E., Bahrick, A. S., & Bahrick, P. E. (1993). Maintenance of foreign language vocabulary and the spacing effect. *Psychological Science, 4,* 316–321.

Baillargeon, R. (2004). Infants' physical worlds. *Current Directions in Psychological Science, 13,* 89–94.

Baillargeon, R., Tremblay, R., & Willms, J. D. (1999). *The prevalence of physical aggression in Canadian children: A multi-group latent class analysis of data from the First Collection Cycle (1994–1995) of the NLSCY.* Applied Research Branch Technical Paper. T-99-2E. Hull, QC: Human Resources Development Canada.

Baker, L. (1989). Metacognition, comprehension monitoring, and the adult reader. *Educational Psychology Review, 1,* 3–38.

Baker, L., & Brown, A. L. (1984). Metacognitive skills of reading. In D. Pearson (Ed.), *Handbook of reading research.* White Plains, NY: Longman.

Balla, D. A., & Zigler, E. (1979). Personality development in retarded persons. In N. R. Ellis (Ed.), *Handbook of mental deficiency: Psychological theory and research* (2nd ed.). Hillsdale, NJ: Erlbaum.

Bandura, A. (1977). *Social learning theory.* Upper Saddle River, NJ: Prentice Hall.

Bandura, A. (1981). Self-referent thought: A developmental analysis of self-efficacy. In J. Flavell & L. Ross (Eds.), *Social cognitive development: Frontiers and possible futures.* Cambridge, England: Cambridge University Press.

Bandura, A. (1982). Self-efficacy mechanism in human agency. *American Psychologist, 37,* 122–147.

Bandura, A. (1986). *Social foundations of thought and action: A social cognitive theory.* Upper Saddle River, NJ: Prentice Hall.

Bandura, A. (1989). Human agency in social cognitive theory. *American Psychologist, 44,* 1175–1184.

Bandura, A. (1997). *Self-efficacy: The exercise of control.* New York: Freeman.

Bandura, A. (2000). Exercise of human agency through collective efficacy. *Current Directions in Psychological Science, 9,* 75–78.

Bandura, A., Ross, D., & Ross, S. A. (1961). Transmission of aggression through imitation of aggressive models. *Journal of Abnormal and Social Psychology, 63,* 575–582.

Bandura, A., Ross, D., & Ross, S. A. (1963). Imitation of film-mediated aggressive models. *Journal of Abnormal and Social Psychology, 66,* 3–11.

Bandura, A., & Schunk, D. H. (1981). Cultivating competence, self-efficacy, and intrinsic interest through proximal self-motivation. *Journal of Personality and Social Psychology, 41,* 586–598.

Bangert-Drowns, R. L., Kulik, C. C., Kulik, J. A., & Morgan, M. (1991). The instructional effect of feedback in test-like events. *Review of Educational Research, 61,* 213–238.

Banks, J. A. (1991). Multicultural literacy and curriculum reform. *Educational Horizons, 69*(3), 135–140.

Banks, J. A. (1994). *An introduction to multicultural education.* Needham Heights, MA: Allyn & Bacon.

Banks, J. A. (1995). Multicultural education: Historical development, dimensions, and practice. In J. A. Banks & C. A. M. Banks (Eds.), *Handbook of research on multicultural education.* New York: Macmillan.

Banks, J. A., & Banks, C. A. M. (Eds.). (1995). *Handbook of research on multicultural education.* New York: Macmillan.

Barbetta, P. M. (1990). GOALS: A group-oriented adapted levels system for children with behavior disorders. *Academic Therapy, 25,* 645–656.

Barbetta, P. M., Heward, W. L., Bradley, D. M., & Miller, A. D. (1994). Effects of immediate and delayed error correction on the acquisition and maintenance of sight words by students with developmental disabilities. *Journal of Applied Behavior Analysis, 27,* 177–178.

Barchfeld, P., Sodian, B., Thoermer, C., & Bullock, M. (2005, April). *The development of simple and complex experiment generation from primary school to late adolescence.* Poster presented at the biennial meeting of the Society for Research in Child Development, Atlanta, GA.

Barga, N. K. (1996). Students with learning disabilities in education: Managing a disability. *Journal of Learning Disabilities, 29,* 413–421.

Barkley, R. A. (1996). Linkages between attention and executive functions. In G. R. Lyon & N. A. Krasnegor (Eds.), *Attention, memory, and executive function.* Baltimore: Brookes.

Barkley, R. A. (1998). *Attention-deficit hyperactivity disorder: A handbook for diagnosis and treatment* (2nd ed.). New York: Guilford Press.

Barnes, D. (1976). *From communication to curriculum.* London: Penguin.

Barnett, J. E. (2001, April). *Study strategies and preparing for exams: A survey of middle and high school students.* Paper presented at the annual meeting of the American Educational Research Association, Seattle, WA.

Barnett, J. E., Di Vesta, F. J., & Rogozinski, J. T. (1981). What is learned in note taking? *Journal of Educational Psychology, 73,* 181–192.

Baron, J. B. (1987). Evaluating thinking skills in the classroom. In J. B. Baron & R. J. Sternberg (Eds.), *Teaching thinking skills: Theory and practice.* New York: Freeman.

Baroody, A. J. (1999). Children's relational knowledge of addition and subtraction. *Cognition and Instruction, 17,* 137–175.

Barron, B. (2000). Problem solving in video-based microworlds: Collaborative and individual outcomes of high-achieving sixth-grade students. *Journal of Educational Psychology, 92,* 391–398.

Bartley, A. W. (1997). Enhancing the validity of portfolio assessment in preservice teacher education. *The Alberta Journal of Educational Research, 43,* 99–113.

Basinger, K. S., Gibbs, J. C., & Fuller, D. (1995). Context and the measurement of moral judgment. *International Journal of Behavioral Development, 18,* 537–556.

Bassok, M. (1990). Transfer of domain-specific problem-solving procedures. *Journal of Experimental Psychology: Learning, Memory, and Cognition, 16,* 522–533.

Bassok, M. (1996). Using content to interpret structure: Effects on analogical transfer. *Current Directions in Psychological Science, 5,* 54–58.

Batson, C. D., & Thompson, E. R. (2001). Why don't moral people act morally? Motivational considerations. *Current Directions in Psychological Science, 10,* 54–57.

Battin-Pearson, S., Newcomb, M. D., Abbott, R. D., Hill, K. G., Catalano, R. F., & Hawkins, J. D. (2000). Predictors of early high school dropout: A test of five theories. *Journal of Educational Psychology, 92,* 568–582.

Battistich, V., Solomon, D., Kim, D., Watson, M., & Schaps, E. (1995). Schools as communities, poverty levels of student populations, and students' attitudes, motives, and performance: A multilevel analysis. *American Educational Research Journal, 32,* 627–658.

Battistich, V., Solomon, D., Watson, M., & Schaps, E. (1997). Caring school communities. *Educational Psychologist, 32,* 137–151.

Baumrind, D. (1971). Current patterns of parental authority. *Developmental Psychology Monograph, 4* (1, Pt. 2).

Baumrind, D. (1989). Rearing competent children. In W. Damon (Ed.), *Child development today and tomorrow.* San Francisco: Jossey-Bass.

Baxter, G. P., Elder, A. D., & Glaser, R. (1996). Knowledge-based cognition and performance assessment in the science classroom. *Educational Psychologist, 31,* 133–140.

Bay-Hinitz, A. K., Peterson, R. F., & Quilitch, H. R. (1994). Cooperative games: A way to modify aggressive and cooperative behaviors in young children. *Journal of Applied Behavior Analysis, 27,* 435–446.

Bear, G. G., & Richards, H. C. (1981). Moral reasoning and conduct problems in the classroom. *Journal of Educational Psychology, 73,* 644–670.

Becker, B. J. (1986). Influence again: An examination of reviews and studies of gender differences in social influence. In J. S. Hyde & M. C. Linn (Eds.), *The psychology of gender differences: Advances through meta-analysis.* Baltimore: Johns Hopkins University Press.

Bédard, A.-C., Nichols, S., Barbosa, J. A., Schachar, R., Logan, G. D., & Tannock, R. (2002). The development of selective inhibitory control across the life span. *Developmental Neuropsychology, 21*(1), 93–111.

Bédard, J., & Chi, M. T. H. (1992). Expertise. *Current Directions in Psychological Science, 1,* 135–139.

Behrmann, M. (2000). The mind's eye mapped onto the brain's matter. *Current Directions in Psychological Science, 9,* 50–54.

Beirne-Smith, M., Ittenbach, R. F., & Patton, J. R. (2002). *Mental retardation* (6th ed.). Upper Saddle River, NJ: Merrill/Prentice Hall.

Belfiore, P. J., & Hornyak, R. S. (1998). Operant theory and application to self-monitoring in adolescents. In D. H. Schunk & B. J. Zimmerman (Eds.), *Self-regulated learning: From teaching to self-reflective practice.* New York: Guilford Press.

Bellezza, F. S. (1986). Mental cues and verbal reports in learning. In G. H. Bower (Ed.), *The psychology of learning and motivation: Advances in research and theory* (Vol. 20). San Diego, CA: Academic Press.

Bender, T. A. (1997). Assessment of subjective well-being during childhood and adolescence. In G. D. Phye (Ed.), *Handbook of classroom assessment: Learning, achievement, and adjustment.* San Diego, CA: Academic Press.

Bennett, R. E., Gottesman, R. L., Rock, D. A., & Cerullo, F. (1993). Influence of behavior perceptions and gender on teachers' judgments of students' academic skill. *Journal of Educational Psychology, 85,* 347–356.

Benware, C., & Deci, E. L. (1984). Quality of learning with an active versus passive motivational set. *American Educational Research Journal, 21,* 755–765.

Beran, T. N. (2006a). A construct validity study of bullying. *Alberta Journal of Educational Research, 52*(4), 238–247.

Beran, T. N. (2006b). Characteristics of victims of bullying: Implications for research. In J. A. Zebrowski (Ed.), *New research on social perception* (pp. 75–94). New York: Nova Science Publishers.

Beran, T. N. (2006c). Managing school bullying: Charting stormy waters. *Alberta Counsellor, 28*(2), 10–14.

Beran, T. N., Hughes, G., & Lupart, J. (2008). A model of achievement and bullying: Analyses of the Canadian National Longitudinal Survey of Children and Youth Data. *Educational Research, 50*(1), 25–39.

Beran, T. N., & Li, Q. (2007). The relationship between cyber-bullying and school bullying. *Journal of Student Wellbeing, 1*(2), 15–33.

Beran, T. N., & Tutty, L. (2002). Children's reports of bullying and safety at school. *Canadian Journal of School Psychology, 17*(2), 1–14.

Bereiter, C. (1994). Implications of postmodernism for science, or, science as progressive discourse. *Educational Psychologist, 29*(1), 3–12.

Bereiter, C. (1995). A dispositional view of transfer. In A. McKeough, J. Lupart, & A. Marini (Eds.), *Teaching for transfer: Fostering generalization in learning.* Mahwah, NJ: Erlbaum.

Bereiter, C. (1997). Situated cognition and how to overcome it. In D. Kirshner & J. A. Whitson (Eds.), *Situated cognition: Social, semiotic, and psychological perspectives.* Mahwah, NJ: Erlbaum.

Berk, L. E. (1994). Why children talk to themselves. *Scientific American, 271,* 78–83.

Berk, L. E. (2000). *Child development* (5th ed.). Boston: Allyn & Bacon.

Berkowitz, M. W., Guerra, N., & Nucci, L. (1991). Sociomoral development and drug and alcohol abuse. In W. M. Kurtines & J. L. Gewirtz (Eds.), *Moral behavior and development: Vol. 3. Application.* Hillsdale, NJ: Erlbaum.

Berndt, T. J. (1992). Friendship and friends' influence in adolescence. *Current Directions in Psychological Science, 1,* 156–159.

Berndt, T. J., Hawkins, J. A., & Jiao, Z. (1999). Influences of friends and friendships on adjustment to junior high school. *Merrill Palmer Quarterly, 45,* 13–41.

Berndt, T. J., & Keefe, K. (1996). Friends' influence on school adjustment: A motivational analysis. In J. Juvonen & K. R. Wentzel (Eds.), *Social motivation: Understanding children's school adjustment* (pp. 248–278). Cambridge, England: Cambridge University Press.

Berndt, T. J., Laychak, A. E., & Park, K. (1990). Friends' influence on adolescents' academic achievement motivation: An experimental study. *Journal of Educational Psychology, 82,* 664–670.

Berthelot, J. M., Ross, N. & Tremblay, S. (2001). Factors affecting Grade 3 student performance in Ontario: A multilevel analysis. *Education Quarterly Review, 7,* 25–36.

Berzonsky, M. D. (1988). Self-theorists, identity status, and social cognition. In D. K. Lapsley & F. C. Power (Eds.), *Self, ego, and identity: Integrative approaches* (pp. 243–261). New York: Springer-Verlag.

Beyer, B. K. (1985). Critical thinking: What is it? *Social Education, 49,* 270–276.

Bialystok, E. (1994a). Representation and ways of knowing: Three issues in second language acquisition. In N. C. Ellis (Ed.), *Implicit and explicit learning of languages.* London: Academic Press.

Bialystok, E. (1994b). Towards an explanation of second language acquisition. In G. Brown, K. Malmkjær, A. Pollitt, & J. Williams (Eds.), *Language and understanding.* Oxford, England: Oxford University Press.

Bialystok, E. (2001). *Bilingualism in development: Language, literacy, and cognition.* Cambridge, England: Cambridge University Press.

Bidell, T. R., & Fischer, K. W. (1997). Between nature and nurture: The role of human agency in the epigenesis of intelligence. In R. J. Sternberg & E. L. Grigorenko (Eds.), *Intelligence, heredity, and environment* (pp. 193–242). Cambridge, England: Cambridge University Press.

Bidwell, N. (1997). The nature and prevalence of bullying in elementary schools. Research report #97–06. Regina, Saskatchewan: Saskatchewan School Trustees Association (SSTA).

Biemiller, A. (2001). Teaching vocabulary: Early, direct, and sequential. *American Educator, 25,* 24–29.

Biemiller, A., Shany, M., Inglis, A., & Meichenbaum, D. (1998). Factors influencing children's acquisition and demonstration of self-regulation on academic tasks. In D. H. Schunk & B. J. Zimmerman (Eds.), *Self-regulated learning: From teaching to self-reflective practice* (pp. 203–224). New York: Guilford Press.

Bierman, K. L., Miller, C. L., & Stabb, S. D. (1987). Improving the social behavior and peer acceptance of rejected boys: Effect of social skill training with instructions and prohibitions. *Journal of Consulting and Clinical Psychology, 55,* 194–200.

Binder, L. M., Dixon, M. R., & Ghezzi, P. M. (2000). A procedure to teach self-control to children with attention deficit hyperactivity disorder. *Journal of Applied Behavior Analysis, 33,* 233–237.

Binns, K., Steinberg, A., Amorosi, S., & Cuevas, A. M. (1997). *The Metropolitan Life survey of the American teacher 1997: Examining gender issues in public schools.* New York: Louis Harris and Associates.

Bjorklund, D. F. (1987). How age changes in knowledge base contribute to the development of children's memory: An interpretive review. *Developmental Review, 7,* 93–130.

Bjorklund, D. F., & Coyle, T. R. (1995). Utilization deficiencies in the development of memory strategies. In F. E. Weinert & W. Schneider (Eds.), *Research on memory development: State of the art and future directions.* Hillsdale, NJ: Erlbaum.

Bjorklund, D. F., & Green, B. L. (1992). The adaptive nature of cognitive immaturity. *American Psychologist, 47,* 46–54.

Bjorklund, D. F., Muir-Broaddus, J. E., & Schneider, W. (1990). The role of knowledge in the development of strategies. In D. F. Bjorklund (Ed.), *Children's strategies: Contemporary views of cognitive development.* Hillsdale, NJ: Erlbaum.

Bjorklund, D. F., Schneider, W., Cassel, W. S., & Ashley, E. (1994). Training and extension of a memory strategy: Evidence for utilization deficiencies in high- and low-IQ children. *Child Development, 65,* 951–965.

Blake, S. B., & Clark, R. E. (1990, April). *The effects of metacognitive selection on far transfer in analogical problem solving tasks.* Paper presented at the annual meeting of the American Educational Research Association, Boston.

Blasi, A. (1980). Bridging moral cognition and moral action: A critical review of the literature. *Psychological Bulletin, 88,* 593–637.

Blasi, A. (1995). Moral understanding and the moral personality: The process of moral integration. In W. M. Kurtines & J. L. Gewirtz (Eds.), *Moral development: An introduction*. Boston: Allyn & Bacon.

Block, J. H. (1983). Differential premises arising from differential socialization of the sexes: Some conjectures. *Child Development, 54*, 1335–1354.

Block, J. H., & Burns, R. B. (1976). Mastery learning. In L. Shulman (Ed.), *Review of research in education* (Vol. 4). Itasca, IL: Peacock.

Bloom, B. S. (1981). *All our children learning*. New York: McGraw-Hill.

Bloom, B. S., Englehart, M. D., Furst, E. J., Hill, W. H., & Krathwohl, D. R. (1956). *Taxonomy of educational objectives. The classification of educational goals: Handbook I. Cognitive domain*. New York: David McKay.

Blumenfeld, P., Hamilton, V. L., Bossert, S., Wessels, K., & Meece, C. (1983). Teacher talk and student thought: Socialization into the student role. In J. Levine & U. Wang (Eds.), *Teacher and student perceptions: Implications for learning*. Hillsdale, NJ: Erlbaum.

Blumenfeld, P. C. (1992). The task and the teacher: Enhancing student thoughtfulness in science. In J. Brophy (Ed.), *Advances in research on teaching: Vol. 3. Planning and managing learning tasks and activities*. Greenwich, CT: JAI Press.

Blumenfeld, P. C., Marx, R. W., Soloway, E., & Krajcik, J. (1996). Learning with peers: From small group cooperation to collaborative communities. *Educational Researcher, 25*(8), 37–40.

Bochenhauer, M. H. (1990, April). *Connections: Geographic education and the National Geographic Society*. Paper presented at the annual meeting of the American Educational Research Association, Boston.

Boettcher, J. (2008). Finding their voice. *Technology Horizons in Education (T.H.E.) Journal*, March. Retrieved August 22, 2008, from http://www.thejournal.com/articles/22175.

Boggiano, A. K., & Pittman, T. S. (Eds.). (1992). *Achievement and motivation: A social-developmental perspective*. Cambridge, England: Cambridge University Press.

Bolles, R. C. (1975). *Theory of motivation* (2nd ed.). New York: Harper & Row.

Bong, M. (2001). Between- and within-domain relations of academic motivation among middle and high school students: Self-efficacy, task-value, and achievement goals. *Journal of Educational Psychology, 93*, 23–34.

Borko, H., & Putnam, R. T. (1996). Learning to teach. In D. C. Berliner & R. C. Calfee (Eds.), *Handbook of educational psychology*. New York: Macmillan.

Borkowski, J. G., Carr, M., Rellinger, E., & Pressley, M. (1990). Self-regulated cognition: Interdependence of metacognition, attributions, and self-esteem. In B. F. Jones & L. Idol (Eds.), *Dimensions of thinking and cognitive instruction*. Hillsdale, NJ: Erlbaum.

Born, D. G., & Davis, M. L. (1974). Amount and distribution of study in a personalized instruction course and in a lecture course. *Journal of Applied Behavior Analysis, 7*, 365–375.

Bornholt, L. J., Goodnow, J. J., & Cooney, G. H. (1994). Influences of gender stereotypes on adolescents' perceptions of their own achievement. *American Educational Research Journal, 31*, 675–692.

Bosacki, S. L. (2000). Theory of mind and self-concept in preadolescents: Links with gender and language. *Journal of Educational Psychology, 92*, 709–717.

Boschee, F., & Baron, M. A. (1993). *Outcome-based education: Developing programs through strategic planning*. Lancaster, PA: Technomic.

Bouchard, T. J., Jr. (1997). IQ similarity in twins reared apart: Findings and responses to critics. In R. J. Sternberg & E. L. Grigorenko (Eds.), *Intelligence, heredity, and environment* (pp. 126–160). Cambridge, England: Cambridge University Press.

Bouchard, T. J., Jr., Lykken, D. T., McGue, M., Segal, N. L., & Tellegen, A. (1990, October 12). Sources of human psychological differences: The Minnesota study of twins reared apart. *Science, 250*, 223–228.

Bouffard, T., Marcoux, M., Vezeau, C., & Bordeleau, L. (2003). Changes in self-perceptions of competence and intrinsic motivation among elementary school children. *British Journal of Educational Psychology, 73*, 171–186.

Bousfield, W. A. (1953). The occurrence of clustering in the recall of randomly arranged associates. *Journal of General Psychology, 49*, 229–240.

Boutte, G. S., & McCormick, C. B. (1992). Authentic multicultural activities: Avoiding pseudomulticulturalism. *Childhood Education, 68*(3), 140–144.f

Bower, G. H., Black, J. B., & Turner, T. J. (1979). Scripts in memory for text. *Cognitive Psychology, 11*, 177–220.

Bower, G. H., & Clark, M. C. (1969). Narrative stories as mediators for serial learning. *Psychonomic Science, 14*, 181–182.

Bower, G. H., Clark, M. C., Lesgold, A. M., & Winzenz, D. (1969). Hierarchical retrieval schemes in recall of categorized word lists. *Journal of Verbal Learning and Verbal Behavior, 8*, 323–343.

Bower, G. H., Karlin, M. B., & Dueck, A. (1975). Comprehension and memory for pictures. *Memory and Cognition, 3*, 216–220.

Bowey, J. (1986). Syntactic awareness and verbal performance from preschool to fifth grade. *Journal of Psycholinguistic Research, 15*, 285–308.

Bowman, B. T. (1989). Educating language-minority children: Challenges and opportunities. *Phi Delta Kappan, 71*, 118–120.

Bowman, L. G., Piazza, C. C., Fisher, W. W., Hagopian, L. P., & Kogan, J. S. (1997). Assessment of preference for varied versus constant reinforcers. *Journal of Applied Behavior Analysis, 30*, 451–458.

Boyatzis, R. E. (1973). Affiliation motivation. In D. C. McClelland & R. S. Steele (Eds.), *Human motivation: A book of readings*. Morristown, NJ: General Learning Press.

Bracken, B. A., McCallum, R. S., & Shaughnessy, M. F. (1999). An interview with Bruce A. Bracken and R. Steve McCallum, authors of the Universal Nonverbal Intelligence Test (UNIT). *North American Journal of Psychology, 1*, 277–288.

Bracken, B. A., & Walker, K. C. (1997). The utility of intelligence tests for preschool children. In D. P. Flanagan, J. L. Genshaft, & P. L. Harrison (Eds.), *Contemporary intellectual assessment: Theories, tests, and issues* (pp. 484–502). New York: Guilford Press.

Bradley, L., & Bryant, P. E. (1991). Phonological skills before and after learning to read. In S. A. Brady & D. P. Shankweiler (Eds.), *Phonological processes in literacy*. Hillsdale, NJ: Erlbaum.

Bradley, R. H., & Caldwell, B. M. (1984). The relation of infants' home environments to achievement test performance in first grade: A follow-up study. *Child Development, 55*, 803–809.

Brainerd, C. J., Reyna, V. F., Howe, M. L., & Kingma, J. (1990). The development of forgetting and reminiscence. *Monographs of the Society for Research in Child Development, 55* (Serial No. 222).

Bransford, J. D., & Franks, J. J. (1971). The abstraction of linguistic ideas. *Cognitive Psychology, 2*, 331–350.

Bransford, J. D., Franks, J. J., Vye, N. J., & Sherwood, R. D. (1989). New approaches to instruction: Because wisdom can't be told. In S. Vosniadou & A. Ortony (Eds.), *Similarity and analogical reasoning*. Cambridge, England: Cambridge University Press.

Bransford, J. D., & Johnson, M. K. (1972). Contextual prerequisites for understanding: Some investigations of comprehension and recall. *Journal of Verbal Learning and Verbal Behavior, 11*, 717–726.

Brantlinger, E. (1997). Using ideology: Cases of nonrecognition of the politics of research and practice in special education. *Review of Educational Research, 67*, 425–459.

Braukmann, C. J., Kirigin, K. A., & Wolf, M. M. (1981). Behavioral treatment of juvenile delinquency. In S. W. Bijou & R. Ruiz (Eds.), *Behavior modification: Contributions to education*. Hillsdale, NJ: Erlbaum.

Brenner, M. E., Mayer, R. E., Moseley, B., Brar, T., Durán, R., Reed, B. S., & Webb, D. (1997). Learning by understanding: The role of multiple representations in learning algebra. *American Educational Research Journal, 34*, 663–689.

Britton, B. K., Stimson, M., Stennett, B., & Gülgöz, S. (1998). Learning from instructional text: Test of an individual differences model. *Journal of Educational Psychology, 90*, 476–491.

Brody, G. H., & Shaffer, D. R. (1982). Contributions of parents and peers to children's moral socialization. *Developmental Review, 2*, 31–75.

Brody, N. (1992). *Intelligence* (2nd ed.). San Diego, CA: Academic Press.

Brody, N. (1997). Intelligence, schooling, and society. *American Psychologist, 52*, 1046–1050.

Bronson, M. B. (2000). *Self-regulation in early childhood: Nature and nurture*. New York: Guilford Press.

Brooke, R. R., & Ruthren, A. J. (1984). The effects of contingency contracting on student performance in a PSI class. *Teaching of Psychology, 11*, 87–89.

Brooks, L. W., & Dansereau, D. F. (1987). Transfer of information: An instructional perspective. In S. M. Cormier & J. D. Hagman (Eds.), *Transfer of learning: Contemporary research and applications*. San Diego, CA: Academic Press.

Brooks-Gunn, J., Klebanov, P. K., & Duncan, G. J. (1996). Ethnic differences in children's intelligence test scores: Role of economic deprivation, home environment, and maternal characteristics. *Child Development, 67*, 396–408.

Brooks-Gunn, J., & Paikoff, R. L. (1993). "Sex is a gamble, kissing is a game": Adolescent sexuality and health promotion. In S. G. Millstein, A. C. Petersen, & E. O. Nightingale (Eds.), *Promoting the health of adolescents: New directions for the twenty-first century* (pp. 180–208). New York: Oxford University Press.

Brophy, J. (1999). Toward a model of the value aspects of motivation in education: Developing appreciation for particular learning domains and activities. *Educational Psychologist, 34*, 75–85.

Brophy, J. E. (1986). *On motivating students* (Occasional Paper No. 101). East Lansing: Michigan State University, Institute for Research on Teaching.

Brophy, J. E. (1987). Synthesis of research on strategies for motivating students to learn. *Educational Leadership, 45*(2), 40–48.

Brophy, J. E. (Ed.). (1991). *Advances in research on teaching: Vol. 2. Teachers' knowledge of subject matter as it relates to their teaching practice.* Greenwich, CT: JAI Press.

Brophy, J. E. (1992). Probing the subtleties of subject-matter teaching. *Educational Leadership, 49*(7), 4–8.

Brophy, J. E., & Alleman, J. (1991). Activities as instructional tools: A framework for analysis and evaluation. *Educational Researcher, 20*(4), 9–23.

Brophy, J. E., & Alleman, J. (1992). Planning and managing learning activities: Basic principles. In J. Brophy (Ed.), *Advances in research on teaching: Vol. 3. Planning and managing learning tasks and activities.* Greenwich, CT: JAI Press.

Brophy, J. E., & Alleman, J. (1996). *Powerful social studies for elementary students.* Fort Worth, TX: Harcourt Brace.

Brophy, J. E., & Evertson, C. (1976). *Learning from teaching: A developmental perspective.* Needham Heights, MA: Allyn & Bacon.

Brophy, J. E., & Good, T. L. (1986). Teacher effects. In M. C. Wittrock (Ed.), *Handbook of research on teaching* (3rd ed.). New York: Macmillan.

Brophy, J. E., & VanSledright, B. (1997). *Teaching and learning history in elementary schools.* New York: Teachers College Press.

Brown, A. L., Ash, D., Rutherford, M., Nakagawa, K., Gordon, A., & Campione, J. C. (1993). Distributed expertise in the classroom. In G. Salomon (Ed.), *Distributed cognitions: Psychological and educational considerations.* Cambridge, England: Cambridge University Press.

Brown, A. L., & Campione, J. C. (1994). Guided discovery in a community of learners. In K. McGilly (Ed.), *Classroom lessons: Integrating cognitive theory and classroom practice.* Cambridge, MA: MIT Press.

Brown, A. L., & Campione, J. C. (1996). Psychological theory and the design of innovative learning environments: On procedures, principles, and systems. In L. Schauble & R. Glaser (Eds.), *Innovations in learning: New environments for education.* Mahwah, NJ: Erlbaum.

Brown, A. L., & Palincsar, A. S. (1987). Reciprocal teaching of comprehension strategies: A natural history of one program for enhancing learning. In J. Borkowski & J. D. Day (Eds.), *Cognition in special education: Comparative approaches to retardation, learning disabilities, and giftedness.* Norwood, NJ: Ablex.

Brown, A. L., & Palincsar, A. S. (1989). Guided, cooperative learning and individual knowledge acquisition. In L. B. Resnick (Ed.), *Knowing, learning, and instruction: Essays in honor of Robert Glaser.* Hillsdale, NJ: Erlbaum.

Brown, A. L., Smiley, S. S., Day, J. D., Townsend, M. A. R., & Lawton, S. C. (1977). Intrusion of a thematic idea in children's comprehension and retention of stories. *Child Development, 48,* 1454–1466.

Brown, A. S., Schilling, H. E. H., & Hockensmith, M. L. (1999). The negative suggestion effect: Pondering incorrect alternatives may be hazardous to your knowledge. *Journal of Educational Psychology, 91,* 756–764.

Brown, B. B. (1990). Peer groups. In S. Feldman & G. Elliott (Eds.), *At the threshold: The developing adolescent* (pp. 171–196). Cambridge, MA: Harvard University Press.

Brown, B. B. (1993). School culture, social politics, and the academic motivation of U.S. students. In T. M. Tomlinson (Ed.), *Motivating students to learn: Overcoming barriers to high achievement.* Berkeley, CA: McCutchan.

Brown, B. B., Eicher, S. A., & Petrie, S. (1986). The importance of peer group ("crowd") affiliation in adolescence. *Journal of Adolescence, 9,* 73–96.

Brown, B. B., Feiring, C., & Furman, W. (1999). Missing the love boat: Why researchers have shied away from adolescent romance. In W. Furman, B. B. Brown, & C. Feiring (Eds.), *The development of romantic relationships in adolescence* (pp. 1–16). Cambridge, England: Cambridge University Press.

Brown, L. M., Tappan, M. B., & Gilligan, C. (1995). Listening to different voices. In W. M. Kurtines & J. L. Gewirtz (Eds.), *Moral development: An introduction.* Boston: Allyn & Bacon.

Brown, R., & McNeill, D. (1966). The "tip of the tongue" phenomenon. *Journal of Verbal Learning and Verbal Behavior, 5,* 325–337.

Brown, R. T. (1989). Creativity: What are we to measure? In J. A. Glover, R. R. Ronning, & C. R. Reynolds (Eds.), *Handbook of creativity.* New York: Plenum Press.

Brownell, M. T., Mellard, D. F., & Deshler, D. D. (1993). Differences in the learning and transfer performance between students with learning disabilities and other low-achieving students on problem-solving tasks. *Learning Disabilities Quarterly, 16,* 138–156.

Bruer, J. T. (1997). Education and the brain: A bridge too far. *Educational Researcher, 26*(8), 4–16.

Bruer, J. T. (1999). *The myth of the first three years: A new understanding of early brain development and lifelong learning.* New York: Free Press.

Bruner, J. S. (1961). The act of discovery. *Harvard Educational Review, 31,* 21–32.

Bruner, J. S. (1966). *Toward a theory of instruction.* Cambridge, MA: Harvard University Press.

Bruning, R. H., Schraw, G. J., & Ronning, R. R. (1995). *Cognitive psychology and instruction* (2nd ed.). Upper Saddle River, NJ: Merrill/Prentice Hall.

Bryan, J. H. (1975). Children's cooperation and helping behaviors. In E. M. Hetherington (Ed.), *Review of child development research* (Vol. 5). Chicago: University of Chicago Press.

Bryan, T., Burstein, K., & Bryan, J. (2001). Students with learning disabilities: Homework problems and promising practices. *Educational Psychologist, 36,* 167–180.

Bryant, P., Nunes, T., & Aidinis, A. (1999). Different morphemes, same spelling problems: Cross-linguistic developmental studies. In M. Harris & G. Hatano (Eds.), *Learning to read and write: A cross-linguistic perspective.* Cambridge, England: Cambridge University Press.

Buchoff, T. (1990). Attention deficit disorder: Help for the classroom teacher. *Childhood Education, 67*(2), 86–90.

Buhrmester, D. (1992). The developmental courses of sibling and peer relationships. In F. Boer & J. Dunn (Eds.), *Children's sibling relationships: Developmental and clinical issues.* Hillsdale, NJ: Erlbaum.

Bulgren, J. A., Deshler, D. D., Schumaker, J. B., & Lenz, B. K. (2000). The use and effectiveness of analogical instruction in diverse secondary content classrooms. *Journal of Educational Psychology, 92,* 426–441.

Bulgren, J. A., Schumaker, J. B., & Deshler, D. D. (1994). The effects of a recall enhancement routine on the test performance of secondary students with and without learning disabilities. *Learning Disabilities Research and Practice, 9,* 2–11.

Burger, S., & Burger, D. (1994). Determining the validity of performance-based assessment. *Educational Measurement: Issues and Practices, 13*(1), 9–15.

Burhans, K. K., & Dweck, C. S. (1995). Helplessness in early childhood: The role of contingent worth. *Child Development, 66,* 1719–1738.

Bushman, B. J., & Anderson, C. A. (2001). Media violence and the American public: Scientific facts versus media misinformation. *American Psychologist, 56,* 477–489.

Bussière, P., Cartwright, F., & Knighton, T. (2004). Measuring up: Canadian results of the OECD PISA study. *The Performance of Canada's Youth in Mathematics, Reading, Science and Problem-Solving. 2003 First Results for Canadians Aged 15.* Ottawa: Human Resources and Social Development Canada; Council of Ministers of Education, Canada; and Statistics Canada. Statistics Canada Catalogue no. 81-590-XIE – no. 2.

Bussière, P., Knighton, T., & Pennock, D. (2007). Measuring up: Canadian results of the OECD PISA study. *The Performance of Canada's Youth in Science, Reading and Mathematics. 2006 First Results for Canadians Aged 15.* Ottawa: Human Resources and Social Development Canada; Council of Ministers of Education, Canada; and Statistics Canada. Statistics Canada Catalogue no. 81-590-XIE – no. 3.

Butler, D. L. (1994). From learning strategies to strategic learning: Promoting self-regulated learning by postsecondary students with learning disabilities. *Canadian Journal of Special Education, 9*(4), 69–101.

Butler, D. L. (1995). Promoting strategic learning by postsecondary students with learning disabilities. *Journal of Learning Disabilities, 28*(3), 170–190.

Butler, D. L. (2002). Individualizing instruction in self-regulated learning. *Theory into Practice, 41*(2), 81–91.

Butler, D. L., Elaschuk, C. L., & Poole, S. (2000). Promoting strategic writing by postsecondary students with learning disabilities: A report of three case studies. *Learning Disability Quarterly, 23,* 196–213.

Butler, D. L., & Winne, P. H. (1995). Feedback and self-regulated learning: A theoretical synthesis. *Review of Educational Research, 65,* 245–281.

Butler, R. (1989). Mastery versus ability appraisal: A developmental study of children's observations of peers' work. *Child Development, 60,* 1350–1361.

Butler, R. (1990). The effects of mastery and competitive conditions on self-assessment at different ages. *Child Development, 61,* 201–210.

Butler, R. (1994). Teacher communication and student interpretations: Effects of teacher responses to failing students on attributional inferences in two age groups. *British Journal of Educational Psychology, 64,* 277–294.

Butler, R. (1998a). Age trends in the use of social and temporal comparison for self-evaluation: Examination of a novel developmental hypothesis. *Child Development, 69,* 1054–1073.

Butler, R. (1998b). Determinants of help seeking: Relations between perceived reasons for classroom help-avoidance and help-seeking behaviors in an experimental context. *Journal of Educational Psychology, 90,* 630–644.

Butterfield, E. C., & Ferretti, R. P. (1987). Toward a theoretical integration of cognitive hypotheses about intellectual differences among children. In J. G. Borkowski & J. D. Day (Eds.), *Cognition in special children: Approaches to retardation, learning disabilities, and giftedness.* Norwood, NJ: Ablex.

Byrnes, J. P. (1996). *Cognitive development and learning in instructional contexts.* Boston: Allyn & Bacon.

Calderhead, J. (1996). Teachers: Beliefs and knowledge. In D. C. Berliner & R. C. Calfee (Eds.),

Handbook of educational psychology. New York: Macmillan.

Calfee, R. (1981). Cognitive psychology and educational practice. In D. C. Berliner (Ed.), *Review of research in education* (Vol. 9). Washington, DC: American Educational Research Association.

Calfee, R., & Chambliss, M. J. (1988, April). *The structure of social studies textbooks: Where is the design?* Paper presented at the annual meeting of the American Educational Research Association, New Orleans, LA.

Calfee, R., Dunlap, K., & Wat, A. (1994). Authentic discussion of texts in middle grade schooling: An analytic-narrative approach. *Journal of Reading, 37,* 546–556.

Calfee, R. C., & Masuda, W. V. (1997). Classroom assessment as inquiry. In G. D. Phye (Ed.), *Handbook of classroom assessment: Learning, achievement, and adjustment.* San Diego, CA: Academic Press.

Cameron, J., & Pierce, W. D. (1994). Reinforcement, reward, and intrinsic motivation: A meta-analysis. *Review of Educational Research, 64,* 363–423.

Campbell, A. (1984). *The girls in the gang: A report from New York City.* New York: Blackwell.

Campbell, D. E. (1996). *Choosing democracy: A practical guide to multicultural education.* Upper Saddle River, NJ: Merrill/Prentice Hall.

Campbell, F. A., & Ramey, C. T. (1994). Effects of early intervention on intellectual and academic achievement: A follow-up study of children from low-income families. *Child Development, 65,* 684–698.

Campbell, F. A., & Ramey, C. T. (1995). Cognitive and school outcomes for high-risk African-American students at middle adolescence: Positive effects of early intervention. *American Educational Research Journal, 32,* 742–772.

Campbell, L., Campbell, B., & Dickinson, D. (1998). *Teaching and learning through multiple intelligences* (2nd ed.). Boston: Allyn & Bacon.

Campbell, P. A. (1986). What's a nice girl like you doing in a math class? *Phi Delta Kappan, 67,* 516–520.

Campione, J. C., Brown, A. L., & Bryant, N. R. (1985). Individual differences in learning and memory. In R. J. Sternberg (Ed.), *Human abilities: An information-processing approach.* New York: Freeman.

Campione, J. C., Shapiro, A. M., & Brown, A. L. (1995). Forms of transfer in a community of learners: Flexible learning and understanding. In A. McKeough, J. Lupart, & A. Marini (Eds.), *Teaching for transfer: Fostering generalization in learning.* Mahwah, NJ: Erlbaum.

Canadian Council on Social Development. (2006). The Progress of Canada's Children and Youth, 2006. http://www.ccsd.ca/pccy/2006/pdf/pccy_2006.pdf.

Canadian Institute of Child Health. (1996). *The health of Canada's children: A CICH Profile* (3rd ed.). Ottawa: Author.

Canadian Psychological Association. (1994). *Recommendations from the Canadian Psychological Association for improving the North American safeguards that help protect the public against test misuse.* Ottawa: Author.

Canadian Psychological Association. (1999). *Standards for educational and psychological testing.* Ottawa: Author.

Candler-Lotven, A., Tallent-Runnels, M. K., Olivárez, A., & Hildreth, B. (1994, April). *A comparison of learning and study strategies of gifted, average-ability, and learning-disabled ninth grade students.* Paper presented at the annual meeting of the American Educational Research Association, New Orleans, LA.

Caprara, G. V., Barbaranelli, C., Pastorelli, C., Bandura, A., & Zimbardo, P. G. (2000). Prosocial foundations of children's academic achievement. *Psychological Science, 11,* 302–306.

Capron, C., & Duyme, M. (1989). Assessment of effects of socio-economic status on IQ in a full cross-fostering study. *Nature, 340,* 552–554.

Carey, L. M. (1994). *Measuring and evaluating school learning* (2nd ed.). Needham Heights, MA: Allyn & Bacon.

Carey, S. (1978). The child as word learner. In M. Halle, J. Bresnan, & G. A. Miller (Eds.), *Linguistic theory and psychological reality.* Cambridge, MA: MIT Press.

Carey, S. (1985). *Conceptual change in childhood.* Cambridge, MA: MIT Press.

Carey, S. (1986). Cognitive science and science education. *American Psychologist, 41,* 1123–1130.

Carney, P. (1999). School violence: The school setting is only part of the picture. Psynopsis. Summer. Retrieved from http://www.cpa.ca/psynopsis/violence%2D99.html.

Carney, R. N., & Levin, J. R. (1998). Do mnemonic memories fade as time goes by? Here's looking anew! *Contemporary Educational Psychology, 23,* 276–297.

Carnine, D. (1989). Teaching complex content to learning disabled students: The role of technology. *Exceptional Children, 55,* 524–533.

Carpenter, P. A., & Just, M. A. (1986). Cognitive processes in reading. In J. Orasanu (Ed.), *Reading comprehension: From research to practice.* Hillsdale, NJ: Erlbaum.

Carr, A. A. (1997, March). *The participation "race": Kentucky's site based decision teams.* Paper presented at the annual meeting of the American Educational Research Association, Chicago.

Carr, M., & Biddlecomb, B. (1998). Metacognition in mathematics from a constructivist perspective. In D. J. Hacker, J. Dunlosky, & A. C. Graesser (Eds.), *Metacognition in educational theory and practice* (pp. 69–91). Mahwah, NJ: Erlbaum.

Carr, M., & Borkowski, J. G. (1989). Attributional training and the generalization of reading strategies with underachieving children. *Learning and Individual Differences, 1,* 327–341.

Carr, M., Kurtz, B. E., Schneider, W., Turner, L. A., & Borkowski, J. G. (1989). Strategy acquisition and transfer among American and German children: Environmental influences on metacognitive development. *Developmental Psychology, 25,* 765–771.

Carter, K. R., & Ormrod, J. E. (1982). Acquisition of formal operations by intellectually gifted children. *Gifted Child Quarterly, 26,* 110–115.

Cartledge, G., & Milburn, J. F. (1995). *Teaching social skills to children and youth: Innovative approaches* (3rd ed.). Needham Heights, MA: Allyn & Bacon.

Carver, C. S., & Scheier, M. F. (1990). Origins and functions of positive and negative affect: A control-process view. *Psychological Review, 97,* 19–35.

Casanova, U. (1987). Ethnic and cultural differences. In V. Richardson-Koehler (Ed.), *Educator's handbook: A research perspective.* White Plains, NY: Longman.

Case, R. (1997). The development of conceptual structures. In D. Kuhn & R.S. Siegler (Eds.), *Carmichael's handbook of child development. Vol 2: Perception, cognition, and language* (5th ed.). New York: McGraw Hill.

Case, R., Griffin, S., & Kelly, W. (1999a). Cognitive development in early childhood and children's readiness for schooling. In S. L. Goldbeck (Ed.), *Psychological perspectives on early childhood education: Reframing dilemmas in research and practice.* Hillsdale, NJ: Erlbaum.

Case, R., Griffin, S., & Kelly, W. (1999b). Social class gradients in mathematical ability and their responsiveness to compensatory education. In D. Keating & C. Hertzman (Eds.), *Tomorrow's society, today's children: The health and developmental wealth of nations.* New York: Guilford.

Case, R., & Okamoto, Y., in collaboration with Griffin, S., McKeough, A., Bleiker, C., Henderson, B., & Stephenson, K. M. (1996). The role of central conceptual structures in the development of children's thought. *Monographs of the Society for Research in Child Development, 61*(1, Serial No. 246).

Caseau, D., Luckasson, R., & Kroth, R. L. (1994). Special education services for girls with serious emotional disturbance: A case of gender bias? *Behavioral Disorders, 20*(1), 51–60.

Casey, W. M., & Burton, R. V. (1982). Training children to be consistently honest through verbal self-instructions. *Child Development, 53,* 911–919.

Caspi, A., & Moffitt, T. E. (1995). The continuity of maladaptive behavior: From description to understanding in the study of antisocial behavior. In D. Cicchetti & D. J. Cohen (Eds.), *Developmental psychopathology: Vol 2: Risk, disorder, and adaptation* (pp. 472–511). New York: Wiley.

Caspi, A., Taylor, A., Moffitt, T. E., & Plomin, R. (2000). Neighborhood deprivation affects children's mental health: Environmental risks identified in a genetic design. *Psychological Science, 11,* 338–342.

Casserly, P. L. (1980). Factors affecting female participation in Advanced Placement programs in mathematics, chemistry, and physics. In L. H. Fox, L. Brody, & D. Tobin (Eds.), *Women and the mathematical mystique.* Baltimore: Johns Hopkins University Press.

Cazden, C. B. (1968). The acquisition of noun and verb inflections. *Child Development, 39,* 433–448.

Cazden, C. B. (1976). Play with language and metalinguistic awareness: One dimension of language experience. In J. Bruner, A. Jolly, & K. Sylva (Eds.), *Play: Its role in development and evolution.* New York: Basic Books.

Cazden, C. B., & Leggett, E. L. (1981). Culturally responsive education: Recommendations for achieving *Lau* remedies II. In H. T. Trueba, G. P. Guthrie, & K. H. Au (Eds.), *Culture and the bilingual classroom: Studies in classroom ethnography.* Rowley, MA: Newbury House.

Ceci, S. J., & Williams, W. M. (1997). Schooling, intelligence, and income. *American Psychologist, 52,* 1051–1058.

Centre for Research in Applied Measurement and Evaluation. (1993). *Principles for Fair Student Assessment Practices for Education in Canada.* Edmonton, AB: Author.

Centre of Excellence for Early Childhood Development. (2002). Perceptions and opinions of Canadians regarding aggression among children. Omnibus research report, Montreal, QC.

Chall, J. S. (1983). *Stages of reading development.* New York: McGraw Hill.

Chalmers, J., & Townsend, M. (1990). The effects of training in social perspective taking on socially maladjusted girls. *Child Development, 61,* 178–190.

Chambliss, M. J. (1994). Why do readers fail to change their beliefs after reading persuasive text? In R. Garner & P. A. Alexander (Eds.), *Beliefs about text and instruction with text.* Hillsdale, NJ: Erlbaum.

Chambliss, M. J., Calfee, R. C., & Wong, I. (1990, April). *Structure and content in science textbooks: Where is the design?* Paper presented at the annual meeting of the American Educational Research Association, Boston.

Chan, C., Burtis, J., & Bereiter, C. (1997). Knowledge building as a mediator of conflict in conceptual change. *Cognition and Instruction, 15,* 1–40.

Chandler, M., & Moran, T. (1990). Psychopathy and moral development: A comparative study of delinquent and nondelinquent youth. *Development and Psychopathology, 2,* 227–246.

Chao, R. K. (1994). Beyond parental control and authoritarian parenting style: Understanding Chinese parenting through the cultural notion of training. *Child Development, 65,* 1111–1119.

Chapman, J. W., Tunmer, W. E., & Prochnow, J. E. (2000). Early reading-related skills and performance, reading self-concept, and the development of academic self-concept: A longitudinal study. *Journal of Educational Psychology, 92,* 703–708.

Chen, X., Rubin, K. H., & Sun, Y. (1992). Social reputation and peer relationships in Chinese and Canadian children: A cross-cultural study. *Child Development, 63,* 1336–1343.

Chen, Z. (1999). Schema induction in children's analogical problem solving. *Journal of Educational Psychology, 91,* 703–715.

Cheng, P. W. (1985). Restructuring versus automaticity: Alternative accounts of skill acquisition. *Psychological Review, 92,* 414–423.

Cherry, E. C. (1953). Some experiments on the recognition of speech, with one and with two ears. *Journal of the Acoustical Society of America, 25,* 975–979.

Cheyne, J. A., & Walters, R. H. (1970). Punishment and prohibition: Some origins of self-control. In T. M. Newcomb (Ed.), *New directions in psychology.* New York: Holt, Rinehart & Winston.

Chi, M. T. H. (1978). Knowledge structures and memory development. In R. S. Siegler (Ed.), *Children's thinking: What develops?* Hillsdale, NJ: Erlbaum.

Chi, M. T. H., Feltovich, P., & Glaser, R. (1981). Categorization and representation of physics problems by experts and novices. *Cognitive Science, 5,* 121–152.

Chiappetta, E. L., & Koballa, T. R. (2006). *Science instruction in the middle and secondary schools: Developing fundamental knowledge and skills for teaching* (6th ed.). Upper Saddle River, NJ: Merrill/Prentice Hall.

Chinn, C. A., & Brewer, W. F. (1993). The role of anomalous data in knowledge acquisition: A theoretical framework and implications for science instruction. *Review of Educational Research, 63,* 1–49.

Chomsky, N. (1965). *Aspects of the theory of syntax.* Cambridge, MA: MIT Press.

Chomsky, N. (1972). *Language and mind* (enlarged ed.). San Diego, CA: Harcourt Brace Jovanovich.

Christie, J. F., & Johnsen, E. P. (1983). The role of play in social-intellectual development. *Review of Educational Research, 53,* 93–115.

Christophe, A., & Morton, J. (1998). Is Dutch native English? Linguistic analysis by 2-month-olds. *Developmental Science, 1,* 215–219.

Chui, T., Tran, K., & Maheux, H. (2007, December 11). "Immigration in Canada: A Portrait of the Foreign-born Population." *Census of Canada.* Statistics Canada. Retrieved August 13, 2008, from http://www12.statcan.ca/english/census06/analysis/immcit/index.cfm.

Clapper, J. P. (2007). Prior knowledge and correlational structure in unsupervised learning. *Canadian Journal of Experimental Psychology, 61,* 109–127.

Clark, B. (1997). *Growing up gifted* (5th ed.). Upper Saddle River, NJ: Merrill/Prentice Hall.

Clark, C. C. (1992). Deviant adolescent subcultures: Assessment strategies and clinical interventions. *Adolescence, 27*(106), 283–293.

Clark, E. V. (1971). On the acquisition of the meaning of "before" and "after." *Journal of Verbal Learning and Verbal Behavior, 10,* 266–275.

Clark, J. M., & Paivio, A. (1991). Dual coding theory and education. *Educational Psychology Review, 3,* 149–210.

Clarke-Stewart, K. A. (1988). Parents' effects on children's development: A decade of progress? *Journal of Applied Developmental Psychology, 9,* 41–84.

Clifford, M. M. (1990). Students need challenge, not easy success. *Educational Leadership, 48*(1), 22–26.

Cobb, P., Wood, T., Yackel, E., Nicholls, J., Wheatley, G., Trigatti, B., & Perlwitz, M. (1991). Assessment of a problem centered second-grade mathematics project. *Journal for Research in Mathematics Education, 22,* 3–29.

Cochran, K. F., & Jones, L. L. (1998). The subject matter knowledge of preservice science teachers. In B. J. Fraser & K. G. Tobin (Eds.), *International Handbook of Science Education. Part II.* Dordrecht, The Netherlands: Kluwer.

Cochran-Smith, M., & Lytle, S. (1993). *Inside out: Teacher research and knowledge.* New York: Teachers College Press.

Cognition and Technology Group at Vanderbilt. (1990). Anchored instruction and its relationship to situated cognition. *Educational Researcher, 19*(6), 2–10.

Cognition and Technology Group at Vanderbilt. (1996). Looking at technology in context: A framework for understanding technology and education research. In D. C. Berliner & R. C. Calfee (Eds.), *Handbook of educational psychology* (pp. 807–840). New York: Macmillan.

Cohen, E. G. (1994). Restructuring the classroom: Conditions for productive small groups. *Review of Educational Research, 64,* 1–35.

Cohen, E. G., Lockheed, M. E., & Lohman, M. R. (1976). The center for interracial cooperation: A field experiment. *Sociology of Education, 59,* 47–58.

Cohen, E. G., & Lotan, R. A. (1995). Producing equal-status interaction in the heterogeneous classroom. *American Educational Research Journal, 32,* 99–120.

Cohen, L. B., & Cashon, C. H. (2006). Infant cognition. In W. Damon & R. M. Lerner (Series Eds.), D. Kuhn & R. Siegler (Vol. Eds.), *Handbook of child psychology: Vol. 1. Cognition, perception, and language* (6th ed.) (pp. 214–251). New York: Wiley.

Cohen, P. (2008). The embodied conductor: Concert pianists, diaper dancers, and the fine art of creative variability in performance. In B. M. Shore, M. W. Aulls, & M. A. B. Delcourt (Eds.), *Inquiry in education, volume II: Overcoming barriers to successful implementation* (pp. 165–205). New York: Erlbaum.

Cohen, R. L. (1989). Memory for action events: The power of enactment. *Educational Psychology Review, 1,* 57–80.

Coie, R. L., & Cillessen, A. H. N. (1993). Peer rejection: Origins and effects on children's development. *Current Directions in Psychological Science, 2,* 89–92.

Colby, A., & Kohlberg, L. (1984). Invariant sequence and internal consistency in moral judgment stages. In W. M. Kurtines & J. L. Gewirtz (Eds.), *Morality, moral behavior, and moral development.* New York: Wiley.

Colby, A., & Kohlberg, L. (1987). *The measurement of moral judgment: Theoretical foundations and research validation* (Vol. 1). Cambridge, England: Cambridge University Press.

Colby, A., Kohlberg, L., Gibbs, J., & Lieberman, M. (1983). A longitudinal study of moral judgment. *Monographs of the Society for Research in Child Development, 48*(1–2, Serial No. 200).

Cole, D. A., Martin, J. M., Peeke, L. A., Seroczynski, A. D., & Fier, J. (1999). Children's over- and underestimation of academic competence: A longitudinal study of gender differences, depression, and anxiety. *Child Development, 70,* 459–473.

Cole, N. S. (1990). Conceptions of educational achievement. *Educational Researcher, 19*(3), 2–7.

Colemann-Martin, M. B., Heller, K. W., Cihak, D. F., & Irvine, K. L. (2005). Using computer-assisted instruction and the nonverbal reading approach to teach word identification. *Focus on Autism and Other Developmental Disabilities, 20,* 80–90.

Collaer, M. L., & Hines, M. (1995). Human behavioral sex differences: A role for gonadal hormones during early development? *Psychological Bulletin, 118,* 55–107.

Collier, V. P. (1992). The Canadian bilingual immersion debate: A synthesis of research findings. *Studies in Second Language Acquisition, 14,* 87–97.

Collins, A., Brown, J. S., & Newman, S. E. (1989). Cognitive apprenticeship: Teaching the crafts of reading, writing, and mathematics. In L. B. Resnick (Ed.), *Knowing, learning, and instruction: Essays in honor of Robert Glaser.* Hillsdale, NJ: Erlbaum.

Collins, S., & Arthur, N. (2005). Multicultural counselling competencies: A framework for professional development. In N. Arthur & S. Collins (Eds.), *Culture-infused counselling: Celebrating the Canadian mosaic* (pp. 41–102). Calgary: Counselling Concepts.

Collins, W. A., Maccoby, E. E., Steinberg, L., Hetherington, E. M., & Bornstein, M. H. (2000). Contemporary research on parenting: The case for nature and nurture. *American Psychologist, 55,* 218–232.

Collins, W. A., & Sroufe, L. A. (1999). Capacity for intimate relationships: A developmental construction. In W. Furman, B. B. Brown, & C. Feiring (Eds.), *The development of romantic relationships in adolescence* (pp. 125–147). Cambridge, England: Cambridge University Press.

Combs, A. W., Richards, A. C., & Richards, F. (1976). *Perceptual psychology: A humanistic approach to the study of persons.* New York: Harper & Row.

Cone, T. E., Wilson, L. R., Bradley, C. M., & Reese, J. H. (1985). Characteristics of LD students in Iowa: An empirical investigation. *Learning Disability Quarterly, 8,* 211–220.

Connell, J. P. (1990). Context, self, and action: A motivational analysis of self-system processes across the life span. In D. Cicchetti & M. Beeghly (Eds.), *The self in transition: Infancy to childhood.* Chicago: University of Chicago Press.

Connell, J. P., & Wellborn, J. G. (1991). Competence, autonomy, and relatedness: A motivational analysis of self-system processes. In M. R. Gunnar & L. A. Sroufe (Eds.), *Self processes and development: The Minnesota Symposia on Child Psychology* (Vol. 23). Hillsdale, NJ: Erlbaum.

Connolly, F. W., & Eisenberg, T. E. (1990). The feedback classroom: Teaching's silent friend. *T.H.E. Journal, 17*(5), 75–77.

Connolly, J., & Goldberg, A. (1999). Romantic relationships in adolescence: The role of friends and peers in their emergence and development. In W. Furman, B. B. Brown, & C. Feiring (Eds.), *The development of romantic relationships in adolescence* (pp. 266–290). Cambridge, England: Cambridge University Press.

Cooper, H. (1989). Synthesis of research on homework. *Educational Leadership, 47*(3), 85–91.

Cooper, H., & Valentine, J. C. (2001). Using research to answer practical questions about homework. *Educational Psychologist, 36,* 143–153.

Cooper, H. M., & Good, T. (1983). *Pygmalion grows up: Studies in the expectation communication process.* White Plains, NY: Longman.

Corbett, H. D., & Wilson, B. (1988). Raising the stakes in statewide mandatory minimum competency testing. *Politics of Education Association Yearbook,* 27–39.

Corenblum, B. (1996). Development of identity of Native Indian children: Review and possible futures. *Canadian Journal of Native Studies, 16*(1), 81–103.

Corkill, A. J. (1992). Advance organizers: Facilitators of recall. *Educational Psychology Review, 4,* 33–67.

Cormier, S. M. (1987). The structural processes underlying transfer of training. In S. M. Cormier & J. D. Hagman (Eds.), *Transfer of learning: Contemporary research and applications.* San Diego, CA: Academic Press.

Cornell, D. G., Pelton, G. M., Bassin, L. E., Landrum, M., Ramsay, S. G., Cooley, M. R., Lynch, K. A., & Hamrick, E. (1990). Self-concept and peer status among gifted program youth. *Journal of Educational Psychology, 82,* 456–463.

Corno, L. (1993). The best-laid plans: Modern conceptions of volition and educational research. *Educational Researcher, 22,* 14–22.

Corno, L. (1996). Homework is a complicated thing. *Educational Researcher, 25*(8), 27–30.

Corno, L., & Rohrkemper, M. M. (1985). The intrinsic motivation to learn in classrooms. In C. Ames & R. Ames (Eds.), *Research on motivation in education: Vol. 2. The classroom milieu.* San Diego, CA: Academic Press.

Corno, L., & Snow, R. E. (1986). Adapting teaching to individual differences among learners. In M. C. Wittrock (Ed.), *Handbook of research on teaching* (3rd ed.). New York: Macmillan.

Cote, S., Vaillancourt, T., LeBlanc, J., Nagin, D., & Tremblay, R. (2006). The development of physical aggression from toddlerhood to pre-adolescence: A nationwide longitudinal study of Canadian children. *Abnormal Child Psychology, 34*(1), 71–85.

Cothern, N. B., Konopak, B. C., & Willis, E. L. (1990). Using readers' imagery of literary characters to study text meaning construction. *Reading Research and Instruction, 30,* 15–29.

Cottrol, R. J. (1990). America the multicultural. *American Educator, 14*(4), 18–21.

Courchesne, E., Townsend, J., Akshoomoff, N. A., Saitoh, O., Yeung-Courchesne, R., Lincoln, A. J., James, H. E., Haas, R. H. Schreibman, L., & Lau, L. (1994). Impairment of shifting attention in autistic and cerebellar patients. *Behavioral Neuroscience, 108,* 848–865.

Covington, M. (2000). Intrinsic versus extrinsic motivation in schools: A reconciliation. *Current Directions in Psychological Science, 9,* 22–25.

Covington, M. V. (1987). Achievement motivation, self-attributions, and the exceptional learner. In J. D. Day & J. G. Borkowski (Eds.), *Intelligence and exceptionality.* Norwood, NJ: Ablex.

Covington, M. V. (1992). *Making the grade: A self-worth perspective on motivation and school reform.* Cambridge, England: Cambridge University Press.

Covington, M. V., & Beery, R. M. (1976). *Self-worth and school learning.* New York: Holt, Rinehart & Winston.

Covington, M. V., & Müeller, K. J. (2001). Intrinsic versus extrinsic motivation: An approach/avoidance reformulation. *Educational Psychology Review, 13,* 157–176.

Cowan, N. (1995). *Attention and memory: An integrated framework.* New York: Oxford University Press.

Cox, B. D. (1997). The rediscovery of the active learner in adaptive contexts: A developmental-historical analysis of transfer of training. *Educational Psychologist, 32,* 41–55.

Craft, M. (1984). Education for diversity. In M. Craft (Ed.), *Educational and cultural pluralism.* London: Falmer Press.

Craig, W., & Pepler, D. J. (1997). Observations of bullying and victimization in the schoolyard. *Canadian Journal of School Psychology, 13,* 41–60.

Craig, W. M. (2004). Bullying in Canada. In *Canadian World Health Organization on the Health of Youth in Canada.* Ottawa: Health Canada.

Craik, F. I. M., Routh, D. A., & Broadbent, D. E. (1983). On the transfer of information from temporary to permanent memory. *Philosophical Transactions of the Royal Society of London. Series B, Biological Sciences: Functional Aspects of Human Memory, 302*(1110), 341–359.

Craik, F. I. M., & Watkins, M. J. (1973). The role of rehearsal in short-term memory. *Journal of Verbal Learning and Verbal Behavior, 12,* 598–607.

Creasey, G. L., Jarvis, P. A., & Berk, L. E. (1998). Play and social competence. In O. N. Saracho & B. Spodek (Eds.), *Multiple perspectives on play in early childhood education.* Albany: State University of New York Press.

Crick, N. R., & Dodge, K. A. (1996). A review and reformulation of social information-processing mechanisms in children's social adjustment. *Psychological Bulletin, 115,* 73–101.

Crick, N. R., & Grotpeter, J. K. (1995). Relational aggression, gender, and social-psychological adjustment. *Child Development, 66,* 710–722.

Crockett, L., Losoff, M., & Peterson, A. C. (1984). Perceptions of the peer group and friendship in early adolescence. *Journal of Early Adolescence, 4,* 155–181.

Crook, C. (1995). On resourcing a concern for collaboration within peer interactions. *Cognition and Instruction, 13,* 541–547.

Crooks, T. J. (1988). The impact of classroom evaluation practices on students. *Review of Educational Research, 58,* 438–481.

Crowder, R. (1993). Short-term memory: Where do we stand? *Memory and Cognition, 21,* 142–145.

Crowley, K., & Jacobs, M. (2002). Building islands of expertise in everyday family activity. In G. Leinhardt, K. Crowley, & K. Knutson (Eds.), *Learning conversations in museums* (pp. 333–356). Mahway, NJ: Erlbaum.

Crowley, K., & Siegler, R. S. (1999). Explanation and generalization in young children's strategy learning. *Child Development, 70,* 304–316.

Crowne, D. P., & Marlowe, D. (1964). *The approval motive: Studies in evaluative dependence.* New York: Wiley.

Csikszentmihalyi, M. (1990). *Flow: The psychology of optimal experience.* New York: HarperPerennial.

Csikszentmihalyi, M. (1996). *Creativity: Flow and the psychology of discovery and invention.* New York: HarperCollins.

Csikszentmihalyi, M., & Nakamura, J. (1989). The dynamics of intrinsic motivation: A study of adolescents. In C. Ames & R. Ames (Eds.), *Research on motivation in education: Vol. 3. Goals and cognitions.* San Diego, CA: Academic Press.

Cunningham, A. E. (1990). Explicit versus implicit instruction in phonemic awareness. *Journal of Experimental Child Psychology, 50,* 429–250.

Cunningham, A. E., & Stanovich, K. E. (2003). Reading can make you smarter: The more children read, the greater their vocabulary and the better their cognitive skills. *Principal—What Principals Need to Know about Reading, 83*(2), 34–39.

Cunningham, C. E., & Cunningham, L. J. (1998). Student-mediated conflict resolution programs. In R. A. Barkley, *Attention-deficit hyperactivity disorder: A handbook for diagnosis and treatment* (2nd ed., pp. 491–509). New York: Guilford Press.

Cunningham, C. E., Cunningham, L. J., & Martorelli, V. (1997). *Coping with conflict at school: The collaborative student mediation project manual.* Hamilton, ON: COPE Works.

Cunningham, T. H., & Graham, C. R. (2000). Increasing native English vocabulary recognition through Spanish immersion: Cognate transfer from foreign to first language. *Journal of Educational Psychology, 92,* 37–49.

Curzon, J., Selby, L. & Ryba, K. (2005). Realising the power within: Partnerships with information and communication technology. In D. Fraser, M. Moltzen, & K. Ryba (Eds.), *Learners with special needs in Aotearoa, New Zealand* (pp. 193–219). Southbank, Victoria: Thomson Dunmore.

Cushing, L. S., & Kennedy, C. H. (1997). Academic effects of providing peer support in general education classrooms on students without disabilities. *Journal of Applied Behavior Analysis, 30,* 139–151.

D'Amato, R. C., Chitooran, M. M., & Whitten, J. D. (1992). Neuropsychological consequences of malnutrition. In D. I. Templer, L. C. Hartlage, & W. G. Cannon (Eds.), *Preventable brain damage: Brain vulnerability and brain health.* New York: Springer.

Damon, W. (1988). *The moral child: Nurturing children's natural moral growth.* New York: Free Press.

Damon, W. (1991). Putting substance into self-esteem: A focus on academic and moral values. *Educational Horizons, 70*(1), 12–18.

Danner, F. W., & Lonky, E. (1981). A cognitive-developmental approach to the effects of rewards on intrinsic motivation. *Child Development, 52,* 1043–1052.

Dansereau, D. F. (1988). Cooperative learning strategies. In C. E. Weinstein, E. T. Goetz, & P. A. Alexander (Eds.), *Learning and study strategies: Issues in assessment, instruction, and evaluation.* San Diego, CA: Academic Press.

Dansereau, D. F. (1995). Derived structural schemas and the transfer of knowledge. In A. McKeough, J. Lupart, & A. Marini (Eds.), *Teaching for transfer: Fostering generalization in learning.* Mahwah, NJ: Erlbaum.

Darling-Hammond, L. (1995). Inequality and access to knowledge. In J. A. Banks & C. A. M. Banks (Eds.), *Handbook of research on multicultural education.* New York: Macmillan.

Das, J. P., Naglieri, J. A., & Kirby, J. R. (1994). *Assessment of cognitive processes: The PASS theory of intelligence.* Boston: Allyn & Bacon.

Dauvergne, M., & Johnson, H. (2001). Children witnessing family violence. *Juristat: Canadian Centre for Justice Statistics, 21*(6), 1–13.

Davidson, J. E., & Sternberg, R. J. (1998). Smart problem solving: How metacognition helps. In D. J. Hacker, J. Dunlosky, & A. C. Graesser (Eds.), *Metacognition in educational theory and practice* (pp. 47–68). Mahwah, NJ: Erlbaum.

Davidson, P., Turiel, E., & Black, A. (1983). The effect of stimulus familiarity on the use of criteria and justifications in children's social reasoning. *British Journal of Developmental Psychology, 1,* 49–65.

Davis, G. A., & Rimm, S. B. (1998). Smart problem solving: How metacognition helps. In D. J. Hacker, J. Dunlosky, & A. C. Graesser (Eds.), *Metacognition in educational theory and practice* (pp. 47–68). Mahwah, NJ: Erlbaum.

Davis, G. A., & Thomas, M. A. (1989). *Effective schools and effective teachers.* Needham Heights, MA: Allyn & Bacon.

Deaux, K. (1984). From individual differences to social categories: Analysis of a decade's research on gender. *American Psychologist, 39,* 105–116.

deCharms, R. (1972). Personal causation training in the schools. *Journal of Applied Social Psychology, 2,* 95–113.

Deci, E. L. (1992). The relation of interest to the motivation of behavior: A self-determination theory perspective. In K. A. Renninger, S. Hidi, & A. Krapp (Eds.), *The role of interest in learning and development.* Hillsdale, NJ: Erlbaum.

Deci, E. L. (1998). The relation of interest to motivation and human needs: The self-determination theory viewpoint. In L. Hoffman, A. Krapp, K. Renninger, & J. Baumert (Eds.), *Interest and learning: Proceedings of the Seeon Conference on interest and gender* (pp. 146–163). Keil, Germany: IPN.

Deci, E. L., Koestner, R., & Ryan, R. M. (1999). A meta-analytic review of experiments examining the effects of extrinsic rewards on intrinsic motivation. *Psychological Bulletin, 125,* 627–688.

Deci, E. L., & Ryan, R. M. (1985). *Intrinsic motivation and self-determination in human behavior.* New York: Plenum Press.

Deci, E. L., & Ryan, R. M. (1992). The initiation and regulation of intrinsically motivated learning and achievement. In A. K. Boggiano & T. S. Pittman (Eds.), *Achievement and motivation: A social-developmental perspective.* Cambridge, England: Cambridge University Press.

Deci, E. L., & Ryan, R. M. (1995). Human autonomy: The basis for true self-esteem. In M. H. Kernis (Ed.), *Efficacy, agency, and self-esteem.* New York: Plenum Press.

De Corte, E., Greer, B., & Verschaffel, L. (1996). Mathematics teaching and learning. In D. C. Berliner & R. C. Calfee (Eds.), *Handbook of educational psychology.* New York: Macmillan.

DeGrandpre, R. J. (2000). A science of meaning: Can behaviorism bring meaning to psychological science? *American Psychologist, 55,* 721–739.

de Jong, T., & van Joolingen, W. R. (1998). Scientific discovery learning with computer simulations of conceptual domains. *Review of Educational Research, 68,* 179–201.

Delandshere, G., & Petrosky, A. R. (1998). Assessment of complex performances: Limitations of key measurement assumptions. *Educational Researcher, 27,* 14–24.

Delgado-Gaitan, C. (1994). Socializing young children in Mexican-American families: An intergenerational perspective. In P. M. Greenfield & R. R. Cocking (Eds.), *Cross-cultural roots of minority child development.* Hillsdale, NJ: Erlbaum.

De Lisi, R., & Golbeck, S. L. (1999). Implications of Piagetian theory for peer learning. In A. M. O'Donnell & A. King (Eds.), *Cognitive perspectives on peer learning* (pp. 3–37). Mahwah, NJ: Erlbaum.

DeLoache, J. S., & Todd, C. M. (1988). Young children's use of spatial categorization as a mnemonic strategy. *Journal of Experimental Child Psychology, 46,* 1–20.

DeMarie-Dreblow, D., & Miller, P. H. (1988). The development of children's strategies for selective attention: Evidence for a transitional period. *Child Development, 59,* 1504–1513.

Dempster, F. N. (1985). Proactive interference in sentence recall: Topic-similarity effects and individual differences. *Memory and Cognition, 13,* 81–89.

Dempster, F. N. (1991). Synthesis of research on reviews and tests. *Educational Leadership, 48*(7), 71–76.

Dempster, F. N., & Corkill, A. J. (1999). Interference and inhibition in cognition and behavior: Unifying themes for educational psychology. *Educational Psychology Review, 11,* 1–88.

Derevensky, J. L., & Leckerman, R. (1997). Teachers' differential use of praise and reinforcement practices. *Canadian Journal of School Psychology, 13,* 15–27.

DeRidder, L. M. (1993). Teenage pregnancy: Etiology and educational interventions. *Educational Psychology Review, 5,* 87–107.

Derry, S. J. (1996). Cognitive schema theory in the constructivist debate. *Educational Psychologist, 31,* 163–174.

Derry, S. J., Levin, J. R., Osana, H. P., & Jones, M. S. (1998). Developing middle school students' statistical reasoning abilities through simulation gaming. In S. P. Lajoie (Ed.), *Reflections on statistics: Learning, teaching, and assessment in grades K-12* (pp. 175–195). Mahwah, NJ: Erlbaum.

Desberg, P., & Taylor, J. H. (1986). *Essentials of task analysis.* Lanham, MD: University Press of America.

Deshler, D. D., Alley, G. R., & Carlson, S. A. (1980). Learning strategies: An approach to mainstreaming secondary students with learning disabilities. *Education Unlimited, 2*(4), 6–11.

Deshler, D. D., & Schumaker, J. B. (1988). An instructional model for teaching students how to learn. In J. L. Graden, J. E. Zins, & M. J. Curtis (Eds.), *Alternative educational delivery systems: Enhancing instructional options for all students.* Washington, DC: National Association of School Psychologists.

Deshler, D. D., Warner, M. M., Schumaker, J. B., & Alley, G. R. (1983). Learning strategies intervention model: Key components and current status. In J. McKinney & L. Feagans (Eds.), *Current topics in learning disabilities* (Vol. 1). Norwood, NJ: Ablex.

Deutsch, M. (1993). Educating for a peaceful world. *American Psychologist, 48,* 510–517.

DeVries, R. (1997). Piaget's social theory. *Educational Researcher, 26*(2), 4–17.

DeVries, R., & Zan, B. (1996). A constructivist perspective on the role of the sociomoral atmosphere in promoting children's development. In C. T. Fosnot (Ed.), *Constructivism: Theory, perspectives, and practice.* New York: Teachers College Press.

Dewhurst, S. A., & Conway, M. A. (1994). Pictures, images, and recollective experience. *Journal of Experimental Psychology: Learning, Memory, and Cognition, 20,* 1088–1098.

Diamond, S. C. (1991). What to do when you can't do anything: Working with disturbed adolescents. *Clearing House, 64,* 232–234.

Diaz, R. M. (1983). Thought and two languages: The impact of bilingualism on cognitive development. In E. W. Gordon (Ed.), *Review of research in education* (Vol. 10). Washington, DC: American Educational Research Association.

Diaz, R. M., & Berk, L. E. (1995). A Vygotskian critique of self-instructional training. *Development and Psychopathology, 7,* 369–392.

Diaz, R. M., & Klingler, C. (1991). Toward an explanatory model of the interaction between bilingualism and cognitive development. In E. Bialystok (Ed.), *Language processing in bilingual children.* Cambridge, England: Cambridge University Press.

Dien, T. (1998). Language and literacy in Vietnamese American communities. In B. Pérez (Ed.), *Sociocultural contexts of language and literacy.* Mahwah, NJ: Erlbaum.

diSessa, A. A. (1982). Unlearning Aristotelian physics: A study of knowledge-based learning. *Cognitive Science, 6,* 37–75.

diSessa, A. A. (1996). What do "just plain folk" know about physics? In D. R. Olson & N. Torrance (Eds.), *The handbook of education and human development: New models of learning, teaching, and schooling.* Cambridge, MA: Blackwell.

Dishion, T. J., McCord, J., & Poulin, F. (1999). When interventions harm: Peer groups and problem behavior. *American Psychologist, 54,* 755–764.

Dishion, T. J., Spracklen, K. M., Andrews, D. W., & Patterson, G. R. (1996). Deviancy training in male adolescents' friendships. *Behavior Therapy, 27,* 373–390.

Di Vesta, F. J., & Gray, S. G. (1972). Listening and notetaking. *Journal of Educational Psychology, 63,* 8–14.

Di Vesta, F. J., & Peverly, S. T. (1984). The effects of encoding variability, processing activity and rule example sequences on the transfer of conceptual rules. *Journal of Educational Psychology, 76,* 108–119.

Di Vesta, F. J., & Smith, D. A. (1979). The pausing principle: Increasing the efficiency of memory for ongoing events. *Contemporary Educational Psychology, 4,* 288–296.

Doescher, S. M., & Sugawara, A. I. (1989). Encouraging prosocial behavior in young children. *Childhood Education, 65,* 213–216.

Dole, J. A., Duffy, G. G., Roehler, L. R., & Pearson, P. D. (1991). Moving from the old to the new: Research on reading comprehension instruction. *Review of Educational Research, 61,* 239–264.

Dominowski, R. L. (1998). Verbalization and problem solving. In D. J. Hacker, J. Dunlosky, & A. C. Graesser (Eds.), *Metacognition in educational theory and practice* (pp. 25–45). Mahwah, NJ: Erlbaum.

Donnelly, C. M., & McDaniel, M. A. (1993). Use of analogy in learning scientific concepts. *Journal of Experimental Psychology: Learning, Memory, and Cognition, 19,* 975–987.

Dovidio, J. F., & Gaertner, S. L. (1999). Reducing prejudice: Combating intergroup biases. *Current Directions in Psychological Science, 8,* 101–105.

Downey, G., Bonica, C., & Rincón, C. (1999). Rejection sensitivity and adolescent romantic relationships. In W. Furman, B. B. Brown, & C. Feiring (Eds.), *The development of romantic relationships in adolescence* (pp. 148–174). Cambridge, England: Cambridge University Press.

Dowrick, P. W. (2000). Creating futures through video self-modelling behavioral interventions: Social and academic development in challenging behaviors and autism. *Journal of Intellectual Disability Research, 44,* 310.

Dowson, M., & McInerney, D. M. (2001). Psychological parameters of students' social and work avoidance goals: A qualitative investigation. *Journal of Educational Psychology, 93,* 35–42.

Doyle, A. (1982). Friends, acquaintances, and strangers: The influence of familiarity and ethnolinguistic backgrounds on social interaction. In K. Rubin & H. Ross (Eds.), *Peer relationships and social skills in childhood.* New York: Springer-Verlag.

Doyle, W. (1983). Academic work. *Review of Educational Research, 53,* 159–199.

Doyle, W. (1984). How order is achieved in classrooms: An interim report. *Journal of Curriculum Studies, 16,* 259–277.

Doyle, W. (1986a). Classroom organization and management. In M. C. Wittrock (Ed.), *Handbook of research on teaching* (3rd ed.). New York: Macmillan.

Doyle, W. (1986b). Content representation in teachers' definitions of academic work. *Journal of Curriculum Studies, 18,* 365–379.

Doyle, W. (1990). Classroom management techniques. In O. C. Moles (Ed.), *Student discipline strategies: Research and practice.* Albany: State University of New York Press.

Drake, D. D. (1993). Student diversity: Implications for classroom teachers. *The Clearing House, 66,* 264–266.

Dreikurs, R. (1998). *Maintaining sanity in the classroom: Classroom management techniques* (2nd ed.). Bristol, PA: Hemisphere.

Drevno, G. E., Kimball, J. W., Possi, M. K., Heward, W. L., Gardner, R., III, & Barbetta, P. M. (1994). Effects of active student responding during error correction on the acquisition, maintenance, and generalization of science vocabulary by elementary students: A systematic replication. *Journal of Applied Behavior Analysis, 27,* 179–180.

Driver, R. (1995). Constructivist approaches to science teaching. In L. P. Steffe & J. Gale (Eds.), *Constructivism in education.* Hillsdale, NJ: Erlbaum.

Driver, R., Asoko, H., Leach, J., Mortimer, E., & Scott, P. (1994). Constructing scientific knowledge in the classroom. *Educational Researcher, 23*(7), 5–12.

DuBois, N. F., Kiewra, K. A., & Fraley, J. (1988, April). *Differential effects of a learning strategy course.* Paper presented at the annual meeting of the American Educational Research Association, New Orleans, LA.

Duchardt, B. A., Deshler, D. D., & Schumaker, J. B. (1995). A strategy intervention for enabling students with learning disabilities to identify and change their ineffective beliefs. *Learning Disability Quarterly, 18,* 186–201.

Duit, R. (1991). Students' conceptual frameworks: Consequences for learning science. In S. M. Glynn, R. H. Yeany, & B. K. Britton (Eds.), *The psychology of learning science.* Hillsdale, NJ: Erlbaum.

Dukacz, A., & McCarthy, A. (1995). School Councils: Making them work. Toronto: Catholic Principals' Council of Ontario.

DuNann, D. G., & Weber, S. J. (1976). Short- and long-term effects of contingency managed instruction on low, medium, and high GPA students. *Journal of Applied Behavior Analysis, 9,* 375–376.

Duncker, K. (1945). On problem solving. *Psychological Monographs, 58,* (Whole No. 270).

Dunlap, G., dePerczel, M., Clarke, S., Wilson, D., Wright, S., White, R., & Gomez, A. (1994). Choice making to promote adaptive behavior for students with emotional and behavioral challenges. *Journal of Applied Behavior Analysis, 27,* 505–518.

DuPaul, G. J., Barkley, R. A., & Connor, D. F. (1998). Stimulants. In R. A. Barkley, *Attention-deficit hyperactivity disorder: A handbook for diagnosis and treatment* (2nd ed., pp. 510–551). New York: Guilford Press.

DuPaul, G. J., & Eckert, T. L. (1994). The effects of social skills curricula: Now you see them, now you don't. *School Psychology Quarterly, 9,* 113–132.

DuPaul, G. J., Ervin, R. A., Hook, C. L., & McGoey, K. E. (1998). Peer tutoring for children with attention deficit hyperactivity disorder: Effects on classroom behavior and academic performance. *Journal of Applied Behavior Analysis, 31,* 579–592.

Durkin, K. (1987). Social cognition and social context in the construction of sex differences. In M. A. Baker (Ed.), *Sex differences in human performance.* Chichester, England: Wiley.

Durkin, K. (1995). *Developmental social psychology: From infancy to old age.* Cambridge, MA: Blackwell.

Dweck, C. S. (1975). The role of expectations and attributions in the alleviation of learned helplessness. *Journal of Personality and Social Psychology, 31,* 674–685.

Dweck, C. S. (1978). Achievement. In M. E. Lamb (Ed.), *Social and personality development.* New York: Holt, Rinehart & Winston.

Dweck, C. S. (1986). Motivational processes affecting learning. *American Psychologist, 41,* 1040–1048.

Dweck, C. S. (1999). *Self-theories: Their role in motivation, personality, and development.* Philadelphia: Taylor & Francis.

Dweck, C. S., & Elliott, E. S. (1983). Achievement motivation. In E. M. Hetherington (Ed.), *Handbook of child psychology: Vol. 4. Socialization, personality, and social development* (4th ed.). New York: Wiley.

Dweck, C. S., & Leggett, E. L. (1988). A social-cognitive approach to motivation and personality. *Psychological Review, 95,* 256–273.

D'Ydewalle, G., Swerts, A., & De Corte, E. (1983). Study time and test performance as a function of test expectations. *Contemporary Educational Psychology, 8*(1), 55–67.

Eaton, J. F., Anderson, C. W., & Smith, E. L. (1984). Students' misconceptions interfere with science learning: Case studies of fifth-grade students. *Elementary School Journal, 84,* 365–379.

Eaton, W. O., & Enns, L. R. (1986). Sex differences in human motor activity level. *Psychological Bulletin, 100,* 19–28.

Eccles, J. S. (1989). Bringing young women to math and science. In M. Crawford & M. Gentry (Eds.), *Gender and thought: Psychological perspectives.* New York: Springer-Verlag.

Eccles, J. S., & Jacobs, J. E. (1986). Social forces shape math attitudes and performance. *Signs: Journal of Women in Culture and Society, 11,* 367–380.

Eccles, J. S., Jacobs, J., Harold-Goldsmith, R., Jayaratne, T., & Yee, D. (1989, April). *The relations between parents' category-based and target-based beliefs: Gender roles and biological influences.* Paper presented at the Society for Research in Child Development, Kansas City, MO.

Eccles, J. S., & Midgley, C. (1989). Stage-environment fit: Developmentally appropriate classrooms for young adolescents. In C. Ames & R. Ames (Eds.), *Research on motivation in education: Vol. 3. Goals and cognition.* San Diego, CA: Academic Press.

Eccles, J. S., & Wigfield, A. (1985). Teacher expectations and student motivation. In J. B. Dusek (Ed.), *Teacher expectancies.* Hillsdale, NJ: Erlbaum.

Eccles, J. S., Wigfield, A., Flanagan, C., Miller, C., Reuman, D., & Yee, D. (1989). Self-concepts, domain values, and self-esteem: Relations and changes at early adolescence. *Journal of Personality, 57,* 283–310.

Eccles, J. S., Wigfield, A., & Schiefele, U. (1998). Motivation to succeed. In W. Damon (Editor-in-Chief) & N. Eisenberg (Vol. Ed.), *Handbook of child psychology: Vol. 3. Social, emotional, and personality development* (5th ed.). New York: Wiley.

Eccles (Parsons), J. S. (1983). Expectancies, values, and academic behaviors. In J. T. Spence (Ed.), *Achievement and achievement motivation.* San Francisco: Freeman.

Eccles (Parsons), J. S. (1984). Sex differences in mathematics participation. In M. Steinkamp & M. Maehr (Eds.), *Women in science.* Greenwich, CT: JAI Press.

Eckert, P. (1989). *Jocks and burnouts: Social categories and identity in the high school.* New York: Teachers College Press.

Edens, K. M., & Potter, E. F. (2001). Promoting conceptual understanding through pictorial representation. *Studies in Art Education, 42,* 214–233.

Eeds, M., & Wells, D. (1989). Grand conversations: An explanation of meaning construction in literature study groups. *Research in the Teaching of English, 23,* 4–29.

Eisenberg, N. (1982). The development of reasoning regarding prosocial behavior. In N. Eisenberg (Ed.), *The development of prosocial behavior.* San Diego, CA: Academic Press.

Eisenberg, N. (1987). The relation of altruism and other moral behaviors to moral cognition: Methodological and conceptual issues. In N. Eisenberg (Ed.), *Contemporary topics in developmental psychology* (pp. 165–189). New York: Wiley.

Eisenberg, N., Carlo, G., Murphy, B., & Van Court, N. (1995). Prosocial development in late adolescence: A longitudinal study. *Child Development, 66,* 1179–1197.

Eisenberg, N., & Fabes, R. A. (1991). Prosocial behavior: A multimethod developmental perspective. In M. S. Clark (Ed.), *Review of personality and social psychology* (Vol. 2, pp. 34–61). Newbury Park, CA: Sage.

Eisenberg, N., Lennon, R., & Pasternack, J. F. (1986). Altruistic values and moral judgment. In N. Eisenberg (Ed.), *Altruistic emotion, cognition, and behavior.* Hillsdale, NJ: Erlbaum.

Eisenberg, N., Martin, C. L., & Fabes, R. A. (1996). Gender development and gender effects. In D. C. Berliner & R. C. Calfee (Eds.), *Handbook of educational psychology.* New York: Macmillan.

Eisenberg, N., Miller, P. A., Shell, R., McNalley, S., & Shea, C. (1991). Prosocial development in adolescence: A longitudinal study. *Developmental Psychology, 27,* 849–857.

Eisenberger, R. (1992). Learned industriousness. *Psychological Review, 99,* 248–267.

Elder-Hinshaw, R., Manset-Williamson, G., Nelson, J. M., & Dunn, M. W. (2006). Engaging older students with reading disabilities: Multimedia inquiry projects supported by reading assistive technology. *Teaching Exceptional Children, 39*(1), 6–11.

Elia, J. P. (1994). Homophobia in the high school: A problem in need of a resolution. *Journal of Homosexuality, 77*(1), 177–185.

Elkind, D. (1981). *Children and adolescents: Interpretive essays on Jean Piaget* (3rd ed.). New York: Oxford University Press.

Elkind, D. (1984). *All grown up and no place to go.* Reading, MA: Addison-Wesley.

Elliot, A. J., & McGregor, H. A. (2000, April). Approach and avoidance goals and autonomous-controlled regulation: Empirical and conceptual relations. In A. Assor (Chair), *Self-determination theory and achievement goal theory: Convergences, divergences, and educational implications.* Symposium conducted at the annual meeting of the American Educational Research Association, New Orleans, LA.

Elliot, A. J., & Thrash, T. M. (2001). Achievement goals and the hierarchical model of achievement motivation. *Educational Psychology Review, 13,* 139–156.

Elliott, R., & Vasta, R. (1970). The modeling of sharing: Effects associated with vicarious reinforcement, symbolization, age, and generalization. *Journal of Experimental Child Psychology, 10,* 8–15.

Elliott, S. N., & Busse, R. T. (1991). Social skills assessment and intervention with children and adolescents. *School Psychology International, 12,* 63–83.

Ellis, E. S., & Friend, P. (1991). Adolescents with learning disabilities. In B. Y. L. Wong (Ed.), *Learning about learning disabilities.* San Diego, CA: Academic Press.

Ellis, N. R. (Ed.). (1979). *Handbook of mental deficiency: Psychological theory and research.* Hillsdale, NJ: Erlbaum.

Emmer, E. T. (1987). Classroom management and discipline. In V. Richardson-Koehler (Ed.), *Educators' handbook: A research perspective.* White Plains, NY: Longman.

Emmer, E. T., & Evertson, C. M. (1981). Synthesis of research on classroom management. *Educational Leadership, 38,* 342–347.

Emmer, E. T., Evertson, C. M., Clements, B. S., & Worsham, M. E. (1994). *Classroom management for secondary teachers* (3rd ed.). Needham Heights, MA: Allyn & Bacon.

Emmer, E. T., & Stough, L. M. (2001). Classroom management: A critical part of educational psychology, with implications for teacher education. *Educational Psychologist, 36,* 103–112.

Empson, S. B. (1999). Equal sharing and shared meaning: The development of fraction concepts in a first-grade classroom. *Cognition and Instruction, 17,* 283–342.

Englemann, S., & Carnine, D. (1982). *Theory of instruction: Principles and applications.* New York: Irvington.

Epstein, J. L. (1983). Longitudinal effects of family-school-person interactions on student outcomes. *Research in Sociology of Education and Socialization, 4,* 101–127.

Epstein, J. L. (1986). Friendship selection: Developmental and environmental influences. In E. Mueller & C. Cooper (Eds.), *Process and outcome in peer relationships* (pp. 129–160). New York: Academic Press.

Epstein, J. L. (1996). Perspectives and previews on research and policy for school, family, and community partnerships. In A. Booth & J. F. Dunn (Eds.), *Family-school links: How do they affect educational outcomes?* Mahwah, NJ: Erlbaum.

Epstein, J. S. (1998). Introduction: Generation X, youth culture, and identity. In J. S. Epstein (Ed.), *Youth culture: Identity in a postmodern world.* Malden, MA: Blackwell.

Epstein, R. (1993). Generativity theory and education. *Educational Technology, 33*(10), 40–45.

Ericsson, K. A., & Chalmers, N. (1994). Expert performance: Its structure and acquisition. *American Psychologist, 49,* 725–747.

Eriks-Brophy, A., & Crago, M. B. (1994). Transforming classroom discourse: An Inuit example. *Language and Education, 8*(3), 105–122.

Erwin, P. (1993). *Friendship and peer relations in children.* Chichester, England: Wiley.

Esquivel, G. B. (1995). Teacher behaviors that foster creativity. *Educational Psychology Review, 7,* 185–202.

Etaugh, C. (1983). Introduction: The influence of environmental factors on sex differences in children's play. In M. B. Liss (Ed.), *Social and cognitive skills: Sex roles and children's play.* San Diego, CA: Academic Press.

Evans, E. D., & Craig, D. (1990). Teacher and student perceptions of academic cheating in middle and senior high schools. *Journal of Educational Research, 84*(1), 44–52.

Evertson, C. M., & Emmer, E. T. (1982). Effective management at the beginning of the year in junior high classes. *Journal of Educational Psychology, 74,* 485–498.

Evertson, C. M., & Harris, A. H. (1992). What we know about managing classrooms. *Educational Leadership, 49*(7), 74–78.

Eysenck, M. W. (1992). *Anxiety: The cognitive perspective.* Hove, England: Erlbaum.

Eysenck, M. W., & Keane, M. T. (1990). *Cognitive psychology: A student's handbook.* Hove, England: Erlbaum.

Fabes, R. A., Eisenberg, N., Jones, S., Smith, M., Guthrie, I., Poulin, R., Shepard, S., & Friedman, J. (1999). Regulation, emotionality, and preschoolers' socially competent peer interactions. *Child Development, 70,* 432–442.

Fabos, B., & Young, M. D. (1999). Telecommunication in the classroom: Rhetoric versus reality. *Review of Educational Research, 69,* 217–259.

Fagot, B. I., Hagan, R., Leinbach, M. D., & Kronsberg, S. (1985). Differential reactions to assertive and communicative acts of toddler boys and girls. *Child Development, 56,* 1499–1505.

Fagot, B. I., & Leinbach, M. D. (1983). Play styles in early childhood: Social consequences for boys and girls. In M. B. Liss (Ed.), *Social and cognitive skills: Sex roles and children's play.* San Diego, CA: Academic Press.

Fairchild, H. H., & Edwards-Evans, S. (1990). African American dialects and schooling: A review. In A. M. Padilla, H. H. Fairchild, & C. M. Valadez (Eds.), *Bilingual education: Issues and strategies.* Newbury Park, CA: Sage.

Fall, R., Webb, N. M., & Chudowsky, N. (2000). Group discussion and large-scale language arts assessment: Effects on students' comprehension. *American Educational Research Journal, 37,* 911–941.

Fantuzzo, J. W., King, J., & Heller, L. R. (1992). Effects of reciprocal peer tutoring on mathematics and school adjustment: A component analysis. *Journal of Educational Psychology, 84,* 331–339.

Farwell, L., & Weiner, B. (1996). Self-perception of fairness in individual and group contexts. *Personality and Social Psychology Bulletin, 22,* 867–881.

Feather, N. T. (1982). *Expectations and actions: Expectancy-value models in psychology.* Hillsdale, NJ: Erlbaum.

Feld, S., Ruhland, D., & Gold, M. (1979). Developmental changes in achievement motivation. *Merrill-Palmer Quarterly, 25,* 43–60.

Feldhusen, J. F., & Treffinger, D. J. (1980). *Creative thinking and problem solving in gifted education.* Dubuque, IA: Kendall/Hunt.

Feldhusen, J. F., Treffinger, D. J., & Bahlke, S. J. (1970). Developing creative thinking: The Purdue Creativity Program. *Journal of Creative Behavior, 4,* 85–90.

Feltz, D. L., Chaase, M. A., Moritz, S. E., & Sullivan, P. J. (1999). A conceptual model of coaching efficacy: Preliminary investigation and instrument development. *Journal of Educational Psychology, 91,* 765–776.

Fennema, E. (1987). Sex-related differences in education: Myths, realities, and interventions. In V. Richardson-Koehler (Ed.), *Educators' handbook: A research perspective.* White Plains, NY: Longman.

Ferguson, E. L., & Hegarty, M. (1995). Learning with real machines or diagrams: Application of knowledge to real-world problems. *Cognition and Instruction, 13,* 129–160.

Ferguson, J. M., & Dorman, J. P. (2001). Psychosocial classroom environment and academic efficacy in Canadian high school mathematics classes. *The Alberta Journal of Educational Research, 47*(3), 276–279.

Feuerstein, R. (1979). *The dynamic assessment of retarded performers: The Learning Potential Assessment Device, theory, instruments, and techniques.* Baltimore: University Park Press.

Feuerstein, R., Feuerstein, R., & Gross, S. (1997). The Learning Potential Assessment Device. In D. P. Flanagan, J. L. Genshaft, & P. L. Harrison (Eds.), *Contemporary intellectual assessment: Theories, tests, and issues* (pp. 297–313). New York: Guilford Press.

Fiedler, E. D., Lange, R. E., & Winebrenner, S. (1993). In search of reality: Unraveling the myths about tracking, ability grouping and the gifted. *Roeper Review, 16*(1), 4–7.

Finders, M., & Lewis, C. (1994). Why some parents don't come to school. *Educational Leadership, 51*(8), 50–54.

Finn, J. D. (1989). Withdrawing from school. *Review of Educational Research, 59,* 117–142.

Finn, J. D. (1991). How to make the dropout problem go away. *Educational Researcher, 20*(1), 28–30.

Fischer, K. W., & Bidell, T. (1991). Constraining nativist inferences about cognitive capacities. In S. Carey & R. Gelman (Eds.), *The epigenesis of mind: Essays on biology and cognition.* Hillsdale, NJ: Erlbaum.

Fisher, W. W., & Mazur, J. E. (1997). Basic and applied research on choice responding. *Journal of Applied Behavior Analysis, 30,* 387–410.

Fivush, R., Haden, C., & Adam, S. (1995). Structure and coherence of preschoolers' personal narratives over time: Implications for childhood amnesia. *Journal of Experimental Child Psychology, 60,* 32–56.

Flavell, J. H. (1994). Cognitive development: Past, present, and future. In R. D. Parke, P. A. Ornstein, J. J. Rieser, & C. Zahn-Waxler (Eds.), *A century of developmental psychology.* Washington, DC: American Psychological Association.

Flavell, J. H. (1996). Piaget's legacy. *Psychological Science, 7,* 200–203.

Flavell, J. H., Friedrichs, A. G., & Hoyt, J. D. (1970). Developmental changes in memorization processes. *Cognitive Psychology, 1,* 324–340.

Flavell, J. H., Miller, P. H., & Miller, S. A. (1993). *Cognitive development* (3rd ed.). Upper Saddle River, NJ: Prentice Hall.

Flieller, A. (1999). Comparison of the development of formal thought in adolescent cohorts aged 10 to 15 years (1967–1996 and 1972–1993). *Developmental Psychology, 35,* 1048–1058.

Flora, S. R. (2004). *The power of reinforcement.* Albany: State University of New York Press.

Flynn, J. R. (2007). *What is intelligence? Beyond the Flynn effect.* Cambridge, England: Cambridge University Press.

Foos, P. W., & Fisher, R. P. (1988). Using tests as learning opportunities. *Journal of Educational Psychology, 80,* 179–183.

Ford, D. Y., & Harris, J. J. (1992). The American achievement ideology and achievement differentials among preadolescent gifted and nongifted African American males and females. *Journal of Negro Education, 61*(1), 45–64.

Ford, M. E. (1992). *Motivating humans: Goals, emotions, and personal agency beliefs.* Newbury Park, CA: Sage.

Ford, M. E. (1996). Motivational opportunities and obstacles associated with social responsibility and caring behavior in school contexts. In J. Juvonen & K. R. Wentzel (Eds.), *Social motivation: Understanding children's school adjustment* (pp. 126–153). Cambridge, England: Cambridge University Press.

Fordham, S., & Ogbu, J. U. (1986). Black students' school success: Coping with "the burden of 'acting white.'" *The Urban Review, 18,* 176–206.

Forsyth, J. P., & Eifert, G. H. (1998). Phobic anxiety and panic: An integrative behavioral account of their origin and treatment. In J. J. Plaud & G. H. Eifert (Eds.), *From behavior theory to behavior therapy* (pp. 38–67). Needham Heights, MA: Allyn & Bacon.

Fosnot, C. T. (1996). Constructivism: A psychological theory of learning. In C. T. Fosnot (Ed.), *Constructivism: Theory, perspectives, and practice.* New York: Teachers College Press.

Foster-Johnson, L., Ferro, J., & Dunlap, G. (1994). Preferred curriculum activities and reduced problem behaviors in students with intellectual disabilities. *Journal of Applied Behavior Analysis, 27,* 493–504.

Fowler, S. A., & Baer, D. M. (1981). "Do I have to be good all day?" The timing of delayed reinforcement as a factor in generalization. *Journal of Applied Behavior Analysis, 14,* 13–24.

Fox, L. H. (1981). *The problem of women and mathematics.* New York: Ford Foundation.

Fox, P. W., & LeCount, J. (1991, April). *When more is less: Faculty misestimation of student learning.* Paper presented at the annual meeting of the American Educational Research Association, Chicago.

Frasier, M. M. (1989). Identification of gifted black students: Developing new perspectives. In C. J. Maker & S. W. Schiever (Eds.), *Critical issues in gifted education: Vol. 2. Defensible programs for cultural and ethnic minorities.* Austin, TX: Pro-Ed.

Frater-Mathieson, K. (2004). Refugee, trauma, loss, and grief. In R. Hamilton & D. Moore (Eds.) *Educational interventions for refugee children: Theoretical perspectives and implementing best practice* (pp. 12–34). New York: Routledge.

Frederiksen, J. R., & Collins, A. (1989). A systems approach to educational testing. *Educational Researcher, 18*(9), 27–32.

Frederiksen, N. (1984a). Implications of cognitive theory for instruction in problem-solving. *Review of Educational Research, 54,* 363–407.

Frederiksen, N. (1984b). The real test bias: Influences of testing on teaching and learning. *American Psychologist, 39,* 193–202.

Freedman, K. (1996). The social reconstruction of art education: Teaching visual culture. In C. A. Grant & M. L. Gomez, *Making schooling multicultural: Campus and classroom.* Upper Saddle River, NJ: Merrill/Prentice Hall.

Freedman, S. G. (1990). *Small victories: The real world of a teacher, her students, and their high school.* New York: Harper & Row.

Freeland, J. T., & Noell, G. H. (1999). Maintaining accurate math responses in elementary school students: The effects of delayed intermittent reinforcement and programming common stimuli. *Journal of Applied Behavior Analysis, 32,* 211–215.

French, E. G. (1956). Motivation as a variable in work partner selection. *Journal of Abnormal and Social Psychology, 53,* 96–99.

Friedel, M. (1993). *Characteristics of gifted/creative children.* Warwick, RI: National Foundation for Gifted and Creative Children.

Frisbie, D. A., & Waltman, K. K. (1992). Developing a personal grading plan. *Educational Measurement: Issues and Practices, 11,* 35–42. Reprinted in K. M. Cauley, F. Linder, & J. H. McMillan (Eds.), (1994), *Educational psychology 94/95.* Guilford, CT: Dushkin.

Frost, J. L., Shin, D., & Jacobs, P. J. (1998). Physical environments and children's play. In O. N. Saracho & B. Spodek (Eds.), *Multiple perspectives on play in early childhood education.* Albany: State University of New York Press.

Fuchs, D., Fuchs, L. S., Mathes, P. G., & Simmons, D. C. (1997). Peer-assisted learning strategies: Making classrooms more responsive to diversity. *American Educational Research Journal, 34,* 174–206.

Fuchs, L. S., Fuchs, D., Karns, K., Hamlett, C. L., Dutka, S., & Katzaroff, M. (1996). The relation between student ability and the quality and effectiveness of explanations. *American Educational Research Journal, 33,* 631–664.

Fuller, M. L. (2001). Multicultural concerns and classroom management. In C. A. Grant & M. L. Gomez, *Campus and classroom: Making schooling multicultural* (2nd ed., pp. 109–134). Upper Saddle River, NJ: Merrill/Prentice Hall.

Furman, W., & Simon, V. A. (1999). Cognitive representations of adolescent romantic relationships. In W. Furman, B. B. Brown, & C. Feiring (Eds.), *The development of romantic relationships in adolescence* (pp. 75–98). Cambridge, England: Cambridge University Press.

Gage, N. L. (1991). The obviousness of social and educational research results. *Educational Researcher, 20*(1), 10–16.

Gagné, E. D. (1985). *The cognitive psychology of school learning.* Boston: Little, Brown.

Gagné, R. M. (1985). *The conditions of learning and theory of instruction* (4th ed.). New York: Holt, Rinehart & Winston.

Gaines, M. L., & Davis, M. (1990, April). *Accuracy of teacher prediction of elementary student achievement.* Paper presented at the annual meeting of the American Educational Research Association, Boston.

Gajdamaschko, N. (2005). Vygotsky on imagination: Why an understanding of the imagination is an important issue for schoolteachers. *Teaching Education, 16,* 13–22.

Gallimore, R., & Tharp, R. (1990). Teaching mind in society: Teaching, schooling, and literate discourse. In L. C. Moll (Ed.), *Vygotsky and education: Instructional implications and applications of sociohistorical psychology.* Cambridge, England: Cambridge University Press.

Gallini, J. (2000, April). *An investigation of self-regulation developments in early adolescence: A comparison between non at-risk and at-risk students.* Paper presented at the annual meeting of the American Educational Research Association, New Orleans, LA.

García, E. E. (1992). "Hispanic" children: Theoretical, empirical, and related policy issues. *Educational Psychology Review, 4,* 69–93.

García, E. E. (1994). *Understanding and meeting the challenge of student cultural diversity.* Boston: Houghton Mifflin.

García, E. E. (1995). Educating Mexican American students: Past treatment and recent developments in theory, research, policy, and practice. In J. A. Banks & C. A. M. Banks (Eds.), *Handbook of research on multicultural education.* New York: Macmillan.

Gardner, H. (1983). *Frames of mind: The theory of multiple intelligences.* New York: Basic Books.

Gardner, H. (1995). Reflections on multiple intelligences: Myths and messages. *Phi Delta Kappan, 77,* 200–209.

Gardner, H. (1998, April). *Where to draw the line: The perils of new paradigms.* Paper presented at the annual meeting of the American Educational Research Association, San Diego, CA.

Gardner, H. (1999). *Intelligence reframed: Multiple intelligences for the 21st century.* New York: Basic Books.

Gardner, H. (2000). *The disciplined mind: Beyond facts and standardized tests, the K-12 education that every child deserves.* New York: Penguin Books.

Garibaldi, A. M. (1992). Educating and motivating African American males to succeed. *The Journal of Negro Education, 61*(1), 4–11.

Garibaldi, A. M. (1993). Creating prescriptions for success in urban schools: Turning the corner on pathological explanations for academic failure. In T. M. Tomlinson (Ed.), *Motivating students to learn: Overcoming barriers to high achievement.* Berkeley, CA: McCutchan.

Garner, R., Alexander, P. A., Gillingham, M. G., Kulikowich, J. M., & Brown, R. (1991). Interest and learning from text. *American Educational Research Journal, 28,* 643–659.

Garner, R., Brown, R., Sanders, S., & Menke, D. J. (1992). "Seductive details" and learning from text. In K. A. Renninger, S. Hidi, & A. Krapp (Eds.), *The role of interest in learning and development.* Hillsdale, NJ: Erlbaum.

Garnier, H. E., Stein, J. A., & Jacobs, J. K. (1997). The process of dropping out of high school: A 19-year perspective. *American Educational Research Journal, 34,* 395–419.

Gathercole, S. E., & Hitch, G. J. (1993). Developmental changes in short-term memory: A revised working memory perspective. In A. F. Collins, S. E. Gathercole, M. A. Conway, & P. E. Morris (Eds.), *Theories of memory.* Hove, England: Erlbaum.

Gaudry, E., & Bradshaw, G. D. (1971). The differential effect of anxiety on performance in progressive and terminal school examinations. In E. Gaudry & C. D. Spielberger (Eds.), *Anxiety and educational achievement.* Sydney, Australia: Wiley.

Gauntt, H. L. (1991, April). *The roles of prior knowledge of text structure and prior knowledge of content in the comprehension and recall of expository text.* Paper presented at the annual meeting of the American Educational Research Association, Chicago.

Gayford, C. (1992). Patterns of group behavior in open-ended problem solving in science classes of 15-year-old students in England. *International Journal of Science Education, 14,* 41–49.

Gaynor, J., & Millham, J. (1976). Student performance and evaluation under variant teaching and testing methods in a large college course. *Journal of Educational Psychology, 68,* 312–317.

Gearheart, B. R., Weishahn, M. W., & Gearheart, C. J. (1992). *The exceptional child in the regular classroom* (5th ed.). Upper Saddle River, NJ: Merrill/Prentice Hall.

Geary, D. C. (1998). What is the function of mind and brain? *Educational Psychology Review, 10,* 377–387.

Gelman, R., & Baillargeon, R. (1983). A review of some Piagetian concepts. In J. H. Flavell & E. M. Markman (Eds.), *Handbook of child psychology: Vol. 3. Cognitive development.* New York: Wiley.

Georgas, J., Weiss, L. G., van de Vijver, F. J. R., & Saklofske, D. H. (Eds.) (2003). *Culture and children's intelligence: Cross-cultural analysis of the WISC-III.* San Diego, CA: Academic Press.

Gerst, M. S. (1971). Symbolic coding processes in observational learning. *Journal of Personality and Social Psychology, 19,* 7–17.

Gettinger, M. (1988). Methods of proactive classroom management. *School Psychology Review, 17,* 227–242.

Giaconia, R. M. (1988). Teacher questioning and wait-time (Doctoral dissertation, Stanford University, 1988). *Dissertation Abstracts International, 49,* 462A.

Gick, M. L., & Holyoak, K. J. (1987). The cognitive basis of knowledge transfer. In S. M. Cormier & J. D. Hagman (Eds.), *Transfer of learning: Contemporary research and applications.* San Diego, CA: Academic Press.

Gillies, R. M., & Ashman, A. D. (1998). Behavior and interactions of children in cooperative groups in lower and middle elementary grades. *Journal of Educational Psychology, 90,* 746–757.

Gilligan, C. F. (1982). *In a different voice.* Cambridge, MA: Harvard University Press.

Gilligan, C. F. (1987). Moral orientation and moral development. In E. F. Kittay & D. T. Meyers (Eds.), *Women and moral theory.* Totowa, NJ: Rowman & Littlefield.

Gilligan, C., & Attanucci, J. (1988). Two moral orientations: Gender differences and similarities. *Merrill-Palmer Quarterly, 34,* 223–237.

Gilliland, H. (1988). Discovering and emphasizing the positive aspects of the culture. In H. Gilliland & J. Reyhner (Eds.), *Teaching the Native American.* Dubuque, IA: Kendall/Hunt.

Gillooly, W. B. (1973). The influence of writing-system characteristics on learning to read. *Reading Research Quarterly, 8,* 167–199.

Ginsberg, D., Gottman, J. M., & Parker, J. G. (1986). The importance of friendship. In J. M. Gottman & J. G. Parker (Eds.), *Conversations of friends: Speculations on affective development* (pp. 3–48). Cambridge, England: Cambridge University Press.

Girotto, V., & Light, P. (1993). The pragmatic bases of children's reasoning. In P. Light & G. Butterworth (Eds.), *Context and cognition: Ways of learning and knowing.* Hillsdale, NJ: Erlbaum.

Glanzer, M., & Nolan, S. D. (1986). Memory mechanisms in text comprehension. In G. H. Bower (Ed.), *The psychology of learning and motivation: Advances in research and theory* (Vol. 20). San Diego, CA: Academic Press.

Glasser, W. (1969). *Schools without failure.* New York: Harper & Row.

Glover, J. A. (1989). The "testing" phenomenon: Not gone but nearly forgotten. *Journal of Educational Psychology, 81,* 392–399.

Glover, J. A., Ronning, R. R., & Reynolds, C. R. (Eds.). (1989). *Handbook of creativity.* New York: Plenum Press.

Glucksberg, S., & Krauss, R. M. (1967). What do people say after they have learned to talk? Studies of the development of referential communication. *Merrill-Palmer Quarterly, 13,* 309–316.

Glynn, S. M., Yeany, R. H., & Britton, B. K. (1991). A constructive view of learning science. In S. M. Glynn, R. H. Yeany, & B. K. Britton (Eds.), *The psychology of learning science.* Hillsdale, NJ: Erlbaum.

Goddard, R. D. (2001). Collective efficacy: A neglected construct in the study of schools and student achievement. *Journal of Educational Psychology, 93,* 467–476.

Goddard, R. D., Hoy, W. K., & Woolfolk Hoy, A. (2000). Collective teacher efficacy: Its meaning, measure, and impact on student achievement. *American Educational Research Journal, 37,* 479–507.

Goldenberg, C. (1992). The limits of expectations: A case for case knowledge about teacher expectancy effects. *American Educational Research Journal, 29,* 517–544.

Good, T. L., & Brophy, J. E. (1994). *Looking in classrooms* (6th ed.). New York: HarperCollins.

Good, T. L., McCaslin, M. M., & Reys, B. J. (1992). Investigating work groups to promote problem solving in mathematics. In J. Brophy (Ed.), *Advances in research on teaching: Vol. 3. Planning and managing learning tasks and activities.* Greenwich, CT: JAI Press.

Good, T. L., & Nichols, S. L. (2001). Expectancy effects in the classroom: A special focus on improving the reading performance of minority students in first-grade classrooms. *Educational Psychologist, 36,* 113–126.

Goodenow, C. (1993). Classroom belonging among early adolescent students: Relationships to motivation and achievement. *Journal of Early Adolescence, 13,* 21–43.

Goodnow, J. J. (1992). *Parental belief systems: The psychological consequences for children.* Hillsdale, NJ: Erlbaum.

Gopnik, M. (1997). *The inheritance and innateness of grammars.* New York: Oxford University Press.

Gottardo, A., Collins, P., Baciu, I., & Gebotys, R. (2008). Predictors of grade 2 word reading and vocabulary learning from grade 1 variables in Spanish speaking children: Similarities and differences. *Learning Disabilities Research and Practice, 23,* 11–24.

Gottfredson, D. C. (2001). *Schools and delinquency.* Cambridge, England: Cambridge University Press.

Gottfredson, D. C., Fink, C. M., & Graham, N. (1994). Grade retention and problem behavior. *American Educational Research Journal, 31,* 761–784.

Gottfredson, G. D., & Gottfredson, D. C. (1985). *Victimization in schools.* New York: Plenum Press.

Gottfredson, L. S. (1981). Circumscription and compromise: A developmental theory of occupational aspirations. *Journal of Counseling Psychology Monograph, 28,* 545–579.

Gottfried, A. E. (1990). Academic intrinsic motivation in young elementary school children. *Journal of Educational Psychology, 82,* 525–538.

Gottfried, A. E., Fleming, J. S., & Gottfried, A. W. (1994). Role of parental motivational practices in children's academic intrinsic motivation and achievement. *Journal of Educational Psychology, 86,* 104–113.

Gottfried, A. W., Gottfried, A. E., Bathurst, K., & Guerin, D. W. (1994). *Gifted IQ: Early developmental aspects.* New York: Plenum Press.

Gottlieb, G. (2000). Environmental and behavioral influences on gene activity. *Current Directions in Psychological Science, 9,* 93–97.

Gottman, J. M. (1986). The world of coordinated play: Same- and cross-sex friendship in young children. In J. M. Gottman & J. G. Parker (Eds.), *Conversations of friends: Speculations on affective development* (pp. 139–191). Cambridge, England: Cambridge University Press.

Gottman, J. M., & Mettetal, G. (1986). Speculations about social and affective development: Friendship and acquaintanceship through adolescence. In J. M. Gottman & J. G. Parker (Eds.), *Conversations of friends: Speculations on affective development* (pp. 192–237). Cambridge, England: Cambridge University Press.

Grabe, M. (1986). Attentional processes in education. In G. D. Phye & T. Andre (Eds.), *Cognitive classroom learning: Understanding, thinking, and problem solving.* San Diego, CA: Academic Press.

Graesser, A., & Person, N. K. (1994). Question asking during tutoring. *American Educational Research Journal, 31,* 104–137.

Graham, S. (1989). Motivation in Afro-Americans. In G. L. Berry & J. K. Asamen (Eds.), *Black students: Psychosocial issues and academic achievement.* Newbury Park, CA: Sage.

Graham, S. (1990). Communicating low ability in the classroom: Bad things good teachers sometimes do. In S. Graham & V. S. Folkes (Eds.), *Attribution theory: Applications to achievement, mental health, and interpersonal conflict.* Hillsdale, NJ: Erlbaum.

Graham, S. (1991). A review of attribution theory in achievement contexts. *Educational Psychology Review, 3,* 5–39.

Graham, S. (1997). Using attribution theory to understand social and academic motivation in African American youth. *Educational Psychologist, 32,* 21–34.

Graham, S., & Golen, S. (1991). Motivational influences on cognition: Task involvement, ego involvement, and depth of information processing. *Journal of Educational Psychology, 83,* 187–194.

Graham, S., Harris, K. R., & Fink, B. (2000). Is handwriting causally related to learning to write? Treatment of handwriting problems in beginning writers. *Journal of Educational Psychology, 92,* 620–633.

Graham, S., & Hudley, C. (1994). Attributions of aggressive and nonaggressive African-American male early adolescents: A study of construct accessibility. *Developmental Psychology, 30,* 365–373.

Graham, S., & Weiner, B. (1996). Theories and principles of motivation. In D. C. Berliner & R. C. Calfee (Eds.), *Handbook of educational psychology.* New York: Macmillan.

Granger, D. A., Whalen, C. K., Henker, B., & Cantwell, C. (1996). ADHD boys' behavior during structured classroom social activities: Effects of social demands, teacher proximity, and methylphenidate. *Journal of Attention Disorders, 1*(1), 16–30.

Grant, C. A., & Gomez, M. L. (2001). *Campus and classroom: Making schooling multicultural* (2nd ed.). Upper Saddle River, NJ: Merrill/Prentice Hall.

Green, L., Fry, A. F., & Myerson, J. (1994). Discounting of delayed rewards: A life-span comparison. *Psychological Science, 5,* 33–36.

Greene, B. A. (1994, April). *Instruction to enhance comprehension of unfamiliar text: Should it focus on domain-specific or strategy knowledge?* Paper presented at the annual meeting of the American Educational Research Association, New Orleans, LA.

Greeno, J. G. (1997). On claims that answer the wrong questions. *Educational Researcher, 26*(1), 5–17.

Greenough, W. T., Black, J. E., & Wallace, C. S. (1987). Experience and brain development. *Child Development, 58,* 539–559.

Greenwood, C. R. (1991). Classwide peer tutoring: Longitudinal effects on the reading, language, and mathematics achievement of at-risk students. *Journal of Reading, Writing, and Learning Disabilities International, 7*(2), 105–123.

Greenwood, C. R., Carta, J. J., & Hall, R. V. (1988). The use of peer tutoring strategies in classroom management and educational instruction. *School Psychology Review, 17,* 258–275.

Grennon Brooks, J., & Brooks, M. (1993). *In search of understanding: The case for constructivist classrooms.* Alexandria, VA: Association for Supervision and Curriculum Development.

Gresham, F. M., & MacMillan, D. L. (1997). Social competence and affective characteristics of students with mild disabilities, *Review of Educational Research, 67*, 377–415.

Griffin, S. A., Case, R., & Capodilupo, A. (1995). Teaching for understanding: The importance of the central conceptual structures in the elementary mathematics curriculum. In A. McKeough, J. Lupart, & A. Marini (Eds.), *Teaching for transfer: Fostering generalization in learning.* Mahwah, NJ: Erlbaum.

Griffore, R. J. (1981). *Child development: An educational perspective.* Springfield, IL: Charles C Thomas.

Grinberg, D., & McLean-Heywood, D. (1999). *Perceptions of behavioural competence in depressed and nondepressed children with behavioural difficulties.* Paper presented at the annual meeting of the American Educational Research Association, Montreal, Canada.

Grissmer, D. W., Williamson, S., Kirby, S. N., & Berends, M. (1998). Exploring the rapid rise in Black achievement scores in the United States (1970–1990). In U. Neisser (Ed.), *The rising curve: Long-term gains in IQ and related measures* (pp. 251–285). Washington, DC: American Psychological Association.

Grodzinsky, G. M., & Diamond, R. (1992). Frontal lobe functioning in boys with attention-deficit hyperactivity disorder. *Developmental Neuropsychology, 8*, 427–445.

Gronlund, N. E. (1993). *How to make achievement tests and assessments* (5th ed.). Needham Heights, MA: Allyn & Bacon.

Gronlund, N. E. (2000). *How to write and use instructional objectives* (6th ed.). Upper Saddle River, NJ: Merrill/Prentice Hall.

Gronlund, N. E., & Cameron, I. J. (2004). *Assessment of student achievement* (Canadian ed.). Toronto: Pearson Canada.

Grusec, J. E., & Redler, E. (1980). Attribution, reinforcement, and altruism. *Developmental Psychology, 16*, 525–534.

Gauvain, M. (2001). *The social context of cognitive development.* New York: Guilford Press.

Guay, F., Boivin, M., & Hodges, E. V. E. (1999). Social comparison processes and academic achievement: The dependence of the development of self-evaluations on friends' performance. *Journal of Educational Psychology, 91*, 564–568.

Guerra, N. G., & Slaby, R. G. (1990). Cognitive mediators of aggression in adolescent offenders: 2. Intervention. *Developmental Psychology, 26*, 269–277.

Gunstone, R. F. (1994). The importance of specific science content in the enhancement of metacognition. In P. J. Fensham, R. F. Gunstone, & R. T. White (Eds.), *The content of science: A constructivist approach to its teaching and learning.* London: Falmer Press.

Gunstone, R. F., & White, R. T. (1981). Understanding of gravity. *Science Education, 65*, 291–299.

Guskey, T. R. (1985). *Implementing mastery learning.* Belmont, CA: Wadsworth.

Guskey, T. R. (1994, April). *Outcome-based education and mastery learning: Clarifying the differences.* Paper presented at the annual meeting of the American Educational Research Association, New Orleans, LA.

Gustafsson, J., & Undheim, J. O. (1996). Individual differences in cognitive functions. In D. C. Berliner & R. C. Calfee (Eds.), *Handbook of educational psychology.* New York: Macmillan.

Hacker, D. J. (1998a). Definitions and empirical foundations. In D. J. Hacker, J. Dunlosky, & A. C. Graesser (Eds.), *Metacognition in educational theory and practice* (pp. 1–23). Mahwah, NJ: Erlbaum.

Hacker, D. J. (1998b). Self-regulated comprehension during normal reading. In D. J. Hacker, J. Dunlosky, & A. C. Graesser (Eds.), *Metacognition in educational theory and practice* (pp. 165–191). Mahwah, NJ: Erlbaum.

Hacker, D. J., Bol, L., Horgan, D. D., & Rakow, E. A. (2000). Test prediction and performance in a classroom context. *Journal of Educational Psychology, 92*, 160–170.

Hadaway, N. L., Florez, V., Larke, P. J., & Wiseman, D. (1993). Teaching in the midst of diversity: How do we prepare? In M. J. O'Hair & S. J. Odell (Eds.), *Diversity and teaching: Teacher education yearbook I.* Fort Worth, TX: Harcourt Brace Jovanovich.

Haenan, J. (1996). Piotr Gal'perin's criticism and extension of Lev Vygotsky's work. *Journal of Russian and East European Psychology, 34*(2), 54–60.

Hagen, J. W., & Stanovich, K. G. (1977). Memory: Strategies of acquisition. In R. V. Kail, Jr., & J. W. Hagen (Eds.), *Perspectives on the development of memory and cognition.* Hillsdale, NJ: Erlbaum.

Hagtvet, K. A., & Johnsen, T. B. (Eds.). (1992). *Advances in test anxiety research* (Vol. 7). Amsterdam: Swets & Zeitlinger.

Hakuta, K., & McLaughlin, B. (1996). Bilingualism and second language learning: Seven tensions that define the research. In D. C. Berliner & R. C. Calfee (Eds.), *Handbook of educational psychology.* New York: Macmillan.

Hale-Benson, J. E. (1986). *Black children: Their roots, culture, and learning styles.* Baltimore: Johns Hopkins University Press.

Halford, G. S. (1989). Cognitive processing capacity and learning ability: An integration of two areas. *Learning and Individual Differences, 1*, 125–153.

Hall, R. H., & O'Donnell, A. (1994, April). *Alternative materials for learning: Cognitive and affective outcomes of learning from knowledge maps.* Paper presented at the annual meeting of the American Educational Research Association, New Orleans, LA.

Hallahan, D. P., & Kauffman, J. M. (1994). *Exceptional children: Introduction to special education* (6th ed.). Needham Heights, MA: Allyn & Bacon.

Haller, E. P., Child, D. A., & Walberg, H. J. (1988). Can comprehension be taught? A quantitative synthesis of "metacognitive" studies. *Educational Researcher, 17*(9), 5–8.

Hallinan, M. T., & Teixeria, R. A. (1987). Opportunities and constraints: Black-white differences in the formation of interracial friendships. *Child Development, 58*, 1358–1371.

Halpern, D. F. (1992). *Sex differences in cognitive abilities* (2nd ed.). Hillsdale, NJ: Erlbaum.

Halpern, D. F. (1997a). *Critical thinking across the curriculum: A brief edition of thought and knowledge.* Mahwah, NJ: Erlbaum.

Halpern, D. F. (1997b). Sex differences in intelligence: Implications for education. *American Psychologist, 52*, 1091–1102.

Halpern, D. F. (1998). Teaching critical thinking for transfer across domains. *American Psychologist, 53*, 449–455.

Halpern, D. F., & LaMay, M. L. (2000). The smarter sex: A critical review of sex differences in intelligence. *Educational Psychology Review, 12*, 229–246.

Halpin, G., & Halpin, G. (1982). Experimental investigations of the effects of study and testing on student learning, retention, and ratings of instruction. *Journal of Educational Psychology, 74*, 32–38.

Halvorsen, A. T., & Sailor, W. (1990). Integration of students with severe and profound disabilities: A review of research. In R. Gaylord-Ross (Ed.), *Issues and research in special education* (Vol. 1, pp. 110–172). New York: Teachers College Press.

Hambleton, R. K. (1996). Advances in assessment models, methods, and practices. In D. C. Berliner & R. C. Calfee (Eds.), *Handbook of educational psychology.* New York: Macmillan.

Hamers, J. H. M., & Ruijssenaars, A. J. J. M. (1997). Assessing classroom learning potential. In G. D. Phye (Ed.), *Handbook of academic learning: Construction of knowledge.* San Diego, CA: Academic Press.

Hamilton, R. (2004). Schools, teachers, and education of refugee children. In R. Hamilton & D. Moore (Eds.) *Educational interventions for refugee children: Theoretical perspectives and implementing best practice* (pp. 83–96). New York: Routledge.

Hamilton, R., & Moore, D. (Eds.). (2004). *Educational interventions for refugee children: Theoretical perspectives and implementing best practice.* New York: Routledge.

Hamman, D., Berthelot, J., Saia, J., & Crowley, E. (2000). Teachers' coaching of learning and its relation to students' strategic learning. *Journal of Educational Psychology, 92*, 342–348.

Hamman, D., Shell, D. F., Droesch, D., Husman, J., Handwerk, M., Park, Y., & Oppenheim, N. (1995, April). *Middle school readers' on-line cognitive processes: Influence of subject-matter knowledge and interest during reading.* Paper presented at the annual meeting of the American Educational Research Association, San Francisco.

Hamp-Lyons, L. (1992). Holistic writing assessment for L.E.P. students. In *Focus on evaluation and measurement* (Vol. 2). Washington, DC: U.S. Department of Education.

Hansen, J., & Pearson, P. D. (1983). An instructional study: Improving the inferential comprehension of good and poor fourth-grade readers. *Journal of Educational Psychology, 75*, 821–829.

Hardre, P. L., & Reeve, J. (2001, April). *A motivational model of rural high school students' dropout intentions.* Paper presented at the annual meeting of the American Educational Research Association, Seattle, WA.

Hardy, C., Bukowski, W., & Sippola, L. (2002). Stability and change in peer relationships during the transition to middle-level school. *Journal of Early Adolescence, 22*(2), 117–142.

Harlow, H. F., & Zimmerman, R. R. (1959). Affectional responses in the infant monkey. *Science, 130*, 421–432.

Harnishfeger, K. K. (1995). The development of cognitive inhibition: Theories, definitions, and research evidence. In F. N. Dempster & C. J. Brainerd (Eds.), *Interference and inhibition in cognition.* San Diego, CA: Academic Press.

Harp, S. F., & Mayer, R. E. (1998). How seductive details do their damage: A theory of cognitive interest in science learning. *Journal of Educational Psychology, 90*, 414–434.

Harris, C. R. (1991). Identifying and serving the gifted new immigrant. *Teaching Exceptional Children, 23*(4), 26–30.

Harris, J. R. (1995). Where is the child's environment? A group socialization theory of development. *Psychological Review, 102*, 458–489.

Harris, J. R. (1998). *The nurture assumption: Why children turn out the way they do.* New York: Free Press.

Harris, K. R. (1982). Cognitive-behavior modification: Application with exceptional students. *Focus on Exceptional Children, 15*, 1–16.

Harris, K. R. (1986). Self-monitoring of attentional behavior versus self-monitoring of productivity: Effects of on-task behavior and academic response rate among learning disabled children. *Journal of Applied Behavior Analysis, 19,* 417–423.

Harris, K. R., & Alexander, P. A. (1998). Integrated, constructivist education: Challenge and reality. *Educational Psychology Review, 10,* 115–127.

Harris, M. (1992). *Language experience and early language development: From input to uptake.* Hove, England: Erlbaum.

Harris, M. B. (1997). Preface: Images of the invisible minority. In M. B. Harries (Ed.), *School experiences of gay and lesbian youth: The invisible minority* (pp. xiv–xxii). Binghamton, NY: Harrington Park Press.

Harris, M. J., & Rosenthal, R. (1985). Mediation of interpersonal expectancy effects: 31 meta-analyses. *Psychological Bulletin, 97,* 363–386.

Harrow, A. J. (1972). *A taxonomy of the psychomotor domain: A guide for developing behavioral objectives.* New York: David McKay.

Hart, D. (1988). The adolescent self-concept in social context. In D. K. Lapsley & F. C. Power (Eds.), *Self, ego, and identity: Integrative approaches* (pp. 71–90). New York: Springer-Verlag.

Harter, S. (1975). Mastery motivation and the need for approval in older children and their relationship to social desirability response tendencies. *Developmental Psychology, 11,* 186–196.

Harter, S. (1978). Pleasure derived from challenge and the effects of receiving grades on children's difficulty level choices. *Child Development, 49,* 788–799.

Harter, S. (1982). The perceived competence scale for children. *Child Development, 53,* 87–97.

Harter, S. (1983a). Children's understanding of multiple emotions: A cognitive-developmental approach. In W. F. Overton (Ed.), *The relationship between social and cognitive development.* Hillsdale, NJ: Erlbaum.

Harter, S. (1983b). Developmental perspectives on the self-system. In E. M. Hetherington (Ed.), *Handbook of child psychology: Vol. 4. Socialization, personality, and social development* (4th ed.). New York: Wiley.

Harter, S. (1988). The construction and conservation of the self: James and Cooley revisited. In D. K. Lapsley & F. C. Power (Eds.), *Self, ego, and identity: Integrative approaches* (pp. 43–69). New York: Springer-Verlag.

Harter, S. (1990). Causes, correlates, and the functional role of global self-worth: A life-span perspective. In R. J. Sternberg & J. Kolligian, Jr. (Eds.), *Competence considered.* New Haven, CT: Yale University Press.

Harter, S. (1992). The relationship between perceived competence, affect, and motivational orientation within the classroom: Processes and patterns of change. In A. K. Boggiano & T. S. Pittman (Eds.), *Achievement and motivation: A social-developmental perspective.* Cambridge, England: Cambridge University Press.

Harter, S. (1996). Teacher and classmate influences on scholastic motivation, self-esteem, and level of voice in adolescents. In J. Juvonen & K. Wentzel (Eds.), *Social motivation: Understanding children's school adjustment.* New York: Cambridge University Press.

Harter, S., Whitesell, N. R., & Junkin, L. J. (1998). Similarities and differences in domain-specific and global self-evaluations of learning-disabled, behaviorally disordered, and normally achieving adolescents. *American Educational Research Journal, 35,* 653–680.

Harter, S., Whitesell, N. R., & Kowalski, P. (1992). Individual differences in the effects of educational transitions on young adolescents' perceptions of competence and motivational orientation. *American Educational Research Journal, 29,* 777–807.

Hartley, J., & Trueman, M. (1982). The effects of summaries on the recall of information from prose: Five experimental studies. *Human Learning, 1,* 63–82.

Hartup, W. W. (1983). Peer relations. In P. H. Mussen (Ed.), *Handbook of child psychology: Vol. IV. Socialization* (4th ed., pp. 103–196). New York: Wiley.

Hartup, W. W. (1989). Social relationships and their developmental significance. *American Psychologist, 44,* 120–126.

Hartup, W. W. (1992). Friendships and their developmental significance. In H. McGurk (Ed.), *Contemporary issues in childhood social development.* London: Routledge.

Haseman, A. L. (1999, April). *Cross talk: How students' epistemological beliefs impact the learning process in a constructivist course.* Paper presented at the annual meeting of the American Educational Research Association, Montreal, Canada.

Hasselbring, T. S., & Bausch, M. E. (2006). Assistive technologies for reading. *Educational Leadership, 63*(4), 72–75.

Hatano, G., & Inagaki, K. (1991). Sharing cognition through collective comprehension activity. In L. B. Resnick, J. M. Levine, & S. D. Teasley (Eds.), *Perspectives on socially shared cognition.* Washington, DC: American Psychological Association.

Hatano, G., & Inagaki, K. (1993). Desituating cognition through the construction of conceptual knowledge. In P. Light & G. Butterworth (Eds.), *Context and cognition: Ways of learning and knowing.* Hillsdale, NJ: Erlbaum.

Hattie, J., Biggs, J., & Purdie, N. (1996). Effects of learning skills interventions on student learning: A meta-analysis. *Review of Educational Research, 66,* 99–136.

Hawkins, F. P. L. (1997). *Journey with children: The autobiography of a teacher.* Niwot: University Press of Colorado.

Hawkins, R. D., & Bower, G. H. (Eds.). (1989). *Computational models of learning in simple neural systems.* San Diego, CA: Academic Press.

Hayes, C. B., Ryan, A. W., & Zseller, E. B. (1994, April). *African-American students' perceptions of caring teacher behaviors.* Paper presented at the annual meeting of the American Educational Research Association, New Orleans, LA.

Hayes, S. C., Rosenfarb, I., Wulfert, E., Munt, E. D., Korn, Z., & Zettle, R. D. (1985). Self-reinforcement effects: An artifact of social standard setting? *Journal of Applied Behavior Analysis, 18,* 201–214.

Hayes-Roth, B., & Thorndyke, P. W. (1979). Integration of knowledge from text. *Journal of Verbal Learning and Verbal Behavior, 18,* 91–108.

Health Canada. (2000). Healthy development of children and youth: The role of the determinants of health. Ottawa: Author.

Hearold, S. (1986). A synthesis of 1,043 effects of television on social behavior. In G. Comstock (Ed.), *Public communication and behavior* (Vol. 1). New York: Academic Press.

Hebb, D. O. (1949). *The organization of behavior: A neurophysiological theory.* New York, MacMillan.

Hedges, L. V., & Nowell, A. (1995). Sex differences in mental test scores, variability, and numbers of high-scoring individuals. *Science, 269,* 41–45.

Hegarty, M., & Kozhevnikov, M. (1999). Types of visual-spatial representations and mathematical problem solving. *Journal of Educational Psychology, 91,* 684–689.

Hegland, S., & Andre, T. (1992). Helping learners construct knowledge. *Educational Psychology Review, 4,* 223–240.

Heindel, P., & Kose, G. (1990). The effects of motoric action and organization on children's memory. *Journal of Experimental Child Psychology, 50,* 416–428.

Heller, J. I., & Hungate, H. N. (1985). Implications for mathematics instruction of research on scientific problem solving. In E. A. Silver (Ed.), *Teaching and learning mathematical problem solving: Multiple research perspectives.* Hillsdale, NJ: Erlbaum.

Helton, G. B., & Oakland, T. D. (1977). Teachers' attitudinal responses to differing characteristics of elementary school students. *Journal of Educational Psychology, 69,* 261–266.

Hembree, R. (1988). Correlates, causes, effects, and treatment of test anxiety. *Review of Educational Research, 58,* 47–77.

Hennessey, B. A. (1995). Social, environmental, and developmental issues and creativity. *Educational Psychology Review, 7,* 163–183.

Hennessey, B. A., & Amabile, T. M. (1987). *Creativity and learning.* Washington, DC: National Education Association.

Hess, G. A., Jr., Lyons, A., & Corsino, L. (1990, April). *Against the odds: The early identification of dropouts.* Paper presented at the annual meeting of the American Educational Research Association, Boston.

Hess, R. D., Chih-Mei, C., & McDevitt, T. M. (1987). Cultural variations in family beliefs about children's performance in mathematics: Comparisons among People's Republic of China, Chinese-American, and Caucasian-American families. *Journal of Educational Psychology, 79,* 179–188.

Hess, R. D., & Holloway, S. D. (1984). Family and school as educational institutions. In R. D. Parke, R. N. Emde, H. P. McAdoo, & G. P. Sackett (Eds.), *Review of child development research* (Vol. 7). Chicago: University of Chicago Press.

Heward, W. L. (2000). *Exceptional children: An introduction to special education* (6th ed.). Upper Saddle River, NJ: Merrill/Prentice Hall.

Hewitt, J., Brett, C., Scardamalia, M., Frecker, K., & Webb, J. (1995, April). *Schools for thought: Transforming classrooms into learning communities.* Paper presented at the annual meeting of the American Educational Research Association, San Francisco.

Hewitt, J., & Scardamalia, M. (1996, April). *Design principles for the support of distributed processes.* Paper presented at the annual meeting of the American Educational Research Association, New York.

Hewitt, J., & Scardamalia, M. (1998). Design principles for distributed knowledge building processes. *Educational Psychology Review, 10,* 75–96.

Heymann, S. J., & Earle, A. (2000). Low-income parents: How do working conditions affect their opportunity to help school-age children at risk? *American Educational Research Journal, 37,* 833–848.

Hickey, D. T. (1997). Motivation and contemporary socio-constructivist instructional perspectives. *Educational Psychologist, 32,* 175–193.

Hicks, L. (1997). Academic motivation and peer relationships—How do they mix in an adolescent world? *Middle School Journal, 28,* 18–22.

Hidalgo, N. M., Siu, S., Bright, J. A., Swap, S. M., & Epstein, J. L. (1995). Research on families, schools, and communities: A multicultural perspective. In J. A. Banks & C. A. M. Banks (Eds.), *Handbook of research on multicultural education.* New York: Macmillan.

Hidi, S. (1990). Interest and its contribution as a mental resource for learning. *Review of Educational Research, 60,* 549–571.

Hidi, S., & Anderson, V. (1986). Producing written summaries: Task demands, cognitive operations, and implications for instruction. *Review of Educational Research, 86,* 473–493.

Hidi, S., & Anderson, V. (1992). Situational interest and its impact on reading and expository writing. In K. A. Renninger, S. Hidi, & A. Krapp (Eds.), *The role of interest in learning and development.* Hillsdale, NJ: Erlbaum.

Hidi, S., & Harackiewicz, J. M. (2000). Motivating the academically unmotivated: A critical issue for the 21st century. *Review of Educational Research, 70,* 151–179.

Hidi, S., & McLaren, J. (1990). The effect of topic and theme interestingness on the production of school expositions. In H. Mandl, E. De Corte, N. Bennett, & H. F. Friedrich (Eds.), *Learning and instruction in an international context.* Oxford, England: Pergamon Press.

Hidi, S., Weiss, J., Berndorff, D., & Nolan, J. (1998). The role of gender, instruction, and a cooperative learning technique in science education across formal and informal settings. In L. Hoffman, A. Krapp, K. Renninger, & J. Baumert (Eds.), *Interest and learning: Proceedings of the Seeon Conference on interest and gender* (pp. 215–227). Kiel, Germany: IPN.

Hiebert, E. H., & Fisher, C. W. (1992). The tasks of school literacy: Trends and issues. In J. Brophy (Ed.), *Advances in research on teaching: Vol. 3. Planning and managing learning tasks and activities.* Greenwich, CT: JAI Press.

Hiebert, E. H., & Raphael, T. E. (1996). Psychological perspectives on literacy and extensions to educational practice. In D. C. Berliner & R. C. Calfee (Eds.), *Handbook of educational psychology.* New York: Macmillan.

Hiebert, E. H., Valencia, S. W., & Afflerbach, P. P. (1994). Definitions and perspectives. In S. W. Valencia, E. H. Hiebert, & P. P. Afflerbach (Eds.), *Authentic reading assessment: Practices and possibilities.* Newark, DE: International Reading Association.

Hiebert, J., Carpenter, T. P., Fennema, E., Fuson, K. C., Wearne, D., Murray, H., Olivier, A., & Human, P. (1997). *Making sense: Teaching and learning mathematics with understanding.* Portsmouth, NH: Heinemann.

Hiebert, J., & Wearne, D. (1996). Instruction, understanding, and skill in multidigit addition and subtraction. *Cognition and Instruction, 14,* 251–283.

Higgins, A. (1995). Educating for justice and community: Lawrence Kohlberg's vision of moral education. In W. M. Kurtines & J. L. Gewirtz (Eds.), *Moral development: An introduction.* Boston: Allyn & Bacon.

Higgins, E. L., & Raskind, M. H. (2005). The compensatory effectiveness of the Qicktionary Reading Pen 11 on the reading comprehension of students with learning disabilities. *Journal of Special Education Technology, 20*(1), 31–37.

Hill, C., & Larsen, E. (1992). *Testing and assessment in secondary education: A critical review of emerging practices.* Berkeley: University of California, National Center for Research in Vocational Education.

Hill, K. T. (1984). Debilitating motivation and testing: A major educational problem, possible solutions, and policy applications. In R. Ames & C. Ames (Eds.), *Research on motivation in education: Vol. 1. Student motivation.* San Diego, CA: Academic Press.

Hill, K. T., & Wigfield, A. (1984). Test anxiety: A major educational problem and what can be done about it. *Elementary School Journal, 85,* 105–126.

Hilliard, A., & Vaughn-Scott, M. (1982). The quest for the minority child. In S. G. Moore & C. R. Cooper (Eds.), *The young child: Reviews of research* (Vol. 3). Washington, DC: National Association for the Education of Young Children.

Hinkel, E. (Ed.). (2005). *Handbook of research in second language teaching and learning.* New York: Routledge.

Hinkley, J. W., McInerney, D. M., & Marsh, H. W. (2001, April). *The multi-faceted structure of school achievement motivation: A case for social goals.* Paper presented at the annual meeting of the American Educational Research Association, Seattle, WA.

Hirsch, E. D., Jr. (1996). *The schools we need and why we don't have them.* New York: Doubleday.

Ho, D. Y. F. (1986). Chinese pattern of socialization: A critical review. In M. H. Bond (Ed.), *The psychology of Chinese people.* Oxford: Oxford University Press.

Ho, D. Y. F. (1994). Cognitive socialization in Confucian heritage cultures. In P. M. Greenfield & R. R. Cocking (Eds.), *Cross-cultural roots of minority child development.* Hillsdale, NJ: Erlbaum.

Ho, H.-Z., Hinckley, H. S., Fox, K. R., Brown, J. H., & Dixon, C. N. (2001, April). *Family literacy: Promoting parent support strategies for student success.* Paper presented at the annual meeting of the American Educational Research Association, Seattle, WA.

Hocevar, D., & Bachelor, P. (1989). A taxonomy and critique of measurements used in the study of creativity. In J. A. Glover, R. R. Ronning, & C. R. Reynolds (Eds.), *Handbook of creativity.* New York: Plenum Press.

Hofer, B. K., & Pintrich, P. R. (1997). The development of epistemological theories: Beliefs about knowledge and knowing and their relation to learning. *Review of Educational Research, 67,* 88–140.

Hoffman, M. L. (1970). Moral development. In P. H. Mussen (Ed.), *Carmichael's manual of child psychology* (Vol. 2). New York: Wiley.

Hoffman, M. L. (1975). Altruistic behavior and the parent-child relationship. *Journal of Personality and Social Psychology, 31,* 937–943.

Hoffman, M. L. (1991). Empathy, social cognition, and moral action. In W. M. Kurtines & J. L. Gewirtz (Eds.), *Moral behavior and development: Vol. 1. Theory* (pp. 275–301). Hillsdale, NJ: Erlbaum.

Hogan, D. M., & Tudge, J. R. H. (1999). Implications of Vygotsky's theory for peer learning. In A. M. O'Donnell & A. King (Eds.), *Cognitive perspectives on peer learning* (pp. 39–65). Mahwah, NJ: Erlbaum.

Hogan, K., Nastasi, B. K., & Pressley, M. (2000). Discourse patterns and collaborative scientific reasoning in peer and teacher-guided discussions. *Cognition and Instruction, 17,* 379–432.

Hoge, R. D., & Coladarci, T. (1989). Teacher-based judgments of academic achievement: A review of literature. *Review of Educational Research, 59,* 297–313.

Hoge, R. D., & Renzulli, J. S. (1993). Exploring the link betwen giftedness and self-concept. *Review of Educational Research, 63,* 449–465.

Holley, C. D., & Dansereau, D. F. (1984). *Spatial learning strategies: Techniques, applications, and related issues.* San Diego, CA: Academic Press.

Hollins, E. R. (1996). *Culture in school learning: Revealing the deep meaning.* Mahwah, NJ: Erlbaum.

Holt-Reynolds, D. (1992). Personal history-based beliefs as relevant prior knowledge in course work. *American Educational Research Journal, 29,* 325–349.

Hom, A., & Battistich, V. (1995, April). *Students' sense of school community as a factor in reducing drug use and delinquency.* Paper presented at the annual meeting of the American Educational Research Association, San Francisco.

Hong, Y., Chiu, C., & Dweck, C. S. (1995). Implicit theories of intelligence: Reconsidering the role of confidence in achievement motivation. In M. H. Kernis (Ed.), *Efficacy, agency, and self-esteem.* New York: Plenum Press.

Hong, Y., Morris, M. W., Chiu, C., & Benet-Martínez, V. (2000). Multicultural minds: A dynamic constructivist approach to culture and cognition. *American Psychologist, 55,* 709–720.

Hoover-Dempsey, K. V., & Sandler, H. M. (1997). Why do parents become involved in their children's education? *Review of Educational Research, 67,* 3–42.

Horgan, D. (1990, April). *Students' predictions of test grades: Calibration and metacognition.* Paper presented at the annual meeting of the American Educational Research Association, Boston.

Horgan, D. D. (1995). *Achieving gender equity: Strategies for the classroom.* Needham Heights, MA: Allyn & Bacon.

Houtz, J. C. (1990). Environments that support creative thinking. In C. Hedley, J. Houtz, & A. Baratta (Eds.), *Cognition, curriculum, and literacy.* Norwood, NJ: Ablex.

Howe, C. K. (1994). Improving the achievement of Hispanic students. *Educational Leadership, 51*(8), 42–44.

Hrycauk, W. (1997). The school's team: A principal of a successful school council offers his insights into what makes it tick. *The Alberta Teachers Association* (summer), 6–8.

Hudley, C., & Graham, S. (1993). An attributional intervention to reduce peer-directed aggression among African American boys. *Child Development, 64,* 124–138.

Hughes, J. N. (1988). *Cognitive behavior therapy with children in schools.* New York: Pergamon Press.

Humphreys, L. G. (1992). What both critics and users of ability tests need to know. *Psychological Science, 3,* 271–274.

Hunt, C. (2007). The effect of an education program on attitudes and beliefs about bullying and bullying behaviour in Junior Secondary school students. *Child and Adolescent Mental Health, 12*(1), 21–26.

Hunt, P., & Goetz, L. (1997). Research on inclusive educational programs, practices, and outcomes for students with severe disabilities. *Journal of Special Education, 21,* 3–29.

Hunter, M. (1982). *Mastery teaching.* El Segundo, CA: TIP.

Husman, J., & Freeman, B. (1999, April). *The effect of perceptions of instrumentality on intrinsic motivation.* Paper presented at the annual meeting of the American Educational Research Association, Montreal, Canada.

Huston, A. C. (1983). Sex-typing. In E. M. Hetherington (Ed.), *Handbook of child psychology: Vol. 4. Socialization, personality, and social development* (4th ed.). New York: Wiley.

Huston, A. C., Donnerstein, E., Fairchild, H., Feshbach, N. D., Katz, P. A., Murray, J. P., Rubenstein, E. A., Wilcox, B. L., & Zuckerman, D. (1992). *Big world, small screen: The role of television in American society.* Lincoln: University of Nebraska Press.

Hutt, S. J., Tyler, S., Hutt, C., & Christopherson, H. (1989). *Play, exploration, and learning: A natural history of the pre-school*. London: Routledge.

Hyde, J. (2005). The gender similarities hypothesis. *American Psychologist, 60*(6), 581–592.

Hyde, J. S., Fennema, E., & Lamon, S. J. (1990). Gender differences in mathematics performance: A meta-analysis. *Psychological Bulletin, 107*, 139–155.

Hyde, J. S., & Linn, M. C. (1988). Gender differences in verbal ability: A meta-analysis. *Psychological Bulletin, 104*, 53–69.

Hymel, S., Comfort, C., Schonert-Reichl, K., & McDougall, P. (1996). Academic failure and school dropout: The influence of peers. In J. Juvonen & K. R. Wentzel (Eds.), *Social motivation: Understanding children's school adjustment* (pp. 313–345). Cambridge, England: Cambridge University Press.

Hymel, S., Schonert-Reichl, K. A., & Miller, L. D. (2006). Reading, 'riting, 'rithmetic and relationships: Considering the social side of education. *Exceptionality Education Canada, 16*(3), 149–192.

Hynd, C. (1998). Observing learning from different perspectives: What does it mean for Barry and his understanding of gravity? In B. Guzzetti & C. Hynd (Eds.), *Perspectives on conceptual change: Multiple ways to understand knowing and learning in a complex world* (pp. 235–244). Mahwah, NJ: Erlbaum.

Igoa, C. (1995). *The inner world of the immigrant child*. Mahwah, NJ: Erlbaum.

Igoe, A. R., & Sullivan, H. (1991, April). *Gender and grade-level differences in student attributes related to school learning and motivation*. Paper presented at the annual meeting of the American Educational Research Association, Chicago.

Inglehart, M., Brown, D. R., & Vida, M. (1994). Competition, achievement, and gender: A stress theoretical analysis. In P. R. Pintrich, D. R. Brown, & C. E. Weinstein (Eds.), *Student motivation, cognition, and learning: Essays in honor of Wilbert J. McKeachie*. Hillsdale, NJ: Erlbaum.

Inglis, A., & Biemiller, A. (1997, March). *Fostering self-direction in mathematics: A cross-age tutoring program that enhances math problem solving*. Paper presented at the annual meeting of the American Educational Research Association, Chicago.

Inhelder, B., & Piaget, J. (1958). *The growth of logical thinking from childhood to adolescence* (A. Parsons & S. Milgram, Trans.). New York: Basic Books.

Iwata, B. A., & Bailey, J. S. (1974). Reward versus cost token systems: An analysis of the effects on students and teacher. *Journal of Applied Behavior Analysis, 7*, 567–576.

Jacklin, C. N. (1989). Female and male: Issues of gender. *American Psychologist, 44*, 127–133.

Jacobsen, B., Lowery, B., & DuCette, J. (1986). Attributions of learning disabled children. *Journal of Educational Psychology, 78*, 59–64.

Jacobson, J. L., & Wille, D. E. (1986). The influence of attachment pattern on developmental changes in peer interaction from the toddler to the preschool period. *Child Development, 57*, 338–347.

Jagacinski, C. M., & Nicholls, J. G. (1984). Conceptions of ability and related affects in task involvement and ego involvement. *Journal of Educational Psychology, 76*, 909–919.

Jagacinski, C. M., & Nicholls, J. G. (1987). Competence and affect in task involvement and ego involvement: The impact of social comparison information. *Journal of Educational Psychology, 79*, 107–114.

Janosz, M., Le Blanc, M., Boulerice, B., & Tremblay, R. E. (2000). Predicting different types of school dropouts: A typological approach with two longitudinal samples. *Journal of Educational Psychology, 92*, 171–190.

Jarvis, S., & Seifert, T. (2002). Work avoidance as a manifestation of hostility, helplessness, and boredom. *The Alberta Journal of Educational Research, 48*(2), 174–187.

Jencks, C., & Crouse, J. (1982). Should we relabel the SAT . . . or replace it? In W. Shrader (Ed.), *New directions for testing and measurement: Measurement, guidance, and program improvement* (No. 13). San Francisco: Jossey-Bass.

Jenlink, C. L. (1994, April). *Music: A lifeline for the self-esteem of at-risk students*. Paper presented at the annual meeting of the American Educational Research Association, New Orleans, LA.

Jessup, L., Egbert, J., & Connolly, T. (1995). Collaborative learning—A CET resource. *Journal of Research on Computing in Education, 2*(2), 190–208.

Jimerson, S., Egeland, B., & Teo, A. (1999). A longitudinal study of achievement trajectories: Factors associated with change. *Journal of Educational Psychology, 91*, 116–126.

Johanning, D. I., D'Agostino, J. V., Steele, D. F., & Shumow, L. (1999, April). *Student writing, post-writing group collaboration, and learning in pre-algebra*. Paper presented at the annual meeting of the American Educational Research Association, Montreal, Canada.

Johnson, D. (2004). Online magazines for children and teens. *Reading and Writing Quarterly: Overcoming Learning Difficulties, 20*, 103–107.

Johnson, D. W., & Johnson, R. T. (1985). Classroom conflict: Controversy versus debate in learning groups. *American Educational Research Journal, 22*, 237–256.

Johnson, D. W., & Johnson, R. T. (1988). Critical thinking through structured controversy. *Educational Leadership, 45*(8), 58–64.

Johnson, D. W., & Johnson, R. T. (1991). *Learning together and alone: Cooperative, competitive, and individualistic learning* (3rd ed.). Upper Saddle River, NJ: Prentice Hall.

Johnson, D. W., & Johnson, R. T. (1996). Conflict resolution and peer mediation programs in elementary and secondary schools: A review of the research. *Review of Educational Research, 66*, 459–506.

Johnson, D. W., & Johnson, R. T. (2001, April). *Teaching students to be peacemakers: A meta-analysis*. Paper presented at the annual meeting of the American Educational Research Association, Seattle, WA.

Johnson, D. W., Johnson, R., Dudley, B., Ward, M., & Magnuson, D. (1995). The impact of peer mediation training on the management of school and home conflicts. *American Educational Research Journal, 32*, 829–844.

Johnson, J. S., & Newport, E. L. (1989). Critical period effects in second language learning. *Cognitive Psychology, 21*, 60–99.

Johnson-Glenberg, M. C. (2000). Training reading comprehension in adequate decoders/poor comprehenders: Verbal versus visual strategies. *Journal of Educational Psychology, 92*, 772–782.

John-Steiner, V. (1997). *Notebooks of the mind: Explorations of thinking* (Rev. ed.). New York: Oxford University Press.

John-Steiner, V., & Mahn, H. (1996). Sociocultural approaches to learning and development: A Vygotskian framework. *Educational Psychologist, 31*, 191–206.

Johnstone, A. H., & El-Banna, H. (1986). Capacities, demands and processes—A predictive model for science education. *Education in Chemistry, 23*, 80–84.

Jonassen, D. H., Hannum, W. H., & Tessmer, M. (1989). *Handbook of task analysis procedures*. New York: Praeger.

Jones, D., & Christensen, C. A. (1999). Relationship between automaticity in handwriting and students' ability to generate written text. *Journal of Educational Psychology, 91*, 44–49.

Jones, E. E., & Berglas, S. (1978). Control of attributions about the self through self-handicapping strategies: The appeal of alcohol and the role of underachievement. *Personality and Social Psychology Bulletin, 4*, 200–206.

Jones, G. P., & Dembo, M. H. (1989). Age and sex role differences in intimate friendships during childhood and adolescence. *Merrill-Palmer Quarterly, 35*, 445–462.

Jones, K. M., Drew, H. A., & Weber, N. L. (2000). Noncontingent peer attention as treatment for disruptive classroom behavior. *Journal of Applied Behavior Analysis, 33*, 343–346.

Jones, M. C. (1924). The elimination of children's fears. *Journal of Experimental Psychology, 7*, 382–390.

Jones, M. S., Levin, M. E., Levin, J. R., & Beitzel, B. D. (2000). Can vocabulary-learning strategies and pair-learning formats be profitably combined? *Journal of Educational Psychology, 92*, 256–262.

Joshi, M. S., & MacLean, M. (1994). Indian and English children's understanding of the distinction between real and apparent emotion. *Child Development, 65*, 1372–1384.

Jovanovic, J., & King, S. S. (1998). Boys and girls in the performance-based science classroom: Who's doing the performing? *American Educational Research Journal, 35*, 477–496.

Jozefowicz, D. M., Arbreton, A. J., Eccles, J. S., Barber, B. L., & Colarossi, L. (1994, April). *Seventh grade student, parent, and teacher factors associated with later school dropout or movement into alternative educational settings*. Paper presented at the annual meeting of the American Educational Research Association, New Orleans, LA.

Judd, C. H. (1932). Autobiography. In C. Murchison (Ed.), *History of psychology in autobiography* (Vol. 2). Worcester, MA: Clark University Press.

Juel, C. (1988). Learning to read and write: A longitudinal study of 54 children from first through fourth grades. *Journal of Educational Psychology, 80*, 437–447.

Juel, C., Griffiths, P. L., & Gough, P. B. (1986). Acquisition of literacy: A longitudinal study of children in first and second grade. *Journal of Educational Psychology, 78*, 243–255.

Jussim, L., Eccles, J., & Madon, S. (1996). Social perception, social stereotypes, and teacher expectations: Accuracy and the quest for the powerful self-fulfilling prophecy. In L. Berkowitz (Ed.), *Advances in experimental social psychology*. New York: Academic Press.

Juvonen, J. (2000). The social functions of attributional face-saving tactics among early adolescents. *Educational Psychology Review, 12*, 15–32.

Juvonen, J., & Weiner, B. (1993). An attributional analysis of students' interactions: The social consequences of perceived responsibility. *Educational Psychology Review, 5*, 325–345.

Kagan, J. (1998). Biology and the child. In W. Damon (Editor-in-Chief) & N. Eisenberg (Vol. Ed.), *Handbook of child psychology: Vol. 3. Social, emotional, and personality development* (5th ed., pp. 177–235). New York: Wiley.

Kagan, J., Snidman, N., & Arcus, D. M. (1992). Initial reactions to unfamiliarity. *Current Directions in Psychological Science, 1*, 171–174.

Kahl, B., & Woloshyn, V. E. (1994). Using elaborative interrogation to facilitate acquisition of factual information in cooperative learning settings: One good strategy deserves another. *Applied Cognitive Psychology, 8,* 465–478.

Kahle, J. B. (1983). *The disadvantaged majority: Science education for women.* Burlington, NC: Carolina Biological Supply Co.

Kahle, J. B., & Lakes, M. K. (1983). The myth of equality in science classrooms. *Journal of Research in Science Teaching, 20,* 131–140.

Kail, R. (1990). *The development of memory in children* (3rd ed.). New York: Freeman.

Kail, R. V. (1998). *Children and their development.* Upper Saddle River, NJ: Prentice Hall.

Kamii, C., with L. L. Joseph. (1989). *Young children continue to reinvent arithmetic, 2nd grade: Implications of Piaget's theory.* New York: Teachers College Press.

Kane, R. J. (1983). In defense of grade inflation. *Today's Education, 67*(4), 41.

Kaplan, A. (1998, April). *Task goal orientation and adaptive social interaction among students of diverse cultural backgrounds.* Paper presented at the annual meeting of the American Educational Research Association, San Diego, CA.

Kaplan, A., & Midgley, C. (1999). The relationship between perceptions of the classroom goal structure and early adolescents' affect in school: The mediating role of coping strategies. *Learning and Individual Differences, 11,* 187–212.

Kapperman, G., & Stickerman, J. (2002). A software tutorial for learning the Nemeth Code of Braille mathematics. *Journal of Visual Impairment and Blindness, 96,* 855–857.

Karau, S. J., & Williams, K. D. (1995). Social loafing: Research findings, implications, and future directions. *Current Directions in Psychological Science, 4,* 134–140.

Kardash, C. A. M., & Scholes, R. J. (1996). Effects of preexisting beliefs, epistemological beliefs, and need for cognition on interpretation of controversial issues. *Journal of Educational Psychology, 88,* 260–271.

Karmiloff-Smith, A. (1979). Language development after five. In P. Fletcher & M. Garman (Eds.), *Language acquisition: Studies in first language development.* Cambridge, England: Cambridge University Press.

Karmiloff-Smith, A. (1993). Innate constraints and developmental change. In P. Bloom (Ed.), *Language acquisition: Core readings.* Cambridge, MA: MIT Press.

Karovitch, S. K., Shore, B. M., & Delcourt, M. A. B. (1996). Gifted and nongifted students' reasons for leaving French-immersion programs. *Gifted and Talented International, 11,* 30–33.

Katchadourian, H. (1990). Sexuality. In S. S. Feldman & G. R. Elliott (Eds.), *At the threshold: The developing adolescent* (pp. 330–351). Cambridge, MA: Harvard University Press.

Katkovsky, W., Crandall, V. C., & Good, S. (1967). Parental antecedents of children's beliefs in internal-external control of reinforcements in intellectual achievement situations. *Child Development, 38,* 765–776.

Katz, E. W., & Brent, S. B. (1968). Understanding connectives. *Journal of Verbal Learning and Verbal Behavior, 7,* 501–509.

Katz, L. (1993). All about me: Are we developing our children's self-esteem or their narcissism? *American Educator, 17*(2), 18–23.

Kearins, J. M. (1981). Visual spatial memory in Australian aboriginal children of desert regions. *Cognitive Psychology, 13,* 434–460.

Kehle, T. J., Clark, E., Jenson, W. R., & Wampold, B. (1986). Effectiveness of the self-modeling procedure with behaviorally disturbed elementary age children. *School Psychology Review, 15,* 289–295.

Keil, F. C. (1987). Conceptual development and category structure. In U. Neisser (Ed.), *Concepts and conceptual development: Ecological and intellectual factors in categorization.* Cambridge, England: Cambridge University Press.

Keil, F. C. (1989). *Concepts, kinds, and cognitive development.* Cambridge, MA: MIT Press.

Keil, F. C. (1991). Theories, concepts, and the acquisition of word meaning. In S. A. Gelman & J. P. Byrnes (Eds.), *Perspectives on language and thought: Interrelations in development.* Cambridge, England: Cambridge University Press.

Keil, F. C. (1994). The birth and nurturance of concepts by domains: The origins of concepts of living things. In L. A. Hirschfeld & S. A. Gelman (Eds.), *Mapping the mind: Domain specificity in cognition and culture.* New York: Cambridge University Press.

Keil, F. C., & Silberstein, C. S. (1996). Schooling and the acquisition of theoretical knowledge. In D. R. Olson & N. Torrance (Eds.), *The handbook of education and human development: New models of learning, teaching, and schooling.* Cambridge, MA: Blackwell.

Kelemen, D. (1999). Why are rocks pointy? Children's preference for teleological explanations of the natural world. *Developmental Psychology, 35,* 1440–1452.

Kelley, M. L., & Carper, L. B. (1988). Home-based reinforcement procedures. In J. C. Witt, S. N. Elliott, & F. M. Gresham (Eds.), *Handbook of behavior therapy in education.* New York: Plenum Press.

Kelly, A., & Smail, B. (1986). Sex stereotypes and attitudes to science among eleven-year-old children. *British Journal of Educational Psychology, 56,* 158–168.

Kelly, G. J., & Chen, C. (1998, April). *The sound of music: Experiment, discourse, and writing of science as sociocultural practices.* Paper presented at the annual meeting of the American Educational Research Association, San Diego, CA.

Keogh, B. K., & MacMillan, D. L. (1996). Exceptionality. In D. C. Berliner & R. C. Calfee (Eds.), *Handbook of educational psychology.* New York: Macmillan.

Kermani, H., & Moallem, M. (1997, March). *Cross-age tutoring: Exploring features and processes of peer-mediated learning.* Paper presented at the annual meeting of the American Educational Research Association, Chicago.

Kerr, B. (1991). Educating gifted girls. In N. Coangelo & G. A. Davis (Eds.), *Handbook of gifted education.* Needham Heights, MA: Allyn & Bacon.

Keys, C., & Dowrick, P. W. (Eds.) (2001). *Empowerment and community action for people with disabilities.* Binghamton, NY: Haworth Press.

Khattri, N., & Sweet, D. (1996). Assessment reform: Promises and challenges. In M. B. Kane & R. Mitchell (Eds.), *Implementing performance assessment: Promises, problems, and challenges* (pp. 1–21). Mahwah, NJ: Erlbaum.

Kiewra, K. A. (1989). A review of note-taking: The encoding-storage paradigm and beyond. *Educational Psychology Review, 1,* 147–172.

Kiewra, K. A. (2002). How classroom teachers can help students learn and teach them how to learn. *Theory into Practice, 41*(2), 71–80.

Kim, D., Solomon, D., & Roberts, W. (1995, April). *Classroom practices that enhance students' sense of community.* Paper presented at the annual meeting of the American Educational Research Association, San Francisco.

Kimberg, D. Y., D'Esposito, M., & Farah, M. J. (1997). Cognitive functions in the prefrontal cortex-working memory and executive control. *Current Directions in Psychological Science, 6,* 185–192.

Kimble, G. A. (2000). Behaviorism and unity in psychology. *Current Directions in Psychological Science, 9,* 208–212.

Kindermann, T. A., McCollam, T., & Gibson, E. (1996). Peer networks and students' classroom engagement during childhood and adolescence. In J. Juvonen & K. Wentzel (Eds.), *Social motivation: Understanding children's school adjustment.* Cambridge, England: Cambridge University Press.

King, A. (1992). Comparison of self-questioning, summarizing, and notetaking-review as strategies for learning from lectures. *American Educational Research Journal, 29,* 303–323.

King, A. (1994). Guiding knowledge construction in the classroom: Effects of teaching children how to question and how to explain. *American Educational Research Journal, 31,* 338–368.

King, A. (1997). ASK to THINK - TEL WHY®©: A model of transactive peer tutoring for scaffolding higher level complex learning. *Educational Psychologist, 32,* 221–235.

King, A. (1999). Discourse patterns for mediating peer learning. In A. M. O'Donnell & A. King (Eds.), *Cognitive perspectives on peer learning* (pp. 87–115). Mahwah, NJ: Erlbaum.

King, N. J., & Ollendick, T. H. (1989). Children's anxiety and phobic disorders in school settings: Classification, assessment, and intervention issues. *Review of Educational Research, 59,* 431–470.

Kintsch, W. (1980). Learning from text, levels of comprehension, or: Why anyone would read a story anyway. *Poetics, 9,* 87–98.

Kirkland, M. C. (1971). The effect of tests on students and schools. *Review of Educational Research, 41,* 303–350.

Kirschenbaum, R. J. (1989). Identification of the gifted and talented American Indian student. In C. J. Maker & S. W. Schiever (Eds.), *Critical issues in gifted education: Vol. 2. Defensible programs for cultural and ethnic minorities.* Austin, TX: Pro-Ed.

Kitsantis, A., Zimmerman, B. J., & Cleary, T. (2000). The role of observation and emulation in the development of athletic self-regulation. *Journal of Educational Psychology, 92,* 811–817.

Klein, J. D. (1990, April). *The effect of interest, task performance, and reward contingencies on self-efficacy.* Paper presented at the annual meeting of the American Educational Research Association, Boston.

Kletzien, S. B. (1988, April). *Achieving and non-achieving high school readers' use of comprehension strategies for reading expository text.* Paper presented at the annual meeting of the American Educational Research Association, New Orleans, LA.

Kluger, A. N., & DeNisi, A. (1998). Feedback interventions: Toward the understanding of a double-edged sword. *Current Directions in Psychological Science, 7,* 67–72.

Knapp, M. S., Turnbull, B. J., & Shields, P. M. (1990). New directions for educating the children of poverty. *Educational Leadership, 48*(1), 4–9.

Knapp, M. S., & Woolverton, S. (1995). Social class and schooling. In J. A. Banks & C. A. M. Banks (Eds.), *Handbook of research on multicultural education.* New York: Macmillan.

Knowlton, D. (1995). Managing children with oppositional behavior. *Beyond Behavior, 6*(3), 5–10.

Koegel, L. K., Koegel, R. L., & Dunlap, G. (Eds.). (1996). *Positive behavioral support: Including people with difficult behavior in the community*. Baltimore: Brookes.

Koeppel, J., & Mulrooney, M. (1992). The Sister Schools Program: A way for children to learn about cultural diversity—When there isn't any in their school. *Young Children, 48*(1), 44–47.

Koestner, R., Ryan, R. M., Bernieri, F., & Holt, K. (1984). Setting limits in children's behavior: The differential effects of controlling versus informational styles on intrinsic motivation and creativity. *Journal of Personality, 52*, 233–248.

Kogan, N. (1983). Stylistic variation in childhood and adolescence: Creativity, metaphor, and cognitive style. In J. H. Flavell & E. M. Markman (Eds.), *Handbook of child psychology: Vol. 3. Cognitive development*. New York: Wiley.

Kohlberg, L. (1975). The cognitive-developmental approach to moral education. *Phi Delta Kappan, 57*, 670–677.

Kohlberg, L. (1976). Moral stages and moralization: The cognitive-developmental approach. In T. Lickona (Ed.), *Moral development and behavior: Theory, research, and social issues*. New York: Holt, Rinehart & Winston.

Kohlberg, L. (1981). *The philosophy of moral development: Moral stages and the idea of justice*. San Francisco: Harper & Row.

Kohlberg, L. (1984). *The psychology of moral development: The nature and validity of moral stages*. San Francisco: Harper & Row.

Kohlberg, L. (1986). A current statement on some theoretical issues. In S. Modgil & C. Modgil (Eds.), *Lawrence Kohlberg: Consensus and controversy*. Philadelphia: Falmer Press.

Kohlberg, L., & Candee, D. (1984). The relationship of moral judgment to moral action. In W. M. Kurtines & J. L. Gewirtz (Eds.), *Morality, moral behavior, and moral development*. New York: Wiley.

Kohn, A. (1993). Choices for children: Why and how to let students decide. *Phi Delta Kappan, 75*(1), 8–20.

Kolodner, J. (1985). Memory for experience. In G. H. Bower (Ed.), *The psychology of learning and motivation: Advances in research and theory* (Vol. 19). San Diego, CA: Academic Press.

Koretz, D., Stecher, B., Klein, S., & McCaffrey, D. (1994). The Vermont portfolio assessment program: Findings and implications. *Educational Measurement: Issues and Practices, 13*(3), 5–16.

Kosslyn, S. M. (1985). Mental imagery ability. In R. J. Sternberg (Ed.), *Human abilities: An information-processing approach*. New York: Freeman.

Kounin, J. S. (1970). *Discipline and group management in classrooms*. New York: Holt, Rinehart & Winston.

Kovacs, D. M., Parker, J. G., & Hoffman, L. W. (1996). Behavioral, affective, and social correlates of involvement in cross-sex friendship in elementary school. *Child Development, 67*, 2269–2286.

Krajcik, J. S. (1991). Developing students' understanding of chemical concepts. In S. M. Glynn, R. H. Yeany, & B. K. Britton (Eds.), *The psychology of learning science*. Hillsdale, NJ: Erlbaum.

Krampen, G. (1987). Differential effects of teacher comments. *Journal of Educational Psychology, 79*, 137–146.

Krashen, S. D. (1996). *Under attack: The case against bilingual education*. Culver City, CA: Language Education Associates.

Krathwohl, D. R. (1994). Reflections on the taxonomy: Its past, present, and future. In L. W. Anderson & L. A. Sosniak (Eds.), *Bloom's taxonomy: A forty-year perspective. Ninety-third yearbook of the National Society for the Study of Education, Part II*. Chicago: National Society for the Study of Education.

Krathwohl, D. R., Bloom, B. S., & Masia, B. B. (1964). *Taxonomy of education objectives: Handbook II. Affective domain*. New York: David McKay.

Kucan, L., & Beck, I. L. (1997). Thinking aloud and reading comprehension research: Inquiry, instruction, and social interaction. *Review of Educational Research, 67*, 271–299.

Kuhl, J. (1985). Volitional mediators of cognition-behavior consistency: Self-regulatory processes and actions versus state orientation. In J. Kuhl & J. Beckmann (Eds.), *Action control: From cognition to behavior*. Berlin, Germany: Springer-Verlag.

Kuhl, J. (1987). Action control: The maintenance of motivational states. In F. Halisch & J. Kuhl (Eds.), *Motivation, intention, and volition*. Berlin, Germany: Springer-Verlag.

Kuhl, P. K. (2000). A new view of language acquisition. *Proceedings of the National Academy of Science—USA, 97*, 11850–11857.

Kuhl, P. K., Stevens, E., Hayashi, A., Deguchi, T., Kiritani, S., & Iverson, P. (2006). Infants show a facilitation effect for native language phonetic perception between 6 and 12 months. *Developmental Science, 9*(2), F13–F21.

Kuhn, D. (2001). How do people know? *Psychological Science, 12*, 1–8.

Kuhn, D., Amsel, E., & O'Loughlin, M. (1988). *The development of scientific thinking skills*. San Diego, CA: Academic Press.

Kuhn, D., & Franklin, S. (2006). The second decade: What develops (and how)? In D. Kuhn & R. Siegler (Vol. Eds.), *Handbook of child psychology, Vol. 2: Cognition, perception, and language* (6th ed.) (pp. 953–993). Hoboken, NJ: Wiley. (W. Damon & R. M. Lerner, Series Eds.)

Kuhn, D., Garcia-Mila, M., Zohar, A., & Andersen, C. (1995). Strategies of knowledge acquisition. *Monographs of the Society for Research in Child Development, 60* (Whole No. 245).

Kuhn, D., Shaw, V., & Felton, M. (1997). Effects of dyadic interaction on argumentative reasoning. *Cognition and Instruction, 15*, 287–315.

Kulhavy, R. W., Lee, J. B., & Caterino, L. C. (1985). Conjoint retention of maps and related discourse. *Contemporary Educational Psychology, 10*, 28–37.

Kulik, C. C., Kulik, J. A., & Bangert-Drowns, R. L. (1990). Effectiveness of mastery learning programs: A meta-analysis. *Review of Educational Research, 60*, 265–299.

Kulik, J. A., Kulik, C. C., & Cohen, P. A. (1979). A meta-analysis of outcome studies of Keller's Personalized System of Instruction. *American Psychologist, 34*, 307–318.

Kulik, J. A., Kulik, C. C., & Cohen, P. A. (1980). Effectiveness of computer-based college teaching: A meta-analysis of findings. *Review of Educational Research, 50*, 525–544.

Kupersmidt, J. B., Buchele, K. S., Voegler, M. E., & Sedikides, C. (1996). Social self-discrepancy: A theory relating peer relations problems and school maladjustment. In J. Juvonen & K. R. Wentzel (Eds.), *Social motivation: Understanding children's school adjustment* (pp. 66–97). Cambridge, England: Cambridge University Press.

Kurtines, W. M., Berman, S. L., Ittel, A., & Williamson, S. (1995). Moral development: A co-constructivist perspective. In W. M. Kurtines & J. L. Gewirtz (Eds.), *Moral development: An introduction*. Boston: Allyn & Bacon.

Kyle, W. C., & Shymansky, J. A. (1989, April). Enhancing learning through conceptual change teaching. *NARST News, 31*, 7–8.

LaBar, K. S., & Phelps, E. A. (1998). Arousal-mediated memory consolidation: Role of the medial temporal lobe in humans. *Psychological Science, 9*, 490–493.

Ladd, G. W. (1990). Having friends, keeping friends, making friends, and being liked by peers in the classroom: Predictors of children's early school adjustment? *Child Development, 61*, 1081–1100.

Ladson-Billings, G. (1994a). *The dreamkeepers: Successful teachers of African American children*. San Francisco: Jossey-Bass.

Ladson-Billings, G. (1994b). What we can learn from multicultural education research. *Educational Leadership, 51*(8), 22–26.

Ladson-Billings, G. (1995). Toward a theory of culturally relevant pedagogy. *American Educational Research Journal, 32*, 465–491.

LaFromboise, T., Coleman, H. L. K., & Gerton, J. (1993). Psychological impact of biculturalism: Evidence and theory. *Psychological Bulletin, 114*, 395–412.

Lajoie, S. P., & Derry, S. J. (Eds.). (1993). *Computers as cognitive tools*. Hillsdale, NJ: Erlbaum.

Lamborn, S. D., Mounts, N. S., Steinberg, L., & Dornbusch, S. M. (1991). Patterns of competence and adjustment among adolescents from authoritative, authoritarian, indulgent, and neglectful families. *Child Development, 62*, 1049–1065.

Lamon, M., Chan, C., Scardamalia, M., Burtis, P. J., & Brett, C. (1993, April). *Beliefs about learning and constructive processes in reading: Effects of a computer supported intentional learning environment (CSILE)*. Paper presented at the annual meeting of the American Educational Research Association, Atlanta, GA.

Lampert, M. (1990). When the problem is not the question and the solution is not the answer: Mathematical knowing and teaching. *American Educational Research Journal, 27*, 29–63.

Lampert, M., Rittenhouse, P., & Crumbaugh, C. (1996). Agreeing to disagree: Developing sociable mathematical discourse. In D. R. Olson & N. Torrance (Eds.), *The handbook of education and human development: New models of learning, teaching, and schooling*. Cambridge, MA: Blackwell.

Lan, W. Y., Repman, J., Bradley, L., & Weller, H. (1994, April). *Immediate and lasting effects of criterion and payoff on academic risk taking*. Paper presented at the annual meeting of the American Educational Research Association, New Orleans, LA.

Landau, S., & McAninch, C. (1993). Young children with attention deficits. *Young Children, 48*(4), 49–58.

Landauer, T. K. (1962). Rate of implicit speech. *Perceptual and Motor Skills, 15*, 646.

Lane, D. M., & Pearson, D. A. (1982). The development of selective attention. *Merrill-Palmer Quarterly, 28*, 317–337.

Langer, E. J. (1997). *The power of mindful learning*. Reading, MA: Addison-Wesley.

Langer, E. J. (2000). Mindful learning. *Current Directions in Psychological Science, 9*, 220–223.

Langer, J. A. (2000). Excellence in English in middle and high school: How teachers' professional lives support student achievement. *American Educational Research Journal, 37*, 397–439.

Lanthier, R. P., & Bates, J. E. (1997, March). *Does infant temperament predict adjustment in adolescence?* Paper presented at the annual meeting of the American Educational Research Association, Chicago.

Laosa, L. M. (1982). School, occupation, culture, and family: The impact of parental schooling on the parent-child relationship. *Journal of Educational Psychology, 74*, 791–827.

Lapsley, D. K. (1993). Toward an integrated theory of adolescent ego development: The "new look" at adolescent egocentrism. *American Journal of Orthopsychiatry, 63,* 562–571.

Larson, R. W. (2000). Toward a psychology of positive youth development. *American Psychologist, 55,* 170–183.

Larson, R. W., Clore, G. L., & Wood, G. A. (1999). The emotions of romantic relationships: Do they wreak havoc on adolescents? In W. Furman, B. B. Brown, & C. Feiring (Eds.), *The development of romantic relationships in adolescence* (pp. 19–49). Cambridge, England: Cambridge University Press.

Laupa, M., & Turiel, E. (1995). Social domain theory. In W. M. Kurtines & J. L. Gewirtz (Eds.), *Moral development: An introduction.* Boston: Allyn & Bacon.

Leary, M. R. (1999). Making sense of self-esteem. *Current Directions in Psychological Science, 8,* 32–35.

Lee, C. (2004). Physical punishment of children: A psychological perspective. *Psynopsis, 26*(2), 12.

Lee, C. D., & Slaughter-Defoe, D. T. (1995). Historical and sociocultural influences on African and American education. In J. A. Banks & C. A. M. Banks (Eds.), *Handbook of research on multicultural education.* New York: Macmillan.

Lee, J. F., Jr., & Pruitt, K. W. (1984). *Providing for individual differences in student learning: A mastery learning approach.* Springfield, IL: Charles C Thomas.

Lee, O. (1999). Science knowledge, world views, and information sources in social and cultural contexts: Making sense after a natural disaster. *American Educational Research Journal, 36,* 187–219.

Lee, O., & Anderson, C. W. (1993). Task engagement and conceptual change in middle school science classrooms. *American Educational Research Journal, 30,* 585–610.

Lee-Pearce, M. L., Plowman, T. S., & Touchstone, D. (1998). Starbase-Atlantis, a school without walls: A comparative study of an innovative science program for at-risk urban elementary students. *Journal of Education for Students Placed at Risk, 3,* 223–235.

Legualt, L., Green-Demers, I., & Pelletier, L. (2006). Why do high school students lack motivation in the classroom: Toward an understanding of academic amotivation and the role of social support. *Journal of Educational Psychology, 98*(3), 567–582.

Leher, R. (1993). Authors of knowledge: Patterns of hypermedia design. In S. P. Lajoie & S. J. Derry (Eds.), *Computers as cognitive tools* (pp. 197–227). Mahwah, NJ: Erlbaum.

Leichtman, M. D., & Ceci, S. J. (1995). The effects of stereotypes and suggestions on preschoolers' reports. *Developmental Psychology, 31,* 568–578.

Leinhardt, G. (1994). History: A time to be mindful. In G. Leinhardt, I. L. Beck, & C. Stainton (Eds.), *Teaching and learning in history.* Hillsdale, NJ: Erlbaum.

Leinhardt, G., & Pallay, A. (1982). Restrictive educational settings: Exile or haven? *Review of Educational Research, 52,* 557–578.

Lejuez, C. W., Schaal, D. W., & O'Donnell, J. (1998). Behavioral pharmacology and the treatment of substance abuse. In J. J. Plaud & G. H. Eifert (Eds.), *From behavior theory to behavior therapy* (pp. 116–135). Needham Heights, MA: Allyn & Bacon.

Le Mare, L., & Sohbat, E. (2002). Canadian students' perceptions of teacher characteristics that support or inhibit help seeking. *The Elementary School Journal, 102*(3), 239–253.

Lennon, R., Eisenberg, N., & Carroll, J. L. (1983). The assessment of empathy in early childhood. *Journal of Applied Developmental Psychology, 4,* 295–302.

Lennon, R., Ormrod, J. E., Burger, S. F., & Warren, E. (1990, October). *Belief systems of teacher education majors and their possible influences on future classroom performance.* Paper presented at the Northern Rocky Mountain Educational Research Association, Greeley, CO.

Lentz, F. E. (1988). Reductive procedures. In J. C. Witt, S. N. Elliott, & F. M. Gresham (Eds.), *Handbook of behavior therapy in education.* New York: Plenum Press.

Lepper, M. R. (1981). Intrinsic and extrinsic motivation in children: Detrimental effects of superfluous social controls. In W. A. Collins (Ed.), *Minnesota Symposia on Child Psychology* (Vol. 14). Hillsdale, NJ: Erlbaum.

Lepper, M. R., Aspinwall, L. G., Mumme, D. L., & Chabay, R. W. (1990). Self-perception and social perception processes in tutoring: Subtle social control strategies of expert tutors. In J. M. Olson & M. P. Zanna (Eds.), *Self-inference processes: The Ontario Symposium.* Hillsdale, NJ: Erlbaum.

Lepper, M. R., & Gurtner, J. (1989). Children and computers: Approaching the twenty-first century. *American Psychologist, 44,* 170–178.

Lepper, M. R., & Hodell, M. (1989). Intrinsic motivation in the classroom. In C. Ames & R. Ames (Eds.), *Research on motivation in education: Vol. 3. Goals and cognitions.* San Diego, CA: Academic Press.

Lerman, D. C., & Iwata, B. A. (1995). Prevalence of the extinction burst and its attenuation during treatment. *Journal of Applied Behavior Analysis, 28,* 93–94.

Leroy, C., & Symes, B. (2001). Teachers' perspectives on the family backgrounds of children at risk. *McGill Journal of Education 36,* 45–60.

Lester, F. K., Jr., Lambdin, D. V., & Preston, R. V. (1997). A new vision of the nature and purposes of assessment in the mathematics classroom. In G. D. Phye (Ed.), *Handbook of classroom assessment: Learning, achievement, and adjustment.* San Diego, CA: Academic Press.

Levin, J. R., & Mayer, R. E. (1993). Understanding illustrations in text. In B. K. Britton, A. Woodward, & M. Binkley (Eds.), *Learning from textbooks: Theory and practice.* Hillsdale, NJ: Erlbaum.

Levine, D. U., & Lezotte, L. W. (1995). Effective schools research. In J. A. Banks & C. A. M. Banks (Eds.), *Handbook of research on multicultural education.* New York: Macmillan.

Levitt, M. J., Guacci-Franco, N., & Levitt, J. L. (1993). Convoys of social support in childhood and early adolescence: Structure and function. *Developmental Psychology, 29,* 811–818.

Levitt, M. J., Levitt, J. L., Bustos, G. L., Crooks, N. A., Santos, J. D., Telan, P., & Silver, M. E. (1999, April). *The social ecology of achievement in preadolescents: Social support and school attitudes.* Paper presented at the annual meeting of the American Educational Research Association, Montreal, Canada.

Levy, I., Kaplan, A., & Patrick, H. (2000, April). *Early adolescents' achievement goals, intergroup processes, and attitudes towards collaboration.* Paper presented at the annual meeting of the American Educational Research Association, New Orleans, LA.

Lewis, M. D. (2000). The promise of dynamic systems approaches for an integrated account of human development. *Child Development, 71,* 36–43.

Lickona, T. (1991). Moral development in the elementary school classroom. In W. M. Kurtines & J. L. Gewirtz (Eds.), *Moral behavior and development: Vol. 3. Application.* Hillsdale, NJ: Erlbaum.

Lieberman, L. M. (1992). Preserving special education... for those who need it. In W. Stainback & S. Stainback (Eds.), *Controversial issues confronting special education: Divergent perspectives.* Boston: Allyn & Bacon.

Lillard, A. S. (1997). Other folks' theories of mind and behavior. *Psychological Science, 8,* 268–274.

Lind, G. (1994, April). *Why do juvenile delinquents gain little from moral discussion programs?* Paper presented at the annual meeting of the American Educational Research Association, New Orleans, LA.

Lindberg, M. (1991). A taxonomy of suggestibility and eyewitness memory: Age, memory process, and focus of analysis. In J. L. Doris (Ed.), *The suggestibility of children's recollections.* Washington, DC: American Psychological Association.

Linderholm, T., Gustafson, M., van den Broek, P., & Lorch, R. F., Jr. (1997, March). *Effects of reading goals on inference generation.* Paper presented at the annual meeting of the American Educational Research Association, Chicago.

Linn, B., & Shore, B. M. (2008). Critical thinking. In J. A. Plucker & C. M. Callahan (Eds.), *Critical issues and practices in gifted education: What the research says* (pp. 155–165). Waco, TX: Prufrock Press (jointly published as a Service Publication of the National Association for Gifted Children, Washington, DC).

Linn, M. C., Clement, C., Pulos, S., & Sullivan, P. (1989). Scientific reasoning during adolescence: The influence of instruction in science knowledge and reasoning strategies. *Journal of Research in Science Teaching, 26,* 171–187.

Linn, M. C., & Hyde, J. S. (1989). Gender, mathematics, and science. *Educational Researcher, 18*(8), 17–19, 22–27.

Linn, M. C., & Petersen, A. C. (1985). Emergence and characterization of sex differences in spatial ability: A meta-analysis. *Child Development, 56,* 1479–1498.

Linn, M. C., Songer, N. B., & Eylon, B. (1996). Shifts and convergences in science learning and instruction. In D. C. Berliner & R. C. Calfee (Eds.), *Handbook of educational psychology.* New York: Macmillan.

Linn, R. L. (1994). Performance assessment: Policy promises and technical measurement standards. *Educational Researcher, 23*(9), 4–14.

Linn, R. L., & Gronlund, N. E. (2000). *Measurement and assessment in teaching* (8th ed.). Upper Saddle River, NJ: Merrill/Prentice Hall.

Lipson, M. Y. (1982). Learning new information from text: The role of prior knowledge and reading ability. *Journal of Reading Behavior, 14,* 243–261.

Lipson, M. Y. (1983). The influence of religious affiliation on children's memory for text information. *Reading Research Quarterly, 18,* 448–457.

Liss, M. B. (1983). Learning gender-related skills through play. In M. B. Liss (Ed.), *Social and cognitive skills: Sex roles and children's play.* San Diego, CA: Academic Press.

Little, T. D., Oettingen, G., Stetsenko, A., & Baltes, P. B. (1995). Children's action-control beliefs about school performance: How do American children compare with German and Russian children? *Journal of Personality and Social Psychology, 69,* 686–700.

Littlewood, W. T. (1984). *Foreign and second language learning: Language-acquisition research and its implications for the classroom.* Cambridge, England: Cambridge University Press.

Lloyd, D. N. (1978). Prediction of school failure from third-grade data. *Educational and Psychological Measurement, 38,* 1193–1200.

Lochman, J. E., & Dodge, K. A. (1994). Social-cognitive processes of severely violent, moderately aggressive, and nonaggressive boys. *Journal of Consulting and Clinical Psychology, 62,* 366–374.

Locke, E. A., & Latham, G. P. (1990). *A theory of goal setting and task performance.* Upper Saddle River, NJ: Prentice Hall.

Locke, E. A., & Latham, G. P. (1994). Goal setting theory. In H. F. O'Neil, Jr., & M. Drillings (Eds.), *Motivation: Theory and research.* Hillsdale, NJ: Erlbaum.

Lockhart, R. S., & Craik, F. I. M. (1990). Levels of processing: A retrospective commentary on a framework for memory research. *Canadian Journal of Psychology, 44,* 87–112.

Lodico, M. G., Ghatala, E. S., Levin, J. R., Pressley, M., & Bell, J. A. (1983). The effects of strategy monitoring training on children's selection of effective memory strategies. *Journal of Experimental Child Psychology, 35,* 273–277.

Loeber, R., & Stouthamer-Loeber, M. (1998). Development of juvenile aggression and violence. *American Psychologist, 53,* 242–259.

Loftus, E. F. (1991). Made in memory: Distortions in recollection after misleading information. In G. H. Bower (Ed.), *The psychology of learning and motivation: Advances in research and theory* (Vol. 27). San Diego, CA: Academic Press.

Loftus, E. F., & Loftus, G. R. (1980). On the permanence of stored information in the human brain. *American Psychologist, 35,* 409–420.

Lomawaima, K. T. (1995). Educating Native Americans. In J. A. Banks & C. A. M. Banks (Eds.), *Handbook of research on multicultural education.* New York: Macmillan.

Long, M. (1995). The role of the linguistic environment in second language acquisition. In W. C. Ritchie & T. K. Bhatia (Eds.), *Handbook of language acquisition: Vol. 2. Second language acquisition.* San Diego, CA: Academic Press.

López, G. R. (2001). Redefining parental involvement: Lessons from high-performing migrant-impacted schools. *American Educational Research Journal, 38,* 253–288.

Loranger, A. L. (1994). The study strategies of successful and unsuccessful high school students. *Journal of Reading Behavior, 26,* 347–360.

Lorch, E. P., Diener, M. B., Sanchez, R. P., Milich, R., Welsh, R., & van den Broek, P. (1999). The effects of story structure on the recall of stories in children with attention deficit hyperactivity disorder. *Journal of Educational Psychology, 91,* 251–260.

Lorch, R. F., Jr., Lorch, E. P., & Inman, W. E. (1993). Effects of signaling topic structure on text recall. *Journal of Educational Psychology, 85,* 281–290.

Losey, K. M. (1995). Mexican American students and classroom interaction: An overview and critique. *Review of Educational Research, 65,* 283–318.

Lou, Y., Abrami, P. C., Spence, J. C., Poulsen, C., Chambers, B., & d'Apollonia, S. (1996). Within-class grouping: A meta-analysis. *Review of Educational Research, 66,* 423–458.

Lovell, K. (1979). Intellectual growth and the school curriculum. In F. B. Murray (Ed.), *The impact of Piagetian theory: On education, philosophy, psychiatry, and psychology.* Baltimore: University Park Press.

Lovett, S. B., & Flavell, J. H. (1990). Understanding and remembering: Children's knowledge about the differential effects of strategy and task variables on comprehension and memorization. *Child Development, 61,* 1842–1858.

Lovitt, T. C., Guppy, T. E., & Blattner, J. E. (1969). The use of free-time contingency with fourth graders to increase spelling accuracy. *Behaviour Research and Therapy, 7,* 151–156.

Lowry, R., Sleet, D., Duncan, C., Powell, K., & Kolbe, L. (1995). Adolescents at risk for violence. *Educational Psychology Review, 7,* 7–39.

Lubart, T. I. (1994). Creativity. In R. J. Sternberg (Ed.), *Thinking and problem solving.* San Diego, CA: Academic Press.

Luchins, A. S. (1942). Mechanization in problem solving: The effect of Einstellung. *Psychological Monographs, 54* (Whole No. 248).

Luchins, A. S., & Luchins, E. H. (1950). New experimental attempts at preventing mechanization in problem solving. *Journal of General Psychology, 42,* 279–297.

Lundeberg, M. A., & Fox, P. W. (1991). Do laboratory findings on test expectancy generalize to classroom outcomes? *Review of Educational Research, 61,* 94–106.

Lupart, J. L. (1995). Exceptional learners and teaching for transfer. In A. McKeough, J. Lupart, & A. Marini (Eds.), *Teaching for transfer: Fostering generalization in learning.* Mahwah, NJ: Erlbaum.

Lyon, M. A. (1984). Positive reinforcement and logical consequences in the treatment of classroom encopresis. *School Psychology Review, 13,* 238–243.

Ma, X., & Kishor, N. (1997). Attitude toward self, social factors, and achievement in mathematics: A meta-analytic review. *Educational Psychology Review, 9,* 89–120.

Maccoby, E. E., & Martin, J. A. (1983). Socialization in the context of the family: Parent-child interaction. In E. M. Hetherington (Ed.), *Handbook of child psychology: Vol. 4. Socialization, personality, and social development* (4th ed.). New York: Wiley.

Mace, F. C., Belfiore, P. J., & Shea, M. C. (1989). Operant theory and research on self-regulation. In B. J. Zimmerman & D. H. Schunk (Eds.), *Self-regulated learning and academic achievement: Theory, research, and practice.* New York: Springer-Verlag.

Macguire, M.H., & McAlpine, L. (1996). Attautsikut/Together: Understanding cultural frames of reference. *The Alberta Journal of Educational Research, XLII* (3), 218-237.

Machiels-Bongaerts, M., Schmidt, H. G., & Boshuizen, H. P. A. (1991, April). *The effects of prior knowledge activation on free recall and study time allocation.* Paper presented at the annual meeting of the American Educational Research Association, Chicago.

MacLean, D. J., Sasse, D. K., Keating, D. P., Stewart, B. E., & Miller, F. K. (1995, April). *All-girls' mathematics and science instruction in early adolescence: Longitudinal effects.* Paper presented at the annual meeting of the American Educational Research Association, San Francisco.

Macphee, A. (2004). *Risk factors for depression in early adolescence.* Unpublished master's thesis. University of Calgary, Calgary, AB.

Madden, N. A., & Slavin, R. E. (1983). Mainstreaming students with mild handicaps: Academic and social outcomes. *Review of Educational Research, 53,* 519–569.

Maehr, M. L. (1984). Meaning and motivation: Toward a theory of personal investment. In R. Ames & C. Ames (Eds.), *Research on motivation in education: Vol. 1. Student motivation.* San Diego, CA: Academic Press.

Maehr, M. L., & Meyer, H. A. (1997). Understanding motivation and schooling: Where we've been, where we are, and where we need to go. *Educational Psychology Review, 9,* 371–409.

Maker, C. J. (1993). Creativity, intelligence, and problem solving: A definition and design for cross-cultural research and measurement related to giftedness. *Gifted Education International, 9*(2), 68–77.

Maker, C. J., & Schiever, S. W. (Eds.). (1989). *Critical issues in gifted education: Vol. 2. Defensible programs for cultural and ethnic minorities.* Austin, TX: Pro-Ed.

Mandler, G., & Pearlstone, Z. (1966). Free and constrained concept learning and subsequent recall. *Journal of Verbal Learning and Verbal Behavior, 5,* 126–131.

Manset, G., & Semmel, M. I. (1997). Are inclusive programs for students with mild disabilities effective? A comparative review of model programs. *Journal of Special Education, 31,* 155–180.

Marachi, R., Friedel, J., & Midgley, C. (2001, April). *"I sometimes annoy my teacher during math": Relations between student perceptions of the teacher and disruptive behavior in the classroom.* Paper presented at the annual meeting of the American Educational Research Association, Seattle, WA.

Maratsos, M. (1998). Some problems in grammatical acquisition. In W. Damon (Series Ed.), D. Kuhn, & R.S. Siegler (Vol. Eds.), *Handbook of child psychology: Vol 2. Cognition, perception, and language* (5th ed.). New York: Wiley.

Marcia, J. E. (1980). Identity in adolescence. In J. Adelson (Ed.), *Handbook of adolescent psychology.* New York: Wiley.

Marcia, J. E. (1988). Common processes underlying ego identity, cognitive/moral development, and individuation. In D. K. Lapsley & F. C. Power (Eds.), *Self, ego, and identity: Integrative approaches* (pp. 211–225). New York: Springer-Verlag.

Marcus, G. F. (1996). Why do children say "breaked"? *Current Directions in Psychological Science, 5,* 81–85.

Maria, K. (1998). Self-confidence and the process of conceptual change. In B. Guzzetti & C. Hynd (Eds.), *Perspectives on conceptual change: Multiple ways to understand knowing and learning in a complex world* (pp. 7–16). Mahwah, NJ: Erlbaum.

Markman, E. M. (1977). Realizing that you don't understand: A preliminary investigation. *Child Development, 48,* 986–992.

Markman, E. M. (1979). Realizing that you don't understand: Elementary school children's awareness of inconsistencies. *Child Development, 50,* 643–655.

Marks, H. M. (2000). Student engagement in instructional activity: Patterns in the elementary, middle, and high school years. *American Educational Research Journal, 37,* 153–184.

Marsh, H. W. (1990a). Causal ordering of academic self-concept and academic achievement: A multi-wave, longitudinal panel analysis. *Journal of Educational Psychology, 82,* 646–656.

Marsh, H. W. (1990b). A multidimensional, hierarchical model of self-concept: Theoretical and empirical justification. *Educational Psychology Review, 2,* 77–172.

Marsh, H. W., Chessor, D., Craven, R., & Roche, L. (1995). The effects of gifted and talented programs on academic self-concept: The big fish strikes again. *American Educational Research Journal, 32,* 285–319.

Marsh, H. W., & Craven, R. (1997). Academic self-concept: Beyond the dustbowl. In G. D. Phye (Ed.), *Handbook of classroom assessment: Learning, achievement, and adjustment.* San Diego, CA: Academic Press.

Marsh, H. W., & Yeung, A. S. (1997). Coursework selection: Relations to academic self-concept and achievement. *American Educational Research Journal, 34,* 691–720.

Marsh, H. W., & Yeung, A. S. (1998). Longitudinal structural equation models of academic self-concept and achievement: Gender differences in the development of math and English constructs. *American Educational Research Journal, 35,* 705–738.

Marshall, H. H. (1992). *Redefining student learning: Roots of educational change.* Norwood, NJ: Ablex.

Mash, E. J., & Wolfe, D. A. (1999). *Abnormal child psychology.* Belmont, CA: Brooks/Cole Wadsworth.

Maslow, A. H. (1973). Theory of human motivation. In R. J. Lowry (Ed.), *Dominance, self-esteem, self-actualization: Germinal papers of A. H. Maslow.* Monterey, CA: Brooks/Cole.

Maslow, A. H. (1987). *Motivation and personality* (3rd ed.). New York: Harper & Row.

Masten, A. S. (2001). Ordinary magic: Resilience processes in development. *American Psychologist, 56,* 227–238.

Masten, A. S., & Coatsworth, J. D. (1998). The development of competence in favorable and unfavorable environments. *American Psychologist, 53,* 205–220.

Mastropieri, M. A., & Scruggs, T. E. (2000). *The inclusive classroom: Strategies for effective instruction.* Upper Saddle River, NJ: Merrill/Prentice Hall.

Mastropieri, M. A., Scruggs, T. E., & Butcher, K. (1997). How effective is inquiry learning for students with mild disabilities? *Journal of Special Education, 31,* 199–211.

Masur, E. F., McIntyre, C. W., & Flavell, J. H. (1973). Developmental changes in apportionment of study time among items in a multitrial free recall task. *Journal of Experimental Child Psychology, 15,* 237–246.

Maxmell, D., Jarrett, O. S., & Dickerson, C. (1998, April). *Are we forgetting the children's needs? Recess through the children's eyes.* Paper presented at the annual meeting of the American Educational Research Association, San Diego, CA.

Mayer, R. E. (1974). Acquisition processes and resilience under varying testing conditions for structurally different problem solving procedures. *Journal of Educational Psychology, 66,* 644–656.

Mayer, R. E. (1984). Aids to text comprehension. *Educational Psychologist, 19,* 30–42.

Mayer, R. E. (1985). Implications of cognitive psychology for instruction in mathematical problem solving. In E. A. Silver (Ed.), *Teaching and learning mathematical problem solving: Multiple research perspectives.* Hillsdale, NJ: Erlbaum.

Mayer, R. E. (1986). Mathematics. In R. F. Dillon & R. J. Sternberg (Eds.), *Cognition and instruction.* San Diego, CA: Academic Press.

Mayer, R. E. (1989). Models for understanding. *Review of Educational Research, 59,* 43–64.

Mayer, R. E. (1992). *Thinking, problem solving, cognition* (2nd ed.). New York: Freeman.

Mayer, R. E. (1996). Learning strategies for making sense out of expository text: The SOI model for guiding three cognitive processes in knowledge construction. *Educational Psychology Review, 8,* 357–371.

Mayer, R. E., & Gallini, J. (1990). When is an illustration worth ten thousand words? *Journal of Educational Psychology, 82,* 715–726.

Mayer, R. E., & Wittrock, M. C. (1996). Problem-solving transfer. In D. C. Berliner & R. C. Calfee (Eds.), *Handbook of educational psychology.* New York: Macmillan.

McAdoo, H. P. (1985). Racial attitude and self-concept of young Black children over time. In H. P. McAdoo & J. L. McAdoo (Eds.), *Black children: Social, educational, and parental environments.* Newbury Park, CA: Sage.

McAlpine, L., & Taylor, D. M. (1993). Instructional preferences of Cree, Inuit, and Mohawk teachers. *Journal of American Indian Education, 33*(1), 1–20.

McAshan, H. H. (1979). *Competency-based education and behavioral objectives.* Englewood Cliffs, NJ: Educational Technology.

McCall, R. B. (1994). Academic underachievers. *Current Directions in Psychological Science, 3,* 15–19.

McCallum, R. S., & Bracken, B. A. (1993). Interpersonal relations between school children and their peers, parents, and teachers. *Educational Psychology Review, 5,* 155–176.

McCarty, T. L., & Watahomigie, L. J. (1998). Language and literacy in American Indian and Alaska Native communities. In B. Pérez (Ed.), *Sociocultural contexts of language and literacy.* Mahwah, NJ: Erlbaum.

McCaslin, M., & Good, T. L. (1996). The informal curriculum. In D. C. Berliner & R. C. Calfee (Eds.), *Handbook of educational psychology.* New York: Macmillan.

McClelland, D. C., Atkinson, J. W., Clark, R. A., & Lowell, E. L. (1953). *The achievement motive.* New York: Appleton-Century-Crofts.

McCown, R. R., Driscoll, M., Roop, P., Saklofske, D. H., Schwean, V. L., Kelly, I. W., & Haines, L. P. (1999). *Educational psychology: A learning-centred approach to classroom practice* (2nd Canadian ed.). Scarborough, ON: Allyn & Bacon.

McCoy, L. P. (1990, April). *Correlates of mathematics anxiety.* Paper presented at the annual meeting of the American Educational Research Association, Boston.

McDaniel, M. A., & Einstein, G. O. (1989). Material-appropriate processing: A contextualist approach to reading and studying strategies. *Educational Psychology Review, 1,* 113–145.

McDaniel, M. A., & Masson, M. E. J. (1985). Altering memory representations through retrieval. *Journal of Experimental Psychology: Learning, Memory, and Cognition, 11,* 371–385.

McDaniel, M. A., & Schlager, M. S. (1990). Discovery learning and transfer of problem-solving skills. *Cognition and Instruction, 7,* 129–159.

McDaniel, M. A., Waddill, P. J., & Einstein, G. O. (1988). A contextual account of the generation effect: A three-factor theory. *Journal of Memory and Language, 27,* 521–536.

McDevitt, T. M. (1990). Encouraging young children's listening skills. *Academic Therapy, 25,* 569–577.

McDevitt, T. M., & Ford, M. E. (1987). Processes in young children's communicative functioning and development. In M. E. Ford & D. H. Ford (Eds.), *Humans as self-constructing living systems: Putting the framework to work.* Hillsdale, NJ: Erlbaum.

McDevitt, T. M., Spivey, N., Sheehan, E. P., Lennon, R., & Story, R. (1990). Children's beliefs about listening: Is it enough to be still and quiet? *Child Development, 61,* 713–721.

McGee, L. M. (1992). An exploration of meaning construction in first graders' grand conversations. In C. K. Kinzer & D. J. Leu (Eds.), *Literacy research, theory, and practice: Views from many perspectives.* Chicago: National Reading Conference.

McGill, P. (1999). Establishing operations: Implications for the assessment, treatment, and prevention of problem behavior. *Journal of Applied Behavior Analysis, 32,* 393–418.

McGlynn, S. M. (1998). Impaired awareness of deficits in a psychiatric context: Implications for rehabilitation. In D. J. Hacker, J. Dunlosky, & A. C. Graesser (Eds.), *Metacognition in educational theory and practice* (pp. 221–248). Mahwah, NJ: Erlbaum.

McGue, M., Bouchard, T. J., Jr., Iacono, W. G., & Lykken, D. T. (1993). Behavioral genetics of cognitive ability: A life-span perspective. In R. Plomin & G. E. McClearn (Eds.), *Nature, nurture, and psychology.* Washington, DC: American Psychological Association.

McInerney, R. J., & Kerns, K. A. (2003). Time reproduction in children with ADHD: Motivation matters. *Child Neuropsychology, 9*(2), 91–108.

McKeachie, W. J., Lin, Y., Milholland, J., & Isaacson, R. (1966). Student affiliation motives, teacher warmth, and academic achievement. *Journal of Personality and Social Psychology, 4,* 457–461.

McKeown, M. G., & Beck, I. L. (1990). The assessment and characterization of young learners' knowledge of a topic in history. *American Educational Research Journal, 27,* 688–726.

McLean, L. (1988). Achievement measures made relevant to pedagogy. *McGill Journal of Education, 23,* 243–252.

McLean, L. (1990). Time to replace the classroom test with authentic measurement. *The Alberta Journal of Educational Research, 36,* 78–84.

McLeod, D. B., & Adams, V. M. (Eds.). (1989). *Affect and mathematical problem solving: A new perspective.* New York: Springer-Verlag.

McLoyd, V. C. (1998). Socioeconomic disadvantage and child development. *American Psychologist, 53,* 185–204.

McMillan, J. H., & Reed, D. F. (1994). At-risk students and resiliency: Factors contributing to academic success. *Clearing House, 67*(3), 137–140.

McMillan, J. H., Singh, J., & Simonetta, L. G. (1994). The tyranny of self-oriented self-esteem. *Educational Horizons, 72,* 141–145.

McMullen, K. (2004, December). First results from the 2003 Programme for International Student Assessment. *Education Matters: Insights on Education, Learning, and Training in Canada,* (5). Statistics Canada catalogue no. 81-004-XIE.

McNamara, D. S., & Healy, A. F. (1995). A generation advantage for multiplication skill training and nonword vocabulary acquisition. In A. F. Healy & L. E. Bourne, Jr. (Eds.), *Learning and memory of knowledge and skills: Durability and specificity.* Thousand Oaks, CA: Sage.

McNeil, N. M., & Alibali, M. W. (2000). Learning mathematics from procedural instruction: Externally imposed goals influence what is learned. *Journal of Educational Psychology, 92,* 734–744.

Meece, J. L. (1994). The role of motivation in self-regulated learning. In D. H. Schunk & B. J. Zimmerman (Eds.), *Self-regulation of learning and performance: Issues and educational applications.* Hillsdale, NJ: Erlbaum.

Meece, J. L., & Holt, K. (1993). A pattern analysis of students' achievement goals. *Journal of Educational Psychology, 85,* 582–590.

Mehan, H. (1979). *Social organization in the classroom.* Cambridge, MA: Harvard University Press.

Meichenbaum, D. (1977). *Cognitive-behavior modification: An integrative approach.* New York: Plenum Press.

Meichenbaum, D. (1985). Teaching thinking: A cognitive-behavioral perspective. In S. F. Chipman,

J. W. Segal, & R. Glaser (Eds.), *Thinking and learning skills: Vol. 2. Research and open questions*. Hillsdale, NJ: Erlbaum.

Meichenbaum, D., & Biemiller, A. (1998). *Nurturing independent learners: Helping students take charge of their learning.* Cambridge, MA: Brookline Books.

Meichenbaum, D., & Goodman, J. (1971). Training impulsive children to talk to themselves: A means of developing self-control. *Journal of Abnormal Psychology, 77*, 115–126.

Meloth, M. S., & Deering, P. D. (1994). Task talk and task awareness under different cooperative learning conditions. *American Educational Research Journal, 31*, 138–165.

Mercer, C. D. (1997). *Students with learning disabilities* (5th ed.). Upper Saddle River, NJ: Merrill/Prentice Hall.

Merrill, P. F., Hammons, K., Vincent, B. R., Reynolds, P. L., Christensen, L., & Tolman, M. N. (1996). *Computers in education* (3rd ed.). Needham Heights, MA: Allyn & Bacon.

Messick, S. (1983). Assessment of children. In W. Kessen (Ed.), *Handbook of child psychology* (Vol. 1). New York: Wiley.

Messick, S. (1994). The interplay of evidence and consequences in the validation of performance assessments. *Educational Researcher, 23*(2), 13–23.

Metsala, J., & Walley, A. C. (1998). Spoken vocabulary growth and the segmental restructuring of lexical representations: Precursors to phonemic awareness and early reading ability. In J. L. Metsala & J. L. Ehri (Eds.), *Word recognition in beginning literacy* (pp. 89–119). Mahwah, NJ: Erlbaum.

Metz, K. E. (1995). Reassessment of developmental constraints on children's science instruction. *Review of Educational Research, 65*, 93–127.

Meyer, B. J. F., Brandt, D. H., & Bluth, G. J. (1980). Use of top-level structure in text: Key for reading comprehension of ninth-grade students. *Reading Research Quarterly, 16*, 72–103.

Meyer, K. A. (1999). Functional analysis and treatment of problem behavior exhibited by elementary school children. *Journal of Applied Behavior Analysis, 32*, 229–232.

Meyer, M. S. (2000). The ability-achievement discrepancy: Does it contribute to an understanding of learning disabilities? *Educational Psychology Review, 12*, 315–337.

Meyers, D. T. (1987). The socialized individual and individual autonomy: An intersection between philosophy and psychology. In E. F. Kittay & S. T. Meyers (Eds.), *Women and moral theory*. Totowa, NJ: Rowman & Littlefield.

Michael, J. (2000). Implications and refinements of the establishing operation concept. *Journal of Applied Behavior Analysis, 33*, 401–410.

Middleton, M. J. (1999, April). *Classroom effects on the gender gap in middle school students' math self-efficacy*. Paper presented at the annual meeting of the American Educational Research Association, Montreal, Canada.

Middleton, M. J., & Midgley, C. (1997). Avoiding the demonstration of lack of ability: An underexplored aspect of goal theory. *Journal of Educational Psychology, 89*, 710–718.

Midgley, C., Kaplan, A., & Middleton, M. (2001). Performance-approach goals: Good for what, for whom, under what circumstances, and at what cost? *Journal of Educational Psychology, 93*, 77–86.

Midgley, C., Kaplan, A., Middleton, M., Maehr, M., Urdan, T., Anderman, L., Anderman, E., & Roeser, R. (1998). The development and validation of scales assessing students' achievement goal orientations. *Contemporary Educational Psychology, 23*, 113–131.

Milch-Reich, S., Campbell, S. B., Pelham, W. E., Jr., Connelly, L. M., & Geva, D. (1999). Developmental and individual differences in children's on-line representation of dynamic social events. *Child Development, 70*, 413–431.

Miller, B. C., & Benson, B. (1999). Romantic and sexual relationship development during adolescence. In W. Furman, B. B. Brown, & C. Feiring (Eds.), *The development of romantic relationships in adolescence* (pp. 99–121). Cambridge, England: Cambridge University Press.

Miller, D. L., & Kelley, M. L. (1994). The use of goal setting and contingency contracting for improving children's homework performance. *Journal of Applied Behavior Analysis, 27*, 73–84.

Miller, G. A. (1956). The magical number seven, plus or minus two: Some limits on our capacity for processing information. *Psychological Review, 63*, 81–97.

Miller, L. S. (1995). *An American imperative: Accelerating minority educational advancement*. New Haven, CT: Yale University Press.

Miller, P. H. (1993). Focus on the interface of cognition, social-emotional behavior and motivation. In P. H. Miller (Ed.), *Theories of developmental psychology* (3rd ed.). New York: Freeman.

Miller, R. R., & Barnet, R. C. (1993). The role of time in elementary associations. *Current Directions in Psychological Science, 2*, 106–111.

Millman, J., Bishop, C. H., & Ebel, R. (1965). An analysis of test-wiseness. *Educational and Psychological Measurement, 25*, 707–726.

Mills, G. E. (2000). *Action research: A guide for the teacher researcher.* Upper Saddle River, NJ: Merrill/Prentice Hall.

Minami, M., & Ovando, C. J. (1995). Language issues in multicultural contexts. In J. A. Banks & C. A. M. Banks (Eds.), *Handbook of research on multicultural education*. New York: Macmillan.

Minstrell, J., & Stimpson, V. (1996). A classroom environment for learning: Guiding students' reconstruction of understanding and reasoning. In L. Schauble & R. Glaser (Eds.), *Innovations in learning: New environments for education*. Mahwah, NJ: Erlbaum.

Mintzes, J. J., Trowbridge, J. E., Arnaudin, M. W., & Wandersee, J. H. (1991). Children's biology: Studies on conceptual development in the life sciences. In S. M. Glynn, R. H. Yeany, & B. K. Britton (Eds.), *The psychology of learning science*. Hillsdale, NJ: Erlbaum.

Mintzes, J. J., Wandersee, J. H., & Novak, J. D. (1997). Meaningful learning in science: The human constructivist perspective. In G. D. Phye (Ed.), *Handbook of academic learning: Construction of knowledge*. San Diego, CA: Academic Press.

Mitchell, M. (1993). Situational interest: Its multifaceted structure in the secondary school mathematics classroom. *Journal of Educational Psychology, 85*, 424–436.

Mohatt, G., & Erickson, F. (1981). Cultural differences in teaching styles in an Odawa school: A sociolinguistic approach. In H. T. Trueba, G. P. Guthrie, & K. H. Au (Eds.), *Culture and the bilingual classroom: Studies in classroom ethnography*. Rowley, MA: Newbury House.

Moje, E. B., & Shepardson, D. P. (1998). Social interactions and children's changing understanding of electric circuits: Exploring unequal power relations in "peer"-learning groups. In B. Guzzetti & C. Hynd (Eds.), *Perspectives on conceptual change: Multiple ways to understand knowing and learning in a complex world* (pp. 225–234). Mahwah, NJ: Erlbaum.

Moles, O. C. (Ed.). (1990). *Student discipline strategies: Research and practice*. Albany: State University of New York Press.

Moll, L. C., & Diaz, S. (1985). Ethnographic pedagogy: Promoting effective bilingual instruction. In E. E. García & R. V. Padilla (Eds.), *Advances in bilingual education research*. Tucson: University of Arizona Press.

Moll, M. (2004). *Passing the test: The false promises of standardized testing*. Ottawa: Canadian Centre for Policy Studies.

Moran, C. E., & Hakuta, K. (1995). Bilingual education: Broadening research perspectives. In J. A. Banks & C. A. M. Banks (Eds.), *Handbook of research on multicultural education*. New York: Macmillan.

Morgan, D. P., & Jenson, W. R. (1988). *Teaching behaviorally disordered students: Preferred practices*. Upper Saddle River, NJ: Merrill/Prentice Hall.

Morrow, S. L. (1997). Career development of lesbian and gay youth: Effects of sexual orientation, coming out, and homophobia. In M. B. Harris (Ed.), *School experiences of gay and lesbian youth: The invisible minority* (pp. 1–15). Binghamton, NY: Harrington Park Press.

Mueller, J. H. (1980). Test anxiety and the encoding and retrieval of information. In I. G. Sarason (Ed.), *Test anxiety: Theory, research, and applications*. Hillsdale, NJ: Erlbaum.

Mulcahy, R. F., Marfo, K., Peat, D., & Andrews, J. (1986). *A strategies program for effective learning and thinking (SPELT): Teacher's manual*. Edmonton: Cognitive Education Project, University of Alberta.

Mulcahy, R. F., Marfo, K., Peat, D., Andrews, J., & Clifford, L. (1986). Applying cognitive psychology in the classroom. A learning-thinking strategies instructional program. *Alberta Psychology, 15*(3), 9–13.

Mulcahy, R. F., Peat, D., Andrews, J., Clifford, L., Marfo, K., & Cho, S. (1989). Cognitive education final report. Edmonton: Alberta Education, Government of Alberta.

Munn, P., Johnstone, M., & Chalmers, V. (1990, April). *How do teachers talk about maintaining effective discipline in their classrooms?* Paper presented at the annual meeting of the American Educational Research Association, Boston.

Murdock, T. B. (1999). The social context of risk: Status and motivational predictors of alienation in middle school. *Journal of Educational Psychology, 91*, 62–75.

Murdock, T. B., Hale, N., Weber, M. J., Tucker, V., & Briggs, W. (1999, April). *Relations of cheating to social and academic motivation among middle school students*. Paper presented at the annual meeting of the American Educational Research Association, Montreal, Canada.

Murphy, D. M. (1996). Implications of inclusion for general and special education. *Elementary School Journal, 96*, 469–492.

Murphy, P. K. (2000). A motivated exploration of motivation terminology. *Contemporary Educational Psychology, 25*, 3–53.

Murray, C. B., & Jackson, J. S. (1982/1983). The conditioned failure model of black educational underachievement. *Humboldt Journal of Social Relations, 10*, 276–300.

Nadel, L., & Jacobs, W. J. (1998). Traumatic memory is special. *Current Directions in Psychological Science, 7*, 154–157.

Naglieri, J. A., & Das, J. P. (1997). *Cognitive Assessment System*. Chicago: Riverside Publishing.

Narváez, D. (1998). The influence of moral schemas on the reconstruction of moral narratives in eighth graders and college students. *Journal of Educational Psychology, 90*, 13–24.

Narváez, D., & Rest, J. (1995). The four components of acting morally. In W. M. Kurtines & J. L. Gewirtz (Eds.), *Moral development: An introduction*. Boston: Allyn & Bacon.

National Assessment of Educational Progress. (1985). *The reading report card: Progress toward excellence in our schools; trends in reading over four national assessments, 1971–1984.* Princeton, NJ: NAEP.

Natriello, G., & Dornbusch, S. M. (1984). *Teacher evaluative standards and student effort.* White Plains, NY: Longman.

Navarro, R. A. (1985). The problems of language, education, and society: Who decides. In E. E. García & R. V. Padilla (Eds.), *Advances in bilingual education research.* Tucson: University of Arizona Press.

NCSS Task Force on Ethnic Studies Curriculum Guidelines. (1992). Curriculum guidelines for multicultural education. *Social Education, 56,* 274–294.

Neel, R. S., Jenkins, Z. N., & Meadows, N. (1990). Social problem-solving behaviors and aggression in young children: A descriptive observational study. *Behavioral Disorders, 16*(1), 39–51.

Neisser, U. (1967). *Cognitive psychology.* New York: Appleton-Century-Crofts.

Neisser, U. (Ed.). (1998). *The rising curve: Long-term gains in IQ and related measures.* Washington, DC: American Psychological Association.

Neisser, U., Boodoo, G., Bouchard, T. J., Boykin, A. W., Brody, N., Ceci, S. J., Halpern, D. F., Loehlen, J. C., Perloff, R., Sternberg, R. J., & Urbina, S. (1996). Intelligence: Knowns and unknowns. *American Psychologist, 51,* 77–101.

Nelson, J. R., Smith, D. J., Young, R. K., & Dodd, J. M. (1991). A review of self-management outcome research conducted with students who exhibit behavioral disorders. *Behavioral Disorders, 16,* 169–179.

Nelson, T. O., & Dunlosky, J. (1991). When people's judgments of learning (JOLs) are extremely accurate at predicting subsequent recall: The "delayed-JOL effect." *Psychological Science, 2,* 267–270.

Nelson-Barber, S., & Estrin, E. (1995). Bringing Native American perspectives to mathematics and science teaching. *Theory into Practice, 34,* 174–185.

Newby, T. J., Ertmer, P. A., & Stepich, D. A. (1994, April). *Instructional analogies and the learning of concepts.* Paper presented at the annual meeting of the American Educational Research Association, New Orleans, LA.

Newcomb, A. F., & Bagwell, C. L. (1995). Children's friendship relations: A meta-analysis review. *Psychological Bulletin, 117,* 306–347.

Newman, R. S., & Schwager, M. T. (1995). Students' help seeking during problem solving: Effects of grade, goal, and prior achievement. *American Educational Research Journal, 32,* 352–376.

Newmann, F. M. (1981). Reducing student alienation in high schools: Implications of theory. *Harvard Educational Review, 51,* 546–564.

Newmann, F. M. (1997). Authentic assessment in social studies: Standards and examples. In G. D. Phye (Ed.), *Handbook of classroom assessment: Learning, achievement, and adjustment.* San Diego, CA: Academic Press.

Newmann, F. M., & Wehlage, G. G. (1993). Five standards of authentic instruction. *Educational Leadership, 50*(7), 8–12.

Newport, E. L. (1993). Maturational constraints on language learning. In P. Bloom (Ed.), *Language acquisition: Core readings.* Cambridge, MA: MIT Press.

New Zealand Ministry of Education. (2006). Enabling the 21st century learner: e-Learning action plan for schools 2006–2010. Retrieved August 18, 2008, from http://www.minedu.govt.nz/educationSetors/Schools/Initiatives/ICTInSchools/ICTInitiativesAndProgrammes/EnablingThe21stCenturyLearner.aspx.

Nezavdal, F. (2003). The standardized testing movement: Equitable or excessive? *The McGill Journal of Education, 38,* 65–78.

Nicholls, J. G. (1979). Development of perception of own attainment and causal attributions for success and failure in reading. *Journal of Educational Psychology, 71,* 94–99.

Nicholls, J. G. (1984). Conceptions of ability and achievement motivation. In R. Ames & C. Ames (Eds.), *Research on motivation in education: Vol 1. Student motivation.* San Diego, CA: Academic Press.

Nicholls, J. G. (1990). What is ability and why are we mindful of it? A developmental perspective. In R. J. Sternberg & J. Kolligian (Eds.), *Competence considered.* New Haven, CT: Yale University Press.

Nicholls, J. G., Cobb, P., Yackel, E., Wood, T., & Wheatley, G. (1990). Students' theories of mathematics and their mathematical knowledge: Multiple dimensions of assessment. In G. Kulm (Ed.), *Assessing higher order thinking in mathematics.* Washington, DC: American Association for the Advancement of Science.

Nichols, J. D. (1996). The effects of cooperative learning on student achievement and motivation in a high school geometry class. *Contemporary Educational Psychology, 21,* 467–476.

Nichols, J. D., Ludwin, W. G., & Iadicola, P. (1999). A darker shade of gray: A year-end analysis of discipline and suspension data. *Equity and Excellence in Education, 32*(1), 43–55.

Nichols, M. L., & Ganschow, L. (1992). Has there been a paradigm shift in gifted education? In N. Coangelo, S. G. Assouline, & D. L. Ambroson (Eds.), *Talent development: Proceedings from the 1991 Henry B. and Jocelyn Wallace National Research Symposium on Talent Development.* New York: Trillium.

Nieto, S. (1995). A history of the education of Puerto Rican students in U.S. mainland schools: "Losers", "outsiders," or "leaders"? In J. A. Banks & C. A. M. Banks (Eds.), *Handbook of research on multicultural education.* New York: Macmillan.

Nippold, M. A. (1988). The literate lexicon. In M. A. Nippold (Ed.), *Later language development: Ages nine through nineteen.* Boston: Little, Brown.

Nippold, M. A. (1991). Evaluating and enhancing idiom comprehension in language-disordered students. *Language, Speech, and Hearing Services in the Schools, 22,* 100–106.

Nist, S. L., Simpson, M. L., Olejnik, S., & Mealey, D. L. (1991). The relation between self-selected study processes and test performance. *American Educational Research Journal, 28,* 849–874.

Nix, R. L., Pinderhughes, E. E., Dodge, K. A., Bates, J. E., Pettit, G. S., & McFadyen-Ketchum, S. A. (1999). The relation between mothers' hostile attribution tendencies and children's externalizing behavior problems: The mediating role of mothers' harsh discipline practices. *Child Development, 70,* 896–909.

Noddings, N. (1985). Small groups as a setting for research on mathematical problem solving. In E. A. Silver (Ed.), *Teaching and learning mathematical problem solving: Multiple research perspectives.* Hillsdale, NJ: Erlbaum.

Nolen, S. B. (1996). Why study? How reasons for learning influence strategy selection. *Educational Psychology Review, 8,* 335–355.

Nolen-Hoeksema, S. (2001). Gender differences in depression. *Current Directions in Psychological Science, 10,* 173–176.

Norman, D. A. (1969). *Memory and attention: An introduction to human information processing.* New York: Wiley.

Northup, J., Broussard, C., Jones, K., George, T., Vollmer, T. R., & Herring, M. (1995). The differential effects of teachers and peer attention on the disruptive classroom behavior of three children with a diagnosis of attention deficit hyperactivity disorder. *Journal of Applied Behavior Analysis, 28,* 227–228.

Nottelmann, E. D. (1987). Competence and self-esteem during transition from childhood to adolescence. *Developmental Psychology, 23,* 441–450.

Novak, J. D. (1998). *Learning, creating, and using knowledge: Concept maps as facilitative tools in schools and corporations.* Mahwah, NJ: Erlbaum.

Novak, J. D., & Gowin, D. B. (1984). *Learning how to learn.* Cambridge, England: Cambridge University Press.

Novak, J. D., & Musonda, D. (1991). A twelve-year longitudinal study of science concept learning. *American Educational Research Journal, 28,* 117–153.

Nucci, L. P., & Nucci, M. S. (1982a). Children's responses to moral and social conventional transgressions in free-play settings. *Child Development, 53,* 1337–1342.

Nucci, L. P., & Nucci, M. S. (1982b). Children's social interactions in the context of moral and conventional transgressions. *Child Development, 53,* 403–412.

Numeroff, L. J. (1991). *If you give a moose a muffin.* Toronto, ON: HarperCollins.

Nunner-Winkler, G. (1984). Two moralities? A critical discussion of an ethic of care and responsibility versus an ethic of rights and justice. In W. M. Kurtines & J. L. Gewirtz (Eds.), *Morality, moral behavior, and moral development.* New York: Wiley.

Nussbaum, J. (1985). The earth as a cosmic body. In R. Driver (Ed.), *Children's ideas of science.* Philadelphia: Open University Press.

Nuthall, G. (1996). Commentary: Of learning and language and understanding the complexity of the classroom. *Educational Psychologist, 31,* 207–214.

Oakes, J., & Guiton, G. (1995). Matchmaking: The dynamics of high school tracking decisions. *American Educational Research Journal, 32,* 3–33.

O'Boyle, M. W., & Gill, H. S. (1998). On the relevance of research findings in cognitive neuroscience to educational practice. *Educational Psychology Review, 10,* 397–409.

O'Donnell, A. M. (1999). Structuring dyadic interaction through scripted cooperation. In A. M. O'Donnell & A. King (Eds.), *Cognitive perspectives on peer learning* (pp. 179–196). Mahwah, NJ: Erlbaum.

O'Donnell, A. M., & O'Kelly, J. (1994). Learning from peers: Beyond the rhetoric of positive results. *Educational Psychology Review, 6,* 321–349.

Ogbu, J. U. (1994). From cultural differences to differences in cultural frame of reference. In P. M. Greenfield & R. R. Cocking (Eds.), *Cross-cultural roots of minority child development.* Hillsdale, NJ: Erlbaum.

Ogbu, J. U. (1999). Beyond language: Ebonics, proper English, and identity in a Black-American speech community. *American Educational Research Journal, 36,* 147–184.

Ogden, E. H., & Germinario, V. (1988). *The at-risk student: Answers for educators.* Lancaster, PA: Technomic.

O'Grady, W. (1997). *Syntactic development.* Chicago: University of Chicago.

Ohler, J. (2006). The world of digital storytelling. *Educational Leadership, 63*(4), 44–47.

O'Leary, K. D., Kaufman, K. F., Kass, R. E., & Drabman, R. S. (1970). The effects of loud and soft reprimands on the behavior of disruptive students. *Exceptional Children, 37,* 145–155.

O'Leary, K. D., & O'Leary, S. G. (Eds.). (1972). *Classroom management: The successful use of behavior modification.* New York: Pergamon Press.

Olneck, M. R. (1995). Immigrants and education. In J. A. Banks & C. A. M. Banks (Eds.), *Handbook of research on multicultural education.* New York: Macmillan.

Onosko, J. J. (1989). Comparing teachers' thinking about promoting students' thinking. *Theory and Research in Social Education, 17,* 174–195.

Onosko, J. J. (1996). Exploring issues with students despite the barriers. *Social Education, 60*(1), 22–27.

Onosko, J. J., & Newmann, F. M. (1994). Creating more thoughtful learning environments. In J. N. Mangieri & C. C. Block (Eds.), *Advanced educational psychology: Enhancing mindfulness.* Fort Worth, TX: Harcourt Brace Jovanovich.

Onyskiw, J., & Hayduk, L. (2001). Processes underlying children's adjustment in families characterized by physical aggression. *Family Relations, 50*(4), 376–386.

Ormrod, J. E. (1999). *Human learning* (3rd ed.). Upper Saddle River, NJ: Merrill/Prentice Hall.

Ormrod, J. E., & Jenkins, L. (1989). Study strategies in spelling: Correlations with achievement and developmental changes. *Perceptual and Motor Skills, 68,* 643–650.

Ormrod, J. E., & Wagner, E. D. (1987, October). *Spelling conscience in undergraduate students: Ratings of spelling accuracy and dictionary use.* Paper presented at the annual meeting of the Northern Rocky Mountain Educational Research Association, Park City, UT.

Oskamp, S. (Ed.). (2000). *Reducing prejudice and discrimination.* Mahwah, NJ: Erlbaum.

Osterman, K. F. (2000). Students' need for belonging in the school community. *Review of Educational Research, 70,* 323–367.

O'Sullivan, J. T., & Joy, R. M. (1990, April). *Children's theories about reading difficulty: A developmental study.* Paper presented at the annual meeting of the American Educational Research Association, Boston.

Owens, R. E., Jr. (1996). *Language development* (4th ed.). Boston: Allyn & Bacon.

Packard, V. (1983). *Our endangered children: Growing up in a changing world.* Boston: Little Brown.

Page-Voth, V., & Graham, S. (1999). Effects of goal setting and strategy use on the writing performance and self-efficacy of students with writing and learning problems. *Journal of Educational Psychology, 91,* 230–240.

Pajares, F., & Valiante, G. (1999). *Writing self-efficacy of middle school students: Relation to motivation constructs, achievement, gender, and gender orientation.* Paper presented at the annual meeting of the American Educational Research Association, Montreal, Canada.

Paley, V. G. (1984). *Boys and girls: Superheroes in the doll corner.* Chicago: University of Chicago Press.

Palincsar, A.S. (1986). Metacognitive strategy instruction. *Exceptional Children, 53,* 118–124.

Palincsar, A. S., & Brown, A. L. (1984). Reciprocal teaching of comprehension-fostering and comprehension-monitoring activities. *Cognition and Instruction, 1,* 117–175.

Palincsar, A. S., & Herrenkohl, L. R. (1999). Designing collaborative contexts: Lessons from three research programs. In A. M. O'Donnell & A. King (Eds.), *Cognitive perspectives on peer learning.* Mahwah, NJ: Erlbaum.

Palmer, E. L. (1965). Accelerating the child's cognitive attainments through the inducement of cognitive conflict: An interpretation of the Piagetian position. *Journal of Research in Science Teaching, 3,* 324.

Pang, V. O. (1995). Asian Pacific American students: A diverse and complex population. In J. A. Banks & C. A. M. Banks (Eds.), *Handbook of research on multicultural education.* New York: Macmillan.

Paris, S. G. (1986). Teaching children to guide their reading and learning. In T. Raphael (Ed.), *The contexts of school-based literacy.* New York: Random House.

Paris, S. G. (1988). Models and metaphors of learning strategies. In C. E. Weinstein, E. T. Goetz, & P. A. Alexander (Eds.), *Learning and study strategies: Issues in assessment, instruction, and evaluation.* San Diego, CA: Academic Press.

Paris, S. G., & Ayres, L. R. (1994). *Becoming reflective students and teachers with portfolios and authentic assessment.* Washington, DC: American Psychological Association.

Paris, S. G., & Byrnes, J. P. (1989). The constructivist approach to self-regulation and learning in the classroom. In B. J. Zimmerman & D. H. Schunk (Eds.), *Self-regulated learning and academic achievement: Theory, research, and practice.* New York: Springer-Verlag.

Paris, S. G., Cross, D. R., & Lipson, M. Y. (1984). Informed strategies for learning: A program to improve children's reading awareness and comprehension. *Journal of Educational Psychology, 76,* 1239–1252.

Paris, S. G., & Cunningham, A. E. (1996). Children becoming students. In D. C. Berliner & R. C. Calfee (Eds.), *Handbook of educational psychology.* New York: Macmillan.

Paris, S. G., Lawton, T. A., Turner, J. C., & Roth, J. L. (1991). A developmental perspective on standardized achievement testing. *Educational Researcher, 20*(5), 12–20, 40.

Paris, S. G., & Oka, E. R. (1986). Children's reading strategies, metacognition, and motivation. *Developmental Review, 6,* 25–56.

Paris, S. G., & Paris, A. H. (2001). Classroom applications of research on self-regulated learning. *Educational Psychologist, 36,* 89–101.

Paris, S. G., & Turner, J. C. (1994). Situated motivation. In P. R. Pintrich, D. R. Brown, & C. E. Weinstein (Eds.), *Student motivation, cognition, and learning: Essays in honor of Wilbert J. McKeachie.* Hillsdale, NJ: Erlbaum.

Paris, S. G., & Winograd, P. (1990). How metacognition can promote academic learning and instruction. In B. F. Jones & L. Idol (Eds.), *Dimensions of thinking and cognitive instruction.* Hillsdale, NJ: Erlbaum.

Parke, R. D. (1974). Rules, roles, and resistance to deviation: Explorations in punishment, discipline, and self-control. In A. Pick (Ed.), *Minnesota Symposia on Child Psychology* (Vol. 8). Minneapolis: University of Minnesota Press.

Parks, C. P. (1995). Gang behavior in the schools: Reality or myth? *Educational Psychology Review, 7,* 41–68.

Parnes, S. J. (1967). *Creative behavior guidebook.* New York: Scribner's.

Parsons, J. E., Adler, T. F., & Kaczala, C. M. (1982). Socialization of achievement attitudes and beliefs: Parental influences. *Child Development, 53,* 310–321.

Parsons, J. E., Kaczala, C. M., & Meece, J. L. (1982). Socialization of achievement attitudes and beliefs: Classroom influences. *Child Development, 53,* 322–339.

Pascual-Leone, J. (1976). On learning and development, Piagetian style: II. A critical historical analysis of Geneva's research programme. *Canadian Psychological Review, 17,* 289–297.

Patrick, H. (1997). Social self-regulation: Exploring the relations between children's social relationships, academic self-regulation, and school performance. *Educational Psychologist, 32,* 209–220.

Patterson, C. J. (1995). Sexual orientation and human development: An overview. *Developmental Psychology, 31,* 3–11.

Patton, J. R., Blackbourn, J. M., & Fad, K. S. (1996). *Exceptional individuals in focus* (6th ed.). Upper Saddle River, NJ: Merrill/Prentice Hall.

Paulson, F. L., Paulson, P. R., & Meyer, C. A. (1991). What makes a portfolio a portfolio? *Educational Leadership, 49*(5), 60–63.

Paulson, K., & Johnson, M. (1983). Sex-role attitudes and mathematical ability in 4th, 8th, and 11th grade students from a high socioeconomic area. *Developmental Psychology, 19,* 210–214.

Paxton, R. J. (1999). A deafening silence: History textbooks and the students who read them. *Review of Educational Research, 69,* 315–339.

PBS. (n.d.). "Hernán Cortés arrives in Mexico." *The border.* Retrieved May 15, 2008, from http://www.pbs.org/kpbs/theborder/history/timeline/1.html.

Pedersen, P. (1991). Introduction to the special issue on multiculturalism as a fourth force in counselling. *Journal of Counselling & Development, 70,* 4.

Pellegrini, A. D., & Bartini, M. (2000). A longitudinal study of bullying, victimization, and peer affiliation during the transition from primary school to middle school. *American Educational Research Journal, 37,* 699–725.

Pellegrini, A. D., & Bjorklund, D. F. (1997). The role of recess in children's cognitive performance. *Educational Psychologist, 32,* 35–40.

Pellegrini, A. D., & Horvat, M. (1995). A developmental contextualist critique of attention deficit hyperactivity disorder. *Educational Researcher, 24*(1), 13–19.

Pellegrini, A. D., Huberty, P. D., & Jones, I. (1995). The effects of recess timing on children's playground and classroom behaviors. *American Educational Research Journal, 32,* 845–864.

Pelletier, S., & Shore, B. M. (2003). The gifted learner, the novice, and the expert: Sharpening emerging views of giftedness. In D. C. Ambrose, L. Cohen, & A. J. Tannenbaum (Eds.), *Creative intelligence: Toward theoretic integration* (pp. 237–281). New York: Hampton Press.

Perera, K. (1986). Language acquisition and writing. In P. Fletcher & M. Garman (Eds.), *Language acquisition: Studies in first language development* (2nd ed.). Cambridge, England: Cambridge University Press.

Pérez, B. (1998). *Sociocultural contexts of language and literacy.* Mahwah, NJ: Erlbaum.

Perkins, D. N. (1990). The nature and nurture of creativity. In B. F. Jones & L. Idol (Eds.), *Dimensions of thinking and cognitive instruction.* Hillsdale, NJ: Erlbaum.

Perkins, D. N. (1992). *Smart schools: From training memories to educating minds.* New York: Free Press/Macmillan.

Perkins, D. N. (1995). *Outsmarting IQ: The emerging science of learnable intelligence.* New York: Free Press.

Perkins, D. N., & Salomon, G. (1987). Transfer and teaching thinking. In D. N. Perkins, J. Lochhead, & J. Bishop (Eds.), *Thinking: The second international conference.* Hillsdale, NJ: Erlbaum.

Perkins, D. N., & Salomon, G. (1989). Are cognitive skills context-bound? *Educational Researcher, 18*(1), 16–25.

Perkins, D. N., & Simmons, R. (1988). Patterns of misunderstanding: An integrative model for science, math, and programming. *Review of Educational Research, 58,* 303–326.

Perry, B. D. (2006). Fear and learning: Trauma-related factors in the adult education process. *New Directions for Adult and Continuing Education, 110,* 21–27.

Perry, D. G., & Perry, L. C. (1983). Social learning, causal attribution, and moral internalization. In J. Bisanz, G. L. Bisanz, & R. Kail (Eds.), *Learning in children: Progress in cognitive development research.* New York: Springer-Verlag.

Perry, N. E. (1998). Young children's self-regulated learning and contexts that support it. *Journal of Educational Psychology, 90,* 715–729.

Perry, N. E., Nordby, C. J., & Vandecamp, K. O. (2003). Promoting self-regulated reading and writing at home and school. *The Elementary School Journal, 103*(4), 317–338.

Perry, N. E., Vandecamp, K. O., Mercer, L. K., & Nordby, C. J. (2002). Investigating teacher-student interactions that foster self-regulated learning. *Educational Psychologist, 37*(1), 5–15.

Perry, R. P. (1985). Instructor expressiveness: Implications for improving teaching. In J. G. Donald & A. M. Sullivan (Eds.), *Using research to improve teaching* (pp. 35–49). San Francisco: Jossey-Bass.

Petersen, G. A., Sudweeks, R. R., & Baird, J. H. (1990, April). *Test-wise responses of third-, fifth-, and sixth-grade students to clued and unclued multiple-choice science items.* Paper presented at the annual meeting of the American Educational Research Assocation, Boston.

Peterson, C. (1990). Explanatory style in the classroom and on the playing field. In S. Graham & V. S. Folkes (Eds.), *Attribution theory: Applications to achievement, mental health, and interpersonal conflict.* Hillsdale, NJ: Erlbaum.

Peterson, C., Maier, S., & Seligman, M. (1993). *Learned helplessness: A theory for the age of personal control.* New York: Oxford University Press.

Peterson, L. R., & Peterson, M. J. (1959). Short-term retention of individual items. *Journal of Experimental Psychology, 58,* 193–198.

Peterson, P. L. (1988). Teachers' and students' cognitional knowledge for classroom teaching and learning. *Educational Researcher, 17*(5), 5–14.

Petrill, S. A., & Wilkerson, B. (2000). Intelligence and achievement: A behavioral genetic perspective. *Educational Psychology Review, 12,* 185–199.

Pfiffner, L. J., & Barkley, R. A. (1998). Treatment of ADHD in school settings. In R. A. Barkley, *Attention-deficit hyperactivity disorder: A handbook for diagnosis and treatment* (2nd ed., pp. 458–490). New York: Guilford Press.

Pfiffner, L. J., & O'Leary, S. G. (1993). School-based psychological treatments. In J. L. Matson (Ed.), *Handbook of hyperactivity in children* (pp. 234–255). Boston: Allyn & Bacon.

Pfiffner, L. J., Rosen, L. A., & O'Leary, S. G. (1985). The efficacy of an all-positive approach to classroom management. *Journal of Applied Behavior Analysis, 18,* 257–261.

Phelan, P., Davidson, A. L., & Cao, H. T. (1991). Students' multiple worlds: Negotiating the boundaries of family, peer, and school cultures. *Anthropology and Education Quarterly, 22,* 224–250.

Phelan, P., Yu, H. C., & Davidson, A. L. (1994). Navigating the psychosocial pressures of adolescence: The voices and experiences of high school youth. *American Educational Research Journal, 31,* 415–447.

Philips, D., Schwean, V. L., & Saklofske, D. H. (1997). Treatment effect of a school-based cognitive-behavioural program for aggressive children. *Canadian Journal of School Psychology, 13,* 60–67.

Phillip, R. A., Flores, A., Sowder, J. T., & Schappelle, B. P. (1994). Conceptions and practices of extraordinary mathematics teachers. *Journal of Mathematical Behavior, 13,* 155–180.

Phillips, B. N., Pitcher, G. D., Worsham, M. E., & Miller, S. C. (1980). Test anxiety and the school environment. In I. G. Sarason (Ed.), *Test anxiety: Theory, research, and applications.* Hillsdale, NJ: Erlbaum.

Phillips, D., & Zimmerman, M. (1990). The developmental course of perceived competence and incompetence among competent children. In R. Sternberg & J. Kolligian (Eds.), *Competence considered* (pp. 41–66). New Haven, CT: Yale University Press.

Phinney, J. (1989). Stages of ethnic identity development in minority group adolescents. *Journal of Early Adolescence, 9,* 34–39.

Phye, G. D. (1997). Classroom assessment: A multi-dimensional perspective. In G. D. Phye (Ed.), *Handbook of classroom assessment: Learning, achievement, and adjustment.* San Diego, CA: Academic Press.

Piaget, J. (1928). *Judgment and reasoning in the child* (M. Warden, Trans.). New York: Harcourt, Brace.

Piaget, J. (1929). *The child's conception of the world.* New York: Harcourt, Brace.

Piaget, J. (1952). *The origins of intelligence in children* (M. Cook, Trans.). New York: Norton.

Piaget, J. (1959). *The language and thought of the child* (3rd ed.; M. Gabain, Trans.). London: Routledge & Kegan Paul.

Piaget, J. (1970). Piaget's theory. In P. H. Mussen (Ed.), *Carmichael's manual of psychology.* New York: Wiley.

Piaget, J. (1980). *Adaptation and intelligence: Organic selection and phenocopy* (S. Eames, Trans.). Chicago: University of Chicago Press.

Piersel, W. C. (1987). Basic skills education. In C. A. Maher & S. G. Forman (Eds.), *A behavioral approach to education of children and youth.* Hillsdale, NJ: Erlbaum.

Pigott, H. E., Fantuzzo, J. W., & Clement, P. W. (1986). The effects of reciprocal peer tutoring and group contingencies on the academic performance of elementary school children. *Journal of Applied Behavior Analysis, 19,* 93–98.

Piirto, J. (1999). *Talented children and adults: Their development and education* (2nd ed.). Upper Saddle River, NJ: Merrill/Prentice Hall.

Pine, K. J., & Messer, D. J. (2000). The effect of explaining another's actions on children's implicit theories of balance. *Cognition and Instruction, 18,* 35–51.

Pinker, S. (1987). The bootstrapping problem in language acquisition. In B. MacWhinney (Ed.), *Mechanisms of language acquisition.* Hillsdale, NJ: Erlbaum.

Pintrich, P. R. (2000). Multiple goals, multiple pathways: The role of goal orientation in learning and achievement. *Journal of Educational Psychology, 92,* 544–555.

Pintrich, P. R., & De Groot, E. V. (1990). Motivational and self-regulated learning components of classroom academic performance. *Journal of Educational Psychology, 82,* 33–40.

Pintrich, P. R., & García, T. (1994). Regulating motivation and cognition in the classroom: The role of self-schemas and self-regulatory strategies. In D. Schunk & B. Zimmerman (Eds.), *Self-regulation of learning and performance: Issues and educational applications.* Hillsdale, NJ: Erlbaum.

Pintrich, P. R., García, T., & De Groot, E. (1994, April). *Positive and negative self-schemas and self-regulated learning.* Paper presented at the annual meeting of the American Educational Research Association, New Orleans, LA.

Pintrich, P. R., Marx, R. W., & Boyle, R. A. (1993). Beyond cold conceptual change: The role of motivational beliefs and classroom contextual factors in the process of conceptual change. *Review of Educational Research, 63,* 167–199.

Pintrich, P. R., & Schrauben, B. (1992). Students' motivational beliefs and their cognitive engagement in academic tasks. In D. Schunk & J. Meece (Eds.), *Students' perceptions in the classroom: Causes and consequences.* Hillsdale, NJ: Erlbaum.

Pintrich, P. R., & Schunk, D. H. (2002). *Motivation in education: Theory, research, and applications* (2nd ed.). Upper Saddle River, NJ: Merrill/Prentice Hall.

Piontkowski, D., & Calfee, R. (1979). Attention in the classroom. In G. A. Hale & M. Lewis (Eds.), *Attention and cognitive development.* New York: Plenum Press.

Pipher, M. (1994). *Reviving Ophelia: Saving the selves of adolescent girls.* New York: Putnam.

Pitoniak, M. J., & Royer, J. M. (2001). Testing accommodations for examinees with disabilities: A review of psychometric, legal, and social policy issues. *Review of Educational Research, 71,* 53–104.

Pittman, K., & Beth-Halachmy, S. (1997, March). *The role of prior knowledge in analogy use.* Paper presented at the annual meeting of the American Educational Research Association, Chicago.

Plomin, R. (1989). Environment and genes: Determinants of behavior. *American Psychologist, 44,* 105–111.

Plomin, R. (1994). *Genetics and experience: The interplay between nature and nurture.* Thousand Oaks, CA: Sage.

Plomin, R., Fulker, D. W., Corley, R., & DeFries, J. C. (1997). Nature, nurture, and cognitive development from 1 to 16 years: A parent-offspring adoption study. *Psychological Science, 8,* 442–447.

Plumert, J. M. (1994). Flexibility in children's use of spatial and categorical organizational strategies in recall. *Developmental Psychology, 30,* 738–747.

Poche, C., Yoder, P., & Miltenberger, R. (1988). Teaching self-protection to children using television techniques. *Journal of Applied Behavior Analysis, 21,* 253–261.

Pollard, S. R., Kurtines, W. M., Carlo, G., Dancs, M., & Mayock, E. (1991). Moral education from the perspective of psychosocial theory. In W. M. Kurtines & J. L. Gewirtz (Eds.), *Moral behavior and development: Vol. 3. Application.* Hillsdale, NJ: Erlbaum.

Polloway, E. A., & Patton, J. R. (1993). *Strategies for teaching learners with special needs* (5th ed.). Upper Saddle River, NJ: Merrill/Prentice Hall.

Poole, D. (1994). Routine testing practices and the linguistic construction of knowledge. *Cognition and Instruction, 12,* 125–150.

Popham, W. J. (1990). *Modern educational measurement: A practitioner's perspective* (2nd ed.). Upper Saddle River, NJ: Prentice Hall.

Popham, W. J. (1995). *Classroom assessment: What teachers need to know.* Needham Heights, MA: Allyn & Bacon.

Porath, M. (1988, April). *Cognitive development of gifted children: A neo-Piagetian perspective.* Paper presented at the annual meeting of the

American Educational Research Association, New Orleans, LA.

Porter, A. C. (1989). A curriculum out of balance: The case of elementary school mathematics. *Educational Researcher, 18*(5), 9–15.

Portes, P. R. (1996). Ethnicity and culture in educational psychology. In D. C. Berliner & R. C. Calfee (Eds.), *Handbook of educational psychology*. New York: Macmillan.

Posner, G. J., Strike, K. A., Hewson, P. W., & Gertzog, W. A. (1982). Accommodation of a scientific conception: Toward a theory of conceptual change. *Science Education, 66*, 211–227.

Postman, L., & Underwood, B. J. (1973). Critical issues in interference theory. *Memory and Cognition, 1*, 19–40.

Powell, S., & Nelson, B. (1997). Effects of choosing academic assignments on a student with attention deficit hyperactivity disorder. *Journal of Applied Behavior Analysis, 30*, 181–183.

Power, F. C., Higgins, A., & Kohlberg, L. (1989). *Lawrence Kohlberg's approach to moral education*. New York: Columbia University Press.

Power, F. C., & Power, M. R. (1992). A raft of hope: Democratic education and the challenge of pluralism. *Journal of Moral Education, 21*, 193–205.

Powers, L. E., Sowers, J. A., & Stevens, T. (1995). An exploratory, randomized study of the impact of mentoring on the self-efficacy and community-based knowledge of adolescents with severe physical challenges. *Journal of Rehabilitation, 61*(1), 33–41.

Powers, L. E., Wilson, R., Matuszewski, J., Phillips, A., Rein, C., Schumacher, D., & Gensert, J. (1996). Facilitating adolescent self-determination. In D. J. Sands & M. L. Wehmeyer (Eds.), *Self-determination across the life span: Independence and choice for people with disabilities*. Baltimore: Brookes.

Powers, S. I., Hauser, S. T., & Kilner, L. A. (1989). Adolescent mental health. *American Psychologist, 44*, 200–208.

Prawat, R. S. (1989). Promoting access to knowledge, strategy, and disposition in students: A research synthesis. *Review of Educational Research, 59*, 1–41.

Prawat, R. S. (1992). From individual differences to learning communities: Our changing focus. *Educational Leadership, 49*(7), 9–13.

Prawat, R. S. (1993). The value of ideas: Problems versus possibilities in learning. *Educational Researcher, 22*(6), 5–16.

Premack, D. (1959). Toward empirical behavior laws: I. Positive reinforcement. *Psychological Review, 66*, 219–233.

Premack, D. (1963). Rate differential reinforcement in monkey manipulation. *Journal of Experimental Analysis of Behavior, 6*, 81–89.

Presseisen, B. Z., & Beyer, F. S. (1994, April). *Facing history and ourselves: An instructional tool for constructivist theory*. Paper presented at the annual meeting of the American Educational Research Association, New Orleans, LA.

Pressley, M. (1982). Elaboration and memory development. *Child Development, 53*, 296–309.

Pressley, M. (with McCormick, C. B.) (1995). *Advanced educational psychology for educators, researchers, and policymakers*. New York: HarperCollins.

Pressley, M., Borkowski, J. G., & Schneider, W. (1987). Cognitive strategies: Good strategy users coordinate metacognition and knowledge. In R. Vasta (Ed.), *Annals of child development* (Vol. 4). Greenwich, CT: JAI Press.

Pressley, M., El-Dinary, P. B., Gaskins, I. W., Schuder, T., Bergman, J. L., Almasi, J., & Brown, R. (1992). Beyond direct explanation: Transactional instruction of reading comprehension strategies. *The Elementary School Journal, 92*, 513–555.

Pressley, M., El-Dinary, P. B., Marks, M. B., Brown, R., & Stein, S. (1992). Good strategy instruction is motivating and interesting. In K. A. Renninger, S. Hidi, & A. Krapp (Eds.), *The role of interest in learning and development*. Hillsdale, NJ: Erlbaum.

Pressley, M., Harris, K. R., & Marks, M. B. (1992). But good strategy instructors are constructivists! *Educational Psychology Review, 4*, 3–31.

Pressley, M., Levin, J. R., & Delaney, H. D. (1982). The mnemonic keyword method. *Review of Educational Research, 52*, 61–91.

Pressley, M., Snyder, B. L., & Cariglia-Bull, T. (1987). How can good strategy use be taught to children? Evaluation of six alternative approaches. In S. M. Cormier & J. D. Hagman (Eds.), *Transfer of learning: Contemporary research and applications*. San Diego, CA: Academic Press.

Pressley, M., Woloshyn, V., Lysynchuk, L. M., Martin, V., Wood, E., & Willoughby, T. (1990). A primer of research on cognitive strategy instruction: The important issues and how to address them. *Educational Psychology Review, 2*, 1–58.

Pressley, M., Yokoi, L., van Meter, P., Van Etten, S., & Freebern, G. (1997). Some of the reasons why preparing for exams is so hard: What can be done to make it easier? *Educational Psychology Review, 9*, 1–38.

Price-Williams, D. R., Gordon, W., & Ramirez, M. (1969). Skill and conservation. *Developmental Psychology, 1*, 769.

Pritchard, R. (1990). The effects of cultural schemata on reading processing strategies. *Reading Research Quarterly, 25*, 273–295.

Proctor, R. W., & Dutta, A. (1995). *Skill acquisition and human performance*. Thousand Oaks, CA: Sage.

Pruitt, R. P. (1989). Fostering creativity: The innovative classroom environment. *Educational Horizons, 68*(1), 51–54.

Pulos, S., & Linn, M. C. (1981). Generality of the controlling variables scheme in early adolescence. *Journal of Early Adolescence, 1*, 26–37.

Puntambekar, S., & Hübscher, R. (2005). Tools for scaffolding students in a complex learning environment. What have we gained and what have we missed? *Educational Psychologist, 40*, 1–12.

Purdie, N., & Hattie, J. (1996). Cultural differences in the use of strategies for self-regulated learning. *American Educational Research Journal, 33*, 845–871.

Purdie, N., Hattie, J., & Douglas, G. (1996). Student conceptions of learning and their use of self-regulated learning strategies: A cross-cultural comparison. *Journal of Educational Psychology, 88*, 87–100.

Pushor, Debbie. (2007). *Parent engagement: Creating a shared world*. Invited paper for the Ontario Education Research Symposium, Toronto.

Qin, Z., Johnson, D. W., & Johnson, R. T. (1995). Cooperative versus competitive efforts and problem solving. *Review of Educational Research, 65*, 129–143.

Raber, S. M. (1990, April). *A school system's look at its dropouts: Why they left school and what has happened to them*. Paper presented at the annual meeting of the American Educational Research Association, Boston.

Rabinowitz, M., & Glaser, R. (1985). Cognitive structure and process in highly competent performance. In F. D. Horowitz & M. O'Brien (Eds.), *The gifted and the talented: Developmental perspectives*. Washington, DC: American Psychological Association.

Rachlin, H. (1991). *Introduction to modern behaviorism* (3rd ed.). New York: Freeman.

Radke-Yarrow, M., Zahn-Waxler, C., & Chapman, M. (1983). Children's prosocial dispositions and behavior. In E. M. Hetherington (Ed.), *Handbook of child psychology: Vol. 4. Socialization, personality, and social development*. New York: Wiley.

Radziszewska, B., & Rogoff, B. (1991). Children's guided participation in planning imaginary errands with skilled adult or peer partners. *Developmental Psychology, 27*, 381–389.

Rakow, S. J. (1984). What's happening in elementary science: A national assessment. *Science and Children, 21*(4), 39–40.

Ramey, C. T., & Ramey, S. L. (1998). Early intervention and early experience. *American Psychologist, 53*, 109–120.

Ramsey, P. G. (1987). *Teaching and learning in a diverse world: Multicultural education for young children*. New York: Teachers College Press.

Ramsey, P. G. (1995). Growing up with the contradictions of race and class. *Young Children, 50*, 18–22.

Randall, T., & Macgregor, S. (2005). Online project-based learning: How collaborative strategies and problem solving processes impact performance. *Journal of Interactive Learning Research, 16*(1), 83–107.

Rapport, M. D., Murphy, H. A., & Bailey, J. S. (1982). Ritalin vs. response cost in the control of hyperactive children: A within-subject comparison. *Journal of Applied Behavior Analysis, 15*, 205–216.

Raudenbush, S. W. (1984). Magnitude of teacher expectancy effects on pupil IQ as a function of credibility induction: A synthesis of findings from 18 experiments. *Journal of Educational Psychology, 76*, 85–97.

Rawsthorne, L. J., & Elliot, A. J. (1999). Achievement goals and intrinsic motivation: A meta-analytic review. *Personality and Social Psychology Review, 3*, 326–344.

Reeve, J., Bolt, E., & Cai, Y. (1999). Autonomy-supportive teachers: How they teach and motivate students. *Journal of Educational Psychology, 91*, 537–548.

Reich, P. A. (1986). *Language development*. Upper Saddle River, NJ: Prentice Hall.

Reid, S. (2002). The integration of information and communication technology into classroom teaching. *The Alberta Journal of Educational Research, 48*(1), 30–46.

Reimann, P., & Schult, T. J. (1996). Turning examples into cases: Acquiring knowledge structures for analogical problem solving. *Educational Psychologist, 31*, 123–132.

Reimer, J., Paolitto, D. P., & Hersh, R. H. (1983). *Promoting moral growth: From Piaget to Kohlberg* (2nd ed.). White Plains, NY: Longman.

Reiner, M., Slotta, J. D., Chi, M. T. H., & Resnick, L. B. (2000). Naïve physics reasoning: A commitment to substance-based conceptions. *Cognition and Instruction, 18*, 1–34.

Reisberg, D. (1997). *Cognition: Exploring the science of the mind*. New York: Norton.

Reisberg, D., & Heuer, F. (1992). Remembering the details of emotional events. In E. Winograd & U. Neisser (Eds.), *Affect and accuracy in recall: Studies of "flashbulb" memories*. Cambridge, England: Cambridge University Press.

Reiter, S. N. (1994). Teaching dialogically: Its relationship to critical thinking in college students. In P. R. Pintrich, D. R. Brown, & C. E. Weinstein (Eds.), *Student motivation, cognition, and learning: Essays in honor of Wilbert J. McKeachie*. Hillsdale, NJ: Erlbaum.

Renkl, A., Mandl, H., & Gruber, H. (1996). Inert knowledge: Analyses and remedies. *Educational Psychologist, 31*, 115–121.

Renninger, K. A., Hidi, S., & Krapp, A. (Eds.). (1992). *The role of interest in learning and development*. Hillsdale, NJ: Erlbaum.

Renzulli, J. S. (1978). What makes giftedness? Reexamining a definition. *Phi Delta Kappan, 60*, 180–184.

Resnick, D. P., & Resnick, L. B. (1996). Performance assessment and the multiple functions of educational measurement. In M. B. Kane & R. Mitchell (Eds.), *Implementing performance assessment: Promises, problems, and challenges* (pp. 23–38). Mahwah, NJ: Erlbaum.

Resnick, L. B. (1983). Mathematics and science learning: A new conception. *Science, 220*, 477–478.

Resnick, L. B. (1989). Developing mathematical knowledge. *American Psychologist, 44*, 162–169.

Resnick, M. D., Bearman, P. S., Blum, R. W., Bauman, K. E., Harris, K. M., Jones, J., Tabor, J., Beuhring, T., Sieving, R. E., Shew, M., Ireland, M., Bearinger, L. H., & Udry, J. R. (1997). Protecting adolescents from harm: Findings from the National Longitudinal Study on Adolescent Health. *Journal of the American Medical Association, 278*, 823–832.

Rest, J., Narvaez, D., Bebeau, M., & Thoma, S. (1999). A neo-Kohlbergian approach: The DIT and schema theory. *Educational Psychology Review, 11*, 291–324.

Reusser, K. (1990, April). *Understanding word arithmetic problems: Linguistic and situational factors*. Paper presented at the annual meeting of the American Educational Research Association, Boston.

Reyna, C. (2000). Lazy, dumb, or industrious: When stereotypes convey attribution information in the classroom. *Educational Psychology Review, 12*, 85–110.

Reyna, C., & Weiner, B. (2001). Justice and utility in the classroom: An attributional analysis of the goals of teachers' punishment and intervention strategies. *Journal of Educational Psychology, 93*, 309–319.

Reynolds, M. C., & Birch, J. W. (1988). *Adaptive mainstreaming: A primer for teachers and principals* (3rd ed.). White Plains, NY: Longman.

Reynolds, R. E., & Shirey, L. L. (1988). The role of attention in studying and learning. In C. E. Weinstein, E. T. Goetz, & P. A. Alexander (Eds.), *Learning and study strategies: Issues in assessment, instruction, and evaluation*. San Diego, CA: Academic Press.

Reynolds, R. E., Taylor, M. A., Steffensen, M. S., Shirey, L. L., & Anderson, R. C. (1982). Cultural schemata and reading comprehension. *Reading Research Quarterly, 17*, 353–366.

Ricciuti, H. N. (1993). Nutrition and mental development. *Current Directions in Psychological Science, 2*, 43–46.

Riggs, J. M. (1992). Self-handicapping and achievement. In A. K. Boggiano & T. S. Pittman (Eds.), *Achievement and motivation: A social-developmental perspective*. Cambridge, England: Cambridge University Press.

Rimm, D. C., & Masters, J. C. (1974). *Behavior therapy: Techniques and empirical findings*. San Diego, CA: Academic Press.

Ripple, R. E. (1989). Ordinary creativity. *Contemporary Educational Psychology, 14*, 189–202.

Ritts, V., Patterson, M. L., & Tubbs, M. E. (1992). Expectations, impressions, and judgments of physically attractive students: A review. *Review of Educational Research, 62*, 413–426.

Roberts, G. C., Treasure, D. C., & Kavussanu, M. (1997). Motivation in physical activity contexts: An achievement goal perspective. *Advances in Motivation and Achievement, 10*, 413–447.

Robinson, A. (1991). Cooperation or exploitation? The argument against cooperative learning for talented students. *Journal for the Education of the Gifted, 14*, 9–27.

Robinson, A., Shore, B. M., & Enerson, D. L. (2006). *Best practices in gifted education: An evidence-based guide*. Waco, TX: Prufrock Press (Jointly published as a Service Publication of the National Association for Gifted Children, Washington, DC).

Roblyer, M. D., Castine, W. H., & King, F. J. (1988). *Assessing the impact of computer-based instruction: A review of recent research*. New York: Haworth.

Roderick, M. (1994). Grade retention and school dropout: Investigating the association. *American Educational Research Journal, 31*, 729–759.

Roderick, M., & Camburn, E. (1999). Risk and recovery from course failure in the early years of high school. *American Educational Research Journal, 36*, 303–343.

Roediger, H. L., III, & McDermott, K. B. (2000). Tricks of memory. *Current Directions in Psychological Science, 9*, 123–127.

Rogers, T. B., Kuiper, N. A., & Kirker, W. S. (1977). Self-reference and the encoding of personal information. *Journal of Personality and Social Psychology, 35*, 677–688.

Rogers, W. T., & Yang, P. (1996). Test-wiseness: Its nature and applications. *European Journal of Psychological Assessment, 12*, 247–259.

Rogoff, B. (1990). *Apprenticeship in thinking: Cognitive development in social context*. New York: Oxford University Press.

Rogoff, B. (1991). Social interaction as apprenticeship in thinking: Guidance and participation in spatial planning. In L. B. Resnick, J. M. Levine, & S. D. Teasley (Eds.), *Perspectives on socially shared cognition*. Washington, DC: American Psychological Association.

Rogoff, B. (1994, April). *Developing understanding of the idea of communities of learners*. Paper presented at the annual meeting of the American Educational Research Association, New Orleans, LA.

Rogoff, B., Matusov, E., & White, C. (1996). Models of teaching and learning: Participation in a community of learners. In D. R. Olson & N. Torrance (Eds.), *The handbook of education and human development: New models of learning, teaching, and schooling*. Cambridge, MA: Blackwell.

Rogoff, B., & Waddell, K. J. (1982). Memory for information organized in a scene by children from two cultures. *Child Development, 53*, 1224–1228.

Rohner, R. P. (1998). Father love and child development: History and current evidence. *Current Directions in Psychological Science, 7*, 157–161.

Roopnarine, J. L., Lasker, J., Sacks, M., & Stores, M. (1998). The cultural contexts of children's play. In O. N. Saracho & B. Spodek (Eds.), *Multiple perspectives on play in early childhood education*. Albany: State University of New York Press.

Rortvedt, A. K., & Miltenberger, R. G. (1994). Analysis of a high-probability instructional sequence and time-out in the treatment of child noncompliance. *Journal of Applied Behavior Analysis, 27*, 327–330.

Rosch, E. H., Mervis, C. B., Gray, W. D., Johnson, D. M., & Boyes-Braem, P. (1976). Basic objects in natural categories. *Cognitive Psychology, 8*, 382–439.

Rose, A. J., & Asher, S. R. (1999). Children's goals and strategies in response to conflicts within a friendship. *Developmental Psychology, 35*, 69–79.

Rose, S. C., & Thornburg, K. R. (1984). Mastery motivation and need for approval in young children: Effects of age, sex, and reinforcement condition. *Educational Research Quarterly, 9*(1), 34–42.

Rosenberg, M. (1986). Self-concept from middle childhood through adolescence. In S. Suls & A. Greenwald (Eds.), *Psychological perspectives on the self* (Vol. 3, pp. 107–135). Hillsdale, NJ: Erlbaum.

Rosenshine, B., & Meister, C. (1992). The use of scaffolds for teaching higher-level cognitive strategies. *Educational Leadership, 49*(7), 26–33.

Rosenshine, B., Meister, C., & Chapman, S. (1996). Teaching students to generate questions: A review of the intervention studies. *Review of Educational Research, 66*, 181–221.

Rosenshine, B. V., & Stevens, R. (1986). Teaching functions. In M. C. Wittrock (Ed.), *Handbook of research on teaching* (3rd ed.). New York: Macmillan.

Rosenthal, R. (1994). Interpersonal expectancy effects: A 30-year perspective. *Current Directions in Psychological Science, 3*, 176–179.

Rosenthal, T. L., Alford, G. S., & Rasp, L. M. (1972). Concept attainment, generalization, and retention through observation and verbal coding. *Journal of Experimental Child Psychology, 13*, 183–194.

Rosenthal, T. L., & Bandura, A. (1978). Psychological modeling: Theory and practice. In S. L. Garfield & A. E. Begia (Eds.), *Handbook of psychotherapy and behavior change: An empirical analysis* (2nd ed.). New York: Wiley.

Rosenthal, T. L., & Zimmerman, B. J. (1978). *Social learning and cognition*. San Diego, CA: Academic Press.

Ross, D., & Roberts, P. (1999). Income and Child Well-being: A new perspective on the poverty debate. Canadian Council on Social Development.

Ross, J. A. (1988). Controlling variables: A meta-analysis of training studies. *Review of Educational Research, 58*, 405–437.

Ross, J. A., Hogaboam-Gray, A., & Hannay, L. (2001). Effects of teacher efficacy on computer skills and computer cognitions of Canadian students in grades K-3. *The Elementary School Journal, 102*(2), 141–156.

Rosser, R. (1994). *Cognitive development: Psychological and biological perspectives*. Needham Heights, MA: Allyn & Bacon.

Rotenberg, K. J., & Mayer, E. V. (1990). Delay of gratification in Native and White children: A cross-cultural comparison. *International Journal of Behavioral Development, 13*, 23–30.

Roth, K. J. (1990). Developing meaningful conceptual understanding in science. In B. F. Jones & L. Idol (Eds.), *Dimensions of thinking and cognitive instruction*. Hillsdale, NJ: Erlbaum.

Roth, K. J., & Anderson, C. (1988). Promoting conceptual change learning from science textbooks. In P. Ramsden (Ed.), *Improving learning: New perspectives*. London: Kogan Page.

Roth, W., & Bowen, G. M. (1995). Knowing and interacting: A study of culture, practices, and resources in a grade 8 open-inquiry science classroom guided by a cognitive apprenticeship metaphor. *Cognition and Instruction, 13*, 73–128.

Rothbart, M. K., & Bates, J. E. (1998). Temperament. In W. Damon (Editor-in-Chief) & N. Eisenberg (Vol. Ed.), *Handbook of child psychology: Vol. 3. Social, emotional, and personality development* (5th ed., pp. 105–176). New York: Wiley.

Rothbaum, F., Weisz, J., Pott, M., Miyake, K., & Morelli, G. (2000). Attachment and culture: Security in the United States and Japan. *American Psychologist, 55,* 1093–1104.

Rowe, E. (1999, April). *Gender differences in math self-concept development: The role of classroom interaction.* Paper presented at the annual meeting of the American Educational Research Association, Montreal, Canada.

Rowe, M. B. (1974). Wait-time and rewards as instructional variables, their influence on language, logic, and fate control: Part one—Wait time. *Journal of Research in Science Teaching, 11,* 81–94.

Rowe, M. B. (1987). Wait-time: Slowing down may be a way of speeding up. *American Educator, 11,* 38–43, 47.

Ruben, R. J. (1999). Time frame of critical/sensitive periods of language development. *Indian Journal of Otolaryngology and Head and Neck Surgery, 51,* 85.

Rubin, K. H. (1982). Nonsocial play in preschoolers: Necessarily evil? *Child Development, 53,* 651–657.

Rubin, K. H., Bukowski, W., & Parker, J. G. (1998). Peer interactions, relationships, and groups. In W. Damon (Editor-in-Chief) & N. Eisenberg (Vol. Ed.), *Handbook of child psychology: Vol. 3. Social, emotional, and personality development* (5th ed.). New York: Wiley.

Ruble, D. N. (1988). Sex-role development. In M. H. Bornstein & M. E. Lamb (Eds.), *Developmental psychology: An advanced textbook* (2nd ed.). Hillsdale, NJ: Erlbaum.

Ruble, D. N., & Ruble, T. L. (1982). Sex stereotypes. In A. G. Miller (Ed.), *In the eye of the beholder.* New York: Praeger.

Rudman, M. K. (1993). Multicultural children's literature: The search for universals. In M. K. Rudman (Ed.), *Children's literature: Resource for the classroom* (2nd ed.). Norwood, MA: Christopher-Gordon.

Rueda, R., & Moll, L. C. (1994). A sociocultural perspective on motivation. In H. F. O'Neil, Jr., & M. Drillings (Eds.), *Motivation: Theory and research.* Hillsdale, NJ: Erlbaum.

Ruef, M. B., Higgins, C., Glaeser, B., & Patnode, M. (1998). Positive behavioral support: Strategies for teachers. *Intervention in School and Clinic, 34*(1), 21–32.

Rueger, D. B., & Liberman, R. P. (1984). Behavioral family therapy for delinquent substance-abusing adolescents. *Journal of Drug Abuse, 14,* 403–418.

Ruff, H. A., & Lawson, K. R. (1990). Development of sustained, focused attention in young children during free play. *Developmental Psychology, 26,* 85–93.

Ruffman, T., Perner, J., Olson, D. R., & Doherty, M. (1993). Reflecting on scientific thinking: Children's understanding of the hypothesis-evidence relation. *Child Development, 64,* 1617–1636.

Rumberger, R. W. (1995). Dropping out of middle school: A multilevel analysis of students and schools. *American Educational Research Journal, 32,* 583–625.

Rumelhart, D. E., & Ortony, A. (1977). The representation of knowledge in memory. In R. C. Anderson, R. J. Spiro, & W. E. Montague (Eds.), *Schooling and the acquisition of knowledge.* Hillsdale, NJ: Erlbaum.

Runco, M. A., & Chand, I. (1995). Cognition and creativity. *Educational Psychology Review, 7,* 243–267.

Rushton, J. P. (1980). *Altruism, socialization, and society.* Upper Saddle River, NJ: Prentice Hall.

Russ, S. W. (1993). *Affect and creativity: The role of affect and play in the creative process.* Hillsdale, NJ: Erlbaum.

Ryan, A. M. (2000). Peer groups as a context for the socialization of adolescents' motivation, engagement, and achievement in school. *Educational Psychologist, 35,* 101–111.

Ryan, A. M., & Patrick, H. (2001). The classroom social environment and changes in adolescents' motivation and engagement during middle school. *American Educational Research Journal, 38,* 437–460.

Ryan, A. M., Pintrich, P. R., & Midgley, C. (2001). Avoiding seeking help in the classroom: Who and why? *Educational Psychology Review, 13,* 93–114.

Ryan, R. M., Connell, J. P., & Grolnick, W. S. (1992). When achievement is *not* intrinsically motivated: A theory of internalization and self-regulation in school. In A. K. Boggiano & T. S. Pittman (Eds.), *Achievement and motivation: A social-developmental perspective.* Cambridge, England: Cambridge University Press.

Ryan, R. M., & Deci, E. L. (2000). Self-determination theory and the facilitation of intrinsic motivation, social development, and well-being. *American Psychologist, 55,* 68–78.

Ryan, R. M., & Kuczkowski, R. (1994). The imaginary audience, self-consciousness, and public individuation in adolescence. *Journal of Personality, 62,* 219–237.

Ryan, R. M., & Lynch, J. H. (1989). Emotional autonomy versus detachment: Revisiting the vicissitudes of adolescence and young adulthood. *Child Development, 60,* 340–356.

Ryan, R. M., Mims, V., & Koestner, R. (1983). Relation of reward contingency and interpersonal context to intrinsic motivation: A review and test using cognitive evaluation theory. *Journal of Personality and Social Psychology, 45,* 736–750.

Ryan, R. M., Stiller, J. D., & Lynch, J. H. (1994). Representations of relationships to teachers, parents, and friends as predictors of academic motivation and self-esteem. *Journal of Early Adolescence, 14,* 226–249.

Ryba, K. (2005). School-based research on learning communities. *Computers in New Zealand Schools, 17*(3), 4–6.

Ryba, K., Curzon, J., & Selby, L. (2004). Creating learning partnerships with information & communication technology. In A. Ashman & J. Elkins (Eds.), *Educating children with diverse abilities* (3rd ed.). Sydney, Australia: Prentice Hall.

Ryba, K., & Selby, L. (2005). *Information communication technology for adults with Down syndrome.* Southampton, England: Down Syndrome Educational Trust.

Ryba, K., Selby, L., & Brown, R. (2004). Developing mental imagery using a digital camera: A study of adult vocational training. *Down Syndrome Research and Practice, 9*(1), 1–11.

Sabers, D. S., Cushing, K. S., & Berliner, D. C. (1991). Differences among teachers in a task characterized by simultaneity, multidimensionality, and immediacy. *American Educational Research Journal, 28,* 63–88.

Sadker, M. P., & Miller, D. (1982). *Sex equity handbook for schools.* White Plains, NY: Longman.

Sadker, M. P., & Sadker, D. (1985). Sexism in the schoolroom of the '80s. *Psychology Today, 19,* 54–57.

Sadker, M. P., & Sadker, D. (1994). *Failing at fairness: How our schools cheat girls.* New York: Touchstone.

Sadker, M. P., Sadker, D., & Klein, S. (1991). The issue of gender in elementary and secondary education. In G. Grant (Ed.), *Review of research in education.* Washington, DC: American Educational Research Association.

Sadoski, M., Goetz, E. T., & Fritz, J. B. (1993). Impact of concreteness on comprehensibility, interest, and memory for text: Implications for dual coding theory and text design. *Journal of Educational Psychology, 85,* 291–304.

Sadoski, M., & Paivio, A. (2001). *Imagery and text: A dual coding theory of reading and writing.* Mahwah, NJ: Erlbaum.

Saklofske, D. H. & Schwean, V. (1993). Standardized procedures for measuring the correlates of ADHD in children: A research program. *Canadian Journal of School Psychology, 9,* 28–36.

Salend, S. J. (2008). *Creating inclusive classrooms: Effective and reflective practices* (6th ed.). Upper Saddle River, NJ: Pearson Education.

Salend, S. J., & Taylor, L. (1993). Working with families: A cross-cultural perspective. *Remedial and Special Education, 14*(5), 25–32, 39.

Salomon, G. (Ed.). (1993a). *Distributed cognitions: Psychological and educational considerations.* Cambridge, England: Cambridge University Press.

Salomon, G. (1993b). No distribution without individuals' cognition: A dynamic interactional view. In G. Salomon (Ed.), *Distributed cognitions: Psychological and educational considerations* (pp. 111–138). Cambridge, England: Cambridge University Press.

Saltz, E. (1971). *The cognitive bases of human learning.* Homewood, IL: Dorsey.

Samuel, E., Krugly-Smolska, E., & Warren, W. (2001). Academic achievement of adolescents from selected ethnocultural groups in Canada: A study consistent with John Ogbu's theory. *McGill Journal of Education, 36,* 61–73.

Sanborn, M. P. (1979). Counseling and guidance needs of the gifted and talented. In A. H. Passow (Ed.), *The gifted and the talented: Their education and development. The seventy-eighth yearbook of the National Society for the Study of Education.* Chicago: University of Chicago Press.

Sanchez, F., & Anderson, M. L. (1990). Gang mediation: A process that works. *Principal, 69*(4), 54–56.

Sanders, M. G. (1996). Action teams in action: Interviews and observations in three schools in the Baltimore School-Family-Community Partnership Program. *Journal of Education for Students Placed at Risk, 1,* 249–262.

Sanders, S. (1987). Cultural conflicts: An important factor in academic failures of American Indian students. *Journal of Multicultural Counseling and Development, 15*(2), 81–90.

Sands, D. J., & Wehmeyer, M. L. (Eds.). (1996). *Self-determination across the life span: Independence and choice for people with disabilities.* Baltimore: Brookes.

Sansone, C., Weir, C., Harpster, L., & Morgan, C. (1992). Once a boring task always a boring task? Interest as a self-regulatory mechanism. *Journal of Personality and Social Psychology, 63,* 379–390.

Sapon-Shevin, M., Dobbelaere, A., Corrigan, C., Goodman, K., & Mastin, M. (1998). Everyone here can play. *Educational Leadership, 56*(1), 42–45.

Sarason, I. G. (Ed.). (1980). *Test anxiety: Theory, research, and applications.* Hillsdale, NJ: Erlbaum.

Sarason, S. B. (1972). What research says about test anxiety in elementary school children. In A. R. Binter & S. H. Frey (Eds.), *The psychology of the elementary school child.* Chicago: Rand McNally.

Saskatchewan Professional Development Unit. (2003). *Performance Assessments: A Wealth of Possibilities, Connecting the Pieces.* Saskatoon: Author.

Saskatchewan Schools Trustees Association. (1994). *One incident is too many: Policy guidelines for schools.* SSTA Research Report #94-05.

Sattler, J. (2008). *Assessment of children: Cognitive Foundations*. San Diego, CA: Author.

Sattler, J. M. (2001). *Assessment of children: Cognitive applications* (4th ed.). San Diego, CA: Author.

Sax, G. (1989). *Principles of educational and psychological measurement and evaluation* (3rd ed.). Belmont, CA: Wadsworth.

Scarcella, R. (1990). *Teaching language-minority students in the multicultural classroom*. Upper Saddle River, NJ: Prentice Hall.

Scardamalia, M. (2000). Can schools enter a knowledge society? In M. Sedlinger & J. Wynn (Eds.), *Educational technology and the impact on teaching and learning*. Abingdon, England: Research Machines.

Scardamalia, M., & Bereiter, C. (1996). Computer support for knowledge-building communities. In T. Koschmann (Ed.), *CSCL: Theory and practice of an emerging paradigm* (pp. 249–268). Mahwah, NJ: Erlbaum.

Scardamalia, M. & Bereiter, C. (1999). Schools as knowledge building organizations. In D. Keating & C. Hertzman (Eds.), *Today's children tomorrow's society: The developmental and wealth of nations*. New York: Guilford.

Scardamalia, M., & Bereiter, C. (2003). Knowledge building. In *Encyclopedia of education* (2nd ed.). New York: Macmillan Reference.

Scarr, S., & Weinberg, R. A. (1976). IQ test performance of black children adopted by white families. *American Psychologist, 31*, 726–739.

Scevak, J. J., Moore, P. J., & Kirby, J. R. (1993). Training students to use maps to increase text recall. *Contemporary Educational Psychology, 18*, 401–413.

Schacter, D. L. (1999). The seven sins of memory: Insights from psychology and neuroscience. *American Psychologist, 54*, 182–203.

Schacter, J. (2000). Does individual tutoring produce optimal learning? *American Educational Research Journal, 37*, 801–829.

Schank, R. C. (1979). Interestingness: Controlling inferences. *Artificial Intelligence, 12*, 273–297.

Schauble, L. (1990). Belief revision in children: The role of prior knowledge and strategies for generating evidence. *Journal of Experimental Child Psychology, 49*, 31–57.

Schauble, L. (1996). The development of scientific reasoning in knowledge-rich contexts. *Developmental Psychology, 32*, 102–119.

Schell, T. L., Klein, S. B., & Babey, S. H. (1996). Testing a hierarchical model of self-knowledge. *Psychological Science, 7*, 170–173.

Schermerhorn, S. M., Goldschmid, M. L., & Shore, B. M. (1975). Learning basic principles of probability in student dyads: A cross-age comparison. *Journal of Educational Psychology, 67*, 551–557

Schiefele, U. (1991). Interest, learning, and motivation. *Educational Psychologist, 26*, 299–323.

Schiefele, U. (1992). Topic interest and levels of text comprehension. In K. A. Renninger, S. Hidi, & A. Krapp (Eds.), *The role of interest in learning and development*. Hillsdale, NJ: Erlbaum.

Schiefele, U., Krapp, A., & Winteler, A. (1992). Interest as a predictor of academic achievement: A meta-analysis of research. In K. A. Renninger, S. Hidi, & A. Krapp (Eds.), *The role of interest in learning and development*. Hillsdale, NJ: Erlbaum.

Schiffman, G., Tobin, D., & Buchanan, B. (1984). Microcomputer instruction for the learning disabled. *Annual Review of Learning Disabilities, 2*, 134–136.

Schimmoeller, M. A. (1998, April). *Influence of private speech on the writing behaviors of young children: Four case studies*. Paper presented at the annual meeting of the American Educational Research Association, San Diego, CA.

Schlaefli, A., Rest, J. R., & Thoma, S. J. (1985). Does moral education improve moral judgment? A meta-analysis of intervention studies using the defining issues test. *Review of Educational Research, 55*, 319–352.

Schliemann, A. D., & Carraher, D. W. (1993). Proportional reasoning in and out of school. In P. Light & G. Butterworth (Eds.), *Context and cognition: Ways of learning and knowing*. Hillsdale, NJ: Erlbaum.

Schloss, P. J., & Smith, M. A. (1994). *Applied behavior analysis in the classroom*. Needham Heights, MA: Allyn & Bacon.

Schmidt, R. A., & Bjork, R. A. (1992). New conceptualizations of practice: Common principles in three paradigms suggest new concepts for training. *Psychological Science, 3*, 207–217.

Schneider, W. (1993). Domain-specific knowledge and memory performance in children. *Educational Psychology Review, 5*, 257–273.

Schneider, W., & Pressley, M. (1989). *Memory development between 2 and 20*. New York: Springer-Verlag.

Schneider, W., & Shiffrin, R. M. (1977). Controlled and automatic human information processing: I. Detection, search, and attention. *Psychological Review, 84*, 1–66.

Schoenfeld, A. H., & Hermann, D. J. (1982). Problem perception and knowledge structure in expert and novice mathematical problem solvers. *Journal of Experimental Psychology: Learning, Memory, and Cognition, 8*, 484–494.

Schofield, J. W. (1995). Improving intergroup relations among students. In J. A. Banks & C. A. M. Banks (Eds.), *Handbook of research on multicultural education*. New York: Macmillan.

Scholes, R. J., & Kardash, C. M. (1996, April). *The effect of topic interest on the relationship between text-based interest and importance in text comprehension*. Paper presented at the annual meeting of the American Educational Research Association, New York.

Schommer, M. (1994a). An emerging conceptualization of epistemological beliefs and their role in learning. In R. Garner & P. A. Alexander (Eds.), *Beliefs about text and instruction with text*. Hillsdale, NJ: Erlbaum.

Schommer, M. (1994b). Synthesizing epistemological belief research: Tentative understandings and provocative confusions. *Educational Psychology Review, 6*, 293–319.

Schommer, M. (1997). The development of epistemological beliefs among secondary students: A longitudinal study. *Journal of Educational Psychology, 89*, 37–40.

Schommer-Aikins, M. (2001). An evolving theoretical framework for an epistemological belief system. In B. K. Hofer & P. R. Pintrich (Eds.), *Personal epistemology: The psychology of beliefs about knowledge and knowing*. Hillsdale, NJ: Erlbaum.

Schonert-Reichl, K. A. (1993). Empathy and social relationships in adolescents with behavioral disorders. *Behavioral Disorders, 18*, 189–204.

Schraw, G., & Lehman, S. (2001). Situational interest: A review of the literature and directions for future research. *Educational Psychology Review, 13*, 23–52.

Schraw, G., & Moshman, D. (1995). Metacognitive theories. *Educational Psychology Review, 7*, 351–371.

Schraw, G., & Wade, S. (1991, April). *Selective learning strategies for relevant and important text information*. Paper presented at the annual meeting of the American Educational Research Association, Chicago.

Schubert, J. G. (1986). Gender equity in computer learning. *Theory into Practice, 25*, 267–275.

Schultz, G. F., & Switzky, H. N. (1990). The development of intrinsic motivation in students with learning problems: Suggestions for more effective instructional practice. *Preventing School Failure, 34*(2), 14–20.

Schultz, K., Buck, P., & Niesz, T. (2000). Democratizing conversations: Racialized talk in a post-desegregated middle school. *American Educational Research Journal, 37*, 33–65.

Schultz, K., & Lochhead, J. (1991). A view from physics. In M. U. Smith (Ed.), *Toward a unified theory of problem solving: Views from the content domains*. Hillsdale, NJ: Erlbaum.

Schumaker, J. B., & Hazel, J. S. (1984). Social skill assessment and training for the learning disabled: Who's on first and what's on second? (Part 1). *Journal of Learning Disabilities, 17*, 422–431.

Schunk, D. H. (1981). Modeling and attributional effects on children's achievement: A self-efficacy analysis. *Journal of Educational Psychology, 73*, 93–105.

Schunk, D. H. (1982). Effects of effort attributional feedback on children's perceived self-efficacy and achievement. *Journal of Educational Psychology, 74*, 548–556.

Schunk, D. H. (1983a). Ability versus effort attributional feedback: Differential effects on self-efficacy and achievement. *Journal of Educational Psychology, 75*, 848–856.

Schunk, D. H. (1983b). Developing children's self-efficacy and skills: The roles of social comparative information and goal setting. *Contemporary Educational Psychology, 8*, 76–86.

Schunk, D. H. (1989a). Self-efficacy and achievement behaviors. *Educational Psychology Review, 1*, 173–208.

Schunk, D. H. (1989b). Self-efficacy and cognitive skill learning. In C. Ames & R. Ames (Eds.), *Research on motivation in education: Vol. 3. Goals and cognitions*. San Diego, CA: Academic Press.

Schunk, D. H. (1989c). Social cognitive theory and self-regulated learning. In B. J. Zimmerman & D. H. Schunk (Eds.), *Self-regulated learning and academic achievement: Theory, research, and practice*. New York: Springer-Verlag.

Schunk, D. H. (1990, April). *Socialization and the development of self-regulated learning: The role of attributions*. Paper presented at the annual meeting of the American Educational Research Association, Boston.

Schunk, D. H. (1996). Goal and self-evaluative influences during children's cognitive skill learning. *American Educational Research Journal, 33*, 359–382.

Schunk, D. H. (1998). Teaching elementary students to self-regulate practice of mathematical skills with modeling. In D. H. Schunk & B. J. Zimmerman (Eds.), *Self-regulated learning: From teaching to self-reflective practice* (pp. 137–159). New York: Guilford Press.

Schunk, D. H., & Hanson, A. R. (1985). Peer models: Influence on children's self-efficacy and achievement. *Journal of Educational Psychology, 77*, 313–322.

Schunk, D. H., Hanson, A. R., & Cox, P. D. (1987). Peer-model attributes and children's achievement behaviors. *Journal of Educational Psychology, 79*, 54–61.

Schunk, D. H., & Rice, J. (1989). Learning goals and children's reading comprehension. *Journal of Reading Behavior, 21*, 279–293.

Schunk, D. H., & Zimmerman, B. J. (Eds.). (1994). *Self-regulation of learning and performance: Issues and educational applications*. Hillsdale, NJ: Erlbaum.

Schunk, D. H., & Zimmerman, B. J. (1997). Social origins of self-regulatory competence. *Educational Psychologist, 32,* 195–208.

Schutz, P. A. (1994). Goals as the transactive point between motivation and cognition. In P. R. Pintrich, D. R. Brown, & C. E. Weinstein (Eds.), *Student motivation, cognition, and learning: Essays in honor of Wilbert J. McKeachie.* Hillsdale, NJ: Erlbaum.

Schutz, P. A., & Davis, H. A. (2000). Emotions and self-regulation during test taking. *Educational Psychologist, 35,* 243–256.

Schwarz, B. B., Neuman, Y., & Biezuner, S. (2000). Two wrongs may make a right . . . if they argue together! *Cognition and Instruction, 18,* 461–494.

Schwebel, A. I., & Cherlin, D. L. (1972). Physical and social distancing in teacher-pupil relationships. *Journal of Educational Psychology, 63,* 543–550.

Scruggs, T. E., & Mastropieri, M. A. (1989). Mnemonic instruction of learning disabled students: A field-based evaluation. *Learning Disabilities Quarterly, 12,* 119–125.

Scruggs, T. E., & Mastropieri, M. A. (1992). Classroom applications of mnemonic instruction: Acquisition, maintenance, and generalization. *Exceptional Children, 58,* 219–229.

Scruggs, T. E., & Mastropieri, M. A. (1994). Successful mainstreaming in elementary science classes: A qualitative study of three reputational cases. *American Educational Research Journal, 31,* 785–811.

Seaton, E., Rodriguez, A., Jacobson, L., Taylor, R., Caintic, R., & Dale, P. (1999, April). *Influence of economic resources on family organization and achievement in economically disadvantaged African-American families.* Paper presented at the annual meeting of the American Educational Research Association, Montreal, Canada.

Seidenberg, M. S. (1992). Connectionism without tears. In S. Davis (Ed.), *Connectionism: Theory and practice* (pp. 84–122). New York: Oxford University Press.

Seifert, T. L (1997). Academic goals and emotions: Results of a structural equation model and cluster analysis. *British Journal of Educational Psychology, 67,* 323–338.

Seifert, T. L., & O'Keefe, B. A. (2001). The relationship of work avoidance and learning goals to perceived competence externality and meaning. *British Journal of Educational Psychology, 71,* 81–92.

Seligman, M. E. P. (1975). *Helplessness: On depression, development, and death.* San Francisco: Freeman.

Seligman, M. E. P. (1991). *Learned optimism.* New York: Knopf.

Semb, G. B., & Ellis, J. A. (1994). Knowledge taught in school: What is remembered? *Review of Educational Research, 64,* 253–286.

Semb, G. B., Ellis, J. A., & Araujo, J. (1993). Long-term memory for knowledge learned in school. *Journal of Educational Psychology, 85,* 305–316.

Shachar, H., & Sharan, S. (1994). Talking, relating, and achieving: Effects of cooperative learning and whole-class instruction. *Cognition and Instruction, 12,* 313–353.

Share, D. L. (1995). Phonological recoding and self-teaching: *Sine qua non* of reading acquisition. *Cognition, 55,* 151–218.

Shatz, M., & Gelman, R. (1973). The development of communication skills: Modifications in the speech of young children as a function of the listener. *Monographs of the Society for Research in Child Development, 38*(5, Serial No. 152).

Shavelson, R. J., & Baxter, G. P. (1992). What we've learned about assessing hands-on science. *Educational Leadership, 49*(8), 20–25.

Shavelson, R. J., Baxter, G. P., & Pine, J. (1992). Performance assessments: Political rhetoric and measurement reality. *Educational Researcher, 21*(4), 22–27.

Sheffield, F. D., Wulff, J. J., & Backer, R. (1951). Reward value of copulation without sex drive reduction. *Journal of Comparative and Physiological Psychology, 44,* 3–8.

Sheldon, A. (1974). The role of parallel function in the acquisition of relative clauses in English. *Journal of Verbal Learning and Verbal Behavior, 13,* 272–281.

Shepard, L. A. (2000). The role of assessment in a learning culture. *Educational Researcher, 29*(7), 4–14.

Sherif, M., Harvey, O. J., White, B. J., Hood, W. R., & Sherif, C. (1961). *Inter-group conflict and cooperation: The Robbers Cave experiment.* Norman: University of Oklahoma Press.

Shernoff, D. J., Knauth, S., & Makris, E. (2000). The quality of classroom experiences. In M. Csikszentmihalyi & B. Schneider, *Becoming adult: How teenagers prepare for the world of work.* New York: Basic Books.

Sherrill, D., Horowitz, B., Friedman, S. T., & Salisbury, J. L. (1970). Seating aggregation as an index of contagion. *Educational and Psychological Measurement, 30,* 663–668.

Shih, S. S., & Alexander, J. M. (2000). Interacting effects of goal setting and self- or other-referenced feedback on children's development of self-efficacy and cognitive skill within the Taiwanese classroom. *Journal of Educational Psychology, 92,* 536–543.

Shipman, S., & Shipman, V. C. (1985). Cognitive styles: Some conceptual, methodological, and applied issues. In E. W. Gordon (Ed.), *Review of research in education* (Vol. 12). Washington, DC: American Educational Research Association.

Shore, B. M., Aulls, M. W., & Delcourt, M. A. B. (Eds.). (2008). *Inquiry in education (vol. II): Overcoming barriers to successful implementation.* New York: Erlbaum.

Shore, B. M., Delcourt, M. A. B., Syer, C. A., & Schapiro, M. (2008). The phantom of the science fair. In B. M. Shore, M. W. Aulls, & M. A. B. Delcourt (Eds.), *Inquiry in education, Volume II: Overcoming barriers to successfully implementation* (pp. 93–118). New York: Erlbaum.

Shore, B. M., & Kanevsky, L. S. (1993). Thinking processes: Being and becoming gifted. In K. A. Heller, F. J. Mönks, & A. H. Passow (Eds.), *International handbook of research and development of giftedness and talent* (pp. 131–145). Oxford, England: Pergamon.

Short, E. J., Schatschneider, C. W., & Friebert, S. E. (1993). Relationship between memory and metamemory performance: A comparison of specific and general strategy knowledge. *Journal of Educational Psychology, 85,* 412–423.

Shuell, T. J. (1996). Teaching and learning in a classroom context. In D. C. Berliner & R. C. Calfee (Eds.), *Handbook of educational psychology.* New York: Macmillan.

Shulman, L. S. (1986). Those who understand: Knowledge growth in teaching. *Educational Researcher, 15,* 4–14.

Shulman, S., Elicker, J., & Sroufe, L. A. (1994). Stages of friendship growth in preadolescence as related to attachment history. *Journal of Social and Personal Relationships, 11,* 341–361.

Sieber, J. E., Kameya, L. I., & Paulson, F. L. (1970). Effect of memory support on the problem-solving ability of test-anxious children. *Journal of Educational Psychology, 61,* 159–168.

Siegel, L. S. (1988). Evidence that IQ scores are irrelevant to the definition of reading disability. *Canadian Journal of Psychology, 42,* 201–215.

Siegler, R. S. (1998). *Children's thinking* (3rd ed.). Upper Saddle River, NJ: Prentice Hall.

Siegler, R. S., & Richards, D. D. (1982). The development of intelligence. In R. J. Sternberg (Ed.), *Handbook of human intelligence.* Cambridge, England: Cambridge University Press.

Sigman, M., & Whaley, S. E. (1998). The role of nutrition in the development of intelligence. In U. Neisser (Ed.), *The rising curve: Long-term gains in IQ and related measures* (pp. 155–182). Washington, DC: American Psychological Association.

Simner, M. L. (2000). "A joint position statement by the Canadian Psychological Association and the Canadian Association of School Psychologists on the Canadian press coverage of the province-wide achievement test results." *Canadian Psychological Association.* Retrieved August 14, 2008, from http://www.cpa.ca/documents/joint_position.html.

Simon, H. A. (1974). How big is a chunk? *Science, 183,* 482–488.

Simons, R. J., Meijden, J., deJong, F., Slighte, H., De Corte, E., Lehtinen, E., Hakkarainen, K., Lipponen, L., Vosniadou, S., Kollias, V., Pontecorvo, C., Cesareni, D., Baldassarre, A., Ligorio, B., Caravita, S., & Berlinguer, L. (1999, August). CL-Net: Computer-supported collaborative learning networks in primary and secondary education. In *Comparing systems of computer-supported collaborative learning.* Symposium conducted at the 8th Biennial Conference for Research on Learning and Instruction (EARLI), Göteborg, Sweden.

Simons, R. L., Whitbeck, L. B., Conger, R. D., & Conger, K. J. (1991). Parenting factors, social skills, and value commitments as precursors to school failure, involvement with deviant peers, and delinquent behavior. *Journal of Youth and Adolescence, 20,* 645–664.

Simonton, D. K. (2000). Creativity: Cognitive, personal, developmental, and social aspects. *American Psychologist, 55,* 151–158.

Simonton, D. K. (2001). Talent development as a multidimensional, multiplicative, and dynamic process. *Current Directions in Psychological Science, 10,* 39–42.

Singer, D. G., & Singer, J. L. (1994). *Barney & Friends as education and entertainment: Phase 3. A national study: Can preschoolers learn through exposure to Barney & Friends?* New Haven, CT: Yale University Family Television Research and Consultation Center.

Sizer, T. R. (1992). *Horace's school: Redesigning the American high school.* Boston: Houghton Mifflin.

Skaalvik, E. (1997). Self-enhancing and self-defeating ego orientation: Relations with task avoidance orientation, achievement, self-perceptions, and anxiety. *Journal of Educational Psychology, 89,* 71–81.

Skinner, B. F. (1953). *Science and human behavior.* New York: Macmillan.

Skinner, B. F. (1954). The science of learning and the art of teaching. *Harvard Educational Review, 24,* 86–97.

Skinner, B. F. (1968). *The technology of teaching.* New York: Appleton-Century-Crofts.

Slaughter-Defoe, D. T. (2001). A longitudinal case study of Head Start eligible children: Implications for urban education. *Educational Psychologist, 36,* 31–44.

Slavin, R. E. (1983). When does cooperative learning increase student achievement? *Psychological Bulletin, 94,* 429–445.

Slavin, R. E. (1987). Ability grouping and student achievement in elementary schools: A best-evidence synthesis. *Review of Educations Research, 57,* 293–336.

Slavin, R. E. (1989). Students at risk of school failure: The problem and its dimensions. In R. E. Slavin, N. L. Karweit, & N. A. Madden (Eds.), *Effective programs for students at risk.* Needham Heights, MA: Allyn & Bacon.

Slavin, R. E. (1990). *Cooperative learning: Theory, research, and practice.* Upper Saddle River, NJ: Prentice Hall.

Slavin, R. E., Karweit, N. L., & Madden, N. A. (Eds.). (1989). *Effective programs for students at risk.* Needham Heights, MA: Allyn & Bacon.

Sleeter, C. E., & Grant, C. A. (1999). *Making choices for multicultural education: Five approaches to race, class, and gender* (3rd ed.). Upper Saddle River, NJ: Merrill/Prentice Hall.

Slife, B. R., Weiss, J., & Bell, T. (1985). Separability of metacognition and cognition: Problem solving in learning disabled and regular students. *Journal of Educational Psychology, 77,* 437–445.

Slusher, M. P., & Anderson, C. A. (1996). Using causal persuasive arguments to change beliefs and teach new information: The mediating role of explanation availability and evaluation bias in the acceptance of knowledge. *Journal of Educational Psychology, 88,* 110–122.

Small, M. Y., Lovett, S. B., & Scher, M. S. (1993). Pictures facilitate children's recall of unillustrated expository prose. *Journal of Educational Psychology, 85,* 520–528.

Smetana, J. G. (1981). Preschool children's conceptions of moral and social rules. *Child Development, 52,* 1333–1336.

Smith, C. L., Maclin, D., Grosslight, L., & Davis, H. (1997). Teaching for understanding: A study of students' preinstruction theories of matter and a comparison of the effectiveness of two approaches to teaching about matter and density. *Cognition and Instruction, 15,* 317–393.

Smith, C. L., Maclin, D., Houghton, C., & Hennessey, M. G. (2000). Sixth-grade students' epistemologies of science: The impact of school science experiences on epistemological development. *Cognition and Instruction, 18,* 349–422.

Smith, D. C., & Neale, D. C. (1991). The construction of subject-matter knowledge in primary science teaching. In J. Brophy (Ed.), *Advances in research on teaching: Vol. 2. Teacher's knowledge of subject matter as it relates to their teaching practice.* Greenwich, CT: JAI Press.

Smith, E. E. (2000). Neural bases of human working memory. *Current Directions in Psychological Science, 9,* 45–49.

Smith, H. L. (1998). Literacy and instruction in African American communities: Shall we overcome? In B. Pérez (Ed.), *Sociocultural contexts of language and literacy.* Mahwah, NJ: Erlbaum.

Smith, J., & Russell, G. (1984). Why do males and females differ? Children's beliefs about sex differences. *Sex Roles, 11,* 1111–1120.

Smith, K., Johnson, D. W., & Johnson, R. T. (1981). Can conflict be constructive? Controversy versus concurrence seeking in learning groups. *Journal of Educational Psychology, 73,* 651–663.

Smith, M. U. (1991). A view from biology. In M. U. Smith (Ed.), *Toward a unified theory of problem solving: Views from the content domains.* Hillsdale, NJ: Erlbaum.

Smith, R. E., & Smoll, F. L. (1997). Coaching the coaches: Youth sports as a scientific and applied behavioral setting. *Current Directions in Psychological Science, 6*(1), 16–21.

Smitherman, G. (1994). "The blacker the berry the sweeter the juice": African American student writers. In A. H. Dyson & C. Genishi (Eds.), *The need for story: Cultural diversity in classroom and community.* Urbana, IL: National Council of Teachers of English.

Snarey, J. (1995). In a communitarian voice: The sociological expansion of Kohlbergian theory, research, and practice. In W. M. Kurtines & J. L. Gewirtz (Eds.), *Moral development: An introduction.* Boston: Allyn & Bacon.

Sneider, C., & Pulos, S. (1983). Children's cosmographies: Understanding the earth's shape and gravity. *Science Education, 67,* 205–221.

Snow, C. E. (1990). Rationales for native language instruction: Evidence from research. In A. M. Padilla, H. H. Fairchild, & C. M. Valadez (Eds.), *Bilingual education: Issues and strategies.* Newbury Park, CA: Sage.

Snow, R. E., Corno, L., & Jackson, D., III. (1996). Individual differences in affective and conative functions. In D. C. Berliner & R. C. Calfee (Eds.), *Handbook of educational psychology.* New York: Macmillan.

Solicitor General Canada. (1994). MSG: Weapons in schools study. *Solicitor General Canada.* Retrieved from http://wwwsgc.gc.ca/releases/e19940823.html (no longer available).

Solicitor General Canada. (2000). Youth crime. *Solicitor General Canada.* Retrieved 2005, from http://www.sgc.gc.ca/efact/eyouthcr.html (no longer available).

Sosniak, L. A., & Stodolsky, S. S. (1994). Making connections: Social studies education in an urban fourth-grade classroom. In J. Brophy (Ed.), *Advances in research on teaching: Vol. 4. Case studies of teaching and learning in social studies.* Greenwich, CT: JAI Press.

Spandel, V. (1997). Reflections on portfolios. In G. D. Phye (Ed.), *Handbook of academic learning: Construction of knowledge.* San Diego, CA: Academic Press.

Spaulding, C. L. (1992). *Motivation in the classroom.* New York: McGraw-Hill.

Spear, L. P. (2000). Neurobehavioral changes in adolescence. *Current Directions in Psychological Science, 9,* 11–114.

Spearman, C. (1904). General intelligence, objectively determined and measured. *American Journal of Psychology, 15,* 201–293.

Spearman, C. (1927). *The abilities of man: Their nature and measurement.* New York: Macmillan.

Spencer, M. B., & Markstrom-Adams, C. (1990). Identity processes among racial and ethnic minority children in America. *Child Development, 61,* 290–310.

Sperling, G. (1967). Successive approximations to a model for short-term memory. *Acta Psychologia, 27,* 285–292.

Spicker, H. H. (1992). Identifying and enriching: Rural gifted children. *Educational Horizons, 70*(2), 60–65.

Spires, H. A. (1990, April). *Learning from a lecture: Effects of comprehension monitoring.* Paper presented at the annual meeting of the American Educational Research Association, Boston.

Spires, H. A., & Donley, J. (1998). Prior knowledge activation: Inducing engagement with informational texts. *Journal of Educational Psychology, 90,* 249–260.

Spires, H. A., Donley, J., & Penrose, A. M. (1990, April). *Prior knowledge activation: Inducing text engagement in reading to learn.* Paper presented at the annual meeting of the American Educational Research Association, Boston.

Spivey, N. N. (1997). *The constructivist metaphor: Reading, writing, and the making of meaning.* San Diego, CA: Academic Press.

Sprafkin, C., Serbin, L. A., Denier, C., & Connor, J. M. (1983). Sex-differentiated play: Cognitive consequences and early interventions. In M. B. Liss (Ed.), *Social and cognitive skills: Sex roles and children's play.* San Diego, CA: Academic Press.

Sroufe, L. A. (1983). Infant-caregiver attachment and patterns of adaptation in preschool: The roots of maladaptation. In M. Perlmutter (Ed.), *Minnesota Symposia on Child Psychology: Vol. 16. Development and policy concerning children with special needs.* Hillsdale, NJ: Erlbaum.

Sroufe, L. A., Carlson, E., & Shulman, S. (1993). Individuals in relationships: Development from infancy through adolescence. In D. C. Funder, R. D. Parke, C. Tomlinson-Keasey, & K. Widaman (Eds.), *Studying lives through time: Personality and development* (pp. 315–342). Washington, DC: American Psychological Association.

Stacey, K. (1992). Mathematical problem solving in groups: Are two heads better than one? *Journal of Mathematical Behavior, 11,* 261–275.

Stack, C. B., & Burton, L. M. (1993). Kinscripts. *Journal of Comparative Family Studies, 24,* 157–170.

Stainback, S., & Stainback, W. (1990). Inclusive schooling. In W. Stainback & S. Stainback (Eds.), *Support networks for inclusive schooling: Interdependent integrated education.* Baltimore: Brookes.

Stainback, W., & Stainback, S. (1992). *Controversial issues confronting special education: Divergent perspectives.* Boston: Allyn & Bacon.

Stanley, J. C. (1980). On educating the gifted. *Educational Researcher, 9*(3), 8–12.

Stanovich, K. E. (2000). *Progress in understanding reading: Scientific foundations and new frontiers.* New York: Guilford Press.

Stanovich, K. E. (1999). *Who is rational? Studies of individual differences in reasoning.* Mahwah, NJ: Erlbaum.

Stanovich, K. E. (2004). *Rationality and evolution: The robot's rebellion in the age of Darwin.* Chicago: University of Chicago Press.

Stanovich, K. E. (2007). *How to think straight about psychology* (8th ed.). Boston: Allyn & Bacon.

Stanovich, K. E., & Cunningham, A. E. (1992). Studying the consequences of literacy within a literate society: The cognitive correlates of print exposure. *Memory and Cognition, 20,* 51–68.

Starr, E. J., & Lovett, S. B. (2000). The ability to distinguish between comprehension and memory: Failing to succeed. *Journal of Educational Psychology, 92,* 761–771.

Statistics Canada. (2007, September 7). "Ethnic Diversity and Immigration." *Canada Yearbook 2007.* Retrieved August 13, 2008, from http://www41.statcan.ca/2007/30000/ceb30000_000-eng.htm.

Steffensen, M. S., Joag-Dev, C., & Anderson, R. C. (1979). A cross-cultural perspective on reading comprehension. *Reading Research Quarterly, 15,* 10–29.

Steinberg, L. (1996). *Beyond the classroom: Why school reform has failed and what parents need to do.* New York: Touchstone.

Steinberg, L., Blinde, P. L., & Chan, K. S. (1984). Dropping out among language minority youth. *Review of Educational Research, 54,* 113–132.

Steinberg, L., Elmen, J., & Mounts, N. (1989). Authoritative parenting, psychosocial maturity, and academic success among adolescents. *Child Development, 60,* 1424–1436.

Sternberg, R. J. (1985). *Beyond IQ: A triarchic theory of human intelligence.* Cambridge, England: Cambridge University Press.

Sternberg, R. J. (1996a). Educational psychology has fallen, but it can get up. *Educational Psychology Review, 8,* 175–185.

Sternberg, R. J. (1996b). Myths, countermyths, and truths about intelligence. *Educational Researcher,* 25(2), 11–16.

Sternberg, R. J. (1998). Teaching triarchically improves school achievement. *Journal of Educational Psychology,* 90, 374–384.

Sternberg, R. J. (2005). The triarchic theory of successful intelligence. In D. P. Flanagan & P. L. Harrison (Eds.), *Contemporary intellectual assessment: Theories, tests, and issues.* (2nd ed.) (pp. 103–119). New York: Guilford.

Sternberg, R. J., Forsythe, G. B., Hedlund, J., Horvath, J. A., Wagner, R. K., Williams, W. M., Snook, S. A., & Grigorenko, E. L. (2000). *Practical intelligence in everyday life.* Cambridge, England: Cambridge University Press.

Sternberg, R. J., & Frensch, P. A. (1993). Mechanisms of transfer. In D. K. Detterman & R. J. Sternberg (Eds.), *Transfer on trial: Intelligence, cognition, and instruction.* Norwood, NJ: Ablex.

Sternberg, R. J., & Horvath, J. A. (1995). A prototype view of expert teaching. *Educational Researcher,* 24(6), 9–17.

Stevahn, L., Johnson, D. W., Johnson, R. T., & Real, D. (1996). The impact of a cooperative or individualistic context on the effectiveness of conflict resolution training. *American Educational Research Journal,* 33, 801–823.

Stevahn, L., Oberle, K., Johnson, D. W., & Johnson, R. T. (2001, April). *Effects of role reversal training and use of integrative negotiation for classroom management on conflict resolution in kindergarten.* Paper presented at the annual meeting of the American Educational Research Association, Seattle, WA.

Stevens, J. J., & Clauser, P. (1996, April). *Longitudinal examination of a writing portfolio and the ITBS.* Paper presented at the annual meeting of the American Educational Research Association, New York.

Stevens, R. J., & Slavin, R. E. (1995). The cooperative elementary school: Effects of students' achievement, attitudes, and social relations. *American Educational Research Journal,* 32, 321–351.

Stevenson, H. C., & Fantuzzo, J. W. (1986). The generality and social validity of a competency-based self-control training intervention for underachieving students. *Journal of Applied Behavior Analysis,* 19, 269–272.

Stevenson, H. W., Chen, C., & Uttal, D. H. (1990). Beliefs and achievement: A study of black, white, and Hispanic children. *Child Development,* 61, 508–523.

Stewart, L., & Pascual-Leone, J. (1992). Mental capacity constraints and the development of moral reasoning. *Journal of Experimental Child Psychology,* 54, 251–287.

Stice, E., & Barrera, M., Jr. (1995). A longitudinal examination of the reciprocal relations between perceived parenting and adolescents' substance use and externalizing behaviors. *Developmental Psychology,* 31, 322–334.

Stiggins, R. J. (2001). *Student-involved classroom assessment* (3rd ed.). Upper Saddle River, NJ: Merrill/Prentice Hall.

Stipek, D. J. (1981). Children's perceptions of their own and their classmates' ability. *Journal of Educational Psychology,* 73, 404–410.

Stipek, D. J. (1984). Sex differences in children's attributions for success and failure on math and spelling tests. *Sex Roles,* 11, 969–981.

Stipek, D. J. (1993). *Motivation to learn: From theory to practice* (2nd ed.). Needham Heights, MA: Allyn & Bacon.

Stipek, D. J. (1996). Motivation and instruction. In D. C. Berliner & R. C. Calfee (Eds.), *Handbook of educational psychology.* New York: Macmillan.

Stipek, D. J., & Gralinski, H. (1990, April). *Gender differences in children's achievement-related beliefs and emotional responses to success and failure in math.* Paper presented at the annual meeting of the American Educational Research Association, Boston.

Stodolsky, S. S., Salk, S., & Glaessner, B. (1991). Student views about learning math and social studies. *American Educational Research Journal,* 28, 89–116.

Stone, N. J. (2000). Exploring the relationship between calibration and self-regulated learning. *Educational Psychology Review,* 12, 437–475.

Strike, K. A., & Posner, G. J. (1992). A revisionist theory of conceptual change. In R. A. Duschl & R. J. Hamilton (Eds.), *Philosophy of science, cognitive psychology, and educational theory and practice.* New York: State University of New York Press.

Sue, S., & Chin, R. (1983). The mental health of Chinese-American children: Stressors and resources. In G. J. Powell (Ed.), *The psychosocial development of minority children.* New York: Brunner/Mazel.

Suina, J. H., & Smolkin, L. B. (1994). From natal culture to school culture to dominant society culture: Supporting transitions for Pueblo Indian students. In P. M. Greenfield & R. R. Cocking (Eds.), *Cross-cultural roots of minority child development.* Hillsdale, NJ: Erlbaum.

Sund, R. B. (1976). *Piaget for educators.* Upper Saddle River, NJ: Merrill/Prentice Hall.

Suppes, P., & Macken, E. (1978). The historical path from research and development to operation use of CAI. *Educational Technology,* 18(4), 9–11.

Suttles, G. D. (1970). Friendship as a social institution. In J. G. McCall, M. McCall, N. K. Denzin, G. D. Scuttles, & S. Kurth (Eds.), *Social relationships* (pp. 95–135). Chicago: Aldine de Gruyter.

Sutton-Smith, B. (Ed.). (1979). *Play and learning.* New York: Gardner Press.

Swan, K., Mitrani, M., Guerrero, F., Cheung, M., & Schoener, J. (1990, April). *Perceived locus of control and computer-based instruction.* Paper presented at the annual meeting of the American Educational Research Association, Boston.

Swanborn, M. S. L., & de Glopper, K. (1999). Incidental word learning while reading: A meta-analysis. *Review of Educational Research,* 69, 261–285.

Swanson, D. B., Norman, G. R., & Linn, R. L. (1995). Performance-based assessment: Lessons from the health professions. *Educational Researcher,* 24(5), 5–11, 35.

Swanson, H. L. (1993). An information processing analysis of learning disabled children's problem solving. *American Educational Research Journal,* 30, 861–893.

Swanson, H. L., Cooney, J. B., & Shaughnessy, T. E. (1998). Learning disabilities and memory. In B. Y. L. Wong (Ed.), *Learning about learning disabilities* (2nd ed.). San Diego, CA: Academic Press.

Swanson, H. L., O'Connor, J. E., & Cooney, J. B. (1990). An information processing analysis of expert and novice teachers' problem solving. *American Educational Research Journal,* 27, 533–556.

Tabach, M., Hershkowitz, R., & Schwarz, B. (2006). Constructing and consolidating of algebraic knowledge within dyadic processes: A case study. *Educational Studies in Mathematics,* 63, 235–258.

Tamburrini, J. (1982). Some educational implications of Piaget's theory. In S. Modgil & C. Modgil (Eds.), *Jean Piaget: Consensus and controversy.* New York: Praeger.

Tarver, S. G. (1992). Direct Instruction. In W. Stainback & S. Stainback (Eds.), *Controversial issues confronting special education.* Boston: Allyn & Bacon.

Tate, W. F. (1995). Returning to the root: A culturally relevant approach to mathematics pedagogy. *Theory into Practice,* 34, 166–173.

Taylor, I. A. (1976). A retrospective view of creativity investigation. In I. A. Taylor & J. W. Getzels (Eds.), *Perspectives in creativity.* Chicago: Aldine de Gruyter.

Taylor, J. C., & Romanczyk, R. G. (1994). Generating hypotheses about the function of student problem behavior by observing teacher behavior. *Journal of Applied Behavior Analysis,* 27, 251–265.

Taylor, S. M. (1994, April). *Staying in school against the odds: Voices of minority adolescent girls.* Paper presented at the annual meeting of the American Educational Research Association, New Orleans, LA.

Teachers must hold firm against standardized testing. (2007). *Saskatchewan Bulletin,* 64, 3.

Tennyson, R. D., & Cocchiarella, M. J. (1986). An empirically based instructional design theory for teaching concepts. *Review of Educational Research,* 56, 40–71.

Terr, L. (1991). Childhood traumas: An outline and overview. *American Journal of Psychiatry,* 148, 10–20.

Terwilliger, J. S. (1989). Classroom standard setting and grading practices. *Educational Measurement: Issues and Practices,* 8(2), 15–19.

Tharp, R. G. (1989). Psychocultural variables and constants: Effects on teaching and learning in schools. *American Psychologist,* 44, 349–359.

Tharp, R. G. (1994). Intergroup differences among Native Americans in socialization and child cognition: An ethnogenetic analysis. In P. M. Greenfield & R. R. Cocking (Eds.), *Cross-cultural roots of minority child development.* Hillsdale, NJ: Erlbaum.

Théberge, C. L. (1994, April). *Small-group vs. whole-class discussion: Gaining the floor in science lessons.* Paper presented at the annual meeting of the American Educational Research Association, New Orleans, LA.

Thomas, J. R., & French, K. E. (1985). Gender differences across age in motor performance: A meta-analysis. *Psychological Bulletin,* 98, 260–282.

Thomas, J. W. (1993a). Expectations and effort: Course demands, students' study practices, and academic achievement. In T. M. Tomlinson (Ed.), *Motivating students to learn: Overcoming barriers to high achievement.* Berkeley, CA: McCutchan.

Thomas, J. W. (1993b). Promoting independent learning in the middle grades: The role of instructional support practices. *Elementary School Journal,* 93, 575–591.

Thomas, S., & Oldfather, P. (1997). Intrinsic motivations, literacy, and assessment practices: "That's my grade. That's me." *Educational Psychologist,* 32, 107–123.

Thomas, S. P., Groër, M., & Droppleman, P. (1993). Physical health of today's school children. *Educational Psychology Review,* 5, 5–33.

Thomas, W. P., Collier, V. P., & Abbott, M. (1993). Academic achievement through Japanese, Spanish, or French: The first two years of partial immersion. *Modern Language Journal,* 77, 170–179.

Thompson, A. G., & Thompson, P. W. (1989). Affect and problem solving in an elementary school mathematics classroom. In D. B. McLeod & V. M. Adams (Eds.), *Affect and mathematical problem solving: A new perspective.* New York: Springer-Verlag.

Thompson, R. A., & Nelson, C. A. (2001). Developmental science and the media: Early brain development. *American Psychologist, 56,* 5–15.

Thompson, R. A., & Wyatt, J. M. (1999). Current research on child maltreatment: Implications for educators. *Educational Psychology Review, 11,* 173–201.

Thorndike, R. M. (1997). *Measurement and evaluation in psychology and education* (6th ed.). Upper Saddle River, NJ: Merrill/Prentice Hall.

Thousand, J. S., Villa, R. A., & Nevin, A. I. (1994). *Creativity and collaborative learning: A practical guide for empowering students and teachers.* Baltimore: Brookes.

Tisak, M. (1993). Preschool children's judgments of moral and personal events involving physical harm and property damage. *Merrill-Palmer Quarterly, 39,* 375–390.

Tobias, S. (1977). A model for research on the effect of anxiety on instruction. In J. E. Sieber, H. F. O'Neil, Jr., & S. Tobias (Eds.), *Anxiety, learning, and instruction.* Hillsdale, NJ: Erlbaum.

Tobias, S. (1980). Anxiety and instruction. In I. G. Sarason (Ed.), *Test anxiety: Theory, research, and applications.* Hillsdale, NJ: Erlbaum.

Tobias, S. (1985). Test anxiety: Interference, defective skills, and cognitive capacity. *Educational Psychologist, 20,* 135–142.

Tobias, S. (1994). Interest, prior knowledge, and learning. *Review of Educational Research, 64,* 37–54.

Tobin, K. (1987). The role of wait time in higher cognitive level learning. *Review of Educational Research, 57,* 69–95.

Tomasello, M. (2000). Culture and cognitive development. *Current Directions in Psychological Science, 9,* 37–40.

Tomlinson, C. A., Kaplan, S. N., Renzulli, J. S., Purcell, J., Leppien, J., & Burns, D. (2002). *The parallel curriculum: A design to develop high potential and challenge high-ability learners.* Thousand Oaks, CA: Corwin Press.

Torgesen, J. K., Alexander, A. W., Wagner, R. K., Rashotte, C. A., Voeller, K. K. S., & Conway, T. (2001). Intensive remedial instruction for children with severe reading disabilities: Immediate and long-term outcomes from two instructional approaches. *Journal of Learning Disabilities, 34.*

Torrance, E. P. (1976). Creativity research in education: Still alive. In I. A. Taylor & J. W. Getzels (Eds.), *Perspectives in creativity.* Chicago: Aldine de Gruyter.

Torrance, E. P. (1989). A reaction to "Gifted black students: Curriculum and teaching strategies." In C. J. Maker & S. W. Schiever (Eds.), *Critical issues in gifted education: Vol. 2. Defensible programs for cultural and ethnic minorities.* Austin, TX: Pro-Ed.

Torrance, E. P. (1995). Insights about creativity: Questioned, rejected, ridiculed, ignored. *Educational Psychology Review, 7,* 313–322.

Torrance, E. P., & Myers, R. E. (1970). *Creative learning and teaching.* New York: Dodd, Mead.

Tourniaire, F., & Pulos, S. (1985). Proportional reasoning: A review of the literature. *Educational Studies in Mathematics, 16,* 181–204.

Trawick-Smith, J. (2000). *Early childhood development: A multicultural perspective* (2nd ed.). Upper Saddle River, NJ: Merrill/Prentice Hall.

Tremblay, R. E., Nagin, D.S., Seguin, J. R., Zoccolillo, M., Zelazo, P. D., Boivin, M., Perusse, D., & Japel, C. (2004). Physical aggression during early childhood: Trajectories and predictors. *Pediatrics, 114*(2), 43–50.

Trueba, H. T. (1988). Peer socialization among minority students: A high school dropout prevention program. In H. T. Trueba & C. Delgado-Gaitan (Eds.), *School and society: Learning content through culture.* New York: Praeger.

Tryon, G. S. (1980). The measurement and treatment of anxiety. *Review of Educational Research, 50,* 343–372.

Tschannen-Moran, M., Woolfolk Hoy, A., & Hoy, W. K. (1998). Teacher efficacy: Its meaning and measure. *Review of Educational Research, 68,* 202–248.

Tucker, V. G., & Anderman, L. H. (1999, April). *Cycles of learning: Demonstrating the interplay between motivation, self-regulation, and cognition.* Paper presented at the annual meeting of the American Educational Research Association, Montreal, Canada.

Tudor, R. M. (1995). Isolating the effects of active responding in computer-based instruction. *Journal of Applied Behavior Analysis, 28,* 343–344.

Tulving, E. (1962). Subjective organization in free recall of "unrelated" words. *Psychological Review, 69,* 344–354.

Tulving, E. (1983). *Elements of episodic memory.* Oxford, England: Oxford University Press.

Tulving, E., & Thomson, D. M. (1973). Encoding specificity and retrieval processes in episodic memory. *Psychological Review, 80,* 352–373.

Turiel, E. (1983). *The development of social knowledge: Morality and convention.* Cambridge, England: Cambridge University Press.

Turiel, E. (1998). The development of morality. In W. Damon (Editor-in-Chief) & N. Eisenberg (Vol. Ed.), *Handbook of child psychology: Vol. 3. Social, emotional, and personality development* (5th ed., pp. 863–932). New York: Wiley.

Turiel, E., Smetana, J. G., & Killen, M. (1991). Social contexts in social cognitive development. In W. M. Kurtines & J. L. Gewirtz (Eds.), *Moral behavior and development: Vol. 2. Research.* Hillsdale, NJ: Erlbaum.

Turkheimer, E. (2000). Three laws of behavior genetics and what they mean. *Current Directions in Psychological Science, 9,* 160–164.

Turnbull, A., Turnbull, R., Shank, M., & Leal, D. (1999). *Exceptional lives: Special education in today's schools* (2nd ed.). Upper Saddle River, NJ: Merrill/Prentice Hall.

Turnbull, A. P., Pereira, L., & Blue-Banning, M. (2000). Teachers as friendship facilitators. *Teaching Exceptional Children, 32*(5), 66–70.

Turner, A. M., & Greenough, W. T. (1985). Differential rearing effects on rate visual cortex synapses. *Brain Research, 329,* 195–203.

Turner, J. C. (1995). The influence of classroom contexts on young children's motivation for literacy. *Reading Research Quarterly, 30,* 410–441.

Turner, J. C., Meyer, D. K., Cox, K. E., Logan, C., DiCintio, M., & Thomas, C. T. (1998). Creating contexts for involvement in mathematics. *Journal of Educational Psychology, 90,* 730–745.

Turner, J. C., Thorpe, P. K., & Meyer, D. K. (1998). Students' reports of motivation and negative affect: A theoretical and empirical analysis. *Journal of Educational Psychology, 90,* 758–771.

Tyler, B. (1958). Expectancy for eventual success as a factor in problem solving behavior. *Journal of Educational Psychology, 49,* 166–172.

Tzuriel, D. (2000). Dynamic assessment of young children: Educational and intervention perspectives. *Educational Psychology Review, 12,* 385–435.

Ulichny, P. (1994, April). *Cultures in conflict.* Paper presented at the annual meeting of the American Educational Research Association, New Orleans, LA.

Underwood, B. J. (1948). "Spontaneous recovery" of verbal associations. *Journal of Experimental Psychology, 38,* 429–439.

Underwood, B. J. (1954). Studies of distributed practice: XII. Retention following varying degrees of original learning. *Journal of Experimental Psychology, 47,* 294–300.

Underwood, B. J. (1957). Interference and forgetting. *Psychological Review, 64,* 49–60.

Urdan, T. C. (1997). Achievement goal theory: Past results, future directions. In M. L. Maehr & P. R. Pintrich (Eds.), *Advances in motivation and achievement* (Vol. 10, pp. 99–141). Greenwich, CT: JAI Press.

Urdan, T. C., & Maehr, M. L. (1995). Beyond a two-goal theory of motivation and achievement: A case for social goals. *Review of Educational Research, 65,* 213–243.

Urdan, T., & Midgley, C. (2001). Academic self-handicapping: What we know, what more there is to learn. *Educational Psychology Review, 13,* 115–138.

Urdan, T. C., Midgley, C., & Anderman, E. M. (1998). The role of classroom goal structure in students' use of self-handicapping strategies. *American Educational Research Journal, 35,* 101–122.

U.S. Department of Education. (1992). *To assure the free appropriate public education of all children with disabilities: Fourteenth annual report to Congress on the implementation of the Individuals with Disabilities Education Act.* Washington, DC: Author.

U.S. Department of Education. (1996). *To assure the free appropriate public education of all children with disabilities: Eighteenth annual report to Congress on the implementation of the Individuals with Disabilities Education Act.* Washington, DC: Author.

U.S. Department of Education. (1997). *To assure the free appropriate public education of all children with disabilities: Nineteenth annual report to Congress on the implementation of the Individuals with Disabilities Education Act.* Washington, DC: Author.

Valencia, S. W., Hiebert, E. H., & Afflerbach, P. P. (1994). Realizing the possibilities of authentic assessment: Current trends and future issues. In S. W. Valencia, E. H. Hiebert, & P. P. Afflerbach (Eds.), *Authentic reading assessment: Practices and possibilities.* Newark, DE: International Reading Association.

Valente, N. (2001). "Who cares about school?" A student responds to learning. Unpublished paper, University of New Hampshire.

Vallerand, R. J., Fortier, M. S., & Guay, F. (1997). Self-determination and persistence in a real-life setting: Toward a motivational model of high school dropout. *Journal of Personality and Social Psychology, 72,* 1161–1176.

Van Camp, C. M., Lerman, D. C., Kelley, M. E., Roane, H. S., Contrucci, S. A., & Vorndran, C. M. (2000). Further analysis of idiosyncratic antecedent influences during the assessment and treatment of problem behavior. *Journal of Applied Behavior Analysis, 33,* 207–221.

Van Dooren, W., De Bock, D., Hessels, A., Janssens, D., & Verschaffel, L. (2005). Not everything is proportional: Effects of age and problem type on propensities for overgeneralization. *Cognition and Instruction, 23,* 57-86.

Van Houten, R., Nau, P., MacKenzie-Keating, S., Sameoto, D., & Colavecchia, B. (1982). An analysis of some variables influencing the effectiveness of reprimands. *Journal of Applied Behavior Analysis, 15,* 65–83.

van Kraayenoord, C. E., & Paris, S. G. (1997). Australian students' self-appraisal of their work samples and academic progress. *Elementary School Journal, 97,* 523–537.

van Laar, C. (2000). The paradox of low academic achievement but high self-esteem in African American students: An attributional account. *Educational Psychology Review, 12,* 33–61.

Van Meter, P. (2001). Drawing construction as a strategy for learning from text. *Journal of Educational Psychology, 93,* 129–140.

Van Rossum, E. J., & Schenk, S. M. (1984). The relationship between learning conception, study strategy, and learning outcome. *British Journal of Educational Psychology, 54,* 73–83.

VanSledright, B., & Brophy, J. (1992). Storytelling, imagination, and fanciful elaboration in children's historical reconstructions. *American Educational Research Journal, 29,* 837–859.

Vasquez, J. A. (1988). Contexts of learning for minority students. *Educational Forum, 6,* 243–253.

Vasquez, J. A. (1990). Teaching to the distinctive traits of minority students. *Clearing House, 63,* 299–304.

Vaughn, B. J., & Horner, R. H. (1997). Identifying instructional tasks that occasion problem behaviors and assessing the effects of student versus teacher choice among these tasks. *Journal of Applied Behavior Analysis, 30,* 299–312.

Vaughn, S. (1991). Social skills enhancement in students with learning disabilities. In B. Y. L. Wong (Ed.), *Learning about learning disabilities.* San Diego, CA: Academic Press.

Venn, J. J. (2000). *Assessing students with special needs* (2nd ed.). Upper Saddle River, NJ: Merrill/Prentice Hall.

Verdi, M. P., Kulhavy, R. W., Stock, W. A., Rittschof, K. A., & Johnson, J. T. (1996). Text learning using scientific diagrams: Implications for classroom use. *Contemporary Educational Psychology, 21,* 487–499.

Vermeer, H. J., Boekaerts, M., & Seegers, G. (2000). Motivational and gender differences: Sixth-grade students' mathematical problem-solving behavior. *Journal of Educational Psychology, 92,* 308–315.

Veroff, J., McClelland, L., & Ruhland, D. (1975). Varieties of achievement motivation. In M. T. S. Mednick, S. S. Tangri, & L. W. Hoffman (Eds.), *Women and achievement: Social and motivational analyses.* New York: Halsted.

Villegas, A. (1991). *Culturally responsive pedagogy for the 1990s and beyond.* Princeton, NJ: Educational Testing Service.

Vollmer, T. R., & Hackenberg, T. D. (2001). Reinforcement contingencies and social reinforcement: Some reciprocal relations between basic and applied research. *Journal of Applied Behavior Analysis, 34,* 241–253.

Vorrath, H. (1985). *Positive peer culture.* New York: Aldine de Gruyter.

Vosniadou, S. (1994). Universal and culture-specific properties of children's mental models of the earth. In L. A. Hirschfeld & S. A. Gelman (Eds.), *Mapping the mind: Domain specificity in cognition and culture.* Cambridge, England: Cambridge University Press.

Vosniadou, S., & Brewer, W. F. (1987). Theories of knowledge restructuring in development. *Review of Educational Research, 57,* 51–67.

Voss, J. F. (1974). Acquisition and nonspecific transfer effects in prose learning as a function of question form. *Journal of Educational Psychology, 66,* 736–740.

Voss, J. F. (1987). Learning and transfer in subject-matter learning: A problem-solving model. *International Journal of Educational Research, 11,* 607–622.

Voss, J. F., Greene, T. R., Post, T. A., & Penner, B. D. (1983). Problem-solving skill in the social sciences. In G. H. Bower (Ed.), *The psychology of learning and motivation* (Vol. 17). San Diego, CA: Academic Press.

Voss, J. F., & Schauble, L. (1992). Is interest educationally interesting? An interest-related model of learning. In K. A. Renninger, S. Hidi, & A. Krapp (Eds.), *The role of interest in learning and development.* Hillsdale, NJ: Erlbaum.

Vouloumanos, A., & Werker, J. F. (2007). Listening to language at birth: Evidence for a bias for speech in neonates. *Developmental Science, 10,* 159–164.

Vye, N. J., Schwartz, D. L., Bransford, J. D., Barron, B. J., Zech, L., & The Cognition and Technology Group at Vanderbilt. (1998). SMART environments that support monitoring, reflection, and revision. In D. J. Hacker, J. Dunlosky, & A. C. Graesser (Eds.), *Metacognition in educational theory and practice* (pp. 305–346). Mahwah, NJ: Erlbaum.

Vygotsky, L. S. (1962). *Thought and language* (E. Haufmann & G. Vakar, Eds. and Trans.). Cambridge, MA: MIT Press.

Vygotsky, L. S. (1978). *Mind in society: The development of higher psychological processes.* Cambridge, MA: Harvard University Press.

Vygotsky, L. S. (1987). *The collected works of L. S. Vygotsky* (Vol. 3; R. W. Rieber & A. S. Carton, Eds.). New York: Plenum Press.

Vygotsky, L. S. (1997). *Educational psychology* (R. Silverman, Trans.). Boca Raton, FL: St. Lucie Press.

Waddell, C. (2007). *Improving the mental health of young children.* Discussion paper prepared for the British Columbia Healthy Child Development Alliance. Children's Health Policy Centre, Faculty of Health Sciences, Simon Fraser University. Retrieved from http://www.firstcallbc.org/pdfs/Communities/4-alliance.pdf.

Wade, S. E. (1992). How interest affects learning from text. In K. A. Renninger, S. Hidi, & A. Krapp (Eds.), *The role of interest in learning and development.* Hillsdale, NJ: Erlbaum.

Wade-Woolley, L. C. W., & Wood, C. (2006). Editorial: Prosodic sensitivity and reading development. *Journal of Research in Reading, 29,* 253–257.

Wahlsten, D., & Gottlieb, G. (1997). The invalid separation of effects of nature and nurture: Lessons from animal experimentation. In R. J. Sternberg & E. L. Grigorenko (Eds.), *Intelligence, heredity, and environment* (pp. 163–192). Cambridge, England: Cambridge University Press.

Walberg, H. J., & Uguroglu, M. (1980). Motivation and educational productivity: Theories, results, and implications. In L. J. Fyans, Jr. (Ed.), *Achievement motivation: Recent trends in theory and research.* New York: Plenum Press.

Walker, J. E., & Shea, T. M. (1995). *Behavior management: A practical approach for educators* (6th ed.). Englewood Cliffs, NJ: Merrill/Prentice Hall.

Walker, J. M. T. (2001, April). *A cross-sectional study of student motivation, strategy knowledge and strategy use during homework: Implications for research on self-regulated learning.* Paper presented at the annual meeting of the American Educational Research Association, Seattle, WA.

Walker, L. J. (1991). Sex differences in moral reasoning. In W. M. Kurtines & J. L. Gewirtz (Eds.), *Handbook of moral behavior and development: Vol. 2. Research* (pp. 333–364). Hillsdale, NJ: Erlbaum.

Walker, L. J. (1995). Sexism in Kohlberg's moral psychology? In W. M. Kurtines & J. L. Gewirtz (Eds.), *Moral development: An introduction.* Boston: Allyn & Bacon.

Warren, A. R., & McCloskey, L. A. (1993). Pragmatics: Language in social contexts. In J. Berko Gleason (Ed.), *The development of language* (3rd ed.). New York: Macmillan.

Warren, G. (1979). Essay versus multiple-choice tests. *Journal of Research in Science Teaching, 16*(6), 563–567.

Waters, H. S. (1982). Memory development in adolescence: Relationships between metamemory, strategy use, and performance. *Journal of Experimental Child Psychology, 33,* 183–195.

Watt, D., & Roessingh, H. (2001). The dynamics of ESL drop-out: Plus ça change . . . . *The Canadian Modern Language, 58*(2), 203–222.

Webb, N. M. (1989). Peer interaction and learning in small groups. *International Journal of Educational Research, 13,* 21–39.

Webb, N. M., & Farivar, S. (1994). Promoting helping behaviour in cooperative small groups in middle school mathematics. *American Educational Research Journal, 31,* 369–395.

Webb, N. M., & Farivar, S. (1999). Developing productive group interaction in middle school mathematics. In A. M. O'Donnell & A. King (Eds.), *Cognitive perspectives on peer learning* (pp. 117–149). Mahwah, NJ: Erlbaum.

Webb, N. M., & Palincsar, A. S. (1996). Group processes in the classroom. In D. C. Berliner & R. C. Calfee (Eds.), *Handbook of educational psychology.* New York: Macmillan.

Webber, J., Scheuermann, B., McCall, C., & Coleman, M. (1993). Research on self-monitoring as a behavior management technique in special education classrooms: A descriptive review. *Remedial and Special Education, 14*(2), 38–56.

Wehmeyer, M. L. (1996). Self-determination as an educational outcome. In D. J. Sands & M. L. Wehmeyer (Eds.), *Self-determination across the life span: Independence and choice for people with disabilities.* Baltimore: Brookes.

Weikum, W. M., Vouloumanos, A., Navarra, J., Soto-Faraco, S., Sebastián-Gallés, N., & Werker, J. F. (2007). Visual language discrimination in infancy. *Science, 316*(5828) 1159.

Weiner, B. (1984). Principles for a theory of student motivation and their application within an attributional framework. In R. Ames & C. Ames (Eds.), *Research on motivation in education: Vol. 1. Student motivation.* San Diego, CA: Academic Press.

Weiner, B. (1986). *An attributional theory of motivation and emotion.* New York: Springer-Verlag.

Weiner, B. (1994). Ability versus effort revisited: The moral determinants of achievement evaluation and achievement as a moral system. *Educational Psychologist, 29,* 163–172.

Weiner, B. (2000). Intrapersonal and interpersonal theories of motivation from an attributional perspective. *Educational Psychology Review, 12,* 1–14.

Weiner, B., Russell, D., & Lerman, D. (1978). Affective consequences of causal ascriptions. In J. Harvey, W. Ickes, & R. Kidd (Eds.), *New directions in attribution research* (Vol. 2). Hillsdale, NJ: Erlbaum.

Weiner, B., Russell, D., & Lerman, D. (1979). The cognition-emotion process in achievement-related contexts. *Journal of Personality and Social Psychology, 37,* 1211–1220.

Weinert, F. E., & Helmke, A. (1995). Learning from wise Mother Nature or Big Brother Instructor: The wrong choice as seen from an educational perspective. *Educational Psychologist, 30,* 135–142.

Weinstein, C. E., Goetz, E. T., & Alexander, P. A. (Eds.). (1988). *Learning and study strategies:*

Issues in assessment, instruction, and evaluation. San Diego, CA: Academic Press.

Weinstein, C. E., Hagen, A. S., & Meyer, D. K. (1991, April). *Work smart . . . not hard: The effects of combining instruction in using strategies, goal using, and executive control on attributions and academic performance.* Paper presented at the annual meeting of the American Educational Research Association, Chicago.

Weinstein, C. S. (1979). The physical environment of the school: A review of the research. *Review of Educational Research, 49,* 577–610.

Weinstein, R. S. (1993). Children's knowledge of differential treatment in school: Implications for motivation. In T. M. Tomlinson (Ed.), *Motivating students to learn: Overcoming barriers to high achievement.* Berkeley, CA: McCutchan.

Weinstein, R. S., Madison, S. M., & Kuklinski, M. R. (1995). Raising expectations in schooling: Obstacles and opportunities for change. *American Educational Research Journal, 32,* 121–159.

Weisberg, R. W. (1993). *Creativity: Beyond the myth of genius.* New York: Freeman.

Weiss, L. G., Saklofske, D. H., Prifitera, A., & Holdnack, J. (2006). *WISC-IV Advanced Clinical Interpretation.* San Diego: Elsevier.

Weiss, M. R., & Klint, K. A. (1987). "Show and tell" in the gymnasium: An investigation of developmental differences in modeling and verbal rehearsal of motor skills. *Research Quarterly for Exercise and Sport, 58,* 234–241.

Weissburg, R. P. (1985). Designing effective social problem-solving programs for the classroom. In B. H. Schneider, K. H. Rubin, & J. E. Ledingham (Eds.), *Children's peer relations: Issues in assessment and intervention.* New York: Springer-Verlag.

Welch, G. J. (1985). Contingency contracting with a delinquent and his family. *Journal of Behavior Therapy and Experimental Psychiatry, 16,* 253–259.

Wellman, H. M. (1985). The child's theory of mind: The development of conceptions of cognition. In S. R. Yussen (Ed.), *The growth of reflection in children.* San Diego, CA: Academic Press.

Wellman, H. M. (1988). The early development of memory strategies. In F. Weinert & M. Perlmutter (Eds.), *Memory development: Universal changes and individual differences.* Hillsdale, NJ: Erlbaum.

Wellman, H. M., Cross, D., & Watson, J. (2001). Meta-analysis of theory-of-mind development. *Child Development, 72,* 655–684.

Wellman, H. M., & Gelman, S. A. (1998). Acquisition of knowledge. In W. Damon (Series Ed.), D. Kuhn, & R. S. Siegler (Vol. Eds.), *Handbook of child psychology: Vol. 2. Cognition, perception, and language* (5th ed.). New York: Wiley.

Wentzel, K. R. (1991). Social competence at school: Relations between social responsibility and academic achievement. *Review of Educational Research, 61,* 1–24.

Wentzel, K. R. (1999). Social-motivational processes and interpersonal relationships: Implications for understanding motivation at school. *Journal of Educational Psychology, 91,* 76–97.

Wentzel, K. R., & Wigfield, A. (1998). Academic and social motivational influences on students' academic performance. *Educational Psychology Review, 10,* 155–175.

Werner, E. E. (1995). Resilience in development. *Current Directions in Psychological Science, 4,* 81–85.

Wertsch, J. V. (1984). The zone of proximal development: Some conceptual issues. *Children's learning in the zone of proximal development: New directions for child development* (No. 23). San Francisco: Jossey-Bass.

West, C. K., Farmer, J. A., & Wolff, P. M. (1991). *Instructional design: Implications from cognitive science.* Upper Saddle River, NJ: Prentice Hall.

Western and Northern Canadian Protocol for Collaboration in Education. (2006a). *Rethinking classroom assessment with purpose in mind: Assessment for learning, assessment as learning, assessment of learning.* The Crown in right of the Governments of Alberta, British Columbia, Manitoba, Northwest Territories, Nunavut, Saskatchewan, and Yukon Territory as represented by their Ministers of Education. Retrieved August 14, 2008, from http://www.wncp.ca/assessment/rethink.pdf.

Western and Northern Canadian Protocol for Collaboration in Education. (2006b). *Assessment tool kit.* The Crown in right of the Governments of Alberta, British Columbia, Manitoba, Northwest Territories, Nunavut, Saskatchewan, and Yukon Territory as represented by their Ministers of Education.

White, B. Y., & Frederiksen, J. R. (1998). Inquiry, modeling, and metacognition: Making science accessible to all students. *Cognition and Instruction, 16,* 3–118.

White, J. J., & Rumsey, S. (1994). Teaching for understanding in a third-grade geography lesson. In J. Brophy (Ed.), *Advances in research on teaching: Vol. 4. Case studies of teaching and learning in social studies.* Greenwich, CT: JAI Press.

White, R. (1959). Motivation reconsidered: The concept of competence. *Psychological Review, 66,* 297–333.

Whitley, B. E., Jr., & Frieze, I. H. (1985). Children's causal attributions for success and failure in achievement settings: A meta-analysis. *Journal of Educational Psychology, 77,* 68–616.

Wideen, M., Mayer-Smith, J., & Moon, B. (1998). A critical analysis of the research on learning to teach: Making the case for an ecological perspective on inquiry. *Review of Educational Research, 68,* 130–178.

Wigfield, A. (1994). Expectancy-value theory of achievement motivation: A developmental perspective. *Educational Psychology Review, 6,* 49–78.

Wigfield, A. (1997). Reading motivation: A domain-specific approach to motivation. *Educational Psychologist, 32,* 59–68.

Wigfield, A., & Eccles, J. (1992). The development of achievement task values: A theoretical analysis. *Developmental Review, 12,* 265–310.

Wigfield, A., & Eccles, J. (1994). Children's competence beliefs, achievement values, and general self-esteem: Change across elementary and middle school. *Journal of Early Adolescence, 14,* 107–138.

Wigfield, A., & Eccles, J. (2000). Expectancy-value theory of achievement motivation. *Contemporary Educational Psychology, 25,* 68–81.

Wigfield, A., Eccles, J., MacIver, D., Reuman, D., & Midgley, C. (1991). Transitions at early adolescence: Changes in children's domain-specific self-perceptions and general self-esteem across the transition to junior high school. *Developmental Psychology, 27,* 552–565.

Wigfield, A., Eccles, J. S., & Pintrich, P. R. (1996). Development between the ages of 11 and 25. In D. C. Berliner & R. C. Calfee (Eds.), *Handbook of educational psychology.* New York: Macmillan.

Wigfield, A., & Meece, J. L. (1988). Math anxiety in elementary and secondary school students. *Journal of Educational Psychology, 80,* 210–216.

Wiggins, G. (1992). Creating tests worth taking. *Educational Leadership, 49*(8), 26–33.

Wilder, A. A., & Williams, J. P. (2001). Students with severe learning disabilities can learn higher order comprehension skills. *Journal of Educational Psychology, 93,* 268–278.

Wilkinson, L. C., & Marrett, C. B. (Eds.). (1985). *Gender influences in classroom interaction.* San Diego, CA: Academic Press.

Wilkinson, L. D., & Frazer, L. H. (1990, April). *Fine-tuning dropout prediction through discriminant analysis: The ethnic factor.* Paper presented at the annual meeting of the American Educational Research Association, Boston.

Williams, B., & Newcombe, E. (1994). Building on the strengths of urban learners. *Educational Leadership, 51*(8), 75–78.

Williams, J. P. (1991, November). *Comprehension of learning disabled and nondisabled students: Identification of narrative themes and idiosyncratic text representation.* Paper presented at the annual meeting of the National Reading Conference, Austin, TX.

Willig, A. C. (1985). A meta-analysis of selected studies on the effectiveness of bilingual education. *Review of Educational Research, 55,* 269–317.

Wilson, C. C., Piazza, C. C., & Nagle, R. (1990). Investigations of the effects of consistent and inconsistent behavioral example upon children's donation behaviors. *Journal of Genetic Psychology, 151,* 361–376.

Wilson, J. E. (1988). Implications of learning strategy research and training: What it has to say to the practitioner. In C. E. Weinstein, E. T. Goetz, & P. A. Alexander (Eds.), *Learning and study strategies: Issues in assessment, instruction, and evaluation.* San Diego, CA: Academic Press.

Wilson, M. (1989). Child development in the context of the black extended family. *American Psychologist, 44,* 380–383.

Wilson, P. S. (1988, April). The relationship of students' definitions and example choices in geometry. In D. Tirosh (Chair), *The role of inconsistent ideas in learning mathematics.* Symposium conducted at the annual meeting of the American Educational Research Association, New Orleans, LA.

Wilson, P. T., & Anderson, R. C. (1986). What they don't know will hurt them: The role of prior knowledge in comprehension. In J. Orasanu (Ed.), *Reading comprehension: From research to practice.* Hillsdale, NJ: Erlbaum.

Wine, J. D. (1980). Cognitive-attentional theory of test anxiety. In I. G. Sarason (Ed.), *Test anxiety: Theory, research, and applications.* Hillsdale, NJ: Erlbaum.

Winer, G. A., & Cottrell, J. E. (1996). Does anything leave the eye when we see? Extramission beliefs of children and adults. *Current Directions in Psychological Science, 5,* 137–142.

Wingfield, A., & Byrnes, D. L. (1981). *The psychology of human memory.* San Diego, CA: Academic Press.

Winn, W. (1991). Learning from maps and diagrams. *Educational Psychology Review, 3,* 211–247.

Winne, P. H. (1995). Inherent details in self-regulated learning. *Educational Psychologist, 30,* 173–187.

Winne, P. H. (2006). How software technologies can improve research on learning and bolster school reform. *Educational Psychologist, 41,* 5–17.

Winne, P. H., & Hadwin, A. F. (1998). Studying as self-regulated learning. In D. J. Hacker, J. Dunlosky, & A. C. Graesser (Eds.), *Metacognition in educational theory and practice* (pp. 277–304). Mahwah, NJ: Erlbaum.

Winne, P. H., & Marx, R. W. (1989). A cognitive-processing analysis of motivation with classroom tasks. In C. Ames & R. Ames (Eds.), *Research on motivation in education* (Vol. 3). San Diego, CA: Academic Press.

Winne, P. H., Nesbit, J. C., Kumar, V., Hadwin, A. F., Lajoie, S. P., Azevedo, R. A., & Perry, N.E. (2006). Supporting self-regulated learning with gStudy software: The Learning Project Kit. *Technology, Instruction, Cognition and Learning, 3*, 105–113.

Winner, E. (1988). *The point of words*. Cambridge, MA: Harvard University Press.

Winner, E. (1997). Exceptionally high intelligence and schooling. *American Psychologist, 52*, 1070–1081.

Winner, E. (2000a). Giftedness: Current theory and research. *Current Directions in Psychological Science, 9*, 153–156.

Winner, E. (2000b). The origins and ends of giftedness. *American Psychologist, 55*, 159–169.

Winograd, P., & Jones, D. L. (1992). The use of portfolios in performance assessment. *New Directions for Education Reform, 1*(2), 37–50.

Winzer, M. (1995). *Educational psychology in the Canadian classroom* (2nd ed.). Scarborough, ON: Allyn & Bacon Canada.

Wise, B. W., & Olson, R. K. (1998). Studies of computer-aided remediation for reading disabilities. In C. Hulme & R. M. Joshi (Eds.), *Reading and spelling: Development and disorders*. Mahwah, NJ: Erlbaum.

Wittmer, D. S., & Honig, A. S. (1994). Encouraging positive social development in young children. *Young Children, 49*(5), 4–12.

Wittrock, M. C. (1994). Generative science teaching. In P. J. Fensham, R. F. Gunstone, & R. T. White (Eds.), *The content of science: A constructivist approach to its teaching and learning*. London: Falmer Press.

Wixson, K. K. (1984). Level of importance of postquestions and children's learning from text. *American Educational Research Journal, 21*, 419–433.

Wizer, J. (1995). Small group instruction using microcomputers: Focus on group behaviours. *Journal of Research on Computing in Education, 28*(1), 10–12.

Wlodkowski, R. J., & Ginsberg, M. B. (1995). *Diversity and motivation: Culturally responsive teaching*. San Francisco: Jossey-Bass.

Wodtke, K. H., Harper, F., & Schommer, M. (1989). How standardized is school testing? An exploratory observational study of standardized group testing in kindergarten. *Educational Evaluation and Policy Analysis, 11*, 223–235.

Wolpe, J. (1969). *The practice of behavior therapy*. Oxford, London: Pergamon Press.

Wolters, C. A. (1998). Self-regulated learning and college students' regulation of motivation. *Journal of Educational Psychology, 90*, 224–235.

Wong, B. Y. L. (Ed.). (1991a). *Learning about learning disabilities*. San Diego, CA: Academic Press.

Wong, B. Y. L. (1991b). The relevance of metacognition to learning disabilities. In B. Y. L. Wong (Ed.), *Learning about learning disabilities*. San Diego, CA: Academic Press.

Wood, D., Bruner, J. S., & Ross, G. (1976). The role of tutoring in problem-solving. *Journal of Child Psychology and Psychiatry, 17*, 89–100.

Wood, E., Motz, M., & Willoughby, T. (1997, April). *Examining students' retrospective memories of strategy development*. Paper presented at the annual meeting of the American Educational Research Association, Chicago.

Wood, E., Willoughby, T., McDermott, C., Motz, M., Kaspar, V., & Ducharme, M. J. (1999). Developmental differences in study behavior. *Journal of Educational Psychology, 91*, 527–536.

Wood, E., Willoughby, T., Reilley, S., Elliott, S., & DuCharme, M. (1994, April). *Evaluating students' acquisition of factual material when studying independently or with a partner*. Paper presented at the annual meeting of the American Educational Research Association, New Orleans, LA.

Wood, J. W., & Rosbe, M. (1985). Adapting the classroom lecture for the mainstreamed student in the secondary schools. *Clearing House, 58*, 354–358.

Woolfolk, A. E., & Brooks, D. M. (1985). The influence of teachers' nonverbal behaviors on students' perceptions and performances. *Elementary School Journal, 85*, 513–528.

Woolfolk, A. E., Winne, P. H., & Perry, N. E. (2004). *Educational Psychology* (2nd Canadian ed.). Toronto, ON: Pearson Canada.

Worswick, C. (2001). *School performance of the children of immigrants in Canada: 1994–98*. Ottawa: Statistics Canada. Retrieved March, 2008, from http://www.statcan.ca/bsolc/english/bsolc?catno=11F0019M2001178.

Worthen, B. R., & Leopold, G. D. (1992). Impediments to implementing alternative assessment: Some emerging issues. *New Directions for Education Reform, 1*(2), 1–20.

Wright, L. S. (1982). The use of logical consequences in counseling children. *School Counselor, 30*, 37–49.

Wright, R. (1994). *The moral animal: The new science of evolutionary psychology*. New York: Pantheon Books.

Wright, S. C., & Taylor, D. M. (1995). Identity and the language of the classroom: Investigating the impact of heritage versus second-language instruction on personal and collective self-esteem. *Journal of Educational Psychology, 87*, 241–252.

Wright, S. C., Taylor, D. M., & Macarthur, J. (2000). Subtractive bilingualism and the survival of the Inuit language: Heritage- versus second-language education. *Journal of Educational Psychology, 92*, 63–84.

Yarmey, A. D. (1973). I recognize your face but I can't remember your name: Further evidence on the tip-of-the-tongue phenomenon. *Memory and Cognition, 1*, 287–290.

Yee, D. K., & Eccles, J. S. (1988). Parent perceptions and attributions for children's math achievement. *Sex Roles, 19*, 317–333.

Yell, M. L., Robinson, T. R., & Drasgow, E. (2001). Cognitive behavior modification. In T. J. Zirpoli & K. J. Melloy, *Behavior management: Applications for teachers* (3rd ed., pp. 200–246). Upper Saddle River, NJ: Merrill/Prentice Hall.

Yerkes, R. M., & Dodson, J. D. (1908). The relation of strength of stimulus to rapidity of habit-formation. *Journal of Comparative Neurology of Psychology, 18*, 459–482.

Yokoi, L. (1997, March). *The developmental context of notetaking: A qualitative examination of notetaking at the secondary level*. Paper presented at the annual meeting of the American Educational Research Association, Chicago.

Youniss, J., & Volpe, J. (1978). A relational analysis of children's friendships. In W. Damon (Ed.), *New directions for child development: Vol. 1. Social cognition* (pp. 1–22). San Francisco: Jossey-Bass.

Youniss, J., & Yates, M. (1999). Youth service and moral-civic identity: A case for everyday morality. *Educational Psychology Review, 11*, 361–376.

Yu, S. L., Elder, A. D., & Urdan, T. C. (1995, April). *Motivation and cognitive strategies in students with a "good student" or "poor student" self-schema*. Paper presented at the annual meeting of the American Educational Research Association, San Francisco.

Zahorik, J. A. (1994, April). *Making things interesting*. Paper presented at the annual meeting of the American Educational Research Association, New Orleans, LA.

Zeaman, D., & House, B. J. (1979). A review of attention theory. In N. R. Ellis (Ed.), *Handbook of mental deficiency: Psychological theory and research* (2nd ed.). Hillsdale, NJ: Erlbaum.

Zeidner, M. (1998). *Test anxiety: The state of the art*. New York: Plenum Press.

Zeldin, A. L., & Pajares, F. (2000). Against the odds: Self-efficacy beliefs of women in mathematical, scientific, and technological careers. *American Educational Research Journal, 37*, 215–246.

Ziegler, S., & Rosenstein-Manner, M. (1991). *Bullying at school: Toronto in an international context*. Toronto: Toronto Board of Education, Research Services.

Ziegler, S. G. (1987). Effects of stimulus cueing on the acquisition of groundstrokes by beginning tennis players. *Journal of Applied Behavior Analysis, 20*, 405–411.

Zigler, E. F., & Seitz, V. (1982). Social policy and intelligence. In R. J. Sternberg (Ed.), *Handbook of human intelligence* (pp. 586–641). Cambridge, England: Cambridge University Press.

Zigmond, N., Jenkins, J., Fuchs, L. S., Deno, S., Fuchs, D., Baker, J. N., Jenkins, L., & Couthino, M. (1995, March). Special education in restructured schools: Findings from three multi-year studies. *Phi Delta Kappan, 76*, 531–540.

Zimmerman, B. J. (1998). Developing self-fulfilling cycles of academic regulation: An analysis of exemplary instructional models. In D. H. Schunk & B. J. Zimmerman (Eds.), *Self-regulated learning: From teaching to self-reflective practice* (pp. 1–19). New York: Guilford Press.

Zimmerman, B. J., Bandura, A., & Martinez-Pons, M. (1992). Self-motivation for academic attainment: The role of self-efficacy beliefs and personal goal setting. *American Educational Research Journal, 29*, 663–676.

Zimmerman, B. J., & Risemberg, R. (1997). Self-regulatory dimensions of academic learning and motivation. In G. D. Phye (Ed.), *Handbook of academic learning: Construction of knowledge*. San Diego, CA: Academic Press.

Zirpoli, T. J., & Melloy, K. J. (2001). *Behavior management: Applications for teachers*. Upper Saddle River, NJ: Merrill/Prentice Hall.

Zook, K. B. (1991). Effects of analogical processes on learning and misrepresentation. *Educational Psychology Review, 3*, 41–72.

Zook, K. B., & Di Vesta, F. J. (1991). Instructional analogies and conceptual misrepresentations. *Journal of Educational Psychology, 83*, 246–252.

Zuckerman, G. A. (1994). A pilot study of a ten-day course in cooperative learning for beginning Russian first graders. *Elementary School Journal, 94*, 405–420.

Name Index

A

Abbott, M., 40
Abery, B., 215
Adam, S., 30
Adams, J.K., 32
Adams, P.A., 38
Adams, V.M., 229, 230
Adler, T.F., 95, 240
Afflerbach, P.P., 343, 348
Aidinis, A., 36
Airasian, P.W., 276, 335, 347, 351, 354
Alapack, R., 60
Alderman, M.K., 99
Alderson, K., 59
Alexander, J.M., 234
Alexander, K.L., 251
Alexander, P.A., 31, 137, 147, 165, 169, 173, 180, 184, 239, 254
Alford, G.S., 202
Alibali, M.W., 242
Alleman, J., 68, 166, 238, 244, 261, 275, 344
Allen, K.D., 209
Alley, G.R., 278
Altermatt, E.R., 96
Amabile, T.M., 86, 236
Ames, C., 242, 244
Amett, J.J., 54, 59
Amsel, E., 169, 187
Anand, P., 239
Anderman, E.M., 240, 242
Anderman, L.H., 242
Andersen, C., 176
Anderson, A., 83
Anderson, C.A., 170
Anderson, C.W., 169, 170, 171
Anderson, J.R., 136, 138, 139, 140, 141, 144, 146, 147, 150, 153, 178, 179, 180, 184
Anderson, L.M., 98, 161, 165, 166, 277
Anderson, M.L., 61
Anderson, R.C., 148, 152, 155, 163
Anderson, V., 175, 228, 238
Anderson, C.A., 200
Andre, T., 132
Andrews, D.W., 57
Andrews, J., 60, 278
Anglin, J.M., 36
Ansley, T., 324
Anzai, Y., 184
Araujo, J., 151, 284
Arbreton, A.J., 97
Archer, S.L., 55
Arcus, D.M., 48
Arlin, M., 286, 300
Arnaudin, M.W., 164, 169
Arnold, M.L., 69
Arter, J.A.M., 354
Arthur, N., 87
Artz, S., 203
Asher, S.R., 56
Ashley, E., 30
Ashman, A.D., 283
Ashton, P., 251
Asoko, H., 169
Aspinwall, L.G., 285
Asselin, M., 273
Assor, A., 51, 205
Atkinson, J.W., 223
Atkinson, R.C., 135, 141
Atkinson, R.K., 170, 182
Atria, M., 84
Attanucci, J., 68
Aulls, M., 24, 161

Aulls, M.W., 161
Austin, L.B., 139
Ausubel, D.P., 36, 141, 142, 148, 174, 265
Ayres, L.R., 210, 212, 316, 341, 348

B

Babad, E., 249
Babey, S.H., 50
Bachelor, P., 85
Bachor, D., 353
Baciu, I., 39
Backer, R., 223
Baddeley, A.D., 136
Baek, S., 315, 332
Bagwell, C.L., 58
Bahrick, H.P., 151
Bahrick, L.E., 151
Bahrick, P.E., 151
Bailey, J.S., 122
Baillargeon, R., 22, 203
Baird, J.H., 332
Baker, L., 173, 174
Baltes, P.B., 223
Bandura, A., 51, 195, 197, 198, 199, 200, 204, 205, 206, 208, 210, 214, 240, 244, 245
Bangert-Drowns, R.L., 267
Banks, C.A.M., 249
Banks, J.A., 91, 92, 161, 171, 249
Barber, B.L., 97
Barbetta, P.M., 116
Barchfeld, P., 22
Barhick, A.S., 151
Barkley, R.A., 123, 124, 136, 285, 304
Barkley, R.M., 72, 155, 228
Barnes, D., 161
Barnet, R.C., 109
Barnett, J.E., 172, 173
Baron, J.B., 182, 315
Baron, M.A., 329
Bartini, M., 56
Bartley, A.W., 353
Barva, C., 250
Basiner, K.S., 57, 58
Bassok, M., 180
Bates, J.E., 16, 48
Batson, C.D., 69
Battin-Pearson, S., 97
Battistich, V., 222, 286, 297, 298, 306
Baumrind, D., 48, 69
Bausch, M.E., 272
Baxter, G.P., 315, 347
Bay-Hinitz, A.K., 60
Beal, L., 78
Bebeau, M., 67
Beck, I.L., 265
Bédard, A.-C., 29
Beery, R.M., 99
Behrmann, M., 170
Beirne-Smith, M., 72
Beitzel, B.D., 149
Belfiore, P.J., 202, 209, 212
Bell, J.A., 176
Bellezza, F.S., 148
Bender, T.A., 54
Benet-Martinez, V., 88
Bennett, R.E., 249
Benson, B., 59
Benware, C., 284
Beran, T.N., 61, 204, 273
Bereiter, C., 168, 170, 178, 180, 274, 277
Berends, M., 82

Berglas, S., 225, 226
Berk, L.E., 25, 41, 60, 80
Berkowitz, M.W., 67
Berliner, D.C., 295
Berman, S.L., 69
Berndorff, D., 239
Berndt, T.J., 57
Bernieri, F., 235
Berthelot, J.M., 172, 322
Berzonsky, M.D., 55
Beyer, F.S., 167
Bialystock, E., 34, 38, 39
Biddlecomb, B., 161, 185
Bidell, T., 23
Bidell, T.R., 82
Biemiller, A., 5, 35, 209, 214, 284
Bierman, K.L., 62, 72
Biezuner, S., 161
Binder, L.M., 114
Binet, A., 77
Birch, J.W., 304
Bishop, C.H., 332
Bjork, R.A., 180
Bjorklund, D.F., 29, 30, 31, 136, 143, 148
Black, A., 66
Black, J.B., 163
Black, J.E., 16, 282
Blake, S.B., 180
Blasi, A., 67, 69
Blattner, J.E., 116
Blinde, P.L., 97
Block, J.H., 95, 267
Bloom, B.S., 265
Blue-Banning, M., 297
Blumenfeld, P., 242, 283, 314
Bluth, G.J., 144
Bochenhauer, M.H., 265
Boettcher, J., 273
Boggiano, A.K., 232, 234
Boivin, M., 51, 56
Bol, L., 32
Bolles, R.C., 223
Bong, M., 242
Bonica, C., 59
Bordeleau, L., 54
Borko, H., 8, 298
Borkowski, J.G., 30, 251
Born, D.G., 267
Bornstein, M.H., 16
Boschee, F., 329
Boshuizen, H.P.A., 143
Bossert, S., 314
Bouchard, T.J., 48, 54, 81
Boulerice, B., 97
Bousfield, W.A., 143
Boutte, G.S., 91, 92
Bowen, G.M., 27
Bower, G.H., 142, 144, 149, 157, 163
Bowey, J., 38
Bowman, B.T., 88
Bowman, L.G., 115
Boyatzis, R.E., 226
Boyes-Braem, P., 162
Boyle, R.A., 170
Bracken, B.A., 57, 80, 331
Bradley, L., 37, 38, 39, 233
Bradley, R.H., 85
Brainerd, C.J., 134
Brandt, D.H., 144
Bransford, J.D., 132, 142, 143, 185
Brantlinger, E., 102
Braukmann, C.J., 62

N-1

Brenner, M.E., 184
Brent, S.B., 35
Brett, C., 281
Brewer, W.F., 169, 170
Briggs, W., 296
Bright, J.A., 90
Britton, B.K., 142, 164
Brody, G.H, 69
Brody, N., 78, 79, 80
Bronson, M.B., 208, 211, 212, 222
Brooke, R.R., 116
Brooks, D.M., 120, 295
Brooks, L.W., 179, 180
Brooks, M., 270
Brooks-Gunn, J., 59, 85
Brophy, J., 8, 166, 239, 344
Brophy, J.E., 68, 166, 180, 227, 231, 238, 239, 242, 244, 249, 254, 261, 275
Brown, A.L., 31, 161, 168, 176, 278, 284, 348
Brown, A.S., 314
Brown, B.B., 56, 57, 59, 226
Brown, J.H., 308
Brown, J.S., 166
Brown, L.M., 68
Brown, R., 137, 151, 173, 178, 271
Bruer, J.T., 16, 34, 38
Bruner, J.S., 27
Bruning, R.H., 277
Bryan, J.H., 200
Bryant, P., 36
Bryant, P.E., 37, 38, 39
Buchele, K.S., 226
Buhrmester, D., 56
Bukowski, W., 58
Bulgren, J.A., 149
Bullock, M., 22
Burger, D., 347
Burger, S., 347
Burger, S.F., 5
Burhans, K.K., 249
Burns, R.B., 267
Burtis, J., 170
Burtis, P.J., 281
Burton, L.M., 306
Burton, R.V., 209
Bushman, B.J., 200
Busse, R.T., 60, 202, 212
Bussiere, P., 197, 219
Butler, D.L., 113, 176, 207, 211, 250
Butler, R., 211, 232, 242
Byrnes, D.L., 135
Byrnes, J.P., 113, 246

C

Calderhead, J., 264–265
Caldwell, B.M., 85
Calfee, R., 136, 265, 344
Camburn, E., 97
Cameron, J., 236
Campbell, A., 58
Campbell, B., 80
Campbell, D.E., 299
Campbell, F.A., 85
Campbell, L., 80
Campbell, P.A., 95, 96
Campione, J.C., 168, 284, 348
Candee, D., 67
Candler-Lotven, A., 189
Cannon, E., 250
Cao, H.T., 227
Capodilupo, A., 84
Caprara, G.V., 62
Capron, C., 82
Carey, L.M., 347
Carey, S., 22, 35, 169
Cariglia-Bull, T., 179
Carlo, G., 62, 68
Carlson, S.A., 278
Carney, P., 136, 203
Carnine, D., 268
Carpenter, P.A., 148

Carper, L.B., 115
Carr, A.A., 308
Carr, M., 30, 161, 185
Carraher, D.W., 23
Carroll, J.L., 22
Carta, J.J., 284, 285
Cartledge, G., 72
Cartright, F., 219
Carver, C.S., 211, 229, 240
Casanova, U., 87, 89, 92
Case, R., 23, 29, 78, 81, 84
Caseau, D., 101
Casey, W.M., 209
Cashon, C.H., 22
Caspi, A., 82, 203
Cassel, W.S., 30
Casserly, P.L., 96
Castine, W.H., 270
Caterino, L.C., 140
Cazden, C.B., 36, 91
Ceci, S.J., 82, 160
Cerullo, F., 249
Chaase, M.A., 113
Chabay, R.W., 285
Chall, J.S., 29
Chalmers, J., 69
Chalmers, N., 85, 146
Chambliss, M.J., 169, 265
Chan, C., 170, 281
Chan, K.S., 97
Chand, I., 85, 86
Chandler, M., 67
Chao, R.K., 49
Chapman, J.W., 54
Chapman, S., 175
Chapman, M., 200
Chen, C., 82, 276
Chen, X., 49
Chen, Z., 184
Cheng, P.W., 150
Cherlin, D.L., 136, 295
Cherry, E.C., 135
Chessor, D., 59
Cheung, M., 270
Cheyne, J.A, 124
Chi, M.T.H., 31, 164, 184
Chiappetta, E.L., 272
Chih-Mei, C., 253
Child, D.A., 176
Chin, R., 253
Chinn, C.A., 169, 170
Chiu, C., 88, 247
Chomsky, N., 33, 36
Christensen, C.A., 150
Christie, J.F., 37
Christophe, A., 34
Christopherson, H., 275
Chudowsky, N., 314
Cihak, D.F., 272
Cillessen, A.H.N., 72
Clark, B, 156
Clark, C.C., 58, 59
Clark, E.V., 36
Clark, J.M., 170
Clark, M.C., 144, 149
Clark, R.A., 223
Clark, R.E., 180
Clauser, P., 324
Cleary, T., 203
Clement, C., 23
Clements, B.S., 295
Clifford, M.M., 233, 246, 349
Clore, G.L., 59
Coatsworth, J.D., 99
Cobb, P., 242, 277
Cochran, K.F., 8
Cochran-Smith, M., 9
Cohen, E.G., 277, 283, 284, 285, 286
Cohen, L.B., 22
Cohen, P., 30, 150
Cohen, P.A., 270
Cohen, R.L., 147, 202

Coie, R.L., 72
Colarossi, L., 97
Colavecchia, B., 122
Colby, A., 64, 66
Cole, D.A., 205, 254
Cole, N.S., 41, 261
Coleman, H.L.K., 88
Coleman, M., 209
Coleman-Martin, M.B., 272
Colins, P., 39
Collins, A., 314, 334, 337
Collaer, M.L., 93
Collier, V.P., 40
Collins, A., 166
Collins, S., 87
Collins, W.A., 16, 48, 57, 59
Combs, A.W., 230
Comfort, C., 97
Conger, K.J., 58
Conger, R.D., 58
Connell, J.P., 51, 205, 222, 226
Connolly, F.W., 276
Connor, D.F., 285
Connor, J.M., 95
Conway, M.A., 145
Cooney, J.B., 302
Cooper, H., 123
Cooper, H.M., 251
Corbett, H.D., 314
Corenblum, B., 249
Corkill, A.J., 29, 72, 79, 151
Corley, R., 81
Cormier, S.M., 181
Cornell, D.G., 54
Corno, L., 123, 211, 232, 257, 260
Corrigan, C., 297
Corsin, L., 97
Cote, S., 203
Cothern, N.B., 155
Cottrell, J.E., 169
Cottrol, R.J., 93
Couchesne, E., 155
Covington, M.V., 57, 99, 124, 208, 222, 225, 230, 233, 239, 240, 242, 247, 315, 316
Cowan, N., 135, 139
Cox, B.D., 180
Cox, P.D., 205
Coyle, T.R., 29
Craft, M., 89
Crago, M.B., 90
Craig, D., 341, 349
Craig, W., 204
Craik, F.I.M., 30, 141
Crandall, V.C., 247
Craven, R., 50, 51, 59, 72, 282
Creasey, G.L., 60
Crick, F.I.M., 203
Crockett, L., 58
Crook, C., 283
Crooks, T.J., 349
Cross, D., 22, 32
Cross, D.R., 278
Crouse, J., 324
Crowder, R., 139
Crowley, E., 172
Crowley, K., 26, 183
Crowne, D.P., 227
Crumbaugh, C., 167, 277
Csikszentmihalyi, M., 86, 221, 222, 230, 233
Cunningham, A.E., 31, 38, 54, 99, 166, 178, 226, 249
Cunningham, C.E., 215
Cunningham, L.J., 215
Cunningham, T.H., 40
Curzon, J., 269
Cushing, K.S., 295
Cushing, L.S., 285

D

D'Agostino, J.V., 186
D'Amato, R.C., 82
Damon, W., 51, 57, 60, 68, 69

Dancs, M., 62
Danner, F.W., 238
Dansereau, D.F., 174, 179, 180, 283
Darling-Hammond, L., 8
Das, J.P., 78, 81
Dauvergne, M., 82
Davidson, A.L., 87, 227, 230, 243
Davidson, J.E., 185
Davidson, P., 66
Davis, G.A., 298, 299, 308
Davis, H., 169, 177
Davis, H.A., 211
Davis, M.L., 267
Dawkins, R., 188
De Corte, E., 166, 344
de Glopper, K., 36
de Jong, T., 274
De Lisi, R., 70
Deaux, K., 251, 254
deCharms, R., 234, 254
Deci, E.L., 232, 284
Deering, P.D., 283
DeFries, J.C., 81
DeGrandpre, R.J., 108
De Groot, E.V., 159
Delandshere, G., 352
Delaney, H.D., 149
Delcourt, M.A.B., 40, 161
Delgado-Gaitan, C., 37, 189
DeLoache, J.S., 30
DeMarie-Dreblow, D., 29
Dempster, F.N., 29, 72, 79, 151, 153, 314
Denier, C., 95
DeNisi, A., 223, 245
Derevensky, J., 112, 116
DeRidder, L.M., 54
Derry, S.J., 27, 169, 182, 188, 270
Desberg, P., 264
Deshler, D.D., 149, 256, 278
D'Espositio, M., 135, 157
Deutsch, M., 60, 61, 212, 283, 284
DeVries, R., 58, 70
Dewhurst, S.A., 145
Diamond, S.C., 296
Diaz, R.M., 38
Diaz, S., 40
Dickerson, C., 56
Dickinson, D., 80
Dien, T., 227, 253
diSessa, A.A., 164, 180
Di Vesta, F.J., 136, 151, 173
Dishion, T.J., 57
Dixon, M.R., 114
Dixon, C.N., 308
Dobbelaere, A., 297
Dodge, K.A., 203
Dodson, J.D., 229
Doescher, S.M., 69
Doherty, M., 22
Dole, J.A., 175, 176
Dominowski, R.L., 186
Donley, J., 174
Dorman, J.P., 297
Dornbusch, S.M., 314
Douglas, G., 176, 189
Dovidio, J.F., 92
Downey, G., 59
Dowrick, P.W., 271
Dowson, M., 56, 226, 242
Doyle, W., 56, 122, 226, 242, 275, 295, 298, 299, 300, 301
Drabman, R.S., 122
Drake, D.D., 332
Drasgow, E., 210
Dreikurs, R., 122
Drevno, G.E., 112
Drew, H.A., 126
Driver, R., 165
Droppleman, P., 54
DuBois, N.F., 143, 174
DuCette, J., 256
DuCharme, M., 142

Dudley, B., 212
Dueck, A., 116
Duffy, G.G., 175
Duit, R., 164, 169
Dukacz, A., 308
Duncan, C., 54
Duncan, G.J., 85
Dunlap, G., 126, 235
Dunlap, K., 277
Dunlosky, J., 176
DuPaul, G.J., 284, 285, 286
Durken, K., 55, 95
Dutta, A., 146, 147, 150
Duyme, M., 82
Dweck, C.S., 223, 234, 236, 240, 242, 245, 246, 247, 249, 251, 254

E

Eaton, J.F., 169
Ebel, R., 332
Eccles [Parsons], J.S., 52, 236, 246
Eccles, J., 55, 226, 236, 250
Eccles, J.S., 52, 54, 96, 97, 205, 208, 221, 223, 232, 237, 239, 247, 249, 250
Eckert, P., 56, 59
Edens, K.M., 170
Eeds, M., 277
Egeland, B., 82, 84
Eicher, S.A., 226
Eifert, G.H., 108
Einstein, G.O., 145, 174, 274
Eisenberg, N., 22, 68, 95–96, 241
Eisenberg, T.E., 276
Elaschuk, C.L., 207
El-Banna, H., 183
Elder, A.D., 51, 315
El-Dinary, P.B., 178
Elkind, D., 54, 55, 57
Elliot, A.J., 240, 242
Elliott, A.J., 242
Elliott, E.S., 223, 234, 236, 240, 241, 242, 245, 246, 247, 251
Elliott, R., 200
Elliott, S., 142
Elliott, S.N., 60, 61, 202, 212
Ellis, E.S., 189
Ellis, J.A., 151, 284
Ellis, R., 36
Emmer, E.T., 120, 295, 297, 298, 299, 300, 301
Empson, S.B., 22
Englemann, S., 268
Entwisle, D.R., 251
Epstein, J.L., 58, 90, 308, 309
Epstein, J.S., 58
Erickson, R., 90, 155
Ericsson, K.A., 85, 146
Eriks-Brophy, A., 90
Erikson, E., 53, 55
Ervin, R.A., 284, 286
Erwin, P., 56, 57
Esquivel, G.B., 86
Etaugh, C., 95
Evans, E.D., 341, 349
Everston, C., 254
Evertson, C.M., 295, 299
Eylon, B., 169
Eysenck, M.W., 139, 230

F

Fabes, R.A., 58, 60, 68, 95
Fagot, B.I., 95
Fall, R., 314
Fantuzzo, J.W., 210, 285
Farah, M.J., 135, 157
Farivar, S., 60, 283, 300
Farmer, J.A., 148
Farwell, L., 335
Feather, N.T., 223, 236, 246
Feiring, C., 59
Feld, S., 232

Feldhusen, J.F., 86
Felton, M., 277
Feltovich, P., 184
Feltz, D.L., 113
Fennema, E., 95, 246, 254, 286
Ferguson, J.M., 297
Feuerstein, R., 338
Finders, M., 84, 309
Finn, J.D., 97, 99
Fischer, K.W., 23, 82
Fisher, C.W., 166
Fisher, R.P., 314
Fisher, W.W., 115
Fivush, R., 30
Flavell, H.J., 18, 22, 23, 31, 54, 72, 155, 162
Flavell, J.H., 32
Fleming, J.S., 222, 236
Flieller, A., 22
Flores, A., 8
Florez, V., 306
Flynn, J.R., 82
Foos, P.W., 314
Ford, M.E., 37, 208, 225, 226, 240, 243
Fordham, S., 253
Forsyth, J.P., 108
Fortier, M.S., 221
Fosnot, C.T., 161, 165
Fox, K.R., 308
Fox, L.H., 96
Fox, P.W., 276, 334
Fraley, J.B., 143, 174
Franklin, S., 22
Franks, J.J., 132, 143, 185
Frater-Mathieson, K., 83
Frecker, K., 281
Frederiksen, J.R., 274, 275, 277, 314, 334, 337
Frederiksen, N., 183, 274, 314
Freebern, G., 173
Freedman, S.G., 59
Freeland, J.T., 125
Freeman, B., 244
French, E.G., 226–227
French, K.E., 93, 95
Frensch, P.A., 181, 185
Friebert, S.E., 32
Friedel, J., 250
Friedrichs, A.G., 31
Frieze, I.H., 246
Fritz, J.B., 145
Frost, J.L., 95
Fry, A.F., 114
Fuchs, D., 284
Fuchs, L.S., 284, 285
Fulker, D.W., 81
Fuller, D., 56, 58
Fuller, M.L., 91, 95, 122
Furman, W., 59

G

Gaertner, S.L., 92
Gage, N.L., 5
Gagne, E.D., 137, 140
Gagne, R.M., 147, 268
Gajdamaschko, N., 28
Gallimore, R., 27
Gallini, J., 242
Ganschow, L., 101
Garcia, E.E., 87, 90, 91, 92, 97, 98, 171, 242, 286
Garcia, T., 39, 51
Garcia-Mila, M., 176
Gardner, H., 78, 79–85
Garibaldi, A.M., 98, 99
Garner, R., 137, 173, 238
Garnier, H.E., 97
Gathercole, S.E., 29
Gauntt, H.L., 143
Gauvain, M., 26
Gayford, C., 282
Gaynor, J., 349
Geary, D.C., 16, 226
Gebotys, R., 22, 37, 39

Gelman, S.A., 163
Georgas, J., 105
Gerst, M.S., 202
Gerton, J., 88
Gertzog, W.A., 170
Gettinger, M., 299
Ghatala, E.S., 176
Ghezzi, P.M., 114
Giaconia, R.M., 155
Gibbs, J.C., 56, 58, 64
Gibson, E., 57
Gick, M.L., 180, 181
Gill, H.S., 93
Gillies, R.M., 283
Gilligan, C.F., 67–68
Gilliland, H., 89, 90
Gillingham, M.G., 137
Gillooly, W.B., 38
Ginsberg, D., 57
Ginsberg, M.B., 87, 242, 254
Girotto, V., 23
Glaeser, B., 124
Glaessner, B., 229, 230
Glanzer, M., 144, 148
Glaser, R., 31, 183, 184, 315
Glasser, W., 299
Glover, J.A., 86, 349
Glucksberg, S., 37
Glynn, S.M., 164
Goddard, R.D., 206, 207
Goetz, E.T., 145
Goetz, L., 103
Golbeck, S.L., 70
Gold, M., 232
Goldenberg, C., 249, 250, 252
Goldschmid, M.L., 136
Golen, S., 234
Gomez, M.L., 155
Good, S., 247
Good, T.L., 27, 243, 249, 250–251, 282
Goodenow, C., 49, 226
Goodman, J., 209
Goodman, K., 297
Gopnik, M., 33
Gordon, W., 41
Gottardo, A., 39
Gottesman, R.L., 249
Gottfredson, D.C., 57, 123, 306
Gottfredson, G.D., 123, 298
Gottfredson, L.S., 239
Gottfried, A.E., 221, 222, 236
Gottfried, A.W., 222, 236
Gottlieb, G., 16, 82
Gottman, J.M., 57, 58, 59, 60
Gough, P.B., 39
Gowin, D.B., 174
Gowin, D.G., 174
Grabe, M., 136
Graesser, A., 284
Graham, C.R., 40
Graham, S., 31, 61, 223, 234, 242, 245, 249, 251
Gralinski, H., 246
Grant, C.A., 93, 155
Gray, S.G., 136, 173
Gray, W.D., 162
Green, B.L., 31
Green, L., 114
Green-Demers, I., 238
Greene, B.A., 176
Greene, T.R., 192
Greeno, J.G., 178
Greenough, S.T., 16, 282
Greenough, W.T., 157
Greenwood, C.R., 284, 285
Greer, T., 166
GrennonBrooks, J., 270
Gresham, F.M., 72
Griffin, S.A., 81, 84
Griffiths, P.L., 39
Griffore, R.J., 52
Grinberg, D., 72
Grissmer, D.W., 82

Groer, M., 54
Grolnick, W.S., 222
Gronlund, N.E., 260, 261, 331, 335, 337, 338, 343, 347, 348, 352
Gross, S., 344
Grosslight, L., 169, 177
Gruber, H., 179
Grusec, J.E., 61
Guacci-Franco, N., 56
Guay, F., 51, 56, 221
Guerra, N., 67
Guerra, N.G., 61
Guerrero, F., 270
Guiton, G., 249
Gunstone, R.F., 169, 172
Guppy, T.E., 116
Gurtner, J., 270
Guskey, T.R., 267, 329
Gustafson, M., 235
Gustafsson, J., 78, 285

H

Hackenberg, T.D., 113
Hacker, D.J., 30, 32, 172, 176
Hadaway, N.L., 306
Haden, C., 30
Hadwin, A.F., 210, 211, 212
Haenan, J., 26
Hagan, R., 95
Hagen, A.S., 251
Hagen, J.W., 29
Hagopian, L.P., 115
Hagtvet, K.A., 230, 331
Hakuta, K., 38, 39
Hale, N., 296
Hale-Benson, J.E., 49
Halford, G.S., 31
Hall, R.V., 284, 285
Hallahan, D.P., 101
Haller, E.P., 176
Hallinan, M.T., 57
Halpern, D.F., 76, 93, 94, 101, 181, 186, 187, 254
Halpin, G., 314
Halvorsen, A.T., 103
Hambleton, R.K., 347
Hamers, J.H.M., 344
Hamilton, V.L., 314
Hamilton, R., 84
Hamman, D., 147, 172
Hanesian, H., 36, 141, 142, 148, 174
Hannay, L., 273
Hannum, W.H., 263, 264
Hanson, A.R., 203, 204, 205, 206
Harackiewicz, J.M., 222, 236, 238, 240, 242
Hardre, P.L., 97, 221
Hardy, C., 58
Harlow, H.F., 112
Harnishfeger, K.K., 211
Harold-Goldsmith, R., 52, 96
Harp, S.F., 173
Harper, F., 331
Harpster, L., 211
Harris, A.H., 299
Harris, C.R., 87
Harris, J.R., 58, 73
Harris, K.R., 165, 210
Harris, M.B., 60
Harris, M.J., 52
Harris, K.R., 31
Hart, D., 50, 54
Harter, S., 50, 52, 54, 72, 222, 227, 230, 233
Hartup, W.W., 52, 57
Harvey, O.J., 58
Haseman, A.L., 276
Hasselbring, T.S., 272
Hatano, G., 161, 165, 166, 277, 282, 283
Hattie, J., 176, 189
Hauser, S.T., 55
Hawkings, F.P.L., 192
Hawkins, J.A., 57

Hawkins, R.D., 157
Hayduk, L., 48
Hayes, C.B., 296
Hayes, S.C., 210
Hayes-Roth, B., 144
Hazel, J.S., 72
Healy, A.F., 274
Hearold, S., 70
Hebb, D., 29
Hegland, S., 132
Heindel, P., 147
Heller, J.I., 182, 184
Heller, K.W., 272
Heller, L.R., 285
Helmke, A., 265, 268, 269, 300
Helton, G.B., 49
Hembree, R., 230
Hennessey, B.A., 86, 236
Hermann, D.J., 184
Herschkowitz, R., 136
Hersh, R.H., 65, 66
Hess, G.A., 97
Hess, R.D., 49, 84, 253
Hetherington, E.M., 16
Heuer, F., 228
Heward, W.L., 72, 156
Hewitt, J., 161, 168, 281
Hewson, P.W., 170
Hickey, D.T., 275
Hidalgo, N.M., 90, 306, 309
Hidi, S., 175, 222, 228, 236, 238, 239, 240, 242
Hieberg, E.H., 43, 161, 166, 167, 277, 343, 348
Hiebert, J., 166, 167, 277
Higgins, A., 69
Higgins, C., 124
Higgins, E.L., 272
Hildreth, B., 189
Hill, C., 332, 343, 353
Hill, K.T., 230, 231
Hilliard, A., 88
Hines, M., 93
Hinkel, E., 84
Hinkley, H.S., 308
Hinkley, J.W., 243
Hirsch, E.D., 165
Hitch, G.J., 29
Ho, D.Y.F., 49, 189
Ho, H.-Z., 308
Hocevar, D., 85
Hockensmith, M.L., 314
Hodell, M., 235, 236, 239
Hodges, E.V.E., 51, 56
Hofer, B.K., 176
Hoffman, L.W., 57
Hoffman, M.L., 68, 69, 228
Hogaboam-Gray, A., 273
Hogan, D.M., 282
Hogan, K., 161, 277
Holley, C.D., 174
Hollins, E.R., 91
Holloway, S.D., 49, 84
Holt, K., 235, 240
Holt-Reynolds, D., 5, 165
Holyoak, K.J., 180, 181
Hom, A., 297, 298
Hong, Y., 99, 160, 247
Honig, A.S., 61, 69
Hood, W.R., 58
Hook, C.L., 284, 286
Hoover-Dempsey, K.V., 308
Horgan, D.D., 32, 95, 246
Horner, R.H., 235
Hornyak, R.S., 209, 212
House, B.J., 72
Houtz, J.C., 86
Howe, M.L., 134
Hoy, W.K., 9, 207
Hoyt, J.D., 31
Hudley, C., 61
Hughes, G., 204

Hughes, J.N., 61, 72, 127
Humphreys, L.G., 99
Hungate, H.N., 182, 184
Hunt, C., 84
Hunt, P., 103
Hunter, M., 267
Husman, J., 244
Huston, A.C., 95
Hutt, C., 275
Hutt, S.J., 275
Hymel, S., 62, 69, 71, 97, 226
Hynd, C., 169, 170

I

Iacono, W.G., 81
Igoa, C., 286
Igoe, A.R., 227
Inagaki, K., 161, 165, 166, 277, 282, 283
Inglehart, M., 253
Inglis, A., 5, 214, 284
Irvine, K.L., 272
Isaacson, R., 227
Ittel, A., 69
Iwata, B.A., 122

J

Jackson, D., 257
Jackson, J.S., 251
Jacobs, J., 52, 96
Jacobs, M., 26
Jacobs, P.J., 95
Jacobs, W.J., 157
Jacobsen, B., 256
Janosz, M., 97, 98
Janzen, H., 81
Janzen, T., 81
Jarrett, O.S., 56
Jarvis, P.A., 60
Jarvis, S., 296
Jayaratne, T., 52, 96
Jencks, C., 324
Jenkins, L., 32
Jenkins, Z.N., 61, 72
Jetton, T.L., 173
Jiao, Z., 57
Jimerson, S., 82, 84
Joag-Dev, C., 163
Johanning, D.I., 186
Johnsen, E.P., 37
Johnsen, T.B., 230, 321
Johnson, D., 272
Johnson, D.M., 162
Johnson, D.W., 38, 61, 70, 170, 212, 277, 281, 282, 283, 284
Johnson, H., 82
Johnson, M.K., 142
Johnson, R.T., 61, 70, 212, 277, 281, 282, 283, 284
Johnson-Glenberg, M.C., 145
John-Steiner, V., 27
Johnstone, A.H., 183
Jonassen, D.H., 263, 264
Jones, D., 150
Jones, E.E., 225, 226
Jones, K.M., 126
Jones, L.L., 8
Jones, M.S., 149, 188
Jones, D.L., 353
Joshi, M.S., 49
Jovanovic, J., 96
Joy, R.M., 172
Jozefowicz, D.M., 97
Judd, C.H., 180
Judy, J.E., 180, 184
Juel, C., 39
Junkin, L.J., 50
Jussim, L., 250
Just, M.A., 148
Juvonen, J., 72, 226, 227, 248

K

Kaczala, C.M., 95, 206, 240, 248
Kagan, J., 16, 48
Kahl, B., 175
Kahle, J.B., 96, 254
Kail, R., 29, 31, 80
Kaplan, A., 242, 253, 282
Karau, S.J., 283
Kardash, C.A.M., 187, 238
Karlin, M.B., 142
Karmiloff-Smith, A., 33, 36
Karovitch, S.K., 40
Karweit, N.L., 98
Kass, R.E., 122
Katkovsky, W., 247
Katz, E.W., 35
Katz, L., 51, 53, 113
Kauffman, J.M., 101
Kaufman, K.F., 122
Kavussanu, M., 242
Keane, M.T., 139, 230
Kearins, J.M., 41
Keating, D.P., 96
Keefe, K., 57
Keil, F.C., 163, 164, 169
Kelemen, D., 164
Kelley, M.L., 115, 116
Kelly, G.J., 276
Kelly, W., 81
Kennedy, C.H., 285
Keogh, B.K., 72, 102, 103
Kermani, H., 284
Kerr, B., 335
Keys, C., 343
Khattri, N., 343
Kiewra, K.A., 136, 143, 173, 174, 314
Kilner, L.A., 55
Kim, D., 222, 296, 297
Kimberg, D.Y., 135, 157
Kimble, G.A., 108
Kindermann, T.A., 57, 58
King, A., 66, 161, 175, 186, 212, 282, 283, 285
King, F.J., 270
King, J., 285
King, N.J., 230
King, S.S., 96
Kingma, J., 134
Kintsch, W., 239
Kirby, J., 81
Kirby, S.N., 82
Kirigin, K.A., 62
Kirker, W.S., 143
Kirkland, M.C., 269, 331
Kirschenbaum, R.J., 85
Kishor, N., 51
Kitsantis, A., 203, 206
Klebanov, P.K., 85
Klein, J.D., 247
Klein, S., 347, 353
Klein, S.B., 50
Kletzien, S.B., 144
Klingler, C., 39
Kluger, A.N., 223, 245
Knapp, M.S., 57, 84, 98, 249, 254
Knauth, S., 233
Knighton, T., 197, 220
Koballa, T.R., 272
Koegel, L.K., 126
Koegel, R.L., 126
Koeppel, J., 93
Koestner, R., 230, 232, 233, 234, 235, 236, 237, 239
Kogan, J.S., 115
Kohlberg, L., 64–67, 70
Kohn, A., 235
Kolbe, L., 54
Kolodner, J., 152, 160
Konopak, B.C., 155
Koretz, D., 347, 353
Kose, G., 147
Kosslyn, S.M., 145

Kovacs, D.M., 57
Kowalski, P., 235
Krajcik, J., 283
Krampen, G., 315
Krapp, A., 221, 238
Krashen, S.D., 40
Krathwohl, D.R., 261
Krauss, R.M., 37
Kronsberg, S., 95
Kroth, R.L., 101
Kuczkowski, R., 54, 55
Kuhl, J., 34, 211
Kuhn, D., 22, 169, 176, 187, 277
Kuiper, N.A., 143
Kuklinski, M.R., 250
Kulhavy, R.W., 140, 170
Kulik, C.C., 267, 270
Kulik, J.A., 267, 270
Kulikowich, J.M., 137, 147
Kumar, V., 316
Kupersmidt, J.B., 226
Kurtines, W.M., 62, 69
Kurtz, B.E., 30

L

LaBar, K.S., 228
Ladd, G.W., 226
Ladson-Billings, G., 92, 98, 171, 304, 306
LaFramboise, T., 88
Lajoie, S.P., 27, 270
Lakes, M.K., 96, 254
LaMay, M.L., 76, 93
Lambdin, D.V., 313
Lamon, M., 281
Lampert, M., 167, 277, 281
Lan, W.Y., 233
Landauer, T.K., 137
Lane, D.M., 29
Langer, E.J., 184
Langer, J.A., 9, 306
Lanthier, R.P., 48
Laosa, L.M., 84
Lapsley, D.K., 54, 55
Larke, P.J., 306
Larsen, E., 332, 343, 353
Larson, R.W., 59, 221, 222, 235
Lasker, J., 57
Latham, G.P., 208, 240
Laupa, M., 66
Lawson, K.R., 29
Lawton, T.A., 314
Laychak, A.E., 57
Le Blanc, M., 97
Le Mare, L., 296
Leach, J., 169
Leary, M.R., 51
LeBlanc, J., 203
Leckerman, R., 112, 116
LeCount, J., 276
Lee, C.D., 87, 92
Lee, J.B., 140
Lee, J.F., 283
Lee, O., 160, 170, 171
Lee-Pearce, M.L., 98
Legault, L., 238
Leggett, E.L., 91
Leggett, E.S., 247
Leher, R., 43
Lehman, S., 238
Leichtman, M.D., 160
Leinbach, M.D., 95
Leinhardt, G., 277, 286
Lejuez, C.W., 113
Lennon, R., 21, 32, 68
Lentz, F.E., 116, 122
Lepper, M.R., 124, 235, 236, 239, 270, 285
Lerman, D., 246
Lesgold, A.M., 144, 149
Lester, F.K., 313, 344, 351
Levin, M.E., 149

Levin, J.R., 136, 149, 176, 188
Levine, D.U., 306, 308
Levitt, J.L., 56
Levitt, M.J., 56
Levy, I., 282
Lewis, C., 84, 309
Lezotte, L.W., 306, 308
Li, Q., 204, 273
Liberman, R.P., 116
Lickona, T., 60, 297, 298
Lieberman, L.M., 102
Lieberman, M., 64
Light, P., 23
Lillard, A.S., 253
Lin, Y., 227
Lind, G., 72
Lindberg, M., 148
Linderholm, T., 235
Linn, B., 187
Linn, M.C., 23, 169, 189
Linn, R.L., 331, 335, 338, 347, 348, 352
Lipson, M.Y., 163, 278
Liss, M.B., 95
Little, T.D., 223
Littlewood, W.T., 178
Lochhead, J., 184
Locke, E.A., 208, 240
Lockhart, R.S., 30
Lockheed, M.E., 260
Lodico, M.G., 176
Loftus, E.F., 160
Lohman, M.R., 285
Lomawaima, K.T., 90
Long, M., 38
Lonky, E., 238
Lopez, G.R., 309
Loranger, A.L., 172, 176
Lorch, E.P., 155
Lorch, R.F., 211
Losey, K.M., 90
Losoff, M., 58
Lou, Y., 282, 283
Lovell, K., 22
Lovett, S.B., 32
Lovitt, T.C., 116
Lowell, E.L., 223
Lowery, B., 256
Lowry, R., 54, 57, 200
Lubart, T.I., 86
Luchins, A.S., 157, 184
Luchins, E.H., 157
Luckasson, R., 101
Lundeberg, M.A., 334
Lupart, J., 204, 250
Lykken, D.T., 82
Lynch, J.H., 52, 56, 57
Lyon, M.A., 122
Lyons, A., 97
Lytle, S., 9
Lyyken, D.T., 48

M

Ma, X., 51
Macarthur, J., 40
Maccoby, E.E., 16, 48, 69
Mace, F.C., 202
Macgregor, S., 280
Machiels-Bongaerts, M., 143
MacIver, D., 226
Macken, E., 269
MacKenzie-Keating, S., 122
MacLean, M., 49
MacLean, D.J., 96, 286
Maclin, D., 169, 177
MacMillan, D.L., 72, 102, 103
Madden, N.A., 98, 103
Madison, S.M., 250
Madon, S., 250
Maehr, M.L., 57, 220, 221, 227, 240, 242
Magnuson, D., 212–213

Maier, S., 249
Maker, C.J., 72
Makris, E., 233
Mandl, H., 179
Mandler, G., 143
Manset, G., 102
Marachi, R., 250
Maratsos, M., 37
Marcia, J.E., 55
Marcoux, M., 54
Marcus, G.F., 36
Marfo, K., 278
Markman, E.M., 32, 176
Marks, M.B., 178
Markstrom-Adams, C., 55, 92
Marlowe, D., 227
Marrett, C.B., 96
Marsh, H.W., 50, 51, 53, 54, 59, 72, 243, 246, 282
Marshall, H.H., 132, 166, 276
Martin, C.L., 58, 95
Martin, J.A., 48, 69
Martinez-Pons, M., 204
Marx, R.W., 170, 224, 240, 247, 283
Mash, E.J., 198
Maslow, A., 225
Masson, M.E.J., 151
Masten, A.S., 99
Masters, J.C., 113
Mastin, M., 297
Mastropieri, M.A., 103, 149, 304, 356
Masuda, W.V., 344
Masur, E.F., 32
Mathes, P.G., 284
Matusov, E., 168
Maxmell, D., 56
Mayer, E.V., 114
Mayer, R.E., 137, 173, 179, 180, 182, 183, 184
Mayer-Smith, J., 5
Mayock, E., 62
Mazur, J.E., 115
McAdoo, H.P., 55
McAlpine, L., 90, 92, 286
McAshan, H.H., 260
McCaffrey, D., 347, 353
McCall, C., 209
McCall, R.B., 254
McCallum, R.S., 57, 80
McCarthy, A., 308
McCarty, T.L., 8, 308
McCaslin, M.M., 27, 243
McClelland, D.C., 223
McClelland, L., 223
McCloskey, L.A., 89
McCollam, T., 57
McCormick, C.B., 91, 92
McCown, R.R., 87, 88
McCoy, L.P., 231
McDaniel, M.A., 145, 151, 180, 274
McDermott, K.B., 152, 160
McDevitt, T.M., 32, 37, 253
McDougall, P., 97
McGee, L.M., 277
McGill, P., 115
McGlynn, S.M., 189
McGoey, K.E., 284, 286
McGregor, H.A., 242
McGue, M., 48, 81
McInerney, D.M., 56, 226, 242, 243
McIntyre, C.W., 32
McKeachie, W.J., 227
McKeown, M.G., 265
McLaren, J., 239
McLaughlin, B., 38
McLean, L., 353
McLean-Heywood, D., 72
McLeod, D.B., 229, 230
McLoyd, V.C., 82, 83, 84, 99, 249, 251
McMillan, J.H., 51, 99
McNalley, S., 68
McNamara, D.S., 274
McNeil, N.M., 242
McNeill, D., 151

Meadows, N., 61, 72
Meece, C., 314
Meece, J.L., 206, 230, 235, 240, 242, 248
Mehan, H., 276
Meichenbaum, D., 209, 212, 214
Meister, C., 27, 175
Melloy, K.J., 61, 72, 120, 122, 203
Meloth, M.S., 283
Menke, D.J., 173
Mercer, C.D., 72, 155, 255, 286
Mercer, L.K., 207
Merrill, P.F., 27, 275, 286
Mervis, C.B., 162
Messer, D.J., 170
Messick, S., 331, 337, 343, 347
Mettatel, G., 58, 59
Metz, K.E., 22
Meyer, B.J.F., 144
Meyer, C.A., 353
Meyer, D.K., 241, 251
Meyer, H.A., 220
Meyer, K.A., 126
Middleton, M., 242
Middleton, M.J., 241, 254
Midgley, C., 54, 211, 225, 226, 240, 241, 250, 254
Milburn, J.F., 72
Milch-Reich, S., 72
Milholland, J., 227
Miller, B.C., 59
Miller, C.L., 62, 72
Miller, D., 95
Miller, D.L., 116
Miller, F.K., 96
Miller, G.A., 137
Miller, L., 62
Miller, L.D., 69, 71
Miller, L.S., 82, 90, 97
Miller, P.A., 68
Miller, P.H., 29, 31, 54, 228
Miller, R.R., 109
Miller, S.A., 31, 54
Millham, J., 332, 349
Mills, G., 9
Miltenberger, R.G., 122, 199
Mims, V., 236
Minami, M., 40, 308
Minstrell, J., 275, 277
Mintzes, J.J., 164, 169, 174
Mitchell, M., 238
Mitrani, M., 270
Miyake, K., 49
Moallem, M., 284
Moffitt, T.E., 83, 203
Mohatt, G., 90, 155
Moje, E.B., 282
Moll, L.C., 40, 220
Moon, B., 5
Mooney, C.M., 133
Moore, D., 84
Moran, C.E., 39
Moran, T., 67
Morelli, G., 49
Morgan, C., 211
Morris, M.W., 88
Morrow, S.L., 59
Mortimer, E., 169
Mortiz, S.E., 113
Morton, J., 34
Moshman, D., 211
Motz, M., 172
Mueller, J.H., 230
Mueller, K.J., 222, 240
Muir-Broaddus, J.E., 148
Mulcahy, R.F., 278
Mulrooney, M., 93
Mumme, D.L., 285
Munn, P., 299
Murdock, T.B., 250, 296
Murphy, B., 68
Murphy, D.M., 103
Murphy, H.A., 122

Murray, C.B., 251
Musonda, D., 175
Myers, R.E., 86, 276
Myerson, J., 114

N

Nadel, L., 157
Nagin, D., 203
Nagle, R., 70
Naglieri, J., 81
Nakamura, J., 221, 230, 233
Narvaez, D., 66, 67, 69
Nastasi, B.K., 161, 277
Natriello, G., 314
Nau, P., 122
Navarro, R.A., 40
Neale, D.C., 8
Neel, R.S., 61, 72
Neisser, U., 78, 82, 85, 132
Nelson, B., 235
Nelson, C.A., 82
Nelson, T.O., 176
Nesbitt, J.C., 316
Neuman, Y., 161
Nevin, A.I., 103
Newcomb, A.F., 58
Newcombe, E., 99
Newman, S.E., 166
Newmann, F.M., 99, 187, 238, 324, 334
Newport, E.L., 34, 38
Nezavdal, R., 311
Nicholls, J.G., 51, 232, 242, 247
Nichols, J.D., 123, 282
Nichols, M.L., 101
Nichols, S.L., 249, 250
Nicholson, D., 203
Nieto, S., 97, 99
Nippold, M.A., 35, 36
Nix, R.L., 48
Noddings, N., 182
Noell, G.H., 125
Nolan, J., 239
Nolan, S.D., 144, 148
Nolen, S.B., 211, 240
Nordy, C.J., 207
Norman, D.A., 135
Northrup, J., 118, 120
Nottelmann, E.D., 55
Novak, J.D., 36, 141, 142, 148, 174
Nucci, L.P., 66, 67
Nucci, M.S., 66
Numeroff, L.J., 35
Nunes, T., 36
Nuthall, G., 165

O

Oakes, J., 249
Oakland, T.D., 49
Oberle, K., 212
Obgu, J.U., 253
O'Boyle, M.W., 93
O'Connor, J.B., 301
O'Donnell, A.M., 282, 283
O'Donnell, J., 112
Oettingen, G., 223
Ogbu, J.U., 78, 88, 89
O'Grady, W., 36
Oka, E.R., 278
Okamoto, Y., 23, 29, 83
O'Keefe, B.A., 296
O'Kelly, J., 282, 283
Oldfather, P., 351
O'Leary, K.D., 116, 122
O'Leary, S.G., 115, 116, 122
Oliverez, A., 189
Ollendick, T.H., 230
Olneck, M.R., 308
O'Loughlin, M., 169
Olsen, R.K., 270
Olson, D.R., 22

Onosko, J.J., 187, 277
Onyskiw, J., 48
Ormord, J.E., 5, 32
Ortony, A., 148, 160, 162
Osana, H.P., 188
Oskamp, S., 92
Osterman, K.F., 297
O'Sullivan, J.T., 172
Ovando, C.J., 40, 308
Owens, R.E., 21, 35, 36, 37, 57

P

Packard, V., 54
Page-Voth, V., 245
Paikoff, R.L., 59
Paivio, A., 139, 140, 145
Pajares, F., 206, 254
Palincsar, A.S., 161, 278, 282, 283, 285, 286
Pallay, A., 286
Palmer, E.L., 275
Pang, V.O., 91, 92, 201, 253
Paolitto, D.P., 65, 66
Paris, A.H., 210, 220, 251, 313, 343
Paris, S.G., 54, 99, 166, 178, 208, 212, 220, 226, 249, 251, 278, 282, 313, 316, 341, 343, 348
Park, K., 57
Parke, R.D., 124
Parker, J.G., 56, 57, 58
Parks, C.P., 59
Parnes, S.J., 86
Parsons, J.E., 95, 206, 240, 248
Pascual-Leone, J., 23
Pasternack, J.F., 68
Patnode, M., 124
Patrick, H., 226, 282, 296, 297
Patterson, C.J., 59
Patterson, G.R., 57
Patterson, M.L., 249
Paulson, F.L., 353, 354
Paulson, P.R., 353
Pearlstone, Z., 143
Pearson, D.A., 29
Pearson, P.D., 175
Peat, D., 278
Pellegrini, A.D., 56, 136
Pelletier, L., 238
Pelletier, S., 144, 189
Pellicer, L.O., 98
Penner, B.D., 184
Pennock, D., 197
Penrose, A.M., 174
Pepler, D.J., 204
Pereira, L., 297
Perera, K., 37
Perez, B., 40, 308
Perkins, D.N., 78, 85, 172, 179, 180, 183
Perner, J., 22
Perry, B.D., 83
Perry, D.G., 124
Perry, N.E., 207, 331
Perry, R.P., 239
Perry, M., 96
Person, N.K., 284
Petersen, G.A., 332
Peterson, A.C., 58
Peterson, C., 249
Peterson, L.R., 137
Peterson, M.J., 137
Peterson, P.L., 172
Peterson, R.F., 60
Petrie, S., 226
Petrill, S.A., 82
Petrosky, A.R., 352
Pfiffner, L.J., 115, 122, 123, 124, 136, 304
Phelan, P., 87, 88, 227, 230, 243
Phelps, E.A., 228
Philips, D., 115
Phillip, R.A., 8
Phillips, D., 205, 226

Phinney, J., 55
Phye, G.D., 140
Piaget, J., 7, 16–24, 28, 29, 40, 66, 133, 160, 163
Piazza, C.C., 70, 115
Pierce, W.D., 236
Piersel, W.C., 113
Piirto, J., 72
Pine, J., 347
Pine, K.J., 170
Pinker, S., 35
Pintrich, P.R., 51, 54, 55, 159, 170, 205, 206, 220, 221, 223, 226, 233, 238, 242, 244, 251
Piontkowski, D., 136
Pipher, M., 58
Pittman, T.S., 232, 234
Plomin, R., 48, 81, 83
Plowman, T.S., 98
Plumert, J.M., 30
Poche, C., 199
Pollard, S.R., 62
Poole, D., 334
Poole, S., 207
Popham, W.J., 307, 337, 347, 353, 354
Porath, M., 189
Porter, A.C., 184
Portes, P.R., 82, 84, 97
Posner, G.J., 170, 177
Post, T.A., 192
Postman, L., 153
Pott, M., 49
Potters, E.F., 170
Powell, K., 54
Powell, S., 235
Power, F.C., 70, 299
Power, M.R., 299
Powers, L.E., 201, 215
Powers, S.I., 55
Prawat, R.S., 166, 167, 170, 184
Presseisen, B.Z., 167
Pressley, M., 30, 145, 149, 161, 172, 173, 176, 178, 179, 251, 265, 277, 278
Preston, R.V., 313
Price-Williams, D.R., 41
Printrich, P.R., 176
Prochnow, J.E., 54
Proctor, R.W., 146, 147, 150
Pruitt, R.P., 86
Pruitt, W.K., 267
Pulos, S., 22, 23, 189
Purdie, N., 176, 177, 189
Putnam, R.T., 8, 298

Q

Qin, Z., 282
Quilitch, H.R., 60

R

Raber, S.M., 97
Rabinowitz, M., 31, 183
Rachlin, H., 109, 114, 223
Radke-Yarrow, M., 200
Radziszewska, B., 26
Rakow, E.A., 32
Ramey, C.T., 85, 98
Ramey, S.L., 98
Ramirez, M., 41
Ramsey, P.G., 87, 91, 92
Randall, T., 280
Raphael, T.E., 161, 277
Rapport, M.D., 122
Raskin, M.H., 272
Rasp, L.M., 202
Raudenbush, S.W., 250
Rawsthorne, L.J., 242
Real, D., 61
Reder, L.M., 147, 178
Redler, E., 61
Reed, D.F., 99
Reeve, J., 97, 221
Reich, P.A., 35, 36, 38

Reid, S., 272
Reilley, S., 142
Reimann, P., 180, 182
Reimer, J., 65, 66, 71
Reiner, M., 164
Resnick, L.B., 164
Reisberg, D., 136, 138, 153, 228
Reiter, S.N., 187
Renkl, A., 179, 182
Renninger, K.A., 238
Repman, J., 233
Resnick, D.P., 343
Resnick, L.B., 143, 150, 182, 183, 343
Resnick, M.D., 298
Rest, J., 67, 69
Rest, J.R., 70
Reuman, D., 226
Reusser, K., 183
Reyna, C., 250, 251
Reyna, V.F., 134
Reynolds, C.R., 86
Reynolds, M.C., 304
Reynolds, R.E., 137, 155, 163, 173
Reys, B.J., 27
Ricciutti, H.N., 82
Richards, D.D., 22
Richards, A.C., 230
Richards, D.D., 22
Richards, F., 230
Riggs, J.M., 225
Rimm, D.C., 113
Rincon, C., 59
Ripple, R.E., 86
Risemberg, R., 211
Rittenhouse, P., 167, 277
Ritts, V., 249
Rittschof, K.A.K., 170
Roberts, G.C., 242
Roberts, W., 296
Robinson, T.R., 210
Roblyer, M.D., 270
Roche, L., 59
Rock, D.A., 249
Roderick, M., 97
Roediger, H.L., 152, 160
Roehler, L.R., 175
Rogers, T.B., 143, 332
Rogoff, B., 26, 27, 41, 168
Rogozinski, J.T., 173
Rohrkemper, M.M., 232
Romanczyk, R.G., 107
Ronning, R.R., 86, 277
Roopnarine, J.L., 57
Rortvedt, A.K., 122
Rosch, E.H., 162
Rose, A.J., 60
Rose, S.C., 227
Rosen, L.A., 115
Rosenberg, M., 54
Rosenshine, B., 27, 175, 268, 285, 286
Rosenstein-Manner, M., 60
Rosenthal, R., 52
Rosenthal, T.L., 197, 200, 202
Ross, D., 200
Ross, G., 27
Ross, J.A., 180, 235, 239, 273
Ross, N., 322
Ross, S.A., 200
Ross, S., 239
Rosser, R., 22, 23
Rotenberg, K.J., 114
Roth, J.L., 314
Roth, K.J., 170
Roth, W., 27
Rothbart, M.K., 16
Rothbaum, F., 49
Rowe, M.B., 90, 154, 155
Ruben, R.J., 34
Rubin, K.H., 49, 58, 60
Ruble, D.N., 95
Ruble, T.L., 95
Rueda, R., 220

Ruef, M.B., 124, 126
Rueger, D.B., 116
Ruff, H.A., 29
Ruffman, T., 22
Ruhland, D., 223, 232
Ruijssenaars, A.J.J.M., 344
Rumberger, R.W., 97
Rumelhart, D.E., 148, 160, 162
Rumsey, S., 166
Runco, M.A., 85, 86
Rushton, J.P., 62, 69, 70, 200
Russ, S.W., 86
Russell, D., 246
Ruthren, A.J., 116
Ryan, A.M., 57, 211, 224, 226, 296, 297
Ryan, A.W., 296
Ryan, R.M., 52, 54, 55, 56, 57, 222, 230, 232, 233, 234, 235, 236, 237, 239, 342
Ryba, K., 269, 271, 273

S

Sabers, D.S., 295
Sacks, M., 57
Sadker, D., 54, 95, 96, 335
Sadker, M.P., 54, 95, 96, 335
Sadoski, M., 139, 140, 145
Saia, J., 172
Sailor, W., 103
Saklofske, D., 78, 81
Saklofske, D.H., 84, 115
Salamon, G., 180
Salend, S.J., 84, 272, 308, 309
Salk, S., 229, 230
Salomon, G., 161
Saltz, E., 35
Sameoto, D., 122
Samuel, D., 88
Sanchez, F., 61
Sanders, M.G., 99, 113, 309
Sanders, S., 91, 173
Sandler, H.M., 308
Sands, D.J., 215, 256
Sansone, C., 211
Sapon-Shevin, M., 297
Sarason, I.G., 230, 231
Sarason, S.B., 230
Sasse, D.K., 96
Sattler, J., 78, 80
Sax, G., 331, 349, 351
Scardamalia, M., 161, 168, 274, 281
Scarr, S., 82
Schaal, D.W., 113
Schacter, D.L., 138, 152, 153
Schank, R.C., 238
Schappelle, B.P., 8
Schaps, E., 222, 306
Schatschneider, C.W., 32
Schauble, L., 22, 23, 221, 222
Scheier, M.F., 211, 229, 240
Schell, T.L., 50
Schenk, S.M., 142
Schermerhorn, S.M., 136
Scheuermann, B., 209
Schiefele, U., 221, 222, 238
Schiever, S.W., 72
Schilling, H.E.H., 314
Schimmoeller, M.A., 25
Schlaefli, A., 70
Schlager, M.S., 274
Schliemann, A.D., 23
Schloss, P.J., 122, 203
Schmidt, H.G., 143
Schmidt, R.A., 180
Schneider, W., 30, 147, 148, 150, 183, 251
Schoener, J., 270
Schoenfeld, A.H., 184
Schofield, J.W., 62, 283, 286
Scholes, R.J., 187, 238
Schommer, M., 172, 176, 177, 331
Schonert-Reichl, K., 62, 69, 71, 72, 97
Schrauben, B., 238

Schraw, G., 173, 211, 238
Schraw, G.J., 277
Schubert, J.G., 96
Schult, T.J., 180, 182
Schultz, K., 92, 184
Schulze, S.K., 147
Schumaker, J.B., 72, 149, 256, 278
Schunk, D.H., 54, 147, 203, 204, 205, 206, 209, 214, 221, 223, 226, 233, 240, 245, 246, 247, 251
Schutz, P.A., 211, 240
Schwartz, B., 136
Schwarz, B.B., 161
Schwean, V.L., 115
Schwebel, A.I., 136, 295
Scott, P., 169
Scruggs, T.E., 103, 149, 304, 356
Seaton, E., 83
Sedikides, C., 226
Segal, N.L., 48
Seidenberg, M.S., 33
Seifert, T.L., 296
Seitz, V., 82
Selby, L., 269, 271
Seligman, M.E.P., 249, 256
Semb, G.B., 151, 284
Semmel, M.I., 102
Serbin, L.A., 94
Shachar, H., 282
Shaffer, D.R., 69
Shany, M., 214
Shapiro, A.M., 168
Sharran, S., 282
Shatz, M., 37
Shaughnessy, M.F., 80
Shavelson, R.J., 347
Shaw, V., 277
Shea, C., 68
Shea, M.C., 202
Sheehan, E.P., 32
Sheffield, F.D., 223
Sheldon, A., 36
Shell, R., 68
Shepard, L.A, 314, 344, 348
Shepardson, D.P., 282
Sherif, C., 58
Sherif, M., 58
Shernoff, D.J., 233
Sherwood, R.D., 185
Shields, P.M., 98, 254
Shiffrin, R.M., 135, 141, 150, 183
Shih, S.S., 234
Shin, D., 94
Shirey, L.L., 137, 163, 173
Shirley, L.L., 155
Shore, B.M., 24, 40, 136, 139, 144, 161, 187, 189
Short, E.J., 32
Shuell, T.J., 169, 267
Shulman, L.S., 8
Shumow, L., 186
Siegler, R.S., 18, 22, 23, 31, 80, 183
Sigman, M., 82
Silberstein, C.S., 169
Simmons, D.C., 284
Simmons, R., 180
Simner, M., 322
Simon, H.A., 137, 147, 178
Simon, V.A., 59
Simonetta, L.G., 51
Simons, R.J., 281
Simons, R.L., 58
Simonton, D.K., 82, 86
Singer, D.G., 70
Singer, J.L., 70
Singh, J., 51
Sippola, L., 58
Siu, S., 90
Skaalvik, E., 241
Skinner, B.F., 33, 111, 269
Slaby, R.G., 61
Slaughter-Defoe, D.T., 85, 87, 92
Slavin, R.E., 98, 99, 103, 282, 283

Sleet, D., 54
Sleeter, C.E., 93
Slotta, J.D., 164
Slusher, M.P., 170
Smetana, J.G., 62, 66
Smith, C.L., 169, 177
Smith, D.A., 151
Smith, D.C., 8
Smith, E.E., 136, 157
Smith, E.L., 169
Smith, H.L., 8, 308
Smith, K., 277
Smith, M.U., 229
Smith, R.E., 124
Smith, M.A., 122, 203
Smitherman, G., 89
Smolkin, L.B., 91
Smoll, F.L., 124
Snarey, J., 65, 66
Snidman, N., 48
Snow, C.E., 40, 257
Snow, R.E., 251, 260
Snyder, B.L., 179
Sodian, B., 22
Sohbat, E., 296
Solomon, D., 222, 296, 306
Soloway, E., 283
Songer, N.B., 169
Sosniak, L.A., 133, 166, 167
Sowder, J.T., 8
Spandel, V., 353, 354
Spaulding, C.L., 208, 222, 232, 233, 296
Spearman, C., 79
Spencer, M.B., 55, 92
Sperling, G., 137
Spiel, C., 84
Spires, H.A., 174, 176
Spivey, N., 32
Spracklen, K.M., 57
Sprafkin, C., 95
Sroufe, L.A., 59
Stabb, S.D., 62, 72
Stack, C.B., 306
Stainback, S., 101
Stainback, W., 101
Stanley, J.C., 189
Stanovich, K., 150, 187
Stanovich, K.E., 31, 35, 36, 38, 187
Stanovich, K.G., 29
Stecher, B., 347, 353
Steele, D.F., 186
Steffensen, M.S., 155
Steinberg, L., 16, 97, 220, 227, 253
Stennett, B., 142
Sternberg, R., 78, 189
Sternberg, R.J., 8, 78, 80, 85, 181, 185
Stetsenko, A., 223
Stevahn, L., 61, 212
Stevens, J.A., 201
Stevens, J.J., 324
Stevens, R., 268, 285, 286
Stevens, R.J., 282
Stevenson, H.C., 210
Stevenson, H.W., 82, 84, 226
Stewart, B.E., 96
Stiggins, R.J., 307, 330, 335, 337, 352
Stiller, J.D., 56
Stimpson, V., 275, 277
Stimson, M., 142
Stipek, D.J., 54, 208, 223, 227, 230, 231, 233, 234, 235, 236, 246, 351
Stock, W.A., 170
Stodolsky, S.S., 133, 166, 167, 229, 230
Stone, N.J., 176
Stores, M., 57
Story, R., 32
Stough, L.M., 301
Strike, K.A., 170, 177
Strohmeier, D., 84
Sudweeks, R.R., 332
Sue, S., 253

Sugawara, A.I., 69
Suina, J.H., 91
Sullivan, H., 227
Sullivan, P.J., 113
Sullivan, P., 23
Sun, Y., 49
Suppes, P., 269
Suttles, G.D., 58
Sutton-Smith, B., 56
Swan, K., 270
Swanborn, M.S.L., 36
Swanson, D.B., 337, 343, 347
Swanson, H.L., 189, 301
Swap, S.M., 90
Sweet, D., 343

T
Tabach, M., 136
Tallent-Runnels, M.K., 189
Tamburrini, J., 22
Tappan, M.B., 68
Tarver, S.G., 268, 269
Taylor, A., 82
Taylor, D.M., 40, 90, 92, 286
Taylor, I.A., 85
Taylor, J.C., 107
Taylor, J.H., 264
Taylor, L., 84, 272, 308, 309
Taylor, M.A., 155
Teixeria, R.A., 57
Tellegen, A., 48
Teo, A., 82, 84
Terr, L., 83
Tessmer, M., 263, 264
Tharp, R., 27
Tharp, R.G., 90, 155
Theberge, C.L., 277, 286
Thoermer, C., 22
Thoma, S.J., 67, 70
Thomas, J.R., 93, 95
Thomas, J.W., 32, 176, 212
Thomas, M.A., 298, 299, 308
Thomas, S.P., 54
Thomas, W.P., 40
Thompson, A.G., 233
Thompson, E.R., 69
Thompson, P.W., 233
Thompson, R.A., 48, 82
Thomson, D.M., 151
Thornburg, K.R., 227
Thorndyke, P.W., 144
Thorpe, P.K., 241
Thousand, J.S., 103
Thrash, T.M., 240
Tisak, M., 66
Tobias, S., 222, 228, 230, 238, 239, 254
Tobin, K., 155
Todd, C.M., 30
Tomasello, M., 160
Tomlinson, C.A., 72
Torrance, E.P., 85, 86, 100, 276
Touchstone, D., 98
Tourniaire, F., 22
Townsend, M., 69
Trawick-Smith, J., 37, 41, 49, 55
Treasure, D.C., 242
Treffinger, D.J., 86
Tremblay, R., 203
Tremblay, R.E., 97
Tremblay, S., 322
Trowbridge, J.E., 164, 169
Tryon, G.S., 231
Tschannen-Moran, M., 9, 206, 207
Tubbs, M.E., 249
Tucker, V., 296
Tudge, T.R.H., 282
Tudor, R.M., 270
Tulving, E., 140, 143, 151
Tunmer, W.E., 54
Turiel, E., 66, 68

Turkheimer, E., 16
Turnbull, A., 72, 155, 297
Turnbull, B.J., 98, 254
Turner, A.M., 157
Turner, J.C., 184, 220, 233, 235, 241, 314
Turner, L.A., 30
Turner, T.J., 163
Tutty, L., 61, 204
Tyler, S., 275
Tzuriel, D., 344

U
Ugoroglu, M., 221
Underwood, B.J., 153
Undheim, J.O., 78, 285
Urdan, T.C., 51, 57, 225, 227, 254
Uttal, D.H., 82

V
Vaillancourt, T., 203
Valencia, S.W., 343, 348
Valente, N., 237
Valiante, G., 254
Vallerand, R.J., 221
Van Camp, C.M., 126
Van court, N., 68
Vandekamp, K.O., 207
van den Broek, 211
van de Vijver, F.J.R., 84
Van Etten, S., 173
Van Houten, R., 122
van Joolingen, W.R., 274
van Kraayenoord, C.E., 208
van Laar, C., 253
Van Meter, P., 146, 173
Van Rossum, E.J., 142
VanSledright, B., 68, 166
Vasquez, J.A., 91
Vasta, R., 200
Vaughn, B.J., 235
Vaughn, S., 61
Vaughn-Scott, M., 88
Venn, J.J., 356
Verdi, M.P., 170
Vermeer, H.J., 254
Veroff, J., 223
Verschaffel, L., 166
Vezeau, C., 54
Villa, R.A., 103
Villegas, A., 335
Voegler, M.E., 226
Vollmer, T.R., 113
Volpe, J., 56
Vorrath, H., 61
Vosniadou, S., 233
Voss, J.F., 180, 184, 221, 222, 314
Vye, N.J., 185, 186, 210, 316
Vygotsky, L., 40–41, 160, 165, 166, 213, 274, 284

W
Waddell, C., 230
Waddell, K.J., 41
Waddill, P.J., 274
Wade, S., 173
Wade-Wooley, L.C.W., 38, 174, 238
Wagner, E.D., 32
Wahlsten, D., 82
Walberg, H.J., 176, 221
Walker, J.E., 122
Walker, J.M.T., 222
Walker, K.C., 331
Walker, L.J., 68
Wallace, C.S., 16, 282
Walters, R.H., 124
Wandersee, J.H., 164, 169
Ward, M., 212
Warner, M.M., 278
Warren, A.R., 89
Warren, E., 5

Wat, A., 277
Watahomigie, L.J., 8, 308
Waters, H.S., 32, 145
Watkins, M.J., 141
Watson, J., 22, 32
Watson, M., 222, 306
Wearne, D., 277
Webb, J., 281
Webb, N.M., 60, 161, 282, 283, 285, 286, 300, 314
Webber, J., 233
Weber, M.J., 296
Weber, N.L., 126
Wehlage, G.G., 238
Wehmeyer, M.L., 215, 256
Weikum, W.M., 39
Weinberg, R.A., 82
Weiner, B., 335
Weiner, B., 72, 223, 227, 236, 242, 245, 246, 249, 250, 251
Weinert, F.E., 265, 268, 300
Weinstein, C.E., 251
Weinstein, C.S., 295
Weinstein, R.S., 250, 251
Weir, C., 211
Weisberg, R.W., 86, 212
Weiss, J., 239
Weiss, L.G., 84
Weisz, J., 49
Welch, G.J., 116
Wellborn, J.G., 226
Weller, H., 233
Wellman, H.M., 22, 32, 163
Wells, D., 277
Wentzel, K.R., 56, 62, 227, 240, 243, 244, 296
Werner, E.E., 99
Wertsch, J.V., 26
Wessels, K., 314
West, C.K., 148
Whaley, S.E., 82
Wheatley, G., 242
Whitbeck, L.B., 58
White, B.J., 58
White, B.Y., 274, 275, 277
White, C., 168
White, J., 166
White, R.T., 169, 172, 225
Whitesell, N.R., 50, 235

Whitley, B.E., 246
Wideen, M., 5
Wigfield, A., 54, 55, 58, 205, 221, 223, 226, 227, 230, 236, 237, 238, 240, 296
Wilkerson, B., 82
Wilkinson, L.C., 96
Wilkinson, L.D., 97
Williams, B., 99
Williams, K.D., 283
Williams, W.M., 82
Williamson, S., 69, 82
Willig, A.C., 40
Willis, E.L., 155
Willms, J.D., 203
Willoughby, T., 142, 172
Wilson, C.C., 70
Wilson, M., 306
Wilson, P.S., 161
Wilson, P.T., 148, 152
Wilson, B., 314
Winer, G.A., 169
Wingfield, A., 135
Winn, W., 140
Winne, P.H., 113, 176, 207, 210, 211, 212, 221, 224, 240, 247, 250, 316, 331
Winner, E., 72, 85, 255
Winograd, P., 282, 353
Winteler, A., 221
Winzenz, D., 144, 149
Winzer, M., 101
Wise, B.W., 270
Wiseman, D., 306
Wittmer, D.S., 61, 69
Wittrock, M.C., 172, 179, 180, 183
Wixson, K.K., 276
Wlodkowski, R.J., 87, 242, 254
Wodtke, K.H., 331
Wolf, M.M., 62
Wolfe, D.A., 203
Wolff, P.M., 148
Woloshyn, V.E., 175
Wolters, C.A., 210
Wong, B., 189
Wood, C., 38, 174, 238
Wood, D., 27
Wood, E., 142, 172, 175, 176
Wood, G.A., 59

Wood, T., 242
Woolfolk Hoy, A., 9, 207
Woolfolk, A.E., 120, 295, 331
Woolverton, S., 57, 84, 249
Worham, D., 182
Worsham, M.E., 295
Worswick, C., 253
Wright, L.S., 122
Wright, R., 226
Wright, S.C., 40
Wulff, J.J., 223
Wyatt, J.M., 48

Y

Yackel, E., 242
Yang, P., 332
Yarmey, A.D., 151
Yates, M., 69, 71
Yeany, R.H., 164
Yee, D., 52, 96
Yell, M.L, 210, 212, 215
Yerkes, R.M., 229
Yoder, P., 199
Yokoi, L., 173
Youniss, J., 56, 69, 71
Yu, H.C., 87, 230, 243
Yu, S.L., 51

Z

Zahn-Waxler, C., 200
Zahorik, J.A., 239
Zajac, R., 215
Zan, B., 70
Zeaman, D., 72
Zeidner, M., 230, 231
Zeldin, A.L., 206
Ziegler, S., 60, 202
Zigler, E.F., 82
Zigmond, N., 102
Zimmerman, B.J., 197, 200, 203, 204, 205, 206, 207, 209, 210, 211, 226, 236, 240
Zimmerman, R.R., 112
Zirpoli, T.J., 61, 72, 120, 122, 203
Zohar, A., 176
Zseller, E.B., 296
Zuckerman, G.A., 216

Subject Index

Note: Entries for figures, footnotes and tables are followed by "*f*," "*n*," and "*t*" respectively.

A

ability tests, 324
abstract reasoning, 21
    morality and, 65
accommodation
    see also special needs
    assessment and, 332–334, 333*t*
    learning by, 16–17
accountability, 329
achievement, 78, 82–84, 85
achievement motivation, 223
achievement tests, 323–324, 323*t*
action research, 8
activation, 139
ActivBoard, 272
activity reinforcers, 113
actual developmental level, 25
adolescent egocentrism, 55
adolescents
    see also cognitive development; moral and prosocial development
    capabilities of, 22, 30
    egocentrism and, 22
    growth and, 93
    identity and, 55
    peers and, 55
    romantic relationships and, 59–60
    self-concept and, 54–55
advance organizers, 144
affect, 228–231, 246
affective domain, 261
affiliation, 226–227
age
    see also cognitive development; moral and prosocial development
    attributions and, 247–248
    self-regulation and, 208
age-equivalent scores, 326
aggression
    bullying, 47, 56, 60–84, 204
    modelling and, 203–204
aggressive behaviour, 62
algorithms, 181–183
allophones, 34
alphabetic principle, 38
alternative-response items, 338
analogies, 182
analytic scoring, 346
antecedent responses, 118
antecedents, 126
antecedent stimuli, 118
anxiety, 83, 229–231
    classroom strategies for, 230–231
    facilitating and debilitating, 229
    learning and, 5
    state *vs.* trait, 229
    test, 331
anxiety disorders, 255*t*
appearance, 54, 230
applied behaviour analysis (ABA), 125–126
apprenticeships, 26, 27
approval, 227
argument analysis, 186
articulation, 27
assessments, 311–312
    classroom strategies for, 353
    cognition, metacognition and, 334
    communicating results of, 330
    decision making and, 12
    diagnostic, 315
    diversity and, 330–334, 333*t*, 354–355, 355*t*
    dynamic, 344
    errors in, 318
    formal *vs.* informal, 312–313
    guidelines for, 312, 324
    importance of, 8
    including students in, 347–348
    informal, 334–336
    item analysis and, 349–350
    learning and, 5
    paper-pencil, 312, 313, 337–343
    performance, 313, 343–347
    planning, 336–337
    portfolio, 353–354
    purposes of, 314–316
    qualities of, 316–321, 317*t*
    risk-taking in, 349
    RSVP characteristics of, 316–321, 317*t*
    self-, 348
    standardized (*see* standardized tests)
    summarizing achievement using, 350–352
    traditional *vs.* authentic, 313
    types of, 312–314, 313*t*
assimilation, 17
attachment, 48
attention, 211
    information processing theory and, 29
    lack of, 156*t*
    memory and, 139–140, 147
    modelling and, 202
    working memory and, 135–136
attention-deficit hyperactivity disorder (ADHD), 41, 102*t*, 333
attributions, 99, 245–246
    age and, 247
    effects of, 246, 250
    factors influencing, 247–248
    internal, 270
    internal *vs.* external, 245–246
    mastery orientation *vs.* learned helplessness, 248–249
    productive, 250–252
    teacher, 249–250
attribution theory, 245
authentic activities, 166, 180, 186, 187, 191
authentic assessments, 313
authoritative parenting, 48
autism, 102*t*, 126, 128*t*
automaticity, 139–140, 183, 267
autonomy, 237

B

backup reinforcers, 115
base groups, 284, 301
baselines, 117
behaviour
    see also misbehaviour.
    aggressive, 47, 56, 60–62, 84, 203–204
    assessment and, 312
    attributions and, 246
    in behaviouristic programming, 108
    beliefs and, 51
    choices about, 199
    immoral, 62
    incompatible, 120
    learning and, 196
    maintaining, 124–125
    modelling and, 200, 201–202
    moral reasoning and, 67
    motivation and, 221*f*
    prosocial, 60
    self-concept and, 51
    self-efficacy and, 204–205
    self-regulated, 208–210, 208*f*
    sex and, 201
    shaping, 117
    terminal, 115
    undesirable, 119–124, 125–126
    verbal *vs.* nonverbal, 335
behavioural problems, 102*t*
behaviour analysis, 263
behaviourism, 107–109, 108*t*
    punishment and, 121
    strengths and limitations of, 127–129
behaviourist theory of motivation, 223
behaviour modification, 125
behaviour therapy, 125
beliefs
    culture and, 25
    epistemological, 176, 187, 334
    erroneous (*see* misconceptions)
    memory and, 132*t*
    prior, 169–170
    teachers and, 9
    trumping evidence, 80
belonging, 225
benchmarks, 260
best work portfolios, 354
bias, 335
bilingual education, 40
bilingualism, 39–40
Bloom's taxonomy, 261
body image, 54, 230
body language, 83, 88
boys, 49, 54, 58, 61
    see also sex
brain, 135*f*, 139*f*, 157
bullying, 47, 56, 60–61, 84, 203–204

C

Canada
    achievement statistics in, 219–220
    aggressive behaviour in, 203, 204
    educational mission and vision statement, 63*f*
    immigrants in, 252–253
    language and culture in, 39, 89
    parents in, 308
    schools in, 84
    special needs in, 101
    standardized testing in, 322–323, 324, 331–332
Canadian Achievement Tests (CAT-III), 324
Canadian Cognitive Abilities Test (CCAT), 324
Canadian Test of Basic Skills (CTBS), 324
candle problems, 183
Case's theory of cognitive development, 81
causation, 6
cause–effect relationships, 6–7, 18
central executive, 135
challenges, 230
cheating, 341
checklists, 345, 345*f*
children
    see also cognitive development; linguistic development; moral and prosocial development
    attributions of, 247
    capabilities of, 22
    image management of, 248
    knowledge and, 31
    learning and, 16–18
    natural learning and, 4
    Piaget's theories on, 16–24
    self-concept in, 54
China, 49
choices, 235, 246

citizenship skills, 62, 63f
classical conditioning, 109–110
    classroom strategies for, 111, 119
    operant conditioning vs., 112
classification, 19
    multiple, 20
classroom climate, 295–298
classroom management, 293–302, 305
classrooms
    arranging, 295
    inclusive, 304–305, 305t, see also inclusive classrooms
    learning-conducive, 293–302
    respectful and caring, 295–298
    rules for, 298–299
classwork, extra, 123
cliques, 55, 58
coaching, 27, 202
cocktail party phenomenon, 135
cognition, 29
    assessment and, 334
    attributions and, 246
    hot, 228–229
    motivation and, 232
cognitive ability tests, 324
cognitive apprenticeship, 27
cognitive delays, 102t, 155, 156t, 189
cognitive development
    diversity and, 40–42
    general themes of, 43t
    information processing view of, 29–33
    physical/social environment and, 17
    Piaget's stages of, 18–22, 18f
cognitive domain, 261
cognitive engagement, 220
cognitive processing, 29, 199, 221, 314
cognitive psychology, 131–134
cognitive revolution, 209
cognitive strategy instruction, 277–280
cognitive theory of motivation, 223–224
collaboration, 304–309
collaborative instruction, 276–285
collective self-efficacy, 206, 306
community
    of learners, 167–169, 281, 297–298
    school, 306
    working with, 306
community service, 71
comparison, 233–234
competence, 50
    modelling and, 201
    sense of, 232
    social, 52
competition, 90
completion items, 339
complexity, 27
comprehension monitoring, 176, 178
computer-assisted instruction (CAI), 269–270
computer-based instruction (CBI), 270
computers
    collaborative learning and, 280–281
    e-learning and research on, 273–274
    instruction using, 269–273
    problem solving on, 186
computer-supported collaborative learning (CSCL), 280–281
concept mapping, 144, 174, 174f
concepts, 161, 162
    changing, 169–171, 170t
    contrary-to-fact, 21, 22, see also misconceptions
    organization of, 174
    trivial vs. important, 173
conceptual change, 169–171, 170t
conceptual understanding, 165–166, 192, 274
concrete operations stage, 18, 20–21
    formal operational stage vs., 21t
    preoperational stage vs., 20t
concrete reinforcers, 113
conditioned response (CR), 110
conditioned stimulus (CS), 109–110

conditioning, 107
    classical, 109–111, 112
    operant, 111–117
conferences, 307–308, 307f, 353
confidence interval, 318
connectionist theorists, 33
consequences, 118
    in functional analysis, 126
    logical, 122
    nonoccurrence of, 198, 199
    social cognitive theory and, 197–199
conservation, 19, 20, 20f
conservation of liquid, 20, 20f
construction of reality, 29
constructions, 132, 133f
    conceptual (see concepts)
    knowledge (see knowledge construction)
    multiple, 171
constructivism, 17, 133
    individual, 160
    moral reasoning and, 67
    social, 160–161
construct validity, 321
content validity, 319–320, 337
context, 180
context-free information, 179t, 180
contingency, 112
    group, 115–116
contingency contracts, 116
contingency management, 125
continuous reinforcement, 117, 125
contrary-to-fact concepts, 21, 22
controllability, 245, 251
conventional morality, 64, 65, 65t, 66
convergent evidence, 187
convergent thinking, 85
co-operation, 60, 85, 90
co-operative learning, 116, 281–284
co-operative teaching, 102
core goals, 240
correlational research, 6, 12, 48
correlation coefficient, 318
cortex, 157
creative variability, 150
creativity, 85–86
criterion-references grades, 352
criterion-references scores, 321–322, 325–326, 326f, 328
critical thinking, 186–188
    classroom strategies for, 188, 189–191
    cultural diversity and, 189
    inclusive classrooms and, 189–190, 190t
    types of, 186–188
cueing, 118, 119, 120
    retrieval, 151–152, 153
    verbal, 120
cultural bias, 331
cultural differences, 8, 25, 87
    assessment and, 331–332
    cognitive development and, 41
    co-operation vs. competition, 90
    groupwork and, 161
    higher-level thinking and, 189
    instructional strategies and, 286
    language and, 88–90
    memory and, 155
    motivation and, 252–253
    oral communication and, 37
    personal development and, 49
    private vs. public performance, 90
    sociolinguistic conventions and, 89–90
    strategies for, 87–88, 91–93
    stress and, 83
cultural identity, 87
cultural mismatch, 87
culture shock, 49
cyber-bullying, 204

D

decay, 153
decision making, 187–188

declarative knowledge, 140, 141–143, 141t
deductive reasoning, 20
delay of gratification, 114
democratic ideals, 93
dependent variables, 6
depression, 54
descriptive studies, 6, 12
developmental differences, 330
developmental milestones, 4
developmental portfolios, 354
deviant behaviour, 57, 58–59
diagnostic assessment, 315, 323
dialects, 41, 88–89
dialogue, 166–167
direct instruction, 268–269
disabilities, 101, 102t, 156t
discovery learning, 274–275
discrimination, 118
discussion, 191, 276–277
disequilibrium, 18, 66
distractibility, 29
distributed cognition, 161
distributed intelligence, 80, 161
Distributed Learning Strategy, 273
divergent thinking, 85
diversity
    see also group differences
    assessment and, 354–355, 355t
    behaviours and, 127, 128t
    classroom management and, 303–305, 305t
    cognitive development and, 40–42, 155–156
    critical thinking and, 188–189
    cultural, 87
    examples of, 85–88
    instructional strategies and, 285–287, 287t, 289–290, 289t
    knowledge construction and, 168, 171
    linguistic development and, 40–42
    need for relatedness and, 226–227
    principles/assumptions regarding, 76t
drive, 223
dropping out, 97
dynamic assessment, 344

E

educational psychology, 3
effort, 205, 221, 245, 246, 247, 351–352
egocentric speech, 37
egocentrism, 19, 22, 55
elaboration, 4, 30, 144–145, 148, 175
elaborative interrogation, 175
elaborative rehearsal, 29
e-learning, 273–274
elementary-level students
    see also children; cognitive development; moral and prosocial development
    attributions in, 247
    image management in, 248
Elluminate Live!, 273, 281
Emotions
    see also affect
    classical conditioning of, 110
    moral development and, 68
empathy, 68
encoding, 134, 173, 183–184
English as a Second Language (ELS), 84
entity view, 247, 249
environment, 81, 214
epistemological beliefs, 176, 187, 334
equilibration, 18
equilibrium, 18
equity, 93, 95
Erikson's theories, 53f
erroneous beliefs, 4
essay tasks, 340
esteem, 225
ethnic diversity, 85–88, 252–253
ethnic groups, 87
evaluation
    formative vs. summative, 314
    of paper-pencil tests, 342, 342f

S-2   Subject Index

exceptionalities, 41–42, 102t
exceptional students, 100–104
existential intelligence, 79
expectancy, 236
expectations, 49, 197–198
    classroom strategies for, 238
    motivation and, 223–224, 236–237
    productive, 250–252
    wait time and, 155
experimental studies, 6, 12
experimentation, 165, 186
exploration, 27
expository instruction, 265–274, 266t
expressive language, 34
extended performance, 344
extinction, 110, 119–120, 125
extra credit, 351–352
extrinsic motivation, 221–222
extrinsic reinforcers, 113, 211, 235–236

F

face-saving, 248
failure, 205–206, 246
    attributions and, 241–247
    self-handicapping and, 225–226
failure to store, 153
families
    peer pressure vs., 57
    as socializing agents, 49
feedback, 223, 231, 233, 315, 342
feed forward, 271
figurative language, 36
First Nations, 82, 85
    behaviour diversity and, 127
    cultural differences and, 87
    sociolinguistic conventions and, 89
foreclosure, 55
forgetting, 152–153
formal assessment, 312–337
formal operational egocentrism, 22
formal operations stage, 18, 21–22, 62–66
    concrete operational stage vs., 21t
formative evaluation, 314
friendships, 57–58
functional analysis, 126
functions, 126

G

g (general factor in intelligence), 79, 81
gambler's fallacy, 186
gangs, 58
Gardner's theory of multiple intelligences, 79–80, 79t
gay, lesbian, and bisexual students, 59
gender. See sex
general aptitude tests, 324
generalization, 110, 118
general transfer, 178–179
generativity, 180
genetics, 16, 18, 81
giftedness, 102t, 156, 189
girls
    see also sex
    peer interaction and, 58
    school success and, 84
    self-concept and, 54
    social development and, 56–57
goals
    adolescents and, 55
    behaviour and, 196
    classroom strategies for, 243–244
    core, 240
    in lesson planning, 260–264
    mastery vs. performance, 240–242, 241t
    motivation and, 220–221, 240–244, 241t
    problem-solving, 182
    self-determined, 208–209
    self-handicapping and, 225–226
    self-regulated learning and, 211, 212
    short-term vs. long-term, 261–263
    social, 243
    work-avoidance, 242–243

grade-equivalent scores, 326
grades, 350–353
graphemes, 38
graphemic correspondences (PGCs), 38
group contingency, 115–116
group differences, 75, 76, 81–82
group performance, 344
groups
    base, 284, 301
    parent discussion, 308
groupwork
    co-operative learning and, 281–284
    critical thinking and, 191
    knowledge construction and, 160–161, 167–168, 175
    problem solving and, 184
growth spurts, 4
guided participation, 26
guided peer questioning, 175
guilt, 68, 83

H

halo effect, 335
handicap, 101
hands-on instruction, 274–276
harassment, 60–61
hearing impairments, 102t
help-seeking behaviour, 246
heredity, 16, 18, 81
heuristics, 177–182
hierarchy of needs, 225
higher-level questions, 86, 276
higher-level thinking, 171–172
    classroom strategies for, 189–191
    cultural diversity and, 189
    in inclusive classrooms, 189–190, 190t
high-stakes assessments, 316, 329–330
holistic scoring, 346
homosexuality, 59–60
horizontal décalage, 23
hormones, 93
hot cognition, 228–229
human development, 15–16
hypotheses, 186, 187

I

identity, 55
identity achievement, 55
identity diffusion, 55
ill-defined problems, 181
illusion of knowing, 5, 12, 176
image management, 248
imaginary audience, 54, 57
imitation. See modelling
immersion, 40
immigrants, 252–253
    cultural differences and, 87–88
    school success and, 83
immoral behaviour, 62
improvement, 351
impulsivity, 156t
inability to retrieve, 154
incentives, 199
in-class activities, 275–276
inclusion, 101, 103–104
inclusive classrooms
    assessment in, 355, 355t
    behaviour in, 128t
    cognitive processing and, 156t
    critical thinking in, 189–190, 190t
    instructional strategies in, 286–290, 305t
    knowledge construction in, 171–172, 172t
    motivation in, 255–256, 255t, 256t
    personal, social, and moral development in, 71–73
incompatible behaviours, 120
incremental view, 247
independent variables, 6
individual constructivism, 160
individual differences, 75, 76
induction, 69

inferences, 312
informal assessment, 312–313, 334–336
information. See concepts; knowledge
information and communication technology (ICT), 269–273
information processing analysis, 264
information processing theory, 29–33, 131
inner speech, 25, 209
inquiry-based instruction, 160–161
instruction, 260, 289t
    cognitive strategy, 277–280
    computer-based, 269–273, 280–281
    direct, 268–269
    diversity and, 285–290, 287t
    expository approaches to, 265–274, 266t
    hands-on approaches to, 274–276
    interactive and collaborative, 276–285
    modifying, 301–302
    for on-task learning, 299–301
    planning for, 260–265, 260f
instructional objectives, 260–262, 262t
intelligence, 75, 77
    expectations of, 249
    factors influencing, 82–84
    heredity, environment, and group differences in, 81–82
    measurement of, 77–78
    socioeconomic difference, ability, achievement and, 82
    theories of, 78–81
intelligence tests, 77–78
interactive instruction, 276–285
interests, 238, 239, 271
    classroom strategies for, 239–240
    importance vs., 173
interference, 153
intermittent reinforcement, 125
internal consistency reliability, 318
internalization, 24
interpretive exercises, 340
intrinsic motivation, 211–212, 221–222, 244
intrinsic reinforcers, 113, 235–236
IQ scores, 77–78, 77f, 328
irreversibility, 19
item analysis (p), 349–350
item discrimination (D), 350

J

jigsaw technique, 283
jokes, 37
journals, 8
junior high school students, 54, 59

K

keyword method of mnemonics, 148
knowledge
    see also concepts; memory
    classroom strategies for, 162
    construction of, 160–161, 163–165, see also knowledge construction
    declarative, 140, 141t
    frequently used, 151
    illusion of knowing and, 5
    information processing theory and, 31
    learning strategies and, 176–177
    organization of, 161–163
    prior (see prior knowledge)
    problem solving and, 184–185
    procedural, 140, 146–147
    social groups and, 160–161
    transfer of, 178–181
knowledge base, 143
knowledge construction
    see also learning
    classroom strategies for, 168–169
    concepts, schemas, and personal theories and, 161–163
    effective, 165–168
    groupwork and, 160–161
    misconceptions and, 163–165, 164f, 169–171
Kohlberg's theory of moral reasoning, 64–67, 65t

L

language
    cultural differences and, 88–89
    figurative, 36
    receptive vs. expressive, 34
    second, 38–40
language development. *See* linguistic development
learned helplessness, 248–249
learned industriousness, 247
learning, 152t, 173–177, 174f, 175f
    anxiety and, 5
    assessment and, 5
    assimilation and accommodation in, 17
    behaviourism and, 108–109
    constructive processes in, 160
    constructivist, 17
    co-operative, 281–284
    discovery, 274–275
    effective, 10–12
    erroneous beliefs and, 4
    meaningful, 142–145
    from modelling, 202–203
    motivation and, 220–221, 221f
    natural, 4
    Piaget's theory of, 7, 16–24
    prior knowledge and, 7
    reinforcers in, 113
    repetition and, 4
    rote, 141, 142
    selective, 132
    self-efficacy and, 205
    self-regulated, 211–212
    Vygotsky's theory of, 24–25
learning disabilities, 41
    motivation and, 256
    self-regulation and, 215–216
    sex and, 101
learning strategies, 32, 152t, 173–177, 174f, 175f
    factors affecting, 176–177
    in information processing theory, 29–31
    learning, 177, 177t
lectures, 265–266
lesson planning, 260–265, 260f
    task analysis for, 263–264, 263f
level of potential development, 25
Limited English Proficiency (LEP), 41, 78
linguistic development, 33–40
    diversity and, 40–42
    facilitating, 39–40
    general themes, 43t
    metalinguistic awareness in, 37–38
    oral communication in, 37, 38
    phonological awareness in, 34–35
    second languages and, 38–40
    syntax in, 36–37
    theories of, 33
    vocabulary in, 35–36
    written language in, 38
live models, 200
locus of control, 245, 270
logic, 20, 21
logical consequences, 122
long-term memory, 138–139
    forgetting and, 152–153
    note taking and, 173
    organization of, 162
    prior knowledge and, 137–138, 148
    problem solving and, 185
    retrieval from, 149–152
    types of knowledge and, 140
long-term objectives, 261–263
love, 225
lower-level questions, 276
lying, 67

M

maintenance rehearsal, 137
mass media, 95
mastery, 233
mastery goals, 240–242, 241t
mastery learning, 266–267
mastery orientation, 248–249
matching items, 338
mathematics, 21
maturation, 16
meaningful learning, 142–146, 147, 179t, 180, 189
meaningful learning sets, 142
mean (M), 327, 327f
mediated learning experience, 26
mediation training, 61, 212
memes, 188
memorization, 189
memory, 134–136, 135f
    classroom strategies for, 146–147, 153–155
    constructive processes in, 160
    defined, 134
    diversity and, 155
    forgetting and, 152–153
    long-term, 137–139, 139f, 140–145, 147–149, 153
    metacognition and, 31
    mnemonics and, 148–149
    models of, 134–135, 135f, 139–140
    organization of, 162
    prior knowledge and, 147–149
    processing time for, 154–155
    retrieval and, 149–153
    working (short-term), 136–137, 147–148
mental imagery training, 271
mental retardation, 102t, 155, 156t, 189
mental sets, 184
metacognition, 31–32, 171–172, 185, 189, 211, 271, 334
metacognitive scaffolding, 189, 191f
metalinguistic awareness, 37–38
methylphenidate, 81
minority groups
    see also cultural differences
    expectations and, 249
    identity and, 55
    wait time and, 154
misbehaviour, 303t
    diversity and, 303–305, 305t
    strategies for, 302–305, 303t, 305t
misconceptions, 4, 163–168, 164f, 188
    about important information, 173
    changing, 169–171
mission and vision statements, 63f
mnemonics, 147, 148–149, 151, 156t, 178
modelling, 27, 215
    aggression and, 203–204
    behaviour and, 200
    critical thinking, 187
    effective, 200–202
    learning from, 202–203
    live vs. symbolic, 200
    in social cognitive theory, 199–204
    of success and failure, 206
monitoring, 301
moral and prosocial development, 62–71, 73t
    behaviour and, 69
    classroom strategies for, 69–71
    emotional components of, 68
    factors influencing, 47–50
    Gilligan's theory of, 67–68
    Kohlberg's theory of, 64–67, 65t
moral dilemmas, 64
moral reasoning
    classroom strategies for, 66
    Kohlberg's theory of, 64–67, 65t
    preoperational, 19
moratorium, 55
motivation, 7, 220
    achievement, 223
    affect and, 228–231
    assessment and, 314, 347
    behaviour and, 196
    in behaviourism, 115
    classroom strategies for, 244
    cognition and, 231–232
    computers and, 270
    creativity and, 86
    diversity and, 252–256
    expectancies and values and, 236–238
    extrinsic, 221–222
    goals and, 240–244
    inclusive education and, 255t, 256t
    interests and, 238–240
    intrinsic, 211–212, 221–222
    learning, behaviour and, 220–221, 221f
    modelling and, 203
    needs and, 225–227
    self-perceptions and, 232–236
    self-regulation and, 211
    situated, 220
    theories of, 222–224, 224t
Motivation and Academic Achievement (MAACH) Research Group, 222
motor reproduction, 202–203
multicultural education, 91
multiculturalism. *See* cultural differences
multimedia programs, 272
multiple-choice items, 338–339
multiple classification, 20
multiple constructions, 171
multiple intelligences, 79–80, 79t

N

National Longitudinal Survey of Children and Youth (NLSCY), 48
nature vs. nurture, 16, 18, 81
needs, 225–227
    for affiliation, 226–227
    for approval, 227
    classroom strategies for, 227–228
    for relatedness, 226–227, 296
negative instances, 162
negative reinforcers, 113–114, 121t
negative transfer, 178
negative wait time, 90
neo-Kohlbergian theory, 67
Neo-Piagetian theory of cognitive development, 81
neurons, 157
neutral stimulus, 109, 110
normal curve, 327
normal distribution, 327
norm-referenced grades, 352
norm-referenced scores, 326–328, 327f, 328f
norms, 49, 322
note taking, 5, 136, 173, 178
nutrition, 82

O

objectives, 260–262, 262t
    short-term vs. long-term, 261–263
object permanence, 18, 22
observation, 196
    self-, 209
observational learning effect, 200
on-task learning, 299–301
operant conditioning
    classical conditioning vs., 112
    classroom strategies for, 119
    punishment and, 121
operations, 20
oral communication, 37, 38
organization, 30
    of knowledge, 174
    memory and, 143–144, 144f, 148
outcomes, 260, 261
outlining, 174
overgeneralization, 35, 162
overregularization, 36

P

paper-pencil tests, 312, 313, 337–343
    administering, 341–342
    constructing, 341
    RSVP characteristics of, 342–343
    scoring, 342, 342f
parenting styles, 48, 84

parents, 307–309, 307f
PASS model of intelligence, 81
peer interaction, 26, 28
    adolescents and, 55
    mediation and, 212
    motivation and, 226–227, 243
    personal and moral development and, 50
    school success and, 84
    self-concept and, 51–52, 55
    sex stereotypes and, 95
    social development and, 56–60
peer pressure, 57
peer tutoring, 5, 284–285
percentile ranks, 327
perception, 156t
perception of phonemes, 34, 132
performance
    anxiety and, 229, 230
    attributions and, 246
    individual vs. group, 344
    motivation and, 221
    restricted vs. extended, 344
performance-approach goals, 240, 241–242
performance assessments, 313, 343–348
    choosing, planning, and administering, 343–345
    RSVP characteristics of, 347–348, 348f
    scoring, 345, 345f
performance-avoidance goals, 240, 241–242
performance goals, 240–242, 241t
persistence, 205, 221
personal development, 47, 73t
    factors influencing, 47–50
    inclusive strategies for, 71, 72t, 73t
    sense of self and, 50–56
personal fables, 54
personal interests, 238–239, 271
personal theories, 161, 163, 169
perspective taking, 60
phoneme-explicit teaching and learning, 38
phonemes, 34
phonemic awareness, 38
phonological awareness, 34–35, 38
physical environment, 17
physical proximity, 120
physiological needs, 225
Piagetian theory, 7, 16–24, 81
    applying, 23–24
    current perspectives on, 22–23
    stages of cognitive development in, 18–22
planning, 211
    instructional, 260–265, 260f
    for on-task learning, 299–301
porcupine dilemma, 67–68
portfolios, 210, 325, 353–354, 354f
positive behavioural support, 126
positive feedback, 56, 113
positive instances, 162
positive reinforcers, 113–114, 121t
positive transfer, 178, 180
postconventional morality, 64–66, 65t
power, 201
practicality, 321, 337
    of informal assessment, 336
    of paper-pencil tests, 343
    of performance assessments, 347
practice, 179, 179t, 180, 187, 268
practising for variability, 30
pragmatics, 34, 37, 41, 105
praise, 52, 228
preconventional morality, 64–65, 65t, 67
predictive validity, 320
Premack principle, 113
preoperational egocentrism, 19
preoperational stage, 18, 19–20
    concrete operational stage vs., 20t
PREP program, 81
Preschoolers
    see also children; cognitive development; moral and prosocial development
    attributions of, 247
    moral reasoning of, 65t, 66

    self-concept and, 54
    reinforcement and, 114
presentation punishment, 121
prestige, 201
primary reinforcers, 112–114
principles, 7, 12, 179t, 180
prior knowledge, 7, 23
    learning strategies and, 176
    memory and, 132t, 133, 138, 143, 147–148
    mnemonics and, 148–149
    oral communication and, 37
    retrieval and, 149–150, 174
private speech, 25
private vs. public performance, 90
probabilistic reasoning, 186
problem solving, 61, 181–186
    affect and, 229
    algorithms and heuristics and, 177–182
    as assessment, 340
    classroom strategies for, 185–186
    computers and, 186
    definition of problems and, 181
    factors affecting, 183–185
    self-regulated, 212–213
procedural knowledge, 140, 146–147
proficiencies, 260
programmed instruction, 269
Programme for International Student Achievement (PISA), 219–220
prompts, 118, 173
prosocial behaviours, 60, 200
prosody, 34
psychological punishment, 122–123
psychomotor domain, 261
puberty, 54, 55
public vs. private performance, 90
punishment, 121t
    effective, 121–122
    humane, 123–124
    ineffective, 122–123
    physical and psychological, 122–123
    presentation and removal, 121
    in social cognitive theory, 197, 199
    undesirable behaviour and, 120–124
    vicarious, 198

Q

quality of concept links, 139
questions, 276
    lower-level vs. higher-level, 276

R

race, 55
rating scales, 345, 345f
raw scores, 325
reading, 38
reasoning
    abstract, 21, see also cognitive development
    children and, 22–23
    deductive, 20
    moral, 19, see also moral and prosocial development
    proportional, 21
    scientific, 22
    transductive, 19, 20
recall tasks, 151, 337, 339
receptive language, 34
recess, 123
reciprocal causation, 214–215, 214t
recognition tasks, 151, 337, 338–339
reconstruction, 136
reconstruction error, 152
reconstruction errors, 160
reflection, 27
rehearsal, 29
    declarative knowledge and, 141
    maintenance, 137
reinforcement, 112–114, 269
    attributions and, 247–248
    continuous, 117

    effective, 115–117
    intermittent, 125
    intrinsic, 125
    motivation and, 221
    shaping and, 117
    in social cognitive theory, 197, 199
    timing of, 114
    vicarious, 198
reinforcers, 112
    backup, 115
    concrete, social, and activity, 113–114
    extrinsic vs. intrinsic, 113–114, 125, 236
    motivation and, 211–212
    positive vs. negative, 113–114
    primary vs. secondary, 112–113
relatedness, 226, 296
reliability, 78, 316–319, 317t, 318f, 337
    of informal assessment, 335
    internal consistency, 318
    of paper-pencil tests, 342
    of performance assessment, 347
    test-retest, 317
reliability coefficient, 318
remediation, 267
removal punishment, 121
repetition, 4
reprimands, 122
research, 6–8
    action, 8
    correlational, 6, 12
    descriptive, 6, 12
    experimental, 6, 12
    online, 273–274
    teaching and, 12
resilience, 99
resilient self-efficacy, 206
resilient students, 99
response cost, 122
response disinhibition effect, 200
response facilitation effect, 200
response inhibition effect, 200
responses (Rs), 108, 112
    antecedent, 118
    conditioned vs. unconditioned, 109–110
restricted performance, 344
retention, 202
retrieval, 134
    factors affecting, 149
    forgetting and, 152–153
    from long-term memory, 149–152
    of prior knowledge, 149–150, 174
    problem solving and, 185
    transfer and, 181
retrieval cues, 151–152, 153, 181
review, 268, 314
rewards
    see also reinforcers
    behaviour and, 5
    creativity and, 86
risk-taking, 54, 349
Ritalin, 81
roles, 49
romantic relationships, 59–60
rote learning, 141, 142, 189
routines, 298–299
RSVP characteristics, 316–321, 317t
    of informal assessments, 335
    of paper-pencil tests, 342–343
    of performance assessment, 347–348, 348t
    of portfolio assessments, 353
rubrics, 342, 342f, 345, 346f
rules, 65, 66, 234, 298–299

S

safety, 225
scaffolding, 26, 27, 173, 306
    metacognitive, 189, 191f
    problem solving and, 182
    self-regulation and, 212
schemas, 67, 161, 162–163
schemes, 17, 18

scholastic ability tests, 324
school councils, 308
School Indicators Achievement Program (SAIP), 323
schools, 84
school success, 205–206
    attributions and, 245, 246, 247
    factors influencing, 82–84
    IQ scores and, 78
    student potential and, 84–85
scientific method, 22
scolding, 122
scorer reliability, 318
scoring
    analytic vs. holistic, 346
    of paper-pencil tests, 342, 342f
    of performance assessments, 345, 345f
    of standardized tests, 325–329, 326t, 327f, 328f
scripted co-operation, 283
scripts, 162–163
secondary reinforcers, 112–114
second language, 38–40
selective learning, 132
self-actualization, 225
self-assessments, 212, 348
self-concept, 50f
    in adolescents, 54–55
    behaviour and, 51
    in children, 53–54
    classroom strategies for, 56
    development of, 50–56
    factors influencing, 51–52
    self-efficacy and, 204
self-contained classes, 103
self-determination, 234–236, 254
    in lesson planning, 263
    motivation and, 232
self-efficacy, 7, 9, 51, 99, 204–207, 215
    classroom strategies for, 207
    collective, 206, 306
    development of, 205–206
    motivation and, 223–224, 226, 232, 234, 254
    resilient, 206
self-esteem, 48
    anxiety and, 9, 222
    in children, 54
    motivation and, 226
    peer interaction and, 52, 56, 58
self-evaluation, 210, 211, 316
self-fulfilling prophecies, 250
self-handicapping, 225–226
self-imposed contingencies, 210
self-instructions, 209
self-monitoring, 209, 211, 316
self-motivation, 211
self-observation, 209
self-perceptions, 232–236
self-questioning, 176
self-regulated learning, 211–212, 240
self-regulated problem-solving strategies, 212–213
self-regulation, 196–197, 207–214
    assessments and, 316
    behaviour and, 208–210, 208f
    classroom strategies for, 213–214
    learning and, 211–212
    in lesson planning, 263
    motivation and, 241t
    problem solving and, 212–213
    reciprocal causation and, 214–215, 214t
    special needs students and, 215–216, 215t
self-talk, 25, 209
self-worth, 225–226, 242
semantics, 34, 35
sensation, 132
sense of community, 169, 297–298
sense of competence, 7
sense of school community, 306
sensitive periods, 16, 34
sensorimotor stage, 18
sensory register, 135
sex, 93, 94t
    bullying and, 204
    classroom strategies for, 95–96

differences, 4, 76f, 93, 94t
    mathematics and, 219–220
    moral reasoning and, 67–68
    motivation, goals, and, 253–254
    origins of, 93–96
    socialization and, 68
    special needs and, 100–101
    teacher behaviour and, 96
    values and interests and, 250
sexuality, 60
shame, 68
shaping, 108t, 117, 267, 269
sharing, 60
    ideas, 165
    knowledge construction and, 161
short-answer items, 339
short-term memory. See working memory
short-term objectives, 261–263
situated motivation, 220
situational interests, 238–239
skepticism, 187
SMART Board, 272
social cognitive theory, 195–196, 196t
    classroom strategies for, 198
    modelling in, 199–204
    motivation in, 223–224
    reciprocal causation and, 214–215, 214t
    reinforcement and punishment in, 197–199
    self-regulation in, 207–214
social competence, 52
social constructivism, 24, 160
social conventions, 66
social development, 56, 60, 73t
    classroom strategies for, 60–62
    factors influencing, 47–50
    social skills and, 60–62
social environment, 17
social goals, 243
social groups, 58, 160–161
socialization, 49
social learning theory, 195
socially constructed meaning, 26
social needs, 226–227
social reinforcers, 113
Social Sciences and humanities Research Council of Canada (SSHRC), 232
social skills, 60–62
    peer interaction and, 56
    self-concept, adolescents, and, 54
sociocultural perspective, 23
socioeconomic status (SES)
    expectations and, 249
    group differences and, 82
    motivation, goals, and, 216–255
    school readiness and, 83–84
    school success and, 84
    strategies for, 97–100
sociolinguistic conventions, 89–90
Spearman's theory of intelligence, 79
special needs, 100–104, 102f
    accommodating, 41–42t
    assessments and, 332–334, 333t
    classrooms for, 305t
    cognitive processing and, 155t–156t
    critical thinking and, 189–190
    inclusive classrooms and, 101–104
    motivation and, 255–256
    peer tutoring and, 285
    self-regulation and, 215–216, 215t
specific aptitude tests, 324
specific transfer, 178–179
speech and communication disorders, 102t
speech, 37
stability, attribution and, 245, 249
standard deviation (SD), 327, 327f
standard error of measurement (SEM), 318
standardization, 319
    of information assessment, 335
    of paper-pencil tests, 343
    of performance assessments, 347
standardized tests, 314–323
    accountability and, 329–330

    choosing and using, 324
    test scores in, 325–329, 326t, 327f, 328f
    types of, 323–324, 323t
standard nines, 328
standards, 208–210
standard scores, 78, 327
stanines, 328
state anxiety, 229
stereotypes
    ethnic, 91–92
    sex, 95
Sternberg's triarchic theory, 80, 80f
stimuli (Ss), 108, 109, 112
    antecedent, 118
    neutral, conditioned, and unconditioned, 109
    in positive and negative reinforcement, 113
storage, 134
Strategies Program for Effective Learning and Thinking (SPELT), 278
stress, 82
students at risk, 96
    characteristics of, 96–97
    dropping out and, 97
    resilience and, 99
    strategies for, 97–100
students with special needs, 100–104, 102t
studies. See research
study tips, 10–12
subcultures, 58
subject matter analysis, 263
substance abuse, 57, 98
success. See school success
summarizing, 12, 175, 175f
summative evaluation, 314
superimposed meaningful structure, 149
suspensions, 123–128
symbolic models, 200
symbolic thinking, 19
sympathy, 68
synapses, 157
syntax, 34, 36–37, 38

T

table of specifications, 320, 320f, 337
tabula rasa, 107
targets, 260
task analysis, 263–264, 263f
taxonomies, 260, 261
teacher-developed assessments, 313–314
teacher expectations, 249–252
teachers
    collaborating with, 304–306
    development of, 8–9, 12
teaching. See instruction
Teaching Resources and Continuing Education (TRACE), 226
temperaments, 16, 48
terminal behaviour, 115
test anxiety, 331
test-retest reliability, 317
tests. See assessment; standardized tests
test scores, 325–329, 326t
test-taking strategies, 178
testwiseness, 332
textbooks, 265–266
    electronic, 272
theories, 7, 12
thinking aloud, 212
threats, 230
time
    assessments and, 341
    memory and, 154–155
    reinforcement and, 114
    transfer and, 179t, 180
    use of, 178
time on task, 209
time-outs, 122
token economy, 115
traditional assessment, 313
trait anxiety, 229

trait theorists, 222
trait theory of motivation, 222–223
transductive reasoning, 19, 20
transfer, 178–181
    classroom strategies for, 185–186
    factors affecting, 179–180
    positive *vs.* negative, 178, 180
    principles of, 179*t*
    retrieval and, 181
    specific *vs.* general, 178–179
transferral, 110
transitions, 300–301
traumatic brain injury, 128*t*
traumatic experiences, 83
triarchic theory of intelligence, 80, 80*f*
true/false tests, 338
T-scores, 328
tutoring, 284–285
    peer, 5

U

unconditioned response (UCR), 109
unconditioned stimulus (UCS), 109
undergeneralization, 35, 162
undesirable behaviours, 119–124

United States, 84
universals, 15

V

validity, 319–321, 320*f*
    construct, 321
    content, 319
    of informal assessment, 335
    of paper-pencil tests, 343
    of performance assessments, 347
    predictive, 320
validity coefficient, 320
values
    classroom strategies for, 238
    internalizing, 237
    motivation and, 236–237
verbal cue, 120
verbal mediation, 148
verbal mediator, 148
verbal reasoning, 186
verbal reprimands, 122
vertical décalage, 23
vicarious experiences, 197, 198
vicarious punishment, 198
vicarous reinforcement, 198

visible minorities, 85
visual imagery, 145
visual impairments, 102*t*
vocabulary, 34, 35–36
Vygotsky's theory, 23, 25, 160
    applying, 28
    current perspectives on, 26–28

W

wait time, 90, 154–155
well-defined problems, 181
Western and Northern Canadian Protocol in Education, 312
withitness, 301
work-avoidance goals, 242–243
working memory, 135–137
    limited capacity of, 137
    prior knowledge and, 147–148
    problem solving and, 183
writing, 38

Z

zone of proximal development (ZPD), 25, 270, 344
z-scores, 328

Photo Credits

Page 2: Ken Hammond/USDA/NRCS/Natural Resources Conservation Service; page 5: Mug Shot/Corbis; page 10: Peter Cade/Stone/Getty Images; page 14: Ellen B. Senisi; page 16: Jeff Greenberg/PhotoEdit; page 17 left: Anthony Magnacca/Merrill, right: A.G.E. FotoStock/First Light; page 32: © 2008 Jupiterimages Corporation; page 46: Scott Cunningham/Merrill; page 49: Scott Cunningham/Merrill; page 61: Susan Burger/www.naturalphotohawaii.com; page 74: Tony Freeman/PhotoEdit Inc.; page 77: David Young-Wolff/PhotoEdit; page 81: Mary Kate Denny/Getty Images; page 86: © Charles Gupton; page 90: © 2008 Chris Arend/AlaskaStock.com; page 95: Laurence Gough/Shutterstock; page 106: Michelle D. Bridwell/PhotoEdit Inc.; page 110: Michael Provest/Silver Birdett Ginn; page 115: Susan Burger/www.naturalphotohawaii.com; page 116: Susan Burger Stock; page 120: Tom Watson/Merrill; page 123: Susan Burger Stock; page 130: Scott Cunningham/Merrill; page 133: © 2008 Jupiterimages Corporation; page 152: Susan Burger Stock; page 155: Jeff Greenberg/PhotoEdit Inc.; page 158: Bill Aron/PhotoEdit Inc.; page 161: Bob Daemmrich/The Image Words; page 165: Scott Cunningham/Merrill; page 170: Michael Newman/PhotoEdit; page 173: David Buffington/Getty Images; page 176: © 2008 Jupiterimages Corporation; page 181: Susan Burger Stock; page 183: © 2008 Jupiterimages Corporation; page 194: Ellen B. Senisi; page 205: Jeff Greenberg/PhotoEdit; page 211: Anthony Magnacca/Merrill; page 214: Mary Kate Denny/PhotoEdit; page 218: Ellen B. Senisi; page 222: © 2008 Jupiterimages Corporation; page 224: © 2008 Jupiterimages Corporation; page 229: Creatas/Dynamic Graphics; page 237: Bonnie Kamin/PhotoEdit; page 242: Scott Cunningham/Merrill; page 250: David Young-Wolff/PhotoEdit Inc.; page 253: David Young-Wolff/PhotoEdit Inc.; page 258: Spencer Grant/PhotoEdit Inc.; page 260: Charles Thatcher/Stone/Getty Images; page 264: Michael Newman/PhotoEdit; page 268: Elizabeth Crews Photography; page 274: David Young-Wolff/PhotoEdit Inc.; page 277: Will Hart/PhotoEdit; page 282: David Young-Wolff/PhotoEdit Inc.; page 285: Paul Conklin/PhotoEdit; page 292: Will Hart/PhotoEdit Inc.; page 295: Pierre Tremblay/Masterfile; page 297: Scott Cunningham/Merrill; page 299: Scott Cunningham/Merrill; page 304: Susan Burger Photography; page 310: Pierre Tremblay/Masterfile; page 312: Susan Burger Stock; page 314: Billy Barnes/PhotoEdit; page 317: Michael Newman/PhotoEdit; page 338: Anthony Magnacca/Merrill; page 341: Bananastock/First Light; page 349: Will Hart/PhotoEdit; page 354: Scott Cunningham/Merrill.